# THE IRWIN SERIES IN RISK AND INSURANCE

*Consulting Editor*
DAVIS W. GREGG

# Health Insurance

# Health Insurance

## O. D. DICKERSON
### *Ph.D., C.L.U., C.P.C.U. F.C.A.S.*

Professor of Risk and Insurance
Florida State University

Director and Consultant
Provident Indemnity Life Insurance Co.

Member
American Academy of Actuaries

 Third Edition · 1968
RICHARD D. IRWIN, INC., Homewood, Illinois
IRWIN-DORSEY LIMITED, Nobleton, Ontario

Third Edition

*First Printing, August, 1968*

Library of Congress Catalog Card No. 68–19499

*Printed in the United States of America*

*To*
Oliver Donald Dickerson
*and*
Miriam Stanger Dickerson
*without whom neither this book*
*nor its author*
*would have come into being*

# Preface

During the long process of revising this book, the author has reached the conclusion that it would be better to write about some topic like Greek grammar in which the body of knowledge remains constant long enough for the printer to set the type. Trying to keep up with the field of health insurance is like trying to give a moment by moment description of a long distance road race: one has to move fast and be everywhere at once. Indeed the principle of Heisenberg, that the very act of observation (and description) may change the phenomenon under study, may apply.

While the author was well aware of the many changes that have taken place in the health insurance industry since the second edition was written in 1962–63, he was appalled at the number of changes necessary to bring the book up to date. Particularly appalling were the changes to the changes which were necessary to reflect developments during the year or so of working on the revision.

This edition represents a substantial revision and slight enlargement of its predecessor. Some of the more significant changes include new statistical material, in most cases through 1966 and in a few cases through 1967; the incorporation of the Social Security Amendments of 1965 and 1967; and the discussion of a whole series of developments of the last five years, including the national Medicare system for medical care for the aged and developing areas of coverage such as nursing services, dental and vision care, mental and nervous diseases and the like. Other new developments include the wider availability of comprehensive medical expense insurance on an individual and family basis and long-term disability income insurance on a group basis. Changes in the Public Assistance and Old-Age, Survivors, and Disability Insurance systems and in federal income tax laws have been included through June 30, 1968, as have developments at the level of state regulation.

Until the appearance of the first edition of this book in early 1959, relatively little attention was given to health insurance in educational institutions. Probably this resulted from the almost inevitable time lag between new developments and their reflection in educational programs. Partly, it may be traced to the lack of a definitive up-to-date text on health insurance.

This book was developed primarily to meet the need for a comprehensive college level text in health insurance for colleges and universities and for professional educational programs such as those conducted by the American College of Life Underwriters and the American Institute for

Property and Liability Underwriters. Likewise, many insurance companies and Blue Cross and Blue Shield organizations had need for more extensive text material. An attempt was made to produce a book which would meet the needs of all these groups and also serve as a useful tool in company training programs. It also was designed to serve as a reference for persons in all these categories and for physicians, hospital administrators, government personnel and others interested in medical economics and social security.

The book is divided into four Parts. Part I discusses health insurance in the economic and social framework of society, defines the problem of poor health and examines what may be done about it, introduces many general principles, briefly surveys the types of insurance available to meet the risk, and describes the government programs and private contract provisions. Part II discusses the private coverages available for meeting the costs of medical care, and Part III describes the private coverages primarily designed to meet loss of income. Part IV covers the most significant functions of health insurance carriers: underwriting, rate-making, reserves, claims, distribution, and regulation. In many of these areas it provides a unique coordinated treatment of these function which is not limited to a particular line or type of insurer.

The book fits a three-semester or four-quarter credit course well. With a little supplementation in areas of special interest, it could serve as the main text of a four-semester credit course. On the other hand, all or most of the book could be combined with any standard life insurance text in a four-or-more-semester credit course in life and health insurance. Where health insurance is treated as part of life or casualty insurance, this book will provide a useful collateral reference to supplement and expand the usually cursory treatment given health insurance in texts in these areas.

The viewpoint from which the book was written is that of a sympathetic student of health insurance who has attempted to consider the interests of insurers of all types, of insureds, of the medical profession, and of the general public. An effort has been made to give a sound and dispassionate evaluation of theories, coverages, and practices, yet to avoid editorializing. A great deal of thought and effort has gone into the development of definitions and concepts. Insofar as possible, these have been patterned after the recommendations of the Committee on Health Insurance Terminology and current usage in the business, but in many cases logic dictates a more rigorous conceptualization than current practice reflects. It is hoped that these concepts will serve a useful purpose as the foundation of a more rigorous and consistent use of terminology.

It is manifestly impossible to acknowledge the contributions of all those whose efforts have helped to make this book possible. Authors, colleagues, company executives, association personnel, and students have contributed. However, there are some who deserve special mention. The original inspiration for the book was provided by Professor Dan M. Mc-Gill and the late Dean C. A. Kulp of the University of Pennsylvania, and by Dr. Davis W. Gregg of the American College of Life Underwriters. Dr. Gregg, and Professor Edison L. Bowers of the Ohio State University, gave close attention to the work throughout its entire development and contributed many helpful suggestions.

Dr. Gregg, Dr. Bowers, and James R. Williams and Robert Waldron of the Health Insurance Institute read the drafts of the first two editions and furnished much valuable information. Dr. C. Arthur Williams of the University of Minnesota and Professor Robert S. Felton of Louisiana State University reviewed the first edition immediately before revision for the second was commenced and suggested many improvements at that time.

Manuscript for the revised edition was reviewed by Dr. William Beadles of Illinois Wesleyan University, by Joseph F. Follmann, Jr., director of information and research of the Health Insurance Association of America, John P. Hanna, general counsel of the H.I.A.A., G. Victor Hallman, director of educational publications of the American College of Life Underwriters, and by a series of executives of the Prudential Insurance Company of America. The contributions of all these readers are uncountable.

The first edition, Chapter 19 of the revised edition, and parts of Chapter 21 of this edition were reviewed by Robert W. Osler, former president, Underwriters National Assurance Company, and consultant to insurance companies. Manuscript for the first edition was reviewed by J. Henry Smith, vice president, and a number of other officers of the Equitable Life Assurance Society of the United States. Their contributions are reflected in the revised edition and in this edition. William S. Corey, President, Provident Indemnity Life Insurance Co. helped update the material on industrial insurance in Chapter 14.

Robert J. Myers, chief actuary, Social Security Administration, reviewed and corrected the material relating to Old-Age, Survivors, and Disability Insurance and Public Assistance in all three editions. William Harmelin of the Harmelin Agency, New York, reviewed Chapter 19 of the revised edition and Dr. Frank G. Dickinson, then economist of the American Medical Association and Dr. James E. Dillinger of Florida State University reviewed portions of the manuscript of the first edition.

Dr. Ronald T. Anderson of Florida State University helped significantly with the research for the revised edition, and Daniel R. Hawkes, Eric B. Tilton, Robert S. Ellis, and Maurice F. Curry, Florida State University, did much of the research for this edition.

It is impossible to cite specifically all those who furnished information useful in the revision. However, special thanks are due to the Health Insurance Association of America, the Health Insurance Institute, the Center for Health Administration Studies and the United States Department of Health, Education and Welfare for the wealth of material they provided and for permission to reproduce various charts and graphs.

The financial support of the Relm Foundation, The Florida State University Research Council, and the American Risk and Insurance Association for the research into social security reflected in this edition is acknowledged and appreciated.

To all those mentioned above, explicitly and implicitly, to the author's patient colleagues and long-suffering secretarial staff and to the many others who furnished information, advice and encouragement, many thanks! Special thanks also are due to Barbara and young Oliver who made the author's home a place of beauty, peace, and joy during these hectic months.

In a book dealing with a field so complex and diverse, it is quite impossible completely to please all persons representing so many different viewpoints. The author has endeavored to maintain academic objectivity. None will be more displeased than he when errors and omissions appear. He hopes that all readers and users of the book will feel free to communicate with him in order that future editions more nearly may approach the unattainable goal of perfection, and that in the meantime the book may contribute to a better knowledge and understanding of health insurance.

O. D. DICKERSON

Tallahassee, Florida
*July, 1968*

# Table of Contents

expansion of social insurance. Commercial contracts. Noncancellable contracts. Summary.

## PART IV. Health Insurer Operations

## General Bibliography

## Appendices

## Index

# List of Charts and Tables

## Charts

**Tables**

# Introduction

## Health insurance in first place

A good case can be made that health insurance, long recognized as the fastest growing of the four major branches of insurance, now also is the largest. It has been traditional to divide the insurance business into three major branches: life, property, and casualty. For many years health insurance was considered a branch of casualty insurance, or alternatively as a minor offshoot of life insurance.

About a decade ago, the tremendous growth of health insurance and the intense public interest in protection of this type led to the recognition that health insurance deserves a place as an independent branch of the industry. This has been evidenced by the formation of the Health Insurance Association of America, the Health Insurance Council, and the Health Insurance Institute,[1] by the development of several modern college texts on health insurance,[2] and by the growing emphasis on health insurance in the program of the American College of Life Underwriters.[3]

Indeed, the developing tendency seems to be to group these branches into two major categories: property-liability insurance on the one hand and life-health, sometimes called "personal insurance" or "life-value" insurance, on the other. The development of multiple peril coverages in the property-liability field has made this a reality, and coordinated or integrated programming of life and health coverages is winning increasing recognition and application among professional "life-value underwriters." Awaiting legislative changes is the development of contracts combining life and health coverages in a single policy, other than the inclusion of "total and permanent" disability income benefits in life insurance contracts and of accidental death benefits in health insurance policies. However, those who recall how rapidly such changes took place in property-liability insurance

---

[1] See Chapter 21 for a description of these organizations.

[2] O. D. Dickerson, *Health Insurance* (Rev. ed.; Homewood, Ill.: Richard D. Irwin Inc., 1963 [1st ed. 1959]); Edwin J. Faulkner, *Health Insurance* (New York: McGraw-Hill Book Co., Inc., 1960); Frank J. Angell, *Health Insurance* (New York: Ronald Press Co., 1963).

[3] See Chapter 21 for a brief description of the College and its educational program.

easily can visualize similarly sweeping changes in the regulatory climate of life and health insurance.

Although it is now generally recognized that health insurance is big enough to stand on its own feet, few realize how big the health insurance business is. Few attempts have been made to compare the size of the various branches of the insurance business. This is partly because of differences in methods of reporting and publicizing measures of size. Life insurance data usually refer to insurance in force or assets. Insurance in force figures for other lines of insurance are not published. Assets are not an appropriate measure because there is no way of separating life from health or property from liability. Health insurance publicity has emphasized numbers of persons insured. Such data are not available for the other branches.

In property and liability insurance, the usual measure of volume is premiums earned. These figures differ from premiums written in that they recognize only the premiums devoted to current protection as distinguished from those collected in advance to provide protection in the future.[4] Premium figures are net of dividends and experience credits.

TABLE A

Premiums and Losses by Major Line of Insurance, U.S., 1966
(millions of dollars)

| Line | Premiums Written | Premiums Earned[c] | Losses Incurred |
|---|---|---|---|
| Health[a] | 13,367[b] | 13,431 | 11,068[d] |
| Life and annuities[a] | 16,653[e] | 10,048[e] | 7,353[f] |
| Casualty[g] | 10,063 | 9,719 | 5,817 |
| Property[h] | 8,974 | 8,644 | 4,549 |
| Total | 49,057 | 41,842 | 28,401 |

[a] Premiums of $223 million for disability income riders for life insurance contracts are excluded from life and included in health.
[b] Earned premiums except for insurance companies.
[c] Premiums written plus unearned premium reserve at beginning of year minus unearned premium reserve at end of year.
[d] Losses paid. Losses-incurred data are not available. Includes $223 million of disability income benefits on life insurance riders.
[e] Net of $2,700 million policyholder dividends.
[f] Includes death benefits, matured endowments and annuity payments. Excludes $2,121 million of surrender values and $2,700 million of dividends. Dividends are treated as a reduction in premium. Perhaps some of the surrender values should be included as representing the attainment of the insureds' goals, but there is no way to measure this.
[g] Liability, workmen's compensation, fidelity, surety, and credit.
[h] Fire, marine, inland marine, allied lines, homeowners, commercial multiple peril, auto physical damage, glass, theft, and boiler and machinery.
Source: Institute of Life Insurance, *Life Insurance Fact Book, 1966;* Health Insurance Institute, *Source Book of Health Insurance Data, 1966;* Alfred M. Best Co., *Best's Fire and Casualty Aggregates and Averages, 1967, passim. Health Insurance Review,* August, 1967. Life insurance figures refer to U.S. life insurance companies only.

[4] See Chapter 19 for a discussion of unearned premium reserves. They are larger for life and health than for property and casualty insurance because of the increase of annual claim costs with age.

Life insurance statistics, on the other hand, include dividends with benefits paid and are strictly on a premiums-written basis.

When the conventional standards of other branches of the business are applied to life insurance data, some startling conclusions result. Deducting dividends paid from losses and from premiums reduces the losses-incurred figure below that for health insurance and reduces the premiums written substantially. Life insurance benefits on this basis, including annuity payments and matured endowments but not surrender values, are substantially less than health insurance benefit payments and not too much larger than casualty insurance losses incurred, as shown in Table A.

When written premiums are adjusted to an earned premium basis by subtracting the increase in unearned premium reserves, health insurance again assumes first place, with life insurance premiums falling closer to the level of casualty insurance than to that of health. Thus, health insurance is the largest of the four major branches by two out of three measures, premiums earned and losses incurred. Only in terms of written premiums does life insurance retain its ancient lead. Casualty insurance is in third place and property insurance in fourth place by all three measures.[5] The figures are given in Table A for 1966, the latest year for which all data are available at the time of writing.

### Growth of health insurance

The tremendous growth of the health insurance business has been discussed so often that there is no need to exhaust the topic here. Table B summarizes the growth of the industry from 1948, which is the earliest year for which all data are available, to 1966, the latest year for which all data are available. The number of persons insured for hospital benefits, the most widely held coverage, more than doubled, and the number covered for other medical expense benefits increased several fold. By 1966, 57 million people were covered by major medical and comprehensive insurance, which did not exist in 1948.

Premium income increased almost tenfold and benefit payments more than fourteenfold. These latter figures reflect substantial improvements in the quality of coverage as well as increases in quantity.

Similarly, the number of companies writing health insurance has almost doubled since 1955, as indicated in Table C.

The overall adequacy of health insurance coverage in relation to the

---

[5] The dividing line between property and casualty insurance always has been tenuous and is blurring rapidly. The author has chosen to allocate lines on the basis of the major exposure. Thus auto liability is considered as casualty and auto physical damage as property. Homeowners, commercial multiple peril and boiler and machinery have been classified as property, since the property exposure is the greater.

TABLE B

Growth of Private Health Insurance, 1948–66
(in millions)

| Item | Year 1948 | Year 1966 | Percentage Increase |
|------|------|------|------|
| Persons insured | | | |
| Hospital............................... | 61 | 158 | 159 |
| Surgical.............................. | 34 | 145 | 326 |
| Basic medical........................ | 13 | 117 | 800 |
| Major medical........................ | none | 57 | infinite |
| Loss of income...................... | 33 | 54 | 64 |
| Premiums written..................... | $1,308 | $13,367 | 945 |
| Insurance company, group............ | 386 | 5,564 | 1,341 |
| Insurance company, individual........ | 537 | 2,930 | 446 |
| Blue Cross, Blue Shield, | | | |
| Blue Cross, Blue Shield, independent.. | 385 | 4,933 | 1,181 |
| Benefit payments ......................$ | 772 | $11,068 | 1,334 |
| Insurance companies................. | 442 | 6,511 | 1,335 |
| Blue Cross, Blue Shield, Independent.. | 330 | 4,557 | 1,271 |

Source: Health Insurance Institute; *Health Insurance Review*, August, 1967.

aggregate need is discussed in Chapter 3, and the special problems of extending coverage to the entire population, and supplementing
government programs for the aged, are discussed in Chapter 10. The remaining market potential is tremendous, especially for major medical,
comprehensive medical, and long-term disability income, on both group
and individual bases. The market potential is discussed in various chapters dealing with specific lines and also in Chapter 21.

TABLE C

Number of Insurance Companies Writing Health Insurance
In the United States, by Type of Company and Type of Coverage
December 31, 1956, 1961, 1966

| | 1956 | 1961 | 1966 |
|------|------|------|------|
| Total Companies............................... | 624 | 839 | 1,045 |
| Life......................................... | 371 | 571 | 706 |
| Casualty.................................... | 219 | 226 | 297 |
| Monoline (offering health insurance only..... | 34 | 42 | 42 |
| No. writing group insurance..................... | 338 | 519 | 703 |
| No. writing individual insurance................. | 568 | 748 | 942 |
| No. writing both group and individual insurance.. | 285 | 428 | 603 |
| No. writing major medical expense policies....... | 137 | 221 | 353 |
| No. writing "substandard" policies.............. | N.A. | 67 | 154[a] |
| No. writing guaranteed renewable policies....... | N.A. | 285 | 438[a] |

[a] 1965—latest available data.
Source: Health Insurance Association of America, "Spectator Insurance by States,"
United States Department of Health, Education and Welfare, "1967 Blue Cross and Blue
Shield Fact Book," and Health Insurance Institute.

When it is realized that the great growth of health insurance in the last decade and a half is entirely the product of private enterprise in a competitive environment, and that this growth continues at a rapid rate, there seems little justification for further government interference.

## Human life values

As Huebner,[6] Osler,[7] and others have pointed out, the human life value should be protected from each of the perils that may destroy earning power: death, disability, old age and unemployment. Private unemployment insurance is not yet developed, but the development of an insurance program or an estate plan should recognize all four perils insofar as possible.[8] Perhaps death has taken priority because loss is always total and permanent. However, disability also can produce a total and permanent loss of income, and the loss is greater than that produced by death. The economic loss is greater because the disabled breadwinner still requires food, clothing, housing, and often medical care. The psychological loss also is greater, because, in the absence of really adequate insurance protection, the disabled breadwinner is still alive to observe the decline in his family's fortunes and standard of living.

Usually the proper amount of disability insurance is determined by a process of programming benefits in relation to financial needs in the same way that life insurance benefits are programmed. This process is explained in detail in Chapter 21. However, sometimes it is useful to measure the total economic loss in terms of the human life value. This can serve as a measure of the overall adequacy of insurance protection on an individual or aggregate basis. Moreover, it is the standard response to the client's objection that he is "worth more dead than alive" or "worth more sick than well."

The author never has met anyone who was worth more disabled than healthy, although there are supposed to have been some in this category during the Great Depression. To illustrate this point and demonstrate how to compute a human life value, the case of an actual client will be used. The client, a professional, is age 37. He has no children. His net income *after* business expenses and other work-connected costs and federal income and other wage-related taxes was $16,363 last year,

---

[6] S. S. Huebner, *The Economics of Health Insurance* (Philadelphia: The American College of Life Underwriters, 1962).

[7] Robert I. Mehr and Robert W. Osler, *Modern Life Insurance* (3d ed.; New York: Macmillan Co., 1961).

[8] Huebner and Osler may not have included unemployment in their discussions beyond indicating that life insurance cash values serve as a reserve fund for this and other emergencies. Private unemployment insurance so far has been hightly experimental, but the author believes it is feasible on a limited basis, at least.

or $1,364 per month. Net after-tax income has been increasing at the rate of 5.34 percent compounded for the past few years. In the event of long-term disability, the following monthly disability income benefits would be available, after waiting periods ranging from 30 days to six months:

| | | |
|---|---:|---:|
| Life insurance disability income riders | | |
| Benefits until age 65 | $323 | |
| Benefits until age 60 | 100 | $ 423 |
| Noncancellable disability income insurance | | |
| Benefits to age 65 | 300 | |
| Full benefit to age 60; half benefit thereafter | 100 | 400 |
| Group disability income, benefit to age 65 | | 500 |
| Old-Age, Survivors and Disability Insurance (social security) | | 119 |
| Waiver of premium benefits on life and health insurance | | 145 |
| Total income plus expense saved | | $1,587 |

Any home office underwriter and most agents would claim that any person with an earned income net of taxes of $1,364 a month and disability income insurance of $1,587 per month is overinsured. But, by using the human life value concept, it is possible to show that this client is *under*insured by almost $200,000.

In general, the value of any piece of property is the present value of the future income stream it will produce. Ideally, this should be measured in terms of utility to reflect all the related amenities, but in practice it usually is necessary to deal only with values that can be measured in monetary units. Thus, in computing the value of a human being to himself and his family, intangible values such as love of life, love and affection, and the like are disregarded, and the present value of his net earned income is computed.[9] This is equal to gross income, less business expenses and other work-connected costs such as commuting and income and similar taxes.

The present value is simply that amount which, when invested at compound interest at an assumed interest rate, will produce the net income stream which is projected. There should be *no* discounting for the probabilities of death, disability or unemployment, since it is the potential loss from such risks that one is seeking to measure. For an income stream and interest rate which are expected to remain constant, the present value can be obtained from a compound interest table.[10] If the income is expected to increase or decrease at a constant rate, and the interest rate is expected to remain constant, the appropriate rate of dis-

---

[9] This computation develops the life value to the individual and his family. His life may also have value to others, such as his employer. For a brief discussion of estimating value to the employer, see Chapter 21.

[10] It will be found under some heading such as "$a_{\overline{n}|}$, Present value of $1 per year for *n* years."

count may be found by dividing 1 plus the rate of growth of income by 1 plus the rate of interest.[11] Where the rate of interest varies or the income stream changes at other than a constant rate, it may be necessary to compute the present value of each future year's income separately[12] and sum the separate figures to obtain the present value of the total expected income.

For the client described above, it seems appropriate to assume a lower rate of increase of after-tax income than the 5.34 percent of recent years, in order to reflect the impact of progressive income tax rates and the possibility of earnings growth slowing down as he gets older. A rate of 3 percent seems appropriate. Similarly, a rate of interest of 3 percent seems an appropriate assumption to reflect the rate that can be earned after income taxes. This simplifies the computation of the life value, since the combined effect of the two rates is the equivalent of a zero interest rate. Thus, the life value is simply equal to the future working life multiplied by present after-tax earnings. Since the client plans to work until age 70, the resulting life value is 33 times $16,363 or $539,979, rounded to $540,000. It might be noted parenthetically that this is the life value for disability insurance purposes, reflecting the value of the client to himself and to his family. For life insurance purposes, it is necessary to estimate his value to his family, since after he dies he will not be there to enjoy his value to himself. More realistically, this value can be estimated by deducting from his earnings the amounts he spends on himself. These should include personal consumption expenses, life and health insurance premiums and most saving for old age. A deduction of 25 percent seems appropriate, yielding a life value to his family of $404,984, or $405,000 rounded for life insurance purposes.[13]

This life value of about $540,000 may be compared with the present value of disability income benefits under the contracts described above. It is necessary to discount these for interest, since the benefits will not be received in a lump sum like life insurance benefits, but in periodic installments over the years. When the present value of the promised disability benefits is computed, assuming 3 percent interest, its value works out to $349,572, or $350,000 rounded.[14] Thus the client is $190,000 *under-*

---

[11] Where the result is less than 1, it is appropriate to subtract it from and use a present-value table. Where the result is greater than 1, it is appropriate to subtract 1 from it and use a table "$s_{\overline{n}|}$, Amount of $1 per year for $n$ years."

[12] A present-value table of "The present value of $1 $n$ Years Hence" or $v^n$ is used for one or more years at a time.

[13] The appropriate discount should be developed from an analysis of the family expenditures. Huebner suggests 50 percent as the appropriate deduction from income *before* income taxes. See S. S. Huebner, *The Economics of Life Insurance* (3d ed.; New York: Appleton Century Crofts, Inc., 1959), p. 51.

[14] This figure includes the value of the life income after age 60 and the increase in maturity values of the life insurance at age 65 for the contracts with such provisions.

insured! The present value of the insurance benefits is only 65 percent of the life value. This is true despite the apparent present overinsurance because of the assumption of increasing earnings and of retirement at age 70, while the disability benefits usually cease at 60 or 65 and never increase (in this program).[15]

## Medical expenses

In addition to the total or partial loss of the human life value through loss of income, poor health also involves out-of-pocket expenditures for medical expenses. These include expenses for the services of physicians, surgeons, hospitals, and nurses and for drugs, appliances, blood, and many other goods and services. While medical expense rarely involves costs comparable to the income loss from total disability, these expenses can have a severe impact on family finances. Indeed, there have been workmen's compensation cases where medical benefits alone have exceeded $100,000. Moreover, when the family breadwinner is disabled, these expenses involve losses in addition to the loss of income. Furthermore, these expenses may be incurred by any member of the family or by several members within a short period of time.

Within the past 30 years, the public generally has recognized the importance of medical expense insurance, and the market for basic coverages is approaching saturation except in special markets such as rural residents and the aged. However, a tremendous need and market exist for broad coverages such as major medical and comprehensive insurance. The number of persons protected by contracts of this type still is increasing at the rate of about 10 percent per year.

## Plan of the book

In order to understand and appreciate the vital role of health insurance in the nation's economy and the problems of providing ever more adequate coverage to a constantly increasing proportion of the population on a voluntary basis, it is necessary to study social and economic problems of poor health. Part I, "Health Losses and How They Are Met," is designed to give the student a broad and deep understanding of these problems and of certain features common to all or most health insurance. In

---

[15] For further discussion of the human life value, see Alfred E. Hofflander, "Loss of Income due to Wrongful Death: A Method of Measurement," *Insurance Law Journal,* February, 1965, pp. 92 ff., but beware of typographic errors in formulas, pp. 97–99. Also see Alfred E. Hofflander, Jr., "The Human Life Value: An Historical Perspective," *Journal of Risk and Insurance* Vol. XXIII, No. 3 (September, 1966). For an attempt to measure life values for an average person by age and sex, see Dorothy P. Rice, *Estimating the Cost of Illness* (Health Economics Series, No. 6), Washington, D.C.: U.S. Government Printing Office, 1966.

Chapter 1 the economic losses from poor health are analyzed, first from the viewpoint of society to demonstrate the importance of health losses in the national economy, and then from the viewpoint of the individual to demonstrate their importance in family financial planning and the need for health insurance.

In Chapter 2, the four main methods of treating the risk of health losses, preventive efforts, assumption of risk, transfer of risk, and insurance, are introduced. The significance of various diseases and injuries as producers of health losses is analyzed, and preventive efforts through medical treatment, public health, and loss prevention are described in moderate detail. The chapter concludes with a summary of progress in health improvement.

Chapter 3 gives a description of the techniques of meeting health losses by assumption of risk. In this chapter, health insurance is defined and classified according to a number of dimensions and a conceptual framework is developed to permit understanding the balance of the book.

Chapter 4 is devoted to government programs of social insurance, public assistance and similar devices.

Chapter 5 describes the fundamental legal principles common to all health insurance contracts and explains many contractual provisions which are found in health insurance policies of all types.

Part II deals explicitly with medical expense coverages: hospital, surgical, medical, major medical, and comprehensive. Contracts and coverages of insurance companies, the Blues and the independents, are described, analyzed, and compared. Chapter 9 discusses developments and potential developments in the coverage of expenses not yet usually covered by health insurance such as nursing services, dental and vision care, and treatment of mental and nervous disease. Chapter 10 deals with a series of problems and issues common to the medical expense lines such as competition among types of insurer, coverage of the population, the special problem of the aged, and the control of utilization.

Part III describes and analyzes disability income coverages including life insurance disability benefits and related problems. In Part IV, various insurer functions are described, primarily from the viewpoint of insurer management. However, Chapter 21 is written mainly with the viewpoint of the agent, and secondarily that of the consumer, in mind. The final chapter deals with the climate of insurance regulation as it affects health insurance.

## Summary

Health insurance is both the fastest growing and, by several measures, the largest of the four major branches of insurance in the United States. Health insurance, like life insurance, protects human life values and family finances against the loss of earning power and extra expenses. The potential loss to a family from total disability of the breadwinner is enormous, and insurance protection is essential. This book describes health insurance and health insurer operations in detail after a preliminary analysis of the physical, social, and economic problems of health losses in an uncertain world.

# PART I

# Health Losses and
# How They Are Met

## chapter 1

(Even as you and I!.)—Kipling, *The Vampire*

# The Problem of Health

## Health insurance and society

Despite all his learning, his art, his science, and his religion, man is an animal. Because of his nature, man is exposed to all sorts of dangers from his surroundings and from his evil instincts.[1] This has been true since before the dawn of history. Man's first instinct is self-preservation. In the earliest days this instinct was applied exclusively to the preservation of the life of the individual. As man evolved into a social animal, he came to learn that self-preservation could be accomplished more effectively by working with other men.

As man came to depend upon others for his own protection, he had to extend his concept of self-preservation to progressively larger groups. First the family, then the clan, the tribe, and finally the nation became a part of the "self" of which he was aware and whose preservation became important to him. Today, for the first time, man's scientific accomplishments have reached such a state of development that the destruction of all human life is within the bounds of his power. Thus, today, the concept of self-preservation must be applied to the entire human species.

*Perils.* Dangers against which man must protect himself are the same today as always—different, perhaps, in degree but generally not in kind. Death, disease, bodily injury, and the infirmity of old age may impair his physical well-being and produce pain, suffering, and financial loss. Man's accumulated property, which represents both the product of past human effort and the means of self-preservation when his own physical efforts fail, is subject to damage or destruction from many circumstances

---

[1] The term "instinct" is used here in a broader sense than that employed by some psychologists. The reference here is to fundamental behavior determinants, called "needs" by some authors. Man also has good instincts, which also may produce losses, but that is not the point here at issue.

13

and events beyond his control. These dangers, events, and circumstances are referred to as *perils*. Perils include such things as war, crime, accident, disease, and old age; fire, flood, famine, windstorm, and earthquake; and in modern society losses from social and economic factors beyond the control of the individual, such as unemployment, price fluctuations, lawsuits, and changes in demand and technology.

*Needs.* Man's animal-level needs are few: freedom from pain, food, drink, air, shelter, clothing, sleep, waste disposal, and some kind of sexual satisfaction. By the middle of the 20th century the great mass of mankind had little cause for concern over any of these but the first. The economic progress of society, indeed, had reached such a stage that, in the Western world at least, most men enjoyed an abundance of goods and services which would have been beyond the wildest dreams of their forebears a scant century before. And yet bodily injury, disease, and infirmity continued to take their toll of pain and suffering, very much as always. Indeed, the development of new weapons of tremendous destructiveness posed the threat of mass pain and suffering on a scale never before conceived.

*Security.* Another way of looking at the above ideas is in connection with security. Security involves freedom from loss or risk of loss. The loss may be of an economic or noneconomic nature. Noneconomic losses involve pain, suffering, psychological disturbance, ignorance, fear, sin, regret, grief, and guilt. Economic losses involve an involuntary decrease in value—either of the human life value or of property values. A gift to a relative or the purchase of a new car is not a loss. These actions involve a decrease in economic value, but the decrease is voluntary. There is no risk, and the possibility of such transactions does not ordinarily produce any insecurity.

*Economic security*, then, means freedom from the risk of economic loss. Economic *loss* is an involuntary parting with value. Economic insecurity involves a risk of loss of income or of accumulated wealth from various perils. The perils which may produce such a loss to earned income are death, disability, unemployment, and old age, and with lesser frequency, underemployment, inflation, and imprisonment. Losses to property may result from perils such as fire, flood, windstorm, war, and crime. Attachment for debt and liability claims may produce loss of both property and income.

*Risk.* *Risk* is used here to refer to uncertainty as to loss. There is no comparable term for uncertainty as to gain nor uncertainty as to which one is indifferent. There is a difference between this concept and that of probability of loss. Where loss is certain to occur, as, for example, depreciation, there is no risk. (Sometimes, as in regard to death, risk exists only as to the time of occurrence.) Where loss is certain, probability of loss equals 1.0; risk equals 0. Contrariwise, where loss is certain not to occur, there is no risk; here both probability of loss and risk are equal to 0. Risk is at its maximum to an individual where the probability of loss is equal to 0.5. To an insurer risk is at a maximum where the probability of loss is lowest, but not quite 0.

*Meeting risk.* Ill health produces pain and suffering; it also produces an economic loss. The impact falls upon the earning power of the individual, and the expenses incurred fall upon both his accumulated wealth and his future earnings. Just as men have joined together in their efforts at self-preservation and economic endeavor, so have they joined together to create social devices to reduce the risk of financial losses.

There is a variety of devices which may reduce risk. They include efforts to prevent loss by removing the factors producing or facilitating loss or by reducing the extent of loss which are referred to as *loss prevention*. They also include devices for *assuming the risk* or *transferring the risk* of financial loss from one party to another. The technique of transfer includes such arrangements as hedging, hold-harmless agreements, and public assistance. The final category of devices for reducing risk of financial loss is known as combination or pooling, of which the most important is *insurance*. Insurance comprehends the social devices for reducing risk which involve the principle of pooling or combining separate exposures so that the total risk for the group is reduced by the operation of the law of averages. Health insurance includes all such devices which reduce the risk of financial loss from ill health. It is with such devices that this book is mainly concerned.

## The cost of poor health

Poor health produces two kinds of financial loss. Poor health requires the expenditure of money to pay for treatment in order to minimize suffering, prevent premature death and facilitate the return to health and productivity. Second, ill health impairs the ability of the individual to work, and there is a loss of his social product. Where the person is employed or produces services for others, this loss may be measured in financial terms. Thus poor health produces a loss of earning power and a loss of accumulated wealth or future earnings in order to pay for the costs of treatment.

*Aggregate cost.* In the United States, by 1965 the aggregate of such financial loss resulting from poor health was estimated to be in excess of $50 billion per year. In a year, 4 out of every 5 persons in the population are disabled for at least one day from disease and 1 in every 18 from accidental injury. One person in every seven becomes a hospital patient. The average family has one person hospitalized each three years. The average worker loses about six days of work a year from short-term disability[2] alone. The probability of long-term disability for insured persons, who are presumably healthier than the general population, ranges from about 7½ times the probability of death at age 22 to 2 times at age 62.[3] Table 1–1 indicates the relationship between disability and death rates and gives the relationship between the probability number of 90-day disabilities and the probability of death before age 65, at various ages.

TABLE 1–1

Disability Probability Compared with Probability of Death per 1,000 Lives Exposed

| (1) | (2) | (3) | (4) | (5) | (6) | (7) |
|---|---|---|---|---|---|---|
| | | | | | | Ratio: Probable No. of Dis- |
| | | | | | Probable | abilities |
| | Probability | | Ratio of | | No. of | before Age |
| | of Dis- | | Disability | Probable | Deaths | 65 to Prob- |
| | ability | | Probability | Number | before | ability of |
| | of 90 Days | Probability | to Prob- | of Dis- | Age 65 | Death be- |
| | or more | of Death | ability of | abilities | $\sum\limits_{x}^{65}$ (3) | fore Age 65 |
| Attained | in Year | in Year | Death | before | | |
| Age (x) | Indicated[a] | Indicated[b] | (2) ÷ (3) | Age 65[c] | | (5) ÷ (6) |
| 22................. | 6.64 | 0.89 | 7.46 | 687 | 243 | 2.83 |
| 27................. | 6.57 | 0.98 | 6.70 | 657 | 239 | 2.75 |
| 32................. | 7.78 | 1.18 | 6.59 | 625 | 235 | 2.66 |
| 37................. | 9.81 | 1.68 | 5.84 | 586 | 230 | 2.55 |
| 42.................12.57 | | 2.95 | 4.26 | 537 | 222 | 1.97 |
| 47.................16.76 | | 4.91 | 3.41 | 475 | 208 | 2.28 |
| 52.................22.39 | | 8.21 | 2.73 | 394 | 183 | 2.15 |
| 57.................31.10 | | 13.22 | 2.35 | 283 | 141 | 2.01 |
| 62.................44.27 | | 21.12 | 2.10 | 138 | 68 | 2.03 |

[a] Health Insurance Association of America, *1964 Commissioners Disability Table,* Vol. III, p. 13.
[b] x 18 ultimate rates from Society of Actuaries, *Transactions,* Vol. XI, pp. 393–40.
[c] Computed by approximate methods from source cited in first note above.

Table 1–2 indicates the magnitude of the national expenditure and income loss due to poor health. Although data for all years are not available, the size of the loss and the trend are readily apparent. The figures tend to exaggerate the trend because some items are lacking for the earlier years of the series.

The figures for income loss relate only to the first six months of disability and were obtained from the Social Security Administration estimates of short-term nonoccupational income loss. Thus these figures understate even short-term disability. Workmen's compensation benefit payments

---

[2] That is, disabilities lasting less than six months and the first six months of longer disabilities.

[3] Both incidence rates and duration increase with age, but death rates increase faster. Age-specific rates are computed for a particular age or group of ages.

TABLE 1-2

Estimated Losses from Poor Health, U.S., 1950–67
(in millions)

| Year[a] | Short-Term Non-occupational Income Loss | Medical Care Expenditures | | | | Grand Total |
|---|---|---|---|---|---|---|
| | | Private[b] | Federal | State & Local | Total | |
| 1950. . . . . . . . . . | $ 4,795 | $ 8,501 | $ 1,706 | $1,872 | $12,079 | $16,874 |
| 1951. . . . . . . . . . | 5,473 | 9,379 | — | — | — | |
| 1952. . . . . . . . . . | 5,814 | 10,134 | — | — | — | |
| 1953. . . . . . . . . . | 6,144 | 11,033[c] | 1,160 | 2,878 | 15,079 | 21,223 |
| 1954. . . . . . . . . . | 6,094 | 11,895[c] | 1,132 | 3,140 | 16,167 | 22,261 |
| 1955. . . . . . . . . . | 6,546 | 12,421 | 2,061 | 2,577 | 17,059 | 23,605 |
| 1956. . . . . . . . . . | 7,031 | 14,375 | 1,681 | 2,802 | 18,840 | 25,871 |
| 1957. . . . . . . . . . | 7,363 | 15,602 | 1,995 | 2,931 | 20,528 | 27,891 |
| 1958. . . . . . . . . . | 7,458 | 16,742 | 2,189 | 3,175 | 22,106 | 29,564 |
| 1959. . . . . . . . . . | 7,724 | 18,321 | 2,499 | 3,398 | 24,218 | 31,942 |
| 1960. . . . . . . . . . | 8,555 | 20,339[d] | 2,918 | 3,478 | 26,735[d] | 35,290 |
| 1961. . . . . . . . . . | 8,639 | 21,611 | 3,253 | 3,806 | 28,670 | 37,309 |
| 1962. . . . . . . . . . | 9,622 | 23,480 | 3,712 | 3,926 | 31,118 | 40,740 |
| 1963. . . . . . . . . . | 10,178 | 25,071 | 4,104 | 4,201 | 33,376 | 43,554 |
| 1964. . . . . . . . . . | 10,248 | 28,283 | 4,462 | 4,509 | 37,254 | 47,502 |
| 1965. . . . . . . . . . | 11,270 | 30,692 | 4,818 | 4,900 | 40,410 | 51,680 |
| 1966. . . . . . . . . . | 12,184 | 32,516 | 5,635 | 5,409 | 43,560 | 55,744 |
| 1967. . . . . . . . . . | — | 31,706[e] | 10,286 | 5,882 | 47,874 | — |

[a] Fiscal year ending in year indicated for government expenditures; otherwise calendar year.
[b] Includes net cost of health insurance.
[c] 1953 and 1954 data were not presented in as detailed a form as that for other years and the federal-state breakdown is less precise.
[d] These totals do not include expenditures by philanthrophy, industrial in-plant health services, and certain privately financed hospital construction before 1960.
[e] July 1, 1966 to June 30, 1967.
Source: *Social Security Bulletin,* October, 1956; November, 1960; November, 1961; December, 1961; January, 1962; November, 1962; December, 1962; January, 1963; and January, 1968. Barbara S. Cooper, "Revised Public and Private Expenditures for Health and Medical Care, Fiscal Years 1960–67," Social Security Administration *Research and Statistics Note,* No. 7–1968.

for income replacement were $1,155 million in 1966, and it is estimated that the total income loss for short-term occupational disability is at least one and one-half billion dollars.

Income losses resulting from long-term disability are very large, but an accurate estimate is difficult. If the crude rate of occurrence of long-term disability is taken as 10 per 1,000 workers exposed and the average duration of such long-term disability is assumed to be three years[4] (after the six-month qualification period), this would indicate that in any year there are 30 workers per 1,000 disabled. If this is applied to personal incomes from wages and salaries of $357.4 billion plus $33 billion esti

---

[4] These figures are based on insurance experience and are probably conservative, as insured persons have been medically selected. Some population studies of all ages and sexes show a duration as high as 270 weeks, but many were never in the labor force.

mated portion of income from unincorporated business due to personal services,[5] it would indicate an estimated income loss from long-term disability of $11 billion per year. Adding this to the other losses above indicates a grand total loss of $68.2 billion in 1966.

Even this figure understates the economic loss arising from poor health, since it makes no allowance for partial disability or for the economic value of housewives and others who perform a productive function but are not paid in money for their services. It is estimated that disability causes losses in this category of another $5 billion per year, although some authors suggest higher or lower figures.[6] Moreover, to the extent to which persons do not receive adequate medical care, the figures as to expenditures are lower than they otherwise should be. Certainly, if all persons received the "best" medical care available, these figures would be much higher.

*Cost trends.*    National loss from ill health has been rising for many reasons. Income loss has gone up as incomes have gone up. It is impossible to determine whether there have been any significant changes in the incidence of disability. The available statistics are not good enough. Insurance data seem to indicate that the probability of disability increased in the period from 1850 to about 1925 and then leveled off or declined slightly.

Improvements in death rates need not necessarily be associated with improvements in disability rates. Advances in medical science may succeed in keeping more disabled people alive, so that, as death rates decline, disability rates increase. The method of computing the estimated income loss in Table 1–2 did not attempt to consider changes in disability incidence before 1959. The prior increases reflected only the growth in the labor force and in average earnings.

However, in the area of medical care it is clear that incidence rates (often called "utilization rates") have been rising. This is due to a number of factors, of which the growth in health insurance is an important one. As people get used to the fact that they can expect these costs to be met, they become more likely to incur them. In addition, there has been a general upgrading of public standards as to what constitutes adequate medical care. Today, almost all babies in the United

---

[5] "National Income Supplement," *Survey of Current Business* (Washington, D.C.: U.S. Government Printing Office) Income figures are for the year 1965.

[6] Roy L. Lassiter, Jr., "The Wife's Contribution to Family Income," *Journal of Insurance*, Vol. XXVIII, No. 4 (December, 1961), p. 33, estimates the value of a wife at $3,068 to $11,459 per year. Dorothy P. Rice, in *Estimating the Cost of Illness* (Health Economics Series No. 6 [Washington, D.C.: U.S. Government Printing Office, 1966]), estimates the lost "earnings" of housewives at $2.9 billion and the total economic cost of illness in 1963 at $55.4 billion, by a rather different methodology. She estimates the value of future earnings lost by death at $50 to $60 billion, depending on what rate of discount is used.

States are born in hospitals, for example; only 30 years ago the proportion was about 40 percent. New drugs and antibiotics are being used; often these are very expensive. Utilization of the services of specialists instead of, or in addition to, the family doctor has increased tremendously.

**Unit costs.** In addition to increases in utilization, there have been significant increases in unit costs of medical care. The consumer price index for December, 1967, shows the following price indices based on 1957–59 prices equal to 100.

```
All medical care................................................140.4
Physicians' fees.................................................141.0
Dentist fees.....................................................130.7
Hospital daily service charge....................................211.4
Prescriptions and drugs.......................................... 98.1
```

The index for all consumer prices rose to a record of 118.2 in December, 1967.[7] Thus in the last 10 years hospital rates have increased tremendously—by more than six times as much as consumer prices in general. The only major component of the medical care index which increased less than consumer prices in general in the last several years was prescriptions and drugs. Chart 1–1 portrays the strong uptrend and Table 1–3 gives full details of the price indexes.

CHART 1–1a

*Medical Care Prices*

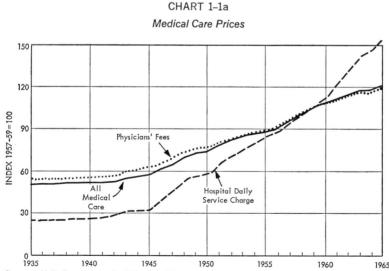

Source: U.S. Department of Health, Education, and Welfare, *Health, Education and Welfare Trends,* 1965, p. S–22.

---

[7] U.S. Department of Labor, Bureau of Labor Statistics, *Consumer Price Indexes for Selected Items and Groups,* December, 1965, to December, 1967.

TABLE 1-3

Medical Care Price Indices

| Calendar year | All medical care | Physicians' fees | | | Dentists' fees | Optometric examination and eye-glasses | Hospital daily service charge[a] | Insurance | | Prescriptions and drugs[d] |
|---|---|---|---|---|---|---|---|---|---|---|
| | | All | Obstet-rical | Surgeons' fees | | | | Hospital-ization[b] | Sur-gical[c] | |
| 1929 | 50.9 | — | 43.2 | — | — | 74.8 | — | — | — | — |
| 1930 | 51.3 | — | 44.2 | — | — | 75.0 | — | — | — | — |
| 1940 | 50.3 | 54.5 | 43.6 | 60.1 | 53.5 | 70.8 | 25.4 | — | — | 69.3 |
| 1942 | 52.0 | 55.8 | 46.4 | 62.4 | 55.0 | 71.9 | 28.0 | — | — | 71.5 |
| 1943 | 54.5 | 59.4 | 51.0 | 66.0 | 57.5 | 75.0 | 30.2 | — | — | 72.0 |
| 1944 | 56.2 | 61.8 | 53.2 | 68.6 | 60.7 | 76.8 | 31.5 | — | — | 72.7 |
| 1945 | 57.5 | 63.3 | 54.3 | 70.6 | 63.3 | 77.8 | 32.5 | — | — | 73.2 |
| 1946 | 60.7 | 66.4 | 57.5 | 73.8 | 67.0 | 79.3 | 37.0 | — | — | 74.6 |
| 1947 | 65.7 | 70.7 | 61.8 | 78.1 | 72.6 | 82.4 | 44.1 | — | — | 80.1 |
| 1948 | 69.8 | 73.5 | 66.0 | 82.0 | 76.5 | 85.9 | 51.5 | — | — | 84.3 |
| 1949 | 72.0 | 74.8 | 66.9 | 83.6 | 79.6 | 88.7 | 55.7 | — | — | 85.6 |
| 1950 | 73.4 | 76.0 | 67.7 | 84.9 | 81.5 | 89.5 | 57.8 | — | — | 86.6 |
| 1951 | 76.9 | 78.8 | 72.0 | 87.2 | 84.6 | 93.6 | 64.1 | 59.4 | — | 89.1 |
| 1952 | 81.1 | 82.3 | 79.7 | 90.6 | 86.4 | 94.7 | 70.4 | 67.3 | — | 89.9 |
| 1953 | 83.9 | 84.5 | 81.4 | 92.5 | 89.2 | 93.7 | 74.8 | 72.7 | — | 90.7 |
| 1954 | 86.6 | 87.0 | 85.2 | 93.6 | 92.2 | 92.5 | 79.2 | 78.0 | — | 91.7 |
| 1955 | 88.6 | 90.0 | 90.8 | 94.6 | 93.1 | 93.8 | 83.0 | 80.1 | — | 92.7 |
| 1956 | 91.8 | 92.7 | 93.8 | 96.0 | 94.9 | 95.3 | 87.5 | 85.1 | — | 94.7 |
| 1957 | 95.5 | 96.7 | 97.3 | 98.2 | 97.2 | 99.0 | 94.5 | 90.1 | — | 97.2 |
| 1958 | 100.1 | 100.0 | 99.9 | 99.7 | 100.2 | 100.0 | 99.9 | 99.4 | — | 100.6 |
| 1959 | 104.4 | 103.4 | 102.8 | 102.2 | 102.7 | 101.1 | 105.5 | 110.5 | 100.5 | 102.2 |
| 1960 | 108.1 | 106.0 | 105.0 | 105.0 | 104.7 | 103.7 | 112.7 | 120.9 | 102.3 | 102.3 |
| 1961 | 111.3 | 108.7 | 107.3 | 106.9 | 105.2 | 107.0 | 121.3 | 130.0 | 106.9 | 101.1 |

| | | | | | | | | | | |
|---|---|---|---|---|---|---|---|---|---|---|
| 1962 | 114.2 | 111.9 | 110.7 | — | 108.0 | 108.6 | 129.8 | 136.0 | 107.9 | 99.6 |
| 1963 | 117.0 | 114.4 | 112.5 | — | 111.1 | 109.3 | 138.0 | 142.7 | 108.8 | 98.7 |
| 1964 | 119.0 | 117.3 | 115.2 | — | 114.0 | 110.7 | 144.9 | — | — | 98.4 |
| 1965 | 122.3 | 121.5 | 117.8 | — | 117.6 | 113.0 | 153.3 | — | — | 98.1 |
| 1966 | 127.7 | 128.5 | 123.0 | — | 121.4 | 116.1 | 168.0 | — | — | 98.4 |
| 1967 (Average) | 136.7 | 137.6 | 132.3 | — | 127.5 | 121.8 | 200.1 | — | — | 97.9 |
| 1967 (Dec.) | 140.4 | 141.0 | 134.6 | — | 130.7 | 123.5 | 211.4 | — | — | 98.1 |

Note: The consumer price index was converted as of January 1962 from the 1947–49 = 100 reference base to the new base 1957–59 = 100. Figures are annual averages except for December 1967.

a Formerly designated "Hospital Room Rates." Includes charge to full-pay adult inpatients for room and board, routine nursing care, and minor medical and surgical supplies.

b Formerly designated "Group Hospitalization."

c December 1958 = 100.

d Limited to prescriptions (an ACP or aspirin, phenacetin, caffeine citrate compound; elixir turpenhydrate with codeine; and buffered penicillin) and over-the-counter drugs (aspirin tablets, milk of magnesia, and multiple vitamin concentrate) prior to March 1960, this prescriptions and drugs index was expanded by linking into the index prescriptions appropriate to each of seven end-use classes (anti-infectives, sedatives and hypnotics, ataractics, antispasmodics, anti-arthritics, cough preparations, cardiovasculars and antihypertensives).

Source: U.S. Department of Labor, Bureau of Labor Statistics; Price Indexes for Selected Items and Groups. See "Medical Care in the Consumer Price Index, 1936–56," Monthly Labor Review, September 1957; Health, Education and Welfare Trends, 1966 ed., p. 111–22.

CHART 1–1b

*Increases in Medical Care and Other Major Groups in
the Consumer Price Index in the United States*

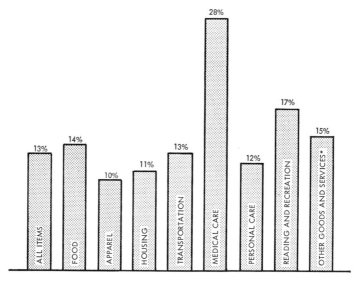

(1957–59 = 100) PERCENT OF INCREASE

* Comprises tobacco, alcoholic beverages, legal services, burial services, banking fees, etc.
Source: *Health Insurance News,* July, 1967 (New York: Health Insurance Institute).

The Health Information Foundation has provided a breakdown for
the periods 1953–58 and 1953–63 of per capita increases in price and use
as shown in Table 1–4.[8] The per capita figures remove the effect of population size changes and are based on their surveys.

The figures on increased use were obtained by deflating the per capita
increases by the appropriate consumer price index figure. They indicate
that while increases caused by price change are twice those caused by
use change overall, they vary widely by service. A similar wide variation
by age was indicated. Increases in use varied from 10 percent at ages
6–17 to 32 percent at ages 35–54.

Of course, the national totals also reflect increases in the population
exposed. Since medical care costs are highest for the youngest and oldest
age groups, changes in the age composition of the population also influence the level of expenditure. The proportion of the population 65
years of age and over has increased steadily from 4.1 percent in 1900
to 9.4 percent in 1965. The proportion at ages 0 to 19 has increased from
33.1 percent in 1945 (the all-time-low census year) to 39.5 percent in
1964 and 1965. There is every indication that these trends will continue

---

[8] The surveys are described more fully below, pp. 30 ff.

TABLE 1-4

Increases in Per Capita Price and Use by Type of Service and Age Group, 1953–58 and 1953–63

| | Percent Increase | | | |
|---|---|---|---|---|
| | *1953–58* | | *1953–63* | |
| *Category* | *Price* | *Use* | *Price* | *Use* |
| All Health Services...................18.4 | 20.3 | 42 | 20 | |
| Physicians..........................17.9 | 5.2 | 33 | 6 | |
| Hospitals...........................33.9 | 26.4 | 90 | 18 | |
| Dentists............................12.3 | 24.7 | 26 | 19 | |
| Drugs.............................. 9.5 | 73.5 | 9 | 121 | |
| Age group | | | | |
| 0–5................................NAᵃ | 44.7 | 36 | 24 | |
| 6–17...............................NAᵃ | 8.9 | 34 | 10 | |
| 18–34..............................NAᵃ | 18.2 | 45 | 22 | |
| 35–54..............................NAᵃ | 14.0 | 43 | 32 | |
| 55–64..............................NAᵃ | 13.4 | 42 | 21 | |
| 65 and over.......................NAᵃ | 46.6 | 41 | 28 | |

ᵃ NA, not available.
Source: *Progress in Health Services,* February, 1960, and November–December, 1965.

TABLE 1-5

Per Capita National Health Expenditures, 1950–66ᵃ

| *Type of Expenditure* | *1950* | *1955* | *1960* | *1965* | *1966* |
|---|---|---|---|---|---|
| Total national health expenditures..........$ 84.49 | $108.67 | $149.25 | $210.12 | $230.69 |
| Health services and supplies............... 78.20 | $103.03 | 139.79 | 192.74 | 212.47 |
| Hospital care............................ 25.25 | 35.72 | 50.04 | 70.94 | 78.36 |
| Physicians' services..................... 18.09 | 22.17 | 31.45 | 44.93 | 47.70 |
| Dentists' services....................... 6.40 | 9.19 | 10.94 | 14.43 | 15.31 |
| Other professional services.............. 2.59 | 3.37 | 4.77 | 4.93 | 5.01 |
| Drugs and drug sundries................. 11.36 | 14.37 | 20.24 | 24.73 | 26.59 |
| Eyeglasses and appliances............... 3.22 | 3.60 | 4.29 | 6.28 | 8.10 |
| Nursing-home care...................... .93 | 1.34 | 2.91 | 6.80 | 7.63 |
| Expenses for prepayment and adminis-tration............................... 1.97 | 3.70 | 4.78 | 6.67 | 8.27 |
| Government public health activities....... 2.37 | 2.27 | 2.28 | 3.58 | 4.11 |
| Other health services.................... 6.02 | 7.30 | 8.09 | 9.44 | 11.39 |
| Total national health expenditures in 1966 pricesᵇ............................... 146.94 | 156.59 | 176.21 | 219.33 | 230.69 |

ᵃ Based on total population, including Armed Forces and Federal civilian employees abroad as of July 1.
ᵇ Based on medical care component of the consumer price index.
Source: Dorothy P. Rice and Barbara S. Cooper, "National Health Expenditures, 1950–66," *Social Security Bulletin,* April, 1968, p. 3.

CHART 1-2

Factors Affecting the Increase in Personal
Health Care Expenditures, 1950 and 1966

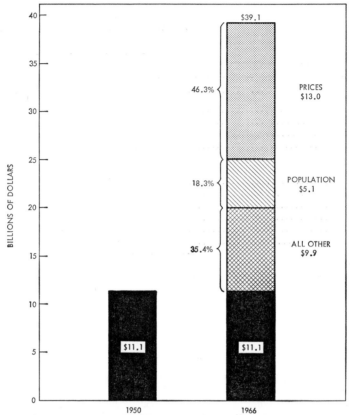

Source   Dorothy   P.   Rice   and   Barbara   S.   Cooper,   "National   Health   Expenditures,
1950–66," *Social Security Bulletin*, April, 1968, p. 3.

for future years. Demographers estimate that, by 1980, 9.4 percent to 9.8 percent of the population will be 65 and over, and 37.1 to 39.4 percent will be under 19.[9]

Table 1–5 shows per capita expenditures for selected years, and Chart 1–2 shows that price increase accounts for 46.3 percent of the increased national expenditure, and population change for 18.3 percent, a total of 64.6 percent. Thus, increased utilization rates and quality improvement account for only slightly more than one third of the national expenditure.

---

[9] U.S. Department of Health, Education, and Welfare. *Health, Education, and Welfare Trends*, 1965 ed., p. S–3. More recent estimates by various methods give the proportion age 65 in 1980 a range from 9.2 to 10.2 percent, and in 1990 from 9.0 to 10.6 percent. Robert J. Myers and Francisco Bayo, *Comparison of Recent Projections of the United States Population*, (Actuarial Note No. 37 [Washington, D.C.: Social Security Administration, Office of the Actuary, 1967]).

TABLE 1-6

U.S. Ratio of Personal Consumption Expenditures for Medical Care to Disposable Personal Income and to the Total Personal Consumption Expenditures

| Year | Personal consumption expenditures for medical care[a] (1) | Disposable personal income (2) | Total personal consumption expenditures (3) | Ratio of Col. (1) to Col. (2) (4) | Ratio of Col. (1) to Col. (3) (5) |
|---|---|---|---|---|---|
| 1948 | $ 7.5 | $189.1 | $173.6 | 4.0% | 4.3% |
| 1949 | 7.8 | 188.6 | 176.8 | 4.1 | 4.4 |
| 1950 | 8.5 | 206.9 | 191.0 | 4.1 | 4.5 |
| 1951 | 9.2 | 226.6 | 206.3 | 4.1 | 4.5 |
| 1952 | 9.9 | 238.3 | 216.7 | 4.2 | 4.6 |
| 1953 | 10.7 | 252.6 | 230.0 | 4.2 | 4.7 |
| 1954 | 11.6 | 257.4 | 236.5 | 4.5 | 4.9 |
| 1955 | 12.3 | 275.3 | 254.4 | 4.5 | 4.8 |
| 1956 | 13.4 | 293.2 | 266.7 | 4.6 | 5.0 |
| 1957 | 14.7 | 308.5 | 281.4 | 4.8 | 5.2 |
| 1958 | 16.0 | 318.8 | 290.1 | 5.0 | 5.5 |
| 1959 | 17.4 | 337.3 | 311.2 | 5.2 | 5.6 |
| 1960 | 18.9 | 350.0 | 325.2 | 5.4 | 5.8 |
| 1961 | 20.0 | 364.4 | 335.2 | 5.5 | 6.0 |
| 1962 | 21.6 | 385.3 | 355.1 | 5.6 | 6.1 |
| 1963 | 23.1 | 404.6 | 375.0 | 5.7 | 6.2 |
| 1964 | 26.0 | 438.1 | 401.2 | 6.1 | 6.5 |
| 1965 | 28.3 | 472.2 | 433.1 | 6.0 | 6.5 |
| 1966 | 30.1 | 508.8 | 465.9 | 5.9 | 6.5 |

[a] Includes expenses for health insurance.

Source: United States Department of Commerce, Health Insurance Association of America, and Health Insurance Institute.

The $30.1 billion of private expenditures for medical care is about 65 percent of total personal consumption expenditures. This proportion had remained stable for many years. From 1929 to 1955 the percentages varied from 4.1 to 4.5. However, since 1951, it has increased in every year except two, as indicated in Table 1–6.

The ratio of personal consumption expenditure for medical care to disposable income has been increasing at about the same rate, leveling off around six percent since 1964.[10]

## The nature of health losses

The loss of income from poor health is about $25 billion per year, of which almost half represents long-term disabilities. No further breakdown of these figures will be attempted. However, from the standpoint of the impact of health losses upon the individual, one should note that

[10] Health Insurance Institute, *1967 Source Book of Health Insurance Data* (New York, 1968). *Social Security Bulletin*, April, 1968.

this figure is almost equal to the $30 billion of private consumer expenditures for medical care.

From the standpoint of the family, the income of the breadwinner is the most important asset. When that income stops and is replaced with a heavy drain of resources, the family is "out of business." If that income can be continued, some way will be found to meet whatever expenses are incurred. They may have to reduce their standard of living, give up some of their installment purchases, or even go into debt. However, in the vast majority of cases, they will be able to get along. On the other hand, if the breadwinner's income stops and is not replaced, no amount of medical care protection will provide food, shelter, and clothing for the family. It is unfortunate that the emphasis of most discussions of health insurance has been only upon one side of the picture, medical expense—the side of lesser importance.

*Private medical care expenditures.* The nature of expenditures for medical care may be considered in somewhat more detail. The breakdown of these expenditures by type serves as a guide in planning the health progress of the nation, and as an important indication of the nature of the impact of these expenditures upon the family. Table 1–7 gives a comparison of the nature of the private expenditures for 1950, 1960, 1965, and 1966.

The first subtotal, "direct and third-party expenditures" represents actual net costs of medical care. Whether it is meaningful to include the net cost of obtaining health insurance (total benefits paid less total premiums received) as a medical expense is a matter about which theorists will differ. The welfare worker or sociologist might consider the cost of health insurance protection a part of the cost of health, but from the standpoint of insurance theory one cannot concur. The sum includes two elements: the operating expense and profit of the insurer, and increases in reserves for future losses. The former represents the cost of risk bearing and risk reducing: a distinct economic function. The latter represents an investment since these reserves, or more properly the assets held to offset them, represent a fund for future medical expenses which increase with age. Thus they are not properly a cost at all. Moreover, much of this item represents costs applicable to well people. Chart 1–3 shows the percentage distribution of medical care expenditures in 1966.

It will be noted that hospital expense continues as the largest element of private expenditure for medical care, with physician's fees making a close second. Drugs and drug sundries are the next most important; these three items together make up almost three fourths of the total. From 1950 to 1966 all increased in absolute amounts, but only hospital expenses, nursing home care, and the "cost of insurance" increased significantly as a proportion of the total. The other items all declined relatively. The reasons for the first have already been indicated; the last would

[TABLE 1-7]

Private Consumer Expenditures for Medical Care and Insurance Protection, U.S., 1950–66
(amounts in millions)

| | 1950 Amount | 1950 Percent | 1960 Amount | 1960 Percent | 1965 Amount | 1965 Percent | 1966 Amount | 1966 Percent |
|---|---|---|---|---|---|---|---|---|
| Total | $8,501 | 100.0 | $18,911 | 100.0 | $28,260 | 100.0 | $30,082 | 100.0 |
| Direct and third-party expenditures | 8,201 | 96.5 | 18,066 | 95.5 | 26,988 | 95.5 | 28,660 | 95.3 |
| Hospital care | 1,965 | 23.1 | 5,188 | 27.4 | 8,463 | 29.9 | 8,772 | 29.2 |
| Physicians' services | 2,597 | 30.5 | 5,309 | 28.1 | 8,184 | 29.0 | 8,608 | 28.6 |
| Dentist services | 961 | 11.3 | 1,974 | 10.4 | 2,773 | 9.8 | 2,959 | 9.8 |
| Other professional services | 370 | 4.4 | 826 | 4.4 | 895 | 3.2 | 905 | 3.0 |
| Drugs and drug sundries | 1,716 | 20.2 | 3,598 | 19.0 | 4,671 | 16.5 | 5,049 | 16.8 |
| Eyeglasses and appliances | 482 | 5.7 | 760 | 4.0 | 1,193 | 4.2 | 1,560 | 5.2 |
| Nursing home care | 110 | 1.3 | 411 | 2.2 | 809 | 2.9 | 807 | 2.7 |
| Net cost of health insurance | 300 | 3.5 | 845 | 4.5 | 1,272 | 4.5 | 1,422 | 4.7 |

Source: Ruth S. Hanft, "National Health Expenditures, 1950–65," Social Security Bulletin, February, 1967, p. 12; Dorothy P. Rice and Barbara S. Cooper, "National Health Expenditures; 1950–66," Social Security Bulletin, April, 1968, p. 3.

CHART 1–3

Distribution of Public and Private Health Expenditures,
by Type of Expenditure, 1966

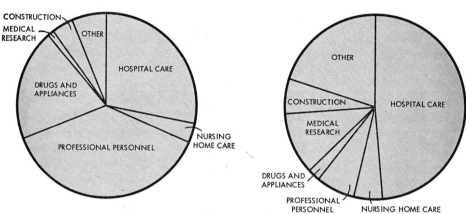

PRIVATE EXPENDITURES
Total —$32.5 Billion

PUBLIC EXPENDITURES
Total —$12.9 Billion

Source: Dorothy P. Rice and Barbara S. Cooper, "National Health Expenditures, 1950–66,"
*Social Security Bulletin,* April, 1968, p. 3.

be expected to increase with the growth of private health insurance. Physicians' fees have declined from the most important to the second most important item. One survey[11] indicated that, of total physicians' services, about 20 percent is for surgery and about 10 percent for obstetrics.

*Public medical care expenditures.* Table 1–8 shows the distribution of public expenditures for medical care in 1959–60, 1965–66, and 1966–67. Examination of these figures indicates that publc health expenditures no longer are preponderantly a state, as distinguished from a federal, function. The institution of Medicare and Title XIX programs and the increased expenditures under veterans' and military programs have increased the federal expenditure to almost twice that of the states in only one year. Moreover, national government financing of medical research has increased twenty-fold since 1950 and is now almost 23 times state research expenditures.

To the extent to which costs of hospital construction exceed depreciation, obsolescence, and withdrawal of existing facilities, this does not represent a current cost but rather an investment for the future. Some investment is, of course, inherent in many of the items which go to make up the category "other community services." Looking behind these figures, all the items except research, hospital construction, and other community services represent direct expenditures for medical care and rehabilitation. Hospital care accounts for almost 50 percent of federal

---

[11] *Progress in Health Services,* February, 1960.

TABLE 1-8

Public Expenditures for Health, U. S., Fiscal Years 1950, 1956 and 1957

(amounts In millions of dollars)

| Type of Expenditure | 1959-60 | | | 1965-66 | | | 1966-67[a] | | |
|---|---|---|---|---|---|---|---|---|---|
| | Total | Federal | State & Local | Total | Federal | State & Local | Total | Federal | State & Local |
| Public expenditures | 6,395.2 | 2,917.6 | 3,477.5 | 11,044.7 | 5,635.6 | 5,409.0 | 15,168.1 | 10,285.9 | 5,882.2 |
| Health and medical services | 5,346.3 | 2,174.8 | 3,171.5 | 8,933.9 | 3,921.8 | 5,012.0 | 13,786.9 | 8,344.8 | 5,442.2 |
| OASDHI (health insurance for the aged) | — | — | — | 63.6 | 63.6 | — | 3,394.6 | 3,394.6 | — |
| Temporary disability insurance (medical benefits)[†] | 40.2 | — | 40.2 | 54.3 | — | 54.3 | 56.0 | — | 55.0 |
| Workmen's compensation (medical benefits)[b] | 420.0 | 9.0 | 411.0 | 630.0 | 11.8 | 618.2 | 685.0 | 12.0 | 673.0 |
| Public assistance (vendor medical payments) | 492.7 | 199.8 | 292.9 | 1,709.9 | 758.0 | 951.9 | 2,318.3 | 1,134.7 | 1,183.6 |
| General hospital and medical care | 1,973.2 | 103.4 | 1,869.8 | 2,720.3 | 146.2 | 2,574.1 | 2,790.8 | 158.3 | 2,632.5 |
| Defense Department hospital and medical Care | 820.1 | 820.1 | — | 1,273.4 | 1,273.4 | — | 1,571.8 | 1,571.8 | — |
| Military dependent's medical care | 60.0 | 60.0 | — | 76.2 | 76.2 | — | 150.8 | 150.8 | — |
| Maternal and child health services | 140.7 | 34.7 | 106.1 | 276.2 | 108.1 | 168.1 | 306.8 | 128.6 | 178.2 |
| School health (educational agencies) | 101.0 | — | 101.0 | 135.0 | — | 135.0 | 140.0 | — | 140.0 |
| Other public health activities | 401.2 | 57.3 | 343.9 | 723.8 | 228.8 | 494.9 | 900.0 | 342.1 | 558.8 |
| Veterans' hospital and medical care | 879.4 | 879.4 | — | 1,175.2 | 1,175.2 | — | 1,271.3 | 1,271.3 | — |
| Medical vocational rehabilitation | 17.7 | 11.2 | 6.6 | 48.0 | 32.4 | 15.5 | 80.5 | 60.4 | 20.1 |
| OEO health and medical care | — | — | — | 48.2 | 48.2 | — | 120.2 | 120.2 | — |
| Medical research | 471.2 | 448.2 | 23.0 | 1,379.7 | 1,318.8 | 61.0 | 1,540.5 | 1,475.4 | 65.0 |
| Medical-facilities construction | 577.7 | 294.7 | 283.0 | 731.0 | 395.0 | 336.0 | 840.6 | 465.7 | 375.0 |
| Defense Department | 40.0 | 40.0 | — | 28.6 | 28.6 | — | 58.5 | 58.5 | — |
| Veterans Administration | 59.6 | 59.6 | — | 86.0 | 86.0 | — | 51.0 | 86.0 | — |
| Other | 478.1 | 195.1 | 283.0 | 616.4 | 280.4 | 336.0 | 731.2 | 356.2 | 375.0 |

a Preliminary estimates.

b Includes medical benefits paid under public law by private insurance carriers and self-insurers.

Source: Barbara S. Cooper, "Revised Public and Private Expenditures for Health and Medical Care, Fiscal Years 1960–67." U.S. Department of Health, Education, and Welfare, Social Security Administration, Research and Statistics Note No. 7–1968.

expenditures and over 40 percent of state expenditures, in contrast to the private sector, as dramatized in Chart 1–3.

## The impact of health losses

The average person loses about two weeks' work from disability each year. The average family expenditure is $370, the average individual expenditure is $112. If everybody incurred these losses according to the average, the problem of financing would not be acute except at the lower income brackets. If every family incurred such losses according to the average for its own income bracket, the problems would be even less. For all income brackets the mean medical expenses are about 5.6 percent of average family income.[12] For the average person the breakdown is $35

TABLE 1–9

Mean and Median Gross Health Charges Incurred by Families for Personal Health Services, by Family Income and Insurance Status, 1963

| Family Income | Mean Gross Charges | | | Median Gross Charges | | |
|---|---|---|---|---|---|---|
| | All Families | In- sured | Un- insured | All Families | In- sured | Un- insured |
| Total, all income groups........$370 | $429 | $201 | $209 | $255 | $111 |
| Under $2,000.................... 228 | 292 | 162 | 86 | 100 | 72 |
| $2,000–$3,499................... 245 | 337 | 144 | 104 | 149 | 79 |
| $3,500–$4,999................... 289 | 322 | 212 | 169 | 186 | 115 |
| $5,000–$7,499................... 407 | 438 | 253 | 255 | 265 | 168 |
| $7,500 and over................ 480 | 501 | 317 | 316 | 333 | 201 |

Source: Ronald Andersen and Odin W. Anderson, *A Decade of Health Services* (Chicago: University of Chicago Press, 1967).

for physicians, $29 for hospitals, $23 for medicine, $15 for dentists, and $10 for other medical expense.

The average expenditure for various family income levels in 1962–63 is indicated by Table 1–9. These data would seem to indicate that, *on the average*, the level of expenditure for medical care increases in direct proportion to ability to pay for it, as evidenced both by income level and by whether or not the family has insurance. Thus it would seem that the typical family would not have any great difficulty in meeting the burden of such costs. However, averages conceal as much as they reveal. It is

---

[12] *Progress in Health Services*, Nov.–Dec., 1965. This is not quite the same as a breakdown of the national totals by dividing by the number of families for two reasons: (1) this survey is based on an actual field probability sample, while the *Social Security Bulletin* data are based on national aggregates; (2) the two studies used somewhat differing definitions.

necessary to investigate the distribution of these costs about their averages in order to assess the impact upon family finances.

*The impact of income losses.* An average loss of about two weeks' income from disability would not be tragic for a typical family. However, the burden of such income loss is not spread uniformly over the population. Accidental injury and disease are largely unpredictable, and the disabilities they produce vary greatly in duration. The vast majority of all disabilities are short. As indicated above, about half the aggregate disability income loss is accounted for by disabilities lasting under six months or the first six months of longer term disabilities. An indication of the magnitude of the longer term loss is given by the number of persons in the population at any time who are disabled and have been disabled for six months or longer. Table 1–10 gives such an estimate for 1963, based on the prevalence rates found in the National Health Survey of 1935–36[13] and the 1949–50 survey of the Census Bureau[14] and adjusted to 1963 population.

TABLE 1–10

Estimated Number of Persons Disabled,[a] U.S., 1963, by Age

| Age | Noninstitutional (000's) | Institutional (000's) | Total (000's) | Percentage of Population |
|---|---|---|---|---|
| Under 25 | 323.3 | 164.8 | 488.1 | 0.56 |
| Ages 25–45 | 1,135.3 | 272.3 | 1,407.6 | 2.99 |
| Ages 45–64 | 1,616.5 | 399.2 | 2,015.7 | 5.33 |
| Age 65 and over | 763.5 | 625.6 | 1,389.1 | 7.95 |
| Total | 2,838.6 | 1,461.9 | 4,300.6 | 2.27 |

[a] Disabled here defined as the inability to carry on major activity.
Source: Dorothy P. Rice, *Estimating the Cost of Illness,* U.S. Department of Health, Education, and Welfare, Public Health Service Publication No. 947–6, May, 1966.

Skolnik prepared estimates in 1964 of the number of persons with long-term disability (more than six months) aged 14 to 64 in order to compare this with the number receiving disability benefits under various public programs. As extrapolated to 1967, this estimates the number with long-

[13] *The National Health Survey, 1935–1936: Significance, Scope and Method of a Nation-wide Family Canvass of Sickness in Relation to Its Social and Economic Setting* (Washington, D.C.: U.S. Public Health Service, Division of Public Health Methods, 1938). See also an earlier study, I. S. Falk, Margaret C. Klim, and Nathan Sinai, *The Incidence of Illness and the Receipt and Costs of Medical Care among Representative Families: Experiences in Twelve Consecutive Months during 1928–1931,* ("Publications of the Committee on the Costs of Medical Care," Report No. 26 [Chicago: University of Chicago Press, 1933]).

[14] Marjorie E. Moore and Barkev S. Sanders, "Extent of Total Disability in the United States," *Social Security Bulletin,* November, 1950; Moore and Sanders, *Estimates of the Prevalence of Disability in the United States,* September, 1950, (Rehabilitation Service Series, No. 317 [Washington, D.C.: Office of Vocational Rehabilitation and Social Security Administration, April, 1955]).

term disability at 3.5 million persons aged 14 to 64, of whom 2.38 million or 68 percent were receiving benefits under public programs, as shown in Table 1–11.

More recent Social Security Survey data show much larger numbers disabled. Based on a mail survey and follow-up interviews with a sub-sample, this study estimated that 6.1 million persons aged 18 to 64, not in institutions, considered themselves "severely disabled"; an additional 5.0 million said they were occupationally disabled (unable to work full time or unable to do the same work as before); and 6.6 million had secondary work limitations. This totals to 17.8 million disabled in some degree for more than six months in the civilian noninstitutional population aged 18 to 64 in 1966. Tables 1–12 and 1–13 give the details of the study. The survey design defined severe disability as inability to work altogether or inability to work regularly. It is believed that the Skolnik figure of 3.5 million is a

TABLE 1–11

Long-Term Disability Benefits—Number of Persons Aged 14–64 Receiving Cash Payments from Public Income-Maintenance Programs: 1939 to 1967

(in thousands, except percent. As of December. Covers persons aged 14–64 with physical or mental disease or impairments that, for more than 6 months, have prevented them from working or following their normal activities on a regular basis)

| Source of Payment | 1939 | 1949 | 1954 | 1959 | 1964 | 1967 |
|---|---|---|---|---|---|---|
| Total disabled.............................. | 2,300 | 2,700 | 2,900 | 3,100 | 3,350 | 3,500 |
| Number receiving payments.............. | 290 | 490 | 865 | 1,290 | 1,915 | 2,380 |
| Percent of total......................... | 12.6 | 18.1 | 29.8 | 41.6 | 57.2 | 68.0 |
| | | | | | | |
| Federal employee retirement.............. | 40 | 80 | 110 | 135 | 170 | 172 |
| State and local government employee | | | | | | |
| retirement.......................... | 10 | 20 | 30 | 35 | 50 | 87 |
| Workmen's compensation................. | 45 | 60 | 70 | 75 | 75 | 75 |
| Veterans' compensation and pension | | | | | | |
| programs[a] ........................... | 160 | 275 | 385 | 330 | 285 | 300 |
| Railroad retirement...................... | 15 | 40 | 45 | 45 | 40 | 40 |
| | | | | | | |
| Old-age, survivors, disability, and health insurance:[b] | | | | | | |
| Worker disability........................ | (d) | (d) | (d) | 335 | 895 | 1,193 |
| Childhood disability..................... | (d) | (d) | (d) | 80 | 185 | 225 |
| | | | | | | |
| Public assistance: | | | | | | |
| Aid to the blind......................... | 40 | 50 | 55 | 55 | 60 | 83 |
| Aid to the permanently and totally | | | | | | |
| disabled[c] .............................. | (d) | (d) | 220 | 340 | 510 | 646 |

[a] Payments to veterans reported as having disability ratings of 70 percent or more.
[b] Worker disability program initiated in 1957; childhood disability (disabled children of disabled workers) in 1958.
[c] Program initiated October, 1950.
[d] Program not in effect.
Source: U.S. Department of Health, Education, and Welfare, Social Security Administration; Social Security Bulletin, October, 1964 and April, 1968; Research and Statistics Note No. 9–1960 and unpublished data.

TABLE 1–12

Prevalence of Long-Term Disability by Severity of Disability and Sex
(number and percent of noninstitutional population aged 18–64, Spring, 1966)

| Severity of Disability | Total | | Men | | Women | |
|---|---|---|---|---|---|---|
| | Number (in millions) | Percent | Number (in millions) | Percent | Number (in millions) | Percent |
| Total[a]................ | 103.0 | 100.0 | 49.0 | 100.0 | 54.1 | 100.0 |
| Disabled longer than 6 months................. | 17.8 | 17.2 | 8.4 | 17.2 | 9.3 | 17.2 |
| Severe.................... | 6.1 | 5.9 | 2.3 | 4.7 | 3.8 | 7.0 |
| Occupational.............. | 5.0 | 4.9 | 2.4 | 4.9 | 2.6 | 4.8 |
| Secondary work limitation.. | 6.6 | 6.4 | 3.7 | 7.6 | 2.9 | 5.4 |

[a] Data from special tabulation of *Current Population Survey*, March, 1966, U.S. Bureau of the Census.

better estimate of those who might be considered disabled sufficiently to be eligible for disability benefits under public or private insurance programs.

Disability lasting more than six months produces a major impact on family finances. The income loss will be half of the annual income or more, if the disabled person was earning income. Even if the disabled person was a housewife, the loss of her services for such an extended period represents a major economic loss. About 73 percent of those disabled noninstitutionalized persons age 14 to 64 in the 1949 study had been in the labor force before the onset of disability. The proportion in the labor force was 86 percent for men and 51 percent for women. Most of the men who had never worked probably had had no opportunity to do so, having been disabled before the working age. These also represent a loss of income— although of potential income only.

The 1949 study showed that the mean duration of disability among the civilian noninstitutional population age 14 to 64 was 270 weeks,[15] but the median was only about five months. The great difference indicates the extreme skewness of the distribution. Most disabilities are short, but most of the persons disabled at a given time have been disabled a long time, and most of the wage loss is accounted for by long-term disability. Table 1–14 gives an estimate of the distribution by duration.

The 50 percent of disabled persons who suffer an income loss of four months' earnings or more are those upon whom the impact of disability is heaviest. In addition to the loss of earnings, they also incur costs for medical care, which tend to increase with increasing disability duration, although less than proportionally. The psychological disintegrating effects

[15] This is higher than the 3½-year estimate on p. 17 above, since the shorter estimate was based on insured lives.

TABLE 1-13
Severity of Disability by Labor Force Status and Sex
(percentage distribution of noninstitutional population aged 18–64
by severity, Spring, 1966)

| Labor Force and Work Status | U.S. Population[a] (in thousands) | Percentage Distribution | | | | | |
|---|---|---|---|---|---|---|---|
| | | Total | Severity of Disability[c] | | | | |
| | | | Non-disabled[b] | All Disabled | Severe | Occupational | Secondary Work Limitation |
| *Total* | | | | | | | |
| Total............. | 103,085 | 100.0 | 82.8 | 17.2 | 5.9 | 4.9 | 6.4 |
| Not in labor force....... | 34,177 | 100.0 | 75.4 | 24.6 | 14.3 | 5.1 | 5.2 |
| In labor force.......... | 68,908 | 100.0 | 86.6 | 13.4 | 1.7 | 4.7 | 7.0 |
| Employed............. | 66,358 | 100.0 | 87.2 | 12.8 | 1.5 | 4.5 | 6.9 |
| Unemployed.......... | 2,550 | 100.0 | 72.5 | 27.5 | 6.9 | 10.3 | 10.2 |
| *Men* | | | | | | | |
| Total............. | 48,982 | 100.0 | 82.8 | 17.2 | 4.7 | 4.9 | 7.6 |
| Not in labor force........ | 4,645 | 100.0 | 53.2 | 46.8 | 35.8 | 2.6 | 8.5 |
| In labor force.......... | 44,337 | 100.0 | 86.0 | 14.0 | 1.4 | 5.2 | 7.4 |
| Employed............. | 42,815 | 100.0 | 86.5 | 13.5 | 1.2 | 5.0 | 7.3 |
| Unemployed.......... | 1,522 | 100.0 | 71.4 | 28.6 | 7.6 | 10.6 | 10.4 |
| *Women* | | | | | | | |
| Total............. | 54,103 | 100.0 | 82.8 | 17.2 | 7.0 | 4.8 | 5.4 |
| Not in labor force....... | 29,532 | 100.0 | 78.9 | 21.1 | 10.9 | 5.5 | 4.7 |
| In labor force.......... | 24,571 | 100.0 | 87.6 | 12.4 | 2.3 | 3.9 | 6.2 |
| Employed............. | 23,543 | 100.0 | 88.3 | 11.7 | 2.1 | 3.6 | 6.0 |
| Unemployed.......... | 1,028 | 100.0 | 74.1 | 25.9 | 5.9 | 9.8 | 10.0 |

[a] Data from special tabulation of *Current Population Survey,* March 1966, U.S. Bureau of the Census.

[b] Includes adults disabled 6 months or less; obtained by subtracting total disabled longer than 6 months from the civilian noninstitutional population aged 18–64.

[c] Disabled longer than 6 months.

Source: Lawrence D. Haber, "Prevalence of Disability among Non-Institutional Adults under Age 65: 1966 Survey of Disabled Adults," U.S. Department of Health, Education, and Welfare, Social Security Administration, *Research and Statistics Note* No. 4–1968.

of disability also increase with duration. Occupational skill is lost, self-confidence declines, and the tendency toward despair increases. A major change in the way of life may be necessary if disability is long continued. If the disabled person was the main income provider for the family, someone else must take over this responsibility, giving up housekeeping or education for the purpose. Family savings are probably insufficient to pay for the heavy expenses of medical care and leave anything over to cushion the income loss. When the wife and mother must give up her main responsibility of supervising the household, either because she is

TABLE 1–14

Duration of Disability by Number of Persons and Percent in the Civilian Noninstitutional Population Aged 14–64, U.S., 1949

| Duration of Disability | Estimated Number Disabled (thousands) | Percent |
|---|---|---|
| 1 week and under..................................... | 1,131 | 24.8 |
| Over 1 week to 1 month.............................. | 690 | 15.1 |
| Over 1 month but under 4 months.................... | 395 | 8.6 |
| 4 months but under 7 months........................ | 246 | 5.4 |
| 7 months to 18 months.............................. | 405 | 8.9 |
| Over 18 months but under 10 years.................. | 1,027 | 22.5 |
| 10 years and over.................................. | 622 | 13.6 |
| Duration not reported.............................. | 3 | 1.2 |
| Total............................................ | 4,569 | 100.0 |

Source: Marjorie E. Moore and Barkev S. Sanders, "Extent of Total Disability in the United States," *Social Security Bulletin,* November, 1950, p. 7.

disabled or because she must go to work to support a disabled husband, the children suffer from lack of care and supervision and become potential recruits for the delinquent or maladjusted population. The family must give up plans for higher education and adapt to a lower standard of living. If its members are forced to rely on public financial aid, their morale and self-reliance decline. They may have to move to low-rent areas, perhaps even slums, and expose their children to the hazards of vice, crime, and disease.

A single person living alone is even worse off than the family man, because there is no one to share his burden and provide love, comfort, and support. He must rely on institutional care or private nursing—either on a charitable basis or at a tremendous cost. Ill, lonely, and nonproductive, he is a burden to himself and society. Truly, the "living death" of long-term disability is the worst of all.

*The impact of medical care costs.* Just as the duration of disability falls unevenly upon individuals and family units, so does the impact of medical care expenditures. Some of this variation is explained by differences in expenditure by age and sex. Table 1–15 gives average expenditures by age and sex from the three Health Information Foundation surveys. Generally, expenditures increase with age and are higher for females than males. This is one reason for the government involvement in health insurance for the aged, discussed in Chapter 4 below. All age groups showed increased expenditures from 1952–53 to 1962–63, but the greatest increases were for the age groups 35–54 and 65 and over. The expenditures of the group under age 6 also increased substantially, almost to equal that for the group aged 6 to 17. The oldest age group had per

TABLE 1–15

Personal Consumption Expenditures for Health by Age and Sex, U.S., 1952–53, 1957–58, and 1962–63

| Age & Sex | Expenditures per Person | | | Percent Increase: 1952–53 to 1962–63 | July–Dec., 1962 National Health Survey |
|---|---|---|---|---|---|
| | *1952–53* | *1957–58* | *1962–63* | | |
| All persons.........$ 66 | | $ 94 | $112 | 69.7 | $129 |
| Under 6............. 28 | | 47 | 48 | 71.4 | 61 |
| 6–17................ 38 | | 49 | 56 | 47.4 | 64[a] |
| 18–34............... 70 | | 98 | 124 | 77.1 | 121[b] |
| 35–54............... 80 | | 108 | 151 | 88.8 | 144[c] |
| 55–64............... 96 | | 129 | 165 | 71.9 | 191[d] |
| 65 and over......... 102 | | 177 | 185 | 81.4 | 208 |
| Males.............. 51 | | 77 | 92 | 80.4 | 111 |
| Females............ 80 | | 111 | 131 | 63.8 | 144 |

[a] 6–16
[b] 17–24
[c] 25–44
[d] 45–64

Source: *Progress in Health Services*, February, 1960, and December, 1965; Elijah L. White, *Personal Health Expenses: Per Capital Annual Expenses, U.S.: July–December, 1962* (National Center for Health Statistics, Series 10, No. 27 [Washington, D.C.: U.S. Government Printing Office, 1966]).

capita expenditures more than three and one half times as great as that for the youngest groups in 1957–58, and in 1962–63, almost four times as great.

Table 1–16 gives the breakdown by type of expenditure for 1962–63.

Chart 1–4 indicates the proportionate distribution of types of charge for various age groups.

TABLE 1–16

Personal Consumption Expenditures for Health by Component, Age, and Sex, U.S., 1962–63

| Age & Sex | All Services[a] | Physicians | Hospitals | Drugs & Medicine | Dentists | Other Medical |
|---|---|---|---|---|---|---|
| All persons......$112 | | $35 | $29 | $24 | $15 | $10 |
| Under 6......... 48 | | 22 | 9 | 14 | 1 | 2 |
| 6–17............ 56 | | 16 | 8 | 11 | 16 | 6 |
| 18–34........... 124 | | 42 | 37 | 17 | 19 | 9 |
| 35–54........... 151 | | 45 | 42 | 32 | 18 | 15 |
| 55–64........... 165 | | 45 | 36 | 40 | 17 | 20 |
| 65 and over...... 185 | | 52 | 52 | 50 | 11 | 20 |
| Males.......... 92 | | 29 | 22 | 20 | 13 | 9 |
| Females........ 131 | | 40 | 35 | 26 | 16 | 12 |

[a]Totals do not always equal the sum of components because of rounding.
Source: *Progress in Health Services*, November–December, 1965.

CHART 1–4

Percentage Distribution of Individual Medical Expenditures according to Type of Service by Age and Sex, U.S., 1963[a]

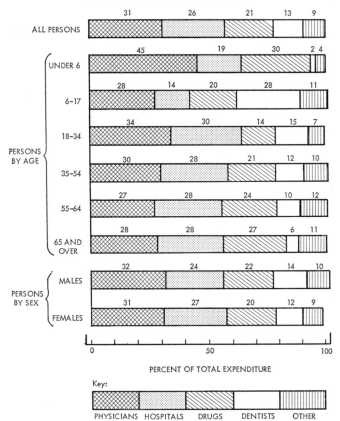

PERCENT OF TOTAL EXPENDITURE

Key:

PHYSICIANS    HOSPITALS    DRUGS    DENTISTS    OTHER

[a] Totals do not add to 100 percent because of rounding.
Source: *Progress in Health Services*, November–December, 1965.

Three consumer studies reveal similar distributions of medical care expenditures among families, by amount, as indicated in Table 1–17.

According to the 1962–63 study, the low-spending third of the families spent only 3 percent of the total, while the high-spending third accounted for 81 percent of total expenditures. Eight percent of the families incurred expenses in excess of $1,000, but this accounted for 36 percent of the total spent by all families. Few families could afford such an amount of expense without disruption of their finances. Chart 1–5 depicts this relationship dramatically.

In the 1957–58 study, the low-spending ($1 to $99) third of the families spent only about 5 percent of the total amount, while the high-

TABLE 1-17

Family Medical Care Expenditures by Amount

| Annual Expenditure per Family (dollars) | Percent of Families | | | Percent of Total Charges | | |
|---|---|---|---|---|---|---|
| | 1953 | 1958 | 1963 | 1953 | 1958 | 1963 |
| Under $50 | 29.8 | 20.2 | 17.8 | 2.3 | 5 | 3 |
| $50–99 | 15.8 | 14.0 | 11.7 | 5.2 | | |
| $100–199 | 20.1 | 20.7 | 18.7 | 13.6 | 21 | 16 |
| $200–299 | 11.8 | 13.5 | 12.8 | 13.7 | | |
| $300–399 | 7.0 | 9.2 | 9.5 | 11.5 | | |
| $400–499 | 4.9 | 5.7 | 6.3 | 10.5 | | |
| $500–749 | 6.3 | 8.3 | 10.0 | 17.9 | 74 | 81 |
| $750–999 | 2.3 | 3.8 | 5.1 | 9.7 | | |
| $1,000–1,999 | 1.6 | 3.9 | 6.5 | 9.4 | | |
| $2,000–over | 0.4 | 0.7 | 1.6 | 6.2 | | |

Source: Ronald Andersen and Odin W. Anderson, *A Decade of Health Services* (Chicago: University of Chicago Press, 1967); and Odin W. Anderson with Jacob J. Feldman, *Family Medical Cost and Voluntary Health Insurance* (New York: McGraw-Hill Book Co., 1956).

expenditure group, again about one third of the total, spent 74 percent of the total.

The 1952–53 study indicates that about 11 percent of the families studied incurred expenditures of $500 or more, and that this made up 43 percent of the total charges. This corresponds pretty closely with the results of previous studies. The Committee on the Costs of Medical Care study showed 10.5 percent of the families bearing 41 percent of the total cost, and an even earlier study in 1918–19 showed that 14 percent of the families bore 41 percent of the total burden.[16]

Thus, according to the most recent study, about 3 percent of the families incur costs of less than $100; and about 19 percent incur costs of less than $300. There are few families who could not meet costs aggregating $100 in a year, and most families easily could meet costs up to $300 in a year. But how can the typical family meet costs of $1,000 and over? Yet one family in 12 incurred costs of this magnitude. One in eight incurred costs of $750 or more, and one in four incurred costs of $500 or more. The uneven incidence of costs points up the necessity for some means of meeting the financial impact of health costs. Of course, few families would incur costs of such magnitude in more than one year in a row. Thus, they could average their costs over time.

Another indication of the impact of family health costs on finances is given by relating these costs to family income. Table 1–18 gives such

[16] United States Bureau of Labor Statistics, *Cost of Living in the United States* (Washington, D.C.: U.S. Government Printing Office, 1924), p. 444.

CHART 1–5

Percent of All Family Expenditures for Health Attributable to Families with Various
Levels of Expenditures, 1963

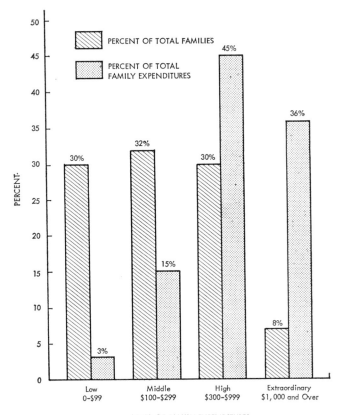

LEVEL OF FAMILY EXPENDITURES

Source: *Progress in Health Services,* November–December, 1965.

a breakdown. Eighty percent of the families incurred expenses of 9
percent or less of family income, after deducting insurance proceeds and
adding in insurance premiums paid. For these families, the cost of medical care should be readily budgetable. But for the 6 or 7 percent of
families which had expenditures exceeding 20 percent of family income,
and especially the 1 or 2 percent whose expenditures exceeded 50 percent, the burden must have been terrific. In evaluating these data, it
should be recognized that including the effect of insurance for the families who carried it tends to make the distribution more uniform and level
out some of the extreme differences. Unfortunately, the data were not
presented in terms of gross charges before considering insurance.

On the average, the amounts spent in relation to family income in-

TABLE 1–18

Net Outlay for All Personal Health Services, including
Insurance, as a Percentage of Family Income, U.S.,
1952–53, 1957–58, and 1962–63.

| Net Health Outlay as a Percent of Family Income | Percent of Families Incurring Various Magnitudes of Health Expenses | | |
|---|---|---|---|
| | 1952–53 | 1957–58 | 1962–63 |
| No Outlay................. 5% | 2% ⎫ | 50% |
| Under 5%................53% | 52% ⎭ | |
| 5–9%....................22% | 26% | 29% |
| 10–19%..................12% | 14% | 13% |
| 20–49%.................. 5% | 5% ⎫ | |
| 50–99%.................. 1% | 1% ⎬ | 7% |
| 100% or over............. 1% | * ⎭ | |

* Less than 0.5 percent.
Source: Ronald Andersen and Odin W. Anderson, *A Decade of Health Services* (Chicago: University of Chicago Press, 1967).

crease with rising income levels but decrease as a percentage of income. In 1963 families with incomes under $2,000 spent 15.7 percent of their income on medical care, while families with incomes over $7,500 spent only 3.8 percent. Table 1–19 shows the pattern in all three surveys.

Another measure of the impact of health costs on the family is provided by the extent to which families have to go into debt in order to meet such costs. The 1952–53 study indicates that 15 percent of American families were in debt for medical services and that 2 percent of families were in debt for amounts of $195 or more. It is somewhat surprising that these figures are not greater, in view of the data presented above as to the magnitude of total expenditure, but it must be recognized that these figures include only debt owed *to* purveyors of medical services. The amount of debt owed to financial institutions and individuals was not

TABLE 1–19

Cash Outlay for Personal Health Services as a
Percent of Family Income, 1953, 1958, and 1963

| Income | Year | | |
|---|---|---|---|
| | 1953 | 1958 | 1963 |
| Under $2,000................11.8 | 13.0 | 15.7 |
| $2,000–3,499................. 6.1 | 8.4 | 8.5 |
| $3,500–4,999................. 5.4 | 6.4 | 6.8 |
| $5,000–7,499................. 4.7 | 5.4 | 5.6 |
| $7,500-over................. 3.0 | 3.9 | 3.8 |
| Total................. 4.8 | 3.5 | 5.0 |

Source: Ronald Andersen and Odin W. Anderson, *A Decade of Health Services* (Chicago: University of Chicago Press, 1967).

revealed; it is probable that such debts for medical services aggregate a considerable amount.

The amounts spent for medical care by families tend to be higher for higher income groups, for families with insurance, for urban families, and for families with older members. The likelihood of debt is greatest among the lower income groups. Families with children tend to have higher expenditures and more frequent debt than those with no children.

**Summary**

Man is exposed to many risks of loss to his person and property, of which poor health from accidental injury or disease is one of the most important. As people have combined their efforts to satisfy other human needs, so have they developed social devices for meeting the need for security against various perils, including that of poor health. These social devices include prevention, transfer of risk, and combination of risks. Insurance is a highly organized device for the reduction of risk, which means uncertainty as to loss, by means of such combination. This book is concerned with insurance against losses from poor health.

Poor health costs this country about $70 billion per year, which is 30 percent loss of income and 70 percent expenditures for medical care. The income loss is about half short term and half long term. The expenditures for medical care are financed about two thirds by private expenditure, about one eighth by state governments, and about one fourth by the federal government.

About 29 percent of the private consumer expenditures for medical care go to hospitals, about 29 percent to physicians, and about 22 percent for drugs and appliances. Most of the federal expenditures go for Hospital Insurance for the aged, veterans' care and public assistance, and most of the state expenditures go for public health programs, especially hospital and medical care for the tubercular and mentally ill.

The average person loses about two weeks' work from disability a year; the average family spends $370 for medical care. If everyone incurred losses according to the average, meeting these losses would not be a problem. However, the losses are very unevenly distributed. Thus a very small percentage of the families bear the preponderant portion of such losses. This inequality of the burden makes it hard to bear and makes social devices for the reduction of risk and spreading of costs very important.

The following chapter discusses the responsibility of society in meeting risk and the main types of devices for meeting risk and examines facilities for providing medical care and the devices designed to prevent or mitigate poor health. Chapter 3 will begin the discussion of devices to meet the financial impact of poor health.

## Selected references

*See the following items from the General Bibliography: 1; 2; 3; 4, ch. 1;
8, ch. 1; 10 ch. 1; 12; 13 chs. 14 & 17; 15, ch. 3; 20, ch. 1; 23, ch. 1; 25,
ch. 1; 27, chs. 3, 4, and 6; 28, ch. 1; 29, chs. 9 & 11.*

AMERICAN MEDICAL ASSOCIATION. *Report of the Commission on the Cost of Medical Care*, Vols. I–IV. 1964.

ANDERSON, ODIN W. *Voluntary Health Insurance in Two Cities.* Cambridge, Mass.: Harvard University Press, 1957.

DAVIS, M. M. *Medical Care for Tomorrow.* New York: Harper & Bros., 1955.

DUBLIN, LOUIS I. *Factbook on Man: From Birth to Death.* 2d ed. New York: Macmillan Co., 1965.

HANFT, RUTH S. "National Health Expenditures, 1950–65," *Social Security Bulletin*, February, 1967, p. 3.

HUEBNER, SOLOMON S. *The Economics of Health Insurance.* Philadelphia: American College of Life Underwriters, 1962.

LASSITER, ROY L., JR. "The Wife's Contribution to Family Income," *Journal of Insurance*, Vol. XXVIII, No. 4 (December, 1961).

NATIONAL SAFETY COUNCIL, STATISTICS DIVISION. *Accident Facts, 1966.* Chicago, 1966.

REED, LOUIS S. "Private Health Insurance: Coverage and Financial Experience, 1940–66." *Social Security Bulletin*, November, 1967, p. 3.

RICE, DOROTHY P. *Estimating the Cost of Illness.* Health Economics Series, No. 6. Washington, D.C.: U.S. Government Printing Office, May, 1966.

RICE, DOROTHY P. AND COOPER, BARBARA S. "National Health Expenditures, 1950–66," *Social Security Bulletin*, April, 1968, p. 3.

RICE, DOROTHY P., AND HOROWITZ, LOUCELE A. "Trends in Medical Care Prices," *Social Security Bulletin*, July, 1967, p. 13.

SKOLNIK, ALFRED M. "Estimated Prevalence of Long-Term Disability, 1954," *Social Security Bulletin*, June, 1955, p. 20.

U.S. DEPARTMENT OF HEALTH, EDUCATION, AND WELFARE, NATIONAL OFFICE OF VITAL STATISTICS. *Health and Demography.* Washington, D.C.: U.S. Government Printing Office, October, 1956.

U.S. DEPARTMENT OF HEALTH, EDUCATION, AND WELFARE, PUBLIC HEALTH SERVICE. *Vital and Health Statistics*, Series 10, Nos. 1–38; Series 12, Nos. 1–9; and the Health Economics Series, Nos. 1–6. Washington, D.C.: U.S. Government Printing Office.

WEEKS, H. ASHLEY. *Family Spending Patterns and Health Care.* Cambridge, Mass.: Harvard University Press (Health Information Foundation).

WILLETT, ALLAN H. *The Economic Theory of Risk and Insurance.* Philadelphia: University of Pennsylvania Press (S. S. Huebner Foundation for Insurance Education), 1951.

## chapter 2

A stitch in time . . .

# Meeting Health Losses:
# Treatment and Prevention

## Social objectives in meeting health losses

*Basic objectives.* The prevention of want has come to be accepted as an important function of society in this modern period. This is evidenced by the development of various devices for relief, public assistance, social and private insurance, as well as many welfare programs which provide benefits in kind. The most important objective of society in regard to health is that *losses* be *kept to a minimum.* This is primarily a matter for preventive techniques such as public health measures and only secondarily a matter for insurance. However, insurance companies can, and often do, participate in public health measures of various types. They have contributed large amounts to research aimed at reducing the toll of death and disability and have conducted extensive advertising campaigns to educate the public to the advantages of early medical care and proper living habits. Moreover, insurance may serve to minimize loss of time from disability by providing the wherewithal for treatment and rehabilitation.

Second, society is concerned with *minimum loss impact.* While the aggregate loss from poor health is staggering, the burden is small compared to the productive capabilities of the nation. If this cost burden were to be spread equally over the entire population, it would not represent a major cost element for any individual. Insurance and similar devices serve the function of spreading the costs of health, equalizing the impact so that the burden is not difficult for any individual or family to bear. Thus they prevent poverty and destitution, which otherwise might result from disability, and help to minimize the other social costs which might result from such poverty. Such costs might include disease, juvenile delinquency, and crime.

Third, society is concerned with *minimum risk-bearing cost.* Where risk cannot be transferred or reduced, it imposes costs which must be met, consciously or otherwise. If a reserve fund is set aside to meet the possible impact of loss, funds are likely to be held idle in bank account balances, or in very low-yield liquid investments. Without this necessity, they could be released for more productive or satisfying purposes. If the risk is merely assumed, with no provision for meeting its impact, fear of loss may produce worry and anxiety which may impair productive efficiency or merely make life more unpleasant. Insurance reduces such risk costs by reducing risk.[1]

Thus, even when no formal risk-bearing device is involved, risk bearing still imposes real costs. Of course, these are difficult to measure, but they are present and significant, nonetheless. When a formal risk-bearing device, such as insurance, comes into the picture, its costs are comparatively easy to measure, since the expenses and profits of the insurer are public information. However, these costs probably are much less than the intangible costs which are incurred when risks are retained or assumed. Society's goal should be to operate its risk-bearing mechanisms in such a way that the total costs, tangible and intangible, are minimized. Insurance represents an extremely efficient, that is, low cost, method of reducing risk for insured persons and in the aggregate.

*Priority in meeting risks.* In establishing priorities as to which risks should be dealt with first, society should give first consideration to high-value risks.[2] Such risks can bring about the "economic death" of an income earner and his dependents. It is the magnitude of the possible loss which imposes the greatest burden on the individual who feels its impact. The aggregate cost to all members of society should not be the criterion. If the value of risk is low and the probability of loss is high, the aggregate social cost will be high, but the impact will be small enough for most people to meet without undue burden. The former emphasis on poliomyelitis in medical research and charitable campaigns is a reflection of the recognition of this principle by society. Here the incidence rate is relatively low, but the magnitude of the individual loss is so great that the problem has captured the interest of large segments of the population. Unfortunately, many varieties of medical care insurance have followed the opposite pattern, insuring against the frequent small loss only. The same criticism applies to most proposals for government health insurance plans, especially those for the aged. The development of major medical and comprehensive insurance was a welcome step in the proper direction.

Among several risks where the value of risk is roughly the same, so-

---

[1] See pp. 45–46 below.

[2] "Value of risk" is a term used by insurance people to refer to the amount of the largest potential loss to which the subject matter is exposed.

ciety should give first priority to those risks in which the probability of loss is highest. Since no risk with such a high value has a probability of occurrence greater than 0.5, this also means that priority of treatment will be given to those risks in which the degree of risk is highest.[3] This is the reason for the recent emphasis on heart disease and cancer in life-conservation efforts.

## Methods of meeting health losses

*General.* Since all human endeavor is exposed to the risk of loss, a variety of techniques has been developed to meet this problem. There are four fundamental approaches: prevention of loss, assumption of risk, transfer of risk, and reduction of risk by combining exposures.[4] Prevention of loss is the best from the social point of view, as none of the others reduces the direct-loss cost to society.[5] Not all loss can be eliminated, and loss-prevention activities must be supplemented by one or more of the other techniques.

*Assumption of risk.* The simplest technique is for the exposed person to assume the risk, to "take his chances." Indeed, this technique may be, and often is, applied to risks of whose very existence the individual is unaware. Where the individual is aware of the existence of the risk, he may supplement this assumption of risk with some provision for meeting loss costs. Such a provision may be made by building up a fund to meet losses and/or charging an additional price for a product or service. Some risks currently can be handled in no other way.

*Transfer of risk.* This involves shifting the possible losses to some other individual or organization which acts as a risk bearer. The risk bearer may be a professional, as in insurance and hedging contracts, or merely any organization to whom competitive pressure makes such shifting possible. Examples of transfer of risk through competition are hold-harmless agreements of various types and waivers of right of recovery in contracts such as leases, bailments, and employment agreements. Public assistance represents a transfer of risk to society and is the main example of transfer of health risks.

*Insurance.* The most difficult to understand of all these techniques is that of reducing risk by combining independent exposures. Insurance

---

[3] Since degree of risk means extent of uncertainty, it is at a maximum to the individual where the probability of occurrence is equal to 0.5.

[4] Three of these are *social* devices. Assumption is an individual device.

[5] As both Huebner and Willett point out, risk, per se, imposes social costs in excess of direct-loss costs. These costs are reduced by the various risk-bearing techniques here described, especially insurance and hedging. See S. S. Huebner, *Life Insurance* (4th ed., New York: Appleton-Century-Crofts, 1950), and Allan H. Willett, *The Economic Theory of Risk and Insurance* (Philadelphia: University of Pennsylvania Press, 1951).

is the outstanding example of this technique and is defined on this basis. Since risk is defined as uncertainty, as independent exposures are combined the number of cases in the sample is increased and the standard deviation is decreased. This is to say that variation about the loss expectation decreases as the number of exposures increases, and risk is reduced. Relative certainty is produced by combining uncertainties. This is the essential element of insurance, but not all such combinations of exposures are called "insurance."

Chapter 3 will be devoted to a classification and description of devices for meeting the financial cost of poor health. This chapter will discuss the preventive measures which reduce the risk of poor health by reducing its probability or severity. First, however, it is appropriate to discuss the meaning of health, the factors producing poor health, and the means at society's disposal for treating poor health.

### The meaning of health

Health is a difficult concept to define. Clearly, it means more than the absence of disease and physical impairment. The World Health Organization charter defines health as a "state of complete physical, mental and social well-being and not merely the absence of disease or infirmity."[6] This state of perfect health rarely is attained. If "perfect" health is considered to be the feeling of ebullient well-being that causes one to "burst into song" with joy, it is achieved only for very brief periods by the healthiest of people. Since "perfect health" is so rare, it is perhaps better to think of health as a scale ranging from death at one extreme to "perfect health" on the other extreme. It is, of course, an oversimplification to relate health, a multivector variate in several dimensions, to a single axis, but it may help in visualizing the problem.[7] Death is readily defined, in most instances,[8] but, moving in the other direction through total disability, partial disability, and minor impairments to an area of "positive" health still establishes no finite definable end point. Rather, it seems that the axis proceeds infinitely toward a conception of health for the individual and the population which never has been experienced in the aggregate and rarely in the individual case. Thus the possibilities for health improvement seem almost infinite.

[6] O. N. Serbein, *Paying for Medical Care in the United States* (New York: Columbia University Press, 1953), p. 17.

[7] Lowell J. Reed, "Principles Applying to the Collection of Information on Health as Related to Socio-environmental Functions," in *Backgrounds of Social Medicine* (New York: Millbank Memorial Fund, 1949).

[8] Dr. J. Russell Elkinton suggests that for moral and legal purposes, death should be defined as the cessation of brain activity rather than the cessation of breathing and heartbeat in view of the development of modern methods of resuscitation. *Pennsylvania Gazette*, May, 1967, p. 5.

*Poor health.* The idea of poor health, used but not yet defined, then would comprehend all conditions falling short of this undefined ideal. If this be the case, everyone has poor health. From a practical standpoint, the concept of poor health must be limited to a state of health at least so poor that it produces a need for treatment or an impairment of productive function. But what is a "need"? If perfection is the goal, any condition for which a remedy is available constitutes a "need" for treatment. This is not much help. For practical purposes, a need for treatment should be defined as a physiological or mental condition which, in the light of current knowledge, the current resources of society, and the opinions of competent physicians, should receive treatment. Thus concepts of needs would be expected to change over time, and indeed they have. Before a need can be translated into action, there must be a recognition of the need. A recognized need becomes a drive in psychological terms or, in popular language, a want or desire. When this want is backed up with purchasing power, one type of capacity, it becomes demand. For such a demand to produce action, there must be a supply of medical services to provide opportunities for satisfaction of the need. The following section will explore the nature of the need for medical services in terms of the factors producing poor health, and the next will discuss the supply of medical services.

The concept of impairment of productive function is also somewhat vague. Productive function may be impaired by serious injury or disease or by chronic, relatively minor, ailments such as fatigue, constipation, indigestion, dull headache, congested nasal passages and nervousness. Again, by such a standard, most people's productive functions are impaired every day. In order to have a practical criterion, the concept should be restricted to impairment so severe as to cause a noticeable restriction of normal activity. Thus, *poor health* may be defined as *any physical or mental impairment which requires treatment in the opinion of accepted medical practice or results in an observable restriction of normal activity.*

Poor health may be produced by injury or by disease. An *injury* is a relatively sudden physical impairment occurring in a violent fashion. It may be produced by accident or by the deliberate act of the person injured or of others. An *accident* is a sudden fortuitous event occurring independently of human intent so as to be unpredictable in the individual instance.[9] A *disease* is a sickness, infection, abnormal growth, mental state, or other loss of function which produces poor health and is not the result of injury. Disease results from a producer agent termed a "pathogen" which may be physical, bacterial, chemical, viral, psychological, or,

---

[9] Accident frequency, however, may be quite predictable in the aggregate. There is a statistical regularity in "chance" events.

all too frequently, unidentifiable. Disease tends to develop over a period of time, while injury occurs almost instantaneously.

*Disability* is the term used to refer to a restriction of activity resulting from poor health. It may lead to an economic loss of two types: loss of earnings and medical care expenditures. Thus disability reults in a loss of earning power or wealth as a result of poor health. The term *disablement* is used to refer to the beginning of the period of disability—the instant at which disability begins.

It will be noted that this involves a chain of events. Human error combines with an unsafe condition to produce an accident, which in turn produces an injury. Or else a pathogen is transmitted by means of a vector or vectors to a potential host and produces a disease. Injury or disease produces poor health, which produces disability, which in turn produces an economic loss of one or both types. Economic loss from disability may be prevented by breaking this chain at any point. Preventive medicine, accident prevention and public health are designed to break this chain at an early point and prevent disability from occurring. Curative medicine is concerned with bringing poor health and disability to a rapid termination. Medical rehabilitation is a part of this technique. Vocational rehabilitation is concerned with similarly minimizing the economic loss, and insurance and assistance are concerned with meeting the impact of such economic losses as do occur. All contribute to the reduction of risk of economic loss and assist in the provision of economic security.

### Factors producing poor health

*Importance.*    The factors producing poor health are worth studying for a number of reasons. From the standpoint of preventive technique, it frequently is necessary to consider each type of accidental injury or disease separately in order to interrupt the chain of events effectively. In establishing social objectives, society should give highest priorities to those injuries or diseases which produce the most severe losses, and, within any degree of severity, should give highest priority to those injuries or diseases that are the most frequent. Such a system of priorities requires a knowledge of the frequency and severity of various diseases and injuries. Finally, from the standpoint of insurance and similar devices, the process of underwriting requires the identification of conditions which predispose to health losses. Thus an analysis of factors producing disability is important in risk selection and rating.

*Rates.*    The concepts of frequency and severity are combined inextricably in any attempt to measure the impact of various types of disability. Any measure of rates of disability involves some definition in terms of severity. The nature of this definition affects the observed total frequency and the relative factor-specific rates.

The term "rate" im
both a numerator and
meaning of the rate. A
nominator in the same
number. This is compar
would be death rates: nu
the number of persons li
unit does not cancel out, t
ple, man-hours lost per 1,00
in the previous chapter on
were of this type: expenditu
noted that these illustrations
rate or probability involves su
to as the "period of exposure.
one year and, when this is the
Thus, if one is asked the proba
will die, one is likely (knowing
in 1,000 or 0.010. This means, of
dying this year; the probability o

50 HEALTH INSURANCE and severity
both frequency and severity
frequency rate times a severity
particular disease is per so m
total loss of time is per
proportion of the pop
it tells depends on
which have go
on whether
possible
stay
is

...ut 10
probability of his
sooner or later is about 1.0.
If the rate is anything other than a pure number and the period is anything other than one year, it is essential to indicate this. Otherwise the
figure is meaningless.

Disability rates frequently are given on three bases. *Incidence rates* or
*frequency rates* indicate the probability of the occurrence of the event
of disablement. In connection with such rates, disablement must be specifically defined. Thus, for example, the probability of hospital admission
is 0.140 for insured persons in the United States; the probability of disability lasting 90 days or more for insured persons aged 40 to 45 in the
United States is 0.01257.

*Severity rates* or duration rates, sometimes called "average severity"
or "average duration," refer to the average severity of disability. This
always will have to be measured in some unit of value or time, and the
base is always some number of persons originally disabled. Where the
number disabled, the denominator of the fraction, is 1, the qualification
frequently is omitted. However, all such omissions are dangerous, as
there may be misunderstanding about what was omitted. For example
the mean length of hospital stay for insured persons in the United States
is almost 7.0 days, or the average cost of a hospital admission is (say)
$280. Similarly, the average duration of disability for an insured person
in the United States disabled at age 35 for at least 1 day is 10 days; for
such a person disabled 6 months, the average (future) duration is 24
months. These illustrations should suffice to indicate the necessity for
clear definition of what kind of a rate one is talking about.

The final type of rate is a *prevalence rate*. This takes into consideration

...ay be looked upon as product of a
...ate. Such a rate tells what the cost of a
...any persons exposed per year, or what the
...so many persons exposed per year, or what
...lation is disabled at a given point of time. What
...the nature of the frequency rates and severity rates
...e into its computation. Whether it tells anything depends
...the author makes all these things clear. For example, it is
...o combine the figures above on hospital admission and average
...if 14 persons per 100 are admitted in a year and the average stay
...seven days, then the average stay per 100 persons per year is 7 × 14 or
98 days. Or the average person is hospitalized 0.98 days per year. Or, at
any point in time, 0.27 percent of the population probably would be hospitalized. It will be remembered that these figures refer to insured persons
in the United States. Similarly, it is possible to take the (arbitrary)
figure of an average cost per admission of $280 and multiply *that* by the
incidence rate of 0.14 and find that the cost of hospitalization is $280 ×
14 or $3,920 per 100 persons exposed per year. Thus $39.20 is the average
cost per person per year. To explore these relationships a little further,
one can divide the cost of $3,920 per 100 persons by the 98 days of
hospitalization per 100 persons and come up with an average cost per
day of $40. The average cost per admission could, then, equally well have
been obtained by multiplying the average cost per day by the average
number of days' stay.[10] Thus a prevalence rate in one unit may be converted into a prevalence rate in another unit, if the necessary data are
available. Prevalence rates do not, of course, give a measure of probability
of occurrence, but may, if appropriately adjusted, give a measure of
probability of (say) a person being in a hospital on a random day.

If one is concerned with the total cost to society, in terms either of
time or of money, prevalence rates may be the best guide. But if one is
concerned with the frequency of severe losses, incidence rates for types
of ill-health which are considered severe must be the guide. Although
the latter approach is the more logical one, some data of each type will
be presented.

*Prevalence rates—all disability.* The 1935–36 National Health survey
data[11] gave prevalence rates (number disabled per 1,000 persons on day
of survey) for various factors producing disability. This study indicated
that acute respiratory conditions, especially colds and influenza, ranked
first as producers of disability. Cardiovascular diseases, rheumatism and

---

[10] Confidentially, that is exactly what the author of this book did. The $40 is
arbitrary but not too far off.

[11] D. E. Hailman, "The Prevalence of Disabling Illness among Male and Female
Workers and Housewives," *Public Health Bulletin*, No. 260 (United States Public
Health Service, Washington, D.C., 1941), from Mortimer Spiegelman, *Significant
Mortality and Morbidity Trends since 1900* (Philadelphia: American College of Life
Underwriters, 1956), p. 9.

allied diseases, mental disorders, and cancer were the next most important in order.

The current National Health Survey, which published data first covering the period July, 1957 to June, 1958, does not tabulate its data in strictly comparable form.[12] Prevalence rates for all disability and for acute

TABLE 2–1

Number of Restricted Activity Days, Bed Disability Days, and
Work- and School-Loss Days per Person per Year
(1958 to 1967, compared with disability prevalence, 1935–36)

| Fiscal Year | Restricted Activity Days | | | Bed Disability Days | | |
|---|---|---|---|---|---|---|
| | Both Sexes | Male | Female | Both Sexes | Male | Female |
| 1958 | 20.0 | 17.7 | 22.2 | 7.8 | 6.9 | 8.7 |
| 1959 | 15.8 | 13.6 | 17.9 | 5.8 | 4.9 | 6.6 |
| 1960 | 16.2 | 14.3 | 18.0 | 6.0 | 5.3 | 6.7 |
| 1961 | 16.5 | 14.6 | 18.3 | 5.8 | 5.0 | 6.6 |
| 1962 | 16.3 | 14.1 | 18.3 | 6.4 | 5.4 | 7.4 |
| 1963 | 16.2 | 14.5 | 17.8 | 6.6 | 5.7 | 7.5 |
| 1964 | 16.2 | 14.5 | 17.8 | 6.0 | 5.3 | 6.8 |
| 1965 | 16.4 | 14.7 | 18.0 | 6.2 | 5.3 | 7.0 |
| 1966 | 15.6 | 14.4 | 16.7 | 6.3 | 5.5 | 7.0 |
| 1967 | 15.4 | 14.1 | 16.5 | 5.6 | 4.9 | 6.3 |

| | Work Days Lost Ages 17 and Over | | | School Days Lost Ages 6–16 | | |
|---|---|---|---|---|---|---|
| | Both Sexes | Male | Female | Both Sexes | Male | Female |
| 1958 | — | — | — | 8.4 | 8.0 | 8.9 |
| 1959 | — | — | — | 5.8 | 5.8 | 5.8 |
| 1960 | 5.6 | 5.5 | 5.6 | 5.3 | 4.9 | 5.6 |
| 1961 | 5.4 | 5.3 | 5.6 | 4.8 | 4.8 | 4.7 |
| 1962 | 5.8 | 5.7 | 5.8 | 5.7 | 5.5 | 6.0 |
| 1963 | 6.1 | 5.9 | 6.6 | 5.6 | 5.3 | 5.9 |
| 1964 | 5.5 | 5.6 | 5.3 | 5.0 | 4.9 | 5.1 |
| 1965 | 5.7 | 5.7 | 5.6 | 5.2 | 4.9 | 5.4 |
| 1966 | 5.8 | 5.9 | 5.6 | 5.2 | 5.1 | 5.3 |
| 1967 | 5.4 | 5.3 | 5.4 | | | |

| | Disability Days | | | |
|---|---|---|---|---|
| | Male Workers | Female Workers | Housewives | All Females |
| 1935–36 | 7.5 | 11.1 | 17.6 | 15.4 |

Source: U.S. Department of Health, Education, and Welfare, *Health, Education, and Welfare Trends,* and *Vital and Health Statistics* (Washington, D.C.: U.S. Government Printing Office), Series 10, No. 25, No. 37, and No. 43.

---

[12] U.S. Department of Health, Education and Welfare, Public Health Service. *Health Statistics from the U.S. National Health Survey* (Washington, D.C.: U.S. Government Printing Office, 1959–61) Series B, Nos. 1–30; National Center for Health Statistics, *Vital and Health Statistics* (Washington, D.C.: U.S. Government Printing Office, 1963–67), Series 10, Nos. 1–44.

conditions are given in terms of days of restricted activity or disability incurred during the year. The most recently published data for total disability days relate to the period July, 1965, to June, 1966.[13]

As indicated in Table 2–1, several definitions of disability are used. These are not mutually exclusive: restricted activity days probably include all work- and school-loss days and all bed disability days, and the latter also overlap. In general, there are more restricted activity days than either bed disability days or work- or school-loss days; the bed disability days exceed the work- or school-loss days by a slight margin. The figures from the 1935–36 National Health Survey, adjusted to a compa-

CHART 2–1

Disability Days per Person per Quarter, by Type of Disability and Sex

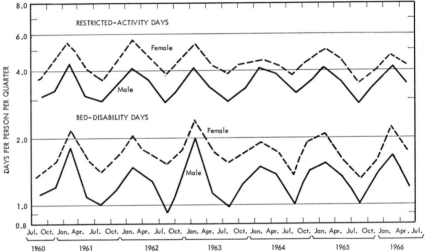

Source: Mary Lou Bauer, *Current Estimates from the Health Interview Survey, United States, July 1965–June 1966* (National Center for Health Statistics, Series 10, No. 37 [Washington, D.C.: U.S. Government Printing Office, 1967]).

rable base, are given for comparison. The definition of disability there was stricter than that for restricted activity days in the current survey, but less strict than the other definitions. Thus, it is not surprising that the figures seem to fall within the range of values from the current study. Chart 2–1 indicates how disability days vary with time and season.

In general, disability rates are higher for females than for males. This is the reverse of the situation in regard to mortality. Apparently the men do not regard themselves as sick quite so readily, perhaps "working until they drop," while the women give way to illness more easily and thus are

[13] National Center for Health Statistics, Series 10, No. 37 (Washington, D.C.: U.S. Government Printing Office, 1967).

able to survive longer. On the other hand, it may be that women are the hardier sex and survive many ailments in a disabled condition while their male counterparts die off. This is an area where further study would be desirable.

A recent report suggests that "culturally determined differences in the attitudes toward what constitutes illness" might be the explanation. The higher disability in women results almost entirely from colds, grippe, pharyngitis, acute gastroenteritis and other minor ailments, while men show a slightly higher incidence of serious life-endangering illnesses.[14] This would tend to confirm the first hypothesis above.

*Prevalence rates, acute conditions.* Current National Health Survey data do not give prevalence rates for acute and chronic conditions on a comparable basis. Table 2–2 gives rates for a variety of acute conditions for restricted activity days, bed disability days, and work- and school-loss days classified by age. Acute conditions are more important producers of disability at the younger ages and at ages over 65. This relationship is found for most of the specific factors. The greater disability for females shows up in the tabulation for work- and school-loss days, and again this applies to most producing factors. Most of the exceptions pertain to injuries rather than sickness.

In general, upper respiratory conditions produce the most disability, followed by other respiratory and infectious and parasitic diseases in turn. Superficially, this would seem to indicate that these conditions should take the highest priority in public health and research efforts at loss prevention. However, this survey counted as disability any period as long as, or longer than, one day. The studies of longer term disability rank these factors far down the list.

Table 2–3 shows total cases, incidence rates, severity rates, and prevalence rates for a more detailed diagnostic classification, for 1964–65 for both sexes and all ages combined. In terms of prevalence, the common cold produced the most restricted activity days, but with an average severity of 0.88 days in bed and 2.36 days of restricted activity, it was one of the least serious conditions. In contrast pneumonia, with very low frequency, restricted activity for 16.36 days, 10.25 in bed, a severity matched only by fractures and dislocations.

*Frequency rates—acute conditions.* The current National Health Survey data include incidence rates for acute conditions only. These are indicated in Table 2–4 and Chart 2–2. The chart shows the decline in incidence of acute conditions with age quite vividly and also indicates the differences in reported rates for the seven survey years. Table 2–4 gives a classification by factors producing disability comparable with the prevalence data in Table 2–2. It would, of course, be possible to

---

[14] Dr. Lawrence E. Hinkle, Jr., quoted in *Safety Maintenance*, June, 1961, p. 27.

TABLE 2–2

Prevalence of Acute Conditions, 1965–66
(Number of restricted activity days, bed disability days, and work and school days lost
per 100 persons per year, both sexes)

| | | Restricted Activity Days | | | |
| | All | Under Age 6 | Age 6–16 | Age 17–44 | Age 45 and over |
|---|---|---|---|---|---|
| All acute conditions................819.5 | 965.2 | 842.5 | 731.8 | 844.3 |
| Infective and parasitic diseases....103.5 | 233.0 | 172.6 | 62.8 | 44.2 |
| Respiratory conditions.............393.5 | 565.2 | 453.9 | 295.4 | 391.2 |
| Upper respiratory..............192.3 | 363.1 | 247.6 | 131.1 | 150.0 |
| Influenza.....................164.0 | 132.9 | 177.3 | 141.8 | 194.1 |
| Other respiratory.............. 37.2 | 69.2 | 29.0 | 22.5 | 47.0 |
| Digestive system conditions....... 35.7 | 33.4 | 24.2 | 35.7 | 45.5 |
| Injuries...........................169.3 | 37.6 | 115.2 | 193.5 | 230.2 |
| All other acute conditions.........117.4 | 96.1 | 76.6 | 144.4 | 125.2 |

| | | Bed Disability Days | | | |
| | All | Under Age 6 | Age 6–16 | Age 17–44 | Age 45 and over |
|---|---|---|---|---|---|
| All acute conditions................365.6 | 445.4 | 403.8 | 341.0 | 331.8 |
| Infective and parasitic diseases.... 54.3 | 112.7 | 83.6 | 40.6 | 23.3 |
| Respiratory conditions.............196.3 | 251.0 | 253.1 | 161.4 | 171.6 |
| Upper respiratory.............. 80.4 | 129.0 | 116.2 | 62.7 | 53.7 |
| Influenza..................... 93.7 | 73.3 | 121.2 | 84.6 | 92.7 |
| Other respiratory.............. 22.1 | 48.7 | 15.7 | 14.0 | 25.3 |
| Digestive system conditions....... 19.6 | 11.6 | 12.8 | 19.6 | 28.2 |
| Injuries........................... 47.0 | 16.1 | 28.3 | 59.3 | 59.8 |
| All other acute conditions.......... 48.4 | 53.9 | 26.0 | 60.2 | 49.0 |

| | Work-Loss Days (Number of Days per 100 "Usually Working" Persons 17+ Years of Age) | | | School-Loss Days (Number of Days per 100 Children 6–16 Years of Age) | | |
| | Both Sexes | Male | Female | Both Sexes | Male | Female |
|---|---|---|---|---|---|---|
| All acute conditions......370.3 | 377.0 | 358.2 | 462.7 | 449.3 | 476.7 |
| Respiratory conditions... 28.7 | 26.0 | 33.6 | 102.1 | 100.3 | 104.0 |
| Upper respiratory conditions.........164.1 | 154.9 | 180.8 | 288.3 | 275.0 | 302.0 |
| Influenza........... 64.1 | 60.1 | 71.3 | 153.3 | 144.7 | 162.1 |
| Other respiratory conditions......... 82.7 | 77.6 | 91.9 | 117.1 | 104.9 | 129.8 |
| Digestive system conditions............ 17.3 | 17.2 | 17.6 | 17.8 | 25.3 | 10.1 |
| Injuries.................. 16.9 | 18.0 | 15.0 | 11.8 | 12.2 | 11.4 |
| All other conditions......121.2 | 148.5 | 71.4 | 24.7 | 28.3 | 21.0 |
| Infective and parasitic conditions............ 39.4 | 29.6 | 57.4 | 35.9 | 33.5 | 38.3 |

Source: U.S. Department of Health, Education, and Welfare, Public Health Service, *Health Statistics from the U.S. National Health Survey* (Washington, D.C.: U.S. Government Printing Office), Series 10, No. 37, pp. 6–9.

derive figures as to average duration by dividing the prevalence rate by the frequency rate and adjusting for the different denominator, as was done in Table 2–3 for all ages and sexes combined. However, there probably are enough statistics in this chapter without this refinement.

CHART 2–2

Incidence of Acute Conditions, 1959–64
(by years of age)

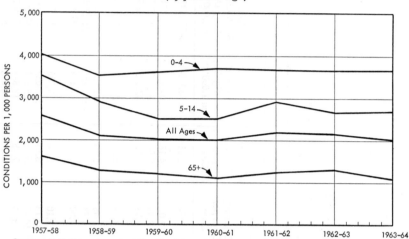

Source: U.S. Department of Health, Education, and Welfare, *Health, Education, and Welfare Trends*, 1965 ed., p. S–14.

*Frequency rates—surgical procedures.* Surgery represents one of the more drastic types of medical procedure. The frequency rates for surgical operations serve as an indication of the relative importance of various factors (Table 2–5).

*Hospitalization: frequency, severity, and prevalence.* Hospital data provide a good measure of relative importance of various ailments. Table 2–6 shows discharge rates (including decedents), average length of stay, and prevalence. Deliveries, respiratory conditions, injuries, digestive conditions, heart disease, and benign neoplasms are the leading conditions requiring hospitalization. Length of stay, however, is greatest for strokes, cancer, diabetes, and heart disease. When the two rates are combined (discharge rate per 1,000 persons times average length of stay equals days per 1,000 persons per year), heart disease, deliveries, respiratory conditions, and fractures and dislocations account for the most hospitalization.

*Prevalence rates, chronic conditions.* Chart 2–3 and Table 2–7 show current data on chronic disability. These figures are not comparable with the data for acute conditions, since they show the number of persons reporting a chronic impairment. However, they do show the importance

TABLE 2-3

Frequency, Severity, and Prevalence of Acute Conditions
(U.S., 1964-65, both sexes)

| Condition Group | Frequency: No. of cases per 100 Persons per Year | Frequency: No. of Cases (in 1,000's) | Severity: Average Bed Disability Days per Case | Severity: Average Restricted Activity Days per Case | Prevalence: Total Bed Disability Days (in 1,000's) | Prevalence: Total Restricted Activity Days (in 1,000's) | Prevalence: Bed Disability Days per 100 Persons per Year | Prevalence: Restricted Activity Days per 100 Persons per Year |
|---|---|---|---|---|---|---|---|---|
| All acute | 212.7 | 400,871 | 1.64 | 3.91 | 658,129 | 1,568,179 | 349.3 | 832.2 |
| Infective and parasitic diseases | 27.5 | 51,886 | 2.01 | 4.18 | 104,033 | 217,191 | 55.2 | 115.3 |
| Common childhood diseases | 8.7 | 16,425 | 2.30 | 5.56 | 37,817 | 91,294 | 20.1 | 48.4 |
| The virus, n.o.s.[a] | 14.7 | 27,681 | 1.53 | 2.88 | 42,305 | 79,689 | 22.5 | 42.3 |
| Other infective and parasitic diseases | 4.1 | 7,779 | 3.07 | 5.94 | 23,911 | 46,208 | 12.7 | 24.5 |
| Respiratory conditions | 116.4 | 219,355 | 1.46 | 3.10 | 321,129 | 680,818 | 170.4 | 361.3 |
| Common cold | 61.1 | 115,132 | 0.88 | 2.36 | 101,255 | 271,791 | 53.7 | 144.2 |
| Other acute respiratory conditions | 16.6 | 31,283 | 1.50 | 2.98 | 47,134 | 93,279 | 25.0 | 49.5 |
| Influenza with digestive manifestations | 3.2 | 6,118 | 1.10 | 2.38 | 6,735 | 14,584 | 3.6 | 7.7 |
| Other influenza | 30.7 | 57,812 | 2.13 | 3.83 | 123,034 | 221,294 | 65.3 | 117.4 |
| Pneumonia | 1.3 | 2,497 | 10.25 | 16.36 | 25,601 | 40,858 | 13.6 | 21.7 |
| Bronchitis | 2.0 | 3,750 | 3.44 | 7.45 | 12,897 | 27,922 | 6.8 | 14.8 |
| Other acute respiratory conditions | 1.5 | 2,762 | 1.62 | 4.02 | 4,473 | 11,090 | 2.4 | 5.9 |

| Condition | | | | | | | |
|---|---|---|---|---|---|---|---|
| Digestive system conditions | 11.2 | 21,049 | 1.60 | 3.89 | 33,646 | 81,879 | 17.9 | 43.5 |
| Dental conditions | 5.1 | 9,663 | 0.63 | 2.20 | 6,095 | 21,277 | 3.2 | 11.3 |
| Functional and symptomatic upper gastrointestinal disorders, n.e.c.[b] | 2.3 | 4,369 | 1.54 | 3.14 | 6,713 | 13,708 | 3.6 | 7.3 |
| Other digestive system conditions | 3.7 | 7,016 | 2.97 | 6.68 | 20,837 | 46,894 | 11.1 | 24.9 |
| Injuries | 29.9 | 56,352 | 1.49 | 5.64 | 84,093 | 318,072 | 44.6 | 168.8 |
| Fractures and dislocations | 3.0 | 5,588 | 4.56 | 19.12 | 25,498 | 106,848 | 13.5 | 56.7 |
| Sprains and strains | 5.0 | 9,425 | 1.50 | 6.67 | 14,687 | 62,899 | 7.8 | 33.4 |
| Open wounds and lacerations | 8.4 | 15,763 | 0.70 | 3.19 | 11,110 | 50,306 | 5.9 | 26.7 |
| Contusions and superficial injuries | 6.2 | 11,720 | 1.34 | 4.09 | 15,742 | 47,993 | 8.4 | 25.5 |
| Other current injuries | 7.4 | 13,856 | 1.23 | 3.61 | 17,056 | 50,025 | 9.1 | 26.5 |
| Other acute conditions | 27.7 | 52,230 | 2.21 | 5.17 | 115,229 | 270,219 | 61.2 | 143.4 |
| Diseases of the ear | 6.4 | 11,969 | 1.14 | 3.01 | 13,588 | 36,043 | 7.2 | 19.1 |
| Headaches | 2.4 | 4,531 | 0.42 | 1.43 | 1,886 | 6,486 | 1.0 | 3.4 |
| Genitourinary disorders | 3.5 | 6,638 | 2.90 | 6.55 | 19,228 | 43,462 | 10.2 | 23.1 |
| Deliveries and disorders of pregnancy and the puerperium | 2.4 | 4,472 | 6.22 | 11.53 | 27,797 | 51,578 | 14.8 | 27.4 |
| Diseases of the skin | 2.9 | 5,398 | 1.69 | 4.84 | 9,125 | 26,114 | 4.8 | 13.9 |
| Diseases of the musculoskeletal system | 2.3 | 4,325 | 2.63 | 8.33 | 11,394 | 36,021 | 6.0 | 19.1 |
| All other acute conditions | 7.9 | 14,898 | 2.16 | 4.73 | 32,211 | 70,515 | 17.1 | 37.4 |

[a] n.o.s., not otherwise specified.
[b] n.e.c., not elsewhere classified.

Source: Alice J. Alderman, *Acute Conditions–Incidence and Associated Disability* (National Center for Health Statistics, Series 10, No. 26 [U.S. Government Printing Office, Washington, D.C., 1965]), p. 16.

TABLE 2-4

Incidence of Acute Conditions,[a] 1961-64
(per 1,000 persons)

| Fiscal Year[b] | Total Acute Conditions | Infective and Parasitic Diseases | Respiratory Conditions | | Conditions of the Digestive System | Current Injuries | | | | All Other Acute Conditions |
|---|---|---|---|---|---|---|---|---|---|---|
| | | | Upper | Other | | Fractures[c] | Open Wounds[d] | Contusions[e] | Other | |
| 1961 | | | | | | | | | | |
| All ages | 2,018.9 | 275.6 | 779.5 | 323.3 | 127.2 | 77.2 | 77.1 | 57.9 | 67.1 | 234.1 |
| 0-4 | 3,733.7 | 725.0 | 1,657.9 | 473.5 | 194.0 | 17.5 | 113.6 | 49.3 | 132.7 | 370.3 |
| 5-14 | 2,555.9 | 502.0 | 1,003.8 | 358.0 | 132.1 | 61.6 | 130.1 | 72.1 | 72.6 | 223.5 |
| 15-24 | 1,885.5 | 108.3 | 670.2 | 377.0 | 160.1 | 98.6 | 77.5 | 70.0 | 60.8 | 263.1 |
| 25-44 | 1,716.1 | 174.1 | 605.0 | 325.2 | 119.8 | 88.4 | 60.3 | 43.2 | 57.1 | 243.1 |
| 45-64 | 1,339.4 | 116.6 | 487.7 | 209.2 | 95.2 | 101.8 | 47.7 | 53.7 | 50.9 | 176.6 |
| 65+ | 1,189.6 | 75.3 | 462.7 | 224.9 | 75.4 | 69.1 | 20.1 | 69.8 | 46.0 | 145.4 |
| 1962 | | | | | | | | | | |
| All ages | 2,222.8 | 271.7 | 779.0 | 497.6 | 123.9 | 71.5 | 81.4 | 62.5 | 73.2 | 261.9 |
| 0-4 | 3,667.4 | 662.9 | 1,502.8 | 554.7 | 210.7 | 30.7 | 110.8 | 62.7 | 162.4 | 369.8 |
| 5-14 | 2,937.4 | 515.6 | 1,057.3 | 688.0 | 117.8 | 56.8 | 126.4 | 74.9 | 67.0 | 233.7 |
| 15-24 | 2,116.7 | 142.2 | 706.5 | 483.6 | 127.6 | 107.5 | 84.9 | 66.5 | 62.2 | 335.8 |
| 25-44 | 1,941.4 | 173.6 | 559.9 | 499.8 | 131.2 | 87.3 | 75.7 | 50.5 | 66.5 | 297.0 |
| 45-64 | 1,515.1 | 107.0 | 538.5 | 366.1 | 84.9 | 73.7 | 48.0 | 56.1 | 53.7 | 187.1 |
| 65+ | 1,278.6 | 51.3 | 484.3 | 292.1 | 90.9 | 53.2 | 25.6 | 75.1 | 55.6 | 150.7 |
| 1963 | | | | | | | | | | |
| All ages | 2,188.2 | 244.0 | 771.4 | 500.2 | 111.8 | 78.6 | 78.9 | 52.2 | 67.4 | 283.7 |
| 0-4 | 3,686.8 | 562.0 | 1,619.3 | 666.2 | 132.1 | 13.3 | 101.4 | 56.6 | 134.8 | 401.1 |
| 5-14 | 2,678.1 | 449.7 | 1,028.9 | 501.6 | 118.9 | 75.2 | 119.6 | 56.7 | 66.4 | 261.0 |
| 15-24 | 2,108.9 | 151.8 | 702.6 | 477.5 | 133.9 | 107.9 | 88.2 | 74.7 | 57.0 | 315.2 |
| 25-44 | 1,938.7 | 159.5 | 550.1 | 543.6 | 114.0 | 86.6 | 76.0 | 36.7 | 59.6 | 312.5 |
| 45-64 | 1,589.5 | 106.4 | 512.0 | 444.3 | 78.1 | 90.3 | 39.8 | 47.5 | 54.2 | 217.0 |
| 65+ | 1,360.8 | 64.7 | 424.7 | 333.9 | 105.6 | 74.4 | 40.0 | 54.1 | 52.6 | 210.7 |

1964

| | | | | | | | | | |
|---|---|---|---|---|---|---|---|---|---|
| All ages | 2,084.8 | 297.5 | 720.1 | 379.5 | 110.9 | 88.1 | 85.2 | 56.1 | 67.8 | 279.6 |
| 0-4 | 3,671.8 | 611.0 | 1,598.0 | 490.0 | 174.5 | 37.9 | 138.6 | 68.2 | 140.5 | 213.1 |
| 5-14 | 2,716.3 | 648.5 | 881.2 | 473.4 | 114.8 | 72.1 | 117.6 | 65.0 | 69.2 | 274.5 |
| 15-24 | 2,071.1 | 191.3 | 654.7 | 380.0 | 131.6 | 126.3 | 96.1 | 56.5 | 75.7 | 358.8 |
| 25-44 | 1,758.1 | 157.5 | 527.2 | 379.4 | 105.4 | 107.5 | 78.4 | 49.1 | 56.8 | 296.8 |
| 45-64 | 1,397.2 | 111.7 | 482.1 | 292.4 | 82.2 | 105.7 | 47.7 | 49.7 | 46.6 | 179.2 |
| 65+ | 1,148.2 | 81.1 | 433.5 | 226.0 | 70.3 | 33.8 | 31.5 | 53.2 | 40.1 | 178.6 |

[a] An acute condition is defined by the National Health Survey as a condition which has lasted less than three months with the exception of certain conditions which are classified as chronic even though the onset was within three months—see the interview questionnaire reproduced in all Series B publications. Minor acute conditions involving neither restricted activity nor medical attention are excluded from the statistics.

[b] Survey year ending June 30 of year shown.

[c] Includes dislocations, sprains and strains.

[d] Includes lacerations.

[e] Includes superficial injuries.

Source: U.S. Department of Health, Education, and Welfare, Public Health Service, *Vital and Health Statistics*, Series 10, No. 15, *Incidence of Acute Conditions, United States, July 1963–June 1964* and unpublished data, *Health, Education, and Welfare Trends*, 1965 ed., p. S-14. All statistics from the U.S. National Health Survey, authorized by Congress in 1956, are based on a continuing sample of the civilian noninstitutional population residing in the United States. Estimates are based on interviews of a minimum of 36,000 households containing approximately 115,000 persons per year. Each statistic is adjusted by two stages of ratio estimation to official Bureau of the Census population figures to make the sample estimate closely representative of the population by age, sex, color, and residence, and to reduce sampling variance.

TABLE 2–5

Frequency of Surgically Treated Discharges from Short-Stay Hospitals, U.S., 1962–63

| Conditions for Which Hospitalized | Surgically Treated Discharges (in 1,000's) | Percent of All Discharges | Discharge Rate per 1,000 Population |
|---|---|---|---|
| All Conditions................................ | 12,836 | 100.00 | 69.00 |
| Malignant neoplasms........................ | 249 | 1.94 | 1.34 |
| Benign and unspecified neoplasms........... | 1,077 | 8.39 | 5.79 |
| Endocrine, allergic, and metabolic disorders... | 135 | 1.05 | 0.72 |
| Diseases of the eye and visual impairments... | 294 | 2.29 | 1.58 |
| Mental, personality disorders, deficiencies, vascular lesions, and other diseases of nervous system and sense organs.......... | 146 | 1.14 | 0.79 |
| Varicose veins (excluding hemorrhoids)....... | 106 | 0.83 | 0.57 |
| Hemorrhoids................................. | 239 | 1.86 | 1.28 |
| Diseases of heart, circulatory system and hypertension............................... | 122 | 0.95 | 0.66 |
| Respiratory conditions....................... | 1,314 | 10.24 | 7.07 |
| Ulcer of stomach and duodenum............. | 117 | 0.91 | 0.63 |
| Appendicitis................................. | 342 | 2.66 | 1.84 |
| Hernia....................................... | 543 | 4.23 | 2.92 |
| Diseases of gallbladder...................... | 340 | 2.65 | 1.83 |
| Other digestive system disorders.............. | 369 | 2.87 | 1.98 |
| Male genital conditions[a]..................... | 231 | 1.80 | 1.24 |
| Female breast and genital disorders[a]......... | 677 | 5.27 | 3.64 |
| Other genitourinary system conditions........ | 395 | 3.08 | 2.13 |
| Deliveries[a]................................... | 3,814 | 29.71 | 20.50 |
| Complications of pregnancy[a].................. | 261 | 2.03 | 1.40 |
| Skin diseases................................ | 162 | 1.26 | 0.87 |
| Conditions of bones and joints............... | 234 | 1.82 | 1.26 |
| Other conditions of musculoskeletal system... | 190 | 1.48 | 1.02 |
| Fractures and dislocations.................... | 730 | 5.68 | 3.92 |
| Other current injuries........................ | 415 | 3.23 | 2.23 |
| All other conditions.......................... | 332 | 2.59 | 1.79 |

[a] Percentages and rates above are based on total population. More meaningful figures for certain sex-specific conditions are given below, based on exposure of the particular sex only.

| Condition | Number of Discharges | Percent of Discharges by Sex | Rate per 1,000 Population |
|---|---|---|---|
| All conditions, male...................... | 3,936 | 100.00 | 44.00 |
| Male genital conditions................... | 231 | 5.87 | 2.58 |
| All conditions, female..................... | 8,900 | 100.00 | 93.00 |
| Female breast and genital............... | 677 | 7.61 | 7.08 |
| Deliveries............................. | 3,814 | 42.85 | 39.85 |
| Complications of pregnancy............. | 261 | 2.93 | 2.72 |
| All other conditions, female............. | 4,148 | 46.60 | 43.34 |

Source: Mary M. Hannaford, *Proportion of Surgical Bill Paid by Insurance* (National Center for Health Statistics, Series 10, No. 31 [Washington, D.C.: U.S. Government Printing Office, 1966]).

of heart disease, arthritis and rheumatism, mental and nervous disorders, and high blood pressure as producers of long-term disability. Paralysis is also important as a cause of disability defined as inability to carry on major activity, which is the most significant indicator of the potential economic loss.

CHART 2-3

Chronic Conditions Causing Activity Limitations, 1962–63

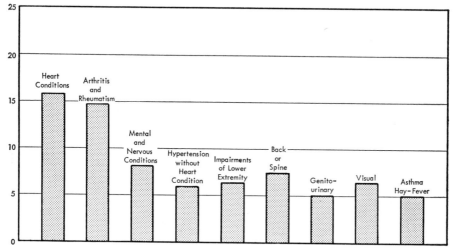

AVERAGE OF FISCAL YEARS 1962 AND 1963

Source: U.S. Department of Health, Education, and Welfare, *Health, Education, and Welfare Trends*, 1965 ed., p. S–15.

About 11 percent of the civilian noninstitutional population suffer some degree of limitation because of chronic impairments. About 2.3 percent are unable to carry on their major activity. This means that about four million people are so disabled, usually for at least three months and often for much longer periods of time. Compared to the work-loss days of 3.7 days per person per year (Table 2–2), which is only about 1.5 percent of a "normal" 250-day work year, this indicates the importance of these chronic diseases as producers of disability. A crude comparison of these two sets of data will show that the leading producers of chronic disability produce a much greater aggregate loss of time than the leading acute conditions. It is a pity that the figures are not published on the same basis so that this could be established rigorously.

The list of major chronic conditions furnishes a better guide toward social effort than one which includes disabilities as short as one day. As a matter of fact, nondisabling conditions are probably more frequent than disabling ones. The most common type of poor health is dental

TABLE 2-6

Total Short-Stay Hospital Discharges, Average Length of Stay and Total Days per 1,000 Persons,
by Sex and Condition for Which Hospitalized, U.S., July, 1963–June, 1964

| Condition for Which Hospitalized | Discharge Rate per 1,000 | | | Average Length of Stay in Days | | | Hospital Days per Year per 1,000 Persons | | |
|---|---|---|---|---|---|---|---|---|---|
| | Both Sexes | Male | Female | Both Sexes | Male | Female | Both Sexes | Male | Female |
| All conditions | 133.7 | 108.3 | 157.5 | 8.4 | 9.9 | 7.4 | 1,123.1 | 1,072.2 | 1,161.8 |
| Infective and parasitic diseases | 2.7 | 2.4 | 2.9 | 8.4 | 6.8 | 9.6 | 22.7 | 16.3 | 27.8 |
| Malignant neoplasms | 3.3 | 3.2 | 3.4 | 15.4 | 16.9 | 14.1 | 50.8 | 54.1 | 47.9 |
| Benign and unspecified neoplasms | 6.2 | 2.6 | 9.7 | 7.3 | 8.3 | 7.0 | 45.3 | 21.6 | 67.9 |
| Diabetes mellitus | 1.4 | 1.1 | 1.7 | 14.1 | 18.2 | 11.5 | 19.7 | 20.0 | 19.6 |
| Other endocrine, allergic, and metabolic disorders | 2.8 | 3.0 | 2.7 | 8.5 | 9.5 | 7.4 | 23.8 | 28.5 | 20.0 |
| Mental, personality disorders, and deficiencies | 2.9 | 2.8 | 3.1 | 12.8 | 15.1 | 10.9 | 37.1 | 42.3 | 33.8 |
| Vascular lesions of the central nervous system | 1.8 | 2.0 | 1.6 | 18.3 | 15.7 | 21.4 | 32.9 | 31.4 | 34.2 |
| Diseases of the eye and visual impairments | 1.8 | 1.5 | 2.0 | 7.5 | 7.8 | 7.3 | 13.5 | 11.7 | 14.6 |
| Other diseases of nervous system and sense organs | 2.4 | 2.3 | 2.5 | 10.4 | 14.0 | 7.3 | 25.0 | 32.2 | 18.3 |
| Diseases of the heart, n.e.c.[a] | 6.4 | 7.7 | 5.2 | 14.0 | 14.5 | 13.4 | 89.6 | 111.7 | 69.7 |
| Hypertension without heart involvement | 1.4 | 1.2 | 1.6 | 8.0 | 8.7 | 7.5 | 11.2 | 10.4 | 12.0 |
| Varicose veins (excluding hemorrhoids) | .7 | — | 1.0 | 8.3 | — | 7.4 | 5.8 | — | 7.4 |
| Hemorrhoids | 1.5 | 1.7 | 1.3 | 8.6 | 8.7 | 8.5 | 12.9 | 14.8 | 11.1 |
| Other circulatory diseases | 2.0 | 2.2 | 1.8 | 11.2 | 11.8 | 10.6 | 22.4 | 26.0 | 19.1 |
| Upper respiratory conditions | 8.3 | 8.3 | 8.3 | 2.5 | 2.5 | 2.6 | 20.8 | 20.8 | 21.6 |
| Other respiratory conditions | 7.8 | 8.1 | 7.5 | 9.3 | 9.8 | 8.8 | 72.5 | 79.4 | 66.0 |
| Ulcer of stomach and duodenum | 3.4 | 4.5 | 2.4 | 11.8 | 13.3 | 9.0 | 40.1 | 59.9 | 21.6 |
| Appendicitis | 2.2 | 2.1 | 2.3 | 6.5 | 7.2 | 5.8 | 14.3 | 15.1 | 13.3 |
| Hernia | 3.3 | 5.5 | 1.3 | 7.7 | 7.1 | 9.9 | 25.4 | 39.1 | 12.9 |

| | | | | | | | | | |
|---|---|---|---|---|---|---|---|---|---|
| Diseases of the gallbladder | 2.8 | 1.5 | 4.2 | 11.6 | 12.4 | 11.3 | 32.5 | 18.6 | 45.2 |
| Other digestive system conditions | 6.7 | 6.0 | 7.3 | 8.6 | 8.4 | 8.7 | 57.6 | 50.4 | 63.5 |
| Male genital disorders | 1.8 | 3.8 | — | 10.7 | 10.7 | — | 19.3 | 40.7 | — |
| Female breast and genital disorders | 4.5 | — | 8.7 | 6.8 | — | 6.8 | 30.6 | — | 59.2 |
| Other genitourinary system conditions | 5.6 | 5.4 | 5.8 | 8.0 | 8.4 | 7.6 | 44.8 | 45.4 | 44.1 |
| Deliveries | 20.5 | — | 39.9 | 4.2 | — | 4.2 | 86.1 | — | 167.6 |
| Complications of pregnancy and the puerperium | 3.2 | — | 6.1 | 3.0 | — | 3.0 | 9.6 | — | 18.3 |
| Diseases of the skin | 1.5 | 1.7 | 1.3 | 7.7 | 8.0 | 7.3 | 11.6 | 13.6 | 9.5 |
| Arthritis, all forms | 1.3 | .9 | 1.6 | 11.6 | 16.9 | 8.7 | 15.1 | 15.2 | 13.9 |
| Conditions of bones and joints, n.e.c.[a] | 2.3 | 2.7 | 2.0 | 12.0 | 12.7 | 11.1 | 27.6 | 34.3 | 22.2 |
| Other conditions of the musculoskeletal system | 2.1 | 2.1 | 2.1 | 7.2 | 8.6 | 5.9 | 15.1 | 18.1 | 12.4 |
| Fractures and dislocations | 5.0 | 5.6 | 4.5 | 13.7 | 11.5 | 16.3 | 68.5 | 64.4 | 73.4 |
| Other current injuries | 7.2 | 9.4 | 5.2 | 7.3 | 6.8 | 8.0 | 52.6 | 63.9 | 41.6 |
| All other conditions and observations | 6.8 | 6.8 | 6.8 | 9.0 | 9.8 | 8.3 | 61.2 | 66.6 | 56.4 |

[a] n.e.c., not elsewhere classified.

Source: Charles S. Wilder, Hospital Discharges and Length of Stay (U.S. Department of Health, Education, and Welfare, National Center for Health Statistics, Vital and Health Statistics, Series 10, No. 30 [Washington, D.C., U.S. Government Printing Office, 1966]).

## TABLE 2-7

### Selected Chronic Conditions Causing Activity Limitations
### (average for two-year period, July, 1961–June, 1963)

| Selected Chronic Conditions[a] | Average Number of Persons with Condition (in Thousands) | | | | Percent Distribution[c] | | | |
|---|---|---|---|---|---|---|---|---|
| | All Degrees of Activity Limitation | With Limitation but Not in Major Activity[b] | Limited in Amount or Kind of Major Activity[b] | Unable to Carry on Major Activity[b] | All Degrees of Activity Limitation | With Limitation But Not in Major Activity[b] | Limited in Amount or Kind of Major Activity[b] | Unable to Carry on Major Activity[b] |
| Persons limited in activity | 22,225 | 6,135 | 11,975 | 4,116 | 100.0 | 100.0 | 100.0 | 100.0 |
| Tuberculosis, all forms | 171 | d | 100 | 46 | .8 | d | .8 | 1.1 |
| Malignant neoplasms | 236 | d | 99 | 108 | 1.1 | d | .8 | 2.6 |
| Benign and unspecified neoplasms | 238 | 63 | 121 | 55 | 1.1 | 1.0 | 1.0 | 1.3 |
| Asthma–hay fever | 1,118 | 388 | 547 | 183 | 5.0 | 6.3 | 4.6 | 4.4 |
| Diabetes | 537 | 99 | 272 | 167 | 2.4 | 1.6 | 2.3 | 4.1 |
| Mental and nervous conditions | 1,701 | 435 | 841 | 425 | 7.7 | 7.1 | 7.0 | 10.3 |
| Heart conditions | 3,567 | 670 | 1,893 | 1,004 | 16.0 | 10.9 | 15.8 | 24.4 |
| Hypertension without heart involvement | 1,330 | 332 | 772 | 225 | 6.0 | 5.4 | 6.4 | 5.5 |
| Conditions of genitourinary system | 1,110 | 295 | 582 | 233 | 5.0 | 4.8 | 4.9 | 5.7 |
| Peptic ulcer | 544 | 145 | 286 | 113 | 2.4 | 2.4 | 2.4 | 2.7 |
| Hernia | 590 | 107 | 365 | 118 | 2.7 | 1.7 | 3.0 | 2.9 |
| Arthritis and rheumatism | 3,300 | 714 | 1,888 | 697 | 14.8 | 11.6 | 15.8 | 16.9 |
| Visual impairments | 1,228 | 179 | 514 | 535 | 5.5 | 2.9 | 4.3 | 13.0 |
| Hearing impairments | 480 | 95 | 201 | 184 | 2.2 | 1.5 | 1.7 | 4.5 |
| Paralysis, complete or partial | 899 | 141 | 324 | 434 | 4.0 | 2.3 | 2.7 | 10.5 |

| | | | | | | | |
|---|---|---|---|---|---|---|---|
| Impairments (except paralysis) of back or spine.......... 1,667 | 459 | 1,047 | 160 | 7.5 | 7.5 | 8.7 | 3.9 |
| Impairments (except paralysis and absence) of upper extremities and shoulders.......... 341 | 72 | 219 | 50 | 1.5 | 1.2 | 1.8 | 1.2 |
| Impairments (except paralysis and absence) of lower extremities and hips.......... 1,374 | 400 | 717 | 257 | 6.2 | 6.5 | 6.0 | 6.2 |

[a] A condition is considered to be chronic if it has lasted for more than three months or if it is one of a list of diverse conditions generally classified as chronic in the interview questionnaire reproduced in *Vital and Health Statistics*, Series 10 publications.

[b] Major activity refers to ability to work, keep house, or go to school.

[c] Percentages may add (a) to more than 100 because a person can report more than one condition as the cause of his limitation; or (b) to less than 100 because only conditions frequently reported are included here.

[d] Figure does not meet standards of reliability or precision.

Source: U. S. Department of Health, Education, and Welfare, Public Health Service, *Vital and Health Statistics*, Series 10, Number 17, *Chronic Conditions and Activity Limitations, United States, July 1961–June 1963; Health, Education, and Welfare Trends*, 1965 ed., p. S–15. All statistics from the U.S. National Health Survey, authorized by Congress in 1956, are based on a continuing sample of the civilian noninstitutional population residing in the United States. Estimates for fiscal years 1962 and 1963 are based on interviews of 80,000 households containing approximately 259,000 persons. Each statistic is adjusted by two stages of ratio estimation to official Bureau of the Census population figures to make the sample estimate closely representative of the population by age, sex, color, and residence, and to reduce sampling variance.

caries, which is said to affect "almost everybody."[15] Surveys of school children have indicated that 90 percent need dental care.

It is important to remember that not all illness produces disability. One study[16] indicated that for males at ages 25 to 64 the total illness rate is 633 per 1,000, while the rate of disabling illness is 358 per 1,000. Thus nondisabling illness occurred at a rate of 275 per 1,000. Even blindness is not always totally disabling. National Health Survey data showed that 29 percent of the totally blind males at ages 15 to 64 years had some employment.

*Frequency rates—long-term disability—insurance data.* Incidence rates for long-term disability by factors producing disability are available only from insurance data. These data are based on experience with se-

TABLE 2–8

Factors Producing Disability by Percentage of Total for Various Benefits and Ages, Eleven Companies, 1946–50, Life Insurance Disability Riders

| | Benefit Type | | | | | | |
|---|---|---|---|---|---|---|---|
| | Waiver of Premiums Only, 6-Month Waiting Period (by ages) | | | | Waiver and $10.00 per Month per $1,000, 90-Day Waiting Period (by age) | | |
| Factor | 20–29 | 30–39 | 40–49 | 50–59 | 30–39 | 40–49 | 50–59 |
| Pulmonary tuberculosis........ | 31.2 | 20.8 | 9.2 | 2.1 | 21.1 | 3.6 | 1.6 |
| Syphilis and sequelae......... | 0.0 | 1.0 | 0.5 | 0.2 | 0.0 | 1.2 | 0.1 |
| Malignant neoplasms.......... | 2.2 | 5.5 | 9.9 | 12.4 | 14.7 | 11.0 | 9.4 |
| Rheumatism, etc.............. | 1.8 | 2.9 | 3.0 | 2.4 | 0.0 | 3.1 | 4.1 |
| Diabetes..................... | 0.0 | 0.1 | 0.8 | 0.9 | 0.0 | 0.7 | 1.5 |
| Mental disorders.............. | 10.0 | 11.1 | 6.6 | 4.6 | 11.0 | 13.2 | 5.7 |
| Diseases of eyes.............. | 0.9 | 0.7 | 1.8 | 1.4 | 0.0 | 1.2 | 1.0 |
| Cardiovascular................ | 3.8 | 16.2 | 38.5 | 56.7 | 9.2 | 31.0 | 51.4 |
| Respiratory (not TB).......... | 0.9 | 1.2 | 2.2 | 1.7 | 1.8 | 0.9 | 3.5 |
| Digestive system............. | 3.0 | 4.9 | 3.8 | 4.0 | 9.2 | 5.4 | 6.7 |
| Nephritis..................... | 2.6 | 0.4 | 0.6 | 0.1 | 0.0 | 0.8 | 1.3 |
| Diseases of bones............. | 2.3 | 3.5 | 2.1 | 0.9 | 0.0 | 4.5 | 2.2 |
| External violence.............. | 20.5 | 14.5 | 9.3 | 4.1 | 9.2 | 11.4 | 3.3 |
| Other........................ | 20.8 | 17.2 | 11.7 | 8.5 | 23.8 | 12.0 | 8.2 |
| Total.................. | 100 | 100 | 100 | 100 | 100 | 100 | 100 |

Source: "Report of the Committee on Disability and Double Indemnity," *Transactions of the Society of Actuaries,* 1952, Reports Number, pp. 137 and 148.

---

[15] M. M. Davis, *Medical Care for Tomorrow* (New York: Harper & Bros., 1955), p. 64.

[16] S. D. Collins, *The Incidence of Illness and the Volume of Medical Services among 9,000 Canvassed Families* (Washington, D.C., 1944), Tables 1 and 4 of Reprint No. 2129 of the *Public Health Reports,* cited in Mortimer Spiegelman, *Significant Mortality and Morbidity Trends since 1900* (Philadelphia: American College of Life Underwriters, 1956), p. 8.

lected insured lives, who are healthier than the general population. Many persons who are disabled from congenital defects or other factors before attaining the age at which insurance is customarily carried never will enter into such tabulations. Moreover, these rates are not really rates of the occurrence of disability; they are *rates of claim* under a particular policy or program and are influenced by the nature of the coverage. However, it is important to remember that the data presented above really represent rates of reporting, rates of diagnosis, and rates of treatment.

Table 2–8 is based upon a comprehensive study by the Society of Actuaries of the experience of eleven companies in the years 1946–50 and indicates the proportion of disability claims at various ages produced by various factors. The data are shown for two types of contract. The first provides a waiver of premium only after six months of disability; the second an income benefit of $10 for each $1,000 of life insurance carried, after a 90-day waiting period. The absolute rates for the latter were higher, due not only to the shorter waiting period but also, to an undetermined degree, to the greater moral hazard attendant upon a policy which provides a cash income.[17] Cardiovascular diseases, malignant neoplasms, mental disorders, tuberculosis, and external violence were the most important factors. The importance of the first two increased with age, while that of the last two decreased.

*Frequency rates: "total and permanent" disability, OASDI.* A good measure of the important causes of long term disability is the experience with disability benefits in the Old-Age, Survivors, and Disability Insurance system under social security. The experience from 1957 to 1963 is shown in Table 2–9. This program picked up many persons who had been disabled prior to the year benefits began, as indicated in the first part of the table. In 1957, 35 percent were disabled less than two years before allowance, 43.9 percent from two to five years, and 21.1 percent more than five years. By 1963, the proportions had changed to 77.8 percent, 20.7 percent, and 1.5 percent, respectively.

In order to be considered disabled, the workers had to be unable to engage in any gainful activity because of a physical or mental impairment expected to result in death or be of long-continued and indefinite duration. This last condition was administratively defined as requiring a prognosis of at least 18 months duration from disablement.

Diseases of the circulatory system were the most important category, especially arteriosclerotic heart disease, including coronary disease. Diseases of the nervous stysem and sense organs accounted for 22 percent of the allowances in 1957, but only 15 percent by 1963. Mental disorders increased from 8 percent in 1957 to 11 percent in 1963. Arthritis accounted for about 6 percent throughout the period. Cancer increased from 6 to 11 percent, as did benign tumors.

---

[17] See chapters 10, 16, and 17 below for discussions of moral hazard.

**TABLE 2-9**

**Worker Disability Allowances, 1957-63 by Duration of Disability and Primary Diagnosis**

| Number of years by which year of onset[a] preceded year of allowance | Year of Disability Allowance | | | | | | | 1957–63 Totals | |
|---|---|---|---|---|---|---|---|---|---|
| | 1957 | 1958 | 1959 | 1960 | 1961 | 1962 | 1963 | No. | % |
| Total number | 165,003 | 184,476 | 178,952 | 179,419 | 241,050 | 286,434 | 224,229 | 1,459,573 | 100% |
| Less than 2 years | 57,723 | 89,112 | 105,691 | 116,021 | 152,432 | 187,698 | 174,352 | 883,029 | 60.5 |
| 2-5 years | 72,455 | 67,330 | 53,282 | 51,646 | 71,049 | 82,484 | 46,489 | 444,735 | 30.4 |
| 6 years or more | 34,825 | 28,034 | 19,979 | 11,752 | 17,579 | 16,252 | 3,388 | 131,809 | 9.1 |

| Diagnostic Group and Primary Diagnosis[b] (number) | Year of Disability Allowance | | | | | | | 1957–63 Totals | |
|---|---|---|---|---|---|---|---|---|---|
| | 1957 | 1958 | 1959 | 1960 | 1961 | 1962 | 1963 | No. | % |
| Total | 165,003 | 184,476 | 178,952 | 179,419 | 241,050 | 286,434 | 224,229 | 1,459,573 | 100% |
| Infective and parasitic diseases | 13,882 | 16,409 | 13,319 | 10,903 | 15,153 | 15,271 | 10,859 | 95,796 | 6.6% |
| Pulmonary tuberculosis | 8,618 | 11,210 | 9,134 | 7,455 | 10,775 | 11,205 | 8,009 | 66,408 | 4.5 |
| Other | 5,264 | 5,199 | 4,185 | 3,447 | 4,378 | 4,055 | 2,850 | 29,388 | 2.0 |
| Neoplasms | 10,642 | 15,309 | 16,043 | 17,739 | 23,103 | 27,632 | 25,042 | 135,510 | 9.3 |
| Malignant neoplasms | 10,041 | 14,637 | 15,523 | 17,159 | 22,185 | 26,455 | 24,125 | 130,125 | 8.9 |
| Benign neoplasms and neoplasms of unspecified nature | 601 | 672 | 520 | 580 | 918 | 1,177 | 917 | 5,385 | .4 |
| Allergic, endocrine system, metabolic, and nutritional diseases | 4,728 | 5,096 | 5,098 | 5,406 | 7,070 | 9,383 | 7,563 | 44,344 | 3.0 |
| Diabetes mellitus | 4,185 | 4,492 | 4,480 | 4,672 | 5,941 | 7,146 | 5,988 | 36,904 | 2.5 |
| Other | 543 | 604 | 618 | 734 | 1,129 | 2,237 | 1,575 | 7,440 | .5 |
| Diseases of the blood and bloodforming organs | 429 | 456 | 374 | 442 | 566 | 739 | 597 | 3,603 | .2 |
| Mental, psychoneurotic, and personality disorders | 13,077 | 20,177 | 19,743 | 17,287 | 26,864 | 37,315 | 24,526 | 158,929 | 10.9 |
| Schizophrenic disorders (dementia praecox) | 6,439 | 11,180 | 10,183 | 7,745 | 14,281 | 19,870 | 12,712 | 82,410 | 5.6 |
| Other | 6,638 | 8,937 | 9,560 | 9,542 | 12,583 | 17,445 | 11,814 | 76,119 | 5.2 |
| Diseases of the nervous system and the sense organs | 36,213 | 38,884 | 33,489 | 32,105 | 44,709 | 45,261 | 32,712 | 263,373 | 18.0 |
| Cerebral hemorrhage | 8,226 | 7,755 | 6,500 | 5,616 | 7,405 | 6,236 | 4,148 | 45,887 | 3.1 |
| Cerebral embolism and thrombosis | 6,312 | 6,898 | 6,792 | 6,705 | 6,014 | 5,414 | 5,180 | 43,315 | 3.0 |
| Certain vascular lesions affecting the central nervous system | 2,542 | 1,935 | 1,531 | 1,624 | 2,359 | 2,974 | 2,351 | 15,316 | 1.0 |
| Multiple sclerosis | 2,241 | 2,791 | 1,813 | 1,623 | 3,442 | 2,642 | 2,072 | 16,624 | 1.1 |

| Diagnostic group[b] | | | | | | | Total | Percent |
|---|---|---|---|---|---|---|---|---|
| Paralysis agitans | 2,850 | 2,504 | 2,285 | 2,247 | 2,625 | 2,600 | 2,006 | 17,117 | 1.2 |
| Epilepsy | 1,238 | 1,763 | 1,583 | 1,601 | 2,698 | 3,145 | 1,968 | 13,996 | 1.9 |
| Certain diseases of the spinal cord, including paralysis resulting from spinal cord injuries | 1,514 | 2,153 | 1,589 | 1,436 | 2,999 | 2,036 | 588 | 12,315 | .8 |
| Encephalopathy (chronic brain syndrome)[c] | 1,955 | 2,434 | 2,176 | 2,160 | 3,842 | 5,143 | 3,165 | 20,875 | 1.4 |
| Diseases of the eye | 4,128 | 4,655 | 3,802 | 3,369 | 5,330 | 5,625 | 4,080 | 30,989 | 2.1 |
| Other | 5,207 | 5,996 | 5,418 | 5,724 | 7,994 | 9,446 | 7,154 | 46,939 | 3.2 |
| Diseases of the circulatory system | 53,527 | 55,240 | 54,262 | 55,855 | 71,860 | 82,015 | 66,468 | 439,227 | 30.1 |
| Rheumatic heart disease of mitral valve | 3,052 | 3,588 | 3,152 | 2,988 | 4,113 | 2,432 | 2,077 | 21,402 | 1.5 |
| Certain heart diseases specified as rheumatic | 545 | 490 | 282 | 281 | 1,081 | 2,947 | 2,346 | 7,972 | .5 |
| Arteriosclerotic heart disease including coronary disease | 29,920 | 32,830 | 34,172 | 35,685 | 43,814 | 49,023 | 41,168 | 266,612 | 18.3 |
| Hypertensive heart disease with clinical type unspecified | 10,217 | 9,542 | 8,704 | 8,439 | 10,933 | 13,578 | 10,516 | 71,929 | 4.9 |
| General arteriosclerosis | 1,371 | 1,468 | 1,558 | 1,779 | 2,754 | 2,493 | 1,978 | 13,401 | .9 |
| Other | 8,422 | 7,322 | 6,394 | 6,683 | 9,165 | 11,542 | 8,383 | 57,911 | 4.0 |
| Diseases of the respiratory system | 13,005 | 13,862 | 15,581 | 16,489 | 20,030 | 23,408 | 19,107 | 121,482 | 8.3 |
| Pneumoconiosis due to silica and silicates (occupational) | 2,985 | 2,010 | 2,573 | 2,842 | 2,335 | 2,089 | 1,546 | 16,380 | 1.1 |
| Emphysema[c] | 8,835 | 10,905 | 11,941 | 12,343 | 15,271 | 17,630 | 14,897 | 91,822 | 6.3 |
| Other | 1,185 | 947 | 1,067 | 1,304 | 2,424 | 3,689 | 2,664 | 13,280 | .9 |
| Diseases of the digestive system | 2,502 | 2,934 | 3,350 | 3,575 | 4,300 | 5,922 | 4,437 | 27,020 | 1.9 |
| Diseases of the genitourinary system | 914 | 1,065 | 1,046 | 1,077 | 1,608 | 2,040 | 1,725 | 9,475 | .6 |
| Diseases of the skin and cellular tissues | 339 | 419 | 450 | 463 | 794 | 1,177 | 719 | 4,361 | .3 |
| Diseases of the bones and organs of movement | 14,974 | 13,681 | 15,196 | 17,124 | 23,241 | 33,751 | 21,744 | 139,711 | 9.6 |
| Rheumatoid arthritis and allied conditions | 5,469 | 5,002 | 4,404 | 4,469 | 6,468 | 7,206 | 5,974 | 38,992 | 2.7 |
| Osteoarthritis and allied conditions | 4,654 | 4,187 | 5,494 | 6,449 | 6,748 | 9,378 | 7,255 | 44,165 | 3.0 |
| Displacement of intervertebral disc | 728 | 829 | 1,098 | 1,483 | 2,165 | 3,888 | 3,139 | 13,330 | .9 |
| Residual deformities of bones and joints[d] | 901 | 953 | 989 | 947 | 1,867 | 3,352 | 522 | 9,531 | .7 |
| Other | 3,222 | 2,710 | 3,211 | 3,776 | 5,993 | 9,927 | 4,854 | 33,693 | 2.3 |
| Congenital malformations | 694 | 887 | 824 | 865 | 1,637 | 2,026 | 1,646 | 8,579 | .6 |
| Accidents, poisonings, and violence[e] | — | — | — | — | — | — | 6,496 | 6,496 | .4 |
| Other[f] | 77 | 177 | 177 | 89 | 125 | 494 | 588 | 1,727 | .1 |

[a] The year of onset of disability is the year in which the applicant was first under a disability, as established by the Social Security Administration.

[b] As grouped in the Manual of the International Statistical Classification of Diseases, Injuries, and Causes of Death.

[c] Special modification of the international code.

[d] Deformities such as malunion or nonunion of a fracture, amputation, or shortened extremity, resulting from traumatic conditions.

[e] First used for 1963 allowances. Over one half of the cases in this newly utilized grouping would have been otherwise tabulated with diseases of the bones and organs of movement, and about one fifth with diseases of the nervous system and sense organs.

[f] Includes diagnoses such as Jacksonian epilepsy, senility, chronic lead poisoning, etc.

Source: Jacob Schmulowitz and Henry D. Lynn, Insured and Disabled Workers under the Social Security Disability Program: Characteristics and Benefit Payments, 1957–1963 (U.S. Department of Health, Education, and Welfare, Social Security Administration Research Report No. 11 [Washington, D.C.: U.S. Government Printing Office, 1966]).

Many health insurance underwriters sell policies with two- or five-year maximum sickness benefits, on the theory that most people are either dead or recovered in two years. These figures refute this idea completely! In 1963, the only year it was tabulated separately, the category of "accidents, poisonings, and violence" accounted for less than 3 percent of allowances. The main causes of really long-term disability are diseases of the nervous system and sense organs and mental, psychoneurotic, and personality disorders. These account for 85 to 90 percent of all benefit awards for OASDI benefits for children disabled before age 18.

*Frequency rates—death.* Just as death may be considered the worst type of poor health, the relative frequency of the factors producing death is a good indication of the importance of these factors from a standpoint of health protection (Table 2–10).

If suicide, which, by definition, does not produce disability, and cirrhosis of the liver are omitted, this list is quite similar to the Social Security data on long-term disability presented in Table 2–9. The two important categories of disability not represented in the factors produc-

TABLE 2–10

Death Rates per 100,000 Population and Proportion of All Deaths from Selected Factors, U.S., 1965, and Preliminary Death Rates, 1966

| Rank Order | Factor | 1965 Rate | 1965 Percent | 1966 Rate (Estimated) |
|---|---|---|---|---|
| | All Causes................................... | 943.2 | 100.0 | 954.2 |
| 1 | Diseases of heart............................ | 367.4 | 39.0 | 375.1 |
| 2 | Malignant neoplasms........................ | 153.5 | 16.3 | 154.8 |
| 3 | Vascular lesions affecting central nervous system................................... | 103.7 | 11.0 | 104.6 |
| 4 | Accidents................................... | 55.7 | 5.9 | 57.3 |
| | Motor vehicle accidents................. | 25.4 | 2.7 | — |
| | Other accidents......................... | 30.4 | 3.2 | — |
| 5 | Influenza and pneumonia ................. | 31.9 | 3.4 | 32.8 |
| 6 | Certain diseases of early infancy........... | 28.6 | 3.0 | 26.1 |
| 7 | General arteriosclerosis..................... | 19.7 | 2.1 | 19.5 |
| 8 | Diabetes mellitus........................... | 17.1 | 1.8 | 18.1 |
| 9 | Other diseases of circulatory system........ | 14.1 | 1.5 | 14.4 |
| 10 | Other bronchopulmonic diseases........... | 13.7 | 1.5 | 14.7 |
| 11 | Cirrhosis of liver............................ | 12.8 | 1.4 | a |
| 12 | Suicide.................................... | 11.1 | 1.2 | a |
| 13 | Congenital malformations.................. | 10.1 | 1.1 | a |
| 14 | Other hypertensive disease................. | 6.0 | 0.6 | a |
| 15 | Homicide................................... | 5.5 | 0.6 | a |
| | All other causes........................... | 92.3 | 9.8 | 136.7 |

a Included in "All other causes."

Source: U.S. Department of Health, Education, and Welfare, Public Health Service, National Center for Health Statistics. *Vital Statistics of The United States, 1964* (Washington, D.C.: U.S. Government Printing Office, 1967), Vol. II, Part A, p. 1–6. *Monthly Vital Statistics Report,* Vol. 15, No. 13 (July 26, 1967), p. 3.

TABLE 2-11

Total Economic Cost: Estimated Direct Expenditures, Indirect Costs of Morbidity, and Present Value of Lifetime Earnings Discounted at 4 Percent, by Diagnosis, 1963

| Diagnosis | Amount (Millions) | | | | Percent Distribution | | | |
|---|---|---|---|---|---|---|---|---|
| | Total | Direct Ex-penditures | Morbidity | Total Mortality | Total | Direct Ex-penditures | Mor-bidity | Total Mortality |
| Total............................................... | $93,500.3 | $22,530.0 | $21,042.2 | $49,928.1 | 100.0 | 100.0 | 100.0 | 100.0 |
| Infective and parasitic diseases................ | 2,135.3 | 501.9 | 858.0 | 775.4 | 2.3 | 2.2 | 4.1 | 1.6 |
| Tuberculosis................................... | 967.6 | 241.4 | 385.2 | 341.0 | 1.0 | 1.1 | 1.8 | .7 |
| Other.......................................... | 1,167.8 | 260.6 | 472.8 | 434.4 | 1.2 | 1.2 | 2.2 | .9 |
| Neoplasms....................................... | 10,589.9 | 1,279.0 | 850.7 | 8,460.2 | 11.3 | 5.7 | 4.0 | 16.9 |
| Allergic, endocrine, metabolic, nutritional diseases.. | 2,623.1 | 902.9 | 539.5 | 1,180.7 | 2.8 | 4.0 | 2.6 | 2.4 |
| Diseases of blood and blood-forming organs...... | 372.6 | 155.9 | 41.3 | 175.4 | .4 | .7 | .2 | .4 |
| Mental, psychoneurotic and personality disorders... | 7,276.6 | 2,401.7 | 4,624.0 | 250.9 | 7.8 | 10.7 | 22.0 | .5 |
| Diseases of nervous system and sense organs..... | 6,795.4 | 1,416.4 | 1,525.5 | 3,853.5 | 7.3 | 6.3 | 7.2 | 7.7 |
| Diseases of circulatory system................. | 20,948.4 | 2,267.3 | 2,919.7 | 15,761.4 | 22.4 | 10.1 | 13.9 | 31.6 |
| Diseases of respiratory system................. | 7,412.8 | 1,581.1 | 3,166.3 | 2,665.4 | 7.9 | 7.0 | 15.0 | 5.3 |
| Diseases of digestive system.................. | 7,837.3 | 4,158.7 | 1,220.1 | 2,458.5 | 8.4 | 18.5 | 5.8 | 4.9 |
| Diseases of genitourinary system.............. | 2,559.9 | 1,210.2 | 497.8 | 851.9 | 2.7 | 5.4 | 2.4 | 1.7 |
| Maternity....................................... | 1,517.2 | 1,391.1 | 32.2 | 93.9 | 1.6 | 6.2 | .2 | .2 |
| Diseases of skin and cellular tissue........... | 450.3 | 248.1 | 128.4 | 73.8 | .5 | 1.1 | .6 | .1 |
| Diseases of bones and organs of movement....... | 2,782.7 | 1,430.0 | 1,225.0 | 127.7 | 3.0 | 6.3 | 5.8 | .3 |
| Congenital malformations....................... | 1,242.7 | 113.0 | 41.8 | 1,087.9 | 1.3 | .5 | .2 | 2.2 |
| Certain diseases of early infancy.............. | 3,103.0 | 30.3 | — | 3,072.7 | 3.3 | .1 | — | 6.2 |
| Symptoms, senility and ill-defined conditions.... | 1,653.7 | 623.7 | 288.5 | 741.5 | 1.8 | 2.8 | 1.4 | 1.5 |
| Injuries........................................ | 11,810.6 | 1,702.8 | 1,810.7 | 8,297.1 | 12.6 | 7.6 | 8.6 | 16.6 |
| Special conditions and examinations............ | 977.6 | 965.8 | 11.8 | — | 1.0 | 4.3 | .1 | — |
| Miscellaneous................................... | 1,411.1 | 150.1 | 1,261.0 | — | 1.5 | .7 | 6.0 | — |

Source: Dorothy P. Rice, *Estimating the Cost of Illness* (Health Economics Series No. 6, U.S. Public Health Service [Washington, D.C.: U.S. Government Printing Office, 1966, p. 109]).

ing death are nervous and mental diseases, and arthritis-rheumatism. Orthopedic impairments are represented by accidents and congenital defects.

If congenital defects and certain diseases of early infancy are omitted, the list corresponds fairly closely to the insurance data on factors producing long-term disability in Table 2–8.

*Total economic cost.* Rice[18] developed a measure of the total economic cost of disability and death, working from aggregate figures. Morbidity costs were determined separately for the institutionalized and noninstitutionalized populations. Estimates were made of number disabled, man-years lost and economic cost (man-years times average earnings). In effect this represents the cost of disability suffered that year as distinguished from that incurred. For mortality losses, however, she estimated the value of earnings lost from the time of death to retirement age, as a measure of losses incurred. Combining these measures with the direct expenditures gives a measure of total economic loss. Each measure was further broken down by diagnosis, yielding a measure of the total economic loss from various diagnoses. Her major results are presented in Table 2–11. Again, circulatory disease, injuries, and neoplasms cause the most loss, together accounting for 46.3 percent of the total loss.

Clearly, any social effort to reduce the toll of death and disability should concentrate upon mental and nervous diseases and on the 10 major producers of death, of which heart disease and cancer are the most important. It is quite possible that suicide (and to a degree homicide) are the correlatives in death of mental disease in disability. Syphilis and tuberculosis have declined rapidly as producers of death, and probably are of lesser importance for disability now than during the period on which the data were based. Rheumatism, arthritis, and hypertension are other important producers of disability, especially at the older ages.

### Facilities for treatment

*Personnel.* There are about 2.6 million professional or skilled persons employed in the "health services industries" in the United States.[19] These include about 1.5 million people employed in specific health occupations of which perhaps two thirds are college or professionally trained. In addition, another 300,000 to 500,000 persons in these health occupations are employed in other industries such as the pharmaceutical industry,

---

[18] Dorothy P. Rice, *Estimating the Cost of Illness* (Health Economics Series No. 6, U.S. Department of Health, Education, and Welfare [Washington, D.C.: U.S. Government Printing Office, 1966]).

[19] Most of the figures in this section are from U.S. Department of Health, Education, and Welfare, Public Health Service, National Center for Health Statistics, *Health Resources Statistics, Health Manpower, 1965* (Washington, D.C.: U.S. Government Printing Office, 1966).

drugstores, and other retail trade, etc. The number employed in the health service industries has increased by about 50 percent since 1950.

Table 2–12 gives estimates of the number employed in various health service occupations in the health field in 1950 and 1965. Also employed in health services are more than 60,000 mechanics and craftsmen, and

TABLE 2–12

Active Health Manpower, 1950 and 1965

| Occupation | Number | | Percent Change 1950–65 |
|---|---|---|---|
| | 1950 | 1965 | |
| Administration of health services............ | a | 31,500–34,000 | a |
| Anthropology and sociology [b]................. | a | 600–800 | a |
| Automatic data processing [b]................. | a | 300 | a |
| Basic sciences in the health field............ | 19,200[c] | 61,900 | +222% |
| Biomedical engineering...................... | a | 7,500 | a |
| Chiropractic and naturopathy................ | 22,000 | 24,000 | +9% |
| Clinical laboratory services.................. | 30,000 | 85,000 | +183% |
| Dentistry and allied services [d]............... | 158,613 | 225,000 | +42% |
| Dietetic and nutritional services [b]............ | a | 7,710 | a |
| Economic research in the health field........ | a | 500 | a |
| Environmental health....................... | a | 32,500–35,000 | a |
| Food and drug protective services........... | a | 16,500 | a |
| Health and vital statistics................... | a | 1,000–2,000 | a |
| Health education........................... | a | 16,700 | a |
| Health information and communication [b].... | a | 5,000 | a |
| Library services in the health field........... | a | 8,000 | a |
| Medical records........................... | 12,000 | 37,000 | +208% |
| Medicine and osteopathy................... | 232,697 | 305,115 | +31% |
| Midwifery................................. | 20,700 | 4,900 | −76% |
| Nursing and related services................ | 718,250 | 1,409,000 | +96% |
| Occupational therapy....................... | 2,000 | 6,000 | +200% |
| Orthopedic and prosthetic appliance making | a | 3,300 | a |
| Pharmacy................................. | 101,100 | 118,000 | +17% |
| Physical therapy........................... | 4,600 | 12,000 | +161% |
| Podiatry.................................. | 6,400 | 7,600 | +19% |
| Psychology............................... | 3,000 | 9,000 | +200% |
| Radiologic technology...................... | 30,800 | 70,000 | +127% |
| Secretarial and office services [b]............. | a | 150,000–250,000 | a |
| Social work [b]............................. | 6,200 | 17,500 | +182% |
| Specialized rehabilitation services........... | a | 5,300–5,900 | a |
| Speech pathology and audiology............ | a | 14,000 | a |
| Veterinary medicine........................ | 15,800 | 23,700[e] | +50% |
| Visual services and eye care................ | a | 40,400 | a |
| Vocational rehabilitation counseling......... | 4,200 | 6,200 | +48% |
| Total.................................. | a | 2,816,125 | +75% [f] |

[a] Data not available.
[b] Employed in the "health field."
[c] 1954.
[d] Including dentists, dental hygienists, assistants, and laboratory technicians.
[e] 1964.
[f] Based on only those occupations for which data were available for both years.
Source: U.S. Department of Health, Education, and Welfare, Public Health Service, National Center for Health Statistics, *Health Resources Statistics, 1965* (Washington, D.C.: U.S. Government Printing Office, 1966).

more than 300,000 service workers such as cooks, kitchen workers, janitors, porters, and maids.

*Physicians* constitute the prime personnel resource for the prevention and care of poor health. They may hold the degree of M.D. (Doctor of Medicine) or D.O. (Doctor of Osteopathy). There are about 278,000 M.D. physicians and about 10,000 osteopaths active in the United States and about 2,500,000 members of other health service oc-

TABLE 2–13

Number of Physicians, Dentists, and Nurses as Compared with
U.S. Population, 1950–65

(population in thousands)

|  | 1950 | 1955 | 1960 | 1965 |
|---|---|---|---|---|
| Total U.S. population[a] | 156,472 | 170,499 | 185,369 | 199,256 |
| U.S. civilian population | 153,635 | 167,038 | 182,348 | 195,811 |
| Total U.S. physicians[b] | 232,697 | 255,211 | 274,834 | 305,115 |
| Total physicians per 100,000 of total population | 149 | 150 | 148 | 153 |
| U.S. civilian physicians in private practice[c] | 168,089 | 169,871 | 179,176 | 190,748 |
| U.S. civilian physicians per 100,000 of civilian population | 109 | 102 | 98 | 97 |
| Total U.S. dentists | 87,164 | 94,879 | 101,947 | 109,301 |
| Total U.S. dentists per 100,000 of total population | 55.7 | 55.6 | 54.9 | 54.8 |
| U.S. active Nonfederal dentists | 75,313 | 76,087 | 82,630 | 86,317 |
| U.S. active Nonfederal dentists per 100,000 civilian population | 49 | 45.6 | 45.3 | 44.1 |
| Total U.S. nurses | 375,000 | 415.300 | 504,000 | 601,000 |
| Total U.S. nurses per 100,000 total population | 239.6 | 243.5 | 271.8 | 301.6 |

a Includes civilians in 50 states, District of Columbia, Puerto Rico, and other U.S. outlying areas, and U.S. citizens living abroad or in armed forces.
b M.D. and D.O.
c In U.S. and District of Columbia.
Source: Derived from Maryland Y. Pennell, *Health Resources Statistics,* U.S. Department of Health, Education, and Welfare, Public Health Service, National Center for Health Statistics (Washington, D.C.: U.S. Government Printing Office, 1965), pp. 46, 100, and 111.

cupations, but the physician is the central figure. The number of physicians has increased greatly in the past half century, from about 120,000 in 1900, and the ratio of physicians to total population has increased slightly since 1950. However, the ratio of civilian physicians located in the United States in private practice to the United States civilian population has declined from 109 per 100,000 to 97 per 100,000 during this period, as shown in Table 2–13.

The nature of activities of physicians has also undergone a profound change. In the early years of the century the majority of physicians were engaged in general practice. Today, more than two thirds are engaged in specialization, as shown in Table 2–14 and Chart 2–4. This tendency has been enforced by the accumulation of knowledge: it is no longer possible for one person to become an expert in all fields of medical care. This increasing specialization has to some degree distorted the prevailing concept of physician-patient relationships. It has been variously estimated that from one third[20] to four fifths[21] of American families have a "family doctor" in a meaningful sense, although there is general agreement everyone should.[22] Many upper-income persons deal directly with a variety of specialists, and many lower-income persons with a variety of clinics—or even the local druggist. The complexity of services and resources available often presents a difficult problem of choice to the individual. Chart 2–4 indicates the distribution of physicians by type of practice and degree of specialization.

General practitioners are of three main types. The personal physician resembles closely the old concept of the "family doctor." He is equipped to diagnose and treat about 80 percent of the illness with which he is presented; the balance is referred to specialists. Another variety is the general physician-internist. He is the same type of person as the personal physician except that he has had several years of advanced training in internal medicine. Thus he is probably the technical superior of members of the first group. The third category is the general physician-specialist. In years gone by, almost all specialists developed from general practitioners. This process continues, and many of this third group are in process of changing from a general practitioner to a full-time specialist. However, many specialists today get their specialized training in residencies right after medical school, and many of the general-specialist group, no doubt, will continue to perform both functions in varying combinations. A combination developing in popularity is that of general practitioner–pediatrician. The author, based on his knowledge of the probabilities discussed earlier in this chapter, relies on a three-man group of two cardiologist-internists and one hematologist-internist. Since there are only 1,040 specialists in cardiovascular diseases in private practice in the country (in 1965; see Table 2–14), not everyone can do this.

---

[20] Davis, *op. cit.*, p. 12.

[21] *Progress in Health Services*, June, 1958. For an overview of the "family doctor problem," see *The Future of the Personal Physician* (New York: Group Health Insurance, Inc. 1964).

[22] See National Commission on Community Health Services (N.C.C.H.S.), *Health Is a Community Affair* (Cambridge, Mass.: Harvard University Press, 1966), pp. 20 ff. See also Rashi Fein, *The Doctor Shortage: An Economic Diagnosis* (Washington, D.C.: The Brookings Institution, 1967), pp. 70 ff. Although limited to physicians' services only, this is by far the best book in medical economics known to the author.

TABLE 2-14

Type of Practice and Primary Specialty of Physicians: 1965

| Primary Specialty | Number of Physicians (M.D.) | | | | | Number of D.O.'s in Private Practice |
| --- | --- | --- | --- | --- | --- | --- |
| | | | Other practice | | | |
| | Total Active | Private Practice | Non-federal | Federal | Training Programs | |
| All specialties............. | 277,575 | 180,752 | 34,403 | 18,912 | 43,508 | 9,996 |
| General practice[a]........... | 83,309 | 65,951 | 4,260 | 4,465 | 8,633 | 8,728[b] |
| Medical specialties......... | 61,860 | 37,408 | 8,504 | 4,671 | 11,277 | 307 |
| Allergy................. | 907 | 811 | 39 | 22 | 35 | 1 |
| Cardiovascular disease.. | 1,867 | 1,040 | 447 | 118 | 262 | 3 |
| Dermatology........... | 3,511 | 2,666 | 230 | 166 | 449 | 17 |
| Gastroenterology........ | 626 | 377 | 97 | 57 | 95 | — |
| Internal medicine....... | 38,115 | 22,432 | 4,732 | 3,356 | 7,595 | 234 |
| Pediatrics[c]............. | 15,719 | 9,726 | 2,446 | 770 | 2,777 | 52 |
| Pulmonary diseases..... | 1,115 | 356 | 513 | 182 | 64 | — |
| Surgical specialties......... | 84,351 | 59,850 | 5,208 | 4,147 | 15,146 | 773 |
| Anesthesiology.......... | 8,621 | 6,050 | 1,076 | 328 | 1,167 | 155 |
| Colon and rectal surgery............... | 647 | 623 | 8 | 5 | 11 | 46 |
| General surgery......... | 27,466 | 17,628 | 1,684 | 1,679 | 6,475 | 254 |
| Neurological surgery..... | 2,038 | 1,251 | 212 | 94 | 481 | 4 |
| Obstetrics and gynecology........... | 16,766 | 12,566 | 917 | 660 | 2,623 | 73 |
| Ophthalmology.......... | 8,380 | 6,672 | 324 | 269 | 1,115 | 146 |
| Orthopedic surgery...... | 7,507 | 5,330 | 305 | 493 | 1,379 | 66 |
| Otolaryngology.......... | 5,307 | 4,173 | 203 | 232 | 699 | [d] |
| Plastic surgery.......... | 1,129 | 857 | 50 | 38 | 184 | — |
| Thoracic surgery........ | 1,463 | 957 | 194 | 115 | 197 | 4 |
| Urology................. | 5,027 | 3,743 | 235 | 234 | 815 | 25 |
| Psychiatry and neurology.... | 20,254 | 9,291 | 5,024 | 1,623 | 4,316 | 27 |
| Child psychiatry......... | 795 | 347 | 235 | 21 | 192 | — |
| Neurology.............. | 2,152 | 760 | 571 | 225 | 596 | 3 |
| Psychiatry.............. | 17,307 | 8,184 | 4,218 | 1,377 | 3,528 | 24 |
| Other specialties............ | 27,801 | 8,252 | 11,407 | 4,006 | 4,136 | 161 |
| Administrative medicine.................. | 4,057 | — | 2,521 | 1,534 | 2 | — |
| Aviation medicine....... | 682 | 41 | 73 | 497 | 71 | — |
| General preventive medicine.............. | 826 | — | 621 | 177 | 28 | — |
| Occupational medicine.. | 1,644 | 389 | 1,150 | 80 | 25 | 2 |
| Pathology[e]............. | 8,458 | 1,896 | 3,737 | 709 | 2,116 | 37 |
| Physical medicine and rehabilitation.......... | 1,053 | 317 | 321 | 209 | 206 | 11 |
| Public health........... | 1,461 | — | 1,254 | 176 | 31 | — |
| Radiology[f]............. | 9,620 | 5,609 | 1,730 | 624 | 1,657 | 111 |

a Includes no specialty and other specialties not recognized.
b Includes 938 with practice limited to manipulative therapy.
c Includes pediatric allergy and cardiology.
d Included in ophthalmology.
e Includes forensic pathology.
f Includes diagnostic roentgenology and therapeutic radiology.

Source: *Health Manpower, 1965,* U.S. Department of Health, Education, and Welfare, Public Health Service, National Center for Health Statistics (Washington, D.C.: U.S. Government Printing Office), p. 103.

CHART 2-4

Specialization of Physicians in Private Practice

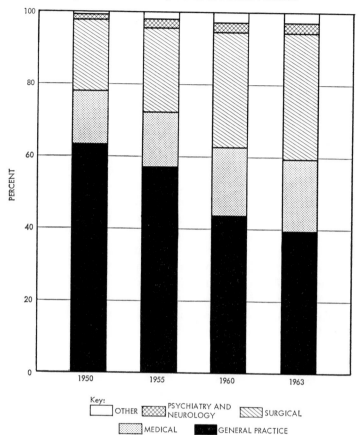

Key:

☐ OTHER   ▨ PSYCHIATRY AND NEUROLOGY   ◪ SURGICAL

▦ MEDICAL   ■ GENERAL PRACTICE

Source: U.S. Department of Health, Education, and Welfare, *Health, Education, and Welfare Trends,* 1965 ed., p. 15.

Specialists provide services which are indispensable to high-quality medical care. With the increasing complexity of medical care, the number of specialists has increased greatly. The most important groups, numerically, specialize in internal medicine, general surgery, psychiatry-neurology, obstetrics-gynecology, pediatrics, and radiology-roentgenology, in that order (Table 2–14). Most specialists are "certified" by examining or qualifying boards approved by the Council on Medical Education and Hospitals of the American Medical Association. Most part-time specialists concentrate in surgery, obstetrics-gynecology, pediatrics, and internal medicine.

The problem of the growing complexity of medical knowledge and the concomitant need for a battery of specialists to work on a single patient probably will be met by the further development of techniques of group practice. Some group practice clinics, like the Mayo Clinic, have developed into huge institutions, but perhaps more significant is the development of many small clinics operated by a team of physicians including several general practitioners and a number of specialists. Sharing offices, personnel and equipment and sometimes organized as partnerships, unincorporated associations with corporate attributes, or even as corporations in states whose law permit, such clinics make quality medical care available without impairing the traditional physician-patient relationship.

Most of these groups operate on the traditional fee-for-service basis, but a number of very large groups, such as the Ross-Loos Clinic, the Kaiser Foundation Health Plans and Health Insurance Plan of New York, operate on a prepayment or insurance basis. Most of the group practice development has been in the West and in smaller communities, but it is developing in the East as well. In eastern hospitals, full-time staffs and out-patient clinics represent a response to the same need.

Originally opposed to the whole idea, the American Medical Association implicitly approved the fee-for-service groups in 1948 and the prepayment plans in 1959, provided that patients retained "free choice of system or plan." These arrangements for group practice seem to represent the "wave of the future."[23]

The distribution of physicians is very uneven. The District of Columbia has 184 physicians in private practice per 100,000 population, and Mississippi has only 58. The distribution of specialists is even more uneven. Most specialists practice in cities and tend to concentrate in large medical centers and among high-income groups.

The overall supply of physicians and osteopaths is considered inadequate to meet either present or future needs for adequate medical care. The ratio of physicians in private practice to civilian population for the nation has declined from 157 per 100,000 population in 1900 to 97 per 100,000 in 1965 (Table 2–13). Of course, with improvements in medical practice and facilities and better transportation, the efficiency of medical

---

[23] For a thorough discussion of group practice, see Herman M. Somers and Anne R. Somers, *Doctors, Patients and Health Insurance* (Washington, D.C.: The Brookings Institution, 1961), pp. 37–43 and *passim*. For an impassioned advocacy of prepaid group practice see William A. MacColl, *Group Practice and Prepayment of Medical Care* (Washington, D.C.: *Public Affairs Press*, 1966). Group practice in general is advocated by the National Commission on Community Health Services, *op. cit.*, pp. 23 ff. See also Fein, *op. cit.*, pp. 94–111. Recently, the Department of Health, Education, and Welfare has been promoting group practice. *Prepayment* group practice is not necessarily part of the wave of the future, despite HEW's interest. See Ch. 10 below

practice has increased. But at the same time, more and more physicians have been engaged in national government employment and medical research, while increasing incomes, health insurance, and new government programs have contributed to an increase in effective demand. There is a growing unanimity of opinion that the present ratio should be maintained if minimum needs are to be met. Merely to maintain the present ratio, 11,000 medical school graduates would be needed by 1975. Only 7,574 graduated in 1966. The gap is filled in part by an influx of foreign physicians as interns and residents. There were more than 44,000 graduates of foreign medical schools in the United States in 1965, and the inflow continued at the rate of 1,600 per year.

Fein[24] estimates the demand for physicians' visits will increase by 22 to 26 percent from 1965 to 1975 and by 35 to 40 percent from 1965 to 1980. The 1965 to 1975 increase is made up as follows:

|  | Percent Increase |
|---|---|
| Population growth | 12.2–14.6 |
| Age-sex changes | 1.0– 1.0 |
| Region and residence changes | 0.5– 0.5 |
| Color | 0.5– 0.5 |
| Education and income | 7.0– 7.5 |
| Medicare (Title XVIII) | 1.0– 2.0 |
| Total | 21.9–25.8 |

This author would estimate 3 to 5 percent for Title XVIII and another 3 to 5 percent for Title XIX (Medicaid), making the increase 27 to 34 percent to 1975 and 40 to 48 percent to 1980.

Expansion of the supply of physicians is limited by the capacity of medical schools. There are only about 84 four-year medical schools and four two-year schools in the country, and they are handicapped in their expansion by shortages of funds and of competent teaching personnel, for whom they must compete with private practice and public and industrial health programs. Expansion of present schools might provide another 1,000 per year, but at least 2,000 will be required from some 20 to 24 new medical schools. Building and staffing medical schools are expensive and time-consuming. Meeting the need requires a massive infusion of resources. Eleven more medical schools are planned by 1968–69.[25] The Health Professions Educational Assistance Act of 1963 is expected to help increase the number of medical school graduates by 7 percent from 1965 to 1975 and by 18 percent by 1980.

---

[24] Fein, *op. cit.*, p. 60. For similar projections see U.S. Department of Health, Education, and Welfare, *A Report to the President on Medical Care Prices* (Washington, D.C.: U.S. Government Printing Office, 1967).

[25] Joseph F. Follmann, Jr., *Health Insurance and the Effectiveness of Health Care* (New York: Health Insurance Association of America, 1967), p. 4.

The total physician supply would increase by 9 percent by 1975 and by 18 percent by 1980.

Thus, despite the continuing inflow of foreign-trained physicians, the supply of physicians will fall short of the demand projections, requiring substantial increases in productivity to meet the demand. Such productivity increases may come in advances in medical science, better organization of medical services such as clinics and group practice, or in the use of paramedical personnel such as the military Medic or Corpsman.[26] In the absence of such productivity increases, further rapid price increase may be expected unless some other way of rationing scarce services can be found.

*Osteopaths* are a group of independent practitioners who supply about the same type of services as do physicians. They are licensed in all states and in most may practice medicine and surgery and prescribe drugs. As time passes, they seem to be giving less relative emphasis to physical manipulation and to resemble physicians more closely. The standards of osteopathic education and hospitals have been raised greatly, and it well may be that, before too long they will be incorporated fully into the body of "organized medicine," as was the case with the homeopaths a few decades ago. Most osteopaths are general practitioners, but a growing proportion are certified in various specialties. They are most concentrated relative to population in the western North-Central states and in the Far West. There are five colleges of osteopathy, all requiring a four-year program for the degree of Doctor of Osteopathy. Three hundred ninety-five degrees were granted in 1964–65. There were 10,000 active osteopaths in private practice in the United States in 1965.

*Dentists* provide health services primarily concerned with the teeth and gums. There are about 93,400 active dentists in the United States, of whom 86,317 are not employed by the federal government. The ratio of such dentists to the U.S. civilian population has declined from 49 per 100,000 in 1950 to 44.1 in 1965. Their distribution is as uneven as that of physicians. The number of active dentists per 100,000 population ranged in 1965 from 80 in the District of Columbia to 20 in South Carolina, and there is no indication of major change since. Utilization of dental services is very closely correlated with income level. Most dentists are in private practice, and most carry on a general practice. However, there are seven recognized specialties, qualification for which requires an additional two or three years of study. The number of specialists is growing. About 7.5 percent of all dentists are specialists, more than half of whom are orthodontists. Like physicians, dentists will probably be in short supply for many years. Present ratios to population will

---

[26] Fein, *op. cit., passim.*

probably be maintained, but there will probably be little increase in the proportion of the population which can expect to receive adequate dental care. The increased utilization of dental assistants, dental hygienists, and other technicians seems to be the most promising avenue for making it possible to treat more patients. Again, the supply of dentists cannot be increased in a hurry, because facilities of dental schools are limited. There are 47 such schools in the country, and these generally have severe problems of staffing and finance. They had 14,021 students in 1965–66 and 3,181 graduates in 1965.

*Nurses* constitute another important category of health personnel. Both the number of nurses and their proportion to the population have increased tremendously in the last half century (see Table 2–13). The number of graduate professional nurses has increased from 12,000 in 1900 to 621,000 in 1965; there are now about 319 nurses per 100,000 persons versus 55 in 1910. However, more than 20 percent of these are part-timers and many—some say as many as half—are not currently actively engaged in nursing: they have withdrawn permanently or otherwise. A 1967 estimate indicates that about 640,000 nurses were in practice, of whom one fourth were part-time workers. About 750,000 are needed at present. The average working life of a nurse is only 17 years. The dropout rate, largely due to marriage, is very rapid in the first few years after graduation but levels off thereafter. Like other health workers, nurses are unevenly distributed throughout the country, and the supply will fall short of the demand during the future decades. Nursing education standards have risen greatly: a larger number each year are enrolled in four-year degree-granting programs. Nursing education is primarily a function of hospitals, which are motivated largely by a desire to meet their own needs.

*Other medical personnel* include practical nursing personnel, by far the largest group; pharmacists; medical laboratory technicians; X-ray technicians; optometrists; dietitians and nutritionists; veterinarians; chiropractors; psychologists; dental hygienists; chiropodists and many others, as shown in Table 2–12. Shortages of personnel exist in most of these fields; in many the shortages are or soon will be acute. Most of these groups provide services which assist the other professional groups to provide health services, although chiropractors and chiropodists are independent practitioners, often competitive with physicians.

The provision of adequate health services requires the cooperation of a team of different specialists. Great as may be the desire, improvement of health services generally must be limited by the supply of competent personnel. Merely providing all parts of the country with a supply of personnel equal to current nationwide averages would demand a tremendous increase in the number of almost all categories.

*Facilities.* *Hospitals* have become the most important organizational facility providing health services. In the last 85 years the hospital has evolved from a charitable institution for those who could not afford care in their own homes to the primary facility for handling severe health impairments. It is currently evolving from an institution providing simple bed-and-board care to one providing a variety of highly complex and specialized services. In addition to purely curative care, these services include health protection, diagnosis, rehabilitation, and

CHART 2-5

Hospital Beds by Type of Control and Type of Service

*Type of Control of Hospital Beds*

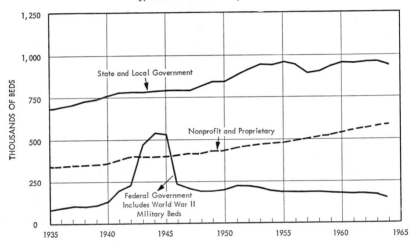

*Type of Service of Hospital Beds*

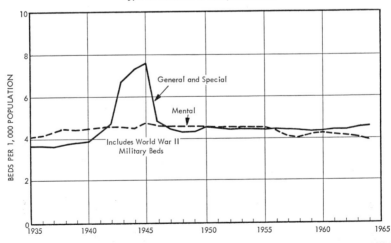

Source: U.S. Department of Health, Education, and Welfare, *Health, Education, and Welfare Trends*, pp. S–31 and S–32.

research. The development of new techniques and new concepts of treatment has accentuated the need for more hospital beds relative to the population and more complex and expensive equipment. While the number of beds has increased in the past 15 years, the ratio to the population has remained almost constant. (See Chart 2–5.)

The necessary investment to provide such facilities has increased tremendously. Physicians must rely more heavily on hospital facilities, since equipment has become so complex and expensive that few can expect to maintain a complete complement in their own offices. Moreover, the increased utilization of specialists has tended to make the hospital the central institution for providing care.

Hospital service has become one of the most important service industries in the country. In 1966, there were 7,160 hospitals with 1,679,000 beds which admitted over 29 million people each year. The average daily number of persons in hospitals was over 1,398,000.

The private nonprofit hospital providing general short-term care is the most numerous type of hospital in the country. Almost half of all hospitals are in this category, and this is the type of institution which most people envision when the term "hospital" is mentioned. However, hospitals of this type provide only a little over 30 percent of the hospital beds in the country. About one third of these nonprofit hospitals are owned by church groups. Private short-term general hospitals make up over 70 percent of the total of short-term general hospitals and provide over two thirds of the beds. The next most important type of short-term general hospital is that provided by state and local governments; these make up about 24 percent of the total number of short-term general hospitals and provide about 21 percent of the beds. Proprietary hospitals are important in number, but relatively unimportant in number of beds (Tables 2–15 and 2–16).

In specialized institutions for the mentally ill and the tubercular, the government hospitals make up the majority by number and provide the vast majority of beds. Preponderantly, these are state and local governmental institutions. Proprietary mental hospitals make up more than 16 percent of the number of mental hospitals but provide less than 1 percent of the beds. Thus, by number of beds, short-term general care is primarily the function of private nonprofit hospitals and secondarily of state and local government hospitals. Care of the long-term institutionalized patient is primarily a state and local government function, with the federal government of second importance. As shown by Table 2–17, the geographic distribution of hospital facilities is quite uneven.

These hospitals represent a tremendous capital investment. The average investment per bed in the voluntary, nonprofit hospitals is $25,785. A recognition that private charity was insufficient to meet the country's growing needs led the federal government to provide financial

TABLE 2–15

Number of Hospitals and Number of Beds, by Type and Control of Hospital, U.S., 1966

| | | General and Special | | Mental and Allied | Tubercu- losis |
| Control | Total | Short Term | Long Term | | |
|---|---|---|---|---|---|
| Number of hospitals: | | | | | |
| Total............................7,160 | | 6,184 | 304 | 513 | 159 |
| Nongovernment..................4,631 | | 4,292 | 165 | 160 | 14 |
| Nonprofit......................3,675 | | 3,440 | 147 | 76 | 12 |
| Proprietary.................... 956 | | 852 | 18 | 84 | 2 |
| Government.....................2,529 | | 1,892 | 139 | 353 | 145 |
| State and local................2,104 | | 1,520 | 126 | 316 | 142 |
| Federal........................ 425 | | 372 | 13 | 37 | 3 |
| Number of beds (in thousands): | | | | | |
| Total............................1,679 | | 874 | 80 | 694 | 31 |
| Nongovernment.................. 618 | | 581 | 19.5 | 16 | 1.5 |
| Nonprofit...................... 563 | | 533 | 18.5 | 10 | 1.5 |
| Proprietary.................... 55 | | 48 | 1 | 6 | 0.09 |
| Government.....................1,061 | | 293 | 60.5 | 678 | 29.5 |
| State and local................ 888 | | 188 | 48 | 623 | 29.0 |
| Federal........................ 173 | | 105 | 12.5 | 55 | 0.5 |

Source: Data adapted from *Hospitals,* Journal of the American Hospital Association, Administrators' Guide Issue, August, 1967, Part II.

TABLE 2–16

Percent of Hospitals and Percent of Beds, by Type and Control of Hospital, U.S., 1966

| | | General and Special | | Mental and Allied | Tubercu- losis |
| Control | Total | Short Term | Long Term | | |
|---|---|---|---|---|---|
| Percent of hospitals: | | | | | |
| Total.........................100% | | 86.4% | 4.2% | 7.2% | 2.2% |
| Nongovernment..............64.6 | | 59.9 | 2.3 | 2.2 | 0.2 |
| Nonprofit..................51.3 | | 48.0 | 2.1 | 1.1 | 0.1 |
| Proprietary.................13.3 | | 11.9 | 0.2 | 1.2 | a |
| Government.................35.3 | | 26.4 | 1.9 | 4.9 | 2.0 |
| State and local.............29.4 | | 21.2 | 1.7 | 4.4 | 2.0 |
| Federal.................... 5.9 | | 5.2 | .2 | .5 | a |
| Percent of beds: | | | | | |
| Total.........................100 | | 52.1 | 4.8 | 41.3 | 1.8 |
| Nongovernment..............36.8 | | 34.6 | 1.2 | 1.0 | .1 |
| Nonprofit..................33.5 | | 31.7 | 1.1 | .6 | a |
| Proprietary................. 3.3 | | 2.9 | .1 | .4 | a |
| Government.................63.2 | | 17.5 | 3.6 | 40.3 | 1.7 |
| State and local.............52.9 | | 11.2 | 28.6 | 37.1 | 1.7 |
| Federal....................10.3 | | 6.3 | 7.4 | 3.2 | a |

a Less than 0.05 percent.
Source: Data adapted from *Hospitals,* Journal of the American Hospital Association, Administrators' Guide Issue, August, 1967, Part II.

## TABLE 2-17

### Hospital Supply and Utilization by Region, 1966

| Region | Hos-pitals | No. of Beds | Est. Pop. (000) | Beds per 1,000 Pop. | Occupancy | | Length of Stay (Days)[a] | Admissions | |
| --- | --- | --- | --- | --- | --- | --- | --- | --- | --- |
| | | | | | Avg. Daily Census | Occupancy Rate | | per 1,000 Pop. | Total |
| New England......... | 420 | 120,999 | 11,224 | 10.8 | 101,085 | 83.5 | 8.2 | 151.2 | 1,696,774 |
| Middle Atlantic......... | 903 | 385,742 | 36,738 | 10.5 | 336,891 | 87.3 | 9.8 | 136.3 | 5,006,902 |
| South Atlantic......... | 915 | 234,543 | 29,220 | 8.0 | 196,673 | 83.9 | 7.6 | 146.3 | 4,275,841 |
| East-North Central...... | 1,180 | 336,104 | 38,480 | 8.7 | 285,010 | 84.8 | 8.2 | 147.9 | 5,689,891 |
| East-South Central..... | 551 | 98,883 | 12,910 | 7.7 | 82,116 | 83.0 | 6.9 | 152.9 | 1,973,400 |
| West-North Central..... | 895 | 140,312 | 15,869 | 8.8 | 111,667 | 79.6 | 8.2 | 168.6 | 2,675,232 |
| West-South Central..... | 935 | 128,834 | 18,768 | 6.9 | 99,696 | 77.4 | 6.6 | 158.6 | 2,976,675 |
| Mountain............. | 442 | 50,306 | 7,804 | 6.4 | 38,419 | 76.4 | 6.7 | 163.4 | 1,275,542 |
| Pacific............... | 919 | 182,935 | 24,843 | 7.4 | 146,934 | 80.3 | 7.0 | 144.1 | 3,580,721 |
| Total............ | 7,160 | 1,678,658 | 195,857 | 8.6 | 1,398,491 | 83.3 | 7.9 | 148.8 | 29,150,978 |

[a] Average of short-term, general and special cases.

Source: Hospitals, Journal of American Hospital Association, Administrators' Guide Issue, August, 1967, Part II.

aid for hospital construction. Almost half the recent hospital construction has been under this program, with federal funds providing 30 to 35 percent of the total costs involved. From 1947 through 1966, this program financed 357,867 new beds, 269,102 in general hospitals, 19,667 in mental hospitals, 34,816 in long-term care units of hospitals, 22,676 in nursing homes, 4,232 in chronic disease hospitals and 7,373 in tuberculosis hospitals at a total cost of $8.3 billion.[27] This has stimulated hospital construction, but the need still is greatly in excess of the supply. A large proportion of the existing plant is obsolete, and replacement is urgently needed. In 1966, only 4,608 of the 7,160 U.S. hospitals were accredited by the Joint Commission on Hospital Accreditation. The nonaccredited hospitals contained 461,533 beds, 27.5 percent of all beds in U.S. hospitals. In some states less than half the hospitals were accredited.[28] Even at present construction rates, shortages probably will continue for a long time, particularly in view of projected population growth and new government financing.

*Nursing homes* provide institutional care of a less intensive nature than hospitals and are an important means of meeting the needs of the convalescent and the chronically ill. Although such homes have increased rapidly in number and to some degree in quality, there is still a need for many more homes and for much higher standards. While well-managed homes can meet many specialized needs adequately and at less cost than hospitals, many present homes are substandard.

An accreditation program has been operating since 1963; it has been conducted by the Joint Commission on Accreditation of Hospitals since 1965. In early 1967, 1,574 extended care facilities, 28 domiciliary facilities, 11 intermediate care facilities and 10 mental facilities had been accredited. Every state had at least 1 and the largest number, 229, was in California.[29] This compares with 12,802 institutions for the aged or chronically ill identified in 1963 as providing nursing care or personal care with nursing.[30] The conditions of eligibility for Medicare benefits also will tend to upgrade these institutions.[31]

*Organized home care* provides a relatively new concept for the care

[27] U.S. Department of Health, Education, and Welfare, Division of Medical Care Administration, *Medical Care Financing and Utilization* (Health Economics Series No. 1-A [Washington, D.C.: U.S. Government Printing Office, 1967]).

[28] *Hospitals*, Administrators' Guide Issue, August 1, 1967.

[29] *Ibid.*

[30] E. Earl Bryant, *Institutions for the Aged and Chronically Ill* (National Center for Health Statistics, Series 12, No. 1. [Washington, D.C.: U.S. Government Printing Office, 1965]).

[31] U.S. Department of Health, Education, and Welfare, Social Security Administration, *Conditions of Participation for Extended Care Facilities*, HIM-3 (Washington, D.C.: U.S. Government Printing Office, 1960).

of the long-term patient. This may be provided by an extension of the hospital administration or by private physicians and connotes continued medical supervision of the patient and guidance of those responsible for his care. Further developments in this area can help relieve the shortage of hospital beds and help provide for the care of such patients in pleasanter surroundings than they could find in an institution. Coverage of such visits by Medicare will help motivate and finance their development.

*Progressive patient care.* This is a new concept of medical care which combines several types of facility with the services of various types of specialist. The basic idea is a classification of patients according to the degree of care needed rather than on conventional bases such as age, sex, or type of ailment.

The usual pattern involves five elements of patient care: an intensive care unit for the critically ill, an intermediate care unit for patients whose condition has stabilized and who require remedial care, a self-care unit for patients who are physically able to care for themselves and who require restorative care or diagnosis, a continuation care unit for long-term patients who require prolonged care, and a hospital-based home care program.[32]

Physical facilities and personnel would be adapted to the particular type of unit. For example, the intensive care unit would involve immediate access to emergency equipment, such as oxygen and transfusion equipment, and 24-hour supervision by staff nurses. As a patient's condition improved he would be moved to the appropriate unit. This concept seems to offer wide scope for improving the quality and coordination of hospital-based medical care, possibly with overall cost savings. The program, of course, involves substantial changes in methods of hospital construction and in the benefit provisions of hospital insurance.[33]

## Public health and loss prevention

The field of loss-preventive efforts in health may be divided into four categories: public health, preventive medicine, rehabilitation, and medical research. In addition to those activities which are specifically aimed at preventing health losses, many other varieties of social effort

---

[32] For further discussion, see Somers and Somers, *op. cit.*, pp. 72–76, and "Symposium on Progressive Patient Care," *Hospitals,* January 16, 1961.

[33] Dr. Karl S. Klicka, quoted in *Accident and Sickness Review,* November, 1961, p. 16. These changes have been appallingly slow. Intensive care units charged around $50 per day in 1962 or 1963. Insurers pay up to the room and board rate and treat the balance of the charge as an extra expense.

contribute toward this end. Any measures which contribute toward an environment where healthy living may flourish contribute to health. Such measures include community planning and housing, adequate nutrition, general and health education, provision of recreational facilities, labor legislation, traffic control and, indeed, almost every social effort to promote the general welfare. More than a mere mention of such activities falls beyond the scope of a book on health insurance.

*Public health.* Public health encompasses the activities for the prevention of disease and the specific promotion of health which are primarily a community responsibility.[34] These activities are carried on by public health departments, by departments of education, or by voluntary groups. The beginning of the American public health movement has been dated variously from 1750 to 1866. While measures for control of certain infectious diseases were initiated earlier, the latter year marked the passage of the first public health law in the United States (New York). The great growth of the public health movement took place in the years 1875–1900 and was characterized mainly by the discovery and application of means for the prevention of communicable diseases. After 1900, voluntary associations and foundations took a much larger share of responsibility. Since 1925, state and federal governments have taken an even larger share. The emphasis is shifting from communicable diseases to chronic illness and accident. This shift is partly the result of success in the earlier fields of concentration.

The functions of public health include the collection and publication of vital statistics, control of communicable diseases, sanitation, provision of laboratory services, maternal and child-health services, and health education. The collection of *vital statistics* in this country leaves much to be desired. Deaths, births, and communicable diseases are reported fairly adequately, but other data on disability and illness have been almost totally lacking. The National Health Survey has remedied this only in part, since data are not presented in a form to provide many important types of information. Often it is necessary to rely on narrow studies of selected groups for information in this area.[35]

*Communicable disease control* is basically a governmental function carried out for the benefit of the whole community. The method of control, generally, is to interrupt the pathogen-vector-host relationship. This may be accomplished by eliminating the pathogen, as in water sanitation; by eliminating the vector, as in insect control; or by im-

---

[34] This definition and much of the following section are based on Wilson G. Smillie, *Preventive Medicine and Public Health* (2d ed.; New York: Macmillan Co., 1953).

[35] U.S. Department of Health, Education, and Welfare, Public Health Service, *United States Statistics on Medical Economics* (Washington D.C.: U.S. Government Printing Office, 1964).

munizing the potential host. Most severe communicable diseases must be reported by the attending physician, and the public health authority acts to impose quarantine requirements, to investigate sources of infection and to institute other control methods. These may include isolation of the patient, immunization and testing of contacts, disinfection and fumigation, carrier control, and/or control of vectors or intermediate hosts. In the community sense, communicable disease control becomes epidemiology, the science which treats of the course, propagation, and control of infectious disease. A broadening concept of epidemiology extends its scope to include noninfectious disease as well.

*Environmental sanitation* is the responsibility of the public health officer, the sanitary engineer, the food chemist, the public health laboratory worker, and the inspector. Areas in which the community has generally accepted some responsibility include water supply and swimming-pool sanitation; waste disposal and treatment, water, air, and radiation pollution control; control of vermin; fumigation, disinfection, and decontamination; food inspection; sanitation of milk; control of food-serving agencies; and sanitary condition requirements in housing and the general environment.

*Laboratory and testing services* provided by the community aid in the diagnosis and control of disease. Mass tuberculosis tests, water and milk supply tests, and venereal disease clinics fall into this category. Tests are provided to identify the pathogen where epidemic threatens.

*Maternal and child-health services* are provided as a means of promoting the health of the coming generation. The younger the age group which is treated, the more effective will be the results. These services include prenatal and maternal care; postnatal and neonatal care, with special attention to premature births; infant hygiene; preschool and child-health services. Important techniques include public health nursing; special provision for crippled children; oral hygiene; and other school health services, including periodic health examinations. A great deal of improvement is possible in the degree to which discovered defects are followed up and treated. All too often, proper corrective action is not taken. This is generally considered an individual responsibility for all except the poorest elements of the population.

*Health education* is important in its own right and also as a means for accomplishing many of the other objectives of public health. The schools are a primary vehicle for such education; indeed, real progress often must wait a generation. To the extent to which preventive medicine is an individual, as distinguished from a professional, responsibility, education in proper techniques is prerequisite to its successful application. Public health control measures can be developed only to the extent that there is public acceptance. Thus health education is necessary for effective control. In addition to the schools, health education for the whole community is attempted through any and all of the media of mass communication. Nongovernment agencies such as foundations and insurance companies have contributed materially to such efforts. Birth-control education is an important aspect of health education, and now must be made available to mothers receiving Aid to Families with Dependent Children.

*Preventive medicine.* Preventive medicine is the function of the individual, professional or otherwise, in promotion of personal and family health. It includes almost all the activities discussed under public health, insofar as medical personnel and their patients may contribute to these objectives. For example, health education by practitioners is probably the most effective means of reaching the mass of adults. In addition, it includes such activities as accident prevention; conservation of vision; use of proper diet to prevent malnutrition, obesity, hypertension, diabetes, and cardiovascular disease; mental hygiene; control of ingestion of food, alcohol, nicotine, marihuana, L.S.D., and similar "goodies"; and industrial hygiene.

While a detailed discussion of these various fields is beyond the scope of this book, the field of accident prevention deserves special consideration. An accident is a sudden, unforeseeable, fortuitous event which is neither predictable nor preventable in the individual case. However, it is possible to identify the factors which produce accidents and reduce the frequency of their occurrence. Moreover, an accident does not lead to a health loss unless it produces an injury. Often it is possible to prevent injury, even though accidents still occur.

Industrial accident prevention has advanced to the status of an exact science, and great progress has been made in reducing loss by proper plant design, machine design and safeguards, protective clothing, and training of workers in safety consciousness and practices. The provision of facilities for proper in-plant treatment has done much to reduce the severity of injuries which still occur.

Motor-vehicle accidents are the most important causes of death because of the severity of injury. While much can be done in terms of highway design, traffic control, and vehicle construction, the development of safer habits of driving is the most important factor in preventing accidents. This is true in regard to other types of accidents and is why this type of effort is classified as being the prime responsibility of individuals. No matter how safe highways and automobiles are made, one still must be concerned with the "nut behind the wheel." Other types of accident which can be reduced by known techniques are drownings, burns, falls, and firearm accidents.

*Rehabilitation.* Rehabilitation may be looked upon as an extension of medical treatment or as a technique for limiting the severity of loss. Treatment is concerned with the cure of physical or mental impairments, while rehabilitation extends beyond mere treatment and is concerned with returning the patient to a state of positive health so that he may become a productive member of society.

Medical rehabilitation is concerned with improving or training the body to permit functions to be carried on, perhaps with the aid of prosthetics, while vocational rehabilitation is concerned with specific training for various occupations. Since 1920, the National Office of Vocational Rehabilitation has been active in this area, providing a system of federal grants-in-aid. In 1943 the program was expanded to provide for medical services as well. The Children's Bureau, the United States Employment Service, the Veterans' Administration, and the Defense Department are also active in rehabilitation. Voluntary associations and foundations have also contributed materially to this effort, as have insurance companies active in the liability, compensation, and disability fields. The earlier rehabilitation can be instituted, the more effective it will be.

Despite the tremendous developments, there is a need for further effort. It has been estimated that there are over two million persons in this country in need of rehabilitation and that over 270,000 a year are added to this total.[36] Rehabilitation of those disabled by mental or nervous diseases is still in its infancy, but the potentials are enormous. The time lag between recovery from injury or illness and the commencement of a rehabilitation program has been the greatest deterrent to adequate rehabilitation. This lag fortunately is being reduced materially as the agencies active in the field become more efficient. In 1965–66, federally aided vocational rehabilitation agencies rehabilitated 154,000 disabled persons for active employment.[37]

Primary responsibility for rehabilitation should rest on the physician who first treats the patient, but specialized facilities are necessary in many cases. The establishment of rehabilitation centers attached to hospitals of various types with more specialized centers for certain severe cases is an urgent objective of any national health program. Only a very small proportion of hospitals currently provides such facilities.

*Medical research.* All the progress made in preventive efforts and in cures has medical research as its foundation. Broadly conceived, it comprehends every investigation into causes, cures, and rehabilitation, by whomever conducted. Past triumphs have been great, as is indi-

---

[36] *Accident and Sickness Bulletins,* April, 1962.
[37] *Health Insurance Review,* September, 1966, p. 14.

cated in the following section. However, there is no foreseeable limit to what future research may accomplish. Society now is faced with diseases in which there are no known pathogens or clear-cut methods of transmission or recognized methods of protecting the host. This includes most of the chronic and degenerative diseases and a great range of minor afflictions and functional disturbances. Mental and nervous diseases are the most important as far as prevalence of disability is concerned, and cardiovascular diseases and cancer are of first importance as producers of death and of tremendous importance in disability. Research gradually is being directed toward the etiology of these diseases. A considerable range of disease is produced by the life situations of the persons involved. Much study is necessary to understand the factors producing such disabilities.

Medical research is conducted primarily in the large hospitals or medical schools but also by commercial concerns such as pharmaceutical and food manufacturers, in special research teams, and by individuals. The federal government, private business, and nonprofit foundations all contribute significantly to the financing. Yet the aggregate effort is very little. The amount spent for medical research is tiny compared to that spent for industrial or military research. Limits of cost impair the research effort despite the huge relative gains that such research has produced and may produce. All too often, financing is limited to too short a period and to too specific a goal. The emphasis of public support is often on "target" research rather than on "basic" research. More of the latter is necessary, particularly in regard to the processes of growth and degeneration of the organism and the interactions of the individual and his environment. It is in such areas that the "pathogens" of much chronic disease will be discovered.

**Health progress**

Since morbidity data are so poor and so often nonexistent, the best measure of health improvement is improvement in death rates. Since death is inevitable, it is only premature death that can be considered as evidence of poor health. While the maximum human life-span which potentially may be attained is not yet known, it certainly is well past the age of normal retirement by current standards. Thus all deaths prior to (say) 65 may be considered as "premature," and the case will not be overstated. Since death rates vary so greatly with age, it is inaccurate to use overall death rates as a measure of mortality improvement, since these ignore the changing age composition of the population. And yet, even on this crude basis, the improvement is startling.

It has been said that the most significant social change of this century, if not of this millennium, is that, for the first time in the history of humanity, the average person can expect to die old rather than to die young. Crude death rates have been lowered from 30 per 1,000 to 10 per 1,000 in a century in the advanced countries. The expectation of life at birth has increased from 47.3 years in 1900 to 70.2 years in the United States in 1965, and age-adjusted death rates have declined from 17.8 per 1,000 to 7.4 per 1,000 in the 20th century alone. However, in much of Africa, death rates around 30 per 1,000 are found. Chart 2–6 shows the differences in life expectancy according to several famous mortality tables.

CHART 2–6

Life Expectancy at Ages 0, 30, and 60 by Various Mortality Tables

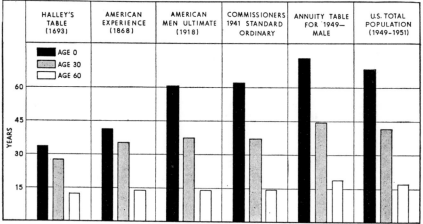

Chart 2–7 indicates vividly the decline in death rates.

Most of this decrease has been at the lower ages as Charts 2–8 and 2–9 indicate. The control of infectious diseases and reductions in infant and maternal mortality have made the greatest contributions. The average remaining lifetime of those already grown to adulthood has not increased so materially. This expectation at age 30 was 34.9 in 1900–1902 and 43.3 in 1965; that at age 50 was 20.8 in 1900–1902 and 25.5 in 1965. Death rates for the infectious diseases declined, while crude death rates for the chronic and degenerative diseases increased.

However, the net effect was some improvement for all age groups. Between 1900 and 1959 age-specific death rates declined by 85 percent for children and young people; by 69 percent for the age group 25 to 44; by 33 percent for the age group 45 to 64; and by 20 percent for those aged 65 and over. The death rates for men have not decreased so rapidly as those for women. Death rates for nonwhites have de-

CHART 2–7

Mortality from All Causes, Actual and Age-Adjusted Rates,[a] U.S., 1900–60[b]

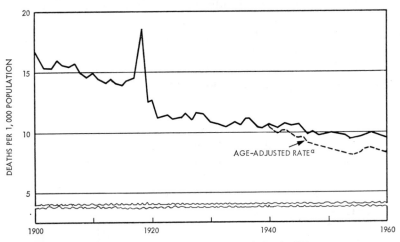

[a] Adjusted to the age distribution of the U.S. population in 1940.
[b] Rates prior to 1933 apply to the death-registration states only. 1959 and 1960 rates are provisional, and 1960 rates have been estimated on the basis of partial-year data.
Source: *Progress in Health Services,* February, 1961.

CHART 2–8

Mortality from All Causes by Age, U.S., 1935–65

*Deaths by Age Groups*

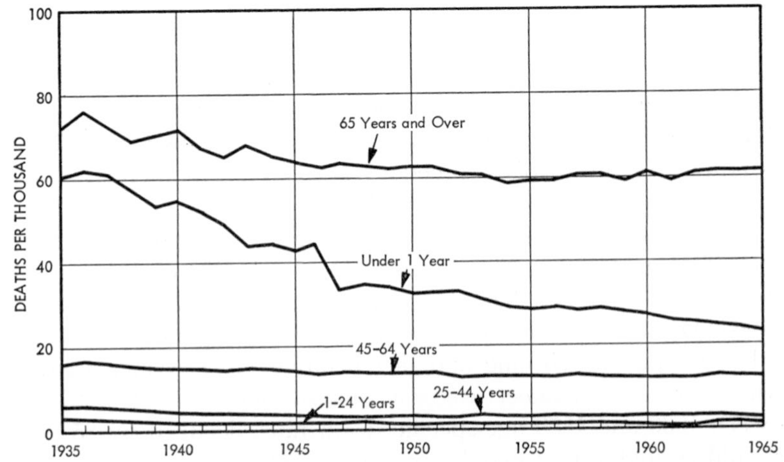

Source: U.S. Department of Health, Education, and Welfare, *Health, Education, and Welfare Trends,* 1965 ed., p. S–8 (Washington D. C.: U. S. Government Printing Office, 1966).

CHART 2-9

Mortality from All Causes by Age, U.S., 1900ª and 1959

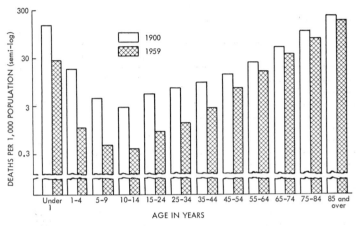

ª Rates for 1900 apply to the death-registration states only.
Source: *Progress in Health Services*, February, 1961.

creased more rapidly than for whites, and the two groups are closer together. (See Chart 2–10 and Table 2–18.)

The increases in crude death rates for the degenerative diseases do not necessarily mean an increase in age-specific rates. For example, the age-specific rate for heart disease has actually declined slightly over the past few decades. Chart 2–11 shows the crude rate down a bit. As more persons are spared the diseases of childhood and young adulthood, they survive to become exposed to the diseases of middle and old age. A larger exposure, with rates the same, means a much

CHART 2-10

Mortality from All Causes by Sex and Color,
U.S., 1900ª and 1959

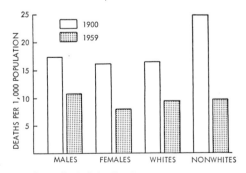

ª Age-adjusted death rates.
Source: *Progress in Health Services* (February, 1961).

TABLE 2–18

Age-Adjusted Death Rates by Color and Sex, U.S., Selected Years, 1900–65

(per 1,000 population)

| Year | Total Male | Total Female | White Male | White Female | Nonwhite Male | Nonwhite Female |
|---|---|---|---|---|---|---|
| 1900 | 18.6 | 17.0 | 18.4 | 16.8 | 28.7 | 27.1 |
| 1905 | 17.8 | 15.7 | 17.6 | 15.4 | 29.7 | 26.9 |
| 1910 | 16.9 | 14.6 | 16.7 | 14.4 | 24.8 | 23.2 |
| 1915 | 15.4 | 13.4 | 15.1 | 13.0 | 23.5 | 22.6 |
| 1920 | 14.7 | 13.8 | 14.2 | 13.1 | 20.4 | 21.0 |
| 1925 | 13.8 | 12.2 | 13.2 | 11.4 | 21.4 | 20.4 |
| 1930 | 13.5 | 11.3 | 12.8 | 10.6 | 21.0 | 19.2 |
| 1935 | 12.9 | 10.4 | 12.3 | 9.8 | 18.5 | 16.1 |
| 1940 | 12.1 | 9.4 | 11.6 | 8.8 | 16.3 | 15.0 |
| 1945 | 11.1 | 8.0 | 10.7 | 7.5 | 14.5 | 11.9 |
| 1950 | 10.0 | 6.9 | 9.6 | 6.5 | 13.6 | 10.9 |
| 1955 | 9.3 | 6.1 | 9.1 | 5.7 | 11.9 | 9.1 |
| 1960 | 9.5 | 5.9 | 9.2 | 5.6 | 12.1 | 8.9 |
| 1965 | 9.4 | 5.7 | 9.1 | 5.3 | 12.4 | 8.5 |
| 1966 | 9.5 | 5.7 | 9.2 | 5.3 | 12.1 | 8.6 |

Source: U.S. Dept. of Health, Education, and Welfare, National Center for Health Statistics, *Vital Statistics of the United States* (Washington, D.C.: U.S. Government Printing Office, 1964), and *Monthly Vital Statistics Report,* Vol. 16, No. 1 (April 14, 1967) and Vol. 16, No. 12 (March 12, 1968).

CHART 2–11

Major Causes of Death

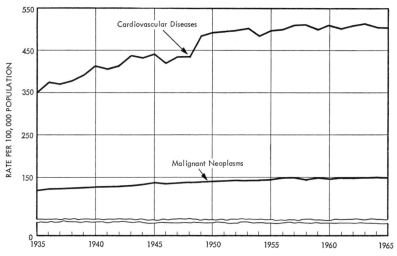

Source: U.S. Department of Health, Education, and Welfare, *Health, Education, and Welfare Trends,* 1965 ed., p. 3.

larger number and proportion of the population disabled or killed by these diseases. The largest increases have occurred in death rates for cancer. Much is not explained by population increase and aging (Chart 2–12).

CHART 2–12

Mortality from Cancer (All Sites), U.S. Death Registration Area of 1900, 1900–60

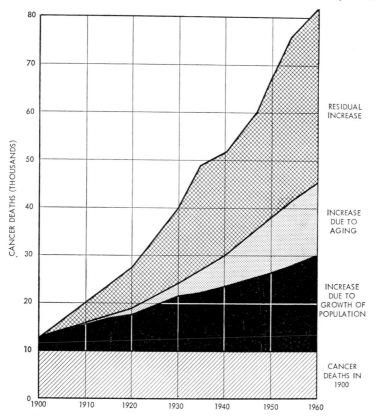

Source: U.S. Department of Health, Education, and Welfare, *Health, Education, and Welfare Trends,* 1965 ed., p. 4.

The most dramatic declines in mortality have taken place in regard to mothers and children. Maternal death rates declined from 608 per 100,000 live births in 1915 to 29.1 in 1966 and a provisional rate of 27.0 in 1967. Infant mortality rates fell from 100 per 1,000 live births in 1915 to 23.7 in 1966 and 22.9 (provisional) in 1967 (See Chart 2–13). This saving has had a material effect on expectancy at birth. However, the nonwhite infant mortality rate was 38.7 in 1966, and 13 countries were known to have lower rates than the United States in 1966–67. The lowest was 13.3 per 1,000 in Sweden compared to 22.9 in the U.S. The U.S. rate decreased only 8.1 percent from 1953–54 to 1963–64, compared to 30 percent in Denmark and 31 percent in Switzerland from comparable bases. The rate in Japan declined 53 percent, from 46.8 to 21.8 per 1,000[38] in 1963–64 and to 18.5 by 1966–67.[39]

The results of these changes in death rates and the reduction of morbidity from contagious disease have profound social implications. As indicated in Chapter 1, the proportion of aged (over 65) in the population has doubled. This has meant greater utilization of medical services, a greater interest in social insurance and pensions and a

CHART 2–13

Fetal, Infant, and Maternal Mortality

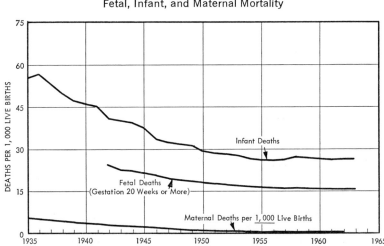

Source: U.S. Department of Health, Education, and Welfare, *Health, Education, and Welfare Trends*, 1965 ed., p. S–12.

greater "security consciousness" in public policy. It also has resulted in heart disease, cancer, and strokes displacing influenza-pneumonia, tuberculosis, and gastritis as leading causes of death.

Expected working life for males at birth increased by 11 years from 1901 to 1958, or more than one third.[40] The expectation of nonworking life also increased by almost half as a result of later labor force entry, earlier retirement and increased longevity. In 1958, for males, the ex-

---

[38] Metropolitan Life Insurance Co., *Statistical Bulletin,* May, 1967, p. 6.

[39] Population Reference Bureau. *World Population Data Sheet, 1968* (Washington, D.C., 1968).

[40] Monroe Lerner and Odin W. Anderson, *Health Progress in the United States, 1900–1960* (Chicago: University of Chicago Press, 1963). Much of the following material is drawn from this source.

pected working life at birth was 42.3, and the expected nonworking life was 24.1. The expectancy at age 20 was for 43.1 years working life and 6.3 years of retirement life, as compared with 39.3 and 2.7 in 1901.

The probability of marital dissolution by death decreased substantially, from 27.4 per 1,000 couples in 1900 to 16.6 per 1,000 (age adjusted) in 1957. The probability of a male age 20 dying in the next 20 years decreased from 133 per 1,000 in 1909–11 to 43 per 1,000 in 1965, a decrease of two thirds.[41] For a man age 45 the decrease was from 376 per 1,000 to 133 per 1,000, or almost two thirds. As one result, the median age of widows has increased from 57.8 in 1900 to 67.6 in 1960.

Similarly, the problem of orphanhood has almost disappeared. The number of full orphans (both parents deceased) declined from 750,000, 2 percent of the child population, to 60,000, 0.1 percent of all children, a decrease of 92 percent. The number of orphans of all types (either one or both parents deceased) decreased from 6.4 million, 16 percent of all children, to 3 million, 4.6 percent of all children, a drop of 53 percent in number and 71 percent in the proportion of children. An increase in the number of families broken by divorce and desertion and never formed due to illegitimacy has more than offset the decrease in families broken up by parental death, however.

Prospects for future increases in longevity depend largely on developments in the prevention and treatment of major cardiovascular-renal disease. A 1957 study showed that the elimination of all deaths caused by infective and parasitic disease (provided age-specific death rates for all other causes remained the same) would add only one year to life expectancy at birth.[42] Elimination of all deaths due to external violence (accidental injury, homicide, suicide, etc.) would add 2.2 years to the average life of males but only 0.9 years to that of females. If all deaths due to the major cardiovascular-renal diseases could be eliminated, about 10.5 years would be added to expectancy at birth and 10 years to average future lifetime at age 60.

In projecting mortality rates for OASDHI actuarial studies, Bayo[43] applied percentage reductions in death rates by age, sex, and cause group and projected a decline from 1959–60 to 2000 of 13.25 to 26.5 percent for males and 13.5 to 27.1 percent for females, producing age-

---

[41] Metropolitan Life Insurance Co., *Statistical Bulletin*, April, 1967, p. 6.

[42] B. Woodhall and Sermore Jablon, "Prospects for Further Increases in Average Longevity," *Geriatrics*, Vol. XII (October, 1957), pp. 586–91, cited in Lerner and Anderson, *op. cit.*, at pp. 323 ff. Mortality data pertain to 1949–51.

[43] Francisco Bayo, *United States Population Projections for OASDHI Cost Estimates* (Actuarial Study No. 62, Department of Health, Education, and Welfare, Social Security Administration [Washington, D.C.: U.S. Government Printing Office, 1966]), p. 10.

adjusted death rates[44] in 2000 of 8.01 to 9.45 per 1,000 for males and from 5.84 to 6.93 per 1,000 for females. The expectation of life at birth was projected at 69.06 to 71.56 for males in the year 2000 and 75.30 to 77.53 for females. As an indication of *present* potential the expectation at birth currently is 74 in Sweden and the Netherlands.

## Summary

Society should give first priority in loss prevention to those factors which produce the most severe losses. Within any degree of severity it should give highest priority to those factors which produce loss most frequently. Nervous and mental diseases, cardiovascular-renal diseases, malignant neoplasms, accidents, and rheumatism all produce death and/or long-term disability very frequently and therefore deserve a high priority.

Physicians and hospitals are society's most important resources in both the treatment and the prevention of poor health. Shortages exist in terms of any real concept of need—in these categories and among other health personnel and facilities.

Loss-preventive activities are limited by scarcity of human and financial resources but are of fundamental importance in any national health program. These activities include public health, preventive medicine, rehabilitation, and medical research. All are important, but research is the cornerstone of all other loss-preventive efforts. Further progress in health preservation and improvement must be accomplished primarily through more intensive research into the factors producing the chronic and degenerative diseases, including mental disease.

While preventive effort has had outstanding success in reducing infant mortality and reducing the toll of communicable diseases, it has done little to increase the maximum span of life. The persons saved from the acute diseases merely succumb eventually to the chronic diseases. It is in regard to these, especially the major cardiovascular-renal diseases, that future intensive efforts must be concentrated.

## Selected references

*See the following items from the General Bibliography: 1; 2; 3; 4, ch. 1; 5, ch. 2; 6, chs. 2, 3, and 4; 7; 8, chs. 4 and 5; 12; 22; 28, chs. 9 and 11.*

AMERICAN HOSPITAL ASSOCIATION. *Hospitals,* Journal of the American Hospital Association. Administrators' Guide Issue, August, 1967.

AMERICAN MEDICAL ASSOCIATION. *The Cost of Medical Care,* Vols. I, II, III, and IV, 1964.

---

[44] Adjusted on the basis of 1960 population age distribution.

AMERICAN MUTUAL ALLIANCE. *Proceedings, Conference on Rehabilitation Concepts.* Chicago, 1963.

ANDERSON, ODIN W., AND LERNER, MONROE. *Measuring Health Levels in the United States, 1950–1958.* New York: Health Information Foundation, 1960.

ANDERSON, ODIN W., AND ROSEN, GEORGE. *An Examination of the Concept of Preventive Medicine.* New York: Health Information Foundation, 1960.

BAYO, FRANCISCO. *United States Population Projections for OASDHI Cost Estimates.* Actuarial Study No. 62, U.S. Department of Health, Education, and Welfare. Washington, D.C.: U.S. Government Printing Office, 1966.

COLLINS, SELWYN D. *Long-Time Trends in Illness and Medical Care.* U.S. Department of Health, Education, and Welfare, Public Health Service, Public Health Monograph No. 48. Washington, D.C.: U.S. Government Printing Office, 1957.

COMMISSION ON CHRONIC ILLNESS. *Chronic Illness in the U.S.,* Vol. II, *Care of the Long-Term Patient.* Cambridge, Mass.: Harvard University Press, 1956.

COOK, FRED J. *The Plot against the Patient.* Englewood Cliffs, N.J.: Prentice-Hall, Inc., 1967.

DAVIS, M. M. *Medical Care for Tomorrow.* New York: Harper & Bros., 1955.

DUNN, HALBERT L. "Points of Attack for Raising the Levels of Wellness," *Journal of the National Medical Association,* Vol. XLIX, No. 4 (July, 1957), p. 225.

FEIN, RASHI. *The Doctor Shortage: An Economic Diagnosis.* Washington, D.C.: The Brookings Institution, May, 1967.

GOFF, PHOEBE H. "Childhood Disability Beneficiaries, 1957–64: Characteristics and Geographic Distribution," *Social Security Bulletin,* February, 1967, p. 14.

HARLOW, ARTHUR H. *et al. The Future of the Personal Physician.* New York: Group Health Insurance, Inc., 1964.

HARRIS, SEYMOUR E. *The Economics of American Medicine.* New York: The Macmillan Co., 1964.

HEALTH INSURANCE ASSOCIATION OF AMERICA. *Health Insurance and the Effectiveness of Health Care,* and *Medical Economic Bulletins.* Chicago, New York, and Washington, D.C., 1967.

KLARMAN, HERBERT E. *Hospital Care in New York City.* New York: Columbia University Press, 1963.

——, *The Economics of Health.* New York: Columbia University Press, 1965.

LERNER, MONROE, AND ANDERSON, ODIN W. *Health Progress in the United States: 1900–1960.* Chicago: The University of Chicago Press, 1963.

LINDER, FORREST E. "The Health of the American People," *The Scientific American,* Vol. 214, No. 6 (June, 1966).

MACCOLL, WILLIAM A., M.D. *Group Practice and Prepayment of Medical Care.* Washington, D.C.: Public Affairs Press, 1966.

MCNERNEY, WALTER J. *et al. Hospital and Medical Economics,* Vols. 1 and 2. Chicago: Lakeside Press, 1962.

NATIONAL COMMISSION ON COMMUNITY HEALTH SERVICES. *Health Is a Community Affair.* Cambridge, Mass.: Harvard University Press, 1966.

SCHMULOWITZ, JACOB, AND LYNN, HENRY D. *Insured and Disabled Workers under the Social Security Disability Program.* U.S. Department of Health, Education, and Welfare, Office of Research and Statistics, Research Report No. 11. Washington, D.C.: U.S. Government Printing Office, 1966.

SMILLIE, WILSON G. *Preventive Medicine and Public Health.* New York: Macmillan Co., 1953.

SOMERS, HERMAN M., AND SOMERS, ANNE R. *A Program for Research in Health Economics.* Health Economics Series, No. 7. Washington, D.C.: U.S. Government Printing Office, 1967.

SPIEGLEMAN, MORTIMER. *Significant Mortality and Morbidity Trends in the United States since 1900.* CLU Brochure. Philadelphia: American College of Life Underwriters, 1964.

U.S. DEPARTMENT OF HEALTH, EDUCATION, AND WELFARE. *Medical Care Prices: A Report to the President.* Washington, D.C.: U.S. Government Printing Office, February, 1967.

———, NATIONAL CENTER FOR HEALTH STATISTICS. *Vital and Health Statistics,* Series 10, Nos. 1–44, Series 12, Nos. 1–9. Washington, D.C.: U.S. Government Printing Office.

———, NATIONAL OFFICE OF VITAL STATISTICS. *Health and Demography.* Washington, D.C.: U.S. Government Printing Office, October, 1956.

———, PUBLIC HEALTH SERVICE. *Health Resources Statistics, 1965.* Health Economics Series, Nos. 1–7. Washington, D.C.: U.S. Government Printing Office, 1966.

**chapter 3**

# Meeting Health Losses:
# The Financial Impact

## Classification of devices

*General.* This chapter will describe the main types of social device for meeting the financial impact of health losses and indicate some of their outstanding characteristics and something of their relative importance. Devices for preventing or reducing loss were considered in the previous chapter. Social devices for meeting the financial impact of risk may be classified according to several bases. They could be classified on a basis of freedom of choice: voluntary measures *versus* compulsory measures. Another basis of classification would be in terms of sponsorship: governmental, community, private business, consumer, employer, and union. Some would see a major distinction between the concepts of prepayment and insurance and attempt to set up a dichotomy on this basis. However, this seems to be a difference of degree more than of kind.

The most important difference is one of kind: of the nature of the social device employed. Here there are three major methods of meeting the financial impact of health losses: assumption, transfer, and insurance. Two of these—transfer and insurance—are devices whereby the risk to the individual may be reduced. In only one—insurance—is there an overall reduction of risk through the combination of individual exposures. This will be the main basis of classification used in this book.

Insurance arrangements, in turn, may be classified according to several bases. The reader will note that these bases are independent so that a given contract or arrangement may be classified according to each independent dimension in order to describe it fully. An outline presentation of the various devices follows.

103

### Devices for Meeting Health Losses

I. Preventive efforts: devices to prevent or minimize loss (These were discussed in Chapter 2.)
   A. Medical care
   B. Public health
   C. Preventive medicine, including accident prevention
   D. Medical and vocational rehabilitation
   E. Medical research
II. Devices for meeting the financial impact of health losses
   A. Assumption of risk—does not reduce risk. An individual device
   B. Transfer of risk—reduces risk for the individual but not for the group; merely shifts the burden, in these cases to the taxpayer
      1. Public assistance
      2. Publicly provided medical care
   C. Insurance—reduces risk by combining individual exposures. Classified according to:
      1. Perils
         a. Accidental injury
         b. Sickness or disease
      2. Types of loss and associated types of benefit
         a. Loss of income—(actual and presumptive)
            (i) Disability income (total and partial)
            (ii) Dismemberment and loss of sight
            (iii) Accidental death
         b. Medical expense
            (i) Hospital
            (ii) Surgical
            (iii) Regular medical
            (iv) Major medical
            (v) Comprehensive
            (vi) Dread disease
      3. Basis of payment
         a. Valued
         b. Reimbursement
         c. Service
      4. Continuance provisions
         a. Noncancellable
         b. Guaranteed renewable
         c. Conditionally renewable
         d. Collectively renewable
         e. Renewable at insurer's option
         f. Cancellable
         g. No provision
      5. Contractual, merchandizing, and underwriting arrangement
         a. Group
            (i) True group
            (ii) Association group

  b. Individual and family
    (i) Limited
    (ii) Industrial
    (iii) Commercial
    (iv) Noncancellable and guaranteed renewable
    (v) Life insurance riders
    (vi) Liability and medical payments
  c. Blanket
  d. Franchise
6. Types of insurer
  a. Insurance companies
    (i) Stock
    (ii) Mutual
  b. Hospital and medical associations
    (i) Blue Cross
    (ii) Blue Shield
  c. Independent plans
    (i) Employer
    (ii) Union
    (iii) Community
    (iv) Consumer
    (v) Group practice
  d. Government
    (i) National
    (ii) State
7. Compulsory versus voluntary
  a. Private
  b. Social
  c. Government subsidized

## Assumption of risk

This technique involves simply accepting the burden of risk and being prepared to meet loss costs when they occur. Risks sometimes are assumed because of ignorance or stupidity, in which case there may be no preparation for loss costs. Where insurance is not possible because the risk does not meet the criteria of insurable risk explained below and there is no way to shift the risk, assumption is the only possibility. Some authorities refer to this technique as "retention."

It is especially difficult to treat perils which represent the working of social and economic forces. Price changes, unemployment, and wars affect many or all exposure units simultaneously. Certain losses, such as death, are certain to occur, and others, such as old age, are extremely likely. Against such perils, it is necessary to build up a reserve fund to meet the loss costs when they occur. This combination of assumption and funding method is also appropriate for the social and economic type perils and is a possible approach to all. Of course, there is no risk which may not be assumed, but this least desirable method should be reserved for risks susceptible to no more satisfactory treatment or where the possible loss is very small. Appropriate use of deductibles and waiting periods permits the assumption of risk of small loss to be combined with insurance against large losses. This combination is much used in medical expense insurance.

### The nature of insurance

Insurance was defined above as a social device to reduce risk by combining independent exposures. Every business corporation which increases its size sufficiently to develop enough independent exposures is utilizing this technique. One might say, loosely, that it is "self-insuring" against such risks, but the term usually is restricted to situations in which the particular risk is sometimes insured by conventional insurers. Indeed, many authors would restrict its usage to situations in which the self-insurer meets all the requirements of a sound insurance plan. This author would prefer to proceed on the basis of a logical distinction and use "self-insurance" to denote every conscious combination of exposures to reduce risk, and to recognize that not every self-insurance plan is sound. In many cases the risks involved do not meet the requirements felt to be necessary for commercial insurance. Nonetheless, some treatment is necessary, and the technique of combination deserves to be called "insurance," even though it may operate imperfectly and only in part. If risk is actually reduced to some degree, the technique is logically and functionally one of insurance. A sound self-insurance plan, however, should have a large enough number of independent exposures so that losses are reasonably predictable. In fact, this is what distinguishes self insurance from assumption of risk.

*Insurance*, then, when defined as a device (or technique) to reduce risk by pooling independent exposures, has its broadest definition and includes self-insurance. If the exposures are not independent, a loss in regard to one exposure may produce a loss in another. If this possibility exists, risk is not reduced necessarily and even may be increased. The statistical theory on which insurance is based presupposes independent samples.

Much confusion as to the proper definition of insurance results from the fact that the term has been used to refer to an institution, a business, and a contract, as well as to a device or technique. The technique, which involves pooling of independent exposures, is utilized by many outside the institutional framework. *Insurance, as an institution*,[1]

---

[1] An institution is defined by sociologists as an *organized* cluster of activity for the purpose of satisfying human needs.

satisfies human needs for security (risk reduction) by transfer of risk combined with pooling. The emphasis here is on the transfer of the risk to an organization within the institution, which performs the risk-bearing function. Transfer of risk involves a shifting of the financial consequences of loss with the concomitant uncertainty to another. As an institution, insurance includes social insurance but excludes self-insurance where there is no transfer of risk.

*Insurance, as a business,* involves a still narrower concept. In this sense, the term means a business, carried on under private auspices, involving transfer of risk and its reduction by pooling exposures. This concept includes stock and mutual insurance companies, reciprocals, Lloyd's associations, and hospital and medical associations but excludes governmental activities. Still more detailed distinctions can be made. For example, the private insurance business would exclude hospital, medical, and professional associations but include all insurance companies and similar organizations. The term "corporate insurance" could be applied to stocks and mutuals only, excluding Lloyd's associations, reciprocals, and fraternals.

*Insurance, as a contract,* refers to an agreement between two or more parties which provides for a transfer of risk in order to pool exposures and reduce risk. The contract must specifically define the parties, the perils, the subject matter, and the term. The specific document evidencing the contract is known as a "policy"; the consideration is the "premium."

The reduction of risk by means of combination is most effective where readily identifiable and predictable perils produce losses definite in time and place according to a statistically controlled pattern, in a large enough group of independent exposures to permit the application of the law of averages. Unfortunately, many perils do not meet these criteria.

### Types of insurance

**General.** As indicated above, health insurance may be classified according to seven independent bases or dimensions: perils; types of loss and benefit; basis of payment; continuance provisions; contractual, merchandising and underwriting arrangement; type of insurer; and compulsory or voluntary arrangement. This method of classification largely represents the work of the Committee on Health Insurance Terminology of the Commission on Insurance Terminology. The Commission on Insurance Terminology was formed several years ago under the auspices of the American Risk and Insurance Association.[2] The

---

[2] Then known as the American Association of University Teachers of Insurance.

Commission and its constituent Committees are composed of professors, authors, and insurance company and trade association executives.

The goals of the commission are to engage in a continuing study of insurance language to evaluate the effectiveness of terms and recommend improvements; to develop and publish a glossary of insurance terms with agreed meanings and to develop a continuing information program to encourage proper usage in cooperation with other groups with similar goals. The fact that the Committee on Health Insurance Terminology was the first of the constituent committees to begin operation is a commentary on the recognition of the need for standard terminology in this area. The major achievement of the committee so far has been the general acceptance of "health insurance" as the term to designate the entire area of insurance that provides lump-sum or periodic payments in event of loss (other than death) occasioned by bodily injury, sickness, disease, or medical expense. Much progress has been made, and the work of the committee continues apace. Much of the following discussion of the various dimensions of health insurance classification represents the fruits of committee discussion. However, many of the decisions have not been agreed upon finally, and if the final decision differs from the presentation in this edition, the author will have to bear the responsibility.

*Perils.* A *peril* is an event which may produce loss. Health insurance contracts are concerned with either or both of two perils: accidental injury and sickness. The term *accident* has been defined as an undesigned (from the point of view of the person affected), sudden and unexpected event that may produce traumatic bodily injury. *Accidental injury* is the term applied to bodily injury produced by accident. The term *sickness* is defined as a disorder of the body or mind, other than the immediate result of traumatic bodily injury. *Sickness, illness* and *disease* are synonomous terms.[3]

Health insurance contracts may protect against losses resulting from both of these perils or from either one alone. However, sickness insurance rarely is written unless accident insurance also is carried with the same insurer.

*Sickness insurance* is defined as a form of health insurance against loss by illness or disease. It provides benefits for loss occasioned by sickness (illness or disease). Illness and disease do not include accidental bodily injury. Sickness insurance may provide benefits in the event of loss

---

[3] A recent court decision held that "disease" is broader than "sickness." The court defined sickness as beginning when one's condition has advanced far enough to incapacitate him. Disease need not incapacitate the individual. *Continental Casualty Co.* v. *Gold*, Florida Supreme Court No. 35,480. On the other hand, sickness can arise from motion as in seasickness and from normal pregnancy, neither of which is a disease.

occasioned by pregnanc[...]
fits for other medical ex[...]

*Accident insurance* is [...]
cidental bodily injury. 1[...]
by accidental bodily inju[...]
form of insurance does [...]
of wounds resulting fron[...]

*Type of loss and ben[...]*
of two major types: loss [...]
ance policies define the [...]
in terms of loss of bodil[...]
ferred to as *disability*. A [...]
minology Committee has [...]
of the insured to functio[...]
may involve a loss of earn[...]
the body, or in the extren[...]

The term *medical expe[...]*
medical care. The term 1[...]
nostic or curative services, supplies, and use of equipment and facilities related to the individual's physical or mental health or bodily condition.

A parallel dichotomy is found in types of contract benefit provisions, although sometimes income and expense benefits are combined in the same policy. This is complicated somewhat by the lump-sum benefits provided in some contracts for dismemberment and accidental death. These represent a presumed loss of income or gainful activity, and thus should be classified as variants of the disability income benefit. Of course, accidental death benefits really represent a form of life insurance, but they frequently are issued in connection with health insurance, and thus must be considered.

*Disability income insurance* is a form of health insurance that provides periodic payments when the insured is unable to work as a result of illness, disease, or injury. It may provide benefits only in the event of accidental bodily injury, only in the event of sickness (although sickness coverage rarely is written except in combination with accident coverage), or may cover both contingencies in one contract. Benefit eligibility is based on a presumed loss of income, but in practice this usually is defined in terms of inability to pursue an occupation.

*Dismemberment insurance* is a form of health insurance that provides payment in event of loss of one or more bodily members or the sight of one or both eyes by accidental bodily injury. Loss of member may be defined in terms of actual severance or as loss of use.

*Accidental death insurance* is a form of insurance that provides payment if the insured individual dies as a result of an accident. Acci-

t insurance frequently are combined
clause and are referred to collectively
ismemberment, sometimes abbreviated as
ent of accidental causation may be expressed
bodily injury or of accidental means. Properly,
e insurance[4] but it is often found in health, as well

smemberment benefits resulting from sickness could be
y insurance contracts, but this does not seem yet to have
empted. Nonaccidental death, of course, is covered (as well
cidental death) in regular life insurance policies. Only a few states
mit insuring against death from nonaccidental causes in a contract
which also provides health benefits. However, there is growing agency
demand for such combination life and health insurance contracts and
many may be developed over the next decade. Health insurance contracts which provide disability income benefits primarily are discussed
in Part III.

*Medical expense insurance* is a form of health insurance which provides benefits for medical care. It provides benefits for expenses of
physicians, hospital, nursing and related health services, and medica-
tions and supplies. It may include benefits for preventive, diagnostic
and rehabilitive services as well as for services associated with curative
treatment. Benefits may be in the form of reimbursement of actual
expense up to a limit, valued or specified sums, or the direct provision
of services. Medical expenses may be paid directly to the purveyor of
services or to the insured.

Medical expense insurance may be classified further according to
the type of expense covered and the extent of coverage. The main subdivisions are hospital, surgical, regular medical, major medical, and
comprehensive benefits. In addition, there are less significant medical
expense benefits such as dread disease, hospital income, "blanket accident," laboratory expense, nursing, and the like, usually written as a
supplement to other coverage. Insurers also make available coverage
of drug expense, nursing home services, dental services, vision care, out-
patient pschiatric services, and preventive and diagnostic services. It is
possible that some day one or several of these may become major
branches of medical expense insurance.

*Hospital insurance* provides benefits for room and board and related
hospital expenses of an ancillary nature. It is written by insurance companies, usually on a reimbursement basis providing benefits up to a
stated number of dollars per day for room and board and up to a stated

---

[4] *Life insurance* is that form of insurance which is designed to protect against
economic loss resulting from death (and/or old age) and often provides other economic benefits to the policy owner.

dollar limit for hospital "extras" or ancillary services. It also is written by Blue Cross associations and a few Blue Shield associations and a number of independents, usually providing semiprivate accommodations on a service basis. Coverage of hospital extras may be on a service or reimbursement basis, often with internal limits. Hospital insurance is discussed in Chapter 6 below.

*Surgical insurance* provides payment for surgeons' fees, according to a schedule in the policy either direct to the surgeon in Blue Shield plans or to the insured in insurance company plans. Unless the insured is in a low-income bracket, he may find his coverage somewhat inadequate in either type of plan, although many insurers now make fairly high schedules available. The physicians maintain their right to charge in accordance with ability to pay and—it is said—may even look upon the existence of insurance as evidence of such ability.

*Regular medical expense insurance* provides payments on account of physicians' charges other than surgeons' fees. It sometimes is referred to as "basic medical expense insurance." Most contracts pay only for visits in the hospital, not for home and office visits. However, some insured plans pay whenever the insured is totally disabled, and a few pay in all instances, sometimes subject to a small deductible, usually the first two or three visits per disability. Plans covering without requiring hospitalization or disability may be extended to cover periodic health examinations and immunizations. Blanket medical expense coverage for individuals sometimes is written, usually as a rider to a disability income policy for accidental injury only. Such a provision covers all medical expenses up to a low overall limit. Surgical and regular medical insurance are discussed in Chapter 7 below.

*Major medical expense insurance* provides a large amount of protection against all medical and related expenses, subject to a deductible usually large enough to make the insured bear a portion of the cost above his basic hospital and surgical policies, if any. The greater the underlying coverage, the greater the deductible should be. In addition, such policies usually require the insured to bear a proportion, such as 15 to 25 percent, of the loss himself. This percentage participation is, rather unfortunately, often termed "coinsurance." This tends to encourage the insured to be reasonable in his utilization of medical services but may require him to bear a rather large loss in extreme cases. Variation among companies in coverage, deductibles, percentage participation requirements, and premiums is extreme. However, this type of contract represents a logical application of the principles of insurance programming to the risk of medical expense and is growing rapidly in use.

*Comprehensive medical expense insurance* represents an extension of this principle to include basic medical and hospital costs. This is like major medical with a very low deductible. The growth of comprehensive in number of persons insured was 9.1 percent in 1966. Policies of this type are issued mainly by insurance companies, and to a somewhat lesser degree by the hospital or medical associations. Some comprehensive contracts are, in effect, a combination of basic hospital, surgical, and medical coverage with major medical in a single policy. Major medical and comprehensive contracts are discussed in Chapter 8 below.

**Basis of payment.**  Disability income, accidental death, and dismemberment benefits usually are paid on a valued basis, but a reimbursement or service basis is more common for medical expense benefits. *Valued benefits* involve an agreement by the insurer to pay to or on behalf of the insured a specified or agreed amount of money upon the occurrence of a defined loss. Whether the actual loss is equal to, more than, or less than the agreed benefit is immaterial; the agreed sum is paid regardless of the extent of the loss.

*Reimbursement benefits* represent an agreement by the insurer to pay to or on behalf of the insured, on the occurrence of a defined loss, an amount of money related to the amount of the loss, but not in excess of a specified maximum amount. Usually the actual loss is reimbursed, subject to the application of provisions such as deductibles and coinsurance, up to the agreed limit. In other lines of insurance, such benefits are referred to as *indemnity benefits,* but since this term has been so abused in health insurance, it is better to avoid it and use the term reimbursement.

*Service benefits* involve an agreement by the insurer to pay, for health care services rendered to its covered persons, certain providers of these services, such as physicians and hospitals, the full or partial cost of the services, or to provide such services itself. When the purveyor of services reserves the right to charge additional amounts to covered persons, these are substantially the equivalent of reimbursement benefits and usually are so referred to. When the agreement provides that no additional charge will be made to any covered person for covered services, the benefits are referred to as being on a *full-service* basis. Where some covered persons receive full-service benefits, and others, usually defined as those having annual incomes above a certain figure, are subject to additional charges, these are referred to as *partial service benefits*. This latter arrangement is the most common in Blue Shield surgical and basic medical insurance, at this time.

**Continuance provisions.**  Health insurance contracts may have a variety of provisions which state the respective rights of the insurer and the insured to continue or discontinue the contract, or they may be silent on this point. There seem to be seven main types of contract, classified according to continuance provisions.

1. *Noncancellable.*  A contract of health insurance that the insured has the right to continue in force by the timely payment of premiums

set forth in the contract for a substantial period of time,[5] during which period the insurer has no right to make unilaterally any change in any provision of the contract while the contrast is in force. The premium may be level from date of issue or increase in accordance with a schedule contained in the contract at issue. The insurer may not modify the premium or coverage while the contract is in force.

2. *Guaranteed renewable.* A contract of health insurance that the insured has the right to continue in force by the timely payment of premiums for a substantial period of time[6] during which period the insurer has no right to make unilaterally any change in any provision of the contract while the contract is in force, other than a change in the premium rate for classes of insureds. The classes of insureds may be based on contract form, territory, age, period of issue, or other objective bases and may or may not be established at the issue of the contract. The term, "Guaranteed continuable," is sometimes used synonymously with the term, "Guaranteed renewable."

3. *Conditionally renewable.* A contract of health insurance that provides that the insured may renew the contract from period to period until a stated or an advanced attained age, subject to the right of the insurer to decline renewal only at anniversary or premium dates and then only for specific reasons such as retirement but other than deterioration of the insured's health, *or* that provides that the insurer relinquishes the right of termination for certain causes, including deterioration of the insured's health. The first of these sometimes is called "non-renewable for stated reasons only."

4. *Collectively renewable.* This term appears in the annual Statement Blank and refers to contracts which guarantee renewal except for all policies of a given type or all such policies in a state of residence.

5. *Renewable at insurer's option.* A contract of health insurance in which the insurer reserves the right to terminate coverage at any anniversary or premium-due date but does not have the right to terminate coverage between such dates.

6. *Cancellable.* A contract that may be terminated by the insurer or insured at any time (subject to the requirements of notice, etc.).

7. *Term.* Contracts where there is no provision relating to termination, except by expiration of the policy term.

The above classification is mutually exclusive and exhaustive and constitutes a true partition. In theory, each of the various types of continuance provision might be used in either group, franchise, or individual

---

[5] The November 30, 1959, report of the National Association of Insurance Commissioners Subcommittee on Definitions of Non Cancellable and Guaranteed Renewable Insurance defined the minimum noncancellable period as until age 50, or if issued after age 44, for at least five years.

[6] The time period described in note 5 applies to guaranteed renewable contracts.

contracts. True group policies do not permit individual termination by the insurer except as a result of change in employee status. The term *commercial contract,* while it carries broader connotations as to methods of merchandising and underwriting, would include policies with provisions of the type defined in (3), (4), (5) and (6) above. Commercial contracts are discussed in Chapter 11, and continuance provisions will be described at greater length in Chapter 12 below.

*Contractual, underwriting and merchandizing arrangement.* It is difficult to find an appropriate name for this basis of classification; it relates in part to contracting parties, in part to underwriting principles and in part to merchandizing method. The basic distinction is one of contractual arrangement: individual and family policies on the one hand and group and blanket contracts on the other, with franchise contracts somewhere in between.

*Group insurance* contracts are contracts made with an employer or other entity to cover a defined named or recorded group of individuals identifiable by reference to their relationship to the entity. The coverage may include dependent members of the families of the covered persons. Premiums may be paid entirely by the employer or other entity, partly by the covered persons, or by the covered persons alone. Eligible groups are limited by state law in some states and by the underwriting criteria of insurers. These limitations and underwriting criteria are applied to the group as a whole and are concerned with the size of group, proportion enrolling, and nature and purpose of the group.

Group medical expense policies provide similar or somewhat more liberal coverage than individual policies, and both are discussed together in Part II. Group disability income policies form a class more clearly distinct from individual disability income contracts and are described in Chapter 15 below. This chapter also includes a further discussion of group underwriting criteria.

Group insurance provides protection generally at a lower cost than individual coverages because of the limitation of adverse selection leading frequently to better loss experience and because of savings in expense. Expense savings result from the economy of a "wholesale"-type operation, from lower commissions, and from the fact that the employer or association performs certain administrative services which would otherwise be performed by the insurer.

In addition, a net saving in taxes occurs because the premiums for a qualified group plan are deductible by the employer and the value thereof is not considered taxable income to the employee. Thus it is more economical for an employer to provide such insurance than to increase wages by an equivalent amount so that the employees could purchase individual policies. The benefits will be partly tax free to the employee.

*Salary continuance plans* represent self-insurance by the employer of the risk of disability income loss by the employee. The plan may be formal or informal; if formal, it may be a part of the employment contract or merely a gratuitous employee benefit. The usual practice is for the employer to pay salary or wages, or a portion thereof, for a limited period of time during disability. In some cases such plans are used to supplement group disability income policies so as to cover the waiting period, increase the amount of benefit, or extend the duration. The fact that the plans are self-insured means that the employees' rights depend on the continuance of employer solvency to a greater degree than under insured plans. Almost invariably, a deduction is made for any workmen's compensation benefits payable.

In 1966, over 12.5 million persons were covered by formal plans, about half of whom were federal, state, and local government civilian employees. Something over one third were covered by private employer plans, with the balance about evenly split between union and employee benefit society plans. Additional millions are covered by informal plans. It is estimated that 90 percent of the labor force has some type of disability income protection.

*Pension plans* are intended primarily to provide retirement benefits, but a growing proportion provide at least some benefit in the event of death or disability. By 1959, 84 percent of union negotiated "pattern" plans and 59 percent of "conventional" plans provided some disability benefit. It is estimated that three fourths of employees under all types of private pension plan have some disability protection. In 1965, 145 out of 151 state and local government plans had disability benefits. Most private plans provided only a return of employee and employer contributions or for the payment of a "disability" pension, actuarially reduced to what such contribution could purchase. If disability occurs at an early age, this can be pitifully small. This represents, essentially, early retirement, and usually a long period of service is required to qualify. In effect this is a means of converting funds accumulated for another purpose into a provision for disability. The national government plans all provide disability protection, as do the retirement plans of the states, and these are somewhat more liberal than private plans. Where disability benefits are in excess of the actuarial value of the accumulation, they usually are not funded, even when the rest of the plan is. The excess benefit upon disability is handled either by "terminal funding" or on a "pay-as-you-go basis." Some pension plans provide for group medical expense insurance and/or Title XVIII, Part B premiums after retirement, sometimes financed by deducting all or part of the premiums from pension benefits. Like group contracts, pension plans may be financed either with an insurance company or on a self-insured basis. In the latter case, the use of a trustee to hold the funds is required and self-insured pension plans are referred to as trusteed plans.

*Blanket contracts* are similar to group contracts in that they cover groups of persons subject to a common hazard. The basic difference between group insurance and blanket insurance is that the persons insured under a blanket insurance policy are not or cannot be individually identified. Hence, individual certificates cannot be issued under a blanket insurance policy as is the case in group insurance. The hazards covered under blanket insurance contracts are usually, although not necessarily, limited to those resulting from accidents. The types of group usually insured under a blanket insurance policy are: passengers of a common carrier, students and faculty at an institution of learning, members of a volunteer fire department, ambulance corps or first-aid unit, scout troop, members of sport team, group of campers, employees of a common employer subject to special hazards incident to their employment, members of an association, and participants in Head Start and other anti-poverty programs.

*Franchise contracts* fall somewhere between group contracts and individual contracts. *Association group contracts* also belong in this middle area. Franchise contracts are issued to individuals under a broad arrangement with an employer or other entity who agrees to make the coverage available to his employees, withholds and/or contributes to premiums, and otherwise facilitates the arrangement. If a sufficient proportion enrolls, group underwriting standards may be employed and the contracts issued to all who apply on a "guaranteed issue" basis. Association group contracts are similar, except that they are issued to members of a professional or trade association, and the covered persons usually remit premiums directly to the insurer. For both of these, rates and underwriting standards usually fall somewhere between the extremes of group and individual.

Franchise arrangements involve the issuance of individual contracts, while association group arrangements may or may not.

*Individual contracts* are contracts made with an individual to cover him and, in certain instances. specified members of his family, usually dependents. The underwriting standards are applied to the individuals concerned, but some contracts are issued with little or no underwriting. For purposes of this book, individual medical expense policies are discussed together with group contracts providing similar benefits, classified by type or extent of benefit, in Part II. Individual disability income policies are classified according to method of marketing or merchandizing in Part III. The main divisions are commercial (Chapter 11); noncancellable and guaranteed renewable (Chapter 12; this distinction is made on the basis of continuance provisions, but the growing importance of this type of contract warrants separate treatment); life insurance waiver of premium and disability income riders (Chapter 13); and limited and industrial policies (Chapter 14).

*Liability insurance* is not properly part of health insurance, but medical payments provisions in liability insurance policies provide indemnification for certain medical expenses arising from accident without regard to liability. The medical payments coverage in automobile liability insurance provides reimbursement up to an agreed amount for medical, surgical, dental, ambulance, hospital, nursing, and funeral expenses incurred by any person from an accident while he is in, on, or alighting from an insured automobile and to the named insured, his spouse, and relatives of either (if resident in the same household) from all automobile accidents. The medical payments coverage in the comprehensive personal liability policy covers similar expenses for anyone injured on the premises or as a result of an act of an insured, except for injuries to insureds. All liability policies provide for payment by the insurer of expenses incurred by the insured for immediate medical and surgical relief to others at the time of an accident. In addition, most of the payment for bodily injury liability damages represents payments for medical expenses and loss of time resulting from disability.

*Types of insurer.* Insurance companies active in the health insurance field include life insurance companies, casualty insurance companies, and monoline or specialty health insurance companies.[7] They usually are organized as corporations, either on a stock basis similar to corporations in other fields of activity, or on a mutual basis where the policyholders exercise the usual rights of stockholders, voting for directors and sharing any "profits" through policyholder dividends. A few special-risk health policies are written by the Underwriters at Lloyd's. For a discussion of these types of insurer, the reader is referred to any good basic insurance text.

Unique to the health insurance field are the hospital and medical associations, Blue Cross and Blue Shield. These are described in Chapters 6 and 7, respectively. The independent plans represent a heterogeneous collection of types of insurer. They have little in common except that they are neither insurance companies nor Blue Cross–Blue Shield organizations. Since they emphasize medical and surgical benefits, they are discussed in Chapter 7. The United States government also sells disability riders to veterans who have government life insurance in force. Competition between insurer types and the relative advantages of each are discussed in Chapter 10.

*Freedom to insure.* Although the subject has been discussed at length, the Committee on Health Insurance Terminology is still trying to find an appropriate term to designate this dimension. Regardless of the name, a distinction must be made between social insurance and private insurance.

---

[7] These must organize as life or casualty companies under the insurance codes, however.

The distinctive characteristic of social insurance as compared to private insurance is its compulsory nature. The government, state or national, requires coverage by law. It may or may not provide the insurance. If it does, it may or may not be on a monopoly basis. Examples of social insurance on a monopoly basis are federal Old-Age, Survivors and Disability Insurance and nonoccupational disability in Rhode Island. Other characteristics, frequently, but not always, found in social insurance systems include a more loose relationship of premiums to benefits; the payment of premiums at least in part by others than the insured; the use of monopolistic insurers; the contribution of government to costs; the lack of need or reduced need for advance funding; the absence of a contract; and the irregularity and unpredictability of benefits, costs, and premiums.

Social insurance is distinguished from public assistance by the payment of premiums which bear some relation to benefits, the existence of a fund and an identifiable group of insured persons, and the fact that benefits are given as a matter of right to the recipients, not as a matter of charity.[8] There is no needs test in a social insurance plan.

Social insurance disability coverage in the United States is somewhat limited, compared to most economically developed foreign countries. This is due, in part, to the high degree of development of private insurance and the prevailing attitude of the people in favor of private enterprise wherever possible. However, social insurance coverage is broader than many realize. The programs now in force in this country include workmen's compensation, state disability or cash sickness insurance, disability benefits under the Railroad Retirement and Unemployment Insurance Acts, the disability provisions of the Old-Age, Survivors, and Disability Insurance program, and the new Title XVIII programs of hospital insurance for the aged. A mere listing of these programs indicates the heterogeneity of the concept of social insurance. Social insurance and related public programs are discussed below in Chapter 4.

### The overall picture

How much of the cost of poor health is met by the various programs discussed above?

*Medical expense.* By fiscal year 1966–67, the first full year of Title XVIII and Title XIX Social Security benefits, about 55 percent of expenditures for personal health care was met by third-party payments. Government programs provided about 30 percent, private health insurance almost 25 percent, and philanthropy about 2 percent, leaving 42 to 45 percent to be paid out of pocket by patients. Table 3–1 and Chart 3–1 show that the

---

[8] See Domenico Gagliardo, *American Social Insurance* (New York: Harper & Bros., 1955), pp. 14–21, for a fuller development of these points.

## TABLE 3-1

### Amount and Percent of Expenditures for Personal Health Care Met by Third Parties, Selected Years, 1950–66
(amounts in millions)

| Year | Personal Health Care Expenditures[a] | Out-of-Pocket Expenditures | | Third-Party Payments | | | | | | | | |
| | | Amount | Percent | Total | | Private Health Insurance | | Government | | Philanthropy and Others | |
| | | | | Amount | Percent | Amount | Percent | Amount | Percent | Amount | Percent |
|---|---|---|---|---|---|---|---|---|---|---|---|
| 1950......... | $11,109 | $ 7,209 | 64.9 | $ 3,900 | 35.1 | $ 992 | 8.9 | $ 2,588 | 23.3 | $320 | 2.9 |
| 1955......... | 15,933 | 9,271 | 58.2 | 6,662 | 41.8 | 2,536 | 15.9 | 3,705 | 23.3 | 421 | 2.6 |
| 1960......... | 23,758 | 13,068 | 55.0 | 10,690 | 45.0 | 4,996 | 21.0 | 5,157 | 21.7 | 537 | 2.3 |
| 1961......... | 25,184 | 13,334 | 52.9 | 11,850 | 47.1 | 5,695 | 22.6 | 5,578 | 22.1 | 577 | 2.3 |
| 1962......... | 27,131 | 14,212 | 52.4 | 12,919 | 47.6 | 6,344 | 23.4 | 5,967 | 22.0 | 608 | 2.2 |
| 1963......... | 29,088 | 15,048 | 51.7 | 14,040 | 48.3 | 6,980 | 24.0 | 6,419 | 22.1 | 641 | 2.2 |
| 1964......... | 32,408 | 17,005 | 52.5 | 15,403 | 47.5 | 7,832 | 24.2 | 6,903 | 21.3 | 668 | 2.1 |
| 1965......... | 35,242 | 18,259 | 51.8 | 16,983 | 48.2 | 8,729 | 24.8 | 7,557 | 21.4 | 697 | 2.0 |
| 1966......... | 39,115 | 19,517 | 49.9 | 19,598 | 50.1 | 9,142 | 23.4 | 9,712[b] | 24.8 | 744 | 1.9 |
| Fiscal 1966–67.. | 41,471.6 | 18,911 | 45.6 | 22,560 | 54.4 | 9,153 | 22.1 | 12,637 | 30.5 | 770 | 1.9 |

[a] All expenditures for health services and supplies other than (1) expenses for prepayment and administration, (2) government public health activities, and (3) expenditures of private voluntary agencies for other health services.

[b] Includes benefit payments under health insurance for the aged (Medicare).

Source: Dorothy P. Rice and Barbara S. Cooper, "National Health Expenditures, 1950–66," *Social Security Bulletin*, April, 1968, p. 3.

proportion of expenditures met by government third-party payments increased from 23 percent in 1950 to 30 percent in fiscal 1966–67, while private health insurance increased from 9 percent to 23.4 percent in 1966 and an estimated 23.5 percent in 1966–67.[9] The proportion of expenditures

CHART 3–1

Personal Health Care Expenditures by Source of Payment, Selected Years 1950–66

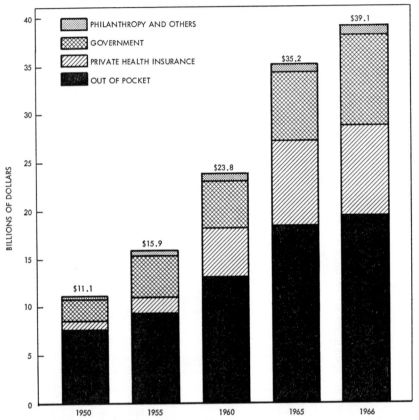

Source: Dorothy P. Rice and Barbara S. Cooper, "National Health Expenditures, 1950–66," *Social Security Bulletin*, April, 1968, p. 3.

met by all third-party payments increased from 35 percent to 55 percent. About one third of all medical care expenditures represent government provisions of one type or another. Of the remaining two thirds, about one third is met by private insurance. The *Social Security Bulletin* presents annual estimates of private consumer medical care expenditures and the

---

[9] Based on estimates for calendar 1967 in *Health Insurance News*, December, 1967. It is believed that the private benefits shown in the table will turn out at least $500,000 too low.

proportion thereof met by private insurance. Table 3–2 indicates the great growth of voluntary health insurance since 1948.

These figures indicate that, despite the rapid increase in expenditures for medical care, the percentage covered by insurance has risen in every year until 1964. The figures tend to understate the proportion of ex-

TABLE 3–2

Private Consumer Expenditures for Medical Care and Percent Met by Voluntary Health Insurance, United States, 1948–1965

(amounts in millions of dollars)

| Year | Total Medical Care Amount | Per-cent | Hospitals Amount | Per-cent | Physicians* Amount | Per-cent | Hospitals and Physicians Combined Amount | Per-cent |
|---|---|---|---|---|---|---|---|---|
| 1948 | 7,407 | 8.2 | 1,689 | 26.9 | 2,490 | 6.1 | 4,179 | 14.5 |
| 1949 | 7,682 | 10.0 | 1,802 | 29.9 | 2,501 | 9.1 | 4,303 | 17.8 |
| 1950 | 8,201 | 12.1 | 1,965 | 34.6 | 2,597 | 12.0 | 4,562 | 20.1 |
| 1951 | 9,072 | 14.9 | 2,334 | 38.4 | 2,697 | 16.9 | 5,031 | 23.7 |
| 1952 | 9,745 | 16.5 | 2,602 | 41.3 | 2,851 | 18.6 | 5,453 | 29.5 |
| 1953 | 10,547 | 18.2 | 2,909 | 44.2 | 3,063 | 20.6 | 5,972 | 32.3 |
| 1954 | 11,318 | 19.3 | 3,167 | 45.5 | 3,336 | 22.1 | 6,503 | 33.5 |
| 1955 | 11,807 | 21.5 | 3,244 | 5.18 | 3,433 | 25.0 | 6,677 | 37.9 |
| 1956 | 13,748 | 21.9 | 3,905 | 51.8 | 3,787 | 26.2 | 7,692 | 38.3 |
| 1957 | 14,932 | 23.3 | 4,221 | 54.6 | 4,101 | 28.5 | 8,322 | 42.1 |
| 1958 | 16,122 | 24.0 | 4,522 | 57.3 | 4,553 | 28.2 | 9,075 | 42.8 |
| 1959 | 17,581 | 25.0 | 4,840 | 60.8 | 5,101 | 28.5 | 9,941 | 43.5 |
| 1960 | 18,066 | 27.7 | 5,188 | 63.7 | 5,309 | 30.0 | 10,497 | 46.2 |
| 1961 | 19,031 | 29.9 | 5,692 | 66.2 | 5,497 | 32.7 | 11,189 | 49.5 |
| 1962 | 20,555 | 30.9 | 6,153 | 68.2 | 6,042 | 33.0 | 12,195 | 50.6 |
| 1963 | 22,028 | 31.7 | 6,912 | 67.2 | 6,406 | 33.6 | 13,318 | 51.5 |
| 1964 | 24,837 | 31.5 | 7,613 | 68.1 | 7,543 | 32.2 | 15,156 | 50.7 |
| 1965 | 26,988 | 32.3 | 8,463 | 68.4 | 8,184 | 32.7 | 16,647 | 51.4 |
| 1966 | 28,660 | 31.9 | 8,772 | 68.3 | 8,608 | 32.9 | 17,380 | 51.9 |

* Including osteopaths.
Source: Louis S. Reed and Dorothy P. Rice, "Private Medical Care Expenditures and Voluntary Health Insurance, 1948–1961," *Social Security Bulletin* (December, 1962), p. 3; Dorothy P. Rice and Barbara S. Cooper, "National Health Expenditures, 1950–66," *Social Security Bulletin* (April, 1968), p. 3; *Research and Statistics Note* No. 7–1968, May 3, 1968.

penditures met by insurance for several reasons. First, workmen's compensation benefits for medical care were not included. These payments equaled $665 million in 1966. Payments under state temporary disability insurance laws for medical care equaled $54 million, and these were not counted either. If this total of $719 million be added to insurance benefits, this increases the percentage met by insurance by 2.5 percent of total expenditures and by 4.1 percent of hospital and physicians' expenditures, bringing the proportions met by insurance to 34.4 and 56.0 percent, respectively.

Second, it is not meaningful to relate insurance benefits to total expenditures. The *Social Security Bulletin* formerly recognized this and attempted to derive a measure of "currently insurable" expenditures. Even this figure, which included all hospital and physicians' expenditures and 10 percent of the costs of drugs and appliances, probably overstated the "currently insurable" loss.

In 1961, as a result of growing optimism as to what is insurable, this computation was dropped. A large proportion of physicians' fees are for single visits for minor ailments or routine prevention and are properly items for the family budget, not for insurance. On this basis it would seem reasonable to conclude that, by today, private insurance covers about four fifths of the severe hospital and physicians' costs. Considering that hospital insurance is not much over 35 years old and medical and surgical coverages are considerably newer, this is a remarkable accomplishment.

TABLE 3-3

Proportion of Health Expenditures Covered by Insurance,
12-Month Period, 1952-53, 1957-58, and 1962-63

| Annual Family Total Gross Medical Expenditures | Total Insurance Benefits as Percent of Mean Gross Total Expenditures according to Level of Family Gross Total Expenditures | | |
|---|---|---|---|
| | *1952-53* | *1957-58* | *1962-63* |
| All insured families.............19 | 24 | 31 |
| Under $50.......................8 | 2 | 2 |
| $50-99..........................6 | 2 | 3 |
| $100-199.......................11 | 7 | 5 |
| $200-299.......................14 | 11 | 13 |
| $300-399.......................20 | 18 | 14 |
| $400-499.......................23 | 21 | 23 |
| $500-749.......................25 | 25 | 28 |
| $750-999.......................24 | 30 | 34 |
| $1,000 and over................23 | 35 | 45 |

Source: *Progress in Health Services.*

Another set of estimates of the portion of medical care bills met by insurance is given by the three Health Information Foundation surveys referred to above.[10] Based on an area probability sample, these estimates differ from those based on national aggregates above. Moreover, the definitions used in the two approaches differed. The Health Information Foundation studies showed that the proportion of expenditures for personal health services met by insurance rose from 19 percent in 1952-53 to 24 percent in 1957-58 and 31 percent in 1962-63 for insured families.

---

[10] P. 30 ff.

These surveys give the proportion of the medical care bill paid for insured families, broken down by type of service and magnitude of expenditure.

Table 3–3 indicates how the proportion reimbursed varies with the magnitude of total expenditure for insured families. In 1952–53, the highest proportion of reimbursement was found in the the $500–$749 bracket. In 1957–58 and 1962–63, the proportion reimbursed increased monotonically with expenditure size to reach its peak in the top bracket. This would seem to indicate that insurance is doing its main job at protecting families from high losses which cannot be budgeted. This result may be due to the growth of major medical and comprehensive coverages.

For hospital bills, 50 percent of the insured families had 80 percent or more of their bills covered in 1952–53 and 62 percent had this proportion covered in 1957–58. The proportion of insured families with 80 percent or more of surgical bills paid by insurance increased from 45 percent to 53 percent. These improvements in the proportion of bills covered by insurance took place despite an increase of 69 percent in the expenditures per person for hospital care and of 27 percent in average charges for all surgical procedures. This would indicate that the quality of health insurance protection is improving as well as the number of persons insured.

*Income loss.* The *Social Security Bulletin* also attempts to estimate the income loss from nonoccupational short-term disability. Table 3–4 gives such estimates for 1948–66 compared with benefit payments of various insurance plans.

When appropriate allowance is made for a waiting period and for the insured sharing the loss, it appears that insurance plans of various types are currently providing benefits equal to about nine tenths of the insurable short-term nonoccupational income loss.[11] Workmen's compensation benefits probably provide coverage of about the same proportion of the short-term occupational loss. However, there is little protection in force against the long-term income loss. Some portion of the individual insurance benefits included in Table 3–3 applies to long-term loss, and some workmen's compensation coverage is available for long-term loss. The other programs tabulated provide relatively little protection for disabilities lasting over six months. Federal Old-Age, Survivors, and Disability Insurance and life insurance disability riders protect only against long-term disability and were not included in the table. OASDI disability benefits were being paid at the rate of $1,939 million per year in 1967.

---

[11] However, this represents an average of over-insured government workers with sick leave, adequately insured employees and individual policy holders and uninsured millions of persons. Formal sick leave plans reimburse about 73–74 percent of lost earnings, which is too high for safety.

TABLE 3-4

Estimated Income Loss from Nonoccupational Short-Term Disability Compared with Insurance Benefit Payments
(amounts in millions of dollars)

| Year | Income Loss[a] | Private Insurance | | Self-Insurance[b] | Compulsory Nonoccupational Disability Laws | | Paid Sick Leave | Total Benefits | Total Benefits as Percent of: | |
| | | Group | Individual | | Private Insurance[c] | Government Funds[d] | | | Total Income Loss | Insurable Loss[e] |
|---|---|---|---|---|---|---|---|---|---|---|
| 1948 | 4,568 | 115.0 | 141.0 | 21.5 | 9.3 | 57.1 | 413 | 757 | 16.6 | 49.8 |
| 1949 | 4,424 | 124.7 | 150.0 | 20.2 | 27.1 | 62.1 | 462 | 846 | 19.1 | 57.3 |
| 1950 | 4,795 | 161.3 | 153.0 | 15.2 | 54.3 | 63.1 | 492 | 939 | 19.6 | 58.8 |
| 1951 | 5,473 | 212.4 | 157.0 | 18.1 | 113.3 | 60.9 | 588 | 1,150 | 21.0 | 63.0 |
| 1952 | 5,814 | 234.6 | 177.0 | 19.7 | 127.8 | 74.5 | 667 | 1,301 | 22.4 | 67.2 |
| 1953 | 6,144 | 241.0 | 209.0 | 16.5 | 139.7 | 90.5 | 713 | 1,410 | 22.9 | 68.8 |
| 1954 | 6,094 | 251.8 | 230.0 | 15.3 | 132.0 | 103.1 | 741 | 1,473 | 24.2 | 72.4 |
| 1955 | 6,546 | 292.0 | 250.0 | 15.2 | 135.2 | 109.4 | 813 | 1,615 | 24.7 | 73.9 |
| 1956 | 7,031 | 357.3 | 278.0 | 16.0 | 151.2 | 113.8 | 884 | 1,800 | 25.6 | 76.5 |
| 1957 | 7,363 | 372.3 | 307.2 | 16.8 | 178.1 | 127.2 | 951 | 1,953 | 26.5 | 79.4 |
| 1958 | 7,458 | 355.9 | 353.4 | 16.1 | 183.7 | 141.4 | 1,034 | 2,085 | 28.0 | 84.0 |
| 1959 | 7,724 | 394.2 | 389.6 | 16.8 | 189.5 | 163.7 | 1,076 | 2,230 | 28.9 | 89.7 |
| 1960 | 8,555 | 424.1 | 392.8 | 18.2 | 196.1 | 172.1 | 1,219 | 2,422 | 28.3 | 84.9 |
| 1961 | 8,639 | 406.8 | 425.9 | 17.5 | 201.4 | 195.2 | 1,310 | 2,557 | 29.6 | 88.8 |
| 1962 | 9,622 | 445.8 | 418.5 | 18.1 | 204.3 | 212.0 | 1,459 | 2,758 | 28.7 | 86.1 |
| 1963 | 10,178 | 454.2 | 447.2 | 17.9 | 198.2 | 243.9 | 1,623 | 2,984 | 29.3 | 87.9 |
| 1964 | 10,248 | 498.9 | 483.9 | 18.2 | 191.4 | 264.4 | 1,621 | 3,078 | 30.0 | 90.0 |
| 1965 | 11,270 | 542.0 | 482.6 | 17.9 | 197.2 | 269.1 | 1,804 | 3,313 | 29.4 | 88.2 |
| 1966 | 12,184 | 602.9 | 512.9 | 18.2 | 208.7 | 273.2 | 1,951 | 3,577 | 29.4 | 88.2 |

[a] Income loss computed by multiplying average earnings per day by seven days by average annual employment, adjusted since 1959 to National Health Survey data.
[b] Self-insurance represents primarily union, union-management, and mutual benefit society plans.
[c] Compulsory private insurance represents benefits provided by private companies under compulsory nonoccupational disability laws, including self-insurance.
[d] Government funds represent federal and state fund nonoccupational disability benefits.
[e] Insurable income loss is computed by the author to exclude 50% of total short-term income loss to allow for a seven-day waiting period and further to reduce the loss one-third to allow for participation by the insured.

_____ , ____ , ____ , Loss Protection against Short-Term Sickness, 1948-61," Social Security Bulletin, January, 1962, p. 11; _____ "Income Loss Pro-

Disability riders provided $169 million of long-term disability benefits in 1966, including waiver of premium. When this is compared to the long-term income loss of $11,000 million, it is clear that approximately 25 percent of long-term disability losses are met by current programs. Thus, while coverage of medical care costs and short-term losses has reached a high degree of development, coverage of the long-term income loss is inadequate.

*Persons covered.* Another measure of the adequacy of insurance is the numbers of persons protected. Health Insurance Institute estimates for 1966 are given in Table 3–5.[12] Chart 3–2 indicates the growth of protection for persons under age 65 since 1940. These figures indicate that substantial numbers of people are protected by voluntary health insurance. However, their meaning is more apparent when they are related to the population or to the number of persons employed. The proportion of the under-65 population covered is 85 percent for hospital expense insurance; 78 percent for surgical; 63 percent for regular medical; and 40 percent for major medical. When it is considered how many in the population are not insurable by usual means because of rural resi-

TABLE 3–5

Number of Persons Protected by Voluntary Health Insurance, December 31, 1966

(amounts in thousands of persons)

| Type of Insuring Organization | Hospital Expense | Surgical Expense | Regular Medical Expense | Major and Comprehensive Medical Expense |
|---|---|---|---|---|
| For Persons under Age 65 | | | | |
| Insurance companies | | | | |
| Group insurance..............67,546 | | 68,574 | 52,901 | 50,884 |
| Individual-policy insurance.....35,729 | | 27,479 | 10,857 | 4,591 |
| Net Total for insurance companies................92,791 | | 86,993 | 59,159 | 55,475 |
| Blue Cross, Blue Shield, and Medical Society plans...........61,556 | | 53,629 | 50,016 | 14,017[a] |
| Independent plans............... 6,596 | | 8,146 | 7,955 | — |
| Total number of policies or certificates....................171,427 | | 157,828 | 121,729 | 69,546[a] |
| Less Persons covered under more than one policy or certificate..... 22,838 | | 20,380 | 10,975 | — |
| Equals total persons protected.....148,589 | | 137,448 | 110,754 | 69,546[a] |
| Percent of Population........ 84.5% | | 78.1% | 63.0% | 39.5%[a] |

[12] H.I.A.A. projected numbers covered by private health insurance on Dec. 31, 1967 were 163 million by hospital insurance, 150 million by surgical, 121 million by basic medical, 57 million by major medical (insurance companies only) and 57 million by disability income insurance.

TABLE 3–5 Continued

| Type of Insuring Organization | Hospital Expense | Surgical Expense | Regular Medical Expense | Major and Comprehensive Medical Expense |
|---|---|---|---|---|
| For Persons 65 Years of Age and over | | | | |
| Insurance companies | | | | |
|   Group insurance.............. | 2,024 | 1,694 | 1,149 | 1,118 |
|   Individual-policy insurance.... | 2,912 | 1,822 | 616 | 149 |
|   Net total for insurance | | | | |
|     companies............... | 4,613 | 3,301 | 1,681 | 1,267 |
| Blue Cross, Blue Shield, and | | | | |
|   Medical Society plans.......... | 4,937 | 3,869 | 3,726 | 335[a] |
| Independent plans............... | 437 | 487 | 479 | |
| Total number of policies or | | | | |
|   certificates.................... | 10,310 | 7,872 | 5,970 | 1,602[a] |
| Less Persons covered under more than one policy or | | | | |
|   certificate...................... | 877 | 605 | 262 | |
| Equals total persons protected.... | 9,433 | 7,267 | 5,708 | 1,602[a] |
|   Percent of population......... | 50.9% | 38.9% | 30.6% | 8.6%[a] |
| For Persons of All Ages | | | | |
| Insurance companies | | | | |
|   Group insurance.............. | 69,570 | 70,268 | 54,050 | 52,002 |
|   Individual-policy insurance.... | 38,641 | 29,301 | 11,473 | 4,740 |
|   Net total for insurance | | | | |
|     companies............... | 97,404 | 90,294 | 60,840 | 56,742 |
| Blue Cross, Blue Shield, and | | | | |
|   Medical Society plans.......... | 66,493 | 57,498 | 53,742 | 14,352 |
| Independent plans............... | 7,033 | 8,633 | 8,434 | — |
| Total number of policies or | | | | |
|   certificates.................... | 181,737 | 165,700 | 127,699 | 71,094 |
| Less persons covered under more than one policy or certificate.... | 23,715 | 20,985 | 11,237 | — |
| Equals total persons protected.... | 158,022 | 144,715 | 116,432 | 71,094 |
|   Percent of Population........ | 81.2% | 74.4% | 59.9% | 36.5% |

[a] Estimated.
Source: Health Insurance Association of America.

dence, impaired health, and lack of financial resources, these proportions are even more impressive. Many of these, of course, have their medical needs taken care of by public assistance and other means. Moreover, not everyone wants health insurance.

As a proportion of the number of persons employed, the figures are even larger. These proportions (after deducting dependents' coverages) are 92 percent for hospital, 81 percent for surgical, 65 percent for regular medical, and more than 50 percent for major medical. Income loss

CHART 3-2

Growth in Health Insurance Provided by Insurance
Companies to Persons under 65

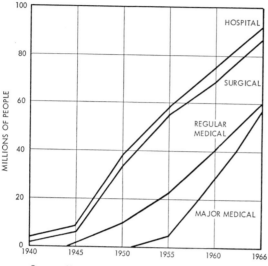

Source: Health Insurance Council.

coverage protects 75 percent of the persons employed. On an overall
basis, then, about 81 percent of the people in the United States have some
form of voluntary health insurance. Of course, such figures indicate nothing about the quality of the protection. This still leaves much to be
desired, especially in the field of income loss. However, by any measure,
private health insurance has done a tremendous job in providing health
protection to the people of the United States on a voluntary basis. If the
future trends continue in the same pattern, the problem of meeting
health costs will be largely solved.

*Medical Expenses and Benefits for Persons 65 and Over.* Data published in June 1968 make it possible to compare medical care expenses
of the aged with benefits from public and private programs for 1966–67,
the first full year of Medicare. Table 3–6 indicates that people age 65 and
over were apparently overinsured for hospital expense in 1966–67 by
approximately $31 million, but uninsured for almost $3.3 billion for other
types of medical expense. This would seem to leave quite a bit of room
for the expansion of private insurance or public programs. Chapter 9
discusses the insurability of medical expenses other than hospital and
physicians' expenses. In general, they are readily insurable on a group
basis, but difficult on an individual basis where opportunity for adverse
selection exists. It is to be hoped that private enterprise can find ways to
meet these needs before public programs are further expanded.

TABLE 3-6
Personal Health Care Expenditures of Persons Age 65 and Over by Type
of Expense and Source of Funds, U.S., 1966–67
(in millions)

| | | Private | | | Public | | |
| Type of Expense | Total | Total | Insurance[a] | Out-of-Pocket[b] | Total | Federal | State-Local |
|---|---|---|---|---|---|---|---|
| Total | 9,156 | 3,774 | 480 | 3,294 | 5,382 | 4,331 | 1,051 |
| Hospital | 4,188 | 348 | 379 | (31) | 3,840 | 3,161 | 679 |
| Physicians | 1,602 | 864 | 101 | 763 | 738 | 675 | 63 |
| Other professional | 425 | 383 | c | c | 42 | 30 | 10 |
| Drugs | 1,232 | 1,139 | c | c | 93 | 46 | 47 |
| Nursing homes | 1,209 | 678 | c | c | 531 | 311 | 220 |
| Other | 500 | 362 | c | c | 138 | 107 | 31 |

[a] Benefits for calendar 1966. This may overstate or understate fiscal 1966–67 benefits.
[b] Residual computed by subtracting 1966 insurance benefits from 1966–67 expenditures.
[c] Not available July 2, 1968.
Source: U.S. Dept. of H.E.W., "Personal Health Care Expenditures of the Aged and Non-Aged, Fiscal Year 1966 and 1967" (Research and Statistics Note No. 11, June 14, 1968); Health Insurance Institute, 1967 Source Book of Health Insurance Data.

## Summary

The financial impact of disability losses may be met by assumption of risk, transfer of risk, or combination of exposures and reduction of risk by insurance. Assumption is the unsatisfactory last resort when other methods fail.

Public assistance and other governmental programs represent transfer of risk to society. Insurance eliminates risk by combining separate exposures. Social insurance is insurance which is compelled by government. It may be provided by government or by private concerns. In the United States social insurance against health losses includes federal Old-Age, Survivors, and Disability Insurance, Hospital Insurance for the Aged, workmen's compensation insurance, and compulsory nonoccupational disability insurance in four states and for railroad workers.

Private insurance may be written on either a group or individual basis and may be provided by insurance companies, Blue Cross, Blue Shield, employee, union, community, or employer plans. Group and individual medical care plans cover hospital, surgical, medical, and major medical expenses. Disability income insurance on a group basis is provided by group insurance, by paid sick leave, and by disability provisions in private pension plans. Individual disability income policies may be classified as limited, industrial, commercial, noncancellable, guaranteed renewable, and life insurance riders.

More than four fifths of the population is covered by medical expense insurance, but such plans meet only about half of the insurable expense. Almost three fourths of the employed have some form of formal income protection. This covers about nine tenths of the short-term insurable income loss, but only about 18 percent of the long-term loss, even after considering social insurance. Thus long-term disability losses are still met largely by public assistance. It is in this area that private insurance faces its greatest challenge and its greatest opportunity for further growth.

## Selected references

*See the following items from the General Bibliography: 6, chs. 1, 5, 6, 7, 9, and 15; 7, chs. 2 and 3; 8, ch. 2; 10, chs. 1 and 2; 11; 15, chs. 43 and 64; 18, pp. 333–64; 19, ch. 21; 21, ch. 11; 23, ch. 2; 25, chs. 2, 3, and 4; 26, ch. 2; 27; 28; 29, chs. 3 and 12; 30.*

HANFT, RUTH S. "National Health Expenditures, 1950–65," *Social Security Bulletin,* February, 1967, p. 3.

HEALTH INSURANCE INSTITUTE. *Source Book of Health Insurance Data, 1967.* New York, 1968.

REED, LOUIS S. "Private Health Insurance and Financial Experience, 1940–1966," *Social Security Bulletin,* November, 1967, p. 3.

———, AND RICE, DOROTHY P. "Private Medical Care Expenditures and Voluntary Health Insurance, 1948–1961." *Social Security Bulletin,* December, 1962, p. 3.

RICE, DOROTHY P. AND COOPER, BARBARA S. "National Health Expenditures, 1950–66," *Social Security Bulletin,* April, 1968, p. 3.

SKOLNIK, ALFRED M. "Income-Loss Protection Against Illness, 1948–66," *Social Security Bulletin,* January 1968, p. 3.

U.S. DEPARTMENT OF HEALTH, EDUCATION, AND WELFARE, NATIONAL CENTER FOR HEALTH STATISTICS. *Vital and Health Statistics,* Series 10, Nos. 1–44; Series 12, Nos. 1–9; and the Health Economics Series, Nos. 1–6. Washington, D.C.: U.S. Government Printing Office.

U.S. DEPARTMENT OF HEALTH, EDUCATION, AND WELFARE, SOCIAL SECURITY ADMINISTRATION, OFFICE OF RESEARCH AND STATISTICS. *State and Local Government Retirement Systems—1965.* Research Report No. 15. Washington, D.C.: U.S. Government Printing Office.

WALDMAN, SAUL. "Income-Loss Protection against Illness," *Social Security Bulletin,* January, 1967, p. 17.

## chapter 4

No doubt but ye are the people.—Kipling, *The Islanders*

# Government Programs

### Introduction

Social insurance is insurance which is compulsory according to law.[1] It must be distinguished from private insurance, which is voluntary and administered by private insurers, and from state or government insurance, which is not compulsory but is provided by a governmental agency. These three types are not mutually exclusive. Social insurance may be written by either a governmental agency or a private company. Thus it may include state insurance and/or private insurance as its mechanism. It overlaps both areas but is not synonymous with either. Pension plans for government employees, veterans, etc. are not considered social insurance.

*Social insurance and public assistance.* Social insurance must be distinguished from public assistance programs, which are not insurance programs at all but merely devices for transferring a risk (or loss) to the government. In social insurance there is a group of covered or insured persons, usually employees, who are the majority of participants. Only a few of these are receiving payment at any time. In public assistance, the

---

[1] Some authorities define "social insurance" differently, some deny that many of these programs deserve the name of insurance, and others point out validly that private insurance is "social" since it serves a social purpose. Nonetheless, the term "social insurance" is used here in this sense. The term "social insurance" does not include devices exclusively for government employees, such as civil service retirement.

The following definitions have been developed by the Committee on Social Insurance Terminology of the Commission on Insurance Terminology.

*Social insurance.* A device for the pooling of risks by their transfer to an organization, usually governmental, that is required by law to provide pecuniary or service benefits to or on behalf of covered persons upon the occurrence of certain predesignated losses under all of the following conditions: 1. Coverage is compulsory by law in virtually all instances; 2. eligibility for benefits is derived, in fact or in effect, from contributions having been made to the program by or in respect of the claimant or the person as to whom the claimant is a dependent; there is no requirement that

only direct participants are the recipients of aid. Social insurance benefits are paid as a matter of right to those who qualify according to the plan. There is neither a means test nor the stigma of charity. Public assistance benefits are paid only to those "in need" according to a means or income test. Social insurance is financed by premium payments (often in the form of earmarked taxes) paid by, or on behalf of, the covered employees, while public assistance is financed from general government revenues. Public assistance payments are difficult to forecast, and most families do not consider them as part of the family security program. If they consider them at all, it is probably as a "last resort" for serious emergency. However, once an individual or family starts collecting benefits, they may become very dependent, and this dependency tends to increase.

*Social and private insurance.* The compulsory nature of social insurance is what distinguishes it from private insurance. As indicated above, it is sometimes, but not always, written by a government agency. The social insurance "contract" consists, usually, of the applicable statute and administrative law and is subject to change, unlike a private insurance contract. In social insurance, the actuarial relationship between premiums, benefits, and the probability of loss need not be as close for each insured and class as is necessary in private insurance. Since participation is compulsory, there will be no adverse selection if some groups are undercharged and others overcharged. Thus it is possible for social insurance to be used as a means for redistributing income through deliberate design of the benefit and premium structure. Where social insurance is written by private insurers under competitive conditions, however, considerations of equity among insureds are similar to those in private insurance.

Similarly, it is not necessary for a social insurance system underwritten by a monopoly fund to collect premiums equal to losses in any given year. Deficiencies may be made up by increasing premiums in following years. Private insurers are rather limited in the degree to which they can do this. For the same reason, reserves are not so necessary for social

---

the individual demonstrate inadequate financial resources, although a dependency status may need to be established; 3. the method for determining the benefits is prescribed by law; 4. the benefits for any individual are not usually directly related to contributions made by or in respect of him but instead usually redistribute income so as to favor certain groups such as those with low former wages or a large number of dependents; 5. there is a definite plan for financing the benefits that is designed to be adequate in terms of long-range considerations; 6. the cost is borne primarily by contributions which are usually made by covered persons, their employers, or both; 7. the plan is administered or at least supervised by the government; 8. the plan is not established by the government solely for its present or former employees.

*Medicare.* A term used to denote the two programs under the Social Security Act that are identified as Hospital Insurance and Supplementary Medical Insurance.

*Contribution* (to a social insurance system). A specific payment or tax made under a social insurance system by a covered person or with respect to covered persons to meet all or a portion of the system's costs.

insurance as for private. While it is desirable that they be large enough to absorb fluctuations, the right to increase future premiums for any and all participants, often most of the population, is a rather sound basis of solvency. The premiums in social insurance are often paid wholly or in part by others than the insured. Sometimes the government may contribute from general revenue to the benefit payments or administration costs.

*U.S. programs.* Four major social insurance programs and one voluntary government subsidized insurance program provide health protection in the United States. These are workmen's compensation, certain nonoccupational disability laws, the disability provisions in federal Old-Age, Survivors, and Disability Insurance and the "Medicare" program of Hospital Insurance and Supplementary Medical Insurance. The nonoccupational disability laws cover railroad workers and industrial and commercial workers in four states. Since the development and characteristics of the various United States programs are so different, they will be discussed separately below.

**Public assistance**

The Social Security Act provides for the operation of a joint federal-state program to provide monthly income and/or vendor payments for medical care to the needy. This system provides benefits for those who are not adequately taken care of by any other program and who can demonstrate a need for help. The impersonality of the program diminishes, in part, the stigma attached to the receipt of charity, and administrative and benefit standards are the same within each state. The national government contributes more than half the cost of the program to states whose plans meet the standards set up in the law. The Social Security Administration approves the programs, and the Treasury Department makes the actual grants-in-aid.

Public assistance payments are classified into seven categories: Aid to the Blind; Aid to the Permanently and Totally Disabled; Medical Assistance; Medical Assistance for the Aged; Aid to Families with Dependent Children; Old-Age Assistance, and General Assistance. The first four of these involve health benefits as such, and vendor payments on behalf of the recipients of the other types of assistance also meet health costs. These vendor payments are made to hospitals, physicians, and others who provide medical care for assistance recipients. Table 4–1 indicates the magnitude of the assistance program in the United States. The national government shares the costs of these programs (except for General Assistance) through grants to the states.

Administrative standards for approval for federal funds include requirements of statewide coverage, centralized administration, signifi-

TABLE 4–1

Public Assistance in the U.S., September, 1967

| Program | Number of Recipients, Dec., 1967 (in Thousands) | Total Benefit Amount (in thousands) | | Average Payment, Dec., 1967 |
| | | Dec., 1967 | Total, Year 1967 | |
| --- | --- | --- | --- | --- |
| *Income programs* | | | | |
| Old-age Assistance............2,073 | | $145,425 | $1,702,086 | $ 70.15 |
| Aid to the Blind................ 82.6 | | 7,474 | 87,711 | 90.45 |
| Aid to the Permanently and | | | | |
| Totally Disabled.............. 646 | | 52,054 | 574,574 | 80.60 |
| Aid to Families with Depend- | | | | |
| ent Children.................5,309 | | 209,736 | 2,263,366 | 39.50 |
| General Assistance............ 782 | | 30,821 | 325,500 | 39.40 |
| Total income programs.....8,074 | | $445,510 | $4,953,215 | — |
| *Vendor payments* | | | | |
| Medical Assistance[a]...........1,187 | | $244,796 | $2,460,749 | $166.72 |
| Medical Assistance for the | | | | |
| Aged[b]....................... 49 | | 4,920 | 61,767 | 102.67 |
| Other federally aided | | | | |
| programs....................N.A. | | 13,580 | 234,705 | — |
| General Assistance............N.A. | | 4,688 | 59,843 | — |
| Total vendor..............N.A. | | $267,984 | $2,817,064 | — |
| Grand total.....................N.A. | | $713,494 | $7,770,279 | — |

Source: *Social Security Bulletin*, January, 1968, and August, 1967.

[a] Figures for the number of recipients and average payments are for April, 1967, and reflect data from 15 of 29 states with programs. The data are from the *Social Security Bulletin*, August, 1967, p. 41.

[b] Figures for the number of recipients and average payments are for April, 1967, and reflect data from 20 states with programs.

cant state (as distinguished from local) financial participation, a "merit system" personnel policy, protection of information concerning individuals, full reporting to the Secretary of Health, Education, and Welfare of other information, fair hearings, prompt benefit payment, and standards for participating institutions. The law also places limits on the restrictions of eligibility requirements in regard to residence, citizenship, and age and requires that benefits be granted only in cases of need which must consider income, property, and the possibility of obtaining financial support from relatives.

*Aid to the Blind.* All of the 54 jurisdictions have approved plans providing Aid to the Blind. About two fifths impose some minimum age requirement, such as 16 or 18. Most impose a residence requirement, and some impose citizenship requirements. A need for aid is presumed to exist if income and other resources, including property owned, are insufficient to provide reasonable subsistence. The states must disregard the first $85 per month of earned income plus one half the excess. In addition the states may disregard up to $7.50 per month of income from any source in computing benefits of the blind, disabled, and aged. Reasonable subsistence usually is based on a theoretical average budget, and many states make payments only up to some percentage (less than 100 percent) of the budget figure. Under some plans the state may recover its expenditures from the recipient's estate. The federal government will pay 31/37 of the first $37 and the "federal percentage," 50 to 65 percent, of the next $38 of average monthly benefit up to an average per recipient of $75. This formula favors those states with low average pensions and low per capita incomes.[2]

*Aid to the Permanently and Totally Disabled.*    Fifty-three jurisdictions, all except Nevada, have plans for the permanently and totally disabled. The requirements for approval of plan and the amount of federal contribution are the same as in the Aid to the Blind program. All plans impose a minimum age requirement of 18 years, and about half impose a maximum age of 65. The other eligibility requirements are approximately the same as under Aid to the Blind. Under both programs there have been substantial liberalizations in eligibility and benefit level since they were instituted. A 1965 amendment provided an exemption of the first $20 per month of earnings of recipients and one-half of the next $60 earned. The average monthly payments for Aid to the Permanently and Totally Disabled have run somewhat lower than those for Aid to the Blind.

*Aid to Families with Dependent Children.*    All 54 jurisdictions have programs for Aid to Families with Dependent Children. These plans provide benefits for children and one or two adults who are caring for the child or children in the event of death, continued absence from home, or physical or mental incapacity of a parent or unemployment of a father. About one fifth of the AFDC cases are due to the disability of a parent.

Under most of the plans the dependent child must be under 18. Under most of the remaining plans he must be under 16, or under 17 if attending school regularly. A 1965 amendment to the Social Security Act allows the states to continue making payments to dependent children, up to the age of 21, who are students regularly attending a school, college, or university or a course of vocational or technical training. Residence requirements usually are more liberal than for the other nationally-supported income assistance programs. In almost all of the states, the child must be in the care of a close relative or in an approved foster home as a result of judicial determination that home conditions are such that he would be better off in a foster home. Payments also may be made for children in nonprofit child-care institutions.

The national government participates in state expenditures under these programs to the extent of 5/6 of the first $18 of average monthly

---

[2] There are special provisions for Puerto Rico, the Virgin Islands and Guam.

payment and the "federal percentage," 50 to 65 percent, of the next $14, to a maximum average of $32 per recipient.

A 1967 amendment created a work incentive program under the control of the Department of Labor. The state welfare agencies would be in charge of referring people to the program. Excluded from the program would be (1) children under age 16 or attending school; (2) any person unable to work in a project for a number of reasons, including advanced age, disability, or distance; (3) any person who must attend another sick or disabled person at home. The welfare agency will provide arrangements for necessary child care.

All people referred to the Department of Labor by the state welfare agencies would be handled under one of three priorities. Priority one would include people found to be satisfactory for employment without additional training. The Secretary of Labor, through all the U.S. employment offices, would try to find employment for these people.

A person whose lack of training was the only thing preventing him from being employed would be provided with training under priority two. He would be given a $30 a month incentive payment. Having finished training, as many people as possible would be referred to regular employment.

A special works project would be provided under priority three for those found unsuitable for training, or for whom jobs could not be found in the economy. The work projects must not result in displacement of regular workers, and must not be of a type that would ordinarily be performed by regular employees. The workers would receive the minimum wage if the work performed is covered by the minimum wage law.

The Secretary of Labor would make arrangements with the public or nonprofit agency that sponsors the project. Thus, the payment to workers would not be from the government, but from the sponsoring agency.

The employee's wages would be subject to normal taxes incurred in employment. If the employee's wages do not equal the grant he would have received plus 20 percent of the wages, a welfare check will be sent to make up the difference. This guarantees the worker a 20 percent raise over the amount of his welfare grants, less the applicable taxes. A person working in such a program will have his case reviewed at least every six months.

If a person referred to such a program refuses to work or undertake training without good cause, and does not return to the program for 60 days, his welfare payments will be terminated. However, dependent children of such parents would still receive vendor and protective payments.

The states will have to meet 20 percent of the total cost of the program for priorities one and two, while priority three jobs will be financed by the welfare agency paying to the employer the entire family benefit up to 80 percent of the wages paid the employee. Thus, the employer would contribute, at the minimum, 20 percent of the payroll plus the employer portion of social insurance taxes. These work projects could, as an example, provide child care for children of mothers under priorities one, two, and three.

The major cause of families receiving AFDC is marital dissolution (with or without formalities). Table 4–2 indicates the status of the father in AFDC families. In 35.5 percent of the nonwhite and 9.7 percent of white families, the father was absent from the home because he never was married to the mother. In 1961 (the latest data available) 37.6 per-

TABLE 4–2

Distribution of AFDC Families by Status of Father, U.S., 1961

| Status of Father | All AFDC Families | White | Nonwhite |
|---|---|---|---|
| Dead................................................ | 7.7% | 8.7% | 6.5% |
| Disabled......................................... | 18.1 | 25.2 | 9.4 |
| Absent from home, total...................... | 66.7 | 57.0 | 78.7 |
| Divorced or legally separated............... | 13.7 | 19.2 | 7.0 |
| Separated without court decree............. | 8.2 | 6.3 | 10.5 |
| Deserting........................................ | 18.6 | 16.2 | 21.5 |
| Never married to mother.................... | 21.3 | 9.7 | 35.5 |
| Imprisoned..................................... | 4.2 | 4.7 | 3.7 |
| Absent for other reason..................... | 5.7 | 0.8 | 0.4 |
| Unemployed.................................... | 5.2 | 6.4 | 3.8 |
| Other status.................................... | 2.2 | 2.7 | 1.6 |

Source: U.S. Department of Health, Education, and Welfare, Welfare Administration, "Characteristics of Families Receiving Aid to Families with Dependent Children," November–December, 1961. Washington, D.C., 1963 (processed).

cent of Negro children and 11.2 percent of white children on AFDC were illegitimate (24.5 percent of all AFDC children).

Moreover, the problem keeps getting worse. The number of children receiving AFDC benefits went from 2,753,000 in 1961 to 3,986,000 in December, 1967, an increase of 44.8 percent. The illegitimate birth rate also keeps hitting new highs, as the legitimate birth rate approaches the all-time lows of the thirties. More than one fourth of nonwhite babies (26.3 percent in 1965 compared to 16.5 percent in 1948) and one white baby in 25 (3.96 percent in 1965, up from 1.63 percent in 1952) are illegitimate.[3] In 1965, 291,200 illegitimate children were born, most to become

---

[3] Nonwhite illegitimate births range from a low of 7.5 percent in Hawaii to a high of 36.5 percent in Delaware. Natality data are from U.S. Dept. of Health, Education, and Welfare, *Vital Statistics of the United States, 1965*, Vol. I, pp. 1–24 and 1–25 (Washington, D.C.: U.S. Government Printing Office, 1967).

part of the 1,649,000 families containing 6,091 individuals receiving AFDC and General Assistance benefits. By no coincidence, the number of children receiving AFDC increased by 146,000 from December, 1964 to December, 1965.[4]

The government has become concerned with the rapid rise in illegitimacy, and is trying to take action to break the cycle of poverty that keeps expanding the AFDC roles. The 1967 Amendments require the states to make family planning (i.e., birth control) services available to all appropriate AFDC families with the national and state governments sharing equally the cost of personnel, equipment and supplies. In addition, authorized appropriations for the maternal and child health programs were increased and 6 percent of this amount was earmarked for family planning ($900,000 in 1969).

The 1967 amendments also limit the national financial participation for payments to children receiving aid to that proportion of the total child population that the number of such AFDC-aided children in the first quarter of 1968 bore to the under-18 population of the state on January 1, 1968.

In another attempt to reduce dependency, the law now provides that earned income of each child who is a full-time student or a part-time student not working full time will not be considered in determining need for assistance. For any other child or adult, the first $30 of income of the group plus one third of the remainder would be exempt. In addition, $5 per month from any source may be disregarded.

In the three programs discussed above, payments to vendors of medical care, including health insurance, are included within the described limits and shared by the national government on the same basis as direct payments to provide income, unless the state has adopted a Title XIX program described below. Until 1960, the same principle applied to Old-Age Assistance, but in that year, special provisions for medical care benefits were added to the Old-Age Assistance program.

*Old-Age Assistance.* All jurisdictions have Old-Age Assistance programs. Beneficiaries must be 65 or over. Residence requirements in state plans are five out of the last nine years and the most recent year in about one third of the states (the strictest permitted by federal law) and more liberal in the others. The provisions for national sharing in income benefits are the same as for Aid to the Permanently and Totally Disabled and Aid to the Blind, except for the special treatment of vendor medical payments.

The special treatment for vendor medical payments for Old-Age Assistance recipients was added by the 1960 amendments to the Social Security Act to tie in with the new program of medical assistance for the aged.

---

[4] *Social Security Bulletin*, April, 1968, p. 63.

There are two methods by which the states may calculate the federal government's share in vendor medical payments. The states may use whichever method results in the largest federal government share.

In the first method, the federal government pays 31/37 of the first $37 of average total payment plus the "federal percentage" (50 to 65 percent, depending on per capita income) of the next $38 of the average total payment plus 15 percent of the average medical vendor payment (up to a maximum of $15).[5] This method yields a higher return in states where the average total payment is below $78.75[6] and where the average vendor payment is equal to or greater than the $15 maximum.

In the second, alternative method, the federal government's share is 31/37 of the first $37 of average total payment plus the federal medical percentage (50 to 80 percent) of the average medical vendor payment (up to a maximum of $15) plus the federal percentage of the next $38 of average total payment.[7] This method usually will produce a higher federal share in states where the average total payment exceeds $78.75.[8]

*Aid to the Aged, Blind, and Disabled.* In 1962 an amendment to the Social Security Act allowed the states to combine their programs for assistance for the aged, the blind and disabled and Medical Assistance for the Aged into a single combined plan. Under this arrangement, the provision of separate and additional federal funds for vendor payments is extended to the blind and disabled. Programs of this type, Aid to the Aged, Blind, or Disabled, were operating in 18 jurisdictions in December, 1967.[9]

*Medical Assistance for the Aged.* The 1960 Kerr-Mills bill provided for the additional federal share of vendor medical payments for recipients of Old-Age Assistance and also instituted a new program of Medical Assistance for the Aged. This was designed to meet the medical care needs of the medically indigent aged, those whose incomes or resources are too high to qualify for public assistance income benefits, but who do not have the resources to meet high medical care costs.

In order to qualify for federal grants, a Medical Assistance for the Aged program must meet the standards applicable to public assistance generally, and also must meet the following criteria: (1) It must provide for the inclusion of both institutional and noninstitutional care. (2) No

---

[5] In this method, the vendor payments may be part of the $38. These percentages are explained below.

[6] One authority says this number should be $75. Exercise for students: which is correct, and why? Show all calculations!

[7] In this method, the first $15 of vendor payments are not part of the $38.

[8] See note 6, above.

[9] In Table 4–1, figures for these programs were broken down into the separate categories.

fee or charge may be imposed as a condition of eligibility. (3) Assistance must be furnished to residents temporarily absent from the state. (4) There must be reasonable standards for eligibility and the amounts of payment. (5) No lien may be imposed or recovery made from the property of a recipient until after the death of such person and his spouse.

If the state includes assistance to individuals who are patients in institutions for mental diseases the plan also must meet the following criteria. The state must: (1) Provide arrangements with state authorities concerned with mental diseases, and institutions, as may be necessary to carry out the state plan. (2) Provide for an individual plan for each patient including periodic review of his medical and other needs. (3) Provide for development of alternate plans of care including appropriate medical treatment to prevent or reduce dependency, or to help the patient attain or retain capacity for self-care. (4) Provide methods of determining the reasonable cost of institutional care for such patients. (5) Show that the state is making satisfactory progress toward developing and implementing a comprehensive mental health program.

Assistance payments may cover part or all of the care and service for persons 65 and over who are not recipients of aid to the aged, blind, or disabled, but whose incomes and resources are insufficient to meet all of their medical care costs. Covered care and services may include in-patient hospital, skilled nursing home, physicians, outpatient or clinic, home care, physical therapy, private duty nursing, dental, laboratory and X-ray, diagnostic screening and preventive services, prescribed drugs, eyeglasses, dentures, and prosthetic devices, and any other medical or remedial care recognized under state law. The national government share of total vendor medical expenditures, including insurance premiums, under Medical Assistance for the Aged programs is equal to the federal medical percentage which varies from 50 to 80 percent, depending on the state's per capita income. There is no dollar limit.

*Medical Assistance* (*Title XIX*). In 1965, in order to provide a more effective medical assistance program for the aged and to extend its provisions to additional needy persons, a separate medical care program was created, Medical Assistance. This program will replace all other existing vendor medical payment programs by January 1, 1970.

Benefit payments cover medical assistance for persons receiving assistance under the programs of aid to families with dependent children, the blind, aged, and the permanently and totally disabled as well as those who would qualify under these programs if their need were sufficiently great.

Inclusion of persons who are not receiving cash assistance but who are unable to meet medical care cost is optional with the states; if such persons are included, comparable groups of aged, blind, disabled, and parents and children also must be included if they need help in meeting medical costs. The amount and scope of benefits for the medically indigent cannot be greater than that of recipients of cash assistance.

Medical Assistance programs must meet the same criteria as the M.A.A. programs previously discussed with the exceptions that no lien may be imposed against the property of a recipient during his lifetime and no recovery of any medical assistance can be made except from the estate of a person who was over 65 at the time he received medical assistance and only after the death of surviving spouse and adulthood or death of minor children.

A minimum Medical Assistance program is required to include at least some institutional and some noninstitutional care, and after July 1, 1967 must include in-patient hospital services (reimbursed at reasonable cost in accordance with standards approved by the Secretary of Health, Education, and Welfare), out-patient hospital services, skilled nursing home services, laboratory and X-ray services, and physicians' services regardless of where they are provided.[10] States may include private duty nursing, dental services, clinic services, prescribed drugs, eyeglasses, dentures, and prosthetic devices, physical therapy and any other medical or remedial care recognized under state law.

Any state which has in effect an approved Medical Assistance program applies the federal medical assistance percentage, instead of the federal percentage or federal medical percentage, to vendor payments under its programs for Old-Age Assistance, Aid to the Blind, Aid to Families with Dependent Children, Aid to the Permanently and Totally Disabled, and Medical Assistance for the Aged.

This option is an incentive to the states to adopt the Medical Assistance program, as the federal medical assistance percentage produces a higher federal government share than either of the other two percentages, in most states.

In January, 1966 seven jurisdictions began operating a Medical Assistance program, and payments for the first month totaled $20.3 million. The average vendor payment for the 15 jurisdictions reporting for April 1967 was $167. By April, 1968, at least 41 states had plans in effect and 16 programs were pending approval in other states.

Table 4–3 indicates the major provisions of the states on which information was available in April, 1968.

The income limits set by most states probably will be similar in nature to those enacted by New York, although lower in amount. In New York, net income is defined as gross income less income taxes, health insurance

---

[10] These five services must be provided for recipients of aid under the income programs. For others eligible, states may provide these five or seven out of the fourteen listed. After July 1, 1970, a state must provide home health services to its cash assistance recipients.

premiums, payments made pursuant to court order, and business expenses. Resources that are exempt and need not be used for medical expenses are a homestead; essential personal property; either life insurance or liquid reserve in the amount of $1,000 per family member for burial services; and savings in amounts equal to one-half of the income exemptions. Certain deductibles are to be imposed in New York for patients who do not have health insurance. In all states, the family's medical expenses, including insurance premiums, are deducted from its income in determining eligibility.

The 1967 amendments set a limit on income levels under this program of 133⅓ percent of the AFDC payments. This will go into effect in 1970, with a limit of 150 percent in the last half of 1968, and a limit of 140 percent in 1969. This was invoked to prevent other states from following New York's example of setting limits so high that a majority of the population is included under the program. In March, 1968, the New York legislature passed and the governor signed a bill reducing income eligibility by about 11 percent. The income limit for a family of four becomes 5,700 and individual counties (who must share in the cost of the program) may petition the state Board of Social Services for a lower income eligibility level.

The figures given in Table 4–3 for income limits are the maximum annual net income amounts that need not be used to pay medical bills for a single person and a family of four respectively. Those with incomes somewhat above these limits may receive partial payment.

All states are required to offer five basic services: in-patient hospital services, out-patient hospital services, skilled nursing home services, laboratory and X-ray services, and physician's services regardless of where they are provided. Most states provide coverage of more types of health service than the minimum required by the Medical Assistance program. These additional coverages vary according to the individual state laws. Most of the states provide dental services, drugs, eyeglasses, and prosthetic devices as well as the five basic services to recipients of Medical Assistance. Details of the laws for which information was available in April, 1968 are given in Table 4–3.

States have until January 1, 1970 to buy in Title XVIII Supplementary Medical Insurance  for persons eligible for Title XIX benefits. There is no federal matching of the states' share of the premium, since it already pays half the total cost. Federal matching amounts will not be available for service which could have been covered by SMI but were not because of a state's failure to buy in.

The national government share of total vendor medical payments under Title XIX is calculated by multiplying the "federal medical assistance percentage" by the total medical payments. This is similar to the "federal percentage" and "federal medical percentage" mentioned above

## TABLE 4-3
### Title XIX—Medical Assistance
### Summary of State Plans, April, 1968

| State | Effective Date | Eligible Classes | Income Limits: Single | Income Limits: Family of 4 | Approximate % Federal Share | Estimated Federal Share (Fiscal 1967; 000 Omitted) | Additional Coverages | Estimated Claimants (Fiscal 1967: 000 Omitted) |
|---|---|---|---|---|---|---|---|---|
| California | 3-1-66 | 1, 2, 3, 4 | $2,000 | $3,800 | 50% | $333,408 | 2, 3, 5, 8 | 2,500 |
| Connecticut | 7-1-66 | 1, 4, 5 | $2,100 | $3,800 | 50 | $ 15,300 | 1, 2, 3, 4, 6, 7, 9 | 297 |
| Delaware | 10-1-66 | 1, 3, 4, 5, 11 | $1,300 | $3,300 | 50 | $ 2,200 | 3, 7, 8 | 112 |
| Georgia | 10-1-67 | 1, 2, 3, 8, 10 | a | a | 81 | $ 33,700 | 3, 8, 10 | 224 |
| Hawaii | 1-1-66 | 1, 4, 5, 6 | $1,440 | $3,000 | 53 | $ 3,096 | 1, 2, 3, 4 | 34 |
| Idaho | 7-1-66 | 1, 2, 3, 9, 10 | a | a | 71 | $ 5,040 | None | 9 |
| Illinois | 1-1-66 | 1, 5, 6, 7, 8 | $1,800 | $3,600 | 50 | $ 43,950 | 1, 2, 3, 4, 7 | 525 |
| Iowa | 7-1-67 | 1, 2, 3, 6, 7, 9 | $1,600 | $3,600 | 60 | $ 21,000 | 1, 2, 3, 10 | 58 |
| Kansas | 6-1-67 | 1, 2, 3, 4, 5, 6, 10 | $1,600 | $3,000 | 58 | $ 45,000 | 1, 2, 3, 4, 10, 11 | 65 |
| Kentucky | 7-1-66 | 1, 7, 11 | $1,620 | $3,420 | 77 | $ 27,944 | 1, 2, 3, 5, 7 | 300 |
| Louisiana | 7-1-66 | 1, 2, 3 | a | a | 76 | $ 27,767 | 2, 3, 4, 5, 7 | 155 |
| Maine | 7-1-66 | 1, 3, 4, 10 | a | a | 70 | $ 5,566 | 1, 4, 5, 7, 10 | 45 |
| Maryland | 7-1-66 | 1, 6, 7 | $1,800 | $3,120 | 50 | $ 16,857 | 1, 2, 4, 7, 8, 10 | 260 |
| Massachusetts | 9-1-66 | 1, 4, 5 | $2,160 | $4,176 | 50 | $ 69,967 | 1, 2, 3, 4, 5, 6, 7, 8, 10 | 380 |
| Michigan | 10-1-66 | 1, 2, 5, 7, 10, 11 | $1,900 | $3,540 | 50 | $ 21,070 | 1, 4, 5, 7 | 330 |
| Minnesota | 1-1-66 | 1, 4, 5 | $1,600 | $2,800 | 60 | $ 41,689 | b | 72 |
| Missouri | 10-13-67 | 1, 2, 3, 10 | a | a | 74 | $ 20,500 | 1, 3, 11 | 225 |
| Montana | 7-1-67 | 1, 2, 3, 9, 10 | a | a | 64 | $ 4,475 | 1, 2, 3, 6, 10 | 17 |
| Nebraska | 7-1-66 | 1, 3, 10 | a | a | 60 | $ 10,499 | 1, 2, 3, 4, 5, 7 | 45 |
| Nevada | 7-1-67 | 1, 2, 3, 9, 10, 11 | a | a | 50 | $ 2,500 | 1, 2, 3, 4, 6, 7, 8, 10 | 15 |
| New Hampshire | 7-1-67 | 1, 2, 3, 4, 5, 6, 7, 9, 10, 11 | $2,088 | $4,056 | 60 | $ 4,325 | 1, 2, 3, 5, 6, 8, 10 | 26 |
| New Mexico | 12-1-66 | 1, 3, 4, 7, 11 | a | a | 71 | $ 4,060 | 1, 3, 4, 5, 7 | 47 |
| New York | 5-1-66 | 1, 3, 4, 8 | $2,900c | $5,300c to 5,700 | 50 | $217,330 | 1, 5, 7 | 2,000 |
| North Dakota | 1-1-66 | 1, 2, 4 | $1,600 | $3,000 | 67 | $ 6,400 | 1, 3, 7 | 17 |
| Ohio | 7-1-66 | 1, 2, 3 | a | a | 52 | $ 18,334 | 1, 3, 5, 7 | 325 |
| Oklahoma | 1-1-66 | 1, 4, 5 | $1,728 | $2,448 | 70 | $ 50,734 | 3, 7, 8 | 19 |

| State | Date | Eligible Classes | Income (individual) | Income (family) | % | Amount | Additional Coverages | Number |
|---|---|---|---|---|---|---|---|---|
| Oregon | 7-1-67 | 1,2,3,10,11 | a | | 54 | $10,298 | 1,2,3,4,5,6,7,8,10,11 | 59 |
| Pennsylvania | 1-1-66 | 1,4,5,6 | $2,000 | $4,000 | 54 | $61,372 | 1,3,5,7 | 583 |
| Rhode Island | 7-1-66 | 1,4 | $2,500 | $4,300 | 56 | $9,302 | 1,2,3,5,7 | 72 |
| South Carolina | 4-1-68 | 1,2,3,6,10,11 | a | a | 80.5 | $12,880 | 1,2,3,8,10 | 78 |
| South Dakota | 10-1-67 | 1,2,3,9,10 | a | | 73 | $6,400 | 1,2,3,10 | 24 |
| Texas | 9-1-67 | 1,2,3,8,10 | a | | 80 | $98,600 | 1,2,3,10,11 | 379 |
| Utah | 7-1-66 | 1,2,3,4,5,6 | $1,200 | $2,640 | 66 | $5,834 | 3,7 | 40 |
| Vermont | 7-1-66 | 1,2,10,11 | a | | 68 | $4,254 | 4,7 | 14 |
| Washington | 7-1-66 | 1,2,4,5,6,11 | $1,680 | $3,000 | 50 | $15,942 | 1,2,3,10 | 250 |
| West Virginia | 7-1-66 | 1,3 | a | | 74 | $15,419 | 1,2,3,7,8 | 140 |
| Wisconsin | 7-1-66 | 1,7 | $1,800 | $3,700 | 58 | $36,020 | 1,2,3,5,7,8,10 | 261 |
| Wyoming | 7-1-67 | 1,2,3,10 | a | | 59 | $638 | 1,2,3,10 | 8 |
| Guam | 7-1-67 | 1,2,4,6,9,11 | $1,500 | $3,000 | 55 | $275 | | 8 |
| Puerto Rico | 1-1-66 | 1,4,5,6 | $1,500 | $2,600 | 55 | $20,167 | 1,2,3,4,5,7,10 | 4 |
| Virgin Islands | 7-1-66 | 1,2,3,4,5,6,7,11 | $2,200 | $3,630 | 55 | $465 | 3,5,7,10 | 1,200 |
| | | | | | | | | 11 |
| TOTAL | | | | | | $1,087,786 | | 9,933 |

a Same as for money payments.
b Minnesota provides "whatever the doctor orders."
c In New York the income limits are higher for wage earners than for nonwage earners.

Key to Additional Coverages
1. Home Nursing Care
2. Dental Services
3. Prosthetics, Drugs, Dentures, Eyeglasses
4. Preventive and Rehabilitative Services
5. Remedial Care
6. Private Duty Nursing
7. Clinic Services
8. Blood Bank Services
9. Maternity Care Centers
10. Ambulance Service
11. Institutions for Mental Care and Tuberculosis

Key to Eligible Classes
1. All persons who receive all or part of their incomes from the federally aided public assistance programs: Medical Assistance for the Aged, Aid to the Blind, Aid to Families with Dependent Children, Aid to the Permanently and Totally Disabled, and Aid to the Aged, Blind and Disabled.
2. Children between 18 and 21 in whose behalf an Aid to Families with Dependent Children payment would be made, except that these individuals are neither disabled nor attending high school or a course of vocational or technical training.
3. All individuals in the above groups who would be entitled to financial assistance except that they do not meet the durational residence requirement of any of the public assistance programs.
4. All persons who, except for having enough income for their daily needs (under state assistance standards), could qualify for public assistance under the federal eligibility requirements.
5. All children (under 21) who could not qualify for public assistance but whose families cannot afford to pay for all or part of the cost of the medical care the children need. (This includes families in which parents are working but do not earn enough to pay for medical expenses.)
6. Other adults (chiefly persons between 21 and 64) whose incomes are insufficient to meet their medical care costs in addition to their maintenance costs. (The costs of their care will be paid entirely from state funds since they are not covered by the federally aided programs.)
7. All persons who, except for having enough income for their daily needs (under state assistance standards), could qualify for public assistance under their state's eligibility requirements.
8. Persons 65 and over who are patients in mental hospitals.
9. All persons who, upon application, would be eligible for financial assistance under one of the federally-aided income programs.
10. Persons in medical institutions who, if they were no longer in such institution, would be eligible for financial assistance under one of the above programs.
11. All children in foster care.

and may range from 50 to 83 percent. These percentages are determined according to a formula related to the per capita income of the state in relation to that of the continental United States.

*The federal share.* The "federal percentage" and the "federal medical percentage" each equal 100 percent minus the state percentage. The state percentage bears the same relationship to 50 percent as the state per capita income squared bears to the national per capita income squared. The "federal percentage" used for the variable portions of income benefits and some vendor payments varies from 50 to 65 percent, while the "federal medical percentage" used for Medical Assistance for the Aged and in some cases for vendor payments under Old-Age Assistance and the combined program ranges from 50 to 80 percent.

The federal medical assistance percentage used for the new Medical Assistance program equals 100 percent minus the state percentage. The state percentage bears the same relationship to 45 percent as the state per capita income squared bears to the square of the average national per capita income for the last three years squared. In formula terms, letting

$F$ = Federal Medical Assistance percentage
$S$ = State percentage (for Medical Assistance)
$Is$ = Average state per capita income
$If$ = Average national per capita income
$F = 100\% - S$

then

$$\frac{S}{45\%} = \frac{(Is)^2}{(If)^2}$$
$$S = \frac{45\% \ (Is)^2}{(If)^2}$$
$$F = 100 - \frac{45\% \ (Is)^2}{(If)^2}.$$
$$50\% \leq F \leq 83\%$$

This formula has the result that a state with per capita income equal to the national average has a federal matching ratio of 55 percent and that a state with per capita income that is at least 4.9 percent above the national average will receive the 50 percent minimum.[10]

These sharing formulae involve an element of "subsidy" from the wealthier states to the poorer states. The lower the per capita income of the state is in relation to the per capita national income, the lower will be the state percentage and the higher the federal percentage. Entering the income figures at their squared values accentuates the differential. This is illustrated by the following figures for 1967 incomes.

---

[10] Robert J. Myers, "Amendments to the Social Security Acts in 1962–65," *Trans-actions, Society of Actuaries*, Vol. XVII, Part 1, p. 464, at 474.

| | Florida | Mississippi | Connecticut |
|---|---|---|---|
| National per capita income | $3137 | $3137 | $3137 |
| State per capita income | 2976 | 1895 | 3865 |
| $Is \div If$ | .9487 | .6041 | 1.2321 |
| $(Is \div If)^2$ | .9000 | .3649 | 1.5181 |
| 45% $(Is \div If)^2$ | 40.50% | 16.42% | 71.15% |
| Federal medical assistance percentage | 59.5% | 83.58% | 28.85% |
| After applying limits | 59.5% | 83.0% | 50% |

There are two other elements of subsidy from the richer states to the poorer in the public assistance program. Not only do the poorer states receive higher proportions of payments in excess of $37 or $18, respectively, and of medical payments, but they are more likely to have low average payments and have a higher proportion of their payments subject to the 31/37 or 5/6 sharing of these lower amounts. Thus, depending on the program, a state with very low income and benefit levels could have the national government paying 31/37 or 5/6 or about 83 percent of its public assistance expenditures.

This is the reason for the special provisions applicable to Guam, Puerto Rico, and the Virgin Islands. In these areas the national government pays half the total expenditures up to a maximum federal payment of $22 in Aid to Families with Dependent Children, up to $37.50 in the other programs, and half of the expenditures for Medical Assistance for the Aged. The vendor medical payments for Old-Age Assistance recipients in excess of $37.50 have additional matching the same as in a state with a federal medical percentage of 50 percent. The federal share for Medical Assistance in these areas is 50 percent, but the limitation of income levels for eligibility for Medical Assistance of 150, 140, and 133 percent does not apply in these areas. Overall dollar maxima for these areas, which are revised periodically, are also provided for in the legislation.

The third element of subsidy from rich to poor states in public assistance results from the source of the national government's tax revenues. Most of these revenues come from income taxes, which are paid largely by corporations and individuals in the higher income states. The personal income tax is graduated so that high-income persons pay higher proportions of income than low-income persons. Combining these three factors indicates the great degree of subsidy built into these programs and emphasizes that they are viewed properly as transfer payments and in no way resemble insurance.

***Recent developments.*** The 1967 Social Security Amendments made few changes in the Title XIX program other than imposing ceilings on the income limits for eligibility. During 1965, 1966, and 1967, 41 states or territories implemented the program and during 1966, 1967, and 1968, Title XIX benefits generally superceded Medical Assistance for the aged, Vendor Payments under the income programs, and, to a degree, General Assistance. Table 4–4 shows the shift dramatically. This will continue

TABLE 4–4

Public Assistance: Number of Recipients of Medical Vendor Payments and Total Medical Vendor Payments, by Program, 1961–68

| Period | Number of Recipients (in Thousands), Federally Aided Programs — Medical Assistance | Medical Assistance for the Aged | Total Amount of Payments (in Thousands) — Total | Federally Aided Programs — Medical Assistance[a] | Medical Assistance for the Aged | Other | General Assistance[b] |
|---|---|---|---|---|---|---|---|
| 1961......... | | 72 | $ 688,297 | ............ | $113,213 | $464,671 | $110,413 |
| 1962......... | | 110 | 924,159 | ............ | 250,830 | 571,001 | 102,328 |
| 1963......... | | 150 | 1,064,664 | ............ | 329,391 | 632,067 | 103,206 |
| 1964......... | | 225 | 1,255,130 | ............ | 444,970 | 699,469 | 110,691 |
| 1965......... | | 280 | 1,480,119 | ............ | 585,501 | 773,555 | 121,063 |
| 1966......... | 1,057 | 48 | 2,007,626 | $1,193,768 | 293,442 | 435,933 | 84,484 |
| 1967......... | | | 2,817,064 | 2,460,749 | 61,767 | 234,705 | 59,843 |
| *1965* | | | | | | | |
| November.... | | 280 | 127,693 | ............ | 52,110 | 65,611 | 9,971 |
| December.... | | 280 | 128,892 | ............ | 52,863 | 66,505 | 9,523 |
| *1966* | | | | | | | |
| January....... | 330 | 251 | 127,886 | 20,450 | 44,956 | 54,379 | 8,101 |
| February...... | 321 | 255 | 131,384 | 19,635 | 47,593 | 55,670 | 8,486 |
| March........ | 389 | 220 | 148,960 | 44,549 | 41,399 | 52,083 | 10,928 |
| April......... | 369 | 218 | 147,244 | 46,718 | 37,458 | 52,049 | 11,019 |
| May.......... | 598 | 190 | 166,185 | 81,353 | 28,183 | 45,692 | 10,956 |
| June......... | 628 | 195 | 180,825 | 97,435 | 28,118 | 44,991 | 10,286 |
| July.......... | 678 | 100 | 153,297 | 100,936 | 17,762 | 24,758 | 9,841 |
| August....... | 715 | 97 | 165,477 | 111,577 | 18,802 | 26,162 | 8,935 |
| September.... | 710 | 66 | 154,347 | 114,068 | 11,616 | 20,625 | 8,038 |
| October....... | 787 | 51 | 160,621 | 126,076 | 5,823 | 20,054 | 8,669 |
| November.... | 893 | 47 | 191,932 | 157,513 | 5,245 | 19,731 | 9,443 |
| December.... | 1,057 | 48 | 197,301 | 165,372 | 5,087 | 20,054 | 6,788 |
| *1967* | | | | | | | |
| January....... | 1,140 | 45 | 179,186 | 148,367 | 5,266 | 23,531 | 5,083 |
| February...... | 1,172 | 49 | 179,764 | 144,628 | 5,082 | 24,842 | 5,313 |
| March........ | 1,272 | 50 | 219,414 | 186,452 | 5,025 | 22,414 | 5,523 |
| April......... | 1,187 | 49 | 231,040 | 497,897 | 5,031 | 22,489 | 5,623 |
| May.......... | c | c | 222,138 | 188,743 | 5,018 | 23,262 | 5,115 |
| June......... | | | 229,960 | 196,721 | 4,649 | 23,327 | 5,263 |
| July.......... | | | 221,531 | 190,454 | 6,472 | 20,277 | 4,328 |
| August....... | | | 262,457 | 232,030 | 5,023 | 20,256 | 5,148 |
| September.... | | | 249,910 | 223,794 | 5,173 | 16,238 | 4,706 |
| October...... | | | 272,461 | 248,896 | 5,013 | 14,333 | 4,217 |
| November.... | | | 280,963 | 258,077 | 5,151 | 13,156 | 4,579 |
| December.... | | | 267,984 | 244,796 | 4,920 | 13,580 | 4,688 |
| *1966* | | | | | | | |
| January...... | | | 304,908 | 281,651 | 5,508 | 13,675 | 4,075 |

a Data incomplete.
b Partly estimated. Excludes Idaho, Indiana, Nebraska and, beginning February 1967, Kentucky and, May 1967, Puerto Rico; data not available.
c Number of recipients, never accurate, was not published for periods after April, 1967.
Source: *Social Security Bulletin*, April, 1968, and prior issues.

until the older programs (except General Assistance) are phased out completely January 1, 1970. Moreover, the number of recipients of Old Age Assistance declined by 86,000 in 1966 as an estimated 50,000 to 60,000 elderly persons, mostly patients in nursing homes, were transferred to Title XIX programs. This was the largest decline since 1962, when the states were implementing the Medical Assistance for the Aged Program.

From 1961 to 1967 the total Public Assistance Vendor Payments quadrupled, and by May, 1968 it looked as though Title XIX payments would be $3.2 billion for fiscal 1967–68 as compared to $2.5 billion in calendar 1967.

**Other federal programs**

*Direct provision.* The federal government provides medical care directly to certain special groups which include members of the armed services and their dependents, veterans, members of the merchant marine, Indians, Alaska natives, the Peace Corps, inmates of federal prisons, and certain persons disabled in federal service. Complete provision is made for members of the armed services on active duty. Almost complete dependents' coverage is provided under the "Medicare"[11] program in both service and civilian facilities. Chronic disease is not covered, and the program is administered by both private insurance companies and Blue Cross and Blue Shield Plans on a cost-plus basis.

The federal government provides domiciliary care and medical care for veterans who have service-connected disabilities. Some nonservice-connected disabilities are completely covered under old legislation for groups such as Spanish-American war veterans, if they are unable to pay for private care. A system of priorities determines the order in which various groups are admitted. Veterans with disabilities also receive cash pensions. These payments total more than $4.3 billion per year.

Medical care for Indians and Eskimos grows out of various treaties. Care is provided only to "indigent" persons, but this includes the vast majority of the groups involved. Provisions include preventive services and dental care as well as medical care and hospitalization.

The United States Public Health Service provides medical care under four divisions. The Division of Hospitals and Medical Care operates programs for merchant marine personnel, Alaska natives, Indians, lepers, Coast Guard personnel, Peace Corps members, Bureau of Employees' Compensation, and narcotic addicts. It also provides "in-plant" medical care for federal civilian employees and for the Bureau of Prisons and the Bureau of Indian Affairs. Limited coverage is provided for a variety of

---

[11] This should be distinguished from the social security programs of Health Insurance and Supplemental Medical Insurance, which are frequently referred to as "Medicare."

groups, including dependents and retired personnel of the groups mentioned. The Division of Foreign Quarantine inspects persons entering the country. Those requiring treatment are handled at the facilities of the Bureau of Hospitals and Medical Care. The Clinical Center of the National Institute of Health is intended for the coordination of laboratory research and treatment of patients and admits patients with the type of disability in which it currently is interested.

Two hospitals in the District of Columbia also provide free or part-pay medical care. Freedmen's Hospital is connected with Howard University and, in practice, provides general hospital care to Negroes. St. Elizabeth's Hospital is a mental and psychiatric hospital which takes care of the mentally disabled from the District of Columbia and the territories.

*Grants-in-aid.* In addition to the public assistance program, grants-in-aid are provided by the federal government for purposes of general and public health and for prevention, control, and treatment of various diseases. Since these activities have been discussed above, it is sufficient here to list the diseases for which grants for prevention and treatment are important. These include tuberculosis, venereal disease, cancer, heart disease, and mental health. The Children's Bureau contributes to maternal and child-health services of the states, and the Office of Vocational Rehabilitation to state programs in its area of concern. In addition, federal grants are available for research, support of education, and hospital construction. These functions, primarily local and state but often aided by federal funds, have been discussed above.

*Special bureaus.* The National Center for Health Statistics surveys the population's health. It attempts to determine the range and scope of types of illness, disability, and birth and death rates.

The Bureau of Family Services oversees the various state public assistance programs under the Social Security Act. It analyzes state plans, approves or disapproves state estimates, acts as an auditor, and has to certify to the Treasurer any grants made to the states.

## Old-Age, Survivors, and Disability Insurance

*Development.* Since 1935, the Social Security Act has been marked by rapid expansion, significant liberalization and widespread public acceptance. The act was amended in important respects in 1939, 1946, 1950, 1952, 1954, 1956, 1958, 1960, 1961, 1965, and 1967. It deals with five major areas of economic and social security: (1) grants to the states for public assistance benefit programs, (2) child and maternal welfare programs, (3) unemployment compensation administration, (4) the federally operated Old-Age, Survivors, and Disability Insurance System, and

(5) Health Insurance for the Aged. The last two are the only federally operated social insurance systems.

The social insurance portion of the law originally covered old age only, but survivors' benefits were added in 1939, and the disability freeze provision was added in 1954. The coverage of disability income for workers between ages 50 and 65 was added in 1956 and extended to provide for added payments to dependents in 1958. The age 50 limitation was removed in 1960, and the disability definition was liberalized slightly in 1965. However, the 1967 amendments give a more restricted definition of disability, clarifying legislative intent after a number of court decisions holding for benefit eligibility in borderline cases.

The movement to include disability had begun as early as 1937 and gained force during and after the war. The Social Security Board prepared actuarial cost estimates for disability benefits as early as 1939. Inclusion of disability benefits was recommended by the Advisory Council on Social Security in 1939 and again in 1948. A bill to include disability benefits was passed by the House of Representatives in 1949. The final version of this legislation, as reported out of the Conference Committee in 1950 and enacted into law, omitted the disability provisions. A variety of proposals was introduced in the next few years, and the disability freeze provisions were finally passed in 1954. Once the ice had been broken, the law was amended rapidly until the present broad coverage was reached in 1967.

*Coverage. Covered employment.* The Old-Age, Survivors, and Disability Insurance program covers almost all employed persons, including the self-employed. The following occupations are excluded:

1. Family employment, except in trade or business by a parent or a child over age 21.
2. Local newsboys under age 18.
3. Student nurses.
4. Student workers in institutions of learning.
5. Students in domestic service in fraternities, sororities, and college clubs.
6. Railroad workers (covered by Railroad Retirement Act).
7. Policemen and firemen covered under an existing retirement system except in some states.
8. Most civilian federal government employees (covered under civil service or special retirement legislation).
9. Certain government employees, mostly elected.

The following occupations are covered under certain circumstances, as follows:

1. Self-employment is covered if net earnings equal $400 per year or more. Certain low-income farmers may obtain coverage based on gross income.

2. Agricultural labor is covered if the worker earns $150 or more or works for 20 days or more for cash pay on a time basis for any one employer in a calendar year.
3. Domestic and casual workers are covered if they earn $50 or more from any one employer in a calendar quarter.

The following may be covered or not on an elective basis:

1. Clergymen (other than members of a religious order who have taken a vow of poverty), if they earn $400 or more a year, are covered as self-employed even if employed unless they elect not to be covered because of conscientious or religious principle.
2. Employees of nonprofit institutions if the employer agrees. Nonagreeing employees are not covered, but all hired after the election are covered.
3. State and local government employees not under a retirement system if the state agrees.
4. State and local government employees already under a retirement system if the state and the majority, or in a few states, some of the employees agree. Other provisions are similar to those regarding nonprofit institutions.
5. Self-employed individuals who, as members of a religious sect, have conscientious objections to insurance, including Social Security, may elect not to be covered.

*Quarters of coverage.* Merely working in covered employment is not enough to qualify for coverage. A certain substantial attachment is required for insured status. This requires a minimum of six quarters of coverage. A quarter of coverage is any quarter in which the worker earned at least $50 in wages.[12] However, if an employee earns the maximum taxable income in any year as an employee, he is credited with four quarters of coverage regardless of the incidence of the income. This maximum was $3,000 per year prior to 1951, $3,600 per year from 1951 to 1954, $4,200 from 1955 to 1958, $4,800 from 1959 to 1965, $6,600 from 1966 to 1967, and $7,800 in 1968 and thereafter. A self-employed person is credited with four quarters for each year in which his self-employment income was equal to or greater than $400.

Periods of military service between September 16, 1940, and January 1, 1957 (provided that the veteran had served at least 90 days and was honorably discharged), are counted as though they were in covered employment at a monthly wage of $160. These periods are not counted if benefits are payable for such period of service under a federal pension system not administered by the Veterans' Administration, except as to service in 1951–56 for those in service after 1956. These periods are not actually credited to the individual's account until a claim is submitted.

---

[12] There are special rules for agricultural workers where wages are reported annually rather than quarterly.

Since January 1, 1957, members of the armed services have been covered the same as other employees and pay the regular contributions. The 1967 amendments gave servicemen wage credits equal to $100 per month more than their base pay, starting in 1968. The extra cost of this is met from general revenue.

*Insured status.* In order for a worker or his dependents to be eligible for disability or retirement benefits, the worker must be fully insured, and for disability benefits he must have 20 quarters of coverage out of the last 40 quarters.[13] In lieu of the latter requirement, workers disabled before age 31 may qualify if they have coverage in half the quarters after age 21 or have six quarters of coverage out of the last 12. In order to be fully insured, a worker must have at least six quarters of coverage and have quarters of coverage equal to one quarter for every year elapsing between his starting and closing dates or have 40 quarters of coverage. The starting date is January 1, 1951, or the first day of the year following the year in which the worker attained age 21, whichever is later. The closing date is the first day of the year in which he was disabled, attained age 65 for men or age 62 for women, or died. The required quarters may be obtained at any time and need not be acquired during the period used for computing the requirement. Quarters obtained before 1951 (back to 1937), before age 21, or after retirement age can be counted.

*Benefits.* All income benefits are based on the primary insurance amount of the insured worker. This is the amount payable to a retired or disabled worker and is computed as a function of the average monthly wage (AMW).

*Average monthly wage.* AMW is computed over a number of years equal to the number of years after 1955 (or the year of attainment of age 26 if later) and before the first year in which the individual died or became disabled while eligible for disability benefits, or reached age 65 (age 62 for women) and was fully insured. Persons who reach these ages before 1961 must count all years through 1960. This number of years is multiplied by 12 to give the number of months, which becomes the denominator of the average monthly wage formula. The covered earnings, up to the maximum per year, for those years (equal to that number) in which covered earnings were highest becomes the numerator.[14] These need not be the same years. The number of years must be at least two and usually will be five or more, especially for retirement benefits. This formula gives effect to the provision for dropping the five years of lowest earnings after 1950 and results in an additional year of low earnings being dropped out for each year of covered employment at higher earn-

---

[13] Certain survivor's benefits are payable when the deceased worker is either currently or fully insured. In order to be currently insured he must have six quarters of coverage out of the last 13 calendar quarters.

[14] In the computation, cents are *dropped*.

ings at and after age 65 (male) or 62 (female) and after 1960. If earnings in the year of death, onset of disability, or retirement are counted, another year of low earnings may be dropped. Earnings before 1955 or before age 26 (but not before 1951) may be counted if desirable. Periods of disability may be excluded from both the numerator and the denominator of the fraction in accordance with the disability freeze provision described below. For persons with high earnings before 1951 and low earnings after 1950 (a relatively small group), a special procedure is applicable.

The maximum income that may be counted toward the average monthly wage is $3,000 per year for years prior to 1951, $3,600 per year for 1951–54, $4,200 for 1955–58, $4,800 for 1959–65, $6,600 for 1966–67, and $7,800 for 1968 and thereafter. The maximum possible average monthly wage is $218. How soon a worker can attain this depends on his date of birth. Workers born after 1946 can reach this figure in 1969. Table 4–5 shows maximum possible AMW for various years of birth.

The 1967 Social Security Act amendments provided for a benefit increase of 13 percent, with a $9.50 minimum increase in the primary insurance amount effective for February, 1968. This 13 percent increase exceeds substantially the rise in the cost of living in the two-year period between January, 1965, when the last general increase was made, and January, 1968. A new formula for the maximum family benefit resulted in greater increases in benefits for some families.

*Primary insurance amount.* The primary insurance amount (PIA) may be computed from the average monthly wage according to any of three methods. Whichever formula produces the largest benefit may be used.

For most workers, the latest method will be best. In order to use this formula, the worker must become entitled to benefits or die after January 31, 1968. The average monthly wage is computed for the appropriate period after January 1, 1951, according to the method described above. The benefit amount is computed from a benefit table that is based approximately on the formula: 71.16 percent of the first $110 of average monthly wage plus 25.88 percent of next $290, plus 21.18 percent of next $150, plus 28.43 percent of the next $100, rounded to the next higher dime and increased for low average monthly wage to grade into the minimum PIA. The minimum PIA is $55, and the maximum PIA is $218. The Primary Insurance Amount is the amount payable (before considering dependents' benefits) to disabled workers and old-age retirement cases, except that for those retiring at ages 62–64, the benefit is subject to a permanent actuarial reduction.

Workers who became entitled to benefits or died before February 1, 1968 use the "1965 law" average method. This method is based approximately on the formula: 62.97 percent of the first $110 of average monthly wage plus 2.9 percent of the next $290, plus 21.4 percent of next $150, rounded to the nearest dollar and increased slightly in some cases for average wages of under $85. This produces the 1965 PIA which is used to enter the benefit table to determine the current PIA, which is about 13 percent greater.

Workers who have at least one quarter of coverage before 1951 may use the "1939 law" average method.[15] Here the average monthly wage is computed for the period starting with 1937 (or age 22 if later). The monthly PIA is determined by computing the original Primary Insurance Benefit under the old formula (but with a dropout of five years) and referring to the table in the law. The original Primary Insurance Benefit is equal to 40 percent of the first $50 of average monthly wage, plus 10 percent of the next $200, all increased by 1 percent for each year before 1951 in which at least $200 was earned in covered employment. Table 4–5 indicates the relationship between the original Primary Insurance Benefit, the 1965 Primary Insurance Amount, and the 1967 Average Monthly Wage, Primary Insurance Amount, and Maximum Family Benefit.

*Disability definition.* To be eligible for disability income benefits, the disability freeze, or income payments as a disabled child age 18 or over of a deceased, disabled, or retired worker, an individual must have a disability so severe that he is unable to engage in any substantially gainful work which exists in the national economy even if such work does not exist in the area where he lives. The impairment must be a medically determinable physical or mental impairment which has lasted six months (except for a disabled child) and can be expected to result in death or which has lasted or can be expected to last for a continuous period of not less than 12 months from inception of disability. Blindness is presumptive total disability for the disability freeze and is defined as central visual acuity of less than 20/200 corrected or a visual angle of 20 degrees or less. Disability must continue for at least six months before benefits may begin for disabled workers and dependents. Determination of disability is made by state agencies, usually state vocational rehabilitation agencies, under contract with the Department of Health, Education, and Welfare.[16]

*Disability freeze.* In order to qualify for the disability freeze benefit, the worker must be fully insured and meet the coverage requirements for disability. The disability freeze provision results in the exclusion of any year which was wholly or partially included in a period of total disability[17] in determining insured status and average monthly wage. Thus a

---

[15] Except for workers who attain age 22 after 1950 and have six quarters of coverage after 1950.

[16] For a discussion of disability evaluation, see Arthur E. Hess, "Five Years of Disability Insurance Benefits: A Progress Report," *Social Security Bulletin,* July, 1962, p. 3.

[17] Such a period must have lasted six months or more.

TABLE 4-5. Old-Age, Survivors, and Disability Insurance Maximum Possible Average Monthly Wage[a]

| Year[b] | Maximum Monthly Wage | Year of Birth | | | | | | | |
|---|---|---|---|---|---|---|---|---|---|
| | | 1896 or Before | 1905 | 1915 | 1925 | 1929[c] and Before | 1930 | 1931 | 1932 |
| 1965 | $400 | $400 | $385 | $385 | $385 | $385 | $388 | $393 | $400 |
| 1966 | 550 | 430 | 400 | 400 | 400 | 400 | 405 | 411 | 418 |
| 1967 | 550 | 460 | 412 | 412 | 412 | 412 | 418 | 425 | 433 |
| 1968 | 650 | 510 | 430 | 430 | 430 | 430 | 437 | 445 | 455 |
| 1969 | 650 | 560 | 446 | 446 | 446 | 446 | 453 | 462 | 472 |
| 1970 | 650 | 610 | 467 | 460 | 460 | 460 | 467 | 476 | 487 |
| 1971 | 650 | 630 | 489 | 471 | 471 | 471 | 480 | 489 | 500 |
| 1972 | 650 | 650 | 510 | 482 | 482 | 482 | 490 | 500 | 510 |
| 1973 | 650 | | 528 | 491 | 491 | 491 | 500 | 509 | 520 |
| 1974 | 650 | | 546 | 500 | 500 | 500 | 508 | 517 | 528 |
| 1975 | 650 | | 564 | 507 | 507 | 507 | 515 | 525 | 535 |
| 1976 | 650 | | 582 | 514 | 514 | 514 | 522 | 531 | 541 |
| 1977 | 650 | | 600 | 520 | 520 | 520 | 528 | 537 | 547 |
| 1978 | 650 | | 617 | 526 | 526 | 526 | 534 | 542 | 552 |
| 1979 | 650 | | 635 | 531 | 531 | 531 | 539 | 547 | 557 |
| 1980 | 650 | | 642 | 543 | 536 | 536 | 543 | 552 | 561 |
| 1981 | 650 | | 650 | 556 | 540 | 540 | 548 | 556 | 565 |
| 1982 | 650 | | | 568 | 544 | 544 | 551 | 560 | 568 |
| 1983 | 650 | | | 579 | 548 | 548 | 555 | 563 | 572 |
| 1984 | 650 | | | 589 | 551 | 551 | 558 | 566 | 575 |
| 1985 | 650 | | | 600 | 555 | 555 | 562 | 569 | 577 |
| 1986 | 650 | | | 610 | 558 | 558 | 565 | 572 | 580 |
| 1987 | 650 | | | 620 | 560 | 560 | 567 | 575 | 582 |
| 1988 | 650 | | | 631 | 563 | 563 | 570 | 577 | 585 |
| 1989 | 650 | | | 641 | 566 | 566 | 572 | 579 | 587 |
| 1990 | 650 | | | 645 | 575 | 568 | 575 | 581 | 589 |
| 1991 | 650 | | | 650 | 583 | 570 | 577 | 583 | 590 |
| 1992 | 650 | | | | 592 | 572 | 579 | 585 | 592 |
| 1993 | 650 | | | | 600 | 575 | 581 | 587 | 594 |
| 1994 | 650 | | | | 607 | 582 | 582 | 589 | 595 |
| 1995 | 650 | | | | 615 | 590 | 590 | 590 | 597 |
| 1996 | 650 | | | | 622 | 598 | 598 | 598 | 598 |
| 1997 | 650 | | | | 629 | 605 | 605 | 605 | 605 |
| 1998 | 650 | | | | 636 | 611 | 611 | 611 | 611 |
| 1999 | 650 | | | | 644 | 618 | 618 | 618 | 618 |
| 2000 | 650 | | | | 647 | 625 | 625 | 625 | 625 |
| 2001 | 650 | | | | 650 | 631 | 631 | 631 | 631 |
| 2002 | 650 | | | | | 638 | 638 | 638 | 638 |
| 2003 | 650 | | | | | 644 | 644 | 644 | 644 |
| 2004 | 650 | | | | | 647 | 647 | 647 | 647 |
| 2005 | 650 | | | | | 650 | 650 | 650 | 650 |

| Year | Maximum Monthly Wage | 1933 | 1934 | 1935 | 1936 | 1937 | 1938 | 1939 | 1940 | 1941 and After |
|---|---|---|---|---|---|---|---|---|---|---|
| 1965 | $400 | $400 | $400 | $400 | $400 | $400 | $400 | $400 | $400 | $400 |
| 1966 | 550 | 421 | 425 | 430 | 437 | 450 | 475 | 475 | 475 | 475 |
| 1967 | 550 | 437 | 442 | 450 | 460 | 475 | 500 | 550 | 550 | 550 |
| 1968 | 650 | 461 | 468 | 478 | 491 | 510 | 537 | 583 | 600 | 600 |
| 1969 | 650 | 480 | 488 | 500 | 514 | 533 | 560 | 600 | 616 | 650 |
| 1970 | 650 | 495 | 505 | 516 | 531 | 550 | 575 | 610 | 625 | 650 |
| 1971 | 650 | 508 | 518 | 530 | 544 | 562 | 585 | 616 | 630 | 650 |
| 1972 | 650 | 519 | 529 | 540 | 555 | 572 | 593 | 621 | 633 | 650 |
| 1973 | 650 | 528 | 538 | 550 | 563 | 580 | 600 | 625 | 635 | 650 |
| 1974 | 650 | 536 | 546 | 557 | 570 | 586 | 605 | 627 | 637 | 650 |
| 1975 | 650 | 543 | 553 | 564 | 576 | 591 | 609 | 630 | 638 | 650 |
| 1976 | 650 | 550 | 559 | 570 | 582 | 596 | 612 | 631 | 640 | 650 |
| 1977 | 650 | 555 | 564 | 575 | 586 | 600 | 615 | 633 | 640 | 650 |
| 1978 | 650 | 560 | 569 | 579 | 590 | 603 | 617 | 634 | 641 | 650 |
| 1979 | 650 | 565 | 573 | 583 | 594 | 606 | 620 | 635 | 642 | 650 |
| 1980 | 650 | 569 | 577 | 586 | 597 | 608 | 621 | 636 | 642 | 650 |
| 1981 | 650 | 572 | 580 | 590 | 600 | 611 | 623 | 637 | 643 | 650 |
| 1982 | 650 | 576 | 584 | 592 | 602 | 613 | 625 | 638 | 643 | 650 |
| 1983 | 650 | 579 | 586 | 595 | 604 | 615 | 626 | 638 | 644 | 650 |
| 1984 | 650 | 582 | 589 | 597 | 606 | 616 | 627 | 639 | 644 | 650 |
| 1985 | 650 | 584 | 592 | 600 | 608 | 618 | 628 | 640 | 644 | 650 |
| 1986 | 650 | 587 | 594 | 602 | 610 | 619 | 629 | 640 | 645 | 650 |
| 1987 | 650 | 589 | 596 | 603 | 612 | 620 | 630 | 640 | 645 | 650 |
| 1988 | 650 | 591 | 598 | 605 | 613 | 622 | 631 | 641 | 645 | 650 |
| 1989 | 650 | 593 | 600 | 607 | 614 | 623 | 632 | 641 | 645 | 650 |
| 1990 | 650 | 595 | 601 | 608 | 616 | 624 | 632 | 642 | 645 | 650 |
| 1991 | 650 | 596 | 603 | 610 | 617 | 625 | 633 | 642 | 646 | 650 |
| 1992 | 650 | 598 | 604 | 611 | 618 | 626 | 633 | 642 | 646 | 650 |
| 1993 | 650 | 600 | 606 | 612 | 619 | 627 | 634 | 642 | 646 | 650 |
| 1994 | 650 | 601 | 607 | 613 | 620 | 627 | 635 | 643 | 646 | 650 |
| 1995 | 650 | 602 | 608 | 614 | 621 | 628 | 635 | 643 | 646 | 650 |
| 1996 | 605 | 604 | 609 | 615 | 622 | 628 | 635 | 643 | 646 | 650 |
| 1997 | 605 | 605 | 610 | 616 | 622 | 629 | 636 | 643 | 646 | 650 |
| 1998 | 650 | 611 | 611 | 617 | 623 | 630 | 636 | 643 | 646 | 650 |
| 1999 | 650 | 618 | 618 | 618 | 624 | 630 | 637 | 644 | 646 | 650 |
| 2000 | 650 | 625 | 625 | 625 | 625 | 631 | 637 | 644 | 647 | 650 |
| 2001 | 650 | 631 | 631 | 631 | 631 | 631 | 637 | 644 | 647 | 650 |
| 2002 | 650 | 638 | 638 | 638 | 638 | 638 | 638 | 644 | 647 | 650 |
| 2003 | 650 | 644 | 644 | 644 | 644 | 644 | 644 | 644 | 647 | 650 |
| 2004 | 650 | 647 | 647 | 647 | 647 | 647 | 647 | 647 | 647 | 650 |
| 2005 | 650 | 650 | 650 | 650 | 650 | 650 | 650 | 650 | 650 | 650 |

[a] Maximum possible AMW for a person with a maximum creditable earnings in each year. Applicable for death, disability, or retirement except for the 1929 and Before column (see note [c] below). Not applicable for female's retirement beyond age 61.

[b] Last year counted in AMW calculation. This usually will be the year *before* death, disability, or retirement, assuming death, disability, or retirement early in year. If person dies or is disabled late in year, but counts that year of earnings, treat as though he were one year younger, i.e., read one column to the right.

[c] Applicable for death and disability and for retirement at age 65 for all persons born before 1930. For retirement beyond age 65, this column is applicable only to persons born in 1929, and other figures would apply for earlier years of birth, back to 1896, as shown for selected years in the table.

TABLE 4–6

Table for Determining Primary Insurance Amount and Maximum Family Benefits

| I 1939 P.I.B. | | II 1965 PIA | III Average Monthly Wage | | IV 1967 Primary Insurance Amount | V Maximum Family Benefits |
|---|---|---|---|---|---|---|
| From | To | | From | To | | |
| — | $15.60 | $ 48.00 or less | — | $ 74 | $ 55.00 | $ 82.50 |
| $15.61 | 16.20 | 49.00 | $ 75 | 76 | 55.40 | 83.10 |
| 16.21 | 16.84 | 50.00 | 77 | 78 | 56.50 | 84.80 |
| 16.85 | 17.60 | 51.00 | 79 | 80 | 57.70 | 86.60 |
| 17.61 | 18.40 | 52.00 | 81 | 81 | 58.80 | 88.20 |
| 18.41 | 19.24 | 53.00 | 82 | 83 | 59.90 | 89.90 |
| 19.25 | 20.00 | 54.00 | 84 | 85 | 61.10 | 91.70 |
| 20.01 | 20.64 | 55.00 | 86 | 87 | 62.20 | 93.30 |
| 20.65 | 21.28 | 56.00 | 88 | 89 | 63.30 | 95.00 |
| 21.29 | 21.88 | 57.00 | 90 | 90 | 64.50 | 96.80 |
| 21.89 | 22.28 | 58.00 | 91 | 92 | 65.60 | 98.40 |
| 22.29 | 22.68 | 59.00 | 93 | 94 | 66.70 | 100.10 |
| 22.69 | 23.08 | 60.00 | 95 | 96 | 67.80 | 101.70 |
| 23.09 | 23.44 | 61.00 | 97 | 97 | 69.00 | 103.50 |
| 23.45 | 23.76 | 62.10 | 98 | 99 | 70.20 | 105.30 |
| 23.77 | 24.20 | 63.20 | 100 | 101 | 71.50 | 107.30 |
| 24.21 | 24.60 | 64.20 | 102 | 102 | 72.60 | 108.90 |
| 24.61 | 25.00 | 65.30 | 103 | 104 | 73.80 | 110.70 |
| 25.01 | 25.48 | 66.40 | 105 | 106 | 75.10 | 112.70 |
| 25.49 | 25.92 | 67.50 | 107 | 107 | 76.30 | 114.50 |
| 25.93 | 26.40 | 68.50 | 108 | 109 | 77.50 | 116.30 |
| 26.41 | 26.94 | 69.60 | 110 | 113 | 78.70 | 118.10 |
| 26.95 | 27.46 | 70.70 | 114 | 118 | 79.90 | 119.90 |
| 27.47 | 28.00 | 71.70 | 119 | 122 | 81.10 | 121.70 |
| 28.01 | 28.68 | 72.80 | 123 | 127 | 82.30 | 123.50 |
| 28.69 | 29.25 | 73.90 | 128 | 132 | 83.60 | 125.40 |
| 29.26 | 29.68 | 74.90 | 133 | 136 | 84.70 | 127.10 |
| 29.69 | 30.36 | 76.00 | 137 | 141 | 85.90 | 128.90 |
| 30.37 | 30.92 | 77.10 | 142 | 146 | 87.20 | 130.80 |
| 30.93 | 31.36 | 78.20 | 147 | 150 | 88.40 | 132.60 |
| 31.37 | 32.00 | 79.20 | 151 | 155 | 89.50 | 134.30 |
| 32.01 | 32.60 | 80.30 | 156 | 160 | 90.80 | 136.20 |
| 32.61 | 33.20 | 81.40 | 161 | 164 | 92.00 | 138.00 |
| 33.21 | 33.88 | 82.40 | 165 | 169 | 93.20 | 139.80 |
| 33.89 | 34.50 | 83.50 | 170 | 174 | 94.40 | 141.60 |
| 34.51 | 35.00 | 84.60 | 175 | 178 | 95.60 | 143.40 |
| 35.01 | 35.80 | 85.60 | 179 | 183 | 96.80 | 146.40 |
| 35.81 | 36.40 | 86.70 | 184 | 188 | 98.00 | 150.40 |
| 36.41 | 37.08 | 87.80 | 189 | 193 | 99.30 | 154.40 |
| 37.09 | 37.60 | 88.90 | 194 | 197 | 100.50 | 157.60 |
| 37.61 | 38.20 | 89.90 | 198 | 202 | 101.60 | 161.60 |
| 38.21 | 39.12 | 91.00 | 203 | 207 | 102.90 | 165.60 |
| 39.13 | 39.68 | 92.10 | 208 | 211 | 104.10 | 168.80 |
| 39.69 | 40.33 | 93.10 | 212 | 216 | 105.20 | 172.80 |
| 40.34 | 41.12 | 94.20 | 217 | 221 | 106.50 | 176.80 |
| 41.13 | 41.76 | 95.30 | 222 | 225 | 107.70 | 180.00 |
| 41.77 | 42.44 | 96.30 | 226 | 230 | 108.90 | 184.00 |
| 42.45 | 43.20 | 97.40 | 231 | 235 | 110.10 | 188.00 |

| I 1939 P.I.B. | | II 1965 PIA | III Average Monthly Wage | | IV 1967 Primary Insurance Amount | V Maximum Family Benefits |
|---|---|---|---|---|---|---|
| From | To | | From | To | | |
| 43.21 | 43.76 | $ 98.50 | $236 | $239 | $111.40 | $191.20 |
| 43.77 | 44.44 | 99.60 | 240 | 244 | 112.60 | 195.20 |
| 44.45 | 44.88 | 100.60 | 245 | 249 | 113.70 | 199.20 |
| 44.89 | 45.60 | 101.70 | 250 | 253 | 115.00 | 202.40 |
| | | 102.80 | 254 | 258 | 116.20 | 206.40 |
| | | 103.80 | 259 | 263 | 117.30 | 210.40 |
| | | 104.90 | 264 | 267 | 118.60 | 213.60 |
| | | 106.00 | 268 | 272 | 119.80 | 217.60 |
| | | 107.00 | 273 | 277 | 121.00 | 221.60 |
| | | 108.10 | 278 | 281 | 122.20 | 224.80 |
| | | 109.20 | 282 | 286 | 123.40 | 228.80 |
| | | 110.30 | 287 | 291 | 124.70 | 232.80 |
| | | 111.30 | 292 | 295 | 125.80 | 236.00 |
| | | 112.40 | 296 | 300 | 127.10 | 240.00 |
| | | 113.50 | 301 | 305 | 128.30 | 244.00 |
| | | 114.50 | 306 | 309 | 129.40 | 247.20 |
| | | 115.60 | 310 | 314 | 130.70 | 251.20 |
| | | 116.70 | 315 | 319 | 131.90 | 255.20 |
| | | 117.70 | 320 | 323 | 133.00 | 258.40 |
| | | 118.80 | 324 | 328 | 134.30 | 263.40 |
| | | 119.90 | 329 | 333 | 135.50 | 266.40 |
| | | 121.00 | 334 | 337 | 136.80 | 269.60 |
| | | 122.00 | 338 | 342 | 137.90 | 273.60 |
| | | 123.10 | 343 | 347 | 139.10 | 277.60 |
| | | 124.20 | 348 | 351 | 140.40 | 280.80 |
| | | 125.20 | 352 | 356 | 141.50 | 284.80 |
| | | 126.30 | 357 | 361 | 142.80 | 288.80 |
| | | 127.40 | 362 | 365 | 144.00 | 292.00 |
| | | 128.40 | 366 | 370 | 145.10 | 296.00 |
| | | 129.50 | 371 | 375 | 146.40 | 300.00 |
| | | 130.60 | 376 | 379 | 147.60 | 303.20 |
| | | 131.70 | 380 | 384 | 148.90 | 307.20 |
| | | 132.70 | 385 | 389 | 150.00 | 311.20 |
| | | 133.80 | 390 | 393 | 151.20 | 314.40 |
| | | 134.90 | 394 | 398 | 152.50 | 318.40 |
| | | 135.90 | 399 | 403 | 153.60 | 322.40 |
| | | 137.00 | 404 | 407 | 154.90 | 325.60 |
| | | 138.00 | 408 | 412 | 156.00 | 329.60 |
| | | 139.00 | 413 | 417 | 157.10 | 333.60 |
| | | 140.00 | 418 | 421 | 158.20 | 336.80 |
| | | 141.00 | 422 | 426 | 159.40 | 340.80 |
| | | 142.00 | 427 | 431 | 160.50 | 344.80 |
| | | 143.00 | 432 | 436 | 161.60 | 348.80 |
| | | 144.00 | 437 | 440 | 162.80 | 350.40 |
| | | 145.00 | 441 | 445 | 163.90 | 352.40 |
| | | 146.00 | 446 | 450 | 165.00 | 354.40 |
| | | 147.00 | 451 | 454 | 166.20 | 356.00 |
| | | 148.00 | 455 | 459 | 167.30 | 358.00 |

TABLE 4–6 (Continued)

| I 1939 P.I.B. | | II 1965 PIA | III Average Monthly Wage | | IV 1967 Primary Insurance Amount | V Maximum Family Benefits |
|---|---|---|---|---|---|---|
| From | To | | From | To | | |
| | | 149.00 | $460 | $464 | $168.40 | $360.00 |
| | | 150.00 | 465 | 468 | 169.50 | 361.60 |
| | | 151.00 | 469 | 473 | 170.70 | 363.60 |
| | | 152.00 | 474 | 478 | 171.80 | 365.60 |
| | | 153.00 | 479 | 482 | 172.90 | 367.20 |
| | | 154.00 | 483 | 487 | 174.10 | 369.20 |
| | | 155.00 | 488 | 492 | 175.20 | 371.20 |
| | | 156.00 | 493 | 496 | 176.30 | 372.80 |
| | | 157.00 | 497 | 501 | 177.50 | 374.80 |
| | | 158.00 | 502 | 506 | 178.60 | 376.80 |
| | | 159.00 | 507 | 510 | 179.70 | 378.40 |
| | | 160.00 | 511 | 515 | 180.80 | 380.40 |
| | | 161.00 | 516 | 520 | 182.00 | 382.40 |
| | | 162.00 | 521 | 524 | 183.10 | 384.00 |
| | | 163.00 | 525 | 529 | 184.20 | 386.00 |
| | | 164.00 | 530 | 534 | 185.40 | 388.00 |
| | | 165.00 | 535 | 538 | 186.50 | 389.60 |
| | | 166.00 | 539 | 543 | 187.60 | 391.60 |
| | | 167.00 | 544 | 548 | 188.80 | 393.60 |
| | | 168.00 | 549 | 553 | 189.90 | 395.60 |
| | | | 554 | 556 | 191.00 | 396.80 |
| | | | 557 | 560 | 192.00 | 398.40 |
| | | | 561 | 563 | 193.00 | 399.60 |
| | | | 564 | 567 | 194.00 | 401.20 |
| | | | 568 | 570 | 195.00 | 402.40 |
| | | | 571 | 574 | 196.00 | 404.00 |
| | | | 575 | 577 | 197.00 | 405.20 |
| | | | 578 | 581 | 198.00 | 406.80 |
| | | | 582 | 584 | 199.00 | 408.00 |
| | | | 585 | 588 | 200.00 | 409.60 |
| | | | 589 | 591 | 201.00 | 410.80 |
| | | | 592 | 595 | 202.00 | 412.40 |
| | | | 596 | 598 | 203.00 | 413.60 |
| | | | 599 | 602 | 204.00 | 415.20 |
| | | | 603 | 605 | 205.00 | 416.40 |
| | | | 606 | 609 | 206.00 | 418.00 |
| | | | 610 | 612 | 207.00 | 419.20 |
| | | | 613 | 616 | 208.00 | 420.80 |
| | | | 617 | 620 | 209.00 | 422.40 |
| | | | 621 | 623 | 210.00 | 423.60 |
| | | | 624 | 627 | 211.00 | 425.20 |
| | | | 628 | 630 | 212.00 | 426.40 |
| | | | 631 | 634 | 213.00 | 428.00 |
| | | | 635 | 637 | 214.00 | 429.20 |
| | | | 638 | 641 | 215.00 | 430.80 |
| | | | 642 | 644 | 216.00 | 432.00 |
| | | | 645 | 648 | 217.00 | 433.60 |
| | | | 649 | 650 | 218.00 | 434.40 |

Source: Social Security Amendments of 1967.

person whose earnings drop off because of disability will not lose his coverage or have his benefit reduced. This is comparable to a waiver of premium benefit in an insurance contract.

*Disability income benefits.* In order to qualify for disability income payments, the disabled worker must have been fully insured and have had 20 quarters of coverage out of the last 40 calendar quarters at the date of disability (with alternate provisions for those disabled before age 31). Payments commence at the end of the seventh full month of disability.

The amount of benefit is the PIA payable to the disabled worker, plus 50 percent for his wife if she has an eligible child under 18 or disabled in her care or is over age 65 at the time of the claim,[18] subject to a maximum of $105 per month, and 50 percent for each eligible child, subject to the maximum family benefit provisions. Benefit payments continue until death, recovery, or age 65 (at which time regular retirement benefits become payable). An eligible child must be under 18 or a full-time student under 22 or disabled since before age 18 and must be unmarried.

*Benefits for disabled children.* Payments to disabled children are made if the child has been totally and permanently disabled continuously since before he reached 18, is unmarried, and either is dependent on a parent (including step and adoptive parents) entitled to OASDI retirement or disability benefits or was dependent at the time of death upon a parent who died insured for survivors' benefits. The child's benefit, to which he would be entitled as a dependent under 18, is paid indefinitely after age 18. The child's benefit is 50 percent of the parent's PIA if the parent is retired or disabled, and if the parent has died, it is 75 percent. A mother with such a disabled child in her care will receive her mother's benefit, which is equal to 75 percent of the deceased worker's PIA or 50 percent of the PIA of a retired or disabled worker, subject to the $105 maximum. Both child's and mother's benefits on account of the child's disability stop when the child recovers, marries, or is adopted by someone other than a stepparent, grandparent, aunt, uncle, brother, or sister.

*Benefits for disabled widows and widowers.* The 1967 amendments added benefits for certain disabled widows and widowers aged 50 to 62. The amount of benefit is reduced for early receipt and ranges from 50 percent of the spouse's PIA at age 50 to $82\frac{1}{2}$ percent at age 65. The disability must commence within seven years of the spouse's death or, for a widowed mother (of an eligible child survivor), within seven years of the end of her eligibility for mother's benefits.

---

[18] Reduced benefits are payable to a wife age 62 to 64 inclusive. The reduction is $8\frac{1}{3}$ for each year or 25/36 percent for each month prior to the age 65, at the time benefits are claimed, and the reduction is permanent. Benefits also are payable to the dependent husband age 62 or over of a disabled female worker in the same amount as for the wife of a disabled male worker.

*Limitations. Family maximum.* The maximum receivable by a family is subject to an overall limit. This may operate to reduce the total payable to a retired or disabled worker and his family, or to the family of a deceased worker. The monthly maximum is equal to 80 percent of the first $436 of average monthly wage plus 40 percent of the balance, but not less than 1½ times PIA.[19] It ranges from $82.50 to $434.40. Table 4-6 shows the maximum family benefit for various primary insurance amounts.

*Benefit termination or reduction.* Disability income payments on account of a disabled person are terminated two months after recovery and may be terminated if the disabled person refuses without good cause to accept rehabilitation services offered by an appropriate state agency. On the other hand, payments may be continued up to one year after return to work as part of a rehabilitation program or trial work period. In the event of a subsequent disability within five years, the six-month waiting period is waived.

For any particular individual retirement beneficiary, dependent of a retirement or disability beneficiary or survivor beneficiary, payments are reduced by one half of the first $1,200 that a beneficiary earns in excess of $1,680 per year and 100 percent of his earnings over $2,880 per year. However, benefits are not withheld for any month in which $140 or less of wages is earned and he did not engage in substantial self-employment. The reduction applies to total family benefits including those for dependents. This retirement test does not apply after the beneficiary attains age 72, nor to a disability beneficiary. The combined disability benefits under OASDI and Workmen's Compensation cannot exceed 80 percent of the worker's average current earnings,[20] with the necessary reductions being made in the OASDI disability benefits. The amount limits so determined are to be readjusted every three years to reflect changes in the average taxable wages of all workers covered by the system.

*Financing.* Old-Age, Survivors, and Disability Insurance is financed by a tax on wages, salaries, commissions and self-employment income up to $7,800 per year for each worker. The tax rate is composed of two elements. Disability income benefits are financed by a tax of .475 percent of wages paid by the employee and a similar sum paid by the employer and by a tax of .7125 percent on the earnings of the self-employed. No increase in this rate is scheduled.

The old-age and survivors benefits are financed by a similar tax of 3.325 percent each, which is scheduled to increase in steps to 4.525 percent in 1973. Self-employed persons pay a tax approximately equal to

---

[19] The calculations are made for the upper limit of the A.M.W. bracket in the table.

[20] Earnings in excess of the tax base are included in computing this average.

three fourths of the combined employer and employee rate, rounded to the nearest one tenth of 1 percent but with a maximum of 7 percent total tax for OASI and DI. The present and future tax rates are given in Table 4-7. The tax law providing for employer and employee contributions is

TABLE 4-7

Old-Age, Survivors, and Disability Insurance and Hospital Insurance Tax Rates

| Year | Employer and Employee | | | Employee | | Self-Employed | | | |
| | OASDI | HI | Total | Total | Amount· | OASDI | HI | To-tal | Amount[a] |
|---|---|---|---|---|---|---|---|---|---|
| 1968............... | 7.6% | 1.2% | 8.8% | 4.4% | $343.20 | 5.8% | .6% | 6.4% | $499.20 |
| 1969–70........... | 8.4 | 1.2 | 9.6 | 4.8 | 374.40 | 6.3 | .6 | 6.9 | 538.20 |
| 1971–72........... | 9.2 | 1.2 | 10.4 | 5.2 | 405.60 | 6.9 | .6 | 7.5 | 585.00 |
| 1973–75...........  | 10.0 | 1.3 | 11.3 | 5.65 | 440.70 | 7.0 | .65 | 7.65 | 596.70 |
| 1976–79...........  | 10.0 | 1.4 | 11.4 | 5.7 | 444.60 | 7.0 | .7 | 7.7 | 600.60 |
| 1980–86...........  | 10.0 | 1.6 | 11.6 | 5.8 | 452.40 | 7.0 | .8 | 7.8 | 608.40 |
| 1987–on...........  | 10.0 | 1.8 | 11.8 | 5.9 | 460.20 | 7.0 | .9 | 7.9 | 616.20 |

[a] Dollar amount paid by taxpayer earning $7,800 per year or more.

the Federal Insurance Contributions Act, now a part of the Internal Revenue Code.

Employers withhold the employee tax on wages up to $7,800 per year and remit quarterly, monthly, or semimonthly the total employee and employer tax along with federal income tax withholdings. Self-employed persons pay tax on their net self-employment income according to Schedule C or F along with their income tax. If a person pays contributions on more than $7,800 per year by working for more than one employer and taxes are withheld, he is entitled to a refund of the tax on amounts in excess of $7,800. This may be taken as a credit on the individual income tax return.

The tax proceeds collected by the Internal Revenue Service are deposited in special federal trust funds and used to pay benefits and administrative expenses of the fund. There is a separate fund for the disability monies. The trust funds are invested in interest-bearing United States government securities. The interest on these funds helps meet the costs of OASDI benefits and administration, and comes from general government revenues.

## Medicare

In 1965, Health Insurance for the Aged was added to the Social Security Act. It provides two separate but complementary health plans for meeting the national problem of adequate medical care for the aged. This program is popularly referred to as Medicare. Medicare represents one of the most important additions made in the history of the Social Security Act. Benefits were first payable July 1, 1966, except for extended care facilities which were covered beginning January 1, 1967.

*Hospital Insurance.* The basic plan, Hospital Insurance, protects aged persons against the costs of hospital and related care. The plan applies to all persons age 65 and over who are eligible for monthly OASDI or Railroad Retirement benefits. In addition, all others who were 65 before 1968 and who are citizens or who are aliens with five years of permanent residence are protected.[21] Those who lack eligibility for OASDI and who will be 65 after 1967 must have three quarters of coverage for each year after 1965 and before age 65. This provision becomes ineffective for men attaining 65 after 1973 and for women attaining 65 after 1971, since at these respective dates the quarters of coverage required for Hospital Insurance will be the same as for OASDI old age benefits.

*Benefits provided.* In-patient hospital services will be furnished for up to 90 days in each "spell of illness."[22] An initial deductible of $40[23] is paid for by the patient and he must also pay one fourth of the in-patient hospital deductible (initially $10) for each day after the 60th day. The 1967 amendments provide each beneficiary with an additional lifetime reserve of 60 days of hospital care with a participation clause requiring the beneficiary to pay $20 daily. The patient also must pay the cost of the first three pints of blood unless it is replaced by a donor. In-patient psychiatric hospital service is included, subject to a lifetime maximum of 190 days.

The services include room and board in semiprivate accommodations, operating room, laboratory tests and X-rays, drugs and dressings, general nursing services, and services of interns and residents in training.

Posthospital extended care will be furnished for up to 100 days with the patient paying one eighth of the in-patient hospital deductible amount (initially $5) for each day after the first 20 days. The patient must have been confined for at least 3 days in a hospital and he must be transferred to the extended care facility within 14 days of his hospital

---

[21] Excluded are certain subversives and retired federal employees (or dependents of such individuals) who are covered under the Federal Employees Health Benefits Act of 1959 (including certain individuals who could have been covered if they had so elected).

[22] A "spell of illness" begins when the individual enters a hospital or extended care facility and ends when he has not been an in-patient of a hospital or extended care facility for 60 consecutive days.

[23] May be adjusted after 1968 to keep pace with changes in hospital costs according to the following method: $40 times ratio of current average per diem rate for in-patient hospital services for the second preceding year to the current average per diem rate for such services for 1966, rounded to the nearest multiple of $4.

discharge while under continued care for the same illness. A patient who is then discharged from the extended care facility can be readmitted to the extended care facility within 14 days of his discharge within the same spell of illness.

Services under extended care services include room and board in semiprivate accommodations, general nursing care, physical, occupational and speech therapy, medical social services, drugs and such services as are generally provided by extended care facilities.

Posthospital home health services are provided for up to 100 visits per spell of illness commencing within 14 days after a person is discharged from a hospital (after at least a 3-day confinement) or extended care facility in the next 365 days before the start of the next spell of illness. The person must be in the care of and under a plan established by a physician within 14 days of discharge from a hospital or extended care facility.

The services covered are basically those for homebound patients and include part-time or intermittent nursing, physical, occupational or speech therapy, medical social services, part-time or intermittent services of a health aide, medical supplies (other than drugs and biologicals), and out-patient hospital services when equipment cannot be brought to the home.

In order to participate, hospitals, extended care facilities and home health agencies must apply to participate and meet certain standards, some quite detailed. By July, 1967, one year after the Medicare program began, 6,857 hospitals with almost 1.2 million beds, 4,160 extended care facilities with more than 291,000 beds and 1,849 home health agencies were participating in the program. Nationally there were 42.4 hospital beds and 15.2 extended care beds per 1,000 enrollees. By state the proportion for hospital beds ranged from 24.2 in Mississippi to 101.5 in Alaska, while that for extended care beds ranged from 3.7 in Mississippi to 40.7 in Connecticut.

*Administration.* Benefits under HI are not paid directly to the beneficiary: they are paid to the providers of the services under regulations prescribed in the Social Security Act.

The law provides that groups or associations of providers of services can nominate a governmental or private agency or organization to act as a fiscal intermediary between them and the federal government. Use of these intermediaries is encouraged because their experience in adjusting health insurance claims should help to prevent overutilization of the services. Such fiscal intermediaries will be expected to determine the amount of payments due upon presentation of bills (within guidelines set by the Secretary of Health, Education, and Welfare), and make payments, serve as consultants to institutions or agencies to enable them to establish and maintain adequate fiscal records, and serve as a channel of communication between the Secretary of Health, Education, and Welfare and the providers of services. The fiscal intermediaries will be reimbursed for their reasonable costs of administration. Because overutilization of services is one of the major concerns associated with this insurance, utilization review committees must be established for hospital and extended care facilities. The American Hospital Association recommended that its members nominate the Blue Cross plans as intermediaries. Blue Cross Association and its member plans were designated as intermediaries for most areas of the country, but Aetna, Travelers and Prudential were assigned small areas, and the Blue Shield plan administers HI in Hawaii (Aetna administers SMI).

In order to assure that the federal government pays only the reasonable costs for the services rendered under the HI program, an accounting system known as RCC—Ratio of Costs to Charges—has been adopted. Under this system, the hospitals have to determine what percentage the charges for aged patients are of the charges for all patients (separately for each type of service). This percentage is then applied to the costs of these services (by type) to determine the hospital's payment from the government for Medicare patients. The purpose of this procedure is to allocate costs equitably between Medicare and other patients and thus keep hospitals from collecting for costs of running maternity wards, pediatric departments, and other services which the aged do not use.[24]

*Financing.* The Hospital Insurance benefits are to be financed through contributions by employers, employees, and self-employed persons computed on the same maximum taxable earnings base as OASDI, that is, $7,800. Unlike OASDI, the Hospital Insurance plan imposes the same rate on self-employed persons as on employees and on employers. Initially this rate was set as .35 percent each for 1966 and it increases to .9 percent in 1987 and thereafter. Table 4–7 shows the tax rates.

According to Social Security actuaries, the contributions developed will be sufficient for the basic plan to be self-supporting. These contributions will be placed in a separate Hospital Insurance Trust Fund administered by its own board of trustees which has the same membership as the OASDI, DI and SMI trust funds and follows the same investment procedures.

In 1969 the contributions under an intermediate cost estimate are expected to total about $4,223 million, out of which $3,636 million will be paid in benefits and $127 million in administrative expenses, while $90 million in interest will be earned on the fund. The fund at the end of

---

[24] See U.S. Department of HEW, Social Security Administration *Principles of Reimbursement for Provider Costs.* Washington, D.C., U.S.G.P.O., 1966, pp. 24 ff. for details.

1969 is expected to be $2,616 million. Table 4–10 (p. 173) shows the actual and estimated progress of the fund.

*Experience.* In 1967, 5,000,968 claims were approved for inpatient care for an average of 13.6 days per claim and an average cost of $48 per day and $655 per claim. Total charges were $3.3 million, and $2.7 million (80.2 percent) was reimbursed after the imposition of deductibles, an average of $526 per claim. In addition, in 1967, the system approved 538,431 outpatient hospital diagnostic claims averaging a reimbursement of $12 each, 312,317 home health claims averaging $66, and 698,209 extended care facility claims averaging $304.

*Supplementary Medical Insurance.* The supplementary plan, Supplementary Medical Insurance Benefits for the Aged, is a voluntary plan available to all persons age 65 and over who are citizens or aliens with five years' permanent residence in the United States.[25]

The premium amount was set initially at a rate of $3 per month per individual with the General Treasury matching this amount. After 1967, the premium rate may be changed annually by the Secretary of Health, Education, and Welfare to reflect the actual past experience and the estimate of that anticipated in the future. The premium rate was increased to $4 per month in April, 1968. For those who do not enroll at the earliest period that they are eligible, the premium rate will be increased by 10 percent for each full year of delay. The premium amount will be deducted, where possible, from OASDI, Railroad Retirement, or Civil Service retirement benefits.

In order to avoid adverse selection against the system, persons wishing to participate must so indicate during specified enrollment periods. Otherwise, individuals in good health might delay enrollment until such time as they had reason to believe their health was deteriorating. Persons attaining age 65 can enroll in the seven-month periods surrounding the months of their birthdays. If one enrolls in the three months preceding his birthday, his effective date of coverage will be the month of his birthday. If he enrolls in the month of his birthday, his effective date of coverage will be the month after his birthday. If he waits until one month after his birthday, his coverage will not begin until the second month after he enrolls. Should he delay enrollment until the second or third month after his 65th birthday, his effective date of coverage will be the third month after his enrollment. If a person fails to enroll during this seven-month period, he may enroll within three years during a "general enrollment period" which is scheduled for January to March of each year. Coverage elected in this way is effective the following July 1.

A person can withdraw from the program at any time, effective at the

---

[25] Excluded are certain subversives.

close of the following quarter, by appropriate notice, or by not paying premiums (providing he is not paying premiums by the benefit deduction method). A person who withdraws from the program can reenroll only once and only during a general enrollment period within three years of his withdrawal.

*Benefits.* The Supplementary Medical Insurance plan (SMI) provides benefits that supplement the protection provided by the basic plan of Hospital Insurance. The cost of any service paid for by the basic plan is excluded from SMI coverages. It covers 80 percent of the cost of the following medical services in excess of a $50 deductible: physician's and surgeon's services in the home, office, and hospital; out-patient psychiatric services; medical and health services, including diagnostic tests other than while an in-patient in a hospital, X-ray, radium and radioactive isotope therapy, surgical dressings, the rental of durable medical equipment, prosthetic devices (other than dental), and ambulance services where necessary due to the patient's condition; and home health services for an additional 100 visits per year similar to those provided under the basic plan, except that there is no requirement of previous hospitalization.

*Exclusions from coverage.* No payment will be made under either HI or SMI for items and services which are not reasonable and necessary for the diagnosis or treatment of illness or injury or to improve the functioning of a malformed body member; where there is no legal obligation for payment by the recipient; those paid for by a government agency; treatment provided outside the U.S. (except certain emergency in-patient hospital services); results of war or an act of war; personal comfort items; routine physical checkups; eyeglasses or eye examinations for the purpose of prescribing, fitting, or changing eyeglasses; hearing aids or examinations therefor; immunizations; orthopedic shoes; custodial care; cosmetic surgery except as required for the prompt repair of accidental injury; charges imposed by immediate relatives; care, treatment, filling, removal, or replacement of teeth or structures directly supporting teeth; and services for which payment is made or expected to be made under a workmen's compensation law or plan of the United States or a state.

*Deductible limitations.* A $50 deductible is imposed each calendar year under SMI. However, an individual paying the $50 deductible during the last three months of the preceding year will not have to pay again in the following year. The purpose of the special carry-over provision is to avoid requiring persons with substantial costs at the end of one year to meet the deductible early in the next year as though they had no prior bills. In addition to the $50 deductible there is a percentage participation provision allowing the plan to pay 80 percent of all "reasonable charges" over the deductible. There is a further calendar year limitation on treatment of out-patient mental, psychoneurotic, and personality disorders. SMI will pay 80 percent of usual benefits of this type with limits of $312.50 or 62½ percent of actual charges, whichever is smaller. The effect of this provision is to limit payment for these services to one half of the incurred expenses (80% of 62½%) or $250 (80% of $312.50), whichever is less. The deductible and percentage participation provisions do not apply to the professional component of in-hospital pathology and radiology fees.

*Administration.* Supplementary Medical Insurance is administered by the Department of Health, Education, and Welfare through carriers such as private insurance companies and Blue Shield plans. Unlike HI, there is no provision for nominations by providers of services. These carriers hold and disburse funds for benefit payments. Because of their knowledge and experience with private insurance, the carriers are in a more favorable position to determine the reasonableness of charges and to assist in controlling utilization. For their services, the carriers will be paid their reasonable costs of administration.

In early 1966, 50 organizations were selected to serve as fiscal intermediaries for SMI for specified areas. Among those selected, 16 were commercial insurers, 33 were Blue Shield plans, and 1 was an independent health insurer. The selected Blue Shield plans serve 60 percent of the nation's Medicare beneficiaries; the insurance companies, 38 percent; and the independent insurer, 1 percent.

The payments of benefits under the supplementary plan are governed by essentially the same procedures and regulations as listed under the basic plan. In the case of hospitals, nursing homes, and home-health agencies who supply services, they will be paid directly by the fiscal intermediary on a reasonable cost basis. As regards physicians and surgeons, the patient may handle the claim himself and present an itemized bill either receipted or not and receive reimbursement for 80 percent of the reasonable charges, after payment of the $50 deductible. If the physician is willing, the patient may assign the claim to him. However, if the physician or other supplier of services accepts an assignment from the patient, his *entire* charge cannot exceed what the intermediary deems to be reasonable in the particular situation. In this case the physician collects 80 percent of his charge in excess of the deductible from the fiscal intermediary and the balance from the patient. On June 29, 1966, the House of Delegates of the American Medical Association passed a resolution requesting and urging physicians to deal directly and only with the patient in billing and not to accept any assignment. However, it now appears that most physicians are willing to accept assignment.

*Experience.* In 1967, 24,364,406 bills for $1,511,829,000, an average of $62 per bill, were covered. Of this, $1,068,000 was reimbursed, an average reimbursement of $44, 70.6 percent of the amount billed. The average surgical bill was $173, reimbursed at 73.8 percent ($127) and the average medical bill was $51, reimbursed at 69.9 percent ($36).

*Adequacy of funding.* There has been much discussion as to the actuarial soundness of the Social Security system. A social insurance plan is different from a private insurance plan in this respect. In social insurance, because participation is compulsory, premium taxes may be increased in the future, or benefits may be reduced. The law specifically indicates that Congress has this right in regard to OASDI. All the funding strictly necessary for social insurance, then, is a revolving fund sufficient to balance short-run variations between premiums and expenditures. The OASDI funds are more than sufficient for this purpose.

However, costs are bound to increase as the program matures and more of the persons who die, become disabled, or retire are covered by the program. Moreover, increasing longevity, particularly at ages over 50, will result in higher benefit costs in relation to the number of persons eligible. The same effect may be produced by an increasing level of income, especially if benefits are increased. The effect of the dropout and disability freeze provisions is to use a higher average monthly wage as a basis of benefit computation than that on which the insured worker paid taxes. It is probable that there will be additional future liberalizations in this respect. This is partially offset, however, by the bias in favor of lower incomes built into the benefit formula. If inflation continues, it is probable that benefit levels will be increased in the future—even for current beneficiaries. This already has happened six times since 1949. When such increases are made, benefit costs are increased without a corresponding increase in past premium rates. Because of these factors, the unfunded or "pay-as-you-go" method of figuring premium taxes greatly understates the ultimate cost of the program. Thus there is considerable danger of undue liberalization because of a lack of recognition of the ultimate costs of benefits already provided but which few, if any, are currently collecting.

Another possible method of funding a social insurance plan is "terminal funding." Under this concept, a large enough fund is maintained to equal the present value of all future benefit costs of beneficiaries in current payment status. In effect, funds are set aside for each beneficiary equal to the present value of an annuity for him. Taxes are maintained at a rate sufficient to provide such funds for each beneficiary. Under such a plan, if the system were terminated, there would always be enough funds to continue payments to all current beneficiaries but nothing for those who had not yet qualified for benefits.

Private insurance and pension plans usually emphasize "full funding." Under this system, a fund is always maintained equal to the difference between the present value of promised future benefits for all insured persons and the present value of future premium (tax) receipts. Past service liability is amortized over the future working lives of employees employed at the inception of the plan, or over a shorter period. If such a plan is terminated, every insured participant could be given a cash value or deferred insurance benefit equivalent to what the taxes he and his employer had paid would purchase.

Such a plan involves the greatest equity between individuals, for each, together with his employer, pays the actuarial cost of the protection he receives. Such a plan would involve a level premium paid on behalf of and by each insured person. If the fundamental assumptions of this plan did not change, this premium would remain level throughout the life of a worker. This level premium would vary with age of entry into the plan and would be very high for newly covered older persons. The fund which would be built up if this funding method were used for the OASI trust fund would be tremendous.[26]

Whether the OASI fund is "actuarially adequate" depends on which criterion of soundness and adequacy one uses. Clearly, it is sound as far as current payments are concerned. Equally clearly, it is far from fully funded. Evaluation of current and future solvency depends on estimates of a number of variables, including employment, earnings, fertility, mortality, disability, retirement, recovery, interest and remarriage rates. Benefit costs under the 1967 law, for the OASI program, are estimated at 8.77 percent of covered payroll according to intermediate cost assumptions on a level equivalent basis to 2040. Tax receipts are estimated at 8.78 percent, leaving a positive actuarial balance of 0.01 percent of payroll.

According to these asumptions, the old-age and survivors insurance trust fund would grow continually in the future, reaching $303 billion in 2025, as shown in Table 4–8. However, the program undoubtedly will have been changed before that time. Since there have been significant changes every two years of late, it is futile to be concerned about contingencies more than half a century in the future.

The Disability Insurance Trust Fund operates independently of the Old-Age and Survivors Insurance Trust Fund. The Social Security Administration has estimated the progress of the disability fund on two bases: a high-cost and a low-cost basis. These were averaged to get an intermediate-cost estimate. Under this estimate the disability provisions would cost 0.95 percent of covered payroll on a level premium basis. Since receipts should equal 0.95 percent of covered payroll, the disability provision may be considered exactly in actuarial balance if these esti-

---

[26] See James A. Hamilton and Dorrance C. Bronson, *Pensions* (New York: McGraw-Hill Book Co., 1958) ch. xi, and Dorrance C. Bronson, *Concepts of Actuarial Soundness in Pension Plans* (Homewood, Ill.: Richard D. Irwin, Inc., 1957), for a fuller discussion of actuarial soundness and degrees of funding.

TABLE 4–8

Progress of Old-Age and Survivors Insurance Trust Fund
(in millions)

| Calendar Year | Contributions | Benefit Payments | Administrative Expenses | Railroad Retirement Financial Interchange[a] | Interest on Fund[b] | Balance in Fund at End of Year[c] |
|---|---|---|---|---|---|---|
| | | | Actual Data | | | |
| 1951.............. | $ 3,367 | $ 1,885 | $ 81 | ... | $ 417 | $ 15,540 |
| 1952.............. | 3,819 | 2,194 | 88 | ... | 365 | 17,442 |
| 1953.............. | 3,945 | 3,006 | 88 | ... | 414 | 18,707 |
| 1954.............. | 5,163 | 3,670 | 92 | −$21 | 447 | 20,576 |
| 1955.............. | 5,713 | 4,968 | 119 | −7 | 454 | 21,663 |
| 1956.............. | 6,172 | 5,715 | 132 | −5 | 526 | 22,519 |
| 1957.............. | 6,825 | 7,347 | 162[d] | −2 | 556 | 22,393 |
| 1958.............. | 7,566 | 8,327 | 194[d] | 124 | 552 | 21,864 |
| 1959.............. | 8,052 | 9,842 | 184 | 282 | 532 | 20,141 |
| 1960.............. | 10,866 | 10,677 | 203 | 318 | 516 | 20,324 |
| 1961.............. | 11,285 | 11,862 | 239 | 332 | 548 | 19,725 |
| 1962.............. | 12,059 | 13,356 | 256 | 361 | 526 | 18,337 |
| 1963.............. | 14,541 | 14,217 | 281 | 423 | 521 | 18,480 |
| 1964.............. | 15,689 | 14,914 | 296 | 403 | 569 | 19,125 |
| 1965.............. | 16,017 | 16,737 | 328 | 436 | 593 | 18,235 |
| 1966.............. | 20,658 | 18,267 | 256 | 444 | 644 | 20,570 |
| 1967.............. | 23,217 | 19,466 | 407 | 508 | 818 | 24,222 |
| | | Short-Range Estimated Data, 1967 Amendments (Increasing Earnings)[e] | | | | |
| 1967.............. | $23,210 | $19,486 | $393 | $508 | $ 797 | $ 24,190 |
| 1968.............. | 23,794 | 22,664 | 488 | 459 | 904 | 25,277 |
| 1969.............. | 27,454 | 24,166 | 435 | 530 | 986 | 28,586 |
| 1970.............. | 28,811 | 25,126 | 448 | 619 | 1,136 | 32,340 |
| 1971.............. | 32,478 | 26,145 | 463 | 601 | 1,386 | 38,995 |
| 1972.............. | 33,905 | 27,161 | 478 | 582 | 1,735 | 46,414 |
| | | Long-Run Intermediate-Cost Estimate (Level Earnings)[f] | | | | |
| 1975.............. | $33,619 | $28,447 | $446 | $450 | $ 1,517 | $ 46,781 |
| 1980.............. | 36,508 | 32,766 | 490 | 300 | 2,536 | 74,876 |
| 1985.............. | 38,870 | 37,304 | 530 | 200 | 3,418 | 98,701 |
| 1990.............. | 41,370 | 41,647 | 576 | 120 | 4,082 | 116,620 |
| 1995.............. | 44,602 | 44,998 | 605 | 60 | 4,688 | 133,683 |
| 2000.............. | 48,247 | 46,938 | 631 | 10 | 5,583 | 159,499 |
| 2010.............. | 54,664 | 52,885 | 704 | −45 | 8,711 | 246,839 |
| 2025.............. | 62,585 | 76,292 | 930 | −90 | 10,933 | 302,846 |

[a] A negative figure indicates payment to the trust fund from the Railroad Retirement account, and a positive figure indicates the reverse.

[b] An interest rate of 3.75 percent is used in determining the level costs under the intermediate-cost long-range estimates, but in developing the progress of the trust fund a varying rate in the early years has been used.

[c] Not including amounts in the Railroad Retirement account to the credit of the Old-Age and

mates prove correct. Disability still represents a small part of the total program.

Table 4–9 gives the estimated progress of the disability insurance trust fund on high employment and 3.75 percent interest assumptions combined with intermediate disability cost assumptions. According to this estimate, the fund will grow steadily in the future.

Under the low-cost estimates the fund continues to increase indefinitely, while under the high-cost estimates it increases to a peak of $6.2 billion in 1960 and declines thereafter. The expectation is that the cost will fall between the two estimates and that the fund will approximately level off at some future date.

As of December, 1967, the assets of the disability insurance trust fund totaled $2,029 million and benefit payments were $169 million that month. There were 1,194,000 disabled workers receiving an average of $98 and the monthly benefits in current payment status were $148 million. Dependents' benefits were also being paid to 234,700 wives and 713,000 children of disabled workers. These amounted to an additional $30.7 million per month, an average of $34 per wife and $31 per child.

The past and projected progress of the DI trust fund is shown in Table 4–9.

Actuarial cost estimates for hospital insurance were prepared on assumptions of increasing earnings levels and increasing hospital costs and indicate the system is in actuarial balance over a 25-year period. Table 4–10 shows the actual and estimated progress of the trust fund under low-, high- and intermediate-cost assumptions. The estimated level cost is 1.38 percent of taxable payroll and the level equivalent of the contribution schedule is 1.41 percent, leaving a margin of 0.03 percent. Whether increases in taxable earnings will provide enough revenue to cover constantly increasing hospital costs remains to be seen. It seems likely that future increases in the maximum taxable earnings will be required as well as the already scheduled increases in rate from a combined employer-employee rate of 0.7 percent in 1966 and 1.0 percent in 1967 to an ultimate combined rate of 1.8 percent in 1987 and after.

---

Survivors Insurance trust fund. In millions of dollars, these amounted to $377 for 1953, $284 for 1954, $163 for 1955, $60 for 1956, and nothing for 1957 and thereafter.

d These figures are artificially high because of the method of reimbursements between this trust fund and the Disability Insurance trust fund (and, likewise, the figure for 1959 is too low).

e Contributions include reimbursement for additional cost of noncontributory credit for military service and for the special benefits payable to certain noninsured persons aged 72 or over.

f Contributions include reimbursement for additional cost of noncontributory credit for military service before 1957. No account is taken in this estimate of the outgo for the special benefits payable to certain noninsured persons aged 72 or over or for the additional benefits payable on the basis of noncontributory credit for military service after 1967 or of the corresponding reimbursement therefor, which is exactly counterbalancing from a long-range cost standpoint.

TABLE 4–9

Progress of Disability Insurance Trust Fund
(in millions)

| Calendar Year | Contribu- tions | Benefit Payments | Adminis- trative Expenses | Railroad Retirement Financial Inter- change[a] | Interest on Fund[b] | Balance in Fund at End of Year |
|---|---|---|---|---|---|---|
| | | | *Actual data* | | | |
| 1957...............| $ 702 | $ 57 | $ 3[c] | ... | $ 7 | $ 649 |
| 1958............... | 966 | 249 | 12[c] | ... | 25 | 1,379 |
| 1959............... | 891 | 457 | 50 | $ −22 | 40 | 1,825 |
| 1960............... | 1,010 | 568 | 36 | −5 | 53 | 2,289 |
| 1961............... | 1,038 | 887 | 64 | 5 | 66 | 2,437 |
| 1962............... | 1,046 | 1,105 | 66 | 11 | 68 | 2,368 |
| 1963............... | 1,099 | 1,210 | 68 | 20 | 66 | 2,235 |
| 1964............... | 1,154 | 1,309 | 79 | 19 | 64 | 2,047 |
| 1965............... | 1,188 | 1,573 | 90 | 24 | 59 | 1,606 |
| 1966............... | 2,022 | 1,784 | 137 | 25 | 58 | 1,739 |
| 1967............... | 2,301 | 1,950 | 109 | 31 | 77 | 2,029 |
| | | *Short Range Estimate, 1967 Amendments (Increasing Earnings)* | | | | |
| 1967............... | 2,313 | 1,956 | 107 | 31 | 72 | 2,030 |
| 1968............... | 3,236 | 2,390 | 129 | 44 | 95 | 2,798 |
| 1969............... | 3,517 | 2,608 | 121 | 22 | 131 | 3,695 |
| 1970............... | 3,629 | 2,740 | 123 | 22 | 171 | 4,610 |
| 1971............... | 3,759 | 2,867 | 127 | 25 | 212 | 5,562 |
| 1972............... | 3,880 | 2,985 | 133 | 29 | 253 | 6,548 |
| | | *Long Range Intermediate-Cost Estimate (Level Earnings)* | | | | |
| 1975............... | 3,555 | 3,157 | 131 | −10 | 232 | 6,877 |
| 1980............... | 3,860 | 3,582 | 133 | −16 | 323 | 9,351 |
| 1985............... | 4,109 | 3,891 | 135 | −18 | 413 | 11,856 |
| 1990............... | 4,372 | 4,113 | 138 | −20 | 519 | 14,854 |
| 1995............... | 4,713 | 4,445 | 143 | −20 | 652 | 18,556 |
| 2000............... | 5,097 | 5,037 | 162 | −20 | 788 | 22,276 |
| 2010............... | 5,774 | 6,562 | 210 | −20 | 906 | 25,222 |
| 2025............... | 6,598 | 7,326 | 233 | −20 | 763 | 21,384 |

[a] A negative figure indicates payment to the trust fund from the Railroad Retirement account, and a positive figure indicates the reverse.

[b] An interest rate of 3.75 percent is used in determining the level costs under the intermediate-cost long-range estimates, but in developing the progress of the trust fund a varying rate in
the early years has been used.

[c] These figures are artificially low because of the method of reimbursements between this
trust fund and the Old-Age and Survivors Insurance trust fund (and, likewise, the figure for 1959
is too high).

Note: Contributions include reimbursement for additional cost of noncontributory credit for
military service before 1957. No account is taken in this table of the outgo for the additional
benefits payable on the basis of noncontributory credit for military service after 1967 or of the
corresponding reimbursement therefor, which is exactly counterbalancing from a long-range
cost standpoint.

TABLE 4-10

Estimated Progress of Hospital Insurance Trust Fund
(in millions)

| Calendar Year | Contributions | Benefit Payments | Administra- tive Expenses | Interest on Fund[a] | Balance in Fund at End of Year |
|---|---|---|---|---|---|
| | | *Actual Data* | | | |
| 1966............ | $ 1,911 | $ 767 | $ 57[b] | $ 34 | $ 1,121 |
| 1967............ | 3,508 | 3,353 | 77 | 51 | 1,073 |
| | | *Low-Cost Estimate* | | | |
| 1967............ | 2,943 | 2,683 | 94 | 45 | 1,332 |
| 1968............ | 3,972 | 2,981 | 104 | 70 | 2,289 |
| 1969............ | 4,223 | 3,336 | 117 | 109 | 3,168 |
| 1970............ | 4,391 | 3,649 | 128 | 142 | 3,924 |
| 1971............ | 4,564 | 3,932 | 138 | 169 | 4,587 |
| 1972............ | 4,732 | 4,215 | 148 | 191 | 5,147 |
| 1973............ | 5,274 | 4,499 | 157 | 215 | 5,980 |
| 1974............ | 5,503 | 4,777 | 167 | 242 | 6,781 |
| 1975............ | 5,695 | 5,055 | 177 | 266 | 7,510 |
| | | *High-Cost Estimate* | | | |
| 1967............ | 2,943 | 2,683 | 94 | 45 | 1,332 |
| 1968............ | 3,972 | 3,190 | 112 | 64 | 2,066 |
| 1969............ | 4,223 | 3,795 | 133 | 86 | 2,447 |
| 1970............ | 4,391 | 4,501 | 157 | 85 | 2,265 |
| 1971............ | 4,564 | 5,292 | 185 | 57 | 1,409 |
| 1972............ | 4,732 | 5,960 | 209 | c | c |
| 1973............ | 5,274 | 6,364 | 223 | | |
| 1974............ | 5,503 | 6,762 | 237 | | |
| 1975............ | 5,695 | 7,161 | 251 | | |
| | | *Intermediate-Cost Estimate* | | | |
| 1967............ | 2,943 | 2,683 | 94 | 45 | 1,332 |
| 1968............ | 3,972 | 3,190 | 112 | 64 | 2,066 |
| 1969............ | 4,223 | 3,636 | 127 | 90 | 2,616 |
| 1970............ | 4,391 | 3,982 | 139 | 108 | 2,994 |
| 1971............ | 4,564 | 4,292 | 150 | 117 | 3,233 |
| 1972............ | 4,732 | 4,602 | 161 | 121 | 3,323 |
| 1973............ | 5,274 | 4,912 | 172 | 125 | 3,683 |
| 1974............ | 5,503 | 5,216 | 183 | 132 | 3,874 |
| 1975............ | 5,695 | 5,522 | 193 | 135 | 3,989 |
| 1980............ | 8,087 | 6,940 | 243 | 203 | 6,454 |
| 1985............ | 9,241 | 8,690 | 304 | 373 | 10,731 |
| 1990............ | 11,627 | 10,843 | 380 | 553 | 15,711 |

[a] An interest rate of 3.75 percent is used in determining the level costs, but in developing the progress of the trust fund a varying rate in the early years has been used, ranging down from 5 percent initially to 4 percent after 1975.

[b] Including administrative expenses incurred in 1965.

[c] Fund exhausted in 1972.

Note: The transactions relating to the noninsured persons, the costs for whom is borne out of the general funds of the Treasury, are not included in the above figures. The actual disbursements in 1966, and the balance in the trust fund by the end of the year, have been adjusted by an estimated $174,000,000 on this account. A similar adjustment was made for 1967 in the amount of $338,000,000 in contributions and benefits but not in the fund.

Actuarial cost estimates are not prepared beyond the immediate future for Supplementary Medical Insurance because of the provision for annual changes in the premium rate. A contingency fund of about $345 million is available from the Treasury if needed, until December 31, 1969. It is not expected that any of this will be required.

In the first full calendar year of operations, 1967, premiums collected were $640 million, more than matched by government contributions of $933 million.[27] Interest earned was $11 million and total revenue was $1,282 million. Benefits paid were $1,187 million and administration expense took $110 million, leaving $412 million in the fund. By February 29, the fund was down to $402 million. The $33\frac{1}{3}$ percent premium increase, effective in April, 1968, should keep the fund solvent.

## Workmen's compensation

Workmen's compensation insurance is the oldest social insurance program. The first workmen's compensation legislation was adopted in Germany in the early 1880's, and by 1910 most European countries had systems in effect. By 1967 at least 117 countries had some form of workmen's compensation program.

Workmen's compensation arose out of the common law defining liability of master to servant. Under this common law system, an employee can recover damages for on-the-job injuries from his employer only if he can prove that the employer's negligence was the proximate cause of the injury. It is actually more difficult for an injured worker to collect damages than it is for an outsider. While the law naturally varies among the states, the general principles are as follows. This law largely still applies where workmen's compensation laws do not.

*The law of employer's liability. Duties of employer.* An employer is liable for injuries to employees only if he was negligent. Negligence is the failure to exercise the care which should be exercised under the circumstances by a reasonable and prudent man. The reasonable care required of an employer includes the furnishing of a reasonably safe place to work; reasonably safe materials, tools, and equipment; reasonably fit, competent, and sober fellow workers; adequate safety rules adequately enforced; and reasonably suitable and sufficient warning of dangers of which the employer has knowledge and the worker does not.

*Defenses of employer.* In order to establish a claim for negligence, the employee has to prove the failure of the employer in one of these

---

[27] For reasons unknown, the government matching is slow and irregular. It must pay interest to the fund for the period involved, however. The over-matching in 1967 did not quite catch up with the under-matching in 1966. For the total period July, 1966, to January, 1968, the government contribution was $24,550,000 less than premiums from participants.

respects. In years gone by, even after this had been established, the claim could still be defeated by one of the three famous defenses of the employer: contributory negligence, the "fellow-servant rule," and the doctrine of assumption of risk.

The defense of *contributory negligence* still may be used in almost any action for negligence. If the defendant (employer) can prove that the plaintiff (employee) was himself negligent and that this negligence contributed to the loss, then the defendant is relieved of liability.

The second defense—the *"fellow-servant"* or "common-employee" rule —provided that if the negligence of a fellow employee, rather than that of the employer himself, was the proximate cause of the loss, the injured employee could not recover from the employer. Rather, his action lay against the fellow worker. The rationale of this rule was that fellow workers in a common shop could supervise each other more adequately than the employer could supervise them.

The third defense—*assumption of risk*—was the most far-reaching of all. This rule of law provided that, in taking a job, an employee assumed all the risks usual and incidental to the job which were of common knowledge or which he could reasonably be expected to discover. Presumably he was paid enough to compensate him for assuming these risks, or he would not continue in the employment. Although almost obsolete in employer's liability cases, this defense still is important in other types of tort claim.

The operation of the three defenses might be illustrated through a series of hypothetical cases involving a railroad brakeman. Prior to the adoption of the knuckle coupler (required in 1911 for interstate commerce) the "link and pin" coupler was used to hook railroad cars together. The brakeman had to lift up the pin with a stick or club and then drop it at the proper moment so that the pin passed through the links and attached the cars together. Suppose the brakeman discarded the club, lifted the pin by hand, missed the link, and got crushed between the cars. In this case he (or his heirs) would be unable to collect because of contributory negligence.

On the other hand, suppose he used the club properly, but the engineer was careless, applied the brakes too suddenly, and flipped the brakeman off the step of the car so that he fell beneath the wheels and lost a leg. In this case he would be unable to collect because of the fellow-servant rule. It was the engineer's fault, not the railroad's.

Finally, suppose that neither the brakeman nor the engineer was negligent but that it was a cold, stormy night, the handrails iced up, the brakeman slipped and fell under the wheels. Then he could not collect because of the doctrine of asumption of risk. Icing handrails are a normal risk of the occupation which the brakeman knew about.

One may wonder just what unique combinations of circumstances were required in order that an injured worker might collect damages under this system. Suffice it to say that this did not occur too often. Even where the employee did win the case, damages were quite small and often delayed through a long process of litigation, and usually the lawyer, operating on a contingent fee basis, got half the proceeds. Effective as this system may have been as a device to limit the risks of employers, as a system for compensating injured employees it was a dismal failure.

*Modifications of the common law.*  The recognition of the defects of the common law negligence system as a means of making sure that injured workers were compensated led to two approaches. One was a modification by statute and court decision of the common law principles discussed above. The other, of course, was the development of workmen's compensation.

The doctrine of contributory negligence was modified by the adoption in some jurisdictions of the principle of comparative negligence, by which the person most at fault is held liable. Some courts have modified it by the doctrine of the "last clear chance," whereby, even if the plaintiff was contributorily negligent, the defendant would still be held liable, if he had one "last clear chance" to avoid the accident.

The fellow-servant rule was modified by the "vice-principal" or "superior-servant" rule, according to which the negligence of a superior servant is considered to be the negligence of the employer or principal. Another modification of this is the "con-association" or "department" rule, whereby the fellow-servant defense cannot be raised if the fellow servant was employed in a different department from the injured employee.

The asumption-of-risk doctrine was weakened by some statutes which provided that the knowledge of an employee of violations of safety regulations by the employer did not constitute a bar to recovery.

Employer's liability acts were passed in many states. These frequently embodied one or more of the above modifications, restated much of the common law, prohibited the employer from requiring the employee to contract away his right to sue, and sometimes extended the right of suit to death cases. This latter change had been adopted independently in many American jurisdictions at an earlier date.

*Development of workmen's compensation.*  The study of the workmen's compensation principle began in this country in 1883 and became intense between 1891 and 1916. The various study committees were almost unanimous in condemning the existing liability systems and in recommending major changes. Bills were proposed as early as 1898 in New York, and a law was passed in Maryland in 1902. This bill was very weak, however, and was declared unconstitutional in 1904. Laws passed in Montana and New York in 1909 and 1910 were declared unconstitutional, but in 1911 seven states passed laws which were upheld, and the movement had gained real impetus.

The basic philosophy of workmen's compensation is liability without fault. Instead of basing the right to collect claims on the common law concept of negligence, the law provides that every employer who comes under the law is required to pay compensation to any worker suffering an injury arising out of and/or in the course of employment.

The rationale is that, to a degree, industrial injuries are an inevitable concomitant of the industrial process. Thus they represent a cost of production which, like other costs of production, should be borne in the first instance by the entrepreneur. Theoretically, such costs are included in the price of the product and passed on to the consumer. While this will probably happen in the long run, in the short run the extent to which such cost increases may be passed on depends on the slope and elasticity of the demand curve for the product.

*Compensation laws. Employments covered.*   The early New York law was held unconstitutional on the grounds that it constituted a deprivation of property without due process of law. New York and a number of other states resolved this difficulty by amending their constitutions and later adopting laws which were compulsory as to employers who came under their provisions. Other states, led by New Jersey, adopted an elective law whereby the employer could elect whether or not to be covered. If he elects out of compensation, he loses his three historic common law defenses. Today, out of 54 laws, 23 are on this elective basis. Usually they provide that coverage is presumed unless either employer or employee specifically elects noncoverage and that the employer does not lose his defenses if it is the employee who elects out.

The analysis of workmen's compensation laws is complicated, since there are no less than 54 laws currently in force in the United States. These include 50 states, the District of Columbia, Puerto Rico, and two special federal statutes for federal civilian employees and longshoremen and harbor workers. Only broad generalizations may be made in the face of such heterogeneity.

Even in compulsory laws, not all employees are covered. Both types of law define specifically the employments to which they apply. The laws of 10 states list specifically the occupations (usually the most hazardous) to which they apply or provide that they cover hazardous or extrahazardous occupations generally. The other laws define covered employment by exclusion, that is, they cover all employment with specific exceptions.

In 40 laws, employees of the state are included; in 12 more they are included in part. Federal government employees are covered by a special statute. All but 7 states and Puerto Rico exclude domestic employment, and 4 of these cover it only in part; 31 exclude agricultural employment and 8 cover it in part; and 27 exclude employees of firms with less than a specified number of employees. This number varies from 2 to 15: the usual limits are 3, 4, and 5.

Most states exclude casual employment, but the definition of the term varies. In some states it means temporary workers; in others, workers not in the usual course of the employer's business or occupation; in others, it means irregular or nonrecurring work. In some states a combination of two of these criteria is used. Other less frequent exclusions are employment by nonprofit institutions, high-salaried employees, outworkers, and a variety of special occupations in various states. In many states an employer not otherwise included under the law may elect voluntary coverage.

For workers not covered by workmen's compensation, the principles of employer's liability still apply, as modified by the legislation and court decisions mentioned above. As a result of these various exclusions and limitations, no more than three fourths of American employees are covered by workmen's compensation. The largest occupational group excluded is probably railroad workers, who are covered by the federal Employers' Liability Act.

*Injuries covered.* The early workmen's compensation laws were intended solely for protection against loss resulting from occupational accident. Gradually the laws have been broadened by interpretation or amendment to include a fairly wide coverage of occupational disease. All but one state (Wyoming) have some specific disease coverage, and even in this state the concept of accidental injury is not defined rigorously. Thirty-two laws cover all occupational disease with only specified exceptions; 19 cover only certain diseases listed in a schedule. Sometimes there is a separate statute for occupational disease, but the tendency seems to be to combine both in a single law.

Disability, whether resulting from an accident or disease, is covered only if it is the result of hazards of the employment. All the laws but six require that the injury be both "in the course of" and "arising out of" employment. Four states require only that it be in the course of employment; one requires only that it arise out of employment; and one will cover either.

"In the course of employment" means that the injury must occur while the worker is doing his duty. "Arising out of employment" requires a producer-product relationship. Injury must be produced by the work or the conditions under which it is performed. These conditions must be peculiar to the work, not just to the general environment. All laws exclude certain injuries which result, in effect, from contributory negligence. Self-inflicted injuries and injuries resulting from intoxication, willful act, violation of the law, violation of work rules, failure to use safety devices, and intent to injure another person are the most common exclusions.

*Benefit provisions.* Workmen's compensation laws require that, if a covered worker is injured according to the definition in the law, the employer must pay benefits according to a statutory scale. There are three types of benefit payments: cash, medical expense, and rehabilitation. Only 33 laws make specific provision for the last. Cash benefits vary with wages and severity of injury and, especially in death cases, with number of dependents.

Disability income benefits: Cash benefits are usually a specified percentage (usually 66⅔ percent) of weekly wages, subject to a maximum and minimum weekly benefit. In all but one state there is a waiting period of two to seven days. In most states the waiting period is waived if disability extends for a longer period: 7 to 49 days. Usually partial disability, whether temporary or permanent, is compensated as though it were temporarily total disability; that is, the total disability benefit is paid for a limited period. This period is in excess of any period for which total disability benefits have been paid. In most states, for permanent partial disability, these benefits are discounted and paid as a lump sum.

The total disability weekly benefit as a percentage of wages varies from 50 to 80 percent, depending on state and, sometimes, number of dependents and marital status. Usually it is between 60 and 66⅔ percent. Maximum weekly benefits in dollars range from a low of $35 to a high of $152.30 in Arizona. Twenty-three laws also impose an overall limit on cash benefit, either in terms of a maximum dollar amount, a maximum number of weeks' benefit, or both. Maximum periods range from 330 to 550 weeks; dollar maxima from $12,000 to $30,000. Thirty-one laws pay for duration of disability with no overall limit, but in some the amount per week is reduced after several years.

Death benefits: In death cases the widow usually receives a smaller portion of wages than does a disabled worker. However, these benefits usually are increased if there are dependent children. The maximum for a family tends to be about the same as for total disability. Benefits for a widow alone range from 32½ to 75 percent of wages; for a widow with dependents, from 66⅔ to 85 percent, subject to dollar minima and maxima. Several states provide a fixed dollar scale, usually of low amount, regardless of wages. The period of benefit may be as short as 300 weeks or as long as the duration of widowhood. Many states have an overall dollar limit in lieu of, or in addition to, the maximum period. Two states have lump-sum benefits in lieu of weekly income. Dollar limits vary from $12,000 to $35,100. All but one state provide burial expenses in amounts ranging from $200 to $1,000. In four laws these are payable only if there are no dependents to receive the regular death benefit.

Medical benefits: Medical benefits are provided in all laws. The injured worker does not receive cash, but expenses are paid on his behalf. In 43 laws there is no limit as to amount. In 24 jurisdictions the law specifically provides unlimited benefits; in the others the administrative agency is authorized to extend the benefits indefinitely. In the remaining 11 laws, there are limits as to dollar cost or period of time, or both. The dollar limits range from $2,400 to $35,000; the time limits from 10 weeks to 5 years. Medical expenses include hospital and surgical fees and, in most cases, appliances also. There usually is no waiting period; benefits are payable from the date of disablement. Medical benefits make up about one third of the total workmen's compensation benefit payments. It has been estimated that over seven and one half million disabilities are treated under this program each year.

Only about one third of the states have specific rehabilitation facilities or departments. Twenty more provide additional benefits or retraining allowances and work through the federal-state vocational rehabilitation program. In 1967, 570,000 disabled persons were served by state vocational rehabilitation services and 174,000 were returned to employment. However, it is estimated that there are more than two million persons now disabled who could be made able to work through vocational rehabilitation and that more than 300,000 persons disabled each year could benefit from vocational rehabilitation. This represents an important area in which major financial and even greater human savings are possible.

A problem related to rehabilitation is that of the second injury. Early laws provided that when a worker suffered a second injury the whole cost of the disability would be charged to the current employer, even if the first disability contributed materially to the loss. Thus if a worker who had lost a leg were employed, the employer ran the risk of disability involving loss of use of the good leg, resulting in a severe cost to him, as this would constitute permanent total disability. Under these circumstances, employers were understandably reluctant to hire workers with a partial disability. Sometimes they would hire such workers only if the worker waived his rights to compensation in event of a second injury attributable to, or complicated by, the first. Only a few states today permit such a waiver. Forty-nine have established second-injury funds. These funds, run by the state, pay the difference between the benefit cost of the second injury alone and that of the total. Among other things, this reduces the financial risk to the employer who hires a partially disabled employee. These funds are financed by a charge on employers for death cases where there are no dependents, by assessments on compensation insurers and self-insurers, or by direct state appropriation, in the order of the frequency of the different methods.

*Administration.* Overall supervision of the compensation system is vested in an appropriate state or federal agency. Claim administration is usually handled through a system of boards, but in one state the courts administer claims. Most of the actual detail is handled by employers and insurers on a direct payment or agreement basis, with the board (or court) handling disputed cases only. Under 13 laws, particularly those with monopoly funds, the board settles every claim. In all states, appeal to the courts is possible. However, the appeal usually may involve questions of law only; the decision of the board or commission as to questions of fact usually is conclusive.

*Financing.* The obligation to pay benefits is imposed on the employer who is primarily responsible. Only a few states require employees' participation in financing and then in small amounts. The cost of administration is usually borne partly by the employer or his insurer and partly by the state, but in some states it is borne entirely by employers through assessments on all insurers (including self-insurers).

*Security of benefit.* While the obligation to pay benefits is imposed on the employer, additional requirements are imposed to make sure that this obligation can be fulfilled. Security for injured workers depends on the certainty with which benefits due will be paid. Every state except Louisiana requires the employer to carry insurance, but most permit self-insurance and sometimes define this so loosely that the requirement becomes almost meaningless. Forty-seven jurisdictions permit self-insurance, and in some the standard is merely the submission of an acceptable balance sheet. Forty-five states permit insurance with private insurers. Eight jurisdictions have monopolistic funds, but two of these permit self-insurance. Eleven states have state funds which compete with private insurers and self-insurance.

The workmen's compensation insurance policy issued by private insurers combines compensation and employer's liability insurance in a single contract. This is because employer's liability is residual; cases which do not fall under compensation will give rise to liability claims. State funds do not write employer's liability, and separate employer's liability contracts are sold by private insurers to cover employers in these states or self-insured employers who want liability coverage. The compensation policy is standard by company agreement. Its insuring agreements read as follows:

The Company agrees with the insured, named in the declarations made a part hereof, in consideration of the payment of the premium and in reliance upon the statements in the declarations and subject to the limits of liability, exclusions, conditions and other terms of this policy:

### INSURING AGREEMENTS

I  Coverage A—Workmen's Compensation

To pay promptly when due all compensation and other benefits required of the insured by the workmen's compensation law.

Coverage B—Employers' Liability

To pay on behalf of the insured all sums which the insured shall become legally obligated to pay as damages because of bodily injury by accident or disease, including death at any time resulting therefrom, sustained in the United States of America, its territories or possessions, or Canada by any employee of the insured arising out of and in the course of his employment by the insured either in operations in a state designated in item 3 of the declarations or in operations necessary or incidental thereto.

The provisions as to defense, settlement and supplementary payments are the same as those in most other liability insurance contracts.

No amount of insurance is specified for workmen's compensation. There is no overall limit as to the insurer's liability, and individual benefits are determined, not by the insurance contract, but by the applicable workmen's compensation and occupational disease laws. A limit of liability is stated in the declarations for Coverage B, Employer's Liability. This limit applies to each accident separately, regardless of the number of persons involved, but for disease coverage it applies to the aggregate disease loss in any one state during the policy period (usually one year). Insuring Agreement II applies primarily to the liability insurance and is typical of other liability insurance policies. The costs of defense and other sums are payable in addition to the actual claim and are not subject to the limit of liability.

The social nature of workmen's compensation insurance is evidenced not only by the fact that the only limit of compensation liability is statutory but also by a series of provisions designed to protect the worker from insolvency, default, or poor administration by the employer. Even where the employer is charged with penalty payments for violation of labor standard or safety laws, the insurer is still liable. In such a case, the insurer may recover such amounts from the employer according to the contract. These provisions for the employee's protection are as follows:

8. Statutory Provisions—Coverage A

The company shall be directly and primarily liable to any person entitled to the benefits of the workmen's compensation law under this policy. The obligations of the company may be enforced by such person, or for his benefit by any agency authorized by law, whether against the company alone or jointly with the insured. Bankruptcy or insolvency of the insured or of the insured's estate, or any default of the insured, shall not relieve the company of any of its obligations under coverage A.

As between the employee and the company, notice or knowledge of the injury on the part of the insured shall be notice or knowledge as the case may be, on the part of the company, the jurisdiction of the insured, for the purposes of the workmen's compensation law, shall be jurisdiction of the company and the company shall in all things be bound by and subject to the findings, judgments, awards, decrees, orders or decisions rendered against the insured in the form and manner provided by such law and within the terms, limitations and provisions of this policy not inconsistent with such law.

All of the provisions of the workmen's compensation law shall be and remain a part of this policy as fully and completely as if written herein, so far as they apply to compensation and other benefits provided by this policy and to special taxes, payments into security or other special funds, and assessments required of or levied against compensation insurance carriers under such law.

The insured shall reimburse the company for any payments required of the company under the workmen's compensation law, in excess of the benefits regularly provided by such law, solely because of injury to (a) any employee by reason of the serious and wilful misconduct of the insured, or (b) any employee employed by the insured in violation of law with the knowledge or acquiescence of the insured or any executive officer thereof.

Nothing herein shall relieve the insured of the obligations imposed upon the insured by the other terms of this policy.

These provisions apply only to the compensation coverage. However, a similar clause states that insolvency of the employer will not be a bar to recovery under Coverage B.

Workmen's compensation premiums are based on a unit of exposure of $100 of payroll. The policy provides for an audit by the insurer of the employer's payroll records shortly after the end of the policy year. Premiums vary with state and occupation and, for the larger cases, with the employer's actual experience.

## Nonoccupational disability laws

*Development.* Since workmen's compensation covers income loss from occupational disability and unemployment compensation covers short-term income loss from unemployment, a natural extension of social insurance is in the area of short-term nonoccupational disability. Interest in this area dates from the 1915–20 period when workmen's compensation laws were spreading rapidly, and a renewed interest was demonstrated during the depression of the 1930's. However, despite the fact that bills were introduced in a number of states during these periods, the first actually passed was by Rhode Island in 1942. Subsequent laws provided coverage for employees of the railroads in 1946, and California passed a law in the same year. Laws were passed by New Jersey in 1948 and by New York and Washington in 1949. The Washington law was defeated in a referendum in 1950. Puerto Rico passed a law in 1968.

All of these laws, except that of New York, grew out of unemployment compensation. The reasons were as follows: Temporary disability produces an income loss similar to that produced by unemployment, and it is logical to treat both under the same program. It is logical to continue the checks from the same fund if an unemployed worker becomes disabled. Further, some states had built up funds in their accounts under the Unemployment Trust Fund from employees' contributions to the unemployment compensation plan. These accumulated funds and contributions could be used to finance the disability coverage. A federal law permitted the release of these accumulated funds for this purpose. New York's law, on the other hand, is an extension of the workmen's compensation law. It was felt that both disability programs should be administered in the same way; there were no accumulations or contributions to help with financing; and the workmen's compensation system permitted private carriers to compete.

*Coverage.* Except under the New York law, the employments covered are the same as under the unemployment compensation act. The railway workers act covers only employees of interstate railroads and related firms, such as the railway express companies. The New Jersey law covers employers of four or more employees in a period of 20 weeks; the California and Rhode Island laws cover employers of one or more; but in California a payroll of at least $100 in at least one quarter is required. The New York law covers employers of one or more workers on each of 30 days in one calendar year. Farm laborers, railroad, and government employees and employees of certain nonprofit organizations generally are excluded under all the state laws. California has the only law to cover farm workers. However, state employees and, optionally, employees of political subdivisions are covered in Rhode Island. In New York all but certain professional employees of nonprofit organizations are covered and so are employees of public authorities at the election of the authority. Domestic servants are excluded in all but New York where four or more such employees are covered. Students in New York and New Jersey, casual workers in New York, and real estate salesmen in California are other categories of persons not covered.

In order to be covered, an employee must have a record of attachment to the labor force. This is expressed in terms of minimum earnings or minimum time worked in covered employment. In New York four consecutive weeks of covered employment are required or 25 days of regular part-time employment; in New Jersey 17 weeks earning at least $15 per week, in covered employment during the base year, is required.

The railroad law requires earnings of $500 in covered employment during the base year; Rhode Island requires earnings of $1,200 in the base year or $20 in each of 20 weeks; and California requires earnings of $300 during the base year.

*Benefits.* Generally the benefits are one half to two thirds of the average weekly wage. The formula or schedule is different for each law. Minimum weekly benefits are $20 in New York (or average weekly wage if less), $25 in California; $22.50 under the railroad law; $12 in Rhode Island; and $10 in the other two laws. Maximum weekly benefit is $50 in New Jersey and New York; $51 under the railroad law; and California and Rhode Island have a fluctuating maximum weekly benefit dependent on the average weekly wage of all individuals in covered employment during the preceding calendar year (two-thirds in California and one-half in Rhode Island). In California such maximum may not fall below $77. Rhode Island provides an additional benefit of $3 per dependent child under 16 years of age up to a weekly total of $12. Maximum duration is

26 weeks after a seven-day waiting period under all laws. The Rhode Island law will pay up to 12 weeks for maternity; New Jersey 8; and the railroad law up to 116 days. The others pay no maternity benefit. California provides hospital coverage of $12 per day for up to 20 days for which there is no waiting period, but currently only for on-the-job injuries, by order of the Governor.

New York covers nonoccupational disability benefits only. The New Jersey law does not pay benefits if workmen's compensation benefits are payable. In California, if temporary workmen's compensation benefits have been paid and the disability benefit is larger, the excess will be paid under the disability law; if permanent compensation benefits are paid, the full disability benefit will be payable. In Rhode Island the total benefit from the temporary disability law and workmen's compensation is limited to 85 percent of the employee's average weekly wage not to exceed $62 per week, not including dependents' benefits. The railroad law covers nonoccupational and occupational disability alike. Railroad workers, of course, do not have workmen's compensation protection. If a worker should be entitled, by some strange turn of events, to workmen's compensation, the excess of disability benefits, if any, is paid. A person who is receiving unemployment compensation benefits is disqualified under all laws and, except in Rhode Island, a person who is ineligible for unemployment compensation is similarly disqualified. In New Jersey, New York, and California, salary or wage continuation plans may reduce the benefit or disqualify completely. New York and New Jersey benefits are similarly reduced by certain public and private pension benefits.

*Financing.* In all but the railroad law, employee contributions are required. The amount is 0.5 percent of the first $60 of weekly wages in New York; 0.5 percent of the first $3,600 of annual wages in New Jersey; 1 percent of the first $3,600 in Rhode Island; 1 percent of $7,400 in California; 0.5 percent of the first $7,800 in Puerto Rico. The employer pays the entire cost (as a part of his unemployment tax) in the railroad plan, and the balance of cost in New York and under private plans in New Jersey and Puerto Rico. In the New Jersey state plan employers pay from 0.10 percent to 0.75 percent of the first $3,600 of annual wages, based on experience rating.

In the railroad plan and the Rhode Island plan, there is a monopolistic government insurer. In California, New Jersey, and Puerto Rico all eligible employers are automatically insured in a state fund until the state approves an acceptable private plan. The private plan may be insured with an insurance company or self-insured. In order for a private plan to be approved, it must be at least as liberal in New Jersey and more liberal in California and Puerto Rico than the state plan. A majority of employees must consent to the private plan in both states. If they do, all employees are covered by the private plan in New Jersey, but only those who consent in California. California will not approve a private plan if it results in substantial adverse selection against the state fund. The definition of substantial adverse selection currently is unrealistically strict.[28] In California, due to the stiff requirements of the 1963 law, private insurers are now writing less than 2 percent of the national coverage. Before the law the private insurers in California paid out nearly one fifth of the total national benefits. In Puerto Rico, private insurers must pay to the state fund enough "to avoid an actuarial disadvantage to the Fund."

In New York the state fund is truly competitive. Positive action of the employer is required in order to insure with a private company or with the fund. Benefits of private plans must be at least the equivalent of the minimums stated in the law. The New York fund is subject to the same regulations and pays the same taxes as do private insurers. In New York about 96 percent of covered employees are covered by private insurance. The employer's premium is reduced by experience rating in New Jersey and in the railroad plan. Private companies may use experience rating.

TABLE 4–11

Benefit Payments, Temporary Disability Insurance Laws, 1948–66
(in millions of dollars)

| | | Type of Insurance Arrangement | | |
|---|---|---|---|---|
| | | Private Plans | | Publicly Operated Funds |
| Year | Total | Group Insurance | Self-Insurance | |
| 1948 | $ 66.4 | $ 9.0 | $ 0.3 | $ 57.1 |
| 1949 | 89.2 | 22.3 | 4.8 | 62.1 |
| 1950 | 117.4 | 41.7 | 12.6 | 63.1 |
| 1951 | 174.2 | 81.1 | 32.2 | 60.9 |
| 1952 | 202.3 | 92.5 | 35.3 | 74.5 |
| 1953 | 230.2 | 102.0 | 37.7 | 90.5 |
| 1954 | 235.1 | 96.2 | 35.8 | 103.1 |
| 1955 | 244.6 | 97.0 | 38.2 | 109.4 |
| 1956 | 265.0 | 109.7 | 41.5 | 113.8 |
| 1957 | 305.3 | 129.5 | 48.6 | 127.2 |
| 1958 | 325.1 | 132.7 | 51.0 | 141.4 |
| 1959 | 353.2 | 135.2 | 54.3 | 163.7 |
| 1960 | 368.2 | 138.1 | 58.0 | 172.1 |
| 1961 | 396.6 | 141.3 | 60.1 | 195.2 |
| 1962 | 416.3 | 143.7 | 60.6 | 212.0 |
| 1963 | 442.2 | 130.6 | 67.6 | 243.9 |
| 1964 | 455.8 | 123.2 | 68.2 | 264.4 |
| 1965 | 466.3 | 124.4 | 72.8 | 269.1 |
| 1966 | 481.9 | 131.2 | 77.5 | 273.2 |

Source: Alfred M. Skolnik, "Income Loss Protection Against Illness," *Social Security Bulletin,* January, 1968, p. 9.

---

[28] See below, p. 542.

All the laws make some provision for paying benefits to workers who become disabled while unemployed. These are paid from the appropriate government fund. In California there is a fund, the interest on which is intended to provide such benefits. If it is insufficient, assessments may be made on all insurers, including the state fund, up to 0.2 percent of taxable wages. In New Jersey there is a comparable fund but the maximum assessment is 0.02 percent of taxable wages. New York set up a fund by a tax of 0.1 percent of wages in the first six months of 1950 which is maintained at $12 million by assessment on insurers once each year if necessary.

Table 4–11 indicates the magnitude of the program and the distribution of benefit payments by type of insurer. The publicly operated funds include Rhode Island and the railroad law, both of which are monopolistic government insurers. The proportion of benefit payments provided by private plans has been declining as the result of a shift towards the state funds in California and New Jersey.

## Summary

Social insurance is insurance which is compulsory by law. It may be written by a government or by a private carrier. It should be distinguished from state insurance, which is insurance (social or otherwise) written by a government insurer. It also should be distinguished from private insurance, which is written on a voluntary basis. There are three main types of social insurance against poor health in the United States at present.

Public Assistance programs attempt to give people who are below or near the poverty level, a minimum income and adequate medical care. The programs are sponsored jointly by the federal and state governments on a matching-of-funds basis.

Workmen's compensation largely has replaced the common law of negligence liability as a means of providing benefits for income loss and medical expense produced by occupational injury and disease. State laws prescribe coverage and benefits, but the insurance largely is written by private insurance companies.

There are five state, and one federal, programs for compulsory nonoccupational disability insurance. The coverage required is substantially similar to that provided by private group insurance, and private companies may write the coverage in three of the states and Puerto Rico.

The federal Old-Age, Survivors, and Disability Insurance program provides a waiver of premium for periods of total disability and income benefits to disabled workers and their eligible dependents and to persons disabled as children and their mothers where they were dependent on a deceased worker or are dependent on a retired or disabled worker. It also provides benefits for certain disabled widows and widowers over age 50.

The popularly termed Medicare program provides compulsory Hospital Insurance for all persons over 65 eligible for OASDI, Railroad Retirement, and certain others under transitional provisions. It is financed by a tax on all earnings in covered employment. It also provides Supplementary Medical Insurance, a voluntary program for people over age 65 financed by a premium (currently $4 per month) which is matched from general national government revenue.

## Selected references

*See the following items from the General Bibliography: 13; 15, chs. 52, 53, and 54; 16, Vol. II Supps. XII A-E and XIII A and B; 19, ch. 25; 29; 30, pp. 50–53.*

ALLEN, DAVID. "Health Insurance for the Aged: Participating Home Health Agencies," *Social Security Bulletin*, Vol. 30, No. 9 (September, 1967), p. 12.

ALTMEYER, A. J. *Formulating a Disability Insurance Program:* Inter-American Committee to Promote Social Security, 1942.

————. *The Formative Years of Social Security.* Madison: The University of Wisconsin Press, 1966.

ARMSTRONG, BARBARA NACHTRIEB. *Insuring the Essentials.* New York: Macmillan Co., Inc., 1940.

AVERBOOK, MARVIN S. "The Malingery Problem in Disability Insurance," *Review of Insurance Studies*, Vol. 11, p. 70.

BACHMAN, GEORGE W. AND MERIAM, LEWIS. *The Issue of Compulsory Health Insurance.* Washington, D.C.: The Brookings Institution, 1948.

BAHMER, ROBERT H. *United States Government Organization Manual 1967–68.* Washington, D.C.: USGPO, 1967.

BALL, ROBERT M. "Health Insurance for People Aged 65 and Over: First Steps in Administration," *Social Security Bulletin*, Vol. 29, No. 2 (February, 1966), p. 3.

BAYO, FRANCISCO. *United States Population Projections for OASDHI Cost Estimates.* U.S. Department of Health, Education, and Welfare, Social Security Administration, Office of the Actuary, Actuarial Study No. 62, Washington, D.C.: USGPO, 1966.

BERKOWITZ, MONROE. *Workmen's Compensation.* New Jersey: Rutgers University Press, 1960.

BLUE CROSS ASSOCIATION. *Blue Cross and Medicare: A Report to the Nation.* Chicago, 1966.

BREWSTER, AGNES W. *Health Insurance and Related Proposals for Financing Personal Health Services.* Washington, D.C.: USGPO, 1958.

BURNS, EVELINE. *Social Security and Public Policy.* New York: McGraw-Hill Book Co., Inc., 1956.

CHAMBER OF COMMERCE OF THE UNITED STATES. *Analysis of Workmen's Compensation Laws.* Washington, D.C., 1967.

CHEIT, EARL F. *Injury and Recovery in the Course of Employment.* New York: John Wiley and Sons, Inc., 1961.

——, AND GORDON, MARGARET S. *Occupational Disability and Public Policy.* New York: John Wiley and Sons, Inc., 1963.

COHEN, WILBUR J. "The First 100 Days of Medicare," *Public Health Report,* Vol. 81, No. 12, December, 1966.

——, *et al.* "Social Security Payments to Noninsured Persons," *Social Security Bulletin,* Vol. 29, No. 9, September, 1966.

COMMERCE CLEARING HOUSE. *Medicare and Social Security Explained.* New York, 1965.

DEVITT, J. E. *et al.* "Social Security Amendments of 1965," Health Insurance Association of America, Individual Insurance Forum, 1966.

DICKERSON, O. D. "Review: 'Social Security and Public Policy' by Eveline Burns," *Journal of Insurance,* Vol. XXIV, p. 99.

——. "The 1965 Social Security Amendments and Private Insurance," *Annals of the Society of Chartered Property & Casualty Underwriters,* September, 1966, p. 227.

DICKENSON, FRANK G. "The Social Security Principle," *The Journal of Insurance,* Vol. XXVII, No. 4, pp. 1–13.

DYERS, JOHN K., JR. "Integration of Private Pension Plans with Social Security," *Journal of the American Society of Chartered Life Underwriters,* Vol. XXI, No. 2 (April, 1967), p. 47.

FARLEY, JARVIS AND BILLINGS, ROGER. "An Approach to a Philosophy of Social Insurance," *Proceedings of the Casualty Actuarial Society,* Vol. XXIX, p. 29.

FEINGOLD, EUGENE. *Medicare: Policy and Politics.* San Francisco: Chandler Publishing Co., 1966.

FROHLICH, PHILIP AND HABER, LAWRENCE D. "Disability Insurance and Public Assistance; A Study of APTD Recipients," *Social Security Bulletin* (August, 1966), p. 3.

GREENFIELD, MARGARET. *Health Insurance for the Aged: The 1965 Program for Medicare.* Berkeley: University of California, Institute of Governmental Studies, 1966.

HABER, LAWRENCE D. *The Disabled Worker Under OASDI.* Washington, D.C.: USGPO, 1964.

HABER, WILLIAM AND COHEN, WILBUR J. *Social Security—Programs, Problems, and Policies.* Homewood, Ill.: Richard D. Irwin, Inc., 1960.

HANCHETT, PAUL E. AND McCOY, GEORGE R. "An Actuarial Appraisal of Congressional Proposals for Hospital Insurance for the Aged," *Journal of Risk and Insurance,* Vol. XXXI, No. 4 (December, 1964), p. 597.

HEALTH INSURANCE ASSOCIATION OF AMERICA. *Title XIX Bulletins.* Chicago, Irregular.

HESS, ARTHUR E. "Medicare's Early Months: A Program Round-Up," *Social Security Bulletin,* Vol. 30, No. 7 (July, 1967), p. 4.

HOBBS, C. W. *Workmen's Compensation Insurance.* New York: McGraw-Hill Book Co., Inc., 1939.

KAPPEL, JOSEPH W. *New Developments and Progress in Health, Education and Welfare.* Washington, D.C.: USGPO, 1961.

LEWAND, FRANK. *Formulation of a Federal Invalidity Insurance Program.* Philadelphia: University of Pennsylvania, 1940.

MALISOFF, HARRY. "Welfare and Social Insurance in a Great Society," *Journal of Risk and Insurance,* Vol. XXXIII, No. 4 (December, 1966), p. 513.

McCAHAN, DAVID. *State Insurance in the United States.* Philadelphia: University of Pennsylvania Press, 1929.

MELONE, JOSEPH J. "Trends in Social Insurance Programs—An International Perspective," *Journal of The American Society of Chartered Life Underwriters,* Vol. XXI, No. 2 (April, 1967), p. 39.

MERIAM, L. *Relief and Social Security.* Washington, D.C.: The Brookings Institution, 1946.

MERRIAM, IDA C. *Social Security Programs in the United States.* Washington, D.C.: USGPO, 1966.

MORGAN, JAMES N. et al. *Income and Welfare in the United States.* New York: McGraw-Hill Book Co., Inc., 1962.

MYERS, ROBERT J. *Actuarial Cost Estimates for Hospital Insurance Act of 1965 and Social Security Amendments of 1965.* U.S. Department of Health, Education, and Welfare, Social Security Administration, Division of the Actuary, Actuarial Study No. 59, Washington, D.C.: USGPO, January, 1965.

————. *Actuarial Cost Estimates for Hospital Insurance Bill.* U.S. Department of Health, Education, and Welfare, Social Security Administration, Division of the Actuary, Actuarial Study No. 57, Washington, D.C.: USGPO, July, 1963.

————. "A Method of Automatically Adjusting Maximum Earnings Base Under OASDI," *Journal of Risk and Insurance,* Vol. XXXI, No. 3 (September, 1964), p. 329.

————. "Role of Social Insurance in Providing Fringe Benefits," *Journal of Risk and Insurance,* Vol. XXXII, No. 2 (June, 1965), p. 267.

————. *Social Insurance and Allied Government Programs.* Homewood, Ill.: Richard D. Irwin, Inc., 1965.

————, AND BAUGHMAN, CHARLES B. *History of Cost Estimates for Hospital Insurance.* U.S. Department of Health, Education, and Welfare, Social Security Administration, Division of the Actuary, Actuarial Study No. 61, Washington, D.C.: USGPO, December, 1966.

————, AND BAYO, FRANCISCO. *Long-Range Estimates for Old-Age, Survivors, and Disability Insurance System 1963.* U.S. Department of Health, Education, and Welfare, Social Security Administration, Division of the Actuary, Actuarial Study No. 58, Washington, D.C.: USGPO, November, 1963.

————. *Long-Range Cost Estimates for Old-Age, Survivors, and Disability Insurance System 1966.* U.S. Department of Health, Education, and Welfare, Social Security Administration, Division of the Actuary, Actuarial Study No. 63, Washington, D.C.: USGPO, January, 1967.

NEWMAN, MONROE. "Issues in Temporary Disability Insurance," *Journal of Insurance,* Vol. XXIV, No. 1, p. 61.

NEW YORK (STATE) DEPARTMENT OF LABOR. *Studies in Disability Insurance.* Special Bulletin No. 224. Albany, 1949.

PETERSON, RAY M. "Misconceptions and Missing Perceptions of Our Social Security System (Actuarial Anesthesia)," *Transactions of the Society of Actuaries,* Vol. XI, No. 31 (November, 1959), p. 812.

SANDERS, BARKEY S. "What Would 'Medicare' Cost?" *Journal of Risk and Insurance,* Vol. XXXII, No. 4 (December, 1965), p. 579.

SCHMULOWITZ, JACOB AND LYNN, HENRY D. *Insured and Disabled Workers under the Social Security Disability Program.* Washington, D.C.: USGPO, 1966.

SCHWARTZ, M. J. "New York Statutory Disability Benefits Law, Coverage, Rates, and Rating Plans," *Proceedings of the Casualty Actuarial Society,* Vol. XXXVI, p. 57.

————. "New York Disability Benefits Law Insurance Experience, 1951–1954," *Proceedings of the Casualty Actuarial Society,* Vol. XLII, p. 8.

SIMONSON, RICHARD C. *Programs of the U.S. Department of Health, Education, and Welfare.* Parts I & II, Washington, D.C.: USGPO, 1964.

SKOLNIK, ALFRED M. "Temporary Disability Insurance Laws in the U.S.," *Social Security Bulletin* (October, 1952), p. 11.

————. "New Benchmarks in Workmen's Compensation," *Social Security Bulletin* (June, 1962), p. 3.

————. "Twenty-five Years of Workmen's Compensation Statistics," *Social Security Bulletin,* Vol. 29, No. 10 (October, 1966), p. 3.

SOMERS, HERMAN MILES AND SOMERS, ANNE RAMSAY. *Workmen's Compensation.* New York: John Wiley and Sons, 1954.

STEWART, WILLIAM H. "The Positive Impact of Medicare on the Nation's Health Care Systems," *Social Security Bulletin,* Vol. 30, No. 7 (July, 1967), p. 9.

THORÉ, EUGENE M. "The Ingratiating Intervention," *Journal of the American Association of University Teachers of Insurance* (March, 1955), p. 40.

TURNBULL, JOHN G. *The Changing Faces of Economic Insecurity.* Minneapolis: The University of Minnesota Press, 1966.

U.S. CONGRESS, HOUSE OF REPRESENTATIVES. *Compilation of the Social Security Laws.* (89th Congress, 1st Session, Document No. 312), Washington, D.C.: USGPO, 1965, Vol. I & II.

————. *Social Security Amendments of 1967 Conference Report.* (90th Congress, Session 1, Report No. 1030), Washington, D.C.: USGPO, 1967.

————. *Social Security Amendments of 1967.* (Public Law 90–248, 90th Congress, H.R.) Washington, D.C.: USGPO, 1968.

U.S. DEPARTMENT OF HEALTH, EDUCATION, AND WELFARE. *New Devolpments and Progress in Health, Education, and Welfare Programs 1961–63.* Washington, D.C.: USGPO, 1963.

U.S. Department of Health, Education, and Welfare, Social Security Administration. *Conditions of Participation for Extended Care Facilities.* Washington, D.C.: USGPO, 1966.

———. *Conditions of Participation for Hospitals,* Washington, D.C.: USGPO, 1966.

———. *Conditions of Participation for Home Health Agencies.* Washington, D.C.: USGPO, 1966.

———. *Conditions for Coverage of Services of Independent Laboratories.* Washington, D.C.: USGPO, 1966.

———. *Health Insurance under Social Security.* Washington, D.C.: USGPO, 1966.

———. *Health Insurance Enrollment under Social Security July 1, 1966.* Washington, D.C.: USGPO, July 1, 1966.

———. *Principles of Provider Reimbursement,* Washington, D.C.: USGPO, 1966.

———. *Social Security Handbook.* Washington, D.C.: USGPO, 1966.

———. *Social Security Programs in the United States.* Washington, D.C.: USGPO, 1966.

———. *Special Payments for People 72 or Over under a Change Made in the Social Security Law in 1966.* Washington, D.C.: USGPO, 1966.

U.S. Department of Labor, Bureau of Labor Standards. *State Workmen's Compensation Laws: A Comparison of Major Provisions with Recommended Standards.* Bulletin No. 212, Washington, D.C.: USGPO, Revised, 1967.

U.S. Railroad Retirement Board. *Annual Reports.* Washington, D.C.: USGPO, annual.

University of Florida Institute on Gerontology. *Medical Care under Social Security: Potentials and Problems.* Gainesville: University of Florida Press, 1966.

Waldman, Saul. "OASDI Benefits, Prices, and Wages: 1966 Experience," *Social Security Bulletin,* Vol. 30, No. 6 (June, 1967), p. 9.

Wenck, Thomas L. "Financing Senior Citizens Health Care: An Alternative Approach," *Journal of Risk and Insurance,* Vol. XXXII, No. 2 (June, 1965), p. 165.

Williams, Walter. "The Social Security and Pension Fund Systems—Their Place in the American Value Structure," *Journal of Risk and Insurance,* Vol. XXXI, No. 3 (September, 1964), p. 431.

Williamson, W. Rulon. "Social Budgeting," *Proceedings of The Casualty Actuarial Society,* Vol. XXIV, p. 17.

———. "Some Backgrounds to American Social Security," *Proceedings of The Casualty Actuarial Society,* Vol. XXX, p. 5.

Witte, Edwin E. *The Development of the Social Security Act.* Madison: University of Wisconsin Press, 1963.

## chapter 5

A matter of Law, not of logic.—Elkin

# Private Health Insurance Contracts

## Introduction

A contract often is defined as "an agreement enforceable by law." The insurance contract represents the agreement between the insurer and the insured. If it is properly drawn and executed, the law will enforce it. It defines the rights and responsibilities of the parties, and the insured must look to the contract for a definition of his protection.

In individual insurance the policy is issued by the company to the individual insured, and the policy, with the application, if attached, and other attached papers, if any, constitutes the entire contract. In group insurance there is a master policy issued by the company to an employer, trustee, or association, and the individual insured's rights are evidenced by a certificate. In insurance written by fraternal and mutual benefit organizations and some nonprofit plans, the charter and/or by-laws of the association may be a part of the contract. In social insurance there is sometimes no policy as such, but the laws establishing the plan and the administrative and court law interpreting them constitute the "contract" which defines the rights and duties of the insured.

Regardless of the formal nature of the arrangement, the obligation of the insurer must be carefully defined and limited by clearly delineating the losses covered and the requirements for coverage and benefit eligibility. This chapter will discuss the fundamental principles applicable to all health insurance contracts. Since various types of coverage are considered in more detail in the following chapters, the treatment here will be rather general. Since the law is more clearly defined in regard to individual policies, these generally will be used for illustration.

193

### Requisites of a valid contract[1]

Except in some social insurance, the health insurance policy is a voluntary contract between private parties and, as such, must meet the requisites of a valid contract at common law.[2] The detailed presentation of insurance or business law is beyond the scope of this book, but it is appropriate to comment briefly on each of these requisites, with emphasis on the law peculiar to insurance contracts.

*Offer and acceptance.* A contract comes into being by the manifestation of mutual assent by the parties. Generally, this is accomplished by the acceptance by one party of an offer made by another. An offer must be definite, and it must be communicated to the other party.

In life and health insurance, where the premium is paid at the time of the application, the application is the offer, and its acceptance by the company, on the exact same terms as applied for, creates a binding contract. Acceptance usually is evidenced by the issuance of the policy. Ordinarily, communication of the acceptance is necessary, but, where the premium has been paid in advance, some courts have held that some other act of the insurer indicating an intent to accept is sufficient. Certainly, constructive delivery by mailing the policy to the insured or the agent is sufficient. Other courts have held that unreasonable delay in rejecting the application and returning the premium implies acceptance. Some have reached a similar conclusion on grounds of negligence, holding that, while there was no acceptance, the insurer is nevertheless liable in tort (a civil wrong for which damages may be claimed) for its negligence in delaying response.

Private companies frequently issue "binding receipts" when the premium is paid in advance. These receipts vary in detail but provide essentially that the applicant is insured from the date of the application (or of the medical exam), provided that the company shall be satisfied that on that date he was insurable for the amount and on the plan applied for. Since this gives coverage only on this condition, it is sometimes more properly called a "conditional receipt." One large company uses the following phraseology, employing the term "conditional receipt" in a different context:

This receipt . . . shall operate as a BINDING RECEIPT only under the conditions hereafter set forth under Paragraph "First."

*First*—If the full first premium in accordance with the published rates of the Company for the form of policy applied for in Questions 7 and 8 has been

---

[1] A requisite is an element without which the contract is void from the beginning.

[2] Five states have codes of contract law, but, even here, case law is of great importance because of the generality of these statutes.

paid at the time of making such application, the insurance subject to the terms and conditions of the policy contract applied for and in use by the Company at this date, shall take effect on the date hereof provided (1) a later effective date is not requested in the application, Part one, (2) the application as completed as agreed therein, (3) the applicant is on this date a risk acceptable to the Company under its rules, limits, and standards, on the plan and for the amount applied for and at the rate of premium declared paid, and (4) the applicant is on this date in good health; otherwise, the payment evidenced hereby shall be returned upon demand and surrender of this receipt.

Second—This receipt shall operate as a conditional receipt if the insurance is not effective coincident herewith under the exact conditions heretofore stipulated or if a policy differing in form, amount or premium from that applied for is offered, in which event no insurance shall be considered in effect under the application herein referred to unless and until the full first premium is paid and a policy actually delivered to and accepted by the applicant during the continued good health of the applicant.

In this case the insurer is considered to have made a conditional offer and the applicant to have accepted it. This makes the contract effective immediately, subject to the condition that the applicant was insurable at the time payment was made.

Even when the premium has been paid in advance, if the company issues a different policy or amount or charges a different rate, this constitutes a counteroffer to the applicant's offer, and there is no contract until he accepts the new offer. The latter situation is covered by the second paragraph of the receipt above, which merely restates the general law. Where the premium is not paid in advance, of course, no receipt is given.

When the applicant does not pay the premium with the application, the issuance of a policy by the company constitutes an offer, which must be accepted by the applicant by paying the premium (or promising such a payment).

*Consideration.* In order for a contract to be binding, there must be consideration (or execution under seal). The consideration is the reason for contracting, which means that something of value must be exchanged for the promise. A contract where the exchange of value for value has already been made is called *executed.* Where something remains to be done by one or more parties, the contract is referred to as *executory.*

An executory contract may be *unilateral,* where only one party still has a promise to perform, or *bilateral,* where both parties have promises outstanding. Since the insurance premium usually is paid in advance, most insurance policies are unilateral contracts. The payment of future premiums is not a promise of the insured, for which he can be haled into court and forced to pay, but merely a condition precedent to performance of the insurer's promise. For this reason and because the performance by the insurer depends on a future event or condition (the occurrence of the loss), the insurance policy is also a *conditional contract*.

Since this future event may or may not occur, depending on chance, the policy is referred to as an *aleatory contract*. An aleatory contract is one where performance by one or more parties depends on chance. Because of this, the consideration need not be proportionate. Gambling contracts also are aleatory contracts. The presence of insurable interest distinguishes the two, as indicated below.

*Reality of consent.* The agreement between the parties must represent a real agreement. There must be a definite understanding, and neither party should be motivated by deceit, force, or undue influence. Specifically, the agreement must be free of mutual mistake, coercion, undue influence, fraud, concealment, misrepresentation, and breach of warranty. The last three of these do not make a contract void but may make it voidable or unenforceable.

*Mutual mistake* involves a situation where both parties are mistaken as to a material fact. Mistakes of *law*, however, will not make a contract voidable. In mutual mistake, courts will relieve the parties of their obligations under the contract or reform it. If the mistake runs to the heart of the contract, the contract is void. For example, if the agent made an error and quoted the premium for a much cheaper policy than the one the insured wanted, and both were under the impression that this was the correct rate for this policy, there would be no contract. The company could not be forced to issue (say) a major medical policy at the rate for hospital insurance, nor could the insured be forced to pay a higher premium than the one quoted to him. In this instance the same conclusions could have been reached on grounds of offer and acceptance.

*Coercion* involves the inducement of a party to contract by force or threat thereof. Such a contract is not valid. For example, if the agent, attempting to deliver a policy, found that the insured had changed his mind and then forced him to pay the premium at gunpoint, the insured would have a right to recover from the company.

*Undue influence* represents a somewhat similar situation: here the pressure results not from force, but from the close relationship of the parties. If, for example, a trusted nephew and adviser persuaded his elderly aunt to purchase large amounts of insurance she did not need, so that he could earn the commission, she would probably be able to recover her premium payments.

*Fraud* represents a misrepresentation of a material fact, knowingly or with reckless disregard so as to imply a deliberate intent to deceive the other party to his deteriment. There must be an actual loss to him resulting from such deception. Proof of such intent is quite difficult, and the injured party usually finds it perferable to seek relief on less rigorous grounds, such as misrepresentation.[3]

*Concealment* involves the withholding of information. In order to avoid liability on grounds of concealment, an insurer must show that the concealment was material, intentional, and, of course, that such a fact was withheld, concealed, or hidden. A fact is considered material if the insurer, had it known the fact, would have declined the application or issued a policy different in type, amount, or rate. The requirement of intent is imposed so that an insured will not be penalized for mere silence. Generally speaking, no intent to conceal can be shown unless the insurer made inquiry, generally by means of the application. An exception is where the fact is so important that the courts will assume that any applicant, no matter how ignorant or stupid, would know that the company wanted the information. For example, the fact that the insured is already dead would fall into this category. If the applicant makes any kind of a positive answer, such as "no" or "none," this is not concealment but a representation. A concealment would involve leaving the space blank or giving (say) a partial list of ailments, omitting one or more.

In order to avoid a contract on grounds of *misrepresentation,* an insurer must show that the statement which was made was both false and material. However, since the applicant made a positive statement, it is not necessary to show that the misrepresentation was intentional. In effect, the law presumes that a person intends to say what he actually does say. The test of materiality is the same as for concealment. In some states the doctrine of misrepresentation has been modified to require intent to deceive for recision of a contract.

A *warranty* is a statement or promise in a contract, which, the parties agree, will have the effect of making the contract voidable in the event of a literal breach. It is not necessary that the breach of warranty be material or intentional: technical falsity is sufficient. Since the effect of such a provision is to penalize an applicant for what may be a completely unintentional or immaterial misstatement, the law has tended to interpret the doctrine of warranty rather narrowly. Most states have adopted statutes which provide that any statement in a policy or application for life or health insurance shall be treated as a representation, even if it purports to be a warranty. This has the effect of prohibiting the use of warranties in these lines.

This gives an illustration of the principle that, wherever possible,

---

[3] See C. C. Cox, *Accident and Health Policy Provisions Manual* (Chicago: privately published, 1960), pp. 79–82, for a good discussion of fraud in connection with health insurance contracts. See also J. E. Greider and W. T. Beadles, *Law and the Life Insurance Contract* (rev. ed.; Homewood, Ill.: Richard D. Irwin, Inc., 1968), pp. 231 ff.

the courts give the benefit of the doubt to the insured when the contract is ambiguous. This is because the insurance policy is a *contract of adhesion*. A contract of adhesion is one which one party has made up and to which the other must adhere if he wants to enter into an agreement. Insurers have drawn up the policy forms, and any ambiguity is resolved in the insured's favor, since he had no power to negotiate regarding wording, punctuation, and the like. To the extent that the contract represents a required statutory language or the regulation of provisions by state insurance departments, the reason for this principle no longer exists. Many courts have recognized this and modified their application of the rule accordingly.

Nonetheless, the insurance policy is said to be a contract *uberrimae fidei*, that is, of utmost good faith. This seems to mean that the parties are held to a higher standard of honesty and integrity than parties to the usual commercial transaction. This is said to apply both to the statements of the applicant and to the promises of the insurer. The doctrine of *caveat emptor* (let the buyer beware), then, does not apply to insurance contracts.

*Capacity of parties.* In order to make a valid contract, a person must be capable. This means that a natural person must be of age[4] and of sound mind; that a corporation must act within the powers of its charter. The principles are the same in regard to insurance contracts as in regard to other contracts, with two exceptions. First, most states require that an insurer be a corporation or an association with essentially corporation-like characteristics and insurance codes limit corporate powers. An insurer may not hide behind a power limitation to avoid paying a claim, if an insured bought the policy in good faith. Second, a number of states have enacted statutes which provide that an individual becomes an adult for purposes of obtaining insurance at an age younger than the customary 21 years. The range of ages is 14½ years to 16 years. The statutes generally refer to insurance on the infant's life, and the extent to which they cover health insurance is questionable. In the absence of such applicable statutes, courts have usually held that an infant may, on attaining adulthood, disaffirm his insurance policy and recover the premiums paid. A few courts require a deduction of the "cost of protection."

*Legality of object.* A contract made for an illegal purpose is unenforceable at law. For practical purposes, legality of object in insurance contracts means that there must be *insurable interest*. Briefly, insurable interest is any such relationship to the subject matter that the assured will suffer a loss if the event insured against occurs. In-

---

[4] This may be by order of a court, by marriage, or by reaching a certain age (age 18 in some states; age 21 in most).

surable interest is required in order to prevent insurance contracts being used as devices for gambling or acting as incentives to crime.

In health insurance income coverages, presumably the same principles apply as in life insurance. Thus insurable interest must exist at the inception of the policy; it is not necessary for it to exist thereafter. This rule should apply to the income coverages, since these are generally *valued policies,* i.e., policies which pay an agreed amount, like life insurance. However, it is probable that, in regard to the expense coverages, which are often written on an indemnity basis, the rule applicable to property insurance would be used.

A contract of *indemnity* is one which reimburses the insured only for his actual loss. In order to avoid confusion, the Committee on Health Insurance Terminology recommends the term *reimbursement* contract, and this term is used generally in this book. In the legal sense, most medical expense policies are contracts of indemnity. In such contracts, insurable interest must exist at the time of the loss; it is immaterial whether it existed previously or not. The law in regard to health insurance is by no means well established, so it is necessary to reason by analogy.[5]

In most cases, health insurance is purchased by the person whose life is insured, and the question of insurable interest does not arise, since every person has an unlimited insurable interest in his own life. Where taken out on the life of another, however, insurable interest in the form of love and affection (presumed in close family relationships) or a pecuniary relationship must exist. The most common case of insurance of the life of another is found in the expense coverages written on the entire family. Here insurable interest may exist either in the form of love and affection or of a pecuniary relation (duty to support).

Other pecuniary relations which have given rise to valid health insurance on the life of another are found in the debtor-creditor relationship and in business insurance. In the former a creditor may insure the life of his debtor against either death or disability. Creditor group disability insurance is growing in importance. In business insurance the firm may insure against disability of a key man, or partners or stockholders of a close corporation may insure each other to provide for business continuation in the event of the disability of one of them.

*Form.* The statute of frauds and its modern equivalents provide, *inter alia,* that all contracts which may not be performed within one year must be in writing. Many health insurance policies would not fall

---

[5] Cf. *Batchelor* v. *American Health Insurance Co.,* 4 *Life Cases* (2d) 182, 234 S.C. 103, 107 S.E. 2–36 (1959) in which a hospital expense contract without any other insurance clause was held to cover in full despite manifest overinsurance. See also *Kopp* v. *Howe Mutual Insurance Co.,* 4 *Life Cases* (2d) 104, 6 Wis. 2d 53, 94 N.W. 2d 224 (1959).

under this rule since it is possible for them to be performed within one year, but as a matter of practice health insurance contracts always are written. Oral contracts of insurance have been upheld in property and liability insurance, usually on a temporary basis, but such contracts arise in practice only where the local agent has binding authority. In health insurance, such authority practically never is given, except for some limited accident contracts.

Since 1912, state laws have imposed certain requirements on the form of individual[6] health insurance contracts. The National Convention of Insurance Commissioners recommended the standard provisions in that year, and most states adopted them by statute or administrative ruling. In 1950 the National Association of Insurance Commissioners (the newer name) recommended a new model law known as the Uniform Individual Accident and Sickness Policy Provisions Law. This law recognized the changes in the business since 1912 and permitted the companies to vary from the prescribed wording either where the statutory language is clearly inappropriate or where the variation is not less favorable to the insured. The law requires that certain provisions be included in every policy and prescribes the wording of others the inclusion of which is optional. Unlike the laws applicable to fire insurance, the wording of the whole contract is not specified. Although this has been advocated widely, especially for hospital policies,[7] the required provisions relate generally to matters concerning claim procedures and the optional clauses to limits on amount of recovery.

The uniform provisions are intended to protect the insured in connection with a contract that is complex and technical and often runs for a substantial period of years, and where there is a heterogeneous collection of benefit provisions and limits. The goal is to establish a degree of uniformity in the "operating provisions of the contracts." The 1912 standard provisions law required that the provision read exactly in the words of the statute, and as individual states enacted variants, this imposed an awkward burden of policy draftsmen and tended to inhibit experimentation. Under the 1950 provisions, this is not so great a problem, since any wording not less favorable to the insured than that prescribed may be used, with the approval of the insurance commissioner.

Forty-eight states, the District of Columbia, and Puerto Rico have enacted the 1950 uniform provisions law, although with some individual variation, and in a few cases substantial additional requirements. These

---

[6] The Ohio statute has been held to cover group credit disability insurance in the recent case of *Green* v. *Credit Life Insurance Co.* 220 N.E. 2d 835.

[7] See Thomas L. Wenck "Standard Hospitalization Insurance Contracts," *Journal of Risk and Insurance*, Vol. xxxi, No. 1 (March, 1964), p. 73, and sources there cited.

variations and special requirements will be discussed more fully below. In Louisiana, the statute specifies provisions which are very close to the provisions in the 1950 law. Alaska has not adopted the 1950 uniform individual provisions law, but individual contracts containing these provisions are acceptable there and approved by the Insurance Department.[8]

The first required uniform provision specifies that the policy, including the endorsements, application, and other papers, if attached, is the entire contract and that changes will not be valid unless approved by an executive officer of the insurer and unless endorsed on or attached to the policy.

In general, the required uniform provisions relate to the respective rights and obligations of the insurer and the insured. The optional provisions relate essentially to permissible limits on the agreements of the insurer.

The various uniform individual provisions will be discussed in following sections, and the complete provisions are found in Appendix A. Most states impose additional requirements by law or administrative ruling. If a contract is issued which departs from the required provisions, generally it will be reformed and interpreted as if the uniform provision were included. The insured, however, might be permitted to rescind it and get his money back.

### Agreements of the insurer

For purposes of analyzing the coverage of various health insurance contracts, it is convenient to use the method developed by C. A. Kulp, whereby the various provisions are discussed under the headings of agreements of the insurer, limits on the insurer's agreements, rights of the insured, agreements of the insured, rights of the insurer, and miscellaneous provisions.

*Defining coverage.* The first thing that must be made clear in any health insurance contract is whose life is covered and when. In individual insurance the policy will state in a schedule the name, address, and other identifying information about the insured or insureds and define the term of the policy. The contract will cover only accidental injury occurring or disease commencing while the policy is in force. In group insurance the master policy will also prescribe the categories of employees or members covered, the dates coverage commences and terminates, and rights as to continuance in the event of separation from

---

[8] See Cox, *op. cit.*, pp. 43–58 and *Proceedings of the National Association of Insurance Commissioners*, 1959, Vol. II, p. 470, for tabulations of the legislation.

the group. The records of the employer will indicate which employees are covered and when and will record employee contributions.

In social insurance the applicable law and administrative rulings will carefully define coverage and specify the requirements therefor. For example, workmen's compensation laws may cover all employees of employers employing two or more workers except domestic, seasonal, casual, and agricultural workers. Federal Old-Age, Survivors, and Disability Insurance covers (against disability) only workers who, at the time of disability, were fully insured and had quarters of coverage equal to 20 out of the last 40 calendar quarters.[9] In workmen's compensation, the employer will keep records as to employment and payroll; in OASDI, the Social Security Administration maintains such records, including tax contributions, based on employer reports.

*Defining the loss.* In addition to indicating who is covered and when, the contract must specify the type of event covered. A workmen's compensation law, for example, will cover only accidental bodily injury or disease arising out of and/or in the course of employment. A limited accident policy may cover only bodily injury produced by accidental means. The insuring clause provides specifically only the first part of the definition of covered loss: the events which produce the loss. The second part of the definition, having to do with the nature of the loss produced, will be discussed below in connection with benefit eligibility. It is necessary to define the loss covered in this dualistic manner in order to prevent the payment of benefits for economic loss which results from factors other than poor health, such as unemployment or old age.

*Problems of defining the loss.* Major problems result from the indefiniteness of the concept of poor health and the subjectivity of disability. Disability and good health are both, in part, states of mind. In the broadest sense, everyone has poor health most of the time. In order to provide benefits only where there is a real need and to keep the costs of the program within reason, it is necessary to define carefully the events leading up to the loss and the resulting loss as well. The narrower the coverage provided (and the lower the premium), the more rigid these definitions must be.

A given physical impairment may disable one person completely, while another more strongly motivated or more pertinacious may continue to work as productively as if not handicapped. It is almost impossible to distinguish between cases in which an individual is unable to work and those in which he merely believes he is unable to work. The requirement of specific events (accident or disease) leading up to

---

[9] The 1967 amendments make coverage easier to obtain for workers under age 31, and it can be obtained with as few as six quarters of coverage.

disability is an attempt to narrow the area of possible misunderstanding and to limit the coverage to the cases it was intended to cover.

In addition, real physical impairment frequently may result from intangible psychological factors. Psychosomatic illness represents a physical impairment produced by emotional factors. Accident-proneness is a similar situation where certain persons seem to be far more subject to accidental injury than the average. These conditions have been tentatively explained by psychologists on two grounds: a desire to escape from reality to the pampered world of the invalid and a desire to punish one's self for real or imagined guilt.

In addition to those persons in whom mental factors bring on genuine physical impairment, there are others who merely imagine that they are ill. The hypochondriac is a familiar feature of the modern scene. Every minor symptom is mentally blown up into a major disease. He is sure to have whatever impairment catches the public fancy.

The foregoing types of situation represent cases in which the person really believes he is disabled, but far more serious is the case in which the claimant deliberately fakes or magnifies his injury in order to collect benefits. The extent of such malingering is difficult to determine, but the more liberal the benefits and the looser the administration of the plan, the greater it will be. Certain limited studies have indicated that it exists to a frightening degree under some programs.

Another difficulty arises from the fact that health insurance is intended to cover an economic loss, but frequently the loss must be defined in noneconomic terms. It would be manifestly impractical to write insurance which covers every decrease in earned income. The contract would cover old age, unemployment, and laziness, as well as disability. Thus it is necessary to specify in the contract both the events leading up to loss and the nature of the loss itself. For a variety of reasons, even in the latter area, an economic loss often is defined in noneconomic terms. Even after the loss has been narrowed down to that produced by poor health as defined, it is common to find the covered loss defined as inability to pursue an occupation, as a specific dismemberment, as admission to a hospital, or as the receipt of physician's services rather than as a loss of income or the incurring of an expense.

These noneconomic definitions are used because of ease of administration or because of a desire to keep costs down. However, they create additional problems, particularly where a fixed sum is payable on the occurrence of a specified contingency regardless of the economic loss involved. It is possible under such circumstances for the insured to make a profit because of the event, particularly after considering the effect of other insurance programs and of the savings in taxes and work-connected expenses of not working versus working. In property insurance it has become customary to define covered loss in economic terms and to reimburse the insured only for actual loss sustained. Where several policies cover, the actual loss is divided between them. This principle of indemnity frequently is not applied in health insurance, and this contributes to moral hazard.

Where this valued policy approach is used, moreover, the amount of agreed benefit is based on past or present values. The loss which occurs is a function of future values, and this increases the likelihood of payments and losses getting out of balance. If more accurate definition of amounts payable can be made through application of economic measures, less stringent limitations and fewer exclusions on noneconomic and arbitrary grounds would be needed in the contract. It is probable that much confusion and resentment on the part of claimants could be eliminated by such a development.

*Methods of defining the loss.* Loss definitions vary greatly among the different varieties of health insurance. This variation results from differences among the various types of loss covered, from differences among types of insurer, and from the fact that no one method of solving the problems described above has gained general acceptance. Thus the discussion in this chapter must be rather general, with detailed treatment reserved for the chapters about the various lines.

In private insurance, the definition of accidental injury has presented problems. Since accident coverage developed first and has always tended to be more liberal than disease coverage, the problem was compounded. This is still quite important in regard to private insurance of income loss, whether the policies are written on a noncancellable, guaranteed renewable, commercial, industrial, or limited basis, and is of some significance in regard to insurance company expense coverages.

The first accident policies, issued more than 100 years ago, provided loosely that losses must be "the result of accident." Since an accident is a sudden fortuitous event, the courts interpreted this type of phrase broadly, and such things as sprains, heart attacks, and strokes were interpreted as being covered. In order to eliminate cases in which disease occurred suddenly and cases in which the injury resulted from deliberate acts of the insured, language such as "loss resulting directly and independently of all other causes from bodily injuries sustained during the term of this policy and effected solely through accidental means" was adopted.

Briefly, the concept of "accidental means" involves the requirement that, in the chain of events leading up to the injury, something accidental must occur. A mere accidental result is not enough. Both the causes and the result must be accidental, that is, sudden and fortuitous. The classic illustration is that injury resulting from deliberately jumping off a wall would not be covered, but if the insured fell or if he slipped in landing, then the means would be accidental, and he could collect. The purposes of this limitation, to exclude cases which are really due to disease, not accident, and cases which involve injury which the insured intended or should have anticipated, are legitimate. However, the application of the clause led to conflicting decisions and much misunderstanding. The distinction was upheld by most courts, but some failed to recognize it, and the law in the area reached such a state that one Justice referred to as a "Serbonian bog." By now only about half the states recognize a distinction between accidental injury and injury by accidental means.[10] As a result, most health insurers have shifted to the newer phraseology, "accidental bodily injuries." This is more liberal to the insured in states which recognize the distinction.

The retention of the phrase "directly and independently of all other causes" serves to eliminate from accident coverage those cases in which preexisting impairment or disease contributes to the loss. Interpreted strictly, this phrase would limit recovery to cases in which the insured was in perfect health at the time of the accident—an impossible standard. In practice, courts have tended to utilize a reasonable interpretation, some resorting to the doctrine of proximate cause, the main, efficient, moving cause of loss. Of course, if disease is produced by accident, the loss will be covered even under the narrower interpretation.

Other types of policy define the eligible events in a variety of ways, and these will be discussed in the applicable chapters.

**Benefit provisions.** The second half of the definition of eligible loss is found in the benefit provisions. After it has been established that the loss was produced by a covered event, in order to collect it still must be established that a particular type of loss occurred.

*Income replacement benefits* are the most important benefit provisions. They may take the form of periodic payments to replace lost earnings or lump-sum payments made shortly after the disability begins. The periodic benefits usually distinguish between total and partial disability, and the lump-sum benefits usually enumerate a whole series of specific losses.

The total disability income benefit requires the definition of total disability. The most common approach here is to define disability in terms of inability to perform the duties of an occupation. One policy, for example, reads thus:

*Total Disability Defined.* The term "total disability," whenever used in this policy, shall mean complete inability of the insured to engage in the insured's regular occupation; except that if during any period of continuous disability . . . any benefit accrues more than sixty months after the date on

---

[10] See Greider and Beadles, *op. cit.*, pp. 207 ff., for an excellent discussion of the accidental means clause. See also A. W. Fossett, "An Accident Is an Accident Is an Accident—Or Is It?" *Health Insurance Review*, March, 1967, p. 19.

which the Insured became disabled, then with respect to that benefit and to any other benefit thereafter accruing during such period of continuous disability the term "total disability" shall mean complete inability to engage in any gainful occupation in which the insured might reasonably be expected to engage having due regard for his training, background and prior economic status.

The first part of this clause defines total disability as inability to engage in the insured's regular occupation. The older policies once applied that definition only. However, it became evident that this was too liberal. Some claimants were collecting full benefits under this definition even while earning more money than ever before in some other occupation.

The companies then adopted a definition which required inability to perform the duties of any occupation for wage, remuneration, or profit. This was too stringent: a literal interpretation would prevent payment if the insured were capable only of selling pencils on a street corner. The courts refused to interpret the clause so strictly and generally interpreted it to mean any occupation for which the insured was reasonably fitted. Thus the companies often have changed their wording to conform to the court interpretation of "any occupation." A typical clause of this newer type may refer to "any gainful occupation for which he is reasonably fitted by education, training, and experience."

The practice, as in the clause quoted, of using the more liberal "his occupation" definition during the first part of the period of disability and then changing to the less liberal is rather common. Five years, however, is unusually long for the liberal definition to apply.

Rather than use the simple phrase "complete inability to engage in" the occupation, the older, and still not uncommon, practice is to require that the injuries "wholly and continuously disable the insured and prevent him from performing any and every duty pertaining to" his occupation. Again, the courts refused to allow the strict interpretation which might have resulted in few benefits being paid. They usually interpreted "any and every" to mean a substantial portion of the duties. Thus the simpler definition in the clause quoted probably implies the same standard that the courts imposed under the older phraseology.[11]

Partial disability usually is defined somewhat as follows:

*"Partial Disability" Defined.* The term "Partial Disability," whenever used in this policy, shall mean such disability as renders the insured able to perform one or more but not all of the duties of his occupation.

Sometimes the negative approach is used, and partial disability is defined as that which prevents the insured "from performing one or more

---

[11] See Gerald S. Parker, "Quality in Disability Insurance," *CLU Journal*, Vol. XVI, No. 1 (Winter, 1962), for a good discussion of insuring clauses.

important daily duties of his occupation." This is the older phrase. Some contracts refer to a loss of some proportion of business time.

Lump-sum benefits are usually found only in private contracts, and then almost exclusively for accidental injury only. Often there is an accidental death benefit, but, since this is not disability insurance, it will suffice to mention it in passing.

Dismemberment and loss of sight benefits are provided for loss of both hands, both feet, one hand and one foot, or the sight of both eyes, in an amount usually referred to as the principal sum or capital sum. This may be a specified amount such as $10,000, or a multiple of the periodic total disability benefit, such as 208 weeks. About half this amount is paid for loss of one hand or foot, and lesser amounts for lesser impairments, according to a brief schedule. Frequently, accident policies carry another list of impairments such as fractures and dislocations and a schedule of lump sums payable for these.

The contract may provide that these specific amounts may be paid in in one of the following ways:

1. In lieu of periodic disability income;
2. In lieu of periodic income at the election of the insured;
3. In addition to disability income paid prior to the dismemberment and in lieu of such income thereafter,
4. Similarly, but at the insured's election, of disability income *or* lump sum after the dismemberment,
5. As a minimum payment, provided that total disability income does not equal such amount, but disability income continued until recovery or benefit termination,
6. In addition to income benefits.

Even where the insured has the election, some policies provide that the lump-sum payment will be made unless he specifically elects otherwise. Since it is generally advisable for the insured to take the periodic income rather than the lump sum, careful attention to the wording of the policy is necessary. The first of these methods is the least liberal, and the third is almost as illiberal, since dismemberment usually follows the injury quite closely. The sixth, fifth, and fourth are the most liberal (in this order) from the claimant's viewpoint. The reason that the periodic income is more desirable should be evident: if the disabled claimant lives more than four years or so, he will collect more in terms of income than the lump sum. The probabilities of this are rather high. Some policies provide that loss of both hands, or both feet, or the sight of both eyes will be presumed to be total and permanent disability. This is a logical approach.

Some policies provide that the benefits will be doubled if the injury is the result of a (carefully defined) travel or other specified type of accident. The economic value of such a provision is debatable; if it has any value, it is to assist in the sale of policies. Some policies go even further, providing triple, quadruple, or other multiple indemnity.

*Medical care benefits.* These benefit clauses may provide for hospital expense, nurses' fees, surgeons' or physicians' fees, or comprehensive medical care. They may be written on either a payment or a service basis. In the latter, common in Blue Cross and Blue Shield plans, payment is made directly by the insurer to the purveyor of service. In the former, there is usually a dollar limit to amount of payment, and benefits may be either on a valued or an indemnity basis. On the valued basis, the agreed amount is paid, regardless of actual expense, if the contingency occurs. On the indemnity basis, the actual expenditures are reimbursed up to the stated limits. Since the variation in such benefits is great, only an example is possible.

A family hospital policy (of an insurance company) provides:

If by reason of "such injury" or "such sickness" the Insured or Member shall be necessarily confined in a duly constituted hospital for which the hospital makes a charge for room and board, the Company will pay the actual expense of such hospital confinement (subject to the elimination period, if any, as provided in the section entitled "Benefits"), but not to exceed the Maximum Daily Hospital Benefit herein specified, and for not exceeding 100 days, as the result of any one accident or any one sickness or disease.

This illustration should be sufficient to indicate the complexity of loss definition and benefit provisions and will suffice for an introductory chapter. More detailed treatment will be found in the chapters following.

### Limits on insurer's agreements

In order to know the nature of the loss covered, to compute premium rates, and to prevent or reduce moral hazard, it is necessary that some limits on the nature and amount of benefit be imposed. The narrower the coverage, the more detailed and stringent these limits must be.[12]

*Time limits on eligibility.* There are two types of time limit on eligible disability frequently found in health insurance contracts. In disease (as distinguished from accident) coverages there is usually a *probationary period,* after the inception of the policy. Sometimes this applies only to certain types of loss, such as preexisting conditions, maternity benefits, elective surgery, etc. Disease originating during this period is not covered; disease originating thereafter is. This is intended to eliminate cases in which the insured purchases a policy knowing that he is coming down with a disease. This is an illustration of "under-

---

[12] See Rex H. Anderson, "Exceptions, Reductions, Limitations—Friend or Foe," Health Insurance Association of America, Individual Insurance Forum, 1965.

writing through the policy" and is less desirable than sound underwriting by conventional means; it is defended as being more economical.

Another time limit is found in accident coverages in regard to the periodic income, death, or specific dismemberment benefits and to medical expense expenditures. This is intended to make certain that the enumerated losses are the result of the accident and not of some later occurrence. In accident blanket medical clauses it is common to provide that the expenditures must be incurred within (say) 26 weeks of the accident to be covered. Dismemberment and loss of sight benefits are paid only if the loss occurs within some period, such as within 90 days of the accident or during 208 weeks if the insured is continuously and totally disabled during the interim. Periodic income benefits are usually paid only if disability commences within some period, such as 30 days, after the accident. Terminology is vague here, but it seems appropriate to refer to such limits as the *benefit period* for the benefit involved. Such periods are not usually found in regard to disease coverages, since the date of disease incidence is rather difficult to determine. However, major medical and comprehensive policies usually specify a maximum benefit period of two years or so, starting with the time that the deductible is satisfied, or with the date of the first expense counted towards the deductible.

*Waiting periods and deductibles.* A *deductible* represents a provision whereby the first portion of the loss, and all losses within this amount, must be borne by the insured. Since most losses are small, such a provision eliminates the substantial claim payments and settlement expenses associated with a great number of small losses. The function of insurance is to reduce the risk of serious loss. It can do this far more efficiently if a deductible is used. Then the small frequent losses can be met by the insured as a matter of family budgeting.

In major medical insurance the deductible takes the form of a dollar amount. In a comprehensive plan it may be quite low, while in other major medical plans it may be quite high, to allow for basic hospital and medical coverage in addition. Sometimes a rather small "corridor" deductible is used, whereby the deductible amount is applied to the excess of expenditures over the amounts collectible under the underlying basic contracts. In major medical the deductible almost always is used, and it is common in the "comprehensive" type of basic medical and hospital policies. It may be expressed either as an amount or as an elimination of the costs of the first one or two days of care or of visits. Sometimes a deductible such as $1 is applied to each day's expenses. This is not infrequent in the "independent" plans.

In connection with the income benefits, the deductible takes the form of a *waiting period*—the exclusion of benefit payments for the first portion of disability. The waiting period may be as short as one day or as long as several years, depending on type of contract and purpose.

In addition to reducing costs and premiums greatly, deductibles also tend to cut down on malingering and other forms of moral hazard—provided that patients do not conspire with purveyors of services to inflate bills and kick back the deductible amount. This is an ever present danger.[13]

*Benefit maxima.*  In order to limit the insurer's total liability, to keep the costs within reason, and to make them predictable, it is necessary either that there be fixed benefit maxima or a device for substantially increasing the insurer's income. Only social insurance schemes have the latter, and then not always. Thus there is almost always a limit to maximum benefit. This is stated separately in the usual contract for each particular benefit.

In income replacement coverages providing periodic income, the maximum usually appears as a maximum period of payment. This is usually a maximum per injury or disease, although sometimes a lifetime aggregate is imposed. It may be expressed in terms of weeks, months, or years or until a specified age or date. Sometimes payments are continued for life, in which case mortality provides the effective limit.

In addition to maximum duration, the contract must express the amount of periodic payment. In private contracts this is expressed in dollars, sometimes with a change after some period to a different amount. In social insurance coverages the amount usually is related to some concept of covered earnings with maximum and minimum limits.

Benefit limits for expense coverages may be in terms of aggregate amount or of time period. Generally, hospital and basic medical benefits are limited in the number of days of treatment or confinement covered and in amount per day or call, while blanket medical and major medical coverages are limited in dollar amount. Specific dismemberment and surgical benefits are usually expressed in dollars according to a schedule of types of injury or operation, although the former may be expressed as a multiple of the weekly or monthly total disability benefit. Service benefits may be limited as to nature and time only.

*Percentage participation.*  The subjectivity of liability and the importance of moral hazard have been touched upon already and will be discussed more fully in a later chapter. The most important safeguard against moral hazard is to make sure that the insured may never profit

---

[13] See Charles P. Hall, "Deductibles in Health Insurance—An Evaluation," *Journal of Risk and Insurance*, Vol. XXXIII. No. 2 (June, 1966), p. 253, and sources there cited for more light on the value of deductibles in controlling utilization.

from the loss. Where the risk is so controllable by the insured as the incurring of medical expense, it is necessary to go further—to try to make sure that the insured bears a portion of the loss himself.

In major medical contracts and in comprehensive contracts the use of a percentage participation clause is common. The device often is called "coinsurance," although this leads to some confusion with the coinsurance clause used in property insurance, which is intended not to reduce moral hazard but to encourage the carrying of adequate amounts of insurance. In life insurance, coinsurance is a type of reinsurance where the reinsurer shares in the investment element as well as the protection portion of the coverage. The typical health insurance contract of this type provides that the insurer will reimburse 75, 80, or 85 percent of all eligible expenses (in excess of the deductible, if any), and the insured must bear the balance. Thus the insured is motivated to exercise care in incurring expenses. Without such a provision, there would be no reason for the insured to use anything but the most expensive services and facilities available.

In individual income replacement contracts, only one company uses such a clause reducing benefits to a stated proportion (75 percent) of the insured's earned income, and this is done only in a contract which is written to accompany life insurance policies. Other companies endeavor to achieve the same effect by applying underwriting standards, but this gives no protection against subsequent decreases in the insured's earnings or against subsequently acquired over-insurance. In contracts where the companies reserve the right of cancellation or non-renewal, this right gives them a way to get off a risk where earnings decline, if the facts come to their knowledge. The only policy provisions that these other companies use provide for a reduction of benefits only to the level of 100 percent of earned income, as discussed below. In group insurance, however, a clause is commonly used which restricts total benefits to a stated percentage of earned income, usually 60 to 75 percent.

*Prorating of benefits.* Four clauses are in common use in individual income replacement contracts which provide for some proportionate reduction in benefit payments. Two of these, dealing with change of occupation and misstatement of age, merely are intended to adjust the benefit level to conform to the proper rating classification. The other two, relating to other insurance and earned income, are designed to limit moral hazard.

The misstatement of age clause provides in effect that the benefit paid will be equal to what the premium the insured is paying would have purchased if the age had been correctly stated. The benefit is adjusted (either up or down) in the proportion that the premium the insured actually paid bears to the premium he should have paid, had the age been correctly stated. This is optional uniform provision 2.

The change of occupation clause, optional uniform provision 1, operates in a similar fashion, except that benefits are never increased: if the insured changes to a less hazardous occupation, the insurer will return the excess unearned premium. However, if he changes to a more hazardous occupation, the benefit is reduced in the proportion that the premium actually paid bears to the premium for the more hazardous occupation.

A similar prorating clause for change of place of principal residence recently was devised by the author for major medical contracts, and it has been approved in at least one state.

The other insurance clauses, optional uniform provisions 4 and 5, apply separately to expense incurred and to other benefits and operate to reduce the benefits payable only if there is in force other valid coverage *of which the company has not been notified* prior to a loss. Essentially, they provide that only such proportion of the benefits under the policy in question shall be paid as the amount cf all coverage of which the company had notice (including the policy itself, of course) bears to the total of all such benefits payable by all insurers, whether or not the company had notice. Thus, if the insured had a policy providing $400 per month income benefit and failed to notify the company of another policy of the same amount, the application of this clause would reduce the payments to $400/$800 of $400, or $200 per month. The formula is:

$$\frac{\text{Benefit in this policy}}{\text{Total benefits in all policies}} \times \begin{array}{c}\text{amount this policy}\\ \text{would pay if it were}\\ \text{the only one in force}\end{array} = \begin{array}{c}\text{Amount paid by}\\ \text{this policy}\end{array}$$

The pro rata premium for the excess coverage not valid must be returned to the insured.

The relation of earnings to insurance clause is permitted only in noncancellable and guaranteed renewable disability income policies. It provides that if the total benefits under all valid loss of time coverage exceed the average monthly earnings of the insured over the previous two years or his current monthly earnings, whichever is greater, then the company will pay only such portion of the amount of benefit due as the amount of such earnings bears to the total benefits under all such policies. For example, if the insured has two policies providing $200 and $300 per month, respectively, but his earnings are only $400 per month, only four fifths of the stated benefit amount would be paid by a policy with such a clause. The formula is:

$$\frac{\text{Average earnings}}{\text{Total benefits in all policies}} \times \text{benefit in this policy} = \begin{array}{c}\text{Amount paid by}\\ \text{this policy}\end{array}$$

This is equal to

$$\frac{\text{Benefit in this policy}}{\text{Total benefits in all policies}} \times \text{average earnings} = \frac{\text{Amount paid by}}{\text{this policy}}$$

This is almost the same as the formula above.

If all policies have such a clause, then the total paid will equal the average earnings. If any policy does not have such a clause, then its benefits will not be reduced, and the insured will collect more than his average earnings. Moreover, the clause may not operate to reduce the total benefits in all contracts below $200 per month or the amount of benefit, if smaller. This clause sometimes is referred to as an "average earnings clause," but in this book this latter term will be reserved for the generic term to include all clauses which reduce or prorate benefits in some relation to average earnings.

The other insurance clause usually is used in cancellable or nonrenewable policies where the insurer has a chance to get off the risk when notified of other insurance. It is little protection for the company under a noncancellable or guaranteed renewable policy. The relation of earnings to insurance clause is common in the latter types of contract, especially where the maximum benefit period is long.

**Coordination of benefit**

The Uniform Individual Policy Provisions laws do not apply to group insurance, and insurers are free to use any type of other insurance clause. Between 1963 and 1965 almost all group contracts were modified to prevent overpayment in relation to total incurred medical expense or in relation to a proportion of the insured's earnings (for long-term income benefits).

The provision for group disability income is discussed in Chapter 15. The commonly used provision for group medical expense contracts results in limiting the total collectible to 100 percent of expenses covered under any of the contracts involved. However, instead of a pro rata approach, the clause provides that the liability of each insurer attaches in a specified order, with each paying the excess, if any, of its coverage over that of its predecessor(s), so that the total paid will not exceed the total allowable expenses. The order of attachment of coverage involves primary coverage taking precedence over dependent; dependent coverage based on a male worker taking precedence over that based on a female worker; and otherwise, attachment in the order of the time coverage commenced. Where a primary policy had a pro rata clause, it would pay the amount for which it ordinarily would be liable under its pro rata clause, and the group contract with the suggested clause would pay the excess up to the total eligible expense or its limit, whichever was lower. Because of its great importance, the clause is reproduced here in full.

## PROVISION FOR COORDINATION BETWEEN
## THIS POLICY AND OTHER BENEFITS

*Benefits Subject to This Provision:*

All the benefits provided under this policy are subject to this provision except those providing any disability income benefits, accidental death and dismemberment benefits, or life insurance benefits, if included.

*Definition:*

(1) "Plan" means any plan providing benefits or services for or by reason of medical or dental care or treatment, which benefits or services are provided by (a) group, blanket or franchise insurance coverage, Blue Cross, Blue Shield, or any other pre-payment plan, or (b) any coverage for students which is sponsored by, or provided through, a school or other educational institution, or (c) any coverage under labor management trustee plans, union welfare plans, employer organization plans or employee benefit organization plans, or (d) individual or family type insurance coverage toward the cost of which any employer shall have contributed or with respect to which any employer shall have made payroll deductions, or (e) any major medical coverage, or (f) any coverage under any governmental program and any coverage required or provided by statute.

The term "Plan" shall be construed separately with respect to each policy, contract, or other arrangement for benefits or services, and separately with respect to that portion of any such policy, contract, or other arrangement which reserves the right to take the benefits or services of other plans into consideration in determining its benefits and that portion which does not.

(2) This "Plan" means that portion of this policy which provides the benefits that are subject to this provision.

(3) "Allowable Expense" means any necessary, reasonable, and customary item of expense at least a portion of which is covered under at least one of the plans covering the person for whom claim is made.

When a Plan provides benefits in the form of services rather than cash payments, the reasonable cash value of each service rendered shall be deemed to be both an Allowable Expense and a benefit paid.

(4) "Claim Determination Period" means calendar year, but if a person is not eligible for benefits under this plan during all of the calendar year, then the claim determination period for such persons as to that year shall be the total period thereof during which he was eligible for benefits.

*Effect on Benefits*

(1) This provision shall apply in determining the benefits as to a person covered under this Plan for any Claim Determination Period if, for the Allowable Expenses incurred as to such person during such period, the sum of

    *a)* the benefits that would be payable under this Plan in the absence of this provision, and

    *b)* the benefits that would be payable under all other Plans in the absence therein of provisions of similar purpose to this provision

would exceed such Allowable Expenses.

(2) As to any Claim Determination Period with respect to which this provision is applicable, the benefits that would be payable under this plan in the absence of this provision for the Allowable Expenses incurred as to such person during such Claim Determination Period shall be reduced to the extent necessary so that the sum of such reduced benefits and all the benefits payable for such Allowable Expenses under all other Plans, except as provided in item (3) below, shall not exceed the total of such Allowable Expenses. Benefits payable under another Plan include the benefits that would have been payable had claim been duly made therefor.

(3) If

　　*a*) another Plan which is involved in item (2) above and which contains a provision co-ordinating its benefits with those of this Plan would, according to its rules, determine its benefits after the benefits of this Plan have been determined, and

　　*b*) the rules set forth in item (4) below would require this Plan to determine its benefits before such other Plan

then the benefits of such other Plan will be ignored for the purposes of determining the benefits under this Plan.

(4) For the purposes of item (3) above, the rules establishing the order of benefit determination are:

　　*a*) the benefits of a Plan which covers the person on whose expenses claim is based other than as a dependent shall be determined before the benefits of a Plan which covers such person as a dependent;

　　*b*) the benefits of a Plan which covers the person on whose expenses claim is based as a dependent of a male person shall be determined before the benefits of a Plan which covers such person as a dependent of a female person;

　　*c*) when rules (*a*) and (*b*) do not establish an order of benefit determination, the benefits of a Plan which has covered the person on whose expenses claim is based for the longer period of time shall be determined before the benefits of a Plan which has covered such person the shorter period of time.

(5) When this provision operates to reduce the total amount of benefits otherwise payable as to a person covered under this Plan during any Claim Determination Period, each benefit that would be payable in the absence of this provision shall be reduced proportionately, and such reduced amount shall be charged against any applicable benefit limit of this Plan.

*Right to Receive and Release Necessary Information*

For the purposes of determining the applicability of and implementing the terms of this provision of this Plan or any provision of similar purpose of any other Plan, Provident Indemnity may, without the consent of or notice to any person, release to or obtain from any other insurance company or other organization or person any information, with respect to any person, which Provident Indemnity deems to be necessary for such purposes. Any person claiming benefits under this Plan shall furnish to Provident Indemnity such information as may be necessary to implement this provision.

*Facility of Payment*

Whenever payments which should have been made under this Plan in accordance with this provision have been made under any other Plans, Provident Indemnity shall have the right, exercisable alone and in its sole discretion, to pay over to any organizations making such other payments any amounts it shall determine to be warranted in order to satisfy the intent of this provision, and amounts so paid shall be deemed to be benefits paid under this Plan and, to the extent of such payments, Provident Indemnity shall be fully discharged from liability under this Plan.

*Right of Recovery*

Whenever payments have been made by Provident Indemnity with respect to Allowable Expenses in a total amount, at any time, in excess of the maximum amount of payment necessary at that time to satisfy the intent of this provision, Provident Indemnity shall have the right to recover such payments, to the extent of such excess, from among one or more of the following, as Provident Indemnity shall determine: any persons to or for or with respect to whom such payments were made, any other insurance companies, or any other organizations.

**Subrogation.**  A few medical expense contracts contain a subrogation provision, requiring an insured to turn over to an insurer any rights he might have to recover damage from a third party, to the extent to which he has been reimbursed by the insurer. Such a provision, in a Blue Cross hospital expense contract, was upheld in the case of *Associated Hospital Service Inc., Appellee* (Wisc. Supreme Ct., No. 31. 7 *Life Cases* (2d)867.) in which Blue Cross was allowed to recover from an auto insurer which had paid the claimant despite notice from Blue Cross of its subrogation claim.

**Recurrent disability.**  Where the benefit maxima and waiting periods or deductibles apply separately to each period of disability, as is common, it is necessary for the contract to make clear just what constitutes a new period of disability and what is considered merely an extension of the previous one. If the second disability is considered to be a new period, the deductible must again be satisfied, but the full benefit amount then becomes available. Otherwise, the benefits commence at once, but are still subject in the aggregate to the original maximum. In noncancellable, guaranteed renewable and commercial policies, the use of a six months' period is common.

The period of recovery may be as short as one day. One large company's group hospital expense policy provides:

Successive periods of hospital confinement shall be considered as having occurred during one period of continuous disability unless complete recovery from the disease or injury causing the previous confinement has taken place before the later confinement commences or unless the later confinement commences after the employee has returned to active work with the Employer and completed one day of continuous active service.

Where there is no waiting period or deductible, the shorter the period of recovery required, the more liberal is the coverage. The shorter the waiting period and the lower the maximum benefit period, the more the clause assumes the character of an extension of coverage and the less the character of a limitation.

*Exclusions and suspension of coverage.* Certain types of loss are usually excluded from coverage. Some, such as exclusion of preexisting conditions or of pregnancy or certain disease for a period of time, are intended primarily as "underwriting through the policy" to relieve the company of responsibility for conditions the knowledge of which might have led the insured to purchase the insurance. Some, such as aviation activities or military service, exclude a risk that the companies consider too great to cover. In the latter case, there is little need for insurance, since government provisions cover both incurred costs and income loss for service-connected disabilities. Insurance cannot soundly cover deliberate acts of the insured, so suicide and self-inflicted injuries are excluded. For the same reasons, benefits for pregnancy and childbirth are usually quite limited or may be excluded entirely. Finally, in order to prevent duplication of coverage and benefit payment, policies often exclude workmen's compensation cases; and health policies exclude accidental injuries. The following excerpts from a guaranteed renewable policy are rather typical:

EXCEPTIONS AND REDUCTIONS

A. *Prior Origin of Disability.* This policy does not cover any disability which is contributed to or caused by (i) accidental injury received prior to the date of this policy or (ii) sickness of which the cause originated prior to the date of this policy; but any disability which commences after the policy has become incontestable . . . will be considered to be the result of causes originating after the date of this policy.

B. *Air Travel.* This policy does not cover any disability which results from being in or on, or from operating, any vehicle or mechanical device for aerial navigation, or from falling or otherwise descending from or with such a vehicle or device; except that this exclusion shall not apply if the Insured is traveling (i) as a passenger in a commercial aircraft on a flight taken for the purpose of transportation (not including any such purpose as crop dusting, seeding, skywriting, racing, testing, exploration, or any other purpose except the sole purpose of transportation) or (ii) as a passenger in an aircraft owned or chartered by the Insured's employer when such aircraft is flown by a professional full time pilot on a flight taken for the purpose of transportation (as limited above) for business purposes only.

C. *Intentionally Self-Inflicted Injury.* This policy does not cover any disability which is contributed to or caused by intentionally self-inflicted injury.

D. *War.* This policy does not cover any disability which results from war (whether declared or undeclared) or any act of war.

E. *Foreign Countries.* This policy does not cover any disability which results from accidental injury sustained, or sickness contracted, outside Canada,

Mexico, or the United States (including territories and possessions of the United States) unless, upon application therefor by the Insured, a foreign travel and residence rider is issued by the Company. Indemnity shall not be payable for any period of disability during which the Insured is not within Canada, Mexico, or the United States (as extended above) unless such a rider is issued by the Company. A foreign travel and residence rider will be issued upon request without additional premium where in the Company's opinion the projected travel or residence will not result in a material increase in risk. An additional premium will be charged for the foreign travel and residence rider if, in the Company's opinion, the projected travel or residence will result in an increased risk; provided, however that the Company reserves the right not to issue such a rider, if in its opinion, the projected travel or residence will result in an uninsurable increase of risk.

F. *Certain Disabilities Deemed Sickness.* Any disability which is contributed to or caused by inguinal, umbilical, or postoperative hernia or by bacterial infection shall be deemed a sickness in interpreting the provisions of this policy, except that pyogenic infection incurred through a wound (including accidental pricks, cuts, abrasions or any similar accidental break in the continuity of the external surface of the body) shall be deemed an injury in interpreting the provisions of this policy.

G. *Concurrent Disabilities.* The Insured shall never be considered to be suffering from two or more disabilities concurrently, nor from both total and partial disabilities concurrently.

It will be noted that most of these items listed exclude certain types of loss. These are referred to as "exclusions." However, the clause relating to war or military service may be of a different nature. This may provide that loss occurring *while* the insured is in military service as defined will not be covered. This type of provision suspends the coverage for a period of time, and it is common to provide for a return of premium for such period. The distinction between exclusions and suspensions of coverage is expressed by some authorities as the distinction between a "results"-type and a "status"-type clause. The first excludes loss resulting from a specified peril, while the latter suspends coverage while a specified "status" exists. A careful reading of the contract is necessary to distinguish one from the other.

House confinement is sometimes required as a prerequisite to collection under loss-of-time policies covering sickness. Sometimes benefits are paid only for house-confining illness; sometimes a reduced benefit is paid for nonconfining sickness, or a shorter duration is covered for nonconfining disability than for confining. At one time the use of house-confinement clauses was the rule in regard to sickness income benefits. Today the clause is rather rare, and it is diminishing in importance with each year that passes.

Other clauses that look like exclusions are merely intended as controls on moral hazard and to define more specifically the event insured against.

Such clauses include the requirement that the insured be under the care of a legally qualified physician other than himself. This is common to almost all health insurance contracts. Policies that cover hospital expense will require admission to a "duly constituted hospital," perhaps as a "registered bed patient." Similar definitions are used in regard to benefits for nursing expense and similar provisions. All these operate to exclude losses not covered by the definition but are intended primarily as claim controls. However, to the extent to which knowledge of such provisions encourages claimants to utilize more expensive types of service than are actually necessary, they may operate to increase claim costs.

### Rights of the insured

The most important right of the insured, of course, is the right to have the promises of the insurer performed. In addition, however, he may have several other important rights. One of the most significant is the right of renewal until a specified age or for life. This will be discussed in detail in connection with noncancellable and guaranteed renewable policies.

Health insurance policies frequently contain provisions for waiver of premium during a period of disability. This may be viewed either as an additional policy benefit or as a right of the insured. It is discussed here for reasons of convenience. The clause is found most frequently in guaranteed renewable policies but is fairly common in other disability and rare in basic medical expense contracts. It provides that if total disability continues for a specified period, commonly three or six months, premiums falling due during such disability will not be charged to the insured. Sometimes the waiver is retroactive to the original date of disablement. Any premium paid for such a period is refunded to the insured.

Noncancellable and guaranteed renewable contracts contain an incontestable clause which reads substantially as follows:

After this policy has been in force for a period of two years[14] during the lifetime of the insured (excluding any period during which the insured is disabled), it shall become incontestable as to the statements contained in the application.

The limitation of the clause to such statements makes impossible the extension of the concept to prohibit contest of a claim as distinguished from contest of the policy. The clause is required only in noncancellable and guaranteed renewable policies.[15]

In contracts other than noncancellable and guaranteed renewable, a

---

[14] Some states permit three years.

[15] See Greider and Beadles, *op. cit.*, pp. 202 ff. for a discussion of how a number of different courts have interpreted the life insurance incontestable clause.

somewhat similar clause is required.[16] It imposes a time limit on certain defenses by requiring a clause which provides that after two years[17] from date of issue, no statement in the application (except a fraudulent misstatement) may be used to void the policy or to deny a claim for disability or other loss commencing after the expiration of the two-year period.

A related clause, required provision 2b, provides that no claim will be reduced or denied on the ground that a disease or physical condition not excluded by name or specific description had existed prior to the effective date of the policy. This is required for noncancellable and guaranteed renewable contracts as well as for other types. This effectively prevents the use of the defense of preexisting condition after two years[18] except for specifically described conditions.

Other rights of the insured commonly include a grace period for payment of premiums of from 7 to 31 days, certain rights in regard to reinstatement, and the right to change beneficiaries. The grace period provision, required provision 3, is as follows:

*Grace Period.* A grace period of thirty-one days will be granted for the payment of each premium falling due after the first premium, during which grace period the policy shall continue in force.

The reinstatement provision, required provision 4, provides that acceptance of a premium by the insurer after lapse will reinstate the policy unless an application for renewal is required. If such an application is required and a conditional receipt tendered, the policy is reinstated on approval by the insurer or automatically at the end of 45 days unless notice of disapproval is sent. The policy, unless endorsed to the contrary, will be on the same terms and conditions as originally, except that it excludes loss for accidental injury occurring prior to reinstatement or sickness commencing prior to or within 10 days after reinstatement. Premiums charged must be applied to periods for which no premium had been paid, and not prior to 60 days before reinstatement except for noncancellable and guaranteed renewable policies. For contracts of this type, back premiums need to be collected to establish the statutory required level premium reserves.

Required provision 12 reserves to the insured the right to change the beneficiary and exercise all rights under the policy unless the insured has made an irrevocable beneficiary designation.

Required provision 8 provides that loss for other than periodic payment claims is payable immediately on receipt of proper proof of loss,

---

[16] These two clauses are alternative forms of required provision 2a. One or the other must appear in every renewable individual policy.

[17] Some states permit three years.

[18] See note 17 above.

and that periodic benefits will be paid not less frequently than monthly. According to required provision 9, claims except for loss of life are payable to the insured. Death claims are paid to the designated beneficiary if any; otherwise to the insured's estate. Benefits of other types accrued at the insured's death may be paid to the beneficiary or the estate at the insurer's option. Optional provision 9 may be thought of as conferring a right on the insured. It provides that any provision of the contract in conflict with the statutes of the state where the insured resides on the effective date is amended to conform to such statute.

## Limits on insured's rights

Several of the uniform provisions seem to represent limits on the rights of the insured. Required provision 11 prohibits legal actions prior to 60 days after proper proof of loss has been furnished or after three years from the furnishing of proof of loss.

Optional provision 3 may be used to prohibit more than one policy of the particular type with the same insurer or coverage in excess of a certain agreed amount. Under this provision, such excess coverage is void and the premium is returned to the insured or his estate.

Optional provisions 10 and 11 permit the exclusion of loss contributed to by the insured's committing a felony or being engaged in an illegal occupation or contracted in consequence of the insured's being intoxicated or under the influence of a narcotic unless administered on the advice of a physician.

Although not a part of the uniform provisions, clauses limiting or prohibiting assignment are not uncommon. On the other hand, an optional portion of required provision 9 provides that the insurer may pay medical expense benefits directly to a hospital or physician unless the insured requests otherwise.

## Rights of the insurer

The most important right of the insurer is the right to cancel the contract or deny renewal. Sometimes this right is limited or circumscribed by certain conditions, and sometimes it is omitted entirely. This topic will be discussed in more detail in the chapter on guaranteed renewable policies.

The uniform cancellation provision, optional provision 8, provides that either the insurer or the insured (after the original term if the insured cancels) may cancel the contract at any time. When the insurer cancels, a minimum of five days' notice is required and the premium is returned for the unexpired term on a pro rata basis. This makes the proportion of premium returned exactly proportional to the unexpired period for which premium has been paid in advance.

When the insured cancels, the cancellation is effective immediately upon receipt of notice by the insurer unless a later date is specified. The premium return is computed on the basis of a short-rate table on file with the insurance department, which provides for a less than pro rata refund. The purpose of this is to make the premium for a short period of coverage on a longer term contract the same as that for a short-term contract.

Required provision 10 gives the insurer the right to require the insured claimant to submit to a physical examination when and as often as it reasonably may require and to make an autopsy when this is not forbidden by law.

Optional provision 7 gives the insurer the right to deduct any unpaid premium or premium note from a claim payment.

### Agreements of the insured

The consideration clause is not strictly an agreement of the insured. The consideration in private contracts is the first premium, which has been paid, and the statements in the application. The payment of subsequent premiums is not a legal obligation on the insured which can be inforced by law; it is merely a condition precedent to continued coverage by the contract. Providing that the statements are part of the consideration merely makes it clear that the policy is issued in reliance thereon and strengthens the hand of the insurer if it disputes the validity of the policy on grounds such as misrepresentation.

The other duties of the insured also are conditions precedent to recovery. They have to do with his duties at the time of loss, and in individual policies are found in the Uniform Individual Policy Provisions.

Notice of claim is required by required provision 5, within 20 days of the occurrence or commencement of loss, or as soon thereafter as is reasonably possible. Notice may be given to the insurer's home or other office or to any authorized agent. It is permissible to include a provision for subsequent notices of claim under disability income policies every six months during the continuance of disability.

Required provision 6 really is a qualification of the insured's duty to file proof of loss. It provides that if the insurer fails to furnish claim forms within 15 days after notice of loss, the insured may submit written proof according to a form of his own devising and that this will comply with the requirement for filing such proof.

Required provision 7 requires this proof of loss within 90 days of the loss or of the termination of the period for which the insurer is liable for continuing loss. If the insured is unable to furnish such proof, failure to do so will not invalidate or reduce a claim if proof is furnished as soon as reasonably possible and within one year after the time it otherwise would be due. Thus, on a contract providing lifetime disability income benefits, proof conceivably could be submitted as late as 15 months after the insured's death. However, there is no decided case in point. Some authorities believe that proof may be required within 90 days after the first benefit period (for example, one month) for which the insurer is liable. It is to the claimant's advantage to submit proof of loss promptly.

## Summary

The insurance contract expresses the rights and obligations of the various parties. Despite the heterogeneity of insurers and policies, the same principles largely apply to all types of insurance. It is necessary that the benefit rights and amounts be clearly defined, that the claim procedure be specified, and that there be a clear understanding of the nature and amount of coverage.

Private insurance contracts must meet the requirements for any contract according to the common law. There must be a valid offer and acceptance, with reality of consent by competent parties. There must be a consideration, the purpose must be legal, and the contract must meet certain requirements as to form. In each of these respects there are certain rules of law peculiar to insurance contracts. The insurance policy is an aleatory, conditional, unilateral contract of adhesion and *uberrimae fidei.*

A contract may be analyzed in terms of the agreements of the insurer, the limits on these agreements, the rights of the insured, the agreements of the insured, and the rights of the insurer. The most important provisions are the agreements of the insurer and the limits thereon. They must define both the situations which give rise to an eligible loss and the nature of the covered loss itself. Limits appear in regard to amount and duration of benefit, prorating clauses, and exclusions. Rights of the insured may include guaranteed renewability, change of beneficiary, and similar provisions. Most of the agreements of the insured and the rights of the insurer have to do with claims.

While there are great differences between individual and group, between private and social, and between types of insurer, essentially the same types of provision must be included in every health insurance contract. Upon the clarity and wisdom of the contract provisions depends the success of the insurance plan.

## Selected references

*See the following items from the General Bibliography: 4, ch. 4 and 5; 5; 7, ch. 4; 10, ch. 3 and 4; 17, ch. 4; 18, pp. 364–84; 19, ch. 9, 10, 11, and 22; 20, ch. 6; 21, ch. 8 and 9; 22, ch. 3; 23; 25.*

ANDERSON, BUIST M. *Vance's Handbook on the Law of Insurance* 3d ed. St. Paul: West Publishing Co., 1951.

ANDERSON, REX H., *et al.* "Exceptions, Reductions, Limitations—Friend or Foe," H.I.A.A. Individual Insurance Forum, 1965.

BAKERMAN, THEODORE. "The Insuring Clause in Personal Accident Income Replacement Insurance: A Study of Some 1953 Policy Provisions," *Review of Insurance Studies,* Vol. II, p. 34.

COX, C. C. *Accident and Health Policy Provisions Manual.* Chicago: privately published, 1960.

DICKERSON, O. D. *Contract Analysis in Health Insurance.* Philadelphia, Pa.: American College of Life Underwriters, 1963.

FOSSETT, A. W. "An Accident Is an Accident Is an Accident—Or Is It?" *Health Insurance Review,* March, 1967, p. 19.

GREIDER, JANICE E., AND BEADLES, WILLIAM T. *Law and the Life Insurance Contract.* Rev. ed. Homewood, Ill.: Richard D. Irwin, Inc., 1968.

HALL, CHARLES P. "Deductibles in Health Insurance: An Evaluation," *Journal of Risk and Insurance,* Vol. XXXIII, No. 2 (June, 1966), p. 253.

HORNE, HAROLD M., AND MANSFIELD, D. BRUCE. *The Life Insurance Contract.* New York: Life Office Management Association, 1938.

KRUEGER, HARRY, AND WAGGONER, LELAND T. *The Life Insurance Policy Contract.* Boston: Little, Brown & Co., 1953.

LAMONT, STEWART M. *Constructing and Construing Policy Contracts.* Health and Accident Underwriters Conference, Chicago, 1932.

————. "The Contract of Personal Accident and Health Insurance," *Proceedings of the Casualty Actuarial Society,* Vol. XVIII, p. 5.

MCGILL, DAN M. *Life Insurance,* Part V. Rev. ed. Homewood, Ill.: Richard D. Irwin, Inc., 1967.

PARKER, GERALD S. "Quality in Disability Insurance," *Journal of the American Society of Chartered Life Underwriters,* Vol. XVI, No. 1 (Winter, 1962), p. 38.

PATTERSON, EDWIN W. *Essentials of Insurance Law.* New York: McGraw-Hill Book Co., 1957.

SOLOMON, EARL RAY. "Overinsurance—Its Control through Contractual Provisions," *Annals of the Society of Chartered Property Casualty Underwriters,* September, 1965, p. 197.

WALKER, ROBERT W. "Writing a Life Insurance Policy," *Journal of Risk and Insurance,* March, 1964, p. 39.

WENCK, THOMAS L. "Standard Hospitalization Insurance Contracts," *Journal of Risk and Insurance,* Vol. XXXI, No. 1 (March, 1964), p. 73.

# PART II

# Expense Coverage

## chapter 6

Excellent herbs had our fathers of old, excellent herbs to ease their
pain.—Kipling, *"Our Fathers of Old"*

# Hospital Insurance

## Introduction

Hospital insurance provides benefits for the expense of hospital room
and board and for various incidental hospital expenses. This is the most
popular type of health insurance in the United States. It is estimated
that about 158,022,000 persons were covered by this type of protection
at the end of 1966.[1] About 97,404,000 persons were covered by insurance
company contracts, about 6,538,000 by Blue Cross and Blue Shield
plans, and about 6,633,000 by independent plans. The great majority of
these people have group coverage. In insurance plans, 69,570,000 persons,
64 percent of the total, were covered under group plans and about
38,641,000 persons were covered under individual policies. About 90 percent of the persons covered under Blue Cross plans had group coverage.
Benefit payments for hospital expense equaled $5,993,000,000 in 1966,
of which $2,991,000,000 was paid by insurance companies, $2,844,000,000
by Blue Cross and Blue Shield, and about $238,100,000 by independent
plans. These figures include payments for hospital expense under major
medical, comprehensive, and extended benefit plans. About 66,897,000,000
of the persons covered were breadwinners; the remaining 91,131,000,000
were dependents.[2]

---

[1] This figure is less than the total of the subcategories, since it is adjusted to
eliminate duplication. Coverage and benefit figures from Louis S. Reed, "Private
Health Insurance: Coverage and Financial Experience, 1940–66," *Social Security
Bulletin,* November, 1968, p. 3. The projected number with hospital insurance as of
December 31, 1967 was 163 million—*Health Insurance News,* December, 1967.

[2] Health Insurance Institute. *1967 Source Book of Health Insurance Data* (New
York, 1968).

## Development

As early as 1880 there were hospital expense prepayment plans in Minnesota and Oregon, and a federal government plan for merchant seamen operated from 1798. Insurance company group plans were offered as early as 1910. Individual hospital insurance coverage was offered for many years, but usually as a relatively unimportant adjunct to loss-of-time benefits.

However, the modern hospital insurance movement really dates from the development of the Baylor University Hospital Plan in 1929. Although the university is located in Waco, Texas, the University Hospital is in Dallas. The impetus to the development was the severe financial straits of the hospital and clinic. A hospital insurance plan was developed and presented to members of a public school teachers' "sick-benefit plan" which had been operating since the early 1920's. The experience of this plan served as a guide to premium rates. The original contract provided 21 days of hospitalization in a semiprivate room for a premium of $0.50 per month. Operating-room use, laboratory service, and drugs and dressings were included. Seventy-five percent enrollment was required. Soon other employee groups, such as newspaper and bank employees, joined the plan.

The Baylor plan attracted nationwide attention, and plans were soon developed in other communities. A strong impetus for development resulted from the efforts of Rufus Rorem, of the Rosenwald Foundation, and from the final report of the Committee on the Costs of Medical Care. By 1932 the communitywide plan began to supplant the individual hospital plan, reducing the chances of competition between plans. In 1933 the American Hospital Association began to encourage the development of such plans and appointed committees to study the field. In 1936 it established the Commission on Hospital Service, which later became the Blue Cross Commission and now has become the Blue Cross Association. This association is the national coordinating agency for Blue Cross plans.

Insurance companies became active in the group hospital field in the 1930's, encouraged by the popularity of Blue Cross and similar plans. As indicated above, the major development has been on a group basis. Today 61.6 percent of persons with hospital insurance are covered by insurance company plans.

## Types of insurer

Insurance companies, Blue Cross and Blue Shield plans, and "independent" plans are active in the hospital insurance business. The insurance companies include both stock and mutual companies, active in the fields of life insurance and casualty insurance, and some health insurance specialist companies.

Blue Cross plans are a unique type of insurer, active only in this field. The first plans were organized by a particular hospital, but such plans were soon largely supplanted by communitywide plans.

With few exceptions, Blue Cross plans are incorporated as nonprofit organizations under special enabling legislation. This legislation exempts nonprofit hospital service corporations from the provisions of state insurance laws, sets certain standards, and recognizes the associations as charitable and benevolent institutions exempt from most state and local taxes.

The initiative for establishing Blue Cross plans has usually come from the hospitals themselves. A primary motive for the initial establishment of most plans like the Baylor one was the pressing financial problems that the hospitals faced during the Great Depression. A ruling by the insurance departments of New York and Ohio that hospital service plans constituted engaging in the business of insurance led to the demand for and eventual passage of special enabling legislation. Today, legislation of this type is in effect in all but eight states.

The fundamental concepts of the Blue Cross philosophy were expressed in a brochure issued by the American Hospital Association in 1933 as: encouraging public welfare, limitation of covered expenses to hospital charges, combination of professional and community interests, free choice of physician and hospital, nonprofit operation, a sound economic basis, and promotion in a cooperative spirit and dignified manner. The American Hospital Association maintains a Blue Cross Approval program to assure plan conformance to these standards.

As "nonprofit" organizations, Blue Cross plans are generally exempt from regulation as insurance companies, and most of them enjoy a tax-exempt status. However, they usually are under the supervision of the state insurance departments. There are 75 such plans in operation in the continental United States and one in Puerto Rico. All are members of the Blue Cross Association. Coverage is available in every state but Hawaii.[3] There are also four Canadian plans serving six provinces and providing benefits that supplement the Provincial Insurance Programs; Canadian plans are associate members of the Blue Cross Association. Plans cover areas ranging from a few counties to two or more states. A typical plan has a board of directors or trustees who represent the hospitals, the physicians of the area, and the general public. Most of the state laws require that the majority of directors be administrators or

---

[3] States having no plan actually located in the state are covered: Alaska by the Seattle plan, South Dakota by the Sioux City, Iowa, plan, and Vermont by New Hampshire.

trustees of member hospitals. While originally selected by the sponsoring hospitals in most instances, the boards frequently are self-perpetuating.

Frequently the sponsoring hospitals guarantee the financial soundness of the plan. In any event the hospitals represent the ultimate risk bearers. The Blue Cross plan contracts with its member hospitals for the provision of services to insured members. More than 7,000 hospitals are under contract with the several plans. These contracts specify the method of payment by the plan to the hospital and the schedule of amounts. Three main methods have been used: (1) a straight per diem amount, based on average costs (sometimes this includes hospital extras; sometimes these are handled separately); (2) payment on the basis of actual charges billed or a portion thereof; and (3) payment based on cost statements submitted by the hospital but not in excess of charges to nonmembers.

Costs may or may not include allocations of overhead, including depreciation, interest, an allowance for contingencies, nurses' training, and care of the indigent, but may not exceed the prevailing charges to nonmembers. This cost method is the most common. The schedule of payments by the plan to the member hospitals is strongly conditioned by the resources of the plan. The schedule of payments to member hospitals always is subject to renegotiation. In the event of overutilization in relation to premium payments and accumulated funds, it is unlikely that the sponsoring member hospitals would let the plan become insolvent. In such an event, it is moral certainty that they would accept a lowered rate of reimbursement for the time being, in order to maintain the fund on a sound basis. On the other hand, should the plan show a growing surplus, raising the payments to member hospitals would be an alternative to increasing benefits to insured members or reducing premiums. Inasmuch as "costs" represent a somewhat nebulous concept, it may be recognized that the hospitals themselves are, in the last analysis, the real insurers. It is they who would bear the losses or enjoy the gains of the plan.

Independent plans have a longer history than do Blue Cross plans. However, they represent a very heterogeneous group, and generalizations are difficult. Most of them are industrial plans sponsored by an employer or union and limiting enrollment to employees or members. Most of these plans emphasize medical and/or surgical benefits, and they will be discussed in a following chapter.

### Benefit provisions and limits

*Insurance company plans—room and board.* The basic hospital expense benefit is the coverage of daily room-and-board charges. Insurance company plans usually provide up to a fixed number of dollars per day, which is generally payable directly to the insured patient. The insured may select any reasonable amount of daily benefit. Newer plans are almost exclusively written on a reimbursement basis; that is, the patient is reimbursed for his actual expenditures up to the stated limit. However, some older plans still in effect and a few currently issued contracts are on a valued basis. Under this type of provision, the stated dollar amount is paid if the patient is admitted to a hospital, without any regard to what his actual costs may be. Such an arrangement is less desirable from the aspect of moral hazard, as it makes it possible to make a profit from hospitalization.

Amounts of benefit available range from $4 to $50 per day. In addition, a few contracts issued on a group basis provide a "service" benefit, which reimburses the entire charge for a specified class of service, such as semi-private.

In 1967, the average daily benefit amount under new group policies issued was about $21 per day. In 1966, plans covering 96.3 percent of the employees provided benefits of $14 or more, and those covering 69.8 percent provided amounts of $20 or more.[4] Amounts varied, in part, to reflect variations in prevailing changes in various areas. The average in 1967 ranged from $16 in Arkansas and Texas to $30 in the District of Columbia. Of course, benefit amounts under existing plans, many issued years ago, would average lower.

The room-and-board charge includes general nursing and a variety of miscellaneous services. The practice of hospitals varies as to what services are included in the daily charge and what are separately charged for as "extras."

The maximum period of hospitalization covered in insurance company plans is most frequently 70 or 120 days, but it may be as short as 30 days or as long as two years. Other popular choices are 31, 60, 90, and 120 days. In new group cases issued in 1967, the most common limit was 70 days. Twenty-six percent of the employees had benefits for 120 days or more. This limit usually applies separately to each disability, but sometimes the limit applies to a contract year or other 12-month period. Where dependents' coverage is included, the limit applies separately, of course, to each insured member.

The typical insurance company group plan covers hospital confinement commencing while the employee is insured under the plan and within three months after termination of insurance coverage if he is continuously totally disabled from termination to admission. Conditions covered under workmen's compensation insurance are excluded under group policies, but sometimes not under individual contracts. The following section

---

[4] Health Insurance Institute, *Group Health Insurance Policies Issued in 1967, Complete Tables.* (New York, 1967).

from an insurance company group hospital policy is fairly typical and indicates the nature of the benefit provisions and limitations. Clause ( *b* ) refers to the coverage of hospital "extras," which will be discussed below.

### HOSPITAL CONFINEMENT BENEFITS

Subject to the terms of this policy, the benefits payable hereunder are as follows:

( *a* ) a daily benefit at the rate to which the employee is entitled in accordance with the foregoing Insurance Schedule, for each day that the employee is confined in the hospital; but in no event shall the daily benefit be payable, during any one continuous period of disability, for more than the applicable maximum period of payment indicated in said Insurance Schedule; and

( *b* ) a benefit in an amount equal to the charges, other than charges for board and room, made by the hospital to the employee in connection with the hospital confinement; but in no event shall the aggregate benefit payable under this clause ( *b* ), during any one continuous period of disability, exceed the sum of (15) times the employee's rate of daily benefit; and no benefits shall be payable under this clause ( *b* ) with respect to any charges incurred after the first (70) days of hospital confinement during any one continuous period of disability; . . .

It is common to define the coverage in more detail by defining a day of coverage either in terms of the hospital's billing procedure or in terms of time elapsed, or both; by defining a continuous period of disability in terms of the same cause or failure to return to active work for a day or more; by requiring a minimum number of hours' admission or a minimum charge for benefit eligibility; by requiring that admission be recommended and approved by a legally qualified physician; by excluding pregnancy, childbirth, and miscarriage except for limited benefits provided in another clause; and defining a hospital so as to exclude nursing homes, convalescent centers, and institutions for the aged, for alcoholics or for drug addicts. There usually are no exclusions as to cause of disability other than occupational disability in group hospital policies.

*Hospital extras.* Hospital "extras" refer to such things as use of operating room or delivery room, anesthetics, X-rays, drugs, dressings, laboratory examinations, physiotherapy, and the like. Some contracts specify the type of such charges. Others, especially group policies, give unrestricted broad coverage up to the policy limits. In the years prior to 1940, it was common to provide a specific limit for each of a list of specific items, such as $25 for X-rays. However, modern policies almost universally employ a blanket limit for all types of expense. This is more liberal to the insured. The majority of contracts seem to dispense with any definition of such eligible expense except that implicit in the exclusions. Elsewhere in the contract, it is common to limit coverage to "necessary and reasonable" expenses. The expense benefit is often expressed as a multiple of the daily room-and-board benefit and may vary from 5 to 20 times the daily rate. Ten and 15 times are the most common ratios.

It is increasingly common to provide full reimbursement of hospital extras up to a certain dollar figure, and to apply a percentage participation clause to additional expenses up to some higher limit. An increasing number of plans, especially group plans, reimburse such expenses with no upper limit except that implicitly indicated by the number of days of coverage.

In new group plans issued in 1967, plans covering 72 percent of the employees provided full reimbursement up to stated limits. These limits usually were between $200 and $400, but a few groups had limits of $700 and over. Plans covering 33 percent of the employees gave full reimbursement with no limit. Plans covering 26 percent of the employees provided benefits subject to percentage participation on some portion of the allowance. For this type of provision, the most common maximum benefit was around $1200.

*Maternity coverage.* Maternity coverage is usually provided by a separate benefit clause and is limited in amount to (say) 10 times the daily room-and-board benefit. This amount may be used either for room and board or for "extras" at the insured's option. Generally the actual costs will exceed this amount, so, in practice, the maternity benefit may be considered a lump-sum payable in the event of childbirth. The following clause from an individual policy provides such a lump-sum benefit.

### MATERNITY COVERAGE

If the Insured's wife shall be confined in a hospital by reason of childbirth or miscarriage, the Company will pay a lump sum equal to ten (10) times the amount of the Maximum Daily Hospital Benefit as set forth for the wife in the section entitled "Benefits," as the result of any one pregnancy, provided this Policy has been in force ten months.

Sometimes a flat dollar limit is specified for maternity benefits, but it is more common in both group and individual contracts to provide a limit expressed as a multiple of the daily room-and-board limit.

Maternity benefits for employees, dependents, or both were provided in 73 percent of new group plans in 1967 which included some form of medical expense coverage.

*Dependents' benefits.* Dependents' coverage is provided in the individual policy either by writing the contract to cover the listed members of a family or by adding them to the policy covering the breadwinner by rider or endorsement. The same methods are available in group policies, but there the rider is more common, since, with no provision for listing the dependents, more careful definition is necessary. In 1967 new group plans, 98 percent of the cases with medical expense coverage provided coverage for dependents.

In family policies it is customary to schedule the insured dependents by name, age, and relationship. In group contracts, the employer's records or the employees' certificates may list insured dependents, but sometimes only the presence or absence of dependent coverage is indicated.

Eligible dependents usually are limited to the insured's spouse and unmarried minor children younger than some specified age such as 18 to 21. Sometimes eligibility continues to a higher age, such as 23, if the dependent is a full-time student. Usually there is a minimum age for coverage, such as 14 days, but sometimes coverage is effective at birth. Sometimes the policy provides that the term "child" will include adopted children, stepchildren, and foster children who live with the insured in a parent-child relationship. Such provisions are more common in group policies than in family contracts, since the scheduling of insured individuals in the family contract defines coverage clearly in any event.

Family policies usually provide that coverage for a child terminates at the end of the policy year during which the child marries or reaches the limiting age. Sometimes the right to convert to an individual policy is spelled out. Of course, if the contract is terminated, coverage of all individuals ceases.

Group contracts generally provide for termination of dependent coverage automatically when the employee fails to make the required premium contribution, when the employee's insurance is terminated, when a dependent becomes employed by the employer and obtains primary coverage, upon the date of a child's marriage or attaining the maximum age, or when a spouse ceases to be married to the employee. Of course, termination of the group policy terminates both employee and dependent coverage.

*Renewal and conversion.*  Much, if not most, individual medical expense insurance is guaranteed renewable to age 65, with the insurer reserving the right to change premium rates by class. The following provision is typical:

GUARANTEED RENEWABLE FOR LIFE

SUBJECT TO ADJUSTABLE PREMIUMS

This policy may be renewed by the timely payment of premiums for the life of the insured and for as long thereafter as his spouse, if a Covered Member hereunder at the time of his death, shall survive. The premiums set forth in the Policy Schedule are based on the Company's table of rates in effect on the Policy Date and will remain in effect unless and until the table of rates is changed in accordance with the next paragraph.

The Company's table of rates may be changed at any time with respect to premiums becoming due on and after the effective date of the change but no change in premium will be made which does not also apply to all other persons covered under policies of this form of the same sex, rating classification and original insuring age. While this policy is continued in force:

1. The Company cannot cancel this policy,
2. The Company cannot refuse to accept any premium for this policy paid before the end of the grace period,
3. The Company cannot add any restrictive rider or endorsement to this policy, and
4. The Company cannot change any provision of this policy.

During 1965 and 1966, several state legislatures amended their requirements relating to family health and accident insurance policies. Louisiana revised statutes which previously had prevented group family health and accident insurance coverage from being continued on family members[5] over 19 years of age, under any circumstances. This new legislation provided that such protection "may be continued" if such family member is mentally retarded or physically impaired to the extent that he (she) is incapable of self-sustaining employment.

Michigan enacted changes which are somewhat stronger than Louisiana's "may be continued" provision. The state law here does not prevent the usage of provisions which set an upper age limit on family members, but the laws do restrict this provision. The new statute provides that an upper-age provision does not apply to a mentally retarded or physically handicapped, unmarried dependent. As in the case of Louisiana, mentally or physically handicapped is defined as the dependent's inability to secure self-sustaining employment.

The New York State Legislature provided that coverage under any form of family health or accident insurance "may be continued" on a family member past his (her) 19th birthday provided he (she) is either a student under age 23 or incapable of securing a self-sustaining occupation. In either case, the family member must remain unmarried. When a family member is no longer able to remain under the protection of the family plan, the law requires that the member be given the right of conversion regardless of insurability. The minimum benefits for the conversion policy are set in the law. However, the particular insurer is relieved of its conversion obligation if the family member already has or is eligible to obtain coverage with similar benefits.

*Exclusions.* Exclusions under individual policies are more extensive than under group contracts. The following list is fairly typical:

### EXCEPTIONS

1. This policy does not cover, and no payment of any kind shall be made for or on account of, any loss with respect to any covered family member, caused or contributed to by any of the following:

---

[5] The term "family member" is used to refer to children of the parents who own the family plan. Family member is used because the author and especially his research assistant think it is better than calling a 22- or 23-year-old person a child.

(*a*) (i) Any injury sustained by any covered family member prior to the date such family member becomes covered under this policy, (ii) any sickness contracted by any covered family member prior to 8 days after such family member becomes covered under this policy unless such sickness had not manifested itself prior to such date or (iii) any sickness contracted by any covered family member resulting from a physical condition existent prior to 8 days after such family member becomes covered under this policy unless such physical condition had not manifested itself prior to such date (this exception is subject to paragraph (*b*) of General Provision 6, entitled "Incontestable");

(*b*) Pregnancy, including resulting childbirth, abortion, miscarriage or any complication arising during the pregnancy or within 6 months after its termination, except to the extent, if any, that coverage is provided under Benefit Provision III;

(*c*) War, whether declared or undeclared, or an act of war;

(*d*) Any injury sustained or sickness contracted by such covered family member while on full-time active duty (other than active duty for training purposes only, for not more than 2 consecutive months) in the armed forces of any country, international organization, or combination of countries (see General Provision 3, entitled "Refund of Unearned Premiums"); or

(*e*) Intentionally self-inflicted injury or self-inflicted injury while insane.

2. This policy does not cover, and no payment of any kind shall be made for or on account of, any hospital confinement or operation which has not been recommended and approved by a legally qualified physician.

3. This policy does not cover, and no payment of any kind shall be made with respect to any covered family member for or on account of, hospital confinement which commences or operation which was performed within 6 months after such covered family member becomes covered under this policy if such confinement or operation is (a) for repair of abdominal hernia, (b) for removal or treatment of hemorrhoids, (c) for removal of tonsils or adenoids, or both, (d) for removal of appendix, or (e) caused or contributed to by any condition of the female generative organs.

4. This policy does not cover, and no payment of any kind shall be made with respect to any covered family member for or on account of, loss incurred

(*a*) while such covered family member is confined in any hospital owned, contracted for, or operated by a national, state or provincial government or any political subdivision thereof, for or on account of the treatment of members or ex-members of the armed forces, or

(*b*) due to any injury or sickness for which benefits are payable under any workmen's compensation or occupational disease law.

The necessity for these exclusions in individual policies should be evident. It is necessary to exclude workmen's compensation cases in order to prevent duplication of coverage and payment. Military service and war, present a catastrophe hazard. Moreover, members of the armed services receive complete medical care at no cost to them. Air travel exclusions seem to be giving broader coverage as familiarity with such exposure increases, and some companies no longer use this exclusion. Mental disorders are being covered with increasing frequency under basic hospital policies, so long as treatment is in a general hospital. The temporary exclusion of certain types of disease, often involving potential elective surgery, is felt to be necessary to prevent adverse selection.

The military and naval service suspension is not necessary under group policies, since the insured must be an employee to retain coverage. The exclusion of certain preexisting conditions is not felt to be necessary in group contracts because of the lack of opportunity for individual selection.

The coverage is usually limited to in-patients, i.e., persons admitted to the hospital and assigned a bed. Sometimes a minimum period of 18 or 24 hours' confinement is required. The purpose of this is to eliminate coverage of minor treatment and diagnosis. Sometimes it may have the reverse effect—to encourage use of the hospital where this is not really necessary. Some policies provide limited out-patient coverage, especially for accidental injury cases and those requiring minor surgery. Often a specific dollar limit is applied to such treatment, sometimes in the form of a multiple of the room-and-board limit.

*Nursing benefits.* Some policies provide a supplementary benefit for nursing expenses. In some cases this covers nurses in the hospital only; in other cases it covers outside the hospital. Such care may be covered for a period as short as 5 days or as long as 180 days. The limit usually applies separately to each disability. Frequently the coverage of nursing expenses is optional, at an extra premium. The following clause, from an individual policy, is fairly typical:

### NURSES' FEES

If on account of such sickness the Insured shall necessarily employ the full-time services of a licensed or graduate nurse not of the Insured's family (other than general duty hospital nurses), in a hospital or elsewhere, beginning

1. while this Policy is in force, or
2. during or immediately following a period for which any other indemnity is payable under this Policy, or
3. within ninety days after the end of this Policy term and during a period of continuous total disability which commenced while the Policy was in force

the Company will pay periodically the actual expenses incurred therefor up to the daily limit specified in the Schedule of Benefits for each day of such nursing service but not exceeding one hundred days for any one sickness.

*Deductibles.* It is becoming increasingly common to utilize a small deductible in basic hospital insurance contracts. Usually this is a flat dollar amount such as $24 or $50. This reduces claim costs and hence premiums and is discussed more fully in Chapter 8.

*Blue Cross plans.*   Blue Cross plans are almost as heterogeneous as insurance company plans. However, the heterogeneity is of a somewhat different nature. Except in North Carolina, there is only one Blue Cross plan operating in any given area. Although some offer a variety of contracts to insured groups, the employee member has no choice as to plan, unless he wishes to purchase an individual policy on a nongroup basis. A nongroup contract is always more expensive than group coverage and often has more restricted benefits.

The Blue Cross concept of group insurance differs from that of the insurance companies. Although negotiation, record keeping, and payroll deductions are handled through the employer, each employee member receives his own policy. This is comparable to what the insurance companies call "wholesale" or "franchise" insurance, a device intended only for small groups. Perhaps because of this difference in concept, some Blue Cross plans have been known to accept groups as small as five employees.

Blue Cross benefits usually are on a service basis rather than a reimbursement basis. The insured member deals directly with the hospital and is billed only for the excess, if any, of his charges over the coverage of his contract.

*Room-and-Board benefits.*   About 56 percent (most widely held certificate) and 75 percent (most comprehensive certificate) of Blue Cross plans provide a full-service benefit, which gives the patient complete coverage for a specified type of accommodation. This is usually semiprivate but may be on a ward, or, more rarely, a private-room basis. These plans tend to be the larger ones, so that almost 70 percent of the persons covered by Blue Cross plans have full-service coverage of room-and-board costs. Usually a stated dollar allowance is payable toward the cost of a room at a hospital not a member of any Blue Cross plan, or toward the cost of a private room. Generally speaking, the larger the plan and the shorter the period of coverage, the more frequently full-service benefits are provided. There are important regional differences as well. The proportion of participants on a service basis varies from a high of 100 percent in the Middle Atlantic states to a low of 9 percent in the New England states.

In 1965, 67.3 percent of all participants had full-service benefits on a semiprivate basis, and 2.5 percent on a ward basis. The remaining 30.2 percent had certificates providing for cash allowances of the same type as in the typical insurance company plan or had benefits subject to coinsurance or a daily deductible. Table 6–1 indicates the distribution of benefits by percent of participants.

The certificates usually define semiprivate accommodations, if at all, in terms of the number of beds per room. Sometimes this definition is left to the member hospitals. A semiprivate room may contain any-

TABLE 6-1

Room Allowance under Blue Cross Basic Certificates by
Type of Remittance as of December 31, 1965

| Room Allowance | Number of Members Covered | Members Surveyed (57.0 million) | Total Blue Cross (61.8 million) |
|---|---|---|---|
| | | *Percent of Members Covered* | |
| **Group** | | | |
| Full semiprivate........................ | 33,492,863 | 58.7% | 54.1% |
| Percent of semiprivate................. | 1,530,570 | 2.7 | 2.5 |
| Full ward............................... | 877,552 | 1.5 | 1.4 |
| Percent of ward........................ | 3,435 | .01 | .01 |
| Dollar amount......................... | 4,697,765 | 8.2 | 7.6 |
| Other.................................. | 4,248,530 | 7.5 | 6.9 |
| **Nongroup** | | | |
| Full semiprivate........................ | 4,796,240 | 8.4 | 7.8 |
| Percent of semiprivate................. | 1,312,992 | 2.3 | 2.1 |
| Full ward............................... | 505,874 | .9 | .8 |
| Percent of ward........................ | 25,760 | .05 | .04 |
| Dollar amount......................... | 4,460,490 | 7.8 | 7.2 |
| Other.................................. | 663,089 | 1.2 | 1.1 |
| **Senior** | | | |
| Full semiprivate........................ | 82,334 | .2 | .1 |
| Percent of semiprivate................. | 179,381 | .3 | .3 |
| Full ward............................... | 57,636 | .1 | .1 |
| Percent of ward........................ | — | — | — |
| Dollar amount......................... | 73,300 | .1 | .1 |
| Other.................................. | 13,321 | .02 | .02 |
| Total known......................... | 57,021,132 | 100% | 92.2 |
| Unknown............................. | 4,831,199 | | 7.8 |
| Total............................. | 61,852,331 | | 100% |
| **Totals** | | | |
| Full semiprivate........................ | 38,371,437 | 67.3% | 62.0% |
| Percent of semiprivate................. | 3,022,943 | 5.3 | 4.9 |
| Full ward............................... | 1,441,062 | 2.5 | 2.3 |
| Percent of ward........................ | 29,195 | .1 | .1 |
| Dollar amount......................... | 9,231,555 | 16.2 | 14.9 |
| Other.................................. | 4,924,940 | 8.6 | 8.0 |
| Total known......................... | 57,021,132 | 100% | 92.2 |
| Unknown............................. | 4,831,199 | | 7.8 |
| Total............................. | 61,852,331 | | 100% |

Source: Blue Cross Association, *Statistical Bulletin No. 8* (Chicago, 1966).

where from 2 to 10 beds, depending on area and hospital. Probably about four is the most common. A ward is any room which contains more than the maximum number of beds considered semiprivate, while a private room has only one bed to a room.

The number of days of full service or cash allowance provided by Blue Cross plans in 1965 ranged from 21 to 365 days with 120 + days by far the most common. Table 6–2 gives a detailed analysis.

TABLE 6–2

Number of Benefit Days Provided under Blue Cross Basic Certificates by
Type of Remittance as of December 31, 1965

| Number of Benefit Days | Number of Members Covered | Percent of Members Covered | |
|---|---|---|---|
| | | Members Surveyed (55.6 million) | Total Blue Cross (61.8 million) |
| Group | | | |
| 21–69 days............................ | 1,585,912 | 2.9% | 2.6% |
| 70–119 days............................ | 6,737,561 | 12.1 | 10.9 |
| 120 + days............................. | 23,970,838 | 43.1 | 38.8 |
| 21–365 days............................ | 3,498,110 | 6.3 | 5.7 |
| Some combination of full and partial benefits adding to: | | | |
| 120 + days........................ | 7,835,532 | 14.1 | 12.6 |
| Less than 120 days............... | 235,149 | .4 | .4 |
| Nongroup | | | |
| 21–69 days............................ | 2,714,441 | 4.9 | 4.4 |
| 70–119 days............................ | 3,026,963 | 5.5 | 4.9 |
| 120 + days............................. | 2,335,561 | 4.2 | 3.8 |
| 21–365 days............................ | 810,290 | 1.5 | 1.3 |
| Some combination of full and partial benefits adding to: | | | |
| 120 + days........................ | 2,237,521 | 4.0 | 3.6 |
| Less than 120 days............... | 191,863 | .3 | .3 |
| Senior | | | |
| 21–69 days............................ | 267,179 | .5 | .4 |
| 70–119 days............................ | 112,435 | .2 | .2 |
| 120 + days............................. | 4,692 | .01 | .01 |
| 21–365 days............................ | 8,345 | .02 | .01 |
| Some combination of full and partial benefits adding to: | | | |
| 120 + days........................ | 15,364 | .03 | .02 |
| Less than 120 days............... | 2,077 | .01 | .01 |
| Total known........................... | 55,589,833 | 100% | 89.9% |
| Unknown.............................. | 6,262,498 | | 10.1 |
| Total................................ | 61,852,331 | | 100% |
| Total | | | |
| 21–69 days............................ | 4,567,532 | 8.2 | 7.4 |
| 70–119 days............................ | 9,876,959 | 17.8 | 16.0 |
| 120 + days............................. | 26,311,091 | 47.3 | 42.5 |
| 21–365 days............................ | 4,316,745 | 7.8 | 7.0 |
| Some combination of full and partial benefits adding to: | | | |
| 120 + days............................ | 10,088,417 | 18.1 | 16.3 |
| Less than 120 days................... | 429,089 | .8 | .7 |
| Total known........................... | 55,589,833 | 100% | 89.9% |
| Unknown.............................. | 6,262,498 | | 10.1 |
| Total................................ | 61,852,331 | | 100% |

Source: Blue Cross Association, *Statistical Bulletin No. 8* (Chicago, 1966).

About 5 percent of plans impose shorter limits during the first one or more years of membership. Such deductions range from 4 to 39 days. In two plans five years of membership is required to attain full coverage, and two years is required in two others. The more comprehensive certificates of these plans provide full immediate coverage.

*Hospital extras.* Hospital extras are covered in all Blue Cross plans. The method of coverage varies. The blanket reimbursement provision to a stated limit as found in insurance company contracts is rare. Some Blue Cross plans cover, without limit, charges for listed types of service incurred during covered periods of hospitalization. Others cover listed charges for specific types of service up to a schedule of dollar limits for each type of service. This approach is less flexible than the use of a blanket limit without internal allocation, and thus is generally less favorable to the insured. Some plans provide full coverage of extras for the first part of the benefit period and thereafter provide partial coverage under a percentage participation arrangement. The usual percentage participation under this type of plan is 50 percent.

The percentage of Blue Cross participants with full and partial coverage for various services is indicated in Table 6–3.

*Maternity benefits.* These are always available, often at an increased premium. One third of the plans provide full-service benefits for a limited number of days, 35 percent provide full-service benefits without limiting the days, and 30 percent pay a stated reimbursement amount, under the most prevalent certificates. Almost all plans impose a probationary period before such coverage is available. Such periods vary from 6 to 12 months, but the vast majority impose a period of 9 months or more. Unlike insurance company group plans, coverage is not extended for nine months after the policy ceases to cover, probably because of the ease of transferring to nongroup coverage. About 26 percent of plans impose a limit of 10 days' benefit; about 5 percent have a flat $75.00 limit and 13 percent a flat $80.00 limit; 4 percent have a seven-day limit; and the balance show little uniformity.

The following summary of the Blue Cross National Contract Benefits is fairly typical of the more liberal Blue Cross plans. This is a group plan available to groups which involve operations in the territories of several local plans and desire uniform coverage.

## NATIONAL CONTRACT

When you or any member of your famliy covered by Blue Cross are admitted to a member hospital, you are each eligible for these benefits: UP TO 120 DAYS CARE PER HOSPITAL CONFINEMENT IN SEMI-PRIVATE AC-COMMODATIONS. (30 DAYS PER CERTIFICATE YEAR FOR NERVOUS OR MENTAL OR T.B.).

TABLE 6-3

Number and Percent of Blue Cross Members Covered for Specified Extra Expenses, U.S., December 31, 1965

## Number Reported Covered

| | Group Full | Group Partial | Nongroup Full | Nongroup Partial | Senior Full | Senior Partial | Supplementary | Total |
|---|---|---|---|---|---|---|---|---|
| Laboratory examinations | 41,806,657 | 2,285,340 | 9,030,659 | 2,290,637 | 330,007 | 54,833 | 0 | 55,798,133 |
| X-ray examinations | 33,078,704 | 2,538,003 | 6,489,199 | 1,983,655 | 143,139 | 52,152 | 0 | 44,284,852 |
| Anesthesia administration | 37,866,690 | 575,007 | 7,833,269 | 1,353,756 | 322,628 | 22,169 | 0 | 47,973,519 |
| Anesthesia supplies | 42,909,916 | 853,327 | 9,759,597 | 1,313,927 | 357,110 | 39,486 | 0 | 55,233,363 |
| Visiting nurse service | 3,589,429 | | 1,190,518 | | 118,876 | | 3,951,385 | 8,850,208 |
| Nursing home care | 2,901,234 | | 593,571 | | 87,727 | | 3,495,612 | 7,078,144 |
| Home care | 2,021,350 | | 723,801 | | 37,547 | | 332,688 | 3,115,386 |

## Percent of Total Blue Cross Membership Reported Covered

| | Group Full | Group Partial | Nongroup Full | Nongroup Partial | Senior Full | Senior Partial | Supplementary | Total |
|---|---|---|---|---|---|---|---|---|
| Laboratory examinations | 67.6 | 3.7 | 14.6 | 3.7 | .5 | .1 | 0 | 90.2 |
| X-ray examinations | 53.5 | 4.1 | 10.5 | 3.2 | .2 | .1 | 0 | 71.6 |
| Anesthesia administration | 61.2 | .9 | 12.7 | 2.2 | .5 | — | 0 | 77.6 |
| Anesthesia supplies | 69.4 | 1.4 | 15.8 | 2.1 | .6 | .1 | 0 | 89.3 |
| Visiting nurse service | 5.8 | | 1.9 | | .2 | | 6.4 | 14.3 |
| Nursing home care | 4.7 | | 1.0 | | .1 | | 5.7 | 11.4 |
| Home care | 3.3 | | 1.2 | | .1 | | .5 | 5.0 |

Source: Blue Cross Association, *Statistical Bulletin No. 8* (Chicago, 1966).

*Renewal Benefits:* A new benefit period begins whenever a period of 90 days lapses between hospital discharge and readmission.

Without Limit: Operating and treatment rooms and equipment; laboratory and X-ray examinations; all drugs and medicines listed in the official formularies; intravenous injections and solutions; dressings, ordinary splints and plaster casts; anesthesia and its administration; oxygen and its administration; basal metabolism tests; electrocardiograms; transfusion supplies and services; physiotherapy.

Full service in member hospital for emergency room care within 24 hours of accident.

Maternity after 270 days of coverage covered in full.

Pre-existing conditions are covered without a waiting period.

Blue Cross Exclusions: Physicians, special duty nurses and ambulance service; rest cures; admissions primarily for diagnostic purposes; care obtained in U.S. Government hospitals or care for injuries or sickness contracted in the military forces or care obtainable without cost from any governmental agency; occupational ailments or injuries; blood or blood plasma; radium and X-ray therapy; special braces or appliances.

Table 6–4 indicates the extent to which Blue Cross plans cover various conditions often excluded or limited.

Originally Blue Cross plans covered only services performed in hospitals. Recently, they have begun to pay benefits for extended care facilities for posthospital and convalescent care for three million members of the automobile unions in 70 Blue Cross plans across the country. Forty-six Blue Cross plans now provide payment for visiting nurse care at home. Some of these are well established, and others are pilot plans or are in the stage of development. Coverage of such home care can reduce covered hospitalization days substantially.

### Special contracts for the aged

The implementation of the national Title XVIII Medicare program in 1966 led to the development of special contracts to supplement Medicare benefits.

Blue Cross plans generally cover the $40 initial deductible, the $10 per day charge from the 61st to 90th day, and the $20 and 20 percent charge for out-patient diagnostic services, and provide additional limits for out-patient diagnosis. Many cover beyond the 90-day Medicare limit and cover drug costs and the cost of care outside the United States. By December, 1966, 4,773,000 persons were covered by supplementary certificates of this type. This compares well with the 5.6 million persons over 65 insured by Blue Cross when Medicare went into effect July 1, 1966.

Insurance companies also offer integrated suplementary plans similar

TABLE 6-4

Blue Cross Coverage of Specified Conditions

| Condition | | Percent |
|---|---|---|
| Nervous and Mental Conditions (74 out of 75 plans reporting) | | |
| Full benefits.....................12 plans | | 16.2 |
| Limited benefits.................53 plans | | 71.6 |
| Excluded........................ 9 plans | | 12.2 |
| Alcoholism (66 out of 75 plans) | | |
| Full benefits.....................20 plans | | 30.3 |
| Limited benefits.................22 plans | | 33.3 |
| Excluded........................24 plans | | 36.4 |
| Drug addiction (61 out of 75 plans) | | |
| Full benefits.....................21 plans | | 34.4 |
| Limited benefits.................20 plans | | 32.8 |
| Excluded........................20 plans | | 32.8 |
| Tuberculosis (71 out of 75 plans) | | |
| Full benefits.....................16 plans | | 22.5 |
| Limited benefits.................37 plans | | 52.1 |
| Excluded........................18 plans | | 25.4 |
| Venereal diseases (62 out of 75 plans) | | |
| Full benefits.....................51 plans | | 82.3 |
| Limited benefits................. 2 plans | | 3.2 |
| Excluded........................ 9 plans | | 14.5 |
| Quarantinable diseases (58 out of 75 plans) | | |
| Full benefits.....................51 plans | | 87.9 |
| Limited benefits................. 3 plans | | 5.2 |
| Excluded........................ 4 plans | | 6.9 |
| Preexisting conditions (71 out of 75 plans) | | |
| No waiting period................20 plans | | 28.2 |
| Waiting period...................47 plans | | 66.2 |
| Excluded........................ 4 plans | | 5.6 |
| Tonsillitis and adenoiditis (49 out of 75 plans) | | |
| No waiting period................ 7 plans | | 14.3 |
| Waiting period...................42 plans | | 85.7 |

Source: Blue Cross Association.

to Blue Cross coverage but usually include medical and surgical benefits as well as hospital benefits. Some offer a major medical contract excess over Medicare, and some offer a hospital income contract that pays a valued benefit per day or week, regardless of other insurance. At the end of 1966, 4,613,000,000 persons over age 65 had some type of insurance company coverage against hospital expenses. It is not known how many had contracts to supplement Medicare and how many merely had kept previously issued contracts in force. Most of the two million covered by group contracts had coverage which provided for coordination with Medicare (i.e., no duplicate benefits), but no breakdown is available as to the 2.9 million persons covered by individual contracts.

## Summary

Hospital insurance covers the expense of hospital room and board and certain other hospital charges. It is the most popular health insurance coverage today, although its development began only a quarter century ago. Hospital policies are issued by insurance companies, by Blue Cross plans, and by independent plans. The vast majority of insurance company plans and a substantial proportion of the Blue Cross plans provide a stated dollar limit per day up to a stated maximum number of days. A few insurance company plans pay a fixed benefit regardless of actual charges, but usually the benefit is on a reimbursement basis. Most Blue Cross plans and a few insurance company policies provide full coverage of room and board on a service benefit basis up to a stated maximum number of days.

Insurance companies usually cover hospital extra charges with few exceptions up to a stated number of times the daily room benefit. Blue Cross plans usually cover a more restricted list of charges with no limit, but some impose specific or overall dollar limits. Both types of contract usually exclude occupational disability which would be covered under workmen's compensation insurance. Blue Cross plans and insurance company individual policies usually exclude a number of other types of loss, while insurance company group policies are virtually free of exclusions, other than coordination of benefit provisions.

## Selected references

*See the following items from the General Bibliography: 3; 4, ch. 11; 6, chs. 8 and 10; 9, chs. 14 and 16; 10, ch. 5; 12, pp. 28–42 and 61–75; 13, ch. 20; 15, chs. 44 and 45; 20, ch. 4; 30.*

BECKER, HARRY (ed.). *Financing Hospital Care in the United States.* 3 vols. New York: McGraw-Hill Book Co., 1954–55.

BLUE CROSS ASSOCIATION. *Blue Cross Guide.* Chicago, 1967.

CUNNINGHAM, ROBERT M., JR. *The Blue Cross Story.* Chicago: Blue Cross Commission of the American Hospital Association, 1958.

EILERS, ROBERT D. *Regulation of Blue Cross and Blue Shield Plans.* Homewood, Ill.: Richard D. Irwin, Inc., 1963.

FITZHUGH, G. W. "Further Developments on Group Hospital Expense Insurance," *Record of the American Institute of Actuaries,* Vol. XXIX, p. 244.

FOLLMANN, J. F., JR. *The Role of Insurance Companies in Financing Hospital Care.* New York: N.Y.: Health Insurance Council, 1967.

GINGERY, STANLEY W. "Special Investigation of Group Hospital Expense Insurance," *Transactions of the Society of Actuaries,* Vol. IV, p. 44.

HUNTER, ARTHUR, AND THOMPSON ALLEN B. "Hospital Service Insurance," *Transactions of the Actuarial Society of America,* Vol. XLIV, p. 5.

KORMES, MARK. "Prolonged Illness Insurance," *Proceedings of the Casualty Actuarial Society,* Vol. XLI, p. 102.

MCNERNEY, WALTER J. *et al. Hospital and Medical Economics.* Vol. I and II, Chicago: Hospital Research and Educational Trust, 1962.

REED, LOUIS S. "Private Health Insurance: Coverage and Financial Experience, 1940–66," *Social Security Bulletin*, November, 1967, p. 3.

ROREM, C. RUFUS. *Non-Profit Hospital Service Plans*. Chicago: Commission on Hospital Service, American Hospital Association, 1940.

TRUSSELL, RAY E. *Prepayment for Hospital Care in New York State*. New York: School of Public Health and Administration, Columbia University, 1960.

U.S. Department of Health, Education, and Welfare, Social Security Administration. *Principles of Reimbursement for Provider Costs*. Washington, D.C.: U.S. Government Printing Office, 1966.

chapter 7

The most unkindest cut of all.—Shakespeare, *Julius Caesar*

# Surgical and
# Medical Insurance

## Introduction

Surgical insurance provides benefits for the expense of surgical operations and related procedures. Medical insurance provides benefits for other types of treatment by physicians. Policies of these types cover large portions of the population. At the end of 1966 it is estimated that 144,715,000 persons were covered by surgical insurance and 116,462,000 by regular medical insurance.[1] The number of persons covered by surgical insurance increased about 27 times from 1940 to 1966, and the number covered by regular medical insurance increased almost 39 times. The persons covered by surgical insurance were divided among types of insurer as follows: insurance companies—90,294,000; Blue Shield and medical society plans—57,498,000; independent plans—8,633,000. The great majority of the Blue Shield coverage was on a group basis, as was more than 70 percent of the insurance company coverage.

About 116,462,000 persons were covered by regular medical insurance, of whom 60,840,000 were covered by insurance company plans, 53,742,000 by Blue Shield and similar plans, and 8,434,000 by independent plans. Most of this was on a group basis; about five sixths of the persons covered by insurance company plans and the vast majority of all others were under group contracts.

In 1966 benefits paid under medical and surgical insurance (including major medical contracts) equaled $2,831,000,000, of which $1,462,000,000

---

[1] Coverage and benefit figures are from Reed, Louis, "Private Health Insurance: Coverage and Financial Experience, 1940–66," *Social Security Bulletin*, November, 1967, p. 3.

Projected coverage figures for December 31, 1967, indicate about 150 million persons covered by surgical insurance and 121 million covered by regular medical— *Health Insurance News*, December, 1967.

was paid by insurance companies, $1,076,400,000 by Blue Shield and Blue Cross, and $292,700,000 by independent plans. About 58,785,000 of the persons covered by surgical insurance had primary coverage; the remaining 85,930,000 were covered as dependents. In regular medical insurance the numbers were 47,158,000 and 69,304,000, respectively.[2]

## Development

Although prepaid medical care contracts can be traced back to 1655 in Montreal, and a number of industrial plans began operating in the United States in the 1880's, the intensive development of the field has been by two types of insurer which entered the field in later times. Limited surgical benefits first appeared in insurance company individual policies in 1903, and medical benefits were first provided in 1910. In group insurance, surgical benefits were first issued in 1928, but the intensive development did not begin until about 1939. Medical expense benefits were first made available in the early 1940's.

County medical societies first sponsored plans in Washington and Oregon in the late 1920's, but the Blue Shield movement may be said to date from the establishment in 1939 of the California Physician's Service on a state-wide basis. This was sponsored by the California Medical Association and offered comprehensive medical services at a subscription rate of $1.70 per month. Enrollment was limited to insureds with an income of less than $3,000 per year, and physicians were reimbursed on a unit basis according to a scale of fees. The unit was the charge for a single office visit, originally $2.50. The physicians agreed to accept pro-rated amounts if the funds proved inadequate, as was soon the case. Both scales of fees and premiums were increased several times until a balance was reached where the fund was self-supporting and the physicians were satisfied with the income they received.

The Michigan State Medical Society began operation in 1939, and in 1940 plans were started in Buffalo and Utica, New York, and in Pennsylvania and North Carolina.

The American Medical Association began studying prepayment in the 1930's, and in 1942 it endorsed the principle of "medical service plans" and set forth certain guiding principles. In the following year the AMA established a Council on Medical Service to act as a clearinghouse for information, to conduct studies, and to assist local plans generally. A set of "Standards for Acceptance" was set up and the AMA issued a "Seal of Acceptance" for approved plans from 1946 to 1954. In 1946 some of the functions of this organization were taken over by the Associated

---

[2] Health Insurance Institute. *1967 Source Book of Health Insurance Data,* New York: 1968.

Medical Care Plans, Inc., whose name was changed in 1950 to Blue Shield Medical Care Plans, Inc. and in 1960 to the National Association of Blue Shield Plans. This is now the certifying body.

As in hospital insurance, the insurance companies lagged behind, despite their earlier start. Medical and surgical coverage were thought of as "frills" to be attached to hospital or income replacement contracts where the prospect could readily afford the premium. However, as the public demonstrated its demand for such protection, the companies moved into the field in volume and have exceeded Blue Shield in rate of growth. As in hospital insurance, the insurance companies now have the bulk of the surgical market, and it seems probable that, as regular medical coverage expands, they will soon write the majority of this business, too.

**Types of insurer**

As in hospital insurance, insurance companies, Blue Shield, and "independent" plans all are active in providing surgical and medical insurance.

*Blue Shield.* Blue Shield occupies approximately the same position here that Blue Cross occupies in the hospital field: it represents the majority of the plans sponsored by the purveyors of services. Insurance companies include those active in both the life and the casualty fields, and almost all types of insurer organization are represented, although stock and mutual companies are dominant.

Blue Shield organizations are, like Blue Cross, local or statewide autonomous groups. The National Association of Blue Shield Plans operates as a service and accrediting agency and authorizes the use of the Blue Shield designation by approved plans.

The fundamental principles of Blue Shield plans call for service benefits, sponsorship by state or county medical associations, physician control of plans without the intervention of any third party, free choice of physician, and freedom of participating physicians to set fees "in accordance with . . . income status and in a manner that is mutually satisfactory."[3] Just how the provision of service benefits is to be reconciled with fees graded according to income is not spelled out. In practice, a variety of compromises between these conflicting objectives has been employed, and the current AMA "Suggested Guides" refer only to "the greatest possible scope of benefits . . . in accord with the economic conditions of the area. . . ."[4]

---

[3] "Ten Principles" adopted by the House of Delegates of the American Medical Association in 1934. Cited in *Voluntary Prepayment Medical Benefit Plan, 1965* (Chicago: The American Medical Association, 1966), p. 11.

[4] *Ibid.*, pp. 220–22.

Throughout this book, the designation "Blue Shield plans" will be used to refer to the collection of medical-surgical benefit plans which are affiliated with the National Association of Blue Shield Plans, approved by medical societies, and/or affiliated or coordinated with Blue Cross plans. There seem to be 78 such plans in the United States at the present time, 12 in Canada, one in Puerto Rico, and one in Jamaica. Seventy of the United States plans have been approved by medical societies, and 65 of these are members of the National Association of Blue Shield Plans. Five medical-society approved plans do not belong to the national association. There is one plan which belongs to the national association which is not medical-society approved, making a total of 68 member plans in the United States (plus one associate). In addition, there are four Blue Cross or Blue Cross coordinated plans which provide medical-surgical benefits but are neither medical-society approved nor members of the National Association of Blue Shield Plans. It is possible that table 7-1 will clarify

TABLE 7-1

Estimated Number of Blue Shield Medical-Surgical Benefit Plans by Status, 1966

| National Association of Blue Shield Plans Status | Medical Society Approval Status | | | Total United States | Foreign | Grand Total |
|---|---|---|---|---|---|---|
| | Approved | Not Approved | | | | |
| | | Blue Cross or Blue Cross Coordinated | Other | | | |
| Member.............67 | | — | 1 | 68 | 1 | 69 |
| Associate...........— | | — | 1 | 1 | — | 1 |
| Affiliate.............— | | — | — | — | 9 | 9 |
| Nonmember......... 5 | | 4 | a | 9 | 1 | 10 |
| Totals...........72 | | 4 | 2 | 78 | 11 | 89 |

a Excluded from table by definition.
Source: American Medical Association, Council on Medical Service, *Voluntary Prepayment Medical Benefit Plans, 1965* (Chicago, 1965); National Association of Blue Shield Plans, *A Directory of Blue Shield Plans* (Chicago, January, 1967).

the situation. These figures count as only one plan in the state of Washington, Washington Physicians' Service, and its 14 coordinated and 6 autonomous local plans. Four local plans in Oregon are not included in the count.

About 54.5 million persons in the United States and 5.5 million in Canada and Jamaica are covered by the plans reporting to the National Association of Blue Shield Plans, Inc. About 3.4 million persons are covered by Blue Cross, a total of about 57.9 million in this country. The United States associations' plans cover about 29 percent of the eligible population. If the 11.2 million other persons served by U.S. plans under fiscal arrangements with government agencies are included, the U.S. Blue Shield plans would be considered to be serving 33 percent of the population in their areas. These plans, together with the "independent" plans, paid 48 percent of the surgical and regular medical benefits paid by all voluntary insurers in 1966.

Organizationally, the Blue Shield plans are more heterogeneous than Blue Cross. There are four general methods of organization: special enabling legislation, general legislation, chartering as regular insurance companies, and provision of supplementary benefits in Blue Cross coverages. Most of the plans of the first two types enjoy a tax-exempt status as nonprofit organizations, as do the Blue Cross or Blue Cross affiliated plans. In some states, stock or mutual insurance companies have been organized by the medical profession in order to avoid the necessity of special enabling legislation. The plans operated by Blue Cross generally make use of a rider attached to the hospital insurance certificate which provides a cash benefit according to a schedule for various surgical and medical procedures. The hospital association is the insurer. In 13 plans in the National Association of Blue Shield Plans and two other medical-society approved plans, this approach is reversed and the Blue Shield Association is issuing hospital insurance.

The plans organized under special or general legislation are nonprofit associations whose boards of directors or trustees are elected in a variety of ways. On the average, more than two thirds of the board members are physicians,[5] so that the medical profession is in a position to exercise control. Contracts with participating physicians may provide for a scaling of fees when the association faces financial stringency, but it is doubtful if the physicians can be said to be the ultimate risk bearers in the sense that the hospitals are for Blue Cross.

Usually the Blue Shield and Blue Cross organizations in an area work very closely together. Frequently, the Blue Cross organization handles administration, enrollment, recording keeping and claims administration for Blue Shield on some type of reimbursement basis.

*Independent plans.* The term "independent" has been used to denote a health insurance plan which is neither a conventional insurance company nor affiliated with the Blue Cross or medical-society approved. The term is something of a misnomer, since it implies that other types of insurer are not independent, which many of them would resent. However, in the sense of being largely free both of insurance code restrictions and of standards of acceptance of the organized hospitals and physicians, these plans are somewhat more independent than their competitors. This independence is reflected in a bewildering heterogeneity of type of plan and organization. So heterogeneous are these plans that generalizations are almost impossible.

---

[5] Sixty-nine percent in 1966, including ex officio physician members.—*The Blue Shield*, December, 1966, p. 2.

TABLE 7-2

Number of Members Enrolled in Independent Health Insurance Plans,
by Benefit and Type, 1964
(enrollment in thousands)

| Type of Benefit | All Plans | Community | Employer-Employee-Union | Medical Society | Private Group Clinic | Dental Plans |
|---|---|---|---|---|---|---|
| | | | *Type of Plan* | | | |
| Any benefit[a] | 10,025.0 | 3,477.9 | 5,711.7 | 10.4 | 276.0 | 549.0 |
| Hospital care | 6,839.9 | 1,859.0 | 4,784.5 | 8.2 | 188.2 | — |
| Physician service | | | | | | |
| Surgical-Obstetrical services | 8,297.1 | 3,110.6 | 4,968.1 | 10.4 | 208.0 | — |
| In-Hospital medical visits | 7,424.8 | 3,100.0 | 4,069.4 | 9.8 | 245.5 | — |
| X-Ray and laboratory, outside hospital | 7,338.6 | 3,063.5 | 4,071.2 | 5.9 | 198.0 | — |
| Office, clinic, health center visits | 6,511.8 | 2,887.6 | 3,384.6 | 5.3 | 234.1 | — |
| Home calls | 5,376.0 | 2,863.4 | 2,314.7 | 5.3 | 192.5 | — |
| Dental care | 1,800.6 | 100.3 | 1,125.6 | — | 25.8 | 549.0 |
| Drugs outside hospital | 2,658.9 | 188.6 | 2,447.9 | 3.3 | 18.9 | — |
| Visiting nurse service | 4,643.1 | 2,900.4 | 1,741.9 | — | .8 | — |
| Special duty nursing | 3,318.3 | 1,339.7 | 1,966.1 | 3.6 | 8.9 | — |
| Eyeglasses | 884.6 | 25.3 | 859.3 | — | — | — |
| Nursing-home care | 961.5 | — | 961.5 | — | — | — |
| Other benefits | | | | | | |
| Appliances[b] | 93.6 | 10.4 | 83.3 | — | — | — |
| Ambulances[b] | 410.8 | 89.9 | 307.3 | 7.5 | 6.2 | — |

[a] Data do not add to totals since most plans provide more than one benefit.
[b] Represents a minimum statement since some other plans probably provided these benefits but did not so specify.

A survey in 1965[6] indicated that there were over 580 independent plans in operation in the United States. The majority of these plans were industrial. Others were consumer-sponsored, community-sponsored, fraternal, and private group clinics. The majority of these offered more or less comprehensive benefits; the balance were limited to hospital and/or surgical coverage.

The industrial plans may be classified further on the basis of sponsorship. This sponsorship may be employer, employee, union, or employer-employee. Most of these confine their membership to a particular employee group. Many of the nonindustrial plans also operate within a limited membership area such as a fraternal society or a particular consumer organization.

In the broad sense, the majority of persons enrolled in all types of in-

---

[6] Louis S. Reed, Anne H. Anderson, and Ruth S. Hanft, *Independent Health Insurance Plans in the United States—1965 Survey* (Washington, D.C.: U.S. Government Printing Office, 1966).

TABLE 7-2 (Continued)    Number of Independent Health Insurance Plans, by Benefit and Type, 1964

| Type of Benefit | All Plans | Community | Employer-Employee-Union | Medical Society | Private Group Clinic | Dental Plans |
|---|---|---|---|---|---|---|
| | | | Type of Plan | | | |
| Any benefit[a] .............. 582 | 43 | 507 | 2[c] | 21 | 9 |
| Hospital care .............. 463 | 34 | 419 | 1 | 9 | — |
| Physician service | | | | | |
| Surgical-Obstetrical services .............. 470 | 33 | 420 | 2 | 15 | — |
| In-Hospital medical visits .................. 337 | 30 | 290 | 2 | 15 | — |
| X-Ray and laboratory, outside hospital ....... 375 | 32 | 328 | 2 | 13 | — |
| Office, clinic, health center visits .......... 338 | 32 | 289 | 2 | 15 | — |
| Dental care ............... 99 | 5 | 80 | — | 5 | 9 |
| Drugs outside hospital .... 142 | 13 | 122 | 1 | 6 | — |
| Visiting nurse service ...... 62 | 13 | 48 | — | 1 | — |
| Special duty nursing ...... 94 | 9 | 81 | 1 | 3 | — |
| Eyeglasses ................ 121 | 1 | 120 | — | — | — |
| Nursing-home care ........ 33 | — | 33 | — | — | — |
| Other benefits | | | | | |
| Appliances[b] ............. 12 | 1 | 11 | — | — | — |
| Ambulances[b] ........... 33 | 2 | 28 | 1 | 2 | — |

a Data do not add to totals since most plans provide more than one benefit.
b Represents a minimum statement since some other plans probably provided these benefits but did not so specify.
c These plans had affiliated with Blue Shield by 1966.
Source: Louis S. Reed, A. D. Anderson, and Ruth S. Hanft, *Independent Health Insurance Plans in the United States*, 1965 Survey (Washington, D.C., U.S. Government Printing Office, 1966).

dependent plans are in plans developed with consumer, including union, backing. In addition to the private group clinics, many of the plans operate on a group-practice basis for one or more benefits. Despite the disapproval or only grudging approval of the American Medical Association, this method of organization seems to be growing in popularity. In 1966, 3.8 million persons were enrolled in plans which provided at least some benefits on a group-practice basis. Table 7–2 indicates the enrollment in the various types of independent plan by type of benefit and the number of plans in 1964. Table 7–3 indicates the proportion of total enrollees who had group-practice type benefits.

A broader survey in 1962 listed 825 independent plans: 682 employer-employee-union sponsored, 24 medical society, 76 community sponsored, 7 dental society, and 36 private group clinics.[7]

---

[7] U.S. Department of Health, Education and Welfare, *Independent Health Insurance Plans, A List By States, June, 1962* (Washington D.C.: U.S. Government Printing Office, 1963). The medical society plans have since disappeared by affiliation with Blue Shield or otherwise.

TABLE 7-3

Number and Percent of Those with Independent Plans Covered by Group Practice
(in millions)

| Type of Plan | Hospital Care | | Surgery | | In-Hospital Medical Visits | | Office, Clinic, or Health Center Visits | |
|---|---|---|---|---|---|---|---|---|
| | No. | Percent | No. | Percent | No. | Percent | No. | Percent |
| All plans..........2,771 | | 41.78 | 3,763 | 45.20 | 3,430 | 45.58 | 4,158 | 59.97 |
| Community.......1,670 | | 85.03 | 2,415 | 68.49 | 2,415 | 68.73 | 2,434 | 72.48 |
| Employer-Employee union..........1,050 | | 22.74 | 1,150 | 24.99 | 780 | 20.65 | 1,500 | 44.76 |
| Private group clinic........... 51 | | 100 | 198 | 100 | 235 | 100 | 224 | 100 |

Source: Louis S. Reed, "Private Health Insurance: Coverage and Financial Experience, 1940–66," *Social Security Bulletin*, November, 1967, p. 3.

The Cooperative Health Foundation of America includes about 20 of the larger consumer-sponsored plans. These are consumer controlled and consumer initiated. They bring together a group of patients and a group of physicians, including specialists, and emphasize completeness of coverage and preventive effort. Overutilization is said to be no problem because of the cooperative nature of the plans and a recognition of consumer responsibility for their success. One might wonder whether this device operates as well in a large city plan as in a small rural one.

**Surgical benefits**

*Insurance company plans.* The typical insurance company plan provides surgical benefits payable to the insured in cash (unless assigned to the surgeon) according to a schedule of operations. The insuring clause in a typical *group policy* provides:

The —— Insurance Company HEREBY AGREES TO PAY the benefits hereinafter described to any employee of —— (herein called the employer) or of an associated company described in this policy, who, as a result of a disease for which the employee is not entitled to benefits under any workmen's compensation law or as a result of an accidental bodily injury which does not arise out of or in the course of employment, undergoes a surgical operation enumerated in the applicable "Schedule of Operations" which is set forth in this policy, provided such operation is performed by a legally qualified surgeon and occurs

(a) while the employee is insured hereunder, or

(b) within a period of three months following termination of the employee's insurance hereunder and during a period of total disability which commences while the employee is insured hereunder.

The foregoing agreement is subject to all of the terms appearing on this and the following pages, which are hereby made a part of this policy.

It will be noted that operations must be performed by a "legally qualified surgeon," and coverage is provided only for accidental injury and disease which are nonoccupational in origin. Since the coverage of occupational disease under workmen's compensation laws varies so greatly from state to state, the limitation is expressed as a disease for which benefits are not payable under a workmen's compensation act. This serves the purpose of avoiding possible gaps in coverage.

The benefit clause of this policy provides that the insurer will reimburse the fees actually charged up to the maximum for that procedure in the applicable schedule of operations as specified in a classification table. The purpose of the classification table is to provide varying benefit amounts to different classes of employees. Usually the basis of classification is the level of employee earnings. The total payment for two or more operations during a single period of disability is stated in the table. This will usually be the same figure as the maximum for the most expensive single operation in the schedule but may be somewhat higher.

The successive or recurrent disability clause provides only that there must be "complete recovery" or a return to work of at least one day. Obstetrical benefits are excluded because they are covered under a separate benefit clause. This contract, like most, is on a reimbursement basis: the benefit equals actual charges incurred up to the maximum in the schedule. The exclusion of operations in government hospitals and other operations for which no fee is charged merely acts to reinforce this principle.

The maximum amounts payable are listed in a schedule of operations. The most frequently used schedules in group insurance have a maximum benefit of $300 to $500, but in high-cost areas or for persons in higher income brackets the schedule maximum may be increased in multiples to $900 or more. The most frequently issued new group policies in 1967 provided a $300 maximum, but 49 percent of the employees were covered by a schedule maximum of $400 or more, and some plans provided a maximum of $1,000 or more. The average for new groups in 1967 was $370. A typical schedule from a *family policy* is reproduced in part below.

## SCHEDULE OF OPERATIONS

This Schedule shows the maximum payments applicable to the respective operations where the Maximum Surgical Expense Benefit is $250.00. For any operation neither specified nor expressly excluded, the Company will determine a maximum payment consistent with the payment for any listed operation of comparable difficulty and complexity, the maximum payment not to exceed such Maximum Surgical Expense Benefit. No coverage is provided under Benefit Provision II and no benefit is provided under this Schedule for dental or obstetrical procedures.

|  | Maximum |
| Description of Operation | Payment |

Abdomen

Appendectomy, freeing of adhesions
or surgical exploration of the
abdominal cavity.......................$125.00
Removal of, or other operation on gall
bladder................................. 187.50
Gastro-enterostomy..................... 187.50
Resection of stomach, bowel or rectum   250.00
Closure of perforated ulcer............... 125.00

Abscesses (See Tumors)

Amputations

Thigh, leg............................... 156.25
Upper arm, forearm, entire hand or
foot.................................... 125.00
Fingers or toes, each..................... 18.75

Breast

Removal of benign tumor or cyst re-
quiring hospital confinement........... 62.50
Simple amputation....................... 125.00
Radical amputation..................... 187.50

Chest

Complete thoracoplasty, transthoracic
approach to stomach, diaphragm,
or esophagus; sympathectomy or
laryngectomy........................... 250.00

Removal of lung or portion of lung........ 250.00

Bronchoscopy, esophagoscopy........... 50.00

Induction of artificial pneumothorax,
initial.................................. 31.25
refills, each (not more than 12)......... 12.50

. . . . . . . . . . . . . .

Tumors

Cutting operation for removal of one or
more benign or superficial tumors,
cysts or abscesses:
Requiring hospital confinement....... 31.25
Not requiring hospital confinement... 12.50
Malignant tumors of face, lip or skin...... 62.50

Varicose Veins

Injection treatment, complete procedure, one or both legs.................. 50.00
Cutting operation, complete procedure, one leg........................... 62.50
both legs............. ................. 93.75

Obstetrical benefits are provided but are governed by a separate benefit clause. Its primary effect is to exclude obstetrical coverage during the first nine months of insurance. The clause provides extended insurance for a period of nine months after termination of coverage. This is the customary approach.

Although this policy provides an allowance for simple delivery, many contracts do not provide such coverage. Some policies exclude maternity benefits altogether, others limit the coverage as here illustrated, and a few provide benefits without restriction except as to amount limits in the schedule. Group surgical may be written separately, but usually the group has other coverage, such as hospital or disability income with the same insurer.

In *individual policies,* surgical coverage is almost invariably available only as an addition to a basic hospital or disability income policy. Thus the benefits are usually provided as one section of a schedule policy or in the form of a rider. Where attached to or a part of a disability income policy covering sickness only, the surgical schedule will cover only operations on account of such sickness. Thus the schedule would not include benefits for treatments of dislocations and fractures. Otherwise, schedules in individual policies are about the same as in group policies. The insuring clause and benefit clause, however, vary considerably from the group policy. A fairly typical surgical benefit clause from an individual hospital-surgical policy is reproduced below:

*II. Surgical Expense Benefit*—If injury or sickness requires any covered family member to undergo an operation while such person is covered under this policy or while the Daily Hospital Benefit is payable under Benefit Provision I with respect to such person, the Company will pay, after applying the Deductible Amount provision, a benefit equal to the amount actually charged for the operation but not more than the maximum payment provided therefor in accordance with the Schedule of Operations. Two or more surgical procedures performed through the same incision or because of the same or related conditions shall be considered as one operation; the maximum payment applicable to such operation shall be whichever one of the maximum payments applicable to such procedures is the largest.

In accident policies, separate benefits for hospital, surgical, and other expenses are not usually provided. In lieu thereof, it is common to find a provision granting a blanket medical reimbursement benefit for accidental injury expenses up to a stated limit. The limit is usually $500 or $1,000. Of course, the insuring clause would also differ. A typical accident expense benefit clause from an individual schedule accident policy is given below.

## EXPENSE OF MEDICAL, SURGICAL, HOSPITAL, AND NURSES' CARE

If such injury shall require, commencing within twenty-six weeks after the date of the accident causing such injury, medical or surgical treatment, hospital confinement or the employment of a trained nurse, the Company will pay, in addition to any other benefit to which the Insured may be entitled, the actual expenses of such treatment, hospital charges and nurses' fees, but not exceeding, for any one accident, the limit specified.

*Dependents' coverage* for surgical expense is available under group contracts in the same fashion as is hospital protection. However, in individual disability income policies coverage of dependents for surgical and medical expense is not too common. By far the most common method of writing surgical coverage on a family basis is to provide this as a rider or optional benefit clause in a family hospital contract. The benefits are very similar to those under group contracts and the dependent coverage provisions are the same as those discussed above in regard to family hospital policies. The surgical insuring clause from a family hospital-surgical policy was reproduced above.

*Exclusions* under group policies are very few. They appear only in the insuring clause, the definition of covered employees and dependents, the provisions relating to term of coverage, the definitions of hospital, and and the requirement that operations be performed by a "legally qualified surgeon." These are not so much exclusions as definitions of the coverage and have all been discussed above. The provisions as to definitions of hospital and term of employee coverage are the same, in general, as the comparable provisions in group hospital policies.

**Blue Shield plans.** Most Blue Shield plans offer service-type benefits, in that payment is made directly to the surgeon rather than to the patient. However, most do not offer full-service benefits except to lower-income groups. Full-service benefits involve an agreement that there will be no additional charge to the insured patient beyond what the policy provides. Only four plans in the National Association of Blue Shield Plans (plus several of the local Washington plans), one other medical-society approved plans and one Blue Cross affiliated plan offer full-service benefits to all subscribers. Indeed these last two often are classified as independents.

Since 1958, a number of Blue Shield Plans have begun providing paid-in-full coverage on the basis of the usual, customary and prevailing charges of individual physicians. By the end of 1967, 48 member plans of the national association were providing such coverage to approximately four million persons. It is estimated that approximately two thirds of the member plans of the national association will have some form of paid-in-full, no income limit coverage available for some groups by 1968. Physicians file their usual fee schedule with the Blue Shield plan and are paid in accordance with this schedule. The maximum fee for each procedure is set high enough to include 90 percent of physicians and 90 percent of fees. The physician collects either his own usual fee or the maximum, based on prevailing fees in the area, whichever is less.

Partial service benefits are much more common. Forty-eight of the N.A.B.S.P. plans and two other medical-society approved plans provide benefits on this basis. Under this arrangement, a patient with an income below some specified amount receives full-service benefits. In other cases, the patient receives credit toward the surgeon's fee for a dollar amount according to a schedule. The patient must pay the balance himself. The income ceilings for full-service benefits vary from $1,500 to $12,000 for an individual and from $2,400 to $12,000 for a family.[8] The median is $6,000 for individuals and $7,500 for families.

Many plans are on a reimbursement basis for all subscribers. Here a stated cash allowance is paid as a credit toward the fee, with the patient paying the balance, if any. Fourteen N.A.B.S.P. plans, two other medical-society approved plans and three Blue Cross plans are on a straight cash indemnity, or reimbursement, basis. This amount is determined according to a schedule. There is no difference between such a plan and the typical insurance company plan except the technicality of direct payment to the physician; and in an insurance plan it almost always is possible to assign benefits to the physician.

In 1966, 4.4 percent of the persons enrolled under Blue Shield plans were covered by full-service benefit contract, or paid-in-full usual, customary and prevailing fee contracts; 63.4 percent by a partial service contract, 24.6 percent by a cash benefit contract and 7.1 percent by a contract to supplement Medicare Part B coverage. It is impossible to obtain data on the portion of subscribers under the partial service plans who fall under the income and net worth limits and thus get full-service coverage. National Blue Shield leaders have suggested that income limits should be high enough to provide full-service benefits for 75 percent of enrollees, but some plans fall far short of this goal. Where a schedule of benefits is included (in all but the full-service plans), the schedule is often comparable to the schedules used in insurance company policies, except that Blue Shield schedules more frequently provide for fees of assistant surgeons and anesthesiologists. Some schedules are quite complex, on the other hand.

In 1964, 54 of the plans participated in a study of the effectiveness of their programs. Overall, it showed that two thirds of surgery, anesthesia, and in-hospital medical claims were paid in full, and 79 percent of patient

---

[8] Three plans also have net worth limits so that the physician may bill excess charges when the patient's net worth or income exceeds the stated figure.

costs were covered. Under the most comprehensive contracts of each plan, 83 percent of the studied-claims were paid in full, and 88 percent of patient costs were covered. The study involved a sampling of 470,000 questionnaires in a six-week period.

Even full-service plans include what amounts to a schedule. However, it is part of the contract with the participating physicians, not the contract with the insured subscribers. Maternity benefits under the most widely held contracts are usually limited to $50 to $150 for a simple delivery, with $75 being the most common benefit. Usually twice this amount is allowed for Caesarean section. The plans usually require a probationary period of nine months or 270 days before maternity benefits are payable and, unlike insurance company plans, do not provide a comparable extension period after coverage terminates. Plans usually have the same types of provision for multiple operations as do insurance company plans.

Dependents' coverage is usually available through Blue Shield plans on both a group and an individual basis.

Exclusions under Blue Shield are often more extensive than under typical insurance company group plans, a situation similar to that in hospital insurance. The following list is somewhat more liberal than typical:

*Blue Shield Exclusions:* Hospital, Dental or Nursing Services, Appliances and Supplies; Rest Cures; services primarily for diagnostic purposes; care obtained in U.S. Government Hospitals or care for injuries or sickness contracted in the military forces or care obtainable without cost from any governmental agency; occupational ailments or injuries; plastic operations for cosmetic or beautifying purposes; preexisting conditions during the first nine (9) months of the contract.

Other types of treatment frequently specially limited include dental surgery, normal childbirth, adenoids, tonsillitis, alcoholism, appendicitis, cancer, contagious disease, drug addiction, female diseases, hemorrhoids, hernia, mental and nervous conditions, self-inflicted injuries, including attempted suicide, tuberculosis, and venereal disease. Frequently the limitation takes the form of a probationary period such as the nine months specified in the list quoted above for preexisting conditions.

### Regular medical benefits

*General.* Medical benefits refer to benefits payable for ordinary physicians' fees for hospital, home, or office visits other than for surgical procedures. They are to be distinguished, on the one hand, from surgical coverage, which protects against the expense of surgeons' fees and, on the other hand, from major medical coverage, which protects against almost all types of medical care, including hospital charges, with few, if any, internal limits. Frequently, medical insurance is referred to as "basic medical," "primary medical," or "general medical" to emphasize the latter distinction. The term "regular medical" will be used generally in this book.

Medical benefits are generally provided, regardless of insurer type, on one of the following three bases: (1) *In-hospital medical.* This provides payments for visits by a physician to the patient while confined in a legally constituted hospital as an in-patient upon the recommendation of a legally qualified physician. No benefits are provided for other physicians' services, nor are surgical fees or fees for postoperative visits by the surgeon usually covered. (2) Total disability medical. This plan is usually written only to cover employed persons, since the fact of total disability is practically impossible to establish for others. The benefits cover charges for visits by a physician whether or not the patient is in a hospital as long as the patient is totally disabled. Sometimes a deductible of the first one or more calls is imposed on claims for visits other than while in the hospital. (3) Nondisability medical. This provides benefits for hospital, home, and office treatments with few exclusions. However, the use of a deductible is rather common. In new group business in 1966, 99 percent of the employees with regular medical benefits were covered for in-hospital calls, 11.0 percent in offices or clinics, and 10.5 percent at home. Nationally it is estimated that private health insurance covers office and home visits for 73.7 million persons, 37.9 percent of the population, and 63.3 percent of those with in-hospital medical. This figure looks high and may include some persons covered only by major medical.

*Insurance company benefits.* In-hospital medical benefits are usually provided for all admissions except maternity cases and surgical cases. The usual plan provides a benefit of $5 per day of hospitalization but amounts of $6 or more are available.

There is a tendency to pay more for a home call than a hospital call, and less for an office call in contracts which cover all three. In group policies this limit usually applies to the aggregate charges, not to the charges for each day. The overall limit is equal to the actual number of days of hospitalization times the daily rate or an aggregate dollar limit, whichever is smaller. The overall limit may be anywhere from 50 to 100 times the daily rate. In individual policies, the limit usually applies separately to each day of hospitalization, or sometimes to each call. Most policies are on an indemnity basis, reimbursing up to the limit. The following benefit clause from an individual schedule sickness policy providing regular medical benefits on an in-hospital basis is fairly typical:

MEDICAL ATTENTION WHILE IN HOSPITAL

(If shown as included coverage in Schedule of Benefits)

If, on account of such sickness and while confined in a hospital as hereinbefore provided the Insured shall receive medical treatment personally administered by a legally qualified physician or surgeon (other than an intern) the Company will pay periodically the actual expense of such medical treatment not exceeding $5.00 per day for not more than 100 days for any one sickness.

This contract would ordinarily be sold only to a person also carrying an accident policy, and in-hospital and other physicians' fees would be included in the blanket accident medical care clause. Such a clause is quoted above in the section on surgical benefits.

Portions of a group rider providing medical benefits on a total disability basis are reproduced below.

If an employee, while insured under this rider, is wholly disabled by a disease for which the employee is not entitled to benefits under any workmen's compensation law or by an accidental bodily injury which does not arise out of or in the course of employment, and thereby prevented from performing any and every duty pertaining to the employee's occupation, and if the employee is given treatment by a legally qualified physician for and during such disability, the Insurance Company shall pay a benefit in an amount equal to the fees actually charged to the employee by the physician for such treatment, but not exceeding the applicable maximum payment determined from the foregoing Table of Benefits.

The following clauses from a group policy rider provide medical benefits regardless of disability or hospitalization:

If an employee, while insured under this rider, is given treatment by a legally qualified physician for a disease for which the employee is not entitled to benefits under any workmen's compensation law or for an accidental bodily injury which does not arise out of or in the course of employment, the Insurance Company shall pay a benefit in an amount equal to the fees actually charged to the employee by the physician for such treatment, but not exceeding the applicable maximum payment determined from the foregoing Table of Benefits.

It is common to exclude workmen's compensation injuries in group policies as in the two examples above. Other common exclusions are pregnancy, childbirth, and miscarriage; dental work and treatment; eye examinations and fitting of glasses; X rays, drugs, dressings, medicines and appliances; and treatment in or from a government hospital or for which no charge is made. It is common to provide that all treatments given on a single day shall be considered one treatment and to exclude from the medical coverage any charges by surgeons after an operation.

Group policies frequently provide an extended coverage period of 90 days or so after coverage otherwise is terminated for medical treatments or surgery, provided the employee is totally disabled during the interim. Some policies include provision for a deductible of the first few dollars of fees or a waiting period which excludes the first one to three treatments for a particular condition. This is particularly common on the nondisability form. It is common to provide in the schedules of benefits for different amounts per day depending on the location of treatment, subject to an overall limit in dollars per disease or injury. For example, a given employee class might have benefits of $5 per visit at the doctor's office, $6 per visit in the hospital, and $7 per visit in the patient's home. The situation in regard to dependents' coverage is the same as in surgical insurance. It is readily available on a group or individual basis.

**Blue Shield benefits.** All Blue Shield plans provide medical as well as surgical benefits. Twelve of the member plans of the National Association of Blue Shield Plans, three other medical-society approved plans and one Blue Cross coordinated plan make medical benefits available in the physician's office or patient's home on a nondisability basis. The other plans make this coverage available on an in-hospital basis only. Most participate in national contracts such as those for federal employees and auto workers.

Either the office and home medical benefits, the entire medical benefit package, or both may be optional at extra premium. Most plans provide several levels of benefit coverage, varying as to amount, duration, or type of benefit.

The Wisconsin Physicians Service may be cited as an example of a plan providing such choice of coverages. It provides four types of basic contract. Plans A and B and the "Century Plan" (for subscribers over age 65) provide schedule benefits as follows:

|  | Plan A | Plan B | Century Plan |
|---|---|---|---|
| Surgical schedule maximum | $300 | $200 | $200 |
| In Hospital Medical, per day (higher amounts for first three days) | $ 4[a] | $ 3[b] | $ 4[c] |
| Maximum number of days | 30 | 30 | 60 |
| Other: Anesthesia | $ 37.50 | $ 25.00 | $ 25.00 |
| Diagnostic X ray | $ 50 | $ 35 | $ 35 |
| Micromic tissue pathology | 0 | 0 | $ 10 |
| Radiation therapy | | | per schedule |

[a] $10 first day; $5.00 second and third day.
[b] $8.00 first day; $4.00 second and third day.
[c] $8.00 first day; $5.00 second and third day.

Alternatively, another option is available providing unscheduled full service benefits up to $1,000 per illness.

*Unscheduled (Special Service) Benefits*—Maximum $1,000 per illness. Benefits paid on basis of reasonable charges of physicians, and charges of assistants and consultants are covered. Benefits available for surgery, Caesarean sections, Porrocaesarean sections, miscarriages, in-hospital medical care, anesthesia, X-ray associated with surgery or maternity, and radiation therapy for proven malignancies. Indemnity of $75 provided for maternity services other than those listed.

At an extra premium, this may be extended by the "Major Illness Endorsement" as follows:

*Major Illness Endorsement*—Extends Special Service Maximum to $10,000 and extends coverage to 100% of reasonable charges for all physicians' services, and 80% of charges for ancillary services such as nursing, drugs, physical therapy, appliances, etc. "Corridor" deductible of $25 per illness must be incurred in a thirty-day period.

This provides major medical benefits for most expenses other than hospital expense and is representative of the broader Blue Shield supplemental plans. These will be discussed in the next chapter.

Some Blue Shield contracts provide benefits for assistant surgeons, and anesthesiologists' fees, and many provide a larger amount of benefit in the first several days of hospital stay when the patient may require more attention than subsequently. Some of these plans use a highly detailed schedule of benefits based on a relative value schedule.[9]

As an illustration of coverage of anesthesiology, pathology, intensive care, and of the nature of a relative value schedule, portions of the benefit schedule used by Blue Shield of Florida for the Federal Employees Health Benefits Program, effective November 1, 1964, are reproduced below. The schedule is in the form of a 69-page booklet, and is based on the California Relative Value Schedule and unit values of $6 for in-hospital medical benefits and $5 for other services. The income limits for full service benefits are $5,000 for an individual and $7,500 for a family in the high-option plan, and $3,000 and $4,000 in the low-option contract. A supplementary major medical contract, described in the next chapter, is available optionally.

A recent survey showed that all U.S. Blue Shield plans provide in-hospital medical benefits, and all but 18 plans require it. Sixty-seven provide first-day coverage. Four have a deductible period for all conditions, and two have one but waive it for listed conditions. In their best local programs nine plans provide in-hospital medical on a prevailing charge basis. Most plans provide higher benefits for the first visit, and 59 offer scheduled intensive care benefits.

Since Blue Shield contracts cover surgical and medical benefits in the same contract the comments on exclusions made above in regard to surgical insurance are equally applicable to medical. Occasionally Blue Shield plans impose stricter limits as to amount or duration of dependents' benefits than on primary coverage, but for the most part, employee and dependent coverage is identical.

---

[9] A relative value schedule is a schedule of the relative economic value of medical, surgical, and related services in units. It is not a fee schedule nor a maximum benefit schedule, but can be converted into one by multiplying the units by a monetary value. These schedules have been developed by state medical societies. They are discussed more fully in Chapter 10.

## SURGERY AND ANESTHESIA

| | | HIGH OPTION Surg. | Anes. | Follow-Up Days | LOW OPTION Surg. | Anes. |
|---|---|---|---|---|---|---|

### CARDIOVASCULAR SYSTEM
#### Heart and Pericardium

*Incision*

| | | Surg. | Anes. | Days | Surg. | Anes. |
|---|---|---|---|---|---|---|
| 2301 | Cardiotomy with exploration or removal of foreign body.................... | 500.00 | 75.00 + T | 90 | 333.00 | 82.00 |
| 2305 | Pericardiotomy with exploration, drainage, or removal of foreign body..... | 500.00 | 65.00 + T | 90 | | |
| 2310 | Pericardiocentesis: puncture of pericardial space for aspiration.............* | 25.00 | | 0 | IC | |
| 2311 | subsequent.............* | 20.00 | | 0 | 10.00 | |
| 2315 | Valvulotomy or commissurotomy................ | 600.00 | 75.00 + T | 120 | 266.00 | 79.00 |
| 2316 | Operation for regurgitation | By Report | 75.00 + T | | 333.00 | 79.00 |
| 2317 | Operation for coronary disease (poudrage).......... | 250.00 | 75.00 + T | 90 | 167.00 | 67.00 |
| | *Excision* | | | | | |
| 2321 | Pericardiectomy........... | 500.00 | 75.00 + T | 90 | 266.00 | 76.00 |
| 2325 | Valvulectomy............. | | | | 333.00 | 79.00 |
| 2326 | Excision of auricular appendage................. | | | | 200.00 | 76.00 |
| | *Introduction* | | | | | |
| 2331 | Catheterization` of the heart (independent procedure)................... | 75.00 | 25.00 + T | 7 | IC | |
| 2332 | Injection for angiocardiograms.................... | 25.00 | 15.00 + T | 7 | 17.00 | |
| 2333 | Retrograde aortography—cut down and pass catheter................. | By Report | 15.00 + T | | 67.00 | |
| | *Destruction* | | | | | |
| 2341 | Cardiolysis............... | | | | 200.00 | 63.00 |
| 2345 | Pericardiolysis........... | | | | 200.00 | 63.00 |
| | *Suture* | | | | | |
| 2351 | Cardiorrhaphy: suture of heart wound or injury...... | 500.00 | 75.00 + T | 90 | 266.00 | 73.00 |
| 2352 | suture 1-A septal defect | By Report | 75.00 + T | | 333.00 | 76.00 |
| 2355 | Pericardiorrhaphy: suture of pericardial wound or injury..................... | 350.00 | 75.00 + T | 90 | 233.00 | 63.00 |

### ANESTHESIA BENEFITS SCHEDULE

1. Regional, intravenous, Inhalation, Intraspinal and Caudal anesthesia service will be payable when administered by a Participating Physician not in charge of the case when the subscriber-patient undergoes compensable surgery as an inpatient or in the hospital outpatient department.
2. Anesthesia Service allowance includes the customary pre and postoperative visits, the administration of the anesthetic and the administration of fluids or blood incident to the anesthesia or surgery.
3. Listed anesthesia Service Fees are payable only when the anesthesia is personally administered by a Participating Physician who remains in constant attendance during the procedure for the sole purpose of rendering such anesthesia service.

4. In procedures where no anesthesia unit is listed, and anesthesia service is required and compensable or the unit is listed as "T," the fee for service is determined according to time by the scale below.

   (a) *High Option Plan* subscribers shall be eligible for anesthesia services on the basis of the Scheduled Anesthesia Allowance plus "Time Units." Time Units shall be computed on the basis of one unit for each fifteen minutes or major part thereof. A Time Unit shall be valued at $5.00 per unit.

   (b) *Low Option Plan:*

First half-hour (or any fraction thereof)...................................13.00
Third and fourth quarter-hour (or major fraction thereof), each............ 5.00
Each succeeding quarter-hour (or major fraction thereof)................. 3.00
Where unusual detention with the patient is essential for the safety and welfare of such patient each quarter-hour (or major fraction thereof)...... 3.00

5. Anesthesia based on time starts with the beginning of anesthesia and ends when the anesthesiologist is no longer in professional attendance (when the patient may safely be placed under customary postoperative supervision.)

6. General Information under Surgery regarding multiple or bilateral surgical procedures is equally applicable to anesthesia procedures.

## PATHOLOGY BENEFITS SCHEDULE

Pathology benefits are limited to tissue examination as shown below

| Code Number | Service | High Option | Low Option |
|---|---|---|---|
| 8901 | Surgical, gross only—no variation........................... | 3.00 | 3.00 |
| 8903 | gross and microscopic, routine............................ | 15.00 | 10.00 |
| 8905 | Gross and microscopic, special (including serial sections).... | IC | 30.00 |
| 8907 | frozen section for establishment of immediate diagnosis during surgery (includes consultation with surgeon and permanent section)........................................ | 25.00 | 20.00 |

## OUTPATIENT EMERGENCY TREATMENT OF MINOR INJURIES

Initial Care Only

| Code Number | Service | High Option | Low Option |
|---|---|---|---|
| 0043 | Concussion, cerebral, uncomplicated....................... | IC | IC |
| 0071 | Puncture wounds.......................................... | IC | IC |
| 0072 | Burn, first degree, initial treatment........................ | IC | IC |
| 0073 | Lacerations (superficial except face) up to 3 inches.......... with sutures Use Code 0381 (FOR FACIAL LACERATIONS AND OTHERS OVER 3 INCHES —USE REPAIR—PLASTIC SURGERY, CODES 0265 to 0267.) 50% of fee is allowable for each additional laceration. | IC | IC |
| 0074 | Poisoning by ingestion (treatment to include gastric lavage, resuscitation therapy and supervision)......................13.00 | | 8.00 |
| 0075 | Snake bite—including cruciate incisions and anti-venom..... | IC | IC |

## MEDICAL BENEFIT SCHEDULE

| Service | Allowance |
|---|---|
| HIGH OPTION ALLOWANCE | |
| Visits and all necessary care, first two inpatient days (Special Medical Benefits)..................................................... | 75.00 |
| Visits and care during the first inpatient day including routine history and physical examination..................................... | 18.00 |
| Visits and care on each subsequent inpatient day.................. | 6.00 |
| Follow-up Hospital Visit necessitating care over and above routine visit* *.................................................... | 12.00 |
| Follow-up Hospital Visit necessitating complete re-examination and reevaluation of patient as a whole, same illness* *.............. | 15.00 |

Follow-up Hospital Visit necessitating complete re-examination and re-evaluation of patient as a whole, new illness* *...............18.00
* * to be documented by submission of a written report. No two of the above mentioned allowances shall be payable simultaneously.

LOW OPTION ALLOWANCE

Visits and all necessary care, first two inpatient days (Special Medical Benefits)....................................................50.00
Visits and care during the first inpatient day including routine history and physical examination......................................12.00
Visits and care on each subsequent inpatient day.................. 5.00

### INTENSIVE CARE SPECIAL MEDICAL BENEFITS

Fee Schedule for First Two Days Care
(In lieu of other Plan payments)

This list of diseases to be documented and evidence of diagnosis and intensive care should appear on the patient's hospital Medical Record and the Doctor's Service Report.

SPECIAL BENEFITS FOR HIGH OPTION ONLY: Benefits allowed for any period of ten days intensive care during an in-hospital stay in the following manner—the below listed amount will be allowed for up to the first two days of intensive care period and the regular daily allowance will be allowed for the remaining eight days. Intensive care required for conditions other than those listed will be given individual consideration, upon documentation. This is a Service Benefit for eligible subscribers.

| | HIGH | LOW |
|---|---|---|
| *A. Diseases of the Nervous System* | | |
| 1. Acute Meningitis..................................................... | 75.00 | 50.00 |
| 2. Cerebral Vascular Accident (Hemorrhage, Thrombosis, Embolization)........................................................................ | 50.00 | 33.00 |
| 3. Myasthenia Gravis, acute onset................................... | 50.00 | 33.00 |
| 4. Acute Poliomyelitis, without bulbar symptoms................... | 50.00 | 33.00 |
|    with bulbar symptoms............................................ | 75.00 | 50.00 |
| 5. Spontaneous Subarachnoid Hemorrhage......................... | 75.00 | 50.00 |
| 6. Acute Encephalitis (Guillain-Barre)............................... | 50.00 | 33.00 |
| *B. Diseases of the Cardiovascular System* | | |
| 7. Coronary Thrombosis—many causes.............................. | 75.00 | 50.00 |
| 8. Cardiac Tamponade, acute with pericardial tap.................. | 75.00 | 50.00 |
| 9. Acute Theumatic Pancarditis..................................... | 50.00 | 33.00 |
| 10. Dissecting Aneurysm of Aorta.................................... | 50.00 | 33.00 |
| 11. Malignant Hypertension with encephalopathy or congestive failure........................................................................ | 75.00 | 50.00 |
| 12. Heart Block with Stokes-Adams Syndrome....................... | 50.00 | 33.00 |
| 13. Ventricular Tachycardia........................................... | 50.00 | 33.00 |
| 14. Ventricular Fibrilation............................................. | 50.00 | 33.00 |
| 15. Acute Congestive Heart Failure................................... | 30.00 | 20.00 |

### RADIATION THERAPY SCHEDULE

Roentgenologic Therapy and Cobalt Bomb Therapy for neoplastic diseases when used alone or in conjunction with surgery:

| | | HIGH | LOW |
|---|---|---|---|
| $10 Per Treatment.....................................Maximum | | 500.00 | 333.00 |

Radium and Radon implant procedures are listed in the Surgical Schedule.

For radioactive Isotope treatments, the Plan Allowance will be on an Individual Consideration (IC) basis for the below listed procedures.

| Code Number | Nomenclature | HIGH OPTION | LOW OPTION |
|---|---|---|---|
| 7515 | Radioiodine treatment of hyperthyroidism—this includes all studies and administration of the radioiodine for a period of 1 year.................................up to | 210.00 | 140.00 |

7516    Radioiodine treatment of functioning carcinoma of the thyroid

7518    Radioiodine treatment of angina and cardiac insufficiency. The same factors apply as below (reference remarks codes 7521, 7523, 7583, and 7584). In other words, the physician doing the radioisotope therapy is expected to consider the patient his own and to follow him during that period of 1 year until he feels that the radioiodine treatment is finished anytime within that particular year.

7521    Intrathoracic administration of collodial radiogold or radio-phosphorus without tap.....................up to    180.00    120.00

7523    with thoracentesis.......................................

7583    Intraperitoneal administration of collodial radiogold or radio-phosphorus without paracentesis...................

7584    with paracentesis........................................

(The above fees (Codes 7583 and 7584) include the history and physical and all other care rendered by the attending physician while in the hospital for this procedure.)

7611    Radiophosphorus for leukemia............................

7617    Radiophosphorus for polycythemia vera.................

## DIAGNOSTIC X-RAY BENEFIT SCHEDULE

(All X-ray services must be documented upon request)

A subscriber receiving diagnostic X-ray examinations when ordered by the attending physician, while a registered bed patient in a hospital, consistent with the condition for which hospitalization is received, or in a physician's office or in the outpatient department of a hospital, when such examination is required as a direct result of an accident and performed within 72 hours of such accident, shall be entitled to benefits for the care received in accordance with the following schedule but not to exceed the fee charged for the procedure performed by a physician who customarily bills for his services.

| Code Number | Service Head and Neck | HIGH OPTION | LOW OPTION |
|---|---|---|---|
| 7000 | Cerebral angiography..................................... | 75.00 | 35.00 |
| 7003 | Encephalography, including preliminary skull............. | 75.00 | 50.00 |
| 7006 | Ventriculography, including preliminary skull............. | 50.00 | 50.00 |
| 7008 | Eye for localization of foreign body...................... | 20.00 | 15.00 |
| 7010 | Mandible................................................ | 15.00 | 15.00 |
| 7012 | Mastoids, with petrous bones........................... | 22.50 | 20.00 |
| 7015 | Maxilla and facial bones............................... | 20.00 | 15.00 |
| 7016 | Nasal bones........................................... | 15.00 | 15.00 |
| 7017 | both 7016 and 7015.............................. | ... | 20.00 |
| 7018 | Optic foramina....................................... | 15.00 | 15.00 |
| 7020 | Paranasal sinuses..................................... | 20.00 | 20.00 |
| 7026 | Skull, complete study (minimum four views)............. | 25.00 | 25.00 |
| 7027 | Skull, partial study................................... | 15.00 | 15.00 |

## Complementary coverage

As of year-end 1966, Blue Shield plans had enrolled more than 3,850,000 persons over age 65 in special programs to complement Medicare. In addition, at least 28 plans allowed members to keep the coverage they had prior to Medicare's Part B and/or as a type of complementary coverage. At least 48 plans still offer basic Blue Shield coverage for persons not having Medicare Part B, but in nine of these, only on a group basis. Thus some four million persons over age 65 still have private coverage with Blue Shield. Considering both the Medicare carrier roles, the U.S. Blue Shield plans serve some 10 million persons over age 65.

The typical Blue Shield contract covers the $50 deductible and the 20 percent participation of Medicare Part B for physicians' services. Some, however, cover the 20 percent but not the $50, and a few cover only the $50. In some cases the $50 deductible amount is covered only if the patient is hospitalized. A few plans impose scheduled maxima for various procedures, and many have a stated lifetime maximum limit, most commonly $10,000, with provision for reinstatement. Some plans also cover private-duty nursing and prescribed drugs. Some Blue Shield plans, however, did not develop specific supplementary plans, citing administrative problems as the reason. In these areas, subscribers 65 and older could retain present coverage despite the duplication with Medicare. In some cases, such coverage was limited to a low-benefit-level surgical schedule with a maximum of $200 or $250.

In some areas a major medical plan is offered, sometimes by Blue Cross and Blue Shield in conjunction, but sometimes, as in Hawaii, by Blue Shield alone. These plans typically reimburse 80 percent of eligible expenses not covered by Medicare, often after a corridor deductible, usually $100. All Medicare deductibles, user charges, etc., may be counted toward meeting the deductible. Maximum benefits range from $5,000 to $15,000, usually with provision for reinstatement.

Some plans provide first-dollar coverage of hospital expense for the first 90 days, but impose a deductible and percentage participation on other expenses. Typical of this approach is the plan of Blue Cross and Blue Shield of Florida. This contract covers a broad range of medical expense, not including, however, private nursing, blood, or drugs outside the hospital.

**Other related benefits**

Insurance companies sometimes issue contracts providing medical care benefits which do not fit into the major categories heretofore discussed but which do not qualify for inclusion with the major medical and comprehensive policies discussed in the next chapter. The *blanket accident* expense provision in the individual schedule accident policy was discussed above. A similar provision is available in group insurance contracts, where it serves as a substitute for or supplement to surgical and medical coverage. Inasmuch as it covers only nonoccupational accidental injury, it is not too satisfactory a substitute. The following clause is from a rider granting such protection:

### EMPLOYEES' ACCIDENT EXPENSE BENEFITS

If an employee, while insured under this section, sustains an accidental bodily injury which does not arise out of or in the course of employment . . .

and if, within ninety days after the date of the accident which caused such injury, any hospital, surgical, or medical services, or the services of a registered graduate nurse, are required by the employee for the treatment of such injury . . . the insurance Company shall pay a benefit . . . but not exceeding $——— in connection with all injuries sustained by the employee through any one accident;

Similar coverage is available for dependents if desired.

*Laboratory and X ray expense* benefits are sometimes provided in insurance company group policies. This cover is generally written as a supplement to hospital insurance and is usually added in the form of a rider. It covers such examinations only when performed other than during a hospital confinement, since examinations in the hospital are covered by the hospital insurance contract. It is rarely written in conjunction with in-hospital medical expense insurance, since it is considered inadvisable to make exception to the general principle of such coverage that benefits are paid for hospital confinement only.

The coverage is provided on an indemnity basis up to the amount set forth in the rider. There may be either a blanket limit for all types of examination or a schedule of specific limits for various types. The amounts tend to be quite low, often only $25 per examination. Higher amounts are written, however. Some companies use a blanket limit for employees and a schedule for dependents. The following benefit clause from a group rider is typical of the employee benefits generally provided:

## EMPLOYEES' LABORATORY AND X-RAY EXPENSE BENEFITS

If an employee, while insured under this section, incurs expenses for a laboratory or x-ray examination for diagnosis of a disease for which the employee is not entitled to benefits under any workmen's compensation law or an accidental bodily injury which does not arise out of or in the course of employment, and if the employee is not entitled to other benefits of any kind under this rider or under the group policy by reason of such examination, the Insurance Company shall pay to the employee an amount equal to the expenses actually incurred by the employee with respect to such examination, but not exceeding $50.00; provided, however, that

(1) no benefit shall be payable with respect to any dental x-ray except in connection with an accidental bodily injury;

(2) no benefit shall be payable with respect to an examination that is not recommended or approved by a legally qualified physician or surgeon; and

(3) no benefit shall be payable with respect to an examination in connection with pregnancy or resulting childbirth or miscarriage.

If two or more such examinations are involved, payment shall be made for each examination in accordance with the foregoing paragraph, but not more than $50.00 shall be payable for all examinations made during any one calendar year, whether involving related or unrelated causes.

A schedule coverage of such expenses for dependents has the same type of benefit clause, except that reference is made to expenses incurred by a dependent, and the limit stated is "the maximum amount in the Schedule of Laboratory and X-ray Benefits set forth below." The exclusions and limits are the same. The schedule ranges from $3 for a bacteria test to $50 for a barium meal and enema X-ray examination.

The maximum benefit is so low that it is questionable whether such fees are proper subject matter for insurance. Similar benefits are often included in Blue Shield and independent plan benefits, especially for diagnostic X ray. If included, they usually are provided as part of the basic coverage, not by rider.

## Independent plan benefits

Independent plans differ so much in organization and type of benefit that it seems best to avoid the surgical-medical dichotomy in discussing their benefits. Indeed, some provide such comprehensive benefits that they might be discussed in the following chapter as readily as here. Generalizations are almost impossible in this area, and space considerations preclude a full treatment.[10] A few of the more interesting plans will be described.

*Industrial plans.* Many industrial plans are sponsored by an employer for his employees only. Some have been very successful and are still vigorous, but others are tainted with memories of "paternalism" and "contract medicine."

One of the most successful is the Kaiser Foundation Health Plan, which began as an industrial plan but evolved into a communitywide plan. Kaiser employees and their dependents make up only about 6 percent of total enrollment. It is organized as a nonprofit corporation, which contracts with 12 hospitals owned by Kaiser Foundation Hospitals, another nonprofit corporation. About 40 out-patient medical centers organized as independent medical partnerships contract to provide medical and surgical services in their areas. The insured individuals may elect annually whether to be covered on a full-service basis through these closed panels or to have a reimbursement type coverage at about the same premium, allowing free choice of physician. The plan provides 111 days of full-service hospital benefits per illness to employees and 60 days of full service and 51 days at half price to dependents; full hospital extras for employees and half price for dependents; full coverage subject to certain fees (which amount to deductibles) for surgery and regular medical benefits (full coverage in hospital), and a variety of services including physical examinations.

---

[10] See Herman M. Somers and Anne R. Somers, *Doctors, Patients and Health Insurance* (Washington, D.C.: The Brookings Institution, 1961), chaps. xii and xvii and Appendix Table A-20 for an excellent discussion of the organization and benefits of independent plans.

The device of providing full coverage, subject to small fees for certain services, such as home and night physician calls, drugs, eyeglasses, and certain elective procedures including maternity, is quite common in independent plans. These charges may apply to all subscribers or only to dependents. They amount to a deductible applied to these items. This is more in accordance with sound insurance principles than the conventional approach of providing first-dollar coverage subject to a fairly low upper limit for such treatment.

The United Mine Workers of America Welfare and Retirement Fund is financed by a royalty on each ton of coal mined, paid by the employers. It is a good example of a union-sponsored plan. It provides very liberal benefits to employed miners; pensioners; unemployed union members; dependents, including dependent parents; and even survivors of deceased miners for one year. The coverage includes hospitalization for the length of time the attending physician thinks necessary, in-patient physicians' services and drugs, specialist services, physical rehabilitation, certain costly drugs, psychiatric diagnosis and short-term mental therapy for good prognosis cases. It uses 10 hospitals owned and operated by a semiautonomous association and supervises the purchase of other services through 10 area medical offices.

*Nonindustrial plans. Private group clinics.* Most private group clinics are small, but some are very large. The largest and best known of those which operate on a prepaid group-practice basis is the Ross–Loos Medical Group of Los Angeles. After vigorous early opposition from the medical profession, it now is listed as a medical-society approved plan and as such was included in the "Blue Shield" statistics above. It is organized as a partnership and provides full-service benefits for surgery and medical treatment in the hospital, office, or home, with no income limits. Coverage includes preventive medicine, diagnosis, eye examinations, refractions, consultation with staff specialists, laboratory tests, diagnostic X ray, and physiotherapy treatments. Dependents' coverage is subject to small fees which amount to deductibles ranging from $0.75 for ordinary laboratory tests to $50 for delivery. Hospital insurance is provided by an associated private insurance company under a contract which provides full coverage in ward or $16 per day for private or semiprivate accommodations, plus other charges including blood and anesthesia up to a combined maximum of $1,500 per disability.

*Consumer cooperatives.* Consumer cooperatives arose originally in rural areas and represented responses to depressed conditions and alleged monopolies by producers and distributors. At the peak of the movement in 1949 there were over 100 cooperatives active in the health field, but by 1959 this had declined to only a few. Cooperative membership is open to the whole community except for very poor risks, and once a member is enrolled he may retain membership status regardless of health.

One of the largest and best known of these is the Group Health Association of Washington, D.C. Its benefits include full-service, semiprivate hospitalization up to 180 days per year or per illness; full coverage of surgical and regular medical subject to small fees for home calls, laboratory tests and injections, physical therapy treatments and X rays.

*Community plans.* This term has been applied to plans sponsored jointly by physicians and consumers. The Kaiser plan discussed above qualifies in this category except for the fact of its industrial initiation. Two of the largest and best known of the community plans operate primarily in New York City. They are the Health Insurance Plan of Greater New York, commonly known as HIP, and Group Health Insurance of New York City, often referred to as GHI.

HIP was originally formed to insure city employees, and these and their families still make up about 60 percent of enrollment. It is a nonprofit corporation which contracts with group-practice centers which are operated by partnerships of physicians. The insured member selects his center, and participating physicians are paid on a capitation basis (so much per member per year) by HIP. They also may engage in private practice. Hospital insurance is provided through affiliation with the New York Blue Cross and must be carried. Thus the plan was listed as Blue Cross affiliated and included in the statistics above.

It gives complete full-service benefits with no income limits except that subscribers with incomes in excess of $6,000 per year for individuals and $7,500 per year for families pay a premium 20 percent higher than others. The full-service benefits are available only to residents of the New York Metropolitan area and Columbia County, with reimbursement benefits available to residents of other areas (mostly those who have moved). Full-service surgical and medical benefits are provided subject to a $2 charge for night calls. Diagnostic services, immunizations, health examinations, specialist care, eye refractions, pathology, radiology, and nursing care are included. Benefits do not include treatment for acute alcoholism, dental care, drugs, appliances, or psychiatric treatment.

GHI, unlike most of the other independents, does not make use of the group-practice technique. It is very like a Blue Shield plan in that physicians are paid on a fee-for-service basis and any physician within the metropolitan area may participate. However, it differs in that it requires the participating physicians to accept the scheduled fee as full payment for almost all out-patient services, regardless of income. Its control is divided equally between laymen and physicians and it is *not* medical-society approved.

Hospital benefits are covered by New York Blue Cross. GHI offers two major contracts. The first, the Semi-Private Plan, provides almost complete medical-surgical full-service coverage for semiprivate patients using participating physicians. The Family Doctor Plan combines virtually free choice of physician for out-patient service, including diagnostic examinations and health checkups, with full-service benefits. Most subscribers are covered by this comprehensive plan. GHI has formed an associated corporation to provide dental insurance on a communitywide basis and has experimented with broad coverage of mental and nervous disease.

*Medical foundations.* A new technique for organization and financing of medical care is the medical foundation. Starting with the organization of the San Joaquin Foundation in California, this movement has spread on the West Coast and more recently in the Middle West. There are about 20 of these foundations in operation. The foundation establishes a pattern of medical-surgical benefits with fee schedules based on the California or other relative value study. The foundations are set up as nonprofit corporations owned by the county medical societies. The benefit schedules are accepted as full payment by the participating physicians, and the foundation contracts with various insurers, both insurance companies and Blue Shield, to provide the insuring mechanism for various groups of insureds.

The foundation negotiates the levels of benefit of the insurance plans and employs personnel to handle claim settlement by draft on the insurers. All claims are given a personal review by one or more physicians in close cooperation with tissue committees, society medical audit committees, and insurer claim departments. Multiple levels of coverage are offered, at, of course, appropriate premium rates.

The goals of the foundations are to distribute quality medical care at prices reasonable both for the patient and the physician, preserve freedom of choice and the personal physician-patient relationship, protect public health, and encourage the development of sound, well-designed financing mechanisms. Future developments will be watched with interest.

### Limitations of basic contracts

The major criticism that should be made of these basic coverages applies equally well to hospital insurance. Many types of expense often are not covered, and the maximum amounts that can be collected are relatively small in comparison to the typical family income level and to the potential magnitude of medical care expenses. Cases in which total expenses have exceeded $10,000 for a single illness or injury are by no means rare. While these basic contracts would help meet the costs of such disabilities, they would fall far short of giving full protection. It is hard to imagine a set of circumstances in which the amount collectible on a basic hospital or a basic surgical-medical plan would exceed $2,000 each.[11] In the event, then, of such a $10,000 loss, the insured would suffer an unin-

---

[11] In a very long hospital stay, one might, but the uninsured area still would not be covered.

sured loss of $6,000. Such an amount would be catastrophic to almost every family budget. The following chapter will be concerned with contracts that provide for major or catastrophic medical care expenses. These contracts have arisen as a result of the recognition of the inherent limits of the basic covers.

## Summary

Surgical and medical insurance protect against charges for surgical operations and ordinary physicians' care, respectively. They are written on both a group and an individual basis by insurance companies, Blue Shield, and "independent" plans. Regardless of insurer type, most contracts provide for benefits according to a schedule of fees for surgical treatment and physicians' charges. However, a good proportion of Blue Shield and independent plan insureds are protected on a full-service basis, and so are a small proportion of the insureds under insurance company plans. Medical insurance is provided on an in-hospital, a total disability, and a nondisability basis. The first is the most common. Almost all the Blue Shield plans and many plans issued by other insurers are on this basis. Dependents' coverage is generally available, although rarer in individual insurance company policies.

Medical and surgical insurance have proved very popular with the public and are contributing greatly to lessen the impact of risk of serious loss from such expenses. However, they are subject to the same criticism as is hospital insurance: they cover only losses which are relatively small compared to the potential costs of a really serious disability. Much higher upper limits could be provided if greater use were made of deductibles to eliminate small claims and the attendant settlement costs. There is some tendency in this direction.

## Selected references

*See the following items from the General Bibliography: 2, chs. 8 and 11; 5, ch. 5; 6; 7, ch. 21; 9, chs. 44 and 45; 14, ch. 5; 22; 23.*

ANDERSON, ODIN W., AND SHEATSLEY, PAUL B. *Comprehensive Medical Insurance.* Health Information Foundation Research Series, No. 9. New York, 1959.

COUNCIL ON MEDICAL SERVICES, AMERICAN MEDICAL ASSOCIATION. *Voluntary Prepayment Medical Benefit Plans.* Chicago, 1965.

EILERS, ROBERT D. *Regulation of Blue Cross and Blue Shield Plans.* Homewood, Ill.: Richard D. Irwin, Inc., 1963.

HUNTER, ARTHUR, AND COLEMAN, JAMES T. "Surgical and Medical Insurance by a Blue Shield Plan," *Transactions of the Society of Actuaries,* Vol. VI, p. 6.

LAMPMAN, ROBERT J., AND MIYAMOTO, S. F. "Effects of Extended Coverage in a Physician-Sponsored Health Insurance Plan," *Journal of Insurance,* Vol. XXVIII, No. 3, p. 1.

NATIONAL ASSOCIATION OF BLUE SHIELD PLANS. *A Directory of Blue Shield Plans.* Chicago, 1967.

———. *Annual Program, Blue Shield Conference.* Chicago, 1965; 1966; 1967.

———. *By-laws and Membership Standards.* Chicago, 1960.

TRUSSELL, RAY E., AND VAN DYKE, FRANK. *Prepayment for Medical and Dental Care in New York State.* New York: Columbia University Press, 1962.

## chapter 8

To its ultimate conclusion in unmitigated act.—Kipling, *The Female of the Species*

# Major Medical and Comprehensive Insurance

## Introduction

Most criticisms of basic hospital, surgical, and medical insurance have centered about the fact that such policies often fall far short of covering the total medical care bill. On the one hand, many types of expenditure are not covered. Coverage of drugs, appliances, prosthetics, blood and plasma, diagnostic services, physical examinations and other preventive medicine, out-patient treatment, nursing services, and many other costs are not provided in most such policies or combinations of policies. Frequently, the policies cover only treatment given in the proper place: usually in a legally constituted hospital.

Moreover, they contain limits, express or implicit, on aggregate amounts payable and on benefits for specific services. Where full-service benefits are provided, they are available only for certain procedures and for limited time periods. Thus these policies may prove grossly inadequate when it comes to meeting the costs of a really serious disability. Even the blanket accident type policy, which imposes few restrictions on eligible types of expense, generally is written with so small a limit that it would not cover a really severe accident. Moreover, it is limited to accidental injuries only. This chapter is devoted to types of insurance that have developed in response to a recognition of the limitations of the basic forms and a desire for adequate coverage.

*Major medical expense insurance* represents contracts that protect against almost all types of medical care expenditure, with few, if any, internal limits and with a high overall limit, from $5,000 to $50,000, or more. Generally, such policies include deductible and/or percentage participation clauses.

*Comprehensive medical expense insurance* contracts are similar to major medical, except for the fact that they provide lower deductibles and sometimes omit or limit the percentage participation feature.

The original concept of the comprehensive contract involved the same concept of broad blanket coverage of all eligible expenses, broadly defined, subject to percentage participation, and with almost no internal limits, but with a small deductible of $25 or $50 instead of a large deductible of $500 or more. This would be the only health insurance policy carried by the insured against the costs of medical care and would do the whole job for him on a logical basis consistent with sound insurance principles. This type of contract sometimes is referred to as a "pure" comprehensive policy.

However, many employees were loath to give up their first dollar coverage of hospital and surgical expenses. In response to this feeling, insurers developed a contract referred to as "modified" comprehensive, which provides first-dollar coverage of hospital and/or surgical expenses up to certain limits, and then covers the excess (perhaps after a small deductible) according to the percentage participation major medical approach.

Chart 8–1, in which type of expense is indicated on the horizontal axis, amount of expense plotted vertically and degree of reimbursement indicated by shading, gives a graphical illustration of the extent of coverage provided by various plans. The basic plans cover only hospital and surgical expense and a few other expenses at 100 percent reimbursement, up to a moderate limit. The major medical policy superimposed on this covers, after a moderate deductible, all other medical expenses, at a 75, 80, or 85 percent reimbursement level up to high limits. The pure comprehensive contract covers all expenses, after a small deductible, at the same reimbursement rate, up to the same high limit. The modified comprehensive plan is the same (in this illustration) except that hospital expenses are covered 100 percent with no deductible up to a moderate limit. Some authorities consider comprehensive policies a variety of major medical, but this author believes comprehensive is sufficiently different to warrant a separate classification.

Another variety of policy, comprehensive as to benefit but not as to peril, is the *dread-disease* type of policy. This appeared first as a "polio" contract but was eventually extended to cover a list of named serious diseases. It covers only the named diseases up to a medium-sized limit like $5,000, without a deductible or percentage participation clause.

All these are of comparatively recent origin. Polio policies appeared first in the late 1940's and were given great impetus by polio epidemics in the first years of the following decade. Major medical appeared as an experimental cover about 1950 but soon gained widespread acceptance. By the end of 1966, about 56.7 million persons were covered by insurance

CHART 8–1

Proportion of Charges Covered under Various Health Insurance Arrangements

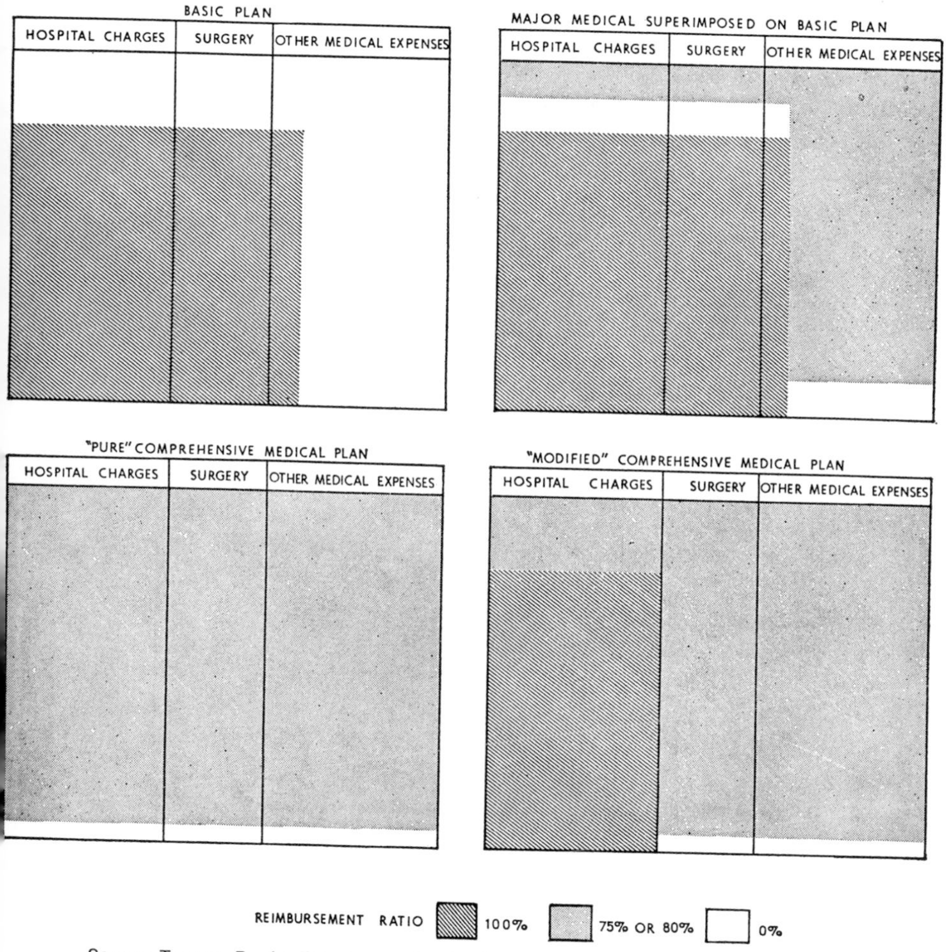

| BASIC PLAN | | | MAJOR MEDICAL SUPERIMPOSED ON BASIC PLAN | | |
|---|---|---|---|---|---|
| HOSPITAL CHARGES | SURGERY | OTHER MEDICAL EXPENSES | HOSPITAL CHARGES | SURGERY | OTHER MEDICAL EXPENSES |

| "PURE" COMPREHENSIVE MEDICAL PLAN | | | "MODIFIED" COMPREHENSIVE MEDICAL PLAN | | |
|---|---|---|---|---|---|
| HOSPITAL CHARGES | SURGERY | OTHER MEDICAL EXPENSES | HOSPITAL CHARGES | SURGERY | OTHER MEDICAL EXPENSES |

REIMBURSEMENT RATIO   ▨ 100%   ▨ 75% OR 80%   ☐ 0%

Source: Towers, Perrin, Forster, and Crosby, Inc.

company major medical and comprehensive contracts.[1] About 21 million were employed persons with primary coverage; the balance were dependents. Insurance companies were the first type of insurer to issue major medical in any quantity, but by 1967 most Blue Cross and 15 Blue Shield plans offered contracts of this type.

Most of the coverage is on a group basis. In 1966, insurance companies covered 52 million persons on a group basis and 4.7 million persons on an individual basis. Major medical contracts covered 39.6 million people in

---

[1] Projected enrollment figures for insurance company major medical and comprehensive insurance indicated 61 million persons were covered December 31, 1967.

group contracts, and 12.3 million people were covered by comprehensive insurance. Most of the individual coverage was major medical, but the exact numbers are not known.

In addition, Blue Cross and Blue Shield contracts covered 10.4 million persons for major medical benefits and 3.9 million for extended basic benefits. Insurance companies were the leaders on the dread-disease field, but six Blue Shield plans offered this coverage in 1966. Chart 8–2 shows

CHART 8–2

Growth in Primary and Dependent Coverage for Insurance Company Major Medical Expense Protection, U.S., 1952–65

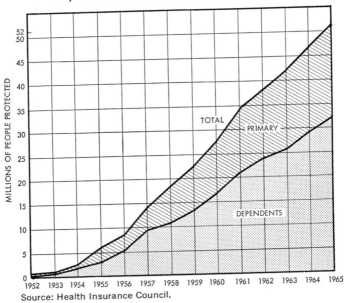

Source: Health Insurance Council.

the growth of insurance company major medical and comprehensive. Table 8–1 gives a detailed analysis and includes the Blue Cross and Blue Shield insureds. Many of the eight million persons insured by independent plans have comprehensive benefits, but how many is not known.

### Major medical benefits

*Covered expenses.* Major medical policies cover almost all types of medical care expenditure with few internal limits.[2] The types of charge

---

[2] The use of a limit on the daily hospital room-and-board benefit is becoming quite common. Such limits usually are around $20 to $50 per day and serve as an added claims control. Many contracts have limits for extended care, room rates, private nursing, or mental and nervous disease, especially out-patient psychiatric treatment.

## TABLE 8-1

| End of Year | Grand Total | Insurance Companies | | | | | Blue Cross–Blue Shield Plans[a] | | |
|---|---|---|---|---|---|---|---|---|---|
| | | Total | Group Policies | | | Individual & Family Policies | Total | Supplementary Major Medical | Comprehensive Extended Benefit |
| | | | Total | Supplementary | Comprehensive | | | | |
| 1951 | ..... | 108 | 96 | 96 | ..... | 12 | ..... | ..... | ..... |
| 1952 | ..... | 689 | 533 | 533 | ..... | 156 | ..... | ..... | ..... |
| 1953 | ..... | 1,220 | 1,044 | 1,044 | ..... | 176 | ..... | ..... | ..... |
| 1954 | ..... | 2,198 | 1,892 | 1,841 | 51 | 306 | ..... | ..... | ..... |
| 1955 | ..... | 5,241 | 4,759 | 3,928 | 831 | 482 | ..... | ..... | ..... |
| 1956 | ..... | 8,876 | 8,294 | 6,881 | 1,413 | 582 | ..... | ..... | ..... |
| 1957 | ..... | 13,262 | 12,428 | 9,290 | 3,138 | 834 | ..... | ..... | ..... |
| 1958 | ..... | 17,375 | 16,229 | 11,072 | 5,157 | 1,146 | ..... | ..... | ..... |
| 1959 | ..... | 21,850 | 20,353 | 13,900 | 6,453 | 1,497 | [a] | [a] | [a] |
| 1960 | 31,161 | 27,448 | 25,608 | 17,285 | 8,323 | 1,840 | 3,713 | 3,020 | 693 |
| 1961 | 39,197 | 34,138 | 31,517 | 22,281 | 9,236 | 2,621 | 5,059 | 4,015 | 1,044 |
| 1962 | 45,751 | 38,250 | 35,053 | 25,301 | 9,752 | 3,197 | 7,501 | 5,068 | 1,735 |
| 1963 | ..... | 42,441 | 38,699 | 28,248 | 10,451 | 3,742 | [b] | [b] | [b] |
| 1964 | ..... | 47,001 | 42,579 | 31,772 | 10,807 | 4,422 | [b] | [b] | [b] |
| 1965 | 66,546 | 51,946 | 47,269 | 35,988 | 11,281 | 4,677 | 14,600[c] | [b] | [b] |
| 1966 | 71,094 | 56,742 | 52,002 | 39,685 | 12,317 | 4,740 | 14,352[d] | 10,409[d] | 3,943[d] |

[a] Comparable data not available for earlier years; data shown are for Blue Cross plans only, except for 1965 and 1966. Data exclude persons covered under polio and dread-disease and prolonged-illness contracts offering coverage only for diseases specified.

[b] Not available.

[c] Data for Blue Cross plans plus an estimated 1,600,000 in Blue Shield plans not affiliated with Blue Cross.

[d] Data jointly developed by Blue Cross Association and National Association of Blue Shield plans on unduplicated number of persons covered.

Source: Reed, Louis S., "Private Health Insurance: Coverage and Financial Experience 1940–66," SSB, November 1967, p. 3.

include hospital charges for room and board and miscellaneous services and supplies, charges by physicians and surgeons for medical treatment and surgery, charges by a physician or anesthetist for administration of anesthesia, charges for professional radiology or physiotherapy, charges for nursing care, laboratory examinations, drugs, medicines, blood and plasma, casts, splints, braces, crutches, prosthetics, oxygen, rental of oxygen equipment, wheelchairs, hospital beds, and iron lungs. Sometimes expenses of transportation to and from a hospital are also included.

Most plans cover these types of expense wherever performed as long as they are ordered or prescribed by a duly licensed physician. Some, however, especially individual contracts, require hospital admission at some time in the course of treatment in order to qualify. One policy, for example, covers expenses incurred in the hospital and for two months before admission and for six months thereafter.

A group policy defines the covered types of expense as follows:

The term "covered expenses" means only such of the following expenses as are incurred by an employee for the therapeutic treatment, while the employee is insured under this rider, of any disease or accidental bodily injury of the employee, and then only to the extent not hereinafter excluded.

(1) The charges made to the employee by a physician for professional medical or surgical services rendered to the employee by the physician; and

(2) The charges made to the employee by a registered graduate nurse other than one who ordinarily resides in the employee's home or who is a member of the immediate family (comprising the employee, the employee's wife or husband, and the children, brothers, sisters, and parents of either the employee or the employee's wife or husband) for professional nursing services rendered to the employee by the nurse; and

(3) the charges made to the employee by a hospital, in its own behalf, for services and supplies required by and rendered to the employee during his hospital confinement in direct connection with the therapeutic treatment of the employee; except that for each day in which the employee occupies private room accommodations, the amount, if any, by which the hospital's charges for board and room for that day exceed —— shall be excluded from covered expenses; and

(4) the charges made to the employee for any of the following services and supplies, to the extent such charges do not duplicate charges included under items (1), (2), and (3) above:

(a) drugs and medicines lawfully obtainable only upon the prescription of a physician;

(b) anesthesia and its administration;

(c) x-ray and laboratory examinations made for diagnostic purposes in connection with the therapeutic treatment of the employee;

(d) x-ray, radium, and radioactive isotopes therapy;

(e) oxygen and its administration;

(f) rental of wheel chair, hospital bed, iron lung, and other durable equipment for the therapeutic treatment of the employee;

(g) artificial limbs and artificial eyes;

(h) professional ambulance service when used to transport the employee directly from the place where he is injured by an accident or stricken by a disease to the first hospital where treatment is given.

Family policies use a similar but sometimes briefer description.

As in any insurance policy, the complete description of the coverage requires a reading of the exclusions. Common major medical policy exclusions are expenses covered under other insurance, pregnancy, childbirth and miscarriage (sometimes covered for limited benefits only), dental expenses, cosmetic surgery,[3] injuries or sickness covered by workmen's compensation, alcoholism, narcotic addiction, nervous and mental diseases,[4] health examinations, travel expenses except as specifically covered, and treatment in government or other noncharge facilities. Extended care and nursing home care is sometimes excluded. If covered, it usually is subject to a limit on the daily room charge and covered only after hospitalization.

Common exclusions relating to peril are war and military service, self-inflicted injuries and attempted suicide, and sometimes aviation activities other than as a fare-paying passenger. Some policies exclude preexisting conditions, at least for a probationary period. Some policies exclude specifically (and others implicitly) expenses which are unreasonable in price or not reasonably necessary to treatment of the disability. The enforcement of such a provision presents difficult problems of claim administration.

The reasons for most of these exclusions have been noted above in other contexts. Major medical policies, defining covered expenses so broadly in the insuring clause, need more exclusions to eliminate optional or elective treatment such as dental treatment and cosmetic surgery. Such exclusions would not be as necessary in (say) a hospital policy, but often are included in such basic contracts, especially when issued on an individual basis.

Group policies often do not exclude military service, since this would take the individual out of the group automatically, nor preexisting conditions because of their inherent freedom from individual selection. However, frequently preexisting conditions are not covered for some period of

---

[3] Dental surgery and cosmetic surgery often are covered if they are required as the result of an accidental injury.

[4] Many major medical contracts, especially group contracts, do cover mental and nervous diseases, sometimes with specific internal limits, especially on out-of-hospital care. The problem of insuring against such losses is discussed in Chapter 9 below.

time free of treatment after an individual joins the group, especially in contracts issued to smaller groups.

*Upper limits.* Most individual upper limits on eligible expense vary from $5,000 to $50,000. The most popular choices are $5,000, $7,500, $10,000, and $15,000. In new group plans issued in 1967, by far the most common was $10,000, covering about two thirds of the insured members. A few plans provide no dollar limit. The limit may apply to each injury or illness separately, or to all injuries or illnesses during a calendar year, or to the aggregate benefits payable to a claimant during his entire lifetime. It is not unusual to find a combination of an aggregate lifetime limit with a per-disability or calendar-year limit. The limit per disability probably is the most common in individual contracts, but the lifetime maximum is most common in group contracts. The use of the benefit-year limits makes possible the mushrooming of a claim to tremendous size. With this type of limit a prolonged illness could result in the company paying the policy maximum limit year after year subject only to an overall limit on expense or duration, if any.

Usually there is some limit on the time within which expenses must be incurred, especially in the each-cause plans. This may run from one to three years or more, with two or three years being probably the most common in the individual each-cause plan and one year in the all-cause plans. This has been referred to as a "benefit period." This term is perhaps unfortunate, as it might lead to confusion with the benefit period in loss-of-time policies where the claim settlement is directly proportionate to the elapsed time.

The use of an aggregate ("lifetime") limit is most common in group insurance where it accounted for about 77 percent of the coverage of new group business in 1967. When it is used, it is common to provide that after (say) $1,000 of benefits have been paid, the original limit may be reinstated if the insured can produce acceptable evidence of insurability, or if he returns to work for a certain period of time.

*Percentage participation.* Not all eligible medical expenses are covered for the full amount in major medical contracts. Policies usually require the insured to bear from 10 to 25 percent of eligible expenses in excess of a specified deductible. The percentage usually is 20 percent or 25 percent in individual policies and 20 percent in group contracts. As indicated above, the purpose of the percentage participation is to encourage the insured to keep losses within a reasonable limit by making him a "coinsurer." The extent to which such provisions will be effective is hard to measure. The impact will vary with the living standards and other resources of the claimant. However, it certainly has some effect, and insurance company personnel seem firmly convinced that some such control on claims is absolutely necessary. Otherwise, it would be to every claimant's advantage to utilize as extensive and expensive health services as possible. The requirement is designed to make possible adequate payment for health necessities without encouraging health luxuries. The limit of benefit described above, it should be noted, applies to the company's maximum payment, not to the maximum covered expenses. Thus, in order to collect the maximum under a $15,000 policy with a $500 deductible and 80 percent reimbursement, a claimant would have to incur eligible expenses of $19,250. He would have to bear $4,250 of expenses himself, a not insubstantial sum.

At least one insurer, Pan-American Life Insurance Co., offers a "Super Ascending Plan" which varies the percent of loss reimbursed with the amount of loss, thus reducing the effective deductible.[5] This major medical plan reimburses eligible medical expense, in excess of basic plan benefits, at the rate of 0 percent of the first $100 (a corridor deductible; see below); 80 percent of the next $2,000; 90 percent of the next $1,500; and 110 percent of the next $7,150. Thus, an insured member who incurred exactly $10,000 of expense in excess of the deductible would be reimbursed exactly for his entire loss, as follows:

$$
\begin{array}{rcrr}
0\% \text{ of } \$ & 100 & = \$ & 0 \\
80\% \text{ of } & 2,000 & = & 1,600 \\
90\% \text{ of } & 1,500 & = & 1,350 \\
110\% \text{ of } & 6,500 & = & 7,150 \\
\hline
\text{Total} & & & \$10,100
\end{array}
$$

The deductible and maximum are on a per disability (each-cause) basis, and the coverage is available only to groups. Basic hospital and medical coverage are also available with similar "disappearing deductibles."

*Deductibles.* These provisions serve two purposes. One is to lower premium costs by insuring only the substantial claims, eliminating the small claims and the expense of handling them. The second is to cut down on moral hazard by eliminating or reducing duplication with other health insurance policies and by making the insured bear the first portion of eligible loss. Deductibles may take a number of forms and may apply on a number of bases.

*Forms.* The *initial deductible* is the most common. This applies to the first portion of medical care expenses, so that the insured must bear expenses up to this amount before the policy begins to pay. This is used almost always in individual and family policies and frequently in group policies. Amounts collected (or paid on behalf of the insured) in basic policies are counted toward the deductible. The deductible may be anywhere from $50 up, on this basis. $500, $750, and $1,000 are the most common amounts in individual policies. Some insurers vary the deductible amount and sometimes also the upper limit in accordance with family in-

---

[5] This was suggested in the previous edition of this book, at p. 280.

come either by policy provision or, more commonly, by underwriting classification.

A *corridor deductible* frequently is used to coordinate the plan with basic insurance policies covering the same insureds. Here the deductible amount is applied to the excess of medical expenses over the amounts covered in the basic contract or contracts. Basic benefits may not be counted toward the deductible in this case, of course. Amounts will usually be lower than on the initial basis. A range of deductible amount of $50–$100 would include most plans. The most common figure in new group business in 1967 was $100. The corridor deductible not only cuts premiums but in effect makes the claimant a coinsurer for a part of the basic plan benefits if he exceeds their limits. It is used mainly in group plans, where it is by far the most common arrangement.

Another approach used to coordinate major medical insurance with underlying contracts is the *integrated deductible*. This is essentially a combination of the two other approaches. Here the deductible is the greater of an agreed dollar amount or the base plan benefits. This provides a varying corridor deductible which equals zero in effect when the base plan benefits equal or exceed the specified amount. This has the advantage of imposing no deductible on the insured when the claim is large and involves types of expense covered under basic contracts. Many insurers now are using the plan in individual as well as group insurance.

The operation of these forms of deductible in combination with 80 percent participation and a $15,000 limit may be clarified by the following illustration:

| | $500 Initial | $100 Corridor | $500 Integrated |
|---|---|---|---|
| Amount of deductible.................... | | | |
| Form of deductible...................... | | | |
| 1. Small loss: | | | |
| a) Amount of loss......................$ 300 | | $ 300 | $ 300 |
| b) Paid by basic contract............... 150 | | 150 | 150 |
| c) Paid by major medical............... 0 | | 40 | 0 |
| d) Borne by insured.................... 150 | | 110 | 150 |
| 2. Large loss: | | | |
| a) Amount of loss..................... 3,000 | | 3,000 | 3,000 |
| b) Paid by basic contract............... 1,500 | | 1,500 | 1,500 |
| c) Paid by major medical............... 2,000 | | 1,120 | 1,200 |
| d) Borne by insured...............($500 profit) | | 380 | 300 |
| 3. Very large loss: | | | |
| a) Amount of loss...................... 20,000 | | 20,000 | 20,000 |
| b) Paid by basic contract............... 4,000 | | 4,000 | 4,000 |
| c) Paid by major medical............... 15,000 | | 12,720 | 12,800 |
| d) Borne by insured.................... 1,000 | | 3,280 | 3,200 |

*Bases.* Deductibles may apply to each disability, to a calendar year, or to a benefit year. Commonly, the deductible and upper limit apply on the same basis, but not always. In the calendar-year or benefit-year deductible, the deductible may apply to each individual separately or to the aggregate expenditures of the family. The deductible amount may be constant or vary with employee classes in group insurance or with earned income in a family plan. About 20 percent of the 1967 new group business had a per cause type deductible, while the balance applied the deductible to all causes during some eligibility period.

Where the deductible applies to *each disability*, it is usually required that the deductible expenses be accumulated within some time period such as six months or one year. Usually the maximum benefit is stated on a per disability basis, and expenses are covered only for the first one to three years. The major objection to this plan is that an individual or, more frequently, a family may incur expenses which aggregate large sums in a short period but which do not exceed the deductible for any one injury or disease.

Where the deductible applies to a *calendar year*, all covered medical expenses incurred by the individual in a calendar year are counted toward the deductible. The deductible is repeated each year in the case of an extended disability.

The *benefit-year* concept works the same way except that any 12-month period may be used to accumulate expenses toward the deductible. The period is referred to as a benefit year because it customarily begins at the inception of a particular disability. Record keeping is complex, as it may be to the insured's advantage to carry forward the benefit year to cover periods beyond the major disability or to carry it back to include periods before.

The use of the family as the unit greatly complicates the administration of the plan, and few policies on this basis have been sold. Some companies have used a variant called a *family budget* deductible, where the company simply reimburses all medical care expenses incurred by the family in a given month in excess of a stated monthly deductible. This may range from $25 to $250, depending on income level. Often the deductible is waived entirely if total expenses exceed a specified (higher) amount. This is simple for the insured to understand. The aggregate family expenditure is held within predictable and budgetable limits. It is customarily used in connection with an aggregate lifetime limit per individual with the usual reinstatement privileges.

Where deductibles are on other than a family basis, it is common to provide that, in the event of accidental injury in a common disaster, the deductible shall be applied only once.

Table 8–2 gives the distribution by number of employees of new group major medical and comprehensive plans issued in 1967 by type and amount of benefit and base of deductible.

**Benefit provisions.**    This should indicate the heterogeneity of major medical policies. It would be pointless to quote provisions as to all types

TABLE 8–2

Distribution of New Group Major Medical and Comprehensive Insurance Company
Coverage by Plan Type and Maximum Benefit, 1967

(number of employees)

| | Major Medical | Compre-hensive | Total | Percent |
|---|---|---|---|---|
| Total Employees.................. | 155,377 | 64,857 | 220,234 | 100.0 |
| All-cause plans.................... | 114,076 | 63,590 | 177,666 | 80.7 |
| Calendar year benefit period— lifetime maximum.............. | 96,821 | 39,748 | 136,569 | 62.0 |
| Calendar year benefit period— each cause maximum.......... | 12,944 | 3,490 | 16,434 | 7.5 |
| Other than calendar year benefit period—lifetime maximum...... | 1,815 | 18,366 | 20,181 | 9.2 |
| Other than calendar year benefit period—each cause maximum.. | 2,496 | 1,986 | 4,482 | 2.0 |
| Maximum benefit amount | | | | |
| $5000............................ | 8,280 | 992 | 9,272 | 4.2 |
| $10,000........................... | 87,213 | 28,996 | 116,209 | 52.8 |
| $15,000........................... | 10,379 | 25,366 | 35,745 | 16.2 |
| $20,000........................... | 7,983 | 900 | 8,883 | 4.50 |
| All others........................ | 221 | 7,336 | 7,557 | 3.4 |
| Each-cause plans.................. | 40,093 | 1,267 | 1,360 | 18.8 |
| Disability required—each cause benefit period—each cause maximum..................... | 0 | 77 | 77 | a |
| Disability required—each cause benefit period—lifetime maximum..................... | 11,868 | 0 | 11,868 | 5.4 |
| Disability not required—each cause benefit period—each cause maximum.............. | 27,647 | 1,136 | 28,783 | 13.1 |
| Disability not required—each cause benefit period—lifetime maximum..................... | 578 | 54 | 632 | 0.3 |
| Maximum benefit amount | | | | |
| $5000............................ | 3,805 | 27 | 3,832 | 1.7 |
| $10,000........................... | 30,307 | 847 | 31,154 | 14.1 |
| $15,000........................... | 2,524 | 393 | 2,917 | 1.3 |
| $20,000........................... | 3,322 | 0 | 3,322 | 1.5 |
| All others........................ | 135 | 0 | 135 | .06 |
| All others........................ | 1,208 | 0 | 1,208 | 0.5 |

a Less than 0.05 percent
Source: Health Insurance Institute, *New Group Health Insurance Policies Issued in 1967—Complete Tables* (New York, 1968).

of upper limit and deductible. However, the applicable provisions from
two policies will be used for illustration.

The following benefit provisions from a family policy provide for a
deductible amount and maximum benefit, both on a per disability basis.

The maximum benefit period may vary, and there is no time limit for accumulating the deductible amount for a given disability.

## BENEFITS

A. The Company will pay benefits equal to 75% of the Covered Expenses in excess of the Deductible Amount which are incurred on behalf of a Covered Person as a result of an accident or sickness; provided

1. Such Expenses are incurred within ___ years after the date such injury is sustained or such sickness first manifests itself; and

2. The Maximum Benefit with respect to a Covered Person as a result of any one accident or sickness and all recurrences and related conditions is as stated in schedule

. . . . . . . . . . . . . . . . . . . . . .

C. Payment of the Maximum Benefit with respect to Covered Expenses incurred on behalf of a Covered Person as the result of one accident or sickness and all recurrences and related conditions shall not preclude the payment of additional benefits with respect to Covered Expenses incurred on behalf of the same Covered Person arising from a different and entirely unrelated accident or sickness.

The applicable provisions from a group rider are reproduced below. They provide for an aggregate lifetime benefit for each insured individual (with the usual provision for reinstatement), with a deductible imposed in each calendar year equal to the sum of a corridor deductible and benefits under the basic group policies.

## EMPLOYEES' MAJOR MEDICAL EXPENSE BENEFITS

The Insurance Company hereby agrees, subject to the terms of the group policy, including this rider, to pay benefits in an amount equal to (75 or 80) per cent of the amount, if any, by which the total covered expenses incurred by an employee in any calendar year exceed the deductible amount applicable for that calendar year; but the aggregate of the benefits payable under this section with respect to any one individual in such individual's entire lifetime (whether or not there has been any interruption in the continuity of the individual's insurance) shall not exceed the maximum benefit (except in accordance with the section entitled "Special Provisions for Establishing a New Maximum Benefit"). The terms "covered expenses" "deductible amount," and "maximum benefit" shall have the meanings assigned to them in the subsection of this section entitled "Definitions and Exclusions." An expense or charge shall be deemed to be incurred on the date on which the particular service or supply which gives rise to the expense or charge is rendered or obtained.

. . . . . . . . . . . . . . . . . . . . . .

The "deductible amount" is made up of two parts, one called the "basic benefits deductible" and the other called the "cash deductible." The "deductible amount" applies in respect of each calendar year.

The "basic benefits deductible," in respect of each calendar year, is an amount equal to the sum of

(1) the total cash value, computed on an equitable basis, of all services and supplies furnished during the calendar year through any "basic benefits" plan or plans under provisions thereof which provide for the furnishing of services or supplies rather than for payments in cash, and

(2) the total payments (whether such payments are contingent on expenses being incurred for services or supplies or whether such payments are contingent on the rendering of services or supplies) provided or available during the calendar year through any "basic benefits" plan or plans;

but only to the extent that such cash value or payments relate to any of the services or supplies which are recognized under this rider for the purposes of covered expenses.

The term "basic benefits" includes benefits, by whatever name called, under or on account of any one or more of the following items in respect of which any employer of the employee shall, directly or indirectly, have either contributed or made payroll deductions: the group policy (exclusive of this rider), any other insurance policy (whether issued by the Insurance Company or by any other insurer), any Blue Cross or Blue Shield plan or other hospital or medical benefit or service plan, any union welfare plan or other employee benefit organization plan, any federal or state or other governmental plan or law.

The "Cash deductible," in respect of each calendar year, is ($100).

If any part (or all) of an employee's "cash deductible" for a calendar year is applied against covered expenses incurred by the employee during the last three months of that calendar year, the employee's "cash deductible" for the next ensuing calendar year shall be reduced by the amount so applied.

The "Maximum benefit" of an employee is ($5,000); except that if an employee has previously been covered as a dependent under the rider providing for Dependents' Major Medical Expense Benefits, the "maximum benefit" as to that employee is limited to the amount, if any, by which ($5,000) exceeds the amount of all benefits paid or accrued in respect of him under said rider, and if and while there is no such excess the employee shall not be insured for Major Medical Expense Benefits insurance in respect of himself under this rider.

The extension of benefits clause is typical of that in other group medical expense policies and usually provides that benefit payments will be continued during a claimant's total disability. Unlike the hospital, surgical, and medical policies, where the period is usually 90 days, major medical policies often cover such expenditures until the end of the calendar year following the year in which contract coverage terminated.

The reinstatement of benefit clause is not so important in connection with a per disability upper limit, since subsequent disabilities are likely to result from a new and different cause. However, it is very important where the upper limit is on a lifetime aggregate basis. It provides that if the insured individual is insurable, the limit will be reinstated to its original amount. Usually there is a minimum benefit payment required before this privilege can be exercised to reduce administrative costs.

A typical reinstatement of benefit provision from a group policy with an aggregate lifetime limit reads as follows:

### SPECIAL PROVISIONS FOR ESTABLISHING A NEW MAXIMUM BENEFIT

If an employee with respect to whom benefits of at least $1,000 have been paid under this rider submits, at no expense to the Insurance Company, evidence of insurability satisfactory to the Insurance Company, the Insurance Company will give its written consent to the ignoring of benefits paid for previous covered expenses in applying the maximum benefit provisions of this rider to benefits payable for covered expenses incurred with respect to the employee after the effective date of such written consent. If such written consent is granted after the employee's insurance under this rider has terminated for any reason, this rider shall, in all particulars, again apply as to the employee to the same extent that it would have applied if the employee had never been insured under this rider before the effective date of such written consent.

## Dread-disease benefits

*Insurance company plans.* The first dread-disease coverage was "polio" coverage, which was first issued in the late 1940's. New policies cover more diseases but are otherwise similar. The typical maximum benefit is $5,000, although $10,000 is common. Sometimes a time limit on benefits is provided, usually three years. The contracts provide high upper limits and cover a broad range of services, including use of iron lungs. In addition to hospital expenses and physicians' and surgeons' fees, most include crutches, braces, drugs and medicines, and transportation to another locality if recommended by a physician. Many also cover physiotherapy; some blood and plasma. There are usually few internal limits. However, many impose such limits on nursing services and ambulance fees. Deductibles or waiting periods are rare in polio policies but more common in other dread-disease policies.

The diseases covered in dread-disease policies vary somewhat but are usually diseases of high severity and low frequency. Heart disease is almost never covered, since its high frequency would add greatly to cost. Almost all such policies cover poliomyelitis, encephalitis, diphtheria, leukemia, tetanus, scarlet fever, smallpox, and spinal meningitis. Many cover rabies and tularemia. A few cover cerebral meningitis and typhoid. A number of companies now are offering cancer policies. These are single-disease contracts very similar to the polio policy and perhaps appeal to the same worry or gambling instincts. There is a growing tendency to include cancer with the other named dread diseases.

In individual insurance, separate policies are issued, but in group contracts the benefits are usually provided as a rider to other types of insurance. As major medical and comprehensive coverage increases, the need and market for these contracts will disappear. Except for coverage of cancer and scarlet fever, a disease of low severity, they are of little value, since many of these diseases are quite rare.[6]

*Blue Shield plans.* Eight Blue Shield plans now issue dread-disease policies, as compared to 13 five years ago. These are usually provided as a rider extending the coverage of the basic Blue Shield surgical-medical plan. In some cases the coverage is jointly issued with the Blue Cross plan. The typical plan covers 10 dread diseases: poliomyelitis, leukemia, diphtheria, scarlet fever, smallpox, tetanus, spinal meningitis, encephalitis, tularemia, and rabies. The typical policy covers to a maximum of $5,000, sometimes allocated as to type of expense and sometimes subject to a two-year maximum period. The types of expense covered are about the same as in insurance company plans.

## Comprehensive plans

*Insurance company group plans.* The term "comprehensive" will be used here to refer to any plan which includes most types of health services in a single plan and provides coverage to very high limits. While no plan can be comprehensive in the sense of being all-inclusive and free of limits, these plans qualify for the term at least as well as policies in other lines of insurance to which the word has been applied, and better than most.

Insurance company comprehensive plans are essentially of two types. The so-called pure comprehensive plan represents an extension of major medical down toward first-dollar coverage and the elimination of underlying coverage. Such a plan might provide for reimbursement of 80 percent of covered medical care expenses in excess of a deductible of $25 or $50 per disability, up to a limit of $10,000 per disability. The coverage usually is not and should not be limited to cases requiring hospital confinement, as such a provision encourages the unnecessary use of such facilities.

The purposes or objectives of comprehensive coverage have been listed as extension of the scope of insurance coverage, discouragement of unnecessary utilization, de-emphasis of small claims, provision of more complete coverage of catastrophic expenditures, avoidance of duplication of coverage and of frequent plan revision, simple plan design, and reasonable cost.[7] This type of plan accomplishes all these objectives well but is subject to the criticism that acceptance will be limited by the tradition of first-

---

[6] Total cases in the U.S. in 1966 were: Poliomyelitis, 113; encephalitis, 3,085; diphtheria, 209; tetanus, 235; smallpox, 0; meningitis (all sites), 3,085; rabies, 1; tularemia, 208; typhoid, 378. Total for all listed here is 7,610 per year, or one case for each 25,568 persons! Data from U.S. Department of Health, Education, and Welfare, *Morbidity and Mortality Weekly Reports*, Vol. 15, No. 53 (November, 1967), p. 2.

[7] R. R. Shinn, "Comprehensive Medical Plans," *Best's Insurance News*, Fire and Casualty Edition, June, 1956, p. 85.

dollar coverage of certain types of expense. This tradition has been long established, especially in hospital and surgical insurance, where Blue Cross and Blue Shield first set the pattern.

Another type of comprehensive plan has been developed which meets this objection but, in so doing, departs somewhat from the sound insurance theory on which the first type plan is based. This type of plan often is referred to as "modified" comprehensive. This approach represents a combination of basic hospital and sometimes surgical coverage with major medical into a single plan. Here there may be no deductible applied to hospital expenses, no percentage participation on (say) the first $250 of covered hospital expenses, and sometimes similar treatment of surgeons' fees. Chart 8–3 outlines the coverage of a plan of this type which does impose a deductible even on hospital expenses. All sorts of combinations are available, of course.

While a modified comprehensive plan is probably more salable in the face of employer and employee conditioning toward first-dollar benefits, it is considerably more expensive than a plan with a small deductible.

For example, in 1954 the annual claim cost was about $6.80 for a hospital room-and-board benefit of $10 per day for a maximum of 90 days for a man in his forties. By eliminating the first-day coverage, the claim cost drops to $6.13, a 13 percent reduction. By eliminating the first five days, the cost drops to $3.80, a 44 percent reduction. Similarly, applying a $50 deductible to miscellaneous hospital expense benefits would make possible providing a $2,000 upper limit at a cost no greater than that of a $100 limit with no deductible. The use of a deductible makes possible much greater coverage at the same cost, or a much lower cost for the same coverage. The experience of one company with the use of a deductible in hospital-surgical coverage has been encouraging. Within eight months of the introduction of these forms, 45 percent of its sales were on a deductible basis.[8] This suggests that acceptance of this concept may be greater than is commonly supposed.

Table 8–3 illustrates a typical group comprehensive plan, except that by now most have a $10,000 maximum benefit, and the premium rate applies as of ca. 1963.

*Individual policies.* Most comprehensive plans are on a group basis. The number of individual (including family) comprehensive contracts in force is still too small to show up in the statistics. However, a number of companies are known to be issuing contracts of this type. One of the most interesting is the "Medical Protector" of Washington National Life. It provides a range of deductibles from $50 to $1,000 (making it a comprehensive or major medical policy respectively) and a range of upper limits up to $27,000. The most liberal comprehensive ($50 deductible) policy

---

[8] Charles N. Walker, "Deductible Hospital Insurance," *Best's Insurance News,* Fire and Casualty Edition, December, 1955, p. 33.

CHART 8-3

A MODIFIED COMPREHENSIVE PLAN MAY PROVIDE

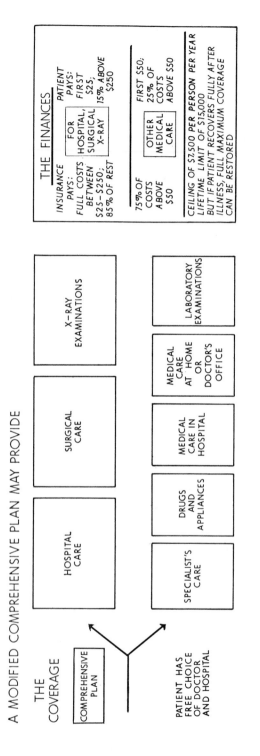

THE COVERAGE

COMPREHENSIVE PLAN

PATIENT HAS FREE CHOICE OF DOCTOR AND HOSPITAL

HOSPITAL CARE

SURGICAL CARE

X-RAY EXAMINATIONS

SPECIALIST'S CARE

DRUGS AND APPLIANCES

MEDICAL CARE IN HOSPITAL

MEDICAL CARE AT HOME OR DOCTOR'S OFFICE

LABORATORY EXAMINATIONS

THE FINANCES

INSURANCE PAYS: FULL COSTS BETWEEN $25-$250; 85% OF REST

FOR HOSPITAL, SURGICAL X-RAY

PATIENT PAYS: FIRST $25, 15% ABOVE $250

75% OF COSTS ABOVE $50

OTHER MEDICAL CARE

FIRST $50. 25% OF COSTS ABOVE $50

CEILING OF $7,500 PER PERSON PER YEAR
LIFETIME LIMIT OF $15,000
BUT IF PATIENT RECOVERS FULLY AFTER
ILLNESS, FULL MAXIMUM COVERAGE
CAN BE RESTORED

TABLE 8-3

Group Comprehensive Medical Expense Insurance Plan including Premium Rates

*Brief Description of Plan*

Expenses covered—reasonable and customary charges for necessary service:

Type A expenses............Hospital room and board (limited to semiprivate charge), special hospital services, surgical fees.

Type B expenses............Physicians' fees other than surgery, X rays and other types of diagnostic services out of hospital, drugs and medicines, professional ambulance service, registered nurses, artificial limbs and eyes.

Benefits:

For each individual covered during calendar year......For Type A expense: Employee pays first $25, plan pays next $225 in full, plan pays 75 percent of excess.

For Type B: expenses: Employee pays greater of first $50 or 1 percent of earnings (reduced by any expenses applied toward $25 deductible under Type A), plan pays 75 percent of excess.

For maternity—Type A and Type B expenses: Normal delivery, $150; Caesarean section, $225; miscarriage, $75. Where there are severe complications, plan pays 75 percent of additional medical expenses incurred because of such complications.

Maximum benefits...........$5,000 in any calendar year; $5,000 aggregate.

Principal expenses not covered..Dental care (except due to accident), eyeglasses, health checkups, expenses paid by government or other employer plan.

*Illustrative Gross Manual Premium Rates*[a]

| Estimated Average Semi-private Room-and-Board Charges Applicable in Area Where Plan Operates | Initial Monthly Premium for Insured Employee Only | Initial Monthly Premium for Dependents |
|---|---|---|
| $15.00............................. | $4.86 | $ 9.95 |
| 20.00............................. | 5.58 | 11.24 |
| 25.00............................. | 6.33 | 12.02 |

[a] These rates would apply to a small group case. For the smallest cases, these premiums would be increased up to 5 percent. For larger group plans the gross premium rate may be reduced by as much as 15 percent. These rates would apply to a group with the following characteristics:

1. All employees covered; less than 30 percent earning $5,000 or more; less than 7 percent earning $10,000 or more.
2. Normal age distribution among employees.
3. Average medical care costs apply for area involved.
4. Thirty-one percent to 40 percent of benefits cover female employees.

Source: Charles A. Siegfried, "Group Medical Expense—Insurance Company" in Davis W. Gregg (ed.), *Life and Health Insurance Handbook* Rev. Ed. (Homewood, Ill.: Richard D. Irwin, Inc., 1964).

provides a $27,000 upper limit on a per disability basis which is reinstated when expenses are not incurred from the same cause for two or more years. It contains internal limits of $32 per day for hospital room and board with no limit on duration, and a surgical schedule with a $3,600 maximum based on the California relative value schedule. Unit values may be selected from $3 to $9. Maximums stated here are based on the $9 value.

Subject to the deductible and schedule, it covers 100 percent of hospital room and board, surgical fees and anesthesia, and convalescent home room and board up to a stated limit per day for up to 60 days. Regular medical expense, drugs, blood and plasma, laboratory tests, nurses services, X rays, medical supplies, and local ambulance services are covered at 80 percent, with physicians' and nurses' services limited by a schedule. An "increase option" makes it possible to increase the dollar value of the units in the schedule without evidence of insurability at current premium rates. This makes possible the adjustment of coverage to changed price levels as a result of inflation or change of residence. The contract is guaranteed renewable until the insured becomes eligible for "Medicare." While this contract contains more internal limits than most modified comprehensive policies, it can provide very liberal benefits, comprehensive in nature and with few exclusions. However, it is expensive. The premium for this attractive package is $536.22 per year for a man aged 35 and spouse and $143.64 for each child up to three. However, medical care itself is expensive and this may be a good way to pay for it. Similar contracts are offered by a number of companies.

### Blue Cross and Blue Shield extended benefits

Major medical coverage is provided by Blue Cross and Blue Shield in conjunction for the nationwide Federal Employee Plan, and for other national accounts such as the autoworkers. In addition it is offered by 43 Blue Cross plans and by 8 Blue Shield plans. However, in some areas, Blue Cross and Blue Shield are the same corporation, and in other areas they are coordinated and offer the identical plan. Eliminating this duplication, there are a total of 47 different major medical plans offered by Blue Cross and/or Blue Shield. Maximum benefits range from $2,500 per year and $5,000 lifetime to $15,000 per year and $30,000 lifetime. There is usually a corridor deductible of $50 to $500 ($100 being the most common), and a percentage participation provision whereby the plans pay 75 or 80 percent of eligible expense. Eligible expense includes not only hospital, but also physicians' services, blood (with three exceptions), nursing care, drugs, and appliances. As an illustration of this approach, the pertinent provisions of the federal employees' plan are reproduced below.

## SUPPLEMENTAL BENEFITS

Subject to the definitions, limitations, and exclusions, each subscriber is entitled to Supplemental Benefits for reasonable and customary charges for necessary covered services and supplies in or out of a hospital prescribed or ordered by a physician, to the extent that such charges are not covered by Basic Benefits. The Plan will determine whether a charge is reasonable and customary by comparing it with charges made for similar services or supplies under similar conditions to persons under like circumstances.

### COVERED SERVICES AND SUPPLIES

* Physicians' services, including surgery, home, office, and hospital visits, and consultations.
* Hospital services; however, any part of the charge for room and board (including special diets and general nursing) in excess of $25 a day (High Option) or $15 a day (Low Option) is not an allowable charge.
* Anesthetics and their administration.
* Oxygen and equipment for its administration.
* Blood transfusions, including the cost of blood, blood plasma, and blood plasma expanders.
* Radiation therapy.
* Diagnostic examinations, including X-ray, laboratory, basal metabolism, electrocardiogram, electroencephalogram, and radioisotope. (Also see Special Benefits Provision, Page 68.)
* Local professional ambulance service to or from a hospital for inpatients, or for outpatient accident care.
* Physical therapy rendered by a qualified professional physical therapist.
* Orthopedic braces (except corrective shoes), crutches, and prosthetic appliances such as artificial limbs and eyes, including their replacement, repair, or adjustment.
* Rental of wheelchair and other durable medical equipment.
* Drugs and medicines obtainable only by written prescription.
* Services of special nurses as follows:
    *In a hospital*—Services of a professional registered nurse (R.N.) or a licensed practical nurse.
    *Outside a hospital*—Services of a professional registered nurse (R.N.) only; except that under unusual circumstances, and upon written certification by the attending physician that the services of a professional registered nurse (R.N.) were necessary but unobtainable, the Plan may determine that the services of a licensed practical nurse are covered services.

### PERCENT OF CHARGES COVERED

The Plan will pay Supplemental Benefits for charges for covered services and supplies in excess of the Deductible within a single Benefit Period of 80 percent under the High Option or 75 percent under the Low Option.

#### except:

*For nervous or mental disorders*—Under both options, the Plan will pay 50 percent of charges in excess of the Deductible for covered services and supplies received in the outpatient department of a hospital or outside of a hospital. However, regular Supplemental Benefits will be provided for drugs and medicines used for the treatment of nervous or mental disorders.

### THE BENEFIT PERIOD

*A Benefit Period begins*—On January 1 and extends through December 31 of that same year.

### THE DEDUCTIBLE

The Deductible is the amount of expense a subscriber must incur in each Benefit Period for covered services or supplies before Supplemental Benefits are payable. To the extent that expenses are paid for by Basic Benefits they cannot be counted toward the Deductible; nor will Supplemental Benefits be paid for the Deductible.

The Deductible is $100 (High Option) and $150 (Low Option) for each subscriber each Benefit Period.

However, under a family enrollment covering three or more subscribers, only two Deductibles have to be satisfied during any Benefit Period.

Further, if two or more subscribers under the same family enrollment are injured in the same accident, only one Deductible need be satisfied each Benefit Period by those injured.

### SPECIAL BENEFIT PROVISIONS FOR DIAGNOSTIC EXAMINATIONS NOT COVERED BY BASIC BENEFITS

To the extent that they are not covered by Basic Benefits, Supplemental Benefits of 80 percent (High Option) or 75 percent (Low Option) will be paid for charges in excess of $20 (High Option) and $25 (Low Option) incurred during a single Benefit Period for the following services in a hospital, in a physician's office or elsewhere:
* X-ray examinations
* Laboratory examinations (except allergy tests and surveys)
* Basal metabolism examinations
* Electroencephalograms
* Radioisotope examinations.

These benefits are paid regardless of whether the subscriber has satisfied the Deductible. The $20 (High Option) or $25 (Low Option) payable by the subscriber may be used to help satisfy the $100 (High Option) or $150 (Low Option) Deductible. If the $100 (High Option) or $150 (Low Option) Deductible has already been satisfied at the time the subscriber receives a service for which the special benefit is payable, Supplemental Benefits will be paid for the charges including the first $20 (High Option) or $25 (Low Option).

### MAXIMUM SUPPLEMENTAL BENEFITS

The maximum Supplemental Benefits payable for each subscriber are:

| HIGH OPTION $30,000 | LOW OPTION $10,000 |
|---|---|

When the maximum Supplemental Benefits of $30,000 (High Option) and $10,000 (Low Option) have been paid for a subscriber, Supplemental Benefits can be reinstated upon submission of evidence, acceptable to the Plan, of the subscriber's insurability.

The Deductible and the above maximums apply only to Supplemental Benefits.

### SUPPLEMENTAL EXCLUSIONS AND LIMITATIONS

* Cosmetic surgery and treatment, except that required to correct accidental injury occurring while covered by this Plan.

Dental care, dental surgery, or dental appliances unless required because of accidental bodily injury occurring while the subscriber is covered under this Plan; except covered oral surgery and in-hospital removal of impacted teeth are not excluded.

Services or supplies required for obstetrical delivery, normal prenatal and postnatal care, or any condition related to pregnancy other than Caesarean delivery or specified complications of pregnancy.

Services or supplies to the extent benefits are available to the subscriber under any other health benefits plan held by reason of law or as a result of employment when the employer:
* contributed toward the cost of the Plan, or
* makes payroll deductions for collection of premium.

Services of a special nurse who is an immediate relative, or member of the household, of the subscriber ("immediate relative" means the spouse, parent, child, brother or sister, by blood, marriage or adoption). However, this exclusion does not apply to the services of such special nurse for one 8-hour shift out of each 24-hour continuous nursing period if satisfactory proof is furnished that she would otherwise be gainfully employed as a nurse.

In addition, 21 plans offer extended benefits on a scheduled basis. Eleven of these are among the plans offering major medical benefits. Thus a total of 57 Blue Cross and Blue Shield plans offer major medical and/or extended benefits.

Some of the extended benefit plans are quite complex with a lengthy schedule of benefits for hospital room and board; hospital extras; physician services in hospital, office, or home; nursing; drugs, etc. Others simply extend the basic hospital or medical coverage for a longer period. An example of the latter approach is the endorsement used by the Colorado Hospital Service. It provides:

### EXTENDED BENEFIT ENDORSEMENTS

In addition to the benefits provided under the basic Blue Cross Comprehensive Certificate for 120 days, an additional 240 days (Endorsement No. 1) or 610 days (Endorsement No. 2) of hospital care will be provided when the subscriber continues to require and receive hospital care for the same or related conditions *except* in cases of pulmonary tuberculosis or nervous and mental diseases. The first date of discharge from the hospital shall terminate the Plan's liability under the Endorsement until the member again qualifies for extended benefits unless the member is admitted to a hospital for the same or related conditions within 90 days of last discharge date. 240 days (Endorsement No. 1) or 610 days (Endorsement No. 2) will be the maximum number of days allowed under this Endorsement for the same or related conditions whether received in one continuous stay or successive stays.

In cases of pulmonary tuberculosis or nervous and mental conditions 90 days (Endorsement No. 1) or 150 days (Endorsement No. 2) will be available in addition to the 30 days provided under the basic certificate.

### Independent plans

Many of the independent plans offer benefits which are quite comprehensive as to amount, type of service, or both. The description of benefits of a few plans in Chapter 7 indicates that many of them approach the broadness of insurance company comprehensive coverage. Some exceed it in certain respects, such as coverage of preventive services such as immunizations and physical examinations.[9]

### Summary

Major medical policies protect against all types of disability and cover almost all types of medical care expenditure. They provide reimbursement of an agreed percentage, usually 75 to 85 percent, of covered expenses in excess of a deductible. The deductible and the maximum benefit

---

[9] Insurance companies provide plenty of free physical examinations, too, but not as contract benefits. All that is necessary is to let an agent know that one might be interested in buying an individual policy.

may apply to each disability or to each insured in a year or on a variety of other bases. They are provided by insurance companies, Blue Cross and Blue Shield.

Dread-disease policies, of which polio insurance was the first, provide protection in large amounts with few restrictions against one or more diseases of high severity but low frequency. They are an unsatisfactory substitute for all risks coverage.

Comprehensive plans provide essentially the major medical type protection extended down to (or almost to) first-dollar benefits. The insurance company plans are either an aggregation of major medical with basic coverages or a major medical policy with a low deductible. The independent plans are on a service basis and provide broad full-service benefits with, however, a number of internal limits. Both major medical and comprehensive plans represent a far more sound approach to health insurance than do the basic contracts. They cover the severe loss and often exclude the small budgetable expenses.

Sound experiments by various mechanisms should be encouraged. The dread-disease policies are sound as to size of benefit, but unsound from a social viewpoint in covering only a limited list of diseases. The danger of such contracts is that they tend to serve, in the minds of insureds, as a substitute for adequate health insurance against all types of disability. If adequate coverage is carried against all types of disability, there is no place in the program for these named-peril contracts.

It seems probable that comprehensive plans gradually will supersede the more limited types of coverage. This probably will occur through a continuation of present tendencies: the increase in benefit periods and maximum amounts in basic contracts and the lowering of deductibles in major medical and the extension to more types of expense. While only about 36 percent of the population have plans of these types today, their extension will probably parallel that of the basic contracts. The present growth rate still is very high. From December, 1965, to December, 1966, the number of persons covered by insurance company major medical increased 10 percent and the number covered by insurance company comprehensive plans increased 11 percent.

It seems likely that in another decade or two most Americans will have almost complete protection against serious medical expenses, on a voluntary basis. If so, this will represent a tremendous triumph of private enterprise or "people's capitalism" over the forces at work in the world which favor the continuous extension of government activity.

### Selected references

*See the following items from the General Bibliography: 4, Ch. 13; 6, chs. 8, 12, 13, and 14; 10, ch. 5; 12, pp. 57–60; 29*

BEVAN, JOHN R. "Comprehensive Medical Insurance—Statistical Analysis for Ratemaking," *Proceedings of the Casualty Actuarial Society*, Vol. 1, p. 111.

BLUE CROSS ASSOCIATION. *Blue Cross Guide*. Chicago, 1967.

CHAMBER OF COMMERCE OF THE UNITED STATES. *Major Medical Expense Insurance*. Washington, October, 1957.

COUNCIL ON MEDICAL SERVICES, AMA. *Voluntary Prepayment Medical Benefit Plans*, 1965. Chicago, 1966.

MILLER, MORTON D. "Gross Premiums for Individual and Family Major Medical Expense Insurance," *Transactions of the Society of Actuaries*, Vol. III, p. 31.

THALER, ALAN M. "Group Major Medical Expense Insurance," *Transactions of the Society of Actuaries*, Vol. III, p. 429.

WALKER, CHARLES N. "Deductible Hospital Insurance," *Best's Insurance News*, Fire and Casualty Edition, December, 1955, p. 33.

## chapter 9

Mental illness, outpatient services, home nursing care, dental care, prescription drugs, and private duty nursing are often excluded. Health insurance should be covering at least 90 percent of all consumer expenditures for health care.—Wilbur J. Cohen, *National Conference on Private Health Insurance, September 28, 1967*

# Toward Broader Coverage

### Introduction

As indicated in Chapter 3 above, private medical expense insurance meets only 32 percent of the national private consumer medical expense, although it meets 68 percent of hospital expenses and 33 percent of physicians' fees. This is a result of the process of development of health insurance which has tended to emphasize the more traumatic types of loss—hospital and surgical expense. But the industry has been criticized, both explicitly and implicitly, for its failure to cover more of the national medical care costs. This naturally has focused attention on the possibility of broadening medical expense insurance coverages to cover more types of expense as well as covering the traditional types of expense more completely.

The recent rapid growth of regular medical expense insurance represents the extension of coverage to cover nonsurgical physicians' fees, but much of this coverage applies only to physicians' calls in the hospital. Major medical and comprehensive contracts cover more types of expense in addition to affording broad coverage of hospital and physicians' fees. Usually such contracts cover blood and plasma, appliances, drugs, and nursing care both in and out of the hospital. In-hospital private-duty nursing services may be covered by a rider to contracts which cover hospital expense. However, the effective coverage of nursing services in general and drugs and appliances is rather limited on an overall basis. The continuing rapid growth of major medical and comprehensive insurance should meet a growing proportion of such costs in the future. Even major medical and comprehensive contracts rarely cover skilled nursing homes, dental and vision care, or preventive medicine in the form of periodic health examinations and immunizations. Coverage of mental and nervous disease often is quite restricted.

Some of these types of expense can be incurred fortuitously in large amounts and represent proper subject matter for insurance. Others are more likely to occur in small amounts on a more or less predictable basis, and coverage of these might be referred to, more properly, as "prepayment." Regardless of the terminology, there is a growing interest in and experimentation with coverage of these types of expense.

In 1967, Secretary of Health, Education, and Welfare John W. Gardner, at the request of the President, convened three conferences dealing with the American health care system. The first of these dealt with the cost of medical care, the second with private health insurance and the third with group practice, especially with prepaid group practice. It was made abundantly clear to representatives of insurance, labor, consumers, physicians, and other conferees that the Johnson administration was vitally concerned with controlling the advance of medical care prices and broadening the coverage of private health insurance both as to proportion of the population covered and the types of expense covered, and that prepaid group practice was believed to be a fruitful vehicle in seeking these goals. It was evident that the administration was telling the industry that it had better intensify its efforts in these directions or else expect further government efforts to expand Title XVIII coverage or otherwise interfere with the market. In March, 1968, before taking office as Secretary of Health, Education, and Welfare, Wilbur J. Cohen referred to private health insurance as "incomplete, inadequate, and not comprehensive enough to meet the medical care needs of the American people." He said he "would like to see us strengthen as far as humanly possible the voluntary health insurance system of this country."

In evaluating the adequacy of private insurance, it is more meaningful to consider only the population under age 65, since the 65-and-over group generally is covered by Title XVIII, and any private insurance is complementary or duplicating. Table 9–1 gives estimates of the number and proportion of persons covered for various types of expense by major age group.

Table 9–2 gives a detailed breakdown of coverage by type of insurer for persons under age 65. In interpreting these data it should be noted that most of those people counted as covered for office and home visits, drugs, nursing, visiting nurse services and nursing home care were covered for such expense only by major medical contracts, and benefits were available only after meeting a substantial deductible. On the other hand, 38.8 million persons under age 65 with supplementary major medical contracts were not counted in estimating the number covered for hospital care, surgical service, in-hospital physicians services and X-ray and laboratory

TABLE 9-1

Number of Persons with Health Insurance Coverage of Various Services,
December 31, 1966

| Type of Service | All Ages | | Under Age 65 | | Aged 65 and Over | |
|---|---|---|---|---|---|---|
| | Number (In Thousands) | Percent of Population[a] | Number (In Thousands) | Percent of Population[a] | Number (In Thousands) | Percent of Population[a] |
| Hospital care..........158,022 | | 81.2 | 148,589 | 84.5 | 9,433 | 50.5 |
| Surgery................144,715 | | 74.4 | 137,448 | 78.1 | 7,267 | 38.9 |
| In-hospital visits........116,462 | | 59.9 | 110,754 | 63.0 | 5,708 | 30.6 |
| X-ray and laboratory examinations†........ 93,459 | | 48.0 | 89,750 | 51.0 | 3,709 | 19.9 |
| Physicians' office and home visits...... 73,706 | | 37.9 | 70,993 | 40.4 | 2,713 | 14.5 |
| Dental care............ 4,227 | | 2.2 | 4,143 | 2.4 | 84 | .4 |
| Prescribed drugs[b]...... 65,544 | | 33.7 | 63,845 | 36.3 | 1,699 | 9.1 |
| Private-duty nursing.... 68,722 | | 35.3 | 66,632 | 37.9 | 2,090 | 11.2 |
| Visiting nurse service... 79,004 | | 40.6 | 76,453 | 43.5 | 2,551 | 13.7 |
| Nursing home care.... 17,814 | | 9.2 | 14,999 | 8.5 | 2,815 | 15.1 |

[a] Civilian population.
[b] Out-of-hospital.
Source: Louis S. Reed, "Private Health Insurance: Coverage and Financial Experience 1940–66," *Social Security Bulletin;* November, 1967, p. 5.

examinations, on grounds that most of them had been counted already. An unknown number has benefits of this type only under major medical contracts, and this number should be added.

An even more striking measure of the degree to which private health insurance is largely limited to hospital and physician services is provided by figures on benefit payments. In 1966, only $310 million was paid for other medical expense, about 3.5 percent of total benefits.[1]

## Nursing and home care

Private-duty nursing is necessary for many severe illnesses and can amount to very substantial sums of money in a short time. Although the development of intensive care units in hospitals may reduce the need for this type of service as a separately billed item in the course of time, the development of such units is still on a small-scale basis. To a lesser degree, nursing home costs and skilled nursing services at home can add up to quite substantial expenditures.

*In-Hospital floor nursing.* General floor nursing in hospitals is provided by a variety of types of personnel ranging from supervisory registered nurses to orderlies and attendants. Since the charges for this

[1] Louis S. Reed, "Private Health Insurance: Coverage and Financial Experience, 1940–66," *Social Security Bulletin,* November, 1967, p. 5.

TABLE 9-2

Private Medical Expense Insurance Enrollment as of December 31, 1966: Number of Persons under Age 65 with Some Coverage of Specified Services or Expense (in thousands)

| Type of Plan | Hospital Care | Surgical Services | Physician Services | | | Dental Care | Prescribed Drugs (Out-of-Hospital)[c] | Private-Duty Nursing | Visiting Nurse Service[d] | Nursing Home Care |
|---|---|---|---|---|---|---|---|---|---|---|
| | | | In-Hospital Visits | X-ray and Laboratory Examinations[a] | Office and Home Visits[b] | | | | | |
| Blue Cross-Blue Shield plans | 60,707 | 53,805 | 50,563 | 26,665 | 13,564 | 16 | 10,400 | 12,400 | 20,750 | 8,300 |
| Blue Cross | 58,635 | 3,161 | 2,971 | e | e | e | e | e | e | e |
| Blue Shield | 2,072 | 50,644 | 47,592 | e | e | e | e | e | e | e |
| Insurance companies | | | | | | | | | | |
| Group policies | 67,546 | 68,574 | 52,901 | 52,000 | 51,000 | 1,960 | 50,700 | 50,000 | 50,000 | 5,900 |
| Individual policies | 35,729 | 27,479 | 10,857 | 9,700 | 5,000 | — | 4,300 | 5,000 | 5,000 | e |
| Unadjusted total | 103,275 | 96,053 | 63,758 | 61,700 | 56,000 | 1,960 | 55,000 | 55,000 | 55,000 | 5,900 |
| Less duplication[f] | 10,484 | 9,060 | 4,599 | 3,085 | 2,800 | — | 2,750 | 2,750 | 2,750 | 177 |
| Net total | 92,791 | 86,993 | 59,159 | 58,615 | 53,200 | 1,960 | 52,250 | 52,250 | 52,250 | 5,900 |
| Independent plans | | | | | | | | | | |
| Community-consumer | 6,196 | 7,838 | 7,047 | 7,324 | 6,482[g] | 2,167 | 2,516 | 3,363 | 5,039 | 5,723 |
| Employer-employee-union | 1,862 | 3,389 | 3,377 | 3,388 | 3,199 | 167 | 297 | 1,539 | 3,408 | 1,128 |
| Private group clinic | 4,295 | 4,263 | 3,447 | 3,760 | 3,071 | 381 | 2,200 | 1,815 | 1,630 | 68 |
| Dental society | 39 | 186 | 223 | 176 | 212 | 610 | 19 | 9 | 1 | 1,060 |
| Gross total | 159,694 | 148,636 | 116,769 | 92,604 | 73,246 | 4,143 | 65,166 | 68,013 | 78,039 | 15,151 |
| Less duplication[h] | 11,105 | 11,188 | 6,015 | 2,854 | 2,253 | — | 1,321 | 1,381 | 1,586 | 152 |
| Net number of different persons | 148,589[i] | 137,448[i] | 110,754[i] | 89,750 | 70,993 | 4,143 | 63,845 | 66,632 | 76,453 | 14,999 |
| Percent of population under age 65[j] | 84.5[i] | 78.1[i] | 63.0[i] | 51.0 | 40.4 | 2.4 | 36.3 | 37.9 | 43.5 | 8.5 |

a In physicians' offices, clinics or health centers. Excludes those covered only in hospital out-patient departments or those covered only in accident or fracture cases or when services are followed by surgery.

b Number covered for all conditions. Excludes those eligible for care only after hospitalization.

c Excludes those covered for drugs only after hospitalization.

d Assumes that all persons covered for private-duty nursing are also covered for visiting nurse service.

e Not estimated separately; in many cases coverage is jointly written.

f As estimated by HIAA for first three services; calculated at 5 percent for X-ray and laboratory examinations, office and home visits, prescribed drugs, private-duty nursing and visiting nurse service, at 3 percent for nursing home care and zero for dental care.

g About 15 percent of this number not covered for home calls.

h Social Security Administration estimate.

i HIAA estimates.

j Based on Census estimate of 175,880,000 as of Jan. 1, 1967.

Source: Louis S. Reed, "Private Health Insurance: Coverage and Financial Experiences, 1940-66," Social Security Bulletin, November, 1967, p. 3.

service are generally included in the basic hospital charge for room and board, these services are covered by hospital, major medical, and comprehensive contracts like other hospital expenses. Similarly, to the extent that insurance covers nursing home services (see below) general duty nursing in these institutions is covered.

*Private-Duty nursing.* Private-duty in-hospital nursing service is, to some degree, elective, but often is medically necessary. Usually the nurse is engaged and paid directly by the patient. Standard fees for eight-hour shifts range from $16 to $24. Where around-the-clock nursing is required, such fees can mount up at an alarming rate.

In 1958, 18 Blue Cross plans provided some coverage of private nursing services under some form of optional extended benefit coverage.[2] Since more plans have extended benefits available at the present time, the number making coverage of nursing services available probably is considerably larger today. Usually, the coverage is subject to limitations in the nature of deductibles, percentage participation, and maximum limits of amount or duration.

In 1955, at least 33 insurance companies made in-hospital private nursing coverage available under hospital contracts. The coverage was limited in terms of the maximum charge per day with a range from $5 to $30, and also limited to a maximum number of days. Similar coverage is available as an optional additional benefit under individual disability income contracts, particularly commercial sickness contracts. Major medical, comprehensive, dread-disease, and blanket accident medical expense coverages include private-duty nursing with other eligible medical expense and cover it like other expenses. Usually the care must be ordered or approved by a physician and the nurse must be a registered professional nurse not related to the claimant. Most such contracts do not include any internal limit on private-duty nursing, but some do. Such limits may be in terms of a schedule, a maximum per day plus an amount or duration limit, or an overall limit on this type of expense. A few apply a stricter percentage participation requirement to this type of expense than to other types.

*Home nursing services.* Similarly, major medical, comprehensive and similar contracts cover nursing services outside the hospital. Some impose special limits or a higher percentage participation by the insured. In 1958, 14 Blue Cross plans provided some coverage for private-duty professional nursing in the home, almost all with specific limits, deductibles, and/or percentage participation. A number of independents, especially the prepaid group practice plans, include some coverage of professional nursing in the home.

---

[2] Joseph F. Follmann, Jr., *Health Insurance and Nursing and Home Care* (New York: Health Insurance Association of America, 1959). Much of the material in this section is based on this study.

*Visiting nurses.* Many convalescent and long-term patients could be cared for more economically in their homes than in hospitals and nursing homes if part-time visiting nurse service were available. Many chronic patients need little in the way of nursing services as such, but need help with household operation, meal preparation, and similar activities if they are to be capable of self-maintenance.

Most visiting nurse services currently are provided by public agencies. Most of the voluntary agencies operate largely on a charity basis. However, they frequently bill the patient for the service where he is able to pay. Several large life insurance companies provided visiting nurse services to their life insurance policyholders from the twenties to the fifties or earlier, but these programs have been terminated because of the development of other agencies which met the same need. The insurance company services were more of a supplementary service and a loss-preventive device than an insurance coverage in the usual sense.

Where the charge is billed to the patient, most major medical, comprehensive, and similar insurance policies will cover such fees. At least five Blue Cross plans, and a number of the independents, including several of the largest, will pay for such part-time nurse services. A number of experiments seem to indicate that such coverage, if administered soundly, actually reduces the overall cost of treatment.[3] Certain administrative safeguards are necessary, such as requiring that care be ordered by a physician, that the nurse be a registered professional one, and that she not be related to the claimant.

The coverage of home health services in Medicare, Part A and Part B, will no doubt encourage the development of such agencies and 1849 were participating in 1967. In 1965, the Health Insurance Council suggested the desirability of extending group contracts to cover home care and suggested guidelines for such contracts. Most insurance contracts designed to supplement Medicare will cover such expense.

*Home care.* Organized home care was described briefly in Chapter 2 as one of the components of "progressive patient care." It involves a coordinated program of physician's, nursing, and social services, and drugs and supplies to permit caring for the chronic or convalescent patient at home. If properly organized, such a program permits adequate care to be given at less cost than in a hospital or other institution. Most of the programs presently in operation are considered experimental or emphasize the treatment of the indigent or nearly so, or both.

Home health services are expected to be more widely available now that their costs are covered by Title XVIII Parts A and B. To the

---

[3] Joseph F. Follmann, Jr., "Prepayment for Public Health Nursing Services," in *Selected Readings for Principles of Individual Health Insurance II* (New York: Health Insurance Association of America, 1961). See also J. F. Follmann, Jr., "Health Insurance and Home Care Programs," *Best's Insurance News,* 1966.

extent that charges are billed to the patient, physicians', nurses', and drug costs would be met by major medical and comprehensive insurance as indicated above. Similarly, some of these services would be covered by Blue Cross and Blue Shield plans, especially under extended benefit provisions. At least one independent, Health Insurance Plan of Greater New York, covers home medical care under an organized program, provided the patient is attended by an HIP physician. Other independent plans covering such home health services include Group Health Cooperative of Puget Sound, Group Health Insurance, in New York, and the Kaiser Foundation Health Plan.[4]

*Practical nurses.* The great demand for nursing services has led to an increased utilization of practical nurses as a supplement to or substitute for registered professional nurses. All states have some provision for licensing such practical nurses, and standards are improving materially. To the extent that they can provide nursing services less expensively, but with a high standard of care, the use of such nurses can reduce the overall costs of medical care. Where practical nurses are used as a part of the general hospital floor nursing services, their services are covered by hospital insurance.

In 1958, six Blue Cross plans provided some coverage of the fees of private-duty practical nurses, and five of these extended the coverage to include home nursing by a practical nurse. The coverage was under some form of optional extended benefits. Most major medical and comprehensive policies limit coverage of nurses' fees to registered professional nurses, but some do not impose this limitation. Most will pay such benefits by administrative procedure where the nursing service seems to be medically necessary, especially if a registered nurse is unavailable.

*Homemaker services.* In many communities, homemaker services are available from social agencies, either public or private. These services involve the full- or part-time services of a trained "homemaker" who can take over the responsibility for housekeeping and child care during the absence or incapacity of the person usually responsible. Such services can make possible home care for an ill wife-mother or elderly person who otherwise would have to be treated in a hospital or nursing home. While not yet clearly recognized as a part of the medical care complex, these services would seem to offer fruitful possibilities for development. Except perhaps as a part of organized home care, as in the HIP program, or as an expense that might be approved administratively under a major medical or comprehensive contract, no insurance coverage is available for such services. It is possible that such coverage could be offered with proper safeguards, at least to the extent to which it reduces amounts which otherwise would be payable under a broad health insurance contract.

---

[4] Joseph F. Follmann, Jr., *Medical Care and Health Insurance* (Homewood, Ill.: Richard D. Irwin, Inc., 1963).

*Meals-on-Wheels.* Programs for providing hot meals to chronically ill or otherwise shut-in persons who live alone have been developed in a number of communities, usually on a charity or semicharity basis. Charges to the recipients vary with income and usually may be waived. These programs reduce the need for institutionalization as well as improve the condition of the recipients. Probably no health insurance contract currently covers the costs of such services, but they well might be paid for under major medical or comprehensive contracts on a noncontractual basis to the extent that they reduce the amount otherwise payable.

## Nursing homes

The skilled nursing home is becoming an ever more important part of the medical care picture as the chronic diseases assume a more important place in the disability complex and as the aging of the population results in more and more persons who need some type of medical care, short of hospitalization. Where such homes actually provide medical care, with genuine nursing services under the supervision of a physician, their costs represent appropriate subject matter for health insurance. However, there are severe problems in attempting to distinguish such a skilled nursing home from an old folks' home or other institution that is primarily a domiciliary or custodial institution.

The recent development of an accreditation program should do much to solve this problem and help to upgrade the quality of nursing homes. In 1963 such a program was instituted by the National Council for Accreditation of Nursing Homes, sponsored by the American Medical Association and the American Nursing Home Association. Detailed standards were developed and institutions were classified as intensive nursing care facility, skilled nursing care facility, and intermediate care facility. The passage of the Social Security amendments of 1965, which provided post-hospital coverage of care in "extended care facilities," made necessary the identification of such institutions and motivated many organizations to build or expand. An extended care facility must be primarily engaged in providing skilled nursing or rehabilitative services, be directed by a physician or registered professional nurse, have at least one full-time registered professional nurse, provide 24-hour nursing service, and meet many other detailed standards.[5] 4,160 extended care facilities were participating in Medicare in 1967.

In 1966, the Joint Commission on Accreditation of Hospitals assumed the function of nursing home accreditation, and by January 1, 1967, the first day of Medicare coverage for "extended care facilities," 1,592 ex-

---

[5] U.S. Department of Health, Education, and Welfare, Social Security Administration, *Health Insurance for the Aged: Conditions of Participation for Extended Care Facilities* (Washington, D.C.: U.S. Government Printing Office, 1966).

tended care facilities had been accredited by the Joint Commission, the American Hospital Association, the National Council for the Accreditation of Nursing Homes, or the California Commission for the Accreditation of Nursing Homes and Related Facilities.[6] There were accredited facilities in every state except Alaska and in the District of Columbia and Puerto Rico. The number of accredited facilities ranged from 1 each in Mississippi and Puerto Rico to 229 in California. In addition, 11 intermediate care facilities, 28 domiciliary facilities, and 10 mental facilities had been accredited.

Many, if not most, major medical contracts will pay benefits for skilled nursing home care required as a result of accidental injury or sickness, but others exclude nursing homes from their coverage either by defining the types of care covered or by specific exclusion. Some impose a daily room charge limit. However, many insurers will pay such benefits in some individual instances, where to do so would result in reducing the claim for covered services such as hospital treatment. The passage of the 1965 Social Security amendments providing nursing home benefits for the over-65 group accentuated the demand for coverage for those under age 65. Many insurers now offer contracts which specifically include the costs of nursing home care.

A 1963 survey showed 32 companies specifically providing nursing home benefits, and 14 others planning to do so. Benefit durations ranged from 30 to 200 days, with 30, 60, and 90 the most common. Daily benefit amounts ranged from $5 to $26.50, with $10, $12.50 and $15 the most frequent. There was no uniformity in defining a nursing home beyond licensing, being primarily for care of the sick, injured, or convalescent patient, providing full-time care, and being under the supervision of a physician or registered professional nurse.

Today, of course, such definition presents little problem to the policy draftsman. It is easy to define an eligible institution as one which has established eligibility in the Health Insurance for the Aged program under Title XVIII of the Social Security Act. A limited 1966 survey showed that all of nine companies offering extended care benefits to people age 65 or more to supplement Medicare required that the facility be approved for Medicare benefits. Three also required accreditation. A much narrower definition which would be simple to administer would be an institution listed as an accredited extended care facility in the latest Guide Issue of *Hospitals*. The Blue Cross and Blue Shield plans have recently begun to cover expenses of "approved" nursing homes in their contract with the United Auto Workers.

Most specific nursing home coverage requires previous hospitalization for one to seven days (most often five) and that confinement be pursuant

---

[6] *Hospitals*, Guide Issue, August 1, 1967, p. 303.

to a physician's recommendation and under his supervision. It is probable that many contracts now will adopt the language of the Social Security Act.

As the quality of nursing homes improves under the pressure of accreditation standards and criteria of approval for Title XVIII and XIX funds, and as these funds and insurance benefits finance the improvement of quality and increase the supply of nursing home beds, utilization will increase, the public image of the nursing home will improve, and nursing home benefits may become a standard feature of basic medical care contracts. Certainly this risk meets every criterion of insurability. It is now common for Blue Cross to cover cost of nursing homes after hospitalization,[7] although those so covered were not counted in Tables 9–1 and 9–2.

## Drugs

The development of antibiotics, hormones, tranquilizers, and other "wonder drugs" has contributed tremendously to effective treatment of disease, to fewer and shorter hospital stays, and to improved general levels of health. But the bill runs high. The total national expenditure for "drugs and sundries" is about $5 billion per year. This represents 16.7 percent of total consumer private medical care expenses, down a little from 20.2 percent in 1950, mainly because drug prices have remained stable while other medical care prices increased. Of this, perhaps 70 percent represents the costs of prescribed drugs. Much of this expenditure represents small amounts ($2.50 to $5 per prescription), spread over the year, and presents little need for insurance coverage. The average per capita expenditure in 1964–65 was $21 for prescribed drugs plus $8.80 for nonprescribed drugs.[8] However, the incidence of drug expense varies widely by families. The 1958 Health Information Foundation study showed 6 percent of the families incurring drug costs in excess of $200 per year.[9]

The problems involved in insuring against the cost of drugs include the difficulty of distinguishing a routine small expenditure from a major one, an optional expenditure from a necessary one, and the possibility of a great increase in utilization where the bill is paid by insurance. Moreover, there are dangers of severe adverse selection since drug expenses are more predictable in the individual instance than expenses for most

---

[7] Louis S. Reed, loc. cit., p. 9.

[8] Joseph F. Follmann, Jr., "Prescription Drug Insurance," Pension and Welfare News, November, 1967.

[9] Odin W. Anderson, Patricia Collette, and Jacob J. Feldman, Family Expenditure Patterns for Personal Health Services, Health Information Foundation Research Series 14 (New York, 1960).

medical services. Many people have chronic conditions which require continued use of high-priced drugs for extended periods of time, often for the rest of their lives. An exclusion of preexisting conditions could protect the insurer, but only at the cost of denying coverage where it is most needed.

Drugs administered in the hospital from the regular pharmacopœia are covered by hospital insurance policies and offer no problem. However, the practice of hospitals varies; many do not include high-priced drugs in their service, and the patient may have to pay for these from his own resources or from a limited benefit for hospital extras.

Insurance company major medical and comprehensive contracts cover expenditures for prescribed drugs as for other eligible medical expenses, subject to their deductible and percentage participation provisions. The same is true of Blue Cross–Blue Shield major medical and extended benefit contracts. Two Blue Cross plans offer separate prescription drug coverage. A number of the independent group practice plans offer relatively broad coverage of drugs. Most impose some deterrents or limits in the nature of small fees for each prescription or limits on the number or cost of prescriptions. A few offer quite broad coverage. Programs have been established by pharmacists in Windsor, Ontario, and by an insurance company in California.[10] The Wisconsin Blue Cross Plan developed a drug program which fixed professional fees, but after government concern over antitrust aspects developed, it was abandoned.[11] These plans are frankly experimental and it remains to be seen whether there is sufficient demand for special coverage of drugs and, if so, whether utilization and adverse selection can be controlled satisfactorily. It would seem that the further development of the insurance company type of pure comprehensive contract would be the best way to handle the problem. This would provide coverage for only the relatively serious costs on the same basis as all other medical expenses. This does not involve the problems of utilization and adverse selection control that are involved in insuring drug expenses separately on a first-dollar basis.

## Dental services

Dental caries probably is the most prevalent of all pathological conditions. Apparently tooth decay, periodontal disease, and loss of teeth start almost as soon as the teeth come in and increase steadily so long as

---

[10] Joseph F. Follmann, Jr., *Drugs, Their Cost and Health Insurance* (New York: Health Insurance Association of America, 1960). See also Nationwide Insurance Company. *The Consumer's Stake in Drugs* (Columbus, Ohio, 1961), and Linda P. Fletcher, "Prepaid Drug Plans Sponsored by Pharmacists," *Journal of Insurance,* March, 1967, p. 81.

[11] Follmann, "Prescription Drug Insurance," *op. cit.*

any teeth are left.[12] Water fluoridation has improved the situation to some degree, but it is probably safe to offer two-to-one odds that a person selected at random will have some indicated need for dental treatment.

However, this probably has been true for most of the history of mankind, and since the severity of the loss is not high, not too many people seem to be worried about the problem. Many states provide limited care through their public health programs, especially to school children,[13] but there is little coverage of dental care expense in conventional health insurance contracts. Most pay only for traumatic injury as the result of an accident. A few pay for any truly operative procedure under surgical contracts, often limited to in-hospital treatment. Blue Cross and Blue Shield plans also frequently include limited coverage, usually somewhat broader than insurance company contracts.

In the last decade, there has been a growing interest on the part of certain union groups, dental associations, employers, and insurance companies in the development of specific dental insurance or prepayment plans. By 1966, it was estimated that 4.2 million persons were covered by plans that provided at least diagnosis, fillings, and extractions. Most of these were independent plans, generally operating in the dental field only, but there were 17 active "Dental Service Corporations" sponsored by dental societies and resembling Blue Shield, with dentists taking the place of physicians.[14] By August, 1967, the Dental Service Corporations had 259 private group contracts in force, with 1.1 million subscribers. In addition, they administered 115 contracts for public programs, mostly Head Start. Many of the independent plans were quite small and often limited their enrollment to narrow employment or union groups. However, several numbered their insureds in the tens of thousands. Tables 9–3 and 9–4 indicate the number of plans in 1963 by sponsorship, enrollment, and scope of service.

Most dental benefit plans cover examinations, fillings, and extractions. They may or may not provide other restorative service or dental care and

---

[12] *Progress in Health Services* (September, 1961) presents interesting data on dental morbidity and utilization of dental services.

[13] For a description of these programs, see U.S. Department of Health, Education, and Welfare, *Digest of State Dental Health Programs, 1961* (Washington, D.C.: U.S. Government Printing Office, 1961).

[14] In 1959 the House of Delegates of the American Dental Association adopted a resolution endorsing group dental care plans and recommending that they be so organized as to permit participation of dentists in private practice. By 1967 there were 17 Dental Service Corporations in operation. For a detailed description of one such plan, see U.S. Department of Health, Education, and Welfare, *The Dental Service Corporation* (Washington, D.C.: U.S. Government Printing Office, 1962). See also Robert D. Eilers, "Dental Service Corporations: Their Place and Problems," *CLU Journal*, Summer, 1964, p. 262, and U.S. Department of Health, Education, and Welfare. *Digest of Prepaid Dental Care Plans, 1963*, Public Health Service Publication No. 585 (Washington, D.C.: U.S. Government Printing Office, 1963).

TABLE 9-3

Number of Persons and Groups with Prepaid Dental Care Coverage, by Scope of Benefits and Administrative Mechanism: U.S., June 30, 1963

| Administrative Mechanism | Total Persons | Total Groups | Minimal Benefits[a] | Basic Benefits[b] | Comprehensive Benefits[c] |
|---|---|---|---|---|---|
| Group practice and clinic.................. | 590,821 | 81 | 25 | 13 | 43 |
| Dental service corporation................... | 213,317 | 28 | — | 4 | 24 |
| Insurance companies | | | | | |
| Health insurers.......... | 152,757 | 131 | — | 28 | 103 |
| Dental insurers.......... | 92,591 | 22 | — | — | 22 |
| Health service corporation................... | 8,190 | 2 | — | 1 | 1 |
| Other.................... | 118,709 | 41 | 11 | 6 | 24 |
| Total............... | 1,176,385 | 305 | 36 | 52 | 217 |

[a] Minimal benefits include diagnostic services and continuing emergency care.
[b] Basic benefits include minimal benefits plus prophylaxis and restorative services.
[c] Comprehensive benefits include basic benefits, plus prosthetic services and in most cases one or more specialty services, e.g., periodontics, endodontics, etc.
Source: U.S. Department of Health, Education, and Welfare, Digest of Prepaid Dental Care Plans, 1963, Public Health Service Publication No. 585 (Washington, D.C.: U.S. Government Printing Office, 1963).

frequently have upper limits, deductibles, or benefit schedules. A major problem in starting a dental insurance plan is the backlog of accumulated need. Many plans require that the enrollee's mouth be put in good condition before coverage begins, or exclude certain restorative services for a year or two or pay reduced benefits for preexisting conditions. Some-

TABLE 9-4

Number of Groups with Prepaid Dental Coverage, by Sponsorship and Administrative Mechanism: June 30, 1963

| Administrative Mechanism | Sponsorship | | | | | |
|---|---|---|---|---|---|---|
| | Union Employer | Employer-Employee | Employer | Co-op | Union | Other |
| Group Practice/Clinic.......... | 61 | 5 | 9 | 3 | 1 | 2 |
| Dental Service Corporation.... | 17 | 1 | 9 | | | 1 |
| Insurance Company | | | | | | |
| Independent Nonprofit...... | 56 | 25 | 24 | | 1 | 25 |
| Commercial................ | 10 | 4 | 8 | | | |
| Health Service Corporation.... | | | 2 | | | |
| Other........................ | 17 | 12 | 7 | | | 5 |
| Total Groups............ | 161 | 47 | 59 | 3 | 2 | 33 |

Source: U.S. Department of Health, Education, and Welfare, Digest of Prepaid Dental Care Plans, 1963, Public Health Service Publication No. 585 (Washington, D.C.: U.S. Government Printing Office, 1963).

times an additional one-shot premium is charged instead of limiting benefits. Many plans exclude or limit orthodontics.

Insurance company activity in the dental field has been limited until recently. By the end of 1966 an estimated two million persons had insurance company group coverage. At least five insurance companies offered coverage on an individual contract basis, one of which is guaranteed renewable.[15] Unlike most of the independent plans, the insurance company plans usually permit free choice of dentist. Most individual policies involve a schedule of benefits, but one uses the pure comprehensive approach of deductibles and percentage participation, except that no deductible is applied to the initial examination, diagnosis, and preparation of a dental chart and treatment plan. One annual examination is permitted thereafter without deductible. The deductible is $25 the first year and $10 per year thereafter. The upper limit is $200 per year per person and $500 per year per family. It *includes* orthodontics and pays 80 percent of fees above the deductible.

Another large company offers a plan to existing group policyholders which pays 75 percent of covered expenses in excess of a calendar year deductible of $25 up to a lifetime maximum of $5,000 and an annual maximum of $1,000. It includes orthodontics, bridgework, palliative treatment, X-rays, and examinations, but not cleaning of teeth.

Thus far, most coverage is on a group basis, with employees sharing in the cost or bearing it all. Group dental contracts are of three types: basic, comprehensive and combination. Basic plans provide scheduled benefits for various procedures on a first-dollar basis with an annual maximum per person of $500 or so. One oral examination and prophylaxis would be covered each six months. Orthodontics usually is excluded.

A typical comprehensive plan would have a deductible of $25 or $50 per family per year or a per individual deductible of $25 the first year and $10 thereafter. Individual maximum benefits might be $200 the first year, $300 the second and $400 thereafter, with family maximums of $500, $750, and $1,000, respectively. The employee would pay 20 percent of the cost of examinations and basic care in excess of the deductible and 40 percent of the cost of denture replacement and orthodontic work. The deductible usually does not apply to examinations, diagnosis, X-ray and prophylaxis. There are no interval limits.

Combination plans combine 100 percent reimbursement of scheduled basic benefits with partial reimbursement of more expensive or elective benefits sometimes after a deductible.

The dental insurance situation seems to resemble that for regular medical insurance about 25 years ago. It well may be that the next edition

---

[15] *Health Insurance Review*, April, 1962, pp. 14, 28. See also J. F. Follmann, Jr., "Dental Insurance Today," *Pension and Welfare News*, June, 1967.

of this book will require a chapter on dental insurance. The insurance companies are providing most of the present coverage, with the Dental Service Corporations in second place. Sound controls apparently can be developed, since the discomfort of dental treatment constitutes a substantial deterrent in itself and the preexisting condition problem is little worse than in other areas such as health insurance for the aged. Devices such as higher first-year premiums and deductibles and lower upper limits and reimbursement percentages should solve this problem of adverse selection. However, the high cost of premiums and of getting the backlog of needed treatment cleared away in the face of such limits will tend to decrease the potential size of the market. Comprehensive dental care is expensive, whether paid for through insurance or otherwise,[16] and many persons will not be able or willing to meet the expense. Of course, where an employer can be persuaded to share the costs, this limitation is less effective. Subject to reasonable deductible and percentage participation provisions, there seems to be no reason why dental services could not be included in employee benefit plans and individual major medical and comprehensive contracts. Utilization data now are readily available as a basis for rate making.[17]

## Vision care

Surgical and medical care of eye disease and injury is covered like other medical and surgical treatment by most health insurance policies. Vision care, which goes beyond this to include the services of optometrists and related professions in the form of eye examinations, refraction tests, and the fitting of glasses, generally is not covered. Like teeth and other parts of the body, eyes seem to deteriorate rather steadily with advancing age. By 65 or so, almost everyone has some degree of vision impairment.[18]

However, there has been relatively little interest in covering the costs of such vision care with health insurance. This probably is because the expenditure is rarely sudden or unpredictable and the cost is not great. The cost for complete service including glasses seems to range from $25 to $100. Since this can be planned for in advance, there is little need for insurance. Assuming a utilization rate of 20 percent, the premium for such insurance would be about $15 per person per year.

---

[16] Some say as high as comprehensive medical care. It ran from $3 to $4 per person per month in 1961.

[17] Two good studies are Herbert J. Grubb, *Dental Health Plans* (Chicago: Continental Casualty Co., 1964), and Helen H. Avnet and Mata K. Nikias, *Insured Dental Care* (New York: Group Health Dental Insurance, 1967).

[18] Joseph F. Follmann, Jr., "Health Insurance and Vision Care," in *Students Guide, Principles of Individual Health Insurance, II* (New York: Health Insurance Association of America, 1966).

However, a few insurance organizations are offering vision care coverage. By 1965, at least eight prepaid vision care plans were operating. These are sponsored by the state optometric associations and somewhat resemble Blue Shield except that they deal with vision services rather than general surgical and medical care. Similar plans had been organized, but were not operating, in 24 other states. One prepaid group panel plan has been operating in New York. One Blue Cross plan and a half dozen independents included coverage of refractions in their contracts, usually on a schedule basis not including the cost of materials. Most insurance companies will include coverage in group contracts, but little demand is reported.

Most coverages are limited to scheduled maximum amounts for each service, and some have deductibles or percentage participation clauses. Moreover, many limit the frequency to (say) one examination and one set of lenses per year and one set of frames each three years. With such safeguards, there should be no difficulty in including vision care under conventional forms of group health insurance. However, the costs and benefits are so low that it probably is uneconomical to insure such costs in a separate individual contract. A lack of interest on the part of the public limits both approaches, but especially the latter. If the premium paying dollars are limited, it seems more appropriate to spend them where they will cover large unpredictable expenses.

## Nervous and mental disease

As indicated above, most medical expense insurance excludes or severely limits benefits for mental and nervous disease. This is due partly to lack of understanding of the problem, lack of knowledge of the risks involved, and the degree to which care for mental illness is either an accepted government function or an option of the claimant. In some cases it is due to past bad experience.

Mental and nervous disease is a broad category which covers a wide range. The psychoses or insanities are rather rare in occurrence but very severe and require intensive treatment over long periods of time. Only about 2 percent of all hospital admissions are accounted for by all psychiatric illness, but the average length of stay in state mental hospitals is eight years. Less severe, but far more prevalent, are the neuroses or psychoneuroses which usually can be treated in psychiatrists' offices or clinics. Least severe are the personality disorders which are difficulties in adjustment that manifest themselves in disturbed behavior, alcoholism, drug addiction, psychosomatic disease, delinquency, sexual deviation, or similar behavior patterns. In an even broader sense, all personality and adjustment deficiencies can be thought of as mental disturbances. In this sense, most of the population is affected.

Insurance is especially suited to cover the severe loss with low probability of occurrence. In accordance with this principle, health insurance contracts tend to cover the more severe manifestations of mental disorder and avoid those of greater frequency and lower severity. Thus most hospital insurance contracts of insurance companies and Blue Cross will pay room and board and hospital extras for mental disease, but only in general hospitals, not in special mental hospitals.[19] Surgical and regular medical contracts will cover treatment on the same basis, in a general hospital only, as the usual approach. This is not as drastic a limitation as might be supposed, since a growing proportion of the mentally ill are now being treated in psychiatric wards of general hospitals. The number of hospitals with such facilities has increased from about 50 to over 600 in the past 25 years. Prompt intensive treatment seems to offer the best prognosis for many severe mental diseases. The average stay in general hospitals for mental disease seems to average somewhere between 13 and 117 days, with 90 percent between 7 and 37 days.

Many major medical and comprehensive contracts and some of the Blue Cross and Blue Shield extended benefit plans provide coverage of mental and nervous disease on the same basis as other illnesses. The deductible and percentage participation provisions operate as controls on utilization. However, experience has indicated that claims can run terrifically high for individual psychiatric treatment on an ambulatory basis. Psychoanalysis is expensive and requires many treatments, and the treatment is often optional with the claimant. Thus, many companies have felt it necessary to impose additional limitations on this type of expense. These limits may take the form of higher percentage participation by the insured, dollar limits per treatment, and/or a limit to the number of treatments per year or an annual dollar limit. In individual contracts even stricter limitations often are imposed because of the greater possibility of adverse selection, and some individual contracts exclude mental and nervous disease entirely. With reasonable limits, the major medical or pure comprehensive approach should be an effective way of broadening health insurance coverage of severe mental disease without paying unnecessary benefits for minor or optional treatment. The availability of funds from this source should aid in the development and application of new curative techniques in this field.[20]

---

[19] A recent study showed 21 Blue Cross group plans do cover such benefits in public institutions usually limited in amount or duration or both. An additional 11 provide such benefits to some subscribers. Fourteen plans exclude all mental illness under the most widely held individual certificate. The others all impose specific limits. National Association of State Mental Health Directors Study No. 79 (Washington, D.C., 1967).

[20] A recent New York study seems to indicate that limited short-term ambulatory and in-hospital psychiatric benefits are readily insurable on a group basis. Helen H. Avnet, *Psychiatric Insurance* (New York: Group Health Insurance, Inc., 1962).

The American Psychiatric Association has strongly recommended that insurance contracts cover all treatment for mental illness emphasizing that the responsibility for establishing the necessity of a specific service rests with the physician in charge.[21] It lists the types of service which should be insured which range from in-patient hospital services to family consultation and recreational therapy. It seems to suggest first-dollar coverage and payment of full prevailing fees and lists a variety of studies which demonstrate the insurability of this risk.[21]

The National Institute of Mental Health also is encouraging insurance coverage of mental and nervous disease. It emphasizes the importance of prompt treatment and insurance coverage of in-patient, out-patient and "partial hospitalization" (i.e. day or night) care. Detailed guidelines have been developed.[22] The new Blue Cross and Blue Shield contract with the United Auto Workers includes comprehensive mental health benefits and the mental health coverage of federal employees has been improved substantially.

**Preventive medicine**

Most insurance company and Blue contracts emphasize the treatment of disease as distinguished from its prevention. Hospital contracts include benefits for laboratory tests and diagnostic X-rays, and special clauses for such services outside the hospital are available under group policies and in many Blue Shield plans. However, such coverage usually is limited to cases where disease seriously is suspected. Deductibles and waiting periods in major medical, comprehensive, and regular medical contracts usually would eliminate payment for routine health examinations, immunizations, and other preventive services, even when the contract did not exclude them specifically. On the other hand, many of the independent plans offering comprehensive coverage make a special point of including such preventive services, claiming that they thus encourage desirable preventive measures and improve the general level of health.

The social desirability of using an insurance or prepayment mechanism for predictable small expenses has not been determined in our society. The insurance company feeling is that regular predictable expenses should be handled by the individuals concerned through family budgeting. This applies both to the costs of minor treatment, including routine drugs and medicines, and to preventive services, such as physical examinations. Experience of insurers with free examinations offered to life

[21] American Psychiatric Association, *APA Guidelines for Psychiatric Services Covered under Health Insurance Plans* (Washington, D.C., 1966). See also APA, *Insurance Coverage for Mental Illness, 1962* (Washington, D.C.: 1962).

[22] U.S. Department of H.E.W. Public Health Service, *Improving Mental Health Insurance Coverage* (Washington, D.C.: USGPO, 1965).

insurance policyholders has indicated that only a small proportion of insureds take advantage of such a privilege. The question is whether the entire insured group should contribute to financing for a few of its members what is an essentially voluntary event.

Proponents of coverage of these minor and voluntary expenses feel that providing such benefits will encourage more adequate medical care for the insured population, especially in prevention. They cite the popularity of time payment for other types of goods and services in modern society. However, it seems that few families are willing to budget more than $25–$40 a month for insurance and/or prepayment. If this be the case, it clearly is more desirable to provide broad coverage with high limits than to insist on coverage of first-dollar expenses at the cost of greatly reducing the maximum benefit. On the other hand, if employers share the cost, employees may desire coverage. When public acceptance and incomes make possible the meeting of higher premium costs, coverage of the minor and voluntary expenditures will be desirable. The answer must await the passage of time.

The American Society of Internal Medicine recently has recommended that health insurance contracts cover comprehensive medical care, including examinations, diagnosis, and preventive care, regardless of location, apparently on a full-fee, first-dollar basis.[23] The new U.A.W. contract with Blue Cross and Blue Shield provides for complete pre- and postnatal care with no 270-day eligibility period.[24]

## Summary

Using the major medical or pure comprehensive approach, there seems to be little difficulty in extending the coverage of health insurance to cover private-duty nursing in and out of the hospital, nursing homes, dental services, vision care, drugs, severe mental illness, or even preventive medicine. On a group basis, with employers sharing the cost, basic benefits without deductibles can be provided. The major question is whether the public demand for such coverage is great enough so that people and employers will be willing to pay the necessary premiums. It may be more economical for most people to handle the minor expenses themselves through family budgeting. But if the public wants and will pay for such coverage, the private insurance industry is able and willing to provide it.

---

[23] American Society for Internal Medicine, *Comprehensive Health Care: Medical Service—Guidelines for Health Insurance* (San Francisco, 1906).

[24] For further discussion of the desirability of insurance coverage of preventive services, see O. D. Dickerson, "Changing Concepts of Health Care Financing," *Journal of the American Society of Chartered Life Underwriters,* Vol. XIX, No. 2 (Spring, 1965) p. 170.

## Selected references

*See the following items from the General Bibliography: 4, chs. 15 and 17; 6; 9, ch. 38; 10, ch. 2; 11, chs. 10–15; 15, ch. 24.*

AMERICAN ACADEMY OF PEDIATRICS. *Health Insurance Guidelines for Infants and Children.* Evanston, Ill.: American Academy of Pediatrics, 1967.

AMERICAN PSYCHIATRIC ASSOCIATION. *APA Guidelines for Psychiatric Services Covered under Health Insurance Plans.* Washington, D.C., 1966.

AMERICAN SOCIETY OF INTERNAL MEDICINE. *Comprehensive Health Care: Medical Service Guidelines for Health Insurance.* San Francisco, 1966.

AVNET, HELEN HERSHFIELD, AND NILIAS, MATA KOUVARI. *Insured Dental Care.* New York: Group Health Dental Insurance, Inc., 1967. Dickerson, O. D. "Changing Concepts of Health Care Financing," *CLU Journal,* Vol. XIX, No. 2 (Spring, 1965), p. 170.

DICKERSON, O. D. "Changing Concepts of Health Care Financing," *CLV Journal,* Vol. XIX, No. 2 (Spring, 1965), p. 170.

EILERS, ROBERT D. "Dental Service Corporations: Their Place and Problems," *CLU Journal,* Vol. XVIII, No. 3 (Summer, 1964), p. 262.

FLETCHER, LINDA P. "Prepaid Drug Plans Sponsored by Pharmacists," *Journal of Risk and Insurance,* Vol. XXXIV, No. 1 (March, 1967).

FOLLMANN, JOSEPH F., JR. *Drugs, Their Cost, and Health Insurance.* Chicago: Health Insurance Association of America, 1960.

―――. "Health Insurance and Nursing Home Care," Health Insurance Association of America, September, 1963.

―――. "Health Insurance and Vision Care," *Best's Insurance News,* 1967.

―――. "Prescription Drug Insurance," *Pension and Welfare News,* November, 1967.

―――. *Prevention of Loss and Rehabilitation.* New York: Health Insurance Association of America, 1962 (Processed).

GRUBB, HERBERT J. *A Statistical Analysis of the Dentists' Supply Company of New York Dental Health Plan.* Chicago: Continental Casualty Company, 1964.

HARMON, EDWIN L. "Extension of Prepayment to Out-of-Hospital Services," *Hospitals, J.A.H.A.,* Vol. 41 (March 1, 1967).

MACINTYRE, DUNCAN M. "Thirty Years of Blue Cross and Blue Shield," *CLU Journal,* Vol. XVIII, No. 3 (Summer, 1964), p. 189.

MITCHELL, GEORGE E., AND SIEVER, MARY L. *Digest of Prepaid Dental Care Plans, 1963.* Washington, D.C.: U.S. Government Printing Office, 1964.

NATIONAL ASSOCIATION STATE MENTAL HEALTH PROGRAM DIRECTORS. *Coverage of Psychiatric Illness under Blue Cross Plans.* Study #79, July 1, 1967.

U.S. DEPARTMENT OF HEALTH, EDUCATION, AND WELFARE, Public Health Service. *Speaking of Prepaid Dental Care—A Glossary of Terms.* Washington, D.C.: U.S. Government Printing Office, 1962.

chapter 10

The attempt to turn a complex problem of the head into a simple
moral question for the heart to answer, is of course a necessary part
of all political discussions—Frank Moore Colby, *The Colby Essays,*
Vol. I

# Medical Expense: Problems and Issues

It easily would be possible to fill an entire book with a discussion of
the problems and issues involved in the economics of medical care and
health insurance. Indeed, many such books have been written.[1] In a book
which attempts to cover the entire area of health insurance, only a limited
treatment can be given to these problems. The main problems and issues
currently facing medical care insurance will be discussed here under the
headings of competition among insurers, population coverage, the special
problem of the aged, and control of utilization. These issues all are inter-
related and they further are involved with problems relating to the organization of medical care and the improvement of health and medical
standards. These latter areas will be discussed only to the extent necessary
for the understanding of the related insurance problems.[2]

### Competition among insurers

*Distinctive characteristics.* Medical expense insurance, as should be
evident by now, long has been characterized by the rivalry or competition between conventional insurance companies and the Blue Cross and
Blue Shield plans and, to a lesser degree, the independents. The description of benefits offered above should by now have made clear that the

---

[1] Many are referred to in the Bibliography and in Selected References and foot-
notes in chapters of this book.

[2] For a discussion of medical care problems in general, and organization and
financing in particular, see Herman M. Somers and Anne R. Somers, *Doctors, Patients
and Health Insurance* (Washington, D.C.: The Brookings Institution, 1961).

differences among different plans and companies within each type of insurer are greater than the differences between insurer types. And yet the argument goes on.

The characteristics which distinguish the Blue Cross and Blue Shield plans are community sponsorship, contract with the purveyors of service, nonprofit operation, service benefits, provision of first-dollar benefits and community rating, as well as experience rating. Enrollment objectives have been suggested as another distinctive characteristic.[3] None of these is completely their province, but in combination these characteristics present a distinctive pattern. Some are competitive advantages; some are of dubious value in the marketplace.

*Community sponsorship* has been an advantage in enrolling members. However, in some areas this is more of a fiction than a fact; to a considerable degree, Blue Cross plans continue to be dominated by hospitals and to a lesser degree by physicians.[4] Blue Shield plans are almost invariably controlled by physicians. Where this is not true or where the plans have sold the public on its major stake in Blue Cross, the policies of the plans have become a matter of state politics and a major element of dissension between opposed groups in the community. Labor union officials, especially, have taken upon themselves the responsibility of speaking for the public, and in some cases have won places on boards of trustees for themselves or other lay personnel. The public recently has taken a tremendous interest in rates and utilization, and in a few areas rivalry has arisen between Blue Cross and the hospitals.[5]

Such difficulties may be too high a price to pay for what is essentially nothing but a public relations device. However, the goodwill and free advertising resulting from this status should not be minimized. It has been suggested that the true measure of community support is the proportion of community population enrolled.[6] If 50 percent is taken as the criterion, only 13 Blue Cross plans and 7 Blue Shield plans qualified in 1966. Counting those served as fiscal intermediary, 11 Blue Shield Plans qualified.

*Contract with the purveyors of service*, the physicians and hospitals

---

[3] Robert D. Eilers, "The Fundamental Nature of Blue Cross and Blue Shield," *Journal of Insurance* (September, 1962), p. 385.

[4] Recent surveys, however, show that Blue Cross plan trustees tend to be representative members equally divided among hospital, medical representatives, and the general public.

[5] See Somers and Somers, *op. cit.*, chaps. xv and xvi and pp. 413–21, for more details on some of these problems. See also Ray E. Trussel and Frank Van Dyke, *Prepayment for Hospital Care in the U.S.* for an excellent study reflecting the depth of public involvement in Blue Cross plans. For a view of the Blue Cross role in utilization review, see below.

[6] Eilers, *op. cit.*, p. 395.

respectively, gives an advantage in that the plans can purchase services for insured members at wholesale rates.[7] Claim administration is facilitated since the purveyors think of it as "their" plan. This attitude also should contribute towards controlling excessive utilization. However, a good case can be made that the participation of a third party in financing contributes more to sound claims procedure than does the unrestrained conscience of the physician.

Physician sponsorship of Blue Shield plans lends an element of strength in gaining public acceptance but presents dangers of overly high claim costs where benefits are on a cash or part-service basis. On the other hand, there is a danger of overutilization where full-service benefits are available. This will be discussed more fully below.

*Nonprofit status.* Most of the Blues legally are nonprofit organizations. This confers major tax advantages over their competitors, even over the nonprofit mutual insurance companies. However, the nonprofit operation is also, partly at least, a fiction. Certainly the plans are no more "nonprofit" than mutual insurance companies, if as much so. As was explained above, by properly adjusting the rate paid to the member hospitals, or participating physicians, the operation can be made to appear as profitable or as unprofitable as its sponsors desire.

However, the nonprofit feature has one major advantage: it relieves the association from the payment of premium and other taxes, which results in a major competitive advantage, even over mutual insurance companies, which are at least equally nonprofit.[8] The nonprofit aspect of

---

[7] Enlightening in this regard are the following questions and answers:
Q. The people who pay are charged extra because some patients can't or won't meet their hospital bill?
A. Yes. The full-pay patient helps pay for the part-pay and no-pay patients. A hospital has to break even somehow. Otherwise it will go bankrupt and close.
Q. Is this one reason Blue Cross expenses are rising?
A. No. Blue Cross pays only what it costs to care for its patients. Charity losses aren't passed on to Blue Cross subscribers. The guy who's taking it in the neck is the patient who pays his own hospital bill and doesn't have Blue Cross.
Q. This includes the patient who has commercial hospital insurance?
A. Yes. The commercial insurance pays him a stated amount and he pays the difference out of his own pocket. If a hospital has to mark up its bill to cover charity losses, there obviously is a bigger difference for him to make up.
John Troan, *Your Hospital Bills.* A series of four interviews with Russell A. Nelson, M.D., President, American Hospital Association (Chicago: Blue Cross Commission, 1960).

[8] A recent change in the Pennsylvania tax law results in the Blue plans paying the same tax (1 percent of premium) as domestic insurance companies. Seven or eight other states tax Blue Cross premiums and a few more tax Blue Shield but not Blue Cross. For an impassioned plea for equal taxation and regulation, see Foster H. Williams, "Blue Cross Preferential Treatment," H.I.A.A. Group Insurance Forum, 1966.

some Blue Shield plans does involve a competitive advantage, but it is not as widespread as in Blue Cross. Some Blue Shield plans are organized as corporate insurers to permit operation without special legislation.

*Service benefits.* A service-type benefit rather than cash payment has long been a major talking point for the proponents of Blue Cross and Blue Shield. However, the percentage of participants covered under this type of contract has declined somewhat in Blue Shield in recent years. It seems that this represents a reaction to the increasing level of physician's fees. However, the recent development of prevailing fee plans is a shift toward full-service coverage. Service-benefit contracts are more vulnerable to cost increases than those imposing specific dollar limits. Especially in the extended benefit plans, the use of deductibles and percentage participation clauses is becoming increasingly common. Apparently, the plans have, in part, found that the control on costs by such limits is as necessary to them as to commercial insurers. While this represents a departure from principle, it may be preferable to the alternatives of the hospitals absorbing the losses or of increasing premium rates in the face of widespread community opposition. On the other hand, the insurance companies are beginning to offer occasional full-service type contracts in carefully selected and controlled circumstances.

*Prepayment.* Many Blue Cross officials have insisted Blue Cross organizations are not in the insurance business—that, rather, they are operating *"prepayment"* plans. Inasmuch as insurance is a social device which reduces risk by pooling, it is hard to see how anyone can claim that the Blues are not engaged in the practice of the insurance technique. The unique nature of prepayment as opposed to insurance has been variously ascribed to the service-type benefit, the lack of an upper limit on benefits, and the coverage of first-dollar costs. It is difficult to justify a distinction on any of these grounds. Some Blue Cross plans do not provide full service-type benefits, and almost all Blue Shield plans are on a partial-service basis. Some insurance company contracts do provide service benefits. In some lines of insurance, such as glass and liability, service benefits are of primary importance. Almost all Blue Cross plans impose some upper limits—if not in terms of dollars, then in terms of number of days' coverage. Sometimes, it is true, hospital extras are covered without limit, but only for the agreed number of days. On the other hand, some insurance benefits—for example, liability defense costs and auto physical damage benefits—are subject to no upper limit.

Despite the emphasis on service benefits, only 4.4 percent of Blue Shield subscribers are enrolled in plans which provide full-service benefits or paid-in-full benefits to all subscribers, regardless of income.

Under Blue Shield partial-service plans, full-service benefit entitlement depends on the income level of the insured and in some cases on the type of service elected. Thus it is difficult, if not impossible, to determine what proportion of benefits actually represent full-service coverage. The tendency has been for plans to shift from a straight reimbursement benefit basis to a partial-service basis, and this should favor an increasing coverage of enrollees on this basis. However, simultaneously, incomes have been rising and families have been moving into brackets where they lose their full-service entitlement. Many plans have raised the income level required for full-service coverage, but this process involves a built-in lag, and it is probable that this factor has tended to decrease the proportion covered on a full-service basis. In any event, the majority of middle-income families and virtually all upper-income families are presently unable to obtain full-service protection from Blue Shield. The recent movement to paid-in-full programs which base payments upon usual, customary, and prevailing fees could overcome this.

The provision of service benefits does facilitate claim settlement and tends to minimize moral hazard by making it almost impossible for a claimant to profit on his loss. However, there is no safeguard against the claimant having another policy from which he collects cash benefits. The insurance companies recently have developed uniform claim forms which simplify claims procedure and facilitate the assignment of benefits. This is almost the equivalent of service benefits.

*First-Dollar coverage.* The best distinction between insurance and "prepayment" has to do with first-dollar costs. It is true that the proper subject matter of insurance is a loss which may have a major financial impact on the insured. To the extent to which any insurance policy pays small regular losses which may be budgeted like other expenses, it is departing from the field where its value is greatest. Moreover, the coverage of such small losses greatly increases the cost, as the expense of settlement procedure is disproportionately great and the premiums must bear their share of overhead and acquisition expense. Yet most insurance policies do bear all losses, both large and small. Only in auto collision, certain marine and inland marine lines, homeowners, windstorm and some types of health insurance is the use of deductibles common.

A contract which covers *only* small budgetable costs and no potentially large losses might be said to be a prepayment contract rather than an insurance contract, but few Blue Cross or Blue Shield personnel would be willing to classify their activities in this category.[9] For the well-to-do, admittedly, any basic hospital or surgical-medical policy covers only losses which are within the ability of the family to meet by other means. This is as true of insurance company policies as of Blue Cross contracts.

---

[9] But this emphasis prevails: "Because the average bill is well under $1,000, your first consideration should be a *basic* program which starts paying at or near the first dollar of cost." *A Buyer's Guide to Health Care Protection.* (Place, date, and publisher not indicated; the introduction states: "This guide is published as a public service by Blue Cross and Blue Shield"; ca. 1961.)

Thus the distinction between prepayment and insurance becomes one of the state of family finances rather than of insurer type. A loss that is well within the ability of one family to meet may be catastrophic to another. For the first family, coverage of a loss of this type might be considered "prepayment"; the second would have to insure against such a potential loss. Many Blue Shield plans involve benefits which will never aggregate more than a rather small sum, such as $1,000, and most pay first-dollar benefits. However, these statements are almost equally true of insurance company plans, and this does not seem to provide a valid basis of distinction. In terms of benefits available, there is little difference between the types of insurer. The extremely rapid growth of major medical seems to indicate that the public can be educated to the need for high upper limits in preference to first-dollar coverage. If the medical care dollar is limited, as it well may be, a growing awareness of this principle will result in a major shift to contracts providing more adequate coverage subject to a small deductible.

*Enrollment objectives.* Eilers sees the Blues' enrollment goals as their "one vital and all-important characteristic."[10] To conform to the objectives of their special enabling statutes, they must attempt to enroll subscribers from the whole population, especially those for whom coverage is not available elsewhere at reasonable rates. Only thus can they justify their privileged status. This means that they must make coverage available to high-cost, low-income groups, such as the aged. Actually, the Blues had led the insurance companies in permitting the aged to continue coverage already in force, but the insurance companies had taken the lead in enrolling new insureds at older ages prior to the advent of Medicare. The special problem of the aged and adjustments to Medicare are discussed more fully below.

*Community rating.* Historically, the Blues practiced community rating. There was little attempt to relate the rate for a group to its own loss probability. Except for differences due to variations in coverage and the presence or absence of dependent coverage, all groups were charged the same. Similarly, individual rates are constructed on a broad base with only the most major classifications as to coverage of spouse and children. The number of children is not considered and often there is no charge for children above the charge for husband and wife with maternity coverage.

Under this concept of a community rate, the premium rate is based on broad averages over large numbers of exposures, largely disregarding differences in loss probability between insured groups. Blue Cross premiums tend to favor families over childless couples, and large families over those with few children, in terms of the loss probabilities involved.

[10] Eilers, *op. cit.,* p. 400.

Insurance companies, on the other hand, tend to relate their premiums more closely to their estimate of the probability of loss involved.[11]

Insurance companies have taken advantage of this by offering somewhat less expensive coverage to small families on an individual basis. On a group basis, by developing a premium based on the experience of the individual group, the insurance companies have been able to capture many of the better risks, leaving the balance to Blue Cross.[12] This is one of the greatest problems that the Blue Cross and Blue Shield plans have had to face: whether to abandon their traditional rating system and the philosophy on which it is based or to face constantly increasing loss costs as the insurance companies keep picking off the better risks. It may cheer them to know that many of the same insurance companies are facing a similar problem in other lines, especially auto insurance, as a result of the operations of exclusive agency companies and others who cater to preferred risks of one type or another.

The combination of the competitive impact of the insurance companies' experience rating with the rising costs of hospitalization has contributed to a relative loss of competitive position for the Blues and constant upward pressure on their premium rates. It also led to a growing proportion of Blue Cross enrollees being on a nongroup basis and to some "alarmingly high" loss ratios,[13] but this has been partly corrected as premiums have been increased in the 1960's. Only nine Blue Cross plans showed a loss for 1965. Only 78 out of 84 reporting Blue Shield plans reported combined loss and expense ratios in excess of 100 percent in 1966, and for three of these, benefit payments alone exceeded earned subscriber dues. Nationally, the combined ratio was 99.2 for Blue Cross and 97.5 for Blue Shield.

The Blues have responded to these pressures by increasing premium rates, increasing the differential of individual rates over group rates, and shifting to an experience rating basis for large groups in most plans. They also have increased the variety of their contracts, provided a wider choice of benefit levels and introduced specific limits, deductibles, and percentage participation.

Blue Cross and Blue Shield proponents claim that community rating

---

[11] In group policies, for reasons of administrative economy and because the employer pays a share of the premium, the number of children beyond the first may be ignored in insurance company plans. However, the rate usually is adjusted to the loss probability of the group.

[12] See below, Chapter 17, for a further discussion of "equity" in rate making and the effects of this selection process. The discussion in Chapter 17 reflects the views of an actuary: the traditional insurance company attitude. For another exposition of the insurance company viewpoint, see J. F. Follmann, *The Role of Insurance Companies in Financing Hospital Care* (New York; Health Insurance Council, 1967), pp. 20–22. See also J. F. Follmann, Jr., "Experience Rating vs. Community Rating," *Journal of Insurance* (September, 1962), p. 403.

[13] Somers and Somers, *op. cit.*, p. 311 ff.

is necessary in order to cover the whole population at reasonable premium rates and that it is necessary for the better risks to subsidize the worse risks, especially the aged and poor, in order that the poor risks can get adequate coverage at a cost they can afford. Meanwhile, the Blues find themselves in the middle—caught between the pressures of insurance commissioners and large group purchasers, including the unions, to hold down costs and utilization and the pressure of hospitals and physicians to cover costs and fees more adequately.

In an impartial study financed by the Health Information Foundation,[14] MacIntyre saw the situation as not very serious. He concluded that much of the discussion is fuzzy and overlaid with emotion-laden catch words and that there is not as much difference between community rating and experience rating as is alleged. Most Blue plans break down their rates into a six-to-nine class structure based on method of enrollment (group, individual and group conversion) and degree of dependent coverage. These classes are prospectively rerated periodically and this amounts to a "rudimentary form of experience rating."

In competition to keep the low-risk groups, many Blue plans are using experience rating,[15] often with a guilty conscience, but such guilt feelings lack strong foundation. Buyers know about experience rating and will insist on it. Increased utilization of experience rating thus becomes a necessity for the Blues. The independents face similar pressure but may be able to avoid much of its impact because of the unique nature of the services many of them render. However, many have taken steps in the direction of experience rating.

MacIntyre felt that the advantages of community rating in covering the aged had been oversold, since even community-rated premiums were too high for many retired people to pay without help. On the other hand, experience rating involves higher administrative costs and unrestrained rate competition forces ever lower profit margins. Both methods have inherent advantages and disadvantages, but experience rating is winning out and "a wider utilization of the technique by the community plans seems advantageous."

True community rating can exist only in a monopoly situation. MacIntyre concludes that:

*It is impossible simply to conclude that "community rating is better" or that "experience rating is better." Continued coexistence, probably with selective reliance on government, is preferable to drastic measures in behalf of or*

---

[14] Duncan M. MacIntyre, *Voluntary Health Insurance and Ratemaking* (Ithaca, N.Y.: Cornell University Press, 1962).

[15] For a discussion of the philosophy and technique of the Blues in experience rating, see George E. McLean, "An Actuarial Analysis of a Prospective Experience Rating Approach for Group Hospital-Surgical-Medical Coverage," *Proceedings of the Casualty Actuarial Society,* Vol. 48, p. 155.

*against either rating system.* . . . Experience rating is infinitely more appealing than community rating in any enterprise-based, individualistic context.[16]

Follmann[17] points out that the concept of a community is undefined. In one sense, any group of sufficient size may be considered a "community," and so all group insurance might be considered to be community rated. On the other hand, all health insurance rates are based on experience and thus "experience rated." Thus the difference in principle fades in practice. That the issue does not disappear seems mainly to be a matter of competition.

**Blue Cross and the medical profession.** A long history of discussion indicates that there is a conflict of opinion between the AMA and Blue Cross plans as to the proper dividing line between hospital and medical insurance. The AMA has strongly insisted that electrocardiographic, metabolic, roentgenographic, and pathologic studies, anesthesia, and physiotherapy are medical rather than hospital services. Accordingly, these should be included in medical insurance, not in hospital insurance. Not all insuring organizations adhere to this distinction. In 1953 the AMA House of Delegates called upon Health Service, Inc., and Medical Indemnity of America, Inc., specifically, and other insurers generally, to refrain from violating the AMA principles in this regard. This position was restated in 1960 and 1961. The AMA is particularly anxious to discourage the corporate practice of medicine, especially by hospitals.[18]

The 1965 Social Security amendments reflected the AMA position and provide that the professional services component of these fees is covered by Part B, Supplementary Medical Insurance. In 1967, the amendments released pathologists' fees for in-hospital tests from the application of the Part B percentage participation and transferred out-patient diagnostic services from Part A to Part B.

**Market shares.** In the last 26 years, insurance companies have increased their share of medical expense insurance at the expense of the Blues and, to an even greater degree, of the independents. All three types of plan increased enrollments during this period as the total number of persons covered by health insurance increased more than thirteenfold. However, their growth rates were very uneven. Insurance companies increased their enrollment in hospital insurance by twenty-sixfold between 1940 and 1966; Blue Cross plans increased elevenfold, and the independents' enrollment almost tripled.

Similarly, in surgical coverage, insurance companies increased enrollment fortyfold; Blue Shield fifty-fivefold; and the independents only

---

[16] MacIntyre, *op. cit.*, p. 290 (MacIntyre's emphasis).

[17] Follmann, *op. cit., Journal of Insurance,* Vol. 29, p. 403.

[18] Council on Medical Service, AMA, *Voluntary Prepayment Medical Benefit Plans* (Chicago, 1965), p. 24.

about threefold. Regular medical coverage was almost entirely written by the independents in 1940, but by 1966 they covered only 6.8 percent of the persons insured; the insurance companies covered 52.2 percent and the Blue Shield plans covered 46.1 percent. The insurance companies still seem to be gaining overall, rapidly in regular medical, and a little more slowly in hospital and surgical coverage. Chart 10–1 indicates the relative market shares of the three major types of insurer in 1966. In terms of premium income, insurance companies increased their share, for all types of medical expense insurance combined, from 48.8 percent in 1948 to

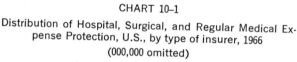

CHART 10-1

Distribution of Hospital, Surgical, and Regular Medical Expense Protection, U.S., by type of insurer, 1966
(000,000 omitted)

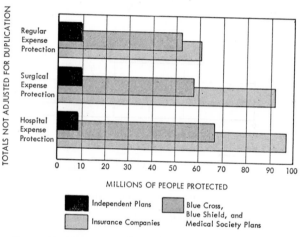

Source: Health Insurance Council and Health Insurance Institute.

53 percent in 1966. Chart 10–2 shows the premium distribution in 1956, 1961 and 1966, and Table 10–1 gives a detailed breakdown.

*Cost comparisons.* It is difficult to make cost comparisons between the types of insurer, since benefits never are strictly comparable. One measure is loss ratios. Generally speaking, assuming the insurers are, on the average, meeting their expenses and staying solvent, the higher the loss ratio the greater is the efficiency of the plan from a social standpoint. The difference between 100 percent and the loss ratio represents operating expenses, changes in reserves, and profit or loss.

The ratio of benefits paid to earned income in 1966 was 93.4 percent for Blue Cross plans, 88.0 percent for Blue Shield plans, 93.1 percent for insurance company group policies, 54.4 percent for insurance company individual policies, and 91.6 percent for the independents. Table 10–1 indicates loss expense and operating profit ratios in more detail. Since Blue Cross and Blue Shield plans pay few taxes and the independents usually pay no premium taxes, their expense ratios should be lower. Without the necessity of paying premium taxes, insurance company premiums would be 2 to 3 percent lower, expense ratios 2 to 3 points lower, and loss ratios 2 to 3 points higher.

From the standpoint of a particular prospect it is meaningless to compare averages. He should compare specific plans and quoted rates. Thus

CHART 10–2

Health Insurance Premiums, U.S. Business, by
Type of Insurer, 1956, 1961, 1966

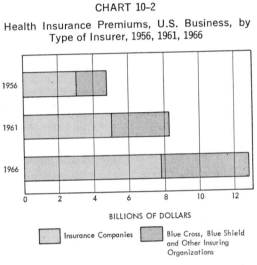

BILLIONS OF DOLLARS

☐ Insurance Companies    ☐ Blue Cross, Blue Shield
and Other Insuring
Organizations

Source: Health Insurance Association of America,
U.S. Department of Health, Education, and Welfare,
and *Health Insurance Review.*

differences between individual insurers are what is meaningful, not differences between types. From the standpoint of society, it would appear at first glance as though the Blue Cross plans are more efficient. However, if some social value is assigned to the taxes that the insurance companies are paying, it may be necessary to revise this tentative conclusion considerably. The author suspects seriously that competition between insurer types will continue and that all three will be in business for a long time to come.

*Territorial coverage.* In territorial coverage, each type of plan has major advantages. The Blue Cross plan usually includes all general hospitals in its area. Thus hospital admission is facilitated, and full coverage is available very readily. The hospital administrators are familiar with the insurer and the plan, and there is no question whether the patient will be able to pay his bills. Similarly, Blue Shield usually enjoys the cooperation of the participating physicians.

TABLE 10-1

Financial Experience of Private Medical Expense Insurance Organizations, 1956
(amounts in millions)

| Type of Plan | Subscription or Premium Income | Claims Expense | | Operating Expense | | Net Underwriting Gain | | Net Income | |
|---|---|---|---|---|---|---|---|---|---|
| | | Amount | % of Premium Income | Amount | % of Premium Income | Amount | % of Premium Income | Amount | % of Total Income |
| Total.......................... | $10,564.1 | $9,141.8 | 86.5 | $1,517.2 | 14.4 | −$94.9 | −0.9 | a | a |
| Blue Cross–Blue Shield........... | 4,327.8 | 3,975.4 | 91.9 | 272.8 | 6.3 | 79.6 | 1.8 | $146.2 | 3.3 |
| Blue Cross..................... | 3,085.9 | 2,882.2 | 93.4 | 152.3 | 4.9 | 52.3 | 1.7 | 99.0 | 3.2 |
| Blue Shield.................... | 1,241.9 | 1,093.2 | 88.0 | 120.5 | 9.7 | 27.3 | 2.2 | 47.2 | 3.7 |
| Insurance companies............ | 5,595.0 | 4,585.0 | 81.9 | 1,205.0 | 21.5 | −195.0 | −3.5 | a | a |
| Group........................ | 3,987.0 | 3,711.0 | 93.1 | 510.0 | 12.8 | −234.0 | −5.9 | a | a |
| Individual..................... | 1,608.0 | 874.0 | 54.4 | 695.0 | 43.2 | 39.0 | 2.4 | a | a |
| Independent plans.............. | 641.3 | 581.4 | 90.7 | 39.4 | 6.1 | 20.5 | 3.2 | 20.5 | 3.2 |
| Community.................... | 237.0 | 218.0 | 92.0 | 17.0 | 7.2 | 2.0 | .8 | 2.0 | .8 |
| Employer-employee-union....... | 370.7 | 332.7 | 89.8 | 20.0 | 5.4 | 18.0 | 4.8 | 18.0 | 4.8 |
| Private group clinics............ | 13.6 | 12.0 | 88.5 | 1.2 | 8.6 | .4 | 2.9 | .4 | 2.9 |
| Dental society................. | 20.0 | 18.7 | 93.5 | 1.2 | 6.0 | .1 | .5 | .1 | .5 |

a Data not available.
Source: Louis S. Reed, "Private Health Insurance: Coverage and Financial Experience, 1940–66," Social Security Bulletin, December, 1967, p. 3.

On the other hand, the insurance companies have the advantage when it comes to wide geographic areas. An insurance company doing a nation-wide business can offer a plan which provides the same coverage for individuals or group members located anywhere in the country or even abroad. A group plan of such a nature may be administered as a unit. If a multilocation employer deals with Blue Cross or Blue Shield, in the absence of special arrangements, he would face a variety of different plans in the various localities. Almost all of the independents are restricted geographically by their very nature.

Each of the major types of insurer has devised methods of meeting the competitive advantage of the other. The insurance companies have developed *hospital admission plans* and *uniform claim forms* under the leadership of the Health Insurance Council. The plans provide a standard procedure whereby the hospital admissions clerk can determine that the patient is insured and what the type and amount of benefits are. Provision is made for convenient verification of such facts and for the assignment of the insurance benefits to the hospital or physician in lieu of an advance deposit. A standard claim form is used to simplify the hospital's and physician's certification of treatment and charges and the employer's certification of loss of time.

There are two methods in use. The older system, still used in several metropolitan areas, involves a card record maintained by the hospital listing the benefits of various group plans in the area. The admissions clerk phones the employer to confirm current coverage. A uniform claim form is used, similar to the last part of the form described below.

In the alternative plan, the certification of benefit system, the employer completes a standard claim form indicating that the employee is covered and describing the nature and amount of benefits. There are separate types of form for individual and group policies.

The forms combine a number of separate forms used previously and include the following sections:

1. Identification data: Name and address of patient, plan under which insured, etc.
2. Certification of insurance benefits, including brief description of nature and amount. This is filled in and signed by the employer, in advance, under the second type plan.
3. Duration of hospital stay and statement of hospital charges. This is filled in and signed by a representative of the hospital as billed, and constitutes the basic claim information for the insurer. The hospital may attach an itemized bill if it prefers.
4. Attending physician statement. This is intended to make sure the treatment was necessary and let the insurer determine whether the condition requiring hospitalization is of origin prior to the effective date of the policy. It is filled in and signed by the attending physician.

5. Condition causing hospital confinement, and description of operation if any. This is necessary in order to determine whether benefits have been partly used up in the past, and also for the medical and surgical coverage, if any.
6. Identification of hospital and signature of certifying official.
7. Authorization to release information. This is signed by the patient, and authorizes the hospital to release information to the insurer.
8. Assignment of insurance benefits. This is signed by the insured and assigns the insurance benefits to the hospital. A statement is included that the patient remains responsible for any charges not covered by the insurance.
9. Information about other insurance.

Thus all necessary information is included on a single uniform form. The only additional forms necessary are the attending physician's statement and the "insured's statement" and "employer's statement" required by some companies. These forms do not involve the hospital administration. The current Health Insurance Council forms are reproduced in Appendix J.

The movement for such a procedure began in 1948 for group policies and in 1952 for individual policies. It has gained widespread acceptance. In May, 1955, the Board of Trustees of the American Hospital Association recommended the use of the standard forms, and the American Medical Association has approved the attending physician's statement. Many individual hospitals and local and regional associations have been actively promoting their use. Most insurance companies have adopted the forms. More than 67 million employees and dependents are covered by the group hospital plans which make use of these procedures.[19] The hospital admission plan and the use of uniform forms have made the admission and claims procedure in insured cases almost as simple as under Blue Cross plans.

Blue Cross and Blue Shield plans have substantial local uniformity in benefit provisions although most offer a choice of several contracts. Their problems have involved the difficulty of competing with insurance companies which can offer a uniform nationwide contract serviced by a single national organization. Blue Cross has attempted to solve this problem by several methods. Health Service, Inc., a stock company wholly owned and controlled by Blue Cross, issues and services multistate group contracts for large employers. The Federal Employees plan was described in Chapter 6 as illustrative of such a Blue Cross contract. Also, the Blue Cross plans have a Local Benefit Agreement which makes it possible for national accounts to be insured for varying local benefits on a national basis.

---

[19] Follmann, *The Role of Insurance Companies in Financing Hospital Care, op. cit.,* p. 25.

The problem of providing coverage for patients who require hospitalization outside the area of a particular plan is met in two ways. The Inter-Plan Service Benefit Bank acts as a clearinghouse and gives the member the benefits of the host plan in the area in which he is hospitalized subject to the maximum number of days in his home plan, which also designates covered ancillary services and authorizes service benefits when the host plan provides only a scheduled benefit.[20] The bank also handles claims of Medicare patients who have Blue Cross complementary coverage. Blue Cross plans provide cash allowances toward the cost of hospitalization in hospitals which are not members of any Blue Cross plan.

Transfer of insured members from plan to plan as they change their residence is facilitated by an Inter-Plan Transfer Program. This provides uniformity of treatment and prevents temporary lapse of coverage.[21]

Blue Shield plans have attempted to meet the problem of providing nationwide coverage by the formation of a stock company, Medical Indemnity of America, Inc. This offers coverage in cooperation with Health Service, Inc., the corresponding Blue Cross organization. The two companies have the same executive officer and have a reciprocal reinsurance agreement whereby each insures a portion of the risk written by the other.[22] There is as yet no effective plan for provision of reciprocal benefits by Blue Shield plans when their members are treated in other areas, but the plans pay scheduled fees to nonparticipating physicians. However, all plans make payment for such services by dealing directly with the physician and patient concerned. A formal agreement for transfer of membership from one plan to another was established in 1953. Blue Shield plans do not generally issue contracts to individuals except to converting members who leave an insured group.

The competition between insurer types and between individual insurers has resulted in a broadening of coverage and a degree of coordination that would have seemed impossible a few decades ago. It has been a strong force in the development of voluntary health insurance, and any proposal which would diminish the area of future competition should be viewed with suspicion as a potential deterrent of future progress.

---

[20] For a devastating account of how this can work in practice, see Chapter 6 in Fred J. Cook, The Plot Against the Patient (Englewood Cliffs, N.J.: Prentice-Hall, Inc., 1967), a vicious attack on almost everything connected with medical care.

[21] In theory. In 1966–67 this author gave up and settled for a return of premium and paid a $400 hospital bill after 6 months of being whipsawed between Philadelphia and Florida Blue Cross.

[22] According to the latest revision of this agreement, each assumes that portion of the total exposure that its policyholder's surplus represents of the total policyholder's surplus of the two companies combined. As much of the liability on the national contracts as possible is assumed by the local plans which handle all claims and servicing. About half the net exposure of the national companies represents excess liability for extended benefit and major medical coverages.

## Population coverage

While it is recognized that voluntary health insurance, especially hospital insurance, has made tremendous progress toward coverage of the entire population, important groups still remain largely unprotected. The advocates of governmental action in the field point to these groups as the justification for the expansion of governmental activity. If pressure of this nature is to be met successfully, the private health insurers should do all that is practical to extend coverage further.

Almost everyone age 65 and over is covered by the H.I. (Part A) Medicare program and the vast majority are covered by Part B (S.M.I.). In addition, about half carry private insurance.

As indicated above, at the end of 1966 almost 85 percent of the population under age 65 and almost 88 percent of the civilian labor force had hospital insurance protection. However, there is great variation among population groups in the proportion covered. In 1966 the variation in proportion of under age 65 population covered by regions was from a low of 72 percent in the West South-Central states to a high of 95 percent in the East North-Central area. Chart 10–3 indicates the variation by state in 1966.

In addition to variation by state, there is considerable variation by degree of urbanization and by employment connection. The coverage is higher in urban areas than in rural areas. The differential is greater for Blue Cross than for insurance companies, so the proportion of covered persons with insurance company plans is higher in rural areas than in cities.

A large proportion of those without insurance are provided for by other public programs. These include 6 million public assistance recipients under age 65, another 11.5 million poor by Social Security Administration standards,[23] and another 15.2 million near-poor, totaling 40 million people who are potentially eligible for Title XIX public assistance benefits. The H.I.A.A. estimated that 7.6 percent of the population under 65 were eligible for public health care programs in 1965, before Title XIX. These included public assistance recipients, armed forces dependents, Indians and Alaska natives, merchant seamen, migratory workers, and persons in institutions. These totaled about 13 million in 1965.[24] Exclusive of public assistance, there are about seven million people under these programs.

---

[23] The index varies by age, sex, family size, and farm-nonfarm residence, from $1,090 per year for a one-person, farm family with female head 65 or over, to $6,960 for a male-headed nonfarm family of seven or more members. Mollie Orshousky, "The Shape of Poverty in 1966," *Social Security Bulletin*, March, 1968, p. 3.

[24] J. F. Follmann, Jr., *Private Health Insurance, 1967.* New York: Health Insurance Association of America, 1967.

CHART 10–3

Percent of Civilian Population under Age 65 with Some Form of
Health Insurance Protection, U.S., 1966

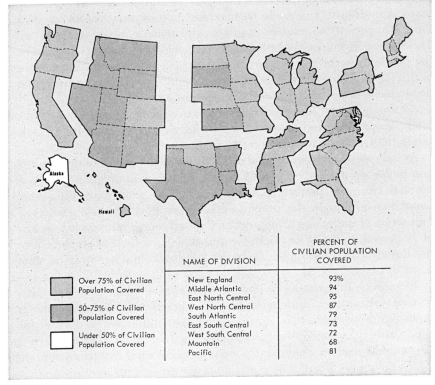

| | NAME OF DIVISION | PERCENT OF CIVILIAN POPULATION COVERED |
|---|---|---|
| Over 75% of Civilian Population Covered | New England | 93% |
| | Middle Atlantic | 94 |
| | East North Central | 95 |
| 50–75% of Civilian Population Covered | West North Central | 87 |
| | South Atlantic | 79 |
| | East South Central | 73 |
| Under 50% of Civilian Population Covered | West South Central | 72 |
| | Mountain | 68 |
| | Pacific | 81 |

Source: Health Insurance Council.

This leaves about 20 million persons uninsured in the U.S. or about 10 percent of the population, at least 75 percent of whom are potentially eligible for Title XIX benefits.

Coverage is highly concentrated among the employed and to a lesser degree among their dependents. The big gaps in coverage are among those not connected with the labor force. Among persons in the labor force and their dependents, coverage is higher in industrial than in nonindustrial occupations and among employees than among the self-employed. There is also an identifiable positive relationship between per capita income by territory and the proportion covered by insurance. Oddly, the relationship is more pronounced for Blue Cross than for insurance company coverage. Coverage is concentrated by age, with the central tendency toward the ages of normal employment and a pronounced concentration in the 25- to 54-year age brackets. Chart 10–4 indicates the variation by age according to Health Information Foundation studies, and Table 10–2 shows

CHART 10-4

Percent of Persons Insured against Costs of Hospital Care by Age,
1953, 1958, 1963

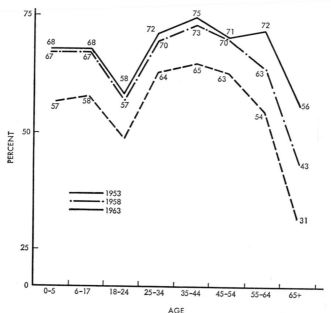

AGE

Source: *Progress in Health Services* (January–February, 1966).

National Health Survey data for hospital and surgical coverage. Slightly more males are insured than females in every age bracket.

Coverage also varies by educational status and income. The 1963 Health Information Foundation study showed only 44 percent of families whose head had from one to four years of elementary schooling insured as compared to 85 percent where the family head had one or more years of college.[25] The proportion insured increases with family income, especially for major medical. Tables 10–3 and 10–4 indicate the striking differences. The difference by race is also notable.

As hospital insurance coverage continues to expand, future progress will become more difficult as the remaining traditional market narrows. Several problems of expanding coverage need to be solved. Intensified selling efforts should make it possible to increase public recognition of the value of such protection. This is particularly important in reaching persons who are not members of groups in which the group insurance principle can be utilized.[26]

---

[25] *Progress in Health Services* (January–February, 1966).

[26] Enrollment of association groups and rural groups through organizations like granges will help meet this problem. See Chapter 15 for a discussion of some of these developments.

## TABLE 10-2

Number and Percent of Persons with Hospital and Surgical Insurance Coverage, by Type of Plan and Age, U.S., July, 1952–June, 1963

(data based on household interviews of the civilian, noninstitutional population)

| Sex | Total Covered | Persons with Hospital Insurance Coverage | | | | Persons with Surgical Insurance Coverage | | | | |
|---|---|---|---|---|---|---|---|---|---|---|
| | | Blue Plan Only | Blue Plan and Other | Other Only | Unknown Type of Plan | Total Covered | Blue Plan Only | Blue Plan and Other | Other Only | Unknown Type of Plan |
| | | | | | *Number of Persons in Thousands* | | | | | |
| Both Sexes: | | | | | | | | | | |
| All ages........ | 128,703 | 49,742 | 8,494 | 61,114 | 9,353 | 119,413 | 45,472 | 5,986 | 59,584 | 8,371 |
| Under 15 years.... | 40,030 | 15,757 | 2,198 | 19,365 | 2,710 | 37,744 | 14,533 | 1,557 | 19,213 | 2,441 |
| 15–24 years....... | 16,979 | 6,236 | 861 | 8,137 | 1,745 | 15,564 | 5,634 | 619 | 7,833 | 1,478 |
| 25–34 years....... | 16,027 | 5,932 | 1,049 | 7,839 | 1,207 | 15,132 | 5,561 | 757 | 7,689 | 1,124 |
| 35–44 years....... | 18,574 | 7,104 | 1,368 | 8,787 | 1,315 | 17,452 | 6,603 | 969 | 8,674 | 1,207 |
| 45–54 years....... | 16,277 | 6,124 | 1,336 | 7,564 | 1,254 | 15,152 | 5,650 | 945 | 7,407 | 1,149 |
| 55–64 years....... | 11,708 | 4,707 | 1,008 | 5,252 | 740 | 10,662 | 4,297 | 698 | 5,024 | 643 |
| 65+ years........ | 9,107 | 3,883 | 673 | 4,169 | 382 | 7,707 | 3,195 | 440 | 3,744 | 328 |
| 65–74 years....... | 6,723 | 2,921 | 509 | 3,004 | 289 | 5,787 | 2,476 | 334 | 2,732 | 244 |
| 75+ years........ | 2,384 | 961 | 164 | 1,165 | 94 | 1,920 | 718 | 106 | 1,012 | 84 |
| | | | | | *Percent Distribution* | | | | | |
| Both Sexes: | 100.0 | 38.6 | 6.6 | 47.5 | 7.3 | 100.0 | 38.1 | 5.0 | 49.9 | 7.0 |
| All ages......... | | | | | | | | | | |
| Under 15 years.... | 100.0 | 39.4 | 5.5 | 48.4 | 6.8 | 100.0 | 38.5 | 4.1 | 50.9 | 6.5 |
| 15–24 years...... | 100.0 | 36.7 | 5.1 | 47.9 | 10.3 | 100.0 | 36.2 | 4.0 | 50.3 | 9.5 |
| 25–34 years....... | 100.0 | 37.0 | 6.5 | 48.9 | 7.5 | 100.0 | 36.7 | 5.0 | 50.8 | 7.4 |
| 35–44 years....... | 100.0 | 38.2 | 7.4 | 47.3 | 7.1 | 100.0 | 37.8 | 5.6 | 49.7 | 6.9 |
| 45–54 years....... | 100.0 | 37.6 | 8.2 | 46.5 | 7.7 | 100.0 | 37.3 | 6.2 | 48.9 | 7.6 |
| 55–64 years....... | 100.0 | 40.2 | 8.6 | 44.9 | 6.3 | 100.0 | 40.3 | 6.5 | 47.1 | 6.0 |
| 65+ years........ | 100.0 | 42.6 | 7.4 | 45.8 | 4.2 | 100.0 | 41.5 | 5.7 | 48.6 | 4.3 |
| 65–74 years....... | 100.0 | 43.4 | 7.6 | 44.7 | 4.3 | 100.0 | 42.8 | 5.8 | 47.2 | 4.2 |
| 75+ years........ | 100.0 | 40.3 | 6.9 | 48.9 | 3.9 | 100.0 | 37.4 | 5.5 | 52.7 | 4.4 |

Source: Carolanne H. Hoffmann, *Health Insurance—Type of Insuring Organization and Multiple Coverage,* U.S. Department of Health, Education, and Welfare, National Center for Health Statistics, Series 10, No. 16.

It is more difficult for selling effort to be directed to these individual prospects, and the very effort increases acquisition costs. Inasmuch as costs of administration are higher for individual policies and adverse selection tends to raise claim costs, it is reasonable to expect a continuing differential between costs of individual policies and group coverage. This accentuates the third obstacle—the fact that many persons are unable to afford adequate health insurance. Low-income groups, particularly the nonwhite, represent the major area of uninsured persons. It seems certain that, if these persons are to obtain coverage on a voluntary basis, some special provisions will be required. Industrial (weekly and monthly pre-

TABLE 10-3

Percent of Families Covered by Any Health Insurance and by Major Medical Insurance by Family Income Level, 1953, 1958, 1963

|  | Percent Covered | | |
| --- | --- | --- | --- |
| *Family Income Level*[a] | *1953* | *1958* | *1963* |
| Any Health Insurance | | | |
| Lower.......................41 | 42 | 51 |
| Middle......................71 | 79 | 78 |
| Upper......................80 | 86 | 89 |
| Major Medical | | | |
| Lower...................... [b] | 1 | 6 |
| Middle..................... [b] | 7 | 22 |
| Upper..................... [b] | 12 | 38 |

[a] Income levels have been adjusted for rising incomes. The intervals for "Lower," "Middle," and "Upper" for each time period are: 1953 = $0–2999, $3000–4999, $5000+; 1958 = $0–3499, $3500–5999, $6000+; 1963 = $0–3999, $4000–6999, $7000+.
[b] Less than ½ of 1 percent.
Source: Health Information Foundation, *Progress in Health Services,* January–February, 1966.

mium) insurance is readily available but many lack the discipline to keep it up, and threats of violence make it difficult to find agents willing to work in certain areas.

Because of its great current interest and because of the various complexities involved, the problem of the aged is discussed separately below.

In regard to low-income groups other than the aged, the problem is less acute, since their rates of utilization are not as high. However, many persons in these groups, such as the unemployed, the disabled, and the institutionalized, are not and never were in a position to obtain coverage through premium payments. At present, Title XIX provides for meeting the costs of hospital and medical care for public assistance recipients and other needy through direct payments to the vendors of medical services.

TABLE 10-4

Percent Distribution[a] of Total Population, by Hospital and Surgical Insurance Coverage, according to Family Income and Race, U.S., July, 1962–June, 1963 (data based on household interviews of the civilian, noninstitutional population)

| | Hospital Insurance | | Surgical Insurance | |
|---|---|---|---|---|
| Family Income and Race | Insured | Not Insured | Insured | Not Insured |
| All incomes | 70.3% | 29.2% | 65.2% | 33.2% |
| White | 73.6 | 25.9 | 68.5 | 29.9 |
| Nonwhite | 45.5 | 53.7 | 40.2 | 58.2 |
| Under $2,000 | | | | |
| Total | 34.1 | 65.2 | 28.8 | 69.5 |
| White | 37.8 | 61.5 | 32.5 | 65.9 |
| Nonwhite | 24.5 | 74.9 | 19.1 | 79.0 |
| $2,000–3,999 | | | | |
| Total | 51.9 | 47.7 | 46.8 | 51.9 |
| White | 55.0 | 44.6 | 50.1 | 48.7 |
| Nonwhite | 38.8 | 60.7 | 33.7 | 65.0 |
| $4,000–6,999 | | | | |
| Total | 79.0 | 20.6 | 73.9 | 24.6 |
| White | 80.2 | 19.4 | 75.2 | 23.3 |
| Nonwhite | 66.4 | 32.8 | 60.2 | 38.5 |
| $7,000–9,999 | | | | |
| Total | 87.3 | 12.3 | 83.2 | 15.7 |
| White | 87.9 | 11.7 | 83.8 | 15.1 |
| Nonwhite | 74.2 | 24.5 | 71.4 | 26.8 |
| $10,000+ | | | | |
| Total | 87.9 | 11.7 | 82.6 | 15.9 |
| White | 88.2 | 11.4 | 82.8 | 15.7 |
| Nonwhite | 80.6 | 19.2 | 76.9 | 22.4 |
| Unknown | | | | |
| Total | 58.7 | 38.8 | 50.9 | 44.3 |
| White | 61.8 | 35.7 | 53.7 | 41.2 |
| Nonwhite | 37.3 | 60.0 | 31.4 | 65.4 |

[a] Insurance status is not known for some, so percentages do not add to 100 percent.
Source: Carolanne H. Hoffmann, *Health Insurance Coverage, U.S., July, 1962–June, 1963*, U.S. Department of Health, Education, and Welfare, National Center for Health Statistics, Series 10, No. 11.

The Social Security law now permits the states to make use of the insurance mechanism to provide such services, with the governmental agency paying premiums. This has been advocated by Blue Cross and Blue Shield personnel, who see their organizations as the ideal vehicles for such an arrangement. Blue Shield now administers Title XIX benefits in 19 states and acts as insurer in one (Texas). The Medicare plan for coverage of armed forces dependents has utilized a similar technique. Except in Texas, the plans are not insurers, however; they merely act as intermediaries in administering claims and paying benefits; receiving a fee for the service. It is encouraging that one insurance company has seen fit to participate in

# TABLE 10-5

Number and Percent of Persons in Total Population, by Hospital and Surgical Insurance Coverage According to Age, Chronic Conditions, and Limitation of Activity, U.S., July, 1962–June, 1963

(Data based on household interviews of the civilian, noninstitutional population; number of persons in thousands)

| Age, Chronic Condition, and Limitation of Activity | Total Popu-lation | Insured by Hospital Insurance | | Insured by Surgical Insurance | |
|---|---|---|---|---|---|
| | | No. | Percent | No. | Percent |
| **All Ages** | | | | | |
| All Persons..................... | 183,146 | 128,703 | 70.3 | 119,413 | 65.2 |
| Persons with no chronic conditions.................... | 101,662 | 71,970 | 70.8 | 66,892 | 65.8 |
| Persons with 1+ chronic conditions.................... | 81,484 | 56,733 | 69.6 | 52,521 | 64.5 |
| With limitation of activity......... | 22,733 | 12,585 | 55.4 | 11,330 | 49.8 |
| **Under 17 Years** | | | | | |
| All Persons..................... | 65,012 | 44,772 | 68.9 | 42,145 | 64.8 |
| Persons with no chronic conditions.................... | 51,924 | 35,723 | 68.8 | 33,568 | 64.6 |
| Persons with 1+ chronic conditions.................... | 13,087 | 9,050 | 69.2 | 8,577 | 65.5 |
| With limitation of activity......... | 1,405 | 847 | 60.3 | 808 | 57.5 |
| **17–24 Years** | | | | | |
| All Persons..................... | 18,930 | 12,237 | 64.6 | 11,163 | 59.0 |
| Persons with no chronic conditions.................... | 11,795 | 7,498 | 63.6 | 6,799 | 57.6 |
| Persons with 1+ chronic conditions.................... | 7,135 | 4,740 | 66.4 | 4,364 | 61.2 |
| With limitation of activity......... | 1,008 | 551 | 54.6 | 501 | 49.7 |
| **25–44 Years** | | | | | |
| All Persons..................... | 45,353 | 34,602 | 76.3 | 32,584 | 71.8 |
| Persons with no chronic conditions.................... | 21,571 | 16,525 | 76.6 | 15,409 | 71.4 |
| Persons with 1+ chronic conditions.................... | 23,782 | 18,076 | 76.0 | 17,175 | 72.2 |
| With limitation of activity......... | 4,426 | 2,755 | 62.3 | 2,637 | 59.6 |
| **45–64 Years** | | | | | |
| All Persons..................... | 36,986 | 27,985 | 75.7 | 25,814 | 69.8 |
| Persons with no chronic conditions.................... | 13,194 | 10,390 | 78.8 | 9,553 | 72.4 |
| Persons with 1+ chronic conditions.................... | 23,792 | 17,594 | 74.0 | 16,261 | 68.3 |
| With limitation of activity......... | 7,649 | 4,683 | 61.2 | 4,278 | 55.9 |
| **65+ Years** | | | | | |
| All Persons..................... | 16,866 | 9,107 | 54.0 | 7,707 | 45.7 |
| Persons with no chronic conditions.................... | 3,178 | 1,834 | 57.7 | 1,563 | 49.2 |
| Persons with 1+ chronic conditions.................... | 13,688 | 7,273 | 53.1 | 6,144 | 44.9 |
| With limitation of activity......... | 8,246 | 3,749 | 45.5 | 3,106 | 37.7 |

Source: Carolanne H. Hoffmann, *Health Insurance Coverage, U.S., July, 1962–June, 1963*, U.S. Department of Health, Education, and Welfare, National Center for Health Statistics, Series 10, No. 11.

the armed forces program. It would seem unfortunate if one type of insurer were to be chosen as the vehicle to the exclusion of all others.

The pressure for any type of action becomes less as coverage expands throughout the population. With 85 percent how having hospital insurance and 11 percent being recipients of various social benefits, the potentially insurable group becomes fairly small as a proportion of the population. It will not be long, if present growth rates continue, before there are few, other than the very poor or sick, who cannot obtain adequate medical expense insurance conveniently and inexpensively.

Surprisingly, a large proportion of persons with activity limitation from chronic disease have medical expense insurance. Table 10–5 shows that more than half the disabled or partially disabled have some health insurance. Serbein,[27] in 1952, fitted several trend lines to enrollment figures as percentages of the population and reached several estimates of the potential growth of hospital insurance. The trend fitted to the postwar years 1946–51 produced a maximum proportion of 62.9 percent of the population covered. This long since has been exceeded. The trend fitted to the period 1940–51 produced a maximum proportion of 89.4 percent in 1960. Assuming no really major change in regard to low-income groups, it is probable that this last estimate reflects the approximate limit of growth.

The problems of population coverage are the same for all lines. Population coverage is greatest for the oldest line, hospital insurance, and least for the newest, major medical. In all cases, there is a strong likelihood that the vast majority of the labor force and their dependents will be covered before long. However, extension to low-income groups, especially of major medical, must await the further development of new sources and methods of financing.

### The special problem of the aged

The problem of providing adequate health insurance for the aged is particularly acute because there are so many of them, their incomes are low, their utilization of medical care is high in both frequency and severity, and most of them are not employed and thus not reachable by standard group enrollment techniques. Despite these obstacles, tremendous progress was made until 1966 towards insuring the aged population, and a substantial proportion still have insurance coverage. Nonetheless, the issue became political and proposals for national government action in this area were hotly debated.

*Demographic and family factors.* There were 18.7 million persons aged 65 and above in the United States in 1965, about 9.3 percent of the total

---

[27] Oscar N. Serbein, *Paying for Medical Care in the United States* (New York: Columbia University Press, 1953), pp. 382 ff.

population. This exceeds previous census estimates and the percentage now 65 and over is greater than any previously projected percentages prior to 1970. The revised projections, new probably considered on the low side, indicate the aged population will reach 20.3 in 1970, 28.8 in 1990, 49.1 in 2025, and 62.8 in 2050. As recently as 1940, the aged made up only 6.8 percent of the population.[28] Largely the result of improvements in health and medical care, this increase poses major problems for the organization and financing of medical care.

As age increases, females outnumber males by ever greater margins since female mortality is lower than male at all ages. For all ages over 65, females outnumber males by a ratio of 56 to 44. This is projected to reach 58:42 by the year 2040, as indicated in Table 10–6.

TABLE 10–6

Actual and Projected Sex Ratio[a] of the U.S. Total and Aged Population

| | Total Population | | Population Aged 65 and Over | |
|---|---|---|---|---|
| Year | Actual | Intermediate Cost | Actual | Intermediate Cost |
| 1900 | 1,045 | — | 1,022 | — |
| 1920 | 1,043 | — | 1,013 | — |
| 1940 | 1,012 | — | 955 | — |
| 1960 | 976 | — | 830 | — |
| 1980 | — | 970 | — | 726 |
| 2000 | — | 975 | — | 692 |
| 2020 | — | 980 | — | 741 |
| 2040 | — | 978 | — | 732 |

[a] Males per 1,000 females.
Source: Francisco Bayo, *U.S. Population Projections for OASDHI Cost Estimates,* U.S. Department of Health, Education, and Welfare, Social Security Administration, Office of the Actuary, Actuarial Study No. 62, p. 35.

Most of these are aged widows. The proportion of both males and females widowed increases substantially with increasing age, especially for females. On Jan. 1, 1963, 65 percent of the females aged 65 and over were widowed and only 21 percent were married with spouse present. The proportion of males widowed was 22 percent at ages 65 and over.[29]

Living arrangements have a significant effect on income needs and on needs and resources for medical care. The 1963 Survey of the Aged indicated that two thirds of those over age 65 were living in families (not

[28] U.S. Department of Health, Education, and Welfare, *Health, Education, and Welfare Trends, 1965* (Washington, D.C.: U.S. Government Printing Office, 1966), p. 3.

[29] All figures are from Lenore A. Epstein and Janet H. Murray, *The Aged Population of the United States* (Washington, D.C.: U.S. Government Printing Office, 1967), Research Report No. 19.

necessarily with a spouse). Most of the remainder were living alone or in lodgings; the balance, 700,000, were in institutions. The aged living with their families are better able to solve medical problems, since they have a relative close at hand who can be turned to in emergencies. Moreover, this family connection may make it easy for them to get along quite comfortably, despite low money incomes. Similarly, the aged living in institutions have most of their medical care needs met.

*Finances.* Incomes of the aged are lower than those of the population in general. Table 10–7 gives median incomes and distribution by income brackets.

TABLE 10-7

Size of Money Income for Family Units Age 65 and Over, Percentage Distribution by Income Interval, 1962

| | | Unmarried Persons | | |
|---|---|---|---|---|
| Total Money Income | Married Couples[a] | Total | Men | Women |
| Total percent............... | 100% | 100% | 100% | 100% |
| Less than $1,000............. | 5 | 44 | 32 | 49 |
| $1,000–$1,499................ | 10 | 22 | 25 | 21 |
| $1,500–$1,999................ | 14 | 13 | 12 | 13 |
| $2,000–$2,499................ | 13 | 8 | 11 | 7 |
| $2,500–$2,999................ | 12 | 4 | 5 | 3 |
| $3,000–$3,999................ | 16 | 4 | 6 | 3 |
| $4,000–$4,999................ | 11 | 2 | 3 | 1 |
| $5,000–$9,999................ | 15 | 4 | 6 | 3 |
| $10,000 and over............ | 5 | b | 1 | b |
| Median Income.............. | $2,875 | $1,130 | $1,365 | $1,015 |

a With at least one member aged 65 or over.
b Less than 0.5 percent.
Source: Lenore A. Epstein, "Income of the Aged in 1962: First Findings of the 1963 Survey of the Aged," *Social Security Bulletin,* March, 1964.

The aged were 18 percent of the poor in 1966 and 15 percent of the near-poor.[30] Fifteen percent of the couples, 32 percent of the single men and 49 percent of the single women were below the Social Security Administration poverty line, and an additional 14 percent of couples, 25 percent of single men and 21 percent of single women fell into the near-poor category, making 29 percent, 57 percent, and 70 percent respectively poor or near-poor by these standards.

The main source of money income for the aged is the Old-Age, Survivors, and Disability Insurance program. The second most important source is employment. About four million persons over 65 are still work-

---
[30] Orshousky, *op. cit.* By 1966, "2 out of 5 households consisting of one aged person or an elderly couple fell below the poverty line."

ing, and they support almost one million nonworking wives. Most persons over 65 have more than one source of money income. Table 10–8 and Chart 10–5 indicate the relative importance of the various income sources. In addition to their money income, many of the aged receive income in kind. This is, of course, true of most of the institutional population who receive free or subsidized housing and often medical care. In addition, most farm residents receive income in kind in the form of farm produce. However, the most prevalent form of income in kind is housing. Many of the aged own their own homes or live with relatives. In either case, they receive housing services at no cost or at considerably less cost than those who have to pay rent. The 1963 survey of the aged revealed that

TABLE 10–8

Sources of Money Income for Family Units Age 65 and Over: Percent Having Income from Specified Sources, 1962

| Sources of Money Income | Married Couples[a] | Unmarried Persons | | |
|---|---|---|---|---|
| | | Total | Men | Women |
| Earnings................................55% | | 24% | 28% | 23% |
| Retirement benefits....................84 | | 67 | 72 | 64 |
| OASDI................................79 | | 62 | 68 | 60 |
| Other public.........................12 | | 7 | 8 | 7 |
| Private group pensions...............16 | | 5 | 10 | 3 |
| Veterans' benefits....................14 | | 8 | 11 | 6 |
| Interest, dividends, and rent............63 | | 48 | 45 | 50 |
| Private individual annuities............. 4 | | 3 | 1 | 3 |
| Unemployment insurance.............. 3 | | 1 | 1 | 1 |
| Public assistance...................... 8 | | 17 | 18 | 17 |
| Contributions from relatives............ 3 | | 5 | 1 | 6 |
| Payments under any public program.....89 | | 80 | 87 | 78 |

[a] With at least one member aged 65 or over.

Source: Lenore A. Epstein, "Income of the Aged in 1962: First Findings of the 1963 Survey of the Aged," Social Security Bulletin, March, 1964.

two thirds of married couples and one third of the single persons owned their own nonfarm homes. Moreover, these homes are more often free of debt than is the case for younger families. The median equity in homes was $10,100 for couples, $7,270 for men, and $7,070 for women. Four out of five couples and three out of five unmarried persons in 1960 had income in kind in the form of home ownership, other rent-free housing, home-grown or free food or free medical care.[31] Such income is estimated to increase the average income of aged couples by $300 to $400 per year.

In addition, the aged usually are in a better financial asset position than younger individuals. Almost three fourths of the couples had financial

[31] Basic Facts on the Health Status of Older Americans (U.S. Cong., Senate Committee Print. [Washington, D.C.: U.S. Government Printing Office, 1961]), p. 23.

assets; the median amount was $3,660. Sixty-eight percent owned life insurance. Seventy-one percent of aged couples had liquid assets; two fifths had such assets in the amount of $2,000 or more.

When evaluating the income situation of the aged, it is important to recognize that needs for income are less for mature families, especially the retired, than for younger families, especially those with children. The number of persons who must be supported from family income decreases

CHART 10-5

Shares of Aggregate Money Income, by Source, of Persons Aged
65 or Over,[a] 1962

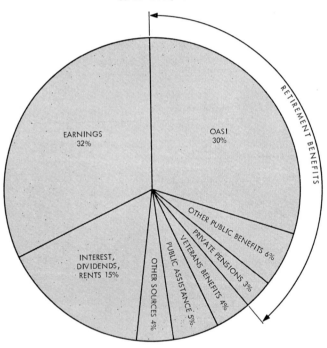

a Including their spouses.
Source: Lenore A. Epstein, "Income of the Aged in 1962: First Findings of the 1963 Survey of the Aged," *Social Security Bulletin*, March, 1964, p. 4.

as the children grow up. The acquisition of consumer durables falls off, and time payments are completed. Eventually the mortgage payments come to an end, releasing considerable income. After retirement, work-related expenses such as commuting, meals away from home, union dues, tools and uniforms are eliminated or reduced sharply.

Moreover, tax liabilities decrease sharply. The social security (FICA) tax no longer is payable, and income tax is reduced or eliminated. Taxpayers over age 65 have an extra $600 personal exemption each, permitting the exclusion of as much as $2,400 of taxable income for a couple both 65 or older. OASDI benefits and similar income are nontaxable; annuities and pensions are partly exempt, and the retirement income credit will reduce the tax burden on annuities and investment income. Finally, what income remains subject to tax is taxed at the lowest bracket rates.

Prospects for income for future generations of aged are considerably better than for those now past retirement age. Many of the latter reached their peak earning years during the Great Depression and had little opportunity to save for old age. Moreover, the OASDI program is just now attaining maturity. Currently, about 89 percent of the aged are receiving OASDI or other public retirement benefits. This is expected to increase to 97 percent for males and 70–75 percent for females by the turn of the century. Moreover, reflecting increased incomes and successive liberalizations of program, the average benefit also will increase substantially.

Similarly, private and nonfederal public pension plans are far from maturity, as over 31 million persons now are covered, but only about 3.5 million are receiving benefit payments. Coverage continues to grow, and pension benefits will constitute a growing proportion of the income of the aged. Moreover, these benefits, like those of OASDI, will be based on the higher and more evenly distributed incomes of recent years.[32]

Summing up, it appears that the financial resources of the aged population are higher than generally believed, but still less than those of the population in general. However, the situation of the aged is improving rapidly, and the disparity to the rest of the population is diminishing.

*Utilization of health services.* It generally is recognized that in almost every respect, persons over 65 show higher frequency and severity of illness, more utilization of services and higher costs and expenditures than do younger persons. Since these facts are generally recognized, it will suffice to cite a few figures here and indicate source material for those who wish to explore the subject further.[33] Charts 10–6 and 10–7 show how disability days and chronic disability increase with age, and Table 10–9 indicates some of the variation in frequency and utilization of health services. This increase takes place consistently with increasing age from a low in the teens. Thus incidence, frequency and utilization figures would be even higher for older segments of the aged group, such as ages 75–84 or 85 and above. Little data are available for the extreme age ranges, but what there is seems to indicate that the problem gets worse continuously until it eventually is solved by death. Other studies sometimes show even higher disability or utilization rates.

---

[32] Cf. *Background Paper on Income Maintenance,* prepared under the direction of the Planning Committee on Income Maintenance (Charles I. Schottland, Chairman), White House Conference on Aging, January 9–12, 1961.

[33] Many of the references cited in Chapters 2 and 16 also give indications of the way disability rates increase with age.

*Availability of Insurance.*  Contrary to popular impression, more than half the people over age 65 had some form of health insurance in 1965, and this proportion was increasing rapidly. Moreover, reasonably adequate new coverage was available for almost all the aged persons who were willing and able to pay a moderate premium. Most of those who could not afford a premium were eligible for Old Age Assistance or Medical Assistance for the Aged.

The private health insurance industry, including the Blues and the

CHART 10–6

Number of Disability Days per Person per Year, by Age and Sex

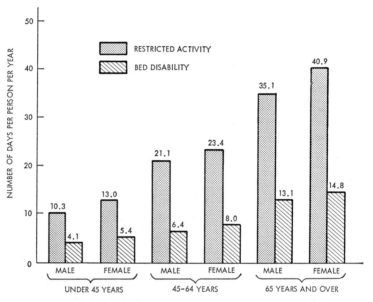

Source: Geraldine A. Gleeson, *Age Patterns in Medical Care, Illness, and Disability, United States, July, 1963-June, 1965* (Washington, D.C., U.S. Government Printing Office, 1966), National Center for Health Statistics Series 10, No. 32, p. 13.

independents, had made tremendous progress in making insurance coverage available to the aged who needed and wanted it and indeed sometimes in marketing it aggressively. There seemed to be at least nine methods of providing health insurance for the aged.[34] Six of these involve group insurance or group enrollment methods, and the others involve individual

---

[34] This is essentially the sevenfold classification first presented by J. F. Follmann, Jr., *Voluntary Health Insurance and Medical Care* (New York: Health Insurance Association of America, 1958), to which the author has added the newest techniques: group enrollment with individual policies (*e.g.,* Continental and Mutual of Omaha) and statewide statutory groups (Connecticut 65).

policies. Most of these still are available for coverage to supplement Medicare.

1. *Continuation of group insurance on employed older workers and their dependents.* All types of insurer and almost every individual company or plan permit this. Most group contracts cover all regularly employed persons without regard to age.

CHART 10–7

Percent of Population with Chronic Limitation of Activity by Age and Geographic Region

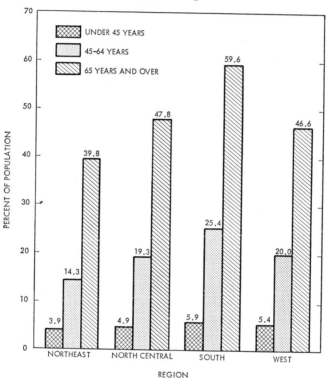

Source: Geraldine A. Gleeson, *Age Patterns in Medical Care, Illness, and Disability, United States, July, 1963-June, 1965* (Washington, D.C.: U.S. Government Printing Office, 1966), National Center for Health Statistics, Series 10, No. 32, p. 16.

2. *Continuation of group insurance on retired workers and their dependents.* Most insurance companies writing group contracts permit the employer or other policyholder to arrange to continue coverage on retired employees and their dependents. The problems involved are the cost of providing the protection and the difficulty of arranging for required employee contributions, if any. The first usually is met by the employer assuming all or most of the extra cost, and/or by reducing the level of

TABLE 10-9

Indices of Health, by Age and Sex

| | All Ages | | Under 45 | | 45 to 64 | | 65 and Over | |
|---|---|---|---|---|---|---|---|---|
| | M | F | M | F | M | F | M | F |
| Hospital discharges per 1,000 population | 102.1 | 153.0 | 78.4 | 150.7 | 149.8 | 146.2 | 190.5 | 183.0 |
| Average stay in hospital (days) | 9.9 | 7.2 | 7.9 | 5.6 | 12.1 | 9.8 | 12.9 | 12.4 |
| Surgical discharges (% of all discharges) | 43.4 | 61.0 | 46.6 | 69.1 | 40.4 | 49.7 | 37.5 | 32.7 |
| No. of physician's visits per person per year | 4.0 | 5.1 | 3.6 | 4.7 | 4.5 | 5.6 | 6.0 | 7.1 |
| Home visits as a percent of total physician visits | 4.6 | 6.0 | 3.2 | 3.3 | 3.6 | 5.1 | 14.0 | 19.5 |
| Restricted activity (days per person per year) | 14.6 | 17.9 | 10.3 | 13.0 | 21.1 | 23.4 | 35.1 | 40.9 |
| Bed disability (days per person per year) | 5.3 | 6.9 | 4.1 | 5.4 | 6.4 | 8.0 | 13.1 | 14.8 |
| Work-loss days among currently employed per person per year | 5.6 | 5.5 | 4.1 | 5.3 | 7.1 | 6.0 | 9.4 | 4.0 |
| Persons with one or more chronic conditions, percent | 44.0 | 47.4 | 34.2 | 36.2 | 63.6 | 67.9 | 81.0 | 84.3 |
| Persons with one or more chronic conditions, unable to carry on major activity, percent | 3.1 | 1.4 | 0.5 | 0.3 | 4.5 | 1.2 | 21.7 | 9.0 |

Source: Geraldine A. Gleeson, Age Patterns in Medical Care, Illness, and Disability, United States, July, 1963–June, 1965 (Washington, D.C.: U.S. Government Printing Office, 1966), National Center for Health Statistics, Series 10, No. 32, pp. 25–50.

benefit. The most common way of arranging for employee contributions is to withhold the employee's share from his pension check.

3. *Conversion from group to individual coverage.* Almost all Blue Cross and Blue Shield plans, a substantial number of the independents, and a growing number of insurance company plans permit members leaving the group to convert to individual coverages. Often there is some requirement as to a minimum period of group coverage, but usually this is relatively short.

The New York Insurance Law was amended in 1959 and 1960 to require all group policies to include conversion privileges, without evidence of insurability at a level premium rate approved by the state. The legislature did not adopt the recommendation that the premium be not greater than the average premium rate under the group contract. The premium rate may take into consideration the age of the insured and for an individual policy may be as high as 120 percent of the state-set rate.

4. *New group coverage for special groups.* The first experiments with group enrollment techniques for retired persons were made with associations of retirees. This permits mass enrollment without selection as to health and provides administrative economies, especially as to acquisition cost. Some of the groups covered in this manner include the National Retired Teachers Association, the New York State Retired Teachers Association, The National Association of Retired Civil Service Employees, "Emeriti," a national association of retired teachers, and the already retired civil service annuitants under the Federal Employees Health Benefits Act. At least one such association, the American Association of Retired Persons, was formed with the main purpose of qualifying for such "group" insurance.

5. *National individual policy-group enrollment plans.* One of the most promising developments of recent years has been the offering of plans that combine group enrollment techniques with individual policies. The original policies first appeared on an experimental basis in 1957 and by 1959 were available to residents of all states. Enrollment campaigns are conducted periodically, for relatively brief periods of time, to prevent undue adverse selection. No health statement is required and preexisting conditions are covered after six months. Where the policy is procured through an agent very low commissions are paid. The insured is given six or twelve monthly premium notices at one time together with pre-addressed envelopes. This greatly reduces costs of premium collection, but probably has an adverse effect on persistency.

6. *State-Wide statutory group plans.* Perhaps the most promising of the developments which made health insurance available to the already aged in the early 1960's was this type of plan, epitomized by "Connecticut 65." It was available in almost one fourth of the states by 1965, and other plans were in the planning stage in a number of others.

The Connecticut plan represents an amazing illustration of the ability of private enterprise to respond effectively and rapidly to a social challenge. The first meetings of an *ad hoc* committee of insurance company executives met in October, 1960. By December the first drafts of the necessary enabling legislation, the plan benefits, premiums, enrollment methods, and insurer organization were drawn up, and work was progressing on liaison with legislators, insurance agents, purveyors of health services, and the public. The enabling act was passed in April and signed by the governor in May. The subscription agreement was signed by the participating insurers by July and advertising began on an intensive scale in August. The first enrollment period was the month of September, 1961, and 21,850 insureds were enrolled. All this took place within one calendar year.[35]

The plan was underwritten jointly by 10 Connecticut companies and 22 other companies which do business in the state. The policyholder was a trustee bank and the insured individuals were members of a "group" formed for this purpose.

The plan emphasized major medical benefits, in recognition of the fact that this type of benefit is most difficult for older people to obtain. However, a basic plan also was issued for those who wanted it. Two major medical benefits were available: a $10,000 lifetime maximum plan with a limit of $5,000 in any one year, and a $5,000 plan with a $2,500 yearly limit. The plan paid 100 percent of the first $250 of hospital expense above the deductible and 80 percent of other medical expense or additional hospital expense. The deductible was $100 plus the benefits of the basic plan, whether or not the insured carried the basic plan. This permitted the major medical plan to "drop down" to cover the occasional major expenses for medical care that are not covered under a basic plan, such as high-priced drugs, blood, etc. The basic plan benefits included hospital room and board up to $12 per day for 31 days per year, hospital extras up to $125 per year, and surgical fees according to a schedule up to a maximum of $360 per year.

If the insured individual carried basic plan insurance plus another basic plan, the plan paid the excess over the other insurance benefits.

7. *New issuance of individual insurance after Age 65.* By 1962 almost all of the Blue Cross and Blue Shield plans and at least 122 insurance companies were issuing new coverage to persons over 65. The insurance company maximum issue ages varied from 69 to 85, and some had no age limit. Of course, on individually issued contracts, certain health standards are required, usually in the form of a health statement. At least 42 companies made basic hospital-surgical coverage available to older persons

[35] Associated Connecticut Health Insurance Companies, *The Story of Connecticut 65 Extended Health Insurance* (Hartford, 1962) (Processed).

on a fully guaranteed renewable for life basis.[36] In addition 11 companies offered hospital income policies on a mass enrollment basis, guaranteed renewable for life, and 8 offered varieties of major medical in guaranteed renewable policies. At least 44 companies offered policies, which, although not guaranteed renewable, specifically prohibited the insurer from cancellation or refusal of renewal on grounds of the insured's health. Many more companies will write insurance for older persons on a commercial basis.

8. *Continuation of individual insurance purchased at younger ages.* At least 175 insurance companies, probably many more, will permit insurance purchased at younger ages to be continued in force after age 65. So will almost every Blue Cross and Blue Shield plan and most of the independents. Blue Cross and Blue Shield individual contracts rarely are terminated for individuals, but premiums are adjustable on a broad class basis. Insurance companies issue both guaranteed renewable and commercial contracts. At least 69 insurance companies were issuing hospital-surgical contracts guaranteed renewable for life in 1963. At least 28 companies issued major medical contracts with a lifetime renewal guarantee.[36] Many issued conditionally renewable basic contracts which provided renewal would not be denied on grounds of deterioration of the insured's health. Since such contracts involve leveling the costs of hospital, surgical, and sometimes medical benefits across the years of premium payments, they require a premium which is higher in the earlier years than would be required for coverage which terminates at retirement age. The excess of the premium over costs in the early years builds up a reserve against higher claim costs in the later years. Thus protection can be continued after age 65 at a lower premium rate than for a policy newly purchased at an advanced age.

9. *Contracts which become paid up at 65.* By 1963, at least eight insurance companies, including some of the industry's leaders, were issuing lifetime guaranteed renewable hospital-surgical contracts on an individual basis which became fully paid up at 65. The benefits were somewhat reduced after 65, but still permitted daily room allowances up to $50 per day for up to 120 days, hospital extras up to $1,000 and surgical schedules up to $1,000.

This type of contract requires an even higher degree of advance funding than the guaranteed renewable type discussed above. Not only must premiums in the early years be sufficient to cover the higher medical care costs of later years, but they must be high enough to build up a reserve at age 65 which will cover all future costs with no further premium payments. Moreover, medical care costs give every indication of continuing to increase, and premiums should include some allowance

---

[36] Health Insurance Institute, *Report on Guaranteed Lifetime Health Insurance* (New York, 1963).

for this. Since the insurer has no way of collecting any premium, let alone an increased premium, after maturity, these contracts are somewhat risky from the underwriting and rate-making viewpoint. However, a number of enterprising companies made them available, and for an insured who could afford the premiums, they represented the ideal way of handling medical care costs after retirement. No company yet, so far as it is known, has had the courage to offer a major medical contract which is guaranteed renewable during the working years and becomes paid up at age 65. Such a contract could be designed and a sound rate probably could be developed, but the high cost would limit the market to higher income prospects. If made excess over Medicare benefits, however, the cost might be within reason.

*Measures of progress.*  By 1962, one insurance company alone had

TABLE 10–10

Proportion of Population with Health Insurance

| Population Group | Percent Insured in Year | | | |
| | 1952 | 1956 | 1959 | 1963 |
|---|---|---|---|---|
| All ages.....................59 | | 69 | 73 | 77 |
| Ages 65–74...................31 | | 44 | 55 | 61 |
| Age 75 and over..............15 | | 24 | 33 | |

Source: H. Lewis Rietz *et al., Statement in Opposition to H.R. 4222* (New York: Health Insurance Association of America, 1961), p. 12; Health Insurance Institute, *Source Book of Health Insurance Data 1964* (New York, 1965), p. 10; statement of C. Manton Eddy, in *Hearings Before the Committee on Finance, U.S. Senate, on H.R. 6675* (Washington, D.C.: U.S. Government Printing Office, 1965), Part 2, p. 553.

two million persons over 65 insured and other insurers covered about eight million more. About 61 percent of the noninstitutionalized population over age 65 had some type of voluntary health insurance by 1963. The number of older persons insured had tripled in nine years and the proportion insured had almost doubled. Table 10–10 indicates the proportion of the population insured in 1952, 1956, 1959, and 1963.

Something of a diagonal progression is apparent. The proportion of age group 65 and over insured in 1963 is a bit higher than that of the whole population in 1952. The proportion of the group aged 75 and over in 1959 is slightly higher than the proportion of the 65–74 group insured seven years earlier. This would indicate that as people get older they tend to retain or replace their health insurance.

*Government action.*  Since 1952, there have been many attempts to amend the Social Security Act to provide medical care benefits to Old-Age, Survivors, and Disability Insurance beneficiaries or to aged beneficiaries. By 1959, the discussion became intense, centering around the Forand bill, H.R. 4700. This would have provided hospital, surgical, and nursing home benefits to aged beneficiaries (including those eligible for benefits but not yet retired) and younger beneficiaries other than disability beneficiaries. By 1960 the proposal had become a major political issue in an election year. Out of a welter of proposed bills, attention finally narrowed down to three. One of these, sponsored by Senator Anderson and strongly supported by Senator Kennedy, in its final version provided hospital, nursing home and home nursing benefits for OASDI beneficiaries over age 68. This was a much watered-down version of the Forand approach. An alternative proposal, sponsored by Senator Javits and supported by Vice-President Nixon, provided for a federal-state subsidy to help aged persons with incomes under $3,000 per year for individuals or $4,500 per year for families to buy health insurance from private insurers. The proposal would have provided a choice among a preventive and short-term plan emphasizing physicians' services, a catastrophic plan providing extended hospital care, and the payment of 50 percent of the premiums on existing private insurance plans. The third proposal was the Kerr-Mills bill which provided for increased public assistance vendor payments under old-age assistance and established the program of Medical Assistance for the Aged. This measure was the only one debated in the House, and the other versions ultimately appeared as proposed Senate amendments to the House-passed bill. The Senate was strongly divided, and inability to get a majority vote in favor of either amendment led to the adoption of the House version with few changes.

The issue became one of the major ones of the 1960 presidential campaign, but little additional light was shed on the problem by all the debate. Early in 1961, President Kennedy recommended that both the Social Security Act and the Railroad Retirement Act be amended to provide medical benefits for aged beneficiaries. The recommendation was introduced in both houses and became known as the King-Anderson bill. It provided 90 days of semiprivate hospital care subject to a deductible of $10 per day (minimum $20; maximum $90) and up to 180 days of skilled nursing home care after hospitalization with a combined limit of 150 "units of service," in which each day of hospital care or each two days of nursing home care constituted a "unit of service." Physicians' services were covered only in the hospital and only for pathology, radiology, physiatry, and anesthesiology when provided by or under arrangement with the hospital. The benefits also included home health services in the nature of nursing care, therapy and part-time homemaker services up to 240 visits per year. Out-patient hospital diagnostic services were covered subject to a deductible of $20. It was to be financed by increasing the taxable wage base to $5,000 per year and raising the tax rates one fourth of 1 percent each for employer and employee. Revised cost estimates led to raising the suggested tax base to $5,200.

On June 14, a modified version of the bill was presented by Senator Anderson on behalf of himself and 25 other senators, including Senator Javits and four other Republicans. Although billed as a "compromise" version, the proposal bore little resemblance to the earlier Javits measures. The proposal was offered in the form of an amendment to the bill for extending and improving public assistance and child welfare, H.R. 10606.

The amendment differed from the earlier King-Anderson proposals in the following respects: a separate trust fund; the blanketing in of all persons reaching age 65 before 1967, to be financed from general revenue; the use of approved nonprofit private organizations selected by providers of services (such as the Blues) as administrative agencies; the use of state agencies as consulting and coordinating units; automatic participation of any accredited hospital; an increase from 0.375 to 0.40 percent in the self-employment tax rate; and a provision for an option whereby individuals who already had insurance with private insurers providing benefits equal to the government benefits plus other benefits could have their insurer reimbursed from the government fund.

Several floor amendments were accepted by Senator Anderson or approved by voice vote. One, submitted by Javits, permitted plans other than individual contracts to offer a 45-day maximum hospital benefit with no deductible in lieu of the 90-day maximum with deductible. The others were of minor import. On July 17, on a motion by the late Senator Kerr, the Senate voted to table the bill, 52 to 48. The vote may have reflected in part the dislike of the senators for irregular procedures. The bill had not been approved either by the House Ways and Means Committee, the traditional starting point for revenue bills, nor by the Senate Finance Committee. Later, Senator Anderson introduced for himself and Senator Javits a "clean" bill, S. 3565, reflecting the floor amendments. This was referred to the Senate Finance Committee, but no action was taken prior to adjournment.

Within about an hour after the voting, President Kennedy appeared on television and declared that almost all the Republicans and a few Democrats had caused the "setback." It was anticipated that the issue of medical care for the aged would be a major issue of the 1962 congressional campaigns, but it was almost completely overshadowed by the Cuban crisis.

In his State of the Union message in January, 1963, President Kennedy again urged passage of the proposal, but he apparently considered it of much less urgency than other proposals, such as tax reform. In his health message early in February, the President referred to the importance of health insurance for the aged under OASDI but reserved the details of his recommendations for a later message.

In a special message on February 21, 1963, he recommended a 36-point "Senior Citizens Program" including many liberalizations in OASDI and a hospital insurance program covering almost all persons over age 65. It provided for three alternative hospital benefits: 90 days benefit with a $10 per day deductible for the first nine days but not less than $20; 180 days benefit with a deductible of the first 2½ days of average costs; or full benefits for 45 days with no deductible. The plan also covered 180 days of skilled nursing home treatment after transfer from hospital; full coverage of hospital out-patient diagnostic services after a $20 deductible and full coverage of up to 240 home health-care visits in a year by community visiting nurses and physical therapists. The proposal did not include the various options of the 1962 bills. Financing was provided by a one fourth of 1 percent tax increase for OASDI and Railroad Retirement employees and employers and an increase in the tax base to $5,200 per year.

On November 22, 1963, President Kennedy was assassinated and President Johnson assumed office. Shortly thereafter he stated his main legislative goals as completing three pending portions of the Kennedy legislative program: a civil rights act, income tax reduction, and health insurance for the aged. The first two of these were achieved in 1964, but the third languished.

On July 7, 1964, the House Committee on Ways and Means reported out H.R. 11865 which increased OASDI benefits and liberalized the program. The committee considered health insurance for the aged but did not even vote on it. The bill passed the House and went to the Senate where a hospital insurance program was added before passage. The bill went to Conference Committee where the House conferees refused to accept the hospital insurance program. The Senate conferees refused to approve the bill without it, and the bill died in the Conference Committee as the 88th Congress adjourned October 3, 1964 so everyone could hurry home to campaign in the 1964 elections.

That debacle resulted in one of the most liberal congresses in history, and the House changed the composition of the Ways and Means Committee to reflect the liberal Democratic majority in the House.[37] On January 7, 1965, the Ways and Means Committee went into executive session to write a bill. They started with H.R. 11865 (88th Congress), the King-Anderson proposals, a Republican proposal for voluntary health insurance for the aged financed from general revenues and premiums

[37] Most but not all of this section is based on Wilbur J. Cohen and Robert M. Ball, "Social Security Amendments of 1965: Summary and Legislative History," *Social Security Bulletin*, September, 1965, p. 3.

paid by the participants, and a proposal dubbed "Eldercare," for broadening Medical Assistance for the Aged and including the blind and disabled. Apparently finding it difficult to decide on the best approach for health benefits for the aged, the Committee reported out a bill including all three: compulsory hospital insurance, voluntary subsidized medical insurance, and broadened Medical Assistance. Moreover, it went much further than previous proposals in increasing OASDI benefits.

The bill was passed by the House on April 8 and sent to the Senate Finance Committee, which held 15 days of public hearings. The committee made a number of changes, and several amendments were made on the Senate floor. After a session in Conference Committee, the bill was approved by both houses and signed by President Johnson on July 30. The OASDI, H.I., and S.M.I. systems, as further amended in 1967, are described in Chapter 4 above.

*Effect on private insurance.*  The 1965 Amendments to the Social Security Acts had a profound impact on the insurers which write health insurance. The normal evolution in policy changes became a revolution during late 1965 and early 1966. In fact, the need for readjustment of benefits and coverages by insurers and the problems involved were so extensive that almost every class of business was affected.

The new programs of Hospital Insurance (H.I.) and Supplementary Medical Insurance (S.M.I.), popularly referred to as Medicare Parts A and B, which were added to the Social Security acts in Title XVIII by the 1965 amendments, effectively preempted the market for medical expense insurance for persons age 65 and older. Coverage under H.I. was extended to virtually all the over-65 population. While coverage under S.M.I. was voluntary, it was evident that a high proportion of those eligible would enroll in this subsidized plan. Indeed, by April 1, 1968 at the close of the second enrollment period, approximately 18.6 million persons, 95 percent of those eligible, had enrolled. In most states, indigent persons were enrolled with the state paying the premiums from public assistance funds.

*Problems.*  Insurers were faced with a number of major decisions. The first question that had to be answered was whether or not there were enough insurable medical expenses not covered under H.I. and S.M.I. to justify offering supplementary medical expense insurance to the over-65 market. Another major problem was what to do with medical expense coverage already in force on the over-65 population. Insurance companies, Blue Cross and Blue Shield, and a variety of independent plans had coverage in force on more than 11 million such persons, and many insurance contracts covering persons under age 65 were guaranteed renewable for life. Millions of the aged had been enrolled in special programs such as the State 65 Plans; the national individual policy group enrollment plans of Continental Casualty, Mutual of Omaha, and Fireman's Fund; and special group plans for retired persons. Most of these contracts provided that the insurer could terminate coverage under certain circumstances. The group enrollment plans similar to Continental's Golden 65 provided that renewal was guaranteed unless the insurer terminated all such policies on the residents of a state. The State 65 plans provided that they could be discontinued if a federal or state program was adopted which made their continuance impractical. Group insurance contracts are almost always on a one year term basis and readily could be modified or terminated. However, millions of aged persons had individual contracts guaranteed renewable for life and thousands more had contracts providing lifetime coverage paid up at age 65. Many others had individual contracts providing coverage beyond age 65 which gave the insurer the right of termination.

When Title XVIII became law, it caused immediate concern to many due to the magnitude of its effects on the insurance industry. This concern was well justified in view of the potential overinsurance and the duplication of benefits for more than 11 million people. Since this situation, if not corrected, might cause illness to be a profitable enterprise, something had to be done quickly.

*Industry activity.* When the passage of Medicare seemed to be certain, the Health Insurance Association of America (H.I.A.A.), together with the American Life Convention (A.L.C.), the Life Insurance Association of America (L.I.A.A.), and the Life Insurers Conference (L.I.C.), appointed an *ad hoc* committee to study the impact of Medicare. They reported on the changes taking place in the industry and made many recommendations. The committee indicated that problems would arise in the following areas: (1) approval of policy changes and language by state insurance departments, (2) avoiding duplication of some or all benefits provided under the government legislation, (3) covering all insureds in full until they individually reached eligibility for the new program, and (4) avoiding adverse selection and overinsurance in connection with in-force business.

The *ad hoc* committee appointed several subcommittees. One such subcommittee was appointed to study the effects of federal Medicare legislation on the regulation of health insurance and to make a report together with suggestions to the National Association of Insurance Commissioners. The committee completed the report October 12, 1965, and mos of its recommendations, after a few modifications, then were adopted by the N.A.I.C. at its regular meeting in Miami during the week of November 27th.

The report recommended that companies should have the right to: (1) exclude from coverage any expense coming within the framework of the federal plans, (2) terminate at age 65 all existing individual policies which are cancellable or renewable at the option of the company,

(3) offer exchange policies which would not duplicate government benefits, with rate adjustments where warranted, (4) offer supplementary coverage in order to cover aged persons' expenses which are not covered under Medicare with due regard to proper determination of premium, (5) place themselves in the role of an excess carrier, while making clear intent as to whether or not the company desires to cover the deductible and percentage participation of the government programs, and (5) choose whether or not they will cover physicians' expenses for persons over 65 who did not elect to enroll for Part B. These recommendations were formally adopted wholly or in part in eight states and generally followed in all of the states.

Another *ad hoc* subcommittee was formed to investigate what specific approaches companies might take to eliminate present and possible future duplication of government benefits. Three basic solutions were formulated. The first was to make the particular contract an "excess coverage" over Medicare, using either a flat amount or any Medicare benefits as a deductible, whichever was the larger. The second proposal was to limit coverage to those items which are not covered wholly or in part by Medicare (this is a very strict approach and leaves very little left to be insured). In fact, some who have advocated this method have suggested that it apply to all government benefits that the insured is or could have been eligible for, whether or not he was enrolled, for example, in Part B. The third approach is an integration method by which an insurance company would pay for all or part of those expenses incurred which were not provided for under Medicare, for example, the first $40 hospital deductible under Part A, the $10 a day hospital charge between the 61st and 90th day, etc. It was suggested by the committee that this last method could be accomplished in two ways, by a "carve out" or by a supplementary approach. In brief, a Carve Out refers to a basic policy which excludes payment of benefits which would duplicate coverage payable under Medicare. This could be accompanied by a rider in many cases (provided the contract permitted or the insured agreed) and usually would be accompanied by a reduction in premiums. Some companies, in anticipation of Medicare, already had written a nonduplication of government benefits clause into their contracts which provided coverage past age 65. In such cases in-force business automatically becomes a Carve-Out plan.

A supplementary approach is one which spells out in a benefit clause what expenses it will cover and for how much according to a schedule. It is designed to circumscribe the Medicare program.

*Group medical expense coverage.* Questionnaires were mailed to the member companies of the H.I.A.A. Of the 101 responding companies (which wrote 87.8 percent of the 1964 group health insurance premium written by insurance companies), 89 companies indicated that they would make coverages available to the aged under outstanding plans, and 85 companies stated that they would make such coverage available for those over 65 under new plans. Only 12 of the respondents indicated that they would not issue any coverage to those over 65 and these companies represent only 0.7 percent of the insurance companies' group volume.

Of the companies which said that they would issue coverage, 67 reported that they would make available supplementary benefits to persons age 65 or older for services or expenditures not paid for under Medicare. However, six of those companies indicated that such coverage would be available only to holders of major medical plans. Fifty-five of the 67 insurers offering supplementary coverages reported that they also would offer to the policyholders a carve-out type of plan, and the remaining 12 indicated they would make available supplementary coverage only. All companies planned to offer the coverage to both in-force and new business.

Generally the supplementary coverages are of a major medical type with lifetime benefit maxima of $5,000 or, less frequently, $10,000, and percentage participation clauses. Eligible medical expenses usually include the Medicare hospital deductible and user charge, hospital room after 90 days, private duty nursing, prescribed drugs and a variety of other expenses not covered by the government plans.

All companies reported that coverage would be offered for groups of 300 lives or more, with a few companies offering coverage to groups as small as 25, or even ten in rare instances. In a few companies such coverage was extended automatically, but the general approach was to do this by request of the insureds only.

Seventy-seven companies indicated they planned to offer an integrated or carve-out plan. Fifty-five of these also offered a supplementary plan while 22 used the carve-out plan exclusively. Those companies which used the carve-out approach did so in several ways. Thirty-one companies indicated that their plans were to implement the program through the use of a "coordination of benefits" provision. Fifty-five companies planned to use a clause which would exclude the duplication of any benefits to which the insured is entitled under Medicare, regardless of whether or not the insured is enrolled for the complete program. Forty-one companies intended to use a provision which excludes any benefits actually paid for under the federal program. The last type of approach used to effect a carve-out plan is a clause which excludes coverage of any expenses covered in part or in full by Medicare. This last method does not leave very much potential expense to cover except certain prescribed drugs and certain private duty nursing benefits. Thirty-four companies, however, were going to offer this type of coverage. Of course, the more strict the exclusion, the harder it was for insurers to replace present coverage with the carve-out version without some loss of business. Negotiations with employers and unions and the explanation of why over-insurance is not good for the group as a whole seem to be essential in implementing the carve-out plan. Insurers already using the H.I.A.A. recommended coordination of benefit clause had only to make sure that Medicare was included in their definition of "other valid coverage" to effect a carve out.

*Individual medical expense coverage.* The individual medical expense policies presented a much more acute problem. Overinsurance and the greater possibility of duplication of Medicare benefits were sure to occur in many cases. All companies which had policies in force which could be cancelled only for nonpayment of premium were faced with a serious dilemma. The same was even more true with the "Paid Up at Sixty-Five" plans which were then in force, although these were relatively uncommon. There was considerable debate also about what to do with the policies of a cancellable nature.

Most insurance companies, as well as other types of health insurers, have discontinued any future issue of contracts which are guaranteed renewable beyond age 65 and contracts which are paid up at 65. On the other hand, some companies, such as Old Equity, are continuing to issue policies which are designed to guarantee coverage for life. These contracts are subject to cancellation only if all policies of that type are cancelled. Also, it is advertised that this type of coverage will pay benefits in addition to benefits which are paid by either other insurance or Medicare.

The approaches being used by many insurers towards individual in-force business have followed the same basic patterns as in group business. This is true even though flexibility is seriously limited because the agreement of the insured to contractual modification is required in guaranteed renewable contracts.

The H.I.A.A. survey referred to above also requested information about individual contracts. One hundred and twenty-two companies, which wrote 48 percent of the individual health insurance premiums in 1964, replied. Ninety-two companies, which wrote 45.9 percent of premiums, would continue to make coverage after age 65 available to persons under policies in force. Eighty-seven would make coverage available on insureds then still under 65, and 88 on insureds then over 65; but 44 and 47 companies, respectively, indicated they would limit such coverage to guaranteed renewable contracts only.

Only 51 companies, however, planned to make coverage available for persons over age 65 in newly issued contracts. Forty-seven of these would issue such coverage to insureds under age 65, and 35 companies would issue such coverage to persons 65 or older.

Twenty-nine companies indicated they would not make any coverage available to persons over age 65, but these represented only 1.5 percent of the premium volume.

Three major approaches to the nature of such coverage were suggested in the questionnaire: (1) Continuation of the usual range of benefits with a carve out of Medicare benefits, (2) flat "indemnity" benefits for each week or day of hospitalization (i.e., a hospital income plan with no Medicare exclusion), and (3) specific supplementary benefits designed to fill the gaps in Medicare.

Fifty-five companies indicated they would use approach (1) for in-force business for insureds not yet 65, and 54 companies would use this for insureds already 65. Fifty would do this for insureds 65 or over on guaranteed renewable policies, but only eight under cancellable policies and nine under policies with limited nonrenewable rights for the insurer.

Forty-eight planned to use approach (2), hospital income, all for insureds 65 and over, and 46 for insureds less than 65.

Fourteen companies indicated they would use approach (3), specific benefits, for in-force contracts, presumably as an exchange contract, nine for insureds not yet 65 and 12 for insureds over 65.

Nineteen companies indicated they would continue coverage on persons over 65 without attempting to avoid duplication of benefit.

For new policies issued to persons under 65 but covering beyond 65, 39 companies would use the hospital income approach, 16 the carve-out approach, 11 the specific benefit approach, and 11 apparently would permit duplication of benefits.

For new issues to persons 65 and over, 30 companies planned to issue hospital income policies, 11 planned to issue specific supplementary benefits, and seven planned some other approach, presumably involving overlap and duplication of benefit. In most cases no age limit for new issue was specified.

*In-Force business.* Exchange to contracts which will not duplicate government benefits was the general approach of many companies. These exchanges were made wherever possible, sometimes without the policy-holder's blessing, when both contract language and the law permit. However, there were some companies which (possibly to maintain good public relations) attempted to make contract exchanges only with those under 65. Some companies contacted all policyholders during 1965 and 1966 to persuade them to switch to a contract guaranteed renewable to age 65 or first date of Medicare eligibility.

The elimination of duplication in the in-force policies by the means of a rider is another method. The reduction in benefits payable applies only to those family members who are also eligible for Medicare. Also, when benefits are reduced because of the rider, the premiums charged to the insured will be reduced as they were under the exchange approach. The rider of this type used by Bankers Life & Casualty reads in part:

The effective date of the benefits provided by this rider shall be the first renewal date following such member's 65th birthday or, if earlier, the date such member becomes eligible to have payments made for hospital confinements of such member under Federal legislation.

A number of companies, such as Equitable and General American, have protected themselves against duplication in their lifetime guaranteed renewable contracts by the use of an integrated deductible. This provides that the deductible amount is the greater of a stated amount or the amount of benefits provided for covered charges under other medical expense coverage provided by any insurance or welfare plan or prepayment arrangement. Such a deductible provision would leave the insurer in the position of an excess insurer.

The conversion privileges which are so common in family medical expense plans do not seem to pose quite as severe a problem in relation to Medicare as the insurance areas already discussed. This is evidenced by the fact that almost all conversion options, which allow a person at 65 to convert to a policy which would provide continuous protection, state that conversion may be only to a policy offered for that purpose at the time of conversion, or that such a conversion may not result in overinsurance, or both. Between these two "conditions," it does not seem that a duplication of Medicare benefits is very likely to result from the exercise of conversion privileges.

In all cases where benefits were reduced immediately or after the insured reaches 65, premiums also were reduced. However, the premiums were not always reduced to the same degree as the benefits, for several reasons. First, the insurance companies were worried about adverse selection, that is, that only the unhealthy policyholders would refuse policy exchange. So, it might be wise to create an extra margin of safety by not reducing premiums on converted coverage too much, or in other words, let the healthy subsidize the unhealthy. The second reason that insurers hesitated to reduce premiums as much as they might is the fact that they feared higher utilization of health facilities as a result of Medicare. It was expected that more aged would enter the hospital and stay longer and therefore accumulate higher bills than ever before. In such a case, an extra margin would be appropriate. Also, in many cases a rate increase would have been required if the Medicare program had not been enacted.

*New issues.* In the area of new business, as in outstanding coverage, there are three basic approaches: (1) a supplementary plan and (2) a carved-out plan. Some companies deliberately duplicated Medicare benefits and in general took a "let the chips fall where they may" attitude. Many companies developed plans which will insure the aged against

TABLE 10-11

Comparison of Expenses Covered under Three Types of Medicare Supplement
(percent of plans covering expense)

| Type of expense | Blue Cross–Blue Shield (37 Plans) | New Commercial Supplement (93 Plans) | Offset-Type Supplement (14 Plans) |
|---|---|---|---|
| Medicare deductible | | | |
| Plan A: $40 deductible.................100% | | 76% | 86% |
| Plan A: $20 deductible for out-patient diagnostic care................ 65 | | 46 | 79 |
| Plan B: $50 initial deductible............ 43 | | 54 | 79 |
| Medicare coinsurance | | | |
| Plan A: $10 per day for 61st–90th day of hospital stay..................100% | | 80% | 86% |
| Plan B: 20% coinsurance................ 65 | | 44 | 79 |
| Plan A: 20% for out-patient diagnostic care....................... 54 | | 41 | 71 |
| Benefits in excess of medicare maximums | | | |
| Plan A: Hospital bed and board for more than 90 days per "spell of illness"............................. 68% | | 82% | 50% |
| Plan A: Hospital extras after 90 days of hospitalization per "spell of illness".. 68 | | 82 | 50 |
| Plan A: Extended care in nursing home.... 30 | | 27 | 29 |
| Plan A: Out-patient psychiatric care above $250 or 50% of expense maximum in one calendar year............. 24 | | 33 | 43 |
| Plan A: Hospital days for psychiatric care above 190....................... 16 | | 43 | 29 |
| Plan B: Post-hospital home care above 100 days.............................. 16 | | 27 | 36 |
| Benefits for coverages not covered by Medicare | | | |
| Private duty nursing care................ 27% | | 78% | 64% |
| Medicines (prescribed for out-of-hospital use).........................27 | | 77 | 64 |

Source: David A. Weeks, "The Effect of Medicare on Retiree Health Insurance," *The Conference Board Record*, January, 1967, p. 19.

many expenses not provided for under the government program such as the deductibles, coverage past the 90th day for hospital expenses, and extended psychiatric services. Table 10–11 indicates the type of new group coverage chosen to supplement Medicare.

*Mass market coverages.* Insurers who had actively solicited over-65 business prior to the enactment of Medicare were presented with major problems. Particularly affected were Mutual of Omaha and Continental Casualty who, along with Fireman's Fund, had offered national individual policy group enrollment plans. More than one million aged persons were enrolled in these plans. Fortunately, these contracts provided that the insurer could terminate coverage if it terminated all policies in force on the residents of a particular state. Both Mutual of Omaha and Continental Casualty developed contracts to be offered both to present and new policyholders 65 and older, but they took quite different approaches.

Mutual of Omaha offered a specific scheduled supplementary plan with three levels of benefits and a hospital income contract to those policyholders who requested change. However, it encouraged all policyholders to retain present coverages. For new issues, it is offering a flexible hospital income plan on a continuous enrollment basis.

Continental Casualty indicated its intention to continue operating aggressively in the over-65 market regardless of Medicare. It is offering a choice of hospital income policies which will pay a cash benefit of either $70 or $110 a week during hospitalization up to 52 weeks. These plans are named the 70-Plus and the 110-Plus plans. Monthly premiums are $8 and $12.50 respectively. A company spokesman stated that "the indemnity approach under Continental's 70-Plus and 110-Plus packages offers the older person the greatest flexibility since it pays him cash to use for medical expenses not covered by Medicare, or to cover the inevitable extra expenses connected with spells of illness." The possible moral hazard in duplicating Medicare Part A benefits, especially during the first 60 days of hospitalization, was not otherwise discussed.

*State 65 plans.* The scope of the benefits provided under the new government legislation so completely preempted the area of coverage of the State 65 plans that all of these plans announced that coverage would be terminated as of July 1, 1966.

In several states, private insurance companies arranged to continue the coverage to under-65 spouses of Medicare recipients. The Equitable Society agreed to do this in New York State and Southland Life in Texas. Nationwide offered such coverage in Ohio, and Occidental did the same in California.

*Blue Cross–Blue Shield.* Blue Cross and Blue Shield have been affected by Medicare in the same ways as have the insurance companies. They have the advantages, however, that most of their business is on a group basis, none is guaranteed renewable, and they are not subject to the Uniform Individual Policy Provisions Law. Choices available are the same as they are for the insurance companies.

Most of the Blue Cross and Blue Shield plans developed contracts designed to supplement Medicare. These, in general, were offered to all insureds, both group and individual enrollment, as a substitute for previous coverage on persons age 65 and older. Most plans terminated coverage completely for persons 65 and older who did not accept the new contract. Many plans also offered these contracts to the general public during an open enrollment period in the spring or summer of 1966.

Most of the contracts were of a specific supplementary nature. The typical Blue Cross plan covers the $40 hospital deductible and the $10 per day user charge from the 61st to the 90th day of hospitalization for out-patient hospital diagnostic expenses. A few cover only the first two items, but some go farther and cover additional items of expense such as full hospital benefits beyond 90 days, to 120, 180, or more days, full out-patient services, services outside the United States, etc. In a few cases private nursing expenses are covered, wholly or in part.

The typical Blue Shield contract covers the $50 deductible and the 20 percent participation of Medicare Part B for physicians' services. Some, however, cover the 20 percent but not the $50, and a few cover only the $50. In some cases the $50 deductible amount is covered only if the patient is hospitalized. A few plans impose scheduled maxima for various procedures and many have a stated lifetime maximum limit, most commonly $10,000, with provision for reinstatement. Some plans also cover private-duty nursing and prescribed drugs. Some Blue Shield plans, however, did not develop specific supplementary plans, citing administrative problems as the reason. In these areas, subscribers 65 and older could retain present coverage despite the duplication with Medicare. In some cases, such coverage was limited to a low-benefit-level surgical schedule with a maximum of $200 or $250.

In some areas a major medical plan was offered, sometimes by Blue Cross and Blue Shield in conjunction, but sometimes, as in Hawaii, by Blue Shield alone. These plans typically reimbursed 80 percent of eligible expenses not covered by Medicare, often after a corridor deductible, usually $100. All Medicare deductibles, user charges, etc., may be counted towards meeting the deductible. Maximum benefits range from $5,000 to $15,000, usually with provision for reinstatement.

*Title XIX.* The impact of the Medical Assistance program of Title XIX on private insurance apparently will be less than initially was feared. Some were concerned that the extension of broad medical benefits on a charity basis to the medically indigent might lead many persons to drop their private coverage. This seemed especially likely where, as in the New York plan, income limits are high and eligible persons can obtain a card certifying their eligibility. However, premiums paid for private insurance are considered in determining the income limits, and this may encourage eligible persons to retain their coverage. It was easy to visualize high lapse rates among low income groups when Title XIX benefits were made available in all states and the public began to understand them. It seemed possible that some unions, all of whose members have low incomes, might wish employers to drop group medical expense contracts and use the funds released for other benefits while the employees relied on Title XIX for medical expense benefits.

These dire results have not eventuated. Most states set income limits much lower than New York's,[38] and the 1967 Social Security Amendments soon will hold the maximum income eligibility for Title XIX benefits to 133⅓% of the income limits for aid to families with dependent children. About one third of the state programs use the same limit for both programs. New York reduced its income limits more than 10 percent in March, 1968.

On the other hand, Title XIX provides that states may utilize private insurers as administrators or insurers for Medical Assistance benefits. In 19 states, Blue Shield is administering Title XIX claims. Only one state, Texas, has insured its Title XIX eligibles with an insurer, Blue Shield, on a "modified prepayment basis."

*Conclusion.* Despite the massive intervention of the national government in taking over a substantial proportion of the health insurance market, private insurers have rallied and responded actively. They have supported the new government programs by acting as administrators and have adjusted their contracts and their practices to the changed situation.

People 65 and over demonstrated their faith in private insurance by retaining existing coverage or by obtaining supplementary coverage by purchases or conversion, to a surprising extent. As Table 10–12 indicates, some 9.4 million persons age 65 and over were covered by private health insurance at the end of 1966 compared to about 11 million at the peak.

Although the full impact of the 1965 Social Security Act Amendments will not be realized for many years, this discussion has attempted to assess the initial impact upon private insurance. Further study is required as events develop, and much research must be done before the full effect on medical care financing, medical practice, and income distribution is determined.

The private insurance industry has demonstrated its resiliency. It should now devote its best efforts to providing adequate health insurance, at reasonable cost, in the areas of the market remaining. It is hoped that the insurance industry can do such a good job of providing sound health insurance on a voluntary basis that further incursions by government into the realm of private enterprise may be avoided.

### Insurance and utilization

In recent years there has been a growing concern with the rising costs of medical care and the rising premium costs of health insurance. Some of this cost increase is attributable to the inflation which the

---

[38] The highest limits for a family of four in order now are New York, $5,300; Rhode Island, $4,300; Massachusetts, $4,176; New Hampshire, $4,056; Pennsylvania, $4,000; California and Connecticut, $3,800; and Illinois and Iowa, $3,000.

Services or Expense (in thousands)

| Type of Plan | Hospital Care | Physician Services | | | | Dental Care | Prescribed Drugs (Out-of-Hospital)[c] | Private Duty Nursing | Visiting-Nurse Service[d] | Nursing-Home Care |
| --- | --- | --- | --- | --- | --- | --- | --- | --- | --- | --- |
| | | Surgical Services | In-Hospital Visits | X-Ray and Laboratory Examinations[a] | Office and Home Visits[b] | | | | | |
| Blue Cross-Blue Shield plans...... | 4,931 | 4,111 | 3,878 | 2,135 | 1,189 | — | 400 | 750 | 1,150 | 2,600 |
| Blue Cross............... | 4,773 | 256 | 241 | e | e | — | e | e | e | e |
| Blue Shield............. | 158 | 3,855 | 3,637 | e | e | — | e | e | e | e |
| Insurance companies: | | | | | | | | | | |
| Group policies............ | 2,024 | 1,694 | 1,149 | 1,000 | 1,000 | 40 | 1,000 | 1,000 | 1,000 | 100 |
| Individual policies......... | 2,912 | 1,822 | 616 | 100 | 100 | — | 100 | 100 | 100 | — |
| Unadjusted total........ | 4,936 | 3,516 | 1,765 | 1,100 | 1,100 | 40 | 1,100 | 1,100 | 1,100 | 100 |
| Less duplication[f]......... | 323 | 215 | 84 | — | — | — | — | — | — | — |
| Net total............. | 4,613 | 3,301 | 1,681 | 1,100 | 1,100 | 40 | 1,100 | 1,100 | 1,100 | 100 |
| Independent plans........... | 437 | 487 | 479 | 511 | 451[g] | 44 | 216 | 261 | 327 | 143 |
| Community-consumer........ | 102 | 137 | 137 | 159 | 159 | 3 | 15 | 76 | 157 | 3 |
| Employer-employee-union...... | 323 | 338 | 330 | 340 | 280 | 8 | 200 | 185 | 170 | 140 |
| Private group clinic......... | 12 | 12 | 12 | 12 | 12 | 12 | 1 | — | — | — |
| Dental society............. | — | — | — | — | — | 21 | — | — | — | — |
| Gross total............... | 9,981 | 7,899 | 6,038 | 3,746 | 2,740 | 84 | 1,716 | 2,111 | 2,577 | 2,843 |
| Less duplication[h]......... | — | — | — | 37 | 27 | — | 17 | 21 | 26 | 28 |
| Net number of different persons covered........... | 9,433[i] | 7,267[i] | 5,708[i] | 3,709 | 2,713 | 84 | 1,699 | 2,090 | 2,551 | 2,815 |
| % of population 65 & over[j]....... | 50.5[i] | 38.9[i] | 30.6[i] | 19.9 | 14.5 | .4 | 9.1 | 11.2 | 13.7 | 15.1 |

a In physicians' offices, clinics, or health centers. Excludes those covered only in hospital out-patient departments or those covered only in accidents or fracture cases or when services are followed by surgery.
b Number covered for all conditions. Excludes those eligible for care only after hospitalization.
c Excludes those covered for drugs only after hospitalization.
d Assumes that all persons covered for private-duty nursing are also covered for visiting nurse service.
e Not estimated separately; in many cases coverage is jointly written.
f As estimated by H.I.A.A. for first three services; considered insignificant for the other services and hence shown as zero.
g About 15 percent of this number not covered for home calls.
h Calculated at 1 percent for all services other than dental care for which duplication is estimated at zero percent.
i H.I.A.A. estimates.
j Based on Census estimate of 18,670,000 as of January 1, 1967.
Source: Louis S. Reed, "Private Health Insurance: Coverage and Financial Experience, 1940-66," Social Security Bulletin, November, 1967, p. 3.

country has been experiencing and is only a part of a larger national problem. Some is the natural result of population increase. Some of the increase represents substantial improvements in the quality of care; some represents more adequate compensation for traditionally underpaid groups such as hospital orderlies. These factors affect unit costs primarily. But total costs have gone up, not only because of increases in unit costs, but because of increased utilization of health services. These increases

TABLE 10-13

Annual Percent Change for All Items and Certain Medical Care Items of the Consumer Price Index 1935–June 30, 1967

| Year | All Items | Medical Care | Hospital Daily Service Charge | Physicians' Fees |
|------|-----------|--------------|-------------------------------|------------------|
| 1935–36.......................... | 1.0 | 0.4 | 0.8 | 0.6 |
| 1936–37.......................... | 3.5 | 0.8 | 2.5 | 0.6 |
| 1937–38.......................... | −1.8 | 0.4 | 2.4 | −0.2 |
| 1938–39.......................... | −1.4 | 0.0 | 0.4 | 0.2 |
| 1939–40.......................... | 0.8 | 0.2 | 0.4 | 0.0 |
| 1940–41.......................... | 5.1 | 0.6 | 2.0 | 0.4 |
| 1941–42.......................... | 10.7 | 2.8 | 8.1 | 2.0 |
| 1942–43.......................... | 6.2 | 4.8 | 7.9 | 6.5 |
| 1943–44.......................... | 1.7 | 3.1 | 4.3 | 4.0 |
| 1944–45.......................... | 2.3 | 2.3 | 3.2 | 2.4 |
| 1945–46.......................... | 8.5 | 5.6 | 13.8 | 4.9 |
| 1946–47.......................... | 14.4 | 8.2 | 19.2 | 6.5 |
| 1947–48.......................... | 7.7 | 6.2 | 16.8 | 4.0 |
| 1948–49.......................... | −1.0 | 3.2 | 8.2 | 1.8 |
| 1949–50.......................... | 1.0 | 1.9 | 3.8 | 1.6 |
| 1950–51.......................... | 8.0 | 4.8 | 10.9 | 3.7 |
| 1951–52.......................... | 2.2 | 5.5 | 9.8 | 4.4 |
| 1952–53.......................... | 0.8 | 3.5 | 6.3 | 2.7 |
| 1953–54.......................... | 0.4 | 3.2 | 5.9 | 3.0 |
| 1954–55.......................... | −0.3 | 2.3 | 4.8 | 3.4 |
| 1955–56.......................... | 1.5 | 3.6 | 5.4 | 3.0 |
| 1956–57.......................... | 3.5 | 4.0 | 8.0 | 4.3 |
| 1957–58.......................... | 2.8 | 4.8 | 5.7 | 3.4 |
| 1958–59.......................... | 0.8 | 4.3 | 5.6 | 3.4 |
| 1959–60.......................... | 1.6 | 3.6 | 6.8 | 2.5 |
| 1960–61.......................... | 1.1 | 3.0 | 7.6 | 2.5 |
| 1961–62.......................... | 1.2 | 2.6 | 7.0 | 2.9 |
| 1962–63.......................... | 1.2 | 2.2 | 6.3 | 2.2 |
| 1963–64.......................... | 1.3 | 2.3 | 5.0 | 2.5 |
| 1964–65.......................... | 1.7 | 2.4 | 5.8 | 3.6 |
| 1965–66.......................... | 2.9 | 4.4 | 9.6 | 5.8 |
| 1966–67.......................... | 2.8 | 7.0 | 19.1 | 7.1 |
| 1967–68[a].......................... | 3.7 | 6.1 | 13.2 | 5.4 |

[a] For all years except 1967, percent changes are based upon the average price indexes for those years. For 1967–68, the price indexes of March were used, and the percent increase was increased one third to obtain the estimated annual rate of increase.

Source: American Medical Association, *Report of the Commission on The Cost of Medical Care*, Vol. I, 1964; U.S. Department of Labor, *Consumer Price Indexes for Selected Items and Groups*, December, 1965 to December 1967; December 1967 to March 1968.

seem to be associated with increased ability to pay and with the growth of health insurance.[39]

In 1966 to 1968 the pace of price increase accelerated under the impact of Medicare and a number of other factors. As indicated in Table 10–13 hospital charges increased by 43.4 percent from the 1965 average to March, 1968, while physicians' fees increased by 21.6 percent. Although the rate of increase may have slowed, it is still cause for concern.

The magnitude of price change over a period of decades is obscured by the Bureau of Labor Statistics' practice of moving its base period decennially to the most recent three years ending with 7, 8, and 9. If an earlier period is selected as a base, the true magnitude becomes apparent. In this example, 1943 was chosen as a base for the following reasons: (a) Although it was a year of war, prices had not yet recovered to their previous highs, but they had recovered largely from the depths of the depression; (b) the general consumer price index has approximately doubled since then; (c) the time span is approximately a quarter century and a third of a normal life span; (d) the author, who graduated from high school and commenced the practice of adulthood that year, remembers it as a year of more or less "normal" prices.[40]

Table 10–14 shows what happens to prices over such a time span.

TABLE 10–14

Selected Consumer Price Indexes, 1943 Base
(1967 Index as percent of 1943 Index)

All items ("cost of living")......................192.9
Medical care (all)...............................250.8
　Physicians' fees (all).........................231.6
　　Obstetrical.................................259.4
　Dentists' fees................................230.1
　Optometric examination and glasses..........162.4
　Hospital daily service charge.................662.6
　Prescriptions and drugs......................136.0

Food............................................199.0
Apparel.........................................180.4
Housing (all)...................................176.1
　Rent..........................................171.1
Transportation..................................208.8
Personal care...................................200.5
Reading and recreation..........................184.8
Other goods and services........................187.0

Source: Bureau of Labor Statistics.

---

[39] See above, Chapter 1, for a discussion of unit cost increases and the growing national health bill, and Chapter 2, for some measures of health progress and for a description of some of the changes in patterns of treatment and medical organization.

[40] For example, 5-cent hamburgers, cokes, ice-cream cones; 3-cent first-class stamps and newspapers; 15-cent cigarettes and milkshakes; 50-cent mixed drinks; and 10-cent (local) beer.

The reasons for these dramatic price increases are evident to anyone with any knowledge of economics: demand has been increasing faster than supply. Rising incomes and expectations and the growth of private health insurance were putting pressure on limited personnel and resources by the mid-sixties. The advent of Title XVIII Medicare and Title XIX Medical Assistance benefits in 1966 merely added fuel to the fire by making available five or six billion additional dollars[41] to compete for an inelastic supply.

The physician shortage was documented in Chapter 2 above. By early 1968, even the American Medical Association, long accused of restricting the supply of physicians, admitted that demand for service had "outstripped both the facilities and personnel to provide them." Its President stated that only an increase in physician manpower could alleviate this cost squeeze.[42] President Johnson, in his "Message on Health in America," transmitted to Congress on March 4, 1968, recommended, as two of his five goals, providing additional health manpower and combating rising health care costs.[43] He proposed a Health Manpower Act of 1968 which would consolidate, expand, and strengthen five existing health training and research programs due to expire in June, 1969. The Acting Secretary of Health, Education, and Welfare, announced a series of Regional Conferences on Health Care Costs to begin in June, 1968. The first was scheduled for Kansas City June 26–27; the second in New England in October and the third in Region VIII in October, 1968.

Hospital demand also has increased, by any measure. Table 10–15 shows that, from 1946 to 1966, while hospital beds increased 62 percent, the average daily census increased 72 percent, and the number of admissions increased 97 percent. That the occupancy rate increased only from 72.1 percent to 76.6 percent is due to a reduction in length of stay from 9.1 to 7.9 days.

More important than increase in demand, however, is the increase in hospital cost per patient day. This has increased from $9.39 in 1946 to $48.15 in 1966 as shown in Table 10–16 and Chart 10–8. This in turn results from two factors: increased utilization of personnel, supplies, and equipment, and increased cost of personnel, supplies, and equipment. The Blue Cross projection in Chart 10–8 in based on the assumption that cost increases in 1966 and 1967 are nonrecurring, reflecting increased pay

---

[41] The figure is impossible to pin down, since there is no way of computing what would have been spent in the absence of the new programs.

[42] Milford O. Rouse, president of the AMA, quoted in *The Blue Shield*, April, 1968, p. 1. The "cost squeeze" did not seem to have hurt physicians seriously. Their *median net* income was almost $29,000 in 1965, five times that of the average production worker.—*The Blue Shield*, February, 1967, p. 4.

[43] The other goals were the reduction of infant mortality, the reduction of accidental deaths, and a nationwide volunteer effort by insurers, physicians, and hospitals to "improve the health of all Americans."

rates for nurses and other personnel, partly the result of the hospitals becoming subject to national minimum wage laws. Chart 10–9 shows that the increase in use of goods and services per day was the most important component of increased expense, followed by population growth, increase in unit costs, and increase in utilization, in that order.

To the extent that rising incomes and broader insurance coverage permit more people to afford necessary and desirable treatment, these devel-

TABLE 10–15

Trends in Hospital Utilization,[a] U.S., 1946–66
(nonfederal short-term general and other special hospitals)[b]

| Year | Hospital Beds Number (in Thousands) | Hospital Beds Per 1000 Population[c] | Average Daily Census Number (in Thousands) | Average Daily Census Per 1000 Population[c] | Occupancy Rate per 100 Beds | Admissions during Year Number (in Thousands) | Admissions during Year Per 1000 Population[c] |
|---|---|---|---|---|---|---|---|
| 1946 | 473 | 3.4 | 341 | 2.5 | 72.1 | 13,655 | 98.7 |
| 1950 | 505 | 3.4 | 372 | 2.5 | 73.7 | 16,663 | 110.9 |
| 1955 | 568 | 3.5 | 407 | 2.5 | 71.7 | 19,100 | 117.7 |
| 1956 | 586 | 3.5 | 425 | 2.6 | 72.5 | 20,107 | 121.6 |
| 1957 | 595 | 3.5 | 438 | 2.6 | 73.6 | 21,002 | 124.7 |
| 1958 | 610 | 3.6 | 451 | 2.6 | 73.9 | 21,684 | 126.5 |
| 1959 | 620 | 3.6 | 462 | 2.6 | 74.5 | 21,605 | 123.7 |
| 1960 | 639 | 3.6 | 477 | 2.7 | 74.6 | 22,970 | 128.9 |
| 1961 | 659 | 3.6 | 489 | 2.7 | 74.2 | 23,375 | 129.0 |
| 1962 | 677 | 3.7 | 509 | 2.8 | 75.2 | 24,307 | 132.3 |
| 1963 | 698 | 3.7 | 530 | 2.8 | 75.9 | 25,267 | 135.4 |
| 1964 | 721 | 3.8 | 550 | 2.9 | 76.3 | 25,987 | 137.2 |
| 1965 | 741 | 3.8 | 563 | 2.9 | 76.0 | 26,463 | 137.9 |
| 1966 | 768 | 4.0 | 588 | 3.0 | 76.6 | 26,897 | 138.8 |
| Percent increase 1946 to 1966 | 62.1% | 18% | 72% | 20% | 6.2% | 97% | 41% |

[a] Excludes newborn infants and nursery accommodations.
[b] Excludes psychiatric and tuberculosis hospitals.
[c] Refers to the civilian population.
Source: American Hospital Association.

opments are desirable. They represent a significant portion of the national rise in living standards and contribute to a higher level of public welfare. Such increased utilization has contributed to the rise in the total national medical care expenditure and to upward pressure on insurance premium rates. Of course, insurance premium rates also have increased to reflect more generous benefit levels in terms of amount, duration, and types of expense covered. This again is basically a desirable development: an improvement in the quality as well as the quantity of health insurance.

*Overutilization.* But above and beyond these extraneous or desirable developments, some of the increases in cost seem to be attributable to unnecessary and undesirable overutilization of health services. In this sense overutilization is something of a euphemism for moral hazard. It may arise from hypochondria, psychosomatic illness, accident proneness, deliberate falsification of sickness or injury, or malingering.[44] Probably more important is the unnecessary use of services, the use of services

TABLE 10-16

Average Cost per Patient-Day, Average Length of Stay
and Average Cost per Patient Stay in Nonfederal
Short-Term General and Other Special
Hospitals, U.S., 1946–66

| Year | Average Cost per Patient Day | Average Length of Stay (Days) | Average Cost per Patient Stay |
|---|---|---|---|
| 1946 | $ 9.39 | 9.1 | $ 85.45 |
| 1947 | 11.09 | 8.0 | 88.72 |
| 1948 | 13.09 | 8.7 | 113.88 |
| 1949 | 14.33 | 8.3 | 118.94 |
| 1950 | 15.62 | 8.1 | 127.26 |
| 1951 | 16.77 | 8.3 | 138.73 |
| 1952 | 18.35 | 8.1 | 148.00 |
| 1953 | 19.95 | 7.9 | 158.47 |
| 1954 | 21.76 | 7.8 | 169.67 |
| 1955 | 23.12 | 7.8 | 179.77 |
| 1956 | 24.15 | 7.7 | 186.11 |
| 1957 | 26.02 | 7.6 | 198.13 |
| 1958 | 28.27 | 7.6 | 214.67 |
| 1959 | 30.19 | 7.8 | 235.66 |
| 1960 | 32.23 | 7.6 | 244.53 |
| 1961 | 34.98 | 7.6 | 267.37 |
| 1962 | 36.83 | 7.6 | 279.91 |
| 1963 | 38.91 | 7.7 | 299.61 |
| 1964 | 41.58 | 7.7 | 320.17 |
| 1965 | 44.48 | 7.8 | 346.94 |
| 1966 | 48.15 | 7.9 | 380.39 |

Source: American Hospital Association and Health Insurance Institute.

which are more expensive than required, and the casual hospital stay of an extra day or so when it is free.

Overutilization takes two forms: increased frequency and duration of use and higher charges than otherwise would be imposed. Full-service plans and open-end plans like major medical are particularly dangerous,

[44] See Chapter 5 above for a brief discussion of these problems and the subjectivity of poor health. See Chapters 17 and 20 below for a discussion of moral hazard in relation to underwriting and claims, respectively.

CHART 10-8

Hospital Cost per Patient-Day, Actual, Trend, and Projections (1961–65 base)

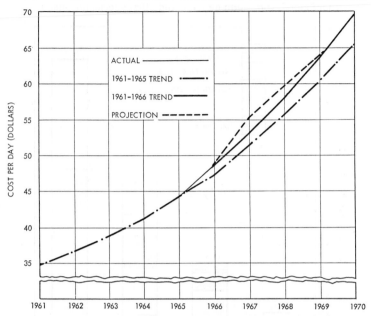

Source: Blue Cross Association, *Blue Cross Reports*, Vol. V, No. 2 (May–June, 1967).

in that they place no limit on the latter type of increase. The dividing line between necessary and unnecessary procedures is vague and ill-defined, and physicians may differ in many individual cases. The proper amount of charge for a given procedure is even more difficult to define with any accuracy. It seems necessary to rely on the good faith and good judgment of physicians and other professionals. Relative value schedules and medical review committees are helpful guides.

Excessive costs may arise from unnecessary admissions, unnecessary use of diagnostic and treatment aids, unnecessarily long periods of stay, and unnecessarily high charges for services rendered. The fact that most hospital policies require admission as an in-patient has contributed to the use of hospitals where other methods of treatment or diagnosis might be adequate. Where hospital insurance is the only medical care insurance carried, the motivation is clear. Moreover, many basic medical and a few surgical and major medical policies require hospital admission as a prerequisite to collection. Excessive charges may arise from the practice of caring for charity patients at less-than-average cost and adding the losses so incurred to the bills of paying patients, especially those with insurance. Title XIX, however, requires payment of the full reasonable costs. Such

CHART 10–9

Hospital Care Expense: Components of Change, 1950–65 Change
(nonfederal, short-term general, and other special hospitals)

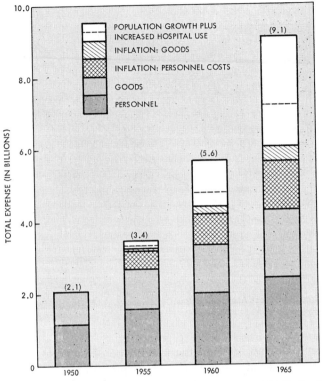

Source: Blue Cross Association, *Blue Cross Reports,* Vol. V, No. 2
(May–June, 1967).

abuses may arise from actions of patients, physicians, and hospitals or insurers.

*Responsibility for overutilization.*[45] *Physicians* may contribute to overutilization in many ways. Almost always the physician must certify the presence of a disability or the need for treatment. Since his relationship with the patient is closer than that with the insurer, his sympathies tend to favor giving the patient the benefit of the doubt where possible. Moreover, the physician may be motivated to modify the diagnosis or recommended treatment to conform to the coverage of insurance policies. Where the policy covers treatment or diagnosis only if performed in a hospital, the physician may order hospital admission even when the con-

---

[45] Much of the material in this section appeared originally in O. D. Dickerson, "The Problem of Overutilization in Health Insurance," *Journal of Insurance,* Spring, 1959, pp. 65 ff. It is reproduced with permission.

dition might well be treated or diagnosed in his office or in a clinic. Where the policy does not cover alcoholism or nervous or mental disease, he may devise some diagnosis such as "exhaustion, malnutrition, avitaminosis."

At least equally prevalent is the tendency to increase the complexity of treatment when the patient has insurance. Instead of restricting tests or treatment to what is clearly indicated to be necessary, he may order "the works." To some extent this may represent a desirable situation in that a better quality of medical care results, but in many cases the only result is to increase claim rates.

In some cases deliberate fraud has been discovered. Bills have been submitted to the insurer for procedures which never took place, or charging for a far more expensive procedure—such as an appendectomy instead of the removal of a wart.[46] Sometimes doctors have actually operated unnecessarily and removed perfectly healthy organs.[47]

Probably the most common abuse is that of the physician charging the patient more when he has health insurance. Physicians have long defended their right to charge their patients in accordance with ability to pay. However, all too frequently they look upon the presence of health insurance as evidence of increased ability to pay rather than as an indication that the patient has already paid for the service.

Gross overcharges are rather rare. However, a small increase in fees for the multitude of less serious procedures can have a substantial impact on claim costs. This effect can come about even when physicians agree upon a schedule of fees. Such schedules tend to be set at the prevailing average level of fees in the community. However, once set, the physicians will tend to charge all insured patients at least as much as the schedule provides for. Since most patients will be insured, this will raise the average; and there will soon come a demand for an increase in the fee schedule so that insurance benefits will at least equal the average. This may happen again and again, and the constant pressure for increased fees may continue until the physicians are charging everyone the same fees (the latest maximum). This subtle upward pressure is probably much more significant than deliberate gouging on the part of physicians. An American Medical Association official has estimated that not more than 5 percent of physicians are guilty of dishonest practices.[48] To an outsider looking in, this figure sounds unhappily high.

---

[46] Milton Silverman, "The High Cost of Chiseling," *Saturday Evening Post,* June 14, 1958, p. 125.

[47] See Roy E. Trussell and Frank Von Dyke, *Prepayment for Medical and Dental Care in New York State* (New York: Columbia University, 1962), pp. 225 ff., for a study where one third of the hysterectomies and almost half the Caesarean sections were evaluated as unjustified.

[48] Silverman, *op. cit.*

*Hospital administrators* must accept their share of responsibility for overutilization. All too often they look upon health insurance primarily as a device to keep their hospitals filled to capacity with paying patients.[49] They tend to put every case in as favorable a light as possible to promote acceptance by the insurer. They cannot evade their responsibility by placing the entire burden on the physician. Hospital trustees establish policies and set standards and should recognize their responsibility to insurers—particularly since the hospitals are the ultimate risk bearers in most Blue Cross plans. They should recognize that the rates charged insured subscribers are directly related to hospital utilization; hence, they should endeavor to keep costs down rather than encouraging maximum use to justify additional hospital construction.

*Insurers* also may contribute to overutilization. Policies which provide fixed cash payments on a valued basis regardless of actual costs or other insurance may permit the claimant to make a profit unless the dollar amounts are quite small. Duplication of benefits presents an even greater problem. Few individual policies provide any safeguard, and frequently such considerations are ignored in underwriting. Where the claimant can collect for the same loss two or three times, the temptation toward abuse is evident.

Unrealistic exclusions actually may contribute to falsification of facts on the part of the patient and his physician. It would be better to provide broad coverage at realistic rates than to provide narrow coverage at cut rates, thereby encouraging evasion. Many policies, even of the major medical type, require hospitalization at some stage of the disability in order to establish eligibility for benefits. Most hospital policies provide coverage for therapeutic and diagnostic procedures only if the claimant is admitted to the hospital as a regular bed patient. Such provisions do much to encourage unnecessary admissions. If coverage were provided for such procedures, even if treatment took place in an out-patient clinic or doctor's office, it is possible that aggregate claim costs would decrease.[50] If the procedure is necessary it will be performed in any event. If the insurance policy covers only the higher cost treatment in the hospital, the procedure usually will be performed there. Formerly, Blue Cross organizations seem to show little interest in keeping claim costs and premiums down. Apparently they became imbued with the idea that their

---

[49] For example, Thomas F. Manley, president of Associated Hospital Service of Philadelphia, claims that the usual unoccupancy rate for hospital beds in the Philadelphia area is 27 percent, yet hospitals keep expanding. This adds to overhead and tends to raise unit costs as well as encouraging unnecessary stays. *Health Insurance Review*, November, 1962, p. 25.

[50] Of course, it might work the other way with the diagnostic service resulting in the detection of illness that otherwise would not be discovered. For a case where this may have happened, see Denwood N. Kelly, "Experience with an Outpatient Diagnostic Program," *Hospitals*, August 1, 1960, p. 50.

main function is to keep an ever-increasing number of hospital beds filled with paying patients. Since the advent of Medicare, however, they all have established some mechanism for claims review.

*The extent of overutilization.* An indication of the extent of overutilization may be obtained by comparing the frequency of utilization of services of insured vis-à-vis uninsured patients. Unfortunately, very few data are available on this basis. An indicated above, the concept of overutilization implies unnecessary services or unreasonable expense. Not all the difference may be presumed to represent the former. An unknown proportion represents necessary services that are performed more frequently when finances permit.

The 1963 Health Information Foundation study, like the earlier two, indicates a consistently higher level of utilization for insured families or persons as compared to those uninsured.[51] Table 10–17 indicates some of these differences.

TABLE 10-17

Utilization of Health Services by Insured and Uninsured Families, 1963

| Type of Cost or Service | Insured Families or Persons | Uninsured Families or Persons | All Families or Persons |
|---|---|---|---|
| Mean gross charges incurred for all personal health services per family | $429 | $201 | $370 |
| Median gross charges incurred for all personal health services per person | 255 | 111 | 209 |
| Net outlay for health service as percent of family income | 5.2 | 3.9 | 5.0 |
| Hospital admissions per 100 person-years, including normal delivery | 15 | 9 | 13 |
| Mean length of hospital stay per admission (days) | 7 | 8.8 | 7.4 |
| Mean hospital days per 100 person-years | 101 | 84 | 96 |
| In-hospital surgical procedures per 100 person-years | 6 | 3 | 4.5 |

Source: Ronald Andersen and Odin W. Anderson, *A Decade of Health Services* (Chicago: University of Chicago Press, 1967).

The only respect in which uninsured persons exceed insured persons in utilization is in the average stay per admission. However, this is more than offset by the higher admission rates of insured persons so that total days of stay per 100 person-years is about 20 percent higher than the rate for uninsured persons.

The distinction between necessary and unnecessary procedures re-

[51] Ronald Andersen and Odin W. Anderson, *A Decade of Health Services* (Chicago: University of Chicago Press, 1967).

quires the evaluation of an expert. Averbrook[52] indicates the effect of requiring an evaluative physical examination for disability income recipients. Twelve percent of those requested to come in for an examination failed to appear, implying that they could not establish disability. Of those who did appear, 55 percent had their benefits reduced materially. He cites an earlier New Jersey study which showed that 25 percent of the persons requested to appear for an examination failed to report. These figures provide an indication of the amount of malingering under a disability income benefit.

The most comprehensive data relating to overutilization comes from a study conducted by the Michigan State Medical Society and the Michigan Hospital Service (Blue Cross).[53] This study analyzed 12,102 consecutive clinical records in 25 Michigan general hospitals. A committee of physicians evaluated each case in order to determine whether the various procedures and admissions were necessary. The total hospital days involved were 76,238; of these, 11,172 were considered unnecessary to the recovery, safety, or reasonable comfort of the patient. This does not imply that the treatments or diagnoses performed were not necessary. In most cases these were felt to be necessary, but in many cases it was not necessary for the patient to occupy a hospital bed for the particular services involved or to stay so long.

Over 28 percent of hospital admissions contained some element of faulty use. The percentage was 36 percent for Blue Cross members, 30 percent for patients with insurance company coverage, and only 14 percent for the uninsured, as indicated by Chart 10–10. Similar results were found in terms of length of stay. Out of 12,102 patients, 1,556 stayed in the hospital longer than was considered necessary. The total days of overstay where 5,231.[54]

The most recent study of the center for Health Administration Studies (formerly the Health Information Foundation) found similar results. Utilization consistently is higher for insured than for uninsured persons, and higher yet where multiple coverage exists. In this study, 7 percent of those surveyed had more than one hospital policy, 6 percent more than one medical policy, and 1 percent more than one major medical policy. Of those with coverage, 11 percent had duplicate benefits for hospital expense, 10 percent for surgical, and 4 percent for major medical.[55] Table

[52] Marvin S. Averbrook, "The Malingery Problem in Disability Insurance," *Review of Insurance Studies,* Summer, 1955, p. 75.

[53] Cited in Harry F. Becker, "Controlling Use and Misuse of Hospital Care," *Hospitals,* December, 1954.

[54] A recent small New York study showed 12 percent unnecessary admissions. See Trussell and Von Dyke, *op. cit.,* pp. 225 ff.

[55] Table 10–2 above shows 6.6 percent duplications between Blue Cross, Blue Shield, and "other" plans for hospital, and 5 percent duplication for surgical. The source is not clear as to the treatment of major medical.

10–18 shows that more services were used by the insured than by the uninsured and even more by those with multiple coverage. Table 10–19 shows a similar variation in whether expenses were incurred and, if so, for how much.

A number of studies seem to indicate that comprehensive medical benefits, particularly in group practice prepayment plans, result in fewer hospital admissions and lower total days per person. One study[56] compared the utilization rates of Blue Cross subscribers who had comprehensive medical-surgical coverage with the Health Insurance Plan of Greater

CHART 10–10

Overutilization and Health Insurance

AMONG
PATIENTS
WITH

NO INSURANCE

COMMERCIAL INSURANCE

BLUE CROSS

HOSPITALIZATION NEEDED
AS RECEIVED                     HOSPITALIZATION UNNECESSARY
                               OR TOO PROLONGED

Source: Harry F. Becker, "Controlling Use and Misuse of Hospital Care," *Hospitals*, December, 1954.

New York with those who had more limited coverage, primarily surgical and in-hospital medical, with Blue Shield. The HIP sample showed admission rates of 77.4 per 1,000 as compared with 95.8 per 1,000 for the Blue Shield group. Average duration was only slightly greater for the HIP group, 7.6 days as compared with 7.2 days, so the average stay per 100 population was much less for the HIP group, 58.8 days as compared

---

[56] *Prepaid Medical Care and Hospital Utilization*, American Hospital Association Chicago, cited in: Paul M. Benson, Eve Balamuth, and Sam Shapiro, "Prepaid Medical Care and Hospital Utilization," *Hospitals*, March 1, 1958.

•

384    HEALTH INSURANCE

TABLE 10–18

Use of Health Services by the Insured and the
Uninsured during 1963, by Percent

| Type of Service | Unin- sured: No Cov- erage | Insured Single Coverage | Multiple Coverage |
|---|---|---|---|
| Hospitalization............ | 6% | 9% | 14% |
| Physician.................. | 57 | 70 | 79 |
| Dentist[a].................. | 28 | 45 | 50 |

[a] Excludes 24 sample persons for whom all information
was not provided in the interview and was not determined
through verification procedures.
Source: Ronald Andersen and Donald C. Riedel, *People
and Their Hospital Insurance* (Center for Health Administration Studies, Research Series No. 23 [Chicago: University
of Chicago Press, 1967]).

with 68.8 days for Blue Shield. This seems to indicate that Blue Shield
patients were using the hospital for less serious conditions, many of which
might have been treated outside the hospital had out-patient insurance
benefits been available.

Somewhat similar results emerged from a 1958 comparison of utilization rates between similar labor union employees enrolled in the Health
Insurance Plan of Greater New York (HIP) and group health insur-

TABLE 10–19

Expenditures for Hospital Care for the Insured
and the Uninsured during 1963, by Percent

| Expenditure | Uninsured | Insured Single Coverage | Multiple Coverage |
|---|---|---|---|
| Any expense during 1963[a] | | | |
| Yes............................... | 13% | 19% | 25% |
| No............................... | 87 | 81 | 75 |
| Total........................... | 100% | 100% | 100% |
| Level of expense during 1963[b] | | | |
| $1–199............................ | 84% | 71% | 56% |
| $200 or more...................... | 16 | 29 | 44 |
| Total........................... | 100% | 100% | 100% |

[a] Includes expense for hospital out-patient as well as in-patient care.
[b] Includes only persons with hospital expense.
Source: Ronald Andersen and Donald C. Riedel, *People and Their Hospital Insurance* (Center for Health Administration Studies, Research Series No. 23 [Chi-
cago: University of Chicago Press, 1967]).

ance (GHI).[57] The HIP enrollees showed lower utilization rates in almost every category. Their overall costs also were lower. This would seem to confirm the value of the group practice method of organization in controlling costs. However, both these studies involved HIP and more study is needed to make a generalization which would be valid for other group practice plans in other areas. Table 10–20 indicates some of the important utilization rates.

A similar comparison among GHI enrollees with comprehensive and limited coverage in 1964 revealed the same type differentials, but these

TABLE 10–20

Utilization of Health Services, Group Health Insurance
and Hospital Insurance Plan, 1958

| Utilization Index | GHI | HIP |
|---|---|---|
| Hospital admissions per 100 persons[a] | 11.0 | 6.3 |
| Mean days of hospital stay per admission | 8.0 | 6.5 |
| Number of days per 100 persons[a] | 87 | 41 |
| Average cost of hospitalization per enrollee[a] | $23 | $13 |
| Hospitalized surgical procedures per 100 persons[a] | 7.6 | 4.3 |
| Nonhospital surgical procedures per 100 persons[a] | 10.1 | 7.3 |
| Average surgical cost, per enrollee[a] | $13 | $ 7 |
| Average number of nonobstetrical physician visits per year[a] | 6.0 | 5.5 |
| Mean total medical care expenditures per year[a] | $154[b] | $139 |

[a] Based on total enrollees whether or not they incurred costs, received treatment, or were hospitalized.

[b] Two high-cost GHI patients were excluded from this average. If they are included the average becomes $165.

Source: Odin W. Anderson and Paul B. Sheatsley, *Comprehensive Medical Insurance* (Research Series 9 [New York: Health Information Foundation, 1959]).

disappeared when the two groups of enrollees were standardized for age and sex distribution.[58]

A study which compared similar groups insured by the Kaiser group practice plan and others showed the following:

|  | Admissions per 1,000 Enrollees | Annual Hospital Days per 1,000 Enrollees |
|---|---|---|
| Kaiser group practice | 90 | 570 |
| Solo practice insured | 135 | 1,032 |

[57] Odin W. Anderson and Paul B. Sheatsley, *Comprehensive Medical Insurance* (Research Series 9 [New York: Health Information Foundation, 1959]).

[58] Helen H. Avnet, *Physician Service Patterns and Illness Rates* (New York: Group Health Insurance, Inc., 1967), pp. 372 ff.

"Among federal employees, those insured by prepaid group practice had hospital utilization [prevalence?] rates 40 percent lower than those covered by other plans."[59]

*Control of utilization.* There are four main methods whereby utilization may be controlled and overutilization may be prevented, and several others are possible. Different types of health insurance plans rely on these in varying degrees; but every plan makes use of at least one, and most plans use more than one.

*Underwriting.* The conventional approach to moral hazard by insurers has been through underwriting. By selecting only those insureds who seem to be relatively free from moral hazard, they attempt to avoid adverse selection and secure a group of risks whose loss levels will be predictable. However, the opportunity for careful selection in the expense coverages is rather limited. The factors bearing on moral hazard are intangible, subjective, and difficult to identify and measure. The vast majority of these coverages are written on a group basis. In group underwriting, selection procedure must be applied to the group as a whole and there must be a clearly dangerous situation in order to make it practical for an insurer to reject a group for moral hazard reasons. When such rejection takes place, it is likely to be in renewal underwriting, and then only after heavy losses have been incurred.

Personnel administering the Blue plans seem to feel that strict underwriting conflicts with their concept of community service. Moreover, if stricter underwriting results in a large proportion of patients without insurance, one of their major objectives would be impaired, that is, making it possible for the purveyors of service to collect their bills readily.

The only area in which selection procedures may be applied with any degree of rigor is in regard to insurance company individual contracts. Here some underwriting is common, but it is usually rather cursory in practice (with the exception of jumbo benefit plans). An objection to strict selection is the current criticism of the health insurance business that large segments of the population, especially the poor, the non-white and rural residents, still are without any protection. More rigorous underwriting would only aggravate this problem and strengthen the case of those who argue for further government participation in the field of health insurance.

Underwriting is not effective even in preventing overinsurance, mainly because of the many different types of health insurance. A combination of any two or more of these may result in duplication of coverage and of benefit payment. Someone who wants more insurance always can find some company to sell it.

*Policy provisions.* The second approach is to make use of policy provi-

---

[59] U.S. Department of Health, Education, and Welfare, Public Health Service, *Promoting the Group Practice of Medicine* (Washington, D.C.: U.S. Government Printing Office, 1967), p. 8.

sions to force the insured to participate in the loss. When he submits a claim, he will be forced to incur expenses himself. Thus he will be motivated to keep the total loss to a minimum. Almost all types of insurers make some use of this technique in one or more of its variants. Most health insurance coverages force the insured to share in the loss by not covering certain types of expenditure. For example, even a combination of basic hospital, surgical, and medical coverages usually will not include nurses' fees, iron lungs, blood and plasma, hormones, and many antibiotics. Since expenses such as these usually accompany the other covered expenses, the insured is sharing in the loss. In addition, almost all policies will contain some exclusions as to essentially voluntary events such as diagnostic services, immunizations, cosmetic and beautifying operations, and dental services. When voluntary events such as these and ordinary pregnancy are covered, they will usually be subject to specific, relatively low limits.

Another method of making the insured share in the loss is through a series of specific limits on various services. This may appear as a limit as to type of service, for example, ward or semiprivate room, or as a limit on dollar expenditure. Almost all the basic coverages include such limits—frequently according to schedules, such as the surgical fee schedules of most surgical contracts and the scheduled coverage of hospital extras in many Blue Cross hospital plans. Some of the comprehensive coverages provided by the "independents" achieve the same effect by imposing a small charge for services, particularly for dependents or for quasi-voluntary expenses. The disadvantage of this approach, particularly when combined with the exclusion of certain expenditures completely, is that the degree to which a loss is covered depends upon an essentially random distribution of charges by type. Thus, a particular insured may find that virtually all, or relatively little, of his expenses are covered, depending on factors largely beyond his control. Such limits and exclusions may encourage a more expensive type of service than is necessary, simply because the more expensive service is fully covered by the policy and the less expensive one is not covered or is severely limited.

Another device, commonly used in regular medical, major medical and comprehensive policies, and to a growing degree in hospital policies, is a deductible. This discourages unnecessary procedures, but has little if any effect on the duration of treatment or the level of charges. Some feel that the possibility of collusion with the practitioner, so that fees are jacked up to allow a rebate of the deductible, virtually destroys its value as a control on claim costs. However, the major purpose of the deductible is not to control overutilization. Its main purpose is to keep losses, expenses, and premiums down by eliminating the expense of investigating, settling, and paying the multitude of small losses which should be budgeted by the typical insured.

Unfortunately, the philosophy of Blue Cross has tended to favor first-dollar coverage—prepayment as opposed to insurance—and it has been difficult to convince the public of the value of this principle, even though it is axiomatic in automobile collision insurance. One objection raised by Blue Cross personnel is that the use of a deductible would impair one of the main objectives of their plans—to see to it that hospitals can collect their bills readily. Labor groups usually seem strongly in favor of first-dollar coverage and have generally opposed plans incorporating the deductible principle. However, the acceptability of deductibles is growing. Most insurance companies and a number of Blue Cross and Blue Shield plans make deductible hospital and surgical-medical policies available.

A final method of forcing the insured to share the loss is through a percentage participation clause. This is commonly included in major medical contracts and comprehensive plans by all types of insurers. Percentage participation is usually combined with the deductible. Since these major medical and comprehensive contracts cover almost all types of injury and disease and almost every form of medical expense, up to high general limits, some such control is considered necessary. In some of the comprehensive plans, where percentage participation does not apply to some forms of expense, such as hospital charges, a specific dollar limit may be used as a substitute.

If not avoided by collusion with purveyors of services, such clauses should be effective in motivating the insured to keep costs down. However, the insured is not the sole and often not the primary person responsible for determining the level of fees. This function is performed largely by physicians and hospitals, and there is always the danger that they may look on such insurance as evidence of greater ability to pay. Perhaps the prudent insured should conceal the fact that he possesses a policy! The biggest objection to the percentage participation clause is that it may force the insured to bear an unduly high amount in a severe case, particularly when combined with the deductible. Perhaps a clause which provides for the percentage paid by the insured to be reduced for successive increments of total expenditure will come into general use someday.[60]

The effectiveness of all the above types of policy provision can be destroyed if the insured has other insurance which will pay benefits for the same loss. This is true whether the other coverage is his own health insurance or is the liability or compensation policy carried by a third party. Duplication of coverage is difficult to detect and prevent. The uniform individual policy provisions law permits prorating only when the insurer has not been notified of the other coverage. When notified, the only recourse is cancellation or nonrenewal. Thus, there is no point in including this provision in a guaranteed renewable policy. The deductible

---

[60] For the first known example, see above, p. 285.

in major medical is designed to avoid duplication with basic policies, but there is nothing to prevent the insured from carrying several such policies if he wishes. Greater control of duplication of benefit will require concerted action by the companies and changes in the uniform individual policy provision laws. Most group medical expense contracts, including Blue Cross, now contain an effective coordination of benefit clause, as indicated in Chapter 5 above.

The Health Insurance Association of America, initially in cooperation with the national Blue Cross and Blue Shield organizations, studied the overinsurance problem for several years and submitted seven reports to the appropriate committee of the National Association of Insurance Commissioners.[61] The first report cited a survey of 12,140 patients in 12 hospitals which indicated that 9.6 percent of the patients who had hospital insurance had two or more contracts. This varied from a high of 16.2 to a low of 5.6 percent when broken down by hospital. On the average, these patients received payments 44 percent greater than their hospital bills. This varied from 23.5 percent to 67.6 percent by hospital.

The third report suggested the amendment of the uniform policy provisions law to permit a more effective other insurance clause. The fourth report recommended such an amendment to permit a new optional provision. The suggested clause provides that the insurer may prorate benefits with other valid coverage which contains an effective prorata provision, but if the other insurance does not then the benefits of such a policy are deducted from both the numerator and denominator of the prorating formula.

The formula relates 110 percent of any necessary and reasonable medical expense which is covered wholly or in part under one or more of the policies incurred during a period of 30 days or more to the total benefits which would be payable by all the "valid coverage." Total payment is limited to what the contract would have paid in the absence of other coverage. Other valid coverage is defined to include group, blanket, franchise, individual, and family coverage, whether provided by an insurance company, Blue Cross or Blue Shield organization, or an independent, or provided by an uninsured welfare plan, government program, or required or provided by statute, and medical payments under liability policies. Third-party liability payments are not included as other valid coverage, but the insurer could use a subrogation clause. There is provision for recovery from the insured of inadvertent overpayments and for payment to other insurers in the event of overpayment by either insurer. The suggested draft legislation was offered for purposes of study and to invite comments from the Commissioners. It was submitted in June,

---

[61] Health Insurance Association of America, *Status Report on Overinsurance,* (1960), *Second* .... (1960), *Third* .... (1961), *Fourth* .... (1962), *Fifth* .... (1962), *Sixth* .... (1963), *Seventh,* .... (1963).

1962. In December, 1962, the N.A.I.C. Subcommittee to Study Overinsurance indicated that it disagreed with the recommendation of the industry. It was not convinced of the necessity of the action, but urged the industry to submit all valid data as to the extent of overinsurance and if necessary to conduct a current systematic survey.

The sixth report presented evidence of the widespread existence of overinsurance and the seventh contained a slightly modified version of the proposed law. This was approved by the Accident and Health Committee on December 4, 1963. It left to the individual states five questions:

1. Whether the legislation should be limited to noncancellable and guaranteed renewable policies.
2. Whether the legislation should contain a subrogation clause.
3. Whether notice of nonduplication provision should be included in the application as well as the policy.
4. Whether a company utilizing such provision should be able to offset its own individually underwritten policies.
5. Whether implementing regulation is necessary.

So far, this proposal has been approved administratively in New Hampshire, but not yet enacted by any legislature. The proposed provisions and instructions read as follows:

Section 1. (Section 3(B)(3) of the Uniform Individual Accident and Sickness Policy Provisions Law) is amended as follows:
OVERINSURANCE: If an accident or sickness or accident and sickness policy or policies previously issued by the insurer to the insured be in force concurrently herewith, making the aggregate indemnity for _____ (insert type of coverage or coverages) in excess of $_____ (insert maximum limit of indemnity or indemnities) the excess shall be void and all premiums paid for such excess shall be returned to the insured or to his estate.
or, in lieu thereof:
Insurance effective at any one time on the insured under *this policy* and a like policy or policies in this insurer is limited to the one [such] policy elected by the insured, his beneficiary or his estate, as the case may be, and the insurer will return all premiums paid for all other such policies.
Section 2. (Section 3(B)(4) of the Uniform Individual Accident and Sickness Policy Provisions Law), is hereby repealed and the following is enacted in lieu thereof.
OVERINSURANCE: If, with respect to a person covered under this policy, benefits for allowable expense incurred during a claim determination period under this policy together with benefits for allowable expense during such period under all other valid coverage (without giving effect to this provision or to any "overinsurance provision" applying to such other valid coverage), exceed the total of such person's allowable expense during such period, this insurer shall be liable only for such proportionate amount of the benefits for allowable expense under this policy during such period as
(I) the total allowable expense during such period bears to
(II) the total amount of benefits payable during such period for such ex-

pense under this policy and all other valid coverage (without giving effect to this provision or to any "overinsurance provision" applying to such other valid coverage)

less in both (I) and (II) any amount of benefits for allowable expense payable under other valid coverage which does not contain an "overinsurance provision." In no event shall this provision operate to increase the amount of benefits for allowable expense payable under this policy with respect to a person covered under this policy above the amount which would have been paid in the absence of this provision. This insurer may pay benefits to any insurer providing other valid coverage in the event of overpayment by such insurer. Any such payment shall discharge the liability of this insurer as fully as if the payment had been made directly to the insured, his assignee or his beneficiary. In the event that this insurer pays benefits to the insured, his assignee or his beneficiary, in excess of the amount which would have been payable if the existence of other valid coverage had been disclosed, this insurer shall have a right of action against the insured, his assignee or his beneficiary, to recover the amount which would not have been paid had there been a disclosure of the existence of the other valid coverage. The amount of other valid coverage which is on a provision of service basis shall be computed as the amount the services rendered would have cost in the absence of such coverage.

For purposes of this provision:

(I) "allowable expense" means 110% of any necessary, reasonable and customary item of expense which is covered, in whole or in part, as a hospital, surgical, medical or major medical expense under this policy or under any other valid coverage.

(II) "claim determination period" with respect to any covered person means the initial period of _____ (insert period of not less than thirty days) and each successive period of a like number of days, during which allowable expense covered under this policy is incurred on account of such person. The first such period begins on the date when the first such expense is incurred, and successive periods shall begin when such expense is incurred after expiration of a prior period.

or, in lieu thereof:

"claim determination period" with respect to any covered person means each _____ (insert calendar or policy period of not less than a month) during which allowable expense covered under this policy is incurred on account of such person.

(III) "overinsurance provision" means this provision and any other provision which may reduce an insurer's liability because of the existence of benefits under other valid coverage.

## INSTRUCTIONS

The foregoing policy provision may be inserted in all (guaranteed renewable and noncancellable as well as guaranteed renewable) policies providing hospital, surgical, medical or major medical benefits. The insurer may make this provision applicable to either or both (a) other valid coverage with other insurers and (b) (except for individual policies individually underwritten), other valid coverage with the same insurer. The insurer shall include in this provision a definition of "other valid coverage" approved as to form by the (commissioner). Such term may include hospital, surgical, medical or major medical benefits provided by group, blanket or franchise coverage, individual and family-type coverage, Blue Cross–Blue Shield coverage and other prepayment plans, group practice and individual practice plans, uninsured benefits provided by labor-management trusteed plans, or union welfare plans, or by employer or employee benefit organizations, benefits provided under governmental programs, workmen's compensation insurance or any coverage required or provided by any other statute, and medical payments under automobile liability and personal liability policies. Other valid coverage shall not include payments made under third party liability coverage as a result of a determination of negligence (but an insurer may at its option include a subrogation clause in its policy). The insurer may require, as part of the proof of claim, the information necessary to administer this provision.

The general adoption of these provisions would go far to solve the overinsurance problem and contribute toward solution of the overutilization problem. It seems fair to the insured, since he probably would receive at least full reimbursement for any expense covered by at least one of his contracts. It is to be hoped that the individual policy provision laws will be amended to permit the use of this type of clause.

*Group pressure.* The third approach is used by consumer-sponsored plans and fraternal insurers. Here they count on self-interest as a cooperative member combined with pressure of other members of the group to keep utilization within bounds. Human nature being what it is, the first of these devices is likely to be of little help. Most persons, when faced with a choice between their own interests and those of a group to which they belong, are unlikely to favor the group too highly. The larger the group, the truer this becomes. The same comment, of course, applies to the physician-insurers in other types of plan. The larger the group becomes, the less effective is this feeling of belongingness and the less effective is the social pressure of other group members. For either to operate with any noticeable degree of success, a feeling of identification with the group is necessary. Thus, this technique is of little value to insurance companies or the Blues.

*Physician control.* Despite the partial effectiveness of the above controls the main reliance must be upon the integrity and good judgment of physicians and, to a lesser degree, of hospital administrators. Since these groups represent the ultimate risk bearers in Blue Shield and Blue Cross respectively, they should be motivated to keep claim costs down. However, the conflict of interest between the purveyor's own pocket and that of the plan in which he is a member frequently may be resolved in his own favor. Where the insurer is a third party, the motivation to control costs is still less. Physician control is the approach used in group-practice plans, especially those providing comprehensive coverage. This may explain the lower utilization rates of H.I.P., for example. This approach is most effective when the physicians are themselves the insurers, and the smaller the group of physicians, the more effective it will be. As plans grow larger, the participating physician is likely to feel less directly concerned with the financial operation of the plan. However, some fear that if the relationship is too direct, the temptation to give less-than-adequate care because of financial considerations may be strong.

Regardless of the type of insurer, all physicians should recognize that voluntary health insurance constitutes the prime defense against the "socialized medicine" which they purport to fear so much. It is hoped that the organized profession will undertake to police its own members so that the minority of physicians does not sabotage the private health insurance movement and make government intervention a certainty.

Data are available showing that hospital administrators and physicians, working together, can do much to reduce overutilization and hospital costs. The Insurance Commissioner of Pennsylvania directed the Blue Cross plans and their member hospitals to institute a series of control measures and indicated that approval of future rate increases and hospital reimbursement contracts would be conditioned on compliance with his directive.[62]

Partly as a result of this, the Philadelphia Blue Cross has developed a number of devices to control utilization. One of the most interesting is a complex formula for hospital reimbursement which varies the rate of reimbursement according to the length of stay. The participating hospitals are divided into categories and the rate of reimbursement varies from 200 percent of the base rate for the first day of stay down to 75 percent for all days in excess of the average. No new unaccredited hospitals are allowed to participate, and present unaccredited hospitals are reimbursed at a rate 10 percent below the normal. There has been some conflict with the member hospitals over this, and the American Hospital Association has lent some weight towards a full-cost reimbursement contract. However, the experiment seems to have achieved at least some of its goals and is worthy of study for future use. There also is a physicians' review board which is backed by the county medical

---

[62] *In the matter of the Filing of Capital Hospital Service, Made November 25, 1957, Adjudication of Francis R. Smith, Insurance Commissioner of the Commonwealth of Pennsylvania* (April 15, 1958). There has been similar pressure in New York and Maryland. See Somers and Somers, *op. cit.*, p. 416.

society. Committees review admission and discharge records and attempt to reduce unnecessary utilization.[63]

The American Medical Association has recognized the need for cost controls. For example, the Annual Report of the AMA House of Delegates in 1954 stated:

> Normal premiums in this field are predicated in a large measure on normal amounts of benefits. If either claim frequency or claim cost increases, the net result is an increased premium. . . . Insurance does not create any new wealth. It merely assists in conservation. Insurance may conserve the ability of an insured person to fulfill his normal financial obligations. It does not enhance his ability to discharge added responsibilities in the form of increased fees. To use insurance as an excuse to revise professional fees upward is but to contribute to the defeat of its purpose. If these indisputable and self-evident facts are not embraced by the entire membership of the profession, then it will have dealt irreparable harm to the whole movement. Also, any such failure might give impetus to whatever demand now exists for forcing rigid benefit schedules on the profession.[64]

The Committee on Insurance and Prepayment Plans of the Council on Medical Service of the AMA adopted the following statement in 1958:

1. The individual physician should advise hospitalization only when definitely indicated for the best care of the patient's condition and should return each patient to his home environment as soon as efficient professional care permits.

    Many hospital staffs have found that an Admission Review Committee has assisted materially in assuring a more efficient utilization of hospital facilities.

2. The subscriber should expect hospitalization only when warranted, thereby avoiding the inevitable rise in premium rates resulting from excessive utilization.

3. The insurance company or prepayment plan should clearly delineate, in the policy, the risks assumed. In the selling of these policies the subscriber should receive a complete explanation of the nature and extent of the coverage provided.

    Prepayment plans, insurance companies, and, in the case of group plans, management and union officials should improve educational procedures to inform subscribers of the advantages of health insurance and dangers of increased cost by unnecessary utilization.

    Efforts should be made to revise coverage so that hospitalization is not the sole requisite for obtaining some types of benefits.

---

[63] Somers and Somers, op. cit., pp. 416–20. See also Anne R. Somers and Herman Miles Somers, "Health Insurance: Are Cost and Quality Controls Necessary" (Washington, D.C.: Brookings Institution Reprint No. 45, 1960).

[64] American Medical Association, Council on Medical Services, Voluntary Prepayment Medical Benefit Plans (Chicago, 1965), p. 32.

4. The hospital administrators should accelerate their studies and seek to improve management practices designed to stabilize hospital costs.[65]

Mechanisms for physician control of utilization are being developed rapidly. They include Medical Society Review Committees, hospital tissue committees, and hospital utilization (audit) committees.

Review committees were formally recognized by medical societies in one or more counties (usually the largest) in 28 states by 1966.[66] Some covered a whole state; some only a single county. Many more were operating actively with tacit approval. These committees serve as fact-finding, advisory, and educational media through which insurers, physicians, and patients can communicate regarding the determination of a reasonable, usual, and customary fee and can sometimes consider other questions of proper utilization. While they have no legal, judicial, or disciplinary power, they can serve as a guide to insurers and exert a subtle pressure on physicians.

Tissue committees are found in every reputable hospital. Composed of staff physicians, including pathologists, they regularly review any tissue removed surgically to prevent the removal of healthy tissue. Their power is great since an adverse report could lead to the denial of staff privileges to an offending physician.

Utilization committees review hospital cases as to medical necessity of admission and duration of stay, overuse or underuse of services, and appropriateness of diagnosis. Their goal is maintenance of high-quality patient care and effective utilization of hospital services to be achieved by an educational approach involving study of patterns of care and encouragement of appropriate utilization.

Such committees, made up of hospital staff physicians, or medical society approved, are required for all hospitals and extended care facilities participating in the Title XVIII Medicare program. It is hoped and expected that these committees will review the utilization by patients under age 65 as well. Blue Cross plans and insurance companies acting as Part A carriers will be able to work through such committees in controlling utilization.

*Control through group practice.* The present administration is moving strongly to encourage the development of multiple specialty group practice plans which can provide coordinated comprehensive medical care in clinics and assume the responsibility for family care. Mainly, the goal is the practice of better medicine and a more effective utilization of health facilities. In particular, it is felt that the fees for in-office

---

[65] American Medical Association, Council on Medical Services, *Voluntary Prepayment Medical Benefit Plans* (Chicago, 1965), p. 33.

[66] Health Insurance Council, *Revised Manual of Currently Active Review Committees in the United States* (New York, 1966).

diagnosis, treatment, and preventive efforts and out-of-hospital diagnostic laboratory expenses act as a deterrent to utilization of out-of-hospital facilities and an encouragement of unnecessary hospital admissions. Such expenses are not covered in about four fifths of basic medical contracts, and major medical contracts are not much help because of their high deductibles. Most group practice clinics operate on a fee-for-service basis, and presently available insurance contracts cover their services for diagnosis and treatment. However, few outstanding contracts cover preventive efforts, and most insureds do not have comprehensive coverage.

The Department of Health, Education, and Welfare seems particularly interested in *prepaid* group practice plans which tend to offer comprehensive benefits, including preventive efforts. The Secretary convened a National Conference on Group Practice on October 19–21, 1967, to "find ways to stimulate the group practice of medicine, based on either prepayment or fee-for-service. (How to promote, not whether.)"[67] Its recommendations pertinent to health insurance are as follows:[68]

> Existing prepayment and financing plans can make the following contributions to group practice development:
> 1. Permit a choice of group practice or solo medicine when plans are established with employee-employer groups;
> 2. Promote carrier marketing and administration of both solo and group practice plans;
> 3. Promote a tie between large-scale prepayment plans and group practice through capitation.
>
> Such activities could conceivably increase group prepayment subscribers six-fold; the resultant 24 million subscribers would provide funds for the clinic, and for hospital expansion and development.
>
> Specific, imaginative suggestions given were these:
> 1. The provision of Federal subsidy for major prepayment group practice plans to allow expansion of facilities and services;
> 2. Training of personnel specifically for use in developing new plans;
> 3. Provision of required capital and operating funds for the creation of new plans;
> 4. Encouragement of major insurance companies to include provision of loans for group practice expansion and development;
> 5. Use of the OEO neighborhood health center concept as a method for expanding group practice, integrated where feasible with existing or new community group practice plans;
> 6. Further use of the retainer mechanism (e.g., nonfee and noncapitation payment) to encourage simplification of payment, and to permit

---

[67] *Promoting the Group Practice of Medicine, op. cit.,* pp. 1–2.

[68] *Ibid.,* pp. 58–59.

flexible, medically acceptable cost reimbursement for the establishment and development of groups;

7. The combination of title 18 and 19 payments, on a capitation basis,
for Medicare beneficiaries who elect to use hospital-based physicians
organized as a group practice;

8. Giving to Blue Cross, Blue Shield and commercial insurance subscribers three choices among plans offering indemnification, capitation,
and intermediate retainer payment so that groups may be developed
under each method.

Group practice prepayment plans are not generally available throughout the country and their growth has slowed in recent years as the
insurance companies, Blue Cross, and Blue Shield have taken larger
shares of the market. Of the 10 largest plans, only 2 have been formed
since 1947.[69]

In 1967 and 1968 exploration of group practice potentialities became
intense. Harvard and Yale medical schools contacted the insurance industry about hospital-based comprehensive plans. Health Insurance Plan
of Greater New York explored dual-choice arrangements; the Public
Health Service planned research on why (whether?) group practice
subscribers use less hospital care, and the H.I.A.A. appointed a series of
committees to study legal, administrative, actuarial, and marketing aspects
of group practice.

Insurers can work with fee-for-service group practice plans simply
by broadening existing types of coverage to include office visits, out-of-
hospital diagnosis, physical examinations, and immunizations. All these
benefits are presently available, but employers and unions must be sold
on their desirability. Some labor unions are already quite interested.

Working with *prepayment* group practice plans seems more difficult,
but several alternatives are available:

1. Dual-choice plans where the worker has the choice of insurance
company coverage or group practice prepayment.

2. Split plans involving insurance company coverage of hospital care
and prepayment group practice for medical care.

3. For all care or for part as in 1 and 2, insurance companies could
handle marketing, finance, administration, premium collection, etc., while
the group practice plan bore the risk.

4. Insurers could share in risk bearing, perhaps bearing the risk of random fluctuations in illness levels while the prepayment plan bears the
risk of faulty utilization. Perhaps this could be accomplished by reinsurance.

5. Insurers could "contract out" certain classes of insureds to group
practice plans on a capitation, retainer, or other financial basis.

[69] Joseph F. Follmann, Jr., "Insurance Companies and the Group Practice of
Medicine," H.I.A.A. *Medical Economics Bulletin* No. 4–67, p. 17.

6. Insurers could provide mortgage money for organizations building group practice clinics.

7. Insurers could provide a financing mechanism for prepayment group practice subscribers who need care outside the geographic area of the plan.

8. Insurance companies themselves could establish group practice clinics, hospitals, and other facilities, and hire the physicians to staff them. They have been doing this with funeral homes for almost a century and they certainly have the money to invest. The American Medical Association would object to this as its ancient anathema, the corporate practice of medicine, but if demonstrably better health care resulted the objection could not be sustained. Perhaps the initial experiments would be more readily acceptable if a nonprofit foundation were used.

The relationships between insurance companies and prepaid group practice that will evolve in the future remain conjectural in the spring of 1968.

*Control by planning.* For the last decade or so, Area Hospital Planning Councils have developed in various areas and have been instrumental in preventing the unnecessary expansion of hospital bed supply. Their success led to the passage, in 1966, of P.L. 89–749, the "Comprehensive Health Planning and Public Health Amendments of 1966." It provides block grants to the states for community health services in conformity with plans developed by a State Health Planning Agency advised by a State Health Planning Council, a majority of whose members are representatives of consumers. The grants may be used to develop the State Health Planning Agency and area planning agencies and for training, studies, and demonstration and development programs by governmental and nonprofit agencies.

The health insurance industry, through the H.I.A.A., actively supported the concept of state- and area-wide comprehensive health planning. The H.I.A.A., through the Health Insurance Council, instituted a public service program known as the Health Insurance Council Community Health Action Planning Program, or HiCHAP for short.[70] Experienced insurance company personnel are to be made available to participate in comprehensive community health planning. Information will be exchanged and disseminated. An insurance company executive was selected for each state, the District of Columbia, and Puerto Rico as state coordinator to act as a control point for making insurance company personnel available.

*Control by government?* Through its grants-in-aid and the strings

---

[70] *Health Insurance Viewpoints,* August, 1967. One wonders, why not HICCHAPP?

attached to them, and more recently through Medicare, the government is exerting an increasing degree of control over the utilization and financing of health services. The conditions of participation for Medicare Part A have forced hospitals to revise accounting and billing procedures, establish utilization committees, integrate racially, and make many other changes.

States administering public assistance programs have published maximum fee schedules. For example, the New York schedule is based on the New York relative value schedule (which is based on the California relative value schedule), with unit fees of $5 for medical services and $4 for surgical. This produces fees which seem to be less than those prevailing in north Florida. One wonders how this is compatible with "free choice of physician" and bringing the poor into the "mainstream of modern medicine."

In President Johnson's 1968 message on health in America, he stated that, since the federal government pays $14 to $16 billion for health expenditures, he was directing the Secretary of Health, Education, and Welfare to submit a "modern plan of organization to achieve the most effective and economical operation of the health program of the federal government." A frightening portent of the direction such a "plan of organization" might take is a 1968 report of an H.E.W. Advisory Committee on Hospital Effectiveness. It recommended that every health service institution be included in the jurisdiction of an areawide health service planning agency; prepare an institutional service plan for the areawide agency, to be updated annually; prepare annually a detailed budget and plan for operations with the medical staff participating and Board of Trustees approving. It recommended that each area planning agency publish an areawide plan and guidelines for determining needs for health services and facilities; that each state health department have a single agency for licensing and regulation of all health care institutions; that the state require prior approval of any significant change in the physical facilities of such institution under a plan approved by the Secretary of Health, Education, and Welfare, which provides for a state health facilities advisory council representing professional and community interests to review such changes; and that both the council and the licensing agency be required to consider the advice and recommendations of the areawide planning agency. It also recommended that each state have an agency for collecting data on the operations of health care institutions and that H.E.W. develop a national standardized administrative reporting system for such data.

The committee's blatant disregard for state's rights, private enterprise, and freedom of choice in its recommendations pertinent to health insurance is so startling that they are reproduced in full:

8. *Recommendation*

Effective at as early a date as the Congress shall find feasible, all federal financing for health facilities and services shall be authorized for health care institutions only in states whose appropriate regulatory agencies governing health service prepayment and health insurance require:

   (a) Non-cancelability of all health prepayment and insurance policies, group and individual, so that each prepaid or insured person or family has the option to maintain the prepayment benefit or insurance policy in force by continued payment either through a group or on an individual basis; however, group practice prepayment plans shall have an option of obtaining for the insured the guaranteed purchase from another carrier of an available policy, reasonably comparable as to benefits and premiums, and

   (b) Reasonable and controlled limits on all carrier retentions, consonant in each case with the type of carrier and the content of the prepayment benefit or insurance policy.

9. *Recommendation*

The Secretary of Health, Education, and Welfare shall establish a commission or committee to work out and recommend a procedure and timetable for requiring by either state or federal law a minimum range of benefits for health prepayment plans and insurance policies including hospital inpatient services, outpatient ambulatory services, extended care services, home care programs, and physicians' services in and out of hospitals. The committee recommends a plan which moves in the direction of requiring that all health insurance shall provide the full range of benefits enumerated above.

In the words of Otto[71] this is a strange way to amend the Constitution of the United States. It is regrettable that this report was not buried somewhere in the National Archives. The report also recommended that a system of federally insured borrowing for capital purposes by health care institutions be established and that reimbursement to all hospitals and other institutions having third party service contracts be based on rates negotiated and agreed to annually.

*Importance.* If overutilization is not controlled, it could bring about the destruction of the voluntary health insurance industry. Pressure on claim costs is constantly upward due to the inflation in medical care costs and the increasing complexity of medical care and the equipment with which it is provided. If overutilization causes further claim costs increases, the combined effect could raise health insurance premiums out of reach of large segments of the market.

Voluntary health insurance was developed primarily to meet the needs of the lower and middle income groups. It is these very groups

---

[71] Ingolf H. E. Otto, "National Insurance Companies and the O'Mahoney Investigation," *CPCU Annals,* Vol. 12, p. 9, at p. 30 (in a somewhat different context).

who are beginning to find premiums an undue burden. If, due to failure to control utilization, the industry fails to meet the needs of these groups, the pressure for further government intervention may become irresistible.

The primary reliance for control of utilization must rest with the physicians. Only trained practitioners can decide accurately what care is necessary and reasonable. Insurers also may contribute materially by working with physicians to establish standards and fees on a basis of voluntary cooperation and by avoiding policy provisions which encourage unnecessary care and duplication of benefits. Yet the primary responsibility must remain with the medical profession. It is hoped that a growing understanding of the nature and importance of health insurance will lead to joint efforts on the part of all parties concerned to control utilization. American ingenuity should be sufficient to preserve the voluntary health insurance movement from destruction at the hands of the dishonest, careless, and morally weak minority.

## Expansion of social insurance

The ink was hardly dry on the Social Security amendments of 1965 when proposals for further expansion of this health care program were heard. Hundreds of bills to that effect were introduced in the 90th Congress, but the only one to receive serious consideration was the President's proposals for the revision of the Social Security system, H.R. 5710. This would have extended the coverage of Title XVIII Medicare benefits to the disabled including children receiving benefits because of disability incurred before age 18 and disabled widows (regardless of age). The house bill, H.R. 12080, eliminated this provision in favor of a study of the health and insurance needs of the disabled.[72] Both the administration and Congress felt that more experience should be gained with the present Title XVIII Medicare system before any substantial change was considered so none was requested by the administration nor seriously considered by either house. This attitude is refreshing.

Several states have considered a bill to make group medical expense insurance compulsory. Legislation to this effect was introduced in New York in 1967, partly motivated by the fear that employers would drop their group insurance programs and rely on New York's generous Title XIX program, the cost of which was already becoming burdensome. It failed to pass and was reintroduced in 1968. The 1968 version of the bill required all employers to provide employees and dependents insurance coverage for 120 days of hospital care, 100 days of home care, and hospital out-patient diagnostic services and care for emergency illness or accidental injury. Insurers would be exempt from premium tax for these

---

[72] See Chapter 4 above for a description of these benefits.

basic benefits, and the state would bear any cost in excess of 4 percent of payroll. The bill never reached the floor of either house and the legislature adjourned May 25, 1968. A New York bill to require hospital insurance for Title XIX participants also died at this time. A similar bill providing for hospital and surgical benefits was considered by the Hawaii legislature in 1967 and was referred to the Legislative Reference Bureau for a study as to the need for it.

It is to be hoped that the continued growth of voluntary private insurance soon will make such legislation clearly unnecessary.

**Summary**

Major problems and issues in medical expense insurance include adjusting to Medicare, the competition between insurer types, the problem of extending coverage to more of the population, the problem of controlling excessive utilization, and threats of further market loss to social insurance.

The alleged unique characteristics of the Blues are their community sponsorship, the use of service-type benefits, nonprofit operation, and the coverage of first-dollar costs. The first is becoming as much of a hindrance as a help in some areas, and the second has been abandoned by many plans in the face of increased utilization. The nonprofit feature remains an important competitive advantage, on the average, but, by more accurate rating techniques, insurance companies are competing effectively, especially for the better groups. Blue Cross plans are experimenting with deductibles to control excessive utilization, and it is possible that such provisions may eventually become common. Thus it appears as though the traditional areas of difference between insurer types are disappearing in the face of competition, growth, and increasing utilization. Each major type of insurer seems to be learning from the other, and they seem to become more similar as time goes by. Competition has been an important factor in promoting progress and should continue to be in the future.

Further coverage of the population can be expected in the normal course of events, but the aged and other low-income or no-income groups present special problems whose solutions require major changes in traditional methods. Many of these changes have taken place, and continued experimentation with new techniques should result in broad coverage of the aged population in few more years. It is hoped that political pressure does not result in the government further preempting an area which private enterprise is quite capable of serving adequately and where tremendous progress has been made in a very few years.

Policy provisions such as deductibles, upper limits, and co-insurance may be effective in controlling excessive utilization. It seems probable that the evident advantage of such provisions, especially the deductible, will become more appreciated and that the emphasis on first-dollar coverage will decline. Control of utilization, however, will remain primarily the responsibility of the medical profession and of hospital administrations. Failure to achieve such control could result in pricing voluntary insurance out of the market and opening the door to government intervention. The private physicians and hospitals should be as strongly interested as are private insurers in preventing such an eventuality.

## Selected references

*See the following items from the General Bibliography: 6; 9, chs. 31, 32, and 36; 10, ch. 17; 11, chs. 6–9; 16, Vol. II; 29, ch. 11.*

AMERICAN MEDICAL ASSOCIATION. "Report of Committee on Medical Care." Commission on the Cost of Medical Care, 1962. Mimeographed.

———. *The Cost of Medical Care,* Vols. I, II, & III. 1964.

ANDERSON, ODIN W. *Comprehensive Medical Insurance.* A study of cost, use, and attitudes under two plans. Health Information Foundation, Research Series 9, 1959.

ANDERSEN, RONALD, AND REIDEL, DONALD C. *People and Their Hospital Insurance.* Chicago: University of Chicago, Center for Health Administration Studies, 1967.

AVNET, HELEN HERSHFIELD. *Physician Service Patterns and Illness Rates.* New York: Group Health Insurance, Inc., 1967.

BABCOCK, KENNETH B. "The Excessive Use of Blue Cross Benefits," *Journal of the American Hospital Association,* July, 1952, p. 49.

BLUE CROSS ASSOCIATION. *Blue Cross Guide.* Chicago, 1967.

———. "Hospital Cost Trends," *Blue Cross Reports,* Vol. V, No. 2 (May–June, 1967).

———. "An Analysis of the Components of Rising Hospital Costs," *Blue Cross Reports,* Vol. V, No. 3 (August–September, 1967).

———. *Year-End Medicare Statements by Health and Government Leaders,* Blue Cross Association Public Relations Bulletin #53, August 10, 1967.

BLUMENFELD, M. EUGENE. "Recent Trends and Innovations in Individual Hospital Insurance," *Proceedings of the Casualty Actuarial Society,* Vol. 48, p. 83.

BRADY, DOROTHY S. *Age and the Income Distribution.* Washington, D.C.: U.S. Government Printing Office, 1965.

BROWN, RAY E. "The Purchase of Health Care—Payments, Controls, and Quality," National Conference on Medical Costs, June 27–28, 1967.

BURKHARDT, LUKAS F. "Das Problem des erhöten Krankheitrisikos der alten Leute in der amerikanischen Sozialversicherung," *Schweizerische Zeitschift für Sozialversicherung,* Vol. 4 (1960).

CANNELLA, SALVATORE. "Variation de la Prime d'Assurance de l'Assistance Pharmaceutique en Fonction de la Participation de l'assure au Coût de l'Assistance," *The ASTIN Bulletin,* January, 1962, p. 30.

CATHLES, L. M. "Big Government and Insurance," H.I.A.A. Group Forum, February 15, 1966.

CHAMBER OF COMMERCE OF THE UNITED STATES. *Poverty: The Sick, Disabled, and Aged.* Washington, D.C.; 1965.

CODY, DONALD D. "Effective Claims Handling—The Major Tool for Progress," H.I.A.A. Group Insurance Forum, 1965.

COHEN, WILBUR J. "Health Insurance and the Government," *Journal of Insurance,* Vol. XXIX, p. 1.

———, AND BALL, ROBERT M. "Social Security Amendments of 1965; Summary and Legislative History," *Social Security Bulletin,* Vol. 28, No. 9 (September, 1965), p. 3.

COOK, FRED J. *The Plot against the Patient.* Englewood Cliffs, N.J.: Prentice-Hall, Inc., 1967.

CRUTHERS, MICHAEL. "The Trouble with Overinsurance," *Medical Economics,* March 8, 1965.

DICKERSON, O. D. "Potential Innovations in Health Insurance," *Journal of Insurance,* Vol. XXVII, p. 7.

———. "Changing Concepts of Health Care Financing," *CLU Journal,* Spring, 1965, p. 170.

———. "Editors Note," *CPCU Annals,* Summer, 1962, p. 98.

———. "The 1965 Social Security Amendments and Private Insurance," *CPCU Annals,* Fall, 1966, p. 227.

EILERS, ROBERT D. *Regulation of Blue Cross and Blue Shield Plans.* Homewood, Ill.: Richard D. Irwin, Inc., 1963.

FARQUHAR, GORDON N. "Major Medical for the Aged—The Connecticut Story," *CLU Journal,* Spring, 1962, p. 174.

FEIGHT, JAMES J. "Blue Cross and the Community Health Problem," *Journal of Insurance,* Vol. XXVII, p. 17.

FLECH, WILLIAM C. "Challenge—The Cornerstone of Progress (Panel Discussion)," H.I.A.A. Group Insurance Forum, 1967.

———. "Costs of Physicians Services," H.I.A.A. Individual Insurance Forum, 1967.

FOLLMANN, JOSEPH F., JR. *Health Insurance and the Effectiveness of Health Care.* H.I.A.A., 1967.

———. *Private Health Insurance, 1967.* H.I.A.A., September, 1967.

———. "The Consumer Interest in Quality Health Care," *Pension and Welfare News,* October, 1967.

———. *The Role of Insurance Companies in Financing Hospital Care.* New York: Health Insurance Council, 1967.

FOODY, WALTER M., JR., AND KLAASSEN, ELDON J. "Financing Medical Care for the Aged," *Journal of Insurance,* June, 1962, p. 221.

GERDES, VICTOR. "Social Security and Family Income Requirements," *Journal of Risk and Insurance*, June, 1966, p. 225.

GOODENOUGH, BENTON H. "Toward More Efficient Systems," National Conference on Medical Costs, June 27–28, 1967.

HALL, CHARLES P., JR. "Deductibles in Health Insurance, An Evaluation," *Journal of Risk and Insurance*, June, 1966, p. 253.

HARMELIN, WILLIAM. "Overinsurance Safeguards," *Life Association News*, June, 1965.

HARRIS, SEYMOUR E. *The Economics of American Medicine*. New York: Macmillan Company, 1964.

HEALTH INSURANCE ASSOCIATION OF AMERICA. "Conserving the Health Insurance Dollar," H.I.A.A. Group Insurance Forum, 1965.

————. *Status Report on Overinsurance* (1960); Second . . . (1960); Third . . . (1961); Fourth . . . (1962); Fifth . . . (1962); Sixth . . . (1963); Seventh . . . (1963).

————. *Medical Economics Bulletin*. No. 1–67, "National Conference on Medical Costs"; No. 2–67, "National Conference on Private Health Insurance"; No. 3–67, "National Conference on Group Practice"; No. 4–67, "Insurance Companies and the Prepaid Group Practice of Medicine"; No. 1–68, "National Conference on Health Care for the Poor"; No. 3–68, "Insurance Companies and the Prepaid Group Practice of Medicine"; No. 4–68, "Association Report to Acting Secretary of Health, Education, and Welfare"; No. 5–68, "Health, Education, and Welfare Committee on Hospital Effectiveness."

*Health Insurance Bulletins*. "Why Hospitals Cost So Much." General Information Ho–5.

HEALTH INSURANCE COUNCIL. *Health Insurance Viewpoints*, Vol. VIII, No. 1 (August, 1967).

————. *Revised Manual of Currently Active Review Committees in the United States*. New York, July, 1966.

HEALTH INSURANCE INSTITUTE. *Guaranteed Lifetime Insurance: For Persons over 65; For Persons under 65*. New York, July 1, 1963.

HESS, ARTHUR E. "Medicare after One Year," *Journal of Risk and Insurance*, March, 1968, p. 119.

HILL, JOHN A. *The Role of Insurance Industry in Community Health Planning*. Health Insurance Council, May, 1967.

INSTITUTE OF LIFE INSURANCE. *Private and Public Pension Plans in the United States*. New York, March, 1967.

JENKINS, SUSAN S. "Medicare and Group Health Insurance (Panel Discussion)," H.I.A.A. Group Insurance Forum, 1966.

KELLEY, BURTON E. "Opportunities for Development," H.I.A.A. Group Insurance Forum, 1965.

LAMPMAN, ROBERT J., AND MIYAMOTO, S. F. "Effects of Extended Coverage in a Physician-Sponsored Health Insurance Plan," *Journal of Insurance*, Vol. XXVIII, p. 1.

LANZA, WILLIAM. "Aspects of Overinsurance against Hospital, Surgical and Medical Expense," *Inspection News*, March, 1965.

LEVINE, SOL; ANDERSON, ODIN W.; AND GORDON, GERALD. *Non-Group Enroll-ment for Health Insurance.* Cambridge, Mass.: Harvard University Press, 1957.

MacCOLL, WILLIAM A. *Group Practice and Prepayment of Medical Care.* Washington, D.C.: Public Affairs Press, 1966.

MacDONALD, DONALD L. "Blue Cross Troubles: A Price of Delusion," *Weekly Underwriter,* November 16, 1956, p. 1134.

MacINTYRE, DUNCAN M. *Voluntary Health Insurance and Ratemaking.* Ithaca, N.Y.: Cornell University Press, 1962.

MAGRAW, RICHARD M. "The Purchase of Health Care—Payments, Controls, and Quality," National Conference on Medical Costs, June 27–28, 1967.

McLEAN, GEORGE E. "An Actuarial Analysis of a Prospective Experience Rating Approach for Group Hospital-Surgical-Medical Coverage," *Proceedings of the Casualty Actuarial Society,* Vol. 48, p. 155.

McNERNEY, WALTER J. "The Role of Prepayment in Achieving Effective Health Services," National Conference on Medical Costs, June 27–28, 1967.

*Medical Economics.* "Fees vs. Time: Hospital and Home Visits," January 24, 1966, p. 94.

MORGAN, J. N.; MARTIN, H. D.; COHEN, W. J.; AND BRAYER, H. E. *Income and Welfare in the United States.* New York: McGraw-Hill Book Co., Inc., 1962.

NATIONAL ASSOCIATION OF BLUE SHIELD PLANS. "Term 1966 'Significant Year' for Blue Shield," *The Blue Shield,* Vol. 3, No. 1 (January 1, 1967).

NATIONAL COMMISSION ON COMMUNITY HEALTH SERVICES. *Health Is a Community Affair.* Cambridge, Mass.: Harvard University Press, 1966.

NEW YORK (STATE) DEPARTMENT OF WELFARE AND OTHER STATE DEPART-MENTS. *Medical Fee Schedule.* H.I.A.A. Title XIX Bulletin 5–66, October 28, 1966.

OWEN, JOCK W. "Hospital Costs—Symptoms or Causes," H.I.A.A. Individual Insurance Forum, 1967.

PETTENGILL, DANIEL W. "Keeping in Tune with the Times: The New Climate for Private Health Insurance," H.I.A.A. Group Insurance Forum, 1968.

PLAISTED, HARRIS M. "Health Insurance and the 'Law of Effect,'" *CLU Journal,* Vol. XVII, No. 3 (Summer, 1963), p. 271.

REED, LOUIS S. *Blue Cross-Blue Shield: Nongroup Coverage for Older People.* Washington, D.C.: U.S. Government Printing Office, 1963.

———. *Financial Experience of Health Insurance Organizations in the United States.* Washington, D.C.: U.S. Government Printing Office, 1966.

———, AND MYERS, KATHLEEN. "Health Insurance Coverage Complementary to Medicare," *Social Security Bulletin,* August, 1967, p. 3.

———. *et al. Independent Health Insurance Plans in the United States.* Washington, D.C.: U.S. Government Printing Office, 1966.

SHANAS, ETHEL. *The Health of Older People: A Social Survey.* Cambridge: Harvard University Press, 1962.

SHINN, RICHARD R. "Adjustment to Medicare by Group Health Plans," H.I.A.A. Group Insurance Forum, 1965.

————. "The Impact of Federal Legislation on Private Health Insurance," H.I.A.A. Group Insurance Forum, 1967.

SOLENBERGER, WILLARD E. "Opportunities for Development (Panel Discussion)," H.I.A.A. Group Insurance Forum, 1965.

SOLOMON, E. RAY. "Overinsurance—Its Control through Contractual Provisions," *CPCU Annals*, Fall, 1966, p. 197.

SPECIAL COMMITTEE ON AGING OF THE U.S. SENATE. *Basic Facts on the Health and Economic Status of Older Americans.* Washington, D.C.: U.S. Government Printing Office, 1961.

SPIEGELMAN, MORTIMER. *Ensuring Medical Care for the Aged.* Pension Research Council, Homewood, Ill.: Richard D. Irwin, Inc., 1960.

TROSPER, JOSEPH F. "Overinsurance—Its Meaning," *Journal of Risk and Insurance*, December, 1964.

TRUSSELL, RAY E. *Prepayment for Hospital Care in New York State: A Report on the Eight Blue Cross Plans Serving New York Residents.* School of Public Health and Administrative Medicine, Columbia University, 1960.

————, AND VAN DYKE, FRANK. *Prepayment for Medical and Dental Care in New York State.* New York: Columbia University, 1962.

U.S. DEPARTMENT OF HEALTH, EDUCATION, AND WELFARE. *Medical Prices.* Washington, D.C.: U.S. Government Printing Office, February, 1967.

————, Public Health Service. *Age Patterns in Medical Care, Illness, and Disability.* Washington, D.C.: U.S. Government Printing Office, 1966.

————, Public Health Service. *The Dental Service Corporation.* Washington, D.C.: U.S. Government Printing Office, 1962.

————, Public Health Service. *Hospital Utilization Studies: Selected References Annotated.* Washington, D.C.: U.S. Government Printing Office, 1962.

————, Public Health Service, Division of Medical Care Administration. *Promoting the Group Practice of Medicine.* Washington, D.C.: U.S. Government Printing Office, 1967.

————, Social Security Administration, Office of Research and Statistics. *The Aged Population of the United States.* Washington, D.C.: U.S. Government Printing Office, 1963.

————, Social Security Administration. *Conditions of Participation for Extended Care Facilities.* Washington, D.C.: U.S. Government Printing Office, 1966.

————, Social Security Administration. *Federal Health Insurance for the Aged: Conditions of Participation—Hospitals.* Washington, D.C.: U.S. Government Printing Office, 1967.

————, Social Security Administration, Office of Research and Statistics. *Private Health Insurance and Medical Care.* Washington, D.C.: U.S. Government Printing Office, 1968.

WANDEL, WILLIAM H. "Overinsurance in Health Insurance," *Journal of Risk and Insurance*, Vol. XXXII, No. 3 (September, 1965), p. 427.

WEEKS, DAVID A. "The Effect of Medicare on Retiree Health Insurance," *The Conference Board Record*, January, 1967, p. 13.

WILLIAMS, FOSTER H. "Blue Cross Preferential Treatment," H.I.A.A. Group Forum, February 15, 1966.

# PART III

# Income Coverages

... to this vast residuum we may with great propriety give the name.—Matthew Arnold, *Culture and Anarchy*

# Commercial Contracts

## Introduction

At the end of 1966 about 54 million workers had some form of disability income protection through voluntary health insurance. This includes about 14 million persons who were covered by paid sick leave or salary continuance plans. These plans represent self-insurance by the employer or the union or welfare fund and will not be discussed further here. About 41 million persons were protected by insurance company plans: 29 million under group contracts and 16 million under individual policies.[1] In medical expense insurance, there is not much difference between the benefits of group and individual insurance. On the other hand, this difference is substantial for the disability income contracts and there are further differences by type of contract classified as to scope of benefits, renewability, and marketing methods. Thus disability income contracts are discussed here separately under the headings of commercial, noncancellable, life insurance riders, limited, industrial, and group. Among the individual contracts, the largest number are written on a commercial basis, but a growing proportion are noncancellable or guaranteed renewable.

The name "commercial" derives not from the type of company writing such contracts nor from the importance of this type of policy but from the nature of the persons to whom such contracts were originally offered. Commercial policies provide more liberal benefits and are issued for higher and less frequent premiums than industrial policies. They originally were intended for the white-collar occupations, while industrial policies

---

[1] Since some people have more than one form of protection, these figures do not add to the total above. Usually the salary continuance plans and the group coverages provide relatively short-term disability income benefits, but long-term group is growing rapidly.

were intended for the occupations involving physical hazard. This distinction is the source of the name.

In health insurance "commercial" means the same thing that "ordinary" means in life insurance—the class of policies which make up the bulk of the business. The term can best be described by indicating what it does not include. It excludes limited and industrial policies, which offer narrower benefits; group insurance, which has a different marketing basis; and guaranteed renewable and noncancellable, which confer one or more important additional rights on the insured. The term is applied only to policies issued by insurance companies.

There has been some objection to the use of the term. Many non-insurance-oriented authors use the term "commercial insurance" to refer to insurance companies as distinguished from the Blues and the independents. Thus there is room for possible misunderstanding where the same word is used in two senses by different writers. However, there is no need for this. It is quite possible to use the term "insurance company" when one means insurance company, and this simple arrangement has much to recommend it.

Others have objected to the usage, in either of the above senses, as being poor public relations in implying a money-making or profit-making connotation. This implication is not valid, since the term derived from an underwriting classification. Moreover, to the extent that insurers do make profits (in the usual sense, mutuals do not and many stock companies suffer losses at times) this is nothing to be ashamed of. Profit making is the main motivating force in a private enterprise economy and should be encouraged, not belittled. At any rate, the term "commercial" has a long history in the business and will have to serve until there is agreement on a better substitute. The life insurance term "ordinary," itself also used in another sense, does not seem to offer an alternative. The term "optionally renewable" is unclear, "renewable with consent of company" is awkward, and "cancellable" is not a happy term.

### Development

Commercial health insurance is the second oldest type of coverage in the health insurance business. Although the first policies issued were of the limited variety, covering travel accidents only, policies covering all types of accident were authorized in England by 1852 and in the United States by 1864. The early policies covered accidental death and total disability only. One such policy provided $2,000 of accidental death benefit and total disability protection of $10 per week for 26 weeks at an annual premium of $10. This premium rate is still the basis of rates for some commercial accident insurance.

From 1865 to 1890, policies became more and more restrictive as the insurance companies attempted to limit their liability and the insureds, with the frequent backing of the courts, to extend it. Many early insurers failed, including all companies underwriting the sickness peril, and today there is only one survivor of the period prior to 1870. Coverage of sickness during this period was provided by fraternal and assessment associations and was not written by insurance companies until 1898.

From about 1890 to 1930 the business developed rapidly. Policies were liberalized to include lifetime disability income benefits, partial disability benefits, specific dismemberment clauses, and a variety of miscellaneous provisions, including the pioneer medical care expense benefits. Restrictions and exclusions became less frequent, the sickness coverage became more important, and claims administration became more liberal. Parallel growth occurred in the development of new types of policy; noncancellable, group, and the life insurance disability clauses became important phases of the health insurance business.

From 1930 until about 1940 there was a period of retrenchment resulting from the impact of the Great Depression. Many companies suffered severe losses, especially on sickness claims under contracts with long benefit periods. The impact on the noncancellable forms and the life insurance disability riders was particularly severe. Many companies ceased writing sickness coverage entirely. Others reduced amounts and benefit periods, tightened up on underwriting and claims procedure, and raised premiums. Tendencies toward fewer and more uniform contracts, simpler occupational classifications, and more accurate rate making were evident.

Since about 1940 there has been another period of rapid growth and development. Group insurance has grown at a tremendous rate, and the various medical care coverages have developed from a minor sideline into the mainstay of the business. Benefits have again been liberalized in amount and duration, and policies made more simple and less restrictive. The entry of many large life insurance companies into the business has had a beneficial effect since they have emphasized simple policy forms and liberal coverage and sounder underwriting. Many companies today use the same policy form for commercial policies as for noncancellable and guaranteed renewable, except for the cancellation and renewal provisions. Others write commercial only. This analysis deals with the pure commercial forms.

## Benefit provisions

*Insuring clause.* It once was common in commercial contracts to have separate policies for accident benefits and sickness benefits or, where both were covered, to have separate insuring clauses. The modern tendency is to have one insuring clause for both accident and sickness benefits. The insuring clause identifies the covered person or persons and establishes the necessary description of the event(s) insured against. The requirement that injury result from "accidental means" usually has been dropped from modern policies. Commercial policies sometimes provide protection against accidental injury in one contract and against sickness in another contract, rather than in a single contract. Even where coverage of both is combined in one contract, there may be separate benefit clauses.

A typical accident insuring clause uses the phrase "accidental bodily injury" instead of the traditional "accidental means" clause and reads as follows:

The ———— Company does hereby insure *John R. Doe,* against loss, as indicated in the Schedule of Coverages, resulting directly and independently of all other causes from Accidental Bodily Injuries sustained during the term of this Policy, subject to all the provisions, conditions, limitations and exclusions herein contained.

There is no definition of accidental bodily injuries in this policy, nor is there a definition of sickness in the companion policy,[2] whose insuring clause reads as follows:

The Company does hereby insure *John R. Doe* against loss, as indicated in the Schedule of Coverages, resulting from sickness contracted and causing loss commencing after the first fourteen days from the date of this Policy but while this Policy is in force, subject to all the provisions, conditions, limitations and exclusions herein contained.

There is provision for a 14-day probationary period. It is common to have a probationary period such as 14 or 15 days in sickness policies but rare in accident contracts.

A description of policy term and the usual consideration clause follows. Most modern policies provide for a choice of coverages from a schedule of benefits.

The insuring clause and schedule of a contract covering both accident and sickness is reproduced below.

*The _____ Company Hereby Insures*
the person named in the Schedule below against certain losses specified in this policy that results from accidental bodily injuries sustained, or sickness contracted, while this policy is in force. The losses insured against include (i) total disability, in accordance with Benefit Provisions 1 and 2, (ii) partial disability in accordance with Benefit Provision 1, and (iii) loss, in accordance with Benefit Provision 3, of life, limbs, or sight, that results from accidental bodily injuries. This insurance is subject to the reductions, exclusions, and all other provisions on this and the following pages.

---

[2] The meaning of these terms is rather well established by legal decisions over the years and it has been said that attempted definition in the contract could lead only to ambiguity or to restricted coverage.

SCHEDULE

| Policy Number | 67309AH | Name of Insured | John Doe |
|---|---|---|---|
| Date of Issue | August 1, 1968 | Monthly Income Benefit for Total Disability | $433.33 |
| Maximum Period of Monthly Income Benefit for Injury | Lifetime | Maximum Period of Monthly Income Benefit for Sickness (but See Monthly Income Benefit, Part C) | 2 Years |
| Elimination Period for Injury | none Days | Elimination Period for Sickness | 7 Days |
| Principal Sum | 5,000 | Premium | 189.25 payable every 12 month(s) |

*Disability income benefits.* The heart of any disability income contract is the benefit clause providing income for periods of total disability.

*Total disability.* Total disability is defined as follows in a disability income contract which covers both accidental injury and disease:

(a) For the purpose of determining the commencement of total disability and thereafter for the first 24 months that the Monthly Income Benefit may be payable during any continuous period of such disability, total disability means only such complete incapacity of the Insured that he is able to perform none of the duties of his occupation, business or employment, and

(b) for the remainder of any such period of continuous disability, total disability means only such complete incapacity of the Insured that he is able to perform none of the duties of any occupation, business or employment for remuneration or profit for which he is reasonably fitted by education, training or experience and such incapacity extends to every such occupation, business or employment;

provided, however, that in no event shall total disability exist for any purpose of this policy during any period in which the Insured is engaged in his or any occupation, business or employment for remuneration or profit.

The "his occupation" definition of disability is used in this policy during the first two years for which disability benefits are paid, and thereafter benefits are payable if the insured is unable to pursue "any occupation . . . for which he is reasonably fitted."

An accidental injury total disability benefit clause often provides lifetime benefits, as follows:

If total disability of the Insured due to accidental bodily injury commences while this policy is in force and within 90 days after the date such injury is sustained, and requires the regular care of a legally qualified physician, other than the Insured himself, the Company will periodically pay the Monthly Income Benefit for each month and, for periods less than a full month, 1/30th of the Monthly Income Benefit for each day, throughout which such total disability continues beyond the Elimination Period for Injury.

If a period of total disability of the Insured due to injury commences while this policy is in force but more than 90 days after such injury is sustained, such total disability shall, for the purposes of this policy, be deemed to have been due to sickness.

The sickness clause is similar, but because short benefit periods are often used, it is necessary to refer to the maximum benefit period, (in no event beyond age 65) and to provide for recurrent disability, as follows:

A. *Continuous Disabilities*—If total disability of the Insured due to sickness commences while this policy is in force and requires the regular care of a legally qualified physician, other than the Insured himself, the Company will periodically pay the Monthly Income Benefit for each month and, for periods less than a full month, 1/30th of the Monthly Income Benefit for each day, throughout which such total disability continues beyond the Elimination Period for Sickness, but no longer than the Maximum Period of Monthly Income Benefit for Sickness, provided that not more than 12 months' benefits shall be payable after the policy anniversary next following the Insured's 64th birthday on account of a period of disability whenever commencing.

B. *Recurrent Disabilities*—If indemnity has been paid in accordance with the foregoing paragraph and if the insured, while this policy is in force, suffers a recurrence of total disability from the same or related cause or causes, the second period of such total disability will be deemed continuous with the first and indemnified as such, unless between the two periods the insured has performed all the duties of a gainful occupation on a full-time basis for at least six consecutive months. If successive periods of total disability do not have the same or related cause or causes, indemnity in accordance with paragraph A of this Benefit Provision will be paid with respect to each such period.

While lifetime benefits for sickness are available, it is very common to issue policies providing much shorter benefit periods and few policies pay beyond age 65. Similarly, while the use of a waiting period of at least one week is almost universal in policies covering sickness, contracts with first-day accident benefits frequently are issued. It is for this reason that separate contracts or clauses are used.

There is, of course, no difference in the economic loss to the family between disabilities produced by accident and those caused by disease. The difference in practice represents the greater ease of underwriting the accident peril and the greater ease of claim settlement where the event is readily recognizable. As a matter of fact, the probability of long-term or permanent disability from disease is much greater than from accident, and it is unfortunate that company underwriting practice results in long-term disease disability being largely uninsured.

*Partial disability.* Partial disability benefits are rarely written for sickness. They are almost never found in a separate sickness policy and are not very common even in the combination forms. Partial disability, from either accident or sickness, sometimes is covered only if it follows a period of compensable total disability. Coverage of partial disability for accidental injury, starting at the time of the accident, however, is common; such coverage for disease is extremely rare. The combination policy quoted above contains the following partial disability benefit clause:

Partial disability means the continuous inability of the Insured because of accidental bodily injury to engage in one or more of the important duties of his occupation. . . .

If, while this policy is in force, the Insured sustains accidental bodily injury which directly and independently of all other causes either within 90 days thereafter or immediately following a period of total disability for which indemnity is payable under paragraph (a) of this part, renders the Insured partially disabled, the Company will pay periodically an indemnity 50% of the monthly indemnity stated in the schedule for the period of such disability but not to exceed 6 consecutive months as the result of any one accident.

**Presumptive disability clauses.** From a logical standpoint, the accidental death and dismemberment benefits may be looked upon as coverage of presumed total disability, either permanant or temporary. These coverages provide a lump-sum settlement in the event of certain losses resulting from accidental injury. Death logically represents the extreme state of disability and is certainly permanent.

It is quite common for disability income policies to include an *accidental death benefit*. This is a carry-over from the early days of the business, when only accidental injury was covered and frequently only certain types of accident. Before it became common to carry substantial sums of permanent life insurance, there was a greater need for coverage of particularly severe risks, such as travel.

Today there seems little logic in carrying insurance against only one type of death when coverage for all types is readily available. The economic loss to the family certainly is no greater when death results from accidental injury than when it results from disease. Indeed, disease usually takes longer to produce death, and the loss is likely to be greater. The best argument that can be made is that in certain younger age groups accidental injuries produce more than half of all deaths, especially of males. Thus it is claimed, at a considerable savings in premium, coverage of a substantial number of deaths at these (young) ages can be obtained. Thus accidental death coverage is a partial substitute for regular life insurance.

It would be better for most insureds to carry term life insurance against all types of death, even if this makes it necessary to carry a smaller amount of coverage. It seems that the basic purpose of insurance is defeated when it becomes necessary to gamble that death will come in the right way. These comments apply equally strongly to the accidental death benefit or "double indemnity" clause issued in connection with life insurance policies. If such insurance is to be issued, it would seem that it properly belongs in the field of life insurance rather than that of health insurance. Someday these two fields may well become one, but in the meantime this overlap is regrettable.

However, many disability income policies do include the accidental death clause, and agents seem to feel that it is a valuable sales producer.

Specific dismemberment benefits provide lump-sum payments for dismemberment, loss of sight, and specified fractures, dislocations, etc. Policies vary greatly as to the basis for such payment, but there are six main types of provision:

1. Lump-sum benefits, where applicable, are paid in lieu of the disability income benefit. The insured has no choice, but must accept the lump sum in full settlement of his claim. Since the lump sum is rarely equal to more than about four years' income benefit, this greatly reduces the amount collectible in most instances.

2. The insured may elect within some reasonable time of the accident whether he will receive the total disability income or the lump-sum benefit. This is more liberal than the first method, since the claimant is not forced to take the lump sum, which is usually much less than the income benefits would be for a permanent disability. However, there is danger that the insured might die shortly after electing the income benefit but too late to collect the accidental death benefit, if any. In such a case, he would have done better with the lump sum, but it is too late. Under both provisions 1 and 2 any income benefits paid prior to dismemberment will be deducted from the lump-sum benefit payment.

3. Lump-sum benefits are paid in addition to disability income up to the time of the dismemberment but in lieu of such benefits thereafter. Since dismemberment usually occurs fairly shortly after injury, this differs little from the first type of provision.

4. The insured may elect, within a reasonable time after dismemberment, whether to settle for the lump-sum dismemberment benefit in lieu of future disability income or to continue receiving the agreed disability income benefit during the continuance of disability. This is similar in effect to the second type of provision described.

5. The lump-sum benefits are a minimum which will be paid for every such loss. This is quite liberal to the claimant, since he is assured of collecting whichever amount turns out to be the larger. Frequently, the additional provision is included that loss of both hands, both feet, or both eyes shall be presumed permanent total disability and entitle him to income benefits for the maximum period in the policy.

6. Lump-sum death and dismemberment benefits will be paid in addition to other benefits payable under the contract including disability income. This is the most liberal to the insured.

Loss of a member may be defined in terms of actual severance or in terms of complete loss of use. The latter is the more liberal, of course. The following fairly typical accidental death and dismemberment benefit clause uses the most liberal approach to payment, paying benefits in addition to all others payable. However, it uses the stricter definition of loss of member. There probably is an inverse relationship here.

### PRINCIPAL SUM INDEMNITY FOR LOSS OF LIFE, LIMBS, OR SIGHT, CAUSED BY ACCIDENTAL BODILY INJURIES

If accidental bodily injury results, directly and independently of all other causes, in any of the following losses by the Insured while this policy is in force and within 180 days after the date of such injury is sustained, the Company will pay the amount specified for such loss, provided that the total amount payable under this Benefit Provision for all such losses resulting from any one accident shall not exceed the Principal Sum. This benefit is payable in addition to any other benefits which may be payable under this policy. Loss of hands or feet means complete severance at or above the wrist or ankle joints respectively. Loss of sight must be entire and irrecoverable.

| *Loss* | *Indemnity* |
|---|---|
| Life.................................................... | The Principal Sum |
| Both hands or both feet or sight of both eyes...... | The Principal Sum |
| One hand and one foot............................... | The Principal Sum |
| Sight of one eye and either one hand or one foot. | The Principal Sum |
| One hand or one foot or sight of one eye.......... | One-half the Principal Sum |

Death or dismemberment must take place within 180 days of the accident. This requirement is intended to make sure that the accident is the proximate cause of death or dismemberment. Many policies are somewhat more liberal in this regard, providing coverage if death occurs either within such a time period (often 90 days) or during a period of compensable total disability.

Some contracts provide additional stipulated benefits for less serious types of injury such as fractures, sprains, and dislocations. The following clause is fairly typical:

### SPECIFIC INDEMNITY FOR SPECIFIED LOSSES

If Weekly Indemnity is provided under this Policy and such injuries shall result in any of the losses enumerated in the following Schedule, the Total amount payable for Weekly Indemnity as may be provided under Parts 1 and 2 shall not be less than the sum set opposite such loss. If more than one such loss shall result from one accident, the Company will pay the largest applicable amount only.

If the Weekly Indemnity for total disability payable under this policy is $25.00, the amounts named in the Schedule shall be payable; if such Weekly Indemnity is greater than $25.00, the amounts to be paid shall be increased proportionately. . . .

*SCHEDULE [Abbreviated]*

For Complete Fracture of Bones:
Skull (except bones of face or nose), both tables...............$325
Thigh (shaft)................................................. 300
For Complete Dislocation:
Hip Joint....................................................$300
Knee Joint (except patella)................................... 150
Bone or Bones of Foot (except toes)........................... 150
By Loss by Removal:
Of one or more entire toes...................................$200
Of one or more fingers (at least one entire phalanx)........... 150

This clause is of the fifth type described above.

While loss of both hands, both feet, or both eyes would be likely to produce total and permanent disability, the other enumerated losses actually produce disability that is either temporary or partial or both. The fractures and dislocations produce temporary disability. Fracture of a major member will probably be total disability and of a minor one, partial. Loss by removal of various members produces partial disability which is permanent. Regardless of these distinctions, however, the policies treat all such losses as total and temporary, paying total disability income for a limited period or else a lump sum.

Some policies treat some of these categories of loss by providing that weekly total disability income benefits will be paid for a limited period as specified or expressing the lump sum as a multiple of the weekly benefit.

*Other benefit provisions.* *Waiver of premium* benefits, while more common in guaranteed renewable contracts, are sometimes found in commercial policies. Waiver is often provided for any premium due during a period of disability, provided that disability lasts at least 90 days. This benefit is the equivalent of an additional disability income benefit in the amount of the premium and helps to cushion the impact of disability on earning power. The clause is similar to that found in many life insurance policies except that life policies usually require a six-month period of disability to qualify. Sometimes, as in the clause quoted below, waiver is not retroactive to the date of disablement but is granted only for premiums falling due after the waiting period.

## WAIVER OF PREMIUMS

The Company will waive the payment of any premium that falls due during a period of total disability for which indemnity is payable, provided total disability has existed uninterruptedly for the 90 days preceding the date such premium falls due.

The *nondisabling injuries* benefit found in some accidental injury policies and occasionally in a combination policy provides coverage for expenses up to a nominal sum for medical expense incurred for treatment of nondisabling injury. It covers only if the claimant is insured for total disability income and is of little value if there is coverage of medical expense under another clause of the contract. It reads as follows:

### NONDISABLING INJURIES BENEFIT

If this Policy provides a benefit payable for total disability and in the event of accidental bodily injuries which result in loss for which no indemnity would otherwise be payable under this Policy, but which shall require treatment by a physician or surgeon, within thirty days after the date of the accident the Company will pay the expense incurred for such treatment, not to exceed the weekly indemnity at the rate hereinbefore specified for total disability for one week.

This benefit is of little value and merely serves to make the list of benefit provisions look more impressive.

Another benefit clause which is all too frequent is the *"double indemnity"* clause. This provides double payment if the insured suffers the right kind of accident. It frequently reads about as follows:

### DOUBLE INDEMNITY FOR SPECIFIED ACCIDENTS

Any amount payable under Parts 1, 2, 5, 6, or 7 of this Policy shall be doubled if such injuries are sustained by the Insured

(1) While a passenger in or upon a public conveyance, except aircraft or other device for air travel, provided by a common carrier for passenger service (including the platform, steps or running board of such conveyance).

(2) While a passenger in an elevator car provided for passenger service other than elevator cars in mines, or are caused

(3) By collapse of the outer walls or the burning of a building if the Insured is therein at the time of the collapse or commencement of the fire,

(4) By the explosion of a steam boiler,

(5) By a hurricane or tornado, or

(6) By a stroke of lightning.

The arguments against insuring only accidental injury or accidental death set forth above apply even more strongly toward insuring against such loss produced by only a limited type of accident. The need of the family is not twice as great for travel accidents as for other more common types. By injecting an element of gambling that the accident will occur the "right" way into the contract, such provisions are said to be useful as sales "gimmicks." The danger, however, is that the insured may purchase a policy with an amount adequate only for the "right kind" of accident. Thus emphasis on such clauses may actually reduce sales. Fortunately, policies providing triple and quadruple indemnity are by now rare, and it is to be hoped that the "double indemnity" clause may soon disappear in the same way.

The reader will have noted the misuse of the term "indemnity" in many of the policy provisions quoted above. In health insurance policy language the term is synonymous with "payment" and does not convey the idea of reimbursement for the actual cash value of a loss. When it is desired to convey this latter idea, such terms as "reimburse" or "pay the actual expenses incurred" are used. It is to be hoped that draftsmen of future policies will be more careful in their choice of terminology. Many modern contracts use the word "benefit."

Other frill benefits which sometimes still appear in health insurance policies are the identification clause and the accumulation clause. The *identification clause* provides that, upon receipt of a telegram or telephone message, the insurer will notify relatives or friends and will defray the expense, up to (usually) $100, of putting the insured in the care of relatives or friends. Claims under this clause were few, and it usually is not included in modern policies.

The *accumulation clause* was a characteristic of the period from 1900 to about 1930. It was intended to encourage renewal and provided for increasing benefits with each successive renewal. Sometimes it applies to only the accidental death benefit; sometimes to all policy benefits. A typical clause reads:

Each consecutive renewal of this policy without default in payment of premium when due, will add 10% to each of the original sums as stated heretofore until such additions shall amount to 50% of such original sums; and thenceforth so long as this policy shall be continuously maintained in force without lapse by the payment of annual premiums in advance of the renewal date, the insurance will be for such original sums plus such accumulations.

Competitively, the value of such a clause was defeated by the development by some companies of a "fully accumulated" policy which started out with 150 percent benefits. Though clauses of this type are very rare in newly issued policies, no doubt many contracts containing them are still in force.

### Exclusions and reductions

*Exclusions.* Exclusions in modern policies generally are fewer than in those of years gone by. Both the accident and the sickness policies usually exclude war or military service, and each excludes losses of the type covered under the other. The exclusion clause from a typical disability income policy reads as follows:

This policy does not cover, and no payment will be made for, disability or other loss caused or contributed to by any of the following:

(*a*) Any injury sustained, sickness contracted, or physical condition existent, prior to the date of issue of this policy unless the sickness or physical condition had not manifested itself prior to such date;

(*b*) War, whether declared or undeclared, or an act of war;

(*c*) Any injury sustained or sickness contracted while the insured is on full-time active duty in the armed forces of any country, international organization, or combination of countries; . . .

(*d*) Travel or flight in any aircraft if the insured has any duties on or relating to such aircraft or flight or is flying in the course of any aviation training or instruction, or any training or maneuvers of any armed forces;

(*e*) Intentionally self-inflicted injury, intentional self-destruction, or self-inflicted injury or self-destruction while insane.

Disability income policies and sickness policies sold to women frequently exclude pregnancy, childbirth or miscarriage. It is quite common for disability income policies to provide that benefits will be paid only for disabilities during which the insured is under the care and/or "regular" attendance of a licensed physician. This requirement is not intended as grounds for a technical defense but merely is designed to assist in the establishment of definite standards as to what constitutes disability. Thus it frequently appears in the insuring or benefit clauses rather than among the exclusions. Since the objective occurrence of an accidental injury is easier to establish than that of a disease, the requirement may be omitted from an accident policy. The courts will generally interpret the requirement of "regular" attendance in the light of what would be reasonably required for the treatment of the disability involved.

*House-confining clauses* were a distinctive feature of policies covering sickness until a few years ago, but they are becoming more rare as time goes by. Such clauses provide that benefits will be paid only "while the insured is continuously confined within doors." Sometimes such policies provide benefits for confining sickness only; sometimes a lower amount or a shorter period of benefit is provided for nonconfining sickness than for confining. The clause has been unpopular with insureds (rightly) and has led to frequent misunderstanding.

In practice, the distinction between confining sickness and nonconfining was made for many years at the point of recovery when the insured ceased to receive medical treatment at home and began to visit the doctor's office. During World War II, physicians limited home visits drastically, and the interpretation of the clause was changed. No comparable objective criterion was developed, and this difficulty of application has contributed to the declining use of the clause. The most common use of the house-confinement provision in modern policies is to provide that benefits will be paid for disability for a limited period, such as six months, regardless of confinement, and will be continued thereafter for life only if the insured is confined to the house. The value of such a benefit depends on the interpretation that is given to house confinement by insurers and, in the last analysis, by the courts. Some courts have ruled that occasional absence from the house for treatment, therapeutic exercise, and recreation do not preclude the claimant from still being considered as "confined."[3]

*Prorating clauses.* As indicated above, there are four clauses sometimes found in health insurance policies which provide for a prorating of benefits. Since the average earnings clause is permissable only in non-cancellable and guaranteed renewable policies, discussion of it will be deferred until the following chapter where these contracts are described in detail.

The clause calling for prorating for change of occupation is more often found in commercial contracts than in guaranteed renewable contracts, despite the protection offered the company by the right of cancellation and/or nonrenewal. The uniform provision is as follows:

*Change of Occupation:* If the insured be injured or contract sickness after having changed his occupation to one classified by the insurer as more hazardous than that stated in this policy or while doing for compensation anything pertaining to an occupation so classified, the insurer will pay only such portion of the indemnities provided in this policy as the premium paid would have purchased at the rates and within the limits fixed by the insurer for the more hazardous occupation. If the insured changes his occupation to one classified by the insurer as less hazardous than that stated in this policy, the insurer, upon receipt of proof of such change of occupation, will reduce the premium rate accordingly, and will return the excess pro rata unearned premium from the date of change of occupation or from the policy anniversary date immediately preceding receipt of such proof, whichever is the more recent. In applying this provision, the classification of occupational risk and the premium rates shall be such as have been last filed by the insurer prior to the occurrence of the loss for which the insurer is liable or prior to date of proof of change in occupation with the state official having supervision of insurance in the state where the insured resided at the time this policy was issued; but if such filing was not required, then the classification of occupational risk and the premium rates shall be those last made effective by the insurer in such state prior to the occurrence of the loss or prior to the date of proof of change in occupation.

While the benefit is reduced if the new occupation is more hazardous, it is not increased if the new occupation is less hazardous. Instead, a proportionate return of premium is made.

The misstatement of age clause is rarely used in commercial policies, since they are usually issued at a flat rate for all common ages of entry. It will be discussed in the following chapter.

The clause prorating for other insurance applies only when notice is not given to the company. It is not very common, even in commercial policies where the insurer can get off the risk by cancellation or nonrenewal. It is reproduced in Appendix A.

---

[3] A recent case ruled that driving a car to a physician's office, visiting one's neighbors and shopping for supplies did not mean that the claimant was not continuously confined within doors—*Shealy* v. *United Insurance Co. of America.* 5 Life CCH (2d) 186 (South Carolina Supreme Court).

## Term, renewal, and cancellation

The typical commercial policy is issued for a term of one year. The term may be expressed in the consideration clause or the insuring clause. Sometimes the clause refers to the premium, date of issue, and term, as set forth in appropriate schedules.

The right of the company to refuse renewal and/or cancel the contract is what distinguishes commercial policies from guaranteed renewable and noncancellable contracts. This renewal clause is frequently combined with the grace period clause. A typical commercial disability income renewal clause provides:

> Unless the Company has given written notice, as provided below, of its intention not to renew, this policy may be renewed, at the expiration of any term during which it has been in force, by payment within the grace period of the premium for a further term. The Company may decline to renew the policy as of any policy anniversary, provided, not less than thirty days before such anniversary, it has mailed to the insured at his last address, as shown by the records of the Company, written notice of its intention not to renew. Nonrenewal of the policy by the Company or the insured shall be without prejudice to any claim originating prior to the effective date of nonrenewal.

The usual grace period in commercial contracts is 31 days, although other periods are sometimes found. The minimum grace periods in the uniform provisions are 7 days for weekly premium policies, 10 days for monthly premium policies, and 31 days for all other policies. The grace period provides for continued coverage beyond the premium due date, unless the company has served notice of intention to deny renewal.

Many contracts in which the company may deny renewal contain a provision for extended coverage of sickness. Usually it provides that benefits will be paid for sickness contracted while the policy is in force provided loss commences within 90 days after termination of the policy by the insurer. However, since the sickness must be "contracted while the policy is in force" and the care or treatment must "occur" within 90 days after termination by the insurer and it must be for a period of continuous compensable loss, the provision adds little to the renewal coverage of the contract.[4]

Many policies today omit the cancellation clause. While they are noncancellable in the dictionary sense of the word, this is of relatively little value to the insured, since the company still can deny renewal. In accordance with industry and National Association of Insurance Com-

---

[4] This clause is required by the California Minimum Benefits Law, Subdivision iii, Section 10291.5(b) (4), *California Insurance Code,* and many insurers include it in their basic contract in preference to using a rider for California policies.

missioners recommendations, all states prohibit the use of the term "non-cancellable" in this context. An increasing amount of coverage is being written on a truly noncancellable guaranteed renewable basis.

The uniform cancellation clause is reproduced in Appendix A. It is very similar to that used in fire and many other types of insurance. Either party may cancel with no reason stated. If the insured cancels, no period of notice is required, and he is charged the short rate. If the company cancels, five days are required before the cancellation is effective, and only the pro rata premium is charged. Of course, cancellation does not affect a claim for a disability which has already been incurred.

Bad public relations because of cancellation and nonrenewal have led to a variety of liberalizations short of the noncancellable and guaranteed renewable contracts described in the next chapter. They include:

1. A contract that provides that renewal will be guaranteed except for certain specified developments, such as change of occupation. The security afforded by such a contract is in direct proportion to the number of such developments and the probability of their occurrence. Contracts of this type are referred to as "non-renewable for stated reasons."

2. A contract providing that renewal will not be refused *solely* because of a change in the insured's physical condition. Since most changes in physical condition are accompanied by changes in occupation, income, or habits, such a clause seems of little value per se. Reliance must be placed on the company's practice rather than upon the contract provision itself. Contracts of the two types above are referred to as "conditionally renewable."

3. A contract providing that it may not be terminated unless all policies in its class (or all in its class and the state of the insured's residence) are terminated. Contracts of this type are referred to as "collectively renewable."

4. The practice of notifying agents that the company will not refuse renewal as above, but with no change in policy provision.

5. The unpublicized practice of overlooking any such change in physical condition.

6. The practice of renewing policies regardless of claim frequency and duration.

7. The practice of merely being generally more liberal in renewal underwriting.

The last four of these are merely company practices and, as such, are subject to change at any time. No matter how pious the current objectives may be, it is questionable how long such practices would be maintained in the face of rising loss ratios. All these responses make some contribution to refuting the charge of lack of reliability in commercial policies, but all fall short of providing the complete security of the noncancellable and guaranteed renewable forms.

## Hospital income policies

While not a new development, the hospital income contract[5] recently has become increasingly popular. It is a difficult creature to classify, since it is a disability income contract intended, in part, to cover hospital expense. The contract pays stated monthly or weekly benefits while the insured is confined in a hospital. It is a valued policy and not a reimbursement contract. Some contracts pay benefits at a reduced rate, often 50 percent, while the insured is confined in a convalescent home following periods of covered hospitalization. There is no coverage of hospital extras as such. The insured is paid in cash, with no waiting period, and can use the money for whatever he wants. For income tax purposes, however, these contracts are treated as medical expense contracts.

The contract is appealing from the standpoint of the insurer since it is relatively inflation proof. Since benefits are valued and there is no coverage of extra expenses, claim rates will be influenced only by hospital admissions and length of stay, not by the cost of services. Moreover, claim administration costs are reduced drastically. It is more difficult to see the appeal from the insured's standpoint. Apparently such contracts usually are purchased to supplement other hospital insurance which is inadequate in amount. Where the other insurance is on a group basis, this may be better than replacing it with a more adequate policy. The convalescent home coverage is a valuable feature which is not generally available.

Coverage is available in amounts from $50 to $1,000 per month or more, with durations up to a year or more per admission. Usually pregnancy, childbirth and miscarriage are not covered but sometimes a stated amount, such as $100, is paid for maternity in lieu of other benefits. Contracts may be on a commercial or guaranteed renewable basis. The contract might have some value as a way of increasing disability income coverage for a person who wants more than insurers are willing to sell him. Of course, it would pay only under the limited circumstances of hospital or convalescent home confinement.

The pertinent benefit provisions from the contract used by one insurer active in this field are reproduced below:

### DEFINITIONS

As used in this policy:

"Hospital" means only an institution operated pursuant to law for the care and treatment of sick and injured persons at the expense of the patient, with organized facilities for diagnosis and major surgery, and 24-hour nursing service

---

[5] Some authorities prefer to call these contracts "hospital indemnity" policies. However, they provide valued benefits, *not* on a reimbursement or indemnity basis, so this term will not be used here. The nomenclature is not yet standardized.

by or under the supervision of nurses having the right to use the title of Registered Nurse. It does not mean a convalescent home, maternity home, nursing home, rest home, or an institution for the treatment of the aged, drug addict, or alcoholic, even though such institution may be licensed by the state in which it is located, nor does it mean a hospital contracted for or operated by the Federal Government if the Insured is not legally obligated to pay the expenses of such hospitalization.

"Injury" means bodily injury caused by an accident which occurs while this policy is in force and which results, exclusive of disease, in loss covered by this policy which is incurred while this policy is in force.

"Sickness" means sickness or disease, other than mental disturbance without demonstrable organic disease, contracted and commencing while this policy is in force and which results in loss covered by this policy which is incurred while this policy is in force. Normal childbirth is not a sickness. "Any one sickness" as used in this policy is defined as either sickness from the same cause at various times or sickness from various causes at the same time.

## RECURRENT SICKNESS

Any one sickness will be construed to have been terminated, and maximum benefits will be restored, at the expiration of any period of 12 consecutive months during which there has been freedom from treatment for the cause or causes of such sickness.

## HOSPITAL INDEMNITY BENEFIT

The Company will pay the "Weekly Hospital Indemnity," specified in the application for each week (or a proportionate part thereof for a fractional part of the week) that the Insured is confined, while this policy is in force, in a hospital as a result of injury or sickness, but not to exceed the number of weeks specified in the application as a result of any one sickness or injury resulting from any one accident.

### Summary

Commercial health insurance is the bulk of the individual health insurance business. It includes all individual contracts which are sold on a monthly or less frequent premium basis, except the limited and guaranteed renewable and noncancellable forms. In the past, separate policies were issued for accidental injury and sickness. Accident policies usually include benefits for both total and partial disability income. Total disability benefits may be paid for life, but partial disability benefits are usually restricted to six months. In addition, many policies include benefits for accidental death and dismemberment, a blanket medical expense benefit, and sometimes double indemnity for certain types of accident. Sometimes frills, such as the nondisabling injury, identification, and accumulation clauses, still are found.

Sickness policies provide disability income, as a rule, only for total disability with no lump-sum benefits. Sickness benefits are rarely available much beyond age 65 and are often as short as one or two years. Today, most contracts cover both accident and sickness in a single policy and often under a single insuring clause with identical waiting periods and limits. Frequently, optional coverage is available for hospital, nurse, surgical, and medical expenses. The typical modern policy covers both accident and sickness and provides a schedule of such benefits from which the insured can select those he desires.

Criticisms of commercial health insurance center about the charges of inadequacy of coverage, undue technicality, high cost, and lack of reliability. Considerable progress has been made in meeting these criticisms, and the industry has done much to improve its product in the last decades. However, there is still room for a great deal of improvement. As contracts offered are improved, commercial contracts are coming more closely to resemble noncancellable and guaranteed renewable contracts.

## Selected references

*See the following items from the General Bibliography: 4, ch. 7; 12, pp. 52–57; 15, ch. 21; 18, pp. 398–407; 20, ch. 2.*

BLANCHARD, RALPH H. *Survey of Accident and Health Insurance.* Bulletins 1–6, Bureau Memorandum No. 62, U.S. Social Security Board, Bureau of Research and Statistics. Washington, D.C.: U.S. Government Printing Office, 1945.

FOLLMANN, JOSEPH F. "The A. & H. Cancellation Problem," *The Spectator,* July, 1955 (special insert).

———. "1952 Analysis of Commercial Accident Insurance," Bureau of Accident and Health Underwriters, *Information Bulletin 194,* September 30, 1952.

———. "The Right of Discontinuance," *Best's Insurance News,* F. & C. ed. (October, 1954), p. 33.

HEALTH INSURANCE ASSOCIATION OF AMERICA. *Individual Accident and Health Insurance.* New York, 1958.

LAIRD, JOHN M. "Personal Accident and Health Insurance," *Transactions of the Actuarial Society of America,* Vol. XXIII, p. 281.

MILLER, JOHN H. "The Development of Individual Health and Accident Insurance," *Journal of the American Society of Chartered Life Underwriters,* December, 1951, p. 5.

chapter 12

There's nothing certain in man's life but this.—Owen Meredith, *Clytemnestra*

# Noncancellable and Guaranteed Renewable Contracts

## Introduction

Noncancellable policies are health insurance contracts which give the insured the unqualified right to continue the policy in force for a substantial period of time by the payment of premiums agreed upon in advance. The premiums may be level for life or may go up with age brackets according to a "step-rate" plan. The term noncancellable, as applied to such contracts, emphasizes only one of their three main characteristics: the absence of a cancellation clause, the right of renewal, and the guarantee of premium rates. All three are necessary in order for the term noncancellable to apply. The common practice of eliminating the cancellation clause from commercial policies does not justify the use of the designation noncancellable for this purpose, and such use is prohibited according to the recommendations of the National Association of Insurance Commissioners.[1] At least 150 insurance companies currently issue disability income coverage on a noncancellable basis.

According to the N.A.I.C. recommendation, the term "guaranteed renewable" is to be used for a contract which guarantees the right of renewal or continuance but reserves to the company the right to change premiums for classes of insureds. This term emphasizes another characteristic but, like noncancellable, it is not completely descriptive. This

---

[1] See the November 30, 1959, *Report of the National Association of Insurance Commissioners Subcommittee on Definitions of Non Cancellable and Guaranteed Renewable Insurance* for details on the agreed meaning of the term. The Report requires that renewal be guaranteed until at least age 50, or at least for five years if issued after age 44. In practice, renewal most commonly is guaranteed until age 60 or 65.

430

type of contract does not provide the unconditional guarantee of a non-cancellable policy but does provide greater security than the commercial forms.

About 138 companies offer income replacement contracts on a non-cancellable basis and about 161 on a guaranteed renewable basis. This approach is far more common for medical expense contracts, however. Many medical expense coverages are issued on a guaranteed renewable basis. Since medical care expenses increase with inflation, this is probably the only safe way for an insurer to provide such coverage with a renewal guarantee. To offer such contracts on a noncancellable basis would require such a high allowance for future inflation that few prospects would be willing to pay the necessary premium. A few companies have offered medical expense insurance on a noncancellable basis, however. In 1966, at least 369 companies issued some form of guaranteed renewable or noncancellable contract.

The growth of the noncancellable and guaranteed renewable business has been outstanding. Premium volume doubled between 1943 and 1949, doubled again from 1949 to 1954, and again doubled from 1954 to 1956. Premiums written were $693,096,646 in 1966. These figures include both disability income and medical expense coverages.

## Development

Although noncancellable disability income insurance was written as early as 1885 in Great Britain, it was not introduced in the United States until 1907. Interest became intense with the entry of the Pacific Mutual in 1918. The basic characteristics of the early forms involved life benefits for total disability only, whether produced by accidental injury or disease; the use of a long waiting period; the elimination of the cancellation clause; and the guarantee of the right of renewal at the agreed premium until an advanced age. This was to be accompanied by strict underwriting, including a medical examination at least as strict as for life insurance. By 1921 at least nine companies were offering noncancellable policies.

Under the impact of competition there was some departure from the earlier principles. Waiting periods were shortened, frills were added to the policies, and underwriting standards were lowered. Many of the companies charged a flat premium regardless of age of issue. Experience soon indicated that such companies were subject to adverse selection, as only the older applicants would buy from them, the younger applicants finding it better to buy from a company whose premiums were graded by age of entry on a level premium basis.

Moreover, the rate basis was itself inadequate. Rates generally had been based on Hunter's Table, which may have been appropriate for life insurance waiver of premium riders but was grossly inadequate for noncancellable income policies. The losses arising from the influenza epidemics of 1918–19 and 1920 and the recession of 1921 made the need for higher rates evident. A report of the Actuarial Committee of the Bureau of Personal Accident and Health Underwriters and several articles in the actuarial journals led to a change to a level premium basis, and some companies adopted disability tables showing higher claim rates. Two companies withdrew entirely from the business. The general mood throughout the 1920's was one of optimism despite this tightening-up. Some contracts were issued with an aggregate limit as to total benefits as early as 1918, and the first policies with a limit per disability appeared in 1921.

The depression soon produced severe losses on noncancellable contracts. Claims increased, premium volume dropped off, and old policies lapsed heavily. Some companies reported tremendous loss ratios. Contracts providing lifetime income benefits produced the heaviest losses, and most companies ceased to write such business. Many withdrew completely from the noncancellable field and some from sickness insurance entirely. The Pacific Mutual was forced into insolvency primarily as a result of its noncancellable business. The companies with aggregate limits of liability or short-term disability duration limits in their policies weathered the storm. Premiums on new policies generally were increased to reflect newly available data, underwriting was tightened up, and limited benefit contracts became the rule.

The general revival of interest in health insurance in the 1940's was reflected by the growth in noncancellable referred to above. In the fifties, many companies began to offer noncancellable and guaranteed renewable disability income contracts for the first time. Many large life insurance companies have entered the noncancellable and guaranteed renewable field. Many of these issue no other type of individual health insurance contract.

## Contract provisions

*Type of policy.* Noncancellable and guaranteed renewable contracts may be divided into two basic categories: those protecting primarily against income loss and those protecting primarily against medical care expenses. The latter provide benefits of the type discussed in the foregoing chapters and usually are on a guaranteed renewable basis which provides for the company's right to change premiums for classes of insureds. The discussion in this chapter will be limited to disability income contracts.

Most noncancellable and guaranteed renewable contracts protect against losses from both accidental injury and disease in a single contract. Some policies covering injury only are sold, but separate sickness or disease contracts are not issued. The policies covering both generally are classified on the basis of the length of the maximum period for which total disability benefits are paid for a single disease. (Very few policies today provide an aggregate lifetime maximum.) Short-term policies provide a sickness benefit of 36 months or less; intermediate-term policies a benefit of from 37 to 99 months; long-term policies from 100 months to 10 years, and extra-long-term policies for over 10 years.

Short-term contracts provide maximum sickness benefit periods of from 26 weeks to three years. The form of contract and presence of supplementary benefits make these policies very reminiscent of commercial policies. They appear to have been developed simply by adding the renewal guarantee to a commercial contract. Most of these policies are available with a lifetime accident benefit, if desired. Most include partial disability for accident only; about a third include accidental death and dismemberment benefits.

Intermediate-term policies almost always provide a maximum sickness benefit of five years. Most provide lifetime accident coverage if desired, and almost all include partial disability benefits for accident. Only about one sixth of these policies cover accidental death and dismemberment.

Long-term policies are usually for a 10-year maximum sickness benefit, although 100 months was common 15 years ago. Lifetime accident benefits usually are available. Most include partial disability benefits for accident only. Dismemberment benefits are quite rare, and accidental death benefits are uncommon. Almost all provide a waiver of premium benefit, while in the shorter term policies about one eighth of the contracts do not include this provision.

By now most companies issue policies with a sickness benefit greater than 10 years, usually to age 65. Only six companies issued such a contract 10 years ago. A few companies issue a life-benefit contract. One of these reduces the benefit 50 percent after age 60 and in any event if the disease is not house confining. Full benefits are paid to age 60 for accidental injury and confining disease. This is the only contract currently issued with a benefit period over three years which includes a house-confining clause. The second life-benefit contract reduces all benefits for sickness by 50 percent after the first year of disability, regardless of confinement. Other life-benefit contracts provide life benefits only if disability commences before age 55. If disability commences after this age, benefits are payable only to age 65, or for 12 months, whichever is greater. Several policies provide maximum sickness benefits of 15 years, 600 weeks, or some other period greater than 10 years.

Many companies issue what is becoming almost a "standard" extra-long-term noncancellable disability income contract. While policy forms and definitions differ and there are variations in supplementary benefits such as lifetime accident, partial disability, and the like, the main benefit structure is relatively uniform. These contracts are all noncancellable and guaranteed renewable to age 65 at guaranteed level premiums. Disability income for sickness is payable from the end of the waiting period until the insured's age 65 or for a shorter period if desired. Lifetime accident benefits may be included, available at optional extra premium, or not available, depending on the company.

The terminal date for benefit payment may be variously defined. Usually it is the policy anniversary nearest age 65, except that if disability occurs after age 64, 12 months' benefits are payable if disability lasts that long. However, lifetime benefits may be payable for disability produced by accidental injury. A few contracts are available with fixed termination ages for benefit payment other than age 65. The benefit termination ages usually are 10, 15, and 20 years greater than age at issue. Only a few insurers offer a complete range of benefit termination ages but others will follow if the demand warrants.

A number of companies issue contracts with benefit periods greater than 10 years from disablement but reduce the benefits somewhere along the line. One provides for reducing benefits to 50 percent with a maximum duration of one year if the insured was not gainfully and regularly employed at least six months (90 days if a housewife) prior to the disability. Others reduce the sickness benefit or both the accident and sickness benefit to 50 percent after a disability duration of one, two, or five years.

*Benefit provisions.* Since most noncancellable and guaranteed renewable policies cover both accidental injury and disease, it is common to make use of a single insuring clause, of which the following is fairly typical of modern practice:

> In consideration of the application, a copy of which is attached to and made a part of this policy, and the payment of the required premiums, Provident Indemnity Life Insurance Company hereby insures the above named Insured subject to the provisions, conditions, exceptions, and limitations contained herein against loss resulting from:
> (1) Sickness of the Insured, first manifesting itself while this policy is in force, hereinafter called "such sickness," or
> (2) Bodily injuries of the Insured caused by an accident occurring while this policy is in force, hereinafter called "such injuries."

Since many companies have different waiting periods and/or different benefit maxima for injury and disease, separate insuring clauses are not uncommon. These are generally comparable to those in commercial policies.

The phrase "accidental bodily injury" or "bodily injury caused by accident" largely has replaced the older "accidental means" terminology. The phrase "contracted and commencing" is often used, instead of "first manifesting itself," as a protection against preexisting conditions.

The total disability benefit is by far the most important, and often the only, benefit provision. A typical benefit clause would read as follows:

*Basic Disability Income Benefits.*

This part is effective only if amount of Initial Monthly Benefit and Extended Monthly Benefit are indicated in the Schedule.

If total disability, requiring the regular attendance of a licensed physician other than the Insured shall commence while this insurance is in force and shall last for longer than the Elimination Period, the Company will pay benefits for the period of such continuous total disability which follows the Elimination Period.

1. At the rate of the Initial Monthly Benefit specified in the Schedule during the Initial Benefit Period, and

2. At the rate of the Extended Monthly Benefit specified in the Schedule for the continuance of such total disability thereafter,

provided that no benefit shall be payable for one continuous total disability for longer than the Maximum Benefit Period specified in the Schedule, nor, in any event, shall more than 12 payments of monthly benefits be payable after the Insured's 64th birthday for any one continuous total disability.

*Schedule:*

Part 3. Basic Disability Income Benefit

Elimination Period

### SCHEDULE:

| Elimination Period | Initial Benefit Period | Initial Monthly Benefit | Extended Monthly Benefit | Maximum Benefit Period |
|---|---|---|---|---|
| *30 days* | *6 months* | *$300.00* | *$200.00* | *5 years* |

The definition of disability is also pertinent:

"Total Disability" means the complete inability of an Insured, as a result of such sickness or such injuries, to engage in his regular occupation, except that, after benefits have been paid under this contract for a continuous period of twenty-four months, "Total Disability" shall mean the complete inability of the Insured, as a result of such sickness or such injuries, to engage in any gainful occupation for which he is reasonably fitted by education, training, and experience and the Company will pay at the rate of the Monthly Benefit specified in the schedule for the continuous period thereafter that the Insured is completely unable to engage in such gainful occupation because of such sickness or such injuries and requires the regular attendance of a licensed physician other than himself, provided that no benefit shall be payable under this policy for any such period for longer than the Maximum Benefit Period specified above, nor, in any event, for any period beyond the Insured's 65th birthday, except as provided under Part 5 hereof.

This contract provides in its schedule of benefits for a benefit period of 1, 2, 5 or 10 years per disability or until the anniversary following age 65. This policy covers total disability only.

A number of insurers[2] offer contracts that provide benefit amounts which increase or decrease at a certain time after disablement. Such step benefits facilitate coordination with other benefits and aid in programing. Typically benefits may increase or decrease at intervals of six months or 1, 2, 5, or 10 years from disablement.

Some insurers offer a "reducing term" or "family income" disability benefit. Under this arrangement, the maximum disability income benefit duration is measured from date of issue rather than from date of disablement. Since the insurer's potential liability decreases over time, this costs much less (for the same number of years) than a contract where benefit duration is measured from disablement. This is useful in meeting a need which decreases with time, such as mortgage payments or child-rearing costs. For example, the coverage part for this benefit from the Provident Indemnity contract is reproduced below. Benefit periods may range from 5 to 30 years by single years.

*Part 4. Family Disability Benefit.*

This part is effective only if the amount of Family Income Disability Benefit is indicated in the Schedule.

If total disability, requiring the regular attendance of a licensed physician other than the Insured shall commence while this insurance is in force and shall last for longer than the Elimination Period for this Part indicated in the Schedule, the Company will pay the monthly income benefit of this part during the total disability of the Insured resulting from injury or sickness and commencing before the end of the income protection period, subject to the provisions, definitions, exceptions and reductions of this policy.

The additional monthly income shall be payable for the period the total disability of the Insured continues beyond the elimination period for this Part but not beyond the end of the Family Income Protection Period. However, if the total disability of the Insured continues beyond the end of the Family Income Protection Period and the additional monthly income has been paid for less than 24 months, the Company will pay the monthly income of this part during the continued total disability of the Insured until such monthly income has been paid for 24 full months, provided in no event shall more than 12 payments of monthly benefits be payable after the insured's 64th birthday for any one continuous total disability.

SCHEDULE:

| Elimination Period | Family Income Monthly Benefit | Family Income Protection Period Expires |
|---|---|---|
| 31 *days* | $200.00 | September 30, 1998 |

---

[2] Monarch, Springfield, General American, Life and Health of St. Louis, and Provident Indemnity, to the author's personal knowledge.

Some policies provide partial disability benefits. Where they do, it is usually for accidental injury only, and then often only if it follows a period for which total disability income is payable. The following benefit clause is fairly typical of partial disability benefits on the most liberal basis issued:

If said injury or said sickness shall result in partial disability which immediately follows a period of total disability for which the Insured is entitled to The Monthly Income, or if said injury shall result in partial disability which does not so follow a period of total disability but which commences while this policy is in force, the Company will pay one-half of the Monthly Income during the continuance of such partial disability, but not for more than six months during any period of continuous disability.

Most noncancellable contracts do not provide scheduled dismemberment benefits which are so common in commercial contracts. Accidental death benefits may be included in the basic contract or added at an optional extra premium. It is common for noncancellable contracts to provide that double dismemberment or blindness will be presumed to be total disability or to provide some additional benefit. The following provision is typical of the latter approach.

*Section B. Disability Caused by Blindness or Dismemberment*

If, while this policy is in force, such sickness or such injuries shall result in the loss of both hands or both feet, or one hand and one foot, or the sight of both eyes, the Company will waive the Elimination Period and will pay, in addition to all other benefits of this policy, an amount equal to the maximum amount payable under this Policy for a period of total disability equal to the Maximum Benefit Period or 24 months, whichever is less. Loss shall mean, with regard to hands and feet, actual severance through or above wrist or ankle joints; with regard to sight, entire and irrecoverable loss.

This means that the total disability benefit will be paid for at least two years, even if the claimant becomes able to work again. Some contracts provide, more liberally, that complete and irrevocable loss of use of both hands or feet will be treated as severance. Where accidental death or dismemberment provisions are included other than as above, they are essentially similar to those found in commercial policies and discussed previously.

Waiver of premium benefits are found in most policies, which is not the case in commercial. Almost always they appear in long-term contracts. The following provision is typical:

*Section A. Waiver of Premiums*

When a continuous total disability of the Insured has lasted for a period of 4 months, or the elimination period if longer, the Company will waive the payment of any premium becoming due during the continuance thereafter of such total disability and prior to the Insured's 65th birthday. After the termination of the period of total disability during which premiums have been waived, the insurance hereunder shall continue in full force until the next quarterly anniversary of the policy, at which time the Insured shall have the right to resume the payment of premiums as provided in this policy.

A comparison of this clause with that quoted in the preceding chapter will indicate the possible variation and emphasize the importance of being familiar with the details of the policy under consideration. Some contracts provide for a refund of any premium paid during the waiting period (four months in the above example; 90 days also is common).

The recurrent disability clause usually is found in noncancellable contracts. It usually provides that if recovery and return to the occupation lasts six months, another disability, even from the same disease, will be considered to be a new disability. This means that a new waiting period will be imposed, a reduction of the insurer's liability, but that a new maximum benefit period will begin. This latter represents an extension of the insurer's liability in all but the policies providing benefits for life or to a fixed future age such as 65. Such a clause was quoted in Chapter 5.

*Cash values and endowment benefits.* Most disability income contracts do not provide cash values. Like a life insurance term-to-age-65 contract, the level premium reserve is exhausted by the end of the policy period. However, in the middle of the period of coverage the reserve equals 3 or 4 times the premium. A few insurers provide for a cash value, based on this reserve, but most do not. The arguments against a cash value are: it rewards the healthy insured who withdraws; the money is needed for claims of the unhealthy who do not withdraw; since it is not required by law it can't be very important; it's too much trouble; we always have done it this way; and there is no demand for it.

However, there does seem to be a demand for some substantial cash values, and a number of insurers offer contracts with endowment benefits, sometimes with cash values and sometimes without. A number of insurers issue contracts or riders providing for the return at age 65 of all premiums paid less the amount of benefits paid up to that time. Since there is no cash value on surrender, these policies have tontine elements. The author once computed rates for a contract providing disability benefits to age 65, which becomes paid up for one year's benefit at age 65, whether or not claims had been paid. It had cash values based on the paid-up benefit. It is easy to develop such a contract. If an endowment benefit is included but no interim cash values are desired, one merely adds a level premium pure endowment[3] to the basic contract and forgets about the cash value of the endowment benefit. If one wants a contract with substantial cash values payable at death or withdrawal,

---

[3] A pure endowment is a benefit payable if and only if the insured survives to a stated future date. It is forfeited upon death.

he simply adds to the basic contract a savings fund contribution which will accumulate to the desired amount at maturity. One big advantage of such cash values is that an automatic premium loan provision can be included so that a premium unpaid at the end of the grace period will be borrowed on the security of the cash value. The endowment benefit can be used to provide retirement income, since the usual life insurance settlement options are included in the contract.

For example, Wilson National Life offers two such contracts. One is designed to produce a retirement income (life income; 10 years certain) equal to 50 percent of the income benefit for disability before age 65. This requires $15,580 for males or $17,390 for females for each $100 per month at age 65. This (at 3½ percent) would require an additional premium of $291.50 for a male age 35. The other form involves the accumulation of $25 per year extra premium for each $100 per month disability benefit. Thus the cash values at age 65 per 100 per month vary from $260 for issue age 55 to $2,789 for issue age 18.

Underwriters National Assurance has introduced an apparently unique return of premium rider. At an extra premium, the rider entitles the insured, each 10 years, provided claims have not exceeded 20 percent of premiums, to receive back 80 percent of premiums including the premiums for the rider less claims which have been paid. If claims exceed 20 percent, the insured can start a new 10-year period upon recovery.

*Other benefit provisions.* There are several approaches to the problem of adjusting benefit amounts to future increases in incomes and living costs. Several American insurers offer a guaranteed insurability rider or increase option. For example, Monarch's guarantee of insurability rider permits the insured, without evidence of insurability, but subject to the company's income limits, to add $100 per month up to four times at ages 25, 28, 31, 34, 37, or 40. Mutual Life of New York issues a similar option but with only four option ages, 25, 30, 35, and 40.[4] Coverage will have the same waiting period and maximum benefit period as the basic contract. The premium is equal to that for an additional $10 per month on the basic plan.

Another approach to the problem is taken by a British insurer, the Crusader Insurance Company, which offers a contract which provides that the maximum benefit amount will increase by 10 percent every five years regardless of the state of the insured's health. This gives protection against inflation after disablement, but doesn't do much to encourage rapid recovery.

Some insurers issue disability income coverage for the insured's wife by rider or coverage part. For example, Provident Indemnity offers the following coverage part.

---

[4] The underinsured author regrets he is already too old for these goodies.

This part is effective only if amount and duration of Wife's Disability Income are indicated in the Schedule and the name and age of the insured's wife are stated in the application.

If total disability of the Insured's wife, requiring the regular attendance of a licensed physician other than the Insured, shall commence while this insurance is in force and shall last for longer than the Elimination Period, the Company will pay benefits for the period of such continuous total disability which follows the Elimination Period provided that no indemnity shall be payable for any one continuous total disability for longer than the Maximum Benefit period specified in the Schedule, nor, in any event, shall more than 12 payments of monthly indemnity be payable after the wife's 64th birthday for any one continuous total disability and provided that, if the insured's wife is described as "Employed" in the Schedule, in consideration of the premium rate at which this contract is issued, it is understood and agreed that if disability commences while the Insured's wife is not gainfully employed on a full time basis away from her residence, the benefit payable under this contract will be reduced to 25 percent of the benefit otherwise payable.

Prior to the renewal date next following the 65th birthday of the Insured's Wife, this Part 6, Wife's Disability Income Benefits, can be renewed by the timely payment of the renewal premium at the Company's premium rate in force at the time of such renewal for Wife's Disability Income Benefits, unless the Company shall have delivered to the Policyowner or mailed to his last known address as shown by the records of the Company written notice of its intention not to renew this Part 6, Wife's Disability Income Benefits, at least 30 days prior to the renewal date.

Wife's Name  *Pauline Provident*  
Schedule:  
Part 6. Wife's Disability Income Benefit

Date of Birth *Sept. 8, 1934*  
Policy Number  *DIP-0000*

| Elimination Period | Is Wife Employed? | Monthly Benefit | Maximum Sickness Benefit Period | Maximum Accident Benefit Period |
|---|---|---|---|---|
| *31 days* | *No* | *$100.00* | *12 months* | *12 months* |

An employed wife may obtain up to $500 per month and 10 years per disability (but not more than the coverage on the husband). A non-employed spouse is eligible for $100 per month for one year.

Most companies offer a variety of other benefits by rider, such as medical expense, accidental death or dismemberment, etc. These are similar to coverages discussed in Part II.

*Exclusions.* Exclusions in noncancellable and guaranteed renewable contracts are comparable to those in the better commercial policies. The following is typical:

## EXCLUSIONS AND BENEFIT REDUCTION

*Exclusions:*

The benefits of this policy shall not be payable for disability caused or contributed to by (*a*) any type of military conflict including war, declared or undeclared, or by any act of war, (b) pregnancy, childbirth, or miscarriage or complications thereof, (c) suicide or attempt thereat, or self inflicted injury, or injuries sustained or sickness which begins while the insured is outside the Home Areas, if such injury is sustained or such sickness begins after the Insured has remained outside the Home Areas for six months or longer, nor shall any payment for any continuous period of disability be made for more than six months while the Insured is outside the Home areas. "Home Areas" means the fifty states of the United States of America, the District of Columbia, Canada, Panama Canal Zone, Puerto Rico and the Virgin Islands.

Any loss which is caused or contributed to by hernia of any kind, illness, disease, bodily infirmity or any bacterial infection other than bacterial infection occurring in consequence of accidental injury on the exterior of the body and within 90 days of such injury will be considered a loss resulting from sickness.

The reference to war "declared or undeclared" is an outgrowth of the Korean affair, in which there was considerable difficulty in interpreting the older war clauses. The limitation on benefits during foreign residence or travel is more important in guaranteed renewable than in commercial. In the latter type of policy the company can always get off the risk if unfavorable conditions develop by canceling or refusing renewal. Contracts which are intended to be issued to women also may exclude pregnancy, childbirth, and miscarriage.

**Reductions.**   The *occupational pro rata clause* is usually not included in guaranteed renewable contracts, particularly in the longer term ones. Long-term sickness disability, the severe risk, is little affected by occupation, partly because underwriting controls usually limit issue to the better occupations. Instead, some policies provide as follows:

*Nonprorating for Change of Occupation.* No reduction will be made in any benefits provided hereunder by reason of any change in the occupation of the Insured nor by reason of his doing any act or thing pertaining to any other occupation.

The *misstatement of age clause* almost always is included. This is especially important where renewal is guaranteed. Otherwise, the company would have to pay the full benefit regardless of the misstatement, if it were discovered after the incontestable clause went into effect. The misstatement of age clause reads as follows:

*Misstatement of Age.* If the age of the Insured has been misstated, all amounts payable under this policy shall be such as the premium would have purchased at the correct age.

The amount of benefit is reduced or increased to equal the amount which the premium actually paid by the insured would have purchased if the age had been correctly stated.

The *other insurance clause* permitted in the Uniform Provisions allows a prorating of benefits only where the insured has failed to notify the company of other insurance. Since there is nothing the insurer can do upon receipt of such notice to reduce its liability, there is no point in including this clause in noncancellable or guaranteed renewable policies.

The *average earnings clause* is found in about half the non-cancellable policies issued. Generally speaking, the longer the benefit period for disability produced by sickness, the more likely is it to be included. It provides as follows in several policies.

Relation of Earnings to Insurance: This provision will not be operative unless the total monthly amount of loss-of-time benefits promised for the same loss under all valid loss-of-time coverage upon an Insured from all sources, whether payable on a weekly or monthly basis, shall exceed the predisability monthly earnings of an insured as herein defined. The term predisability monthly earnings as used in this provision shall mean the greater of (a) the monthly earnings of an Insured at the time disability for which claims is made commences, or (b) his average monthly earnings for the period of 2 years immediately preceding a disability for which claim is made.

If this provision shall be operative, the Company will be liable only for such proportionate amount of the loss-of-time benefits under this policy as the amount of the predisability monthly earnings of an Insured bears to the total amount of monthly benefits for the same loss under all valid loss-of-time coverage upon an Insured at the time disability commences and for the return of such part of the premiums paid during the 2-year period immediately preceding such disability as shall exceed the pro rata amount of the premiums for the benefits actually paid hereunder, but this shall not operate to reduce the total monthly amount of benefits payable under all such coverage upon an Insured below the lesser of (1) $200, or (2) the monthly benefits specified under this policy.

"Valid loss-of-time benefits" shall include any amount received by or due an insured, for the same period from (1) Social Security, Old-Age, Survivors and Disability Insurance; (2) any other state or federal government disability pension or retirement plans; (3) salary paid by the employer; (4) any retirement or pension plan; (5) Workmen's Compensation or any similar law; and (6) any total disability or total and permanent disability provision of any insurance policy.

Unfortunately, this clause operates only to reduce the liability of those companies with such a clause in their policies. If the insured has one or more policies without such a clause, it is still possible for him to collect more than his income. For example, if the insured had a $200-per-month policy in Company A with an average earnings clause and a $300-per-month policy with Company B with no such clause, if a loss was suffered when his average earnings were $250, Company A would pay 250/500 or 50 percent of the benefit amount. Company A would thus pay $100 and Company B, without the clause, would pay the full amount of its monthly benefit, $300. Thus the insured would be collecting $400 per month to cover a $250-per-month loss. Such a situation hardly seems conducive to rapid recovery.

Even if Company B also had such a clause, its liability would be reduced only to $150 per month for a total of $250 per month from the two companies. Since the insured does not have to pay income, social security, or wage taxes on the insurance proceeds and saves the expenses of travel, lunches, and perhaps work clothes and/or tools, he would still find it profitable to be disabled.

For maximum effectiveness, every policy providing disability income must have such a clause. This includes OASDI, workmen's compensation policies, life insurance disability riders, and any salary continuance plan. Since it is extremely unlikely that all such coverages would include an average earnings clause, a company that wants protection from the moral hazard associated with overinsurance should use a clause which provides that the benefits of the policy will be reduced so that the total collected will not exceed (say) 75 percent of average earnings. One life insurance company uses such a clause in contracts sold in combination with life insurance. This will be examined in detail in the following chapter. The use of such a clause in health insurance would not be permissible under present legislation, but legislatures and insurance commissioners should be able to see the logic of such an arrangement if the facts were presented. The reason for limiting liability to 75 percent or less of average earnings is to compensate for the tax and other savings associated with not working and, if such savings are less than (say) 25 percent of income, to make the claimant a coinsurer for a small portion of the loss.

The industry recently has presented a suggestion to the National Association of Insurance Commissioners which would meet the recommendations above.[5] It suggests amending the Uniform Policy Provisions Law to permit a new and stricter optional "Relation of Earnings to Insurance" provision which may be used in commercial as well as noncancellable and guaranteed renewable disability income contracts. It provides for a prorating of benefits with other valid loss-of-time coverage which has a similar clause in the proportion that not less than 60 percent of the insured's average earnings bears to the total of all such coverage. However, if any other contract does not contain an effective relation of earnings to insurance clause, its amount is deducted from both the numerator and the denominator of the prorate ratio. The contract then becomes excess insurance as to such other contract and pays only the excess over the other insurance up to a maximum of 60 percent of the average earnings.

[5] John P. Hanna, *Seventh Status Report on Overinsurance for the Accident and Health Committee of the National Association of Insurance Commissioners,* 1963.

The clause would apply only to benefits after disability had continued for more than 91 days, which would eliminate from 90 to 95 percent of disabilities from its application. This would reduce the expense of applying it and reduce potential policyholder disappointment. There is no provision for a refund of premium. An insurer may use a higher percentage than 60 percent if it wishes.

The suggested clause reads as follows:

*Overinsurance:* After the loss-of-time benefit of this policy has been payable for 90 days, such benefit will be adjusted, as provided below, if the total amount of unadjusted loss-of-time benefits provided in all valid loss-of-time coverage upon the insured should exceed 60% of the insured's earned income; provided, however, that if the information contained in the application discloses that the total amount of loss-of-time benefits under this policy and under all other valid loss-of-time coverage expected to be effective upon the insured in accordance with the application for this policy exceeded 60% of the insured's earned income at the time of such application, such higher percentage will be used in place of 60%. Such adjusted loss-of-time benefit under this policy for any month shall be only such proportion of the loss-of-time benefit otherwise payable under this policy as

    (i) the product of the insured's earned income and 60% (or, if higher, the alternative percentage described at the end of the first sentence of this provision)

bears to

    (ii) the total amount of loss-of-time benefits payable for such month under this policy and all other valid loss-of-time coverage on the insured (without giving effect to the "overinsurance provision" in this or any other coverage)

less in both (i) and (ii) any amount of loss-of-time benefits payable under other valid loss-of-time coverage which does not contain an "overinsurance provision." In making such computation, all benefits and earnings shall be converted to a consistent [weekly or monthly] basis. If the numerator of the foregoing ratio is zero or is negative, no benefit shall be payable under this policy. In no event shall this provision (i) operate to reduce the total combined amount of loss-of-time benefits for such month payable under this policy and all other valid loss-of-time coverage below the lesser of $300 and the total combined amount of loss-of-time benefits determined without giving effect to any "overinsurance provision," nor (ii) operate to increase the amount of benefits payable under this policy above the amount which would have been paid in the absence of this provision, nor (iii) take into account or operate to reduce any benefit other than the loss-of-time benefit.

For purposes of this provision:

    (i) "earned income," except where otherwise specified, means the greater of the monthly earnings of the insured at the time disability commences and his average monthly earnings for a period of two years immediately preceding the commencement of such disability, and shall not include any investment income or any other income not derived from the insured's vocational activities.

(ii) "overinsurance provision" shall include this provision and any other provision with respect to any loss-of-time coverage which may have the effect of reducing an insurer's liability if the total amount of loss-of-time benefits under all coverage exceeds a stated relationship to the insured's earnings.

The following examples illustrate the application of the recommended provision.

If a person is disabled for five months with disability income coverage in both company A and company B of $500 and $300 of monthly income benefit respectively, both policies include the proposed relation of earnings to insurance provision, and the insured's "monthly earnings" as defined in the proposed provision are $1,000, so that 60% of monthly earnings (or $600) is less than the combined benefits otherwise payable under the two policies, the payments would be as follows.

For the first 91 days of disability the proposed relation of earnings to insurance provision is inapplicable. During this period the full combined monthly benefits of $800 are payable regardless of the insured's earnings.

For each month after the first 91 days of disability, policy A pays:

$$\text{Benefits otherwise payable} \times \frac{60\% \text{ of monthly earnings}}{\text{total loss of time benefits}}$$

or

$$\$500 \times \frac{\$600}{\$800} = \$375$$

For each month after the first 91 days of disability, policy B pays:

$$\$300 \times \frac{\$600}{\$800} = \$225$$

The total payment to policyholder is $375 plus $225, or $600 a month. This equals 60 percent of monthly earnings.

If the situation is the same except that policy B does not have a relation of earnings to insurance clause, company B pays full benefits of $300 and the benefits payable by company A are adjusted as follows:

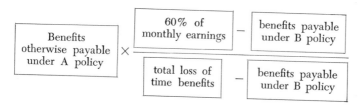

$$A \text{ policy pays } \$500 \times \frac{\$600-\$300}{\$800-\$300}$$

or

$$\$500 \times \frac{\$300}{\$500} = \$300$$

The total payment to policyholder is $300 plus $300, or $600 a month. This equals 60 percent of monthly earnings.

The general adoption of such a contract provision would effectively control overinsurance and permit more generous underwriting limits. The Accident and Health Committee of the National Association of Insurance Commissioners unanimously approved the seventh status report in December, 1963, and urged that the states pass legislation permitting the use of this provision. Bills have been introduced in a number of states, but none has been passed to date. The New Hampshire Commissioner approved the provision by administrative ruling in June, 1964, but this remains the only jurisdiction where it may be used.

Because of the moral hazard involved in insuring disability income for housewives, most insurers will not insure them at all and every insurer which does limits benefits to a small amount and short duration. Employed females are readily insurable, so long as they stay employed. To meet the risk of a female insured leaving the labor force and later claiming substantial disability benefits where there is no economic loss, many insurers use a clause reducing benefits unless the female is gainfully employed outside her home prior to disablement. The following clause is typical:

*Section F. Special Provision for Policy Issued to Employed Woman Policyholder*
In consideration of the premium rate at which this contract is issued, it is understood and agreed that if disability commences while the insured is not gainfully employed away from her residence, the benefit payable under this contract will be reduced to 25 percent of the benefit otherwise payable.

*House-confining clauses* are found in a small proportion of guaranteed renewable policies. With the one exception noted, these are all short-term policies. Aggregate lifetime limits are almost as rare and are mostly found in policies with a short-term sickness benefit. With a short limit on an aggregate basis, these contracts are extremely illiberal.

*Term and renewal.* The distinctive feature of a noncancellable policy is the renewal guarantee. This is not essential from a legal standpoint, since the elimination of the cancellation clause and the expression of the policy term as running to (say) age 65 would have the same effect. It is necessary where the contract is written for a one-year term. It usually is included, whether necessary or not, to prevent any possible misunderstanding and to serve as a talking point for the agent. It reads as follows in one contract:

## NONCANCELLABLE AND GUARANTEED RENEWABLE TO AGE 65 AT GUARANTEED PREMIUMS

This policy is noncancellable and guaranteed renewable by the timely payment of premiums in the guaranteed amount specified in the Policy Schedule until the premium due date on or next following the Insured's 65th birthday, or until eligible for full old age benefits under Title II of the Social Security Act, whichever is earlier, during which time, without the consent of the Insured

1. The Company cannot cancel this policy.
2. The Company cannot refuse to accept any premium for this policy paid before the end of the grace period,
3. The Company cannot add any restrictive rider or endorsement to this policy,
4. The Company cannot change any provision of this policy, and,
5. The Company cannot increase the premium or make any additional charge for this policy.

The continuance of this policy after the Insured's 65th birthday, or after eligible for full old age benefits under Title II of the Social Security Act, whichever is earlier, is subject to the provisions of Part 2, Section E.

*Section E. Continuance of Policy between Ages 65 and 70 While Gainfully Employed, Subject to Company's Right to Decline Renewal*

This policy may be continued for the period between the Insured's 65th and 70th birthdays while he is regularly and gainfully employed on a full-time basis unless the Company shall have delivered to the Insured or mailed to his last known address as shown by the records of the Company written notice of its intention not to renew this policy at least 30 days prior to the premium due date. If the Company accepts a premium covering any period after the Insured's 70th birthday or after he has ceased to be regularly and gainfully employed on a full-time basis, the Company's liability will be limited to a refund of all premiums accepted after age 70 or after he ceased to be gainfully employed. The Insured shall be considered to be employed on a full-time basis if his earned income is sufficient to disqualify him for any benefits under Title II of the Social Security Act.

Premiums payable after the Insured's 65th birthday are not guaranteed as to amount but shall be based on the Company's table of rates for Insured's age 65 and over, which table may be changed with respect to premiums becoming due thereafter.

Sometimes the guarantee extends to the (say) 65th anniversary of birth. Most policies are noncancellable until age 65; age 60 is the next most common provision for men and the most common for women; and a few are noncancellable for life or until "retirement." A guarantee of renewal for life is rare and usually is found only in a policy covering only accidental injury. Some contracts are continuable after age 65 on a guaranteed renewable basis whereby the premium can be adjusted on a class basis. Sometimes the contract may be renewed after age 65 only with the insurer's consent (a commercial basis). There are other variants.

Most policies provide that benefits are not payable past the renewal guarantee date, except that a minimum of 12 months' payments will be made for disability commencing at age 64. Some provide no such limit and rely only on the maximum benefit per disability to limit liability. This approach is most common in the policies guaranteed renewable only to age 60. A growing number of companies permit continuance after age 65 if the insured is employed full time. The policy becomes renewable at the insurer's option, rates are not guaranteed, and the maximum benefit period is one year in the example above.

The incontestable clause is required in noncancellable and guaranteed renewable policies. It frequently accompanies the renewal guarantee and usually reads as follows:

*Incontestable.* After this policy has been in force for a period of two years during the lifetime of the Insured it shall become incontestable as to the statements contained in the application and as to the physical condition of the Insured on the date of this policy.

The consideration and term of the policy are described in a somewhat different fashion than in commercial contracts. The policy may be continuous to the expiration of the renewal guarantee period. In this case the clause is more similar to that found in life insurance policies than to commercial health policies. It reads as follows in one contract:

This policy will take effect this ...... day of .........., 19.... and unless it lapses for nonpayment of premium it will continue to the sixty-fifth anniversary of the Insured's birth, on which date it will expire. If the Company accepts a premium applicable wholly or in part to a period subsequent to the sixty-fifth anniversary of the Insured's birth the policy will continue in force after such anniversary but only until the end of the period for which premium has been accepted.

### Guaranteed renewable contracts

The only essential difference between noncancellable and guaranteed renewable contracts is that under the latter, the premium may be adjusted for classes of insureds or for all insureds under a particular policy form. In general, the benefits available under guaranteed renewable disability income contracts are similar to those under noncancellable contracts. Indeed, a number of companies use identical contracts except for the renewal clause and premium rates. A growing number of insurers are using one standard disability contract form for noncancellable, guaranteed renewable, and optionally renewable, differing only in the renewal provision and premium rate. Noncancellable rates are about

11 percent above guaranteed renewable rates for the same benefits and commercial rates about 10 percent less.

A typical guaranteed renewable clause reads as follows:

### GUARANTEED RENEWABLE TO AGE 65
### SUBJECT TO ADJUSTABLE PREMIUMS

This policy may be renewed by the Insured by the timely payment of premiums until the premium due date on or next following his 65th birthday. The premium set forth in the Policy Schedule is based on the Company's table of rates in effect on the Policy Date and will remain in effect unless and until the table of rates is changed in accordance with the next paragraph.

The Company's table of rates may be changed at any time with respect to premiums becoming due on and after the effective date of the change but no change in premium will be made which does not also apply to all other persons covered under policies of this form of the same sex, rating classification and original insuring age. While this policy is continued in force:

1. The Company cannot cancel this policy,
2. The Company cannot refuse to accept any premium for this policy paid before the end of the grace period,
3. The Company cannot add any restrictive rider or endorsement to this policy, and
4. The Company cannot change any provision of this policy.

The continuance of this policy after the Insured's 65th birthday, or after eligible for full old age benefits under Title II of the Social Security Act, whichever is earlier, is subject to the provisions of Part 2, Section E.

Other companies issue a line of guaranteed renewable contracts which differs considerably from their noncancellable contracts. Still others issue only guaranteed renewable and no noncancellable. Guaranteed renewable premiums may be somewhat lower than noncancellable, since the right to increase them for broad classes of insureds is retained. However, they should not be too much lower, since such increases are unpopular with the customers and expensive to administer. As indicated, about 10 percent lower seems about right. Moreover, if the increases are too great, the healthier insureds will drop out, leaving the insurer with a very unhealthy group. For these reasons, the initial premium should be high enough to minimize the probability of having to institute a subsequent rate increase.

**Summary**

Noncancellable contracts give the insured the unqualified right to continue the policy in force by payment of agreed premiums for a substantial period of time. Their benefits are essentially similar to commercial policies, but the contracts have fewer frills and restrictions. The primary coverage is of loss of income from total disability. Most policies cover both injury and disease in a single policy, but frequently a shorter benefit limit is placed on disability produced by disease. Many contracts are available with disease benefits payable to age 65 or beyond, and most provide at least a 10-year sickness benefit.

Hospital, surgical, and medical benefits are included in some disability income policies by rider, on a truly noncancellable basis. However, most such coverage is provided by separate medical expense policies in which the company reserves the right to change premiums for broad classes of insureds. Income protection contracts are issued by many companies on this guaranteed renewable basis with premiums adjustable by classes. Such policies usually differ from noncancellable only in premium rate and the right to change it.

The long-term noncancellable policies represent the best protection currently available against long-term income loss and, like major and comprehensive medical, seem to represent the "wave of the future."

### Selected references

See the following items from the General Bibliography: 4, ch. 9; 7, ch. 5; 8; 10, pp. 141–49; 15, ch. 21; 18, pp. 398–407; 19, ch. 22.

BIGGS, D. E. "Permanent Health Insurance," Post, September 23, 1965, p. 1493.

———. "Permanent Health Insurance," Policy Holder, April 14, 1967, p. 511.

DICKERSON, O. D. Guaranteed Renewable Disability Insurance. Ann Arbor, Mich.: University Microfilms, Inc., 1957.

———. "Insurance against Long-Term Disability," Journal of the American Society of Chartered Life Underwriters, Fall, 1960, p. 345.

FARLEY, JARVIS P. "A 1940 View of Non-Cancellable Disability Insurance," Proceedings of the Casualty Actuarial Society, Vol. XXVII, p. 40.

HANNA, JOHN P. Seventh Status Report on Overinsurance. Health Insurance Association of America, 1962.

MILLER, JOHN H. "History and Present Status of Non-Cancellable Accident and Health Insurance," Proceedings of the Casualty Actuarial Society, Vol. XXI, p. 235.

SOLOMON, E. R. "Overinsurance—Its Control through Contractual Provisions," Annals of the Society of Chartered Property Casualty Underwriters, Fall, 1966, p. 197.

## chapter 13

Proud rider on so proud a back.—Shakespeare, *Venus and Adonis*

# Life Insurance Riders

## Introduction

Life insurance contracts have the primary function of protecting against financial loss resulting from premature death. As a secondary function, all permanent life insurance involves elements of saving which help to provide for the alternative event of old age. Because death and disability are so intimately related, being produced by the same perils and producing a similar loss to the family, it is logical to expect to find protection against both provided in the same contract. When such disability provision is made, it generally is in the form of a rider or supplementary contract, rarely as a part of the basic policy.

There are two main types of disability provision found in, or added to, life insurance policies. The most common is a provision for the waiver of the life insurance premiums in the event of total and "permanent" disability. Less common is a rider providing for the payment of an income benefit to the disabled insured.

Disability benefits paid by life insurance companies under life insurance contracts equalled $169 million in 1966. This represents $130 million in disability income and $39 million in waived premiums. Premium income for disability benefits was $223 million. These figures exclude health insurance benefits, government life insurance, savings banks, and fraternal and assessment associations.

The accidental death benefit (or double indemnity provision) in life insurance contracts does not represent disability protection. It is life insurance, not health insurance, and will not be discussed further in this book.

## Development

Total and permanent disability provisions in life insurance contracts first appeared in Germany in 1876. In the United States such provisions were included in the contracts of fraternal societies as early as 1877. A typical provision was for waiver of premiums and payment of one half the face with the balance staying in force until death or recovery. The first insurance company provision was issued by the Fidelity Mutual in 1896. It gave the insured a choice of either waiver of premiums or an annuity such as the face value would purchase on a "disability annuity" basis. This annuity was higher than could be purchased by a healthy life at an equivalent age. Straight waiver provisions were introduced by the Travelers in 1906 and the New York Life in 1910. A series of actuarial studies of foreign and fraternal experience was published in these years, and Hunter's Table became the commonly used basis for premium rates. By 1914 about half of the companies were issuing some type of disability benefit.

Early policies defined disability as the state of being "wholly and permanently disabled by bodily injury or disease, so that he [the insured] is and will be permanently, continuously and wholly prevented thereby from performing any work for compensation or profit." Some provided that blindness or double dismemberment would be presumed to be total and permanent disability. Most offered only a waiver of premium benefit, but a substantial number also offered one or more of the following benefits:

1. Payment of the face of the policy in installments. (This payment was without any interest and cost the company only $736 for 20 years or $861 for 10 years, per $1,000 of face amount at 3½ percent interest.)
2. Lump-sum payment of the face. This was usually provided only for disability due to accidental injury and sometimes only for certain types of accident.)
3. Payment of the face in the form of an ordinary life annuity. (This allowed the companies a substantial recovery from the greater mortality of disabled lives.)

None of these provisions offered very much to the insured beyond waiver, and frequently they were included in the basic policy at no extra charge beyond the extra premium for the waiver feature.

The first substantial income benefits appeared about 1915. The first policies provided for a payment of 10 percent of the face annually, the life insurance remaining in force. By 1917, at least two companies had shifted to a monthly basis and paid 1/120 of the face each month. By 1920, the typical provision was changed to pay 1/100 or 1 percent of the face each month. This is still the most common relationship.

The early contracts had required a physician's prognosis of permanence of disability, but in the 1920's a new definition was introduced. Under this clause, disability was presumed permanent after 90 days. Thus the contracts were insuring against all total disability with a duration over three months, not just permanent disability. The effect of this on claim rates was greatly underestimated.

Some companies began to issue contracts providing for a monthly disability annuity of 2 percent of the face. Underwriting standards were lowered, sales boomed, and insuring clauses were liberalized. Some companies adopted the far more liberal "his occupation" definition of disability. Finally, a few companies began to pay disability income benefits retroactively from the original date of disablement, instead of from the end of the waiting period. Income clauses were sold to women and children and on nonmedical and substandard policies.

The 1926 report of the Society of Actuaries showed much higher rates of disability, and a few companies increased premiums as a result. By 1928, all but one of the largest 65 companies had some type of disability income clause. In 1929 a N.A.I.C. committee recommended standardization of benefit provisions, but this report, like the rate revisions, came too late. The depression had begun.

Losses began to rise rapidly, and companies restricted their writings, tightened up their policy provisions, and raised premium rates. One company raised premiums three different times in 1930 alone. By 1932, companies began to withdraw the benefit entirely as far as new issues were concerned. As in noncancellable, heavy losses were suffered, and this painful experience remained fresh in company executives' minds for a generation.

A sizable minority of companies continued to write disability income coverage with a number of changes. Disability had to occur prior to age 55 rather than age 60; monthly income was reduced to $5 per $1,000 of face amount; the waiting period was increased to six months with no retroactive benefits except for waiver; rates were increased and underwriting made much more strict. In group insurance, disability income coverage virtually ceased to exist. Experience on the new clauses written after 1932 was generally profitable, but, because of the backlog of old business, most companies continued to show losses on the line for many years. Those which did not continue in the business suffered the heaviest losses, since they did not have the newer business to offset losses on the old. The aggregate business did not begin to show a profit consistently until the 1950's. In the past 25 years, quite a number of companies have again begun to issue a $10-per-month income benefit with, however, a provision for maturity of the contract as an endowment with no further income payments at (usually) age 65.

## Benefit provisions

*Individual insurance—waiver of premium.* Practically every United States life insurance company issues waiver of premium benefits. Several companies, including two of the largest, include a waiver of premium benefit as a part of all standard life insurance contracts. The typical company, however, writes waiver benefits on about half of the life insurance issued.

The definition of disability is usually the "any occupation" definition. One company uses a loss of earned income definition, and one uses "any . . . occupation for which he (the insured) is or may be suited by education, training or experience." As indicated above, this is the interpretation which many courts have placed on the phrase "any occupation." Some use a "his occupation" definition for the first few years and then "any for which fitted." A modern definition of total disability is as follows:

*Definition of Total Disability*

Total disability means disability which: (*a*) resulted from bodily injury or disease; (*b*) began after the issue date of this policy and before the policy anniversary nearest the Insured's 60th birthday; (*c*) has existed continuously for at least six months; and (*d*) prevents the Insured from engaging for remuneration or profit in an occupation. During the first twenty-four months of disability, occupation means the occupation of the Insured at the time such disability began; thereafter it means any occupation for which he is or becomes reasonably fitted by education, training, or experience.

The total and irrecoverable loss of the sight of both eyes, or of the use of both hands, or both feet, or of one hand and one foot shall be considered total disability even if the Insured shall engage in an occupation.

The majority of companies provide, as in the clause quoted, that blindness or loss of both hands, both feet, or one hand and one foot is presumed to be total disability. Most of these use the phrase "loss of use of," but a substantial number require "severance."

The insuring and benefit clauses are combined in most such provisions. The following is typical of modern practice.

*The Benefit*

The Company will waive the payment of all premiums becoming due during the total disability of the Insured.

The dividends, policy values, and other benefits of this policy shall be the same as if premiums waived has been paid in cash.

It is most common to provide that disability must occur before age 60, although about half the companies impose a limit of age 55 for females. Coverage may begin at age 5, 10, or 15, or this reference may be omitted and coverage of the younger ages avoided by means of underwriting.

It should be noted that all premiums are waived during disability, not just those falling due after the expiration of the waiting period. This is different from the disability income provision and from most waiver of premium provisions in health insurance policies. Almost all companies require six months of disability in order for the waiver benefit to take effect, but at least two require only a four-month period.

As long as disability commences during the period of coverage, all premiums are waived while it continues, even those falling due after age 60. Of course, if the policy is an endowment contract, the face is payable to the insured at maturity, and the contract then terminates. Where the policy is a term insurance contract, most companies continue protection until the end of life. This is equivalent to converting the policy to an ordinary life contract, except that it reverts to a term basis if the insured recovers. In some companies the conversion is formal and final. This is the usual provision even if there is no renewal or conversion provision in the term life insurance contract. On recovery, the insured must pay the higher premiums of the ordinary life contract.

The exclusions are those typical of health insurance generally: war and self-inflicted injury. The following clause is typical:

Disability resulting directly from wilfully and intentionally self-inflicted injury and disability resulting from an act of war or from any of the special hazards incident to service in the military, naval, or air forces of any country at war, declared or undeclared, are risks not assumed by the Company under this provision.

Some companies also exclude one or more of the following: injury received while committing an assault or felony, while riding in a submarine, air travel except as a fare-paying passenger of a scheduled line, riot, military aircraft, or injury or disease occurring outside the United States and Canada. The misstatement of age clause in the basic life policy applies; other prorating clauses are usually not included in disability riders, nor would they be applicable to waiver benefits.

*Individual insurance—income benefits.* About one-third of United States life insurance companies issue a disability income provision. Most of these issue a benefit of $10 per month per $1,000 of face amount of life insurance. At least two companies issue a $20 benefit, one of which reduces to $10 after age 60. Most of the companies with a $10 benefit make payments only to age 65 (or sometimes 60), and then the policy matures as an endowment. This means that disability income payments cease, the face amount is payable, subject to usual settlement options, and the contract is terminated. Sometimes income ceases at age 65 and the policy is paid up, but no endowment benefit is paid.

Some companies, however, pay $10 per month to age 65, and then reduce the benefit to $5 per month and pay this amount for life. One pays for life, even if the life policy matures earlier. One company pays benefits for 10 years and then the policy matures.

The most common single type of provision is for a $10 income payable to age 65, at which time the policy matures as an endowment. Where income benefits are issued, premium waiver is included, and it is common to combine the two benefits under a single insuring clause. The following portions of a disability income rider are typical of the most common type of provision. The contract covers disability commencing before age 60, which is the most common, although age 55 is not rare.

*Payment of Monthly Income:* The Company will, during the continuance of such disability, pay to the insured, or, at the election of the Company, if such disability is due to or is accompanied by mental incapacity, to any beneficiary under the policy for the benefit of the insured, a monthly income of one percent of the Sum Insured under the policy, exclusive of any paid-up additions thereto, for the sixth and each succeeding completed month of such disability until the anniversary of the policy on which the age of the insured at nearest birthday is sixty-five years or until prior maturity or termination of the policy, provided, however, that in no case shall any monthly income be paid for the first five months of disability, nor for any fractional part of a month of disability, nor for any period of disability more than six months prior to the date of receipt at the Home Office of the Company of written notice of claim hereunder; and

*Maturity of Policy as an Endowment:* if a payment of monthly income as provided above is payable during the month preceding the anniversary of the policy on which the age of the insured at nearest birthday is sixty-five years and if, on the said anniversary, the insured is alive and continues to be disabled as defined herein the Company will, on the said anniversary, pay to the insured a final disability payment equal to the difference between the Sum Insured and the reserve under the policy and such additional sum as is sufficient together with the aforesaid final disability payment to equal the Sum Insured plus the value of any paid-up additions, any dividends, and any dividend accumulations and less any indebtedness on the policy, the payment of which sums will thereby mature the policy as an endowment. Such maturity of the policy as an endowment shall, except as to any provisions of the Optional Methods of Settlement which may be effective, discharge the Company from all liability under this provision and under the policy and terminate all rights under this provision and under the policy.

It is perhaps illogical to look upon maturity as an endowment as an additional benefit. Actually, $1,000 of proceeds, if applied under a life income option (10 years certain) will produce only about $6 per month for life for a male age 65. At age 60 it would produce only $5.34. Thus, from the company's standpoint, the endowment payment is the equivalent of reducing the company's liability by at least 40 percent. However, since the insured has the option of taking cash or some other settlement option not involving mortality contingencies, adverse selection will probably largely offset such savings. The less healthy insureds are unlikely to select the life income option.

This rider, as is common, requires that disability centinue at least six months to be compensable, but pays the first check at the end of the sixth month. This is really the equivalent of a five-month waiting period or, more precisely, a six-month period with a one-month retroactive payment. Some companies impose a four- or six-month waiting period, but the above is by far the most common.

Most contracts provide that disability benefits will not reduce the amounts otherwise payable under the contract, including dividends and nonforfeiture values.

The definition of disability and the exclusions usually are the same as those used in waiver of premium benefits.

Disability income is not sold in connection with industrial life insurance, but waiver of premium and/or dismemberment benefits sometimes are sold. Often separate industrial disability policies are available from insurers which write industrial life.

*Group insurance.* Three types of disability provisions are commonly found in group life insurance policies. The most liberal of these is a provision for payment of the face of the certificate (usually in installments). This was commonly issued until about 1932 and again apparently is returning to favor. This clause generally provides for payment of the face in the event of total and permanent disability prior to age 60. Usually the face of the certificate is paid in installments over a short period, such as 60 months. This provision is again becoming more common, especially in Canada.

The next most liberal, and currently the most commonly issued, provision is for a lifetime waiver of premiums. This has been the most frequently issued coverage since about 1938. It provides that, in the event of total and permanent disability incurred prior to age 60, the insurance will be continued beyond the period for which the employer pays premiums. Usually the waiver of premium extends for a succession of one-year periods, subject to written notice of continuance of disability each year. Sometimes total and permanent disability is presumed in the case of blindness and double dismemberment.

The least liberal clause was issued mainly between 1932 and 1938. It provides for an "extended death benefit." This amounts to a one-year waiver of premium. If the employee is disabled before (usually) age 65, the death benefit remains in force during one year of continuous disability. On group insurance in force a few years ago, the maturity benefit was used for 38 percent of the lives insured, the extended death benefit for 23 percent, and the waiver of premium for 39 percent.[1]

Group insurance policies usually use the "any occupation" definition of disability, but some make use of the type of definition which changes from "any occupation" to "any occupation for which fitted" after a number of years as in the individual policy quoted above.

---

[1] Davis W. Gregg, *Group Life Insurance* (3d ed., Homewood, Ill.: Richard D. Irwin, Inc., 1962), pp. 73–77.

*Mutual Benefit Life—a unique approach.*  A disability income contract which occupies a place midway between noncancellable insurance and life insurance riders is issued by the Mutual Benefit Life Insurance Company of Newark, New Jersey. This is a separate contract, not a rider, but is issued only in combination with life insurance issued by the same company. The amount of maximum disability benefit is limited to $10 per $1,000 of life insurance in the accompanying policy ($5 per $1,000 for women).

This company entered the disability business in 1929, at a time when most companies were already feeling the impact of the depression. It is the only major insurer to show profits consistently through the depression years on disability business. It employs a unique definition of disability, has an average earnings clause[2] with teeth, and has a number of other special features.

Disability is defined as a reduction in earned income of 75 percent or more resulting from accidental injury or sickness. This reduction must continue for four months in order to qualify for benefits. Premiums are waived retroactively to the date of disablement, and income benefits are paid after the four months. The definition of total and permanent disability reads as follows:

> The insured will be regarded as totally disabled when, by reason of accidental bodily injury or by sickness, his average monthly earned income for a period of four months has not exceeded one-fourth of his former earned income (average monthly for the twelve months immediately preceding such four months), and such disability will be regarded as permanent while the earned monthly income of the insured, on account of such injury or sickness, does not exceed the said one-fourth.

The average earnings clause reads as follows:

### REDUCTION OF BENEFITS

> If the insured shall be regarded as totally disabled under the provisions hereof, and the monthly income benefit to which he shall be entitled hereunder, and under other Supplementary Disability Policies issued to him by the Company, together with the income benefits, if any, to which he shall be entitled, by reason of bodily injury or disease, under insurance in any other company or association of whatever kind, shall exceed in the aggregate seventy-five per centum of his former earned income, ascertained as herein provided, the monthly income provided for herein shall be reduced so that the total monthly income under this and such other insurance, if any, shall not exceed seventy-five per centum of such former earned income. In event of such reduction future premiums hereon will be equitably reduced, and the company

---

[2] The term "average earnings clause" is used generically to include clauses like this one as well as the present and proposed "relation of earnings to insurance" clauses discussed above.

will pay an equitable part of the Cash Surrender Value hereof, computed as of a date immediatedly preceding disability. If at the time of such reduction, there shall be an election to have the premiums remain at their original amount, and to leave with the Company the portion of the Cash Surrender Value referred to above, and if the Company is thereafter notified that the income benefits to which the Insured was entitled under insurance in other companies or associations at the time of approval of proofs as herein provided, have been reduced or terminated, the monthly income benefits which may become due hereunder after such notification, by reason of his then disability, will be redetermined as herein provided. In event of such election, and of the Insured's recovery from his then disability, the monthly income benefit provided for herein will be restored to its original amount, subject to all the provisions hereof.

A general adoption of a definition of disability and average earnings clause similar to the above would do a great deal to remove the difficulty in determining the existence of disability and to eliminate the moral hazard of overinsurance. This is not merely a prorating clause. It provides for the reduction of benefits in this contract by an amount sufficient to make sure that total insurance proceeds do not exceed 75 percent of the insured's earned income. The entire reduction could come from this policy alone; indeed, it is possible for the benefits under this contract to be reduced to zero. Equity is maintained in such cases by the provision for payment of cash-surrender values. Very few health insurance contracts or riders provide cash values. For this contract, they are computed on the basis of Hunter's Table and are rather low. Presumably, if the insured had policies with several companies with such average earnings clauses, the benefits of each policy would be reduced proportionately. One other company uses a somewhat similar clause in its life insurance disability income rider.

The company originally used a clause worded somewhat differently which provided for determining the company's liability only at the time of proof of loss. It was company practice, however, to recompute the benefit if other policy benefits were reduced or terminated, and now this provision is a part of the clause. The clause has been applied in only about 3 percent of disability claims. This is attributed to a combination of conservative underwriting by the company and the recent uptrend in incomes.

Unfortunately, despite the strong arguments for the use of an average earnings clause, most companies have not adopted one. However, at least three other American companies and a number of Canadian ones are now using some type of average earnings clause in life insurance riders. Generally, these resemble more closely the type used in guaranteed renewable policies than the Mutual Benefit type.

Other unique features of the Mutual Benefit contract are the absence of a war clause and a provision for the insured to pay an increased premium and the difference in reserves if he changes to a more hazardous occupation. If the company is not notified of such a change, the benefit is reduced, as in health insurance contracts generally.

## Uses and limitations

The major problem in regard to life insurance disability riders is their limited economic effectiveness as protection against the costs of long-term disability. While waiver of premium riders are sold in connection with about 40 percent of life insurance issued, the amount of benefit is rather small. Merely waiving life insurance premiums does not put any new money into the family income stream. Waiver, however, does make it possible to maintain life insurance in force and does free other income (if any) for use in meeting the family budget.

Waiver benefits perform an important function in a health insurance program. In the event of permanent disability, most health insurance policies do not pay benefits past age 65. This leaves the problem of income in the later years to be solved by other means. Deferred pension rights and Old-Age, Survivors, and Disability Insurance benefits will contribute to this retirement income but are unlikely to be adequate for a middle-class standard of living. If a man is disabled at a young age the pension payments may be pitifully small. If the program contains life insurance with a waiver provision, the proceeds will accrue at retirement just as if the insured were active and paying premiums. Thus these contracts enable the insured to solve the problem of income beyond age 65, whether or not he is disabled.

Disability income benefits are sold in connection with only about 4 percent of new life insurance policies. Thus most of the population is not purchasing such protection. Moreover, the amount any individual can obtain is limited by the maximum ratio between the amount of disability income and the face amount of life insurance carried. Income benefits are not often sold with term insurance. To obtain a disability income of $600 per month, an insured would have to buy $60,000 of permanent insurance. This is more than a typical insured with an income of, say, $700–$800 a month is likely to feel he can afford. Moreover, if any of the insurance is in companies which do not issue disability income, the total amount of life insurance needed is even greater. Moreover, many life companies have low underwriting limits which drastically curtail the amount which may be purchased.

Both these difficulties stem from the memory of the poor experience of the depression. Because of this, companies feel that the amount of disability income on a single life must be drastically limited. Restricting it to a specified percentage of the life insurance in the same company serves this purpose. Moreover, the memory of the depression has made many company executives less than enthusiastic about disability income. Several of the largest companies, which incidentally suffered the most severe losses during the depression, do not issue it at all.

Life insurance disability income coverage has a number of advantages over separate health insurance policies. It is guaranteed renewable (and is sometimes incontestable). Benefits are payable for life, or else the policy matures as an endowment. Thus it provides income beyond age 65, which most health insurance policies, especially noncancellable and guaranteed renewable, do not. The premium tends to be less than for a noncancellable policy with comparable benefits. This is because of the longer waiting period, lower loading for expenses in the disability rider, since the basic life policy helps to cover the expenses, and because many companies use disability tables showing lower rates of disability than those used for noncancellable contracts. Contingency loadings also are likely to be lower. The cost of a disability rider usually will fall between that of a separate noncancellable policy and that of a commercial contract with comparable benefits and waiting periods.

It would seem desirable that the issuance of disability income riders be greatly extended. This could be accomplished through a combination of relaxed limits on amounts issued and more aggressive sales efforts. The limit of issue might be raised to $15 or $20 per $1,000 of permanent life insurance, or disability income might be issued in connection with term, family income, and similar contracts. Safeguards against over-insurance could be maintained by strict underwriting as to the relation of insurance to earnings at the time of issue, coupled with the use of an average earnings clause of the Mutual Benefit Life type.

One obstacle to more aggressive selling is the feeling that a potential rejection for disability income may ruin the life insurance sale. Several techniques have been employed by some companies to avoid this problem. One method is for the life underwriter to get all the necessary information for disability income and then offer an alternative contract containing the coverage at the time of delivery. Where the applicant is not eligible, he does not even learn that he has been considered. Other companies consider every life insurance application an application for disability income as well and issue the alternative policy as a matter of routine. Of course, in some cases, selling disability income coverage may *help* the sale of life insurance.

## Summary

Life insurance disability riders are of two types. The most common provides only for waiver of premium on the basic life insurance contract. While this does not provide any disability income as such, it releases other resources and makes it possible to continue the protection and investment features of the life insurance policy. Thus provision for premature death and old age are not impaired by disability.

462    HEALTH INSURANCE

Disability income benefits are much less frequent but of greater total financial value. The most common provision involves a benefit of $10 per month for each $1,000 of life insurance payable until age 65, at which time the policy matures as an endowment. A few contracts pay a lesser amount per month per $1,000, sometimes for life. These riders fit the economic needs of the insured well and are generally a little cheaper than guaranteed renewable policies.

Their usefulness to the general population is limited by the requirement of heavy accompanying life insurance purchases and the companies' failure to promote their sale aggressively. The general adoption of an average earnings clause like that used by a few companies would go far to eliminate the moral hazard which the insurers fear.

### Selected References

*See the following items from the General Bibliography: 8; 14, ch. 2; 15, ch. 22; 17; 19, ch. 12; 15, pp. 234–36.*

GREGG, DAVIS W. *Group Life Insuranec.* 3d ed. Homewood, Ill.: Richard D. Irwin, Inc., 1962.

GREIDER, JANICE E., AND BEADLES, WILLIAM T. *Law and the Life Insurance Contract*, chap. 7. Rev. ed. Homewood, Ill. Richard D. Irwin, Inc., 1968.

HORNE, HAROLD M., AND MANSFIELD, D. BRUCE. *The Life Insurance Contract*, chap. 12. New York: Life Office Management Association, 1938.

KNIGHT, CHARLES KELLEY. *Advanced Life Insurance*, chap. 14. New York: John Wiley & Sons, Inc., 1926.

LAIRD, JOHN M. "Should Disability Be Subject to Pro Rate?" *Transactions of the Actuarial Society of America*, Vol. XXX.

——— (Chairman). "Fourth Report of the Committee Appointed by the A.L.C. to Study the Total and Permanent Disability Benefits in Life Insurance Contracts," *Proceedings American Life Convention*, Vol. XXIV, p. 403; also the third report, Vol. XXIII, p. 186.

McGILL, DAN M. *Life Insurance*, chap. 38. Rev. ed. Homewood, Ill.: Richard D. Irwin, Inc., 1967.

MILLER, JOHN H. "The Impact of New Disability Coverages on the Life Insurance Companies," *Journal of the American Association of University Teachers of Insurance*, March, 1952, p. 29.

MUDGETT, BRUCE D. *The Total Disability Provision in American Life Insurance Contracts.* Philadelphia: University of Pennsylvania Press, 1915.

SOCIETY OF ACTUARIES. "Report of Committee on Disability and Double Indemnity," *Transactions of the Society of Actuaries*, 1952 Reports Number, p. 70.

WALKER, R. W. "Writing a Life Insurance Policy," *Journal of Risk and Insurance*, March, 1964, p. 39.

YAMAMOTO, J. FUMIO. "Disability in the Past Five Years." Philadelphia: University of Pennsylvania, 1932. (Master's thesis; mimeographed.)

chapter 14

*It's clever, but is it art?*—Kipling, *The Conundrum of the Workshops*

# Limited and Industrial Contracts

## Introduction

All health insurance contracts necessarily impose limits. The term "limited," however, is used only for those which impose restrictions, exclusions, or limitations considerably greater than those found in commercial policies. The most frequent limitations apply to type of accident or disease and to period of coverage. Limited policies include railway and aviation ticket accident policies, newspaper policies, automobile accident policies, annual travel accident policies, and a variety of other specialized forms. It is estimated that over 20,000,000 persons are covered by travel or special-hazard policies.

Industrial health insurance contracts are the health insurance concomitant of industrial life insurance policies. They are similar to commercial forms, except that the amount and duration of benefit are lower and the premiums are payable weekly or monthly to an agent who calls at the home of the insured. They are often called "weekly premium policies." Companies selling industrial health policies almost always also sell industrial life policies, and the agent handles both.

The agent is a collector as well as a salesman. He is charged each week with the premiums due on the block of business assigned to him. This premium with which he is charged is referred to as a "debit," and, by extension, the term has come to be used to refer to the group of policies, to the territory in which the policyholders are located, and to the policyholders themselves. A typical debit represents a weekly premium of from $400 to $1,200, depending on territory, company, and the race of the policyholders. A typical territory is four to six blocks square but may be as small as a single apartment house or as large as a county, depending on population density.

The premium is payable weekly or monthly, and the policy term runs from week to week or month to month. However, the policy is continu-

463

ous until expiration or cancellation. The policyholder usually is allowed four weeks' grace period before the coverage is suspended for nonpayment of premium. While the premiums are in arrears, the policy is "out of benefit," but reinstatement is simple and informal unless the policyholder has an unfavorable claim record. The policyholder's payments are recorded in a small premium receipt book which remains in his (or usually her) possession and also in a record book maintained by the agent.

In some companies the agent's records are transferred weekly to a branch-office copy of his book. Frequently a premium discount is allowed if premiums are paid directly to the office, but sometimes only at the end of a year if there has been no lapse. Some agents are successful in training the people on their debit to pay two to five weeks at a time in advance. The ideal arrangement is to have them pay five weeks' premiums on the first of each month. This makes "carrying the book" a less confining job, and, since the policy holder gets eight weeks ahead each year, it reduces the probability of lapse.

## Development

Limited accident policies were the first type of health insurance policy to be issued by insurance companies. The pioneer company in England was the Railway Passenger's Assurance Company, which was chartered in 1848. The first American company was the Franklin Health Assurance Company of Massachusetts, but the real development of the business dates from the founding of the Travelers Insurance Company in 1863. This is the only one of the early insurers which has survived.

While more general policies, the first "commercial" contracts, soon were issued, the travel accident policy remained the backbone of the business for many years. By 1866 there were over 60 companies writing accident insurance, most specializing in railway ticket policies. The Travelers took the lead in forming a new corporation, the Railway Passengers Assurance Company of Hartford. This company was owned by the 10 leading companies and consolidated the ticket accident business.

By 1871, none of the 70 companies organized prior to 1869 remained. Travelers took over the ticket accident business in 1871 and in 1878 merged with the Railway Passengers. Since that time, other companies have, of course, entered the travel accident field. The business continues to be profitable. Except for the development of new types of policy and some broadening of benefits, there has been little change in the past half century.

Industrial health insurance developed from two sources. One was the industrial life insurance companies, which gradually extended their coverage to health insurance during the first two decades of this century. The other was the "friendly societies," mutual aid associations patterned on the English model, which specialized in sickness coverage. Many of these were mutual insurance companies in all but name, collecting "dues" from their members on a weekly basis. Many of these early societies were reorganized as insurance companies and extended their coverage to the life field.

### Benefits—limited policies

Limited policies are characterized by an emphasis on accidental death and dismemberment, a multiplicity of specific indemnities, and multiple indemnity provisions if the accident happens in the right way. Further generalization is difficult, and it will be better to analyze a few of the types of policy specifically.

*Aviation ticket policies.* The aviation ticket policy is by far the most popular of the limited contracts. It is sold mainly at counters or by coin machines located in airports. The standard of underwriting is somewhat lower than that employed in connection with railway ticket policies. The policy covers only injuries sustained as a result of accidents while a passenger is on a scheduled airline or nonscheduled U.S. common carrier airlines. Prior to the Vietnam affair certain U.S., Canadian, and British Military aircraft were covered, but they now are excluded. It also covers accidents in transit to an airport by airport bus or limousine (but not taxicab), while riding in a substitute and/or water vehicle provided at airline expense and while on the premises of an airport, all during or in connection with "the next one-way or round-trip flight."

The benefit amount for a round-trip or foreign flight is 75 percent of that for a one-way domestic flight. The instructions for purchase vary with the type of machine, but all involve the applicant filling out and signing a very brief application, including the address of the beneficiary, and inserting an appropriate number of quarters into the machine. The machine retains the application and the money; the policy, including the duplicate application, is mailed to the beneficiary. She is more likely to need it than the insured is, since the policy covers only death and dismemberment and from $1,000 to $5,000 of medical care expenses. The policy is not cancellable but expires automatically at the end of the flight, or at the expiration of 90 days. The contract provides that nonrenewable air-trip accident insurance with this company in excess of $100,000/$75,000 principal sum is void.

The contract is available in amounts from $20,000 to $100,000 of principal sum at a premium rate of 25 cents per $10,000. The amount of coverage has been increased three times in the past decade or so, from

$5,000 to $6,250 to $7,500 to $10,000, at no change in premium rate. Modern contracts are still broader than those of most past years, despite recent cutbacks.

The principal sum is paid for death, double dismemberment of loss of sight, half the principal sum is paid for single dismemberment, and one fourth for loss of the sight of one eye. In addition it provides reimbursement for medical, surgical, hospital and nurses' services up to $50 for each $1,000 of principal sum resulting from a covered accident. Since these are the only benefits, the contract is primarily one of accidental death insurance. The only exclusions pertain to war, suicide or attempt thereat, and commission of illegal acts by an insured.

A few years ago, three major insurers shared almost the entire aviation accident insurance market. First in the field was Associated Aviation Underwriters, which is an underwriting pool made up of about 40 domestic stock insurance companies. It is managed jointly by Chubb and Son and the Marine Office of America, two large insurance brokerage firms. Its aviation accident insurance business was sold over counters in airports by agents and also by machines which were owned by a life insurance holding company, Life Companies, Inc., which received 50 percent of the net profit on the aviation accident business as rental for the machines. The second insurer in the field was Continental Casualty Company, which initiated the over-the-counter type of operation in 1948. Its sales were handled through an organization known as Airport Sales, Inc, a wholly owned subsidiary. Continental recently has sold its interest in this company. Another important insurer is Mutual of Omaha, which sells its air travel business through Tele-Trip Co., Inc., a wholly owned subsidiary. Associated Aviation Underwriters and Continental had a reciprocal agreement, whereby each sold the insurance of the other, over the counter, when customers want more than the maximum $75,000 coverage. Such excess coverage is about 20 percent of total premium volume. Mutual of Omaha makes similar excess coverage available through its affiliate, United Benefit Life Insurance Co. The business produces in excess of $10,000,000 of annual premium.

A few years ago, Associated Aviation Underwriters withdrew from the field, and its business was taken over by the Fidelity and Casualty Company of New York, of the Continental Insurance group.

Automatic aviation accident coverage is offered by both American Express, through a blanket contract with Bankers Life and Casualty, and Diners Club, through a blanket contract with Beneficial Standard. The cardholder requests coverage by sending in a form, and thenceforth he is covered automatically whenever he charges a flight to his account. A premium of $3 per trip is charged through the credit card company. On family trips, if a collective charge is made, only one family member (head, wife, or eldest child, in that order) and one $3 premium is payable, but each member may be insured by charging each ticket separately, at a $3 premium per person.

Coverage is similar to the contracts described above except that any common carrier is covered for transit to and from an airport, non-scheduled airlines and airport premises are not covered, there is no medical expense benefit, and the principal sum is always $100,000, whether the flight is domestic or foreign, one-way or round trip.

*Ticket accident policies.* The ticket accident policy covers all types of accident for limited periods of time. The term "ticket" has two connotations. It is issued in railway stations and similar places by the carrier's ticket agent and by regular insurance agents. Second, the bottom of the policy form has a number of lines, similar to tickets. The period of coverage is indicated by cutting off the sections which do not apply, leaving the correct policy term and premium on the last existing line. A typical contract insures against loss "solely through external violent and accidental means." Its main benefit provision is as follows:

## LOSS OF LIFE OR LIMB

If such injuries shall result, directly and independently of all other causes, within ninety days after the date of accident, in any of the losses enumerated in this Part, the Company will pay the sum set opposite such loss in Column A if the injuries are sustained by the Insured while riding as a passenger in or upon a public conveyance (other than aircraft) provided by a common carrier for passenger service and propelled by mechanical power on land or water, or will pay the sum set opposite such loss in Column B if such injuries are sustained elsewhere; but under this Part not more than one (the larger) of the amounts specified will be paid for injuries resulting from one accident.

| For Loss of | Column A | Column B |
|---|---|---|
| Life (payable to estate of Insured as beneficiary)............................. | $5,000 | $3,000 |
| Both Hands or Both Feet..................... | 5,000 | 3,000 |
| Either Hand or Foot.......................... | 2,500 | 1,500 |

"Loss" shall mean with regard to hands and feet, actual severance through or above wrist or ankle joints.

The contract emphasizes its major benefit: payment of the face for death or double dismemberment resulting from travel accidents. Half this sum is paid for loss of one hand or one foot. Sixty percent of these amounts are paid if the loss occurs as a result of a more frequent type of accident; and, if the insured is not lucky enough to get killed or lose the proper members, he may collect in lieu of the lump sum the princely amount of $25 per week for up to 52 weeks of total disability for a travel accident, or $15 for an ordinary accident.

These contracts are issued with no underwriting and rely on policy provisions to control other insurance (prohibited) and occupational and extraordinary hazard (excluded, largely). The following list of exclusions leaves the reader wondering what, if anything, the insured can collect for:

## EXCLUSIONS

The insurance hereunder shall be void as to persons employed in mines, or in subaqueous work, or on iron or steel construction work, or on railroads, steam boats, or other passenger or freight conveyances while on duty, or on vessels of any kind while on duty; and persons maimed, crippled, or deformed, blind in one or both eyes, or deaf, or insane; or if, at the time this policy becomes effective, the person whose name is written upon the stub hereof is insured under any other Accident Ticket Policy in this Company. When this insurance is void the Company will return on demand the premium paid. This insurance shall not cover disappearance nor injuries (except drowning) of which there is no visible contusion or wound on the exterior of the body of the Insured, nor shall it cover injury, fatal or non-fatal, caused directly or indirectly, wholly or partly, by any of the following: medical or surgical treatment, hernia, disease in any form, gas or poison, sunstroke or freezing, firearms, or explosives of any kind, horse, automobile, motorcycle or bicycle racing, lacrosse, football, skiing, polo, hockey, fighting, riot, war or any act of war or suffered by the Insured while in the military or naval service of any country at war, suicide, sane or insane, or injuries inflicted intentionally by the Insured, or sustained by the Insured while resisting arrest or fleeing from justice, or while getting on or off any moving conveyance or trying so to do, or while in or on any part thereof not provided for the use of passengers, or while in or on any aircraft or other device for air travel, or in falling or otherwise descending therefrom or therewith, or while operating or handling any such aircraft or device.

The insurance under this Policy shall not cover any person under the age of eighteen years nor over the age of seventy years. Any premium paid to the Company for any period not covered by this Policy will be returned upon request.

Incidentally, the maximum amount issued is $5,000, as in the illustration. Thus adequate coverage cannot be obtained either by increasing the amount or by buying another policy. Other travel accident contracts are available with higher limits and broader coverage, but all represent extensions of this basic coverage.

*Newspaper policies.* The newspaper policy is even more interesting. It is not so called, as might be assumed, because it is printed on newsprint but because it is sold (or sometimes given away) with a newspaper subscription. The premium is paid either directly to the insurance company or is collected by the newsboy along with the payment for the newspaper. The newsboy is not a licensed insurance agent, but then neither is the machine that sells the aviation and railway ticket policies. The companies are currently trying to get their insureds to replace the old 7-cent policy with the newer and more liberal 10-cent policy. This premium covers for one week. An earlier policy, issued for a "registration fee" of $1 and the agreement to continue as a reader of the newspaper, provides death and specific dismemberment benefits from $2,500 to $12,500 for loss resulting directly, independently and exclusively of all other causes from bodily injuries effected solely through external, violent, and accidental means and sustained by the insured.

By the wrecking or disablement of any railroad passenger car or passenger steamship or steamboat or street railway car, elevated railway car, or subway car in or on which the Insured is traveling as a fare-paying passenger, in a place regularly provided for the sole use of fare-paying passengers.

If death or dismemberment results from "the wrecking or disablement of a taxicab, public omnibus or automobile stage, which is being driven or operated at the time of such wrecking or disablement by a licensed driver plying for public hire and in which the Insured is traveling as a fare-paying passenger" the maximum amount payable is $2,500. If the source of loss is "the wrecking or disablement of a private automobile (motor cycles excepted) or horse-drawn vehicle of the exclusively pleasure type in which the insured is riding or driving" the maximum benefit is $1,250. It is reduced to a maximum of $1,000 if the injury is produced:

(*a*) By the burning of a theatre, school, municipal building or church while the Insured is therein and provided the Insured is therein at the beginning of the fire and is burned by such fire or suffocated by the smoke therefrom.

(*b*) By being struck or run over while walking or standing in or on a public highway, by any automobile or any vehicle then being propelled by steam, cable, electricity, naphtha, gasoline, horse, compressed air or liquid power (excluding injuries sustained while working in a public highway; or while on a railroad right of way).

(*c*) By being struck by lightning.

(*d*) The result of accidental drowning while swimming at a public bathing beach during the time that a life-saver is on duty, and not otherwise.

(*e*) By the wrecking of a passenger elevator (elevator in mines excepted) in which the Insured is riding as a passenger.

(*f*) By the collapsing of the outer walls of a building (except buildings in course of construction, wrecking or repair).

To collect the maximum sum, $12,500, the insured has to get himself killed or doubly disabled by the wrecking or disablement of a railroad car, etc. It is not sufficient that he be involved in a travel accident; the vehicle itself must be wrecked. Only one fifth of the maximum amount is paid for such a serious loss if it occurs as a result of a public automobile accident, and only one tenth if it is a private automobile. For other common types of accident, the amount is 8 percent of maximum, and for accidents other than those enumerated there is no coverage. If the insured is not lucky enough to lose his sight or have a member severed, he may collect $25 or $10 per week during total disability, up to 15 weeks.

The exclusions further narrow the coverage of the contract:

This insurance does not cover as follows: (1) Suicide or attempt thereat while sane or insane; (2) While riding or driving in races or any driver or occupant of any automobile in any race or speed contest anywhere or while testing any automobile on any race track or speedway; (3) While engaged in military or naval service; (4) Any law enforcement officer while on duty; (5) Operating employees of fire departments or railroads while on duty; (6) While intoxicated or under the influence of, or affected by, or resulting directly or indirectly from intoxicants or narcotics; (7) While violating law; (8) Any loss contributed to or caused by any sickness, disease or mental or or bodily infirmity.

This insurance does not cover any accident unless sustained in the United States or Canada.

The occurrence of any of the losses mentioned in Parts One, Two, Three or Four shall at once terminate the insurance effected by this policy, and indemnity for more than one of such losses will not be paid under any circumstances.

The insurance under this policy shall not cover any person who is blind, deaf, or crippled or who has lost a limb or the sight of an eye. In all such cases, the limit of the Company's liability shall be the amount of the premium paid, which will be returned.

Indemnity as payable hereunder shall only be payable for the period that the Insured is under the professional care and regular attendance of a licensed physician or surgeon, other than himself.

. . . . . . . . . . . . . . . . . . . .

No indemnity will be paid for disability caused by any other means or under other conditions than those specified herein. In event of the specific loss no idemnity shall be paid for loss of time.

While this policy is somewhat more liberal than the classic of the humorists which pays benefits only if the insured is "gored by a purple bull at midnight on main street," it falls somewhat short of complete protection. The same comment applies to most newspaper contracts.

*Automobile accident contracts.* These policies cover the risk of injury from various types of auto accident. Some cover only while "riding in" an auto; some "while cranking, adjusting, or changing a tire" on a private passenger auto; and some are even broader. One of the broadest covers "while riding in a taxi-cab, motor bus or automobile, or being struck or run down by an automobile or being injured through the burning or explosion of an automobile." Some policies provide weekly benefits for total disability, and some include hospital benefits or blanket medical, but most are limited to accidental death and dismemberment.

To some degree, the market for such a policy has been reduced by the common practice of including medical payments coverage in auto policies. This coverage provides blanket reimbursement for medical care and funeral expenses for any person injured in an insured auto and for any insured injured by or in any auto. Of course, these medical payments do not pay lump-sum or periodic disability benefits. Several of the largest companies have gone even further in this direction. They are including in the auto policy, as an optional coverage, provisions for an accidental death benefit and disability income for life for injuries resulting from auto accidents. This coverage is equivalent to that of the automobile accident contract and more liberal than many such policies.

A recent but short-lived upsurge in the sale of auto accident contracts occurred when certain auto manufacturers began giving away policies to purchasers of cars. The gimmick was intended to emphasize the safe construction of the auto and may have impressed a few customers, who did not realize that auto accident policies can be purchased for $12.50 or less a year. Dealers of other companies soon realized this and were able to point this out to the customers or, in some cases, to "give away" a policy themselves.

The latest development in this field has been the sale of automobile or broader travel accident contracts through vending machines located at service stations, motels, hotels, and bus terminals. One such contract provides $5,000 accidental death and dismemberment benefits for injuries sustained while riding in an automobile, bus, or train. A 50-cent premium provides coverage for seven days, and an insured may purchase as many as four such contracts. Another provides an accidental death benefit of $7,500 and blanket medical expense coverage of $500 at a premium of $1 per week.

Agents and agents' associations have objected strongly to such methods of marketing, but if the contracts prove popular, this probably will be of little avail. Some states, such as Ohio, do require that the machines must be serviced by licensed insurance agents and countersigned (by facsimile) by a licensed resident agent. These programs have not worked well and most have been abandoned. Apparently auto travelers are in too much of a hurry to stop for insurance or do not consider auto travel dangerous. After all, only 52,500 people are killed by auto accidents in the United States in a year (1966).

Another related development is the sale of travel accident contracts through the credit card facilities of oil companies. One contract offered by this method and underwritten by a large insurer provides accidental death and dismemberment benefits of $10,000 and $1,000 blanket accident medical expense coverage for a premium of $2.25 per month. It includes accidents occuring while traveling in automobiles, trains, ships, private yachts, and commercial airliners. The accidental death and dismemberment coverage is doubled if the accident occurs on a weekend or holiday, according to a logic which escapes this author.

*Annual travel accident contracts.* As people get tired of feeding coins into slot machines, clipping coupons and filling out applications, they are turning to annual travel accident contracts which can be renewed (usually subject to the insurer's consent) just by paying another premium. These contracts are particularly attractive to those who travel frequently, since they are much more economical than the short-term contracts sold at places where travelers congregate.

They may be divided into three categories: automobile travel accident contracts, special aviation travel accident contracts and general travel accident contracts. The automobile accident contracts are similar in all respects to those discussed above and require no further comment.

One insurer, Associated Aviation Underwriters, offers a range of annual contracts which emphasize the aviation exposure. Its basic contract, by successive endorsement at higher premium, may be extended from coverage of worldwide scheduled airline flights as a passenger; to all common carrier (including land and water) coverage; to riding as passenger on any scheduled or nonscheduled aircraft with a FAA standard airworthiness certificate including Military Air Transport Service (MATS); and to include flying as pilot, student pilot or crew member. Injuries in private automobiles are not covered. Benefits in all cases may include accidental death and dismemberment, blanket medical expense and disability income for a maximum of 52 weeks.

The general travel accident contracts are issued by a number of insurers. They generally cover either all common carrier accidents, or include as well all accidents in conveyances operated on land or water, and being struck by such conveyances. The aviation passenger coverage may include MATS coverage and, more rarely, nonscheduled airline travel or private planes. In no case does it cover loss sustained while serving as an aircraft pilot, crew member, or student pilot.

The contracts all include accidental death and dismemberment benefits and most include blanket medical expense benefits, limited in some instances to hospital and nurse fees. Some include disability income benefits of six months or one-year maximum, but one will pay disability income for a maximum of 100 months.

Travel accident coverage may be obtained by a "double indemnity" (or triple or higher) rider on a regular commercial accident contract. In all cases, it is open to the criticism that disease and nontravel accidents, which together produce death and disability much more frequently than travel accidents, are not covered.

*Limited hospital income contracts.* Hospital income contracts were described above. These contracts are inherently limited to disability income while hospitalized. More recently, there has appeared an even more limited version: a hospital income contract which pays benefits only during hospitalization resulting from accidental injury. One such contract pays $1,000 per month (or $33.33 per day) for hospitalization resulting from accident. It is noncancellable and guaranteed renewable and the premium is "only" $5 per month. Contracts of this type are a poor substitute for adequate medical expense insurance and are hardly a bargain at any price.

*Special-risk contracts.* Special-risk contracts include a heterogeneous collection of policies written to cover special situations. They might be classified to include contracts which cover unusual and unconventional sets of circumstances; contracts offering coverage on an experimental basis for high-loss risks previously not insurable; and contracts covering relatively conventional activities which previously were not covered by health insurance.[1] Mostly they are written on standard forms at special premium rates, but sometimes it is necessary to develop a special type-written policy.

Contracts are available covering an entrepreneur hiring an actor or other celebrity against loss resulting from nonappearance at a scheduled performance resulting from injury or illness. The contract may cover merely the value of the performer's time, or it may protect the producer against loss resulting from the cancellation of the performance. This may exceed the actual salary or fee by manyfold.

Special-risk contracts have been written to protect flagpole sitters, auto racing on ice, divers, human flys, steeplejacks and such things as a pianist's fingers, an actress's legs, or a singer's voice. Special aviation accident contracts are available for test pilots, cropdusters, and submarine technicians, and similar coverage is written for other hazardous occupations. Such contracts are usually written through a "special risks" department of the insurance company, and the rates and coverage are largely handled on a judgment basis. The more unusual risks are likely to be placeable only at Lloyd's of London.

Policies are available to cover creditors of an institution; school children and campers at school and in camp; members of school, amateur, and professional athletic teams; contestants in sporting events; members of volunteer fire departments; and so forth. These contracts are more

---

[1] Armand Sommer, "Limited and Special Risk Contracts," in *Life and Health Insurance Handbook,* Davis W. Gregg (ed.) (2d ed.; Homewood, Ill.: Richard D. Irwin, Inc., 1964).

closely related to group insurance and will be discussed in more detail in the following chapter. Tuition refund insurance, a special business coverage, is discussed in Chapter 21.

*Limited sickness policies.* The polio, cancer, and dread-disease contracts discussed earlier are examples of limited sickness policies. They are clearly limited to the named diseases but, because of the high limits and freedom from restriction as to type of loss, were discussed under the heading of major medical and related contracts. Limited sickness policies providing for loss of income and sometimes lump-sum benefits have been sold in the past, and a few still may be available. Contracts occasionally have been issued covering a long list of diseases which practically never have been reported in the United States. Fortunately, this type of practice has declined greatly.

## Benefits—industrial policies

The benefits provided in industrial policies are essentially similar to those found in commercial policies. However, they are more likely to emphasize total disability income and contain fewer frills. This is not due to the greater sophistication of the purchasers but to the desire to keep costs down. Accidental death and dismemberment coverage usually is issued by the same companies in connection with their life insurance policies. Thus there is no need to include these benefits in health policies. Some, however do include them. Most industrial policies cover sickness as well as accidental injury. This is a reflection of their Friendly Society background. Moreover, the sales emphasis is largely on sickness rather than accident.

The insuring clause of an industrial policy is similar to that of a commercial contract. The insuring clause and premium clause of a recently developed contract are reproduced below.

PROVIDENT INDEMNITY LIFE INSURANCE COMPANY (Hereinafter Called the Company) hereby insures the person designated as the Insured in the Policy Schedule above against: (1) total disability resulting directly, and independently of all other causes, from injury and (2) total disability commencing while this policy is in force resulting from sickness; subject, however, to a reduction in benefits at age 65 as provided in Paragraph B of Part 7 on page three of this policy and to all of the other provisions and limitations hereinafter contained.

*Definition of Injury.* The term injury as used in this policy shall mean an accidental bodily injury sustained by the Insured while this policy is in force.

*Definition of Sickness.* The term sickness as used in this policy shall mean a sickness or disease contracted by the Insured while this policy is in force.

## PREMIUMS, GRACE PERIOD, RENEWABILITY

*Payment of Premiums.* This Policy is issued for:

a) a term of one week if the Policy Schedule indicates the premium is payable weekly, or

b) a term of one month if the Policy Schedule indicates the premium is payable monthly,

in consideration of the payment of the premium stated in said Policy Schedule on or before the Date of Issue. Subject to the renewal provisions of this Policy it may be renewed:

a) if the premium is payable weekly for additional terms of one week by the payment of a like weekly premium on or before Monday of each succeeding week, or within the grace period; or

b) if the premium is payable monthly, for additional terms of one month by the payment of a like monthly premium on or before the same day of each succeeding month, or within the grace period.

All premiums are payable at the Home Office of the Company or to a duly authorized agent, but failure of an agent to collect the premium when due shall not excuse the nonpayment thereof. Payment of the premium will not be valid unless entered in the Premium Receipt Book by the agent or an employee of the Company at the time of receipt.

*Grace Period.* Unless not less than thirty days prior to the premium due date the Company has delivered to the Insured or has mailed to his last address as shown by the records of the Company written notice of its intention not to renew this policy beyond the period for which the premium has been accepted, a grace period of one month (31 days) will be granted for the payment of each premium falling due after the first premium, during which grace period this policy shall continue in force.

*Renewal at Option of Company.* The acceptance of any renewal premium for this policy shall be optional with the Company.

*Refund on Direct Payment of Premiums:* If, while premiums are not in default beyond the Grace Period, notice is given to an Office of the Company that premiums will in future be paid directly to such an Office, and if premiums are so paid continuously for a period of one year without default beyond the Grace Period, the Company will, at the end of such year, refund 10 percent of the total of the year's premiums so paid.

This contract provides daily benefits but, in some contracts, disability income is payable only for a full week or a number of full weeks of disability and there is no payment for fractional weeks. There is some moral hazard in such a provision, since it hardly tends to encourage recovery during the last few days of a week. However, this is partially, at least, offset by savings in administration costs. Since the weekly benefit is typically $10 or $20, it is hardly worth the trouble of attempting to measure more closely the period of disability. However, benefits as high as $50 per week or $10 per day are offered. The provisions as to premium payment are typical of industrial policies. The burden of payment is placed on the insured and failure of the agent to call is no excuse.

For many years it was common for industrial life policies to limit the amount payable if death occurred during the first years of the policy. Today, life policies are almost always issued on a "full immediate benefit" basis, but some industrial health policies still make use of the principle of reduced benefits in the early years. The reason, of course, is that these policies are issued with practically no underwriting. The applicant does complete a brief application, but there is no physical examination and frequently no inspection to check up on the agent's and applicant's veracity. Industrial life policies occasionally have been issued on the life of a dead person.

A typical modern disability income benefit clause is reproduced below:

*Total Disability.* If sickness shall totally disable the Insured so as to prevent him from performing each and every duty pertaining to his occupation or any other gainful occupation for which he is reasonably qualified by education, training or experience and cause him to be under the regular care and attendance of a legally-qualified physician, the Company will pay at the rate of the Daily Benefit for the period of such disability, but not exceeding 182 days during any one period of disability, or during any one policy year.

*Hospital Confinement.* If by reason of sickness the Insured shall be confined in a hospital as an in-patient, the Company will double the Daily Benefit payable under this Part for each day of such hospital confinement; provided, however, the Daily Benefit will not be doubled for more than 60 days of hospital confinement during a policy year nor for more than 60 days of hospital confinement for any one sickness or disease, which shall include all complications arising therefrom or recurrences thereof.

This contract provides a daily benefit with no waiting period and a 182 day maximum per period of disability and per policy year. The accident disability benefit is identical. Six months is the typical benefit period but industrial policies range from 8 weeks to one year.

Some industrial policies cover hospital and/or surgical benefits. Where surgical benefits are included, it is on a schedule basis comparable to that in commercial policies, except that the maximum payable for a single operation is likely to be somewhat smaller. A $150 schedule is about the highest obtainable on an industrial basis.

Hospital benefits may be provided as a part of a disability income policy or as a separate contract. When part of a disability income contract, the hospital benefit is usually the simple provision that twice the regular benefit will be paid for disability during which the insured is confined to a hospital as in the example above. The period is, of course, limited. Sometimes the separate policies are on the same basis, providing a benefit of (say) $50 a week while hospitalized. Sometimes a daily benefit is provided comparable to that in commercial and group contracts. The amount, however, is rarely more than $21 per day, and coverage of extra expenses is uncommon. Often, unlike most hospital policies, industrial contracts are not on an indemnity basis. The agreed benefit usually is payable in the event of hospitalization regardless of the actual amount of expense. This is reasonable, since the daily benefit will almost always be less than the cost of a hospital room, or even a bed in a ward.

The Provident Indemnity contract quoted above contains limited specific death and dismemberment benefits, as follows:

If injury shall result directly, and independently of all other causes, in one of the following total losses within 90 days from the date of the accident, the Company will pay a single sum for such loss as stipulated and determined below in lieu of all other benefits under this policy except any disability benefits paid or payable to the date of such loss:

| Specific Total Losses | A Single Sum Equal to Daily Benefits for: |
|---|---|
| Accidental Death | 182 Days |
| Both Hands | 182 Days |
| Both Feet | 182 Days |
| One Hand and One Foot | 182 Days |
| Sight of Both Eyes | 182 Days |
| Either Hand | 91 Days |
| Either Foot | 91 Days |
| Sight of One Eye | 46 Days |

Total loss shall mean, with respect to hands and feet, actual severance at or above the wrist or ankle joints; with respect to eyes, the entire and irrecoverable loss of sight thereof. Indemnity will be paid for only one of the specific total losses (the greatest) resulting from any one accident.

*Exclusions.* The exclusions and limits in industrial policies are stricter than those in commercial contracts but more liberal to the insured than in most limited policies. The following, from the disability income policy quoted above, are typical.

### Maternity Benefit

If after 10 months from the Policy Date the Insured shall be disabled due to pregnancy, childbirth or miscarriage, or complications therefrom, the Company will pay, in lieu of all other benefits under this policy, a single sum equal to Daily Benefits for 14 days which shall constitute payment in full under this policy for any one pregnancy.

## Limited Benefit for Mental Disease or Disorder

*TOTAL DISABILITY AND CONFINEMENT INDOORS.* If sickness is a mental disease or disorder and shall totally disable the Insured so as to prevent him from performing each and every duty pertaining to his occupation or any other gainful occupation for which he is reasonably qualified by education, training or experience and cause him to be confined indoors or in a hospital under the regular care and attendance of a legally-qualified physician, the Company will pay at the rate of the Daily Benefit for the period of such disability, but not exceeding 21 days during any one period of disability.

The requirement for confinement indoors shall be interpreted to allow necessary visits to the physician's office or hospital for treatment, and, by direction of the attending physician, periods of rest on the porch or in the yard of the house or building in which the Insured is confined.

## Limitations and Exclusions

A. This policy does not cover loss or disability:
   (a) caused by war, or any act of war, whether war be declared or undeclared;
   (b) caused by pregnancy, childbirth or miscarriage, or complications therefrom, except as provided in Part 5 of this policy;
   (c) injury sustained or sickness contracted outside the continental United States and Canada;
   (d) suicide or any attempt at suicide, while sane or insane, or by intentionally self-inflicted injury;
   (e) injury resulting from the Insured's being engaged in an illegal occupation, participation in an assault, or commission or attempted commission of a felony;
   (f) the Insured's participation in a riot or insurrection;
   (g) the Insured's being intoxicated or under the influence of narcotics unless administered on the advice of a Physician;
   (h) caused by a mental disease or disorder except as provided in Part 6 of this Policy.
B. Benefits for disability commencing or loss occurring after the Insured's 65th birthday shall be reduced fifty percent.

*Other provisions.* The grace period usually is five weeks. Most states require a minimum grace period of 30 days on individual policies, and, since industrial companies keep all records on a weekly basis, this means five weeks. Sometimes the period is expressed as 30 days but is enforced only on a five-week basis. Many companies, however, provide as follows:

Grace Period—If any renewal premium is due and unpaid for five successive Mondays this Policy becomes lapsed automatically at the close of business on the fifth Monday, and shall not be renewable by payments of further premiums, except as provided in the Reinstatement Provision.

The Uniform Individual Policy Provisions law applies to industrial insurance, and these provisions are found in such policies. The misstatement of age clause almost always is included. Other prorating clauses are rare. Industrial policy premiums are not graded by occupation. Thus the occupational prorate clause is unnecessary. Where benefits are on a valued basis and low in amount, there is little occasion for other insurance or average earnings clauses.

The cancellation clause is often omitted, but with a policy term of one week, the right to decline to renew gives the company virtually the same freedom as if it were included. A few industrial health policies have been issued which are guaranteed renewable and/or incontestable, but this is rare.

### Uses and limitations

A cynic might say that the major question about limited and industrial policies is what, if anything, they are good for. The coverage provided by most is so limited as to type of injury or as to amount of benefit, or both, as to lead one to question the value of the contract. This is not to imply that the contracts are a "gyp." The premiums are very low, and it is probable that, after due allowance is made for the high relative costs of handling small premium amounts and often small benefit amounts, these contracts are no more profitable for the companies than other types of insurance. Actually, the potential loss, although unlikely, is so great in relation to premium that many companies do not wish to handle the limited lines at all. Where, as in the aviation policy for example, it takes the premium from 40,000 policies to equal the amount of one total loss (with *no* allowance for expenses), a tremendous volume is necessary in order for the law of averages to operate.[2]

Industrial policies provide a means for a person of low income and poor savings habits to obtain a minimum amount of short-term disability protection at a cost within his weekly budget. While there are very few persons who actually cannot afford commercial premium rates, there are many who think they cannot. It is far easier for such a person to agree to pay (say) 50¢ a week than (say) $5 every three months. While the relative cost of industrial insurance is high in proportion to its benefits because of the expenses of collection and record keeping, it cannot be denied that the device has made it possible for millions to obtain insurance.[3] Most of these would not have obtained coverage

---

[2] To an insurer, risk may be measured by the coefficient of variation of total losses. This is equal to the ratio of the standard deviation to the mean, and its value is proportionate to $p/q$ where $q =$ probability of loss and $p =$ probability of no loss. It approaches maximum value as $q$ approaches 0.

[3] No information exists as to the volume of industrial health insurance. However, in 1966, 88 million industrial life policies were in force, for $39.7 billion of protection which produced $1.4 billion in premium.—*1967 Life Insurance Fact Book* (New York: Institute of Life Insurance, 1967).

on any other basis. Things in small packages cost a lot relatively. Even coal would be pretty expensive if it were purchased by the pound, delivered to the door, and "sold again" every week.

Much of the market for industrial insurance is also served by group insurance, and, as the group principle grows, the relative amount of industrial insurance will continue to decline. As incomes rise, eventually the absolute volume also probably will decline. But, for the present, there are many persons who cannot or will not obtain coverage on any other basis. These groups include housewives, dayworkers, employees of small firms, the unemployed, public assistance and relief recipients, and students. Industrial and limited policies are the only type available to most of these persons, and industrial better meets their needs. They are better off, on the average, with a policy which covers all types of injury and sickness, even if the amounts are low, than they would be with a policy paying large amounts for the spectacular but unlikely types of injury.

The arguments for the limited policy are more difficult to establish, since commercial, guaranteed renewable, and group policies cover almost all accidents. As has been indicated above, it is contrary to sound insurance principles to select one or more types of peril for insurance and to leave the others unprotected. This is particularly undesirable when the perils selected are among the least likely to produce loss. The only reasonable justification for such a policy is to fill a gap in existing coverage. Where a person is covered with life and health insurance, which, for example, excludes all aviation accidents from coverage, the aviation accident policy provides a worthwhile device to give coverage for brief periods of exposure. Where other coverage is inadequate in amount, there is some justification for carrying limited policies for periods of brief and unusually dangerous exposure. However, air travel and railway travel are not unusually dangerous. On a mile-for-mile basis, it is probably considerably more hazardous for most people to drive to work than to travel between cities on either type of carrier.

The major disadvantage of limited policies is their tendency to mislead the insured. Emphasis on large amounts of benefit and a long list of covered events may leave him with the impression that he is adequately protected against all types of poor health. Generally this is so far from the truth as to be almost ridiculous. Moreover, these contracts appeal to the gambling instinct of the insured, and, even where he recognizes the fact that they are so far from complete coverage, he is likely to give in to temptation and purchase such a contract in preference to broader coverage.

Aviation accident policies make a good gift for a fiancée. They show that one loves her at least $20,000 worth and are cheaper than flowers.

The special-risk policies do, of course, meet an important economic

need in covering exposures which otherwise may be completely uninsurable. In some cases, they may materially assist an employer in
finding someone willing to undertake an exceptionally hazardous activity.

The late O'Mahoney Committee[4] investigations focused considerable
attention on the air travel accident insurance business.[5] The Committee
was concerned with the small number of insurers in the market, allegations of unfair competition in attempting to exclude new entrants and
the low loss ratios and high rentals paid to airports for space. The
allegations as to unfair competition seem to have been refuted substantially. The small number of insurers is at least partly attributable
to the fact that losses are very rare and that benefits are terrifyingly
large in relation to premium. There is enough exposure for only a limited number of insurers to be able to obtain a reasonable spread of risk.
If a 150-passenger jet were to crash, with each passenger insured for
the maximum, $100,000, the total loss would be 15 million dollars. Few
insurers are in a position to assume such a liability. It would take the
premium income from six million maximum benefit policies to provide
this amount, with no allowance for expenses or profit.

While such a catastrophe, with all passengers insured with one insurer for the maximum, is unlikely, it always is a possibility. One such
loss could wipe out all the profits from years of operation and convert
the present low loss ratio to an extremely high one.

The typical airport rental is 13 percent of premiums written, subject
to a dollar minimum. The percentage does not seem excessive. The
competition for airport space has taken the form of bidding for leases
with high minimum rentals. In some instances, these have turned out
to be 100 percent or more of actual premiums collected. Obviously, no
insurer can afford many such leases and it is to be hoped that the
revelations of the Committee will lead to more restrained bidding for
business in this fashion, and that city officials and others in control of
airports will recognize that charging unreasonably high space rentals
is inconsistent with the public policy objective that insurance rates
should be reasonable.

At the December, 1962, meeting of the National Association of Insurance Commissioners, the chairman of the Subcommittee on Rentals
Paid at Terminals (of the Accident and Health Committee) proposed

---

[4] More properly, the Subcommittee on Antitrust and Monopoly, Committee on
the Judiciary, U.S. Senate.

[5] *The Insurance Industry* (Report of the Committee of the Judiciary, Report 1834,
U.S. Senate. 86th Cong., 2d sess. [Washington, D.C.: U.S. Government Printing
Office, 1960]). *The Insurance Industry* (Hearings before the Subcommittee on Antitrust and Monopoly of the Committee on the Judiciary, U.S. Senate. 85th Cong., 2d
sess. Part 1, Aviation Insurance [Washington, D.C.: U.S. Government Printing Office,
1959]).

an arrangement for limiting competition in bidding for space. Questions as to the antitrust aspects of this were raised, and the subcommittee recommended further study.

## Summary

Industrial policies provide small amounts of insurance on a weekly premium basis. Other than this and the limitation of benefits to 52 weeks or less, they are quite similar to commercial policies. They continue to serve a worthwhile economic function, despite the fact that their market is being cut down by the growth of group insurance and by the general rise in income.

Limited policies cover either very short periods or only limited types of accident (or sometimes sickness) or both. The ticket accident policy covers all types of accident for brief periods but provides primarily lump-sum benefits. Its purpose is to provide coverage during short periods of extra risk, but many people already have adequate coverage, and travel, especially by rail, is a relatively safe type of activity. The aviation and automobile accident policies cover only one type of accident each. They may be effectively used to fill a gap in existing coverage or to supplement the amount during periods of unusual risk. However, there is no such gap as to auto accident. Premiums expended for such policies were better spent for broad coverage, even if it is necessary to purchase much smaller amounts of insurance. The newspaper policy is, at best, an innocuous device to help sell newspapers; at worst, a snare and delusion that leads insureds to think they are adequately protected. As the better policies, providing adequate benefits for all types of health loss, develop, the market for these limited forms will diminish.

## Selected references

Very little material is available which bears specifically on limited and industrial policies. Many of the items listed in the General Bibliography and in the Selected References for Chapter 9 make some passing reference or devote a few pages to these lines.

See the following items from the General Bibliography: 4, ch. 17; 10, ch. 6; 15, ch. 24; 18, pp. 364–65; 19, ch. 20; 21, ch. 12.

UNITED STATES CONGRESS, SENATE. *The Insurance Industry*, U.S. Senate Report 1834, report of the Committee of the Judiciary (86th Cong., 2d sess.). Washington D.C.: U.S. Government Printing Office, 1960.

————. *The Insurance Industry*, Hearings before the Subcommittee on Antitrust and Monopoly of the Committee on the Judiciary, U.S. Senate (85th Cong., 2d sess.), Part 1, Aviation Insurance. Washington, D.C.: U.S. Government Printing Office, 1959.

# chapter 15

# Group Contracts

## Introduction

*Contractual arrangement.* Group insurance represents an arrangement whereby a group of persons is covered by a single contract with an insurer. Group insurance policies are, in effect, three-party contracts. While technically they represent a contract between an insurer and an employer, union, or other insured, they are actually for the benefit of third parties, such as employees or union members. The insured individuals and their families are not parties to the contract, yet they do acquire certain rights under it. These rights are usually evidenced by a certificate issued to each individual employee. Legally, the employee or member is in the position of a "third-party beneficiary." Although the term is not used, his dependents or beneficiaries might be considered "fourth-party beneficiaries." While not parties to the contract, all these people do acquire legally enforceable rights under it.

*Group underwriting principles.* An outstanding, if not essential, characteristic of group insurance is that the process of selection is applied to the group as a whole, and standards of insurability usually are not imposed upon individual members provided they enroll promptly. Adverse selection is prevented by certain inherent characteristics of insurable groups and by certain contract provisions.

The prime requisite for an acceptable group is that there must be an overriding purpose for its existence other than the desire to obtain insurance. Most insured groups are employees of a common employer or group of employers or members of a union or group of unions. The insured policyholder may be the employer, the union, or a trustee for one or more employers or unions. There has been some slight deviation from this principle in the writing of voluntary groups such as professional associations, trade associations and Granges.

Most acceptable groups are made up of persons who are workers of one type or another, and this presumes some degree of health. There is a "flow" of workers through the group—older workers retire or die, and younger workers replace them. This tends to keep average costs relatively low and stable which encourages newly eligible members to enroll for the group coverage. Of course, where coverage is extended beyond retirement, some increase in cost occurs, but this often is mitigated by providing reduced benefits after retirement and/or by the employer assuming all the extra cost.

A proper spread of risk is assured and adverse selection is minimized by contract provisions which require a minimum number in the group and minimum proportions of those eligible; determine benefit amounts according to a formula rather than by individual choice; require evidence of insurability under certain conditions such as enrollment after the initial eligibility period; and require that an employee be "actively at work" in order to obtain new or increased coverage. For long term disability income, this may require a period of several weeks, or even months, prior to inception of coverage. Additional protection is provided the insurer by the right to increase rates and the right of cancellation of the group.

More detailed discussion of underwriting will be reserved for Chapter 17.

*Advantages of group insurance.* Group insurance has a lower cost partly because claim rates sometimes have been lower than under individual policies. This speaks well for the quality of underwriting and the efficacy of the safeguards against adverse selection. Moreover, there are important savings in expenses. One big saving is in acquisition costs. Commissions are much less in percentage of premium than in individual contracts.[1] A sound group plan will be simple and economical in administration. Premium collections are handled by the employer or other insured, and remittance is made in a lump sum to the insurance company. Great economies are thus possible in record keeping.

Part of the saving in insurance company expense results from the greater efficiency in handling the coverage on a "wholesale" basis and part because the employer performs functions which the insurer would perform in individual insurance. To a large degree, these functions cost less in the aggregate when performed by the employer. For example, the payroll deduction of premium contributions often can be performed merely by setting one more instruction for the payroll computation process. Where this is handled by machine, the only increased cost is a little more setup time.

Where the group is an employee group, the employer usually must contribute at least part of the premiums. In most states, this is a re-

---

[1] See below, for a discussion of group commission arrangements.

quirement for "true" group insurance. This increases the employee interest in the plan, makes for better employee relations, and provides a mechanism for absorbing inequalities in cost to employees, possible premium increases, and future dividends or premium refunds.

*State laws.* Legally, group health insurance is whatever the applicable state law says it is. Thirty-four states have laws defining group health insurance in terms of the types of group eligible and most of these specify the minimum number of members. The minimum number ranges from two to 10, with 10 the most common. Sixteen of these also require minimum percentage participation—usually 100 percent if the employer pays the whole premium and 75 percent if the employee contributes. Sixteen states and the District of Columbia do not have specific legislation, but one (Maryland) has regulations which serve the same purpose. In all states the insurance companies establish their own underwriting standards, subject to the minimum, if any, of the state law.

*Group health coverages.* Most group health insurance covers nonoccupational disability only, because the employer also buys workmen's compensation insurance which covers occupational disability. Group health insurance is a complement to, not a substitute for, workmen's compensation. Generally, group health policies exclude disability produced by any accident arising out of and in the course of employment. This is the definition of coverage usually found in workmen's compensation laws. It is impossible to generalize thus about the disease coverage of various laws, so most group health policies exclude any sickness or disease covered by any workmen's compensation law. Frequently, where it cannot be readily determined whether the disability is occupational, the group health insurer will pay the claim but reserve the right to be reimbursed if it turns out that workmen's compensation covers.

Group health insurance includes the following areas or lines:

1. Disability income
2. Accidental death and dismemberment
3. Hospital expense
4. Surgical expense
5. Medical expense
6. Major medical
7. Polio, cancer and dread disease
8. Comprehensive medical care
9. Group travel accident
10. Diagnostic and X ray.

Table 15–1 indicates the magnitude of the major types of group health insurance written by insurance companies at the end of 1966.

## TABLE 15-1
### Group Health Insurance Coverage, 1966

| Kind of Coverage | Issued during Year | | In Force at End of Year | | Premiums and Considerations during Year |
|---|---|---|---|---|---|
| | Number of Master Policies | Number of Individuals Covered[a] | Number of Master Policies | Number of Individuals Covered[a] | |
| Group wage replacement (including group credit health insurance)...60,080 | | 2,943,000 | 424,650 | 28,698,000 | $1,052,000,000 |
| Group hospital expense | | | | | |
| Employee coverage...28,670 | | 1,711,000[b] | 152,490 | 21,376,000 | 745,000,000 |
| Dependent coverage...27,670 | | 2,868,000[b] | 144,770 | 35,877,000 | 1,058,000,000 |
| Group surgical expense | | | | | |
| Employee coverage...28,610 | | 1,839,000[b] | 152,970 | 21,789,000 | 231,000,000 |
| Dependent coverage...27,580 | | 3,080,000[b] | 144,990 | 36,162,000 | 430,000,000 |
| Group medical expense | | | | | |
| Employee coverage...25,590 | | 1,561,000[b] | 125,550 | 15,786,000 | 133,000,000 |
| Dependent coverage...24,410 | | 2,667,000[b] | 118,060 | 25,945,000 | 114,000,000 |
| Group major medical expense—supplementary to basic plans | | | | | |
| Employee coverage...22,830 | | 1,412,000[b] | 95,460 | 14,399,000 | 198,000,000 |
| Dependent coverage...22,340 | | 2,316,000[b] | 93,500 | 25,286,000 | 221,000,000 |
| Group major medical expense—comprehensive (no basic plans)[c] | | | | | |
| Employee coverage...6,240 | | 426,000[b] | 33,830 | 4,646,000 | 322,000,000 |
| Dependent coverage...5,680 | | 746,000[b] | 31,330 | 7,671,000 | 419,000,000 |
| Group accidental death and dismemberment...30,420 | | 2,126,000 | 171,250 | 28,533,000 | 131,000,000 |
| Total | | | | | $5,054,000,000 |

[a] The number of individuals covered represents the sum of the number reported by the companies, with no attempt to remove duplication among companies.

[b] These new business figures may exclude some individuals covered who are age 65 and over.

[c] Note: Master policies and certificates providing more than one coverage were counted for each kind of coverage. It should be noted, however, that the data for group comprehensive major medical expense insurance have not been included in the hospital, surgical, or medical expense lines, although such insurance does provide protection for each of those expenses.

Source: Health Insurance Association of America, *Group Insurance Coverages in the United States—1966* (New York, 1967).

The benefit provisions and limitations of all but the first two of these have been discussed in previous chapters. In these areas there is little difference between the benefits of group and individual insurance, so the two types of coverage were discussed together. This chapter, thus, will be limited to an analysis of the group master contract and the disability income and death and dismemberment benefits. In addition, it will discuss briefly franchise and blanket health insurance, which are compromises between group and individual insurance and are sold to small groups. Disability provisions in group life insurance were discussed in Chapter 13 and salary continuance and pension plans were discussed briefly in Chapter 3.

**Development.** Group insurance began in 1890, but the first policy issued to a regular commercial employer was not written until about 1910, and the coverage did not develop very much until World War I. The growth rate has been quite rapid since 1930. Disability income and accidental death and dismemberment were the first covers issued, followed by hospital, surgical, medical, major medical and comprehensive in turn.

By 1966 about 29 million persons were covered for disability income under 425 thousand master policies. About 29 million employees were covered by accidental death and dismemberment under about 171 thousand master policies. The premium volume was $1,052 million and $131 million, respectively.

### Master contract

*Insuring and benefit clauses.* The *disability income* insuring clause is usually quite simple. The following is typical:

The company hereby agrees to pay a weekly benefit, in an amount determined from the Insurance Schedule in this policy, to any insured employee of ———— (herein called the Employer), or of an Associated Company listed in this policy, for any period during which such employee shall be wholly disabled by a disease for which the employee is not entitled to benefits under any workmen's compensation law, or by an accidental bodily injury which does not arise out of or in the course of employment, and shall be prevented by such disability from performing any and every duty pertaining to the employee's occupation; provided, however, that:

(a) not more than ———— weeks' benefits shall be paid for any one period of disability, and no benefit shall be paid for the first ———— days of any disability.

The types of injury and disease are defined as nonoccupational in the manner discussed above. This clause refers to injuries that "arise out of *or* in the course of employment." This is the more common wording in group policies. Some policies, however, use the phrase "arise out of *and* in the course of employment" which is the usual definition in workmen's compensation laws. The use of "or" in a group policy is a broad exclusion and thus less liberal to the insured person since an injury arising in the course of, but not out of, employment probably would not be covered either by the group contract or by workmen's compensation.[2] The exclusion of sickness or disease covered by any workmen's compensation law is typical of group contracts.

The definition of disability refers to "any and every duty of the employee's occupation." This is the broadest type of occupational definition. Since all covered persons are employees and since benefit periods are short, there is no reason to use a stricter definition.

The insuring clause provides for a maximum benefit period and for a waiting period. While accident benefits may be paid for the first day of disability, the use of a waiting period for sickness is almost universal. It may range from 3 to 14 days, but 7 days is by far the most common. If the contract treats accidental injury and disease the same, the waiting period is simply inserted in the blank space. If different waiting periods are imposed, an additional phrase would be typed in so that the clause would read, for example, "no benefit shall be paid for the first *seven* days of any disability *resulting from such disease, nor for the first three days of any disability resulting from such injury.*"

The maximum benefit period is most frequently 13 weeks, but 26-week, 52-week, and even longer durations are becoming more common. Long-term group may cover to age 65. It is discussed below in detail. In new short-term group cases in 1967, 58.3 percent of employees had a 13-week maximum; 36.2 percent, a 26-week limit; and 1.45 percent, a 52-week maximum. Actuaries refer to the combination of waiting periods and benefit duration by a three-number system. The first number is the first day for which benefits are payable for accidental injury, the second the corresponding day for disease benefits, and the third the maximum duration in weeks. Thus a "1–8–13" plan provides first day accident benefits; a one-week waiting period for disease, and a 13-week maximum duration. This is the most popular plan currently, followed by 1–8–26, 1–4–26, 8–8–26, 8–8–13, 1–4–13, and 1–8–52, in that order. Policies with maximum durations of 104 weeks are written, and the tendency is toward the longer periods. Retroactive waiting periods have been written in some policies but generally have been abandoned because of the high moral hazard. One recent development is to waive the waiting period and pay immediate benefits if the insured is hospitalized.

Other *limits on the insurer's agreement* are very brief. The following is typical:

(b) no benefit shall be paid for any period during which the employee is not under the care of a legally qualified physician;

---

[2] See above, p. 178, for a discussion of the meaning of these phrases.

(c) successive periods of disability separated by less than two weeks of active work on full time shall be considered one period of disability unless the subsequent disability is due to an injury or disease entirely unrelated to the causes of the previous disability and commences after return to active work on full time.

The Insurance Company also agrees to pay such weekly benefit to any insured female employee for any period, not exceeding six weeks, during which such employee shall be wholly disabled by a pregnancy or resulting childbirth or miscarriage and shall be prevented by such disability from performing any and every duty pertaining to the employee's occupation; provided, however, that no benefit shall be for any period during which the employee is not under the care of a legally qualified physician, and that, if the employee becomes insured after ——— no benefit shall be payable with respect to any period of disability due to a pregnancy which results in a childbirth or miscarriage within nine months following the date the employee becomes insured under this policy.

The recurrent disability clause requires two weeks of active work to constitute a new disability. This is the most common provision. Some policies exclude pregnancy, childbirth, and miscarriage entirely. Others, as here, impose a limit such as six weeks' benefit. The blank space in the clause is filled out by inserting a date, usually 30 days after the group plan goes into effect. Thus existing pregnancies are covered only in newly installed plans.

The *amount of weekly benefit* is set forth for various classes of employee in a schedule of insurance. The following provision is typical:

The amount of insurance (Weekly Benefit) for each employee shall be determined from the "Insurance Table" below; provided, however, that in no case shall the amount of weekly benefit for any employee exceed ———% of his weekly rate of basic earnings (on the basis of the number of hours per week customarily worked by the employee), the weekly benefit, if not a multiple of 50¢, to be taken to the next higher 50¢.

Provision is made for excluding part-time employees, and space is left for excluding others. Such groups excluded might include casual and seasonal workers. A minimum period of service often is required before an employee is covered. The typical period is 90 days, although 30 days is not uncommon. Employees actively at work at the installation of the contract usually are covered immediately.

Changes in the amount of insurance based on changes in classification are automatic in noncontributory policies; in contributory policies the employee sometimes must request such a change. Of course, he always must authorize or accept any increased payroll deduction. If it is an increase, the request must be made within 31 days of the classification change, or the insurance company may require evidence of insurability.

The amount of weekly benefit is determined by some method which precludes individual selection. The most common type of plan determines weekly benefit according to an earnings scale. For example, a schedule might be set up as follows:

| Basic Weekly Earnings | Weekly Benefit |
|---|---|
| Less than $50.00 | $30.00 |
| $ 50.00– 69.99 | 40.00 |
| 70.00– 89.99 | 50.00 |
| 90.00–109.99 | 60.00 |
| 110.00–129.99 | 70.00 |
| 130.00–159.99 | 80.00 |
| 160.00–189.99 | 90.00 |
| 190.00–219.99 | 100.00 |
| *220.00 and over | 110.00 |

In order to avoid moral hazard, the benefit amount should not exceed about two thirds of average wages. Many plans use a schedule which provides about 50 percent. It is desirable to have a maximum benefit regardless of earnings. Fifty dollars per week is the most common such maximum, but contracts providing as high as $2,000 per month have been written for select groups. About 33.6 percent of the new group plans written by insurance companies in 1967 provided maxima greater than $75 per week.

Sometimes a basis other than basic earnings is used. Length of service and position class have been employed, especially where earnings fluctuate greatly, as under a commission basis of compensation. The length of service basis has the objection that length of service is more highly correlated with age than are the other bases. Thus the highest amounts of insurance are provided on the older employees, where the probability of disability is greatest. Some plans, particularly those negotiated by labor unions, provide a flat benefit for every employee. Any plan which uses a basis other than earnings must be designed carefully to make sure that benefits are not too high in relation to the earnings of the lower paid employees. The flat benefit plan is particularly dangerous in this respect, and the amount must be kept quite low to avoid potential over-insurance. In collectively bargained plans in 1958, only one fifth of the employees with flat benefit plans had such benefits of $40 per week or more.

*Accidental death and dismemberment* benefits in group policies are very similar to those in individual policies, as discussed above. Unlike other group health coverages, these are often written on a full occupational basis. Thus these benefits would be paid in addition to any payments under workmen's compensation. Moral hazard is considered to be much less in death and dismemberment insurance than in the other lines, since this would involve suicide or deliberate self-mutilation. Hence this potential overinsurance is not viewed with undue alarm. As indicated above, the frequency of such losses is quite low. However, in some industries, costs are high enough to limit sales.

A typical benefit clause reads as follows:

If any employee . . . suffers any of the losses described below, as a result of bodily injuries sustained solely as a result of external, violent and accidental means, directly and independently of all other causes and within ninety days from the date of such injuries, the Company shall pay to the employee, if living, otherwise to the beneficiary, the amount of insurance specified for such loss in the following Schedule of Benefits.

The accidental means clause has been discussed above. The phrase "external and violent" adds little to the definition since courts almost always ignore it. The requirement that such losses be incurred "directly and independently of all other causes" is intended to exclude cases where disease, preexisting or otherwise, contributed to the loss. The schedule of payments for various dismemberments is comparable to that found in individual policies. The largest principal sum ordinarily written is that of the accompanying group life insurance policy or $10,000, whichever is less. However, in large groups, much larger limits may be written. Relating the amount of accidental death benefit to the amount of life insurance solves the problem of deciding on a classification of employees for this benefit, but any means may be used which precludes individual selection. Sometimes a schedule is included in the same way as for disability income. Sometimes the maximum amount is graded down as occupational hazard increases, so as to keep the cost about the same for various classes of employees.

*Term, renewal, and cancellation.* Group policies usually are continuous, running until cancelled, although technically most are written for a one-year term. The *effective date* usually is agreed upon in advance, but the policy may not go into effect until the risk is accepted by the insurer, the initial premium is paid, and the minimum participation requirements are met. The payment of subsequent premiums is a condition precedent to continuation of coverage. However, a grace period of 31 days is provided.

*Termination* of the group contract usually is automatic for default in premium payment beyond the grace period, and the insurer may cancel on any premium due date if the minimum participation requirements are not met. The customary minimum is 25 lives (but may be as low as five), and 75 percent of those eligible if the group plan is contributory. Thirty-one days' notice usually is required for such cancellation. Although it hardly is necessary in view of the insurer's right to raise future rates, some policies give the insurer the unrestricted right of cancellation. In all cases, the employer may discontinue at any time by so notifying the insurer.

The *effective date* of the *employee's insurance* is the date on which he becomes eligible in a noncontributory plan, provided that he is actively at work at that time. This requirement serves to exclude those who are sick at the time of eligibility and is similar in purpose to the individual policy exclusion of preexisting conditions but much more liberal. If he is not regularly performing the duties of his occupation, the insurance is effective upon his return to active work. Some policies do not impose the requirement that he be regularly performing the duties of his occupation. In dependents' coverage under medical care plans, insurance usually is not effective if the dependent is in the hospital on the date of eligibility.

Where the plan is contributory, the employee must elect coverage. This is accomplished by a written request. If this request is made before 31 days after the date of eligibility, the insurance is effective on the date of eligibility or the date of the request, whichever is later. If the request is made more than 31 days after the date of eligibility, the insurance is not effective until the insurance company accepts him, based on evidence of insurability that he may be asked to submit.

The date of eligibility is the effective date of the group contract for those employed at that time. For new employees it may be the date of hiring, or after a specified eligibility period.

*Dependents' coverage* in group medical care policies usually is limited to spouse and dependent children within a given age range such as 14 days to 19 years. In contributory plans the employee must request coverage, and, if he fails to do so and later changes his mind, evidence of the dependent's insurability must be furnished. The following are the appropriate provisions from a group hospital policy:

(1) the word "dependent" shall mean only an employee's unmarried child at least fourteen days of age but under nineteen years of age, or an employee's wife, neither of whom is insured or eligible for benefits as an employee under the group policy; no person shall be considered as a dependent of more than one employee;

(2) the word "child" shall, in addition to the employee's own children, include such stepchildren, foster children, and other children as depend upon the employee for support and live with the employee in a regular parent-child relationship.

## EFFECTIVE DATE OF INDIVIDUAL INSURANCE

An employee shall become insured with respect to each of his dependents on the latest of the following dates:

On the effective date of this rider, or on the effective date of the employee's insurance under the group policy, or on the date the employee makes written request to the Employer for insurance under this rider, or on the date the child or wife ceases to be insured or eligible for benefits as an employee under the group policy, or, in the case of a child, on the date the child attains the age of fourteen days, or, in the case of a wife, on the date of her marriage to the employee.

Where an employee fails to make written request for dependents' coverage within 31 days of eligibility for it, evidence of the dependent's insurability is required, at his expense, and the dependent is not covered unless and until the company accepts the evidence as satisfactory.

*Termination of an employee's insurance* is automatic upon termination of employment in disability income and accidental death and dismemberment coverages. This includes changing to a classification outside the plan, being laid off, granted leave of absence, and retiring. Individual coverage also terminates when maximum benefits have been paid. If the employer and employee continue to pay premiums, the insurance usually may remain in force during a period of disability.

In contributory plans, coverage terminates if the employee fails to make the required contribution. Of course, coverage terminates when the master contract is discontinued.

In medical care coverages, the situation is the same, with two exceptions. Coverage does not terminate with payment of maximum benefits (except a lifetime maximum in major medical), since the employee is still covered for a new disability. Dependents' coverage, of course, terminates when the employee's coverage terminates. It also terminates when the dependency status ceases to exist as, for example, where a wife gets a divorce or a child reaches age 19. The second difference is that medical care policies, as indicated above, usually provide for extended insurance benefits. The extension generally runs for three months and is effective only if the employee was disabled at the time his insurance ceased. In major medical contracts the period may be a year or longer, but continuous total disability is required. Female employees and dependent wives are usually entitled to maternity coverage for nine months after termination of the insurance. This makes up for the initial nine months of insurance coverage during which such protection is generally not granted, in effect making the insured event conception rather than birth.

*Premiums and records.* Premiums usually are paid monthly but may be paid on a less frequent basis. The employer reports to the company on either of two bases. In a *home-office accounting* system, used in smaller groups, the employer sends a list of new employees, changes in coverage, and terminations to the insurer each month. The insurer maintains a card for each insured employee and prepares the premium bill on the basis of these records.

In a *self-accounting* system, individual employee records are maintained only by the employer. The employer summarizes the data and reports the aggregates to the insurer. Usually the employer computes the premiums as well. Generally all changes are considered to occur as of the first of the month following the actual date of change. The policy usually provides that clerical error or oversight will not invalidate insurance which should be valid according to the plan, nor continue insurance which should be terminated. The insurer reserves the right to inspect the books and records of the employer as a check on record keeping and reporting. The provisions of a typical group disability income policy as to premiums and records are as follows:

## PREMIUM CALCULATIONS—EXPERIENCE RATING

Premiums shall be calculated at the rate of ———— for each Ten Dollars of weekly benefit in force, subject to such reductions or increases as the Insurance Company may make under its experience rating plan in use at the time of the respective changes in premium rates. Any reduction in premium rate shall be retroactive for the twelve months preceding its effective date, and a consequent refund of premium shall be made to the Employer. No increase in premium rate shall be retroactive, and no increase in premium rate shall become effective less than twelve months after the effective date of any previous increase in premium rate.

Any insurance becoming effective shall be charged for from the first day of the policy month coinciding with or next following the date the insurance takes effect. Premium charges for any insurance terminated shall cease as of the first day of the policy month coinciding with or next following the date the insurance terminates. If premiums are payable quarterly, semiannually, or annually, premium charges or credits for a fraction of a premium paying period required by the foregoing terms of this paragraph shall be made on a pro-rata basis for the number of policy months between the date premium charges commence or cease and the end of the premium paying period.

## DATA REQUIRED

The ———— shall keep a record with respect to each employee insured under this policy, showing the employee's name, sex, age or date of birth, the amount of insurance, the date insurance became effective, the amount of any increase or reduction in the insurance and the date it became effective, the date insurance terminated, and such other data as may be necessary to carry out the terms of this policy.

Most group policies provide for *dividends or experience rating*. A mutual company will allow dividends on group policies in about the same way as on individual policies. In order to compete effectively with the mutuals, the stock companies have developed experience-rating plans. The provisions of a group policy for experience rating were reproduced above. Premium reductions are retroactive, but increases are not, and rates may not be increased during the first policy year. Experience-rating refunds sometimes are contingent upon renewal of the master policy, while dividends usually are not.

Regardless of the nature of the adjustment, it attempts to consider the same factors. Generally speaking, the ideal refund would equal the accumulated premiums paid by the case, less the accumulated losses, expenses, and dividends paid, less a retention for contingencies and the insurer's profits. In smaller groups, however, full credibility cannot be given to the experience of the individual case, and it is necessary to develop formulas which vary credibility with group size. Essentially, a weighted average of individual and class experience is used, with the weight given the individual case increasing with size of group. The problems of allocating expense, especially overhead, to individual policies or classes is quite difficult. Thus dividend and experience-rating formulas become quite complex and vary greatly in detail from one insurer to another. These formulas will be discussed more fully in Chapter 18.

*Certificates* are issued to each employee. Those certificates are not a part of the contract and do not make the employee a party to it. However, they serve as evidence of insurance, give a summary of the coverage to which he is entitled, and state the person(s) to whom benefits are payable. As indicated above, the employee does acquire rights under the contract as a third-party beneficiary. These certificates are prepared by the insurer, but in self-administered plans the actual issue operation is performed by the employer.

*Claims provisions.* Most contracts require written *notice of loss* within 20 days of the commencement of claim. Some, however, do not impose any time limit. This seems to be the developing tendency and is justified by the fact that the employee naturally will be motivated to collect his claim as soon as possible. There is a tendency to postpone notice until near the limit where a limit is expressed. The company generally reserves the right to examine the person of the claimant as often as reasonably necessary.

Accidental death policies require the designation of a *beneficiary.* To cover cases where insured or beneficiary is incompetent, the designation is not made, the beneficiary predeceases the insured, or where other benefits are unpaid at death, many policies make use of a facility of payment clause. This permits the insurer to pay benefits to a guardian or committee or to a relative of specified close relationship, which in turn permits the insurer to obtain a valid release when the payee is a minor, *non compos mentis,* or otherwise incompetent or incapable of executing a valid receipt and release.

### Franchise insurance

Franchise insurance is comparable to wholesale insurance in the life field. The minimum membership requirements are smaller than for group insurance, and individual policies are issued to each person. The policies are all of the same form but may vary as to amounts and kind of coverage.

Generally, there is some individual underwriting, often in the form of a nonmedical application from each applicant. This requirement may be waived if the plan meets requirements as to percentage enrollment reasonably close to those used in group insurance. Usually at least 50 percent must enroll to get the benefit of "guaranteed issue," which means that individual standards of insurability are not imposed.

The term "franchise" also has been applied to plans whereby individual policies are sold through individual solicitation and underwriting under a payroll deduction or salary allotment plan. This is what is usually called "salary savings insurance" in the life insurance field.

Professional association group franchise insurance is also sold. This is a plan whereby individual policies are sold to members of professional societies, such as physicians, schoolteachers, etc. The solicitation and underwriting are handled on an individual basis, but sometimes, if at least 50 percent of the group joins the plan, some group underwriting standards are employed. Where these enrollment conditions are met, it is common to waive the customary individual policy exclusion of preexisting conditions.

Similar coverage is available to members of trade associations of small businessmen. Trade association group franchise insurance covers not only the officers, partners, and proprietors, but also their eligible employees.

The insurer usually agrees that no individual policy may be modified or discontinued. However, the right to modify or discontinue the entire group is reserved. The cost of franchise insurance will fall between that of individual and group insurance in most cases. However, two states specifically prohibit rate differentials between individual insurance and franchise. Usually franchise policies may be continued after leaving the group by changing to an individual premium basis.

All sorts of credit card plans are offering health insurance to their cardholders on a group or franchise basis. Playboy Club offers two plans, underwritten by Beneficial Insurance Group. One combines up to $100,000 accidental death benefit with up to $1,500 hospital income and the other combines $500 or $1,000 per month with regular medical expense of $5 per call in hospital, office, or clinic, and $8 for home calls. The insured's wife and children also may be covered for 10 percent of the husband's accidental death benefit. Contracts are guaranteed renewable to age 65 or effective age of Medicare coverage. The contract may be placed through an agent who then receives a commission, where state law permits.

Carte Blanche offers a hospital income plan underwritten by Combined Insurance Company of America which provides $30 per day hospital income for adults and $10 per day for children. Pregnancy, childbirth, and miscarriage are covered after the contract has been in force 10 months, with a limit of seven days per pregnancy. An accumulation clause provides a 5 percent increase in benefit each second year until the amount is increased 25 percent at the 10th anniversary. The group contract is guaranteed renewable but the insurer may adjust premiums annually, and Carte Blanche may terminate the group contract at any time.

## Blanket insurance

Group and franchise insurance both involve identification of insured persons by name. In self-administered group plans these records are kept by the employer; nonetheless, they must be maintained. Blanket insurance, on the other hand, does not specifically identify the insured persons. The insurance covers all members of a defined (or definable) group only while they are members of the group. The individual members constantly change, but the policy covers whoever happens to incur a loss while a member.

Usually there are no individual certificates, as under group insurance. State laws vary very greatly as to the requirements for blanket insurance, and it is almost impossible to generalize. It is permitted expressly or by implication in all states, but one prohibits the use of the name. Types of group eligible for blanket insurance include the following:

Passengers of a common carrier
Members of an athletic team
Students of a school
Participants in Head Start programs
Campers at a camp (and in transit)
Employees of a common employer for extraordinary occupational hazard
Members of a volunteer fire department
Members of a first-aid or ambulance squad or volunteer police department
Volunteer workers for a nonprofit community welfare organization
Debtors of a creditor
Spectators at sports or entertainment events
Other associations having a common interest
Other substantially similar groups

Where state law does not permit writing a particular type of group on a blanket basis, it may be handled on a group or franchise basis, with the necessary paper work increasing the cost. Another technique similar to franchise is to issue an individual policy to one member and to provide by endorsement that all the listed members also are insured under the policy for the same benefits.[3]

Blanket insurance usually is limited to accidental death and dismemberment benefits and blanket accident medical expense, covering injuries

---

[3] Questions have been raised as to the propriety of this arrangement. The legal effect would seem to be the same as if an individual contract had been issued to each member. The author has observed this method used for camper accident coverage.

incurred while a member of the group or under the defined circumstances. Contracts covering students at a school or college or campers at a camp may extend to cover sickness as well as accidental injury, but because of the broader benefits, it is more common to insure such groups on a group or franchise basis so that covered individuals may be identified more readily. Sports team contracts usually cover only accidental death and dismemberment and blanket accident medical expense for accidents occurring while participating in sports events or practice, or traveling for that purpose.

## Credit disability insurance

Credit disability insurance is written in connection with a consumer installment debt to pay the installments due to the creditor, on behalf of the insured borrower when the borrower is disabled. The potential market for this form of insurance is quite large. Consumer installment debt in the United States totaled $60.9 billion in March, 1966. In 1965, at least 135 companies were writing group or individual credit insurance: 31 wrote both, 66 wrote group only, and 26 wrote individual only. Premiums written in 1965 were $83 million for group credit disability, $29 million individual, and $113 million total.

Credit insurance may be written on a group, blanket, or individual basis, but in any case group underwriting techniques are employed. When a group contract is used, the creditor institution is the insured and the borrowers receive certificates evidencing their coverage. The creditor usually makes money on the transaction through dividends or experience rating credits which accrue to it. When individual contracts are used, the individual borrowers are the insureds and receive individual policies. The lending institution is the agent and receives commissions for the sale of the insurance through one or more of its employees who hold agents' licenses.[4] In either case, premiums are charged to the borrower.

Credit disability insurance is available to financial institutions and retail merchants who sell on the installment plan. This includes banks, credit unions, finance companies, small loan companies, appliance and automobile dealers, and department and furniture stores. The types of loan insured include secured and unsecured personal loans, direct loans for the purchase of consumer hard goods, installment sales contracts of various types, home improvement loans, and even obligations to purchase

---

[4] Texas is an apparent exception. An April 26, 1968 statement by the Texas Board of Insurance and the Regional Administration of National Banks stated that "Since a life insurance company cannot appoint a corporation (including national banks) to act as an agent within the State of Texas, there should be no way in which an insurance company would remit directly or indirectly to the bank."

mutual fund shares. The loans covered usually are short or medium term. The N.A.I.C. model bill defines credit insurance as being limited to loans of five years' duration or less. It is reproduced as Appendix H.

Credit disability insurance contracts provide that in the event of total disability, usually defined in terms of inability to engage in any occupation for wage or profit, installment payments will be made to the creditor on behalf of the insured. The contracts vary in the method of defining the loss and determining the benefit payment. The most common approach is to pay 1/30 of the monthly installment due for each day of total disability after a waiting period. Sometimes, benefits are retroactive back to the first day of disability if the insured debtor is totally and continuously disabled throughout the waiting period. Waiting periods vary from 3 to 30 days.

A variant is to provide for a payment equal to the monthly installment whenever the claimant is totally disabled on a due date after the expiration of the waiting period. A third approach is to provide for the payment of the entire outstanding loan in the event of total and *permanent* disability. Permanent disability may be defined as any disability which lasts a substantial period of time such as 90 days, or a prognosis of permanence or long and indefinite continuation may be required from the attending physician. In some cases, only blindness or dismemberment is covered. In any event, the maximum benefit is the amount of the loan outstanding.

The premium usually is paid in a single sum at the inception of the contract so that it can be added to the loan. The rate depends on the benefit provisions, duration, and waiting period and usually is expressed as a function of the initial amount of the loan. Rates are higher for individual contracts than for group.

Despite the fact that it seems to benefit the lender as much as the borrower, credit disability insurance serves a useful function, since very few people carry an adequate disability income program. Those who are adequately covered by disability insurance would have no need of it, however. On the other hand, a person who finds it impossible to obtain enough disability income insurance because of insurer underwriting limits may find credit insurance useful as a temporary supplement. It might be especially valuable to a professional man such as a physician or dentist purchasing expensive equipment on the installment plan, since overhead expense insurance usually doesn't cover such payments.

Credit insurance has been criticized because of a number of alleged abuses. These include the sale of insurance in amounts excessive in relation to the size of the loan, pyramiding of insurance in cases of refinancing; failure to refund premiums in the event of cancellation or prepayment; overcharging for the insurance; failure to notify the borrower of the amount, cost or sometimes the existence of the insurance;

nonpayment of claims; coercion and tie-in sales; and the sale of insurance by unlicensed agents. Since the lending institution benefits from high rates in either commissions, dividends or experience rate credits, there is a tendency for a sort of reverse competition to develop somewhat akin to the situation with airport space rentals for air travel insurance. N.A.I.C. committees have studied these problems and made a number of recommendations to correct the abuses. These will be discussed in Chapter 22 below.

### Long-term group disability income

The major problem of short-term group insurance is adequacy of coverage. Less than two fifths of the labor force is covered by group disability income insurance. Adding those covered by formal salary continuance plans raises the proportion to only about 57 percent. About 20 percent of the labor force have individual contracts; for all types of protection combined the proportion is 74.6 percent. Thus large segments of the population have no protection against income loss. While group insurance can be expected to grow, it is limited by its very nature to groups of employees or others of a size sufficient to meet underwriting criteria. The development of franchise insurance and the extension of the concept of group insurance to include trade associations, employee and professional associations, and trade-union groups have helped meet this problem. Further development along these lines should go far toward providing coverage for more members of the population.

From the standpoint of adequacy of benefits, group insurance is even more limited. Thirteen weeks is the most common duration for income benefits, and coverage for more than 52 weeks' benefit is relatively rare. Disability beyond the first six months, as indicated above, represents more than half the total income loss, and the impact of these extended disabilities is most severe. The public recognition of this exposure is growing, as evidenced by the constant broadening of disability benefits in federal Old-Age, Survivors and Disability Insurance. The OASDI program currently pays benefits to disabled workers (and their dependents) with as little as one and one-half years of covered employment. Maximum benefits are $218 for a worker with no children and $434.40 for a family, and these levels can be attained in 1969 for workers born in 1941 or later who have sufficiently high earnings. This largely has preempted the field for long-term group benefits for the lower income groups. Social insurance and group insurance both are concerned with providing a basic amount of protection for employed persons and their dependents. They represent, in effect, alternative approaches to the same problem.

Long-term disability insurance on a group basis is offered by a large number of insurers to select groups, but no information is available as to how much is in force.[5] However, coverage is being extended rapidly. In new group insurance issued in 1966, 35.9 percent of employees covered in plans providing disability income had long-term benefits. Short-term benefits covered 77.4 percent so that 13.4 percent of employees had both types of benefit.

This is high-quality coverage. Nine tenths of the employees covered by new group plans installed in 1967 provided maximum benefits to age 65 for both accidental injury and sickness. More than seven eighths of the employees were in plans which provided a maximum monthly benefit of $1,000 or more. Waiting periods ranged from one month to two years to coordinate with underlying short-term group contracts or salary continuance plans. Table 15–2 gives a detailed breakdown of the 1967 new business.

There are two main approaches to long-term disability income. One, executive group, often miscalled "key man" is intended for higher income employees only.[6] Eligibility for coverage depends on having an income in excess of a stipulated amount and benefits are paid with no regard to OASDI. These plans produce an average maximum benefit of $500 or more.

Typical is the plan of Provident Life and Accident for executives. A typical arrangement might restrict eligibility to employees earning more than $650 per month. A monthly benefit schedule is so designed as to cover up to 50 percent of basic salary up to $12,000 per year and one third of salary for the excess. Benefits are not reduced to offset OASDI or workmen's compensation benefits. (Occupational injuries are covered.) Since the benefit formulas for these types of social insurance replace a larger portion of the lower amounts of average wages and are subject to dollar maxima, this plan, restricted to higher income groups, does not need protection against duplication of benefits. Instead, it raises the overall level of benefit for the high-income worker to approximate that which the lower income worker gets from social insurance alone. Benefits are payable both for accidental injury and disease until age 65, after a waiting period which may be as short as 90 days.

Unlike most long-term group, this contract is noncancellable. The contract, in event of termination of employment or of the group contract, gives a covered employee the right to convert, without evidence of insurability, to an individual noncancellable and guaranteed renew-

---

[5] One actuary estimated that five million persons were covered by group long-term disability insurance in 1966.

[6] The Internal Revenue Code provisions prohibiting discrimination in favor of higher paid employees apply to group life insurance and pensions, but not to health insurance.

TABLE 15–2

Distribution of Number of Employees Having Long-Term[a] Disability Income Coverage
by Duration of, Commencement of, Maximum and Average
Monthly Income Benefits, and Size of Group, 1967

| | Number of Employers | | | | | |
|---|---|---|---|---|---|---|
| | *Size of Group* | | | | | |
| | *Less than 25 Number* | *25–99 Number* | *100–499 Number* | *500 or More Number* | *Total Number* | *Percentage of Total* |
| Total Employees................291 | 3,529 | 8,168 | 20,456 | 32,444 | 100 | |
| **Maximum Benefit Period** | | | | | | |
| *Accident    Sickness* | | | | | | |
| To age 65    5 years.......... 58 | 575 | 117 | 663 | 1,413 | 4.4 | |
| To age 65    To age 65......... 41 | 2,155 | 7,172 | 19,793 | 29,161 | 89.9 | |
| Lifetime    5 years.......... 24 | 87 | — | — | 111 | .3 | |
| Lifetime    To age 65........ — | 93 | 200 | — | 293 | .9 | |
| All others....................168 | 619 | 679 | — | 1,466 | 4.5 | |
| **Commencement of Benefit** | | | | | | |
| 30 days or 1 month............114 | 565 | 413 | 550 | 1,642 | 5.1 | |
| 90 days or 3 months........... 48 | 1,917 | 3,192 | 1,266 | 6,423 | 19.8 | |
| 180 days or 6 months.......... — | 532 | 3,719 | 11,822 | 16,073 | 45.5 | |
| All others....................129 | 515 | 844 | 6,818 | 8,306 | 25.6 | |
| **Maximum Monthly Benefit** | | | | | | |
| Less than $500................130 | 88 | 240 | — | 458 | 1.4 | |
| $500–749...................... 45 | 531 | 534 | 1,203 | 2,313 | 7.1 | |
| 750–999....................... 75 | 422 | 450 | — | 943 | 2.9 | |
| 1000–1249..................... — | 2,258 | 6,456 | 1,213 | 9,927 | 30.6 | |
| 1250–1499..................... — | 54 | 236 | — | 290 | .9 | |
| 1500 and over................. 41 | 176 | 252 | 18,040 | 18,509 | 57.1 | |
| **Average Monthly Benefit** | | | | | | |
| Less than $200................ 28 | 126 | 712 | — | 866 | 2.7 | |
| $200–299......................131 | 936 | 1,927 | 1,203 | 4,197 | 12.9 | |
| 300–399....................... 88 | 1,108 | 1,764 | 3,986 | 6,946 | 21.4 | |
| 400–499....................... 44 | 786 | 2,176 | 5,044 | 8,050 | 24.8 | |
| 500–599....................... — | 482 | 1,104 | 4,875 | 6,461 | 19.9 | |
| 600 and over.................. — | 91 | 485 | 5,348 | 5,924 | 18.3 | |

[a] Long term applies to benefit durations of two years or more, but most frequently five years or longer.

Source: Health Insurance Institute, *New Group Health Insurance Policies Issued in 1967* (New York, 1967).

able contract *as of original date of issue* (or of benefit increase). This is made possible by crediting the terminating employee with his share of the level premium reserve under the group contract. The right of conversion is limited to the period of coverage under the group contract, that is, prior to age 65. The group contract is issued without evidence of individual insurability, providing group underwriting standards are met. These include a requirement that the employer contribute at least 50 percent of the premiums. The maximum benefit amount issued is $2,500 per month. Premium rates are guaranteed, except as to new entrants and increases of benefit amount. This is level premium noncancellable disability income insurance on a group basis, a new and probably unique development.

The other approach is to cover almost all employees, but to use a coordination of benefit provision to make benefits excess over OASDI and workmen's compensation or over all other insurance. Avoiding duplication with OASDI benefits has become almost mandatory since the 1965 and 1967 amendments to the Social Security Act. Most insurers now use a coordination of benefit provision in all long-term group disability income plans except where eligibility is limited to higher paid employees. The plans covering all employees often have high benefit maximums, but average benefits are from $200 to $400 per month.

The group coordination of benefit (C.O.B.) provisions are much stricter than those currently permissible in individual contracts. Benefits are reduced so that the total under all coverages does not exceed a stipulated percentage (sometimes as low as 60 percent) of the insured's earnings. A typical group C.O.B. clause is reproduced below.

Benefits shall be reduced by any amount received by or due the employee from the following sources for the same period:
1. Social Security;
2. Any other state or federal government disability or retirement plan;
3. Salary paid by the employer;
4. Any retirement plan with the employer;
5. Workmen's Compensation or any similar law; and
6. Any total disability or total and permanent disability provision of any insurance policy.

However, such reduction shall not act to reduce the total amount from all such sources, including the group policy, below 60 percent of the employee's basic monthly earnings immediately prior to the disability, or $1,200, whichever is the lesser.

Some companies do not offset for individual insurance where the employer does not withhold premiums. This is mainly to avoid the administrative problems in identifying such coverage and determining the amount and duration of its benefits.

There are problems in determining the appropriate rate credit for such an offset provision, since OASDI benefit amounts depend on so many variables. Group cases large enough for full experience rating will develop proper rates as experience matures. However, for smaller cases and in bidding on new business, insurers will have to develop a table of rate credits, varying with age, sex, earnings, and number of dependents, to determine the proper premium reduction.

Fireman's Fund is using an unusual clause in some of its association group contracts which reads as follows:

The Company reserves the right, at the time of original application or on any annual premium due date, to reduce the Monthly Indemnity applied for or owned in this Company if such amount together with other disability income insurance owned or applied for in other companies is in excess of the smaller of the following two maximum amounts; (a) 60% of the Insured's average total monthly income during the 24 month period immediately preceding such premium due date or, (b) a total of $1,600 per month.

In the opinion of the writer, and in the opinions of state regulatory authorities, this clause would not reduce benefits, in the absence of official action of the insurer to reduce the amount of coverage and the premium prior to disablement. The phrase "other companies" probably would not include the U.S. government.

An advantage of making benefits excess over OASDI is that as OASDI benefits are increased in the future,[7] the insurer's liability under the long-term disability plan correspondingly will decrease. A disability income plan probably will show cost increases during the first few years (or even decades) as the plan matures. A plan paying the excess over social security could use the savings from social security liberalizations, to offset all or part of these cost increases. However, some method would have to be devised to make sure the workers applied for OASDI benefits. This can be accomplished by referring in the C.O.B. clause to benefits due or for which the claimant is eligible, rather than to benefits paid.

A severe problem in arranging complete disability income protection is income after age 65 if permanent disability occurs at an early age. Most disability income benefits cease at age 65, and most pension plans pay an actuarially reduced annuity based on age at disablement which often is pitifully small. One solution is individually owned endowment or retirement income life insurance with waiver of premium, but this is very expensive.

Another solution is for a group health insurance contract to provide for continuing employer and employee contributions just as though the employee were still working. A number of insurers now offer such a plan. One company, the Teacher's Insurance and Annuity Association, deals only with colleges, universities, independent schools, foundations, libraries, and scientific and research institutions. It provides a waiver of premium benefit for the T.I.A.A./C.R.E.F. annuity, and assumes both employer and employee contributions. (All T.I.A.A./C.R.E.F. annuities are on a money purchase basis.) Thus the employee ultimately receives the

---

[7] This has happened every 2.125 years since 1950.

amount of pension he would have received if he had continued working, at current salary, until age 65. Disability income benefits also are available whether or not the institution has an annuity plan. Disability is defined as "the inability of the employee, by reason of sickness or bodily injury, to engage in any occupation for which the employee is reasonably fitted." Benefits begin after a six-month waiting period and continue until age 65. Benefits are reduced by any amount received as benefits under workmen's compensation and OASDI. The monthly income benefit may not exceed 60 percent of the employee's salary up to $1,000 and 40 percent of the excess, or $1500 in any event. In groups of less than 200 employees, lower dollar limits are imposed. An optional feature provides an annual 3 percent increase in monthly disability income and pension contributions, giving the disabled employee an annual "raise" and protecting him from rising costs of living.

## Summary

Group insurance is sold to employer- and union-sponsored groups of workers through a master contract issued to an employer, union, or trustee. Underwriting, rating, and administration are handled on a group basis, with consequent major cost savings. Accidental death and dismemberment benefits are similar to those in individual policies. Disability income benefits generally have a three-to-seven-day sickness waiting period and provide maximum benefit periods of 13 or 26 weeks. It is necessary for the master contract to include detailed provisions as to the beginning and termination of coverage of employees and dependents. The employee is given a certificate which evidences his insurance but does not make him a party to the contract.

Despite warnings in previous editions of this book[8] private health insurers did not move rapidly enough with long-term disability insurance, and social insurance has substantially preempted the field for lower income workers. Thus long-term group contracts must be limited to higher income employees or be written as excess over OASDI. Nonetheless, they are growing in popularity and provide quite liberal protection in both duration and amount. Some are as good as individual noncancellable contracts and some are even better in some respects.

## Selected references

*See the following items from the General Bibliography: 4, chs. 18 and 19; 9; 10, ch. 7; 12, pp. 42–46; 15, chs. 28, 31, 33, 34, and 35; 18, pp. 354–84; 19, ch. 18; 20, chs. 3 and 7; 21, ch. 13.*

---

[8] O. D. Dickerson, *Health Insurance* (1st ed.; Homewood, Ill.: Richard D. Irwin, Inc., 1959) p. 285; repeated verbatim on p. 411 of the revised edition, 1963.

CRAIG, JAMES D. "Group Health Insurance," *Proceedings of the Casualty Actuarial Society,* Vol. VII, p. 78.

FOLLMANN, J. F., JR. "Growth of Group Health Insurance," *Journal of Risk and Insurance,* Vol. XXXII, p. 105.

FORDE, LOIS E. "Group Disability Insurance Plans," *Management Record,* Vol. XV (March, 1954), p. 90.

*Group Insurance Forums and Proceedings* of the Health Insurance Association of America and Health and Accident Underwriter's Conference. Entire proceedings devoted to group health insurance. Since 1951, annual.

HEALTH INSURANCE ASSOCIATION OF AMERICA. *Member Company Survey on Groups of Less than 25 Lives.* New York: Health Insurance Association of America, 1960.

―――. *New Group Health Insurance Policies Issued in 1967.* New York, H.I.A.A., 1967.

HIPP, GEORGE H.; PEARSON, JOHN E., AND LAVIGNA, SHERMAN J. "Marketing Opportunities and Problems of Companies with Less than $10 Million Group Health Premium," *Tenth Annual Group Insurance Forum,* Health Insurance Association of America, February 16, 1966.

KEDZIE, DANIEL P. *Consumer Credit Insurance.* Homewood, Ill.: Richard D. Irwin, Inc., 1957.

LACROIX, H. F. "A Discussion of Group Accident and Health Insurance," *Proceedings of the Casualty Actuarial Society,* Vol. XXXVI, p. 17.

NICHOLS, KENNETH C. "Long Term Disability." H.I.A.A. Group Insurance Forum, 1963.

PERKINS, ALFRED W. "Insurance Buyers Hear Reasons behind Growth of Long Term Disability Plans," *The National Underwriter,* December 16, 1966, p. 14.

POWELL, JAMES E. "Long-Term Disability—The Next Great Area of Protection," *Health Insurance Review* (1963 Sales and Service Number), p. 12.

SARASON, HARRY M. "Association Insurance," *Journal of Insurance,* December, 1961, p. 79.

SEYBOLD, GENEVA. *Personnel Practices in Factory and Office.* New York: National Industrial Conference Board, 1954.

SOCIETY OF ACTUARIES, EDUCATION AND EXAMINATION COMMITTEE. *Part 8 Study Notes: Group Insurance.* Chicago (processed).

STIEGLITZ, HAROLD. *Fringe Benefit Packages.* New York: National Industrial Conference Board, 1954.

*Health Inquiry Hearings, 83rd Congress.* U.S. Congress, House Committee on Interstate and Foreign Commerce. Washington, D.C.: U.S. Government Printing Office, 1953–54 (8 parts).

U.S. DEPARTMENT OF LABOR, BUREAU OF LABOR STATISTICS. *Analysis of Health and Insurance Plans under Collective Bargaining.* Bulletin No. 121. Washington, D.C.: U.S. Government Printing Office (periodical).

WILLIAMS, C. ARTHUR, JR. "College Faculty Accidental Injury and Sickness

Plans: A Preliminary Report," *Review of Insurance Studies,* Vol. II, p. 29.

————. "College Faculty Accidental Injury and Sickness Plans: Some Variations by Size and Type of College," *Review of Insurance Studies,* Vol. II, p. 117.

WILSON, HORACE H. "Let's Take a Stand—Mass Marketing," Health Insurance Association of America. Group Insurance Forum, 1966.

## chapter 16

*To evil habit's earliest wile*
*Lend neither ear nor glance nor smile—*
*Choke the dark fountain ere it flows,*
*Nor e'en admit the camel's nose.*

—Lydia Huntley Sigourney, *The Camel's Nose*

# Disability Income Problems and Issues

## Coordination with OASDI

The most pressing problem facing writers of disability insurance is avoiding overinsurance, particularly since the expansion of OASDI disability benefits under the 1965 and 1967 Social Security amendments. The 1965 amendments to the Social Security Act not only created Medicare but also liberalized the definition of disability and increased the amount of benefits payable for it by liberalizing the benefit formula, increasing the earnings base, and increasing the maximum family benefits. The 1967 amendments increased benefits another 13 percent and increased the maximum family benefit for average monthly wage (A.M.W.) over $370. For A.M.W. of $650, the increase was 18 percent. They also reduced the period required for insured status for disability benefits to as little as 1½ years at the younger ages. There has been relatively little discussion of the effects of these changes on private insurance, perhaps because of the attention devoted to Medicare. Moreover, many feel the problem to be less pressing because of the delayed impact of the earnings base increase. However, many do not seem to understand the full impact of these amendments.

*The Problem.* The definition of disability now is inability to perform any gainful work which is available in the worker's area or generally in the national economy, which is expected to continue for a period of one year from disablement, or to result in death. There are still the requirements for a six-month waiting or elimination period and that the claimant be fully insured under the OASDI program.

Consequently, *more persons* than ever before will be eligible to receive *larger amounts* of benefits. It follows that there will remain a smaller amount of uninsured average monthly income, hence, a lesser amount available for the private insurance industry to protect through its own disability income programs. This presents little problem in the higher

TABLE 16–1

Relationship between Take-Home Pay and Disability Income Benefit

| | | Annual | | | Monthly | | Margin for Private Insurance | |
|---|---|---|---|---|---|---|---|---|
| Number of Children | Gross Annual Earnings | Federal Income Tax[a] | Em-ployee FICA Tax[a] | Take-Home Pay | D.I. Benefit | (1) Wife and Child | (2) Wife and Two Children |
| (1)............... | $7,800 | $851.80 | $343.20 | $550.42 | $434.40 | $116.02 | |
| (2)............... | " | 737.80 | " | 561.02 | 434.40 | | $126.62 |
| (1)............... | 7,200 | 749.20 | 316.80 | 511.17 | 408.00 | 103.17 | |
| (2)............... | " | 635.20 | " | 520.67 | 415.20 | | 105.47 |
| (1)............... | 6,600 | 646.60 | 290.40 | 471.92 | 379.80 | 92.12 | |
| (2)............... | " | 541.80 | " | 480.65 | 395.60 | | 85.05 |
| (1)............... | 6,000 | 552.00 | 264.00 | 432.00 | 355.00 | 77.00 | |
| (2)............... | " | 450.00 | " | 440.50 | 374.80 | | 65.70 |
| (1)............... | 5,400 | 460.20 | 237.60 | 391.85 | 330.00 | 61.85 | |
| (2)............... | " | 363.60 | " | 399.90 | 354.40 | | 45.50 |
| (1)............... | 4,800 | 374.00 | 211.20 | 351.07 | 307.20 | 43.87 | |
| (2)............... | " | 264.00 | " | 360.40 | 322.40 | | 38.00 |
| (1)............... | 4,200 | 279.00 | 184.80 | 311.35 | 280.80 | 30.55 | |
| (2)............... | " | 174.00 | " | 320.10 | 280.80 | | 39.30 |

[a] Rate in effect April 15, 1968. While the 10 percent income tax surcharge is in effect taxes will be higher and take-home pay and the margin for private insurance will decrease. The already scheduled increases in the FICA Tax will have the same effect.

income brackets because there is an upper limit to the disability benefit payments under Social Security, but for lower income groups there is little margin between D.I. benefits and take-home pay.

Maximum benefits of $434.40 will be payable to disabled workers with three or more dependents and A.M.W. of $650. Although older workers cannot attain this A.M.W. until 2006, or age 76, whichever comes first, their A.M.W. can increase fairly rapidly. Young workers, however, (born in 1941 or later) can attain an A.M.W. of $650 by 1969.

Table 16–1 shows the amounts left for private insurance at various wage levels. The table was obtained by subtracting from the gross annual earnings the appropriate federal income taxes and social security

(FICA) taxes, dividing the result by 12 in order to derive the monthly take-home pay, and finally deducting from this figure the amount of Disability Income (D.I.) payments. In the development of the table, certain assumptions were made. They were (1) the 10 percent optional standard deduction, (2) the filing of a joint return with spouse, (3) one dependent child in the first case and two children in the second case, (4) the breadwinner not self-employed, and (5) the breadwinner eligible for the maximum benefits available considering his average monthly wage for OASDI to be equal to current monthly earnings. To the extent that current monthly earnings exceed the A.M.W. for OASDI, a greater margin for private insurance will exist.

*Individual disability income coverage.* As illustrated in Table 16–1, the new OASDI provisions effectively preempt the market for private long term disability income business in the lower income brackets. For a family man earning less than $6,000 a year, there is hardly enough uninsured income left to make it worthwhile for insurers to provide such coverage on an individual basis. If companies did provide coverage for such a small amount of income, they would have to: (1) do so at a loss, (2) charge a rather high premium, or (3) simply overinsure by offering more coverage than there was income to cover. The problem lies in the high expenses of putting business in force, many of which do not vary substantially with policy size. If an adequate expense loading were included in the premium, the expense element would be a high percent of premium. If the margin were not adequate, the insurer would be losing money. Higher average policy size involving overinsurance hardly seems to be an acceptable solution.

Individual policies already in force present a problem, since in many cases, the new amendments to the law have produced overinsurance. In other cases, such as the single man with no dependents, there is not now overinsurance, but should he get married and have children without substantial increase in salary, overinsurance would be almost certain to result.

In 1965, the H.I.A.A. *ad hoc* committee appointed two subcommittees to study the impact of the disability changes on the health insurance business. The individual subcommittees made several suggestions as to how writers of individual loss-of-time coverages could solve many of the difficulties created by the Social Security amendments. Some of their suggestions were that some companies attempt to modify their policy definition of total disability to make it consistent with the Social Security definition; that insurers reconsider their underwriting limits in order to protect themselves against potential overinsurance problems again in the future; that companies modify their policies so that benefits will be reduced at or about the time the insured would become eligible for the D.I.

benefits; that companies include the D.I. benefits in the definition of "other valid coverage" in the relation of earnings to insurance clauses; that companies attempt to exclude any similar benefits which are provided under any national, state, or other governmental plan.

There is little that insurers can do to protect themselves against over-insurance in respect to their present policyholders. Nothing whatever can be done to modify noncancellable contracts. If overinsurance results in high claim levels, premiums could be increased for outstanding guaranteed renewable contracts, but the policies cannot be modified. In the case of cancellable contracts, coverage modifications can be made, but the change of coverage on all outstanding business would be quite expensive. Of course, cancellable policies could be terminated or reduced in amount where overinsurance is discovered in individual instances. Usually this would be discovered only at the time of claim, which might be too late. The H.I.A.A. survey, in the spring of 1966, revealed no pattern of adjustment of outstanding business.[1]

For new business there are three possible approaches: (1) the inclusion of OASDI benefits in the "Relation of Earnings to Insurance" clause, (2) the dollar-for-dollar deduction of Social Security benefits from what is payable under the private insurance policy, and (3) tighter underwriting restrictions designed to prevent any future problems in this area. Almost all companies will tighten up on their underwriting when the effect of the 1965 and 1967 Amendments is understood fully. A variety of rules of thumb was reported in Spring, 1966.

The presently permissible relation of earnings to insurance clause is not very effective, even when government benefits are included in "other valid coverage." Moreover, it is permissible only in noncancellable and guaranteed renewable contracts. Only the benefits of contracts which contain the clause are reduced and not other benefits including OASDI.[2] Despite the limited effectiveness of the presently permissible clause, it is expected that more companies will use it, in response to the 1965 amendments.

Because of the limitations of this clause, a few companies are trying a more drastic approach. Gulf Life uses a relation of earnings to insurance clause which defines valid loss-of-time coverage as coverage provided by any governmental agency or by any organization subject to regulation by insurance law or by insurance authorities of any state of the United States or any province of Canada. It provides that if the insured's monthly earnings are less than 150 percent of the total benefits under all coverages, the income payable under the policy will be reduced to an amount which

---

[1] See above, pp. 361 ff. for a discussion of this survey.

[2] See above, pp. 442 ff. for a description of these clauses.

bears the same ratio to the amount otherwise payable as the monthly earnings bear to 150 percent of total benefits. This amounts to a prorating to two-thirds of income. Although this provision appears more stringent than Optional Provision 6 of the Uniform Individual Policy Provisions Law, contracts containing it have been approved in all states in which the company operates.

Only one instance is known of the use of method 2. Illinois Mutual Life and Casualty is using a clause to avoid the duplication of OASDI benefits which reads:

The amount of Accident or Sickness Total Disability Monthly Indemnity payable in any calendar month will be reduced by the amount of any Social Security Disability or Retirement Benefits payable to the insured the same calendar month, including any allowance payable for a spouse or other dependents.

The contracts with this provision do not include a conventional relation of earnings to insurance clause. The company reports no difficulty in getting contracts with this clause approved. The premium is reduced to reflect probable OASDI benefits.

Another method by which duplication of the new, or any future, government benefits could be avoided is by the adoption of the proposed relation of earnings to insurance provision recommended by the N.A.I.C. and approved administratively only in New Hampshire. This clause would protect the insurance company from duplication of loss-of-time benefits whether the insured was receiving payments from other insurance or from a government program. It permits a pro rata reduction of benefits payable in the proportion that a specified percentage (as low as 60 percent) of the insured's average earnings bears to the total benefits in all valid coverages, deducting from both numerator and denominator the amount of any other valid coverage which does not have a relation of earnings to insurance clause. This clause could reduce benefits under the contract containing it to zero.[3]

At best, however, it will be many years before the laws of enough states are changed so that such a provision could be used generally. Thus the main reliance must be on underwriting for some time to come.

*Group disability income coverage.* Since most group contracts cover for short periods, for example, 13 or 26 weeks, and since group plans are so flexible and easily modified, the problems caused by OASDI are both few and slight. The *ad hoc* subcommittee appointed to study the effects of the 1965 Social Security amendments on group disability income

---

[3] See above, pp. 443 ff. for a description of this clause and E. R. Solomon, "Control of Overinsurance by Contract Provision," *Annals of the Society of C.P.C.U.*, Vol. 19, No. 3, p. 197, for the outlook for enactment of these laws.

coverage suggested that insurers of groups review their present definitions of total disability and make them consistent with the government one, possibly limiting coverage to six months or modifying long-term coverage so that it would take a supplementary approach to OASDI benefits and that any companies not using a coordination of benefits clause, should do so.

Many companies writing long-term group disability income contracts were using coordination of benefit clauses already, and these usually included, by some wording, OASDI benefits as other valid coverage. The H.I.A.A. survey indicated that 28 companies, writing 37.8 percent of the insurance company group premium, already had a coordination of benefit provision. Seventeen companies, representing 31.4 percent of premiums, were making adjustments in coverage or underwriting, and six companies, writing 6.3 percent of premium, were considering such adjustments. Fifty-seven companies, representing 18 percent of the group premium volume, apparently had taken no action.

As indicated above, group coordination of benefit (C.O.B.) provisions are much stricter than those permissible in individual contracts. Under these clauses benefits are reduced so that the total under all coverages does not exceed a stipulated percentage (sometimes as low as 60 percent) of the insured's earnings. A typical group C.O.B. clause was reproduced on page 503 above. Under a clause of this type, the entire reduction in payment can come from the group policy and it actually may end up paying nothing. In order to avoid this possibility, many insurers include a provision for some minimum benefit, such as $20 per month or $10 per week.

As indicated above, it is necessary to develop a system for prospective rate credits for an OASDI offset provision. Such a system must take into account the probability that each employee will be insured by OASDI for disability benefits. This will vary by age and sex, but will be much higher than previously because of the liberalized requirements for disability insured status introduced by the 1967 Social Security Amendments. Then, the probable amount of benefit will have to be calculated. This will depend on Average Monthly Wage, which varies with age, sex, and current wage. The probable amount of benefit also will depend on dependent status. This can also be handled by a probability approach, varying by age and sex. For each age-sex-earnings level group, the formula would be:

| Prospective Rate Credit | = | Probability of Insured Status | × | Proportion of Premium Applicable to Benefit after 6 months | × | Probable P.I.A. | × | 50% of Probable Number of Eligible Dependents |
|---|---|---|---|---|---|---|---|---|

The summation of this for all the age-sex-earnings level groups would yield the dollar credit to be deducted from the premium quotation.

For small groups, of course, information as to actual coverage status, earnings history, and number and ages of children and spouse can be obtained and rate credits can be computed based on actual data rather than a probability model. Perhaps enough has been said to indicate the complexity of coordination between private insurance and OASDI.

## How much social insurance?

The central problem of social insurance is how much of it the country should have. Opinions range from suggestions that the whole thing be abandoned in favor of public assistance to proposals for complete cradle-to-grave coverage. No matter what one's personal philosophy may be, he must recognize that in modern society it has become unfashionable (and political suicide) to let people starve in the streets. Human beings, fortunately in view of what they face, are basically optimists. It is contrary to human nature to make adequate provision for all future contingencies which may impair family security. Only the most perceptive will be adequately motivated to do this on a voluntary basis. Only the economically fortunate will be able to afford the costs of private insurance.

Yet there is a strong tradition in favor of voluntary methods. In a capitalistic competitive economy it has been accepted that, insofar as possible, individuals should provide for their own welfare, by meeting all the costs which they incur, out of their own resources. This tradition of individual responsibility is a part of the American heritage, and provisions for meeting risk costs should follow the same principle. In keeping with this tradition, relief in kind has given way largely to cash relief; out-and-out relief to public assistance; and public assistance has been viewed as a stop-gap measure to meet the inadequacies of programs of social insurance.

Security and freedom from want are held to be rights of the individual which he earns through his productive efforts for himself and his family. Group insurance and social insurance are looked upon as the reward for labor effort expended—not as the doles of a paternalistic society. Individual insurance, where the costs are met entirely out of personal resources, represents the most complete form of individual responsibility for meeting risk through cooperative efforts. Thus the principles of this economic and social system would appear to favor individual insurance and savings as the preferred method of meeting risk, with group insurance, social insurance, and public assistance being progressively less desirable alternatives.

*Public assistance versus social insurance.* The argument for using public assistance instead of social insurance is one of economy: since public assistance is paid only to those who can demonstrate need, benefit payments will be less. This probably is true, but several factors must be considered before jumping to conclusions. If public assistance should become the accepted method for society to provide economic security to its members, much of the stigma attached to "charity" would disappear. This already is happening despite the retention of the needs test. Welfare recipients are organizing in order to protect their "rights." It may be assumed that under such circumstances the needs test would be so watered down, or the concept of "needs" so broadened, that it would lose all meaning.

A second consideration is one of administrative cost. While the record keeping associated with social insurance (wage records, etc.) is substantial (2 percent in OAS and 5 to 6 percent in DI), public assistance involves even higher costs. The application of any meaningful type of means or needs test cannot be handled by rule of thumb. It requires an expensive administrative mechanism. Third, the means of financing associated with the two devices differ. Public assistance is financed out of general tax revenues, which, on the federal level at least, are so unduly progressive as to impair individual incentive. To burden the taxpayers with the costs of a complete social security program on such a financing basis would impair further the functioning of the economy. On the other hand, social insurance is financed by premiums or taxes which usually are a flat percentage of covered payroll—neither progressive nor regressive. To the extent that the employer passes these costs on to consumers, it is probably as a constant percentage of the price of the product. Thus the employer's contribution when passed on becomes a sales tax, again neither progressive nor regressive.[4] There is some progression in the OASDI benefit formula, in that benefits are a higher percentage of lower earnings than of higher. However, this progression is slight compared to that of the federal income tax.

A fourth argument in favor of insurance as opposed to assistance is visibility of costs. Social insurance is financed by earmarked taxes or premiums, and it should be evident that, if the fund is in balance, increased benefits must be financed by increased premiums or taxes. This is partic-

---

[4] A progressive rate schedule (for taxes or otherwise) is one which applies successively higher rates to successively higher increments of the base. A regressive schedule applies successively lower rates to successively higher increments of the base. If the whole of payroll is considered as the base, the OASDI tax is slightly regressive, but the benefit formula is even more so, making the system as a whole somewhat "progressive." Neither of these concepts has anything to do with progress or the reverse. Many authorities consider sales taxes as regressive but this is logically impossible without shifting one's frame of thought to another base, such as income. But sales taxes are not income taxes!

ularly true when the insured worker himself pays all or a part of the premium. Unfortunately, this direct connection between benefits and taxes is less obvious in OASDI than it might be because of the immaturity of the system. However, the recent increases in taxes should have made this point evident to many. The "something-for-nothing" philosophy, certainly, is less of a danger in an insurance program than in one of public assistance.

Public assistance should be considered a residual program to provide the minimum necessities of subsistence to those whom private means and social insurance have failed to cover. There will always be those who, because of incapacity or for other reasons, have never been attached to the labor force long enough to qualify for insurance. However, if these numbers are small, it might be more economical to finance their benefits through the insurance system than maintain two separate systems. This would not preclude the retention of a needs test for such "uninsured benefits" or a lower level of benefit for such persons. The level could be, perhaps, the statutory minimum for social insurance.

*The place of social insurance. Risks.* But, others will ask, why have social insurance at all? The answer is that there are certain contingencies which produce losses so frequent or so severe that most private individuals cannot cope with them. One of these is old age, which affects perhaps three fourths of the labor force[5] and requires the accumulation of large amounts of money to provide retirement benefits. Participation in this financing by the employer and/or the power of government compulsion seems to be generally accepted. Unemployment is not considered insurable by private methods, and social insurance or assistance is the only resort. Premature death of a person with dependents and industrial injury have also been generally accepted as proper subject matter for social insurance. In the last decade, long term disability and medical care expenses for the aged have been added. It is in the area of health that most of the unresolved questions remain. The extent of public assistance, social insurance, and private insurance against the losses resulting from poor health has been discussed in Chapter 4.

*Amount of benefit.* Once it has been decided against what risks social insurance will insure, there are a number of subsidiary questions. One's answer will depend on personal philosophy as well as upon objectively determinable factors. In answering all such questions, the concept of individual freedom must be kept in mind. Social insurance is, by definition, compulsory. Compulsion, by definition, interferes with freedom. How far should this interference be carried? Moreover, compulsion as to the disposition of people's incomes may interfere seriously with the economic incentives which have made this country strong. How far should

---

[5] That is, about three fourths survive until old age becomes a problem.

this interference be carried? How much can the country risk its future growth in order to pay for its future security?

Most thinking Americans would answer that society wants to interfere no more than necessary with individual freedom and economic incentives. Then they would argue for years over what is "necessary." The concept which has gained the widest acceptance, at least in terms of "lip service," is the concept of a *floor of protection*. Under this concept, social insurance should cover only those risks of fundamental economic importance to the family and should provide benefits at a level sufficient to sustain a minimum but decent standard of living.

The standard should be higher than that provided by public assistance, which should provide incomes just above the subsistence level. However, the income provided by social insurance should be low enough to discourage malingering and low enough to encourage individual savings and private insurance to supplement it. Social insurance coverage then becomes a minimum reward for a minimum attachment to the labor market. Greater attachment to the labor force results in higher benefits, but still low enough that only the most unambitious family will consider them adequate.

The current social insurance system is founded on this "floor of protection" concept. Social insurance is supposed to cover the entire labor force and its dependents against the risks insured. All but the least ambitious and least productive employees will have group insurance provided through either employers, unions or associations to supplement social insurance. This will provide additional protection against the risks of death, disability, and old age for employees of most firms. Private insurance will be available further to supplement the protection for the self-employed and the majority of employees who will want greater coverage than social and group insurance together will provide.

*Persons covered.* As one moves from public assistance to social insurance, group insurance, and individual insurance, he finds progressively fewer persons covered for progressively higher aggregate benefits. This concept may be illustrated by a triangle where level of benefit is plotted vertically and number covered horizontally (Chart 16–1).

It seems that the many recent increases in OASDI benefit levels have constituted a significant departure from the "floor of protection" concept. While a maximum P.I.A. of $218 per month hardly seems high, it must be recognized that a family of three or more may collect as much as $434.40 per month. This is more than some families earn when actively working. Workmen's compensation benefits may range as high as $150 a week.[6] This is one of the highest "floors" on record. Nonoccupational

---

[6] Most states have maximum benefits of $50 per week or less, however.

CHART 16–1

The Williamson[a] Triangle

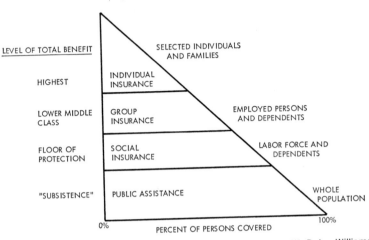

| LEVEL OF TOTAL BENEFIT | | SELECTED INDIVIDUALS AND FAMILIES |
| HIGHEST | INDIVIDUAL INSURANCE | |
| LOWER MIDDLE CLASS | GROUP INSURANCE | EMPLOYED PERSONS AND DEPENDENTS |
| FLOOR OF PROTECTION | SOCIAL INSURANCE | LABOR FORCE AND DEPENDENTS |
| "SUBSISTENCE" | PUBLIC ASSISTANCE | WHOLE POPULATION |

0%                        PERCENT OF PERSONS COVERED                        100%

[a] The original use of this illustration was attributed by C. A. Kulp to W. Rulon Williamson.

disability income benefits may be as high as $70 per week or more under the California act—again a rather high amount. While economic security is desirable, it is necessary to recognize the costs involved.

*Costs of social security.* The cost of social security can be illustrated by picturing a "typical" worker and family. He earns $650 a month and has a wife and two children. The deductions from his pay are as follows, assuming he lives in California and not considering the "temporary" income tax surcharge:

| | |
|---|---|
| Federal income tax | $ 70.98 |
| FICA (social security) | 28.60 |
| Nonoccupational disability | 6.17 |
| Total deductions | $105.75 |
| Take-home pay | $544.25 |
| Total social insurance contributions | $ 34.77 |
| Social insurance contributions as percent of take-home pay | 6.4% |

In addition, his employer pays on his behalf:

| | |
|---|---|
| FICA | $28.60 |
| Unemployment compensation (Assuming 3.1 percent rate after experience rating (applicable to the first $3,800 per year per employee) | 9.82 |
| Workmen's compensation (about 1.0 percent) | 6.50 |
| Total social insurance contributions by employer | $44.92 |
| Total social insurance contributions by employer and employee combined | $79.69 |
| Total contributions as percent of employee's take-home pay | 14.6% |

Assuming that the employer's social insurance contributions could and would be used to raise wages, might our employee not prefer a 14.6 percent increase in take-home pay, from $544.25 to $623.94? If the FICA taxes were at their ultimate level, to be reached under present legislation for present benefit levels in 1987, the cost would be much higher. The FICA tax would be $38.35 each for employer and employee. Total deductions would be $170.17, take-home pay only $479.83. Total employees'

TABLE 16–2

Past and Future OASDHI Tax Rates and Bases
(employer and employee combined)

| Year | Combined Tax Rate | Earnings Base | Maximum Combined Tax | Income Tax Amount[a] |
|---|---|---|---|---|
| Past | | | | |
| 1937–49..................... 2.0 | | $3,000 | $ 60.00 | — |
| 1950....................... 3.0 | | 3,000 | 90.00 | — |
| 1951–53..................... 3.0 | | 3,600 | 108.00 | — |
| 1954....................... 4.0 | | 3,600 | 144.00 | — |
| 1955–56..................... 4.0 | | 4,200 | 168.00 | — |
| 1957–58..................... 4.5 | | 4,200 | 189.00 | — |
| 1959....................... 5.0 | | 4,800 | 240.00 | — |
| 1960–61..................... 6.0 | | 4,800 | 288.00 | — |
| 1962....................... 6.25 | | 4,800 | 300.00 | — |
| 1963–65..................... 7.25 | | 4,800 | 348.00 | — |
| 1966....................... 8.4 | | 6,600 | 554.40 | 646.60 |
| 1967....................... 8.8 | | 6,600 | 580.80 | 646.60 |
| Future, 1967 Law | | | | |
| 1968....................... 8.8 | | 7,800 | 686.40 | 729.80 |
| 1969–70..................... 9.6 | | 7,800 | 748.80 | 729.80 |
| 1971–72.....................10.4 | | 7,800 | 811.20 | 729.80 |
| 1973–75.....................11.3 | | 7,800 | 881.40 | 729.80 |
| 1976–79.....................11.4 | | 7,800 | 889.20 | 729.80 |
| 1980–86.....................11.6 | | 7,800 | 904.80 | 729.80 |
| 1987 on.....................11.8 | | 7,800 | 920.40 | 729.80 |

[a] 1967 Income Tax, assuming: wife and one child, 10% standard deductions, filing joint return, no income by wife, not including the "temporary" income tax surcharge.
Source: Robert J. Myers, *Actuarial Cost Estimates for the Old-Age, Survivors, Disability, and Health Insurance System as Modified by the Social Security Amendments of 1967* (Washington, D.C.: U.S. Government Printing Office), pp. 3, 4.

contributions would be $44.52—9.3 percent of take-home pay. The total contribution of employer and employee would be $99.19. This would be equal to 20.7 percent of take-home pay. Would the worker prefer the security or a cash increase of $99.19—20.7 percent of his take-home pay? This is not to question the proportion of income that properly may be devoted to security purposes, only the proportion that should properly be so devoted on a *compulsory* basis.

Table 16–2 shows how the Social Security tax has increased to such an extent that in 1969 the Social Security tax will be greater than income tax for a married couple filing a joint return earning $650 a month or less. In years after 1969 until 1985 this disparity between income and Social Security tax will grow until the difference will be $190.60.

### Further expansion of social insurance

*Extension of OASDI permanent disability insurance.* Most people do not realize the vast expansion that the social security system has undergone within the last few years. The number of persons receiving benefits from social security has increased dramatically. Chart 16–2 shows the effects the various amendments have had on increasing the number of beneficiaries under the program. It is still too early to tell the effect of the expanded disability eligibility definition under the 1967 amendments, but the only effect it can possibly have is to increase the number of beneficiaries again.

Perhaps the best indication one may use of the expansion in the system is to compare the different acts and their respective benefits. Chart 16–3 and Table 16–3 show all the acts with their major provisions as to benefit amount. The wage base has jumped from $3,000 to $7,800, while the minimum primary insurance amount has gone from $10 to $55, and the maximum primary insurance amount has gone from $85 to $218. The maximum family benefit has increased from $85 per month to $434.40.

The benefit formula has been changed somewhat, mainly by increasing the percentage of average monthly wage ( A.M.W. ) in the existing law by a uniform percentage multiplier but the general effect has been to benefit the middle income worker in all the amendments. Table 16–4 gives the various formulas. The percentage increases were 7 percent in 1958 and 1965 and 13 percent in 1967. The average monthly wage originally included all working years, but now the five lowest years may be dropped in order to produce a higher A.M.W.

In the 1965 and 1967 amendments, the increased benefit levels, combined with the increased earnings base, produced a tremendous increase in benefit amounts. The maximum primary insurance amount ( P.I.A. ) was increased by 112 percent from 1939 to 1961 as median earnings increased by 280 percent. From 1961 to 1967 the maximum P.I.A. increased by 72 percent, while median earnings increased an estimated 24 percent.

Perhaps the best way to analyze the benefit amount increases is to express them as percentages of median earnings, as in Table 16–3. The major jump occurred in the earnings base. This had been periodically increased to keep pace with median earnings of male four-quarter workers, ranging from 96.5 percent to 112 percent from 1950 to 1961. If past patterns had been adhered to it would have been increased from $4,800 to $5,400 in 1964 and to $6,000 in 1967. This would have just matched the increase in earnings. However, the attention of Congress was occupied by

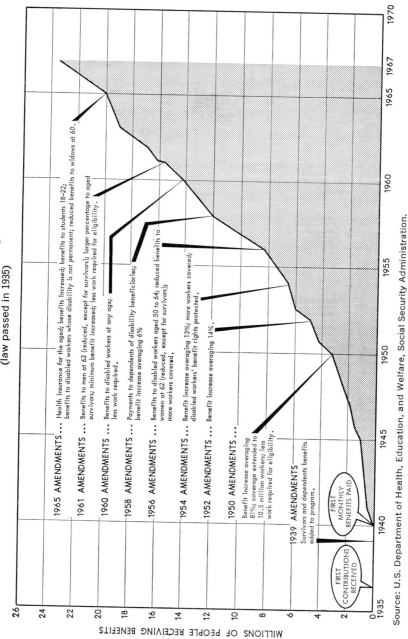

CHART 16–2

History of the Social Security Program
(law passed in 1935)

MILLIONS OF PEOPLE RECEIVING BENEFITS

1965 AMENDMENTS ... Health insurance for the aged; benefits increased; benefits to students 18–22; benefits to disabled workers whose disability is not permanent; reduced benefits to widows at 60.

1961 AMENDMENTS ... Benefits to men at 62 (reduced, except for survivors); larger percentage to aged survivors; minimum benefit increased; less work required for eligibility.

1960 AMENDMENTS ... Benefits to disabled workers at any age; less work required.

1958 AMENDMENTS ... Payments to dependents of disability beneficiaries; benefit increase averaging 6%

1956 AMENDMENTS ... Benefits to disabled workers aged 50 to 64; reduced benefits to women at 62 (reduced, except for survivors); more workers covered.

1954 AMENDMENTS ... Benefit increase averaging 13%; more workers covered; disabled workers' benefit rights protected.

1952 AMENDMENTS ... Benefit increase averaging 14%.

1950 AMENDMENTS ... Benefit increase averaging 81%; coverage extended to 10.5 million workers; less work required for eligibility.

1939 AMENDMENTS Survivors and dependents benefits added to program.

FIRST MONTHLY BENEFITS PAID

FIRST CONTRIBUTIONS RECEIVED

Source: U.S. Department of Health, Education, and Welfare, Social Security Administration.

CHART 16-3

OASDI Earnings Base, Maximum Family Benefit, Maximum and Minimum Primary Insurance Amounts Compared with Median Earnings

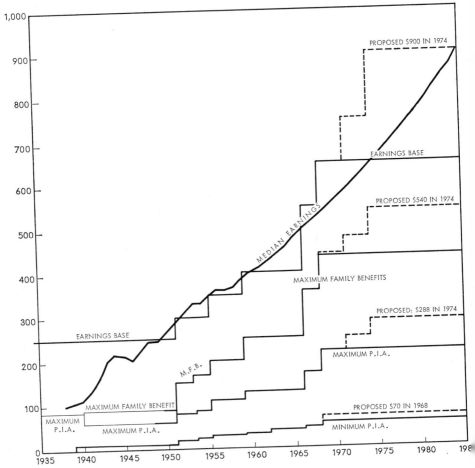

the King-Anderson proposals, and the House-passed social security bill, increasing the earnings base to $5,400, died in Conference Committee in 1964. The 1965 amendments overcompensated and increased the base to 115 percent of median earnings, and the 1967 amendments jumped this to 127 percent. This can be explained only as a deliberate change in policy, financing most of the increased OASDI benefits and much of the H.I. benefits from taxes paid by and on behalf of workers earning more than $4,800 per year.

This, combined with successive benefit amount increases totaling 21 percent, pushed maximum benefits to their highest levels, as a percent of median earnings, since 1942, when earnings were only $163 per month.

TABLE 16-3

Monthly Minimum and Maximum Benefit Provisions under
OASDI and Earnings Base Compared to Median Earnings

| Year of Legisla-tion | Median Earn-ings[a] | Earnings Base | | Minimum Primary Benefit | | Maximum Primary Benefit | | Minimum Maximum Family Benefit | | Maximum Maximum Family Benefit | |
|---|---|---|---|---|---|---|---|---|---|---|---|
| | | $ | %[b] | $[d] | %[b] | $[d] | %[b] | $[g] | %[b] | $[f,g] | %[b] |
| 1935........$102[c] | | 250 | 245[c] | 10 | 9.8 | 85 | 83.3 | — | — | — | — |
| 1939........ 108 | | 250 | 231 | 10 | 9.3 | 60[e] | 55.6 | 25 | 23.1 | 85 | 78.7 |
| 1950........ 268 | | 300 | 112 | 20 | 7.5 | 80 | 29.8 | 40 | 14.9 | 150 | 56.0 |
| 1952........ 311 | | 300 | 96.5 | 25 | 8.0 | 85 | 27.3 | 45 | 14.5 | 168.75 | 54.3 |
| 1954........ 321 | | 350 | 106 | 30 | 9.1 | 108.5 | 32.8 | 50 | 15.1 | 200 | 60.4 |
| 1958........ 369 | | 400 | 108 | 33 | 8.9 | 127 | 34.4 | 53 | 14.4 | 254 | 68.8 |
| 1961........ 412 | | 400 | 97.1 | 40 | 9.7 | 127 | 30.8 | 60 | 14.6 | 254 | 61.6 |
| 1965........ 479 | | 550 | 115 | 44 | 9.2 | 168 | 35.1 | 66 | 13.8 | 368 | 76.8 |
| 1967........ 510 | | 650 | 127 | 55 | 10.8 | 218 | 42.7 | 82.5 | 16.2 | 434.40 | 85.2 |
| 1968[h]....... 510 | | 650 | 127 | 70 | 13.7 | 221 | 43.3 | 105 | 20.6 | 440.40 | 86.4 |
| 1971[h]....... 561 | | 750 | 134 | 70 | 12.5 | 248 | 44.2 | 105 | 18.7 | 480 | 85.6 |
| 1974[h]....... 617 | | 900 | 146 | 70 | 11.3 | 288 | 46.7 | 105 | 17.0 | 540 | 87.5 |

[a] Median earnings for male four-quarter wage and salary workers in covered employment. Earnings in excess of the earning base partly estimated. Data for 1937–65 from Social Security Bulletin, Annual Statistical Supplement, 1965, p. 33. Projected for 1966–74 on basis of a 3.21 percent compound annual growth rate, the average annual increase from 1954–65.
[b] Percent of median earnings in year enacted (1935–67) or year prior to proposed effective year (1968–74).
[c] Data not available. Figure is for 1938.
[d] Payable to disabled or retired worker (before reduction for retirement before age 65).
[e] Assumes that 50 years of coverage is the maximum possible.
[f] Total benefit payable to retired worker and dependents or to all survivor beneficiaries.
[g] Maximum provision of 80 percent of average monthly wage also applies, but application may not reduce benefit to less than $25 for the 1939 law, $40 for the 1950 law, $45 for the 1952 law, $50 or one and a half times the primary insurance amount for the 1954 law, and $20 plus primary insurance amount or one and a half times the primary insurance amount for the 1958 law. In some cases, slightly larger amounts can be paid as the result of the provision for rounding benefit amounts (to next higher 10 cents for each beneficiary).
[h] Proposed but not enacted in 1967, to be effective in year shown.

Maximum primary insurance amount, which had been around 30 percent of median earnings, jumped to 35.1 percent in 1965 and 42.7 percent in 1967.

Similarly, the maximum maximum family benefit, which had ranged from 54.3 percent of median earnings to 68.8 percent from 1950 to 1965, was increased to 76.8 percent in 1965 and 85.2 percent in 1967. The only benefit amounts which were not increased more rapidly than earnings (which themselves increased more rapidly than prices during this pe-riod) were the minimum primary insurance amount and the minimum maximum family benefit. The minimum P.I.A. increased only from 9.8 percent of median earnings in 1937 to 10.8 percent in 1967. The minimum maximum family benefit which had ranged from 14.4 to 15.1 percent was increased to 16.2 percent of median earnings in 1967.

Thus, despite the expressed concern for "social adequacy" in benefit

## TABLE 16–4

### OASDI Benefit Formulas under the Social Security Act and Its Amendments

| Formula Enacted in | Monthly Retirement Benefit | |
| --- | --- | --- |
| | Basis | Percentages Applied |
| 1935.............. | Cumulative wage credits | ½% of first $3,000 plus ¹⁄₁₂% of next $42,000 plus ¹⁄₂₄% of next $84,000. |
| 1939.............. | Average monthly wage[a] (A.M.W.) up to $250 after 1936 | 40% of first $50 plus 10% of next $200, all increased by 1% for each year of coverage. |
| 1950.............. | A.M.W.[a] up to $300 after 1950 | 50% of first $100 plus 15% of next $200. |
| 1952.............. | A.M.W.[a] up to $300 after 1950 | 55% of first $100 plus 15% of next $200. |
| 1954.............. | A.M.W.[a] up to $350 after 1950, excluding four or five years of lowest earnings | 55% of first $110 plus 20% of next $240. |
| 1958.............. | A.M.W.[b] up to $400 after 1950, excluding five years of lowest earnings. | 58.85% of first $110 plus 21.4% of next $290. |
| 1965.............. | A.M.W. up to $550 after 1950 excluding five years of lowest earnings | 62.9% of first $110 plus 22.9% of next $290 plus 22.4% of next $150. |
| 1967.............. | A.M.W. up to $650 after 1950 excluding five years of lowest earnings | 71.16% of first $110 plus 25.88% of next $290 plus 24.18% of next $150 plus 28.43% of next $100. |

[a] Total credited earnings divided by months elapsed after year of attainment of age 21 or after "starting year" shown, whichever is more favorable.
[b] Total credited earnings divided by elapsed months for a number of years equal to number in the measuring period.
Source: Robert J. Myers, *Social Insurance and Allied Government Programs* (Homewood, Ill.: Richard D. Irwin, Inc., 1965), p. 49.

levels and "helping people get above the poverty line," the Congress abandoned the "floor of protection" concept and increased benefits more for the well-to-do than for the poor.

Despite the tremendous expansion in coverage and benefit amount which already has taken place, one may expect proposals for further expansion in the future. Sure to be requested are the following changes in OASDI, which were administration proposals in 1967, most of which passed the Senate.

1. An increase in benefit formula of 9 or 10 percent by 1970. (In 1967, the administration and Senate wanted a 15 percent increase but only got 13 percent. At a rate of inflation of 3 to 3½ percent per year, they will want an additional 7 or 8 percent as a cost of living adjustment.)
2. An increase in earnings base to $9,000 a year in 1970 and $10,800 in 1974. (This will generate enough revenue to finance the benefit increases

and a few other expansions and will automatically increase maximum benefits.)

3. Benefits for disabled widows, regardless of age, of 82½ percent of P.I.A.

4. Increased minimum benefits of $70 for an individual and $105 for a family. (Probably higher minimum dollar amounts will be requested for 1970.)

5. A special minimum benefit of $4 for each year in covered employment up to 25 years.

6. Benefits for parents of retired and disabled workers.

Increased social security taxes are already putting pressure on take-home pay. Workers respond by seeking wage raises which contribute to cost-push inflation, which leads to a demand for higher social security benefits. Admittedly, as dollars depreciate, benefit levels must keep pace, but the country should face up to a decision as to the proper role of social security. Already the market for long-term disability benefits is cut off except for people earning more than $8,000 a year. The problem is similar with life insurance and private pension plans, but the study of this must appear elsewhere.

*A dynamic OASDI system.* Myers[7] has suggested a system of auto-matically changing the earnings base by tying it to some economic indi-cator so that it would not take an act of Congress to adjust benefit levels to changing economic conditions. In order to stimulate some thought, the following illustration (*not* proposal) shows how such a system might work (see Table 16–5). It is designed to reproduce present maximum benefit levels in 1974. Between enactment and 1974 would be a tran-sitional period during which payments would be the higher of those provided in present law and those provided in the illustration. This period is required for median earnings to catch up with the $650 earn-ings base of the 1967 amendments. Most benefit provisions are a function of the earnings base, which is defined as 110 percent of the median earnings of four-quarter male workers three years previously as promul-gated by the Secretary of Health, Education, and Welfare annually. Minimum benefits would be affected immediately, but most other amounts would not be affected for several years.

While this is offered as an illustration to provoke further study and *not* as a proposal, some thought did go into the choices:

1. The median earnings of four-quarter male workers is the appro-priate base. Use of this gives the retiring and retired a share in the growth of the economy which a price-index base does not.

2. The 110 percent reflects an assumed 3.2 percent rate of increase in median earnings and is designed to approximate the current year level.

---

[7] Robert J. Myers, "A Method Automatically Adjusting the Earnings Base under OASDI," *Journal of Risk and Insurance*, September, 1964, p. 329.

TABLE 16-5

Illustrative OASDI Benefits, Dynamic System

| | | Amount in 1974 | |
| | | Dynamic | |
| Item | Formula | System | 1967 Law |
|---|---|---|---|
| Earnings base (E.B.)......... | 110% of 1972 Median Earnings ($598) | $658 | $650 |
| Minimum primary insurance amount (P.I.A.)............ | 12% of Earnings Base | 79[a] | 55 |
| Maximum P.I.A.............. | 33⅓% of E.B. | 220 | 218 |
| P.I.A...................... | Minimum P.I.A. plus 25% of excess of Average monthly wage (A.M.W.) over minimum P.I.A. | | |
| | e.g.: A.M.W. | | |
| | $ 79 | 79 | 57.70 |
| | 100 | 85 | 71.50 |
| | 200 | 110 | 101.60 |
| | 300 | 135 | 128.30 |
| | 400 | 159 | 158.20 |
| | 500 | 185 | 178.60 |
| | 600 | 210 | 204.00 |
| | 650 | 222 | 218.00 |
| Maximum family benefit..... | 150% of P.I.A. | | |
| Minimum maximum family benefit................... | 150% of minimum P.I.A. = 18% of E.B. | 118 | 82.50 |
| Maximum maximum family benefit................... | 150% of maximum P.I.A. = 50% of E.B. | 333[b] | 434.40 |

[a] All calculations, including intermediate calculations, are rounded *up* to nearest dollar.
[b] Ineffective until ca. 1984 when E.B. $\cong$ $873 and maximum P.I.A. $\cong$ $437.

3. It is very expensive to increase minimum benefits since millions of people are affected. The 12 percent is between the 10.8 percent of the 1967 law and the 13.7 percent proposed by the administration and passed by the Senate. If earnings rise, this minimum amount will increase every year as tax receipts increase. At the 3.2 percent rate, median earnings would be $900 and minimum P.I.A. would be $108 by 1985.

4. One third of current median earnings is enough for a compulsory system. With a wife's benefit of 50 percent a retired couple would get 50 percent of current median earnings.

5. If the law is to limit workers with A.M.W. below $179 to 150 percent of P.I.A. as their maximum family benefit (M.F.B.), as it now does, it should do the same at higher A.M.W., leaving some function for voluntary insurance and pension plans.

6. The P.I.A. formula is simple, approximates present levels, and will not require periodic adjustment. If past experience is valid, median earnings will increase every year and so will *every* beneficiary's benefit amount. This should be good politically.

7. By 1984 or so, M.F.B., which now ranges from 150 percent of

P.I.A. at A.M.W. of $178 and below to 215.84 percent at $436, then down to 199.27 percent at $650, will be 150 percent for everybody.

It is hoped that this illustration will encourage further study of such a dynamic system, especially cost studies. It also would be valuable to consider the philosophical question regarding the proper relationships between current earnings levels and minimum and maximum social insurance benefits.

*Extension of nonoccupational disability laws.* Another proposal is for the compulsory coverage of short-term nonoccupational disability in the states which do not have such laws. More than half the states have decided specifically against passage of such laws in the past 10 years, but the last has not been heard from their proponents. For example, bills were introduced in the legislatures of Hawaii in 1967 and Puerto Rico in 1968. The Hawaii legislature appropriated funds for a study as to whether such a law was desirable. The Puerto Rico bill was passed by the legislature on May 31, 1968 and signed by the Governor. The bill is patterned after the California U.C.D. law. Private insurers could provide coverage if the benefits were more liberal than those of the statutory plan but they would have to protect the fund from an "actuarial disadvantage due to the establishment of the private plan." The plan is financed by a one percent tax on wages up to $7,800 per year, half paid by the employer and half by the employee.

The growth of group disability income insurance would, one might expect, weaken arguments for such laws. However, in 1949 this was used in New York as an argument *for* a compulsory law: since most employers carried it anyway, it would not be too great an imposition to require it of all. It has been suggested that an important reason why more states have not passed such laws is an inability of legislators to agree on whether to take the approach of New York emphasizing private insurance or the state fund approach used in varying degrees in the other programs.[8]

If such plans are adopted in other states, it is hoped that they will follow the New York plan, which interferes least with private enterprise. As evidenced in Rhode Island, there is a tendency for a statutory plan, intended as a minimum, to end up as a maximum. There is little private group disability income insurance in that state. On the other hand, where statutory benefits are written by private insurers, there is ample room for private initiative to produce plans much broader than the statutory minimum. This is particularly true where they do not have to face unfair competition from subsidized state funds. The extremes which such unfair competition can take are discussed below.[9]

---

[8] Robert Tilove, "Experience under State Disability Benefit Laws," *Proceedings,* New York University Eleventh Annual Conference on Labor, 1958, in William Haber and Wilbur J. Cohen (eds.), *Social Security: Programs, Problems and Policies* (Homewood, Ill.: Richard D. Irwin, Inc., 1960), p. 440.

[9] See below, pp. 694 ff.

## Commercial contracts

Kulp[10] cites the main criticisms of commercial health insurance as the following four points: it does not meet the needs of the average man; it is too technical; it costs too much; and it is not dependable. There is some merit in each of these criticisms.

Individual insurance can never be expected to *cover the entire population*. The weak and ill, the aged, the impecunious, and the isolated are not insurable for reasons of hazard, ability to pay, or accessibility. Thus individual insurance, at least so far as new sales are concerned, will continue to be concentrated among the younger, healthier, better income class, and urban groups.

Group insurance can extend further to cover some persons who are individually uninsurable and to extend coverage to lower income groups, but not to no-income groups unless someone can be found to pay the premium. Some progress has been made through associations, such as Granges, toward insuring the rural population on a group basis. The unemployed and the retired, including those already disabled, present underwriting problems that it is probably unfair to expect voluntary methods to solve. Unless they plan to return to the labor force, they have no need for disability income insurance.

The other aspect of the needs of the average man is the *adequacy of coverage*. Here it must be conceded that great gaps remain. Most producers of income are not adequately protected against the risk of long-term disability. Very few have protection against long-term disability produced by sickness. The major obstacles to providing this coverage result from moral hazard. Better selection by insurers can reduce the magnitude of this but there will still be adverse selection.

That health insurance forms are *technical* and frequently *misunderstood* cannot be denied. The risk insured is so complex and subjective that accurate and rigid definition of coverage is essential if losses are to be predictable. However, much of the complexity results from an archaic distinction between perils in terms of the types of benefits offered. The heterogeneity of the typical accident policy benefits is unnecessary and of little value to the insured. Coverage of accidental death, if written at all, should be written in connection with life insurance, not health insurance.

A simple policy, covering all disability regardless of source under a single insuring clause and defining the loss in terms of reduction of earned income could eliminate this benefit complexity and the need for distinguishing between accident and disease. Such a concept has proved practical in workmen's compensation insurance and is used in one disabil-

---

[10] C. Arthur Kulp, *Casualty Insurance* (3d ed.; New York: Ronald Press, 1956), p. 391.

ity contract issued by a life insurance company in combination with life insurance.[11] Better selection could make possible the elimination of some of the exclusions and restrictions commonly used. A simpler contract would result, one which would go much further toward serving its fundamental purposes—protection against severe loss of income.

High costs in health insurance result from several factors: the high incidence of disability, especially for small losses; the high severity of loss; the moral hazard; and the expenses of operation of the insurers. Premiums can be reduced by attacking these factors in a number of ways. Incidence rates can be reduced through the use of appropriate deductible and waiting period provisions which exclude the multiplicity of small losses. Severity can be reduced by requiring the insured to share a part of the loss and by intelligent claims procedure, including an emphasis on rehabilitation.

The use of an average earnings clause with teeth in it would contribute toward reducing severity and combating moral hazard. Better underwriting can also cut down on moral hazard. Expenses of operation would be reduced by each of the above developments, especially the use of deductible provisions. Not only the benefit payments but also the high costs of settling small claims might be eliminated.

To the extent that pure premiums are reduced by such methods, gross premiums will be reduced by a greater amount, since many expenses, such as commissions and premium taxes, are a direct proportion of premium. Another way in which costs of operation can be reduced is through the payment of unlevel commissions instead of a flat percentage of each renewal premium.[12] The entry of life insurance companies into the health insurance field has greatly contributed to a change to this method of operation. Expenses per policy also could be reduced materially by improving persistency. When most costs must be recovered in a short period of years because of low persistency, unit costs inevitably are high.

The fourth criticism—lack of dependability—hinges on the right of the insurer to cancel or to refuse renewal. It is difficult to determine what proportion of policies terminate on these bases. Studies have generally been limited to cancellation without including nonrenewal and have often been weighted heavily with policies covering accident only, where reasons for cancellation are not so great as in sickness or combination policies. Recent studies have also taken place in a period of prosperity when insurers' claim rates are low and their practices correspondingly generous.

Various authors have estimated the average rate of cancellation and nonrenewal as between 0.5 percent and 2 percent per year.[13] While these

---

[11] See above, pp. 458 ff.

[12] See below, p. 640.

[13] An H.I.A.A. study showed a rate of 0.52 percent per year; 2 percent of the policies in which claims were paid were nonrenewed or canceled. H.I.A.A., Individual Accident and Health Insurance (New York, 1958).

figures sound small, of a group of insureds entering at age 25 and exposed to such a rate of cancellation and nonrenewal, only 74 percent would be left at age 65 if the rate were 0.75 percent per annum and only 45 percent if the rate were 2 percent.[14] In either case, the proportion who would lose their policies before normal retirement age seems high. If it were possible also to consider the decrement produced by death and voluntary lapse, a much smaller proportion would maintain their coverage until retirement. Actually, the average life of a commercial policy is about 11 years.

Regardless of the actual proportion of cancellations and nonrenewals, the existence of the right cannot fail to impair the insured's feeling of security in his policy. To the extent that policies are canceled or renewal is denied because of deterioration in the insured's health, he loses his protection at the very time he needs it most and at a time when he cannot obtain another policy. Moreover, there is a great variation between companies in the extent of cancellation. One study showed a range of proportions of business canceled in a year from 0.1 to 9.0 percent. The insured who is unfortunate enough to deal with a company with such a high rate of cancellation would have to be a veritable superman to keep his policy until he needed it.

Insurer representatives cite a number of reasons why the right of cancellation is necessary. Besides deterioration of health and excessive claims, they include misrepresentation in the application; fraud, collusion, or malingering; moral hazard; insanity; overinsurance; change of occupation or country of residence; cancellation of entire class of policies or of agency; expiration of age limits; exhaustion of benefits; expiration of policy term; inadequate premium rate; and "insured just plain cantankerous and difficult to deal with." While many of these are legitimate reasons from the company viewpoint, they seem to work a hardship on the insured except where benefits, age limits, or policy term has been exhausted.

There are other ways to control physical and moral hazard. Sounder underwriting, longer waiting periods, and adequate premiums in the first instance would remove most occasions for cancellations. A clause limiting total benefits from all companies to a reasonable proportion of earned income would protect from overinsurance and the associated moral hazard.

In response to the complaints of insureds and to public criticism, a number of devices have been utilized to improve the situation. Most companies by now are eliminating the cancellation clause while still reserving the right to refuse renewal annually. This adds little in the way of protection but makes it possible for a not too scrupulous agent to refer to the

---

[14] This assumes a level rate of cancellation and nonrenewal. Actually, the rate probably would be higher in the early years, lower in the middle years, and high again as age and claim rates advanced.

policy as "noncancellable." Inasmuch as this term has been reserved for decades for a policy which was not only noncancellable but guaranteed renewable, such a description is misleading, if not downright dishonest. All states prohibit such use of the term "noncancellable," but it is virtually impossible to control what the agent says in a face-to-face interview. More effective devices have been motivated in part by the introduction of laws in many states narrowing the terms of cancellation and nonrenewal. North Carolina passed a law in 1955 which required a period of notice of up to two years of cancellation, and several other states have somewhat similar legislation although not so drastic. Companies have employed many techniques to defend themselves against such complaints and legislation short of a noncancellable guaranteed renewable contract.

## Noncancellable contracts

The problems and issues in noncancellable and guaranteed renewable health insurance are somewhat similar to those in other lines of health insurance. There is no current issue in regard to insurer type: only insurance companies issue such contracts. The problem of moral hazard (referred to in regard to the expense coverages as overutilization) exists here, perhaps in greater measure. The problem of how extensively the population can be covered exists in theory only; so far only the surface has been scratched. In regard to meeting adequately the needs of the average man, the better noncancellable contracts are among the best in the income replacement field. The contracts are simpler, easier to understand, and more free of frills than commercial contracts. The charge of lack of reliability does not apply at all to noncancellable contracts.

The basic issue in regard to noncancellable is whether contracts providing adequate duration and amount of benefit can safely be issued to the mass market. Since the insurer cannot terminate the contract once it has been issued, a number of new problems arise from the company standpoint.

First, underwriting must be stricter and more accurate. In commercial contracts, companies may reunderwrite at each policy anniversary or at each claim. In guaranteed renewable they may increase rates on a class basis. In noncancellable, neither remedy is possible. Thus much more careful selection is necessary at the time of issue. It is common to require a physical examination in connection with policies which provide the longer sickness benefit periods. While such techniques can be fairly effective as regards physical hazard, particular attention to moral hazard is necessary. Care must be taken to make sure that the aggregate coverage in all companies and with all types of policy is reasonably below the insured's net earned income.

Second, since the rights of cancellation, nonrenewal, and increasing premium do not exist, the company must protect itself from unfavorable changes by appropriate policy provisions. The use of an average earnings clause provides some such protection against declines in income, but, as indicated above, the currently used clause is still rather weak, and only one state permits the use of the N.A.I.C. approved clause. The provision for prorating on change of occupation would seem to be desirable from this standpoint, but, since the major types of loss in guaranteed renewable are long-term sickness, which is little affected by occupation, many companies eliminate such a clause. Indeed, some authorities feel that the occupational prorate clause is incompatible with the concept of guaranteed renewability. Some contracts require permits or riders for such things as foreign travel or residence.

Third, the rate of disability incidence increases sharply with age for a group of policyholders. Furthermore, the average duration increases with age. Close to the end of the period of coverage, the probability of loss reaches its maximum, and, for a contract with a benefit expressed as a fixed number of years or for life, so does the average severity. Thus pure term premiums increase sharply with age. Where maximum benefit duration is to a stated future age, the reverse situation prevails, as the cutoff age is approached. In this case pure premium and gross premiums sometimes decrease with age in the last few years.

In commercial policies most of this effect can be removed by the process of renewal underwriting. The curve of premium increase is flattened out, and it is possible to issue contracts at a premium rate which is the same for all the common ages of entry. In guaranteed renewable and noncancellable, the difference in premiums among the ages is too great for this. Premiums must be graded with entry age, and the premium must be high enough in the early years to build up a reserve against the higher claim costs of the later years. Thus there are level premiums and level premium reserves similar to those found in life insurance policies. The necessity for this level premium results in a higher premium rate to the insured. This is the price he must pay for a guarantee that his protection will continue in force until he needs it.

For many years, noncancellable premiums were computed on an inadequate rate basis. This was one of the major factors responsible for the heavy losses of the depression period. Better data now are available, and most companies seem to have adopted adequate premium rates. There are great differences between the rates charged by different companies, reflecting their varying appraisals as to the accuracy of these data and their varying appraisals as to the effect of a potential future depression on claim rates. The difference in premium between a commercial and a guaranteed renewable policy providing substantially similar benefits ranges from about 10 to 100 percent, depending on company and policy. In participating contracts, dividends often decrease this differential. Generally speaking, the longer the benefit period and the longer the waiting period, the less is the difference.

As indicated above, policies are available with benefits payable for injury or disease for relatively long benefit periods—for 10 or 15 years or to age 65 or beyond. There has not yet been time to evaluate the experience on contracts with longer benefit periods than 10 years, and the companies are, to some degree, operating in the dark. However, with adequate rating, underwriting, and policy controls, there is no reason that this risk cannot be safely written. So far, the experience has been satisfactory.

Because of the higher anticipated losses due to the renewal guarantee and the necessity of building up a reserve in the early years, guaranteed renewable policies carry higher premium rates than do commercial policies. Prospects who recognize the situation should be as willing to pay this extra amount for greater security of protection just as they do in life insurance, where the difference between a term and a permanent policy is well recognized. As appreciation of this principle grows and incomes increase, more and more of the population will be willing and able to pay the higher cost of better protection. Similarly, as cancellations and non-renewals become less frequent in commercial policies, their costs will increase, and the differential will narrow. As indicated above, the use of graded commission rates cuts acquisition costs. Since most noncancellable policies are written on this basis, this represents a favorable cost factor and makes the premium difference somewhat less than it otherwise would be. However, as more commercial policies are issued on an unlevel commission basis, this will become of lesser importance.

**Summary**

There have been many proposals for extension of the social insurance system against disability. The main ones have been for broadening benefit eligibility in OASDI and extending the nonoccupational disability laws to more states. There is also constant pressure to liberalize coverage and increase benefits.

All such proposals should be viewed with caution and with the recognition that social insurance, by definition, interferes with freedom. Such proposals should be evaluated with adequate recognition of the ultimate costs involved, and methods of financing and administration should be selected so as to give the greatest possible encouragement to self-reliance and private enterprise.

Criticisms of commercial health insurance center about the charges of inadequacy of coverage, undue technicality, high cost, and lack of reliability. Considerable progress has been made in meeting these criticisms, and the industry has done much to improve its product in the last decades. However, there is still room for a great deal of improvement. As contracts offered are improved, commercial contracts are beginning to resemble noncancellable and guaranteed renewable contracts.

The problems of issuing noncancellable and guaranteed renewable contracts center on rate adequacy, underwriting standards, and moral hazard. Failure to solve these problems satisfactorily resulted in heavy losses during the great depression, but now many companies seem to feel that the situation is under control. The main need seems to be a stronger average earnings clause. The fact that renewal is guaranteed until older ages, at which disability costs are quite high, requires a higher premium for noncancellable contracts. This tends to make the market more limited than for commercial forms, but it seems likely that more and more persons will be willing and able to pay for permanent protection in the future.

### Selected references

See the following references from the General Bibliography: 4, ch. 16; 6, ch. 14; 11, chs. 4 and 5; 13, chs. 4, 5, 18, and 23; 15, chs. 52 and 54; 29, chs. 3, 4, 7, 11, and 18.

BALL, ROBERT M. "Policy Issues in Social Security," Social Security Bulletin, Vol. 29, No. 6 (June, 1966), p. 3.

DICKERSON, O. D. "The 1965 Social Security Amendments and Private Insurance," Annals of the Society of Chartered Property Casualty Underwriters, September, 1966, p. 227.

MYERS, ROBERT J. "A Method of Automatically Adjusting the Maximum Earnings Base Under OASDI," Journal of Risk and Insurance, Vol. XXI, No. 3 (September, 1964), p. 329.

———. Social Insurance and Allied Government Programs. Homewood, Ill.: Richard D. Irwin, Inc., 1965.

———. "Status of the Social Security Program in the Mid-Sixties and Its Possible Future Trends," Journal of the American Society of Chartered Life Underwriters, Vol. XX, No. 4, p. 346.

———. Summary of Social Security Amendments of 1967, 90th Congress, 1st Session. Washington, D.C.: U.S. Government Printing Office, 1967.

U.S. CONGRESS. Public Law 90–248, "Social Security Amendments of 1967." Washington, D. C.: U.S. Government Printing Office, 1968.

U.S. CONGRESS, HOUSE. President's Proposals for Revision in the Social Security System. Hearings before the Committee on Ways and Means. 4 parts. Washington, D.C.: U.S. Government Printing Office, 1967.

———. Social Security Amendments of 1967. House Report No. 544. Washington, D.C.: U.S. Government Printing Office, 1967.

U.S. Congress, House. *Actuarial Cost Estimates for the Old-Age, Survivors, Disability, and Health Insurance System as Modified by the Social Security Amendments of 1967.* Washington, D.C.: U.S. Government Printing Office, 1967.

U.S. Congress, Senate. *Social Security Amendments of 1967, 90th Congress, 1st Session.* Hearings before the Committee on Finance, 3 parts. Washington, D.C.: U.S. Government Printing Office, 1967.

U.S. Department of Health, Education, and Welfare. Social Security Administration. *The Economic Status of the Retired Aged in 1980: Simulation Projections.* Washington, D.C.: U.S. Government Printing Office, 1967.

# PART IV

# Health Insurer
# Operations

## chapter 17

Many are called but few are chosen—*Matt. xxii:14*

# Underwriting

## Introduction

The underwriting process involves selection, classification, and rating of risks. Its fundamental purpose is to make sure that the group insured has the same probability of loss and probable amount of loss, within reasonable limits, as the universe on which premium rates were based. In individual insurance this process is applied to individual applicants, while in group insurance it is applied to potential groups. In social insurance there is no formal underwriting process as such. However, the coverage and eligibility provisions of social insurance laws serve a similar purpose.

Since premium rates are based on expectation of loss, the underwriting process must classify subject matter into classes with about the same expectation of loss. The units with the highest expectation of loss will probably be uninsurable; the others must be classified into classes which will be charged appropriate premium rates. In order to make the following discussion of underwriting and ratemaking understandable, it is necessary to pause to develop certain concepts.

## Some concepts

*Probability and expectation of loss.* *Probability* is apparently an indefinable concept, although many attempts have been made to give it reality. This intuitive concept is used to refer to the likelihood of occurrence of an event, usually one in the future. This implies that there is an element of uncertainty as to the future. If there were not, it would never be necessary to speak of probability; it would suffice to be able to say, with this perfect knowledge, that "$x$ will occur" or "$x$ will not occur." As a matter of fact, not only is there uncertainty as to whether a future event will occur, but usually there also is uncertainty as to all the factors which influence the probability of its occurrence. Thus, in all practical investigations, it is necessary to work with estimated probabilities.

Probabilities may be estimated on the basis of reasoning. This involves taking the ratio of the possible ways in which an event may occur to all the ways it may occur or not occur as the measure of probability. Such an estimate is known as an *a priori probability*. However, cases in which there is such knowledge of the possible ways in which an event may happen and it is possible validly to assume that each possible way is equally likely are rare. More commonly, it is necessary to base the estimate of probability on the relative frequency with which an event has occurred in the past. Such estimates are called *statistical probabilities*. Insofar as the science of statistics is concerned with prediction, it must, of necessity, provide techniques for estimating such probabilities. Insurance usually must rely on statistical probabilities.

A third method of estimating probabilities is the *analytic* or *engineering* approach. This involves an analysis of the factors determining the event such as the flash point of flammable vapors, the speed with which a door burns through or the oxygen content of a substance. These physical measurements may be compared with those of standard materials and ignition and damagability probabilities may be estimated. Analyses of this type form the basis of fire insurance schedule rating and are useful in all underwriting.[1]

The *probability of loss* is the likelihood that a loss will occur in a finite future period, based on the relative frequency with which it has occurred in the past. The measure of probability is a scale ranging from 0, certainty of nonoccurrence or impossibility, to 1.0, certainty of occurrence.

This is an abstract concept which is translated into more meaningful terms by the concept of the *expected number of losses*. This is the product of the probability of loss and the number of units exposed to loss and represents the most probable number of losses expected in the group. Of course, this concept is valid only for a group of exposure units. Multiplying the expected number of losses by the average *loss per unit* will give the *expectation of loss* in dollars. This step may be unnecessary when the exposure unit already is in dollar terms.

Since the probability of loss and the expectation of loss are estimates only, it is important to know the degree of reliance that can be placed upon them. Statistical devices have been developed for measuring the probability of actual results departing from the expected by various amounts. In general, it can be said that the accuracy of an estimate increases as the number of cases increases. This is often referred to as the "law of averages" or "law of large numbers." The term *standard error* is

---

[1] See Kenneth L. McIntosh, "The Rationale of the Fire Schedule," *Annals of the Society of C.P.C.U.*, Summer, 1960, p. 1 and Fall, 1960, p. 117.

used in statistics to denote the probable range of deviation from an estimate. There are many formulas for computing such standard errors, but the development of these is beyond the scope of this work.

*Hazard.* In endeavoring to estimate probabilities of loss in advance of the event, underwriters examine the hazards to which a given unit of subject matter is exposed. Hazards are conditions which may increase the probability—or probable severity—or facilitate the occurrence of a loss: or, more simply, they are loss-producing propensities associated with a given exposure. Unfortunately, some authors have used the term "hazard" synonymously with "peril." A careful examination of its usage in such perfectly proper phrases as "moral hazard" indicates that the term, hazard, refers not to the event which is primarily responsible for producing loss but to some situation or condition of a facilitative nature. Hazards have been classified into three categories: physical, moral, and legal.

*Physical hazard* refers to the loss-producing propensities associated with the tangible physical characteristics of the subject matter and its environment. It may be illustrated by medical impairments in health insurance or by occupancy in fire insurance.

*Moral hazard* refers to the intangible loss-producing propensities of the individual assured. Its characteristics are more difficult to illustrate, since such intangibles are difficult to define and identify. Any situation or circumstance that might indicate a desire on the part of the assured that the loss occur is evidence of moral hazard. Dishonesty, carelessness, lack of pertinacity, and ignorance on the part of the assured are elements of moral hazard. Some authors have distinguished between moral hazard, which refers to situations of potential dishonesty and the like, and *morale* hazard, which refers to potential carelessness. However, such a distinction is not particularly useful in practice, and it is frequently impossible to distinguish one from the other. It seems to be more a difference of degree than of kind.

*Legal hazard* is also an intangible. It refers to the loss-producing propensities of the local legal environment. While of great importance in insurance against legal liability, legal hazard is also significant in other areas. The legal definition of such concepts as fire or accident may differ from one jurisdiction to another for example.

*Subject matter and exposure.* The *subject matter* of insurance is that which is exposed to loss from a given peril—that which is insured. It may be a human life, an individual item of property, or the whole aggregation of property rights of an individual. In health insurance it is either the individual life or the lives making up a group.

The term *exposure* has been used in two of the definitions above. It refers to the state or condition of being subject or vulnerable to loss from a given peril or perils. It may be defined as a condition of susceptibility or vulnerability to loss. Exposure exists when the probability of loss exceeds zero. Hazards relate to exposure, inasmuch as they increase the probability of loss being produced. Without exposure, there can be no hazard.

The unit in which the subject matter is measured for purposes of computing probability of loss, expectation of loss, and premium is called the *exposure unit*. It may be a physical unit such as a life or an automobile; a measure such as square feet of floor space; or a unit of value or insurance measured in dollars. In health insurance it is usually a single life but may be a unit of benefit.

*Adverse selection.* In a sense, the underwriting process has as its main objective the prevention of adverse selection. Adverse selection refers to the process whereby, in the absence of adequate controls, the persons who obtain insurance will tend to be those who want it most—those with a greater probability of loss than average. While not necessarily operative in every individual instance, experience has demonstrated amply that this process operates with groups of applicants. For example, despite the fact that many persons are disabled from birth or from an early age and cannot obtain health insurance and despite the companies' underwriting efforts, morbidity tables of insured lives usually show higher rates than do tables based on the population in general. While the explanation above was based on the purchase of insurance, adverse selection occurs in other cases: in surrenders, in selection of benefit options, and wherever insureds or claimants can exercise choice. More technically, it may be defined as any process whereby the exercise of choice by insureds or beneficiaries leads to higher loss levels than average.

If it were possible to insure a random sample of persons from the population, the level of losses would correspond to that expected from population data, and further underwriting would be unnecessary. An insurer, for example, could expect sound results if it insured every person walking down a certain street. However, this would work only as long as it kept it a secret. When the news got out, all the "sick, lame, and lazy" from miles around, who otherwise would not be there, would congregate to get insurance. Adverse selection is controlled in part by selection by the insurer and in part by policy provisions which limit coverage or benefits. This latter technique is referred to as "underwriting through the policy." In general, it is less preferable than sound selection in the first instance.

## Underwriting standards

Standards of acceptability vary with the type of insurance. They are strictest for individual insurance and least strict for social insurance. They are concerned essentially with an evaluation of various hazards which affect the probability of loss. These hazards will be discussed in connection with individual insurance, and then the special features of group and social insurance will be described.

*Individual insurance.* The probability of loss and the average severity are affected by age, sex, occupation, health, type and amount of benefit, income and cost factors, and moral hazard.

*Age* affects disability rates differently, depending on the type of benefit involved. For almost all types of benefit, both frequency and severity increase with advancing age, but the rate of increase varies greatly. For long-term disability, the increase is almost as rapid as that found in death rates. For the expense coverages and short-benefit-period income replacement contracts the increase is not marked until about age 55.

Thus, noncancellable and guaranteed renewable policies, life insurance disability riders and major medical policies usually are issued with net level premiums graded according to age at entry into the plan. Other types of policy often have a flat premium for the usual ages of entry, say 18 to 55, with sharply higher rates for policyholders renewing or entering at higher ages. Generally speaking, disability income policies are not available at ages materially greater than age 65; and many companies do not issue them beyond age 55 or 60. At least 24 companies issue at ages 66–71, and 12 others to 75–76, however. There is little need for income replacement coverages at advanced ages, since most persons then depend on retirement income and relatively few persons have an earned income to insure.

However, there is great need for expense coverages. The term premiums are rather high; and there is a problem of adverse selection at these ages. Adequate coverage at reasonable rates involves guaranteed renewable policies which provide for funding the benefit costs throughout the insured's working life. Many group policies now provide considerable protection for retiring persons. The individual policies currently available are usually limited as to amount of coverage and frequently to hospital, surgical and medical only. The methods used to extend medical expense insurance to older age groups were discussed in Chapters 6 to 10. At least 52 companies issue hospital expense insurance at ages 69 and above and at least 96 issue contracts to supplement Medicare.

*Sex* is important in regard to disability rates, as well as in other respects. Strangely enough, despite the fact that females show consistently lower death rates, they show higher disability rates according to most studies.[2] This is true even even for policies which exclude coverage of pregnancy, miscarriage, abortion, and other "female trouble." It is difficult to decide which is the healthier sex. One hypothesis is that females are healthier in

---

[2] But not for OASDI disability benefits. The reason for this is not known, but it may relate to the immaturity of the experience, or to the strict definition of disability.

that the ailments which kill the men merely disable the women. The alternative explanation is that women succumb to illness more readily and their lives are saved by early treatment, while the "hardier" male "works till he drops." The reader may take his (or her) choice.

Underwriters feel that there is greater moral hazard in connection with women, since they, usually not being the breadwinners, can more readily take advantage of poor health as an excuse to stay home or in the hospital at company expense. Of course, women who are not employed outside the home are ineligible for any type of disability income insurance. Since there is always the danger that an employed woman may retire from the labor market to become a (supposedly unproductive) housewife, companies are reluctant to insure females for income replacement policies.[3] Where issued, such policies provide for shorter and lower income benefits than would be issued to men and often contain a clause reducing benefits if the woman is not regularly employed outside the home prior to disablement. Noncancellable and guaranteed renewable disability income policies, including the life insurance riders, often are not available to women. The longest sickness benefit available to a female on a noncancellable form currently is ten years. A few insurers will insure housewives for a $100 per month disability income benefit limited to one or two years. For all types of policy, females generally are charged a higher rate than males, even if the maternity risk is excluded. Where such coverage is included, rates for the child-bearing ages are even higher.

*Occupation* obviously affects the probability of disablement, especially as regards the peril of accidental injury. Certain occupations are considered uninsurable for individual insurance. Such occupations as test pilot, steeplejack, sandhog, and the like are beyond the purview of ordinary policy forms. Persons may, however, be able to obtain coverage from the "special-risks" department of an enterprising company or through the underwriters at Lloyd's. Such risks are judgment-rated, and the premiums may be very high.

Companies classify the insurable occupations into groups of about the same average claim cost and have a scale of premium rates applicable to the various classes. The number of classes may vary from two (uninsurable versus insurable) to over 30, depending on the type of company and the types of policy sold. Both the Bureau of Accident and Health Underwriters and the Health and Accident Underwriters Conference[4] developed systems of classification, but many companies make use of their own systems. A study several years ago of the systems of 25 companies in the guaranteed renewable business showed at least 10 different

---

[3] However, social insurance usually covers female workers on the same basis as male workers.

[4] These organizations now have been merged into the Health Insurance Association of America, but the systems still are used widely.

systems. There is a tendency to use systems with fewer classes and most companies today use five classes or fewer. Probably the most frequently used system is based on the old Conference classification with five classes running from AAA to C.

The complexity of occupational classification is greatest in the commercial policies. Limited and industrial contracts usually are sold at the same (relatively high) rate to all occupations except certain very hazardous ones which are excluded by policy provisions. Noncancellable policies and life insurance disability riders are usually sold only to the better occupational classes. One company in the noncancellable field lists the most hazardous occupation it will cover (Class D) as "Clerk, shipping, light duties only."

The expense coverages usually are sold with very little variation in premium according to occupation. Many of these contracts provide that benefit payments will be excess over any workmen's compensation benefits available, which, for most employees in most states, amounts to an exclusion of the occupational hazard.

The statement was made above that occupations must be classified according to average claim cost. This concept takes into consideration both probability of disability and average severity. Both are affected by occupation. Occupational hazard directly affects the probability of accidental injury and certain types of occupational and quasi-occupational disease. However, the effect on severity is probably even more significant. A given type of injury may completely disable a person whose occupation calls for the exercise of great physical skill, such as a surgeon, while it may hardly affect (say) a salesman. Persons who are engaged in manual labor probably will be away from work longer for a given ailment than will office workers.

Furthermore, the type of occupation affects moral hazard. Aside from occupations which are themselves evidence of low moral standards, such as professional bookmakers, there are many occupations involving irregular hours, irregular earnings, and/or the lack of a fixed place of business. It is very easy for persons with such occupations to feign or exaggerate disability. Such occupations include entertainers, authors, teachers, sole proprietors, and professional men. Where the income from the occupation is also sensitive to the business cycle, greater hazard exists. In addition, the traditions and attitudes of members of the occupation and the social and environmental influences associated with it will affect the attitude of the claimant and probably the level of claims. The occupational classifications described above are intended to reflect, as far as possible, the combined effect of these various factors on average claim cost.

*Health.* Obviously the current and future health of the applicant is important. Future health status cannot, of course, be determined accurately in the individual case. It is necessary to evaluate the probability of future disability on the basis of present condition and past health history. Of course, an applicant who is disabled or undergoing treatment at the time of application is not eligible for insurance against losses resulting from the currently existing disability. If the impairment is minor, the policy may be issued, the underwriter relying on the provisions in the policy relating to pre-existing disease and the probationary period to protect the company. However, this is not considered good practice. If the impairment is more serious, the application will be postponed, declined, or rated up or a rider will be used.

A history of past illness or accident will be given weight depending on the severity of the original ailment, the degree of permanent impairment, and the length of time which has elapsed since recovery. This is important for accidental injury coverages as well as for policies covering sickness. Certain types of impairment tend to increase the probability of accidental injury or the severity of the resulting disability. For example, epilepsy and vertigo would increase the probability of accident; diabetes, hemophilia, overweight, or cardiovascular conditions would increase the severity of injury or length of resultant disability.

The underwriter must be especially careful regarding chronic ailments where the probability of recurrence is high. On the other hand, acute conditions, even if quite serious, may be disregarded if recovery has been good, there is no permanent impairment, and a reasonable time has elapsed without recurrence. Thus a chronic condition such as asthma or phlebitis will be regarded more seriously than a history of (say) pneumonia or appendicitis.

Conditions which are chronic and also produce severe losses will be considered most strictly and often declined altogether. Heart disease, acute hypertension, and cancer fall into this category. However, some cancer cases, such as cancer of the skin, may be considered for insurance after a "cure" has been effective for five years or more with no recurrence.

Family health history is sometimes taken into consideration. It is common for an application to call for information on the age and health status of parents, siblings, and spouse, if living, and for age at death and cause of death, if dead. While such data are far from conclusive by themselves, they may often shed light on the case and, in combination with other factors, contribute toward a decision.

Build, which refers in effect to the relationship between weight and height, is of considerable significance. Extremes of weight will be avoided or given special treatment. Generally overweight beyond 15–20 percent of the average for the age or marked underweight is unacceptable for standard insurance at standard rates. From a health standpoint the ideal weight is about 20 pounds or 10 percent less than average. When overweight is associated with hypertension or other circulatory difficulty, it is much more dangerous. Extreme underweight is considered more serious for health insurance than for life insurance because it may imply poor general health with possible association with various diseases which produce disability more frequently than death. Extreme height is also considered dangerous.

*Area.* Other factors which affect physical hazard to some degree include habitat, habits, and race. In the past it was common for residence in certain areas within the United States to be subject to increased premiums. At present, there is little differentiation within the United States, except for certain medical expense benefits, but underwriters view foreign residence, especially in the tropics, with disfavor. Some policies cover only within the United States and Canada. The increasing mobility of the population and the decrease in local differences have contributed to these changes. Location is sometimes considered in the rating process in group insurance, where the location of the firm and its employees is likely to remain fixed.

*Habits.* Habits of drug addiction or excessive use of alcohol are, of course, very significant. These affect both physical and moral hazard and will usually lead to rejection. Sometimes special treatment is accorded to an individual who participates in particularly hazardous sports. Aviation activities are not usually considered serious in underwriting, since it is common for policies to exclude aviation accidents except those incurred in normal commercial flight.

*Race.* Race rarely is officially considered in the underwriting process, lest the companies be subject to charges of unfair discrimination. The New York law specifically prohibits such discrimination in insurance rate or practice. However, the nonwhite races show considerably higher morbidity than does the white race, and underwriters are quite aware of this. Generally speaking, little effort is expended in soliciting nonwhite applicants, except for industrial policies, which carry a higher premium rate. Some insurers, however, specialize in nonwhite markets, and their rates reflect their own experience. In the underwriting process, race alone will not be considered grounds for rejection, but all other standards probably will be applied more strictly to persons of nonwhite races. There is, of course, no logical argument against racial differences in premium rate or in underwriting standards. Statistics are rather impartial, and different treatment based on the facts is not unfair discrimination. However, the whole subject seems to be loaded with emotion, and it is one which the companies prefer to avoid. The problem is diminishing in importance as differences in morbidity among the races decrease.

*Type and amount of benefit.* A fundamental determinant of actual observed claim rates, of course, is the type of policy and the type and amount of benefit. The definition of disability itself is important in this respect. This may be in terms of inability to pursue an occupation, defined according to the "his occupation," "any occupation," or "any occupation for which suited" basis. In expense coverages it may be in terms of the incurring of an expense and/or the admission to a hospital or treatment by a physician. For some benefits it will be presumptive disability for certain specific disablements. Since most disabilities are of short duration, the length of the waiting period or the amount of the deductible will be a primary determinant of the magnitude of claim rates. Small claims will be eliminated entirely, and larger ones reduced in magnitude.

Entirely aside from the differences in rates due to different definitions of covered events, differences in type and amount of benefit will produce different claim rates. This is a reflection of moral hazard. For example, under exactly the same definition of disability and waiting period, higher claim rates result for a disability income benefit than for a waiver of premium benefit. Generally speaking, the greater the prospective benefit in terms of both amount and duration, the greater will be the claim rate, other things being equal. Particular difficulties arise where the potential benefit exceeds the loss. Here the insured can make a profit from disability, and the motivation for malingering, especially slow recovery, is greatest.

The underwriter's primary concern with differences in disability definition is one of exercising care to make sure that underwriting criteria appropriate for one type of insurance are not applied thoughtlessly to other types. For example, much of the difficulty during the great depression with noncancellable policies and life insurance disability riders was the result of issuing coverage of this type according to underwriting standards developed for life insurance waiver of premium or for commercial health insurance. Where a policy or rider is noncancellable or guaranteed renewable, much higher standards must be applied in the first instance, since the company has no opportunity to get off the risk subsequently. Similarly, stricter standards must be applied to contracts providing high benefits in regard to amount or duration or both. Higher standards must be applied for policies covering sickness than for those covering accidental injury alone.

As a result of these differences, in practice, the strictest underwriting standards are applied to the long-term noncancellable and guaranteed renewable income policies and to life insurance disability riders. Among the expense covers, similar high standards are applied to major medical contracts, especially if guaranteed renewable.

Commercial disability income and hospital, surgical, and basic medical policies are issued with less careful underwriting. Industrial policies, where benefit amounts and durations are small, are still less carefully underwritten, and underwriting is almost completely foregone in the limited policies. The careful reader will note that the more carefully underwritten types of policy are usually the freest from exclusions and restrictions in the contract. Conversely, in the less carefully underwritten forms, these restrictions often perform the function of "underwriting through the policy."

*Relation of insurance to loss.*  The primary safeguard of the underwriter against moral hazard is a reasonable relationship between the insurance benefit and the amount of potential net loss after taxes. By this is meant that the benefit should never exceed and rarely equal the net loss. Where the net loss is exceeded by the insurance benefit, moral hazard and claim rates will be high. Indeed, this will probably result even where the net loss is exactly reimbursed, since many persons will prefer the receipt of insurance benefits to the rigors of working for a living. Thus underwriters feel that the situation is sound only if the insured shares in the loss. This may be achieved by limited benefit amounts, by limitations on amount of insurance issued, by not covering certain types of loss, and by policy provisions limiting the amount which may be collected in relation to the loss.

In expense coverages other than major medical, the objective is usually met by a combination of specific limits, limited coverage and exclusions. The amount of benefit for each type of expense is stated in the policy, and this amount is usually somewhat less than the going rate in the area. A claimant with a $15-a-day hospital benefit will not be motivated to malinger if his room actually is costing him $20 per day. Moreover, even the insured with all three types of basic contract will find certain types of expenses not covered. These are likely to include nurses' fees, drugs, appliances, prosthetics, blood and plasma, etc. Some may be covered by rider, but the typical claimant will find that he still has to bear a substantial portion of the total expense. Thus he participates in meeting the loss.

In major medical the main reliance is on exclusions and percentage participation. Often dental services, services in government hospitals, services primarily for rest or diagnosis, and the like are not covered. Policies commonly include deductible and percentage participation provisions, to force the insured to participate in the loss. The main purpose of the deductible is to prevent duplication of benefits with underlying basic policies. Aside from this, its direct effect on moral hazard probably is minor. The percentage participation or coinsurance clause, however, has a direct effect on moral hazard by requiring the insured to bear 15 to 25 percent of losses above the deductible. With a policy providing high limits of liability and few exclusions, this is felt to be necessary.

In income replacement contracts, the main reliance is on limiting the amount of benefit in relation to earned income. In income replacement contracts in general, companies will issue policies so that the total benefits in all companies does not exceed two thirds to three fourths of earned income for medium-income levels. There should be some margin between benefit level and net take-home pay, since in addition to saving income and other withheld taxes, the claimant is relieved of expenses of transportation, work clothes and equipment, etc. After considering all these factors, he should still collect a benefit less than the net income loss. Otherwise, there will be little motivation for recovery. An appropriate standard for participation would be 80–85 percent of *after-tax earned income*. Most insurers attempt to hit this goal by applying varying percentages to gross income.

For higher incomes, long-benefit durations, noncancellable and guaranteed renewable policies, and life insurance disability riders, even stricter standards are applied. Most companies have absolute limits of issue on a single life—anywhere from $500 to $2500 per month. In addition to these limits of issue, they may have a higher limit of participation, which expresses the maximum total insurance from all companies in which they will participate. This may be as high as $2,500 per month, but most insurers have limits of $1,500 per month or less. In policies where renewal can be refused, these limits sometimes are backed up by a clause permitting a prorating of benefit for other insurance of which the company is not notified. Such a provision is of little value in noncancellable or guaranteed renewable policies.

In noncancellable and guaranteed renewable policies the Relation of Earnings to Insurance provision often is used, particularly where the benefit duration is long. This prorates the benefit so that, if all companies had the clause, the total collected would be equal to average earnings for the period prior to disability. Since many companies do not use the clause and since it makes no provision for the savings in taxes and other expenses, it is of limited value. Prorating provisions rarely are used in the expense coverages, and there is no protection in the usual policy against duplication of benefits. Probably safeguards against such a situation will be developed in the future as the business matures. Recent suggestions for stricter clauses of these types were discussed above.[5]

*Moral hazard.* Moral hazard is a particularly severe problem in health insurance. The subjectivity of the disability risk and the difficulties in defining the insured events have been discussed above. The character of the insured is one of the most important determinants of claim rates. Insurers must contend with psychosomatic illness, accident-proneness, hypochondria, and just plain laziness, as well as deliberate malingering. In addition to the primary safeguard of limiting the amount of benefit to something less than the amount of loss, companies employ certain criteria in the selection process designed to limit moral hazard.

Specific warning signs upon which underwriters rely for indications of possible moral hazard include the following situations. Where the applicant voluntarily approaches the company for insurance, he is immedi-

---

[5] Pp. 389 ff.; 442 ff.

ately suspect. It is felt that there is a better-than-average chance that he has knowledge of some condition which will make the insurance particularly valuable to him. Where the occupation is characterized by unstable earnings, work performed at home, irregular and seasonable work, or any connection with illegal or dubious activities, underwriters will be hesitant to approve the risk. Of course, disability income insurance is not written for those who are not earning income from their own efforts. Any business or personal history of fraud, cheating, or bad debts indicates a poor risk. Extramarital entanglements, dishonest or questionable business practices or ethics, questionable associates, criminal activity, and poor personal habits all present danger signals. Poor personal habits include gambling, excessive drinking, drug addiction, and the like. Any evidence of cheating or misrepresentation in the application also will be given great weight.

**Group insurance.**   In group insurance, the underwriting standards are similar to those in individual insurance, because these factors all affect the probability of loss and its probable amount. However, since the standards must be applied to groups rather than to individuals, their application is quite different. Group underwriting is concerned with the characteristics of the group, and the standards refer to type of group; size of group; industry; sex and race composition; economic level, location, and surroundings of the group; and the nature of the policy coverage in terms of benefit type and level, spread of risk, and administration. Initial underwriting is usually liberal; the right to increase rates in the future and to underwrite again at each annual renewal date gives the insurers protection.

*Type of group.*   In order to get a good sample of the universe, it is important that the group be one which exists independently of the need for insurance. Were a group to be formed solely for the purpose of obtaining insurance, it probably would experience as severe adverse selection as under individual policies. The motives for belonging or not belonging to the group must be stronger than the desire to obtain or avoid obtaining insurance.

Second, the group should be of such a nature that there is a regular "flow" of persons through the group. New younger members should be continually joining and older members moving out. Otherwise the average age of the group is bound to increase, with consequent increases in claim rates, premiums, and adverse selection. Third, the group should, if possible, be one whose members are, by definition, fairly healthy. Moreover, the group should promise low expenses of administration and a high probability of persistency.

The enumeration of these desirable characteristics of the group indicates why employee groups are so highly favored. In addition to meeting these criteria, employee groups are often healthier than average because of health standards for hiring imposed by the employer. Other types of group which are acceptable include trade unions, professional associations, trade associations, state police and national guard units, and farmer's cooperatives. These are all, essentially, groups which possess a substantial attachment to the labor force in one way or another.

The type of group also will affect the ease of administration of the plan, which will in turn influence costs. In employee groups the employer frequently assumes a large part of the administrative burden, keeping premium rates low. In multiemployer, union, and association groups this cannot be achieved as readily. There is danger that records may be inadequate and that changes in personnel might cause low stability in the group. Taft-Hartley trust groups, often involving more than one employer and sometimes more than one union, may require special efforts to set up an effective administration process. Special problems arise where the contributions are based on unit of product or hours worked. There is always the danger that premiums will prove inadequate in a period of recession. Benefit levels, set by union contract, will not decline; and claim rates well may go up as workers with dubious job prospects get sick more easily or recover more slowly.

*Size of group* is of importance, in that the larger the group in number, the more likely the law of averages is to operate effectively. The minimum-size group is now generally 10 lives, although a few years ago 50 was considered the minimum. Some types of insurer, especially the Blue Cross and Blue Shield associations, utilize a lower criterion, but these associations usually issue individual policies and should perhaps be considered to be issuing franchise insurance. The usual minimum for franchise insurance for insurance companies is five lives, but may be as low as three.

*Industry* is of less importance than might be expected, since most group policies are issued on a nonoccupational basis. However, some industries require special treatment because of a higher nonoccupational morbidity. When 24-hour coverage is issued, of course, many industries that are treated as standard for nonoccupational coverage must be rated up.

*Composition of group* is important. An unduly high proportion of female lives is unfavorable from both the underwriting and the rating standpoints. Similarly, a high proportion of older members or of nonwhites is viewed with disfavor. If the composition of the group is changing rapidly through high turnover, this is a danger signal. Not only may this change the underwriting characteristics of the group, but it imposes additional administrative costs. Provisions for a probationary period before new workers are covered will minimize this problem.

The *economic level, location, and surroundings* of the group affect claim rates and must be considered in underwriting. A low-income group will be subject to lower living standards and experience poorer health. A high-income group will tend to spend more for medical services, especially on a unit basis. The type of worker and his alternative economic opportunities affect moral hazard. In hospital and other expense coverages, the prevailing level of charges in the locality will affect the claim rate. So will the community attitude toward insurance and medical care, although this is difficult to measure.

*Policy coverage* is of underwriting significance in a number of ways. The type of benefit and its level in relation to earnings are of importance here just as in individual insurance. In evaluating these, it must be recognized that the policy is usually only a part of a comprehensive plan for employee benefits, and it must be considered in connection with other group policies, salary continuation plans, and workmen's compensation insurance. Overlapping and duplication of group policies should be avoided carefully, and care should be exercised that the total benefits available from all sources bear a safe level in relation to the economic loss suffered. The policy formula for determining the amount of benefit to which a member is entitled should take into consideration differences in earning and spending levels among classes of employee. This is why the determination of these benefit levels is usually made on a basis of earnings class. Of course, the formula should be set up so as to preclude selection by individuals as to amount of benefit. Coordination of benefit provisions should be included in all group contracts.

The *spread of risk* within the group is primarily a function of the proportion of eligible members who are insured. In noncontributory plans it is common procedure to require 100 percent participation. In contributory plans such a requirement is impractical, and it is common to require 75 percent participation. Some companies are currently experimenting with requirements of 60 or even 50 percent in employee-pay-all plans issued through professional associations. In policies providing dependents' coverage, the same percentage requirements are usually applied to the proportion of eligible dependents as are applied to eligible employees.

Eligibility for coverage, like the amount of benefit, should be determined by criteria which prevent adverse selection. Where an employee fails to join the plan within (say) 31 days of the time he becomes eligible, he usually is required to submit evidence of insurability when he changes his mind.

*Previous experience of group.* In many group cases, the insurer will not be the first one on the risk. Many "new" group cases actually represent a change of insurer. In such cases, careful consideration of prior experience is important. The group may be changing insurers because of unsatisfactory claims history. In some cases it may be changing to avoid a rate increase, or because the maximum has been paid for some favorite employees. In the worst instances, the previous insurer may have declined to renew the case. Experience has been particularly bad with groups of public employees (especially county and municipal) and with groups composed mainly of seasonal employees such as construction companies, food processing companies and resort businesses.[6] Groups which change insurers frequently are not profitable for any insurer and should be avoided.

The underwriter should insist on obtaining a complete record of incurred losses with the previous insurer. It is not enough to get data on claims paid. The claims reserves set up to cover liability incurred but not yet paid make up a substantial proportion of the total loss record. Incurred and not paid claims may make up from 30 to 55 percent of one years' total claims, which means from 43 to 122 percent of paid claims at year end.[7] Attitudes of insurers towards furnishing such data vary. Where they cannot be obtained from the previous insurer, they must be obtained from the insured. Where neither previous insurer nor insured will furnish claims data, the underwriter should assume the worst and proceed accordingly.

Even though the experience of the previous insurer was unsatisfactory, it may be possible to accept the group at a reasonable premium by introducing underwriting safeguards such as percentage participation provisions, deductibles, specific internal limits, and provisions to prevent duplication of benefit. Sometimes the attitudes of employer, employees, union and the medical profession in the area can be improved by thorough communication and frank discussion.

*Small group, association group and franchise.* Where size or nature of group, percentage of enrollment or opportunity for individual selection departs from accepted group underwriting standards, special attention is necessary. This will occur in small group and franchise plans almost by definition, and frequently in association group plans. The underwriting standards applied to such groups will be a blend of group and individual standards. The more the group approaches the characteristics of true group insurance, the more the underwriting will be conducted according to group standards. Conversely, the closer the characteristics of the group to individual insurance, the more the underwriter must apply underwriting standards to the individual member rather than to the group as a whole. Particular care must be used where high benefits are made available to officers and employers—especially long-term group disability income. One technique is a special actively-at-work requirement, of several days, weeks, or even months prior to inception of coverage.

*Blue Cross and Blue Shield.* Blue Cross and Blue Shield group underwriting is similar to that of insurance companies, but their standards are usually a little more liberal in a few respects. Most insurers of either type

---

[6] Brooks Chandler, "Underwriting of New Groups," H.I.A.A. Group Insurance Forum, 1959.

[7] Donald S. Cody, "Renewal Underwriting—Problems and Procedures," H.I.A.A. Group Insurance Forum, 1959.

will write groups as small as five, but some of the Blues have written even smaller groups. Insurance companies usually require employer participation in premium payments, while the Blues usually will write employee-pay-all groups. The Blues are not as strict about requiring 75 percent participation in contributory plans and where the enrollment percentage is high enough are more liberal than insurance companies in permitting a choice of levels of benefit.[8]

To the extent that Blue Cross and Blue Shield plans accept individual enrollment, they usually do so with little if any individual underwriting. Without an agency force in the usual sense of the word, they are handicapped in reaching the individual market and apparently are unwilling to incur the acquisition expenses that would be required by intensive efforts in this area. Thus, most of their nongroup enrollees represent conversions of previous group coverage. Blue Cross and Blue Shield plans obtain individual enrollment by a variety of methods, varying from plan to plan and time to time. These include community-wide enrollment campaigns, sometimes requiring a certain minimum enrollment percentage or sometimes limited to relatively brief periods. Either or both these limits tend to reduce adverse selection. In 1954, almost three fourths of the Blue Cross plans maintained procedures for continuous open enrollment. Since few apply individual standards of insurability, there must be considerable adverse selection.[9]

*Social insurance.* There is no formal underwriting in social insurance. However, most social insurance plans have definite, clearly identifiable criteria of eligibility for coverage, which resemble and employ the same principles as group insurance. For example, in the OASDI disability income coverage, to be eligible for coverage a worker over age 31 must be fully insured, and have 20 quarters of coverage out of the last 40. Coverage is compulsory for all who meet these tests; thus there is no adverse selection. The eligibility provisions require substantial and recent attachment to the labor market, thus eliminating many in poor health. Benefit amounts are based on a formula which pitches benefits substantially lower than earnings, thus discouraging moral hazard. Adverse selection as to coverage and as to amount of insurance is impossible.

In workmen's compensation and nonoccupational disability programs similar, but not so strict, eligibility and benefit provisions operate. Private companies writing these types of coverage apply underwriting criteria similar to those for voluntary group insurance. All in all, it may be said

---

[8] George E. McLean, "An Actuarial Analysis of a Prospective Experience Rating Approach for Group Hospital-Surgical-Medical Coverage," *Proceedings of the Casualty Actuarial Society,* Vol. 48, p. 155.

[9] See Sol Levine; Odin W. Anderson; and Gerald Gordon, *Non-Group Enrollment for Health Insurance* (Cambridge: Harvard University Press, 1957) for a comprehensive discussion of Blue Cross practices in nongroup enrollment.

that the underwriting of social insurance is rather similar, in essence, to the underwriting of noncontributory group insurance.

## Courses of action

*General.* Basically, there are three courses of action an insurer may take regarding a potential insured. The applicant may be rejected altogether, insured at regular rates on a regular policy form, or insured at substandard rates or on restricted policy forms.

In *group insurance* it is very rare for a group to be rejected altogether. The rate structure is flexible enough so that almost any group can be handled for some combination of benefits and eligibility and at some rate. Of course, the applicant may be unsatisfied with the proposal and lose interest. Where an insurer completely refuses to handle a group, it will be where the nature of the group is such that the insurer feels the law of averages will not operate satisfactorily or where the administration promises to be so complex as not to be worth the trouble. Generally speaking, however, most group cases can be underwritten with the proper combination of policy provisions. Thus the process of underwriting inevitably affects materially the problem of rating and policy writing. This is natural in an area where policies are individually rated and often individually designed for a specific case.

It is in the area of *individual insurance* that the variety of techniques for handling substandard risks is greatest. In recent years there have been great advances in underwriting substandard business, and the proportion of applicants declined outright has diminished greatly. About 80–90 percent of applicants are eligible for standard insurance at standard rates, and only a quite small proportion is completely ineligible. Techniques for substandard risks include waivers, extra premiums, limitation of the type of policy which will be issued and "specified condition underwriting." They are applied to about 15 percent of applicants.

The use of *waivers* is the most common method of handling physical impairments. A waiver or impairment rider is an endorsement or rider on a policy which excludes from coverage any loss arising from a named disease or physical impairment or occurring to a specified part of the body. By excluding the particular type of loss which makes the case substandard, full coverage may be issued for other types of loss at standard rates. Generally, the waiver is broader than the condition with which the underwriter is specifically concerned. For example, an applicant with a history of kidney stones might be offered a policy excluding all diseases of the kidney or genitourinary tract. This is felt to be necessary because the kidney stone condition might aggravate another related disease and also because there is a danger that a claimant might seek to avoid the rider by alleging a slightly different disease. However, the broadness of many exclusion riders seriously impairs the value of the coverage. Despite this, there is no reduction in premium for a ridered policy. Underwriters claim that the existence of the impairment is likely to prolong many disabilities even from entirely unrelated ailments. Conditions which may commonly require waivers include allergies, asthma, back injuries, eczema, hay fever, hernia, migraine, and tuberculosis.

The use of *extra premiums* has been unusual in health insurance, except for occupational hazards, as indicated above. Recently, many insurers have been experimenting with extra premiums for health impairments, despite the fact that there is not yet a sufficient body of experience on which to base such rates.[10] Conditions for which extra premiums are fairly frequently charged include underweight, overweight, loss of specific members, blindness, and deafness. Some insurers will consider extra premium full coverage for conditions as serious as syphilis, multiple sclerosis, and chronic leukemia, at least for hospital insurance. Often the extra premium will be computed separately for accidental injury and sickness. Various numerical rating scales have been developed to assist in determining the amount of extra premium, but much of this still represents essentially arbitrary judgment.

One reason that extra premiums cannot safely be used more frequently instead of waivers is that, for many impairments, the obtaining of treatment and its duration are substantially under the control of the insured. This is the case for many chronic ailments and for conditions correctable by elective surgery. There is no extra premium short of the full amount of the potential claim which is adequate to handle such an increased risk.

Federal Life and Casualty recently introduced a series of new policies for the applicants with histories of conditions such as cancer, cardiac disease, tuberculosis, and ulcers. It hopes to find a wide market among persons with policies with exclusion riders, persons who are considered uninsurable, and persons whose policies have been cancelled. Information on rate level is not available at the time of writing.

*Modification of type of policy* is the third major approach to underwriting substandard cases. Where an application is borderline, it may be felt that a more limited coverage than that applied for may be issued safely. This limitation may take the form of issuing accident-only coverage, lower amounts, shorter maximum benefit periods, on a commercial rather than a guaranteed renewable basis, or with a longer waiting period. The latter device is particularly valuable for a history of minor chronic ailments and for cases where there is a danger of moral hazard related to possible seasonal unemployment.

*Specified Condition Underwriting* represents, in effect, a combination

---

[10] At least 163 insurers were using extra premiums for impaired risks in 1966. —"Today's Trends . . . for Tomorrow," *Health Insurance Review* (1967 Sales and Service Number), p. 20.

of two or more of the above techniques. In its usual application, it represents what might be called a "partial waiver" for a specified physical condition. Instead of excluding the condition or the entire area of the body completely, the rider limits benefits for the specified condition more severely than benefits for other conditions. This may be accomplished by imposing a lower maximum benefit, a higher deductible, a longer waiting period or a higher percentage participation by the insured.

Usually, there will be a required period of symptom-free good health before the applicant will be considered for such coverage. Sometimes there also is an extra premium. Usually the condition for which benefits are limited is defined more narrowly than the condition excluded under the conventional waiver arrangement. This seems to be a desirable approach in that it permits considerable flexibility and provides limited coverage for conditions that might not be eligible for full benefits at any premium rate. Another approach is a temporary exclusion of a specific condition which either expires automatically or may be removed with the insurer's consent after a specified period of time.

The insured never should be given a choice between two alternative methods of handling the case, as, for example, between a waiver and an extra premium. Such a choice presents too great a possibility of adverse selection.

**The underwriting process**

*Sources of information.* The sources of information which a company may utilize in underwriting include the application, agent's report, inspection report, physician's examination, intercompany data, reports from attending physicians, and, in renewal underwriting and in some group cases, the previous insurance experience of the risk.

As indicated above, the strictness of underwriting varies greatly with the type of policy. Only in long-term noncancellable and guaranteed renewable contracts and life insurance disability riders will all these sources be utilized. At the other extreme, in connection with limited policies, the only source generally used is an extremely brief application which includes little more than the name and address of insured and beneficiary and a description of the policy applied for. This section will discuss each of these sources, but the reader should recognize that, for many lines, the underwriting is much less complete and strict than this discussion might imply.

The *application* consists of a statement by the insured of certain pertinent information about himself and a description of the policy applied for. It is usually quite detailed and complete for noncancellable and guaranteed renewable insurance, and progressively less so for commercial, industrial, and limited. In its most complete form it will include the applicant's name, address, date of birth, height, weight, occupation, business, and employer. It will also call for information as to monthly income and health insurance carried with this and other insurers or pending. Sometimes the life insurance carried must also be listed, especially if there are any disability riders. Usually the policies must be described completely in regard to type, company, amount, date issued, and waiting period or deductible. The applicant must state whether any life, health, or accident insurer ever rejected or modified his application, canceled or refused to renew a policy, or refused payment of a claim.

A second portion of the application has to do with the applicant's current and past health and often that of his family. This will be filled out by the agent along with the first part of the application when there is to be no medical examination. It may be specifically designated Part II of the application or combined with the first part. Where there is a medical examination, these questions are asked and the answers filled in by the medical examiner. Some companies have both the agent and the medical examiner ask these questions. In either event, both parts of the application are usually made a part of the contract. Often this is made clear to the applicant by adding a statement at the end of the application whereby he must state that the above answers are complete and true to the best of his knowledge and belief and that he understands and agrees that they are material to his acceptance as a policyholder. It is to be hoped that most applicants read and understand this.

The health questions relate to a series of specific diseases and medical and surgical procedures and ask whether the applicant now has, or ever has had, these listed conditions. In addition, there are a number of general questions such as whether he has had within the past five or 10 years any medical or surgical advice or treatment or any departure from good health. Specific details such as month, year, nature of ailment and treatment, name and address of physician or surgeon, and prognosis are requested. Questions as to family health history may be included. Generally these relate to parents and siblings and call for age and state of health, if living, and age at death and cause of death, if dead.

In group insurance the application is signed by the employer, and the information has to do with the number of employees, their distribution by age, sex, race, and occupation, the location of the various plants, and, of course, the nature of the coverage applied for. Sometimes information is required on earnings and age and sex of dependents. Often it will be supplemented by studies made by the insurer's group representative. Of course, there are no questions relating to the health of prospective insured members.

The *agent's report* is a statement by the agent, frequently on the back of the application. It states that he has asked all the questions required; what premium has been collected, if any; what the applicant's earned income is; how the business was obtained; how long the agent has known the applicant; and how they met. It may ask whether other applications for life or health insurance are pending, whether the new insurance is intended to replace any other policy, and whether the agent unqualifiedly recommends the applicant for insurance. It may call for the names and addresses of two or three intimate friends. This last item is useful not only as underwriting information but also as a source of additional prospects for the agent.

The *inspection report* serves as a check on the accuracy and completeness of the statements of the applicant and the agent. It may be obtained from an inspection department of the company, from a credit agency, or from an agency specializing in insurance inspections. It involves inquiries in the neighborhood of the applicant's home and at his place of employment and checks of public records, such as military, hospital, police and credit records. If properly conducted, it will reveal information about earnings, occupation, habits, hobbies, spare-time activities, past health history, sex life and work absences, which the agent is rarely able to obtain.

The *medical examination* is the best source of information about the current health of the insured but also is quite expensive. Therefore, it is used as a regular thing only in applications for long-term noncancellable policies, life insurance disability riders and major medical at higher ages. In some other types of insurance it is used in doubtful cases, while in limited policies it is almost unheard of. The examination is quite similar to that used for life insurance and includes pulse and blood pressure readings and frequently urinalysis. For very large policies, more detailed examinations involving x-rays and electrocardiograms occasionally may be used. The examination is not a foolproof safeguard against adverse selection. The applicant may go to considerable effort to appear at his best by means of rest, diet, and medication and there have even been cases where a different individual has been substituted for examination purposes or to provide a urine sample.

The *attending physician's report* is used where the individual application and/or examiner's report reveals conditions, past or present, about which more information is desired. Of course, professional ethics prevent a physician from divulging such information without the consent of the patient. Companies use standard authorization forms which may be signed by the applicant at the time of the original application, at the time of the medical examination, or at a special visit by agent or company representative. The prudent agent makes it a practice to obtain an authorization with the application to save trouble in the future.

*Intercompany data* are utilized where the application or inspection reveals that the applicant has been declined, rated up, canceled, ridered, or nonrenewed. In group cases which are being transferred from one insurer to another, the claim history of the previous insurer will be particularly valuable. Often this can be obtained from the employer more readily than from the first insurer. In individual insurance the information available will usually relate only to physical defects discovered. This may be obtained from the other company directly or from intercompany agencies, such as the Medical Information Bureau or the Hooper-Holmes Bureau. These bureaus collect, tabulate, and make available information about physical impairments discovered by any of their member companies. While they do not keep records of the other company's action on the case, sometimes this may be obtained directly. In addition, public sources such as court records may be checked by the home-office underwriter as well as by the inspector.

*Responsibilities in underwriting.* Underwriting may be divided into three phases: field underwriting, lay underwriting, and medical underwriting. *Field underwriting,* primarily the responsibility of the agent, is of great importance in individual insurance but of less significance in group insurance. The first stage of field underwriting is prospecting. The agent should endeavor to develop a market where he will find good risks, free of moral hazard, and in good physical condition, and of substantial financial strength. The agent must be careful to get accurate information in the application, especially in regard to questions about the applicant's health and health history. The applicant is rarely in a position to judge what is important, and skillful questioning may be necessary to reveal the full story. An agent who has been soundly trained can save himself and his company a great deal of trouble and bad public relations by minimizing unnecessary rejections. However, the progress which has been made in substandard underwriting must be kept in mind. Today, many applicants who would have been declined a few years ago can be written substandard.

*Lay underwriting* is the responsibility of the home-office underwriting department. Junior underwriters decide on the majority of applications and refer special cases to senior underwriters or the medical department for final decision. The underwriting process involves assigning the applicant to the proper rate class for occupation and deciding whether the case should be standard, substandard, or rejected. The lay underwriter is particularly concerned with occupational physical hazard and with moral hazard but must weigh all factors and decide how to treat the case on the basis of the net balance.

*Medical underwriting* refers to the evaluation of the applicant's medical examination and health history. This is handled by a branch of the medical department, except that clear-cut cases may be passed upon directly by the lay underwriter, saving time and money. The medical underwriter, a physician, should be available for consultation in all debatable cases. Of course, in group insurance and for limited policies where medical information is not gathered, medical underwriting does not take place.

*Renewal underwriting.* Except in the noncancellable and guaranteed renewable policies and the life insurance riders, the insurer has an opportunity to reevaluate its insureds periodically. The practice of companies varies greatly in this regard. Presumably, the policies which are issued with the provision or with the understanding that renewal will not be denied for reasons having to do with changes in the health of the individual insured are not subject to this process to any material degree.

However, renewal underwriting is concerned with more than the health history of the insured. Changes in occupation, income, residence, or habits may have made him an undesirable insured. However, knowledge of such changes comes to the insurer primarily at the time a claim is submitted, and it may appear as though it is canceling or refusing to renew for physical reasons, even where it is motivated quite differently. Sometimes information of such changes may come to the insurer as a result of an application for reinstatement of a lapsed policy or an application for new insurance.

Where the cancellation clause is not included in the policy—a practice which is becoming more and more common—the insurer must defer any action until the next renewal date. Where the cancellation clause exists, the company has its choice of acting immediately or at the renewal date. In either event, the decision usually is reached shortly after the question comes up.

As indicated above, some companies limit their use of the right of cancellation or nonrenewal to situations other than changes in the personal health of the insured. Some go even further and exercise the right only where the insured himself has done something to indicate that he is a poor risk. Such things might include sharp claim practices, taking up a dangerous sport or hobby, or entering an uninsurable occupation. Sometimes policies are terminated because the maximum benefit has been paid for a chronic disease or permanent injury.

Other insurers make extensive use of the right of termination, canceling, or refusing renewal if, in the judgment of the underwriter, the risk has declined in desirability to the point that it would be unprofitable to continue it upon the books.[11] In reaching such a decision it must be kept in mind that it costs money to put a policy on the books and that this expense has already been incurred and largely paid on existing policies. Thus a more liberal standard should be applied to renewal underwriting than to new applications. The uniform provisions require written notice at least five days before the effective date of cancellation or the due date of the

---

[11] See above, p. 530, for some of the reasons insurers cancel or refuse renewal.

renewal premium, as the case may be. In many states rights of cancellation or nonrenewal are further limited by law.

As an alternative to termination, many companies make a practice of offering to renew the policy subject to an impairment rider or other modification. Rates may be increased, as for change of occupation, amounts reduced to conform to a decline in earnings, maximum duration reduced, or the waiting period lengthened.

In group insurance, renewal underwriting is carried out at almost every renewal. The risk is reexamined each year in terms of loss ratios, changes in the character or composition of the risk, current enrollment, and employment conditions in the industry. The insurer has the right to change the premium rate on any anniversary. In the larger cases, experience rating is applied, through a dividend formula or directly.

The insurance company and the policyholder jointly may agree to change the schedule of benefits or any other provision of the contract. Frequently, some relatively minor change, such as a longer waiting period or a higher deductible, may make an unprofitable case satisfactory. Only where the insured fails to agree to such recommended changes or where participation drops below agreed minima is a case likely to be terminated by action of the insurer.

### Reinsurance

*General.* Reinsurance represents the extension of the insurance principle to insurers themselves. The primary insurer purchases insurance from another company, which protects it against all or a part of the losses against which it is insuring its policyholders. The original company is called the "ceding company"; the second company is the "reinsurer." The process is referred to as "cession of reinsurance," and, where the reinsurer itself reinsures, this process is called "retrocession."

*Reasons for reinsurance.* The reasons why reinsurance contracts are negotiated include the following: (1) The ceding company may wish to protect itself against losses in individual cases beyond a certain amount, yet competition may require it to offer policies providing coverage in excess of these amounts. The larger and stronger the ceding company, of course, the less likely it is to require this type of protection. (2) The ceding company may wish protection against catastrophe losses in a certain line of insurance, such as aviation accident or polio insurance. (3) The ceding company may wish protection against mistakes in rating and underwriting in entering a new line of insurance such as major medical. The reinsurer not only would share the risk but might be quite helpful in giving advice as to proper rates and procedures. (4) A company expanding at a rapid rate might find reinsurance an effective way of limiting the "surplus drain" resulting from the redundancy of the unearned premium reserve requirements.[12] (5) A customer might insist on reinsurance of a large case in order to strengthen the security of the original contract or to permit another insurer it favors to participate in the business. This latter is especially common in group cases.

Reinsurance is not too highly developed in the health insurance business. It has only recently become generally available in noncancellable and guaranteed renewable policies, and reinsurers require a fairly high retention.[13] (6) An insurer may wish to withdraw from a line or go out of business. Excess of loss reinsurance is especially difficult to obtain. In group cases it is rarely used except when requested by a large policyholder. It is most common for new small companies and in lines such as aviation accident, major medical and dread-disease policies, which have a combination of high individual limits, low premium rates, and a potential catastrophe hazard. The recent growth of major medical and long-term disability income insurance has increased the demand for reinsurance.

*Types of reinsurance. Contractual arrangement.* Reinsurance may be either facultative or treaty. *Facultative reinsurance* involves a separate negotiation of the reinsurance on each individual risk, which the reinsurer may either accept or decline. Similarly, the ceding company offers only those particular cases for which it desires coverage. *Treaty reinsurance,* on the other hand, involves a continuing contractual relationship between the ceding company and the reinsurer. The treaty may be automatic or facultative.

An *automatic treaty* provides that every risk meeting certain criteria will be reinsured. Neither the ceding company nor the reinsurer has any choice. A *facultative treaty* provides for a compromise between the automatic treaty and the pure facultative arrangement. Here the contract calls for a continuing relationship and spells out the details of how the reinsurance will be effected, but the ceding company selects the risks it wants to submit, and the reinsurer has the option of accepting or declining individual cases. Other variants sometimes are found. A facultative obligatory treaty permits the ceding company to select risks which the reinsurer *must* accept.

*Sharing of loss.* Reinsurance may be classified in another way: in regard to how the risk is shared between the ceding company and the reinsurer. There are two main types of arrangement: "share" reinsurance and "excess of loss" reinsurance.

*Share reinsurance* involves the reinsurer's sharing an agreed or determinable portion of the risk on each individual case. In group insurance, incidentally, the individual case is considered to be the individual life, not

---

[12] See p. 606 below for an explanation of the "surplus drain" phenomenon.

[13] The retention is the share of the risk retained (that is, not reinsured) by the ceding insurer.

the group. One type of share reinsurance provides for a fixed share of each case to be reinsured. This is referred to as "fixed share," "quota share," or "pro rata reinsurance." For example, 50 percent of every case falling into the classes covered by the contract might be reinsured, no matter how small the amount involved.

*Surplus share reinsurance,* on the other hand, provides that the excess of the amount insured over a stated absolute amount will be reinsured. Once the amount reinsured is determined, all losses on the case, large and small, are shared in the proportion of the respective amounts insured, just as in the fixed share arrangement. Some plans call for a varying proportion to be reinsured, depending on the size of the risk. This represents a compromise between the two other approaches. There may be first, second, or more treaties.

*Excess of loss reinsurance* involves no sharing of specific cases. In this type of arrangement, the reinsurer agrees to pay all losses in excess of an agreed amount. The premium is more difficult to determine for this, since the probability of a large loss is usually much less than the probability of a small loss. The reinsurer may meet losses in excess of an agreed amount on a single life, in which case the contract is referred to as excess single loss or "per risk excess" reinsurance.

Another approach is to have the reinsurance apply to any loss in excess of an agreed amount resulting from a single accident or epidemic involving (say) four or more lives. This is called "excess aggregate loss," "disaster," or "catastrophe reinsurance." A third approach, somewhat rarer than the above, is excess loss ratio reinsurance. Here the reinsurer reimburses the ceding company for any losses in excess of an agreed proportion of the premium received on a given class of business. Sometimes this is referred to as "stop-loss" reinsurance, and sometimes as "perfect nonsense."

## Problems and issues

The problems and issues in health insurance underwriting have been discussed above, either throughout this chapter or in chapters 9, 10, and 16. They include the avoidance of adverse selection and overlapping coverages, the control of moral hazard, largely through a reasonable relationship between the amount of insurance and the potential loss, and the problems of extending coverage in terms of covering more members of the population, especially the aged and lower-income groups, and in making more adequate benefits available generally. In addition, there are problems of overutilization and increased cost, with their impact upon the practice of medicine and upon hospital administration. These, however, are partly problems in claim relationships and will be more fully discussed in Chapter 20.

## Summary

Underwriting involves the process of selection, classification, and rating and is intended to make sure that the risks insured display the same expectation of loss as that on which premium rates are based. While standards and procedures differ considerably as between individual, group, and social insurance, all types require certain underwriting safeguards.

The probability of loss and average claim cost are affected by age, sex, occupation, health, race, location, type of policy, and the relation of insurance to the potential loss. Moral hazard is especially important in health insurance and is controlled both by observing certain criteria of acceptance and by policy provisions and underwriting procedures which require the insured to share in the loss.

An insurer may accept a case at standard rates, reject it altogether, or issue the policy on a substandard basis. Substandard policies may be at special premium rates, subject to exclusion riders, or limited in amount, duration, or type of benefit.

The underwriting process is divided into three stages: field, lay, and medical underwriting. The sources of information available may include the application, the agent's report, report of the medical examiner and attending physician, the inspection report, and intercompany data. Renewal underwriting is similar to initial underwriting except that more liberal standards are used because of express or implied obligations to policyholders, issue expense, and public relations.

Reinsurance is simply the process whereby the original insurer insures his own risk with another company. It may be effected on a facultative or treaty basis on either a share or excess of loss basis. It serves to protect the original company from unduly heavy losses.

All the problems of health insurance are underwriting problems or closely related to underwriting. They are discussed throughout the book.

## Selected references

*See the following items from the General Bibliography: 4, ch. 22; 7, ch. 6; 8, ch. 8; 10, ch. 10; 12 pp. 46–49; 14, ch. 6; 15, ch. 17; 16; 17, ch. 7; 18, ch. 16; 19, chs. 13 and 14; 20, chs. 8, 9, and 10; 21, ch. 19; 22, chs. 9, 10, and 11; 30, pp. 28–34.*

ALTMAN, JOSEPH. *Underwriter's Medical Guide for Accident and Sickness Insurance.* Cincinnati, Ohio: National Underwriter Co., 1953.

BLUMENFELD, M. EUGENE. "Recent Trends and Innovations in Individual Hospital Insurance," *Proceedings of the Casualty Actuarial Society,* Vol. XLVIII, p. 83.

CHANDLER, BROOKS. "Underwriting of New Groups," H.I.A.A. Group Insurance Forum, 1959.

CODY, DONALD D. "Renewal Underwriting—Problems and Procedures," H.I.A.A. Group Insurance Forum, 1959.

COX, CHRISTOPHER J. "Substandard Accident and Sickness," H.I.A.A. Individual Insurance Forum, 1959.

CRANE, HOWARD G. "Commercial Accident and Health Insurance from the Standpoint of the Reinsurance Company," *Proceedings of the Casualty Actuarial Society*, Vol. XXI, p. 303.

DINGMAN, HARRY W. *Risk Appraisal* (rev. ed). Cincinnati, Ohio: National Underwriter Co., 1954.

HEALTH AND ACCIDENT UNDERWRITERS CONFERENCE. Underwriting Forums. Annual, 1947–55.

HEALTH INSURANCE ASSOCIATION OF AMERICA. "Panel Discussion—Exceptions, Reductions, Limitations—Friend or Foe?" H.I.A.A. Individual Insurance Forum, 1965.

HEALTH INSURANCE ASSOCIATION OF AMERICA. "Symposium on Substandard—Why, How and Results," H.I.A.A. Individual Insurance Forum, 1960.

———. *Member Company Survey on Coverage for Groups of Less than 25 Lives*. New York: H.I.A.A., 1960.

LAIRD, JOHN M. "Non-Cancellable Accident and Health Insurance Underwriting Problems," *Proceedings of the Casualty Actuarial Society*, Vol. VII, p. 302.

LEVINE, SOL; ANDERSON, ODIN W.; and GORDON, GERALD. *Non-Group Enrollment for Health Insurance*. Cambridge: Harvard University Press, 1957.

MACDONALD, ROY A. *Underwriting Sub-Standard A. & H. Insurance*. Cincinnati, Ohio: National Underwriter Co., 1951.

MCLEAN, GEORGE E. "An Actuarial Analysis of a Prospective Experience Rating Approach for Group Hospital-Surgical-Medical, Coverage," *Proceedings of the Casualty Actuarial Society*, Vol. 48, p. 155.

MUNICH AMERICAN REASSURANCE COMPANY. *Reinsurance and Reassurance*, Vols. I–IV. New York: Munich Reinsurance Company, 1963–66.

WALRAVEN, J. HESSER. *Accident and Sickness Field Underwriting Guide*. Cincinnati, Ohio: National Underwriter Co., 1956.

WICKMAN, J. M. *Evaluating the Health Insurance Risk*, Cincinnati, Ohio: National Underwriter Company, 1965.

# chapter 18

Tomorrow's Fate, though thou be wise,
Thou canst not tell nor yet surmise.—Edward FitzGerald, *Omar Khayyam*

# Rate Making

## General principles

The process of rate making involves the study of experience and the setting up of premium rates for the various classifications of insureds. A premium rate is the charge made for insurance per unit of exposure. The premium that an insured pays is the product of the premium rate and the number of units of exposure insured by the contract.

## Goals of rate making

The rate should be adequate, reasonable, and equitable. Adequacy requires that it be sufficient to cover the cost of claims for the insured group, cover the expenses of operation of the company, provide a reserve for contingencies, and yield a profit sufficient to attract capital into the industry. Reasonableness means that it should not be unduly high. Competition is strong enough in most lines of insurance to make sure that this objective is met. Equity requires that each insured be charged a rate which reflects, as closely as is practicable, the probability of occurrence and the probable severity of loss to which he is subject.

At first thought, it might seem that equity would be achieved by charging all insureds the same rate. Thus losses would be shared among the insured group in direct proportion to the exposure. However, if the probability of loss and/or probable amount of loss differs materially from one insured to another, this process involves undercharging some insureds and overcharging others. When this comes to be recognized, the insureds who are being overcharged will withdraw from the group and find another method of meeting their need for security.[1] This might

---

[1] In exceptional cases, where the insurer with broad rate classes has extremely low

involve dealing with another insurer, self-insuring, or merely assuming the risk themselves. As soon as this takes place, the insurer, with the better risks no longer in the group, will find that losses are no longer being covered by premium income. Thus it will be necessary to increase premium rates. This process will continue until the only insureds left are the worst risks and the final premium rate is quite high. Only in a program in which insurance is compulsory is it possible to maintain an inequitable rate structure for any extended period.

**Premium computation**

*General.* The gross premium rate is divided into two portions, pure premium and loading. The pure or net premium represents the anticipated cost of the benefit payments. The loading represents additions to the pure premium for expenses, the effect of withdrawals, and taxes, plus an allowance for contingencies, sometimes the accumulation of reserves, and profits. In the language of mathematics,

$$
\begin{aligned}
G &= \text{Gross premium rate} \\
P &= \text{Net premium rate} \\
\lambda \text{ (lambda)} &= \text{Loading (per unit) and} \\
G &= P + \lambda.
\end{aligned}
$$

The pure premium may be thought of as the product of the claim frequency rate or probability of loss and the average severity of the claim, or average claim value. For some benefits, such as accidental death, the average claim value is an absolute dollar amount. More frequently, however, it depends on variables such as the level of expenses incurred or the duration of disability or hospital confinement. The claim frequency also may be referred to as the "claim rate" or the probability of occurrence of the event insured against. For some benefits the pure premium may be derived directly from loss data without separately computing the probability of loss and the severity, but conceptually it is better to keep them distinct.

In actuarial notation, if

$$
\begin{aligned}
r &= \text{Rate of disability (as defined for the particular} \\
&\quad \text{benefit) or probability of loss, and} \\
s &= \text{Average severity, then} \\
P &= rs
\end{aligned}
$$

For some policies involving the payment of an income benefit, the average severity may be expressed as the present value of an annuity due and designated by the symbol $\ddot{a}^1$. An annuity is a series of payments,

rates because of better selection or lower expenses, the relatively overcharged insured still may find it advantageous, on an absolute basis, to remain in the insured group. The same comment applies to group insurance where an employer contributes substantially to premium payments.

and the symbol refers to its present value. In the case of a disability annuity, the future payments are discounted to take account of interest, probability of death and probability of recovery. The superscript i indicates a disability annuity. The diaeresis indicates that it is an annuity *due;* that is, that the first payment is due immediately, rather than at the end of the period.

For most types of benefit the frequency rate varies considerably by age. This is particularly true of long-term income and major medical benefits. For this type of benefit, it often is advisable to compute the rate of disability separately for each age of exposure. When this is done, the subscript x is added to the symbol r to indicate the age of exposure. Thus $r_x$ means the rate of disability (for the benefit under consideration) for lives exposed at age x, and $r_{30}$ means the rate for age 30.

Similarly, for the long-term income benefits, the severity rate (expressed as a disability annuity due) varies with the age at which disability commences and must be computed separately for each age. The same subscript is used and the benefit is expressed as $\ddot{a}_x^i$. Where periods are short and interest does not enter into the computation, the average severity per unit of benefit exposed is expressed as $s_{(x)}^i$. The parentheses are used to distinguish this from another method of notation.

Where the rate of disability and/or the severity vary considerably by age, the pure term premiums will, of course, also vary with age. Thus it is necessary to have a notation which will indicate the age involved. The symbol for the term premium is $P_x^1$, where x is the age exposed. The superscript 1 is used to indicate that the premium is a term insurance premium. Frequently, the term premiums are converted into level premiums for each age of entry, in a fashion similar to that used in life insurance. The net level premium for each age of entry (x) is indicated by the symbol $P_x$, and the gross level premium by $G_x$.

The reader should not be discouraged or intimidated by the use of mathematical notations. These merely represent a convenient language for expressing some of the relationships involved—a sort of shorthand. Like any other language, it must be learned, but it affords considerable advantages in communication after it is learned. The reader who finds it difficult to think symbolically may ignore the notation if he desires. The meaning of each concept will be stated and its derivation and application will be explained in words as well as in mathematical language. However, the more complex concepts are difficult to explain clearly in ordinary language, and the reader who will take the time to master the notation will find that the learning process is expedited.

*Loss ratio method.* The discussion of premium computation up to this point has referred to the "pure premium" method of computation, whereby pure premiums are computed by dividing losses by exposures.

Losses, of course, involve the concept of severity as well as frequency. In actual computation, frequency and severity rates may be developed separately or claim costs, encompassing both frequency and severity in a single rate, may be used.

The "loss ratio" method, on the other hand, does not derive pure premiums directly but makes use of a comparison of actual and expected losses to derive a modification of an existing premium structure. Of course, the two approaches are mathematically equivalent, but the loss ratio method is often used in practice on a relatively crude overall basis. The general formula for a loss ratio calculation is

$$P_n = P_o \frac{A}{E},$$

where $P_n$ and $P_o$ are the new and old premiums, respectively, A is actual losses, and E is expected losses. The formula may be appiled to either pure or gross premiums, and actual and expected losses may be expressed in a variety of forms—in terms of aggregate losses for the insured group, losses per unit of exposure (that is, pure premiums), or loss ratios.

Loss ratios refer to the ratio of losses to some other measure. The most frequent use of the term is to refer to the ratio of losses incurred to premiums earned.[2] However, sometimes the term refers to the ratio of actual to anticipated claims where anticipated claims refer to the claims expected according to the assumptions underlying the existing premium. Sometimes the claims in dollars are compared to the "net amount available for claims," which is equal to earned premium less expenses and reserve allocations. Claims plus expenses may be compared to total earned premium. In most of these methods, it is possible to express losses or claims in terms of dollars or in terms of number of cases. In using the loss ratio method, any of these approaches may be appropriate, so long as the numerator and denominator are consistent. The unit cancels out, and a pure ratio of actual to expected losses remains. This indicates the modification to be applied to the current premium.

### Sources of data

Some of the complexities of determining and expressing rates of disability and severity were discussed in Chapter 2. There are many types

---

[2] Losses incurred include allowances for anticipated future claims payments on losses which have taken place and should be distinguished from losses paid, which include only payments to date. Similarly, premiums earned reflect the actual period of protection provided under a contract and should be distinguished from premiums written, which reflect actual receipts including premiums to be applied to future periods of protection.

of rate, many units in which they can be expressed, and many other variations. The subjectivity inherent in the concept of poor health further complicates the utilization of what data are available. The type and amount of benefit, for example, may be the primary determinants of the magnitude of the rate. Generally speaking, morbidity data suitable for premium computation for this country are not available.

Population studies are usually on a prevalence basis and do not develop separate frequency and severity rates. With a few exceptions, insurance data are limited in scope and usefulness, since they so frequently are based on experience under a certain type of benefit, of a particular company, or both. The principal sources of statistics are as follows:  .

Statistics showing experience under *individual health insurance* policies were published by the Bureau of Accident and Health Underwriters, covering accident insurance for the years 1931–40 and 1948–51. It also has published statistics of hospital, nurse, and surgical expense benefits for the period 1939–41, and of personal sickness benefits for the years 1952 and 1953. Several studies by a committee of the Society of Actuaries have been published, and these are of great value.[3] In addition, most companies have developed data based on their own experience.

*Life insurance company data* have been developed through two intercompany studies of disability riders issued in connection with life insurance policies. These studies were prepared by committees of the Actuarial Society of America and the Society of Actuaries in 1926 and 1952. The benefits studied usually commenced after a waiting period of three to six months and coverage terminated at age 55 or 60. Thus, in order to use these data for other types of disability income benefit, it was necessary to extend the data downward for shorter waiting periods and to extrapolate them for higher ages of coverage. The 1926 study,[4] with such modifications, long served as the main basis for computing premiums for relatively long-term disability income benefits. The most commonly used of these modifications has been the modification of the Class 3 (the class which showed the highest claim rates) figures from the 1926 study developed by the Health and Accident Underwriters Conference. This is commonly referred to as the "Conference Modifica-

---

[3] Society of Actuaries, "Report of the Committee on Experience under Individual Accident and Sickness Insurance—Experience under Individual Accident and Sickness Policies, 1955–57" *Transactions of the Society of Actuaries,* 1959 Reports Number, p. 123; "Committee on Experience under Individual Health Insurance—Experience under Individual Loss of Time Policies, 1955–59," *Transactions of the Society of Actuaries,* 1961 Reports Number, p. 101; 1960–61, *TSA 1963* Reports Number, p. 117; 1960–63 *TSA 1965* Reports Number, p. 62. Reports on individual medical expense policies are found in the 1963 and 1965 reports.

[4] Actuarial Society of America, *Report of Committee on Disability Experience* (New York, 1926).

tion."[5] The data[6] from the 1952 study were used extensively from 1955 to 1965, especially for life insurance riders and guaranteed renewable policies of long-benefit durations. Commutation columns for the 1952 data have been published.[7] The Society of Actuaries also conducts double indemnity studies which have a bearing on the accidental death benefit. Hospital, surgical, and maternity tables based on intercompany data also are available.[8]

The *1964 Commissioners Disability Table* was adopted by the Accident and Health Committee of the National Association of Insurance Commissioners as a minimum reserve standard[9] for disability income contracts in December 1964. The report recommended that the states implement this standard in 1965 by administrative ruling or legislation where necessary. Insurers certainly will use these standards as a check on premium adequacy and probably for premium computation.

The table was based on the first year of total disability for claims incurred in 1958–61 by 17 companies. Termination rates after the first year were those of the 1952 study for benefits 2 and 3 combined. Very extensive tables have been published including commutation columns, valuation net premiums, and active and disabled life reserves based on 2½ and 3 percent interest and the 1958 C.S.O. Mortality Table.[10]

*Group insurance* statistics have been published regularly since 1947 in reports of the Committee on Group Morbidity of the Society of Actuaries,[11] and a number of reports of single-company experience have been published. These include experience under disability income; hospital, surgical, and medical expense; major medical; and comprehensive benefits. Most companies which are active in the group field maintain their own statistics and tend to rely on these rather than on intercompany data. However, the intercompany data are very useful to a company newly entering a line. Of course, they must be adjusted for trends in benefit cost and for differences in underwriting standards of the company

---

[5] Health and Accident Underwriters Conference, *Conference Modification of Class 3 Disability Table for Calculation of Reserves on Non-Cancellable Accident and Health Insurance* (Chicago, 1941).

[6] Society of Actuaries, "Report of Committee on Disability and Double Indemnity," *Transactions of the Society of Actuaries*, 1952 Reports Number, p. 70.

[7] Manuel R. Cueto, "Monetary Values for Ordinary Disability Benefits," *Transactions of the Society of Actuaries*, Vol. VI, p. 108. (Also published separately by the Society of Actuaries with extended tables.) Commutation columns are an actuarial device to facilitate computation of rates and reserves.

[8] Edwin L. Bartleson and James J. Olsen, "Reserves for Individual Hospital and Surgical Expense Insurance," *Transactions of the Society of Actuaries*, Vol. IX, p. 331.

[9] See Chapter 19 for a description of active and disabled life reserves.

[10] Health Insurance Association of America, *1964 Commissioners Disability Table* (New York, 1965).

[11] *Transactions of the Society of Actuaries* reports numbers, annual.

using them. The group studies exclude occupational disability, and allowance must be made for this if 24-hour coverage is to be issued on either a group or an individual basis.

*Population statistics* are of little value for insurance purposes. They do not reflect either the adverse selection on the part of the policyholders or the selection of the insurer, and it is very difficult to predict the combined effect of these two factors. Moreover, they are frequently collected and published on a basis which greatly limits their utility. They may make no distinction as to age, sex, or occupation; or they may be on a prevalence basis that fails to separate frequency and severity; or exposure data may be lacking entirely, making the computation of rates impossible. However, some of these data, as well as those published by Blue Cross, Blue Shield, or "independent" insurers may be of considerable value in developing rates for new coverages where better data are lacking.

**Term premium computation**

As indicated above, the pure premium may be thought of as the product of the rate of disability and the average severity of a claim. The form in which these data are developed varies widely by type of benefit, so that it will be necessary to discuss the different types of benefit separately. Moving from the most simple to the most complex, the process will be discussed under the headings of "Accidental Death and Dismemberment," "Medical Care Benefits," and "Disability Income Benefits." For the time being, the discussion will be restricted to one-year term premiums which reflect only the benefit and expense costs for the current year.

*Accidental death and dismemberment.* These benefits involve the most simple premium computation, since the claim severity does not vary. The claim severity is the principal or capital sum for death or double dismemberment or a specified fraction thereof for lesser dismemberments. For ease of tabulation, dismemberment claims are not included in the annually published reports of the Group Mortality and Morbidity Committee. Since these claims are only about 6 to 10 percent of total accidental death and dismemberment claims and since this proportion varies little from year to year, it is easy to add a margin to the reported accidental death rates to allow for dismemberment claims. This margin may be varied to reflect minor differences in dismemberment benefits under particular classes of policy. Assuming a margin of 6 percent of total net premium, the net premium formula for age x and a principal sum of $1,000 becomes

$$P^l_x = \frac{\$1,000}{0.94} q^{ad}_x$$

where $q_x^{ad}$ is the accidental death rate of age x. Accidental death rates vary little by age at common entry ages. Therefore, it is usual to charge the same premium for all ages at entry. The most recent study, based on accidental death riders on ordinary life insurance in 1951–56, shows graduated rates per 1,000 lives exposed declining from 0.424 at age 1 to 0.198 at age 9; increasing to a peak of 0.583 at age 19; declining thereafter to 0.286 at ages 33–35 and thereafter rising consistently with age, The level of age 19 is not reached again until age 64.[12]

Theoretically, the premium for group contracts should be an average rate computed on a basis that takes into consideration the anticipated age distribution of the life-years of exposure for the company. In practice, a somewhat cruder method of selecting an appropriate pure premium is used. Thus, selecting an accidental death rate of 0.470 (say) as appropriate for all ages of entry up to age 55 (coverage limited to accidental deaths occurring before age 65) would yield a premium equal to

$$P = \frac{\$1,000 \cdot 0.47}{0.94} = \frac{\$0.50 \text{ or } 50\cancel{c} \text{ per } 1,000 \text{ of principal}}{\text{sum, before loading}^{13}}$$

*Medical care benefits. Hospital benefits.* For these benefits the average severity varies considerably, with type, amount, and maximum duration of benefit, sex, and age. In order to make possible the computation of premiums for various durations of benefit, tables known as "continuance tables" have been developed. These indicate the distribution of hospital confinement by duration in days. In developing such basic tables, age generally is not considered. However, it is not uncommon to differentiate between adults and children, between those persons age 65 and over and those under age 65, to distinguish between the sexes of adults, and to compute tables separately for surgical, obstetrical, and other admissions. Such a table makes it possible to compute average expected duration for any combination of benefit period and waiting period. When the exposure (in terms of active life-years) on which the table is based is known, it is also possible to compute frequency rates and average claim costs per insured life. Since the latter is what is generally desired, it is common to compute claim costs directly from the continuance table and exposure data. Table 18–1 is an example of such a continuance table. It refers to adult females, surgical admissions only.

---

[12] Society of Actuaries, "Report of Committee on Disability and Double Indemnity," *Transactions of the Society of Actuaries* 1958 Reports Number, p. 45.

[13] This rate allows no margin for contingencies or adverse selection. A graduated accidental death table with built-in margins for these, based on the 1951–56 study, is given in Norman Brodie and William J. November, "A New Table for Accidental Death Benefits," *Transactions of the Society of Actuaries*, Vol. XI, p. 749. The margin varies from 30 to 51 percent. This table was separately published by the Society of Actuaries with monetary values in 1962 and is known as the *1959 Accidental Death Benefits Table.*

TABLE 18–1

Hospital Continuance Table—Adult Female Surgical Admissions
per One Million Exposures

| Days n (1) | No. Cases Confined Exactly n Days (2) | No. Cases Confined n Days or More $\sum\limits_{n}^{120} (2)$ (3) | No. Days of Hospitalization Suffered Through nth Day $\sum\limits_{0}^{n} (3)$ (4) |
|---|---|---|---|
| 1 | 6,001 | 83,418 | 83,418 |
| 2 | 8,563 | 77,417 | 160,835 |
| 3 | 6,864 | 68,854 | 229,689 |
| 4 | 5,750 | 61,990 | 291,679 |
| 5 | 5,655 | 56,240 | 347,919 |
| 6 | 5,702 | 50,585 | 398,504 |
| 7 | 5,574 | 44,883 | 443,387 |
| 8 | 5,532 | 39,309 | 482,696 |
| 9 | 5,076 | 33,777 | 516,473 |
| 10 | 4,412 | 28,701 | 545,174 |
| 11–120 | 24,289 | | |

The construction of such a table is relatively simple. The study of experience yields the number of admissions distributed according to the length of stay. This is adjusted to a basis of 1,000,000 exposures and becomes column 2 of the table. Column 3 is the sum of column 2 from the bottom of the table to the day in question and represents the number of admissions per 1,000,000 exposures hospitalized for exactly n days or more. Column 4 is the sum of column 3 from the first day to the day in question and represents the total number of days of hospitalization up to the end of the nth day.

With such a table, the computation of the pure premium becomes a rather simple calculation. The pure premium for a benefit of $1 a day for a policy paying 10 days' maximum per admission is $0.545 (545,174 ÷ 1,000,000). This may be multiplied by the actual daily benefit rate to arrive at the premium for a particular contract. The table could be used to compute premiums for contracts with deductibles expressed in numbers of days by deduction of the appropriate value from column 4 for the deductible period. However, most deductible hospital contracts use a dollar deductible which requires the use of a somewhat more complex method.

Of course, this particular table gives the premium for surgical admissions only. A similar calculation, from the appropriate tables, would be required to produce the premium for obstetrical and general hospital admissions, and the sum of three would give the premium for all types of admission. This approach is particularly valuable for a full-service type contract, where the benefit cost per patient day may vary with the type of admission. Each separate pure premium per dollar of daily claim cost may be multiplied by the separate average cost for that type of admission and the total summed to get the total pure premium. Where a flat dollar benefit is paid, this refinement generally is considered unnecessary and continuance tables are constructed for all types of admission combined.

A basic group hospital table has been developed and published. It is based on insurance company experience with group hospital expense insurance.[14] The annual studies of actual claim experience now are reported in terms of the percentage of expected loss according to this table.

*Hospital extras.* The treatment of claim costs for hospital extras may vary considerably from one insurer to another. In the full-service contracts, where most insureds have complete or almost complete coverage for such benefits, they may be added to the average daily hospital cost and treated the same as the room-and-board component of pure premium. Where the room-and-board benefit is expressed in dollar terms and the hospital extra expense benefit is subject to a maximum such as 10 to 20 times the daily rate or a flat dollar figure, the premium calculation must allow for variations in this benefit.

It is common to use a continuance table or tables only for the room-and-board component of pure premium, and to analyze the hospital extras separately for the various types of contract offered. An average benefit per insured member per year is computed and added to the room-and-board component to get total pure premium. Hospital extra average claim costs were developed in the 1957 group hospital study for various maximum benefit amounts and room-and-board limits.[15]

Under both service and reimbursement types of contract it is customary to handle the maternity benefits separately, since these will be limited in most cases and such coverage may be eliminated from some contracts. Often room-and-board and extra expenses are combined for maternity cases.

Blue Cross associations, operating in a relatively limited area, need not be concerned with geographical variations in claim costs if they are using statistics based on their own experience. However, insurance companies operating over a wide geographical range may wish to make such allowances. Since the dollar room-and-board benefit is usually set

[14] Stanley W. Gingery, "A Reinvestigation of Group Hospital Expense Insurance Experience," *Transactions of the Society of Actuaries,* Vol. XII, p. 564 at 682–3.

[15] *Ibid.* at pp. 576–681.

at or below average actual charges, these local variations are not too important for this benefit. However, such variations may affect greatly the average level of claims under the hospital extra expense benefit, where the limit is rather high, and premium differentials may be used to reflect this. Moreover, these claim rates are affected by differences in hospital billing procedures.

All types of insurer should be hesitant at accepting statistics of past claim costs as the main guide to future premium rates. The trend in average claim costs clearly has been upward, and a conservative rate maker will want some allowance in the premium for a continuation of such a secular trend.

While it is known that both frequency and severity of hospital claims increase with age, this increase is generally ignored for rate-making purposes by Blue Cross except for the distinction between adults and children. Under contracts which continue coverage beyond retirement age it is necessary to allow for the sharp increase in claim costs at this time either by reducing benefit amounts and durations, increasing premiums, advance funding, or some combination of these. In group insurance a special loading may be used in initial rating where too large a proportion of the insured group is of advanced age. Individual guaranteed renewable contracts require a level premium for each age of entry, as explained below.

*Surgical benefits.* Surgical benefits involve calculations somewhat less complex than those for hospital benefits, since the duration of confinement does not affect claim costs. The various schedules of surgical benefit in use are rather similar, and claim costs will be determined primarily by the particular schedule involved. The group intercompany studies show claim costs under rather standard $150, $200 and $300 maximum schedules. Several special studies have been published showing the relative frequency of various procedures and total charges independent of the benefit schedule,[16] and most companies will have developed data of this type based on their own experience.

It is possible to make use of such studies to develop premiums for a schedule different from that on which the general studies are based and from one the company currently is using. The process involves a fairly detailed analysis of a sizable sample of claims to determine what the average claim cost would be under the standard schedule and under the new schedule. The ratio of the latter to the former may then be applied to premium rates under the old schedule, to yield a premium for the new schedule.

---

[16] For the most recent and probably the most comprehensive, see Morton D. Miller, "1957 Study of Group Surgical Expense Insurance Claims," *Transactions of the Society of Actuaries,* Vol. X, pp. 359–504.

For example, if an insurer planned to use a schedule which provided a maximum benefit of $500 instead of $200 as in the "standard" schedule, it could compute the increase in premium required as follows:

| Procedure (Code No.) | Average Benefit Cost | | Relative Frequency[17] of Procedure | Benefit Cost Component per 1,000 Procedures | |
|---|---|---|---|---|---|
| | Old Schedule | New Schedule | | Old Schedule | New Schedule |
| | (1) | (2) | (3) | (4) | (5) |
| Craniotomy (9020) | 190 (assumed) | 398 | $\frac{36}{97,088} = .3708$ | [(1) × (3)] $ 70.50 | [(2) × (3)] $ 147.80 |
| Appendectomy (6040) | 131 | 147 | $\frac{3930}{97,088} = 40.474$ | $5,302.10 | $5,949.70 |

The process would be completed for each procedure or procedure group. Then the totals in columns 4 and 5 would be compared. The ratio of column 5 total to column 4 total would give the ratio of benefit costs per claim in the new schedule to that in the old. For example, the relative costs indicated for appendectomy and craniotomy are $\frac{6097.3}{5372.6} =$ 113.5, an increase in average benefit cost of 13.5 percent. This amounts to an average of the increase in benefit cost for each of the procedures, weighted by the relative frequency of each procedure. Since there are hundreds of procedures, the computation is time-consuming. However, it may be simplified by considering only the 10 to 15 most frequent procedures, since these account for most of the premium. If there were reason to believe that the probability of having an operation would be affected by the change in schedule, further adjustment would be required.

The process is carried out usually at least four times: for adult males; adult females; maternity and obstetrical claims; and children. The illustrative figures above are for all nonobstetrical claims combined. Often an additional distinction is made between female employees and dependent spouses. As in hospital insurance, no further distinction is generally made in regard to age, except where coverage is to be extended to extreme ages, in group policies where an undue proportion of the exposure is at the higher ages, or in individual guaranteed renewable contracts.

Companies operating over a wide geographical range may wish to take into consideration geographical differences in benefit costs. This becomes more important as the maximum benefit increases and is most important for the full-service type contracts. However, these are primarily issued by Blue Shield and independent plans which are concentrated in a rather small area.

---

[17] *Ibid., passim.* The relative frequency is the probability of *this* procedure for a claimant who has some type of operation.

*Medical expense insurance.* Medical expense insurance is relatively new, and data are scarce. The experience of several companies with various types of medical expense benefit has been published and may serve as a basis for premium computation. Generally speaking, initial rates were set largely on a judgment basis, and modifications have usually been made on a loss ratio basis. This method is also used by many insurers offering surgical and medical benefits under a single contract, such as the Blue Shield organizations.

*Major medical benefits.* Major medical benefits are the most recent type of health insurance, and most data pertain to individual company studies. One of these, published in 1951,[18] analyzed the experience of a large life insurance company's employees and provided the basis for most initial pure premium calculations. As experience becomes greater, most companies active in the field are developing and utilizing their own statistics. Generally speaking, claim costs are developed by five-year age groups for male and female employees, dependent wives, and children for the combinations of deductibles and upper limits in use. Employee claim costs increase greatly with age, and dependent claim costs increase considerably. Thus it becomes necessary to make use of a step-rate or level premium approach. In individual policies a level premium is computed,[19] while in group insurance the age distribution of the insured members is considered in the premium structure.

Claim costs also increase with income. Income level enters into the rate-making process in group insurance but rarely in individual. The underwriting process in individual insurance should include an adjustment of deductible and upper limit consistent with income level. In group policies, a schedule of deductibles, or, more rarely, upper limits may take care of this process. Then, when claim costs are developed for the various upper-limit and deductible combinations based on actual experience, income differentials will be considered automatically. Moreover, there is considerable correlation of income level with age, and premiums graded by age largely will reflect variations by income level. In some group plans an addition is made to premium when an unduly large number of insureds earn more than (say) $10,000 per year.

Adjustment of the premium rate computation is, of course, necessary for different amounts and different methods of applying the deductible and upper limit. An analysis of a representative sample of claims will indicate the nature and magnitude of these adjustments. Variations in

---

[18] Alan M. Thaler, "Group Major Medical Expense Insurance," *Transactions of the Society of Actuaries*, Vol. III, p. 48. See also Morton D. Miller "Gross Premiums for Individual and Family Major Medical Expense Insurance," *Transactions of the Society of Actuaries*, Vol. VII, p. 1.

[19] See below, pp. 587 ff., for a discussion of level premium computation.

the percentage participation (coinsurance) requirement will also affect the level of claims, but probably considerably less than proportionately. This is a question which requires more study and analysis. Geographical variation will also affect claim costs, as in the basic medical care benefits, and to a much greater degree. Of course, not all companies recognize all these factors in their rate structures, but, as experience develops, the tendency seems to be to include more factors and develop more equitable, although more complex, rate structures.[20]

*Comprehensive medical expense benefits.* Since comprehensive benefits include hospital, surgical, basic medical, and major medical, initial premium rates were developed from those for the separate benefits. The first intercompany experience was published in 1962,[21] and other studies have appeared subsequently.[22] Tabular claim costs vary with the applicability of deductible, amount of deductible, participation percentage, amount of fully covered hospital expense, age and sex, coverage of dependents, area, private room limit, integration with California Unemployment Compensation Disability benefit, and amount of maternity benefit. Ratios of actual to tabular claims are published periodically. Premiums may be derived for a particular plan by adjusting its tabular cost for experience and projected trend.

*Disability income benefits.* In disability income benefits, an agreed amount is paid for each period of disability. Thus the severity of claims depends directly on the duration of disability within the limits of coverage as defined by the waiting period and maximum benefit period. Where the maximum benefit period is longer than one year, the interest on the future benefit payments should be considered, and the average claim becomes the present value of a disability annuity due. For benefit periods of a year or less, interest is disregarded, and many companies disregard it for benefit periods of several years.

The duration of disability may be expressed in terms of a continuance table similar to that used for the duration of hospital claims above. Where the exposure is known and interest is to be ignored, such a table

---

[20] For a discussion of the problems of analyzing experience and developing major medical premiums, see Charles A. Siegfried, "Some Considerations Involved in the Analysis of Major Medical Expense Insurance Experience," *Transactions of the Society of Actuaries*, Vol. X, pp. 505–30. For an example of as study of one insurer see Lowell M. Dorn, "New York Life Morbidity Experience under Individual and Family Major Medical Policies," *Transactions of the Society of Actuaries*, Vol. XV, p. 275.

[21] S. W. Gingery and R. W. Mellman, "An Investigation of Group Major Medical Expense Insurance," *Transactions of the Society of Actuaries*, Vol. XIII, p. 513.

[22] Burton E. Burton and Daniel W. Pettingill, "Development of Expected Claim Costs for Comprehensive Medical Expense Benefits and Ratios of 1959 and 1960 Actual Experience Thereto," *Transactions of the Society of Actuaries*, Vol. XV, p. 10 and discussion, p. 49; Committee on Experience under Group Health Insurance, "Group Comprehensive Medical Expense Benefits Insurance," *Transactions of the Society of Actuaries*, 1965 Reports Number, p. 186 and 1966 Reports Number, p. 143.

may be used directly for premium computation. In some cases the table will be developed for various ages of exposure and in other cases for all exposed ages grouped together. The latter approach is common in group insurance. The classic example of such a table is the conference

TABLE 18–2

Continuance Table Based on Conference Modification of Class
(3) Disability Rates: Disablement Commencing at Age 40 per
100,000 Lives Exposed

| Days<br>m | No. Disabled<br>Exactly m<br>Days | No. Disabled<br>m Days or<br>Longer | No. Days of<br>Disability<br>Suffered Through<br>mth Day<br>$S^0_{(40)}/\frac{m}{365} =$ |
|---|---|---|---|
|  |  | $\sum\limits_{m}^{\omega} (2)$ | $\sum\limits_{1}^{m} (3)$ |
| (1) | (2) | (3) | (4) |
| 1................1,410 | | 32,810 | 32,810 |
| 2................1,810 | | 31,400 | 64,210 |
| 3................2,010 | | 29,590 | 93,800 |
| 4................2,120 | | 27,580 | 121,380 |
| 5................2,020 | | 25,460 | 146,840 |
| 6................1,830 | | 23,440 | 170,280 |
| 7................1,510 | | 21,610 | 191,890 |
| 8................1,480 | | 20,100 | 211,990 |
| 9................1,210 | | 18,620 | 230,610 |
| 10................1,090 | | 17,410 | 248,020 |
| ... | .... | ..... | ...... |
| 70.................. 38 | | 1,800 | 572,667 |
| 71.................. 36 | | 1,762 | 574,429 |
| 72.................. 34 | | 1,726 | 576,155 |
| 73.................. 32 | | 1,692 | 577,847 |
| 74.................. 31 | | 1,660 | 579,507 |
| 75.................. 30 | | 1,629 | 581,136 |
| 76.................. 29 | | 1,599 | 582,735 |
| 77.................. 27 | | 1,570 | 584,305 |
| 78.................. 26 | | 1,543 | 585,848 |

Source: Health and Accident Underwriters Conference.

modification of the Class 3 disability tables derived from the Society of Actuaries study in 1926. A portion of this table is reproduced in Table 18–2.

This table is similar to the hospital continuance table (Table 18–1). Columns 1 and 2 of this table correspond to columns 1 and 2 of the hospital table. Column 4 is developed from column 3, which represents the number disabled m days or longer. Column 3 is formed by summing column 2 from the end of the table up to m, and column 4 is developed by summing column 3 from the first day through m. Thus it represents the total number of days which will be paid for disability of m days or less duration.

This can be used directly to compute premiums. For example, to find a premium at age 40 for a 70-day benefit following a 7-day waiting period, one just subtracts the amount of disability for 7 days, 191,890, from the amount suffered through the 77th day, 584,305, and divides by the exposure, 100,000. This equals $3.92415 for a benefit of $1 per day. It is easy to adjust this for any amount of benefit.

In standard actuarial notation, the symbol $s_{(x)}^{n/t}$ indicates the average or expected period of disability during the first t years following the first n years of disability. This is equivalent to the disability incurred in the first t + n years less that incurred in the first n years. (Using n to indicate the number of years and m to indicate the number of days implicitly makes m = 365n.) The values are expressed in terms of 100,000 lives exposed and are specific for disablement commencing at age x (40 in the illustration.)

In the illustration, the premium for a benefit of 70 days following a 7-day waiting period,

$$P^{\frac{7}{365}/\frac{77}{365}} \cong s_{(40)}^{\frac{7}{365}/\frac{77}{365}} \div 100{,}000$$

$$\cong \frac{s_{(40)}^{0/\frac{77}{365}} - s_{(40)}^{0/\frac{7}{365}}}{100{,}000}$$

$$\cong \frac{584{,}305 - 191{,}890}{100{,}000}$$

$$\cong \$3.92$$

Where premiums are paid annually in advance, it is common to discount this value for one-half year interest and mortality. Where premiums are payable monthly, this refinement usually is omitted. This method combines severity with frequency and yields the premium directly. For the possible use of the reader, a more modern basic continuance table is reproduced as Table 18–3. This shows lower claim rates for short durations and higher for long durations than the Conference Modification. The figures in Table 18–3 correspond to those in column 2 of Table 18–2.

Sometimes the continuance table is converted into a table showing premium costs directly for the various durations. This is accomplished merely by multiplying the amount of disability in days by the appropriate amount of benefit, and expressing the result as an annual premium cost per (say) $1 of benefit a week. It may be more convenient to have the results in the form of monthly premiums. This merely involves dividing by 12 if no allowance is to be made for interest and collection expense. Table 18–4, used frequently in group insurance, is

## TABLE 18-3

## 1964 Commissioners Disability Table; Basic Continuance Table: Lives Disabled from Date of Disablement, by Duration; 100,000 Active Lives Exposed at Each Age

| Duration: Yr. | Mo. | Day | Age at beginning of policy year in which disablement occurs | | | | | | | | | | |
|---|---|---|---|---|---|---|---|---|---|---|---|---|---|
| | | | 22 | 27 | 32 | 37 | 42 | 47 | 52 | 57 | 62 | 67 | 72 |
| 0 | | 8 | 10807 | 10579 | 11604 | 12621 | 13721 | 14957 | 16384 | 18115 | 20162 | 22704 | 26014 |
| | | 9 | 10295 | 10173 | 11082 | 12085 | 13178 | 14414 | 15849 | 17592 | 19648 | 22198 | 25546 |
| | | 10 | 9807 | 9691 | 10583 | 11571 | 12656 | 13891 | 15331 | 17084 | 19146 | 21704 | 25087 |
| | | 11 | 9342 | 9232 | 10107 | 11079 | 12155 | 13387 | 14830 | 16591 | 18657 | 21222 | 24637 |
| | | 12 | 8899 | 8794 | 9652 | 10608 | 11674 | 12901 | 14346 | 16112 | 18180 | 20751 | 24196 |
| | | 13 | 8477 | 8377 | 9218 | 10157 | 11212 | 12433 | 13878 | 15647 | 17716 | 20292 | 23763 |
| | | 14 | 8075 | 7980 | 8803 | 9725 | 10768 | 11982 | 13425 | 15196 | 17264 | 19845 | 23339 |
| | | 15 | 7692 | 7502 | 8407 | 9312 | 10342 | 11547 | 12987 | 14759 | 16824 | 19410 | 22924 |
| | | 16 | 7327 | 7242 | 8029 | 8916 | 9932 | 11128 | 12565 | 14336 | 16397 | 18987 | 22517 |
| | | 17 | 6983 | 6902 | 7668 | 8537 | 9543 | 10730 | 12159 | 13927 | 15983 | 18576 | 22119 |
| | | 18 | 6659 | 6582 | 7323 | 8174 | 9173 | 10350 | 11769 | 13532 | 15582 | 18177 | 21729 |
| | | 19 | 6353 | 6280 | 6993 | 7827 | 8821 | 9986 | 11395 | 13151 | 15194 | 17789 | 21348 |
| | | 20 | 6055 | 5995 | 6678 | 7494 | 8486 | 9637 | 11036 | 12784 | 14819 | 17412 | 20975 |
| | | 21 | 5793 | 5726 | 6384 | 7181 | 8167 | 9305 | 10692 | 12431 | 14457 | 17046 | 20611 |
| | | 22 | 5536 | 5472 | 6107 | 6886 | 7863 | 8990 | 10363 | 12092 | 14108 | 16690 | 20255 |
| | | 23 | 5293 | 5232 | 5846 | 6609 | 7574 | 8688 | 10047 | 11766 | 13772 | 16345 | 19908 |
| | | 24 | 5063 | 5005 | 5599 | 6347 | 7298 | 8400 | 9743 | 11453 | 13449 | 16010 | 19569 |
| | | 25 | 4846 | 4790 | 5366 | 6098 | 7035 | 8125 | 9451 | 11153 | 13138 | 15685 | 19238 |
| | | 26 | 4641 | 4587 | 5145 | 5862 | 6785 | 7863 | 9171 | 10865 | 12838 | 15370 | 18916 |
| | | 27 | 4447 | 4395 | 4935 | 5638 | 6545 | 7612 | 8902 | 10588 | 12548 | 15065 | 18603 |
| | | 28 | 4253 | 4213 | 4738 | 5425 | 6318 | 7371 | 8644 | 10321 | 12268 | 14769 | 18298 |
| | | 29 | 4089 | 4041 | 4550 | 5223 | 6101 | 7140 | 8396 | 10054 | 11998 | 14483 | 18000 |
| 1 | | | 3923 | 3877 | 4372 | 5029 | 5895 | 6918 | 8158 | 9816 | 11737 | 14206 | 11710 |
| 2 | | | 1412 | 1396 | 1618 | 1961 | 2417 | 3048 | 3820 | 4931 | 6462 | 8550 | 11860 |
| 3 | | | 664 | 657 | 778 | 981 | 1257 | 1676 | 2239 | 3110 | 4427 | 6324 | 9629 |
| 4 | | | 367 | 363 | 432 | 547 | 730 | 1020 | 1447 | 2158 | 3317 | 5182 | 8690 |
| 5 | | | 231 | 229 | 273 | 347 | 476 | 692 | 1029 | 1630 | 2656 | 4472 | 8137 |

| | | | | | | | | | | |
|---|---|---|---|---|---|---|---|---|---|---|
| 162 | 161 | 192 | 245 | 343 | 515 | 793 | 1327 | 2264 | 4022 | 7731 |
| 125 | 124 | 149 | 190 | 270 | 417 | 659 | 1145 | 2017 | 3706 | 7355 |
| 105 | 104 | 126 | 161 | 231 | 365 | 587 | 1039 | 1850 | 3488 | 7004 |
| 93 | 92 | 112 | 144 | 208 | 334 | 537 | 970 | 1729 | 3309 | 6675 |
| 85 | 84 | 103 | 133 | 191 | 310 | 505 | 919 | 1633 | 3148 | 6365 |
| 79 | 78 | 96 | 125 | 180 | 295 | 481 | 877 | 1558 | 2999 | 6070 |
| 75 | 74 | 91 | 119 | 172 | 283 | 463 | 842 | 1491 | 2865 | 5789 |
| 72 | 71 | 87 | 115 | 166 | 274 | 451 | 825 | 1467 | 2822 | 5709 |
| 69 | 68 | 84 | 111 | 161 | 267 | 440 | 811 | 1445 | 2783 | 5634 |
| 66 | 66 | 81 | 107 | 155 | 260 | 431 | 797 | 1425 | 2746 | 5563 |
| 64 | 64 | 79 | 104 | 152 | 254 | 422 | 785 | 1406 | 2711 | 5496 |
| 62 | 62 | 77 | 101 | 148 | 248 | 415 | 773 | 1389 | 2679 | 5433 |
| 60 | 60 | 74 | 99 | 145 | 243 | 407 | 763 | 1372 | 2648 | 5375 |
| 58 | 58 | 73 | 96 | 142 | 238 | 401 | 752 | 1356 | 2620 | 5320 |
| 56 | 57 | 71 | 94 | 139 | 234 | 394 | 743 | 1341 | 2593 | 5269 |
| 55 | 55 | 69 | 92 | 136 | 230 | 389 | 734 | 1327 | 2567 | 5221 |
| 53 | 54 | 68 | 90 | 134 | 226 | 383 | 725 | 1312 | 2542 | 5178 |
| 52 | 53 | 66 | 89 | 131 | 223 | 378 | 716 | 1299 | 2519 | 5137 |
| 51 | 52 | 65 | 87 | 129 | 219 | 372 | 707 | 1286 | 2497 | 5100 |
| 39 | 40 | 51 | 70 | 107 | 185 | 319 | 617 | 1131 | 2203 | 4512 |
| 32 | 33 | 44 | 61 | 93 | 163 | 285 | 552 | 1010 | 1961 | 4004 |
| 27 | 29 | 39 | 55 | 85 | 149 | 260 | 501 | 910 | 1756 | 3532 |
| 24 | 26 | 35 | 50 | 78 | 138 | 240 | 459 | 825 | 1578 | 3096 |
| 21 | 24 | 32 | 47 | 73 | 128 | 222 | 422 | 750 | 1415 | 2695 |
| 19 | 22 | 30 | 44 | 68 | 120 | 206 | 388 | 681 | 1265 | 2325 |
| 18 | 20 | 28 | 41 | 64 | 112 | 191 | 357 | 618 | 1125 | 1987 |
| 16 | 19 | 26 | 38 | 60 | 105 | 178 | 328 | 558 | 995 | 1677 |
| 15 | 18 | 25 | 36 | 57 | 98 | 166 | 302 | 504 | 874 | 1397 |
| 14 | 16 | 23 | 34 | 54 | 93 | 155 | 278 | 455 | 762 | 1146 |
| 13 | 15 | 22 | 32 | 51 | 87 | 144 | 255 | 409 | 658 | 928 |
| 12 | 14 | 21 | 30 | 48 | 82 | 134 | 234 | 366 | 563 | 734 |
| 12 | 14 | 19 | 29 | 46 | 77 | 125 | 215 | 326 | 475 | 571 |

Source: Health Insurance Association of America, 1964 Commissioners Disability Table, Vol. III, Committee Recommendations and Basic Tables.

TABLE 18-4

1947–49 Basic Morbidity Table for Males, Group Accident and Sickness Insurance

| Duration | Tabular Cost per $1 of Weekly Benefit for Duration of Disability t or Less | | Duration | Tabular Cost per $1 of Weekly Benefit for Duration of Disability t or Less | |
|---|---|---|---|---|---|
| t | Annual | Monthly | t | Annual | Monthly |
| 1 day............... | $0.0279 | $0.0023 | 17 weeks............ | $0.7030 | $0.0586 |
| 2 days.............. | .0553 | .0046 | 18 weeks............ | .7160 | .0597 |
| 3 days.............. | .0820 | .0068 | 19 weeks............ | .7284 | .0607 |
| 4 days.............. | .1078 | .0090 | 20 weeks............ | .7402 | .0617 |
| 5 days.............. | .1326 | .0110 | 21 weeks............ | .7515 | .0626 |
| 6 days.............. | .1564 | .0130 | 22 weeks............ | .7623 | .0635 |
| 7 days.............. | .1790 | .0149 | 23 weeks............ | .7726 | .0644 |
| 8 days.............. | .1999 | .0167 | 24 weeks............ | .7825 | .0652 |
| 9 days.............. | .2191 | .0183 | 25 weeks............ | .7920 | .0660 |
| 10 days............. | .2365 | .0197 | 25 weeks............ | .8011 | .0668 |
| 11 days............. | .2519 | .0210 | 26 weeks, 3 days..... | .8049 | .0671 |
| 12 days............. | .2659 | .0222 | 27 weeks............ | .8099 | .0675 |
| 13 days............. | .2788 | .0232 | 28 weeks............ | .8184 | .0682 |
| 14 days............. | .2908 | .0242 | 29 weeks............ | .8266 | .0689 |
| 15 days............. | .3021 | .0252 | 30 weeks............ | .8345 | .0695 |
| 16 days............. | .3129 | .0261 | 31 weeks............ | .8422 | .0702 |
| 17 days............. | .3233 | .0269 | 32 weeks............ | .8496 | .0708 |
| 18 days............. | .3333 | .0278 | 33 weeks............ | .8568 | .0714 |
| 19 days............. | .3430 | .0286 | 34 weeks............ | .8638 | .0720 |
| 20 days............. | .3524 | .0294 | 35 weeks............ | .8706 | .0725 |
| 21 days............. | .3615 | .0301 | 36 weeks............ | .8772 | .0731 |
| 22 days............. | .3703 | .0309 | 37 weeks............ | .8836 | .0736 |
| 23 days............. | .3788 | .0316 | 38 weeks............ | .8899 | .0742 |
| 24 days............. | .3870 | .0322 | 39 weeks............ | .8960 | .0747 |
| 25 days............. | .3949 | .0329 | 40 weeks............ | .9020 | .0752 |
| 26 days............. | .4025 | .0335 | 41 weeks............ | .9078 | .0756 |
| 27 days............. | .4099 | .0342 | 42 weeks............ | .9135 | .0761 |
| 28 days............. | .4171 | .0348 | 43 weeks............ | .9191 | .0766 |
| 29 days............. | .4241 | .0353 | 44 weeks............ | .9246 | .0770 |
| 30 days............. | .4309 | .0359 | 45 weeks............ | .9300 | .0775 |
| 31 days............. | .4375 | .0365 | 46 weeks............ | .9352 | .0779 |
| 32 days............. | .4439 | .0370 | 47 weeks............ | .9403 | .0784 |
| 33 days............. | .4501 | .0375 | 48 weeks............ | .9453 | .0788 |
| 34 days............. | .4561 | .0380 | 49 weeks............ | .9502 | .0792 |
| 35 days............. | .4619 | .0385 | 50 weeks............ | .9550 | .0796 |
| 6 weeks............. | .4977 | .0415 | 51 weeks............ | .9598 | .0800 |
| 7 weeks............. | .5265 | .0439 | 52 weeks............ | .9645 | .0804 |
| 8 weeks............. | .5505 | .0459 | 52 weeks, 3 days..... | .9665 | .0805 |
| 9 weeks............. | .5718 | .0476 | 53 weeks............ | .9691 | .0808 |
| 10 weeks............ | .5914 | .0493 | 54 weeks............ | .9736 | .0811 |
| 11 weeks............ | .6099 | .0508 | 55 weeks............ | .9780 | .0815 |
| 12 weeks............ | .6274 | .0523 | 56 weeks............ | .9824 | .0819 |
| 13 weeks............ | .6440 | .0537 | 57 weeks............ | .9867 | .0822 |
| 13 weeks, 3 days..... | .6508 | .0542 | 58 weeks............ | .9909 | .0826 |
| 14 weeks............ | .6598 | .0550 | 59 weeks............ | .9950 | .0829 |
| 15 weeks............ | .6749 | .0562 | 60 weeks............ | 0.9991 | 0.0833 |
| 16 weeks............ | 0.6893 | 0.0574 | | | |

Source: Morton D. Miller, "Group Weekly Indemnity Continuation Table Study," *Transactions of the Society of Actuaries*, Vol. III (1951), p. 55.

of this type. Only the final columns are given, since these are all that is required for premium calculation. All ages of exposure are combined.

According to this table, the annual premium for a $1 per week benefit with maximum period of 70 days (10 weeks) after a waiting period of 7 days is obtained by subtracting the tabular claim cost for a 7-day benefit, 0.1790, from that of an 11-week benefit, 0.6099. This equals 0.4209. If this is multiplied by 7 it yields the net premium for a benefit amount of $1 per day of $2.9463.

This result differs from the illustration above, where the comparable premium equaled $3.92, because the former was specific to age 40, while the latter represents all ages of exposure. Moreover, the tables were drawn from different types of exposure under different types of policy and represent periods of exposure about 25 years apart.

Where benefits are payable over a period of years, the average claim cost becomes the present value of a disability annuity due, since it is no longer equitable to ignore interest. Such an annuity represents a benefit payable periodically to a disabled annuitant until he dies or recovers or until the maximum benefit is paid. The present value is computed by discounting each future payment for interest, mortality, and the probability of recovery. Commonly, probabilities of death and recovery are combined into termination rates, which are then used to compute the present value in the same way as death rates are used in a conventional life annuity. The term premium then becomes $P_x^1 = r_x \ddot{a}_x^1$, where $r_x$ is the rate of disability and $\ddot{a}_x^1$ is the present value of the disabled life annuity due. The development of this in terms of actuarial notation is beyond the scope of this volume.[23]

## Level premium computation

Up to this point the discussion has been confined to the development of term premiums. These represent the cost of protection for a single year. Where the term premiums vary greatly with age, as in long-term disability income policies and major medical contracts, it becomes impractical simply to use the average term premium for all ages of entry. This would involve overcharging the younger insureds and undercharging the older ones, with consequent adverse selection. Moreover, the more steeply the term premiums increase with age, the more significant the factor of interest becomes.

There are several approaches to this problem. One is to use premiums which increase with each annual renewal, so that the insured is always paying the current term rate. Another is to have the premium increase each (say) five years according to a step-rate plan. The dis-

---

[23] See Cueto, *op. cit.*, for a rather sophisticated explanation of the process. In practice, the discount for one-half year interest and mortality usually is included, as discussed above.

advantage of these is that, as renewal premiums rise, so will the lapse rate, with consequent adverse selection. Another approach would be to reduce progressively the benefits of the policy, permitting the premium to remain the same. This is likely to produce considerable customer dissatisfaction as well as adverse selection. However, this occurs automatically in disability income contracts paying benefits to a fixed future age or date such as age 65, and no one seems to mind.

The fourth approach is to compute a level premium which will be payable throughout the period of coverage. This involves establishing a reserve on the insurance for each policyholder and accumulating an equivalent amount of assets as the excessive payments of earlier years are accumulated to provide for the excessive costs of protection in later years.[24] Fairness would seem to demand that the policyholder's equity be recognized by making the contract explicitly or implicitly noncancellable or guaranteed renewable or by granting a cash value to those who surrender or are refused renewal by the company.

Most contracts where such level premiums are used either guarantee renewal or contain the provision that renewal will not be refused because of the health of the individual insured. Cash values are extremely rare, however. Most companies seem to feel that the lapse rate is high enough already without encouraging further lapses by granting any surrender value. Moreover, premiums may be discounted in advance for future withdrawals.

The computation of level premiums is similar to the process used in life insurance. The term premiums are discounted for interest and mortality to derive a net single premium. This is then divided by the present value of an annuity due for the premium-paying period in order to obtain the net level premium. As in life insurance, commutation columns have been developed to simplify the process of computation, but the derivation and use of these are beyond the scope of this book.

In long-term guaranteed renewable medical expense coverage, it becomes necessary to allow for future increases in the cost of medical care. If such increases in average benefit cost are projected at a high enough rate of increase and far enough into the future, the resulting level premium for a young insured may be more than that for an older insured.[25] For example, the premium for a man buying coverage at age 40 in 1968 might be higher than that for a man buying equivalent

---

[24] Technically, the reserve is set aside for the block of business, not for the individual, since the latter theoretically would involve a prognosis of each individual's future health costs. Unless the premium is sufficient to provide offsetting assets, the establishment of the reserve will decrease the insurer's surplus. See below, pp. 606–609 for a discussion of the level premium reserve.

[25] M. Eugene Blumenfeld, "Recent Trends and Innovations in Individual Hospital Insurance," *Proceedings of the Casualty Actuarial Society*, Vol. XLVIII, p. 83.

coverage in 1968 at age 55. However, it would be less than the projected premium for a man buying the same coverage at age 55 in 1983. The assumption of constantly increasing benefit cost makes premiums, reserves, and related values specific to the year of policy issuance as well as to the age. Such an assumption also may produce premiums which are too high to be competitive.[26]

**Pure premium classification**

In order to achieve equity among policyholders, it is necessary that classes be established to reflect differences in the probability of loss and probable amount of loss. Sometimes the classification process takes place during the computation of premiums from the experience data, as indicated above. In such a case, the data are divided according to the classification criteria, and separate pure premiums are computed for each class.

In many cases, however, the data are too few for there to be any great credibility if there are many subdivisions. In such cases the pure premium is computed for a "standard" case, and differentials are applied to this "standard" in order to develop premiums for other classes. For example, premiums might be computed for males of the best occupation class, and then extra charges might be added for females and for more hazardous occupations. Regardless of the techniques used, the result will be a set of premium rates applicable to various classifications. The method of handling these classifications differs considerably between individual and group insurance.

*Individual insurance.* In individual insurance, each individual or family will be charged the premium rate applicable to his classification. The bases of classification vary with the type of policy under consideration. In limited accident policies there is only one insurable class, and all insureds pay the same rate. The policy excludes certain hazardous occupations and activities. In industrial policies the premium will vary with sex and (usually) with age. In commercial disability income policies the premium varies with sex and occupation and less often with age except beyond (say) age 45. Noncancellable and guaranteed renewable disability income policies and life insurance disability riders usually have level premiums graded according to age of issue, higher premiums for women (if written at all), and are further graded by occupation.

The basic medical care policies (hospital, surgical, and medical) usually do not have premium differentials for age, except at advanced

---

[26] E. Paul Barnhart, "Adjustment of Premiums under Guaranteed Renewable Policies," *Transactions of the Society of Actuaries,* Vol. XII, p. 472 at 484.

ages and to distinguish between adults and children. However, premium rates may be graded by age, and usually are on noncancellable and guaranteed renewable forms. They usually do have higher premiums for women, certainly if maternity and obstetric benefits are included. Premiums may vary with occupation, but usually do not.

Major medical policy premiums are usually graded by age for male and female separately, but all children are charged the same rate. The premiums are on a level premium basis in most cases, and higher rates are charged for the more hazardous occupations. Underwriting rules generally require higher deductibles for higher family income classes, but the premium structure as such only occasionally recognizes income. Many insurers now vary major medical premiums by territory or area.

*Group insurance.* In group insurance the problem is not one of assigning individuals to appropriate classifications but of determining an equitable premium to charge the insured group as a whole. Since the insurer has the right to revise rates for the group annually and since the larger groups are subject to experience rating or entitled to dividends, there is less need than there would be otherwise for accuracy in initial rating. The initial rating is designed to determine a tentative rate which will be revised periodically. Sometimes it seems that the initial rate is designed primarily to attract business rather than to produce a profit in the first year. Indeed, annual statements of many insurers show heavy losses on group health insurance year after year.

Generally, group rates are computed from basic experience tables developed for male workers in moderate-sized groups in nonhazardous occupations. Then they are increased to allow for dependent coverage, excessive female representation in the group, extra-hazardous industry, and an excessive proportion of older insureds, and discounted for larger size of group. For major medical insurance the income distribution of the employees is considered, and an extra charge is imposed if an undue proportion of insureds are at high-income levels. No female or age charges are required for accidental death and dismemberment. For the medical care coverages, especially major medical, differentials to reflect geographical differences in claim costs are common.

The extra charge for dependent coverage is independent of industry or age, and female coverage is implicit in the definition of dependent. Insurance companies use three bases of computing and applying these extra charges for dependents:

1. Single-rate basis—one extra charge for dependent coverage, regardless of the number of dependents.
2. Two-rate basis—one class for a single dependent, and one class for more than one dependent.
3. Three-rate basis—one class—spouse only; one class—child or children only; one class—spouse and child or children.

Blue Cross and Blue Shield plans usually use the first of these bases. Unlike the individual "family group" policies, there is no extra charge under any of these bases for children beyond the first. The more refined the rate structure, the more equitable the plan becomes as between different employees. However, the record keeping becomes correspondingly more complex. These factors must be equated; obviously, the larger the proportion of the premium paid by the employer, the less important equity between employees becomes. In an employer-pay-all plan the crudest rate base for dependent coverage will be adequate.

## Loading

"Loading" is the term used to refer to the amount added to pure premium to provide for expenses of operation, contingencies, and profit. The determination of an appropriate loading for the expense items is primarily a matter of cost accounting. The various expenses should be allocated to the various types of policy on as equitable a basis as possible. Direct expenses, such as commissions and premium taxes, should vary rather directly with the amount of premium. Investment expenses generally are deducted from investment income, and claim adjustment expenses are added to claims.

General administrative expenses must be allocated among the various classes of business on some fair basis. Many lines are treated like casualty insurance, with the loading a constant percentage of gross premium. This is particularly true where level commissions are payable to the agent throughout the life of the contract. Where unlevel commissions are used, it is more common to load in the form of a constant plus a percentage, in a fashion similar to that used in life insurance. For guaranteed renewable policies and life insurance riders it is common to develop a gross premium formula which recognizes the time incidence of the various types of expense and discounts them for mortality and interest and (usually) lapsation in order to produce a gross level premium. With a computer, net and gross premiums may be produced simultaneously.[27]

The proper allowance for contingencies and profit is difficult to determine. In order for the industry to survive, it must provide a satisfactory return on capital invested and produce enough earnings to permit expansion. The contingency funds should be large enough to absorb all likely fluctuations in claim rates. The older and more established the line, the greater the volume of business and the smaller the average

[27] O. D. Dickerson, "Mortgage Disability Insurance—A Case Study in Risk Theory," *Annals of the Society of Chartered Property Casualty Underwriters,* Summer, 1963, p. 163.

claim in relation to premium; and the larger the resources of the issuing company, the lower the contingency allowance in premium need be. Sometimes a specific allowance for contingencies is included; more frequently the same effect is produced by having a margin of safety in each of the factors involved in the premium computation. The margin of safety in participating policies or group policies subject to experience rating may properly be larger than in nonparticipating contracts. In addition to allowing for general contingencies, it may be wise to allow for secular trend, particularly in the expense covers where the trend is clearly upward. On the other side of the picture is the well-known phenomenon that disability income claim rates increase materially in

TABLE 18-5

Group Health Insurance Premium Discounts

| Monthly Premium before Adjustment | Percentage Reduction from Manual Rate |
|---|---|
| $  500–   750............................................. | 3 |
| 750– 2,500............................................. | 5 |
| 2,500– 3,000............................................. | 6 |
| 3,000– 3,500............................................. | 7 |
| 3,500– 4,000............................................. | 8 |
| 4,000– 5,000............................................. | 9 |
| 5,000– 7,500............................................. | 10 |
| 7,500–10,000............................................. | 11 |
| 10,000–15,000............................................. | 12 |
| 15,000–20,000............................................. | 13 |
| 20,000–25,000............................................. | 14 |
| 25,000 or more........................................... | 15 |

periods of depression. It is well to allow a certain margin of safety for this eventuality.

The process of loading is essentially the same under group and individual policies, except that the actual levels of loading reflect differences in cost between group and individual. Manual rates are computed for small groups, and additional discounts in premium are allowed the larger groups. Table 18-5 is typical of the discount schedules used. However, variation between companies is great, since initial premium levels and loss and expense figures differ.

### Dividends and experience rating

*General.* Mutual companies are owned and controlled by their policyholders, and the policyholders are entitled to share in the profits of the company through policy dividends. However, most individual health insurance policies have been issued on a nonparticipating basis.

Thus the holders of these policies do not share in ownership or profits. The entry of most of the large mutual life insurance companies into the health insurance business has given considerable impetus to the issuance of participating policies. However, because of the upward trend of medical care costs, dividends are more likely on disability income contracts than on medical care contracts.

Group health insurance policies issued by mutual companies are almost always on a participating basis, and the policyholders may expect to receive dividends. In order to compete more effectively with the mutual companies, the stock companies have developed a variety of schemes for retrospective and prospective premium refunds and discounts which are intended to reflect the profitability of the individual group case. Recently, so have many Blue Cross and Blue Shield plans. These schemes are referred to as "experience rating devices." They are used retrospectively to determine refunds and prospectively for renewal rating (usually upward). In prospective renewal rating for medical expense benefits, a trend factor should be used to reflect anticipated increases in unit charges.

The concepts underlying both dividends and experience rating are similar, but may differ somewhat in basic philosophy. The primary object of experience rating is to rerate the business in conformity with the financial stability of the insurer and its competitive position in the industry. In addition, the mutual company, in its dividend apportionment, will attempt to distribute its available earnings to various classes of policyholders in proportion to their respective contributions to these earnings. This difference in philosophy will tend to produce differences in the contributions of various classes to contingency reserves and profits. However, competition will tend to produce a fairly uniform pattern of resultant rates. Whatever the basic philosophy, the process should take into consideration the contribution of the policyholder or class to surplus, the degree of pooling of losses and expenses necessary between policyholders or classes, and the total surplus available for distribution.

Theoretically, the appropriate dividend or premium refund is equal to the accumulated premiums paid less the accumulated losses, expenses, and contributions to contingencies and (for a stock company) profits of each individual case. For the larger group cases it is practical to develop this amount for each case on an asset share basis. This involves the accumulation from original date of issue of actual premiums to which interest earnings may be added. From these are deducted accumulated actual losses incurred and accumulated expenses directly incurred and allocated to the case, including allowances for contingencies and sometimes for profit. From this the total dividends paid on the case in the past are deducted, and the result is the amount available for distribution. Interest earnings are usually ignored for health insurance because most coverages are on a term basis. However, on policies written on a level premium basis they are of sufficient magnitude to warrant consideration.

*Individual policies.* It is impractical to perform such an asset share computation for each individual policy. However, policies may be grouped into classes of similar type, duration, and, perhaps, age at issue, and asset shares attributable to the class may be computed. The actual dividend formula should be simple in application and will usually be a direct proportion of premium, varying only with type of policy and perhaps duration. The asset share calculation serves as a guide to this formula rather than producing it directly. Usually dividends are not paid until policies have been in force for two or three years.

*Small groups—tabular method.* For small group cases, an approach similar to that used in individual insurance is employed. The amount distributable to such groups will be determined by asset share calculations applied to classes of groups, and the apportionment will be made according to tables which reflect only a limited number of variables. These refunds are expressed as a percentage of premium, and the factors may include amount of premium, claim rate, and policy duration as well as type of coverage. In these small groups the individual loss experience will have a rather low credibility. Moreover, the expenses, especially for acquisition, will be relatively higher than in large groups. However, because these groups have not received a large premium discount for size, the redundancy in premium may be greater proportionally than for many large groups.

*Larger groups—asset share formulas.* The asset share approach will be applied to larger groups and often to classes of smaller groups and individual policies. As indicated above, the formula used will attempt to determine the fair share of divisible surplus to be allocated to each group and class. The process is complicated by four major problems— expense allocations, contingency charges, loss limits and insurance charges, and credibility.

The problem of expense allocation is primarily one of cost accounting. The final formula should be relatively simple in application. For smaller groups it may be merely the application of single percentage and constant charges to the premiums developed. A separation will generally be made between acquisition and other expenses. For larger groups some expenses such as commissions and premium taxes may be charged directly, and overhead charges will be allocated on one or more of the following bases: cost per contract, cost per certificate, cost per claim, or cost per dollar of premium. Acquisition expenses may be treated separately and often are amortized over a period of years. The charge for contingencies and the insurance charge often are included with expenses in the final distribution formula.

The proper amount that each case should contribute to contingencies and profits is difficult to determine. It has been suggested that the over-all goal of a company should be to have such contingency reserves equal to 50 percent of one year's premiums. This goal may take a new company a long time to attain. Greater allowances for contingencies should be made for groups where industrial hazard exists and for lines where premium is low in relation to the magnitude of a single claim.

Few groups are so large that they should be placed on a self-rating basis where they pay their own losses regardless of magnitude plus a fee to the insurer for service. In almost every case, there should be some limit on the maximum level of losses which will be considered in the rate-adjustment formula. This may be achieved by imposing such a limit on an aggregate basis or on the maximum single claim.

Since group policies rarely involve large single claims, it is more common to impose this limit on an aggregate basis. This might be expressed as a percentage of gross manual premium, perhaps ranging from 140 percent for the smaller groups to 110 percent for the larger groups. Any such loss limit requires the computation of an insurance charge which serves the purpose of spreading the cost of claims in excess of the limit among all cases in the class. In addition to making year-to-year costs more predictable for the policyholder, such limits also reduce the possibility of a negative surplus (deficit) becoming so large that the policyholder will prefer starting over with another company to making up the losses in the future. Such a changeover would subject him to charges for new acquisition costs, but this might be preferable to going many years without premium refunds. The magnitude of the insurance charge for the loss limit will depend on the frequency distribution of losses and the level of the limit selected. The method of computing such a charge is beyond the scope of this book.

Credibility refers to the statistical reliability of the experience of a group or class. The actual loss ratio may be thought of as a ratio derived from a sample. The true loss ratio of the universe of all possible samples may be estimated from this sample ratio. The possible sample ratios will form a frequency distribution about the true value, and statistical theory enables the actuary to estimate the true value from the particular sample. This distribution will be quite broad for small cases, and only limited credence may be given to it as an estimate of the true value. In a very large case, the distribution of sample ratios will be quite narrow, and 100 percent credibility will be approached.

The degree of credibility will vary with the size of the sample in terms of life-years of exposure and theoretically with the frequency of expected losses. Where several lines are "packaged" for premium adjustment purposes, the combined credibility will be greater than that of each individual coverage. In practice, a table of credibility factors will be worked out for various sizes of group (measured in terms of lives exposed or of premium volume). This table indicates the weight to be attached to the loss experience of the group (not in excess of the loss limit). The complement of this is the weight attached to the expected losses or to the averages for the whole class. For example, in a case with a credibility factor equal to 70 percent, the losses considered in the premium adjustment formula would be 70 percent of the actual losses and 30 percent of the expected losses. Expected losses are derived from underlying pure premium for the class and line involved. Because of the loss limit and the credibility factor, it is possible for a group to qualify for a premium refund even when it has actually produced a loss to the company. Conversely, a group does not receive full credit for losses which are less than expected. This is not a matter of inequity: it is the essence of the insurance process.

The actual premium adjustment formulas are closely guarded company secrets. However, all will involve consideration of premiums paid, incurred losses modified by loss limits and credibility, and direct and allocated expenses, including allowances for contingencies and perhaps profits. The premium adjustment is usually made retroactively, but it is becoming more and more common also to make prospective adjustments. Where retrospective adjustments have been large and consistently in one direction for a fairly long period, it becomes possible to make adjustments of future premiums in the same direction. However, since conditions may change, it is advisable to use more conservative assumptions in prospective adjustments, allowing a margin for future adverse developments. Of course, even after such prospective rate credits, the premium is still subject to retrospective adjustment at the end of the year.

*Adjustment of guaranteed renewable rates.* The problems involved in adjusting rates for classes of insureds under guaranteed renewable contracts are somewhat similar to those of adjusting rates for groups, but more complicated. Most if not all guaranteed-renewable adjustments have been upward, and it looks as though this will be the situation for the foreseeable future, especially for hospital and major medical contracts.

The problem of rate adjustments is complicated by the necessity of preserving the level premium equity of the insured in his contract.[28] The revision should preserve the original classification as well since this usually is guaranteed in the contract. Maintaining level premium equity requires charging a rate less than that indicated for new entrants at the insured's attained age. This can be produced either by computing an increment to be added to the original rate to reflect higher future costs, or by recomputing the original rate, as of original age of entry, using

---

[28] See Barnhart, *op. cit.*, p. 472. This is a somewhat controversial subject. See also the discussion of Barnhart's paper, *op. cit.* at p. 499.

the original assumptions for periods prior to the date of revision and the new assumptions thereafter.

The revised rate should not be so high as to "freeze out" the insured, thus impairing the renewal guarantee, nor should it be so high as to lead to substantial adverse selection on the part of the insured. However, any increase will present problems of public and agent relations. These problems can be minimized by setting the original rate high enough so that revision appears unlikely under the original cost assumption and by revising rates as soon as revision appears to be necessary so that no single increase is excessive. Certainly it is not wise for an insurer to wait until it suffers actual losses on a block of contracts.

Rate revision may be made necessary by inflation in medical costs, increases in utilization with advancing age which are greater than expected, or by insufficient original claim cost estimates. Each of these situations indicates a somewhat different method of adjustment. In each case, however, the job is at least as difficult as computing rates for a new contract. After each such rate revision, the insurer will have at least one additional set of rate classes based on time of entry or duration of contract.

## Summary

Rate making is the process of developing premium rates which are adequate, reasonable, and equitable. It involves the computation of pure premiums for various coverages and classes and loading these pure premiums for expenses, profits, and contingencies, to produce gross premiums. The pure premium may be thought of as the product of the probability of loss (frequency) and the average amount of claim (severity), per unit of exposure.

For some lines of insurance, the severity is the amount of benefit; for others it depends on the magnitude of expenses incurred or the duration of disability or hospital confinement. Where benefits are payable over a period of years, interest and mortality enter into the determination of severity, which is expressed as the present value of a disabled life annuity due.

Where time is an important determinant of severity it is common to develop continuance tables which make possible the computation of premiums for various combinations of waiting period and maximum benefit period. For other lines, average claim costs may be computed directly for standard benefits and modifications applied for other benefit schedules or limits.

Where pure one-year term premiums increase sharply by age, it is necessary to discount for interest and mortality and develop net level premiums. In individual insurance, premiums are developed for various classes of insureds on a basis of sex, occupation, and sometimes age. In group insurance, premiums are developed for a standard group, and adjustments are made for industry, sex, and age distributions differing substantially from standard.

Gross premiums are developed from pure premiums by adding a loading for expenses, profits, and contingencies. In group insurance, size discounts are offered the larger groups to reflect the savings in acquisition and administrative costs involved. Some individual policies and most group policies are entitled to premium adjustments in the form of dividends or experience rating. In group insurance these adjustments may be made prospectively as well as retrospectively. The factors entering into such computations are the same as those entering into initial premium determination, except that they are applied to the actual experience of the group or class rather than to the expected experience based on a priori considerations.

The process of rate making is complicated by the difficulty of obtaining reliable data, the subjectivity of disability, and differences in underwriting and claim practices among various companies. For these reasons, it is quite inadvisable to utilize data derived from the experience of other companies or under other policies without making adequate allowance for such differences and allowing an adequate margin for possible unfavorable developments. A great deal of judgment must be utilized, and in the present state of knowledge sound rate making is as much an art as a science.

## Selected references

*See the following items from the General Bibliography: 4, ch. 25; 7, ch. 7; 8, chs. 5 and 6; 9, chs. 11, 12, and 25; 10, ch. 11; 14, ch. 7; 15, chs. 25 and 36; 17, chs. 5 and 6; 18, chs. 17 and 18; 19, chs. 5, 6, and 8; 20, chs. 11 and 12; 21, chs. 20 and 21; 22, chs. 5 and 6.*

ACTUARIAL SOCIETY OF AMERICA. *Report of Committee on Disability Experience.* New York, 1926.

BARNHART, E. PAUL. "Adjustment of Premiums under Guaranteed Renewable Policies," *Transactions of the Society of Actuaries,* Vol. XII, p. 472.

———. "Continuance Functions," *Transactions of the Society of Actuaries,* Vol. XI, p. 649.

———. "Some New Tables for Major Medical and Disability Benefits," *Transactions of the Society of Actuaries,* Vol. XIII, p. 497.

BARTLESON, EDWIN L., AND OLSEN, JAMES J. "Reserves for Individual Hospital and Surgical Expense Insurance," *Transactions of the Society of Actuaries,* Vol. IX, p. 334.

BEVAN, JOHN R. "Comprehenive Medical Insurance," *Proceedings of the Casualty Actuarial Society,* Vol. L, p. 111.

BLUMENFELD, M. EUGENE. "Recent Trends in Individual Hospital Insurance," *Proceedings of the Casualty Actuarial Society,* Vol. XLVIII, p. 83.

BRODIE, NORMAN, AND NOVEMBER, WILLIAM J. "A New Table for Accidental Death Benefits," *Transactions of the Society of Actuaries,* Vol. XI, p. 749.

BURTON, BURTON E., AND PETTINGILL, DANIEL W. "Development of Expected Claim Cost for Comprehensive Medical Expense Benefits and Ratios of 1959 and 1960 Actual Experience Thereto," *Transactions of the Society of Actuaries,* Vol. XV, p. 11.

CAMMACK, E. E. "Premium and Reserves for Non-Cancellable Accident and Health Policies," *Proceedings of the Casualty Actuarial Society,* Vol. VII, p. 267.

CRAIG, JAMES D. "The Actuarial Basis for Premiums and Reserves in Personal Accident and Health Inurance," *Proceedings of the Casualty Actuarial Society,* Vol. XVII, p. 50.

CUETO, MANUEL R. "Monetary Values for Ordinary Disability Benefits," *Transactions of the Society of Actuaries,* Vol. VI, p. 108.

DICKERSON, O. D. "Mortgage Disability Insurance—A Case Study in Risk Theory," *Annals of the Society of Chartered Property Casualty Underwriters,* Summer, 1963, p. 163.

DORN, LOWELL M. "New York Life Morbidity Experience under Individual and Family Major Medical Policies," *Transactions of the Society of Actuaries,* Vol. XV, p. 275.

FACKLER, E. B. "Net Premiums and Reserves for Policies Giving Installment Disability Benefits," *Transactions of the Society of Actuaries,* Vol. XII, p. 241.

FAIRBANKS, ALFRED F. "Notes on Non-Cancellable Health and Accident Ratemaking," *Proceedings of the Casualty Actuarial Society,* Vol. XLII, p. 89.

FARLEY, JARVIS P. "A 1940 View of Non-Cancellable Disability Insurance," *Proceedings of the Casualty Actuarial Society,* Vol. XXVII, p. 40.

FAUST, J. EDWARD. "The Actuarial Aspects of Blue Cross Plans," *Proceedings of the Casualty Actuarial Society,* Vol. XLVI, p. 177.

FITZHUGH, GILBERT W. "Group Accident and Health Insurance Morbidity," *Transactions of the Actuarial Society of America,* Vol. XXXVIII, p. 221.

————. "Group Life and Disability Insurance on the One-Year Term Premium Basis," *Transactions of the Actuarial Society of America,* Vol. XLVI, p. 238.

FOODY, WALTER M., AND KLAASSEN, ELDON J. "Financing Medical Care for the Aged," *Journal of Insurance,* June, 1962, p. 226.

GINGERY, STANLEY W. "A Reinvestigation of Group Hospital Expense Insurance Experience," *Transactions of the Society of Actuaries,* Vol. XII, p. 564.

GINGERY, S. W., AND MELLMAN, R. J., "An Investigation of Group Major Medical Expense Insurance Experience," *Transactions of the Society of Actuaries,* Vol. XIII, p. 513.

GRANGE, G. W. K., AND MILLER, JOHN. "Cash Benefits for Extended Disability," *Transactions of the Actuarial Society of America,* Vol. XLIX.

GUERTIN, ALFRED N. "Life Insurance Premiums," *Journal of Risk and Insurance,* March, 1965, p. 23.

HEALTH AND ACCIDENT UNDERWRITERS CONFERENCE. *Conference Modification of Class 3 Disability Table for Calculation of Reserves on Non-Cancellable Accident and Health Insurance.* Chicago: 1941.

HEALTH INSURANCE ASSOCIATION OF AMERICA. *Relative Value Study Index* (Processed).

———. *1964 Commissioners Disability Table,* 3 vols. New York: 1965.

HENDERSON, ROBERT. "Monetary Values for Disability Benefits Based on Class 3 Experience," *Transactions of the Actuarial Society of America,* Vol. XXX, p. 463.

HEZLETT, EDWARD H. "Premiums and Reserves for Temporary and Total Disability Benefits Incorporated in Life Contracts," *Transactions of the Actuarial Society of America,* Vol. XXIV, p. 92.

HOUGHTON, ANTHONY J. "Continuance Study of Hospital Claims on Individually Underwritten Lives Age 65 and Over," *Transactions of the Society of Actuaries,* Vol. XV, p. 530.

HUNTER, ARTHUR. "Disability Premiums and Reserves under Policies Providing for Monthly Income at Disability," *Transactions of the Actuarial Society of America,* Vol. XXX, p. 373.

———, AND PHILLIPS, JAMES T. *Disability Benefits in Life Insurance Policies.* New York: Actuarial Society of America, 1937.

JORDAN, CHESTER W. *Life Contingencies.* Chicago: Society of Actuaries, 1952.

KORMES, MARK. "Patterns of Serious Illness Insurance," *Proceedings of the Casualty Actuarial Society,* Vol. XLVIII, p. 121.

KULP, C. ARTHUR. "The Rate Making Process in Property and Casualty Insurance—Goals, Techniques, and Limits," *Law and Contemporary Problems,* Autumn, 1950.

LATIMER, MURRAY W. "Costs of Hospital Benefits for Retired Employees," *Proceedings of the Casualty Actuarial Society,* Vol. XLVIII, p. 13.

MCLEAN, GEORGE E. "An Actuarial Analysis of a Prospective Experience Rating Approach for Group Hospital-Surgical-Medical Coverage," *Proceedings of the Casualty Actuarial Society,* Vol. XLVIII, p. 155.

MILLER, MORTON D. "Group Weekly Indemnity Continuation Table Study," *Transactions of the Society of Actuaries,* Vol. III, p. 31.

———. "Gross Premiums for Individual and Family Major Medical Expense Insurance," *Transaction of the Society of Actuaries,* Vol. VII, p. 1.

———. "1957 Study of Group Surgical Expense Insurance Claims," *Transactions of the Society of Actuaries,* Vol. X, p. 359.

MILLIMAN, W. A. "Insurance of the Expense of Medical Service," *Transactions of the Actuarial Society of America,* Vol. XLI, p. 114.

OTTESON, PAUL M. "Group Accident and Health Therapeutic Benefits—Measurement of Loss Costs for Rate-Making Purposes," *Proceedings of the Casualty Actuarial Society,* Vol. XLVI, p. 116.

PIKE, BERTRAM. "Some Considerations in Determining Incurred Claims Used in the Computation of Dividends under Group Accident and Health Insurance," *Transactions of the Society of Actuaries,* Vol. X, p. 630.

SEIGFRIED, CHARLES A. "Some Considerations Involved in the Analysis of Major Medical Expense Insurance Experience," *Transactions of the Society of Actuaries,* Vol. X, p. 505.

SOCIETY OF ACTUARIES. *Transactions of the Society of Actuaries,* reports number, annual, 1947 to date.

———, EDUCATION AND EXAMINATION COMMITTEE. *Part 8 Study Notes: Group Insurance.* Chicago, 1956.

STEINHAUS, HENRY W. "Commutation Functions for Individual Policies Providing for Hospital, Surgical, and Medical Care Benefits after Retirement," *Proceedings of the Casualty Actuarial Society,* Vol. XLVI, p. 251.

chapter 19

Reserved for some end or other.—Lord Clive

# Reserves

## Function of reserves

Reserves are balance sheet accounts set up to reflect actual and potential liabilities under outstanding insurance contracts.[1] Since insurance premiums are collected in advance and losses are paid out over a period of time, an insurer, assuming premiums initially were adequate, always will have in its possession assets to which it has full legal title but which are earmarked for the payment of claims in the future.[2] It would be unsound from an actuarial as well as an accounting viewpoint to look upon these assets as the property solely of the insurer or its owners. In effect, they represent funds belonging to the policyholders. Thus an accurate valuation of the company at the time of preparation of financial statements and an accurate portrayal of its profit position require that balance sheet accounts be set up to reflect this liability to policyholders.

It is important that these reserves be valued as accurately as possible. Essentially, reserves should represent the present value of all future payments to be made by the insurer on all business in force less the present value of all future income which will be available toward these payments. However, since future payments depend upon the occurrence of fortuitous events, they cannot be valued with complete accuracy but must be estimated. Another function served by reserves is to facilitate

---

[1] This definition does not include valuation reserves, such as reserves for depreciation. These are not liabilities; they represent direct deductions from the value of the related asset. The modern tendency is to avoid the use of the term *reserve* in this sense. Reserves are not ledger accounts. Some authorities distinguish reserves from other liabilities on the basis that the amount of the liability requiring a reserve is not known but must be estimated by actuarial procedures.

[2] A particular new contract or block of business usually will show a negative cash flow for the first several years, but reserves nevertheless must be set up to reflect the insurer's liabilities under these contracts.

602

the computation of prospective and retrospective rate adjustments in group cases. To the extent that the insurer's obligations on account of the policy year under consideration have not been discharged fully, reserves must be set up and charged to the insured before rate credits may be granted.

## Types of reserve

From the accounting standpoint there are three types of reserve: insurance reserves, expense reserves, and surplus reserves. Insurance reserves and expense reserves are true deferred liabilities. Insurance reserves represent the present value of claims payable in the future. Expense reserves represent the present value of expenses payable in the future.

Surplus reserves are not liabilities but surplus accounts set up to allow for possible unfavorable future developments. They represent portions of surplus appropriated to special accounts, so that the balancing assets will not be distributed as profits but retained as a margin of safety for the protection of the insurer and its policyholders. These accounts bear such titles as "Reserve for Contingencies," "Reserve for Fluctuations of Morbidity," "Reserve for Revaluation of Assets," and the like. They are properly considered as part of the insurer's surplus, but not as amounts available for current distribution.

Expense reserves bear such titles as "Claim Expense Reserve," "Reserve for Federal Income Tax Payable," and the like. Except for the claim expense reserve, they are similar to accounts found in the statements of companies in other lines of business.

There are two main types of insurance reserve: premium reserves and loss (or claim) reserves. Premium reserves are set up to reflect the liability of the insurer for losses which have not yet occurred but for which premiums have been paid. Essentially, they represent premiums which have been received but are as yet unearned; that is, the promised protection has not yet been granted. Loss reserves, on the other hand, represent the liability of the insurer for events which have already taken place but for which settlement is not yet complete. These include losses which have occurred but for which notice has not yet been received, cases in process of investigation, settlement or litigation, and cases where liability is admitted but benefits are payable over a period of time.

Annual statements required by state insurance departments classify reserves somewhat differently. Health insurance statements may be made on either the combined Life and Accident and Health Blank or the Fire and Casualty Company "Miscellaneous" Blank. Most filings are on the combined blank, and this discussion will be largely confined to it.

The reserve figures will appear in Exhibit 9—*Aggregate Reserve for Accident and Health Policies* and in Exhibit 11, *Policy and Contract Claims.* Exhibit 9 is in two parts. Part A. *Active Life Reserve* has to do with reserves for losses for which premiums have been received but which are not yet incurred. This includes the premium reserve. It provides four lines for various items. The four specified are the *Unearned Premium Reserve, Additional reserves* (for guaranteed renewable and similar policies), *Reserve for future contingent benefits,* and *Reserve for rate credits.*

Part B of Exhibit 9 includes the balance of the loss reserves. It is headed *Claim reserve* and includes *Present value of amount not due on claims, Reserve for future contingent benefits* and one blank line for possible other claim reserves. Exhibit 11 is headed *Policy and Contract Claims* and includes life as well as health. Part 1 includes the *Liability End of Current Year* which consists of claims *Due and Unpaid, In Course of Settlement,* and *Incurred but Unreported.* Exhibit 9 provides a column for total reserves and five columns for a breakdown by lines: group; collectively renewable and individual. Individual is broken down into noncancellable, quaranteed renewable, non-renewable for stated reasons only, other accident only, and all other. Exhibit 11 is broken down only between group and other. The casualty blank is essentially similar but differs in detail.[3] The discussion of the various reserve items will follow the logical classification presented initially rather than the format of the Convention Blank, which is subject to periodic change.[4]

### Premium reserves

Premium reserves represent liabilities for events which have not yet taken place. Usually they are classified into three categories: the pro rata unearned premium reserve, the additional reserve for guaranteed renewable policies, and reserves for future contingent benefits. Each of these, of course, may be divided into subcategories and by lines of insurance.

*Pro rata unearned premium reserve.* Premiums are paid in advance but earned by the insurer over the policy period as the protection is provided. The unearned portion represents a liability to the policyholders which will be discharged in the future in one of several ways:

---

[3] The items required for this blank (Part 3A) are as follows: (a) *Claims Adjusted or in Process of Adjustment,* which includes the reported portion of *Amounts Not Yet Due* plus the *Due and Unpaid* and *Claims in Course of Settlement;* (b) *Claims Incurred but Unreported,* which is similar to the same reserve in the life blank but also includes the unreported portion of *Amounts Not Yet Due* and the *Reserve for Deferred Mortality and Similar Benefits;* and (c) *Unpaid Loss Adjustment Expense,* which is peculiar to this blank.

[4] Indeed, it was necessary to rewrite this entire section in galley proof to reflect changes effective in 1968.

by granting future protection (i.e., through the promise to pay future claims to those who incur losses), by returning premium in the event of cancellation, or by reinsuring the business with another insurer. Any of these methods of discharging the liability will cost the insurer money, so the reserve is necessary.

State laws and regulations generally require that the pro rata unearned premium reserve equal the entire unearned portion of gross premiums received. Another way of expressing the same idea is that the reserve must equal all premiums received which apply to periods beyond the valuation date. It involves a great deal of effort to apportion the premium under every policy separately, and so state laws generally permit the use of shortcut methods which sacrifice a measure of accuracy for ease of computation. However, some insurers prorate each individual premium, especially for group business, when the effect of a few policies may be great. With modern electronic data-processing systems, this is not difficult. More commonly, only the largest groups will be treated this way, and the balance of the business handled on an overall basis.

A less accurate method, but much easier to apply, is the monthly pro rata system. Here it is assumed that premiums are received at a uniform rate throughout the month or, in effect, that each is received on the 15th of the respective month. Thus, at year-end date, December policies have been in force half a month, November policies one and one-half months, etc. A variant is to assume that all fall due on the first of the month. Premiums are apportioned this way with proper adjustment for variations in the premium-paying period.

A variant of this method is to handle premiums received on the first of the month separately, and to apply the monthly pro rata system to the balance. This is common for group business where premium due dates may concentrate at the first and 15th of the month. Assuming that they all fall due on the 15th would result in inaccuracy.

A commonly used approximate method is simply to assume that premiums are falling due regularly throughout the year and that half of the last premiums received—whether annual, semiannual, quarterly, or monthly—is earned, and the balance unearned. The use of the annual or monthly pro rata method will result in the reserve being too low if the volume of business is growing, and too high if the volume is declining, as compared to the more accurate method.

When premiums are paid more than one year in advance (rare in health insurance), 100 percent of premiums beyond the current policy year is held in reserve. These are separately reported in the statement as "Premiums Received in Advance." Retroactive premium refunds and rate credits due must also be offset by a 100 percent reserve. These are current liabilities.

Basing the reserve on gross rather than net premiums implies the assumption that expenses, like losses, are spread uniformly over the life of the policy. This is, of course, incorrect. By far the greatest portion of expenses is incurred at, or shortly after, the issuance of a policy. Commissions, underwriting, policy writing, and group installation expenses are largely incurred and paid roughly at the time of issue. Since these expenses have already been paid, it is unnecessary to set up a reserve for their future payment. However, state laws require reserving on a gross premium basis. Thus the reserve is larger than it otherwise need be, and the earnings and surplus of the insurer are understated as a result.

For a rapidly growing company, particularly a small one, the constant drain on surplus produced by setting up reserves on new business may result in the rate of expansion being curtailed. Of course, when the premiums are ultimately earned, the excessive reserves will be released to surplus. One way around this limitation is to reinsure a portion of the company's business. Reinsurance premiums will be based on net rather than gross premiums, and the ceding company can take reserve credit for the portion of the business ceded. The ceding insurer need not carry reserves on the business ceded, and thus its liabilities are reduced by more than the reinsurance premium. This problem of "surplus drain" is, of course, not peculiar to health insurance; indeed, it is more acute in lines such as fire insurance, where premiums are customarily paid for three or five years in advance.

*Additional reserve for guaranteed renewable policies.* Guaranteed renewable and noncancellable policies generally provide that renewal is guaranteed at a level premium until age 60 or 65. Since pure premiums increase with age, a reserve similar to that in a term-to-65 life insurance policy is necessary. Where renewal is guaranteed to a higher age, or for life, the reserve is essentially similar but generally larger. The excess of net level premiums over annual claim costs in the early years is accumulated with interest and then dissipated in the later years to provide for the excess of claim costs over net premiums. This reserve is variously referred to as the "active life reserve," the "level premium reserve," the "policy reserve," or the "additional reserve for guaranteed renewable insurance." Such a reserve should be set up for all contracts where the insurer has no right of cancellation or nonrenewal because of the insured's health and for all other contracts with premiums competed on the net level premium basis.

The reserve may be viewed prospectively as the present value of future benefits minus the present value of future premium payments and expressed as: $_nV_x = A_{x+n} - P_x \cdot \ddot{a}_{x+n}$, where $A_{x+n}$ represents the net single premium for the benefit at the attained age, $P_x$ represents the net annual level premiums payable, and $\ddot{a}_{x+n}$ represents the present value of an annuity due of one dollar for the balance of the premium-paying period—life in this illustration. Where the premium-paying period is less than life, appropriate subscripts will be added to the formula.

Another generally used expression is the present value of the future net level premiums at the attained age minus the present value of the future net premiums payable (based on age of issue). This is the equivalent of the above, since the present value of future net attained age level premiums must be equal to the net single premium at the attained age. This makes it possible readily to compute the reserve by subtracting the issue age net level premium from the attained age net level premium and multiplying by the present value of an annuity due for the remaining premium-paying period. In the notation: $_nV_x =$ $(P_{x+n} - P_x)\ddot{a}_{x+n:\overline{t-n}|}$, where $x + n$ is the attained age at valuation and $x + t$ is the limiting age of premium payment.

The reserve also may be computed retrospectively. It is equal to the accumulated value of premiums paid less the accumulated cost of insurance. Computing this involves either successive computation for each year the insurance has been in force or the use of commutation columns. This is beyond the scope of this book. The reserve is the same whether computed retrospectively or prospectively. It can be demonstrated that the two approaches are mathematically equivalent and produce identical numerical results.

The formulas above produce terminal reserves. For life insurance policy valuation it is common to use the mean reserve, which represents the mean of the initial and terminal reserve. The initial reserve is the reserve at the beginning of the policy year immediately after the premium is paid and is equal to the previous year's terminal reserve plus the net premium. Thus the mean reserve equals the previous year's terminal reserve plus the net premiums plus the current year terminal reserve, all divided by 2. This is the recommended[5] method for health contracts, but an alternative method is the use of the mid-terminal reserve, which is equal to the mean of the terminal reserves for the current and preceding year. This is used when the pro rata unearned premium reserve also is required or set up for guaranteed renewable policies. This is equal (on an annual pro rata basis) to half the annual gross premium, while the mean reserve exceeds the midterminal reserve by half the annual net premium. Thus the total of the two reserves for guaranteed renewable policies is greater than the mean reserve by half the annual loading. The redundancy in the pro rata unearned premium reserve applies to guaranteed renewable policies when this method is

---

[5] Health Insurance Association of America, *1964 Commissioners Disability Tables,* Vol. 3, p. 9. See also Eduard H. Minor, "Loss of Time Health Insurance Reserves Based on the 1964 Commissioners Disability Table, *Transactions of the Society of Actuaries,* Vol. XVII, p. 368.

used. Other alternative valuation methods permitted include mid-terminal reserves plus *net* unearned premium reserves, prospective valuation based on net premium, and various approximate methods.

Since the expenses of the first year are quite heavy, setting up the various reserves is likely to produce a considerable drain on surplus. This is avoided or minimized by most companies by using a preliminary term method of reserve computation. While the details may be complex, the principle behind this valuation method is simple. Essentially, the reserve set up at the end of the first year is the reserve that would be required if the policy were a one-year term policy, i.e., usually zero. Thereafter, the reserve is equal to the level premium reserve that would be produced for a policy issued at an age one year greater than the actual age at issue. Thus the reserve begins to build up one year later than it normally would, but it builds up at a more rapid rate. This is necessary so that when the reserve reaches its peak, some years before termination of coverage, it will be about the same as though the level premium reserve method were used. Two-year preliminary term methods are also commonly used.

Tables of disability rates, disabled life annuities, and mortality rates must be used in connection with an assumed rate of interest to calculate the level premium reserve for disability income contracts. The 1964 Commissioners Disability Table was adopted by the National Association of Insurance Commissioners as a recommended minimum standard for disability rates and annuity values. The recommended standard includes any mortality table permitted for life insurance valuation and an interest rate no higher than the currently permissible rate for life insurance contracts.

For reserves on guaranteed renewable and noncancellable hospital, medical, and surgical expense contracts, the N.A.I.C. approved as a recommended standard the report of a special industry committee known as "Task Force Four."[6] The report recommends that active life reserves be established and that the 1956 Intercompany Hospital and Surgical Tables be used as a minimum for such benefits. Tables were included for a 90-day maximum hospital room-and-board benefit; several dollar limits for hospital extras, a $100 maximum surgical benefit, and a $1 maternity benefit. The tables include net premiums and reserves for the first 15 policy years for these benefits, for contracts providing coverage to age 65. These tables may be adjusted to reflect coverage differences or subsequent changes in average claim costs. Without such adjustment, the resulting reserves probably would not be adequate to

---

[6] The full report, including tables, appears as an appendix to Edwin L. Bartleson and James J. Olson, "Reserves for Individual Hospital and Surgical Expense Insurance," *Transactions of the Society of Actuaries*, Vol. IX, p. 334.

cover the present level of hospital and physician fees, let alone that anticipated in the future. The report recommends that a two-year preliminary term valuation method be permitted.

Legislative requirements for the additional reserve for guaranteed renewable policies are found only in a few states. Usually they apply only to noncancellable contracts, guaranteed renewable contracts and contracts where renewal may not be refused because of changes in the insured's health. However, other policies in which the net term premium increases substantially with age but gross premiums are level would produce such a reserve. Technically, it is not necessary to set up such a reserve for reasons of solvency, since companies could avoid the deferred liability by canceling or refusing renewal. However, to avail themselves extensively of this right would be very poor business. Therefore many companies set up level premium reserves for such policies on a voluntary basis, and many states require that this be done by administrative ruling. The necessity for such a reserve is minimized by the fact that expenses are high in the early years when claim rates (hopefully) are low, and vice versa. Even if not strictly necessary, the maintenance of such a reserve will make possible more accurate determination of underwriting results.

*Reserve for future contingent benefits.* Group hospital and surgical policies usually and individual hospital policies sometimes provide for an extension of maternity and obstetrical coverage for nine months after termination of insurance coverage. Some states require this extension in all contracts on which the insurer may deny renewal. Group medical care policies in general may provide for an extension of coverage of 30–90 days for other injuries or diseases. Since the event has not yet occurred but the premium has been paid, the estimated liability for such claims should be included as a premium reserve.

However, by far the largest portion of this reserve is required for maternity and obstetrical coverage, and, if the insured event be considered to be conception, it can be argued that the event has already occurred and the reserve should be a loss reserve. Annual statement requirements permit treating it either way in Exhibit 10.

The amount of the appropriate reserve may be estimated by relating actual claims for such deferred benefits during the previous year to the insurance in force at year-end (or to an average in force for the last nine months of the year), and applying this percentage to the same base for the current year. In group insurance it is common to set up such reserves on the assumption that all insurance containing such extended benefits is expiring on December 31. This assumption is made because there is at least a potentiality that all insurance in force could be canceled by either company or insured on short notice. The method of estimating the value of the reserve is the same, except that all maternity and obstetrical claims are included, not just those under expired policies. This, of course, results in a much larger reserve figure.

### Loss reserves

*Methods of computation.* Since loss reserves (often called "claim reserves") represent the liability for events which have already occurred, it is logical to compute their value on a prospective basis, applying some type of value estimate to known or estimated numbers of losses. This approach is generally followed in health insurance. The retrospective method of estimating loss reserve liability which is required by law for many types of casualty insurance is not generally required for health insurance. This method involves reserving the difference between expected losses (computed by a loss ratio technique) and losses actually paid. Since it is based on a (not necessarily valid) assumption of premium adequacy, it does little to guarantee accurate valuation.

There are five main methods of computing loss reserves based on the prospective approach: individual case estimate, average value, tabular and formula methods, and the development or runoff method. The first of these involves making an estimate of the expected future payments on each individual claim. Where the claim is fixed in amount, as for accidental death and dismemberment, or where it may vary greatly so that considerable judgment is called for, this method may be appropriate. For the great mass of claims, however, this technique is unduly time-consuming and expensive.

The average value technique involves the computation of average claim values for a recent sample of completed claims and applying this to the actual or estimated number of claims or of notices received. Where applied to notices, it is referred to as the "notice average" method.

The use of tabular values is a variant of the average value method. Tables of claim continuance and disabled life annuities are available for certain types of benefit and represent the best basis of valuing claims where duration is an important determinant of severity. Any of these may be applied to each claim individually (the seriatim method) or to a group or class (the grouping method).

In the formula method, developed claims from past experience are expressed as a percent of some base such as premiums in force at statement date or a few months earlier. This percentage then is applied to the current year base to estimate the claim reserve for the end of the current year.

The runoff or development method involves tallying claim amounts by month incurred and month paid. As experience accumulates, factors are developed which can be used to project the eventual payout, month by month into the future. Multiplying by a monthly interest factor produces the present value of each month's future payout and the total of these equals the reserve.

*Present value of amounts not yet due on claims.* This reserve represents the present value of expected claim payments to be made for benefit periods after the valuation date on claims which have been incurred prior to the valuation date. It does not include liability for claims currently due, or for the accrued portion of claims in course of settlement and incurred but unreported. It includes pro rata "unaccrued" amounts for benefit periods which begin before the valuation date and continue beyond it. For example, a benefit of $70 per week where the week had run two days at valuation time would be divided into $50 of "amounts not yet due on claims" and $20 of "due and unpaid." For many types of benefit not yet due, average values are the best basis for estimating the amount.

For disability income benefits, continuance tables or disabled life annuity tables will be used, depending on the potential benefit duration. Continuance tables reflect only probable future duration of benefit payment, while the disabled life annuity values also reflect the interest factor. The National Association of Insurance Commissioners has recommended minimum standards for disabled life reserves under noncancellable, guaranteed renewable and level premium policies, and many states have adopted such requirements. The N.A.I.C. minimum standard calls for valuing claims according to the 1964 Commissioners Disability Table and an interest rate not exceeding the maximum rate permitted in life insurance valuation. For claims with a duration from disablement of less than two years and for unreported and contested claims, an insurer may use its own methods.

As duration of disability increases, recovery rates decrease more rapidly than mortality rates increase up to quite advanced attained ages. Because of this, disability annuity values increase with increasing duration of disability for many years. Thus a revaluation of outstanding claims is necessary at each statement date. Many companies will maintain separate records by month of disablement, permitting the use of monthly annuity values. For claims of less than one year's duration, average values independent of age at disablement often are used. For longer durations, it is common to segregate the annuity values according to age at disablement, often in five-year groups.

The statement requirements now clearly lable this a claim reserve which is proper, since it provides for losses which already have taken place. The regulations permit methods of computation which do not distinguish between this reserve and claims "due and unpaid." Especially where policy maximum benefit durations are short, it may be more convenient to use methods of computation which combine the two items.

*Claims due and unpaid.* This is the amount required to pay all claims approved and due at the valuation date. It represents a current liability the amount of which is determined and presents no valuation problem except the necessity of prorating current benefit periods to separate "due and unpaid" from "not yet due," as indicated above. Since claims generally are paid as soon as approved, the amount of this reserve is usually rather small, and often is zero.

*Claims in course of settlement.* This item includes claims which are being processed, for which proof is being awaited, and the rare cases in course of litigation, and it reflects the amount which will be payable with respect to any period up to and including the valuation date. Where the amount of potential claim is unusually large, the individual case estimate may be the best method of valuation, as it permits the exercise of judgment by actuaries, attorneys and others involved. For the great majority of cases, a series of average values will be the better method. Formula factors may be applied to the premiums in force at year-end, but it seems that this method is inherently less accurate than applying average values to the number of outstanding claims.

*Claims incurred but unreported.* This reserve represents the company's liability for claims which have not yet been reported for losses which have already occurred. Losses should be considered to have occurred at the commencement of disability, not the expiration of the waiting period. Thus, for long waiting period disability income contracts there may be many claims outstanding with no benefit yet due, but with a large future liability. The liability for incurred but unreported claims must be split into its accrued and unaccrued parts. The unaccrued part is included with "The Present Value of Amounts Not Yet Due on Claims." Obviously, some variety of average value factor must be used. The easiest method is to derive from the experience of the past one or two years average values for claims of this type and ratios of the number of such claims to some convenient base, such as year-end insurance in force. Then these factors may be applied to the current base to derive estimates of the value of unreported claims.

An alternative method, which is more complex but perhaps more accurate, is known as the "development" method. A record is maintained of all claims according to date "incurred" and date paid. A study of such a tabulation over several years permits the actuary to estimate the proportion of claims for each past month which have been incurred but not yet paid. All methods of estimating unreported claims represent the application of a good deal of judgment. The lapse of time between valuation date and the actual preparation of the statement may permit more accurate evaluation as the experience develops.

*Loss reserves and premium adjustments.* In group cases which are entitled to retroactive premium adjustments according to a dividend or experience rating plan, it is necessary to estimate the liability of the company for losses incurred but unpaid. This estimated liability must be added to losses paid in computing the refund to be allowed. The types of loss and the methods of computation are essentially similar to those discussed above.

Logic would seem to indicate that the same method be used for estimating losses under a particular group policy as are used for the business or line as a whole. However, considerations of competition, convenience and expediency may dictate somewhat different methods. If the group is large enough and experience for a number of years is available, the actual experience of the group may be taken into consideration. It is desirable that the process be routinized as much as possible so that the computation can be handled by clerical personnel and need not claim the attention of the actuary.

**Other reserves**

*Claim expense reserves.* Unlike the reserves discussed above, which provide for future claim payments, this reserve provides for future expenses. It is related to future claims and may be computed as a percentage of loss reserves derived from past experience. An alternative method is to apply average claim adjustment expense values to the estimated number of unpaid claims outstanding. Sometimes the two methods are combined.

In applying these methods, allowance should be made for the uneven incidence of claim expenses. For example, on approved claims much of the total expense already has been paid, while on unreported claims the entire amount is payable in the future. It is common to deal with different types of claim separately, as the amount and incidence of expense may vary considerably between (say) hospital expense and dismemberment claims.

This reserve is required for the casualty blank but not for the life blank.

*Other expense reserves.* Reserves are commonly set up for other deferred liabilities, primarily expenses accrued and unpaid. A reserve for taxes would be an illustration of such a reserve. These accounts are similar to those found in statements of other types of business and do not require further comment.

*Reserve for dividends payable.* On participating policies, particularly those issued on an individual basis, dividends may be payable throughout the year following the year in which they were earned. Such dividends payable should be set up as a liability. The value may be determined directly from the calculation of dividends payable from surplus available for distribution or derived by applying average dividend rates to the business eligible for such dividends. Which method is preferred will depend on the original method of determining the dividend and upon the degree to which the policy holders keep their insurance in force. The reserve should also include dividends currently due and unpaid, and experience rating refunds payable.

*Reserves under compulsory disability laws.*    In addition to the other types of reserve discussed here, insurance written under compulsory disability laws may require other special types of reserve. One type is necessary under the New York law, which provides for assessments of insurers to provide for administrative expense and for benefit costs for the disabled unemployed. Both assessments are based on the total taxable payrolls of the groups insured by the particular company. The reserve for the expense assessment is the amount estimated to be due the following March 31. The reserve for the disabled unemployed includes both the estimated assessment for the current year and a reserve for future periods of greater unemployment. Some companies treat their assessments as taxes and provide for them under expense reserves.

Another special reserve which may be set up under certain compulsory disability laws is a reserve to provide for future declines in premium income. Under some of these laws, premiums are expressed as a percentage of covered payroll, and it is likely that in periods of recession premium income would decline more rapidly than claim payments.

*Contingency reserves.*    These are voluntary reserves and represent portions of surplus rather than true liabilities. They are especially important in health insurance because of the subjectivity of the hazard and the susceptibility of claim rates to economic conditions.

In periods of inflation, benefit costs for medical care coverages are likely to rise more rapidly than premium income, and, in periods of depression, incidence and severity rates under disability income policies may rise materially. It is important to accumulate reserves during periods of good earnings to provide a cushion against such developments. Moreover, health insurance claims vary with the season of the year. There is also the possibility of catastrophic losses through epidemics and natural and man-made disasters.

It is largely a matter of judgment as to what level of contingency reserves should be set up. An analysis of potential claims under assumed unfavorable conditions may serve as a guide to the desirable level. It has been widely suggested that a desirable ultimate objective would be the maintenance of such reserves equal to 50 percent of annual premium income. One state, Missouri, suggests such reserves for group health insurance in a circular letter from the insurance commissioner. The minimum objective is to set aside each year 2 percent of net premiums but not more than 10 percent of that amount necessary to reach a goal of 50 percent of net premiums. The 1959 Federal Life Insurance Company Income Tax Law[7] permits an insurer to deduct 2 percent of group health insurance premiums from taxable income for such reserve purposes.

*Mandatory security valuation reserve.* This reserve is a special type of contingency reserve specifically required by law. It is increased each year according to a prescribed method until its amount equals 1 percent of the value of amortizable bonds and 20 percent of the value of other securities owned. This reserve helps to cushion fluctuations in surplus and operating results resulting from changes in the security markets. Investment losses may be charged to this reserve as they are incurred and the reserve may be replenished over the years.

### Summary

There are three main types of reserve carried by insurance companies: insurance reserves, expense reserves, and contingency reserves.

Insurance reserves include premium reserves, which provide for losses not yet incurred, and loss reserves, which provide for losses incurred but not paid.

Premium reserves include the pro rata unearned premium reserve, the additional reserve for guaranteed renewable insurance, and the reserve for future contingent benefits. The first of these usually is computed on a pro rata basis, the second according to disability and mortality tables, and third on an average value basis.

Loss reserves include reserves for claims not yet due, due and not paid, in course of settlement, and incurred but not reported. The amounts may be estimated on an individual case basis, according to average values or by means of tabular values.

Expense reserves, like insurance reserves, are true liabilities and are similar to deferred liabilities carried by other types of business. The claim expense reserve represents the liability for future claim expense on claims already incurred and may be computed as a function of the claim reserve or on an average value basis. Special reserves are often maintained for assessments under compulsory disability laws and for dividends payable to policyholders.

Contingency reserves represent appropriated surplus to provide for possible unfavorable developments in the future.

An accurate computation of reserves is necessary to state accurately the financial position and operating results of the company and to protect

---

[7] P.L. 86–69, 26 U.S.C. 809 (d) (6).

the company and its policyholders against weakness or insolvency in the future.

### Selected references

*See the following items from the General Bibliography: 4, ch. 25; 7, ch. 8; 8, ch. 7; 10, ch. 12; 14, ch. 7; 15, ch. 12; 16, Vol. I, ch. 15; 17, chs. 5 and 6; 18, pp. 598–607; 19, ch. 7; 20, chs. 11 and 12; 21, ch. 23; 22, ch. 7.*

BARTLESON, EDWIN L., AND OLSEN, JAMES J. "Reserves for Individual Hospital and Surgical Expense Insurance," *Transactions of the Society of Actuaries,* Vol. IX, p. 334.

BRAGG, JOHN M. "Health Insurance Claim Reserves and Liabilities," *Transactions of the Society of Actuaries,* Vol. XVI, p. 17.

CONROD, S. F. "Valuation of Non-Cancellable Accident and Health Insurance Policies," *Proceedings of the Casualty Actuarial Society,* Vol. XXXII, p. 27.

HEALTH INSURANCE ASSOCIATION OF AMERICA. *1964 Commissioners Disability Table.* 3 vols. New York, 1965.

HIPP, GRADY. "Present Status of Reserves on Non-Cancellable Disability Insurance," *Proceedings of the Casualty Actuarial Society,* Vol. XIV, p. 190.

MINOR, EDUARD H. "Loss of Time Health Insurance Reserves Based on the 1964 Commissioners Disability Table," *Transactions of the Society of Actuaries,* Vol. XVII, p. 368.

PIKE, BERTRAM. "Some Considerations in Determining Incurred Claims Used in the Computation of Dividends under Group Accident and Health Insurance," *Transactions of the Society of Actuaries,* Vol. X, p. 630.

"Report of Committee on Mortality for Disabled Lives," *Proceedings of the Casualty Actuarial Society,* Vol. XXXV, p. 56.

TARBELL, T. F. "Incurred But Not Reported Claim Reserves," *Proceedings of the Casualty Actuarial Society,* Vol. XX, p. 275.

THOMPSON, GRAHAM C. *Reserve Considerations in Writing Non-Cancellable Insurance.* New York: Bureau of Accident and Health Underwriters, 1953.

## chapter 20

Pass the hat for your credit's sake, and pay, pay—pay!—Kipling, *The Absent-Minded Beggar*

# Claims

## Function and importance of claim administration

The purpose of insurance is to provide protection and security. In the last analysis this is accomplished by the payment of claims to insureds who suffer covered losses. The payment of claims represents the delivery of the product of the insurance industry. The primary function of claim administration is to deliver this product by paying all legitimate claims promptly, pleasantly and in accordance with the provisions of the contract. This should be done in such a way that the claimant remains a satisfied customer who will influence future sales favorably. The record of a company in paying claims is probably the most important single determinant of good will.

The insured buys the policy with the objective of having his claims paid promptly and cheerfully. Where circumstances do not permit immediate and full settlement, it is important that he be made to understand the reasons why. If the payment is made grudgingly or if there is argument over small differences, dissatisfaction will result. If the insurance has been sold and explained properly, there should be few difficulties in reaching a settlement which leaves the claimant completely satisfied. However, all too frequently, the claimant does not understand the character and extent of his coverage, and claim administration must include a process of education which should be courteous, patient, and diplomatic. The goal of claim administration should be to settle every claim on an equitable basis.

However, equitable settlement does not imply overpayment or the payment of claims that are not within the coverage of the contract. The second function of claim administration is to make sure that only honest claims, covered by the policy and correct in amount, are paid. This is necessary in order that the actual loss experience of the insurer will

617

reflect the expected loss experience which served as the basis of premium computation. If illegitimate claims are paid or if legitimate claims are overpaid in amount, actual losses will exceed the expected, and the insurer's profit or even solvency may be impaired. Even if premiums are increased to cover such overpayment and illegitimate payment, the honest policyholders of normal health will be forced to subsidize a dishonest and hazardous minority.

Because of the fact that most claims are for small amounts, a little malingering or overpayment on the many small claims will have a more severe impact on losses than would great overpayments on the few very severe claims. Thus claim administration must be so designed as to safeguard the insurer against laxity in small claims just as in large. Of course, the larger the deductible or waiting period, the fewer small claims will be presented, and the lower the upper limit or maximum duration, the fewer large claims. The greatest care is needed for noncancellable and guaranteed renewable policies where there is little chance of getting off the risk.

### The process of claim settlement

*General.*    There are four main steps in claim settlement: notice, proof of loss, investigation, and payment. The details of these steps vary with the type of insurance. The process is most clearly defined in regard to individual insurance, and the discussion will be centered on this type. Special circumstances and procedures in Blue Cross–Blue Shield plans, group insurance, and social insurance will be discussed later.

*Individual insurance.   Notice.*    The first step in the claim process is the furnishing of notice of injury or disease to the insurer. The Uniform Provisions state that such notice must be furnished within 20 days of the occurrence or commencement of loss covered by the policy or as soon thereafter as is reasonably possible. While the policy provision calls for written notice, many companies accept oral or telephoned notice. In addition, some companies use an optional addition to this provision which calls for notice of continued disability each six months under policies providing benefits payable for two years or more. If the insured delays in giving such notice, he may forfeit his right to benefits for periods more than six months prior to the date of filing.

*Proof of loss.*    Upon receipt of notice of claim, the insurer must furnish claim forms for proof of loss to the insured within 15 days, according to Uniform Provision 6. If the company fails to furnish such forms, the insured may submit proof in writing of the occurrence, character, and extent of loss. Uniform Provision 7 requires the insured to furnish the proof of loss to the insurer, in writing within 90 days of the occurrence of loss other than disability income and within 90 days of the termination of the period for which the company is liable for income losses.[1]

The agent may have a great deal, a little, or nothing to do with claim settlement, depending on the practices of the insurer involved. Independent property-casualty agents often are permitted to settle small claims on their own authority under these lines, and insurers of this type sometimes extend such authority to health insurance claims.

At the other extreme, many insurers centralize all claim administration, record keeping and collections in home or regional offices, and the agent concerns himself almost exclusively with selling.

In most instances, company practice falls between these extremes, and the agent may be called upon to assist the claimant with notice of loss, filling in claim blanks and the like. Many agents, even if they take no part in the actual claim adjustment process, still make it a point to deliver claim checks whenever possible. This builds goodwill and often leads to future sales.

Uniform claim forms for the proof of loss for medical care coverages are in general use. These were discussed in Chapter 10 in connection with group insurance hospital admission plans. Somewhat similar procedures are used in individual hospital insurance. The Health Insurance Council has developed standard claim forms and a standard hospital admission system for individual insurance. This is referred to as the "Benefit Identification and Certification System."

In this program the patient carries a card which is presented to the hospital upon admission. It identifies the insurer, insured and policy number. The hospitals stock and file, when appropriate, a standard Hospital Information Request Form (HIRF–1), which is sent to the insurance company, requesting information as to coverage and level of benefit. The insurer responds by sending either, the Benefit Certification Form (BCF–1), which certifies coverage and guarantees payment up to the described maximum benefits or the Benefit Identification Form (BIF–1) identifies benefit maximums but does not guarantee payment because of some question of policy restrictions and limitations or possible prior payments, or by notice of lack of coverage. The reverse side of the BCF–1 and BIF–1 forms is the Individual Hospital Insurance Form (IHF–1), which is used by the hospital to certify the actual stay and charge. It also provides space for the patient to assign benefits to the hospital if he so desires and to authorize the hospital to release information to the insurer if required. This serves as the basis for claim payment by the insurer. Where such forms are used, benefits usually are

---

[1] See above, p. 222, for a brief discussion of various interpretations of this clause.

assigned to the hospital or physician, and payment is made direct. Where this is not done, proofs of loss for the medical care coverages usually must be accompanied by actual bills or photo copies.

Accidental death forms usually include an affidavit by the beneficiary, a statement by the physician as to time and cause of death, and statements from the undertaker and witnesses of the accident.

Short-period disability income forms usually are not filed until disability has terminated and usually are limited to brief statements from the insured and his physician. Sometimes a statement is required from the employer certifying to actual loss of time. Long-period disability income forms are similar but usually more extensive. Generally, there is a preliminary statement similar to the short-benefit-period form, one or more reports as to continuance of disability, and an affidavit from insured and physician when disability ends. For most cases the preliminary claim blank serves as the proof of loss, but for more severe cases a formal proof may be required upon termination of liability.

*Investigation.* The process of investigation takes place between the initial notice and the final payment. Frequently a good deal of the process is carried out before the insured files final proof of loss. In addition to the notice and proof, a number of sources of information are open to the insurer.

The importance of the corroboration of the insured's statement by the report of the attending physician and, if applicable, the hospital, is obvious. The diagnosis of illness or injury is sufficient, in connection with the information as to treatment and time of disability, to establish the validity of most claims. Records of past experience will indicate the pattern of treatment and probable duration of most disabilities, and, where the case fits the pattern, the claim rarely will be questioned. Where the claim deviates markedly from the norm or where questions of preexisting condition or misrepresentation arise, further investigation is called for.

Inspection reports may be obtained from company representatives, independent adjusters, or mercantile inspection agencies.

These reports should be obtained as soon after disablement as practicable. Where waiting periods are long, it may be wise to obtain information before the company actually becomes liable if it appears as though the disability is likely to be of long duration. The inspection will check on the insured's residence, date of birth, employment, and nature and extent of disability. It is necessary to inquire into the insured's activities during the period of claimed total disability to make sure these activities are not inconsistent with claims of total disability. Logical sources of information include neighbors, business associates, and competitors. Care should be exercised to avoid antagonizing or embarrassing the claimant through this process. Moreover, excessive use of inspections results in unnecessary expense to the company.

The employer may supply information as to the cause of disability and dates of absence from work as well as to the insured's occupation. Many employers require an authorization from the employee before they will release such information. In addition to the statement from the attending physician obtained as a part of the proof of loss, the insurer may want further information. If specialists or consultants have been employed, statements from them probably are desirable. Of course, this is privileged information and cannot be released without authorization. The preliminary claim forms usually contain authorizations directed to physicians and employers to release such information.

Where conflicting information is revealed or where the company suspects malingering or misrepresentation, it may have the claimant examined by its own physician. This may vary from a routine examination to a very detailed process complete with diagnosis, prognosis, and evaluation of treatment in process. Uniform Provision 10 gives the insurer the right of physical examination or autopsy.

Where a preexisting condition is suspected, it may be necessary to obtain information from other physicians who have treated the claimant in the past.

Hospital records may also supply important information as to prior history as well as to the current disability. Again, authorization from the claimant is necessary. Consultation with other companies with whom the claimant is or has been insured is appropriate in some instances. Other sources sometimes used include Social Security records, Defense Department records, board of health reports, and even immigration records.

It should be noted that the investigation is concerned with more than just the facts surrounding the current claim. Many policies exclude coverage of preexisting disease for a limited period of time, and some exclude named preexisting diseases during the entire period of coverage. Thus the claimant's health history should be checked for evidence of previous treatment. Moreover, the investigation should check on the statements in the application. If there have been material misrepresentations, these may serve as grounds for rescission of the policy.

Questions about other insurance which might cover the loss are directed to the insured and employer (in group cases) and to the hospital and the attending physician on the latest Group Hospital Admissions Form (HAP–4), Individual Hospital Insurance Form (IHF–1) and Attending Physician's Statement (APSC). Where such other insurance exists, it is necessary to contact the other insurers involved if the contract contains an other insurance provision. All of these forms are reproduced in Appendix J.

*Payment.* The final step in the procedure is payment of the claim. This may be paid in full or adjusted or prorated according to policy provisions. Uniform Provision 8 requires "immediate" payment on presentation of proof of loss for benefits not dependent on time of disability or treatment. For benefits payable periodically, the policy must stipulate the time interval for payment, which may not be less frequent than monthly.

Payment ordinarily is made to the insured if living, otherwise to the beneficiary, if any, or the insured's estate. Uniform Provision 9 spells this out, and companies may include as optional provisions a facility of payment clause and/or an assignment clause. The former provides that benefits payable to the insured's estate or to a minor beneficiary up to $1,000 may be paid to a relative by blood or marriage and that such payment will discharge the company's liability. The latter provision is of more significance: it permits assignment of proceeds to hospitals and physicians. As indicated above, this procedure is quite common for medical care benefits. Determination of the amount and duration of benefit payment will be discussed below under the heading of "Possible Courses of Action."

*Group insurance.* The procedure in group insurance is essentially similar to that discussed above but differs in detail. Since the majority of group insurance claimants have limited financial resources, it is important that payments be made promptly. Procedures are designed with this objective and are generally simpler than in individual insurance. Claim forms are usually available directly from the employer. The uniform claim forms for medical care coverages have been discussed above in Chapter 10. Claim forms for loss-of-time benefits are stocked by the employer. They provide for statements from the employer that the employee-claimant lost time as a result of nonoccupational disability; from the attending physician as to inability to work, nature of disability, and prospective duration; and from the claimant, identifying himself and describing the disability.

The group contract may provide for administration of claims by the insurer or by the employer. Self-administration of claims is less common than self-administration of coverage and accounting records because of the need for greater specialized training for claims work. Self-administration of claims will require the services of at least one trained full-time employee.

In the normal insurer-administered system, the employee obtains claim forms from a representative of the employer. Each fills out his appropriate portion of the form, and the physician's statement is added if required. Where the claim is for accidental death, the employer usually will initiate the process and obtain a proof of death to accompany it. The employer forwards the completed claim forms to the local claim office of the insurer. The local office reviews and approves most claims and sends the checks to the employees through the employer.

Claims for large amounts or unusual circumstances may be sent to the home office for approval. This is most likely under accidental death and dismemberment and major medical coverages. Where the claim is for hospital or income benefits that continue for a considerable time, many companies have a simple continuing claim form which the employee periodically submits through the employer. Local claim offices report information on claims paid to the central office daily or weekly. At the central accounting office (usually the home office), records of the group's claims are maintained for premium adjustment purposes.

Under self-administration of claims, certain employees of the employer are permitted to approve claims and sign drafts on the insurer. Usually there is provision for countersignature by an officer of the employer company and/or limits on the size of claim that can be approved. Death, dismemberment, and major medical claims are usually excluded from self-administration because of their size and complexity. Daily reports of claim settlements and the supporting papers are sent to the local claims office of the insurer, which makes the claims entries and sends reports to the home office. In rare cases, the employer will have to contact the insurer about an unusual claim situation, but the routine procedure suffices for the vast majority of claims.

**Blue Cross–Blue Shield.** Since Blue Cross, Blue Shield, and many independent plans are sponsored by the purveyors of medical services, claim procedures differ somewhat from insurance company practice. The claim usually is presented through the physician or hospital, who maintains a supply of claim forms. The insured may fill out the form, but more commonly this is handled by the physician or hospital. The insured merely submits evidence of coverage, and the purveyors of service do the rest. Payment of insured amounts is made directly by the association to the physician or hospital, and the insured is billed by them for any excess.

**Social insurance.** Disability benefit claims under OASDI are handled like other OASDI claims. The insured applies at the nearest Social Security district office. Here he is given forms which must be filled out and accompanied by medical evidence that he is disabled so that he cannot perform any substantially gainful work, that disability has lasted six months or more, and that it is expected to continue six more months. It is important to submit this evidence even if not currently entitled to benefits, in order to have the wage and coverage accounts "frozen." Moreover, this will facilitate benefit payments in the future. Where the applicant is entitled to benefits currently, promptness is even more important: he is not entitled to benefits for any month prior to the month in which application is made. Determination of disability is made by a state agency, usually the agency which handles vocational rehabilitation.

Claim administration under workmen's compensation and compulsory disability insurance laws, where the insurance is written by private companies, is handled very much like group insurance, subject to possible review by the appropriate state agency. This is the workmen's compensation board for workmen's compensation and for the New York disability law; the unemployment compensation bureau under the California and New Jersey laws. Where the insurance is provided by a state or federal agency, the procedure is very much like that for OASDI claims. There is usually provision for appeal of disputed cases to a board of review.

### Possible courses of action

*Payment.*    There are two basic courses of action open to the insurer when confronted with a claim: it may pay the claim or contest it. If the claim is to be paid, there are several possibilities which will be discussed in turn. About 95 percent of claims presented are paid.

1. *Payment of incurred loss in full.*    This is the most common procedure. It is estimated that from 70 to 85 percent of claims are paid in full. The main problem in handling these claims is making sure that the payments are made promptly and courteously. If the amount is paid grudgingly or payment is unduly delayed, the claimant may be as dissatisfied as if the insurer had cut down the amount.

2. *Adjustment to conform to policy limits.*    When the claim exceeds the policy limits or includes items not insured, it must be "adjusted." This means that payment is made only in the amount to which the claimant is entitled by the terms of his contract. This might include the recognition of a deductible or waiting period where the claim as presented did not recognize this provision.

3. *Prorating according to policy provisions.*    As indicated above, there are provisions which may be included in health insurance contracts which may call for reducing the amount payable. Major medical and comprehensive policies usually include percentage participation or coinsurance clauses which call for reimbursing only 75 or 80 percent of eligible loss. Noncancellable and guaranteed renewable policies providing disability income benefits may include a provision for prorating in relation to earned income. All types of contract may include provisions for prorating the benefit amount for other insurance of which the company is not notified, change of occupation, or misstatement of age. Some policies provide for reduced benefits for illness which is not house confining, and some reduce benefits after a certain age, such as 60 or 65. A

kind of prorating may also occur where partial disability is claimed as total. Some contracts prorate for change of residence.

Some insurers request the claimant merely to indicate the total incurred expenses and they then compute the amount payable. Others expect the claimant to compute the amount claimed. Under the latter system, when a claim is adjusted or prorated, it may mean that there has been a failure in communication or that the claim was not properly presented in the first place. This means either that the insured failed to understand his policy or that he is making an attempt to cheat the company. The first of these can largely be prevented by better explanation of coverage at the time of sale and delivery, and the latter by more effective underwriting. It is desirable to reduce situations calling for adjustment or prorating as much as possible, as these are fruitful sources of misunderstanding and ill will. It is important that the insured be made to understand why he is not receiving the amount he asked for and to feel that he is being treated fairly. This calls for tact, courtesy, and diplomacy on the part of the claim administrator.

4. *Coordination of benefits.* Most group contracts now contain the H.I.A.A. model coordination of benefits provision. The disability income provision[2] has the effect of making the group coverage excess over all "other valid coverage." Thus, it is necessary to determine what benefits are available from OASDI, pensions, salary continuation and individual insurance to determine how much is payable. The group insurer will pay the excess over other benefits up to a stated percentage (usually 60 to 75 percent) of earnings. Whenever the benefit payments in other coverage change in amount, the group insurer's liability must be recalculated.

The medical expense provisions[3] require the determination of the order of benefit application to establish whether the insurer is primary or excess. If primary, the insurer pays without regard to the C.O.B. provision; if secondary, it pays the excess over the benefits with the primary plan up to 110 percent reimbursement of all items of eligible expense under either plan, or its own plan limit, whichever is less. Any unused limit in the excess coverage is available, in effect, as an additional limit during the balance of the claim determination period, usually a calendar year, benefit year, or policy year.

Many major medical contracts contain an integrated or corridor deductible provision which requires adjustment on an excess basis.

5. *Expenses not reasonable, necessary, usual or customary.* Almost all major medical and many basic medical expense contracts limit coverage to reasonable and customary charges for necessary care for bodily

---

[2] See above, p. 503.
[3] See above, p. 213.

injury or disease. Sometimes, claims under such contracts must be adjusted to eliminate payment for unnecessary care or routine physical examinations or to reduce payment to the agreed percentage of reasonable and customary charges. Many claims departments rely on relative value schedules together with experience data on fee variation by area as a guide to the reasonableness of fees. When charges exceed this reasonable figure by a sufficient margin, the physician is requested to explain the fee. Sometimes a local medical review committee can help in determining whether care was necessary or fees were reasonable or customary.

6. *Rehabilitation payments.* Sometimes an insurer may make payments for rehabilitation in excess of the policy limits. For example, it might be to the insurer's advantage to pay for a certain operation, for vocational training, or for prosthetic appliances to permit the insured to get back to work and cease drawing benefits. Sometimes a company may agree to continue benefits in reduced amount if the claimant returns to work part time, or agree not to impose another waiting period if his efforts to return to work are unsuccessful.

Some insurers include specific rehabilitation benefits in their disability income policies,[4] and major medical contracts will cover most rehabilitation expenses.

Recently many companies have been experimenting with a program offering rehabilitation benefits, beyond those of the regular contract, as an inducement to undertake and complete rehabilitation. Some pay the cost of the rehabilitation; some advance a lump sum in lieu of disability income which otherwise probably would be payable in a future six-month period; others make advance or additional payments, limiting the total liability to the product of the monthly benefit amount and number of months' maximum benefit period remaining. All provide that benefits will continue during trial work periods, but some reduce benefits by some proportion of actual earnings. Some companies execute a formal contract[5] modifying the policy benefits in these fashions, while others rely on an informal letter of understanding.[6]

Where long-term benefits are in force and the worker is young, rehabilitation will save the companies money and restore the disabled to dignity. However, great care is necessary in such cases. There should be a reasonable likelihood of success and the best relations between com-

---

[4] For two examples, see William Harmelin, "The Humanistic Approach," *Life Association News*, February, 1967, p. 53.

[5] For example, see A. W. Adee, "The Value of Rehabilitation to Health Insurance" in *Principles of Individual Health Insurance II* (New York: Health Insurance Association of America, 1966), p. 46.

[6] For an example of this approach, see John G. Kelly, "Insurance and Rehabilitation of the Disabled," *CLU Journal*, July, 1967, p. 49.

pany and claimant are necessary for a successful outcome. The social advantages are obvious, but insurers should be hesitant to spend their policyholders' or stockholders' money beyond contractual obligations unless the probability of success is good and the liability of which the insurer will be relieved is considerable.

7. *Lump-sum settlements.* These represent voluntary settlements by the insurer in the same way that the rehabilitation payments do. An agreed lump-sum settlement is made in return for the claimant's agreement to waive the right to future disability income. Great care should be exercised in regard to such settlements. There is a temptation to the claim administrator to settle if he can do so for less than the reserve on the claim. However, the reserve represents an average value, and it will not be the average claimant who is interested in a lump-sum settlement. There will be considerable adverse selection, since the claimant is often in a better position than the company to judge his chances of recovery. Care must be exercised to make sure that such settlements do not encourage false or exaggerated claims. Moreover, lump-sum settlement is often not to the insured's advantage, unless he can make use of the funds to provide for rehabilitation or to accomplish a major change in living arrangements so that he can get along on a lower income. State insurance departments often view lump-sum settlements with a jaundiced eye.

**Contest of claim.** Where the company does not feel that a claim should be paid, it will deny liability. This usually results in a contested claim, which stands a good chance of ending up in court. There are two basic grounds for contest: the claimant did not suffer the loss, or the policy does not cover. The policy may not cover for two reasons, either because the particular type of loss is excluded or because the policy was not in force at the time of the loss. The policy might not be in force at the time of the loss because the loss occurred before the inception or after the termination of coverage, or it might be that the policy was never in force because of fraud, misrepresentation, etc., in the making of the contract.

*Loss not incurred.* The occurrence of the loss insured against depends upon the claimant's being disabled within the meaning of the contract or incurring expenses for covered medical care. Determining the existence of disability is difficult because of the subjectivity of the concept. One man may remain at home because of an impairment that another virtually would ignore. The fact that the insured did remain at home is significant but not conclusive. Whether disability exists and, if so, whether it is total will be determined according to the statements of the insured, the opinion of his physician, the actual record of absence from employment, and the nature of the disability in relation to the duties of his occupation. Determination of disability of a self-employed claimant is especially difficult since it is difficult to tell whether he actually is active in his business. This is especially true for a family business. The exact circumstances necessary to establish disability depend upon the wording of the benefit clause, which may refer to "his," "any," or "any occupation for which suited." If the policy covers only confining disability, the wording of this clause must be considered.

In partial disability the benefit clause usually calls for inability to perform "one or more important daily duties" of the occupation, but some policies call for "inability to perform a majority of the duties." Often, partially disabled persons will be employed and paid on a full-time basis; hence the problems of moral hazard are evident.

The company must rely primarily on the statements of the claimant and the physician. It is also necessary to check on the continuance of disability. The actual return to work or the date in the physician's statement as to when disability terminated is the usual closing date of benefit payment, but sometimes other evidence may indicate that recovery was earlier. The case records of insurance companies read like a good detective story. Many interesting stratagems have been employed to prove that disability does not exist.

In the medical care coverages the determination of whether the loss occurred is somewhat simpler because there is usually a bill from the purveyor of service, which serves as objective evidence of the expenditure. However, there are certain problems that may arise. One is the question as to whether the facility where the claimant was treated is really a hospital. Generally, confinement in rest, nursing, and convalescent homes is not covered. Insurers usually will not raise this question if the occasion for admission is a surgical operation or other treatment that would ordinarily be performed in a regular hospital.

Most policies providing either medical care or disability income benefits require that the claimant be under the care and treatment of a physician other than himself. Since state laws and standards vary greatly, uniform treatment cannot be applied to osteopaths, chiropractors, naturopaths, and others without an M.D. degree.

Most contracts call for settlement of medical care fees on a reimbursement basis. It is necessary that evidence of the actual amount of the charge be submitted, and cases have been known in which a fee was inflated and the excess shared with the insured. Major medical and some other policies provide that only the "usual and customary" charges for the services will be reimbursed. Under both these situations, the claim administrator should be alert for claims whose amounts are seriously out of line with the general practice in the area. The development of relative value schedules and, occasionally, advisory fee schedules by medical societies has gone far to provide objective standards of reasonableness.[7]

---

[7] For a listing, see Health Insurance Association of America, *Relative Value Study Index* (Processed).

Many medical societies have grievance or review committees which deal, among other things, with complaints about excessive fees. The general problem of overutilization was discussed in Chapter 10 above.

*No coverage in policy.* Because of the difficulties of proving that the loss did not take place, most insurers prefer to contest, if at all, on grounds that the loss is not covered by the policy. This may be because the particular loss was excluded or because the policy itself was not in force at the time of the loss.

Loss Excluded. The exclusions in various types of health insurance policy have been discussed above. Generally, specific exclusions such as war, ridered impairments, sickness under accident policies, and the like are not difficult to apply. The two common exclusions which are likely to produce the most difficulty are the probationary period and the preexisting condition exclusion.

Probationary periods are found in many commercial policies, especially in regard to sickness claims. The application of this exclusion is primarily one of determining when the loss began. It is not difficult to determine the date of an accidental injury, but the date of origin of a sickness is difficult to establish. About the only practical way of upsetting the contention of the insured and his physician in this regard is to find records of treatment for the same condition before the alleged commencement of disability.

The preexisting condition exclusion presents similar problems of administration. While the company does not have to prove that the insured knew of his impairment, it is common practice to avoid enforcing this provision where it appears that he was really unaware of his condition and it could have been discovered only by medical opinion. However, where the company does wish to enforce the exclusion, it is relatively easy to do so, since all it need show is that the impairment existed and was the proximate cause of the loss. The company must depend for evidence primarily upon records of physicians or hospitals relating to previous treatment or medical examinations. So-called "routine" examinations shortly before the issuance of the policy should be investigated carefully.

Policy not in Force. The company may also contest on the grounds that the policy was not in force at the time of the loss. This may be because it was not yet effective, because it had terminated or lapsed, or because it was invalid because of misrepresentation or concealment at issue. The determination of dates of coverage and lapse is not difficult; the major problem arises in determining the date of loss, as discussed above in connection with the probationary period.

Denial of liability on the grounds of misrepresentation in the application or concealment is somewhat more difficult. It is necessary to show that the insurer was misinformed as to a material fact and, in concealment cases, that this was intentional on the part of the applicant. Noncancellable and guaranteed renewable policies contain a provision making the policy incontestable as to statements in the application after it has been in force for three or sometimes two years. The Uniform Provisions limit the right of rescission to three years unless the misstatement was fraudulent, and exclusions for preexisting conditions may not be enforced after the three-year period unless the condition is excluded by name or specific description. Thus defenses of this type must generally be raised within three years of issue to be effective.[8]

It is even more difficult to defend successfully on grounds of fraud. This involves a conscious intent by the insured to deceive the company to its detriment, which is extremely difficult to prove in court. It is difficult enough to get a jury to believe that the insurer was deceived where there was a complete application and more difficult where there was a physical examination. It is even more difficult to convince a jury that this deceit was intentional, since the claimant can always plead ignorance or misunderstanding. Even where fraud can be proved, rescission of a policy usually requires the insurer to refund all premiums back to the date of original issue.

After the insurer has decided to contest a claim and on what grounds, it still does not rush into court. Juries are notoriously unsympathetic to insurance companies, and it is better to avoid a court action where possible. The best procedure is to accumulate all possible evidence and show enough of it to the claimant to convince him that it is better to withdraw the claim. Where outright fraud is believed to exist, a combination of delay and bluffing tactics may be effective.

Where these methods do not result in withdrawal of the claim, it is wise to consider a compromise settlement. There may be a real difference of opinion as to whether the charges were reasonable. Because so many of these things are subjective, there is room for a compromise settlement in a good proportion of cases. Where the company can settle for less than the probable court award plus costs of defense, it is to its advantage to do so, but care should be taken to avoid encouraging excessive claims. Insurers rarely let a case get to court if they can avoid it, and they go so far as to prosecute a claimant for fraud only in the rarest instances.

### Responsibility of the parties in claim adjustment

Each of the various parties involved in the claim adjustment process should meet certain responsibilities in order to achieve the type of claim adjustment which will be both a credit to the industry and a protection of insurer assets. These parties are the insured, the agent, the under-

---

[8] In many states, the limit is two years.

writer, the policy writer, company management, the claim adjuster, the inspector, the physician, the hospital, and the employer.

The *insured* has the obligation to pay premiums promptly, to notify the company of loss, supply proper proof, and cooperate in the investigation. If he meets these obligations and has the mental attitude to regard his insurance fairly, a prompt and satisfactory settlement will usually result.

However, it is the responsibility of company personnel, especially *agents and brokers*, to see to it that the insured is made aware of his responsibilities. Agents should make sure that the policy is explained adequately at the time of sale and especially at the time of delivery. The insured will have forgotten most of the detail of the original sales presentation. This explanation should include not only the main benefit provisions but the limits and exclusions and the insured's duties at the time of loss.

At the time of claim the agent should assist the policyholder in giving notice, obtaining supporting data, and filing proof. He often will deliver the claim check. In addition to those duties which involve assisting the insured, agents have a responsibility to the company. Careful field underwriting will eliminate most cases involving moral hazard and greatly reduce future claim problems. At the time of claim, the agent should bend every effort to make sure that only valid claims, reasonable in amount, are submitted.

The *home office underwriter* should also be on the alert for evidence of moral hazard. Underwriting should be performed at the time of issue, not at the time of claim. The policy-writing process can also contribute to more effective claims administration. If the coverage is soundly designed and the wording clear and unambiguous, claim settlement will be facilitated. The company management must determine a proper claims philosophy, establish overall procedures for implementing it, and exercise control to see that it is carried out.

*Claim adjusters* should be thoroughly trained in their work and closely supervised by management. Coordination of their function with the sales force is desirable. The inspector should carry on his investigation in such a way as to obtain accurate information, yet consider the feelings and sensibilities of the claimant. The inspection agency and the insurer should cooperate closely.

The *physician and hospital* are important sources of information, and much reliance must be placed on the data they supply. In the medical care coverages their charges are among the chief determinants of the amount of claim. The medical profession, which has always claimed the right to establish fees in accordance with ability to pay, must recognize that the private practice of medicine and the private insurance business are tied closely together. They should be educated to this fact, so that a working agreement can be reached so that the prudent, who have made provision in advance for medical care expenditures, will not be penalized for their foresight by being charged a higher fee. Even where the entire bill is met by insurance, such a practice will cost the policyholders more in the form of higher premiums. Provisions for direct payment to physicians and hospitals under uniform claim and assignment procedures should go a long way toward eliminating overcharges and overinsurance.

The *employer* of the claimant is an important source of information and in group insurance may assume most of the work of settlement. A clear understanding of the nature of the coverage and of his responsibilities is desirable.

## Summary

The function of claim administration is to pay all legitimate claims promptly, pleasantly, and in accordance with the terms of the contract. This represents the delivery of the product of the industry, and the attitudes engendered are a prime factor in future goodwill. Yet a company must not pay illegitimate claims or overpay. If it does, it is overcharging the legitimate policyholders and may even impair the security of their contracts.

The four main steps in claim settlement are notice of loss, investigation, proof of loss, and payment. Procedures in group insurance are simpler than in individual insurance. Sometimes claim administration is handled by the employer. In social insurance the procedure involves about the same steps but is greatly conditioned by the nature of the agency administering the plan. In Blue Cross and Blue Shield plans the procedure is similar, except that payment is made directly to the hospital or physician, with the claimant being billed for any balance.

Possible courses of action include payment and contest of claim. Most claims (95 percent) are paid. Payment may be in full, adjusted to conform to policy limits, or prorated in accordance with policy provisions. Sometimes extra-contractual payments are made for rehabilitation or lump-sum settlements made in lieu of disability income payments. If the claim is to be contested, it may be on grounds of nonexistence of disability or noncoverage of the policy. The policy may not cover because of specific exclusions, loss occurring before or after the policy period, or because the policy is invalid owing to misrepresentation. Even where it is decided to contest a claim, informal procedures and compromise settlements are generally preferable to court action.

Claim administration involves almost everyone connected with the insurance contract. The various parties should understand their responsibilities and exercise restraint and good judgment. If this is done, misunderstandings over claims can be kept to a minimum, and public relations can be greatly improved.

## Selected references

*See the following items from the General Bibliography: 4, ch. 23; 7, ch. 9; 8, ch. 9; 10, ch. 13; 16, Vol. I, ch. 16; 20, chs. 8, 9, and 10; 22, ch. 12.*

ERICSON, ARTHUR A. *The Group Health Insurance Claim.* New York: Roberts Publishing Co., 1965.

HEALTH INSURANCE ASSOCIATION OF AMERICA. *Relative Value Study Index* (Processed).

HUNTER, ARTHUR. "Treatment of Claims for Total and Permanent Disability," *Transactions of the Actuarial Society of America,* Vol. XXII, p. 442.

KELLY, JOHN G. "Insurance and Rehabilitation of the Disabled," *CLU Journal,* July, 1967, p. 49.

METCALF, ROBERT K. "Disability Viewed Claimwise," *PALC,* Vol. XXVI, p. 95.

MORRISON, DOUGLAS N., AND WESSELS, WALLACE. *Claim Administration, Life and Health Insurance.* Omaha: International Claim Association, 1966.

## chapter 21

> With the gratifying feeling that our duty has been done!—W. S.
> Gilbert, *The Gondoliers*

# Distribution

### The unmet need

Despite the tremendous growth of health insurance in recent years, a broad potential market remains. As indicated in Chapter 3, private insurance programs meet more than half the total expense of hospital and physicians' charges. Less than one third of the short-term income loss is met by insurance and no more than 20 percent of the long-term loss. Other types of medical care expenditure generally are not covered. Thus there is still room for great expansion in the types of policy now generally issued. The market for major medical still has tremendous potential and that for long-term disability income insurance is wide open. Only about 72 million persons are covered by major medical policies and 15 to 20 million by long-term disability income policies. This represents only about 36 percent of the population covered by major medical and about 20 to 25 percent of the labor force covered by long-term disability income insurance. There is plenty of room for future growth.

Like life insurance, health insurance requires extensive sales efforts in order to reach most of the market. Except for aviation accident contracts, very little is purchased at the initiative of the buyer.

### The distribution process

*Methods of selling.* Health insurance is sold by agents, brokers, and direct mail, backed up by advertising. In group insurance, salaried group representatives assist the agents and brokers, and the home office actuarial and underwriting departments participate in preparing group proposals for some cases.

*Insurers.* Health insurance is sold by insurance companies, by Blue Cross and Blue Shield associations, and by independent plans. Social insurance sometimes is provided by governmental organizations. Most of what is said in this chapter applies to insurance company sales methods and to a lesser degree to the Blues.

The independent plans are so heterogeneous that little generalization is possible. Their distribution setup may resemble that of insurance companies or may be almost automatic, as in social insurance.

Government insurers generally do not engage in selling efforts. Where membership is compulsory, there is no need, and where they compete with private insurers, they are usually content to accept only the cases which seek them out. An exception was the extensive advertising campaign during the initial enrollment for Title XVIII, Part B Medicare benefits in 1966.

Insurance companies in the health insurance field include life companies, casualty companies, and specialist monoline health insurers. The life companies write life insurance and annuities, and usually the health lines are of secondary importance in their activities. However, some push health insurance very actively, and about 85 percent of the insurance company health business is written by life companies.

Casualty companies also write compensation, liability, and certain "casualty property" lines such as theft, power plant, and glass insurance. Many of them are also active in the fidelity and surety bonding business. In these companies health insurance is likely to be considered as a line of not too great importance. Many life companies have a casualty-property running mate and vice versa. Usually in such a group or fleet of companies, health insurance is written by the life company. The specialist insurers devote their entire sales effort to health insurance. They resemble life companies most closely, and several have entered the life business as an outgrowth of their health insurance business.

*Agents and brokers.* The life companies use the same agency force for health insurance as for their other lines. Their agents owe primary loyalty to the one company and tend to emphasize it in their presentations. Casualty companies and the monoline specialists rely on the independent general insurance agent and broker to a greater degree than do the life companies. However, most companies of all types are willing to accept brokerage business from general insurance agents and brokers, or "surplus" or "excess" business from life insurance agents of other companies.

In casualty insurance, as in property insurance, the agent or broker is considered to "own" the business. That is, he has the right to change the policy from one insurer to another at expiration. Most life insurance companies provide for some degree of vesting of renewal commission in the event of termination of agency connection. This gives the agent protection similar to that obtained through the ownership of expirations.

Since health insurance used to be considered a casualty line, the traditional attitude has carried over to some degree. However, the influence of the life insurance companies is changing this picture. The increasing use of level premiums graded by age at issue, noncancellable and guaranteed renewable contracts, incontestable and "time limit on certain defenses" clauses, probationary periods, and nonlevel commissions[1] have led to a recognition that change of insurer is usually to the disadvantage of the insured.

Some life companies sell health insurance policies in combination with life insurance, using a single application and combined premium billing where state laws permit.

General insurance agents and brokers sometimes use health insurance as a leader or "door-opener." Almost everyone is a prospect, and the high claim frequency of the basic medical expense policies makes for a quick demonstration to the clientele of the value of insurance "in action."

However, it seems more logical that health insurance should be sold in connection with life insurance. Both involve the protection of earned personal income and existing wealth against extraordinary losses. Both represent long-term risks, and health policies are increasingly being written on a long-term basis, often with renewal guaranteed. Health policies are in effect incontestable, like life insurance, and usually are issued by the same companies. The process of programming health insurance is very similar to that of programming life insurance, and the two should be coordinated. Life policies provide some disability protection by riders; the entire life insurance program may be upset by disability unless adequate safeguards are included; and health insurance may reduce the need for life insurance for some purposes such as last-illness expenses. The process of programming will be discussed below.

*Direct mail and advertising.* Some companies, especially specialist insurers, have developed a successful direct mail health insurance business. The commercial traveling men's associations and specialist companies catering to such groups as government employees and teachers are the most noteworthy. These companies rely heavily on advertising and on word-of-mouth recommendations by existing members as well as on the endorsement of sponsoring organizations. Often their expense ratios are fairly low, despite the costs of mail and advertising, but the policyholder must dispense with the personal service of the local agent. Recently a number of insurers have offered direct mail coverage through oil companies and credit card organizations.

Other insurers use advertising in varying degrees. In addition to direct mail, newspapers, magazines, radio, and television are employed by some companies. The regulation of advertising by the national and state governments and by voluntary efforts of the companies will be discussed in the following chapter.

---

[1] Nonlevel commissions involve a high first-year acquisition expense. Every time an insured changes policies, he must incur this expense again.

*The Blues.*  Blue Cross and Blue Shield organizations employ about the same methods of selling as do insurance companies, except that they make use of salaried representatives rather than commissioned agents and brokers. However, they refer to the process as "enrollment" rather than as "selling." Their organizations are comparable to the exclusive agency insurance companies in some of the casualty and property lines, except, of course, that they operate in a limited geographical area. Generally they do not solicit individual business with any intensity. Solicitation is limited to fair-sized groups. Individual applicants, other than conversions from group, are accepted sometimes only for brief periods once or twice a year. Enrollment periods are limited in an attempt to minimize the adverse selection that might be expected from applicants who seek coverage on their own initiative.

*Group contracts.*  In group insurance the agent or broker makes the initial contact with the prospect and sells him on the idea of considering a group policy. At this point he often calls in the group representative, who is a salaried employee of the company. The group representative generally takes control of the sales process from this point on. It is necessary to get information about the type of coverage in which the prospect is interested, other group plans in effect, and the necessary data regarding the employees to be covered. This will include the age, sex, and salary distribution and usually some estimate of the number of employees with dependents, and often the age and sex of the dependents. The group representative should be familiar with the type of group insurance carried by other employers and with the prevailing attitudes of labor unions in the area.

The group representative works out a formal proposal for the employer, giving a brief description of the coverages, cost estimates for employer and employee, retention illustrations and suggested schedules of coverage amounts and contributions. If the plan is not standard or if the case is very large, the home office may prepare special rates. If the proposal is extremely complicated, it may be prepared in the home office. The representative then presents the plan to the employer and attempts to close the case. Frequently, proposals from other insurers also are being considered, and it may be necessary to revise the proposed plan several times before agreement is reached. The original agent will cooperate in this process and endeavor to facilitate the closing of the sale, but the main burden is on the group representative.

After the sale is made, the plan must be installed. Where the plan is contributory, it is necessary to explain and "sell" it to the required proportion of eligible employees (usually 75 percent) before the plan can go into effect. Descriptive literature and forms must be prepared. The representative may meet with groups of supervisors and/or employees to explain the plan and prepare publicity releases for company and local newspapers and/or display material for bulletin boards. When the employees have signed up, certificates are issued on the basis of the sign-up cards, the premium payment is made, and the plan goes into effect. A wise agent will collect enough toward the premium to bind the case as soon as possible in the transaction, often at the signing of the application of the master group policy. The group man also must instruct the personnel department as to proper procedures for maintaining records and handling claims. As indicated above, these functions may be performed largely by the employer or by the insurer, depending on the size of the case and the wishes of the parties.

*Credit insurance.* Credit life and health insurance is marketed in two ways: in the form of group insurance and by individual policies. When an individual policy plan is used, an officer or employee of the bank, savings and loan association, or other institution is appointed as an agent of the insurer and licensed. However, the commissions usually accrue to the institution rather than to the individual.

In the case of group credit insurance, a master group policy is issued to the institution sponsoring the plan and commissions for its sale are payable to the regular, full-time, licensed agent who placed the group contract. No commission is payable to the institution on account of insurance becoming effective upon individuals under the group policy. However, dividends or experience rating credits usually do accrue to the institution.

*Other sales methods.* Industrial insurance agents must collect premiums as well as sell insurance. The industrial method of operation was described above in Chapter 14. The industrial agent is supervised much more closely than the ordinary life or health agent and his status usually is that of an employee, rather than an independent contractor.

Fraternal associations sometimes sell insurance to their members through the secretary of the lodge or a designated deputy in the local lodge. Some, however, have developed agency organizations similar to those of other insurers. Sometimes other clubs and associations contract with an insurance company to provide group, blanket, or individual insurance to the members. In these cases, some official of the club often assumes some enrollment responsibility and may be licensed as an agent and compensated by a flat salary or commission.

Travel accident contracts, as indicated in Chapter 14, may be sold by railroad ticket agents, by agents in booths at airports, or by machine. In each case, some licensed agent must handle the business. The carrier's employee must be licensed as an agent of the insurer. Licensed agents must service the vending machines and they receive commissions on the business produced. Of course, the owner of the machine and of the space also must be compensated. Although dependent on volume, these payments are considered rents, not commissions.

***Types of field organization.*** Insurer field operations may be classified as general agency, branch office, direct reporting and direct writing. All but the last of these involve sales personnel in the field and the systems may be further classified according to whether the representation is exclusive or nonexclusive.

The general agency system involves a general agent who is an independent contractor authorized to represent the insurer in a particular territory. He may or may not have an exclusive franchise in the area. He receives the maximum commission paid and contracts with soliciting agents to represent him (or the insurer) in the sales process. The general agent's income is the difference between the commission he receives from the insurer and that which he pays the soliciting agent. Sometimes the soliciting agents contract directly with the insurer, and the general agent gets an additional commission called an "override" (or "overwrite") on the business they produce.

The general agent is responsible for recruiting and training agents, and often for collection of premiums, handling policy changes and providing claims service. Some have limited authority to adjust and pay claims. The general agent usually pays his own overhead and salary costs out of his commission income, although increasingly, especially for new general agents, the insurer pays special allowances for these purposes.

The branch office system involves a branch manager who is a salaried employee of the insurer. The insurer pays the expense of operating the branch office and contracts directly with the soliciting agents. Either formally or informally, the branch manager's salary depends on the volume and premium income.

The direct reporting system dispenses with general agencies or branch offices and involves the agent dealing directly with the insurer's home office. This system is practical only for smaller insurers with business concentrated in a limited area. In effect, this is the system used by most of the Blues.

Direct writing dispenses entirely with the field force and involves the insured dealing directly with the insurer's home office. This method is used by mail-order and specialty insurers and by small local mutuals and some fraternal organizations.

Exclusive agency relationship involves the agent agreeing to represent only one insurer or agreeing to give the great bulk of the business he produces to that insurer. Insurers like the Blues with salaried sales representatives use this system, as do some of the largest automobile insurers,[2] some of which are moving into the health field in force.

Most life insurers use a semiexclusive agency arrangement with their full-time agents for both life and health contracts. The agent agrees to

---

[2] Such as State Farm, Nationwide and Allstate. These often are miscalled "direct writers."

submit to the insurer all cases where the insurer has appropriate contracts available. Business which the insurer does not handle, or for which it offers a substandard or rated-up contract, and other cases where competition requires, may be submitted to another insurer on a brokerage basis. This is known as surplus or excess business.

In the property-casualty insurance business, most agents operate on a nonexclusive or "independent" basis. They are free to represent several competing insurers and apportion the business as they wish. Many such insurers, however, require a minimum production from each agent. When these insurers write health insurance, they usually use their standard agency contracts and system. Usually, the insurer provides much less in the way of office space, clerical and telephone service and the like to independent agents than to exclusive agents.

*Commissions.* Group representatives and the "solicitors" of the Blues usually are compensated by either a straight salary or a salary plus bonus. Agents and brokers, on the other hand, are compensated by commission arrangements. There are two methods of establishing commission scales: the level and the nonlevel basis. The level basis involves commission rates which remain the same during the life of the policy, while the nonlevel basis involves a high first-year commission and lower renewal commissions. The first is the casualty insurance approach; the second the life insurance approach. To a considerable degree, the type of insurer will determine the choice of commission arrangement. Most life companies, however, will allow an agent to switch to a level commission basis if he wishes, so that commissions are level for ten years.

In comparing commissions, it should be noted that not only the rate is important. The degree of vesting in the event of death, disability, retirement, or termination of agency contract affects the value of the commission. Moreover, the scale must be considered in relation to the amount of work the agent is expected to do in the form of continuing service, collecting premiums, and handling claims. Practice in this regard varies greatly among companies.

Generally, the level commission is 20–25 percent for the soliciting agent each year. Level commissions usually are fully vested under the concept that the agent "owns his renewals" and may, if he wishes, shift the business to another company.[3] Brokers usually receive the same commissions as agents, but they may get a higher rate or greater vesting to compensate for lack of certain benefits such as pension rights. Some in-

---

[3] As indicated above, such shifting is rarely to the advantage of the insured and may involve a significant disadvantage especially under noncancellable and guaranteed renewable contracts or where the insured has some health impairment. While shifting hurts the insured less under contracts with level commissions than under contracts with nonlevel commissions, it is generally undesirable.

surers charge a policy fee of $5 to $10 at issue. Part of this usually goes to the agent.

A typical general agent's override commission is 5 to 10 percent each year, but with only half this vested from the second through the tenth year and none thereafter. The general agent is responsible for handling (and paying for) service and premium collections, and the reduced vesting makes it possible for a company to finance these activities if the general agent terminates his contract. In a branch office system the branch manager usually will get a salary plus bonus. However, he may get an override commission of about 5 percent instead of these. Under this system the company bears the cost of service and premium collection.

A typical nonlevel commission scale for commercial business would call for a 40 percent first-year commission, 20 percent the second year, and 10 percent thereafter. For guaranteed renewable business the first-year rate often is higher and the renewal rate tends to be lower. This reflects the presumed higher persistency of this type of business. A typical scale might be 50, four 10's, and indefinite 5's. Some companies do not pay renewal commissions beyond the 10th year but may pay service fees for agents still under contract. There are many variations in the amount of commissions and the vesting provisions.

The general agent's override commissions are lower under the nonlevel than under the level scale. A typical arrangement might call for 5 to 10 percent first year, fully vested, followed by 3 percent vested and 2 percent unvested for the next nine years, and 2 percent vested and 3 percent unvested thereafter. Broker's commissions usually are not payable for more than 10 years but usually are fully vested. Almost all noncancellable and guaranteed renewable business and a large proportion of other individual business is now being sold under nonlevel commission plans.

In group insurance, the nonlevel commission scale is general, but some insurers will pay an equivalent level scale instead if the agent requests. In addition, group commission rates are graded down as the size of the case increases. This helps make possible the "size discounts" in premium described above. Table 21–1 is representative of current practice in soliciting agent's commissions. Where a group plan is changed substantially or increased, the additional premium is treated as new business, and the first-year rate applies starting at the top of the table again. However, renewals on such new business often are paid at the rate for the total premium in force.

Blanket, franchise and association group commissions may range from less than true group to the equivalent of the rate for individual business depending on the sales and administrative effort required of the agent. Some insurers pay no commission or a lower commission than usual for group conversion business. This is intended to offset the adverse selection involved in such conversions and discourage the agent from seeking them out. However, the adverse selection may be made worse if only a few of those eligible convert. Generally, the least healthy will be the first to exercise their conversion rights.

In addition to commissions, a variety of fringe benefits is provided for full-time agents. These may include pensions, group life and health insurance and the like. Many insurers also pay bonuses to agents based on extra production, persistency or sometimes on the loss ratio or underwriting profit on the agent's block of business.

Financing arrangements are common for new full-time agents and are generally similar to those used in life insurance. Most plans pay an agreed

### TABLE 21-1
#### Typical Group Commission Schedule

| Amount of Annual Premium | Commission Rates (Percentage of Premium) | | |
| --- | --- | --- | --- |
| | Nonlevel Basis | | Alternative Level Basis |
| | 1st Year | Years 2 to 10 | Years 1 to 10 |
| First $ 1,000.................. | 20.0 | 5.0 | 6.5 |
| Next    4,000.................. | 20.0 | 3.0 | 4.7 |
| Next   15,000.................. | 15.0 | 1.5 | 2.85 |
| Next   10,000.................. | 12.5 | 1.5 | 2.6 |
| Next   10,000.................. | 10.0 | 1.5 | 2.35 |
| Next   20,000.................. | 5.0 | 1.5 | 1.85 |
| Next   50,000.................. | 2.5 | 1.0 | 1.15 |
| Next  150,000.................. | 1.0 | 0.5 | 0.55 |
| Next  250,000.................. | 0.25 | 0.1 | 0.115 |
| Over  500,000.................. | 0.1 | 0.1 | 0.1 |

Source: Scale in use at time of writing for most life and health insurance by a large mutual insurer.

monthly salary, against which commissions are offset, if earned. The proportion which must be offset increases with the agent's length of service and eventually he switches to a straight commission basis. Financing plans may run from 90 days to four years, depending on the insurer's philosophy and practice. The use of a drawing account whereby the agent assumes the responsibility of repaying all advances out of commissions or otherwise is becoming rare.

*The sales process.* The process of selling usually is considered to consist of the activities of prospecting, the approach, the presentation, and the close. While there is no point in attempting to reproduce in this chapter all the principles of personal salesmanship, some discussion of these activities as applied to the selling of health insurance is appropriate.

Both the life and the general insurance underwriter will find that their existing clientele constitute their best source of prospects for health insurance. In the course of developing and reviewing life insurance programs and property-liability insurance surveys, there is an excellent opportunity to broaden the process to include health insurance. In prospecting among nonclientele groups, in general the same criteria which qualify a prospect for life insurance also qualify him for health insurance.

It should be noted that underwriting standards for many of the better types of health insurance are higher than those for life insurance, so more careful prospecting and field underwriting are necessary. For this reason, some underwriters prefer to defer the actual submission of the application for health insurance until the life policy is paid for and in force. Thus they avoid the risk of losing the whole sale when the applicant is disappointed because he does not qualify for one policy.

The techniques of preapproach and approach are similar to those used in the sale of life insurance. Life or general insurance agents may find the use of direct mail to existing clients particularly useful in building up a volume of health insurance. As indicated above, the life insurance programming process or the general insurance survey is a natural approach to the presentation of health insurance.

The presentation and closing processes are also similar to those used in life insurance. The underwriter may sell policies, packages, or programs. The latter method is clearly superior for the better class of prospects and will be discussed below in considerable detail. However, the package presentation, when based on a new and outstanding type of policy which fills a real need, is very effective as a means of developing new clientele. It may lead naturally into a complete programming operation where the opportunity is disclosed.

Closing is similar to the same process in life insurance. The medical examination may be used in the same way where it is required. It is probably easier to convince the prospect of the need for speed in putting the policy in force in health insurance than in life insurance. This is true because it is psychologically easier for him to visualize himself disabled than dead.

*Field underwriting and persistency.* The importance of careful selection of risks as a determinant of the insurer's loss ratios and therefore profit was discussed above in Chapter 17. As a "field underwriter" the agent participates in this selection process and thus affects his company's profit and, in the aggregate, the cost of health insurance to the public.

But selection of insureds has an equally important effect on insurer profits through the expense portion of the premium. Aside from loss ratios, the most important determinant of the profitability of a single contract or of a block of business is its persistency—how long it stays in force. First, the lives who drop out are the healthier and the group left may have high claims.

Moreover, as indicated above in Chapters 18 and 19, most of the expenses incurred by an insurer on a particular contract are incurred at the time of issue. These include the expenses of the high first-year commission (most contracts call for nonlevel commissions), the inspection reports, perhaps a medical examination, policy writing and issue and setting up the records for the contract. These expenses, together with the contract's share of claims for the first accounting period, the pro rata unearned premium reserve, and possibly an additional reserve for guaranteed renewable insurance,[4] substantially exceed the first-year premium received. This means that the insurer loses money during the first several years on every case written. During the first year there may be a negative cash flow and there will almost always be a net loss after considering accrual items such as the pro rata unearned premium reserve. If the contract terminates at this time, the insurer will suffer a loss. Indeed, it takes several years for the insurer to recover the high first-year expenses and a lapse any time within these years will produce a loss. This process results in a drain on surplus which must be replenished in later years when the premium exceeds the charges for losses, expenses, and additions to reserves. In the meantime, the insurer is losing interest on the deficiency. These losses fall on the insurer's profits in the short run, but in the long run they must be covered by premium income. Thus low persistency operates to raise the cost of health insurance to the public.

Various mathematical models may be set up to demonstrate this phenomenon under various assumptions. According to one such model,[5] the insurer reaches a positive cash-flow position on a particular policy which stays in force in the second policy year. However, when interest on the deficit and the share of losses on lapsing contracts are considered, a positive cash flow is not reached until the third year. Without considering interest and lapse, the accrued deficit on the whole block of business is wiped out by the end of the 11th year; considering them, it is not wiped out until the end of the 15th year. This model makes no allowance for a planned profit margin in the premium rate. With such an allowance, which leads to a higher premium, the break-even points would be somewhat sooner. The figures above are based on "intermediate" persistency assumptions. With an assumption of "good" persistency, the deficit (allow-

---

[4] Most insurers use a preliminary term valuation basis so as to eliminate this item as a charge against first-year premium.

[5] John H. Miller, "The Price of Failure," *Selected Talks from Eleventh Annual Accident and Sickness Spring Meeting, 1960.* Life Insurance Agency Management Association. A model is a device to test results of a process by making certain simplified but realistic assumptions as to the values and quantities involved in the process and tracing the results over a period of operational time. In this case, the values assumed include premium level and volume, first-year and subsequent losses and expenses and similar factors. These figures are combined with various lapse rates to show the effect on the insurer's surplus position and profit.

ing for interest and lapse) is wiped out by the ninth year. With "poor" persistency, the deficit is larger at the end of the 15th year than at the end of the first and still is growing.

Out of 1,000 policies issued, with good persistency, 328 remain in force at the end of the 15th year and the insurer's profit is $15,378. With "intermediate" persistency, 239 remain in force and the insurer breaks precisely even. With "poor" persistency, only 172 policies are in force, and the cumulative loss is $13,267.

Persistency similarly affects the agent's commission. Good persistency results in commissions 14 percent higher than "intermediate," and "poor" persistency results in commissions 12 percent lower than intermediate.

Another model[6] shows cash flow turning positive in the second quarter for both "high" and "low" persistency. The deficit is wiped out at the end of the third year under "high" persistency, but not until the fifth year with "low" persistency. When it is assumed that policies are issued over a period of 20 years at a constant rate, it takes 6 years to attain a profit position with "high" persistency and 18 years with "low" persistency. The insurer's 20-year profit on a single block of 1,250 policies is $262,400 with "high" persistency and only $39,950 with low persistency. On a business of 1,250 policies per quarter for 20 years, the cumulative net gain after 20 years is $2,263,620 with high persistency and only $90,030 with low persistency.[7]

Thus the agent can improve his own profit position and that of his company by working towards high persistency among his insureds. This can be accomplished by selecting prospects who have stable incomes and personalities, by carefully fitting the coverage to the client's needs and ability to pay and by aiding the company in premium collection when necessary. Occasionally this may involve "reselling" the client on the need for the protection. The responsibilities of home office and field management in encouraging persistency by sound product design, careful selection and training of agents, good claims practice and good billing procedure (including notices to the agent when payment is delayed) are obvious.

### Programming health insurance

*General.* There are three main ways of selling insurance: policy selling, package selling, and program selling.

---

[6] Health Insurance Association of America.

[7] This discussion implicitly has assumed that the insurer involved was a stock company. In the case of a mutual, the premium rate would be higher, and the break-even point could be reached sooner if policy dividends were not paid in the early years. Much of the "profit" of a mutual eventually would be distributed to the policy-holders as dividends.

Policy selling involves selling a policy on its own merits, with little consideration of the needs of the prospect. This approach is epitomized by the agent who pushes the "special—just out today." In the early days of life and health insurance, where it could be assumed that the typical prospect had little or no insurance and any coverage was better than none, this approach may have had some merit, but it is clearly obsolete today.

Package selling involves the presentation of coverage to meet a single need such as mortgage protection. It is possible that an adequate program can be built up by this process, but this is unlikely. The dangers of gaps and overlaps in coverage and incorrect priorities should be obvious.

Programming, on the other hand, represents the professional approach to selling life and health insurance. All needs are considered in connection with resources available to meet them, and a complete plan of protection is worked out. Unfortunately, while programming techniques have reached a high state of development in life insurance, less attention has been devoted to programming health insurance. Yet long-term disability and large medical bills can have a more severe impact on the family than death or retirement and, unlike retirement, may occur at any time.

Life and health needs should be programmed as a part of the same process, for several reasons. In case of death, disability, or retirement, the main loss is a loss of income. The peril which causes the loss is relatively immaterial. Disability may completely upset the life insurance and retirement program unless adequate safeguards are included. Both logic and the professional concept of life underwriting require that the program include adequate protection against all three risks—death, disability, and old age. Moreover, provision for adequate income after retirement age if disability occurs early in life requires, in the present state of the arts, a combination of the two types of coverage.

The process of programming involves five steps: (1) an analysis of needs; (2) an analysis of existing insurance and other resources; (3) an analysis of ability to pay for more protection; (4) the development of the program based on these three analyses; and (5) putting the program into effect. In addition, the program should be reviewed and brought up to date periodically.

The programming sale usually involves at least two interviews. The first interview is a fact-finding interview, in the course of which the necessary information for the analyses is developed. This interview is also part of the presentation, in that the needs of the family for insurance protection are developed and the prospect is motivated to take some action. In the second interview the completed program is presented, and the closing of the sale takes place. Of course, either of these may turn into several interviews before its purposes are achieved.

In the fact-finding interview it is desirable to have both the prospect and his wife present. Most underwriters prefer to analyze needs as the first step after "selling" the couple on the desirability of the whole process. The technique is to kill and disable the prospect in imagination and develop with the family what the needs would be for immediate cash and for income in the future. In establishing the amounts needed, it is well to be conservative, so that the resulting program will bear a reasonable relationship to ability to pay.

After these needs have been established and estimated as accurately as possible, the facts about existing insurance, OASDI, pension, and other resources are obtained. Where possible, it is a good idea to obtain the actual policies. This greatly facilitates the analysis and almost guarantees that the prospect will follow through and permit the closing interview to take place.

Finally, some indication of ability to pay is sought. Some underwriters ask direct questions relating to how much the family is saving. An experienced underwriter will learn to estimate the probable costs of a program and may ask, "If you really wanted to, could you 'save' (say) $20 more a week?" Other underwriters prefer to estimate ability to pay on the basis of their observation of the income of the prospect and his standard of living.

In developing the program for final presentation, it may be well to prepare alternative recommendations at different costs. Some underwriters prefer to prepare an alternative plan which costs less by cutting down on the provision for one or more needs. Retirement income is usually the first need to be sacrificed, since this can always be taken care of later if the client stays alive and healthy and continues to earn money. Other underwriters prefer to present a minimum program and then "trade up," indicating how much more can be accomplished at a slightly greater outlay.

*Cash Needs.* Personal needs include needs for cash at death or disability and income for the future for personal and family, as distinguished from business, purposes. Each of the commonly recognized needs will be discussed in turn, with emphasis on the health insurance aspects as distinguished from the life insurance aspects. For every life insurance need there is a parallel health insurance need.

Cash needs are needs which call for lump-sum amounts at death or disability or at some future date. These may include "clean-up" funds, mortgage funds, and funds for emergencies, including the meeting of medical care expenses.

*"Clean-up" funds* are required at death to meet expenses of last illness; funeral; lot and stone; debts; federal estate taxes, state inheritance and estate taxes, and current income taxes; and estate settlement fees. Health insurance providing adequate protection against medical care expenditures can cover the last-illness need and reduce the amount of life in-

surance required for clean up. Life insurance is not appropriate for the last-illness need since the cost cannot be estimated with any degree of accuracy. Moreover, a reasonably adequate estimated amount of life insurance could cost more than a major medical contract providing 5 to 10 times as much protection.

*Mortgage protection* involves insurance designed to meet mortgage payments in the event of death or disability. In the event of death, life insurance (usually a policy which is a combination of reducing term and whole life) provides cash to pay off the mortgage. Disability income insurance can be used to provide funds to meet the mortgage payments in the event of disability. A policy should be selected with a waiting period of about 30 days and a period of maximum benefit sufficient to cover the anticipated duration of mortgage payments. It should be noted that mortgage payments often include amounts for property insurance and real estate taxes which will continue even after the mortgage is paid off. Provision for these expenses should be included under income needs. The mortgage payments themselves *can* be included as part of basic family income but the different duration suggests a separate policy. A number of insurers now offer a sort of "reducing term" mortgage disability policy, where the maximum duration is expressed as a stated number of years from date of issue rather than from date of disability. Usually, these periods may be selected only as multiples of five years, but a few insurers are now on the market with a contract offering such coverage to any single future age desired, up to age 65. Group policies also are available to borrowers from lending institutions. These cover the exact amount and duration and do not involve individual underwriting.

The need for *emergency funds* is always present. A portion of life insurance proceeds should be set aside, usually under an interest option, to provide for emergencies after the breadwinner's death. Life insurance cash values and other savings should be available for emergencies during the breadwinner's life. The amount which should be maintained in such emergency funds depends upon the potential needs in conjunction with the family's resources. An adequate program of medical care insurance, especially major medical, on all members of the family will cover the most serious likely emergency and reduce the need for setting aside principal to protect against such contingencies. Similarly, the family should carry adequate liability and property insurance and at least enough life insurance on each family member to cover the "clean-up" need. It is important to allow for such life, health, liability and property premiums in estimating income needs at death, disability or retirement of the breadwinner.

In planning the family's medical care insurance, emphasis should be given to the large potential loss rather than the small, frequent loss. Major medical coverage with an adequate upper limit should take the first priority. If family resources are sufficient to absorb the participation in losses necessitated by the deductible and percentage participation provisions in the major medical contract, it probably is economical to handle these expenses through the budget rather than through basic medical care insurance. Thus the overhead costs of insurance are avoided. However, unless a "comprehensive" policy with low deductible can be obtained, most families will want some additional protection. Generally, comprehensive contracts are available only on a group basis as explained in Chapter 8.

Applying the principle of protecting against the large losses first, the family next may want to consider hospital, surgical, and basic medical expense in that order. Another factor to consider in regard to these basic coverages is the probable extent of utilization. A young family which envisions a number of births in the next few years may find that these coverages will pay for themselves in maternity benefits alone. For families past the childbearing period, only those with the least resources will be likely to find basic medical care expenses beyond the reach of the family budget. Of course, where the employer pays all or a good part of the premium, as in group insurance, it probably will be economical to carry basic benefit coverages.

*Income needs.* Income needs refer to the needs of the family for income at the death, disability, or retirement of the breadwinner. They are usually considered under the categories of readjustment income, family period income, "social security gap" period income, and life income.

In life insurance programming it has long been customary to analyze these needs and develop and present the program for meeting them by means of a graph. On this graph, the period of years beginning at the present is plotted horizontally, and the monthly income is plotted vertically. Thus it is possible to visualize the entire income program at one time. It has not been customary to plot the program for retirement similarly, since this is so simple in most cases that a mere tabulation is adequate.

Disability income programming should be handled in the same way. Since disability needs terminate at retirement, to be replaced by retirement needs, and since most disability income policies do not provide benefits beyond retirement age, it may be convenient to plot the disability and retirement programs on a single graph. A color code can be used to distinguish benefits payable only if disabled from those payable for retirement regardless of disability. However, if there are many policies, separate charts may be required. Because of the importance of variations in waiting period, it is desirable to use a larger horizontal scale for the first year of disability in order to make the chart easy to read. Chart 21–1 is an example of such a graph.

The process of determining the needs of the family in case of disability of the breadwinner is about the same as that of establishing the needs in case of premature death. The family sets its own needs in relation to present income and living standard levels, considering what changes might be necessary in the event of disability. It should be noted that the income needs will be greater in amount for disability than for death, since the breadwinner still lingers on as a consumer.

*Readjustment income* is designed to continue income to the family at a level equal or close to former take-home pay for a year or two following disability or death. Sometimes several steps down are provided to permit gradual adjustment to the level of income provided during the child-rearing period. This author feels that unless earned income is very high, a need for readjustment income benefits indicates that the level of income benefits for the next period has been set too low, and that too great a readjustment of the standard of living will be required. Often group disability income insurance with short waiting periods and short maximum benefit periods will be available to meet this need.

*Family period income.* In case of disability, like death, a higher income will be required for some period until the children are grown. Unlike death, however, disability may not prevent the conception of additional children. Thus the period during which this extra income will be required may be extended by the birth of more children after the event as well as before.

When there are eligible children in the family (under age 18, or themselves disabled before 18 and unmarried) additional OASDI disability and survivors' benefits are payable both to the children and to the mother. If the programmer decides to count on these benefits for disability income,[8] this increment may provide sufficient extra family period income to meet the need, since it can be as great as $216.60 per month with two or more children. If not, it may be necessary to supplement the other coverage with a contract providing disability income benefits for a limited period. Ideally, the maximum disability income period for this purpose should be expressed as the balance of a fixed period (for example, 23 years) from issue or to a stated future age (for example, 49). However, as indicated above, many companies do not issue contracts which provide benefits to a fixed future age other than 65. Most of those which are available at the time of writing (early 1968) provide durations (from date of issue) only in a limited number of multiples of five years. Thus, precise programming is, at the moment, impossible, except with the contracts of two companies,[9] to the author's knowledge.

*Social security gap.* When the last eligible child reaches age 18, both

---

[8] The author feels they *should* be counted on in every case, but others have differed as explained below, pp. 658–59.

[9] Occidental Life and Provident Indemnity Life.

his OASDI benefit and that of the mother terminate unless he continues in school, in which case his benefit, but not his mother's, continues to age 22. The disability benefit payable to the family drops to that for the worker himself, his Primary Insurance Amount (P.I.A.). When his wife reaches age 62, she becomes entitled to a wife's benefit of 37½ percent (75 percent of 50 percent) of his P.I.A. If she waits until she is 65, she receives 50 percent of his P.I.A. Thus there is a period of reduced OASDI benefits, the "social security gap," in disability programming as in programming death benefits. However, the amount of the gap is not as great since the worker lives to collect his own benefit. A policy paying disability benefits until some convenient age of the wife between 62 and 65 may be used to level income over this period. Currently, the maximum wife's benefit is $105 per month, and the maximum child's benefit is $109, so that the decrease in benefit cannot exceed $214 per month. Unfortunately, no company yet has a contract under which benefits increase when OASDI benefits decrease.[10] However, several companies offer a step benefit contract under which benefits may increase (or decrease) after a stated period from disablement.

*Income after retirement age.* For life income, most disability income policies are inappropriate. Usually benefits are not payable past age 65. However, this need is met in part by OASDI benefits, which will continue after retirement. Technically, the disability benefits are replaced by old-age benefits, but this is almost immaterial to the beneficiary, since the amounts are the same unless the wife's benefit is elected to start before age 65 and is reduced permanently.

There may be private pension benefits which vest in event of disability, either in full or in reduced amount in the form of an immediate or a deferred pension benefit. Aside from this possibility, reliance should be placed on the same life, endowment, retirement income, or annuity contracts which are intended to cover retirement needs if disability does not occur. Waiver of premium provisions usually will be available on the insurance policies and should be carried as a standard procedure. This is also important in order to prevent the life insurance program from being upset by disability. In many, if not most, annual premium deferred annuity contracts, such disability waivers are not available. In such a case, additional disability income insurance may be carried to provide for continuing the annuity deposits during disability, if underwriting limits permit.

Providing retirement income is the most expensive part of a comprehensive personal insurance program. This is true whether or not disability takes place. Most clients rely on a private or public employee pension plan for some of their planned retirement income. Most such plans

---

[10] That prospect must wait until after revision of this book has been completed.

provide for an actuarially reduced pension in the event of disability which is permanent as defined by the plan. Usually this starts at the time the disability qualifies as permanent, and the amount may be very small if age at disablement is young. Moreover, most such plans do not provide any disability benefit (other than a return of the employee's contributions with interest) if disability occurs before some specified period of employment, sometimes as long as 20 years. Thus, if disablement occurs before the disability benefit "vests," the client will have a big gap in his retirement program.

This problem may be met, in part, by using life insurance riders to meet the disability income needs. Most of these provide that the underlying life policy matures as an endowment when disability income benefits terminate. Thus the full face amount is available at that time instead of just the cash value. This makes possible a greater amount of income under the contract's life income option.

Another solution is to use disability income contracts or life insurance riders which provide for a life income. However, few do (except for accidental injury), and fewer yet on a noncancellable basis free of restrictive limitations. Thus, finding the appropriate contract involves considerable shopping.

A general solution awaits the development of new types of insurance contract. One answer would be the general adoption in private pension plans of provisions for continuing pension contributions and benefits regardless of disability. Only a few insurers currently offer this arrangement and few pension plans include it. However, it is possible to use a long-term group disability income policy to pick up the pension contributions of both employer and employee. The disabled employee would incur income tax on the benefits used for pension contributions but this would result in less income tax on the retirement benefits.

Another solution would be the general offering of life income disability income contracts. Most insurers are very reluctant to consider this because of the high moral hazard. The risk is a fake or exaggerated claim in the 50's or early 60's. By getting disabled at the right time, the claimant acquires a life income that he will lose forever if he makes the error of staying healthy until coverage terminates at age 65. The memory of the terrible experience of insurers with life benefit contracts during the depression years reinforces this attitude.

One solution would be a disability income contract that provides an income after age 65 that varies in duration, or better, in amount with the time of onset of continuous disability. It might provide, for example, that the benefit paid after age 65 is equal to that percent of the contractual benefit which is equal to three times the difference between age 60 and the age at the onset of continuous total disability. Then the benefit after age 65 would equal 100 percent for disabilities before age 27, 50 percent for disability occurring at 43 and nothing after 65 for disablement occurring after age 60. A contract of this type would avoid most of the moral hazard associated specifically with life benefits and would meet the insured's needs rather well. The longer the insured lived, worked, and saved before disablement, the more of his retirement program would be met through pension plans or other savings and the less he would need from the disability insurance.[11]

**Other needs.** Other needs may include *educational funds* and insurance on other members of the family. These needs are easy to meet in case of death, but very difficult to meet in the case of disability. There is no disability income policy currently available which provides for benefits deferred until the time a child enters college. Such a policy should have a ready market, and there is no actuarial reason why such a policy could not be written. It is to be hoped that the product-planning department of some insurers will recognize this need.[12] One approach to this need at present is to carry extra disability income insurance on the father's life all through the early life of the child, so as to be covered for education. If disability occurs well before the child reaches college age, the benefits would be available for other purposes or could be invested and held until needed.

Another approach, although expensive, is to carry a short-term endowment policy on the life of the father with a waiver of premium clause. Or the endowment contract could be on the child's life with a payor clause added waiving premiums in event of death or disability of the father. Both these approaches accumulate the educational funds even if the father lives and is not disabled. A fourth approach is to use an ordinary life policy on the father's life with waiver and disability income rider. If the father dies, the face of the contract will provide the needed funds. If he is disabled, the disability income benefits can be accumulated and invested and if he lives and stays healthy, the cash value will provide a part of the needed funds.

Similarly, *disability income* insurance is virtually unobtainable *for housewives.* A few companies will issue $100 or $200 per month with a maximum duration of one year. Yet the need is obvious. If a housewife is disabled, her work must be performed by expensive hired help. If there are young children, the cost may be very great.[13] The reason such cover-

---

[11] As an actuary, the author notes that the reducing amount of life benefit would tend to reduce the increase of premiums with age of issue and flatten the reserve curve. Someday he hopes to design and rate such a contract. One insurer recently has introduced a contract that pays benefit for life if disability commences before age 55, but pays only to age 65 if disability commences between 55 and 65. Under such a contract, one would anticipate a rather high claim rate at ages 50 to 54.

[12] See footnote 10 above.

[13] Roy L. Lassiter, "The Wife's Contribution to Family Income," *Journal of Insurance* (December, 1961), p. 33, estimates the value of a wife with young children at $11,459 per year or $150,960 present value assuming constant prices.

age is not available is, of course, the companies' fear of moral hazard and the difficulty of determining what constitutes total disability for a house-wife. Perhaps this is not as great as feared. It seems policies could be issued safely in small amounts with careful underwriting. This area deserves further exploration. The only possible solution in today's market is for the wife to buy a noncancellable guaranteed renewable policy with no average earnings clause while she is employed, preferably before marriage. Even then, the maximum benefit duration probably will be no more than five years according to the practice of most insurers. Moreover, many such contracts reduce benefits by 50 to 75 percent if the female is not gainfully employed outside the home immediately prior to disability.

*Type of contract.*   The type of policy to use is partly a matter of philosophy. Generally speaking, life insurance disability income riders will be somewhat more economical than separate disability income policies, partly because of the strict definition of disability. However, the long waiting period may require that they be supplemented with short-benefit-period or step-benefit disability income policies. A number of companies offer contracts where benefits may reduce after six months. This also could fill the gap. Often a group policy will be available to meet this need.

Consideration should be given to the diversity of maximum benefit durations under such riders. Where they are attached to endowment or retirement income policies, the disability income terminates when the policy matures. Newer riders attached to life policies also often include a provision for maturity of the contract and termination of income benefits at some age such as 60 or 65. This is particularly likely to be the case where the income is $10 per $1,000 of life insurance. Other riders may provide a benefit payable for life. Where possible, all life riders and endowment benefits should be arranged to mature at the same time—usually the date at which retirement is planned if disability does not occur. Where this is not possible, the underwriter must recognize how the income amount will change at maturity. If needs reduce at some age prior to planned retirement date, it may be possible to arrange policy maturity to conform to this change. In any event, the program should include the selection of appropriate settlement options at maturity.

Since the disability rider rarely will provide more than $10 per $1,000 of permanent life insurance and may be available on some existing policies at only $5 per $1,000 or not at all, it is a rare case where these riders can meet the complete need for disability income protection. Most clients cannot afford enough permanent life insurance to provide adequate disability protection solely by life riders. Those who can usually are limited by the life companies' underwriting limits.

Thus, usually it will be necessary to make use of separate disability income policies. Until a few years ago, it was necessary to choose between adequate benefit durations for disability income and the noncancellable feature. Contracts incorporating both simply were not available. However, a good number of companies are now issuing contracts with long maximum benefit periods on a noncancellable basis.

This author is a strong believer in the noncancellable or guaranteed renewable principle and believes that the extra cost is worthwhile to the client. However, for clients who cannot qualify for noncancellable or guaranteed renewable contracts, or where cost is an impelling factor, commercial contracts of the better companies probably will be satisfactory. Often these are now available on a conditionally renewable basis, which is a step in the right direction.

The underwriter should resist firmly the temptation to cut down the premium cost by arranging the program so that adequate benefit durations are provided only for accidental injury. Most disability is produced by disease, and the program would be as weak as a life insurance program which relied on the double indemnity clause to provide adequate coverage.

The selection of waiting period should be made after due consideration of any salary continuation agreement or plan at the place of employment and of the resources available to the family. The longer the waiting period, the lower will be the cost for the insurance. As in regard to the basic expense coverages discussed above, it is possible to save the overhead expenses as well as the claim costs for the portion of loss excluded from coverage.

Where the client insists he cannot afford the premium for the program and it is necessary to "cut back," a longer waiting period should be the first approach. The second choice should be to reduce benefit amounts overall, and shorter maximum durations should be the last resort. The main function of insurance is to protect against the serious loss, even though it is less likely than smaller losses.

In building up a disability income program, it is necessary to think about the underwriting issue and participation limits of the insurers. In order to avoid having applications declined for this reason, it is wise to obtain the coverage first where the limit is strictest and then progressively move to other types in order. Thus one should, in general, obtain life insurance riders first since underwriting limits are lowest for these, followed in turn by noncancellable, guaranteed renewable, commercial, group and travel accident.

*An illustrative program.*  Insofar as possible, existing insurance and other benefits available should be fitted together with new coverage so as to meet the income needs of the family. Chart 21–1 indicates a typical program. It portrays the following situation: John Smith, born in 1933, has a wife, Mary, the same age, and one child, Johnny, born in 1960. His salary is $1,350 per month before taxes. He has no disability income protection, when approached by the underwriter except OASDI. He always

CHART 21-1

Illustrative Disability and Retirement Program
Monthly Income for "John and Mary Smith"

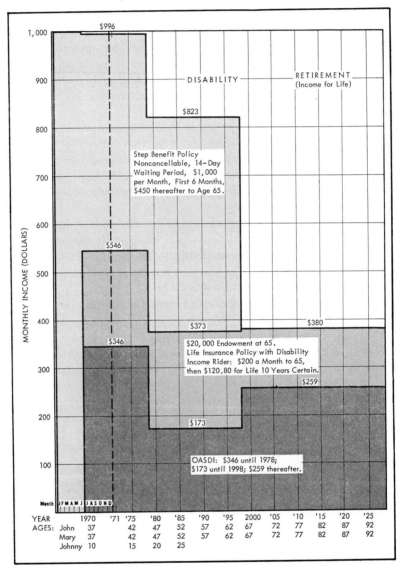

has earned the maximum average monthly wage. He has $20,000 of life insurance on an endowment at 65 policy and a $50,000 term contract.

His OASDI Primary Insurance Amount is equal to the maximum for his date of birth and equals $172.90 if he is disabled or dies early in 1970, increasing gradually under the 1967 Social Security Act to reach $205.00 if he is disabled at age 64 early in 1997. (Tables 4–5 and 4–6, pp. 154–57.) His OASDI disability benefits will be $346 per month until Johnny is 18 in 1978, $173 per month until Mary is 65 in 1998, and $259 per month thereafter. Alternatively, Mary could have her wife's benefits commence earlier at a reduced amount (75 percent at age 62) for a total of $238 for life. If Johnny stays in school, his child's benefit of $86.50 will continue until his age 22.

The underwriter's recommendation is as follows: Add a $200-per-month disability income rider to John's $20,000 endowment at 65 policy. A waiver provision should be added, if not already included. This will provide $200 per month after a six-month waiting period until age 65, at which time the policy matures. The proceeds, on a life income option, 10 years certain, will provide $120.80 for life. As an alternative approach, a waiver of premium rider on the life contract and a separate $200 non-cancellable disability income contract with a six-month waiting period would provide equivalent coverage in this case. However, if the life policy were whole life rather than endowment, the maturity value at age 65 would be less under this arrangement. The underwriter also recommends a new noncancellable disability income policy with a 14-day waiting period providing $1,000 per month for the first six months and $450 per month thereafter until age 65. At issue age 36 in 1969, the premium is $225.00 for the first six months and $276.75 for the $450-per-month balance to age 65, a total of only $501.75 for the policy.[14]

The complete disability program provides income as follows:

| | | |
|---|---:|---:|
| First two weeks of disability......................... | | nothing |
| Next six months (readjustment) | | |
|     From noncancellable policy................. | $1,000 | |
|         Total............................. | | $1,000 |
| Next 7½ years (family period) | | |
|     From OASDI............................. | $ 346 | |
|     From life insurance rider.................... | 200 | |
|     From noncancellable policy................. | 450 | |
|         Total............................. | | $ 996 |
| For next 22 years, until age 65 (social security gap) | | |
|     From OASDI............................. | $ 173 | |
|     From life insurance rider.................... | 200 | |
|     From noncancellable policy................. | 450 | |
|         Total............................. | | $ 823 |
| After age 65 for life | | |
|     From OASDI............................. | $ 259 | |
|     From life insurance settlement option....... | 121 | |
|         Total............................. | | $ 380 |

For the sake of simplicity, it is assumed that mortgage payments are included in the basic monthly income. The mortgage will be paid off before John and Mary are 65, reducing the amount needed thereafter.

---

[14] Provident Indemnity preliminary noncancellable rates.

The program is still quite weak as to retirement income, especially if John is disabled early in life. If he keeps working long enough for his present employer, the company pension plan will help to take care of this. As soon as his finances permit, John should obtain more permanent life insurance with waiver of premium provisions. This would guarantee the life insurance cash values and dividends at age 65 to provide more retirement income. He could convert his term contract or buy new insurance depending on his finances, his insurability and the amount of life insurance required.[15]

After this is accomplished he might consider less pressing needs such as a contract to provide funds for Johnny's education if John becomes disabled or dies. Life insurance and possibly dismenberment insurance on the other family members also might be considered. Ideally, there should be some way of obtaining a disability income insurance contract on a child who is not currently earning an income, providing protection against the loss of future earning power through disability; since such a contract does not exist, accidental dismemberment insurance is recommended as a partial substitute.

In this illustration, OASDI benefits were treated as basic with the other coverages superimposed on them. This is a standard practice in programming life insurance death and retirement benefits. This author favors this approach because of the parallelism with the life insurance program and the fact that it makes it possible to combine disability and retirement provisions on a single graph for purposes of analysis and presentation. Moreover, the author is concerned mainly about the severe long-term disability which would qualify for OASDI benefits.

Other authors point out, validly, that the OASDI disability definition is somewhat stricter than that of most life and health policies in that it requires a prognosis of at least 12 months' duration and inability to pursue any occupation. Thus they advocate treating the life rider and health policy benefit as basic and using the OASDI for less fundamental needs such as education, readjustment, and emergency needs.[16]

This author prefers the other approach for the reasons above, and also because the high OASDI benefits during the family period are too significant in amount to ignore. Moreover, more and more insurers consider these benefits in connection with their participation limits. This approach

---

[15] He also needs more death protection now, but this is supposed to be an illustration of *health* insurance programming. In a coordinated program, recommendations would be included for more life insurance, perhaps a reducing term contract or a family income policy. See Robert I. Mehr and Robert W. Osler, *Modern Life Insurance* (3d ed., New York: The Macmillan Co., 1961), chs. xv and xvi, for a discussion of coordinated programming.

[16] *Cf.* Robert W. Osler, *Programming Health Insurance* (Philadelphia: American College of Life Underwriters, 1966.) (Reprinted with revisions from the *Life and Health Insurance Handbook*).

makes for a smaller, but therefore easier, sale. One should not rely exclusively on OASDI benefits, of course. In this illustration, for example, John would have $1000 per month during the readjustment period, $650 per month thereafter to age 65, and the same $380 after age 65 if he did not qualify for OASDI disability income benefits.[17]

Most programs will not be so simple, but this should suffice as an illustration of the technique. Unfortunately, the exact combinations of waiting period and maximum duration that are required for careful programming are not always available. Maximum benefit periods of 5, 10, and 15 years or to age 60 or 65 are readily available. However, these are so limited that many programs may involve some gaps or overlaps in the income provided. Close programming of mortgage payments also requires more flexibility in maximum duration than most companies' contracts provide. It is to be expected that more flexible policies will be developed as the practice of programming becomes more common and the demand is demonstrated.

*Medical care expenses.* Of course, the complete health insurance program also must consider the coverage of medical expense. Here it is important to make sure that all family members are covered and that the upper limits are adequate. There is no standard method of presentation. A second page of the program might indicate the names and ages of the various members, the types of coverage, and the maximum amounts available. It might be well to indicate the date of termination of coverage according to the renewal provisions of the policies. The tabular method of presentation, suggested as one possibility, is illustrated in Table 21–2.

A color code may be used to distinguish individual from group coverages and to distinguish existing insurance from recommended new insurance. Alternatively, two such tables may be prepared, one showing the existing situation and the other showing the situation after the recommended insurance is purchased. The use of some such standard presentation will help to avoid gaps and overlaps.

*Taxation of health insurance.* Health insurance receives favorable income tax treatment from the viewpoint of the insured taxpayer. Intelligent insurance programming requires a knowledge of the tax factors affecting insurance. This discussion will not attempt to describe the general tax law or the taxation of life insurance, but will point out some of the main principles regarding the taxation of health insurance.

Generally speaking, personal insurance premiums are not deductible, and personal insurance benefits are not taxable income. This rule applies to personal health insurance except that special rules apply to medical expenses. Medical expenses are deductible to the extent to which they

---

[17] By the time he had been disabled a few years he probably could qualify for the disability freeze, at least.

TABLE 21–2

Medical Care Insurance for "John and Mary Smith"

| Coverage | Family Member | | |
|---|---|---|---|
| | John, 35 (Present Age) | Mary, 35 (Present Age) | Johnny, 10 (Present Age) |
| **Major medical** | | | |
| Upper limit | $15,000 | $15,000 | $15,000 |
| Deductible | $500 | $500 | $500 |
| Coinsurance percent | 80 | 80 | 80 |
| Age when coverage ends | 65 | 65 | 22 |
| **Hospital expense** | | | |
| Number of days | 70 | 70 | 70 |
| Dollars per day | $10 | $10 | $10 |
| Maximum extra expenses | $150 | $150 | $150 |
| Age when coverage ends | 65 | 65 | 19 |
| **Surgical expense** | | | |
| Maximum amount | $250 | none | none |
| Age when coverage ends | 60 | | |
| **Medical expense** | | | |
| Maximum per call | none | none | none |
| Number of calls | | | |
| Where calls covered | | | |
| Age when coverage ends | | | |
| **Blanket medical accident only** | | | |
| Maximum amount | $100 | none | none |
| Age when coverage ends | 60 | | |
| **Dread disease** | | | |
| Maximum amount | none | none | none |
| Age when coverage ends | | | |
| **Diagnostic expense** | | | |
| Maximum amount | $25 | none | none |
| Age when coverage ends | 60 | | |
| **Accidental death and dismemberment** | | | |
| Maximum amount | $10,000 | none | none |
| Age when coverage ends | 70 | | |

exceed 3 percent of adjusted gross income, not counting expenses for drugs as medical expense except to the extent they exceed 1 percent of adjusted gross income. In determining the amount of deductible medical expenses, benefits received on health insurance policies to cover such expenses must be offset against the deductible expenses, but premiums for such policies may be included as deductible expenses.[18] Premiums for disability income and accidental death and dismemberment insurance no longer are deductible, and life insurance premiums are not deductible. Where a contract provides benefits of these types and for medical expense benefits, only the portion of premium for the medical expense benefits is deductible and the allocation must be reasonable and set forth

---

[18] U.S. Internal Revenue Code, Sec. 213.

in the contract or a statement from the insurer. Half of such medical expense premiums up to $150 per return[19] may be deducted without regard to the 3 percent limitation. Premiums for Medicare (SMI) Part B are deductible, but the FICA tax for Medicare Part A hospital insurance is not. A hospital income plan is considered a medical expense policy even though it is on a valued rather than reimbursement benefit. Of course, these deductions may be taken only if the taxpayer itemizes deductions instead of taking the optional standard deduction.

For businesses, necessary and proper business expenses may be deducted from income for tax purposes. Where health insurance constitutes such an expense, the premiums may be deducted. This is true whether there is a group plan, an individual policy plan, or benefits are self-insured,[20] and even if the insured owns the policy. A corporation may deduct such premiums as business expenses, even when they apply to officers who are also stockholders, but a partnership may not on its principals, nor may a sole proprietor on himself. Benefits paid directly by an employer (as under a self-insured or salary continuation plan) are deducted as paid. The health insurance premiums paid by an employer, except for accidental death and dismemberment coverage, do not constitute taxable income to the employee. However, the benefits received are subject to tax in some degree, as indicated below.

Benefits paid for medical care are included in income only to the extent that they reimburse for medical expenses deducted in prior years. Benefits resulting from an employer-paid premium for medical expense insurance are included in income to the extent to which they over-reimburse for all medical expense (including transportation, all drugs, etc.) during the tax year. Of course, they must be offset against any itemized deduction for medical expense as described above.

Benefits not related to absence from work, such as accidental death and dismemberment benefits, are not included in gross income and thus come in tax free, even if paid for by the employer.

---

[19] Strangely, by filing separate returns, a husband and wife could each deduct half his premiums up to $150 for medical expense insurance for himself and his dependents for a total of $300. However, unless husband and wife had about equal income, they might lose more than they would gain by this device.

[20] However, there must be a "plan" for employees. It may cover one or more employees who must have notice or knowledge of the plan reasonably available to them. The plan need not be in writing nor be legally enforceable.—Internal Revenue Code, Sec. 106; Reg. Sec. 1.105–5. A plan for officers only recently was upheld in Sanders & Sons Inc., T. C. Memo 1967–146, July 17, 1967, but another recently was held not a "plan for employees" but a plan for stockholders, Alan B. Larkin, 48 T. C. No. 59. The court held that medical expenses paid by the corporation for its employees were dividends with the unhappy result that they were not deductible by the corporation and were taxable income to the recipient. The plan covered "such employees that the officers at their discretion consider should be covered" but benefits were in fact paid only for employees who were stockholders.

Where there is a plan, insured or otherwise, for continuing salary or providing other income benefits to disabled employees, such income is excluded from the individual's income for tax purposes up to $100 per week. Amounts above this must be included. The exclusion is computed on a daily basis. Income for the first week of disability may not be excluded unless the employee is hospitalized at least one day. During the first 30 days of disability no exclusion is available unless the amount of sick pay during this period is 75 percent or less of regular pay and the amount excluded is limited to $75 per week. The employee may exclude such "sick pay" whether he receives it directly from the insurer or from the employer.[21] Of course, the employee may exclude, as personal insurance, any amount of benefit attributable to his own contribution to premium.

The tax aspects of business insurance are discussed below in connection with the specific uses.

## Business uses

Business life insurance, to protect business against loss resulting from the death of key men and to assure the continuation of the business in the event of the death of an owner, is readily available and generally sold. Disability of a key man or owner involves a loss, which is just as serious as that resulting from death, to the business, the family or other owners. Nonetheless, this type of insurance is not widely sold. The only ascertainable reason is the lack of familiarity of underwriters with the needs and with the techniques for meeting them. The various types of business health insurance will be discussed under the headings of key man, business continuation, overhead expense, and tuition refund insurance.

*Key man.* Key-man insurance is designed to indemnify the employer for the loss of income and/or extra expense occasioned by the death or disability of a key man and to strengthen the firm's credit standing. A key man is any employee who contributes materially to the success of the business. He may be an executive, a salesman, a researcher, or any employee who makes a unique contribution and is difficult to replace. The loss to the employer may come in any of four ways: the irreplaceable loss in earnings when the key man cannot contribute; the temporary loss of earnings while the key man is temporarily disabled or while a replacement is being hired and trained; the extra cost of hiring and training a replacement; and the expense of continuing salary to the key man while he is disabled. Disability income insurance on the life of the key man will protect against such losses. Where it is intended to reimburse the business for losses of the first three types, the insurance proceeds will be

---

[21] U.S. Internal Revenue Code, Secs. 104 and 105.

payable to the firm. Where it is intended to finance a salary continuation agreement the benefits may be made payable to the key man directly, since there may be tax advantages in this arrangement.

Often it is desirable to use life insurance to provide for key-man protection of the employer and simultaneously to fund a deferred compensation plan. Where key-man life insurance is provided, especially in a plan where deferred compensation is involved (which calls for *permanent* life insurance), it may be desirable to fund the key-man disability benefits with a life insurance rider. However, the long waiting period and strict disability definition of the life rider may suggest a separate noncancellable disability income contract.

Tax factors are a consideration in determining whether the key-man disability insurance benefits should be payable to the employer or the employee.

If the insurance is payable to the firm, the premiums are not deductible by the firm, but the proceeds come in tax free to the firm,[22] and the firm may deduct the benefits it pays to the employee.

If the insurance is payable to the employee, the premiums are deductible by the firm. The firm neither receives nor pays taxes on the benefits, but, is, of course, relieved of the need to continue salary.

In either case, premiums paid by the firm are not taxable as income to the employee,[23] but benefits received are taxable to the extent they exceed the $100 per week[24] exclusion described above.

Which of these arrangements is the more desirable will depend, in part, on the firm's present and estimated future earnings' position and tax rates. Generally speaking, a firm should have two contracts, one payable to the firm to reimburse its own losses and one payable to the employee to replace his salary. The first will be owned by the firm and the latter may be owned by either firm or employee. Either may be an individual or group contract.

**Business continuation.**    Business continuation insurance provides a means of financing the continuation of a business at the death or disability of an owner. Whether the form of organization is a sole proprietorship, a partnership, or a corporation, the problems are similar. When an owner is disabled, provision should be made to keep the business operating during a short-term disability and to provide for the purchase of the business by a successor or successors in the event of permanent disability.

---

[22] This is the prevailing opinion, supported by strong logical arguments. Cf. William Hamelin and Morris R. Friedman, *Disability Insurance in the Business Buy-Out Agreement* (Indianapolis: Rough Notes Co., 1963), pp. 55–57.

[23] This is clearly the case where the employee is not a stockholder. Where he is a stockholder, the tax situation is not clear, especially when he is a major stockholder and key man insurance is not carried on the employees. By analogy to life insurance, however, the statement should hold.

[24] This exclusion depends on the existence of a "plan," but a policy is a plan.

*Proprietorship.* In the sole proprietorship both problems may be the same. Whether a member of the family or an outside manager assumes the responsibility of management, he must be compensated, while the sole proprietor continues to need the income he had been drawing from the business. Disability income insurance on the life of the sole proprietor will provide the financing to make this possible. Since this is personal insurance, the income will be tax-free to the proprietor. Of course, the premiums are not deductible as a business expense. Often, overhead expense insurance, described below, also should be carried.

Another approach, rarely utilized, is to develop employees who are willing to pay the premiums on life and disability income insurance on the employer's life. Then, when the proprietor dies or is permanently disabled, the proceeds can be used to buy out his interest, and the employees become the new owners. An endowment policy with premium waiver and disability income rider could provide a means of financing that would guarantee the employees the ownership of the business whether the sole proprietor dies, is disabled, or retires. This is probably the ideal approach, but not many firms will have such a competent and forward-thinking group of employees. Of course, the employees may have a problem in raising the money to pay premiums. In many cases, the proprietor's interest in securing the benefits of business continuation to his heirs might make it worthwhile to raise their salaries to help with the premium financing.

Another approach is to make a similar arrangement with one or more competitors for a reciprocal buy-out at death or permanent disability. Each would then own and be the beneficiary of a policy on the life of the other, as in the cross-purchase plan described below.

*Partnerships.* Disability does not dissolve a partnership as death does, but it may present equally severe problems. The partner usually is a key man, and key-man and overhead expense insurance may be indicated. Moreover, there will be an obligation to continue the share of the partner in profits even if he is disabled, unless the agreement provides otherwise or a court order dissolving the partnership or reducing the disabled partner's share of earnings is obtained. If disability continues, sooner or later the well member or members will want to obtain complete control of the firm.

The remaining partners constitute the natural market for the partnership interest of the disabled partner, just as for the deceased partner. The proper handling of disability in the buy-out agreement presents several problems.

Who buys the insurance and pays the premiums is perhaps the first question. Each partner could own the insurance on his own life as personal insurance with the buy-out funded from regular partnership earnings. This solves the problem of disability income but not the problem of buying out the interest. Another approach is the cross-purchase plan where each partner owns and pays for the insurance on each of the others in accordance with their respective shares of the business. Where there are more than two partners, this leads to a multiplicity of policies. This can be avoided, where the insurer will permit, by having one policy on each partner, jointly owned by the other partners. An even simpler approach is to have a trustee named as owner of all the policies as trustee for the partners as their interests appear.

A third approach is to have the firm as owner and premium payer. This approach makes it difficult to allocate the premium payments in proportion to what each partner will receive in a buy-out since the charge to partnership funds normally would be in proportion to present interests. Of course, if interests are equal this presents no problem. Also, this "entity" approach presents problems of equity where the partners' ages (and thus premium rates) differ significantly. However, it is usually not difficult to work this out in practice.

Regardless of who owns the insurance, premiums are not deductible and benefits are not taxable to the recipient as such. However, if the firm is beneficiary of the disability insurance benefits and these flow through the firm, there may be adverse tax effects. In such a case, the payments to the disabled partner not attributable to his share in tangible assets are taxable to him as "guaranteed payments" at ordinary income tax rate. The firm, however, may deduct such payments as a business expense, giving a tax advantage to the other partners. Where the benefits are paid directly to the disabled partner, they are neither taxable to him nor deductible by the firm, even if the firm owns the policy.

Which of these plans will be selected depends on the relative weight attached to the considerations enumerated above. Another factor to consider is how the life insurance buy-out plan is set up. Where possible, the two should be parallel.

Another problem is determining when buy-out should become effective. Most writers on the subject seem to feel that after disability has continued a moderate period (say two or three years) that subsequent payments should be considered installments on the purchase price of the partnership interest. The choice of period will depend in part on the nature of the business. Equity would seem to demand that some portion would be considered as interest or share of profit on the portion not yet purchased, but the literature is not clear as to any "standard" solution. It has been suggested that two separate policies be carried, one for the "income" payments before buy-out and the other for the buy-out installments in order to obtain the most advantageous tax treatment. However, unless the two contracts paid benefits for the same time period, the buy-out contract would need a longer waiting period than is generally available.

To this author, the ideal arrangement would seem to be a combination of the life and health aspects of the buy-out funded by a permanent life insurance contract with disability income rider. The disability income payments could serve in lieu of, or as a part payment of, the disabled partner's share of the profits, depending on the size of his interest. The agreement could provide for a reduced share of profits for inactive partners. If disability continues until the contract matures as an endowment (age 55, 60, or 65) according to the disability rider, the face becomes payable and funds all, or a part of, the buy-out, just as though the partner had died or retired. If payable directly to the partner, the disability payments probably would be tax-free, any additional current payments would be taxable as ordinary income, and the purchase price at maturity taxable as capital gain to the extent it exceeds his cost basis. This capital gain treatment would apply to the amount funded by the insurance and to additional amounts otherwise funded. In order to spread the capital gain tax liability, it might be wise to arrange for installment payments of the buy-out price. (This problem does not come up in case of death, since a decedent's assets take a new basis at death.)

*Corporations.* The problem and solution to disability of a close corporation stockholder are similar to those of a partner. There are five alternatives as to ownership of the insurance.

First, the stockholder-employee could use personal insurance. This is even less advantageous than under the partnership since he must pay premiums with income after personal taxes and sometimes after corporate taxes (to the extent his income consists of dividends).

Second, the corporation could buy key-man insurance payable to the employee, making the premium deductible to the corporation and the benefits taxable to the employee above the $100-per-week exclusion. Of course, this exclusion is available only for stockholders who also are employees.

Third, key-man health insurance could be purchased with the employer as owner and beneficiary. Premiums are not deductible, benefits paid to the corporation are tax-free,[25] and payments to the disabled employee are deductible as salary when made (and taxable to him to the extent they exceed $100 per week).

Fourth, the corporation may purchase health insurance to buy out the disabled stockholder's interest. This is referred to as an entity or stock-redemption arrangement. Premiums are not deductible, and benefits come into the corporation tax-free. Payments to the disabled stockholder for his stock are not deductible by the corporation but are taxable to the stockholder only to the extent they exceed his basis and then at capital gains rates.

Fifth, the health insurance for buy-out may be owned by the other

---

[25] See footnote 22, above.

stockholders on a cross-purchase arrangement. This would not be desirable for the income payments before buy-out because the disabled stockholder is not an employee of the other stockholders. Thus they would lose the deductions of payments to him. Probably, however, the proceeds might be tax-free to the disabled stockholder if paid directly to him and clearly identified as buy-out funds.

It is a little easier to handle this installment buy-out because the stock is easily divisible, and a formula can be used for current value if no market quotation is available.

The arguments on cross-purchase versus entity buy-outs are the same as for partnerships with the exceptions noted above.

To this author, the situation seems to call for a solution similar to that suggested above for a partnership, except with the corporation owning the insurance. There should be an agreement calling for payments in lieu of salary until some age such as 60 of at least $100 per week to take advantage of the favorable tax provisions. The agreement could be funded with ordinary life insurance with a disability rider to mature the contract as an endowment at (say) 60. Disability income benefit payments in excess of the $100 per week (or other agreed figure) could be applied to the purchase of the disabled shareholder's stock, a few shares at a time, at *current* market or agreed value. The $100 per week would be tax-free and the proceeds of stock sale would be taxable at the capital gains rate to the extent these payments represented a gain over cost basis. The disabled shareholder would continue to vote and receive dividends on the stock he still owned. By this method, he would have a diminishing voice in the affairs of the corporation.[26]

When the life insurance contract matures in accordance with the provisions of the disability income rider (say age 60), the face could be applied to buy all or much of the remaining stock at current prices. If the insurance is insufficient to buy all the stock, the balance can be redeemed over a period of time. If the proceeds are more than sufficient, the agreement could provide for the excess to inure to the corporation or to the shareholder as desired. There are many possible variants, but an approach along these lines seems fairest to all concerned.

For all types of business continuation insurance, a problem arises in obtaining adequate amounts of disability insurance to fund the plan. A partial solution would be to buy additional endowment life insurance with waiver provisions to complete the purchase at age 60 or 65. A more

---

[26] Of course, the active stockholders probably would prefer to gain complete control immediately. This probably could be accomplished by an installment sale arrangement whereby title to the stock would pass immediately and payment in the future would reflect both purchase installments and interest on the remaining debt. This question should be discussed thoroughly in the negotiations leading up to the drafting of the buy-out agreement.

adequate solution will await the development of sounder concepts of insurable interest and larger participation and issue limits by insurers. As long as there will be a real and significant loss to the various parties, even after considering the disability insurance, there should be little moral hazard. Underwriters should recognize this different interest and permit adequate amounts to be issued.[27] Another solution would be the development of new types of contract to provide a better solution than is possible with presently available coverages.

*Valuation.* In all cases, the buy-out agreement should specify the price or valuation method. The best arrangement is to specify a valuation method and then use it to determine the price each year.

**Business overhead expense.** A fairly recent development in the disability insurance business is the use of overhead expense insurance. This reimburses anyone legally liable for the overhead expenses which necessarily continue when a sole proprietor is disabled. It also is available for small partnerships, but not for corporations since a corporate stockholder is not legally liable for the debts of the business. The solution for a corporation is key man insurance.

Ordinary disability income insurance can be purchased, under most companies' underwriting rules, only in amounts somewhat less than net earned income after income taxes. If a sole proprietor or partner is disabled, his losses will be greater than this. He will have to maintain his office or shop and pay rent, heat, light, and similar overhead expense. Premiums paid for insurance to cover these expenses are deductible as necessary business expenses. To qualify for the deduction, the contract must be designed specifically to reimburse actual expenditure for such expenses. The conventional (valued) disability income policy will not qualify. Of course, the benefits are taxable as income but will be offset by the actual expenses incurred.

The maximum period of benefit need not be very long in a policy for this purpose. If the disability is of long duration, the business probably will be sold, or arrangements will be made for its continuation by hired personnel. A period of one or two years would seem adequate.

Many companies have developed special policies for this purpose. They provide benefits on a reimbursement basis for expenses actually incurred for which the sole proprietor or partner is legally liable, subject to an upper limit. Waiting periods may range from 14 to 60 days. Maximum benefit periods commonly run from six months to two years.

The policies list the types of expense covered. These usually include rent, electricity, water, heat, employees' salaries, and depreciation and

---

[27] Guardian Life recently announced it will issue up to $4,500 per month, $1,500 disability income and $3,000 per month for buy-out. The latter, however, is limited to a one year benefit period after a one-year waiting period.

may include other items, such as laundry, telephone, membership dues, and accountants' services. Some provide that other normal and customary expenses incident to the operation of the office or business will be covered. It will be noted that this coverage serves a purpose similar to that of business interruption (fire) insurance.

Professional businesses have the greatest need for coverage of this type, since the earnings of the principal are often the only source of income. However, other types of sole proprietorship may have some need. Generally speaking, the more dependent the business is on the professional skill and services of the proprietor, the greater is the need for the policy. The occupations which have been covered by such policies include accountants, architects, attorneys, barbers, beauty shops, brokers, chiropodists, chiropractors, dentists, filling stations, electricians, garage mechanics, insurance and real estate agents, manufacturers' agents, optometrists, orthodontists, osteopaths, physicians, and plumbers, among others.

*Tuition refund.* Tuition refund insurance is also similar to business interruption insurance against fire and allied perils. It protects operators of private schools and summer camps against loss of income from decreases in enrollment or the closing of camp or school as a result of exposure of students or campers to specified diseases. The amount of indemnity is the reduction in gross earnings for the balance of the season or semester less the expenses of operation which do not continue. The policies usually cover listed diseases only. The lists are similar to those covered under dread-disease policies. Although this coverage has a limited market, it is very valuable to the types of business for which it is designed.

A similar form is available to reimburse parents of campers for loss of camp fees when their child has to stay or return home from camp because of an injury or sickness he incurs.

### Summary

Despite the rapid growth of private health insurance, the potential market is still very large. Health insurance is marketed through agents, brokers, salaried representatives, and direct mail. Life, casualty, and monoline insurance companies, Blue Cross, Blue Shield, independent insurers, and government agencies all provide protection in this area. In group insurance a salaried group representative has primary responsibility for developing the presentation and closing the case, and the home or regional office may participate in developing the proposal and the rates.

The representatives of the Blues and the group representatives usually receive a salary plus bonus. Agents and brokers are compensated on either a level or a nonlevel commission scale. The nonlevel commission scale is similar to that used in life insurance and is by far the more common.

The sales process includes the activities of prospecting, the approach, the presentation, and the close. It is similar to the process in life insurance, and the health insurance and life insurance programs should be closely coordinated. Programming is the process of developing a complete plan for insurance protection based on analyses of the client's needs, existing coverages, and ability to pay.

Programming involves at least two interviews. In the first, fact-finding, interview, the data for the analysis of needs, existing coverage, and ability to pay are obtained from the prospect and his wife. In the second, closing, interview the program is presented to the prospect, and he is sold the new coverage required.

The programming of disability income insurance is similar to the programming of life insurance. A graph showing monthly income provided over the future years is a useful tool in developing the program and presenting it to the prospect. Needs for income for the readjustment period, the child-rearing period, and life income for the insured and his spouse must be considered. The programming of insurance against medical care expenditures can be most conveniently handled by a table showing the amounts in force on the various family members, together with recommended new coverage.

The business needs for which health insurance provides important protection are similar to those which have long been recognized for life insurance. They include key-man and business continuation needs. In addition, overhead expense and tuition refund insurance represent two areas where health insurance performs an important economic function in protecting against losses of short duration.

Health insurance programming is necessary to provide truly professional service to an underwriter's clients. In addition to performing a valuable service for this clientele, the underwriter should find the process very profitable. The market is huge and barely has been touched.

### Selected references

*See the following items from the General Bibliography: 4, ch. 26; 5, ch. 3; 7, ch. 10; 8, ch. 10; 10, chs. 14 and 15; 12; 16, Vol. I, ch. 17; 18, ch. 19; 19, chs. 26 and 27; 20, chs. 13 and 14; 21, ch. 27; 22, chs. 13, 22, and 23; 30, pp. 58–67.*

BROWN, ROBERT A., JR. "The Role of Disability Income Insurance in the Business Continuation Plan," *Journal of the American Society of Chartered Life Underwriters*, Winter, 1953, p. 60.

DORNFELD, KIVIE. "Taxation Affecting Health Insurance," *Journal of the American Society of Chartered Life Underwriters*, Fall, 1964, p. 359.

HARMELIN, WILLIAM. "Disability—the Oft-Neglected Hazard in Buy and Sell Agreements," *CLU Journal*, Winter, 1965, p. 46.

HARMELIN, WILLIAM, AND OSLER, ROBERT W. *Business Uses of Health Insurance*. Philadelphia: American College of Life Underwriters, 1966.

HARMELIN, WILLIAM, AND FRIEDMAN, MORRIS R. *Disability Insurance in the Business Buy-Out Agreement*. Rev. ed. Indianapolis: The Rough Notes Co. Inc., 1963.

HUEBNER, S. S. *The Economics of Life Insurance*. 3rd. Ed. New York: *Appleton-Century-Crofts*, Inc., 1959.

————. *The Professional Concept in Life Underwriting*. Philadelphia: American College of Life Underwriters, 1962.

HUTCHESON, MITCHELL. "What about Disability Income?" *CLU Journal*, Spring, 1955, p. 146.

KEDZIE, DANIEL P. *Consumer Credit Insurance*. Homewood, Ill.: Richard D. Irwin, Inc., 1957 (The Consumer Credit Insurance Association).

LASSITER, ROY L., JR. "The Wife's Contribution to Family Income," *Journal of Insurance*, December, 1961, p. 33.

LEVINE, SOL; ANDERSON, ODIN W.; AND GORDON, GERALD. *Non-Group Enrollment for Health Insurance*. Cambridge: Harvard University Press, 1957.

MILLER, JEROME S. *Selling Accident and Health Insurance*. New York: Prentice-Hall, Inc., 1953.

MILLER, JOHN H. "The Price of Failure," *Selected Talks from Eleventh Annual Accident and Sickness Spring Meeting 1960*. Life Insurance Agency Management Association.

OSLER, ROBERT W. *Programing Health Insurance*. Philadelphia: American College of Life Underwriters, 1966.

SULLIVAN, HAROLD L. *Needs and the Life Underwriter*. C.L.U. Brochure. Philadelphia: American College of Life Underwriters, 1947.

WILLIAMS, C. ARTHUR, JR. (ed.). *Small Business Uses of Individual Life and Health Insurance*. Minneapolis: University of Minnesota, 1960.

## chapter 22

> Government, even its best state, is but a necessary evil.—Thomas
> Paine, *Common Sense*

# Regulation

### The background of state regulation

The insurance business is intimately connected with the public welfare and, as such, is subject to the regulation of the various states under statutory authority and the police power. For many years, from the decision in *Paul* v. *Virginia*[1] in 1869 to the *U.S.* v. *South-Eastern Underwriters Association*[2] case in 1944, it was held that insurance was not commerce and therefore was not properly subject to federal regulation. This decision was reversed in the latter (S.E.U.A.) case, which held that the association had violated the Sherman Antitrust Act by combining for rate-making purposes and by certain other practices.

The entire historic pattern of insurance regulation was upset by this decision, and it was almost a year before the situation was somewhat clarified by the passage of P.L. 15 (79th Congress),[3] known as the McCarran-Ferguson Act. This law provided that continued regulation and taxation of insurance by the several states was in the public interest and that the Sherman Act, the Clayton Act, the Federal Trade Commission Act, and the Robinson-Patman Act should not apply to insurance until January 1, 1948,[4] and thereafter only "to the extent that such business is not regulated by state law." An exception was made in regard to cases involving boycott, coercion, or intimidation by specifically excluding such cases from these limitations on federal jurisdiction.

Following the passage of this act, the National Association of In-

---

[1] 8 Wall. 168 (1869).

[2] 322 U.S. 533.

[3] Public Law No. 15, 79th Cong., 1st Sess. (1945), 58 Stat. 33, 15 U.S.C. Secs. 1011–15.

[4] The moratorium was extended six months to June 30, 1948, by P.L. No. 238, 80th Cong., 1st Sess. (1947).

surance Commissioners instituted a series of meetings to prepare recommendations for strengthening state regulation. The insurance industry organized the All-Industry Committee to prepare similar recommendations in a form that would be acceptable to all segments of the business. As a result, state laws were strengthened, new legislation passed in many states, and a more thorough and uniform system of regulation evolved. Cooperation between companies for purposes of statistical studies and rate making is now permissible, if adequately regulated by the states. However, health insurance rates are not specifically regulated nor are they made cooperatively. There is cooperation in the collection and publication of statistics and the development and publication of morbidity tables and valuation net premiums.

There has been a little further action by the government in this area.[5] The right of the states to continue to collect premium taxes was upheld in *Prudential Insurance Co.* v. *Benjamin*[6] and the general right of the states to regulate insurance was upheld in *Robertson* v. *California*.[7] These cases were not brought by the national government, but by an insurer and an agent, respectively.

## Objectives of regulation

The objectives of state regulation include policyholder protection, production of revenue for the states, and retaliation against discrimination by other states against domestic companies. The most important element of policyholder protection is maintaining the solvency of insurers. The retaliation objective is not so important as formerly, in view of the progress made, largely by the efforts of the National Association of Insurance Commissioners and cooperating industry groups, in developing uniform state laws.

The revenue objective seems to be a little difficult to follow from a standpoint of logic. Insofar as taxation of insurance companies is required to finance their regulation, it seems justifiable, but taxation beyond this point seems to be an outstanding example of discriminatory excise

---

[5] A few actions have been taken by the Department of Justice. The first was in March, 1951, against the Cleveland Insurance Board in a case of alleged boycott. A more recent case is *New Orleans Insurance Exchange* v. *United States,* 148 F. Supp. 915, aff'd. 355 U.S. 22, reh. den. 355 U.S. 908. The FTC action in regard to insurance advertising is a more recent case in point (see pp. 685 ff.). See also Thomas J. Gilhooley, "The Extent of the Present Regulation of Insurance by the Federal Government," paper presented at the Association of Life Insurance Counsel Meeting, December 8, 1959. For an excellent summary of the entire subject, see Arthur C. Mertz, *The First Twenty Years* (Chicago: National Association of Independent Insurers, 1965).

[6] 328 U.S. 408 (1946).

[7] 328 U.S. 440 (1946).

taxation of the type decried by many students of public fiscal policy.[8] Not only does a premium tax discriminate against particular businesses and localities, but it deliberately taxes the prudent for the production of general revenue which is used, to a considerable degree, to provide for the imprudent.

It would seem much more logical for the taxing authorities to encourage individuals to make sound provision for their own protection by permitting the deduction of insurance premiums for individual income tax purposes. This privilege, already granted to businesses, would be a much better way of handling the situation than present provisions for deducting only uninsured casualty losses, in excess of a $100 deductible. This latter privilege is of little help, once a really catastrophic loss has occurred. The recent change in the Internal Revenue Code permitting deductions of half of medical expense insurance up to $150 per return without regard to the 3 percent limit is a laudable step in the right direction.

Kimball[9] suggests somewhat broader goals for insurance regulation. These may be divided into internal and external goals. The internal goals include insurer *solidity*, which is something more than mere solvency, and *aequum ad bonum*, which is something more than reasonableness, equity, and fairness.[10]

The external goals include the larger purposes of society: political structure and attitudes, economic and social policies and basic moral values. These affect insurance regulation just as they affect all social action. Some of these goals which have influenced insurance regulation in this country are democracy, liberty, local protectionism, federalism, socialization of risk, and freedom of enterprise.[11]

### Health insurance organizations

No study of health insurance can be complete without mention of the many organizations which have contributed so much towards de-

---

[8] See, e.g., Committee for Economic Development, *Taxes, National Security, and Economic Growth* (January, 1954), p. 21; National Association of Manufacturers, *A Tax Program for Economic Growth* (January, 1955), pp. 39, 43. However, if the state has a general sales tax, and the rate of premium tax is equivalent to the sales tax and in effect substitutes for it, there may be no discrimination.

[9] Spencer L. Kimball, "The Goals of Insurance Regulation: Means versus Ends" *Journal of Insurance* (March, 1962), p. 19.

[10] In Kimball's paradigm, reasonableness refers to the whole body of policyholders; equity to fair treatment of groups or policyholders vis-à-vis one another; and fairness to the treatment of the individual insured.

[11] For a broader discussion of the influence of social policy on insurance, *see* Spencer L. Kimball, *Insurance and Public Policy* (Madison: University of Wisconsin Press, 1960) and "Insurance and the Evolution of Public Policy," *CPCU Annals* (Summer, 1962), p. 127.

veloping the health insurance industry and improving its standards of quality and service to the public. It may seem inappropriate to discuss these organizations in a chapter entitled "Regulation," but short of writing a separate chapter, this seems to be the best place to discuss them. All of these organizations contribute to improving the insurance business, its personnel, or its relationships with the public. Thus, they serve to reduce the need for regulation of the industry by government. Indeed, Kulp has categorized the activities of organizations of insurers and insurer executives as "self-regulation."[12]

***Organizations of insurers and executives.*** The main trade association in the health insurance field is the Health Insurance Association of America. Its origins may be traced back many years. The Bureau of (Personal) Accident and Health Underwriters and the Health and Accident Underwriters Conference were established early in this century as an outgrowth of earlier associations. Early efforts were directed toward the interchange of information and statistics, the development of standard occupational classification manuals, and control of practices such as the use of policy frills and restrictions and twisting.

As the need arose, these associations also were instrumental in fostering sound legislation and aiding in the defeat of other measures. They had some success in standardizing policy provisions, collecting and publishing statistics, and developing classification manuals. For some time the Bureau and Conference published advisory policy forms and the Bureau recommended premium rates, but these practices were discontinued after the S.E.U.A. decision.

In 1954, as a response to criticism of the health insurance business, and recognizing the rapid growth of the business, their common interests and objectives and to avoid unnecessary duplication of effort and expense, these two associations and five others[13] joined together as the Joint Committee on Health Insurance. They set up "task forces" which conducted studies of a number of problem areas. One recommendation was for the formation of a new trade association. This association, the Health Insurance Association of America, was organized in April, 1956. It includes the members of the two earlier associations as well as many companies which had not belonged to either. It took over the functions, offices, and staffs of the Bureau and Conference and established offices in Chicago, New York, and Washington. Currently, it includes

---

[12] C. Arthur Kulp, *Casualty Insurance* (3rd ed.; New York: The Ronald Press Co., 1956), p. 533. "*Self-Regulation* means regulation of the business policies and activities of individual insurer members by an insurer group."

[13] The American Life Convention, American Mutual Alliance, Association of Casualty and Surety Companies, Life Insurance Association of America and the Life Insurers Conference.

more than 330 insurance companies which write about 80 percent of the insurance company health insurance business. All these companies have subscribed to the H.I.A.A. Code of Ethical Standards.[14]

The Health Insurance Institute was organized to serve as a central source of health insurance information for the public on behalf of insurance companies through a variety of publications and information programs. The Institute distributes news about health insurance to all of the media of communication. It analyzes health insurance statistics for writers, economists, and others, and assists writers and researchers in the preparation of articles dealing with health insurance. The Institute also prepares educational material for teachers, students, and women's groups and collects data for use by librarians, educators, labor unions, employer associations, government officials and bureaus, civic organizations, and hospital and medical groups.

The Health Insurance Council, composed of seven associations,[15] including those of the Joint Committee, has conducted a vigorous program directed toward greater understanding and cooperation between the insurance business and the providers of medical care. It acts as a central source of information and counsel to physicians and hospitals and others in the health care field. It maintains liaison at the national level with the American Medical Association and American Hospital Association and at the state and local levels with the local medical and hospital associations. Its work in developing hospital admission plans and uniform claim forms was discussed in Chapters 10 and 20 above. It has viewed with interest the development of relative value schedules for medical services and the establishment of insurance review committees in the county medical societies. It operates through a series of committees on medical relations, hospital relations, uniform forms, allied health services, and technical advice. There also are committees in each state and many localities.[16]

The Blue Cross Association and the National Association of Blue Shield Plans have been described above.

Many other insurance trade associations, although not primarily devoted to health insurance, pay considerable attention to it in their activities. These include the International Federation of Commercial Travelers Insurance Organizations, the Life Insurance Association of America, The

---

[14] See Appendix E.

[15] The H.I.A.A., the other associations from the Joint Committee on Health Insurance, the Association of Life Insurance Medical Directors, and the International Claim Association. The American Insurance Association has since replaced the Association of Casualty and Surety Companies.

[16] E. J. Faulkner, "The Health Insurance Council Acts," *H.I.A.A. Group Insurance Forum,* 1960. "Tremendous Progress Is Reported for Health Insurance Council," *Health Insurance Review* (May, 1962), p. 6.

American Life Convention, the Life Insurer's Conference, the American Insurance Association, and the American Mutual Insurance Alliance. The International Claim Association, the Life Office Management Association, the Insurance-Accounting and Statistical Association, the Home Office Life Underwriters Association, the Institute of Life Insurance, and the Life Insurance Agency Management Association also devote considerable attention to health insurance. The Life Insurance Medical Research Fund supports research directed towards life conservation and health improvement. It is particularly active in supporting heart research.

*Agents' associations.* The main agents' organization in the health insurance field is the International Association of Health Underwriters. It includes state and local associations and conducts a program of public relations, legislative activity, and an educational program through the Disability Insurance Training Council. Its members must subscribe to a code of ethics prescribing high standards of conduct.[17]

The National Association of Life Underwriters, the national organization of life insurance agents, devotes considerable program time to health insurance and sponsors the Life Underwriters Training Council Program, which includes the subject of health insurance.

*Educational organizations.* The American College of Life Underwriters is an independent, nonprofit, educational institution. Its broad purpose is to serve as an institution of higher learning for persons who participate in the process of insuring human life values. This, of course, includes health insurance. It administers an educational and examination program and awards the Chartered Life Underwriter (C.L.U.) Diploma and designation to those who meet its high standards of education, experience, and character. Health insurance personnel are eligible for the C.L.U. Diploma and designation and the C.L.U. Associate Diploma[18] and designation on exactly the same basis as life insurance personnel. Health insurance is included throughout the C.L.U. examination program on an integrated basis.

The American College also conducts a Certificate Course Program, in several specialized areas, and a continuing education program. A Certificate Course in Health Insurance was first offered on a pilot basis in 1961–62 and the Disability Insurance Training Council has adopted this as its recommended course and is actively promoting it.

The American Institute for Property and Liability Underwriters, Inc., is a similar nonprofit educational institution. Its purposes are to establish and administer standards for the professional designation Chartered Property Casualty Underwriter (C.P.C.U.) and to encourage and foster train-

---

[17] See Appendix F.

[18] This designation no longer is being granted except to candidates who matriculated on or before June 1, 1966.

ing in educational institutions in professional property and casualty underwriting. Its requirements as to examinations, character, education, and experience are similar to those of the American College. Health insurance is included in the examination program leading to the C.P.C.U. designation.

The Insurance Institute of America is a corporation separate from the American Institute, but shares officers, staff, and facilities with the Institute. It administers an educational program encouraging educational institutions to offer courses and conducts a national examination program which includes health insurance in its subject areas. While not required as a prerequisite, I.I.A. study is recommended as preparation for the more advanced C.P.C.U. program.

The educational activities of the Health Insurance Association of America, the Life Underwriters Training Council, and the Disability Insurance Training Council were mentioned above.

*Professional associations.*    The Society of Actuaries combines the functions of a professional association and a designation-granting educational institution. It conducts a program of examinations leading to the designations of Associate of the Society of Actuaries (A.S.A.) on the completion of the first five examinations, and Fellow of the Society of Actuaries (F.S.A.) on completion of the entire series of ten examinations. Health insurance is included in the examination requirements and many papers about health insurance appear in the *Transactions.* Several important studies of health insurance have been conducted by committees of the Society.

Similarly, the Casualty Actuarial Society is the professional association and designation-granting body in the field of casualty and property actuarial science. Its examination program permits qualification for the designation Associate of the Casualty Actuarial Society (A.C.A.S.) on completion of the first five examinations and Fellow of the Casualty Actuarial Society (F.C.A.S.) on the successful completion of four more. Health insurance is included in the subject matter of the examinations and in articles in the *Proceedings.*

The American Academy of Actuaries is the single body organized to represent the whole of the actuarial profession in the United States. It was formed in 1965 to embrace all existing qualified actuaries in the United States. By December, 1966, it had more than 2,100 members. It is hoped that membership in this body will become generally accepted by the public and by regulators as the criterion of actuarial qualification.

The American Society of Chartered Life Underwriters is the professional organization for holders of the C.L.U. designation. It conducts the annual C.L.U. Institutes, maintains a program of continuing education for its members in cooperation with the American College of Life Underwriters, and publishes *The Journal of the American Society of Chartered Life Underwriters.*

The Society of Chartered Property Casualty Underwriters is the professional society for C.P.C.U.'s. It conducts an Annual Seminar and regional institutes and local clinics and publishes *The Annals of the Society of C.P.C.U.* All of these societies are active in the development and encouragement of high standards of professional ethics and most have adopted formal codes of ethics.

### Areas and mechanics of state regulation

*Areas.* The areas of state regulation comprehended under the general category of policyholder protection include regulations concerning the formation and incorporation of insurers; admission of out-of-state (foreign) companies; standards of solvency in terms of size of capital and surplus; adequacy of reserves; permissible media for investment; requirements of periodic reports and examinations; and provision of means for conservation and liquidation of companies whose solvency is endangered.

The public is further protected by laws regulating the qualifications of agents and brokers and prohibiting certain practices; prohibiting misleading and false advertising and representations; defining standards of fair competition; prescribing policy forms or requiring approval; limiting company expenses; and regulating rates[19] and the activities of intercompany organizations.

*Mechanics—the insurance commissioner.* The mechanics of state regulation are usually handled by an insurance department under an official usually termed the "Insurance Commissioner," but sometimes "Superintendent" or "Director." Sometimes the department is a branch of some other state department, such as banking.[20] The commissioner usually has the power to grant or withhold licenses to do business; examine the financial condition and practices of carriers; require periodic statements; act as depository of securities and as conservator or liquidator of companies when necessary; investigate complaints and initiate investigations; and undertake activities which are necessary and incidental to these. His duties involve the enforcement of all the insurance laws of the state and the administration of his department.[21]

Space precludes a complete analysis of state laws regulating insurance. Some of the more important provisions affecting health insurance

---

[19] But not for health insurance. See below, pp. 684–85.

[20] This is the case in twelve states at present.

[21] The definitive study of the Insurance Commissioner and his powers is Edwin W. Patterson, *The Insurance Commissioner in the United States* (Cambridge, Mass.: Harvard University Press, 1927).

will be discussed here. Health insurance is, of course, also subject to many legislative provisions applicable to the insurance industry as a whole. For current legislation in a particular state and for the provisions applicable to the business in general, the reader is referred to the latest edition of the state insurance code involved.

*The National Association of Insurance Commissioners.* Coordination and uniformity of regulation among the various states have been promoted by the National Association of Insurance Commissioners. This organization was founded in 1871 as the National Convention of Insurance Commissioners, and its membership consists of the insurance commissioners of the states and territories. It operates through an executive committee, 15 other standing committees, and a number of special committees. Studies are often conducted by a particular state insurance department at N.A.I.C. request.

Its decisions have no legal status but are merely recommendations to the insurance departments. However, its persuasive powers have been quite effective, and a great deal of uniformity has resulted. The N.A.I.C. recommendations often serve as a model for legislation and administrative standards in the various states and give the individual state the advantage of thorough study which many states would not be able to provide by themselves. Some of its notable accomplishments are the standard fire policy, uniform financial statements, uniform rules for valuing securities, the establishment of the "zone" system for triennial examinations of companies, Uniform Policy Provisions laws, the uniform Unauthorized Insurer's Service of Process Act, the "all-industry" rate-regulation laws, and studies of problem areas such as cancellation and overinsurance.[22]

### Specific provisions affecting health insurance

*Organization, admission, and solvency of companies.* Health insurance has never been established within the trichotomy of types of insurer established by state insurance laws. It may be written by casualty companies, life companies, or monoline specialists. A monoline company may organize under either the casualty or the life section of the law.

While the laws defining health insurance and the health insurance business vary somewhat in language from state to state, they all define it, in substance, as "insurance against loss resulting from sickness or from bodily injury, or death by accident, or both."

The laws require the drawing-up of a charter giving, among other things, the name and location of the company, the lines of insurance planned, the powers of the corporation and its officers, and the method of

---

[22] The *Proceedings of the N.A.I.C.*, published each year, record the actions of the N.A.I.C. and its committees and are a fruitful source of data for students of insurance.

internal organization. If the company is to be a stock company, the amount of paid-in capital must be stated. This must conform to the minimum requirements of the state law.

In most states the requirement for writing health insurance is from $100,000 to $1,000,000 of capital plus a surplus equal to 50 percent of the minimum capital. Requirements for advertising of incorporation, certificates of intention, and bylaws are similar to those for other types of corporation.

For mutual companies the requirements have to do with a minimum number of applications and premiums for insurance and a minimum amount of surplus. In some states, such as New York, these requirements are so strict that it is almost impossible to form a mutual company. Some states require deposits of securities with the insurance commissioner as an additional safeguard. These may range from 25 to 100 percent of the minimum capital required. When these requirements have been met and directors and officers have been chosen, the company may commence doing business. The laws may impose different requirements by line of insurer. Usually an insurer desiring to enter the health insurance field has the choice of organizing as a life company, a casualty company, or a monoline (health) insurer.

All insurance companies doing business in a state must be licensed or "authorized." Generally, the requirements for licensing a domestic company are the same as for its organization. Sometimes the licensing requirements, unlike the organization requirements, are the same for stocks and mutuals. Requirements for licensing out-of-state (foreign) insurers are essentially similar to the standards required for domestic companies, but they may be more or less strict.

Occasionally, the states require deposits of securities by foreign and alien insurers and may fail to give credit for deposits in other states. Such requirements may have a quite restrictive effect in the aggregate. An N.A.I.C. committee has recommended legislation limiting such deposits, but such legislation has not been adopted to any extent.

Regulation of reserves, investments, and methods of valuation contribute toward insurer solvency. The first of these will be discussed specifically below. In addition, insurance commissioners have the power and duty to take steps to conserve the assets of companies which are on dangerous financial grounds. They may and do examine the companies' statements and actual operations and, in case of actual or impending insolvency, may limit writing of new business or actually step in as conservator, liquidator, or rehabilitator of the company involved.

*Policy provisions and filing.*  All states regulate the policy forms for individual health insurance. The Uniform Individual Policy Provisions Law recommended by the N.A.I.C. in 1950 has been enacted in 48 states, the District of Columbia, and Puerto Rico. Louisiana has a similar law, and while no law has been enacted in Alaska, contracts with the Uniform Provisions are routinely approved by the Insurance Department.

These provisions have been discussed above and are reproduced in full in Appendix A. The law requires 12 provisions which are designed primarily to protect the interests of the insured after a loss. They include such provisions as requirements for notice and proof of loss, time of proofs and payment of claims, time limits on certain defenses, and change of beneficiary.

In addition, the law provides for 11 optional provisions. These need not be included unless the company so desires. However, if they are included, they must be in the language of the statute or in language not less favorable to the insured. They provide for such things as change of occupation, misstatement of age, other insurance, relation of insurance to earnings, and cancellation. It should be noted that, unlike the Standard Provisions Law of 1912 which it replaced, the new law makes it possible for a company to use different wording for both the required and the optional provisions as long as this is at least as favorable to the insured. Thus the new law provides a desirable element of flexibility.

In addition to prescribing the uniform provisions, the law contains certain other requirements. These relate to typography, to the application, to who may be covered (individuals and families only) and the like.

Most states do not have similar requirements for group policy provisions. A model law was prepared by the Health and Accident Underwriters Conference and approved by the N.A.I.C. However, this has been enacted in only a few states. Its requirements as to policy provisions are much less detailed than the Uniform Individual Provisions, and it primarily is concerned with a definition of group insurance. The latest model law, as approved by the H.I.A.A., is reproduced in Appendix B. A number of states impose additional requirements beyond the uniform individual provisions. Most of these are minor. New York has unique legislation relative to cancellation and continuation which will be discussed below. Other limits on cancellation and nonrenewal are discussed below.

California has a "minimum benefits law." This provides that no policy will be approved if "irrespective of the premium charged therefor any benefit of the policy is, or the benefits of the policy as a whole are, not sufficient to be of real economic value to the insured."[23] In addition to this somewhat vague requirement, the law specifically prohibits approval of policies including, for example, unintelligible, uncertain, or ambiguous provisions; more than triple indemnity; and abnormally restricted benefits for one type of disability as compared to others. The law is quite detailed, and one may question the advisability of imposing such detailed require-

---

[23] *Deering's Insurance Code,* Ann. 1955 Supp. (and Insurance Code 1955), Sec. 10291.5.

ments on top of the Uniform Provisions Law. If every state had such a set of different criteria, the situation would be intolerable. It would seem that better results might be achieved by intercompany action backed up by flexible administrative regulation. Rigid standards are not desirable in an industry which is in a stage of rapid evolution. Another California statute empowers the commissioner to withdraw approval of individual hospital, medical, and surgical forms if benefits are unreasonable in relation to premium. The commissioner issues standards for approval. The initially promulgated standards[24] provided that benefits were reasonable if the loss ratio was at least 50 percent if the premium exceeds $7.50 per person or 35 percent otherwise. Insurers must file experience reports. If the aggregate loss ratio is high enough the company is considered in compliance; otherwise the commissioner may investigate each form separately.

Laws in 50 jurisdictions require the filing of health insurance policy forms. Usually, the classifications and rates also must be filed. Seven of these laws require advance approval of the policy before issue; about 35 provide for automatic approval if no action is taken within a time limit such as 30 days. The remainder provide that the forms may be used unless subsequently disapproved by the commissioner. Some laws specify standards for disapproval, including such things as benefits unreasonable in relation to the premium charged; unjust, unfair, inequitable, or misleading provisions; or sales methods involving misleading or inadequate description of the policy provisions. The California law is a uniquely detailed example of such standards.

In addition to purely statutory standards for policy forms and approval, there are several other guides for company and commissioner action. The *Official Guide* was promulgated by the N.A.I.C. in cooperation with the Bureau and Conference. The latest edition was published in 1947, and, with the adoption of the Uniform Provisions, much of it is somewhat out of date.

However, it is understood that it is still applicable to the extent not superseded by the new legislation. It was originally intended to facilitate uniformity in interpreting and applying the 1912 Standard Provisions Law. But it goes considerably beyond this by establishing rules relating to such things as labeling limited policies; prohibiting identification benefits; requiring clear statements of provisions relating to renewal, house confinement, and attendance of physician; provision for military service; prohibiting exclusions of "chronic disease"; and the like.[25]

Other recommendations of the N.A.I.C. include the *Statement of Principles—Personal Accident and Health Insurance*. This was drawn up by

---

[24] *California Administrative Code,* Article 1.9.

[25] For a copy of the *Official Guide,* see David McCahan (ed.), *Accident and Sickness Insurance* (Philadelphia: University of Pennsylvania Press, 1954). (Now published by Richard D. Irwin, Inc.).

an industry committee and adopted by the N.A.I.C. in 1948. It is even broader than the *Official Guide* and is concerned with the number of policy forms; clarity of policy language; reasonable policy exclusions; substantial scope of coverage; and use of elective provisions, multiple indemnities, qualifying and waiting periods, and confinement provisions. It also goes into considerable detail regarding specific policy provisions and exclusions and establishes standards for advertising and solicitation material. It is reproduced in Appendix D. A more recently recommended procedure deals with giving prominence to provisions regarding renewability and cancellation.

A purely voluntary guide to the preparation of policies and practices in the industry is the Health Insurance Association of America *Code of Ethical Standards*. This was adopted unanimously in May, 1957, and represents a blending of codes adopted in 1954 by the Bureau and Conference. Compliance with this code is required for membership in the H.I.A.A. The code requires each member company to pledge itself (among other things) to offer only insurance providing effective and real protection against loss and to use clear and direct language without unreasonable restrictions and limitations. The code is included in Appendix E.

*Reserves and rates.* State laws generally impose requirements for the maintenance and valuation of reserves. The types of reserve carried by insurance companies and the nature of the convention blank have been described in Chapter 19.

The requirement for unearned premium reserves is usually stated broadly as "the unearned portions of the gross premiums charged on unexpired risks." The basis of reserving is further defined as premiums in force at year-end. This is determined by adding premiums written during the year to premiums in force at the beginning of the year and deducting premiums cancelled, expired, and reinsured. Some states permit mutual companies to deduct from this the portion of premium which represents loading for dividends. Most laws specify the annual pro rata method of computation as the primary method of calculation but permit the use of more accurate methods.

The all-industry rate regulation bills passed in response to P.L. 15 and the S.E.U.A. decision were not made applicable to health insurance. It was felt that the health insurance business was so different from the property and casualty business that rate regulation was not justified. The heterogeneity of policies and types of insurer, the intense competition on a nationwide basis, and the absence of cooperation and regulation of rates in the past were cited as evidence of this fact. Since rates are not specifically regulated and approved by the states, there is some legal question as to the extent to which insurers may cooperate in rate making.

As indicated above, there is no rate-making association in the health insurance business at present.

Although rates are not regulated as such, they must be filed with the insurance department in 33 states. One reason for this is to facilitate the application of prorating provisions. Seventeen state laws provide that policies shall not be approved "if the benefits provided therein are unreasonable in relation to the premium charged." In 31 states, the District of Columbia and Puerto Rico credit disability forms must be approved under a law similar to the "relationships of benefits to premium" law. Pennsylvania has a law applying to all individual health insurance. Five states require the filing of estimated loss experience by policy form, and all states require the filing of actual loss experience. While there is no necessary connection between these requirements and the unreasonable-benefit laws, the industry fears that some such connection may be urged in the future. In a number of states, the commissioners seem to make a reasonable rate structure a criterion for approving the policy form.

*Unlicensed out-of-state insurers.*   A difficult problem of state regulation involves the operation of out-of-state insurers. When these companies "do business" in a state by establishing offices and employing agents, they become subject to the regulation of that state. Under such circumstances, they must be licensed by the state in which they are doing business and must meet the standards discussed above. However, the degree of contact which is necessary to subject an insurer to regulation by a state in which it is not domiciled is difficult to establish, and regulation is difficult. State laws attempt to deal with this problem by prohibiting unauthorized insurers from doing business, prohibiting persons acting as agents for such companies, and prohibiting such companies from advertising, using the courts, and the like.

Despite laws of this type, the regulation of out-of-state insurers presents difficult problems, particularly when they operate exclusively by mail. The Post Office Department has broad powers to control the use of the mails, but these are usually exercised only where there is evidence of fraud. Since 1965, the department has been actively pursuing mail fraud cases involving insurance with initial emphasis on high-risk auto insurance. Some convictions and many indictments have been obtained. The Federal Trade Commission in 1950 promulgated a set of "Trade Practice Rules" regarding the advertising and sale of mail-order insurance. Most of these rules were aimed at the health insurance business, although they applied to insurance in general. These were replaced by the 1956 Trade Practice Rules, which were rescinded in 1962.

One problem regarding out-of-state insurers is that of providing a legal forum for insureds without requiring them to bring action in the state of the insurer's domicile. Forty-six states, the District of Columbia, and Puerto Rico have passed the Unauthorized Insurers Service of Process Act recommended by an all-industry committee and the N.A.I.C. This law provides that service may be made on the insurance commissioner of the state as agent for the out-of-state insurer.

Fourteen states have passed the N.A.I.C. recommended Uniform Reciprocal Licensing Law. This provides that the insurance commissioner may revoke the certificate of authority of a domestic company adjudged to be operating without a license in any other state which has enacted the law.

A Wisconsin statute[26] enacted in 1961 provides for the regulation and taxation by the state of Wisconsin of unlicensed out-of-state insurers. The constitutionality of this statute was upheld by the Wisconsin Supreme Court in 1966.[27] The U.S. Supreme Court dismissed the appeal for "want of a substantial federal question."

*Advertising.* The Federal Trade Commission code dealing with advertising by health insurers represented the first attempt of the Commission to regulate the practices of insurers in detail, other than actions regarding coercion and boycott. All states and Puerto Rico have passed an N.A.I.C. model bill defining and providing penalties for unfair methods of competition and deceptive acts and practices. This bill is applicable to all types of insurance. This type of fair trade practice act is intended to preempt the area and prevent FTC regulation.

The FTC commenced an investigation of health insurance advertising in 1954 as a result of a "flood of letters." In 1954 and 1955 the FTC formally issued complaints against 41 companies, alleging the use of false or deceptive advertising. The complaints were based on 1953 advertising copy which the companies had submitted voluntarily. The complaints alleged misrepresentation as to extent of coverage, beginning time of coverage, required health status of applicant, maximum benefit limits, cost of policy, and termination provisions.

The companies raised the following defenses: (1) the complaints were based on advertising of two years previous, which had long since been withdrawn from use; (2) there was no evidence that applicants actually had been misled; (3) the advertising was regulated by state law and had in some cases been specifically approved by state authorities; (4) the statements were misleading only when quoted out of context; (5) there had been no intention to mislead. Trade associations, backed by the N.A.I.C., filed briefs in the ensuing litigation, denying the federal jurisdiction.

The industry adopted voluntary advertising standards. The N.A.I.C. developed Rules Governing Advertisements of Accident and Sickness In-

---

[26] Sec. 201.42, *Wisconsin Statutes.*

[27] *Ministers Life and Casualty Union v. Haase.*

surance, approved in December, 1955 and amended in December, 1956. This recommended regulation is intended as a guide to state regulatory authorities, and it is hoped that its general application will solve the problem. It has been adopted officially in 31 states and is used as a guide in other states. This recommended regulation is printed in Appendix C. The FTC held a conference to consult with industry and N.A.I.C. representatives and promulgated its own code in early 1956, which was later rescinded as noted below.

In addition to denying the charges, the companies also denied the jurisdiction of the FTC. This question seems to hinge on the interpretation of the phrase of P.L. 15 which provides that federal laws shall apply "to the business of insurance to the extent that such business is not regulated by state law." Apparently, this means that there must be adequate state statutes covering unfair competition and misleading advertising which provide adequate authority and machinery for enforcement. It is apparently not necessary that these laws have been passed prior to the passage of P.L. 15 nor that they be inconsistent with the FTC Act.

Most of the cases eventually were dropped, but three got as far as the U.S. Supreme Court. In two of these cases,[28] the Court held that the FTC did not have authority to regulate these companies' advertising programs since they "did business" in the states in question and those states had adequate fair-trade practice acts and methods of enforcement. For a time it looked as though the FTC had been ousted effectively from any jurisdiction over health insurance advertising.

However, the third case[29] involved somewhat different facts. The insurer in this case transacted all its business by mail from its home office in Nebraska and did not employ local agents. Thus it did not technically "do business" in other states and could be regulated only by the state of domicile. The Court of Appeals for the Eighth Circuit held that the FTC had no jurisdiction since the Nebraska statute covered unfair trade practices "in any other state" as well as "in this state."

However, the U.S. Supreme Court reversed this decision on the grounds that the McCarran-Ferguson Act requires effective regulation "by the state in which the deception is practiced and has its impact." The judgment was vacated and the case remanded to the Eighth Circuit for further proceedings. In January, 1962, the Eighth Circuit Court of Appeals ruled unanimously that the FTC has jurisdiction over direct-

---

[28] *American Hospital and Life Ins. Co.* v. *FTC*, 23 F. (2d) 719 (1957); *National Casualty Co.* v. *FTC*, 245 F. (2d) 833 (1957), affirmed 357 U.S. 560 (1958).

[29] *Travelers Health Association* v. *FTC*, 262 F. (2d) 241 (1959), reversed by 362 U.S. 293 (1960).

mail insurance. The effect is to affirm a cease-and-desist order prohibiting the insurer from making certain statements in its advertising in states other than Nebraska and Virginia, where it is licensed.

In June, 1962, the FTC rescinded its 1956 trade practice rules which had been directed at health insurance advertising. It was expected that it would move to develop rules specifically applicable to direct-mail insurance advertising, to which its jurisdiction now seems to be limited. The recent *Ministers* case, mentioned above, suggests that the states, by regulating the actions of out-of-state insurers, may be able to preempt even this limited jurisdiction.

In 1964, as expected, the FTC promulgated its *Guides for the Mail Order Insurance Industry*. It is reproduced as Appendix I.

### Special provisions for group, blanket, and franchise insurance

Group and blanket insurance are usually, and franchise insurance may be, dealt with separately in the state insurance laws. In general, the laws are concerned with defining the nature of the coverage and the types of "group" to which it may be issued and requiring certain policy provisions. The latter is not necessary with franchise insurance, since the Uniform Individual Policy Provisions Law applies.

*Group insurance.* About 34 states have some type of law specifically dealing with group insurance. These laws vary in detail but resemble the model group bill originally prepared by the Health and Accident Underwriters Conference in 1948 and revised in 1950 and 1954. The latest version, as approved by the H.I.A.A. in 1957, is reproduced in Appendix B. An earlier model bill was approved in 1940 by the N.A.I.C. This is similar but varies in detail. Sixteen states now prescribe minimum percentage enrollment requirements, and 18 states do not, but do define group insurance. The remaining 16 states and the District of Columbia have no group health law. Of the 32 states with group laws, seven require a minimum size group of five persons; 17 require a minimum of 10; and four require a minimum of two. The other six do not impose a minimum.

The types of group which may be written include employees or associations of employees of a common employer or of affiliate employers; employees of government agencies; members of a labor union or group of unions; other substantially similar groups; and dependents of such employees or members. Some laws, like the Association Model, specifically provide for trustees of employer or employee associations and unions as insureds.

Thirty-two states impose some requirements as to policy provisions in group health insurance. The requirements imposed by a majority of these states include provisions for issuance of certificates to member employees; for definition of the contract; that statements will be representations and not warranties; for remittance of premiums; and for addition of new employees. A few states require provisions dealing with proofs of loss and payment of claims similar to those required for individual insurance, and 12 states specifically require provisions similar to those of individual policies to the extent that these are appropriate for group insurance. Most states require filing of group policies and rates as for individual insurance.

New York imposes a minimum initial premium rate on group business. The law provides that no group contract may be issued within or outside the state by an insurer doing business in New York unless it appears to be "self supporting on reasonable assumptions as to morbidity or other appropriate claim rate, interest and expense." Rates and supporting experience must be filed with the Superintendent, who may impose a minimum rate if necessary. No specific minimum rate has been promulgated, but some insurers have been asked to justify apparently low rates. This acts as a restraint on unbridled competition nationally because of the extra-territorial aspect of the requirements.

*Blanket insurance.* Forty-four states have specific provision for the writing of blanket insurance, but all states permit it to be written. The laws usually prescribe the types of group which may be written, as described in Chapter 15. In 10 states and the District of Columbia the statutory definition of blanket is the same as that of group. Requirements for filing and policy provisions are similar to those for group insurance.

*Franchise insurance.* Franchise insurance involves individual policies issued to members of small groups, and the policy forms are the same as those for individual insurance. Twelve states have adopted the N.A.I.C. recommended definition of franchise insurance, and seven have similar definitions. These definitions involve the issuance of the same form of policy to five or more employees or 10 or more trade association, professional association, or union members, where premiums are paid by or through the employer, union, or association. The amounts and kind of coverage may vary between the individual members of the group, but the same form of an individual policy must be used. There is little other regulation specifically directed at franchise insurance. The H.I.A.A. recommended definition is reproduced as Appendix G.

*Credit insurance regulation.* For most types of health insurance, rate regulation is not necessary because competition operates effectively to hold down rates. However, in at least two areas, each involving something of a "captive market," a sort of "reverse competition" seems to operate. One of these areas, aviation accident insurance, was discussed in Chapter 14. Here, competition tends to take the form of ever-higher bids for space rental from the airports.

A similar situation prevails in consumer credit life and health insurance. Here the lender has virtually a "captive market" and competition tends to take the form of increasing commissions or experience dividends. In fact, sometimes higher rates are charged the borrowers to make this possible.[30] There also have been complaints about "tie-in sales" and the use of compulsory insurance to get around the usury laws.

In order to correct this situation, the N.A.I.C., in 1958, adopted a model bill. This has been amended twice, most recently in December, 1960. It provides for disclosure of the type and cost of the insurance, limits the type, term, and amount of insurance, provides for refunds on renewal or refinancing, and requires that all contracts and rates must be filed with the insurance commissioner, who may disapprove the filing if the benefits are not reasonable in relation to the premium. It is reproduced as Appendix H.

By January 1, 1967, 31 states, the District of Columbia, and Puerto Rico had enacted the model bill or similar legislation and 20 had issued regulations implementing it. A number of states have promulgated prima facie rates. If a contract calls for rates equal to or less than the prima facie rate, it is deemed acceptable. In 18 states the wording of the section relating to premiums and benefits provides for disapproval if "premium rates charged or to be charged are excessive in relation to benefits." This wording was recommended by the A.L.C., H.I.A.A., and L.I.A.A. The Virginia statute makes no mention of premiums, so the department may not disapprove a policy on such grounds.

In June 1967 the N.A.I.C. adopted a proposed uniform form for insurers to report their experience under various types of credit insurance. In December, 1967 an Industry Advisory Committee submitted a report of an industry-wide study of experience. The study was accepted and further study was requested.

*Taxation of health insurance companies.* Health insurance companies are subject to the same type of tax as other insurers and other types of business. However, there are two special areas of taxation which deserve particular comment. One of these—the state premium tax—was discussed above. The usual rate is 2 percent. In addition, there are a variety of special taxes and fees payable by insurers and agents, often connected with licensing.

The other situation in which health insurance constitutes a somewhat special case is in regard to the federal income tax. A portion of the business is taxed like life insurance and a portion like casualty insurance. The method of taxation of life insurance companies has been changed many times. Prior to 1921 the companies were taxed like other corporations, except that additions to reserves were included as expenditures. The 1921 law recognized the fiduciary nature of the life insurance business

---

[30] *Proceedings of the National Association of Insurance Commissions,* 1957, p. 121.

and attempted to tax only the portion of investment income not directly attributable to policyholders' investment. This objective was maintained until the 1959 changes, effective for tax year 1958, in a series of revisions which used a variety of formulas. Some of these formulas involved applying the regular corporate rate to the net investment income not attributable to the policyholders' investment, and others attempted to achieve the same aim by applying a lower rate to the entire net investment income. For several years prior to 1958, the Congress each year extended the "Mills Law," which resulted in an effective tax rate of about 7.8 percent on net investment income. If this had not been extended, the effective rate would have been about 11.6 percent, according to the formula of the 1942 law, which would have applied automatically.

The Life Insurance Company Income Tax Act of 1959 introduced a fundamental revision of the principles on which the income taxation of life insurance companies was based. The law is quite complex—so much so that detailed discussion here is not possible.

Very briefly, it provides that life insurance companies are taxed at regular corporate rates (currently 22 percent of the first $25,000 plus 48 percent of the excess) on taxable investment income, on half the excess of the underwriting gain over taxable investment income and on the other half of the excess of underwriting gain over taxable investment income when and if it is paid out as dividends to stockholders. The recently enacted "Great Society Surcharge" will result in effective corporate rates of 24.2 percent and 52.8 percent in 1968 and 23.1 percent and 50.4 percent in 1969 according to the June, 1968 legislation. It is likely, however, that the 1968 rates will be continued, at least through 1969, and probably until the next recession.

Taxable investment income is determined by splitting net investment income into "the policyholder's share" and "the company's share." Only the latter is taxed. Underwriting gain is the excess of premiums, taxable investment income, and all other income except capital gains over all expenses, claims, increases in reserves, surrender values, endowment benefits and policyholder dividends paid. Capital gains are taxed at 25 percent of the excess of net long-term gains over net short-term losses.[31]

Companies writing health insurance may be taxed as life insurance companies or as insurance companies other than life. If the life insurance reserves and reserves on all types of noncancellable and guaranteed

---

[31] This discussion is necessarily brief. For more detail see Allen L. Mayerson, "The Life Insurance Income Tax Act of 1959," *CLU Journal* (Spring, 1960), p. 171, and Malcolm E. Osborn, (same title) *CLU Journal.* (Winter, 1962), p. 74. The corporate tax probably will be increased by a surcharge effective July 1, 1967. See also John C. Fraser, "Mathematical Analysis of Phase I and Phase II of 'The Life Insurance Income Tax Act of 1959,'" *Transactions of the Society of Actuaries,* Vol. XIV, p. 51. See also Thomas G. Nash, *Federal Taxation of Life Insurance Companies* (New York: Matthew Bender & Co., 1965).

renewable policies are more than 50 percent of all reserves, the company is taxed as a life company. The tax is computed as explained above. The company's nonlife insurance business, including cancellable health insurance, enters into the computation of gain from operations as discussed above. Since most of the health insurance business is written by life companies, the taxation of other types of insurance company will not be discussed.

## Problems and issues

Many of the recent developments in the regulation of health insurance have been discussed above. The F.T.C. advertising investigation, the general adoption of the Uniform Provisions and Unauthorized Insurer's laws, and the developments in the field of social insurance have been covered. Some recent developments and unresolved issues in health insurance regulation include the growing tendency to limit the cancellability of policies, insurer objections to "overregulation," and the problem of achieving uniformity of regulation. These will be discussed below. Other problems and issues regarding regulation, including attempts to control overinsurance and utilization, have been discussed at length above.

*Cancellation and conversion.* Several states have passed laws limiting the cancellability of health insurance policies by requiring notice of cancellation in one extreme case for as much as two years in advance in some circumstances. Many other states have considered such legislation, and bills to this effect have been introduced into the U.S. Congress from time to time. These laws and proposals have grown out of complaints from policyholders regarding cancellation, some of which are justified. However, investigations reveal that many are due to misunderstanding.

The strictest law is that of North Carolina, which grew out of a study of cancellation in that state. The North Carolina law requires that the insurer may refuse to renew only by giving prior written notice of from 30 days to two years depending on the length of time the policy has been in force. The period is 30 days during the first year and reaches the maximum after eight years in force.

Nine states[32] do not permit cancellation by the insurer during the term of the policy (usually one year). In 9 states,[33] reference to the insurer's right of nonrenewal (and cancellation if any) must be displayed prominently on the face of the policy and/or the filing back. Ten states permit

---

[32] Alabama, Arkansas, Montana, Ohio, Oklahoma, South Carolina (after six months in force), South Dakota, West Virginia, and Wisconsin. In Ohio and, as an optional provision in Wisconsin, the insured may cancel.

[33] Alabama, Georgia, Maine, Maryland, Minnesota, Oklahoma, South Carolina, West Virginia, and Wisconsin.

nonrenewal only on the anniversary of the policy or of its reinstatement.[34] Most of these states, and a number of others, require a greater period of notice of cancellation or nonrenewal than is required by the Uniform Provisions, usually 30 days.

The Georgia law provides that, on cancellation, the insurer must tender a refund of 75 percent of the difference between the premiums paid and total claims paid unless the termination is because of the insured reaching the stated age limit (not less than 60) or changing to an uninsurable occupation.

Several laws bearing on this problem were adopted in New York in 1958 and 1960. They apply generally to both insurance companies and hospital and medical associations. They require that individual and family policies provide for a 10-day examination period within which the policyholder may cancel with refund of the entire premium;[35] that the policy state the age limit (if any) for renewal; that after 90 days in force the insurer may not cancel but only refuse renewal at each policy anniversary on 30 days' written notice.

After two years, the permissible reasons for nonrenewal of hospital, surgical and basic medical policies are limited to fraud, moral hazard, overinsurance, discontinuance of class of policies and such other reasons as the Superintendent of Insurance may approve. Refusal to renew because of deterioration of the insured's health is specifically prohibited. In addition, family hospital and surgical policies must provide for a right of conversion to an individual policy without evidence of insurability for persons who cease to be eligible as family members under the family policy.

Group hospital and surgical policies must[36] provide a right of conversion for persons who cease to be eligible as employees, members, or dependents, as the case may be, to comparable individual contracts without evidence of insurability. Conversion must be made within 31 days by payment of a quarterly or less frequent premium, and the privilege may be denied if the policyholder has other coverage or is eligible for other group coverage which would result in overinsurance or duplication of benefit.

The law gives the Superintendent the power to specify a maximum at the option of the employee, but not in excess of the coverage of the group contract for the employee or his dependents. The three options

---

[34] Alabama, Arkansas, Georgia, Massachusetts, Montana, Ohio, Oklahoma, South Dakota, West Virginia, and Wisconsin.

[35] Eleven other states have enacted provisions for this 10-day examination period, and many insurers include provisions for this privilege in all their contracts.

[36] Under the 1958 (Metcalf) legislation this was optional with the group policyholder (e.g., employer). Under the 1960 (Russo) legislation, it is compulsory for all policies issued, modified, altered, or amended after January 1, 1961.

are: (1) hospital room and board of $10 per day for 21 days, $100 hospital extras, and a $200 maximum surgical schedule, (2) $15.00 for 30 days, extras of $150, and $250 surgical, and (3) $15 for 70 days, $150 extras, and $300 surgical.

The conversion privilege also is available to dependents on the death of the employee.

The law gives the superintendent the power to specify a maximum net level premium for conversion policies (of each benefit level) covering persons of age 60 and older who were covered for at least two years under the group policy. The gross premium may not exceed 120 percent of such net level premium based on age of conversion.

Initial industry response to the North Carolina law indicated that many insurers withdrew from the state and others increased premiums or decreased benefits. It remains to be seen whether voluntary limitation of exercise of cancellation rights by the companies and the increased availability of guaranteed renewable and noncancellable policies will forestall other efforts to enact laws curtailing or eliminating the right of cancellation.

*Overregulation.* This type of law is an illustration of what has been variously referred to as overregulation or unrealistic regulation. The California minimum benefits law and the vague requirement that benefits be reasonable in relation to premiums are other examples. Even more serious is the multitude of measures introduced into state legislatures at every session. Many of these impose requirements which would put the business in a strait jacket. It would seem wiser if detailed regulation could be left to joint action of the insurance commissioners and the industry. In a rapidly developing business a great deal of flexibility is necessary. Unwise and too extensive regulation can impede progress and unnecessarily raise the costs to policyholders.

Perhaps the outstanding example of abuse of regulatory authority in the history of insurance has occurred in California. As indicated in Chapter 4, the California Unemployment Compensation Disability (nonoccupational disability) Law provides that private insurers may provide coverage equal to or greater than the legislative standard, provided that their operations do not result in substantial adverse selection against the state fund.

A law enacted in 1961[37] raised the maximum benefit to $70 per week and provided for further increases or decreases (but not below $70) depending on average weekly total wages in a base period. It also provided for increasing the wage base in $500 annual increments to reach $5,600 per year in 1965 (since increased to $7,400).

More importantly, it reinstated the substantial adverse selection pro-

---

[37] Assembly Bill 234, passed June 16, 1961.

vision (which had been in abeyance for some years) and directed the Director of Employment to prescribe reasonable tests for such substantial adverse selection based on the sex, age, and wage distributions of employees.

The director proposed standards which could hardly be considered reasonable by any stretch of linguistics. They provided that no private insurance plan would be approved (or its approval continued) if it deviated by more than 5 percent in its sex, age, and wage distribution from the average of all employees covered by the U.C.D. law. The regulation was bitterly opposed by the H.I.A.A. and the Life Insurance Association of America but was promulgated with very little change on November 3, 1961.

The official regulation provided that private plans must have not less than 95 percent of the state average for female lives,[38] not less than 90 percent of the state average for workers over age 50, and not less than 93 percent of the state average of persons with earnings under $3,600 per year, all based on the proportion of benefits paid. If an insurer deviates in *any one* of these regards (for all its U.C.D. business in the state) it will be denied approval without any credit for exceeding the standard in other respects. Out of 58 insurers then writing California U.C.D. business, only three met all three tests.

The associations and insurers appealed the regulation and hearings were held in December, 1961. Eventually, the Appeals Board approved the regulation, taking its final action on April 13, 1962. The industry appealed to the courts and obtained a preliminary injunction on April 27 postponing the effectiveness of the regulation until the court had considered the matter. The industry contended that the regulation was not "reasonable" and that making it apply to previously approved plans was contrary to the intent of the legislature. Indeed, it seemed to be taking of property without due process of law.

Subsequent legal steps initiated by representatives of labor brought the issue to the Supreme Court, which ordered the Director of Employment to carry out the regulation pending a full trial hearing. Arguments were heard in late October, 1962, and a decision was rendered in early December. The decision was reported to be unanimous and upheld the regulation. As if this were not strange enough, the Court also issued a press release which referred to the private insurers "skimming off the cream" of the U.C.D. business. It was estimated that more than one million workers would lose the extra benefits provided by private insurers and revert to the minimum benefits of the state plan.

Regardless of the outcome of this particular case, it serves as an ex-

---

[38] For example, the statewide average was 38.61 percent of benefits paid on female lives. An insurer who had less than 95 percent of this or 36.68 percent paid on female lives would not be approved according to this criterion.

ample of abuse of regulatory authority where administrative government uses its delegated authority to accomplish by its own authority what it cannot accomplish in the legislature. It illustrates well the dangers of unwise delegation of legislative authority to the executive and the dangers of overregulation in general.

*Uniformity of regulation.* Another problem is achieving uniformity among the states. The N.A.I.C. recommendations have gone far in this direction, but they have not always been accepted. In many matters of detail, state requirements differ so that it becomes difficult, if not impossible, for a company to make use of uniform policies and rates on a nationwide basis.

Uniformity is desirable not only to keep down operating costs but also to conform with population mobility and to make the judicial interpretation of contract provisions generally applicable. Moreover, lack of uniformity may retard desirable developments.

The question that the nation must face is whether an acceptable degree of uniformity can be obtained by voluntary state action. If present trends towards nonuniform, excessive, and unrealistic regulation continue unchecked indefinitely, the only alternative may be an abandonment of the entire system of state regulation in favor of regulation by the national government. Most industry representatives today would not welcome such a development, but they might well change their minds if the situation got bad enough.

Uniformity is the strongest argument for national regulation, but there are other valid points which may be raised in its favor. These include the wasteful duplication of effort under state regulation; the local viewpoint reflected in state regulation; and the waste resulting from inefficient and politically dominated administration.

The arguments on the other side consist essentially of denials of the importance of these points, emphasis on improvements taking place, and philosophical arguments directed to the values of a federal rather than a centralized government.

The McCarran Act puts the burden on the states to regulate insurance adequately. Currently, the industry seems in favor of state regulation and is cooperating in this endeavor. However, unless the inadequacies and deficiencies of state regulation are corrected, renewed pressure for national regulation may be expected to arise in more than one quarter.

## Summary

The insurance business is regulated by the states under the provisions of the McCarran Act, which provides that such regulation is in the public interest and federal laws will not apply to insurance except to the extent that the business is not regulated by the states. The objectives of insurance regulation are primarily the protection of policyholders, mainly by maintaining the solvency of insurers and the production of revenue for the state treasury. The latter is rarely emphasized in public discussions but should not be underestimated as a political force.

Insurance regulation is administered by the insurance departments of the states under an official usually known as the "Insurance Commissioner." The National Association of Insurance Commissioners has contributed greatly toward intelligent and uniform regulation. The industry also carries out a great deal of self-regulation, now largely through the Health Insurance Association of America.

Areas in which the regulation of health insurance is distinctive include the organization, admission, and solvency of companies; policy provisions and filing; regulation of out-of-state insurers; reserve requirements and rate filings; advertising; and taxation. The regulation is most thorough in regard to individual insurance, but most states also have special provisions relating to group, blanket, and franchise insurance.

Some of the remaining unresolved issues in health insurance regulation relate to continuance of coverage; excessive and unrealistic regulation; and whether uniform regulation can be achieved without resorting to the power of the federal government.

## Selected references

*See the following items from the General Bibliography: 4, ch. 24; 8, ch. 11; 9, ch. 26; 10, ch. 9; 14, ch. 5; 22, chs. 14 and 15.*

CENTER, CHARLES C. AND HEINS, RICHARD M. (eds.). *Insurance and Government,* Vol. II, Nos. 1–5. Madison: University of Wisconsin Insurance Series, 1960.

Cox, C. C. *Accident and Health Policy Provisions Manual.* Chicago: North American Co. for Life, Accident and Health Insurance, 1960.

FOLLMAN, JOSEPH F., JR. "Cooperative Endeavor in the Accident and Health Field," *CLU Journal* (June, 1952), p. 285.

FRASER, JOHN C. "Mathematical Analysis of Phase I and Phase II of 'The Life Insurance Company Income Tax Act of 1959'," *Transactions of the Society of Actuaries,* Vol. XIV, p. 51.

HEALTH INSURANCE ASSOCIATION OF AMERICA. *Digest of Accident and Health Laws and Regulations,* and Supplements. New York, irregular.

HERMAN, EDWARD S. "The Federal Trade Commission Insurance Proceedings," *Review of Insurance Studies,* Vol. II, p. 91.

KIMBALL, SPENCER L. "The Goals of Insurance Law: Means Versus Ends," *Journal of Insurance,* March, 1962, p. 19.

———. *Insurance and Public Policy.* Madison: University of Wisconsin Press, 1960.

——— AND PFENNIGSTORF, WERNER. "Administrative Control of the Terms of

Insurance Contracts: A Comparative Study," *Indiana Law Journal,* Winter, 1965, p. 143.

KIMBALL, SPENCER L. AND PFENNIGSTORF, WERNER. "Legislative Control of the Terms of Insurance Contracts," *Indiana Law Journal,* Vol. XXXIX, p. 675 (1964).

MAYERSON, ALLEN L. "The Life Insurance Company Income Tax Act of 1959," *CLU Journal,* Spring, 1960, p. 171.

MERTZ, ARTHUR C. *The First Twenty Years, Chicago: National Association of Independent Insurers,* 1965.

NASH, THOMAS G. *Federal Taxation of Life Insurance Companies.* New York: Matthew Bender & Co., 1965.

OSBORN, MALCOLM E. "The Life Insurance Income Tax Act of 1959," *CLU Journal,* Winter, 1962, p. 94.

WENCK, THOMAS L. "Standard Hospitalization Insurance Contracts," *Journal of Risk and Insurance,* March, 1964, p. 73.

# General Bibliography

# General Bibliography*

## Books and brochures

1. ANDERSEN, RONALD AND ANDERSON, ODIN W. *A Decade of Health Services.* Chicago: University of Chicago Press, 1967.
2. ANDERSON, ODIN W., COLLETTE, PATRICIA, AND FELDMAN, JACOB J. *Changes in Family Medical Care Expenditures and Voluntary Health Insurance: A Five Year Resurvey.* Cambridge, Massachusetts: Harvard University Press, 1963.
3. ANDERSON, ODIN W., WITH FELDMAN, JACOB J. *Family Medical Costs and Voluntary Health Insurance: A Nationwide Survey.* New York: McGraw-Hill Book Co., Inc., 1956.
4. ANGELL, FRANK J. *Health Insurance.* New York: The Ronald Press, 1963.
5. BARTLESON, EDWIN L., et al. *Health Insurance: Provided through Individual Policies.* Chicago: The Society of Actuaries, 1963.
6. CHAMBER OF COMMERCE OF THE UNITED STATES. *A Look at Modern Health Insurance.* Washington, 1954.
7. CONTINENTAL-NATIONAL INSURANCE INSTITUTE. *Health Insurance.* Chicago, 1961.
8. DICKERSON, O. D. *Long-Term Guaranteed Renewable Disability Insurance.* Chicago: Health and Accident Underwriters Conference, 1955.
9. EILERS, ROBERT D. AND CROWE, ROBERT M. (ed.) *Group Insurance Handbook.* Homewood, Ill.: Richard D. Irwin, Inc., 1965.
10. FAULKNER, EDWIN J. *Health Insurance.* New York: McGraw-Hill Book Co., 1960.
11. FOLLMANN, JOSEPH F., JR. *Voluntary Health Insurance and Medical Care.* New York: Health Insurance Association of America, 1958.
12. ———. *Medical Care and Health Insurance.* Homewood, Ill.: Richard D. Irwin, Inc., 1963.
13. GAGLIARDO, DOMENICO. *American Social Insurance.* New York: Harper & Bros., 1955.
14. GREGG, DAVIS M. *Group Life Insurance.* 3d ed. Homewood, Ill.: Richard D. Irwin, Inc. (The S. S. Huebner Foundation for Insurance Education), 1962.
15. ——— (ed.) *Life and Health Insurance Handbook.* 2d ed. Homewood, Ill.: Richard D. Irwin, Inc., 1964.
16. HEALTH INSURANCE ASSOCIATION OF AMERICA. *Principles of Individual*

---

* These references pertain to the general area of health insurance. See also selected references on specific topics listed at the end of each chapter.

*Health Insurance I*, Student's Guide and Instructor's Guide. New York: 1966.

17. HERRICK, KENNETH W. *Total Disability Provisions in Life Insurance Contracts.* Homewood, Ill.: Richard D. Irwin, Inc. (The S. S. Huebner Foundation for Insurance Education), 1956.

18. KULP, C. ARTHUR. *Casualty Insurance.* 3d ed. New York: Ronald Press Co., 1956.

19. MACLEAN, JOSEPH B. *Life Insurance.* 9th ed. New York: McGraw-Hill Book Co., 1962.

20. McCAHAN, DAVID (ed.) *Accident and Sickness Insurance.* Philadelphia: University of Pennsylvania Press (S. S. Huebner Foundation for Insurance Education), 1953.

21. MEHR, ROBERT I. AND OSLER, ROBERT W. *Modern Life Insurance.* 3d ed. New York: Macmillan Co., 1961.

22. MICHELBACHER, G. F. *Multiple-Line Insurance.* New York: McGraw-Hill Book Co., 1957.

23. NATIONAL UNDERWRITER COMPANY. *Handbook of Health Insurance.* Cincinnati, 1962.

24. OSBORNE, GRANT M. *Compulsory Temporary Disability Insurance in the United States.* Homewood, Ill.: Richard D. Irwin, Inc. (The S. S. Huebner Foundation for Insurance Education), 1958.

25. OSLER, ROBERT W. *Guide to Health Insurance.* Indianapolis: Rough Notes Co., 1967.

26. PICKRELL, JESSE F. *Group Health Insurance.* Rev. ed. Homewood, Ill.: Richard D. Irwin, Inc. (The S. S. Huebner Foundation for Insurance Education), 1961.

27. SERBEIN, OSCAR N. *Paying for Medical Care in the U.S.* New York: Columbia University Press, 1953.

28. SOMERS, HERMAN M. AND ANNE R. *Doctors, Patients and Health Insurance.* Washington: The Brookings Institution, 1961.

29. TURNBULL, JOHN G., WILLIAMS, C. ARTHUR, AND CHEIT, EARL F. *Economic and Social Security.* 3d ed. New York: Ronald Press Co., 1967.

30. WERBEL, BERNARD G. *Werbel's Health Insurance Primer.* New York: Werbel Publishing Co., Inc., 1966.

# Appendices

# The 1950 Uniform Individual
# Accident and Sickness Policy
# Provisions Law: N.A.I.C.

Section 1. DEFINITION OF ACCIDENT AND SICKNESS INSURANCE POLICY.

The term "policy of accident and sickness insurance" as used herein includes any policy or contract covering the kind or kinds of insurance described in .......................... (*insert here the section of law authorizing accident and sickness insurance*).

(*Note: If the insurance law of the state in which this draft is proposed for enactment does not have a section specifically authorizing the various types of insurance which may be written, this section should be modified to define accident and sickness insurance as "insurance against loss resulting from sickness or from bodily injury or death by accident, or both."*)

Section 2. FORM OF POLICY.

(A) No policy of accident and sickness insurance shall be delivered or issued for delivery to any person in this state unless:

(1) the entire money and other considerations therefor are expressed therein; and

(2) the time at which the insurance takes effect and terminates is expressed therein; and

(3) it purports to insure only one person, except that a policy may insure, originally or by subsequent amendment, upon the application of an adult member of a family who shall be deemed the policyholder, any two or more eligible members of that family, including husband, wife, dependent children or any children under a specified age which shall not exceed nineteen years and any other person dependent upon the policyholder; and

(*Note: In states having community property systems derived from the civil law it is suggested that in the foregoing subparagraph the words "an adult member" be replaced with "the head."*)

(4) the style, arrangement and over-all appearance of the policy give

no undue prominence to any portion of the text, and unless every printed portion of the text of the policy and of any endorsements or attached papers is plainly printed in light-faced type of a style in general use, the size of which shall be uniform and not less than ten-point with a lower-case unspaced alphabet length not less than one hundred and twenty-point (the "text" shall include all printed matter except the name and address of the insurer, name or title of the policy, the brief description if any, and captions and subcaptions); and

(5) the exceptions and reductions of indemnity are set forth in the policy and, except those which are set forth in section 3 of this act, are printed, at the insurer's option, either included with the benefit provision to which they apply, or under an appropriate caption such as "EXCEPTIONS," or "EXCEPTIONS AND REDUCTIONS," provided that if an exception or reduction specifically applies only to a particular benefit of the policy, a statement of such exception or reduction shall be included with the benefit provision to which it applies; and

(6) each such form, including riders and endorsements, shall be identified by a form number in the lower left-hand corner of the first page thereof; and

(7) it contains no provision purporting to make any portion of the charter, rules, constitution, or by-laws of the insurer a part of the policy unless such portion is set forth in full in the policy, except in the case of the incorporation of, or reference to, a statement of rates or classification of risks, or short-rate table filed with the (*Commissioner*).

(B)  If any policy is issued by an insurer domiciled in this state for delivery to a person residing in another state, and if the official having responsibility for the administration of the insurance laws of such other state shall have advised the (*Commissioner*) that any such policy is not subject to approval or disapproval by such official, the (*Commissioner*) may by ruling require that such policy meet the standards set forth in subsection (A) of this section and in section 3.

*Section 3.*    ACCIDENT AND SICKNESS POLICY PROVISIONS.

(A) *Required Provisions*

Except as provided in paragraph (C) of this section each such policy delivered or issued for delivery to any person in this state shall contain the provisions specified in this subsection in the words in which the same appear in this section; provided, however, that the insurer may, at its option, substitute for one or more of such provisions corresponding provisions of different wording approved by the (*Commissioner*) which are in each instance not less favorable in any respect to the insured or the beneficiary. Such provisions shall be preceded individually by the caption appearing in this subsection or, at the option of the insurer, by such appropriate individual or group captions or subcaptions as the (*Commissioner*) may approve.

(1)   A provision as follows:

**Entire Contract; Changes:** This policy, including the endorsements and the attached papers, if any, constitutes the entire contract of insurance. No change in this policy shall be valid until approved by an executive officer of the insurer and unless such approval be endorsed hereon or attached hereto. No agent has authority to change this policy or to waive any of its provisions.

(*Note: When enacted in states which prohibit amendment of a policy form by means other than attached printed rider upon a separate piece of paper the new law should contain (but not as a required policy provision) an added section defining "endorsement" in such a manner as to make the new law consistent with current statutes.*)

(2)   A provision as follows:

**Time Limit on Certain Defenses:** (a) After three years from the date of issue of this policy no misstatements, except fraudulent misstatements, made by the applicant in the application for such policy shall be used to void the policy or to deny a claim for loss incurred or disability (as defined in the policy) commencing after the expiration of such three year period.

(The foregoing policy provision shall not be so construed as to affect any legal requirement for avoidance of a policy or denial of a claim during such initial three year period, nor to limit the application of section 3 (B), (1), (2), (3), (4) and (5) in the event of misstatement with respect to age or occupation or other insurance.)

(A policy which the insured has the right to continue in force subject to its terms by the timely payment of premium (1) until at least age 50 or, (2) in the case of a policy issued after age 44, for at least five years from its date of issue, may contain in lieu of the foregoing the following provision (from which the clause in parentheses may be omitted at the insurer's option) under the caption "INCONTESTABLE":

After this policy has been in force for a period of three years during the lifetime of the insured (excluding any period during which the insured is disabled), it shall become incontestable as to the statements contained in the application.

(b) No claim for loss incurred or disability (as defined in the policy) commencing after three years from the date of issue of this policy shall be reduced or denied on the ground that a disease or physical condition not excluded from coverage by name or specific description effective on the date of loss had existed prior to the effective date of coverage of this policy.

(3)   A provision as follows:

**Grace Period:**  A grace period of . . . . . . . . . (*insert a number not less than "7" for weekly premium policies, "10" for monthly premium policies and "31" for all other policies*) days will be granted for the payment of each premium falling due after the first premium, during which grace period the policy shall continue in force.

(A policy which contains a cancellation provision may add, at the end of the above provision,

subject to the right of the insurer to cancel in accordance with the cancellation provision hereof.

A policy in which the insurer reserves the right to refuse any renewal shall have, at the beginning of the above provision,

Unless not less than five days prior to the premium due date the insurer has delivered to the insured or has mailed to his last address as shown by the records of the insurer written notice of its intention not to renew this policy beyond the period for which the premium has been accepted, ).

(4)   A provision as follows:

**Reinstatement:**  If any renewal premium be not paid within the time granted the insured for payment, a subsequent acceptance of premium by the insurer or by any agent duly authorized by the insurer to accept such premium, without requiring in connection therewith an application for reinstatement, shall reinstate the policy; provided, however, that if the insurer or such agent requires an application for reinstatement and issues a conditional receipt for the premium tendered, the policy will be reinstated upon approval of such application by the insurer or, lacking such approval, upon the forty-fifth day following the date of such conditional receipt unless the insurer has previously notified the insured in writing of its disapproval of such application. The reinstated policy shall cover only loss resulting from such accidental injury as may be sustained after the date of reinstatement and loss due to such sickness as may begin more than ten days after such date. In all other respects the insured and insurer shall have the same rights thereunder as they had under the policy immediately before the due date of the defaulted premium, subject to any provisions endorsed hereon or attached hereto in connection with the reinstatement. Any premium accepted in connection with a reinstatement shall be applied to a period for which premium has not been previously paid, but not to any period more than sixty days prior to the date of reinstatement.

(The last sentence of the above provision may be omitted from any policy which the insured has the right to continue in force subject to its terms by the timely payment of premiums (1) until at least age 50 or, (2) in the case of a policy issued after age 44, for at least five years from its date of issue.)

(5) A provision as follows:

**Notice of Claim:** Written notice of claim must be given to the insurer within twenty days after the occurrence or commencement of any loss covered by the policy, or as soon thereafter as is reasonably possible. Notice given by or on behalf of the insured or the beneficiary to the insurer at ................ (*insert the location of such office as the insurer may designate for the purpose*), or to any authorized agent of the insurer, with information sufficient to identify the insured, shall be deemed notice to the insurer.

(In a policy providing a loss-of-time benefit which may be payable for at least two years, an insurer may at its option insert the following between the first and second sentences of the above provision:

Subject to the qualifications set forth below, if the insured suffers loss of time on account of disability for which indemnity may be payable for at least two years, he shall, at least once in every six months after having given notice of claim, give to the insurer notice of continuance of said disability, except in the event of legal incapacity. The period of six months following any filing of proof by the insured or any payment by the insurer on account of such claim or any denial of liability in whole or in part by the insurer shall be excluded in applying this provision. Delay in the giving of such notice shall not impair the insured's right to any indemnity which would otherwise have accrued during the period of six months preceding the date on which such notice is actually given.)

(6) A provision as follows:

**Claim Forms:** The insurer, upon receipt of a notice of claim, will furnish to the claimant such forms as are usually furnished by it for filing proofs of loss. If such forms are not furnished within fifteen days after the giving of such notice the claimant shall be deemed to have complied with the requirements of this policy as to proof of loss upon submitting, within the time fixed in the policy for filing proofs of loss, written proof covering the occurrence, the character and the extent of the loss for which claim is made.

(7) A provision as follows:

**Proofs of Loss:** Written proof of loss must be furnished to the insurer at its said office in case of claim for loss for which this policy provides any periodic payment contingent upon continuing loss within ninety days after the termination of the period for which the insurer is liable and in case of claim for any other loss within ninety days after the date of such loss. Failure to furnish such proof within the time required shall not invalidate nor reduce any claim if it was not reasonably possible to give proof within such time, provided such proof is furnished as soon as reasonably possible and in no event, except in the absence of legal capacity, later than one year from the time proof is otherwise required.

(8)   A provision as follows:

**Time of Payment of Claims:** Indemnities payable under this policy for any loss other than loss for which this policy provides any periodic payment will be paid immediately upon receipt of due written proof of such loss. Subject to due written proof of loss, all accrued indemnities for loss for which this policy provides periodic payment will be paid . . . . . . . . . . . . . . . . . . . . (*insert period for payment which must not be less frequently than monthly*) and any balance remaining unpaid upon the termination of liability will be paid immediately upon receipt of due written proof.

(9)   A provision as follows:

**Payment of Claims:** Indemnity for loss of life will be payable in accordance with the beneficiary designation and the provisions respecting such payment which may be prescribed herein and effective at the time of payment. If no such designation or provision is then effective, such indemnity shall be payable to the estate of the insured. Any other accrued indemnities unpaid at the insured's death may, at the option of the insurer, be paid either to such beneficiary or to such estate. All other indemnities will be payable to the insured.

(The following provisions, or either of them, may be included with the foregoing provision at the option of the insurer:

If any indemnity of this policy shall be payable to the estate of the insured, or to an insured or beneficiary who is a minor or otherwise not competent to give a valid release, the insurer may pay such indemnity, up to an amount not exceeding $. . . . . . . . . . . . (*insert an amount which shall not exceed $1000*), to any relative by blood or connection by marriage of the insured or beneficiary who is deemed by the insurer to be equitably entitled thereto. Any payment made by the insurer in good faith pursuant to this provision shall fully discharge the insurer to the extent of such payment.

Subject to any written direction of the insured in the application or otherwise all or a portion of any indemnities provided by this policy on account of hospital, nursing, medical, or surgical services may, at the insurer's option and unless the insured requests otherwise in writing not later than the time of filing proofs of such loss, be paid directly to the hospital or person rendering such services; but it is not required that the service be rendered by a particular hospital or person.)

(10)  A provision as follows:

**Physical Examinations and Autopsy:** The insurer at its own expense shall have the right and opportunity to examine the person of the insured when and as often as it may reasonably require during the pendency of a claim hereunder and to make an autopsy in case of death where it is not forbidden by law.

(11)  A provision as follows:

**Legal Actions:** No action at law or in equity shall be brought to recover on this policy prior to the expiration of sixty days after written proof of loss has been furnished in accordance with the requirements of this policy. No such action shall be brought after the expiration of three years after the time written proof of loss is required to be furnished.

(12)  A provision as follows:

**Change of Beneficiary:** Unless the insured makes an irrevocable designation of beneficiary, the right to change of beneficiary is reserved to the insured and the consent of the beneficiary or beneficiaries shall not be requisite to surrender or assignment of this policy or to any change of beneficiary or beneficiaries, or to any other changes in this policy.

(The first clause of this provision, relating to the irrevocable designation of beneficiary, may be omitted at the insurer's option.)

### (B)  *Other Provisions*

Except as provided in paragraph (C) of this section, no such policy delivered or issued for delivery to any person in this state shall contain provisions respecting the matters set forth below unless such provisions are in the words in which the same appear in this section; provided, however, that the insurer may, at its option, use in lieu of any such provision a corresponding provision of different wording approved by the (*Commissioner*) which is not less favorable in any respect to the insured or the beneficiary. Any such provision contained in the policy shall be preceded individually by the appropriate caption appearing in this subsection or, at the option of the insurer, by such approriate individual or group captions or subcaptions as the (*Commissioner*) may approve.

(1)  A provision as follows:

**Change of Occupation:** If the insured be injured or contract sickness after having changed his occupation to one classified by the insurer as more hazardous than that stated in this policy or while doing for compensation anything pertaining to an occupation so classified, the insurer will pay only such portion of the indemnities provided in this policy as the premium paid would have purchased at the rates and within the limits fixed by the insurer for such more hazardous occupation. If the insured changes his occupation to one classified by the insurer as less hazardous than that stated in this policy, the insurer, upon receipt of proof of such change of occupation, will reduce the premium rate accordingly, and will return the excess pro-rata unearned premium from the date of change of occupation or from the policy anniversary date immediately preceding receipt of such proof, whichever is the more recent. In applying this provision, the classification of occupational risk and the premium rates shall be such as have been last filed by the insurer prior to the occurrence of the loss for which the insurer is liable or prior to date of proof of change in occupation with the state official having supervision of insurance in the state where the insured resided at the time this policy was issued; but if such filing was not required, then the classification of occupational risk and the premium rates shall be those last made effective by the insurer in such state prior to the occurrence of the loss or prior to the date of proof of change in occupation.

(2)   A provision as follows:

**Misstatement of Age:** If the age of the insured has been misstated, all amounts payable under this policy shall be such as the premium paid would have purchased at the correct age.

(3)   A provision as follows:

**Other Insurance in This Insurer:** If an accident or sickness or accident and sickness policy or policies previously issued by the insurer to the insured be in force concurrently herewith, making the aggregate indemnity for ............... (*insert type of coverage or coverages*) in excess of $............... (*insert maximum limit of indemnity or indemnities*) the excess insurance shall be void and all premiums paid for such excess shall be returned to the insured or to his estate.

Or, in lieu thereof:

Insurance effective at any one time on the insured under a like policy or policies in this insurer is limited to the one such policy elected by the insured, his beneficiary or his estate, as the case may be, and the insurer will return all premiums paid for all other such policies.

(4)   A provision as follows:

**Insurance with Other Insurers:** If there be other valid coverage, not with this insurer, providing benefits for the same loss on a provision of service basis or on an expense incurred basis and of which this insurer has not been given written notice prior to the occurrence or commencement of loss, the only liability under any expense incurred coverage of this policy shall be for such proportion of the loss as the amount which would otherwise have been payable hereunder plus the total of the like amounts under all such other valid coverages for the same loss of which this insurer had notice bears to the total like amounts under all valid coverages for such loss, and for the return of such portion of the premiums paid as shall exceed the pro-rata portion for the amount so determined. For the purpose of applying this provision when other coverage is on a provision of service basis, the "like amount" of such other coverage shall be taken as the amount which the services rendered would have cost in the absence of such coverage.

(If the foregoing policy provision is included in a policy which also contains the next following policy provision there shall be added to the caption of the foregoing provision the phrase "—EXPENSE INCURRED BENEFITS." The insurer may, at its option, include in this provision a definition of "other valid coverage," approved as to form by the (*Commissioner*), which definition shall be limited in subject matter to coverage provided by organizations subject to regulation by insurance law or by insurance authorities of this or any other state of the United States or any province of Canada, and by hospital or medical service organizations, and to any other coverage the inclusion of which may be approved by the (*Commissioner*). In the absence of such definition such term shall not include group insurance, automobile medical payments insurance, or coverage provided by hospital or medical service organizations or by union welfare plans or employer or employee benefit organizations. For the purpose of applying the foregoing policy provision with respect to any insured, any amount of benefit provided for such insured pursuant to any compulsory benefit statute (including any workmen's compensation or employer's liability statute) whether provided by a governmental agency or otherwise shall in all cases be deemed to be "other valid coverage" of which the insurer has had notice. In applying the foregoing policy provision no third party liability coverage shall be included as "other valid coverage.")

(5) A provision as follows:

**Insurance with Other Insurers:** If there be other valid coverage, not with this insurer, providing benefits for the same loss on other than an expense incurred basis and of which this insurer has not been given written notice prior to the occurence or commencement of loss, the only liability for such benefits under this policy shall be for such proportion of the indemnities otherwise provided hereunder for such loss as the like indemnities of which the insurer had notice (including the indemnities under this policy) bear to the total amount of all like indemnities for such loss, and for the return of such portion of the premium paid as shall exceed the pro-rata portion for the indemnities thus determined.

(If the foregoing policy provision is included in a policy which also contains the next preceding policy provision there shall be added to the caption of the foregoing provision the phrase "—OTHER BENEFITS." The insurer may, at its option, include in this provision a definition of "other valid coverage," approved as to form by the (*Commissioner*), which definition shall be limited in subject matter to coverage provided by organizations subject to regulation by insurance law or by insurance authorities of this or any other state of the United States or any province of Canada, and to any other coverage the inclusion of which may be approved by the (*Commissioner*). In the absence of such definition such term shall not include group insurance, or benefits provided by union welfare plans or by employer or employee benefit organizations. For the purpose of applying the foregoing policy provision with respect to any insured, any amount of benefit provided for such insured pursuant to any compulsory benefit statute (including any workmen's compensation or employer's liability statute) whether provided by a governmental agency or otherwise shall in all cases be deemed to be "other valid coverage" of which the insurer has had notice. In applying the foregoing policy provision no third party liability coverage shall be included as "other valid coverage.")

(6)   A provision as follows:

**Relation of Earnings to Insurance:**   If the total monthly amount of loss of time benefits promised for the same loss under all valid loss of time coverage upon the insured, whether payable on a weekly or monthly basis, shall exceed the monthly earnings of the insured at the time disability commenced or his average monthly earnings for the period of two years immediately preceding a disability for which claim is made, whichever is the greater, the insurer will be liable only for such proportionate amount of such benefits under this policy as the amount of such monthly earnings or such average monthly earnings of the insured bears to the total amount of monthly benefits for the same loss under all such coverage upon the insured at the time such disability commences and for the return of such part of the premiums paid during such two years as shall exceed the pro-rata amount of the premiums for the benefits actually paid hereunder; but this shall not operate to reduce the total monthly amount of benefits payable under all such coverage upon the insured below the sum of two hundred dollars or the sum of the monthly benefits specified in such coverages, whichever is the lesser, nor shall it operate to reduce benefits other than those payable for loss of time.

(The foregoing policy provision may be inserted only in a policy which the insured has the right to continue in force subject to its terms by the timely payment of premiums (1) until at least age 50 or, (2) in the case of a policy issued after age 44, for at least five years from its date of issue. The insurer may, at its option, include in this provision a definition of "valid loss of time coverage," approved as to form by the (*Commissioner*), which definition shall be limited in subject matter to coverage provided by governmental agencies or by organizations subject to regulation by insurance law or by insurance authorities of this or any other state of the United States or any province of Canada, or to any other coverage the inclusion of which may be approved by the (*Commissioner*) or any combination of such coverages. In the absence of such definition such term shall not include any coverage provided for such insured pursuant to any compulsory benefit statute (including any workmen's compensation or employer's liability statute), or benefits provided by union welfare plans or by employer or employee benefit organizations.)

(7)   A provision as follows:

**Unpaid Premium:** Upon the payment of a claim under this policy, any premium then due and unpaid or covered by any note or written order may be deducted therefrom.

(8)   A provision as follows:

**Cancellation:** The insurer may cancel this policy at any time by written notice delivered to the insured, or mailed to his last address as shown by the records of the insurer, stating when, not less than five days thereafter, such cancellation shall be effective; and after the policy has been continued beyond its original term the insured may cancel this policy at any time by written notice delivered or mailed to the insurer, effective upon receipt or on such later date as may be specified in such notice. In the event of cancellation, the insurer will return promptly the unearned portion of any premium paid. If the insured cancels, the earned premium shall be computed by the use of the short-rate table last filed with the state official having supervision of insurance in the state where the insured resided when the policy was issued. If the insurer cancels, the earned premium shall be computed pro-rata. Cancellation shall be without prejudice to any claim originating prior to the effective date of cancellation.

(*Note: In some states by statute termination of the in force status of the policy alone may not prejudice any claim for loss arising during and out of a disability which commenced while the policy was in force. The language here is susceptible of an interpretation consistent with such statutes.*)

(9)   A provision as follows:

**Conformity with State Statutes:** Any provision of this policy which, on its effective date, is in conflict with the statutes of the state in which the insured resides on such date is hereby amended to conform to the minimum requirements of such statutes.

(10)   A provision as follows:

**Illegal Occupation:** The insurer shall not be liable for any loss to which a contributing cause was the insured's commission of or attempt to commit a felony or to which a contributing cause was the insured's being engaged in an illegal occupation.

(11)   A provision as follows:

**Intoxicants and Narcotics:** The insurer shall not be liable for any loss sustained or contracted in consequence of the insured's being intoxicated or under the influence of any narcotic unless administered on the advice of a physician.

(*Note: Paragraphs (10) and (11) are suggested for states which desire such provisions.*)

### (C) Inapplicable or Inconsistent Provisions

If any provision of this section is in whole or in part inapplicable to or inconsistent with the coverage provided by a particular form of policy the insurer, with the approval of the (*Commissioner*), shall omit from such policy any inapplicable provision or part of a provision, and shall modify any inconsistent provision or part of the provision in such manner as to make the provision as contained in the policy consistent with the coverage provided by the policy.

### (D) Order of Certain Policy Provisions

The provisions which are the subject of subsections (A) and (B) of this section, or any corresponding provisions which are used in lieu thereof in accordance with such subsections, shall be printed in the consecutive order of the provisions in such subsections or, at the option of the insurer, any such provision may appear as a unit in any part of the policy, with other provisions to which it may be logically related, provided the resulting policy shall not be in whole or in part unintelligible, uncertain, ambiguous, abstruse, or likely to mislead a person to whom the policy is offered, delivered or issued.

### (E) Third Party Ownership

The word "insured," as used in this act, shall not be construed as preventing a person other than the insured with a proper insurable interest from making application for and owning a policy covering the insured or from being entitled under such a policy to any indemnities, benefits and rights provided therein.

### (F) Requirements of Other Jurisdictions

(1) Any policy of a foreign or alien insurer, when delivered or issued for delivery to any person in this state, may contain any provision which is not less favorable to the insured or the beneficiary than the provisions of this act and which is prescribed or required by the law of the state under which the insurer is organized.

(2) Any policy of a domestic insurer may, when issued for delivery in any other state or country, contain any provision permitted or required by the laws of such other state or country.

### (G) Filing Procedure

The (*Commissioner*) may make such reasonable rules and regulations concerning the procedure for the filing or submission of policies subject to this act as are necessary, proper or advisable to the administration of this act. This provision shall not abridge any other authority granted the (*Commissioner*) by law.

*Section* 4.   CONFORMING TO STATUTE.

### (A) *Other Policy Provisions*

No policy provision which is not subject to section 3 of this act shall make a policy, or any portion thereof, less favorable in any respect to the insured or the beneficiary than the provisions thereof which are subject to this act.

### (B) *Policy Conflicting with This Act*

A policy delivered or issued for delivery to any person in this state in violation of this act shall be held valid but shall be construed as provided in this act. When any provision in a policy subject to this act is in conflict with any provision of this act, the rights, duties and obligations of the insurer, the insured and the beneficiary shall be governed by the provisions of this act.

*Section* 5.   APPLICATION.

(A)   The insured shall not be bound by any statement made in an application for a policy unless a copy of such application is attached to or endorsed on the policy when issued as a part thereof. If any such policy delivered or issued for delivery to any person in this state shall be reinstated or renewed, and the insured or the beneficiary or assignee of such policy shall make written request to the insurer for a copy of the application, if any, for such reinstatement or renewal, the insurer shall within fifteen days after the receipt of such request at its home office or any branch office of the insurer, deliver or mail to the person making such request, a copy of such application. If such copy shall not be so delivered or mailed, the insurer shall be precluded from introducing such application as evidence in any action or proceeding based upon or involving such policy or its reinstatement or renewal.

(B)   No alteration of any written application for any such policy shall be made by any person other than the applicant without his written consent, except that insertions may be made by the insurer, for administrative purposes only, in such manner as to indicate clearly that such insertions are not to be ascribed to the applicant.

(C)   The falsity of any satement in the application for any policy covered by this act may not bar the right to recovery thereunder unless such false statement materially affected either the acceptance of the risk or the hazard assumed by the insurer.

(*Note: Section 5, or any subsection thereof, is suggested for use in states which have no comparable statutes relating to the application.*)

*Section* 6.   NOTICE, WAIVER.

The acknowledgment by any insurer of the receipt of notice given under any policy covered by this act, or the furnishing of forms for filing proofs of loss, or the acceptance of such proofs, or the investigation of any claim thereunder still not operate as a waiver of any of the rights of the insurer in defense of any claim arising under such policy.

*Section 7.    AGE LIMIT.*

If any such policy contains a provision establishing, as an age limit or otherwise, a date after which the coverage provided by the policy will not be effective, and if such date falls within a period for which premium is accepted by the insurer or if the insurer accepts a premium after such date, the coverage provided by the policy will continue in force subject to any right of cancellation until the end of the period for which premium has been accepted. In the event the age of the insured has been misstated and if, according to the correct age of the insured, the coverage provided by the policy would not have become effective, or would have ceased prior to the acceptance of such premium or premiums, then the liability of the insurer shall be limited to the refund, upon request, of all premiums paid for the period not covered by the policy.

*Section 8.    NON-APPLICATION TO CERTAIN POLICIES.*

Nothing in this act shall apply to or affect ( 1 ) any policy of workmen's compensation insurance or any policy of liability insurance with or without supplementary expense coverage therein; or ( 2 ) any policy or contract of reinsurance; or ( 3 ) any blanket or group policy of insurance; or ( 4 ) life insurance, endowment or annuity contracts, or contracts supplemental thereto which contain only such provisions relating to accident and sickness insurance as ( a ) provide additional benefits in case of death or dismemberment or loss of sight by accident, or as ( b ) operate to safeguard such contracts against lapse, or to give a special surrender value or special benefit or an annuity in the event that the insured or annuitant shall become totally and permanently disabled, as defined by the contract or supplemental contract.

(*Note: This provision may, if desired, be modified in individual states so as to be consistent with current statutes of such states.*)

*Section 9.    VIOLATION.*

Any person, partnership or corporation willfully violating any provision of this act or order of the (*Commissioner*) made in accordance with this act, shall forfeit to the people of the state a sum not to exceed $............ for each such violation, which may be recovered by a civil action. The (*Commissioner*) may also suspend or revoke the license of an insurer or agent for any such willful violation.

(*Note: This provision is to be used only in those states which do not have similar legislation now in effect.*)

*Section* 10. JUDICIAL REVIEW.

Any order or decision of the (*Commissioner*) under this act shall be subject to review by appeal (writ of certiorari) to the .............. Court at the instance of any party in interest. The filing of the appeal (petition for such writ) shall operate as a state of any such order or decision until the Court directs otherwise. The Court may review all the facts and, in disposing of the issue before it, may modify, affirm or reverse the order or decision of the (*Commissioner*) in whole or in part.

(*Note: This provision is to be used only in those states which do not have similar legislation now in effect.*)

*Section* 11. REPEAL OF INCONSISTENT ACTS.

(*Note: This section should contain suitable language to repeal acts or parts of acts presently enacted and inconsistent with this act. The repealing section should contain an appropriate exception with regard to section 12 of this act.*)

*Section* 12. EFFECTIVE DATE OF ACT.

This act shall take effect on the ............. day of .............., 19...... A policy, rider or endorsement, which could have been lawfully used or delivered or issued for delivery to any person in this state immediately before the effective date of this act may be used or delivered or issued for delivery to any such person during five years after the effective date of this act without being subject to the provisions of sections 2, 3, or 4 of this act.

Prepared by Health Insurance Association of America, October 4, 1957

# Group Accident and Sickness Insurance

(a) Group accident and sickness insurance is hereby declared to be that form of accident and sickness insurance covering groups of persons as defined below, with or without one or more members of their families or one or more of their dependents, or covering one or more members of the families or one or more dependents of such groups of persons, and issued upon the following basis:

(1) Under a policy issued to an employer or trustees of a fund established by an employer, who shall be deemed the policyholder, insuring employees of such employer for the benefit of persons other than the employer. The term "employees" as used herein shall be deemed to include the officers, managers, and employees of the employer, the individual proprietor or partner if the employer is an individual proprietor or partnership, the officers, managers, and employees of subsidiary or affiliated corporations, the individual proprietors, partners and employees of individuals and firms, if the business of the employer and such individual or firm is under common control through stock ownership, contract, or otherwise. The term "employees" as used herein may include retired employees. A policy issued to insure employees of a public body may provide that the term "employees" shall include elected or appointed officials. The policy may provide that the term, "employees" shall include the trustees or their employees, or both, if their duties are principally connected with such trusteeship.

(2) Under a policy issued to an association, including a labor union, which shall have a constitution and by-laws and which has been

organized and is maintained in good faith for purposes other than that of obtaining insurance, insuring members, employees, or employees of members of the association for the benefit of persons other than the association or its officers or trustees. The term "employees" as used herein may include retired employees.

(3) Under a policy issued to the trustees of a fund established by two or more employers in the same or related industry or by one or more labor unions or by one or more employers and one or more labor unions or by an association as defined in (a) (2) which trustees shall be deemed the policyholder, to insure employees of the employers or members of the unions or of such association, or employees of members of such association for the benefit of persons other than the employers or the unions or such association. The term "employees" as used herein may include the officers, managers and employees of the employer, and the individual proprietor or partners if the employer is an individual proprietor or partnership. The term "employees" as used herein may include retired employees. The policy may provide that the term "employees" shall include the trustees or their employees, or both, if their duties are principally connected with such trusteeship.

(4) Under a policy issued to any person or organization to which a policy of group life insurance may be issued or delivered in this (state) to insure any class or classes of individuals that could be insured under such group life policy.

(5) Under a policy issued to cover any other substantially similar group which, in the discretion of the Commissioner, may be subject to the issuance of a group accident and sickness policy or contract.

(b) Each such policy shall contain in substance the following provisions:

(1) A provision that, in the absence of fraud, all statements made by applicants or the policyholder or by an insured person shall be deemed representations and not warranties, and that no statement made for the purpose of effecting insurance shall avoid such insurance or reduce benefits unless contained in a written instrument signed by the policyholder or the insured person, a copy of which has been furnished to such policyholder or to such person or his beneficiary.

(2) A provision that the insurer will furnish to the policyholder for delivery to each employee or member of the insured group, a statement in summary form of the essential features of the insur-

ance coverage of such employee or member and to whom benefits thereunder are payable. If dependents are included in the coverage, only one certificate need be issued for each family unit.

(3) A provision that to the group originally insured may be added from time to time eligible new employees or members or dependents, as the case may be, in accordance with the terms of the policy.

(c) Any group accident and sickness policy may on request by the group policyholder provide that all or any portion of any indemnities provided by any such policy on account of hospital, nursing, medical or surgical services may, at the insurer's option, be paid directly to the hospital or person rendering such services; but the policy may not require that the service be rendered by a particular hospital or person. Payment so made shall discharge the insurer's obligation with respect to the amount of insurance so paid.

Adopted by the National Association of Insurance Commissioners, November 28–December 2, 1955, and Revised December, 1956

# Rules Governing Advertisements of Accident and Sickness Insurance

WHEREAS the insurance laws of this state and particularly (refer to specific sections of law) prohibit the transmission of information in the form of advertisements or otherwise in such a manner or of such substance that the insurance buying public may be deceived or misled thereby; and

WHEREAS said insurance laws establish only general standards by which advertisements in the field of individual, group, blanket and franchise accident and sickness insurance should be prepared, disseminated and regulated; and,

WHEREAS it is considered proper and desirable to implement and interpret the general statutory standards and to adopt proper procedures to expedite enforcement thereof by this office; now therefore

IT IS ORDERED that the following standards for advertisements of such accident and sickness insurance as well as the administrative and enforcement procedures hereafter enumerated be and are hereby adopted as a formal and official rule (ruling) of this department:

Section 1. DEFINITIONS

A. An advertisement for the purpose of these rules shall include:
  (1) printed and published material and descriptive literature of an insurer used in newspapers, magazines, radio, and TV scripts, billboards and similar displays; and
  (2) descriptive literature and sales aids of all kinds issued by an insurer for presentation to members of the public, including

723

but not limited to circulars, leaflets, booklets, depictions, illustrations, and form letters; and

(3) prepared sales talks, presentations and material for use by agents and brokers, and representations made by agents and brokers in accordance therewith.

B. Policy for the purpose of these rules shall include any policy plan, certificate, contract, agreement, statement of coverage, rider or endorsement which provides accident or sickness benefits, or medical, surgical or hospital expense benefits whether on a cash indemnity, reimbursement, or service basis, except when issued in connection with another kind of insurance other than life, and except disability and double indemnity benefits included in life insurance and annuity contracts.

C. Insurer for the purpose of these rules shall include any individual, corporation, association, partnership, reciprocal exchange, interinsurer, Lloyds, fraternal benefit society, and any other legal entity engaged in the advertisement of a policy as herein defined.

D. These rules shall also apply to agents and brokers to the extent that they are responsible for the advertisement of any policy.

Section 2.   ADVERTISEMENTS IN GENERAL

Advertisements shall be truthful and not misleading in fact or in implication. Words or phrases the meaning of which is clear only by implication or by familiarity with insurance terminology shall not be used.

Section 3. ADVERTISEMENTS OF BENEFITS PAYABLE, LOSSES COVERED OR PREMIUMS PAYABLE

A. Deceptive Words, Phrases or Illustrations

Words, phrases or illustrations shall not be used in a manner which misleads or has the capacity and tendency to deceive as to the extent of any policy benefit payable, loss covered or premium payable. An advertisement relating to any policy benefit payable, loss covered or premium payable shall be sufficiently complete and clear as to avoid deception or the capacity and tendency to deceive.

Explanation:

(1) The words and phrases "all," "full," "complete," "comprehensive," "unlimited," "up to," "as high as," "this policy will pay your hospital and surgical bills" or "this policy will replace your income," or similar words and phrases shall not be used so as to exaggerate any benefit beyond the terms of the policy, but may be used only in such manner as fairly to describe such benefit.

(2) A policy covering only one disease or a list of specified diseases shall not be advertised so as to imply coverage

beyond the terms of the policy. Synonymous terms shall not be used to refer to any disease so as to imply broader coverage than is the fact.

(3) The benefits of a policy which pays varying amounts for the same loss occurring under different conditions or which pays benefits only when a loss occurs under certain conditions shall not be advertised without disclosing the limited conditions under which the benefits referred to are provided by the policy.

(4) Phrases such as "this policy pays $1,800 for hospital room and board expenses" are incomplete without indicating the maximum daily benefit and the maximum time limit for hospital room and board expenses.

B. Exceptions, Reductions and Limitations

When an advertisement refers to any dollar amount, period of time for which any benefit is payable, cost of policy, or specific policy benefit or the loss for which such benefit is payable, it shall also disclose these exceptions, reductions and limitations affecting the basic provisions of the policy without which the advertisement would have the capacity and tendency to mislead or deceive.

Explanation:

(1) The term "exception" shall mean any provision in a policy whereby coverage for a specified hazard is entirely eliminated; it is a statement of a risk not assumed under the policy.

(2) The term "reduction" shall mean any provision which reduces the amount of the benefit; a risk of loss is assumed but payment upon the occurrence of such loss is limited to some amount or period less than would be otherwise payable had such reduction clause not been used.

(3) The term "limitation" shall mean any provision which restricts coverage under the policy other than an exception or a reduction.

(4) Waiting, Elimination, Probationary or Similar Periods
When a policy contains a time period between the effective date of the policy and the effective date of coverage under the policy or a time period between the date a loss occurs and the date benefits begin to accrue for such loss, an advertisement covered by Section 3B shall disclose the existence of such periods.

(5) Pre-existing Conditions
(a) An advertisement covered by Section 3B shall disclose the extent to which any loss is not covered

if the cause of such loss is traceable to a condition existing prior to the effective date of the policy.

(b) When a policy does not cover losses traceable to pre-existing conditions no advertisement of the policy shall state or imply that the applicant's physical condition or medical history will not affect the issuance of the policy or payment of a claim thereunder. This limits the use of the phrase "no medical examination required" and phrases of similar import.

## Section 4. NECESSITY FOR DISCLOSING POLICY PROVISIONS RELATING TO RENEWABILITY, CANCELLABILITY AND TERMINATION

An advertisement which refers to renewability, cancellability or termination of a policy, or which refers to a policy benefit, or which states or illustrates time or age in connection with eligibility of applicants or continuation of the policy, shall disclose the provisions relating to renewability, cancellability and termination and any modification of benefits, losses covered or premiums because of age or for other reasons, in a manner which shall not minimize or render obscure the qualifying conditions.

## Section 5. METHOD OF DISCLOSURE OF REQUIRED INFORMATION

All information required to be disclosed by these rules shall be set out conspicuously and in close conjunction with the statements to which such information relates or under appropriate captions of such prominence that it shall not be minimized, rendered obscure or presented in an ambiguous fashion or intermingled with the context of the advertisement so as to be confusing or misleading.

## Section 6. TESTIMONIALS

Testimonials used in advertisements must be genuine, represent the current opinion of the author, be applicable to the policy advertised and be accurately reproduced. The insurer, in using a testimonial, makes as its own all of the statements contained therein, and the advertisement including such statements is subject to all of the provisions of these rules.

## Section 7. USE OF STATISTICS

An advertisement relating to the dollar amounts of claims paid, the number of persons insured, or similar statistical information relating to any insurer or policy shall not be used unless it accurately reflects all of the relevant facts. Such an advertisement shall not imply that such statistics are derived from the policy advertised unless such is the fact.

## Section 8. INSPECTION OF POLICY

An offer in an advertisement of free inspection of a policy or offer of a premium refund is not a cure for misleading or deceptive statements contained in such advertisement.

## Section 9. IDENTIFICATION OF PLAN OR NUMBER OF POLICIES

A. When a choice of the amount of benefits is referred to, an advertisement shall disclose that the amount of benefits provided depends upon the plan selected and that the premium will vary with the amount of the benefits.

B. When an advertisement refers to various benefits which may be contained in two or more policies, other than group master policies, the advertisement shall disclose that such benefits are provided only through a combination of such policies.

## Section 10. DISPARAGING COMPARISONS AND STATEMENTS

An advertisement shall not directly or indirectly make unfair or incomplete comparisons of policies or benefits or otherwise falsely disparage competitors, their policies, services or business methods.

## Section 11. JURISDICTIONAL LICENSING

An advertisement which is intended to be seen or heard beyond the limits of the jurisdiction in which the insurer is licensed shall not imply licensing beyond those limits.

## Section 12. IDENTITY OF INSURER

The identity of the insurer shall be made clear in all of its advertisements. An advertisement shall not use a trade name, service mark, slogan, symbol or other device which has the capacity and tendency to mislead or deceive as to the true identity of the insurer.

## Section 13. GROUP OR QUASI-GROUP IMPLICATIONS

An advertisement of a particular policy shall not state or imply that prospective policyholders become group or quasi-group members and as such enjoy special rates or underwriting privileges, unless such is the fact.

## Section 14. INTRODUCTORY, INITIAL OR SPECIAL OFFERS

An advertisement shall not state or imply that a particular policy or combination of policies is an introductory, initial or special offer and that the applicant will receive advantages by accepting the offer, unless such is the fact.

Section 15.  APPROVAL OR ENDORSEMENT BY THIRD PARTIES

A. An advertisement shall not state or imply that an insurer or a policy has been approved or an insurer's financial condition has been examined and found to be satisfactory by a governmental agency, unless such is the fact.

B. An advertisement shall not state or imply that an insurer or a policy has been approved or endorsed by any individual, group of individuals, society, association or other organization, unless such is the fact.

Section 16.  SERVICE FACILITIES

An advertisement shall not contain untrue statements with respect to the time within which claims are paid or statements which imply that claim settlements will be liberal or generous beyond the terms of the policy.

Section 17.  STATEMENTS ABOUT AN INSURER

An advertisement shall not contain statements which are untrue in fact or by implication misleading with respect to the insurer's assets, corporate structure, financial standing, age or relative position in the insurance business.

SPECIAL ENFORCEMENT PROCEDURES FOR RULES GOVERNING THE ADVERTISEMENT OF ACCIDENT AND SICKNESS INSURANCE

(1) *Advertising File:* Each insurer shall maintain at its home or principal office a complete file containing every printed, published or prepared advertisement of individual policies and typical printed, published or prepared advertisement of blanket, franchise and group policies hereafter disseminated in this or any other state whether or not licensed in such other state, with a notation attached to each such advertisement which shall indicate the manner and extent of distribution and the form number of any policy advertised. Such file shall be subject to regular and periodical inspection by this department. All such advertisements shall be maintained in said file for a period of not less than three years.

(2) *Certificate of Compliance:* Each insurer required to file an annual statement which is now or hereafter becomes subject to the provisions of this rule (ruling) must file with this department together with its annual statement, a certificate executed by an authorized officer of the insurer wherein it is stated that to the best of his knowledge, information and belief the advertisements which were disseminated by the insurer during the preceding

statement year complied or were made to comply in all respects with the provisions (of the insurance laws of this state as implemented and interpreted by this rule—ruling) (of this rule—ruling). It is requested that the chief executive officer of each such insurer to which this rule (ruling) is addressed acknowledge its receipt and indicate its attention to comply therewith.

Effective date of this rule (ruling) is 90 days from date hereof.

Dated this _____ day of _____

Signature _____

## appendix D

Approved by the N.A.I.C., December 15, 1948, and Recommended by That Association as a Guidepost for Insurance Commissioners and Industry

# Statement of Principles—Personal Accident and Health Insurance

I. Principles for construction of policy forms:

a. Number of Policy Forms. Under the influence of constantly changing economic and social conditions the needs of the insurance-buying public vary to a considerable degree. It is highly desirable that the forms of coverage and the types of policies offered should meet those needs, but it is equally desirable that the number of different policies written be kept within practicable limits. No useful purpose is served by making available an infinite variety of policies reflecting only inconsequential differences in coverage.

b. Policy Language. Policies should be prepared in clear, direct and unambiguous language. The policy must be a clear expression of the insurer's undertaking.

c. Insuring Agreements and Exclusions. The insuring agreements when read with the exclusions and conditions should constitute an express promise to pay within the limits of the insurer's intended undertaking. Policy exclusions should be given sufficient prominence to assure their recognition.

d. Scope of Coverage to Be Substantial. No accident or sickness insurance contract should be issued unless it provides protection against substantial hazards. Policies which insure only against exposures of rare occurrence are seldom justified.

Policies which insure against accidents or sickness generally, and which are not clearly limited to certain types of accidents or diseases, should not contain any definitions, restrictions or ex-

730

clusions which take out of the coverage, or reduce benefits for hazards which custom and experience have determined to be normal insurable risks. Limited policies insuring only against accidents or diseases of a certain type or types should give a broad coverage within the field which they cover.

Policies may contain a general limitation of coverage to non-occupational hazards and to hazards for which the insured is not entitled to compensation under any workmen's compensation law. The subject matter of this section I–d and the subject matter of Part III are closely related, and should be considered together.

e. Limited Policies. The term "limited policies" should be used to refer to policies providing coverage only within a specified field. The following principles should be applicable to limited policies: (1) the policy should express clearly the specified field covered; and

(2) the policy should clearly show on its face and filing back that it is a limited policy; and

(3) the aggregate of the hazards covered should be of sufficiently frequent occurrence to justify the sale of the policy.

f. Titles and Descriptions. An insurer may identify the policy by a name, title, or symbol of its own choice, but the name used should not be such as to give a misleading impression of the coverage.

The word "non-cancellable" may be used in or immediately following the title, but only if the policyholder has the right to continue the policy for a specified period of not less than five years or to a specified age not less than fifty and not less than five years older than the age of the insured at the date of issue of the policy. If the word "non-cancellable" appears in or immediately follows the title, the period during which the policyholder has the right to continue the policy should be shown. Any further description on the face or on the filing back of the policy generally serves no useful purpose and should not be required.

g. Mail Policies. Policies sold by mail should be governed by the same principles applying to all other types of policies.

II. Principles applying to particular policy provisions and their use:

a. Accident Policy Exclusions. Certain types of exclusions are proper and are common to all types of general coverage accident policies. Since accident policies are designed to cover only loss resulting from bodily injuries caused by an accident, such policies properly may exclude, for example, loss caused or contributed to be disease, by hernia, or by suicide or self-destruction or any attempt thereat (sane or insane). Also because of the unusual hazard not contemplated by the normal premium charge, other examples or proper exclusions are while in military (land, sea, or air) service, war or any act of war, while traveling or flying in any aircraft, or minimum and maximum age limits. The limited policies such as the usual automobile accident policy may of course include exclusions for risks not covered; for example, while the automobile is being used in a race or speed test, or while riding in, or driving, or working on, or adjusting an automobile for compensation or hire.

Examples of similar special policies that require appropriate exclusions include air travel policies, ticket accident policies, policies covering boy scouts in camp, non-occupational policies, policies designed especially for athletes, artists or singers, farmers, nurses, coal miners, railroad employees, aircraft pilots or crew members, and other special coverage policies where the field covered is clearly defined and varying exclusions are necessary in connection with such policies, but they should not be unduly restrictive.

There are certain types of accident policies that are sold with little or no underwriting, such as policies sold by machines and ticket travel accident policies designed for sale through ticket agents in transportation offices, which may properly contain exclusions, such as minimum and maximum age limits, persons maimed or deformed, persons engaged in exceptionally hazardous pursuits and similar exclusions. The Standard Provisions Law provides for additional exclusions relating to violating law and intoxicants or narcotics. An impaired risk may be insured subject to a waiver attached to or endorsed on the policy excluding indemnity for loss caused by or resulting from the impairment.

The foregoing examples of policies and exclusions are merely illustrative. There are other proper coverages and exclusions depending on the type of policy involved.

b. Sickness Policy Exclusions. Policies of sickness insurance are designed to protect only for loss caused by disease during the term of the policy and properly exclude disease contracted prior to its effective date and loss resulting from bodily injuries caused by an accident. Because of the unusual hazard not contemplated by the normal premium charge, other examples of proper exclusions are disease contracted during or while in military (land, sea or air) service, minimum and maximum age limits, and venereal disease. For the same reason policies of sickness insurance designed for issuance to female risks may properly exclude loss due to pregnancy, childbirth or miscarriage or to disease or derangement of the female generative organs.

There should be no such general exclusion as "chronic disease" or "organic disease." Risks who have impairments or who have had chronic or recurrent diseases may be insured subject to a waiver attached to or endorsed on the policy, excluding indemnity for loss caused by or resulting from the particular impairment or disease.

Policies providing hospital, medical, nurse, and surgical benefits or expense alone or in any combination thereof present special problems which the general principles outlined in Parts II and III of this Statement should be applied. Policies providing both accident and sickness insurance should be prepared in a manner not inconsistent with the principles above set forth.

c. Elective Provisions. Every benefit provision of an accident or sickness policy should constitute an express promise to pay. Policies should not contain provisions of the elective indemnity type which make it possible in certain cases for claimants to make elections or fail to make elections that ultimately prove to be against their best interest.

d. Multiple Indemnities. Where an accident policy provides indemnities of varying amounts for the same loss for injury sustained in different types of accidents, such policy is said to provide multiple indemnities. Multiple indemnities for loss resulting from injuries occurring in other than ordinary accidents may be provided only where the field in which such special injuries occur is well defined and clearly stated. If a policy provides different amounts for loss under different conditions, the larger amount shall not be given more prominence than the smaller amount.

e. Qualifying Periods and Waiting Periods. Qualifying (or elimination or probationary) and waiting periods are proper and necessary in some policies as an underwriting precaution to protect the company from diseases or conditions to which the insured has been exposed. Waiting periods likewise are proper both as a means of programming the policyholder's disability insurance with other disability benefits available to him and as a means of reducing the premium charge for such policies. Therefore, and due to the many and varied uses for such periods, no limitations of their use are feasible.

f. Disability and Confinement Clauses. An accident policy shall not predicate liability for time indemnity upon any kind of confinement. A sickness policy may predicate liability for time indemnity upon a requirement for house confinement. Weekly premium payment type industrial policies may properly require bed confinement.

Policies of accident insurance may provide indemnity at the full rate of total disability and at a reduced rate and term for partial disability. Policies of sickness insurance may provide indemnity at the full rate for confinement and at a reduced rate and term for total disability which does not necessitate such confinement. Companies should pay at the full rate under such policies for substantial confinement where the Insured is necessarily totally disabled and unable to leave the house except for necessary visits to the doctor's office or to hospitals, and policies should so state by providing that confinement shall not be terminated by reason of the transportation of the Insured, at the direction of his doctor, to or from a hospital or the doctor's office for necessary treatment.

Policies may require regular treatment by a physician or surgeon but payment shall not be conditioned upon any specified frequency of visits or attendance. The beginning of a disability period may not be conditioned upon date of receipt of claim notice by the insured.

III. Principles for the preparation of advertising and solicitation material:

1. Advertising shall truthfully and fairly represent the benefits provided by the policy and shall be designed to avoid the drawing of untrue and misleading conclusions therefrom.
2. Statements or representations of fact shall be true in fact and capable of definite proof.
3. An offer of free inspection of a policy is not a cure for misleading statements in advertising.
4. If a policy provides different benefits as to amount or time for the same loss occurring under different circumstances or from different causes, the smaller benefits payable shall be given the same prominence as the larger benefits.
5. If reduced benefits are in effect at certain age limitations, the advertising shall so state.
6. No advertising which contains a list of diseases covered by the policy shall repeat reference to such disease by the use of synonymous terms, nor list diseases which are rarely or never found in the class of persons covered by the terms of the policy, now shall such advertising emphasize payment of benefits for diseases which occur only infrequently.
7. Statements that agents' commissions are saved shall not be made if other equivalent acquisition expenses are in fact incurred.
8. The phrase "No Medical Examination Required" or similar

phrases shall not be used to create the impression that impaired risks will be insured.

9. References to "generous benefits" or "liberal benefits" or similar phrases to imply generosity or liberality beyond the terms of the policy contract shall not be made.

10. Such phrases as "complete protection," "full coverage," "all coverage," shall not be used where possible benefits do not sustain their accuracy.

11. Advertising shall contain no exaggerations relating to time within which claims are paid (within 24 or 48 hours, etc.), nor imply that a company frequently and routinely pays specified sums for any type of accident or sickness when in truth only certain specified accidents are covered.

12. No advertising shall state or imply that only a specific number of policies will be sold or that a time limit is fixed for the discontinuance of the sale of the particular policy advertised, unless such statement is literally true.

13. No advertisement shall state or imply that all costs of hospitalization or medical expense or that all income will be replaced by benefits unless the policy is without limitations or restrictions in any form.

14. No advertising shall indicate that a policy covers a pre-existing disease unless such is a fact.

15. Advertising which purports to give a full explanation of the policy coverage shall refer to the fact that the policy does contain exceptions and reductions or limitations if any.

16. Statistics on a national basis covering all accidents or all illnesses shall not be used to imply that the policy covers all such accidents and illnesses.

Adopted May 1957

# Health Insurance Association of America: Codes of Ethical Standards

Each member company pledges itself:

1. To offer only insurance providing effective and real protection against such loss as the policy is designed to cover.
2. To write its policies in clear and direct language without unreasonable restrictions and limitations.
3. To advertise its policies in such manner that the public can readily understand the protection offered, and not use advertising which has the tendency or capacity to mislead or deceive.
4. To select, train, and supervise personnel of integrity in a manner which will assure intelligent, honest, courteous sales and service.
5. To engage only in sales methods, promotional practices and other transactions which give primary consideration to the needs, interest, and continued satisfaction of the persons insured.
6. To endeavor to establish the insurability of persons at the time of application in every instance where such insurability is a factor in the issuance or continuance of the insurance or in the liability of the insurer.
7. To pay all just claims fairly, courteously, and promptly, with a minimum of requirements.
8. To continue research and experimentation in order to meet the changing needs of the public.
9. To engage in keen, fair competition so the public may obtain the protection it needs at a reasonable price.

## appendix F

# International Association of Health Underwriters: Code of Ethics

TO:

Hold the selling of health insurance as a profession and a public trust, and to do all in my power to maintain its prestige.

Keep the needs of my prospect and his family above all else.

Respect my client's trust in me, and never do anything which could betray that trust or confidence.

Give all service possible where service is needed.

Present policies factually and accurately, giving all information to my prospect which may be essential to his best interests.

Use no advertising which may be false or misleading or may in any way imply coverage not actually given.

Increase my knowledge of health insurance by constant study and observation, to devote myself to the selling of it by looking upon it as a career, and to know and abide by the insurance laws of my state.

Be fair and just to my competitors, attempt no twisting, and make no statements which do injustice to another company or competitor.

Treat both my prospect and my company fairly by submitting applications which give all information pertinent to the underwriting of a policy.

Be loyal to my associates, my agents, and my company.

*I subscribe to and will uphold this code.*

## appendix G

Prepared by Health Insurance Association of America, April 3, 1957.

# Franchise Accident and
# Sickness Insurance

Accident and sickness insurance on a franchise plan is hereby declared to be that form of accident and sickness insurance issued to:

(1) Five or more employees of any corporation, co-partnership, or individual employer or any governmental corporation, agency or department thereof; or

(2) Ten or more members, employees, or employees of members of any trade or professional association or of a labor union or of any other association having had an active existence for at least two years where such association or union has a constitution or bylaws and is formed in good faith for purposes other than that of obtaining insurance;

where such persons, with or without their dependents, are issued the same form of an individual policy varying only as to amounts and kinds of coverage applied for by such persons under an arrangement whereby the premiums on such policies may be paid to the insurer periodically by the employer, with or without payroll deductions, or by the association or union for its members, or by some designated person acting on behalf of such employer or association or union. The term "employees" as used herein shall be deemed to include the officers, managers and employees and retired employees of the employer and the individual proprietor or partners if the employer is an individual proprietor or partnership.

**appendix H**

Adopted by the Subcommittee, November 28, 1960, New York, N.Y.

# N.A.I.C. Model Bill to Provide for the Regulation of Credit Life Insurance and Credit Accident and Health Insurance

BE IT ENACTED BY THE STATE OF _____
(adapt caption and formal portions to local requirements and statutes)

1. *Purpose:*

    The purpose of this Act is to promote the public welfare by regulating credit life insurance and credit accident and health insurance. Nothing in this Act is intended to prohibit or discourage reasonable competition. The provisions of this Act shall be liberally construed.

2. *Scope and Definitions:*

    A. Citation and Scope

    (1) This Act may be cited as "The Model Act for the Regulation of Credit Life Insurance and Credit Accident and Health Insurance."

    (2) All life insurance and all accident and health insurance in connection with loans or other credit transactions shall be subject to the provisions of this Act, except such insurance in connection with a loan or other credit transaction of more than five years duration; nor shall insurance be subject to the provisions of this Act where the issuance of such insurance is an isolated transaction on the part of the insurer not related to an agreement or a plan for insuring debtors of the creditor.

    B. Definitions

    For the purpose of this Act:

(1) "Credit life insurance" means insurance on the life of a debtor pursuant to or in connection with a specific loan or other credit transaction;

(2) "Credit accident and health insurance" means insurance on a debtor to provide indemnity for payments becoming due on a specific loan or other credit transaction while the debtor is disabled as defined in the policy;

(3) "Creditor" means the lender of money or vendor or lessor of goods, services, or property, rights or privileges, for which payment is arranged through a credit transaction, or any successor to the right, title or interest of any such lender, vendor, or lessor, and an affiliate, associate or subsidiary of any of them or any director, officer or employee of any of them or any other person in any way associated with any of them;

(4) "Debtor" means a borrower of money or a purchaser or lessee of goods, services, property, rights or privileges for which payment is arranged through a credit transaction;

(5) "Indebtedness" means the total amount payable by a debtor to a creditor in connection with a loan or other credit transaction;

(6) "Commissioner" means _____ (Insurance Supervisory Authority of the State).

3. *Forms of Credit Life Insurance and Credit Accident and Health Insurance:*

Credit life insurance and credit accident and health insurance shall be issued only in the following forms:

A. Individual policies of life insurance issued to debtors on the term plan;

B. Individual policies of accident and health insurance issued to debtors on a term plan or disability benefit provisions in individual policies of credit life insurance;

C. Group policies of life insurance issued to creditors providing insurance upon the lives of debtors on the term plan;

D. Group policies of accident and health insurance issued to creditors on a term plan insuring debtors or disability benefit provisions in group credit life insurance policies to provide such coverage.

4. *Amount of Credit Life Insurance and Credit Accident and Health Insurance:*

A. Credit Life Insurance

(1) The initial amount of credit life insurance shall not exceed the total amount repayable under the contract of indebtedness and, where an indebtedness is repayable in substantially equal installments, the amount of insurance shall at no time exceed

the scheduled or actual amount of unpaid indebtedness, whichever is greater.

(Note: If desired the following provisions may be added as subsections (2) and (3).

(2) Notwithstanding the provisions of the above paragraph, insurance on agricultural credit transaction commitments, not exceeding one year in duration may be written up to the amount of the loan commitment, on a non-decreasing or level term plan.

(3) Notwithstanding the provisions of Paragraph A (1) of this or any other subsection, insurance on educational credit transaction commitments may be written for the amount of the portion of such commitment that has not been advanced by the creditor.

B. Credit Accident and Health Insurance

The total amount of periodic indemnity payable by credit accident and health insurance in the event of disability, as defined in the policy, shall not exceed the aggregate of the periodic scheduled unpaid installments of the indebtedness; and the amount of each periodic indemnity payment shall not exceed the original indebtedness divided by the number of periodic installments.

5. *Term of Credit Life Insurance and Credit Accident and Health Insurance:*

The term of any credit life insurance or credit accident and health insurance shall, subject to acceptance by the insurer, commence on the date when the debtor becomes obligated to the creditor, except that, where a group policy provides coverage with respect to existing obligations, the insurance on a debtor with respect to such indebtedness shall commence on the effective date of the policy. Where evidence of insurability is required and such evidence is furnished more than thirty (30) days after the date when the debtor becomes obligated to the creditor, the term of the insurance may commence on the date on which the insurance company determines the evidence to be satisfactory, and in such event there shall be an appropriate refund or adjustment of any charge to the debtor for insurance. The term of such insurance shall not extend more than fifteen days beyond the scheduled maturity date of the indebtedness except when extended without additional cost to the debtor. If the indebtedness is discharged due to renewal or refinancing prior to the scheduled maturity date, the insurance in force shall be terminated before any new insurance may be issued in connection with the renewed or refinanced indebtedness. In all cases of termination prior to scheduled maturity, a refund shall be paid or credited as provided in Section 8.

6. *Provisions of Policies and Certificates of Insurance: Disclosure to Debtors:*

    A. All credit life insurance and credit accident and health insurance shall be evidenced by an individual policy, or in the case of group insurance by a certificate of insurance, which individual policy or group certificate of insurance shall be delivered to the debtor.

    B. Each individual policy or group certificate of credit life insurance, and/or credit accident and health insurance shall, in addition to other requirements of law, set forth the name and home office address of the insurer, the name or names of the debtor or in the case of a certificate under a group policy, the identity by name or otherwise of the debtor, the premium or amount of payment, if any, by the debtor separately for credit life insurance and credit accident and health insurance, a description of the coverage including the amount and term thereof, and any exceptions, limitations and restrictions, and shall state that the benefits shall be paid to the creditor to reduce or extinguish the unpaid indebtedness and, wherever the amount of insurance may exceed the unpaid indebtedness, that any such excess shall be payable to a beneficiary, other than the creditor, named by the debtor or to his estate.

    C. Said individual policy or group certificate of insurance shall be delivered to the insured debtor at the time the indebtedness is incurred except as hereinafter provided.

    D. If said individual policy or group certificate of insurance is not delivered to the debtor at the time the indebtedness is incurred, a copy of the application for such policy or a notice of proposed insurance, signed by the debtor and setting forth the name and home office address of the insurer, the name or names of the debtor, the premium or amount of payment by the debtor, if any, separately for credit life insurance and credit accident and health insurance, the amount, term and a brief description of the coverage provided, shall be delivered to the debtor at the time such indebtedness is incurred. The copy of the application for, or notice of proposed insurance, shall also refer exclusively to insurance coverage, and shall be separate and apart from the loan, sale or other credit statement of account, instrument or agreement, unless the information required by this subsection is prominently set forth therein. Upon acceptance of the insurance by the insurer and within thirty (30) days of the date upon which the indebtedness is incurred, the insurer shall cause the individual policy or group certificate of insurance to be delivered to the debtor. Said application or notice of proposed insurance shall state that upon acceptance by the insurer, the insurance shall become effective as provided in Section 5.

    E. If the named insurer does not accept the risk, then and in such event the debtor shall receive a policy or certificate of insurance setting forth the name and home office address of the substituted insurer and the amount of the premium to be charged, and if the amount of premium is less than that set forth in the notice of proposed insurance an appropriate refund shall be made.

7. *Filing, Approval and Withdrawal of Forms:*

    A. All policies, certificates of insurance, notices of proposed insurance, applications for insurance, endorsements and riders delivered or issued for delivery in this State and the schedules of premium rates pertaining thereto shall be filed with the Commissioner.

    B. The Commissioner shall within thirty (30) days after the filing of any such policies, certificates of insurance, notices of proposed ininsurance, applications for insurance, endorsements and riders, disapprove any such form if the benefits provided therein are not reasonable in relation to the premium charge, or if it contains provisions which are unjust, unfair, inequitable, misleading, deceptive or encourage misrepresentation of the coverage, or are contrary to any provision of the Insurance Code or of any rule or regulation promulgated thereunder.

    C. If the Commissioner notifies the insurer that the form is disapproved, it is unlawful thereafter for such insurer to issue or use such form. In such notice, the Commissioner shall specify the reason for his disapproval and state that a hearing will be granted within twenty (20) days after request in writing by the insurer. No such policy, certificate of insurance, notice of proposed insurance, nor any application, endorsement or rider, shall be issued or used until the expiration of thirty (30) days after it has been so filed, unless the Commissioner shall give his prior written approval thereto.

    D. The Commissioner may, at any time after a hearing held not less than twenty (20) days after written notice to the insurer, withdraw his approval of any such form on any ground set forth in subsection B above. The written notice of such hearing shall state the reason for the proposed withdrawal.

    E. It is not lawful for the insurer to issue such forms or use them after the effective date of such withdrawal.

    F. If a group policy of credit life insurance or credit accident and health insurance

       (i) has been delivered in this State before the effective date of this Act, or

      (ii) has been or is delivered in another State before or after the effective date of this Act,

    the insurer shall be required to file only the group certificate and notice of proposed insurance delivered or issued for delivery in this State as specified in subsections B and D of Section 6 of this Act and such forms shall be approved by the Commissioner if they conform with the requirements specified in said subsections and if the schedules of premium rates applicable to the insurance evidenced by such certificate or notice are not in excess of the insurer's schedules of premium rates filed with the Commissioner; provided, however, the premium rate in effect on existing group policies may be continued until the first policy anniversary date following the date this Act becomes operative as provided in Section 12.

G. Any order or final determination of the Commissioner under the provisions of this section shall be subject to judicial review.

8. *Premiums and Refunds:*

   A. Any insurer may revise its schedules of premium rates from time to time, and shall file such revised schedules with the Commissioner. No insurer shall issue any credit life insurance policy or credit accident and health insurance policy for which the premium rate exceeds that determined by the schedules of such insurer as then on file with the Commissioner.

   B. Each individual policy, or group certificate shall provide that in the event of termination of the insurance prior to the scheduled maturity date of the indebtedness, any refund of an amount paid by the debtor for insurance shall be paid or credited promptly to the person entitled thereto; provided, however, that the Commissioner shall prescribe a minimum refund and no refund which would be less than such minimum need be made. The formula to be used in computing such refund shall be filed with and approved by the Commissioner.

   C. If a creditor requires a debtor to make any payment for credit life insurance or credit accident and health insurance and an individual policy or group certificate of insurance is not issued, the creditor shall immediately give written notice to such debtor and shall promptly make an appropriate credit to the account.

   D. The amount charged to a debtor for any credit life or credit health and accident insurance shall not exceed the premiums charged by the insurer, as computed at the time the charge to the debtor is determined.

   (Note: Where a state prohibits payments for insurance by the debtor in connection with credit transactions, the following paragraph may be included.)

   E. Nothing in this Act shall be construed to authorize any payments for insurance now prohibited under any statute, or rule thereunder, governing credit transactions.

9. *Issuance of Policies:*

   All policies of credit life insurance and credit accident and health insurance shall be delivered or issued for delivery in this state only by an insurer authorized to do an insurance business therein, and shall be issued only through holders of licenses or authorizations issued by the Commissioner.

10. *Claims:*

    A. All claims shall be promptly reported to the insurer or its designated claim representative, and the insurer shall maintain adequate claim files. All claims shall be settled as soon as possible and in accordance with the terms of the insurance contract.

    B. All claims shall be paid either by draft drawn upon the insurer or by check of the insurer to the order of the claimant to whom payment of the claim is due pursuant to the policy provisions, or upon direction of such claimant to one specified.

    C. No plan or arrangement shall be used whereby any person, firm or corporation other than the insurer or its designated claim representative shall be authorized to settle or adjust claims. The creditor shall not be designated as claim representative for the insurer in adjusting claims; provided, that a group policyholder may, by arrangement with the group insurer, draw drafts or checks in payment of claims due to the group policyholder subject to audit and review by the insurer.

11. *Existing Insurance—Choice of Insurer:*

    When credit life insurance or credit accident and health insurance is required as additional security for any indebtedness, the debtor shall, upon request to the creditor, have the option of furnishing the required amount of insurance through existing policies of insurance owned or controlled by him or of procuring and furnishing the required coverage through any insurer authorized to transact an insurance business within this state.

12. *Enforcement:*

    The Commissioner may, after notice and hearing, issue such rules and regulations as he deems appropriate for the supervision of this Act. Whenever the Commissioner finds that there has been a violation of this Act or any rules or regulations issued pursuant thereto, and after written notice thereof and hearing given to the insurer or other person authorized or licensed by the Commissioner, he shall set forth the details of his findings together with an order for compliance by a specified date. Such order shall be binding on the insurer and other person authorized or licensed by the Commissioner on the date specified unless sooner withdrawn by the Commissioner or a stay thereof has been ordered by a court of competent jurisdiction. The provisions of Sections 5, 6, 7, and 8 of this Act shall not be operative until ninety (90) days after the effective date of this Act, and the Commissioner in his discretion may extend by not more than an additional ninety (90) days the initial period within which the provisions of said sections shall not be operative.

13. *Judicial Review:*

Any party to the proceeding affected by an order of the Commissioner shall be entitled to judicial review by following the procedure set forth in _____.

14. *Penalties:*

In addition to any other penalty provided by law, any person, firm or corporation which violates an order of the Commissioner after it has become final, and while such order is in effect, shall, upon proof thereof to the satisfaction of the court, forfeit and pay to the State of _____ a sum not to exceed $250.00 which may be recovered in a civil action, except that if such violation is found to be willful, the amount of such penalty shall be a sum not to exceed $1,000.00. The Commissioner, in his discretion, may revoke or suspend the license or certificate of authority of the person, firm or corporation guilty of such violation. Such order for suspension or revocation shall be upon notice and hearing, and shall be subject to judicial review as provided in Section 13 of this Act.

15. *Separability Provision:*

If any provision of this Act, or the application of such provision to any person or circumstances, shall be held invalid, the remainder of the Act, and the application of such provision to any person or circumstances other than those as to which it is held invalid, shall not be affected thereby.

## appendix I

# Federal Trade Commission
# Guides for the Mail Order
# Insurance Industry

Definitions:

A. "Advertisement" for the purpose of these Guides shall mean any of the following material when used in connection with solicitation of the original purchase of a policy, or renewal or reinstatement thereof:

(1) Any printed or published material, descriptive literature, statements or depictions of an insurer used in newspapers, magazines, radio and TV scripts or presentations, billboards, and similar displays, and

(2) Descriptive literature and sales aids of all kinds issued or caused to be issued by an insurer or by an insurer's agent or broker for presentation to members of the public, including, but not limited to, circulars, leaflets, booklets, depictions, illustrations, form letters, and policy forms.

B. "Policy" for the purpose of these Guides shall include any policy, plan, certificate, contract, agreement, statement of coverages, rider or endorsement which provides insurance benefits for any kind of loss or expense.

C. "Insurer" for the purpose of these Guides, shall include any individual, corporation, association, partnership, reciprocal exchange, interinsurer, Lloyd's, fraternal benefit society, and any other legal entity, engaged in the advertisement and sale of a policy as herein defined.

### Guide 1. Deception (General).

No advertisement shall be used which because of words, phrases, statements or illustrations therein or information omitted therefrom has the capacity and tendency to mislead or deceive purchasers or prospective purchasers, irrespective of whether a policy advertised is made available to an insured prior to the consummation of the sale, or an offer is made of a premium refund if a purchaser is not satisfied. Words or phrases which are misleading or deceptive because the meaning thereof is not clear, or is clear only to persons familiar with insurance terminology, shall not be used.

*Guide 2.  Advertisement of Benefits, Losses Covered or Premums Payable.*

A. *Disclosure as to exceptions, reductions and limitations.*

No advertisement shall refer to any loss covered or benefit provided by an insurance policy, period of time for which any benefit is payable, or the cost of a policy, without clearly and conspicuously disclosing in close conjunction therewith such exceptions, reductions and limitations relating thereto as will fully relieve the advertisement of all capacity to deceive.

The disclosure requirements of this Guide 2 are not applicable to advertisements which mention only the general kind of insurance (e.g. "life," "accident," "hospitalization"), give no information as to losses covered, benefits or premiums, and serve the purpose of merely inviting inquiries or a show of interest on the part of the recipients.

As used in this Guide—

The term "exception" means any provision in a policy whereby coverage for a specified hazard is entirely eliminated. It is a statement of risk not assumed under the policy.

The term "reduction" shall mean any provision which reduces the amount of the benefit; a risk of loss is assumed but payment upon the occurrence of such loss is limited to some amount or period less than would be otherwise payable had such reduction clause not been used.

The term "limitation" means any provision which restricts the duration or extent of coverage, losses covered, or benefits payable under the policy other than an exception or a reduction.

(1) *Waiting, elimination, probationary or similar periods.*  When there is a time period between the effective date of a policy and the effective date of coverage under the policy, or a time period between the date a loss occurs and the date benefits begin to accrue for such loss, such fact must be clearly and conspicuously disclosed in close conjunction with any reference to such coverage or benefits made in any advertisement.

(2) *Benefits contingent on conditions.*  When a policy pays varying amounts of benefits for the same loss occurring under different conditions or which pays benefits only when a loss occurs under certain conditions, any reference to such benefits in an advertisement must be closely accompanied by clear and conspicuous disclosure of such different or limited conditions as are applicable.

(3) *Pre-existing conditions.*  If a policy provides any limitations on the coverage of a loss if the cause of such loss is traceable to a condition existing prior to the effective date of the policy, or prior to any other particular time, any reference to the policy coverage of the loss made in any advertisement must be closely accompanied by clear and conspicuous disclosure of such limitations. (See also Guide 3.)

(4) *Deceptive words or phrases.*

(a) No words, terms or phrases shall be used as descriptive of the coverage provided by a policy which misrepresent the extent of such coverage. Words such as "all," "full," "complete," "unlimited," and words of similar import must not be used to refer to any coverage which under the terms of the policy is subject to exceptions, reductions, or limitations. Other words, terms, or phrases representing or implying broad insurance coverage must not be used as descriptive of losses covered or benefits provided by a policy which are subject to exceptions, reductions, or limitations without disclosure of the applicable exceptions, reductions or limitations as required by Part A of this Guide 2.

(b) The terms "hospitalization," "accident," or "life" must not be used as descriptive of an insurance policy which provides benefits for only unusual or unique sicknesses, accidents, or causes of death unless in close conjunction with such terms clear and conspicuous disclosure is made of such coverage (e.g. "leukemia hospitalization," "death by drowning").

(c) Words or phrases such as "up to," "as high as," etc., shall not be used as descriptive of the dollar amount payable for any kind of represented losses or expenses unless the policy provides benefit payments up to such amounts in all cases for such losses or expenses actually sustained by a policyholder, or there is full and conspicuous disclosure in close conjunction with such words or phrases of either (1) the complete schedule of payments provided by the policy, or (2) the specific loss or expenses for which the represented dollar amount is provided by the policy; and also disclosure that benefits provided by the policy for losses or expenses of the kind represented vary in amount depending on the particular kind of loss or expense incurred, if such is the case, as for example, "Policy provides surgical benefits which vary in amount depending on kind of operation performed. For example, pays up to $150 for operation to remove lung," and there is also disclosure of such other exceptions, reductions or limitations as required by Part A of this Guide 2.

(d) An advertisement must not contain representations such as "This policy pays $1,800 for hospital room and board expenses" without clear and conspicuous disclosure in close conjunction therewith of the maximum daily benefit and the maximum time limit for such hospital room and board expense.

(e) An advertisement must not represent the weekly, monthly, or other periodic benefits payable under a policy without clearly and conspicuously disclosing in close conjunction with such representation the limitation of time over which such benefits will be paid or of the number of payments or total amount thereof which will be made if, by the terms of the policy, payment or benefits for any loss or aggregate of losses is limited to time, number, or total amount.

(5) *Age limitation.* Any reference in an advertisement to any insur-

ance coverage or benefits which by the terms of the policy are limited to a certain age group must be closely accompanied by clear and conspicuous disclosure of such fact.

B. *Deception as to coverage and additional benefits.*

(1) A policy covering only one disease or certain specified diseases must not be advertised in such manner as to imply coverage beyond the terms of the policy, either by use of synonymous words or terms to refer to any disease or physical conditions so as to imply broader coverage, or by other means.

(2) An advertisement must not represent, directly or indirectly, that a policy provides for the payment of certain benefits in addition to other benefits when such is not the fact.

### Guide 3.  *Health of Applicant or Insured.*

No advertisement shall be used which represents or implies—

(1) That the condition of the applicant's or insured's health prior to, or at the time of issuance of a policy, or thereafter, will not be considered by the insurer in determining its liability or benefits to be furnished for or in the settlement of a claim when such is not the fact (see also part A(3) of Guide 2); or

(2) That no medical examination is required if the furnishing of benefits by an insurer under a policy so represented is or may be contingent on a medical examination under any condition; or

(3) That no medical examination is required, even though such is the case, without conspicuously disclosing in close conjunction therewith all the conditions pertaining to or involving the insured's health under which the insurer is not liable for the furnishing of benefits under a policy.

### Guide 4.  *Disclosure of Policy Provisions Relating to Renewability, Cancellability or Termination.*

A. No advertisement shall refer, directly or by implication, to renewability, cancellability, or termination of a policy or a policy benefit, or contain any statement or illustration of time or age in connection with any benefit payable, loss, eligibility of applicants, or continuation of a policy, unless in close conjunction with such reference, statement or illustration there is clear and conspicuous disclosure of the material provisions in the policy relating thereto.

B. No advertisement shall represent or imply that an insurance policy may be continued in effect indefinitely or for any period of time, when, in fact, said policy provides that it may not be renewed or may be cancelled by the insurer, or terminated under any circumstances over which insured has no control, during the period of time represented.

### Guide 5.  *Testimonials, Appraisals Analyses.*

No testimonial, appraisal or analysis shall be used in any advertisement which is not genuine, does not represent the current opinion of the author, does not accurately describe the facts, does not correctly reflect the present practices of an insurer, is not applicable to the policy or insurer advertised or is not accurately reproduced. (Note: An insurer makes as his own all statements contained in any testimonial which he uses in his advertisement, and the advertisement including such statements is subject to all of the provisions of these Guides.)

### Guide 6.  Deceptive Use of Statistics.

A. No advertisement shall be used in which representations are made as to the time within which claims are paid, the dollar amount of claims, the number of claims paid or the number of persons insured under a particular policy or otherwise, or which contains other statistical information relating to any insurer or policy, unless such advertisement accurately reflects all the relevant facts. The advertisement shall not imply that the statistics are derived from a policy advertised unless such is the fact.

B. No advertisement shall be used which misrepresents that claim settlements by an insurer are liberal or generous beyond the terms of a policy.

### Guide 7.  Identification of Plan or Number of Policies.

A. No advertisement shall offer a choice of the amount of benefits without clearly and conspicuously disclosing that the amount of benefits provided depends upon the plan selected and that the premium will vary with the amount of benefits.

B. No advertisement shall refer to various benefits which may be contained in two or more policies, other than group master policies, without clearly and conspicuously disclosing that such benefits are provided only through a combination of such policies.

### Guide 8.  Deception as to Introductory, Initial or Special Offers.

No representation shall be made in an advertisement, directly or by implication, that a policy or combination of policies is an introductory, initial, special or limited offer and that applicants will receive advantages not available at a later date, unless such is the fact.

### Guide 9.  Misrepresentation as to Licensing, Approval or Endorsement of Insurer, Policy or Advertisement.

No advertisement shall represent directly or by implication—

(1) That an insurer, or any policy or advertisement thereof, has been licensed, approved, endorsed or recommended by any governmental agency or department, unless such is the fact;

(2) That an insurer, or a policy or an advertisement thereof, has been approved, endorsed or recommended by any individual, group of individuals, society, association, or other organization, unless such is the fact.

### Guide 10.  Deception as to "Group" or "Quasi-Group" Policies.

No advertisement shall represent, directly or indirectly, that prospective policyholders become group or quasi-group members and as such enjoy special rates or underwriting privileges ordinarily associated with group insurance as recognized in the industry, unless such is the fact.

### Guide 11.  Allocation of Benefits Under a "Family Group" Policy.

No advertisement shall refer to a benefit payable under a "family group" policy when the full amount of such benefit is not payable upon the death or disability, etc., of only one member of the family unless clear and conspicuous disclosure of such fact is made in the advertisement.

### Guide 12.  Deceptive Use of Trade Names, Service Marks, etc.

There shall not be used in an advertisement any trade name, service mark, slogan, symbol, or other device which has the capacity and tendency to mislead or deceive prospective purchasers as to the true identity of the insurer or its relation with public or private institutions.

### Guide 13.  Disparagement.

No advertisement shall be used which, directly or indirectly, falsely disparages competitors, their policies, services, or business methods.

### Guide 14.  Misrepresentation Concerning the Insurer.

No advertisement shall be used which, directly or by implication, has the capacity and tendency to mislead or deceive prospective purchasers with respect to an insurer's assets, corporate structure, financial standing, age, or relative position in the insurance business, or in any other material respect.

## appendix J

# Health Insurance Council Claim Forms

**HOSPITAL INFORMATION REQUEST FORM**
Individual and Family Hospital Expense Insurance

INSTRUCTIONS TO HOSPITAL:

1. Complete this form in duplicate. Give complete answers to all questions.

2. Have patient sign Authorization to Release Information.

3. Have insured sign the "Authorization to Pay Insurance Benefits" clause below.

4. Consult your directory of insurance companies for address to which form is to be sent.

5. If Company is not listed in the directory request information card from the patient.

6. Mail original to the Insurance Company — a copy should be retained for your file.

7. This form is a self-mailer — fold and mail.

When this notice is received at the designated office of the insurance company, they will send you, in duplicate, information concerning the policy and its benefits. Upon discharge of patient from the hospital, fill out the Individual Hospital Insurance Form (IHF-1) and return it to the insurance company.

The Authorization to Pay Insurance Benefits on the Individual Hospital Insurance Form (IHF-1) should be signed before patient's release.

**Notice of Hospital Admission**
**(To be Completed by Hospital on Admission)**

Name of Policyholder_____ Policy No._____

Name of Patient if a
Dependent of Policyholder _____Date to be admitted _____, 19_____

Address _____State _____

Is condition due to injury or sickness arising out of patient's employment?                    Yes _____No _____

Attending Physician's Name and Address_____

Is condition due to pregnancy?          Yes_____No _____

Admitting Diagnosis (Please be specific) _____

_____

Has patient suffered from same or related condition previously?                    Yes _____ No _____

If sickness, what is initial date of origin?_____, 19_____Date of injury?_____, 19_____

Name of Hospital_____

Hospital Case No._____ City _____ State_____

Date _____By _____
                                                                                   Hospital Admission Officer

AUTHORIZATION TO RELEASE INFORMATION: I hereby authorize the above named hospital to release the information requested on this form.

Date _____, 19_____Signed_____
                                                                                   Patient (Parent if a Minor)

AUTHORIZATION TO PAY INSURANCE BENEFITS: I hereby authorize payment directly to the above named hospital of the Hospital benefits otherwise payable to me but not to exceed the balance due of the hospital's regular charges for this period of hospitalization. I understand I am financially responsible to the hospital for charges not covered by this assignment.

Date_____, 19_____Signed_____
                                                                                   Policyholder

HIRF-1 (1965)

**IDENTIFICATION** (To be presented to the Hospital in Duplicate)

## INDIVIDUAL AND FAMILY HOSPITAL BENEFIT IDENTIFICATION FORM

TO_____Hospital

_____is insured for Hospital Expense Benefits

(in behalf of his dependent_____), subject to the terms of

policy_____ issued by_____. The effective date of coverage of

the policy was_____. The insurance will be inforce for _____days from the date of
completion of this form.

 Notice to Company:  If the description of benefits is not adaptable to your insurance, an appropriate format may
 be substituted.

| BENEFITS FOR OTHER THAN MATERNITY CASES | BENEFITS FOR MATERNITY CASES |
|---|---|
| A.  Hospital Room and Board (including general nursing service). Actual Hospital charges up to $_____ for each day of hospitalization up to_____days. | Hospital Room and Board (including general nursing service) and other Hospital Services. Actual Hospital charges up to $_____ |
| B.  Other hospital charges for hospital care and treatment (excluding charges for nurses and physicians services and take home drugs)   $_____ | OR |
| | 1.  Hospital Room and Board (including general nursing service) $_____ for each day of hospitalization up to _____days. |
| | and |
| | 2.  Other hospital charges for hospital care and treatment (excluding charges for nurses and physicians services and take home drugs)   $_____ |

### MINIMUM HOUR REQUIREMENTS

The Minimum Hour Hospitalization requirement will be met if_____

This is not a guarantee that payment will be made. It is a statement of the inforce status of the policy and the maximum
benefits provided by the policy. Payment of these benefits is subject to the policy restrictions and limitations, and also to
any prior payment.

Insurance Company

Address

| Signed | Name and Title | Phone | Date |
|---|---|---|---|

BIF-1 (62)

CERTIFICATION (To be presented to Hospital in duplicate)

INDIVIDUAL AND FAMILY HOSPITAL BENEFIT CERTIFICATION FORM

| NOT VALID IF USED AFTER | DATE |
| --- | --- |

TO_____Hospital
This is to certify that_____is insured for Hospital.
Expense Benefits (in behalf of his dependent_____) under
Hospital Expense Policy No._____Issued by_____

    Notice to Company: If the description of benefits is not adaptable to your insurance, an appropriate format
    may be substituted.

| BENEFITS FOR OTHER THAN MATERNITY CASES | BENEFITS FOR MATERNITY CASES |
| --- | --- |
| A. Hospital room and board (including general nursing service). Actual Hospital charges up to $_____ for each day of hospitalization up to _____days. | Hospital room and board (including general nursing service) and other hospital services. Actual charges up to $_____ |
| | OR |
| B. Other hospital charges for hospital care and treatment (excluding charges for nurses and physicians services and take home drugs) $_____ | 1. Hospital Room and Board (including general nursing service) $_____ for each day of hospitalization up to _____days. |
| | 2. Other hospital charges for hospital care and treatment (excluding charges for nurses and physicians services and take home drugs) $_____ |

MINIMUM HOUR REQUIREMENTS

The Minimum Hour Hospitalization requirements will be met if_____

The insurance company issuing this form agrees, subject to execution by the policyholder of the authorization to pay insurance benefits on the reverse side of this form, to make payment to the hospital named above, the hospital benefits otherwise payable to the policyholder but not to exceed the balance due of the hospital's regular charges for this period of hospitalization.

Insurance Company

Address

| Signed | Name and Title | Phone |
| --- | --- | --- |

BCF-1 (62)

INDIVIDUAL HOSPITAL INSURANCE FORM

Spaced for Typewriter — Marks for Tabulator Appear on this Line

| Hospital Complete and Furnish Copy To | Address |
|---|---|
| Name of Policyholder | Policy Number(s) |

| Address | Street and Number | City | State or Province |
|---|---|---|---|

Name of Patient (if other than policyholder) | Age

| Date Admitted | Time Admitted | AM PM | Date Discharged | Time Discharged | AM PM |
|---|---|---|---|---|---|

Other Insurance Indicated by Hospital Records. If YES name of Company

☐ NO   ☐ YES

Complaint

Date of First Symptoms

Diagnosis from Records (if injury give date, place of accident)

Operations or Obstetrical Procedures Performed (Nature and Date)

**HOSPITAL CHARGES**   (Complete this section or attach copy of itemized bill showing information below.)

| ROOM AND BOARD | ☐ Ward | Days at $ | TOTAL | $ | | | |
|---|---|---|---|---|---|---|---|
| | ☐ Semi-Private | Days at $ | TOTAL | $ | | TOTAL CHARGES | $ |
| | ☐ Private | Days at $ | TOTAL | $ | | | $_____ |
| | ☐ Other | | | $ | | | $_____ |
| OTHER CHARGES | OPERATING OR DELIVERY ROOM | | | | | | $_____ |
| | ANESTHESIA | | | | | | |
| | X-RAY | | | | | | |
| | LABORATORY | | | | | | |
| | EKG BMR | | | | | | |
| | PHYSICAL THERAPY | | | | | | |
| | AMBULANCE | | | | | | |
| | MEDICAL AND SURGICAL SUPPLIES | | | | | | |
| | PHARMACY (Except Take Home Drugs) | | | | | THIS FORM APPROVED BY THE HEALTH | |
| | INHALATION THERAPY | | | | | INSURANCE COUNCIL AND ACCEPTED BY | |
| | INTRAVENOUS SOLUTION | | | | | THE AMERICAN HOSPITAL ASSOCIATION | |
| | | TOTAL | $ | | | FOR USE BY HOSPITALS (see explanatory instructions). | |

HOSPITAL

ADDRESS

SIGNED BY

TAKEN FROM RECORDS ON _____ 19____

AUTHORIZATION TO RELEASE INFORMATION: I hereby authorize the above named hospital to release information requested on this form.

Date_____ 19____   Signed_____

Patient (Parent if a Minor)

AUTHORIZATION TO PAY INSURANCE BENEFITS: I hereby authorize payment directly to the above named hospital of the Hospital benefits otherwise payable to me but not to exceed the hospital's regular charges for this period of hospitalization. I understand I am financially responsible to the hospital for charges not covered by this authorization.

Date_____, 19____   Signed_____

Policyholder

IHF-1 [1962]

**ATTENDING PHYSICIAN'S STATEMENT – HEALTH INSURANCE CLAIM – GROUP OR INDIVIDUAL**   APSC

*Spaced for Typewriter — Marks for Tabulator Appear on this Line*

PATIENT'S NAME AND ADDRESS

AGE

INSURED'S NAME IF PATIENT IS A DEPENDENT

NAME OF INSURANCE COMPANY

POLICY NUMBER

IF GROUP INSURANCE GIVE NAME OF POLICYHOLDER
(i.e., Employer, Union or Association through whom insured)

AUTHORIZATION TO RELEASE INFORMATION: I HEREBY AUTHORIZE THE UNDERSIGNED PHYSICIAN TO RELEASE ANY INFORMATION ACQUIRED. IN THE COURSE OF MY EXAMINATION OR TREATMENT.

DATE_____19_____          SIGNED (PATIENT, OR PARENT IF MINOR)_____

AUTHORIZATION TO PAY: I HEREBY AUTHORIZE PAYMENT DIRECTLY TO THE UNDERSIGNED PHYSICIAN OF THE SURGICAL AND/OR MEDICAL BENEFITS, IF ANY, OTHERWISE PAYABLE TO ME FOR HIS SERVICES AS DESCRIBED BELOW BUT NOT TO EXCEED THE REASONABLE AND CUSTOMARY CHARGE FOR THESE SERVICES. I UNDERSTAND THAT I AM FINANCIALLY RESPONSIBLE FOR THE CHARGES NOT COVERED BY THIS AUTHORIZATION.

DATE_____19_____          SIGNED (INSURED PERSON)_____

(1A) DIAGNOSIS AND CONCURRENT CONDITIONS
(IF FRACTURE OR DISLOCATION, DESCRIBE NATURE AND LOCATION) *

(B) IS CONDITION DUE TO INJURY OR SICKNESS ARISING OUT OF PATIENT'S EMPLOYMENT?   IF "YES" EXPLAIN     YES ☐   NO ☐

(C) IS CONDITION DUE TO PREGNANCY?   IF "YES" WHAT WAS APPROXIMATE DATE OF COMMENCEMENT OF PREGNANCY?   YES ☐   NO ☐   DATE          19

(2A) WHEN DID SYMPTOMS FIRST APPEAR OR ACCIDENT HAPPEN?   DATE.........................19....

(B) WHEN DID PATIENT FIRST CONSULT YOU FOR THIS CONDITION?   DATE.........................19....

(C) HAS PATIENT EVER HAD SAME OR SIMILAR CONDITION?   IF "YES" STATE WHEN AND DESCRIBE   YES ☐   NO ☐

(3A) NATURE OF SURGICAL OR OBSTETRICAL PROCEDURE, IF ANY (Describe Fully)

DATE PERFORMED ...........................19....

(B) CHARGE TO PATIENT FOR THIS PROCEDURE INCLUDING POST-OPERATIVE CARE   $..............

(C) IF PERFORMED IN HOSPITAL, GIVE NAME OF HOSPITAL   INPATIENT ☐   OUTPATIENT ☐

(4) GIVE DATES OF OTHER MEDICAL (NON-SURGICAL) TREATMENT, IF ANY   CHARGE * PER CALL

OFFICE......................................... $..............

HOME......................................... $..............

HOSPITAL......................................... $..............

NURSING HOME......................................... $..............

TOTAL (NON-SURGICAL) CHARGES  $..............

(5) WHAT OTHER SERVICES, IF ANY, DID YOU PROVIDE PATIENT? (ITEMIZE, GIVING DATES AND FEES)

(6) WERE REGISTERED PRIVATE DUTY NURSE (R.N.) * SERVICES NECESSARY?   YES ☐   NO ☐

(7) IS PATIENT STILL UNDER YOUR CARE FOR THIS CONDITION? IF "NO" GIVE DATE YOUR SERVICES TERMINATED   YES ☐   NO ☐   DATE          19

(8A) HOW LONG WAS OR WILL PATIENT BE CONTINUOUSLY TOTALLY DISABLED (Unable to work)?   FROM...................19... THRU...................19...

(B) HOW LONG WAS OR WILL PATIENT BE PARTIALLY DISABLED?   FROM...................19... THRU...................19...

(C) WAS HOUSE CONFINEMENT NECESSARY? IF "YES" GIVE DATES   YES ☐   NO ☐   FROM     19     THRU     19

(9) TO YOUR KNOWLEDGE DOES PATIENT HAVE OTHER HEALTH INSURANCE OR HEALTH PLAN COVERAGE? IF "YES" IDENTIFY   YES ☐   NO ☐

DATE          SIGNATURE (ATTENDING PHYSICIAN)          DEGREE          TELEPHONE

STREET ADDRESS          CITY OR TOWN          STATE OR PROVINCE          ZIP CODE

*OPTIONAL          Approved by Council on Medical Service, AMA November 1964

**GROUP HOSPITAL INSURANCE FORM** *TO BE PRESENTED TO THE HOSPITAL IN DUPLICATE*

*Spaced for Typewriter — Marks for Tabulator Appear on this Line*

To _____ Hospital. This certifies that _____ is insured for the following

Group Hospital Benefits (in behalf of his dependent _____ ) By

(Name)          (Relationship)

_____
(Name of Insurer)

| BENEFITS FOR OTHER THAN MATERNITY CASES | BENEFITS FOR MATERNITY CASES |
|---|---|
| A. HOSPITAL ROOM AND BOARD (INCLUDING GENERAL NURSING SERVICES) ACTUAL HOSPITAL CHARGES UP TO $_____ FOR EACH DAY OF HOSPITALIZATION UP TO _____ DAYS. | HOSPITAL ROOM AND BOARD (INCLUDING GENERAL NURSING SERVICE) AND OTHER HOSPITAL SERVICES . . . ACTUAL CHARGES UP TO $_____. OR |
| | 1. HOSPITAL ROOM AND BOARD (INCLUDING GENERAL NURSING SERVICES) $_____ FOR EACH DAY OF HOSPITALIZATION UP TO _____ DAYS |
| B. OTHER HOSPITAL CHARGES FOR HOSPITAL CARE AND TREATMENT (EXCLUDING CHARGES FOR NURSES' AND PHYSICIANS' SERVICES AND TAKE HOME DRUGS) $_____ | 2. OTHER HOSPITAL CHARGES FOR HOSPITAL CARE AND TREATMENT (EXCLUDING CHARGES FOR NURSES' AND PHYSICIANS' SERVICES AND TAKE HOME DRUGS) $_____ |

THE MINIMUM HOUR HOSPITALIZATION REQUIREMENT WILL BE MET IF _____

| GROUP POLICYHOLDER | ADDRESS | PHONE |
|---|---|---|

| BY (Name and Title) | ABOVE CERTIFICATION VALID FOR ONLY SEVEN DAYS FROM THIS DATE (Exception — Maternity Cases) | DATE |
|---|---|---|

| HOSPITAL COMPLETE FOLLOWING AND FURNISH COPY TO | ADDRESS |
|---|---|

| NAME OF PATIENT | AGE | DATE ADMITTED | TIME ADMITTED AM PM | DATE DISCHARGED | TIME DISCHARGED AM PM |
|---|---|---|---|---|---|

IF PATIENT HAD OTHER THAN SEMI-PRIVATE ROOM, INDICATE SEMI-PRIVATE DAILY RATE   $    OTHER INSURANCE INDICATED BY HOSPITAL RECORDS. IF YES, NAME OF COMPANY   ☐ NO   ☐ YES

DIAGNOSIS FROM RECORDS (If Injury, Give Date and Place of Accident)

OPERATIONS OR OBSTETRICAL PROCEDURES PERFORMED (Nature and Date)

HOSPITAL CHARGES (Complete This Section or Attach Copy of Itemized Bill Showing Information Below).

| ROOM AND BOARD | | | | | | |
|---|---|---|---|---|---|---|
| ☐ WARD | DAYS AT $ | TOTAL | $ | | TOTAL CHARGES | $ |
| ☐ SEMI-PRIVATE | DAYS AT $ | TOTAL | $ | | | |
| ☐ PRIVATE | DAYS AT $ | TOTAL | $ | | | $ |
| ☐ OTHERS | | | $ | | | $ |

| OTHER CHARGES | | |
|---|---|---|
| OPERATING OR DELIVERY ROOM | |
| ANESTHESIA | |
| X-RAY | |
| LABORATORY | |
| EKG BMR | |
| PHYSICAL THERAPY | |
| AMBULANCE | |
| MEDICAL AND SURGICAL SUPPLIES | |
| PHARMACY (Except Take Home Drugs) | |
| INHALATION THERAPY | |
| INTRAVENOUS SOLUTIONS | |
| TOTAL | $ |

THIS FORM APPROVED BY THE HEALTH INSURANCE COUNCIL AND ACCEPTED BY THE AMERICAN HOSPITAL ASSOCIATION FOR USE BY HOSPITALS (see explanatory instructions).

| HOSPITAL | ADDRESS |
|---|---|
| TAKEN FROM RECORDS ON          19 | SIGNED BY |

AUTHORIZATION TO RELEASE INFORMATION:    I hereby authorize the above named hospital to release the information requested on this form.

Date_____, 19___ Signed_____

*Patient (Parent if a Minor)*

AUTHORIZATION TO PAY INSURANCE BENEFITS: I hereby authorize payment directly to the above named hospital of the Group Hospital Benefits herein specified and otherwise payable to me but not to exceed the hospital's regular charges for this period of hospitalization. I understand I am financially responsible to the hospital for charges not covered by this authorization.

Date_____, 19___ Signed_____

*(Insured)*

MAP-4 (1961)                                                    PRINTED IN U.S.A.

# Index

# Index

*This book has been set in 10 and 9 point
Caledonia, leaded 2 points. Part numbers and
Part and Chapter titles are in 16 point Helvet-
ica Medium; Chapter numbers are in 12 point
Helvetica Bold. The size of the type page is
27 × 46 picas.*